Psychology

AN INTRODUCTION
TENTH EDITION

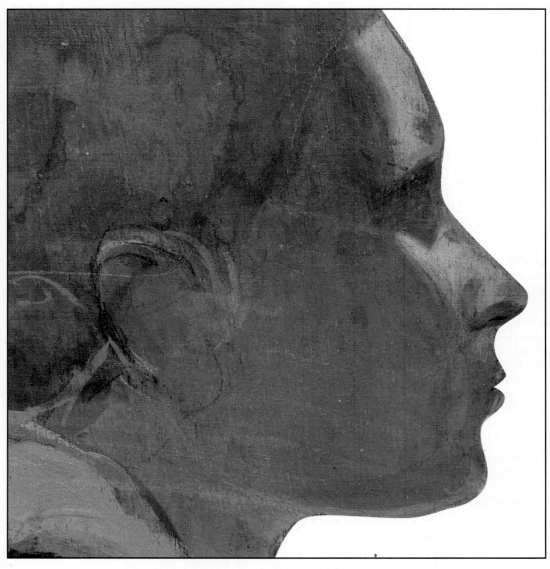

Charles G. Morris
University of Michigan

with

Albert A. Maisto
University of North Carolina at Charlotte

PRENTICE HALL
Upper Saddle River, New Jersey 07458

Library of Congress Cataloging-in-Publication Data

Morris, Charles G.
    Psychology : an introduction / Charles G. Morris.—10th ed.
        p.   cm.
    Includes bibliographical references (p.   ) and indexes.
    ISBN 0-13-676537-8
    1. Psychology.   I. Title.
BF121.M598   1999
150—dc21   98-14514
                                                            CIP

Editorial Director: Charlyce Jones-Owen
Editor in Chief: Nancy Roberts
Executive Editor: Bill Webber
Development Editor: Roberta Meyer
Director of Development: Susanna Lesan
Assistant Vice President of Production and
    Manufacturing: Barbara Kittle
Senior Managing Editor: Bonnie Biller
Assistant Managing Editor: Mary Rottino
Project Manager: Maureen Richardson
Manufacturing Manager: Nick Sklitsis
Prepress and Manufacturing Buyer: Tricia
    Kenny

Creative Design Director: Leslie Osher
Art Director and Interior Design: Carole
    Anson
Cover Design: Tom Nery
Cover Art: Deborah Healy
Director, Image Resource Center: Lori
    Morris-Nantz
Photo Research Supervisor: Melinda Reo
Image Permission Supervisor: Kay Dellosh
Photo Research: Barbara Salz
Director of Marketing: Gina Sluss
Marketing Manager: Mike Alread
Editorial Assistant: Tamsen Adams

Photo credits appear on pp. 689-690, which constitute a continuation of the copyright page.

This book was set in 11/12 Goudy by TSI Graphics and was printed and bound by RR Donnelley and Sons Company. The cover was printed by The Lehigh Press, Inc.

©1998, 1996, 1993, 1990, 1988, 1985, 1982, 1979, 1976, 1973
by Prentice Hall, Inc.
Simon & Schuster/A Viacom Company
Upper Saddle River, New Jersey 07458

Printed in the United States of America
10 9 8 7 6 5 4 3 2 1

ISBN 0-13-676537-8 (College)
ISBN 0-13-436104-0 (School)
ISBN 0-13-090503-8 (Professional)

Prentice-Hall International (UK) Limited, London
Prentice-Hall of Australia Pty. Limited, Sydney
Prentice Hall Canada, Inc. Toronto
Prentice-Hall Hispanoamericana, S.A., Mexico
Prentice-Hall of India Private Limited, New Delhi
Prentice-Hall of Japan, Inc. Tokyo
Simon & Schuster Asia Pte. Ltd., Singapore
Editoria Prentice-Hall do Brasil, Ltda., Rio de Janeiro

BRIEF CONTENTS

CONTENTS

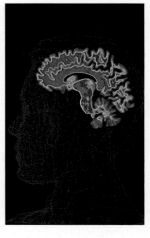

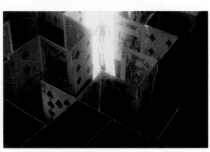

FEATURE BOXES

Preface

This is the twenty-fifth anniversary of *Psychology: An Introduction*. It is hard to remember or even to imagine life without this book. The book is so much a part of my life that at times I have found myself thinking of my age in editions: "How old are you?" "Oh, nine editions going on ten." Inevitably, my family has been an important part of the whole process. Several years ago, when I was talking at the dinner table about some revision problems, my youngest son piped up "Dad, how many times are you going to revise the book until you get it right?" I probably replied "About ten. Now eat your beans." And sure enough, here I am at the tenth edition.

The task of capturing recent developments in psychology and reporting them in a brief form that is accurate, interesting and understandable is an extraordinary challenge, but it is more than made up for by the excitement of discovery and the joy of accomplishment. On each edition I have been blessed with editors who have come up with exciting, creative new ways of doing things; the energy and enthusiasm they have brought to the revision process has been invigorating. And the field of psychology itself has changed so much over the years, and so many of the recent discoveries are truly exciting, that it's still fun to be able to pull it all together every three years in interesting, readable prose. In fact, I was reading *The New York Times* one morning recently and I came across the headline "Studies of Brain Find Marijuana Can Have the Same Effect as Other Drugs." It's probably a sign of life in the editorial "fast lane" that my first thought was "Wow, I wonder if we should cover that in the chapter on altered states of consciousness!" I'm firmly convinced that I will never be able to read a newspaper, magazine or professional journal without scissors in hand. What, then does the Tenth Edition have to show for all this effort? Every chapter has been updated to reflect the most important research findings since the last edition. In addition, we have added the following new features:

NEW IN THE TENTH EDITION

Applying Psychology

This new series of boxes presents activities, introduces strategies for personal change, and provides information for students seeking assistance with personal or family problems. Thus, we tell students what kinds of behaviors might indicate an alcohol-abuse problem (Chapter 4); how to improve their memories (Chapter

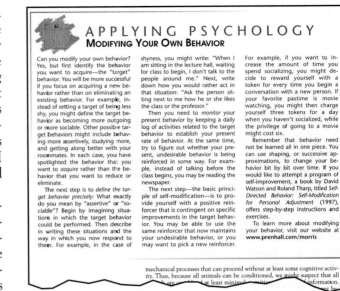

6); and how to deal with exam stress at college (Chapter 12). The therapies chapter (Chapter 14) provides a long list of self-help organizations for all types of problems, along with addresses and phone numbers.

Enduring Issues

A new feature in this edition is the inclusion of five issues that have intrigued psychologists for decades: To what extent is behavior caused by processes that occur inside the person as opposed to factors outside the person **(person-situation)?** What is the relative

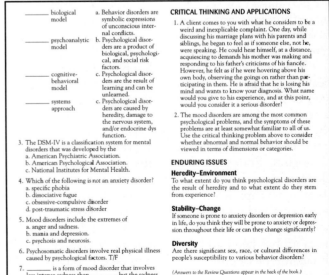

importance of **heredity and environment?** To what extent do people remain relatively unchanged throughout their lives **(stability-change)?** In what respects do people differ significantly from one another based on such things as gender, race, ethnicity, and culture **(diversity)?** And finally, what is the relationship between our experiences and biological processes **(mind-body)?** These enduring issues are first described in Chapter 1, and each chapter ends with several questions that ask the reader to reconsider the issue in light of what has been learned in that chapter.

While there is much that is new in this edition, my original goals for this book remain unchanged: to present a scientific, accurate, and thorough overview of psychology in engaging language that the average student can easily comprehend; to be current without being trendy; and to write clearly about psychology and its applications without being condescending. Three unifying themes still run throughout the text: (1) Psychology is a science; (2) human behavior and thought are diverse, varied, and affected by culture; and (3) the study of psychology involves active thinking, questioning, and problem solving. In addition, the tenth edition retains all of the features that have always made *Psychology: An Introduction* highly accessible to students.

PSYCHOLOGY IS A SCIENCE

Every edition of this text has reflected the fact that psychology is the scientific study of behavior and mental processes, and this new edition is no exception. Key topics are presented in a balanced, scientific manner, incorporating both classic studies and the most recent developments. There are more than 500 new references to recent work in the field. For example, the introductory chapter has a new section on evolutionary psychology, a more thorough discussion of research methods and control procedures, and a stronger focus on ethical issues in research with both humans and animals.

The Biological Basis of Behavior (Chapter 2) has been thoroughly rewritten and now includes a discussion of the most recent research in neurogenesis, a new section on evolutionary psychology, a new discussion of the nature-nurture debate, and a clear discussion of the latest brain imaging methods and their usefulness to psychologists. **States of Consciousness (Chapter 4)** includes a new discussion of interesting topics related to sleep, a new application box on insomnia, and consideration of the latest research on the biological basis of consciousness. Recent research on the biological basis of memory has been added to **Memory (Chapter 6).** The discussion of **Cognition and Language (Chapter 7)** has been changed to reflect contemporary cognitive theory and the discussion of language and cognition in nonhu-

mans has been greatly updated. **Intelligence and Mental Abilities (Chapter 8)** includes new material on the effects of early intervention programs, consideration of all the most current tests, and up-to-date coverage of the nature versus nurture debate. **Motivation and Emotion (Chapter 9)** has been moved forward to precede life span development. The discussion of emotion has been greatly expanded and includes the latest cross-cultural research. Human sexuality receives more attention, including a new section describing the latest research on sexual orientation. **Personality (Chapter 11)** now includes a discussion of the complexity of nature/nurture and personality development and an expanded discussion of the *Big Five* trait theory of personality. **Stress and Health Psychology (Chapter 12)** includes new material on the rapidly expanding field of health psychology and psychoimmunology (particularly relating to cancer, disease and heart disease) and the relationships between social support and health, a new discussion of coping with stress in college, and an enhanced discussion of posttraumatic stress disorder. New research examining the biological factors involved in psychological disorders is discussed in **Psychological Disorders (Chapter 13),** and a discussion of the effectiveness of medication and psychotherapy appears in **Therapies (Chapter 14).**

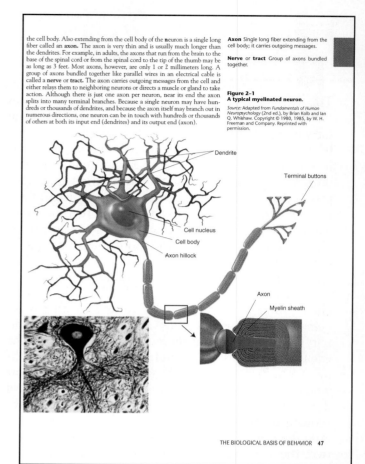

the cell body. Also extending from the cell body of the neuron is a single long fiber called an **axon.** The axon is very thin and is usually much longer than the dendrites. For example, in adults, the axons that run from the brain to the base of the spinal cord or from the spinal cord to the tip of the thumb may be as long as 3 feet. Most axons, however, are only 1 or 2 millimeters long. A group of axons bundled together like parallel wires in an electrical cable is called a **nerve** or **tract.** The axon carries outgoing messages from the cell and either relays them to neighboring neurons or directs a muscle or gland to take action. Although there is just one axon per neuron, near its end the axon splits into many terminal branches. Because a single neuron may have hundreds or thousands of dendrites, and because the axon itself may branch out in numerous directions, one neuron can be in touch with hundreds or thousands of others at both its input end (dendrites) and its output end (axon).

Axon Single long fiber extending from the cell body; it carries outgoing messages.

Nerve or **tract** Group of axons bundled together.

Figure 2–1
A typical myelinated neuron.
Source: Adapted from *Fundamentals of Human Neuropsychology* (2nd ed.), by Brian Kolb and Ian Q. Whishaw. Copyright © 1980, 1985, by W. H. Freeman and Company. Reprinted with permission.

Dendrite

Terminal buttons

Cell nucleus

Cell body

Axon hillock

Axon

Myelin sheath

THE BIOLOGICAL BASIS OF BEHAVIOR 47

Race A subpopulation of a species, defined according to an identifiable characteristic (i.e., geographic location, skin color, hair texture, genes, facial features).

Diversity can exist within a culture as well as across cultures. Here, a fan of Madonna has parked his truck near an ancient mosque in Mali, northern Africa.

Even within a dominant culture diversity exists in the form of *subcultures*, "cultural patterns that distinguish some segment of a society's population" (Macionis, 1993, p. 75). Texans, psychology professors, persons with AIDS, African American women, homeless people, and teenagers all form subcultures within U.S. society. These subcultures have their own norms, values, and rituals, which may or may not be similar to those of the dominant culture. Moreover, many nations (such as the United States) are composed of various peoples with different backgrounds and traditions. Although we identify certain ideas, products, and behaviors as distinctly "American," we are actually a nation of great diversity—within our borders there are many well-formed subcultures of immigrants and their families. In later chapters, we discuss how cultural differences affect psychological processes, including our motivation to achieve, the way we express emotion, and a whole range of social behaviors.

Race and Ethnicity

Most people (including some psychologists) speak of Asians, Latinos, Native Americans, African Americans, Caucasians, and Pacific Islanders as distinct races, implying fundamental differences among these peoples. A **race** is usually defined as a subpopulation of a species (in this case, humans) who share some biological and genetic similarities and who have reproduced among themselves (Betancourt & López, 1993; Diamond, 1994; Macionis, 1993). Furthermore, members of different races generally have distinct physical characteristics, such as hair color or type, skin pigmentation, and facial features. At one time it might have been reasonable to talk about races as distinct groups, given the isolated geographic regions some peoples occupied and the identifiable physical characteristics they developed in adapting to those regions. Today, however, many scientists do not consider race a valid scientific concept because humans have so frequently migrated, intermarried, and commingled. Consequently, genetic characteristics that were once specific to a group of individuals in a particular region were spread widely across a much larger area. All contemporary societies are populated by people with rich genetic mixtures, so it is difficult to argue that human beings now differ substantially on a genetic basis. Furthermore, the physical characteristics that were once thought to "define" membership in a racial group are somewhat arbitrary. Race classification has often been based on melanin (the substance that produces differences in the color of skin, hair, and eyes), but humans could just as easily be classified along several other dimensions. For example, some people have a genetic resistance to malaria and others do not; some people can digest milk products and others cannot; and some people have fingerprint patterns that form spirals, whereas others have patterns that form loops and still others exhibit patterns that form arches (Diamond, 1994). We could posit any number of different "races" based on these other classification schemes.

Because race is so difficult to define, psychologists have ...

HUMAN DIVERSITY

For today's students and instructors of introductory psychology, diversity is more than simply an issue for discussion and debate; it is a daily reality. Within a single classroom, students may vary in age from 16 to 60. Some come to their first psychology course having experienced poverty, racism, or sexism. Others have had to adjust to a new culture and language. The challenge confronting any textbook author is to satisfy a heterogeneous audience without becoming "trendy" or unscientific. Over the last several years, the body of research examining issues of diversity has grown to significant levels. As a result, I have expanded the consideration of diversity throughout this new edition, both diversity within the North American population and diversity across cultures worldwide.

The Ninth Edition discussed diversity in a separate chapter. In contrast, the Tenth Edition integrates research dealing with aspects of gender and cultural similarities and differences into every chapter, wherever appropriate. We introduce this topic in Chapter 1, with a new section on human diversity including feminism, ethnicity, and sexual orientation as well as an expanded consideration of cross-cultural research and biases. New material on cultural influences on memory is presented in **Chapter 6;** human diversity and cross cultural themes get much greater attention in the discussion of language, categorization and decision making (**Chapter 7**); and **Chapter 8** includes new sections on gender and cultural differences related to intelligence, academic performance and mental abilities. Diversity also receives more attention in our discussion of motivation and emotion (**Chapter 9**) particularly in the discussion of aggression and emotional expression.

ACTIVE THINKING, QUESTIONING, AND PROBLEM SOLVING

Education involves far more than just memorizing information. A successful course in general psychology (and, for that matter, most other disciplines) helps students develop their ability to analyze, to ask questions, to evaluate the ideas of others, and ultimately to form their own ideas. Teaching active, critical thinking has long been a major objective of the courses I teach and of this text, and it remains a basic theme in the Tenth Edition which contains numerous critical thinking features based on cognitive research about effective learning from textbooks.

Every chapter starts with **Think About It!** questions that are designed to stimulate thinking about the material in the chapter. Students have told us that the questions serve as advance organizers while piquing their interest in the material that follows. Each question is repeated in the margin opposite the text discussion where the related issue is addressed.

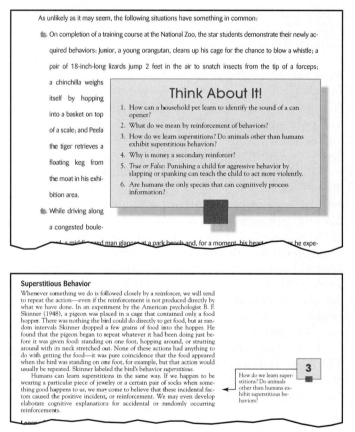

As unlikely as it may seem, the following situations have something in common:

🐾 On completion of a training course at the National Zoo, the star students demonstrate their newly acquired behaviors: Junior, a young orangutan, cleans up his cage for the chance to blow a whistle; a pair of 18-inch-long lizards jump 2 feet in the air to snatch insects from the tip of a forceps; a chinchilla weighs itself by hopping into a basket on top of a scale; and Peela the tiger retrieves a floating keg from the moat in his exhibition area.

🐾 While driving along a congested boule-

Think About It!

1. How can a household pet learn to identify the sound of a can opener?
2. What do we mean by reinforcement of behaviors?
3. How do we learn superstitions? Do animals other than humans exhibit superstitious behaviors?
4. Why is money a secondary reinforcer?
5. *True or False:* Punishing a child for aggressive behavior by slapping or spanking can teach the child to act more violently.
6. Are humans the only species that can cognitively process information?

...d a middle-aged man glances at a park bench and, for a moment, his heart ... he expe-

Superstitious Behavior

Whenever something we do is followed closely by a reinforcer, we will tend to repeat the action—even if the reinforcement is not produced directly by what we have done. In an experiment by the American psychologist B. F. Skinner (1948), a pigeon was placed in a cage that contained only a food hopper. There was nothing the bird could do directly to get food, but at random intervals Skinner dropped a few grains of food into the hopper. He found that the pigeon began to repeat whatever it had been doing just before it was given food: standing on one foot, hopping around, or strutting around with its neck stretched out. None of these actions had anything to do with getting the food—it was pure coincidence that the food appeared when the bird was standing on one foot, for example, but that action would usually be repeated. Skinner labeled the bird's behavior *superstitious.*

Humans can learn superstitions in the same way. If we happen to be wearing a particular piece of jewelry or a certain pair of socks when something good happens to us, we may come to believe that these incidental factors caused the positive incident, or reinforcement. We may even develop elaborate cognitive explanations for accidental or randomly occurring reinforcements.

| | **3** |

How do we learn superstitions? Do animals other than humans exhibit superstitious behaviors?

Most chapters include at least one box describing a controversial issue in the field of psychology. Each of these **Controversies** boxes ends with several thought-provoking questions designed to encourage students to reconsider their own position on the issues. Do the brains of males and females differ significantly (Chapter 2)? How do we see objects and shapes (Chapter 3)? Does biofeedback work (Chapter 5)? Is our language male-

CONTROVERSIES
THE INSANITY DEFENSE

Particularly horrifying crimes—assassinations of public figures, mass murders, and serial murders, for instance—have often been attributed to mental disturbance because it seems to many people that anyone who could commit such crimes must be crazy. But to the legal system, this presents a problem: If a person is truly "crazy," are we justified in holding him or her responsible for criminal acts? The legal answer to this question is a qualified *yes*. A mentally ill person *is* responsible for his or her crimes unless he or she is determined to be *insane*. What's the difference between being "mentally ill" and being "insane"? Insanity is a legal term, not a psychological one. It is typically applied to defendants who, when they committed the offense with which they are charged, were so mentally disturbed that they either could not distinguish right from wrong or could not control the act—it was an "irresistible impulse."

Actually, when a defendant is suspected of being mentally disturbed, another important question must be answered before that person is brought to trial: Is the person able to understand the charges against him or her and to participate in a defense in court? This issue is known as *competency to stand trial*. The person is examined by a court-appointed expert and, if found to be incompetent, is sent to a mental institution, often for an indefinite period. If judged to be competent, the person is required to stand trial. At this point the defendant may decide to plead not guilty by reason of insanity—which is an assertion that *at the time of the crime* the defendant

lacked substantial capacity to appreciate the criminality of his or her action (know right from wrong) or to conform to the requirements of the law (control his or her behavior).

Despite popular belief to the contrary, the insanity plea is rare, arising in less than 1 percent of serious criminal cases. But it became controversial when it was successfully used by John Hinckley, the man who attempted to assassinate President Ronald Reagan in 1981. Many people were very upset that Hinckley, whose action had been clearly captured on videotape, seemed to escape punishment for his crime by pleading insanity in a jurisdiction (Washington, D.C.) that required the prosecution to prove beyond a reasonable doubt that *he was sane*. (In contrast, most states, as well as the federal courts, place the burden on the defense to prove that the *defendant is insane*.) Since his trial, Hinckley has been confined in a mental hospital.

When a defendant enters an insanity plea, the court system relies heavily on the testimony of forensic psychologists and psychiatrists to determine the mental state of the defendant at the time of the crime. Because most such trials feature well-credentialed experts testifying both for the defense and for the prosecution, the jury is often perplexed about which side to believe. Furthermore, there is much cynicism about "hired-gun" professionals who receive large fees to appear in court and argue that a defendant is or is

Is the person able to understand the charges against him or her and to participate in a defense in court?

Theodore J. Kaczynski, the serial terrorist known as the Unabomber was sought by the FBI for 17 years. Kaczynski pleaded guilty to three killings to avoid a trial in which his lawyers had planned to argue that he was mentally ill.

not sane. The public, skeptical about professional jargon, often feels that psychological testimony allows dangerous criminals to "get off." Actually, those who successfully plead insanity—like John Hinckley—often are confined longer in mental hospitals than they would have been in prison if convicted of their crimes. Therefore, the insanity plea is not an easy way out of responsibility for a crime.

Questions

1. What is your position on the question of whether insanity should ever be considered a legal defense for criminals?

2. In some states, a person can be found *both* guilty and mentally ill. Such people are sentenced to normal prison terms but must be provided with psychological or psychiatric treatment if they need it. Do you think this is a good alternative to the insanity plea? Why, or why not?

---

dominated (Chapter 7)? Should psychological research routinely report gender differences (Chapter 8)? Can illusions keep you healthy (Chapter 12)? Is the insanity defense defensible (Chapter 13)?

The critical perspective also pervades the narrative of the text. In many cases I examine a topic from different angles, showing that there isn't always a "right" answer or approach to a psychological issue or problem. We also show how new research and new theories have changed the way that psychologists think about and understand important psychological processes, thus reinforcing the idea that what we "know" today may turn out to be wrong tomorrow! Throughout the book, **Highlights** boxes describe the implications of significant research.

Finally, each chapter ends with a number of **Critical Thinking and Applications** questions that require students to analyze, evaluate, and interpret some of the basic themes of the chapter.

ACCESSIBLE TO STUDENTS

Writing Style

Throughout every edition of my text I have kept in mind that my final audience consists primarily of college undergraduates. Having taught undergraduates for more than 35 years, I realize that it is essential to make a text-

book as accessible and helpful as possible. I have retained the clear, straightforward writing style to which students and reviewers have responded so positively over the years. And for this edition, the entire manuscript was rewritten, carefully edited, and rewritten again to convey ideas as clearly and concisely as possible. Once again the text contains plenty of examples relevant to today's undergraduates. The tone is conversational without resorting to slang.

Pedagogy

The attention to pedagogy integrated in every chapter has always made this book a student favorite. Cognitive psychology research has proved that structure and elaborate rehearsals can improve reading comprehension and retention. As a result, a chapter-opening **Overview** provides students with a road map for each chapter, then reinforces and helps organize material for students when major headings reappear as the basic structure for end-of-chapter **Summaries.** Within each chapter, **Summary Tables** of key concepts provide concise reviews of the most important concepts (for example, defense mechanisms, types of memory, theories of personality, and the structures and functions of the brain). **Key terms** are printed in boldface and defined in the margin where they first appear. The result is that students don't just process lists of unrelated facts, but instead have a cognitive map in which to contextualize, better understand, and more effectively relate and recall concepts. By answering the **Review Questions** at the end of each chapter students can test themselves before moving ahead.

_____ biological model
_____ psychoanalytic model
_____ cognitive-behavioral model
_____ systems approach

a. Behavior disorders are symbolic expressions of unconscious internal conflicts.
b. Psychological disorders are a product of biological, psychological, and social risk factors.
c. Psychological disorders are the result of learning and can be unlearned.
c. Psychological disorders are caused by heredity, damage to the nervous system, and/or endocrine dysfunction.

3. The DSM-IV is a classification system for mental disorders that was developed by the
a. American Psychiatric Association.

CRITICAL THINKING AND APPLICATIONS

1. A client comes to you with what he considers to be a weird and inexplicable complaint. One day, while discussing his marriage plans with his parents and siblings, he began to feel as if someone else, not he, were speaking. He could hear himself, at a distance, acquiescing to demands his mother was making and responding to his father's criticisms of his fiancée. However, he felt as if he were hovering above his own body, observing the goings on rather than participating in them. He is afraid that he is losing his mind and wants to know your diagnosis. What name would you give to his experience, and at this point, would you consider it a serious disorder?

2. The mood disorders are among the most common psychological problems, and the symptoms of these problems are at least somewhat familiar to all of us. Use the critical thinking problem above to consider whether abnormal and normal behavior should be viewed in terms of dimensions or categories.

SUMMARY TABLE		
MAJOR NEUROTRANSMITTERS AND THEIR EFFECTS		
Acetylcholine (ACh)	Generally excitatory	Affects arousal, attention, memory, motivation, movement. Too much: spasms, tremors. Too little: paralysis, torpor.
Dopamine	Inhibitory	Inhibits wide range of behavior and emotions, including pleasure. Implicated in schizophrenia and Parkinson's disease.
Serotonin	Inhibitory	Inhibits virtually all activities. Important for sleep onset, mood, eating behavior.
Norepinephrine	Generally excitatory	Affects arousal, wakefulness, learning, memory, mood.
Endorphins	Inhibitory	Inhibit transmission of pain messages.

Synaptic vesicles Tiny sacs in a terminal button that release chemicals into the synapse.

Neurotransmitters Chemicals released by the synaptic vesicles that travel across the synaptic space and affect adjacent neurons.

Receptor site A location on a receptor neuron into which a specific neurotransmitter fits like a key into a lock.

Art and Design

Finally, in keeping with the time-honored truism that "a picture is worth a thousand words," special attention has been given in this edition to the visual appearance of the book. New figures and photographs have been carefully selected to complement the text material. Cartoons have been added to provide some levity and to lighten the presentation.

SUPPLEMENTS

It is increasingly true today that, as valuable as a good textbook is, it is still only one element of a comprehensive learning package. Throughout the many editions of my book, Prentice Hall and I have labored to produce not only a well-written text, but also a full range of supplemental learning tools. The supplements package that accompanies the Tenth Edition is the most comprehensive and impressive yet.

For Instructors

INSTRUCTOR'S RESOURCE MANUAL (0-13-095717-8) by Alan Swinkels, St. Edward's University, and Tracy Giuliano, Southwestern University. For each chapter the manual contains a Chapter Outline; a list of Learning Objectives which correspond to the exercises in the Study Guide; Lecture Suggestions describing additional topics of interest; suggested Demonstrations and Activities such as class projects and experiments; and Student Assignments including reports and out-of-class exercises. Additionally, each chapter contains a list of the ABC News videos, multimedia resources, and transparencies available to accompany the text plus Handouts for use with the Demonstrations and Activities.

TEST ITEM FILE (0-13-095714-3) by Gary Piggrem, DeVry Institute of Technology. Contains over 4000 multiple choice, true/false, and essay questions. To facilitate instructors in creating tests, each question is page referenced to the textbook, is described as either factual,

conceptual, or applied, and is identified as being new, from the previous edition, or revised. We will continue our effort to improve and expand the Test Item File for future editions, and as always I welcome your comments, suggestions, and teaching feedback. Send them directly to: Charles G. Morris, Department of Psychology, University of Michigan, Ann Arbor, MI 48109-1109.

PRENTICE HALL CUSTOM TESTS for Windows, Macintosh and DOS platforms. The questions in the Test Item File are available on all three platforms and allow instructors complete personal flexibility in building and editing their own customized tests. Advances in the most recent version of this software now allow instructors to load their tests onto the World Wide Web or a Local Area Network in an on-line testing format.

> Windows PH Custom Test (0-13-095707-0)
> DOS PH Custom Test (0-13-095713-5)
> Macintosh PH Custom Test (0-13-095711-9)

TOLL-FREE TELEPHONE TEST PREPARATION SERVICES. Prentice Hall offers a telephone test preparation service through which instructors can call a special, toll-free number and select up to 200 questions from the printed Test Item File available with the text. The test and an alternate version (if requested), and answer key are mailed or faxed within hours of the initial request.

PH COLOR ACETATE TRANSPARENCIES for Introductory Psychology Series V (0-13-095708-9)—contains illustrations, figures and graphs from *Psychology: An Introduction Tenth Edition* as well as images from a variety of other sources.

POWERPOINT SLIDES for *Psychology: An Introduction, Tenth Edition.* Scores of illustrations, figures and graphs from the text have been downloaded and made accessible via the popular Powerpoint program from Microsoft. Instructors can edit or otherwise customize these images and slides and project them onto a screen while delivering lectures or clip them for Web-based learning systems.

PRESENTATION MANAGER FOR INTRODUCTORY PSYCHOLOGY (0-13-095705-4). Contains the same images as the Powerpoint slides but also contains a Lecture Maker that allows instructors to assemble and sequence these images, laser disc segments, digital graphics, and interactive animations in computer-driven lectures.

TWO SUPPLEMENTARY LASERDISCS are available. LaserPsych for Introductory Psychology (0-13-735382-0) and the Auxiliary Laser Disc for Psychology (0-02-409612-1) provide an abundance of still graphics, demonstrations, animations, and video segments from classic experiments to enhance lecture presentations.

NEWSLINK for Introductory Psychology. This is an exclusive, Internet-based electronic clipping service that brings daily delivery of information linked to introductory psychology from major newspapers from around the world to your computer.

 ABC NEWS/PH VIDEO LIBRARY. Prentice Hall has assembled a collection of feature segments from award-winning news programs. The following libraries are currently available to qualified adopters:

Introductory Psychology Series III consists of segments from award-winning news programs such as "ABC Nightly News," "Nightline," "20/20," "Prime Time Live," and "The Health Show." Summaries of questions, designed to stimulate critical thinking for each segment, are included in the Instructor's Resource Manual.

The Alliance Series: The Annenberg/CPB Collection. The Alliance Series in the most extensive collection of professionally produced videos available with any introductory psychology textbook. Selections include videos in the following Annenberg series: The Brain, The Brain Teaching Modules, Discovering Psychology, The Mind, and The Mind Teaching Modules. Contact your local Prentice Hall representative for details.

TEACHING PSYCHOLOGY, 2/E (0-13-735143-7); (73514-2) by Fred W. Whitford (Montana State University) Serves as a guide for new instructors or teaching assistants to manage the myriad complex tasks required to teach effectively from the start. The Second Edition has been updated to include coverage of regional teaching of psychology conferences and organizations, and a new section on using the Internet and online services to enhance teaching.

CRITICAL THINKING RESOURCE MANUAL (0-13-735697-8); (73569-6) This instructor supplement offers intriguing questions, exercises, and activities for each of the major topics of the introductory course. It is divided into three types of resources: questions, exercises, and extended activities, presenting scenarios from the student perspective. The format facilitates copying and use as class handouts. Also available in class quantities for students, shrinkwrapped to text.

For Students

STUDY GUIDE WITH PRACTICE TESTS (0-13-095718-6) by Joyce Bishop, Golden West College. Each chapter contains an Overview to introduce students to the chapter; Class Notes Outline with space for students to take notes from the text and during lecture; a Learning Objectives exercise to test students' understanding of the main themes; a multiple choice Pretest and Posttest for gauging students' progress; Short Essay Questions to develop writing skills; Language Support Section for extra support in English; and Flash Cards of vocabulary terms.

NEW YORK TIMES THEME OF THE TIMES SUPPLEMENT FOR INTRODUCTORY PSYCHOLOGY. Prentice Hall and The New York Times have joined forces to bring students a complimentary newspaper supplement containing recent articles pertinent to introductory psychology. These articles augment the text material and provide real-world examples. Updated twice a year.

COMPANION WEBSITE with Course Monitor Edition. http://www.prenhall.com/morris An interactive website is available for instructors and students who use Psychology: An Introduction, Tenth Edition. Visitors will find a range of interactive resources, including a free, interactive student study guide; a virtual discussion group/chat area, and related links and resources. The quizzes available in every chapter can be e-mailed to instructors or teaching assistants and be viewed, graded and recorded through special function available in the Course Monitor Edition upgrade.

PSYCHOLOGY: AN INTRODUCTION, INTERACTIVE EDITION. (0-13-095709-7) An exciting new multimedia companion version of Psychology: An Introduction, Tenth Edition is available as a supplemental learning aid for students or as a stand-alone textbook replacement. This dual-platform CD-ROM features the full content of the textbook, plus an interactive study guide and a wealth of multimedia teaching and learning devices.

Supplemental Texts

Any one of these texts can be packaged with Psychology: An Introduction, Tenth Edition at a reduced price:

GUIDE TO THE BRAIN: A GRAPHIC WORKBOOK (0-13-365982-8) Prepared by Mark B. Kristal (SUNY Buffalo), this study aid helps students learn the names and locations of the most important structures and locations of the brain and nervous systems.

PSYCHOLOGY ON THE INTERNET '98/'99: A STUDENT'S GUIDE (0-13-646159-X) Prepared by Jeffrey Platt of North Iowa Area Community College. This is a hands-on Internet tutorial features web sites related to psychology. Designed to enhance the effectiveness of the textbook, it helps students capitalize on all the resources that the Internet and World Wide Web have to offer. Available free with every new book purchased from Prentice Hall.

HOW TO THINK LIKE A PSYCHOLOGIST: CRITICAL THINKING IN PSYCHOLOGY (0-02-378392-3) by Donald McBurney, University of Pittsburgh. This 128-page paperback supplementary text uses a question-answer format to explore some of the most common questions students ask about psychology.

FORTY STUDIES THAT CHANGED PSYCHOLOGY, 3E (0-13-922725-3) by Roger Hock, Mendocino College. Presenting the seminal research studies that have shaped modern psychological study, this supplement provides an overview of the research, its findings, and the impact these findings have had on current thinking in the discipline. A special combination package with the text is available.

ACKNOWLEDGMENTS

As always, I am immensely grateful for the assistance I received from the many people who reviewed the previous edition and suggested improvements for this edition. I am deeply indebted to the small team of content specialists who provided detailed technical feedback, helped me to revise certain areas, and served as overall consultants for individual chapters. Their contributions are largely responsible for the thoroughness of this revision.

> Denys deCatanzaro, McMaster University (Chapter 9, Motivation and Emotion)
>
> John Jahnke, Miami University (Chapter 6, Memory)
>
> Phillip S. Lasiter, Florida Atlantic University (Chapter 2, The Biological Basis of Behavior)
>
> Stephan Mayer, Oberlin College (Chapter 11, Personality)
>
> Ronald Nowaczyk, Clemson University (Chapter 12, Stress and Health Psychology)
>
> Wesley Schultz, California State University, San Marcos (Chapter 15, Social Psychology)

Let me also thank those individuals who completed user surveys and chapter reviews. Their comments and suggestions were an enormous help to me.

> Steve Arnold, Northeast Community College
>
> Susan K. Johnson, University of North Carolina, Charlotte

> Don McCoy, University of Kentucky
>
> Jerald S. Marshall, University of Central Florida
>
> Michael Ruchs, Baker College
>
> Morgan Slusher, Essex Community College
>
> Harold G. Souheaver, East Arkansas Community College

Several other people contributed in special ways to this edition and deserve recognition. My daughter, Anne Wagner, went over every chapter in the Ninth Edition comparing the text to the chapter ending material; her numerous corrections have helped to ensure that the corresponding material in this edition matches up. To Anne, my two sons Jon and Matt, and to my long-suffering wife Penny, I can't thank you enough for your support and love and understanding over the past 25 years. You really did have a father and husband—though it didn't seem like it at times! My brother, Stephen Morris, tracked down every bibliographic reference in the Ninth Edition, thus helping to ensure that our references in this edition are more complete and accurate.

Special, heartfelt thanks go to my colleague Al Maisto who joined me as co-author on this edition. Al's excellence in undergraduate teaching and his devotion to his students earned him the prestigious *Carnegie Foundation Professor of the Year* award in 1997. Al has worked tirelessly at my side for the last year, making suggestions for changes, acting as a sounding board for new ideas, absorbing the vast amount of resource material that had accumulated since the pervious edition, helping to shape the plans for revision of every chapter, and then actually sitting down and writing the initial draft of the new manuscript. I am very much in his debt, as is every reader of this edition. I look forward to a long and productive partnership and friendship in the years to come.

Al and I would also like to express our deep gratitude to the outstanding team of people at Prentice Hall, all of whom made major contributions. We are immensely grateful to Roberta Meyer who brought a new level of professionalism to this edition. Much that is good and exciting here is due to her enthusiasm and creativity. My long-time friend Bill Webber returned home to Prentice Hall as Psychology Editor after wandering afield for some years and he brought an invigorating dedication and commitment to this edition, not to mention his excellent ideas for new features. Bill's assistant, Tamsen Adams helped with many of the administrative details involved in this project. Al Maisto's graduate assistant, Sherri McKee provided invaluable help with many research tasks.

The production of the Tenth Edition was managed by Bonnie Biller and Mary Rottino, and directly supervised by Maureen Richardson, whose dedication, expertise, and quiet persistence assured an end product of very high quality, delivered on schedule! Thanks also to manufacturing buyer Tricia Kenny, and to Lisa Marie Brassini who coordinated various aspects of the ancillary program for this edition. Carole Anson did a super job on the design of both the interior and the cover, and with the help of photo researcher Barbara Salz, the tenth edition has many new and interesting photographs. Finally, special thanks to Michael Alread for directing the marketing campaign for the book.

Al Maisto would like to thank the many students whose insatiable curiosity through the years has served as his inspiration, for they have kept his love of teaching alive. He would also like to thank his colleagues at the University of North Carolina at Charlotte who served as critical sounding boards throughout the drafting of many of the chapters. In particular, the Learning chapter and the history section of Chapter 1 benefited from the comments offered by Scott Terry and George Windholtz. Discussions of feminist theory were improved by the insights of Laura Duhan Kaplan. Lynn Frasure, on several occasions, kept the Honors Program Office running smoothly so that Al could work on the book without interruption. Finally, and most importantly Al wishes to thank his wife Phyllis for her enthusiastic support of his work. In addition to offering astute comments on the manuscript, she often served as both mother and father for their children, Aaron and Rebecca. Her patience, energy, devotion, and tolerance were extraordinary. Without her love and support, Al's contribution to this book would not only not have been possible, but would have been without meaning.

Charles G. Morris
Albert A. Maisto

To the Student

GETTING THE MOST OUT OF
PSYCHOLOGY, AN INTRODUCTION

With over 600 pages of text in 15 chapters on topics from brain physiology to social psychology, this text can appear daunting, but embedded throughout are tools to help you master the material in each chapter. Before we review these features, we strongly recommend that you read two of the feature boxes.

Read These First

Throughout *Psychology, An Introduction,* you will find a series of boxes that apply concepts in psychology to real life situations. Two of these *Applying Psychology* boxes can help you to do your best in this or any other course. We urge you to read these boxes first, before you begin Chapter 1.

> *Improving Your Memory for Textbook Material,* page 249.
>
> *Coping with Stress at College,* page 485.

Study Tools

Every chapter starts with an **Overview** which is your road map to the chapter. Read through the overview to get a sense of the structure and major topics discussed in the chapter. The **Think About It!** questions are designed to stimulate thinking about the material in the chapter. These can help you organize your thoughts in advance about the material that follows. Each appears in the margin opposite the text discussion where the related issue is discussed.

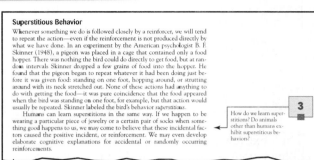

Superstitious Behavior

Whenever something we do is followed closely by a reinforcer, we will tend to repeat the action—even if the reinforcement is not produced directly by what we have done. In an experiment by the American psychologist B. F. Skinner (1948), a pigeon was placed in a cage that contained only a food hopper. There was nothing the bird could do directly to get food, but at random intervals Skinner dropped a few grains of food into the hopper. He found that the pigeon began to repeat whatever it had been doing just before it was given food: standing on one foot, hopping around, or strutting around with its neck stretched out. None of these actions had anything to do with getting the food—it was pure coincidence that the food appeared when the bird was standing on one foot, for example, but that action would usually be repeated. Skinner labeled the bird's behavior superstitious.

Humans can learn superstitions in the same way. If we happen to be wearing a particular piece of jewelry or a certain pair of socks when something good happens to us, we may come to believe that these incidental factors caused the positive incident, or reinforcement. We may even develop elaborate cognitive explanations for accidental or randomly occurring reinforcements.

> How do we learn superstitions? Do animals other than humans exhibit superstitious behaviors? **3**

As you read a chapter, a list of **key terms** and definitions appears in the margin of every page. Study these as you go along rather than waiting until you have finished reading the chapter. You will be actively learning the important concepts in each chapter as you move from section to section. Focus too on the **summary tables** which organize concepts into a manageable format. After you have read a chapter, read the **summary.** See if you can define the key terms that appear in boldface, and then test yourself by answering the **review questions.**

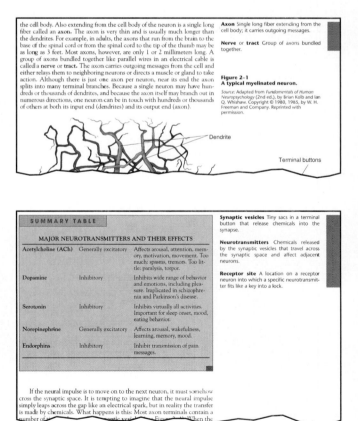

the cell body. Also extending from the cell body of the neuron is a single long fiber called an **axon.** The axon is very thin and is usually much longer than the dendrites. For example, in adults, the axons that run from the brain to the base of the spinal cord or from the spinal cord to the tip of the thumb may be as long as 3 feet. Most axons, however, are only 1 or 2 millimeters long. A group of axons bundled together like parallel wires in an electrical cable is called a **nerve** or **tract.** The axon carries outgoing messages from the cell and either relays them to neighboring neurons or directs a muscle or gland to take action. Although there is just one axon per neuron, near its end the axon splits into many terminal branches. Because a single neuron may have hundreds or thousands of dendrites, and because the axon itself may branch out in numerous directions, one neuron can be in touch with hundreds or thousands of others at both its input end (dendrites) and its output end (axon).

Axon Single long fiber extending from the cell body; it carries outgoing messages.

Nerve or **tract** Group of axons bundled together.

Figure 2–1
A typical myelinated neuron.
Source: Adapted from *Fundamentals of Human Neuropsychology* (2nd ed.), by Brian Kolb and Ian Q. Whishaw. Copyright © 1980, 1985, by W. H. Freeman and Company. Reprinted with permission.

Dendrite

Terminal buttons

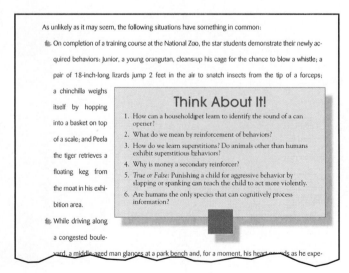

As unlikely as it may seem, the following situations have something in common:

🐾 On completion of a training course at the National Zoo, the star students demonstrate their newly acquired behaviors: Junior, a young orangutan, cleans up his cage for the chance to blow a whistle; a pair of 18-inch-long lizards jump 2 feet in the air to snatch insects from the tip of a forceps; a chinchilla weighs itself by hopping into a basket on top of a scale; and Peela the tiger retrieves a floating keg from the moat in his exhibition area.

🐾 While driving along a congested boulevard, a middle-aged man glances at a park bench and, for a moment, his heart pounds as he expe-

Think About It!

1. How can a household pet learn to identify the sound of a can opener?
2. What do we mean by reinforcement of behaviors?
3. How do we learn superstitions? Do animals other than humans exhibit superstitious behaviors?
4. Why is money a secondary reinforcer?
5. *True or False:* Punishing a child for aggressive behavior by slapping or spanking can teach the child to act more violently.
6. Are humans the only species that can cognitively process information?

SUMMARY TABLE		
MAJOR NEUROTRANSMITTERS AND THEIR EFFECTS		
Acetylcholine (ACh)	Generally excitatory	Affects arousal, attention, memory, motivation, movement. Too much: spasms, tremors. Too little: paralysis, torpor.
Dopamine	Inhibitory	Inhibits wide range of behavior and emotions, including pleasure. Implicated in schizophrenia and Parkinson's disease.
Serotonin	Inhibitory	Inhibits virtually all activities. Important for sleep onset, mood, eating behavior.
Norepinephrine	Generally excitatory	Affects arousal, wakefulness, learning, memory, mood.
Endorphins	Inhibitory	Inhibit transmission of pain messages.

Synaptic vesicles Tiny sacs in a terminal button that release chemicals into the synapse.

Neurotransmitters Chemicals released by the synaptic vesicles that travel across the synaptic space and affect adjacent neurons.

Receptor site A location on a receptor neuron into which a specific neurotransmitter fits like a key into a lock.

If the neural impulse is to move on to the next neuron, it must somehow cross the synaptic space. It is tempting to imagine that the neural impulse simply leaps across the gap like an electrical spark, but in reality the transfer is made by chemicals. What happens is this: Most axon terminals contain a number of [synaptic vesicles] (Figure 2–1). When the

The next few pages are a guide to using these tools to enhance your learning. Begin by previewing the first chapter. These techniques will help you to study any subject. Please turn to page 1.

PREVIEW THE CHAPTER Previewing prepares you to receive information in an organized way. Properly done, it will help you read faster and comprehend better. To preview a chapter, read the outline, "Think About It!", all the key terms, and the summary.

ASK QUESTIONS Then, ask yourself the "Think About It" questions as you read the chapter. This technique stimulates thinking and learning, as you actively search for answers while you read.

USE CHARTS, GRAPHS, AND PHOTOGRAPHS In every chapter, charts, graphs, and summary tables will help you to organize information, and photographs will help you visualize concepts.

STUDY IN CHUNKS Researchers have discovered that we remember the first and last things we learn far better than the material in the middle. Breaking up your studying into many short sessions creates many more beginnings and endings and it also reduces fatigue.

TAKE STUDY BREAKS Your brain needs time to process information. Taking study breaks every 20 to 40 minutes gives your brain the time it needs to process the new information. Without this time for processing, the information may disappear quickly, long before you need to recall it for an exam. Begin with short breaks of about 5-10 minutes each, adding a longer break of about 30 minutes after a couple of hours.

REVIEW OFTEN One of the earliest memory researchers, Hermann Ebbinghaus, discovered that the rate of forgetting is highest during the first hour after learning new information.

Psychology
AN INTRODUCTION
TENTH EDITION

1 The Science of

Psychology

Rey Ramos graduated from Harvard University, *magna cum laude,* and was accepted by Harvard Medical School—against all odds. Rey grew up in the South Bronx, an urban ghetto where young males are more likely to go to jail than they are to graduate from high school, and early, violent death is not uncommon. All any-one asked of Rey was that he stay out of trouble and stay alive. As a young boy, he was considered a problem child, out of control. In eighth grade, Rey's principal told his mother that her son was being ex-pelled and reassigned to a program for students with learning problems.

Think About It!

1. What are the major areas or subdivisions of psychology?
2. What is psychology?
3. What is the scientific method, and how does it apply to psychology?
4. How has psychology addressed human diversity, especially issues relating to gender, racial and ethnic, and cultural differences?
5. What methods are used by psychologists to conduct their research?
6. Is it ethical for psychologists to use people in psychological experiments without telling them? What about experiments on humans?
7. What is the difference between a psychologist and a psychiatrist?

Rey: *"My Mom just started crying, you know, in front of him, and I saw that. And I felt ashamed of myself."*

Rey entered ninth grade determined to turn his life around. His math teacher recognized his change in attitude—and his ability in math.

Math "*When he got here, I knew he wasn't joking around*
teacher: *anymore. He knew this was it. This was where it starts*
new."

Rey: "*And I started feeling good about this one teacher who*
said good things about me, and that made me feel
good."

Rey also excelled in science. But the high school he attended, considered one of the worst in New York City and since shut down, offered little. Rey enrolled in a special science program at local colleges and graduated first in his class. It was his biology teacher who first suggested to Rey that he might be "Harvard material."

Biology "*I was trying to push him to believe in himself and*
teacher: *do something, because I felt he was incredible.*"

Rey accepted the challenge. In his Harvard application he wrote, "The four years I invest in Harvard will probably be the most important four years of my life. I will waste no time while I attend Harvard University." True to his word, Rey maintained a 3.4 grade point average, enlisted in ROTC, joined a Latino fraternity, and worked part-time. At graduation, he looked back.

Rey: "*My father always said you can't change anything; destiny has everything written for you. And I told him no. I rebelled against that, and I told him I was going to make my own destiny, and so far I've never heard him say that line to me again.*"

Rey planned to marry Maiysha, his childhood sweetheart, that summer, enter Harvard Medical School in the fall, and fulfill his lifelong dream of returning to the South Bronx as a doctor.

Rey Ramos's story is the American Dream. Indeed, he was chosen to represent "The American Spirit" on *NBC Nightly News* (June 13, 1997). How did Rey Ramos escape from the "mean streets" to the Ivy League and a future as an M.D.? What can psychology tell us about his success story? About intelligence and motivation in general? About the many factors that shape who we become?

1 What are the major areas or subdivisions of psychology?

WHAT IS PSYCHOLOGY?

Psychologists are interested in every aspect of human thought and behavior (see Table 1-1). One way to grasp the breadth and depth of psychology is to look at the several major subdivisions of the field.

The Fields of Psychology

DEVELOPMENTAL PSYCHOLOGY Developmental psychologists study human mental and physical growth from the prenatal period through childhood,

TABLE 1-1

AMERICAN PSYCHOLOGICAL ASSOCIATION DIVISIONS (1996)

The two major organizations of psychologists in the United States are the American Psychological Association (APA), founded over 100 years ago, and the American Psychological Society (APS), founded in 1988. Members of both groups work in a wide variety of areas. The following list of divisions of the APA reflects the enormous diversity of the field of psychology.

DIVISION*

1. General Psychology
2. Teaching of Psychology
3. Experimental Psychology
5. Evaluation, Measurement, and Statistics
6. Behavioral Neuroscience and Comparative Psychology
7. Developmental Psychology
8. Society for Personality and Social Psychology
9. Society for the Psychological Study of Social Issues (SPSSI)
10. Psychology and the Arts
12. Clinical Psychology
13. Consulting Psychology
14. The Society for Industrial and Organizational Psychology
15. Educational Psychology
16. School Psychology
17. Counseling Psychology
18. Psychologists in Public Service
19. Military Psychology
20. Adult Development and Aging
21. Applied Experimental and Engineering Psychologists
22. Rehabilitation Psychology
23. Society for Consumer Psychology
24. Theoretical and Philosophical Psychology
25. Experimental Analysis of Behavior
26. History of Psychology
27. Society for Community Research and Action
28. Psychopharmacology and Substance Abuse
29. Psychotherapy
30. Psychological Hypnosis
31. State Psychological Association Affairs
32. Humanistic Psychology
33. Mental Retardation and Developmental Disabilities
34. Population and Environmental Psychology
35. Psychology of Women
36. Psychology of Religion
37. Child, Youth, and Family Services
38. Health Psychology
39. Psychoanalysis
40. Clinical Neuropsychology
41. American Psychology—Law Society
42. Psychologists in Independent Practice
43. Family Psychology
44. Society for the Psychological Study of Lesbian and Gay Issues
45. Society for the Psychological Study of Ethnic Minority Issues
46. Media Psychology
47. Exercise and Sport Psychology
48. Peace Psychology
49. Group Psychology and Group Psychotherapy
50. Psychology of Addictive Behaviors
51. Society for the Psychological Study of Men and Masculinity

*There are no divisions 4 or 11.

For information on a division, e-mail the APA at division@apa.org, or locate them on the Internet at http://www.apa.org/division.html.

Source: The American Psychological Association.

For a minority student from an inner-city neighborhood, adjusting to life at a predominantly white college can be stressful.

adolescence, adulthood, and old age. *Child psychologists* focus on infants and children. They are concerned with such issues as whether babies are born with distinct personalities and temperaments, how infants become attached to their parents and caretakers, the age at which sex differences in behavior emerge, and changes in the meaning and importance of friendship during childhood. *Adolescent psychologists* specialize in the teenage years, and how puberty, changes in relationships with peers and parents, and the search for identity can make this a difficult period for some young people. *Life-span psychologists* focus on the adult years, and the different ways individuals adjust to partnership and parenting, middle age, retirement, and eventually death.

Developmental psychologists would see Rey Ramos's change of direction in eighth grade in part as a reflection of his level of cognitive and emotional development. At earlier ages, the same experience would have not had the same impact. At age 3, he probably would have been frightened by his mother bursting into tears. If he had been assigned to a slow-learner class at age 8, he might have known that he'd been "bad," but he would not have understood how or why. By age 12, his ability to analyze the connection between actions and consequences was much sharper. As a young adult now, Rey seems to have a strong sense of identity and purpose; he is ready to make a commitment to his girlfriend. But development does not suddenly stop at this point. Many chapters of his life story—establishing himself in his profession, parenthood, evaluating what he has made of his life in middle age, and facing the challenges of old age—have not yet been written.

PHYSIOLOGICAL PSYCHOLOGY Physiological psychologists investigate the biological basis of human behavior, thoughts, and emotions. *Neuropsychologists* are primarily interested in the brain and the nervous system. Why can't you taste food when you have a stuffy nose? What happens when a person has a stroke? *Psychobiologists* specialize in the body's biochemistry, and how hormones, psychoactive medications (such as antidepressants), and "social drugs" (such as alcohol, marijuana, or cocaine) affect people. Do changes in hormone levels—at puberty, before menstruation, at menopause—cause mood swings? Exactly how does alcohol act on the brain? *Behavioral geneticists* investigate the impact of heredity on both normal and abnormal traits and behavior. To what degree is intelligence hereditary? what about shyness? Do illnesses such as alcoholism and depression run in families? To what extent are differences in the way men and women think, act, and respond to situations rooted in biology?

Some of the most exciting work in contemporary psychobiology concerns the effect of stress on health. We know that Rey Ramos grew up in a dangerous neighborhood; we can imagine that he faced many frustrations in his struggle to change directions as a teenager and that he had to adjust to an almost totally new environment at Harvard—all sources of stress. Will this stress eventually take a toll on his health? Research shows that some racial and ethnic groups are more vulnerable to certain conditions than others. For example, African Americans are at high risk for hypertension. Is this because of a genetic weakness (as is sickle-cell anemia, also more prevalent among African Americans); because African Americans are more likely than other groups in the United States to be poor and live in unsafe neighborhoods like Rey's; or because even middle-class African American professionals are viewed with suspicion and have direct experience of prejudice—ranging from small insults to police brutality—and so may live in a state of constant vigilance?

EXPERIMENTAL PSYCHOLOGY Experimental psychologists conduct research on basic psychological processes, including learning, memory, sensation, perception, cognition, motivation, and emotion. They are interested in answering such questions as: How do people remember, and what makes them forget? How do people make decisions and solve problems? Do men and women go about solving complex problems in different ways? Why are some people more motivated than others?

Rey Ramos apparently has a "flair for numbers" and he clearly excels at science. Experimental psychologists might be interested in discovering exactly how his style of thinking differs from that of other people. Does he process mathematical and scientific information in an unusual way? Does he perhaps have an unusually good memory for such information, and if so, how does his memory differ from yours and mine? During childhood and adolescence, Rey probably was given a number of aptitude, achievement, and intelligence tests. Do such test actually measure important cognitive skills such as the ability to make decisions and solve problems or are they more a measure of cultural knowledge? And finally, what motives drive Rey to achieve and excel?

PERSONALITY PSYCHOLOGY Personality psychologists study the differences among individuals in such traits as anxiety, sociability, self-esteem, the need for achievement, and aggressiveness. Psychologists in this field attempt to determine what causes some people to be optimists and others to be pessimists, and why some people are outgoing and sociable whereas others are more reserved. They also study whether there are consistent differences between men and women on such characteristics as amiability, anxiety, and conscientiousness.

From our brief introduction to Rey Ramos, we can infer that he is sociable: at Harvard, he made friends and deepened his relationship with his fiancé, Mayesha. He appears to have a strong need to achieve and a healthy level of self-esteem. Where did these characteristics come from? his early childhood experiences? the realization, in ninth grade, that he could take control of "his destiny"? Is he as competitive in sports as he is in academics? as self-confident in an art gallery as he is in a laboratory? If he realizes his dream, returns to the Bronx with his M.D., and spends years trying to deal with the desperate needs of his patients on the one hand, and the lack of adequate funding and up-to-date facilities on the other, will he remain an optimist? A major issue for personality psychologists is whether a given characteristic is a stable personality trait or simply a response to the social situation.

A psychologist talking with a client. About half of all psychologists specialize in clinical or counseling psychology.

CLINICAL AND COUNSELING PSYCHOLOGY When asked to describe a "psychologist," most people think of a therapist who sees patients (or "clients") in his or her office, a clinic, or a hospital. This popular view is half correct. About half of all psychologists specialize in clinical or counseling psychology. *Clinical psychologists* are interested primarily in the diagnosis, cause, and treatment of psychological disorders. *Counseling psychologists* are concerned primarily with "normal" problems of adjustment that most of us face at some point, such as choosing a career or coping with marital problems. Clinical and counseling psychologists often divide their time between treating patients and conducting research on the causes of psychological disorders and the effectiveness of different types of psychotherapy and counseling.

One of the deepest controversies in psychological treatment today pits drug therapy against psychotherapy. The development of new medications—beginning with antipsychotic drugs such as Thorazine, antianxiety drugs or tranquilizers such as Valium, and most recently antidepressive medications such as Prozac—reflects advances in our knowledge of the genetic and/or biochemical basis of many psychological disorders. No one debates that these drugs can be highly effective in relieving symptoms, especially with schizophrenia (delusions, hallucinations, disorganized speech, and extreme withdrawal) and depression (feelings of hopelessness, lethargy, difficulty thinking, and preoccupation with death or suicide). Advocates of drug therapy foresee a day when psychotherapy will become obsolete. But many others disagree. Opponents argue, first, that drug therapy addresses the symptoms of psychological disorder, but not the causes. Even if a biochemical imbalance triggered the disturbance, psychotherapy is needed to help individuals understand the events surrounding the onset and to deal with marital problems, strained family relationships, broken friendships, and disrupted work records *caused* by the disorder. Second, all medications have side effects; the more powerful the medication the more likely some individuals will have extreme reactions. Third, severely disturbed patients often stop taking medication. Conversely, patients may overrequest and doctors may overprescribe antidepressive and antianxiety medication for normal, temporary problems in living. Most mental health professionals agree that drug therapy is not a substitute for psychotherapy; rather the two work best in combination.

As a child, Rey Ramos was described as "out of control." A clinical psychologist who saw him at age 8 or 10 might have diagnosed his problem as "hyperactivity" (now called attention-deficit/hyperactivity disorder, or ADHD), a childhood disorder, seen mostly in boys, characterized by restlessness, impulsive behavior, and inability to focus on one subject or activity for very long. In the 1970s, the treatment of choice might have been the drug Ritalin, a stimulant that—paradoxically—slows down hyperactive children, apparently by increasing their powers of concentration (Barkley, 1990). Hailed as a "miracle cure" when first introduced, Ritalin soon drew criticism. Short-term use may help some children diagnosed with ADHD, but long-term use does not sustain improvements. Critics (e.g., McGuinness, 1985) ask if many children were medicated simply because they were acting like boys (and found school more restrictive than girls do), or because they had not learned middle-class concepts of proper classroom decorum.

SOCIAL PSYCHOLOGY   Social psychologists study how people influence one another. They explore such issues as first impressions and interpersonal attraction, how attitudes are formed and maintained or changed, prejudice, conformity, and whether people behave differently when they are part of a group or crowd than they would on their own.

As a teenager living in a tough, urban neighborhood, Rey Ramos no doubt experienced considerable peer pressure to become a member of a gang. Gangs seem to be an institution in poor neighborhoods. Why? Many of Rey's contemporaries probably gave in to this pressure; Rey didn't. Again, why? As a Latino at one of America's most prestigious universities, he probably encountered prejudice. Classmates may have assumed that, because he was a member of a minority, he was admitted to Harvard as part of an affirmative action program, not because of his academic achievements. The Latino fraternity Rey joined probably helped him to maintain ethnic pride in the face of such prejudice. Do ethnically based social organizations promote mutual tolerance, or do they contribute to maintaining social distance?

INDUSTRIAL AND ORGANIZATIONAL (I/O) PSYCHOLOGY   Industrial and organizational (I/O) psychologists are concerned with such practical issues as selecting and training personnel, improving productivity and working conditions, and the impact of computerization and automation on workers. Is it possible to determine in advance who will be an effective salesperson or airline pilot, and who will not? Do organizations tend to operate differently under female as opposed to male leadership? Research shows that work groups with high morale usually are more productive than those with low morale; are there specific strategies that managers can use to improve group morale?

In medical school, Rey Ramos will spend much of his time in hospitals, on rotations, as an intern, and finally as a resident. Hospitals and other large organizations frequently hire I/O psychologists as consultants to advise them on ways to increase efficiency, humanize a sterile environment, boost the morale of patients as well as staff, and so on.

Enduring Issues

Given this wide array of interests, what holds psychology together? What do psychologists who study organizations, psychological disorders, memory and cognition, behavioral genetics, or attachment in infants have in common? What distinguishes psychologists from other scientists (and nonscientists) who observe and seek to understand human beings?

In part, psychologists are drawn together by their common interest in a number of fundamental questions about behavior that cut across their areas of specialization. We identify five of these enduring issues below.

PERSON—SITUATION To what extent is behavior caused by processes that occur inside the person (such as thoughts, emotions, motives, attitudes, values, personality, and genes)? In contrast, to what extent is behavior controlled or caused or triggered by factors outside the person (such as incentives, cues in the environment, and the presence of other people)? We will encounter these questions most directly in our consideration of behavior genetics, learning, emotion and motivation, personality, and social psychology, though they will arise elsewhere as well.

HEREDITY—ENVIRONMENT For decades, psychologists have been debating the degree of influence that heredity (genetics) and environment or experience have on behavior. This is the famous "nature vs. nurture" debate. This issue appears in our discussions of behavior genetics, intelligence, development, personality, and abnormal psychology, though it will arise elsewhere as well.

STABILITY—CHANGE To what extent do people stay relatively unchanged throughout their lives? How much do we change? Can you "teach old dogs new tricks"? Is the child "father to the man"? Or is each day a new beginning with the possibility for significant change? Developmental psychologists are especially interested in these questions, though their interest is shared by psychologists who specialize in personality, adjustment, abnormal psychology, and therapy as well as other areas.

DIVERSITY Another topic of increasing interest to many psychologists is diversity—the extent to which "Every person is in certain respects (a) like all other people, (b) like some other people, (c) like no other person" (Kluckhohn & Murray, 1961, p. 53). Throughout the book we will encounter these questions: Does our understanding apply equally well to every human being? Or does it apply only to men or women, or only to particular racial or ethnic groups, or particular societies? Do we perhaps need "different psychologies" to account for the wide diversity of human behaviors?

Psychology The scientific study of behavior and mental processes.

Scientific method An approach to knowledge that relies on collecting data, generating a theory to explain the data, producing testable hypotheses based on the theory, and testing those hypotheses empirically.

"Your father's a suit, and when you grow up you'll be just a suit, too."

Mind—Body   Finally, many psychologists are fascinated by the relationship between what we experience (such as thoughts and feelings) and biological processes (such as activity in the nervous system). This mind-body issue will arise most clearly in our discussions of psychobiology, sensation and perception, altered states of consciousness, emotion and motivation, adjustment/health psychology, and disorders/therapy, though you will find it in other chapters as well.

So despite their apparent differences, psychologists are drawn together in part because of their common interest in enduring questions such as these. In addition, psychologists share a common belief that the scientific method is the most promising way to gain insight into the causes of behavior, as we will see in the next section of the chapter.

Psychology as Science

2 What is psychology?

Psychology is the science of behavior and mental processes. The key word in this definition is *science*. Although psychologists share the average person's interest in behavior and the unseen mental processes that shape it, they rely on the **scientific method** when searching out answers to psychological questions. They collect data through careful, systematic observation; attempt to explain what they have observed by developing theories; make new predictions based on those theories; and then systematically test those predictions through additional observations and experiments to determine whether they are correct. Thus, like all scientists, psychologists use the scientific method to *describe, understand, predict,* and eventually, to achieve some measure of *control* over what they study. (The scientific method is not for scientists only; see *Highlights*.)

3 What is the scientific method, and how does it apply to psychology?

Take, for example, the issue of males, females, and aggression. Some people believe that males are naturally more aggressive than females. Others contend that this is merely a stereotype, or at least that it is not always true. How would psychologists approach this issue? First, they would want

HIGHLIGHTS
CRITICAL THINKING: A FRINGE BENEFIT OF STUDYING PSYCHOLOGY

❧ Gifted children are less well adjusted than other children.

❧ Opposites attract.

❧ Subliminal messages on self-help audiotapes have beneficial effects.

Do you agree with these statements? Many people answer "yes" without a moment's hesitation on the grounds that "Everybody knows that." Critical thinkers, however, question common knowledge.

What exactly is critical thinking? It is the process of examining the information we have and then, based on this inquiry, making judgments and decisions. When we think critically, we define problems, examine evidence, analyze assumptions, consider alternatives, and ultimately find reasons to support or reject an argument. To think critically, you must adopt a certain state of mind, one characterized by objectivity, caution, a willingness to challenge other people's opinions, and—perhaps most difficult of all—a willingness to subject your own deepest beliefs to scrutiny. In other words, you must think like a scientist.

The ability to think critically is learned behavior. Many people, including quite a few introductory psychology students, view psychology as nothing more than common sense "dressed up" with fancy jargon. But in fact, psychology is based on data resulting from carefully designed research. Reading about the research in this text, some of which questions common knowledge, will sharpen your own critical thinking skills. You don't have to take our word for this (in fact, you shouldn't). Several studies of graduate students

in psychology, medicine, law, and chemistry found that psychology students improved their reasoning abilities the most during their first 2 years of study (Lehman, Lempert, & Nisbett, 1988; Nisbett et al., 1987).

Psychologists use a number of strategies in questioning assumptions and examining data. Here, we will use the rules of psychological investigation to judge whether the second statement above, "Opposites attract," is correct.

1. *Define the problem or the question you are investigating.* (Do opposites attract each other?)

2. *Suggest a theory or a reasonable explanation for the problem.* (People who are dissimilar balance each other out in a relationship.)

3. *Collect and examine all the available evidence.* In doing so, be skeptical of people's self-reports, as they may be subjectively biased. If data conflict, try to find more evidence. (Research on attraction yields no support for the idea that opposites attract, whereas many studies confirm that people of similar looks, interests, age, family background, religion, values, and attitudes seek each other out.)

4. *Analyze assumptions.* (Because balancing different people's strengths and weaknesses is a good way to form a group, it is probably a good basis for personal relationships as well, and that is why people of opposite temperaments are naturally attracted to each other. Yet research evidence shows that this assumption is false. Why

should similars attract? One important reason is that they often belong to the same social circles. Research suggests proximity is a big factor in attraction.)

5. *Avoid oversimplifying.* (Don't overlook the evidence that people of similar temperaments find living together rather difficult in some ways. For example, living with someone who is as tense as you are may be harder than living with someone of calm temperament—your opposite.)

6. *Draw conclusions carefully.* (It seems safe to conclude that, in general, opposites don't attract, but there are specific exceptions to this general rule.)

7. *Consider every alternative interpretation.* (People may cite cases that conflict with your conclusion. Remember, however, that their arguments are based on subjective observations and a far narrower database than attraction researchers have used.)

8. *Recognize the relevance of research to events and situations.* (If you have been thinking of dating someone whose temperament seems quite different from yours, you may decide, on the basis of what you now know, not to rush into things but to go more slowly, testing your own observations against your knowledge of research findings.)

By the way, psychological research has demonstrated that the other two statements are also false.

Theory Systematic explanation of a phenomenon; it organizes known facts, allows us to predict new facts, and permits us to exercise a degree of control over the phenomenon.

Hypotheses Specific, testable predictions derived from a theory.

to find out whether men and women actually differ in aggressive behavior. A number of research studies have addressed this question, and the evidence seems conclusive: Males do behave more aggressively than females, particularly when we're talking about physical aggression (Eagly & Steffen, 1986; Wright, 1994). Perhaps girls and women make nasty remarks or yell, but boys and men are far more likely to fight. Having established that there are sex differences in physical aggression, and having described those differences, the next step is to explain them. A number of explanations are possible. Physiological psychologists would probably ascribe these differences to genetics or body chemistry; developmental psychologists might look to the ways a child is taught to behave "like a boy" or "like a girl"; and social psychologists might explain the differences as a function of cultural constraints against aggressive behavior in women.

Each of these explanations stands as a **theory** about the causes of sex differences in aggression; each attempts to distill a few principles from a large number of facts. And each theory allows us to make a number of new **hypotheses,** or predictions, about the phenomenon in question—in this case, aggressive behavior. For example, if gender differences in aggression arise because males have a greater amount of the male hormone testosterone than females do, then we would predict that extremely violent men have higher levels of testosterone than do men who are generally nonviolent. If sex differences in aggression stem from early training, then we would predict that there would be fewer sex differences in aggression in families where parents did not stress gender differences. Finally, if sex differences in aggression reflect cultural constraints against aggression in women, then we would predict that removing or reducing those prohibitions would result in higher levels of aggressive behavior among women.

Each of these predictions or hypotheses can be tested through research, and the results should indicate whether one theory is better than another at accounting for known facts and predicting new facts. If one or more of the theories is supported by research evidence, it should be possible to control aggressive behavior to a greater degree than was possible before. For example, if people with higher levels of testosterone are indeed more aggressive, then, theoretically, it should be possible to make a highly aggressive person less aggressive by lowering the overall level of testosterone in that person's body.

SCIENCE VS. NONSCIENCE   Our discussion of sex differences in aggression helps to illustrate how psychology differs from various nonscientific explanations of human behavior. For example, common sense is a collection of untested cultural assumptions and sayings that cover almost any situation. Common sense holds that "opposites attract." In fact, research shows that people are attracted to people who are like themselves in characteristics they consider important, such as looks, social status, or sense of humor. Common sense holds that extremely intelligent people are social misfits and eccentrics. In fact, research shows that highly intelligent people tend to be stable, popular, and well-adjusted. As you will see, these and other findings in psychology often contradict "common sense."

Philosophy and religion deal with such important issues as ethics, human values, aesthetics, and the nature of life—issues that cannot be resolved through research, but rather are matters of faith or logic. Psychology does not seek to compete with or replace philosophy and religion. Psychologists strive to describe and explain human thought and behavior. But questions of what is right or wrong, good or evil, are value judgments, and beyond the scope of science.

Astrology, palm-reading, fortune-telling, and the like often portray themselves as "sciences," but their practices and theories are not based on evidence and research. Rather they are **pseudosciences** (or imitation sciences). There is no evidence, from the sciences of psychology or astronomy, that the movement of the stars has any impact on human behavior (Kelly & Saklofske, 1994). Nonetheless, psychologists *would* be interested in why some people believe in astrology whereas others do not, and how reading a horoscope affects a person's attitudes and behavior. For example, a psychologist might present people with different horoscopes—one saying they will meet Mr./Ms. Right this month, the other that it will be Mr./Ms. Wrong—and observe how they describe a blind date. The psychologist's goal would be to investigate the power of persuasion, not the movement of the stars.

We have seen how psychology as a social science differs from common sense, philosophy, religion and various pseudosciences. In the next section, we will see how psychology also differs from other behavioral sciences.

OTHER SOCIAL SCIENCES   Psychology is not alone in applying the scientific method to the study of behavior. Indeed, the behavioral sciences—psychology, sociology, anthropology, political science, economics, and history—are so closely related that it is often hard to tell where one ends and the next begins. For example, all of them would regard a campus protest in response to a racial incident worthy of study. And, while all of them would use the scientific method, the questions they would ask and hypotheses they would use to guide their research would differ.

A *sociologist* might ask how the behavior of crowds differs from the behavior of small groups or individuals. On the surface, demonstrations appear to be spontaneous and free form; but closer analysis shows that crowds develop and enforce their own codes for behavior, select leaders, improvise a division of labor, and so on. Far from being random, behavior in crowds is purposeful or goal-oriented, even though the crowd may seem irrational to bystanders.

An *anthropologist* might ask whether Western protests have any parallel in other types of societies. Many small, traditional societies resolve disputes through ritual combat. The "warring" parties select a time and place to meet, adorn themselves for combat, line up opposite one another, and hurl insults—and sometimes throw spears and shoot arrows—at their enemy. If someone on either side is seriously injured, however, both parties withdraw and the "war" is "called off." Similarly, demonstrators in Western societies usually announce their plans in advance, adorn themselves with symbols of their cause (t-shirts, hats, etc.), "arm" themselves with placards, line up opposite the "enemy," chant slogans, and nearly always disband if someone is badly hurt.

Political scientists, who study the distribution of power, might ask who organized the protest, whether they are allied with other groups and organizations, and whose power will be diminished if they achieve their goals. *Economists* are mainly concerned with the production, distribution, and consumption of goods and services. They might ask what the demonstrators seek to obtain and why they chose to use this means to pursue this goal. An *historian* would compare this event to past demonstrations and social movements, and ask why it is taking place here and now.

A psychologist surveying the same situation would be most interested in how individuals in the crowd behave and why they behave that way. Is their participation an expression of their political attitudes and values? Or is there some underlying motive for attending the protest (such as making friends or establishing an identity as a "rebel")? Do most of the people at this particular protest also go to other protests, and if so, why?

Pseudoscience A theory or body of knowledge that portrays itself as a science but is not based on empirical observation or is inconsistent with broader scientific theory.

The world-famous primatologist, Jane Goodall, has spent most of her adult life observing chimpanzees in their natural environment in Africa.

At one time, the boundaries between these disciplines were hard and fast. Psychologists and sociologists saw themselves as offering competing views of why human beings are as they are; historians did not exchange ideas with anthropologists; and undergraduates were required to select a single major, either political science or economics or sociology. In recent years, however, interest in interdisciplinary studies has grown, as have combined majors in the social sciences.

THE GROWTH OF PSYCHOLOGY

Psychology has a long past but a short history. Dating back to the time of Plato and Aristotle, people have wondered about human behavior and mental processes. But not until the late 1800s did they begin to apply the scientific method to questions that had puzzled philosophers for centuries. Only then did psychology come into being as a formal, scientific discipline separate from philosophy.

Charles Darwin (1809–1882) was not a psychologist. Yet more than any other individual, he was responsible for the idea that human behavior and thinking might be a subject for scientific inquiry. Before Darwin, human beings had considered themselves separate from all other creatures—occupying a special place between the angels and the beasts—and as such, above the laws of nature. Science was the study of the natural world. In contrast to planets, plants, and cells, human beings possess consciousness and exercise free will and self-determination. Hence the study of human beings belonged to the realm of philosophy and metaphysics. In the *Origin of Species* (1859) and *The Descent of Man* (1871), Darwin marshaled evidence that like all other forms of life on our planet, human beings *evolved* through a process of natural selection. If human beings are a product of evolution, maybe we too are subject to the laws of nature and therefore can be studied, analyzed, and understood scientifically.

Looking back, more than a century later, it is difficult to grasp just how radical Darwin's ideas were. Darwin developed his theory of evolution as a young man, but did not publish his "dreadful secret" for 20 years. Darwin feared—correctly, as it turned out—that he would be vilified, ridiculed, and misinterpreted. More than two decades would pass before the theory of evolution gained widespread acceptance among scientists, much less the general public. We will discuss Darwin's theory in more detail in Chapter 2, The Biological Basis of Behavior. The key point here is that he inspired a number of young thinkers to apply the scientific method to our own species, paving the way for modern psychology.

Wilhelm Wundt and Edward Bradford Titchener: Structuralism

The first formal psychological laboratory was founded in 1879 by Wilhelm Wundt, a physiologist and philosopher at the University of Leipzig in Germany. His goal was to develop techniques for uncovering the natural laws of the human mind. At the outset, Wundt did not attract much attention; only four students attended his first lecture. By the mid-1890s, however, his classes were filled to capacity.

Wundt's primary interest was perception. When we look at a banana, for example, we immediately think, "Here is a fruit, something to peel and eat." But these are associations based on past experience. All we really *see* is a long, yellow object. Wundt and his students set out to strip perception of all its associations to find the most fundamental elements, or "atoms," of thought. They trained themselves in the art of *objective introspection*, recording in minute detail their thoughts, feelings, heartbeat, and respiration rates

Wilhelm Wundt

when listening to a metronome, for example. This may sound crude today, but Wundt's insistence on measurement and experimentation marked psychology as a science from the beginning.

Perhaps the most important product of the Leipzig lab was its students, who carried the new science to universities around the world. Among them was Edward Bradford Titchener. British by birth, Titchener was appointed professor of psychology at Cornell University, a post that he held until his death in 1927.

Psychology, Titchener wrote, is the science of consciousness—"physics with the observer kept in." In physics, an hour or a mile is an exact measure. To the observer, however, an hour may seem to pass in seconds, whereas a mile may seem endless. Titchener broke consciousness down into three basic elements: physical sensations (what we see), feelings (such as liking or disliking bananas), and images (memories of other bananas). Even the most complex thoughts and feelings can be reduced to these simple elements. Titchener saw psychology's role as identifying these elements and showing how they can be combined and integrated. Because it stresses the basic units of experience and the combinations in which they occur, this school of psychology is called **structuralism.**

William James: Functionalism

William James was the first American-born psychologist. As a young man, James earned a degree in physiology and studied philosophy in his spare time, unable to decide which interested him most. In psychology he found the link between the two. In 1875, James offered a class in psychology at Harvard. He later commented that the first lecture he ever heard on the subject was his own. James held that Wundt's "atoms of experience"—pure sensations without associations—simply do not exist in real-life experience. Our minds are constantly weaving associations, revising experience, starting, stopping, jumping back and forth in time. Perceptions, emotions, and images cannot be separated, James argued; consciousness flows in a continuous stream. If we could not recognize a banana, we would have to figure out what it was each time we saw one. Mental associations allow us to benefit from previous experience. When we get up in the morning, get dressed, open a door, or walk down the street, we don't have to think about what we are doing; we act out of habit. James suggested that when we repeat something, our nervous systems are changed so that each repetition is easier than the last.

With these insights, James arrived at a **functionalist theory** of mental life and behavior. Functionalist theory goes beyond mere sensation and perception to explore how an organism learns to function in its environment.

Sigmund Freud: Psychodynamic Psychology

Sigmund Freud, unlike the other figures we have introduced, was a doctor. Although his first love was research, he also maintained a private medical practice. A neurologist by training, Freud noticed that many of his patients' nervous ailments appeared to be psychological rather than physiological in origin. He came to believe that unconscious desires and conflicts lay at the root of their symptoms. Freud's clinical discoveries led him to develop a comprehensive theory of mental life that differed radically from the views of American psychologists.

Freud held that human beings are not as rational as they imagine and that "free will" is largely an illusion. Rather, we are motivated by unconscious instincts and urges that are not available to the rational, conscious

Structuralism School of psychology that stresses the basic units of experience and the combinations in which they occur.

Functionalist theory Theory of mental life and behavior that is concerned with how an organism uses its perceptual abilities to function in its environment.

William James

Sigmund Freud

Psychodynamic theories Personality theories contending that behavior results from psychological dynamics that interact within the individual, often outside conscious awareness.

Behaviorism School of psychology that studies only observable and measurable behavior.

part of our mind. To uncover the unconscious, he developed a technique (called *psychoanalysis*) in which the patient lies on a couch, recounts dreams, and says whatever comes to mind (free association). Somewhat like an archeologist, the psychoanalyst sorts through half-remembered scenes, broken trains of thought, and the like and attempts to reconstruct the past experiences that shape the patient's present behavior. Freud held that personality develops in a series of critical stages during the first few years of life. If we successfully resolve the conflicts that we encounter at each of these stages, we can avoid psychological problems in later life. But if we become "fixated" at any one of these stages, we may carry related feelings of anxiety or exaggerated fears with us into adulthood. Freud maintained that many unconscious desires and conflicts have their roots in sexual repression. A 5-year-old boy, Freud argued, desires his mother and dreams of destroying his father, whom he sees as his rival for her affection. Yet at the same time, he loves—and fears—his father. These two feelings give rise to the "Oedipal conflict" (so named for the Greek myth in which Oedipus unknowingly murders his father and marries his mother, and becomes King). Ideally the boy is able to repress these feelings, to push them out of consciousness, but they may resurface later, for example, when he selects a marriage partner.

Freud's **psychodynamic theory** was as controversial at the turn of the century as Darwin's theory of evolution was 25 years earlier. His Victorian contemporaries were shocked, not only by his emphasis on sexuality, but also by his suggestion that we are often unaware of our true motives, and thus are not entirely in control of our thoughts, desires, and behavior. Yet Freud's lectures and writings attracted considerable attention in the United States as well as Europe; he had a profound impact on twentieth-century arts and philosophy, as well as psychology.

The view that unconscious conflicts within the individual influence much human thought and action is known today as *psychodynamic psychology*. Psychodynamic theory, as expanded and revised by Freud's colleagues and successors, laid the foundation for the study of personality and psychological disorders, and remains influential today.

John B. Watson

John B. Watson: Behaviorism

Challenging structuralist, functionalist, and psychodynamic theories, the American psychologist John B. Watson argued that the whole idea of mental life was superstition, a relic left over from the Middle Ages. In "Psychology as a Behaviorist Views It" (1913), Watson contended that you cannot define consciousness any more than you can define a soul. And if you cannot locate or measure something, it cannot be the object of scientific study. For Watson, psychology was the study of observable, measurable behavior—and nothing more.

Watson's view of psychology, known as **behaviorism,** was based on well-known experiments conducted by the Russian physiologist Ivan Pavlov. Pavlov had noticed that the dogs in his laboratory began to drool as soon as they heard their feeder coming, even before they could see their dinner. He decided to find out whether salivation, which appeared to be an automatic reflex, could be shaped by learning. He succeeded by first pairing the sound of a bell with the presence of food and then eventually ringing the bell without introducing any food. Pavlov concluded that all behavior is a learned response to some stimulus in the environment. He called this training *conditioning*.

Could the same type of conditioning be applied to people? In a famous experiment, Watson worked with "Little Albert," a secure, happy baby who had no reason to fear soft, furry white rats. Each time the child reached out to pet the rat that Watson offered him, Watson made a loud, frightening noise. Before long, Albert became terrified of white rats (Watson & Rayner, 1920). Watson came to the conclusion that an infant is a *tabula rasa* (Latin for "blank slate") on which experience may write virtually anything.

> Give me a dozen healthy infants, well-formed, and my own specialized world to bring them up in, and I'll guarantee to take any one at random and train him to become any type of specialist I might select—doctor, lawyer, artist, merchant chief and, yes, even beggar man, and thief, regardless of his talents, penchants, tendencies, abilities, vocations, and race. (Watson, 1924, p. 104)

When first published in the 1920s, Watson's orthodox scientific approach (if you cannot see it, and measure it, forget about it) found a receptive audience. Watson was also interested in showing that fears could be *eliminated* by conditioning. Mary Cover Jones (1924), one of his graduate students, successfully reconditioned a boy who showed a fear of rabbits (not caused by laboratory conditioning) to overcome this fear. Her technique, which involved presenting the rabbit at a great distance and then gradually bringing it closer while the child was eating, is similar to conditioning techniques by psychologists today.

Mary Cover Jones

B. F. Skinner: Behaviorism Revisited

B. F. Skinner became one of the leaders of the behaviorist school of psychology. Like Watson, Skinner fervently believed that psychologists should study only observable and measurable behavior (Skinner, 1938, 1987, 1989, 1990). He, too, was primarily interested in changing behavior through conditioning—and in discovering natural laws of behavior in the process. But Skinner added a new element to the behaviorist repertoire: *reinforcement.* He rewarded his subjects for behaving the way he wanted them to behave. For example, an animal (rats and pigeons were Skinner's favorite subjects) was put into a special cage and allowed to explore it. Eventually, the animal reached up and pressed a lever or pecked at a disk on the wall, whereupon a food pellet dropped into the box. Gradually, the animal learned that pressing the bar or pecking at the disk always brought food. Why did the animal learn this? Because it was reinforced, or rewarded, for doing so. Skinner thus made the animal an active agent in its own conditioning. Behaviorism dominated academic psychology in the United States well into the 1960s.

Gestalt Psychology

Meanwhile, a group of psychologists in Germany was attacking structuralism from another direction. Max Wertheimer, Wolfgang Köhler, and Kurt Koffka were all interested in perception, but particularly in certain tricks that the mind plays on itself. Why, they asked, when we are shown a series of still pictures flashed at a constant rate (for example, movies or "moving" neon signs), do the pictures seem to move? The eye *sees* only a series of still pictures. What makes us *perceive* motion?

Phenomena like these launched a new school of thought, **Gestalt psychology.** Roughly translated from German, *Gestalt* means "whole" or "form." When applied to perception, it refers to our tendency to see patterns, to distinguish an object from its background, to complete a picture from a few cues. Like William James, the Gestalt psychologists rejected the structuralists' attempt to break down perception and thought into their elements. When we look at a tree, we see just that, a tree, not a

Existential psychology School of psychology that focuses on the meaninglessness and alienation of modern life, and how these factors lead to apathy and psychological problems.

Humanistic psychology School of psychology that emphasizes nonverbal experience and altered states of consciousness as a means of realizing one's full human potential.

Cognitive psychology School of psychology devoted to the study of mental processes in the broadest sense.

Evolutionary psychology An approach to, and subfield of, psychology that is concerned with the evolutionary origins of behaviors and mental process, their adaptive value, and the purposes they continue to serve.

series of isolated leaves and branches. Gestalt psychology paved the way for the modern study of perception (see Chapter 3).

Existential and Humanistic Psychology

Existential psychology draws on the philosophy put forward in the 1940s by the French philosopher, playwright, and novelist Jean-Paul Sartre and others. Existential psychologists are concerned with the search for meaning in an indifferent or hostile world, where religion and tradition have lost the authority to define the purpose of life, leading to alienation and apathy. Psychoanalyst Rollo May, for example, held that modern Americans are lost souls—a people without myths and heroes. R. D. Laing, another existentialist, believed that we must reevaluate our attitude toward psychotic behavior: Such behavior, far from being abnormal, constitutes a reasonable, normal response to an abnormal world. Existential psychology guides people toward an inner sense of identity, which allows them to take responsibility for their actions and, in the process, to achieve freedom.

Humanistic psychology is closely related to existential psychology. Both schools insist that people must learn how to realize their human potential. But where existential psychology emphasizes restoring an inner sense of identity and willpower, humanistic psychology focuses on the possibilities of nonverbal experience, the unity of mind, altered states of consciousness, and "letting go."

The existential and humanistic viewpoints have not been widely accepted in American psychology, but they raise questions that are still relevant to explanations of personality and the treatment of psychologic disorders.

Cognitive Psychology

One of the newest fields in psychology, which began to grow in the 1960s, has also been one of the most influential. **Cognitive psychology** is the study of our mental processes in the broadest sense: thinking, feeling, learning, remembering, making decisions and judgments, and so on. Thus cognitive psychologists are especially interested in the ways in which people "process"—that is perceive, interpret, store, and retrieve—information.

In contrast to the behaviorists, cognitive psychologists believe that mental processes can and should be studied scientifically. Although we cannot observe cognitive processes directly, we can observe behavior and make inferences about the kinds of cognitive processes that underlie that behavior. For example, we can read a lengthy story to people and then observe the kinds of things that they remember from that story, the ways in which their recollections change over time, and the sorts of errors in recall they are prone to make. On the basis of systematic research of this kind, it is possible to gain insight into the cognitive processes underlying human memory.

Although relatively young, cognitive psychology has already had an enormous impact on almost every area of psychology (Sperry, 1988, 1995). Even the definition of psychology has changed. Psychology is still the study of human "behavior," but psychologists' concept of "behavior" has been expanded to include thoughts, feelings, and states of consciousness.

Evolutionary Psychology

The most recent addition to psychology is the evolutionary perspective. **Evolutionary psychology,** as the names suggests, focuses on the evolutionary origins of behavior patterns and mental processes, exploring what adaptive value they have and what functions they serve (DeKay & Buss, 1992; Wright, 1994). All of the views introduced so far seek to explain modern humans, or *Homo sapiens*; evolutionary psychologists ask how did human beings get to be the way we are? They study such diverse topics as helping others (altruism), mate selection, and jealousy. By studying such phenomena in different species, different habitats, different cultures, and different times, and by comparing males and females, evolutionary psychologists have expanded our understanding of cultural and gender differences, in particular (DeKay & Buss, 1992; Scarr, 1993). The basic principle underlying evolutionary biology and psychology is called *reproductive success*: simply put, all species are genetically "programmed" to produce offspring who successfully reproduce themselves. Biologists have identified two basic reproductive strategies: one is to produce a very large number of offspring and leave them to mature on their own, with the possibility that a few will survive (as fish and turtles do). The other is to have a small number of offspring and to protect and nurture them so that most will survive (the pattern among mammals, especially humans and their close relatives the great apes).

These basic principles help to explain jealousy, for example. People in all cultures experience jealousy. How is jealousy adaptive? Evolutionary psychologists link jealousy to reproductive success, which explains why men and women experience jealousy somewhat differently. Because men cannot be certain that they are the biological fathers of their children, they are more likely to experience jealousy regarding their partner's sexual fidelity. They are also more likely to be promiscuous, because the more liaisons they have, the more likely they will father offspring. In contrast, women, as childbearers, know for certain which children are their own. As a rule, women bear only one offspring at a time, and devote years to rearing that child. Hence, they are more likely to experience jealousy regarding the potential loss of their partner's commitment and investment in raising offspring (Daly & Wilson, 1988; Symonds, 1979, cited in DeKay & Buss, 1992).

Evolutionary psychology does not seek to replace or supplant other theories of human thought and behavior, but rather adds another dimension to our understanding (Archer, 1996). The evolutionary perspective may become increasingly important as advances in behavioral genetics add to our scientific understanding of human beings.

Multiple Perspectives of Psychology Today

For many years, psychologists clashed over the merits of the various approaches to psychology. Contemporary psychologists are less likely to advocate one theoretical perspective to the exclusion of all others (Friman et al., 1993). Rather, psychologists today tend to see them as complementary, with each approach contributing in its own way to our understanding of human behavior.

Consider the study of aggression. Psychologists no longer limit their explanations to the behavioral view (aggressive behavior is learned as a consequence of reward and punishment) or the Freudian perspective (aggression is an expression of unconscious hostility toward a parent). Instead, most contemporary psychologists trace aggression to a number of factors, including long-standing adaptations to the environment (evolutionary psychology) and the influences of culture, gender, and socioeconomic status on how people perceive and interpret events—"That guy is making fun of me" or "She's asking for it"—(cognitive psychology).

Likewise, physiological psychologists no longer limit themselves to identifying the genetic and biochemical roots of aggression, but study how heredity and the environment *interact*.

Sometimes these theoretical perspectives mesh beautifully, with each one enhancing the others; at other times adherents of one approach challenge their peers, arguing for one viewpoint over all the others. But all psychologists agree that the field advances only with the addition of new evidence to support or challenge existing theories.

Where Are the Women?

As you read the brief history of modern psychology, you may have concluded that the founders of the new discipline were all men. But did psychology really have only fathers and no mothers? If there were women pioneers, why are their names and accomplishments missing from historical accounts?

In fact, psychology has profited from the contributions of women from its beginnings. Women presented papers and joined the national professional association as soon as it was formed in 1892 (Furumoto & Scarborough, 1986). Often, however, they faced discrimination. Some colleges and universities did not grant degrees to women, professional journals were reluctant to publish their work, and teaching positions were often closed to them (O'Connell & Russo, 1990; Russo & Denmark, 1987; Stevens & Gardner, 1982).

Despite these barriers, a number of early women psychologists made important contributions, and were acknowledged by at least some of the men in the growing discipline of psychology (see *Highlights*).

The apparent absence of women from the history of psychology is only one aspect of a much bigger and more troubling concern: the relative inattention to human diversity that has characterized psychology through most of the 20th century. Only recently have psychologists looked closely at the ways in which culture, gender, race, and ethnicity can affect virtually all aspects of human behavior. In the next section of the chapter, we will begin our examination of this important topic.

HUMAN DIVERSITY

Most contemporary psychologists agree that a fuller understanding of human behavior and mental processes will result from appreciating the rich diversity in behavior and mental processes that exists within the human species.

Let us suppose you accept the foregoing argument. Still, you may ask: Why should *I* be interested in learning about human diversity? The answer is all around you. Our major cities are populated by people from diverse backgrounds, with diverse values and goals, living side by side. But proximity does not always produce harmony; sometimes it leads to aggression, prejudice, and conflict. Understanding the behavior of people from diverse backgrounds gives us the tools to reduce some of these interpersonal tensions. The differences between males and females are also important to understand. Advertisers' images of the sexes are widely accepted, yet they may have little basis in fact. For example, stereotypes about how the "typical male" looks and acts or the "accepted social roles" for females often lead to confusion and misunderstandings between the sexes. Knowing the scientific bases of human diversity will allow you to separate fact from fiction in your daily interactions with people. Moreover, once you understand how and why groups differ in their values, behaviors, approaches to the world,

HIGHLIGHTS
MISSING: WOMEN IN PSYCHOLOGY

In 1906, James McKeen Cattell published *American Men of Science,* which, despite its title, included a number of women, among them 22 female psychologists. Cattell rated three of these women as among the 1,000 most distinguished scientists in the country: Mary Whiton Calkins (1863–1930), Christine Ladd-Franklin (1847–1930), and Margaret Floy Washburn (1871–1939).

Their accomplishments were particularly impressive at a time when discrimination kept women and their work in the background. Ladd-Franklin and Calkins were admitted to all-male graduate schools only after men interceded on their behalf. Washburn transferred from Columbia to Cornell, where the opportunities for women were greater (Furumoto & Scarborough, 1986). Only Calkins and Washburn went on to have academic careers. Though both taught at distinguished schools (Calkins at Wellesley and Washburn at Wells and Vassar), neither gained a place on the faculty of a major research institution. All three grappled with the competing demands of family and career. Denied a doctorate from Harvard because of her sex—although the university's most eminent psychologist, William James, described her as his brightest student—Mary Whiton Calkins developed an influential system of self-psychology (Furumoto, 1980). She also developed a significant research tool used in the study of memory, and in 1891 she inaugurated the psychology laboratory at Wellesley College.

Unlike Calkins, Christine Ladd-Franklin received a Ph.D., but only in 1926—more than 40 years after she had completed the degree requirements—when Johns Hopkins finally lifted its restrictions against granting doctoral degrees to women.

Although women are increasing in number and influence in psychology, women's experiences as psychologists are still considerably different from those of men.

Although she developed an influential theory of color vision, Ladd-Franklin never received a permanent academic position, largely because of the prevailing prejudice against women combining a professional career with marriage and motherhood (Furumoto & Scarborough, 1986).

In contrast to Calkin and Ladd-Franklin, Margaret Floy Washburn received her Ph.D. in psychology from Cornell soon after completing her degree requirements. She subsequently taught at Wells and Vassar for 34 years. Washburn went on to write several important books, including *Movement and Mental Imagery* (1916), which anticipated current research on the role of imagery in directing thought and activity.

Today women receive over half of the Ph.D.s granted in psychology (*Chronicle of Higher Education,* 1995; Pion et al., 1996) and perform key research in all of psychology's subfields. You will find their work referred to throughout this text. Terry Amabile has studied creativity, in particular the positive effect exposure to creative role models can have on people. Karen DeValois studies color vision. Elizabeth Loftus studies memory; her work has uncovered how unreliable eyewitness accounts of a crime can be. Carol Nagy Jacklin has studied the role that parents' expectations can play in girls' (and boys') perceptions of the value of mathematics. Judith Rodin's research examines eating behavior, in particular bulimia and obesity. Eleanor Maccoby, Alice Eagly, and Jacqueline Eccles are prominent among the growing number of women and men who are studying sex differences in a variety of areas, such as emotionality, influenceability, math and verbal ability, and helping behavior. Throughout this text we will be looking at this work to see what part biology and society play in differences in the behavior of women and men.

Although women are increasing in number and influence in psychology, women's experiences as psychologists are still considerably different from those of men (Pion et al., 1996). Women graduate students tend to receive less financial support from their institutions than men do (Cohen & Gutek, 1991; Pion et al., 1996). After graduation, men are more likely to secure full-time employment in psychology and to be employed by the government and business, whereas women more often work in schools (APA 1991a; Stapp & Fulcher, 1984 cited in Cohen & Gutek, 1991). The most recent available statistics indicate that the median annual salary for male psychologists is $58,700, whereas that for female psychologists is $50,300 (National Science Foundation, 1994, cited in Pion et al., 1996). Encouragingly, salary differences are smaller among more recent graduates (Cohen & Gutek, 1991).

Gender The psychological and social meanings attached to being biologically male or female.

To understand human behavior fully, we must appreciate the rich diversity of human beings throughout the world.

4 How has psychology addressed human diversity, especially issues relating to gender, racial and ethnic, and cultural differences?

thought processes, and responses to situations, you will savor the diversity around you. Finally, the more you comprehend the extent of human diversity, the more you will appreciate the many universal features of humanity.

Throughout this book we will explore similarities and differences among *individuals* and among *groups* of people. For example, we will examine differences in personality characteristics, intelligence, and levels of motivation; we will look at similarities in biological functioning and developmental stages. We will also consider the research on males and females and members of different cultural and ethnic groups.

Gender

Male and *female* refer to one's biological makeup, the physical and genetic facts of being one sex or the other. Some people (e.g., Unger & Crawford, 1992) use the term *sex* to refer exclusively to biological differences in anatomy, genetics, or physical functioning and **gender** to refer to the psychological and social meanings attached to being biologically male or female. This distinction can be difficult to maintain, however, since we are all biological beings interacting in a social world. Because distinguishing what is biologically produced from what is socially influenced is almost impossible, in our discussion of these issues we will use the terms *sex* and *gender* interchangeably.

In contrast, the terms *masculine* and *feminine* have distinct psychological and social meanings. "Masculine" preferences, attributes, and interests are those that are typically associated with being a male in our society, whereas "feminine" preferences, attributes, and interests are those associated with

Gender stereotypes General beliefs about characteristics that are presumed to be typical of each sex.

Gender roles Behaviors that we expect each gender to engage in.

Culture The tangible goods and the values, attitudes, behaviors, and beliefs that are passed from one generation to another.

Our expectations concerning gender roles often reflect traditional gender stereotypes. What were your first reactions to these photos?

being a female. These terms are based on people's perceptions about the sexes (and indeed, about themselves) rather than on biological facts.

GENDER STEREOTYPES Many popular beliefs concerning differences between the sexes are based on **gender stereotypes:** characteristics that are assumed to be typical of each sex. For example, in most cultures, men are seen as dominant, strong, and aggressive, whereas women are viewed as affectionate, emotional, and soft-hearted (Williams & Best, 1990).

Beyond our stereotypes about what males and females "typically" are like, we have general beliefs about **gender roles,** behaviors that we expect males and females to engage in. For example, common gender roles for women in many cultures are to take care of children and family, cook meals, and do laundry. Men, on the other hand, are expected to hold a paying job, provide resources, and drive the car whenever the family goes somewhere.

Generalizations are undeniably an important "cognitive shorthand"; the point about stereotypes is that they are *over*generalizations. Habitually relying on stereotypes rather than paying attention to an individual's personal characteristics can lead to mistaken impressions, false beliefs, and misbegotten conclusions about a person. Because our stereotypes about men and women are so firmly fixed and so potentially damaging, they need to be examined scientifically. One group of psychologists has been doing exactly that. We discuss the work of feminist psychologists later in this section.

Culture

Culture refers to the tangible goods produced in a society, such as art, inventions, literature, and consumer goods. But it also refers to *intangible* processes such as shared beliefs, values, attitudes, traditions, and behaviors that are communicated from one generation to the next within a society (Barnouw, 1985). These cultural values, traditions, and beliefs in turn give rise to characteristic rules or norms that govern the behavior of people in that society, including what foods they eat, whom they may marry, and what they do on Saturday nights.

Race A subpopulation of a species, defined according to an identifiable characteristic (i.e., geographic location, skin color, hair texture, genes, facial features).

Even within a dominant culture diversity exists in the form of *subcultures*, "cultural patterns that distinguish some segment of a society's population" (Macionis, 1993, p. 75). Texans, psychology professors, persons with AIDS, African American women, homeless people, and teenagers all form subcultures within U.S. society. These subcultures have their own norms, values, and rituals, which may or may not be similar to those of the dominant culture. Moreover, many nations (such as the United States) are composed of various peoples with different backgrounds and traditions. Although we identify certain ideas, products, and behaviors as distinctly "American," we are actually a nation of great diversity—within our borders there are many well-formed subcultures of immigrants and their families. In later chapters, we discuss how cultural differences affect psychological processes, including our motivation to achieve, the way we express emotion, and a whole range of social behaviors.

Race and Ethnicity

Most people (including some psychologists) speak of Asians, Latinos, Native Americans, African Americans, Caucasians, and Pacific Islanders as distinct races, implying fundamental differences among these peoples. A **race** is usually defined as a subpopulation of a species (in this case, humans) who share some biological and genetic similarities and who have reproduced among themselves (Betancourt & López, 1993; Diamond, 1994; Macionis, 1993). Furthermore, members of different races generally have distinct physical characteristics, such as hair color or type, skin pigmentation, and facial features. At one time it might have been reasonable to talk about races as distinct groups, given the isolated geographic regions some peoples occupied and the identifiable physical characteristics they developed in adapting to those regions. Today, however, many scientists do not consider race a valid scientific concept because humans have so frequently migrated, intermarried, and commingled. Consequently, genetic characteristics that were once specific to a group of individuals in a particular region were spread widely across a much larger area. All contemporary societies are populated by people with rich genetic mixtures, so it is difficult to argue that human beings now differ substantially on a genetic basis. Furthermore, the physical characteristics that were once thought to "define" membership in a racial group are somewhat arbitrary. Race classification has often been based on melanin (the substance that produces differences in the color of skin, hair, and eyes), but humans could just as easily be classified along several other dimensions. For example, some people have a genetic resistance to malaria and others do not; some people can digest milk products and others cannot; and some people have fingerprint patterns that form spirals, whereas others have patterns that form loops and still others exhibit patterns that form arches (Diamond, 1994). We could posit any number of different "races" based on these other classification schemes.

Because it is so difficult to define "race" exactly, most psychologists have abandoned the term as a fundamental scientific concept (e.g., Dole, 1995), although racial categories are still used by social scientists and public officials for demographic purposes or for purposes of formulating public policy. (Think of the many forms you've completed that asked you to check off a box identifying yourself as a member of one racial group or another.) Race still has a role in psychology, however, because it can form an important part of a person's self-identity. Identifying with a socially or politically recognized racial group—for example, feeling strongly about oneself as an Asian American—can affect an individual's behavior, attitudes, and cognitive processes. This type of self-identification is even more apparent in the related concept of ethnicity.

Diversity can exist within a culture as well as across cultures. Here, a fan of Madonna has parked his truck near an ancient mosque in Mali, northern Africa.

Whereas race refers to an individual's biological heritage, **ethnicity** refers to a common cultural heritage that is shared by a group of people. Members of an ethnic group may have common ancestors, language, or religion or feel a kinship based on traditional social practices. For example, a person of Cuban ancestry living in Florida may share the traditions and viewpoints of her compatriots in Cuba (the ethnic group to which she belongs), all the while residing in Florida (the cultural setting where these behaviors are taking place).

What effect does ethnicity have on behavior? **Ethnic identity** refers to that aspect of one's self-concept that is based on identifying oneself as a member of a particular ethnic group. Our Cuban American friend may feel strongly about her ethnic background and build on that identification as a foundation for her overall self-concept. In turn, this view of herself can influence her choice of friends (she may seek out other Cubans), the activities she engages in (she may participate in activities associated with her ethnic group), and her cognitions about herself (seeing herself as a person who is Cuban first and a resident of the United States second). Research shows that a strong sense of ethnic identity is linked to high self-esteem (Phinney, 1996), but only when the individual also feels a positive association with the mainstream culture he or she is living in. In other words, holding a strong ethnic identity and being assimilated to the larger culture (e.g., seeing oneself as a Cuban in the United States) is a positive combination.

Psychology and Human Diversity

In recent years psychologists have taken steps to ensure that psychology reflects the richness and diversity of the human population (Phinney, 1996). To meet this end, the American Psychological Association established a number of divisions (see Table 1-1) to promote the representation and appreciation of diverse perspectives.

FEMINIST CHALLENGES Division 35, *The Psychology of Women*, was founded to promote feminist research, theories, education, and practice to improve the lives of girls and women. Psychologists who have embraced the feminist perspective have challenged many of the accepted theories of human behavior. Many feminist psychologists have argued that before the emergence of **feminist theory,** psychology reflected only a male perspective of human behavior—essentially excluding the views of half the human species (Rabinowitz & Sechzer, 1993).

As the number of female psychologists has grown so have their questions about psychological theories, research, and clinical practices (see *Highlights*). Feminist psychologists make three main points. First, much of the research supporting key psychological theories, such as moral development, was based on all-male samples. Measured against "universal male" standards, females often were found "lacking." Thus on tests of moral development, adolescent boys usually score higher than girls. The reason, as Carol Gilligan (1982) pointed out, may be that they think about moral issues in different ways: males tend to emphasize impartial rules and principles, while females are more concerned with people's feelings. Second, reports of gender differences tend to focus on the extremes, exaggerating small differences and ignoring much greater similarities (Tavris, 1992). For example, boys and girls score about the same on tests of mathematical ability (Hyde & Linn, 1988; Lumis & Stevenson, 1990). Only when one looks at mathematically gifted students do boys come out ahead. But this finding has received far more attention than the overlap in male/female ability. Third,

Ethnicity A common cultural heritage, including religion, language, and/or ancestry, that is shared by a group of individuals.

Ethnic identity That aspect of an individual's self-concept that is based on his or her awareness of being a member of a particular ethnic group.

Feminist theory Feminist theories offer a wide variety of views on the social roles of women and men, the problems and rewards of those roles, and prescriptions for changing those roles.

Sexual orientations Refers to the direction of one's sexual interest toward members of the same sex, the other sex, or both sexes.

the questions psychologists ask and the topics they study reflect what they consider to be important. Because psychology was dominated by men for so long, many issues of primary concern to women, including domestic violence, pregnancy, and childbirth, received little attention (DeAngelis, 1991a). For example, developmental psychology was long considered a "step child" of general psychology; indeed, courses in child development were usually taught in departments of home economics or education (Kessen, 1965). Not until the late 1950s and early 1960s was development recognized as an important branch of psychology. As another example, researchers have found that the rate of depression soars among adolescent girls (but not boys); this phenomenon has received very little attention from researchers.

Beyond research and theory, contemporary feminist psychology has begun to influence every facet of psychological practice by seeking mechanisms to empower women in the community, by advocating action to establish policies that advance equality and social justice, and by increasing women's representation in global leadership.

SEXUAL ORIENTATION   Division 44, "Society for the Psychological Study of Lesbian and Gay Issues," focuses psychological research on the diversity of human **sexual orientations,** that is, whether one's sexual interest is directed toward members of the same sex, the other sex, or both sexes. Psychologists have only begun to investigate the many sensitive issues associated with this dimension of human diversity—including such topics as the origins of sexual orientation (LeVay & Hamer, 1994), brain differences between heterosexual and homosexual men (Swaab & Hoffman, 1995), and the impact of allowing gays and lesbians in the military (Jones & Koshes, 1995).

ETHNIC AND MINORITY ISSUES   Division 45, *The Society for the Psychological Study of Ethnic Minority Issues,* was founded to encourage research and promote the application of psychological knowledge to our understanding of ethnic and minority issues. This increased sensitivity toward issues of ethnic minorities has enabled psychologists to develop a better appreciation for the unique challenges faced by individuals from various ethnic backgrounds. For example, research has shown that African Americans are more likely to be unnecessarily admitted to psychiatric hospitals than whites (Friedman, Paradis, & Hatch, 1994), while other research has shown that some forms of mental disorders are more prevalent among ethnic minorities (Beidel, Turner, & Trahger, 1994; Brown, Eaton, & Sussman, 1990). Although researchers have only begun to identify the psychological processes associated with ethnicity (Betancourt & Lopez, 1993), simply increasing awareness can help psychologists be more sensitive and knowledgeable in the treatment of clients from diverse ethnic backgrounds (Rogler, Cortes, & Malgady, 1991).

Unfortunately most ethnic minorities are still underrepresented among the ranks of psychologists. For example, African Americans receive only about 3% of the Ph.D.s in psychology, with a similar percentage being earned by Hispanic Americans (Smith & Davidson, 1992). To alleviate this problem, the American Psychological Association is currently examining mechanisms aimed at increasing minority representation among psychologists (*Trends in Education,* 1995).

The relatively small number of ethnic minorities in psychology has not stopped them from achieving prominence and making significant contributions to the field. Kenneth Clark, for example, a former president of the American Psychological Association, received national recognition for his important work on the effects of segregation on black children. His research was cited by the Supreme Court in the *Brown v. Board of Education* decision of 1954 that outlawed school desegregation in the United States. Over 50 years later, psychologists are still exploring the effects of racial prejudice.

Very little research has been done on differences in psychological processes from one society and culture to another, but this neglect is also beginning to be remedied. A special effort has been made in this text to address concerns about gender, sexual orientation, race, and culture, and to report on research that bears on these issues. For example, we will consider findings on the physiological effects of racism (in Chapter 12, Stress and Health Psychology); the effects of sexist language (in Chapter 7, Cognition and Language); the influence of culture on academic achievement (in Chapter 8, Intelligence and Mental Abilities); and on emotional expression (in Chapter 9, Motivation and Emotion), and how gender and culture combine to affect many aspects of development (Chapter 10, Life Span Development).

In the next section, we see how psychologists are also working to uncover and overcome biases in psychological research that are related to gender, race, and ethnicity. The field of psychology is broadening its scope to probe the full range and richness of human diversity, and this text mirrors that expansive and inclusive approach.

UNINTENDED BIASES   The gender, race, or ethnicity of the experimenter (in the past, usually a white male) may introduce subtle, unintended biases. For example, some early research concluded that women were more likely than men to conform to social pressure in the laboratory (e.g., Crutchfield, 1955). However, research now reveals no gender difference in this area when the experimenter is female (Eagly & Carli, 1981). Similarly, evidence suggests that the results of research with African American subjects may be significantly affected by the race of the experimenter (Graham, 1992). Data on race and IQ scores have been widely misinterpreted as "demonstrating" innate racial inferiority. Advocates of this view rarely note that African Americans score higher on IQ and other tests when the person administering the test is also African American (Graham, 1992). Similarly, do feminist theories, developed by and tested primarily with white, college-educated women, apply to women of color (Yoder & Kahn, 1993)?

Biases, whether intended or not, also influence clinical psychologists. As we noted earlier, African Americans are far more likely to be unnecessarily admitted to psychiatric hospitals than are whites (Friedman, Paradis, & Hatch, 1994). When health care professionals are shown identical case studies, they are more likely to diagnose alcoholism or schizophrenia if the patient is identified as black, but depression if the patient is identified as white.

The systematic reappraisal of research studies and the methods used in conducting them have caused many psychologists to question the view of the scientist as an impartial or value-free observer (Riger, 1992). Though research methods and the scientific process strive for objectivity, subjective values—whether they derive from race, gender, or cultural background—influence human behavior, whether the human in question is the designer of or the participant in research. We look now at the methods psychologists use to study human behavior.

RESEARCH METHODS IN PSYCHOLOGY

Because psychology is a science, psychologists must collect data systematically and objectively. To accomplish this, they use a variety of research

5

What methods are used by psychologists to conduct their research?

Naturalistic observation Research method involving the systematic study of animal or human behavior in natural settings rather than in the laboratory.

Observer bias Expectations or biases of the observer that might distort or influence his or her interpretation of what was actually observed.

methods, each of which has advantages and disadvantages compared to the others. In this section, we examine some of the techniques psychologists frequently use in their research, including naturalistic observation, case studies, surveys, correlational research, and experimental research.

Naturalistic Observation

Psychologists rely on **naturalistic observation** to study human or animal behavior in its natural context instead of under imposed conditions in the laboratory. One psychologist with this real-life orientation might observe behavior in a school or a factory; another might actually join a family to study the behavior of its members; still another might observe monkeys in their natural habitats instead of in cages. The primary advantage of naturalistic observation is that the behavior observed in everyday life is likely to be more natural, spontaneous, and varied than that observed in a laboratory.

For example, W. H. Whyte (1956) wanted to learn how people living in a suburban community chose their friends. By reading the social column in the local newspaper, he learned when parties were being given and who was invited to each one. After collecting such data for some time, Whyte noticed that there were definite friendship patterns in the community. *Proximity*—people's nearness to one another—seemed to be important in determining which people became friends. Whyte concluded that all things being equal, people are more likely to make friends with those who live nearby—something he could not have discovered in a laboratory.

When people are unaware that they are being watched, they behave naturally. A one-way mirror is therefore sometimes used for naturalistic observation.

Whyte restricted his observations to one specific behavior: going to parties. It is not always possible, however, to make such restrictions. Psychologists using naturalistic observation have to take behavior as it comes. They cannot suddenly yell "Freeze!" when they want to study what is going on in more detail. Nor can psychologists tell people to stop what they are doing because it is not what they are interested in researching.

Another potential problem with naturalistic observation is **observer bias.** Any police officer will tell you how unreliable eyewitnesses can be. Even psychologists who are trained observers may subtly distort what they see to make it conform to what they were hoping to see. For this reason, contemporary observational studies often use videotapes that can be analyzed and scored by researchers who do not know what the study is designed to find out. Another potential problem is that psychologists may not observe or record behavior that seems to be irrelevant. Therefore, it is sometimes preferable to rely on a team of trained observers who pool their notes. This strategy often generates a more complete picture than one observer could draw alone.

Unlike laboratory experiments that can be repeated over and over again, each natural situation is a one-time-only occurrence. Therefore, psychologists prefer not to make general statements based on information from naturalistic studies alone. They would rather test the information under controlled conditions in the laboratory before they apply it to situations other than the original one.

Despite these disadvantages, naturalistic observation is a valuable tool. After all, real-life behavior is what psychology is all about. Naturalistic observation often provides new ideas and suggests new theories, which can then be studied more systematically and in more detail in the laboratory. This method also helps researchers keep their perspective by reminding them of the larger world outside the lab.

Case Studies

Another research method, similar to naturalistic observation, is the **case study** method. A researcher using this method observes the real-life behavior of one person or just a few people at a time. Case studies helped Sigmund Freud develop his psychological theories and refine his therapeutic techniques. One of his patients was a 5-year-old boy whom he called "Little Hans" (Freud, 1909). Little Hans had a terrible fear of horses, which Freud later concluded stemmed from his fear of his father and sexual longing for his mother. This case not only confirmed Freud's suspicion that even very young children have sexual desires but also his belief that strong emotions that are pushed out of consciousness may surface in disguised form and cause psychological distress. Another famous psychologist, Jean Piaget, developed a comprehensive theory of cognitive development by carefully studying each of his three children as they grew and changed during childhood; his theory of cognitive development is described in Chapter 10, Life Span Development.

Like naturalistic observation, case studies can provide valuable insights but also have some significant drawbacks. Observer bias is as much a problem here as it is with naturalistic observation. Moreover, because each person is unique, it is impossible to know whether we can confidently draw general conclusions from a single case. Nevertheless, case studies figure prominently in psychological research. For example, the famous case of Phineas Gage, who suffered severe and unusual brain damage, led researchers to identify the front portion of the brain as important for the control of emotions and the ability to plan and carry out complex tasks (see Chapter 2). The case study of another brain-damaged patient (Milner, 1959), called "H. M.," who could remember events that preceded the injury but nothing that happened after it, prompted psychologists to suggest that we have several, distinct kinds of memory, an idea we will explore in Chapter 6.

Surveys

In some respects, surveys address some of the shortcomings of naturalistic observation and case studies. In **survey research,** a carefully selected group of people is asked a set of predetermined questions in face-to-face interviews or in questionnaires. Perhaps the most familiar surveys are the polls taken before major elections: For weeks or months before the election, we are bombarded with estimates of the percentage of people likely to vote for each candidate. But surveys are used for other purposes as well. For example, a 1991 survey determined that 61 percent of the adults questioned by telephone believed that advertisers embedded subliminal messages in their ads, and 56 percent were convinced that such messages make people buy things they do not want (Lev, 1991). (There is no scientific evidence to support these beliefs.) According to another 1991 survey, 38 percent of the American women polled said they had been "the object of sexual advances, propositions, or unwanted sexual discussions from men who supervised [them] or could affect [their] position at work" and that only 10 percent of that group

Case study Intensive description and analysis of a single individual or just a few individuals.

Survey research Research technique in which questionnaires or interviews are administered to a selected group of people.

Correlational research Research technique based on the naturally occurring relationship between two or more variables.

Two homeless men: one in Tokyo, the other in New York City. Researchers might use a correlational study to understand the conditions under which passersby are more likely to stop and help such people. The same study undertaken in both countries might reveal significant cross-cultural differences, or it might show that Japanese and Americans respond similarly to the homeless.

had reported the incident at the time (Kolbert, 1991). This survey—and others more recently—indicates that sexual harassment in the workplace is both widespread and underreported.

Surveys may generate a great deal of interesting and useful information at relatively low cost, but to be accurate, the survey questions must be unambiguous and clear, and the people surveyed must be selected with great care. Moreover, the results can be seriously distorted if people are reluctant to talk about or admit to certain feelings, beliefs, or behaviors.

Naturalistic observations, case studies, and surveys can provide a rich set of raw data that describes behaviors, beliefs, opinions, and attitudes. But these research methods are not ideal for making predictions, and they are not at all well suited to explaining, or determining, the causes of behavior.

Correlational Research

A psychologist, under contract to the Air Force, is asked to predict which applicants for a pilot training program will make good pilots. An excellent approach to solving this problem would be **correlational research.** The psychologist might select several hundred trainees, give them a variety of aptitude and personality tests, then compare the results to their performance in training school. This approach would tell him whether there is some characteristic or set of characteristics that is closely related to, or correlated with, eventual success as a pilot.

Suppose he finds that the most successful trainees score higher than the unsuccessful trainees on mechanical aptitude tests and that they are also cautious people who do not like to take unnecessary risks. The psychologist has discovered that there is a *correlation*, or relationship, between these traits and success as a pilot trainee: High scores on tests of mechanical aptitude and caution predict success as a pilot trainee. If these correlations are confirmed in new groups of trainees, then the psychologist could recommend with some confidence that the Air Force consider using these tests to select future trainees.

This psychologist has *described* a relationship between skill as a pilot and two other characteristics, and as a result he is able to use those relationships to *predict* with some accuracy which trainees will and will not become skilled pilots. But he has no basis for drawing conclusions about cause and effect. Does the tendency to shy away from risk taking make a trainee a good pilot? Or is it the other way around: Learning to be a skillful pilot makes people cautious? Or is there some unknown factor that causes people to be both cautious and capable of acquiring the different skills needed in the cockpit? Correlational data do not permit the researcher to *explain* cause and effect.

Despite limitations, correlational research often sheds light on important psychological phenomena. In this book you will come across many examples of correlational research: people who are experiencing severe stress are more prone to develop physical illnesses than people who are not; children whose parent(s) have schizophrenia are more likely to develop this disorder than are other children; and when someone needs help, the more bystanders, the less likely it is that any one of them will come forward to offer to help.

These interesting findings allow us to make some predictions, but most psychologists eventually want to move beyond simply making predictions. They want to understand the *causes* of phenomena. To explain psychological phenomena psychologists most often use experimental research.

Experimental Research

A psychology instructor notices that on Monday mornings most students in her class do not remember material as well as they do later in the week. This psychologist has discovered a correlation between the day of the week and memory for course-related material. Based on this correlation, she could predict that next Monday and every Monday after that the students in her class will not absorb material as well as on other days. But she wants to go beyond simply predicting her students' behavior; she wants to understand or explain why their memories are poorer on Mondays than on other days of the week.

Based on her own experiences and some informal interviews with students, she suspects that students stay up late on weekends and their difficulty remembering facts and ideas presented on Mondays is due to lack of sleep. This hypothesis appears to make sense, but the psychologist wants to prove that it is correct. To gather evidence that lack of sleep actually causes memory deficits, she turns to the **experimental method.**

Her first step is to pick **subjects** or **participants,** people whom she can observe to find out whether her theory is right. She decides to use student volunteers. To keep her results from being influenced by sex differences or intelligence levels, she chooses a group made up of equal numbers of men and women who scored between 520 and 550 on the verbal section of their College Boards.

Next, she designs a memory task. She needs something that none of her participants will know in advance. If she chooses a chapter in a history book, for example, she runs the risk that some of her participants will be history buffs. Given the various possibilities, the psychologist decides to print a page of geometric shapes, each labeled with a nonsense word. Circles are "glucks," triangles, "rogs," and so on. She will give the students half an hour to learn the names, then take them away and ask them to assign those same labels to geometric shapes on a new page.

The psychologist also needs to know which participants are sleep-deprived. Simply asking people whether they have slept well is not ideal: Some may say "no" so they will have an excuse for doing poorly on the test, others may say "yes" because they do not want a psychologist to think they are so unstable they cannot sleep. And two people who both say they "slept well" may not mean the same thing by that phrase. So the psychologist decides to intervene—that is, to control the situation more closely. Everyone in the experiment, she decides, will spend the night in the same dormitory. They will be kept awake until 4:00 A.M., and then they will be awakened at 7:00 A.M. sharp. She and her colleagues will patrol the halls to make sure that no one falls asleep ahead of schedule. By *manipulating* the amount of time the subjects sleep, the psychologist is introducing and controlling an essential element of the experimental method: an **independent variable.** The psychologist believes that the students' ability to learn and remember labels for geometric shapes will depend on their having had a good night's sleep. Performance on the memory task (the number of correct answers) thus becomes the **dependent variable.** According to the hypothesis, changing the independent variable (the amount of sleep) should also change the dependent variable (performance on the memory task). Her prediction is that this group of subjects, who get no more than 3 hours of sleep, should do quite poorly on the memory test.

At this point, the experimenter begins looking for loopholes in her experimental design. How can she be sure that poor test results mean that the participants did less well than they would have done had they had more sleep? For example, their poor performance could be the result simply of knowing that they were being closely observed. To be sure that her

Experimental method A research technique in which an investigator deliberately manipulates selected events or circumstances and then measures the effects of those manipulations on subsequent behavior.

Subjects or participants Individuals whose reactions or responses are observed in an experiment.

Independent variable In an experiment, the variable that is manipulated to test its effects on the other, dependent variables.

Dependent variable In an experiment, the variable that is measured to see how it is changed by manipulations in the independent variable.

Experimental group In a controlled experiment, the group subjected to a change in the independent variable.

Control group In a controlled experiment, the group not subjected to a change in the independent variable; used for comparison with the experimental group.

Experimenter bias Expectations by the experimenter that might influence the results of an experiment or its interpretation.

experiment measures only the effects of inadequate sleep, the experimenter creates two groups, containing equal numbers of males and females of the same ages and with the same College Board scores. One of the groups, the **experimental group,** will be kept awake, as described, until 4:00 A.M. That is, they will be subjected to the experimenter's manipulation of the independent variable—amount of sleep. Members of the other group, the **control group,** will be allowed to go to sleep whenever they please. If the only consistent difference between the two groups is the amount of sleep they get, the experimenter can be much more confident that if the groups differ in their test performance, the difference is due to the length of time they slept the night before.

Finally, the psychologist questions her own objectivity. Because she believes that lack of sleep inhibits students' learning and memory, she does not want to prejudice the results of her experiment; that is, she wants to avoid **experimenter bias.** So she decides to ask a neutral person, someone who does not know which subjects did or did not sleep all night, to score the tests.

The experimental method is a powerful tool, but it too has limitations. First, many intriguing psychological variables, such as love, hatred, or grief, do not readily lend themselves to experimental manipulation. And even if it were possible to induce such strong emotions as part of a psychological experiment, this would raise serious ethical questions. In some cases, psychologists may use animals rather than humans for experiments. For example, an experimenter might study the effects on infant monkeys of separation from their mothers (Harlow, 1958). But some subjects, such as the emergence of language in children or the expression of emotions, cannot be studied with other species. Second, because experiments are conducted in an artificial setting, participants—whether human or nonhuman animals—may behave differently than they would in real life.

Multimethod Research

Each of the research methods we have discussed has both advantages and disadvantages. Therefore, most psychologists use several methods to study a single problem. For example, someone interested in studying creativity might begin her research by giving a group of college students a creativity test that she invented to measure their capacity to discover or produce something new. Next she would compare the students' scores with their scores on intelligence tests and with their grades to see if there is a *correlation* between them. Then she would spend several weeks *observing* a college class and *interviewing* teachers, students, and parents to correlate classroom behavior and the adults' evaluations with the students' scores on the creativity test. She would go on to test some of her ideas with an *experiment* using a group of students as subjects. Finally, her findings might prompt her to revise the test, or they might give the teachers and parents new insight into particular students.

Interestingly, there are some indications that male and female researchers have somewhat different preferences in their choice of research methods (Moses, 1991). Many women researchers report that they feel uncomfortable conducting laboratory experiments that isolate psychological processes and study them out of their natural context. Moreover, some issues of special interest to many female psychologists—rape, incest, sexual abuse, domestic violence—cannot be studied effectively in a laboratory; they are best understood in context. Thus, traditionally, many female researchers have been drawn more to naturalistic observation, case study, and correlational research methods than to laboratory experiments.

BASIC METHODS OF RESEARCH

Research Method	Advantages	Limitations
Naturalistic Observation		
Behavior is observed in the environment in which it occurs naturally.	Provides a great deal of firsthand behavioral information that is more likely to be accurate than reports after the fact. The subject's behavior is more natural, spontaneous, and varied than behaviors taking place in the laboratory. A rich source of hypotheses as well.	The presence of an observer may alter the participants' behavior; the observer's recording of the behavior may reflect a preexisting bias; and it is often unclear whether the observations can be generalized to other settings and other subjects.
Case Studies		
Behavior of one person or a few people is studied in depth.	Yields a great deal of detailed descriptive information. Useful for forming hypotheses.	The case(s) studied may not be a representative sample. Can be time-consuming and expensive. Observer bias is a potential problem.
Surveys		
A large number of participants are asked a standard set of questions.	Enables an immense amount of data to be gathered quickly and inexpensively.	Sampling biases can skew results. Poorly constructed questions can result in answers that are ambiguous, so data are not clear. Accuracy depends on ability and willingness of participants to answer questions accurately.
Correlational Research		
Employs statistical methods to examine the relationship between two or more variables.	May clarify relationships between variables that cannot be examined by other research methods. Allows prediction of behavior.	Does not permit researchers to draw conclusions regarding cause-and-effect relationships.
Experimental Research		
One or more variables are systematically manipulated, and the effect of that manipulation on other variables is studied.	Strict control of variables offers researchers the opportunity to draw conclusions about cause-and-effect relationships.	The artificiality of the lab setting may influence subjects' behavior; unexpected and uncontrolled variables may confound results; many variables cannot be controlled and manipulated.

The Importance of Sampling

One obvious drawback to *every* form of research is that it is usually impossible, or at least impractical, to measure every single occurrence of a characteristic. No one could expect to measure the memory of every human being, to study the responses of all individuals who suffer from phobias (irrational fears), or to record the maternal behavior of all female monkeys. No matter what research method is used, whenever researchers conduct a study, they examine only a relatively small number of people or animals of the population they seek to understand. In other words, researchers almost

Sample Selection of cases from a larger population.

Random sample Sample in which each potential participant has an equal chance of being selected.

Representative sample Sample carefully chosen so that the characteristics of the participants correspond closely to the characteristics of the larger population.

always study a small **sample** and then use the results of that limited study to generalize about larger populations. For example, the psychologist who was trying to predict success in pilot training assumed that the trainees he was studying were representative of future groups of trainees. The psychology instructor who studied the effect of lack of sleep on memory assumed that her results would apply to other students in her classes (past and future), as well as to students in other classes and at other colleges.

How realistic are these assumptions? How confident can researchers be that the results of research conducted on a relatively small sample of people apply to the much larger population from which the sample was drawn? A classic example of faulty generalization occurred during the 1948 presidential election. The morning after the election, newspaper headlines proclaimed Thomas E. Dewey the winner. In fact, Harry S Truman had been elected. What happened? These headlines were based, not on election results, but on a telephone survey of voters. At that time, telephones were a luxury; as a result, the sample was biased toward wealthy voters. The majority of voters, who did not own telephones, had voted overwhelmingly for Truman. This famous blunder has become a beacon—a flashing yellow light—warning researchers to avoid biased samples and faulty generalizations.

Social scientists have developed several techniques to deal with sampling error. One is to select subjects at random from the larger population. For example, the researcher studying pilot trainees might begin with an alphabetical list of all trainees and then select every third

A classic case of biased sampling: An exuberant Harry S Truman holds a newspaper that mistakenly announced a victory by Thomas Dewey over Truman in the 1948 presidential election.

name or every fifth name on the list to be in his study. These participants would constitute a **random sample** from the larger group of trainees because at the outset every trainee had an equal chance of being chosen for the study.

Another way to make sure that conclusions apply to the larger population is to pick a **representative sample** of the population being studied. For example, researchers looking for a representative cross-section of Americans would want to ensure that the proportion of males and females in the study matched the national proportion, that the number of participants from each state matched the national population distribution, and so on.

Even with these precautions, however, unintended bias may influence psychological research. This issue has received a great deal of attention recently, particularly in relation to women and African Americans, as discussed below (e.g., Denmark, 1994; Gannon et al., 1992; Graham, 1992; Riger, 1992).

Human Diversity and Research

Historically, most psychological researchers have been white American males, and most subjects used in psychological research have been white

American male college students. For decades, hardly anyone thought about the underlying assumption that the results of these studies would also apply to women, to people of other racial and ethnic groups, and to people of different cultures. Psychologists have now begun to question that assumption explicitly. Are women more likely to help a person in distress than men are? Are African Americans more vulnerable to certain types of mental illness than white people, and vice versa? Do the Japanese view children's ability to learn in the same way Americans do?

Research indicates that the answer to such questions often is "no"; people's gender, race, ethnic background, and culture often have a profound effect on their behavior. Research has found consistent cultural differences in aggression (Triandis, 1994), memory (Mistry & Rogoff, 1994), some forms of nonverbal communication (Johnson, Ekman, & Friesen, 1975), and other behaviors. Similarly, men and women display differences in a variety of traits including aggression (Eagly & Steffen, 1986) and their skill at perceiving or reading another person's expressions of emotion (Hall, 1984).

AVOIDING CULTURAL BIAS.   A major concern for clinical psychologists is how to avoid cultural bias in diagnosing mental disorders. Behavior that is considered abnormal in one culture may be considered normal in others. A woman tells a psychologist she was up all night caring for her second baby by her spirit husband. (Her children are grown and there is no baby in her home.) Is this woman hallucinating? If she were American, or French, or Japanese, a psychologist would conclude she was. In the Saora tribe of India, however, people take for granted that some women are wooed, wed, and impregnated by supernatural lovers (Elwin, 1955). Suckled at night, the children are never seen. In her own culture this woman may be no more "mentally ill" than we are in our culture for believing that germs, which we never see, cause disease.

The most recent edition of the American Psychiatric Association's *Diagnostic and Statistical Manual of Mental Disorders*, the *DSM-IV*, addresses the issue of cultural bias. A "Glossary of Culture-Bound Syndromes" identifies behavior that is considered normal in other cultural contexts, such as "ghost sickness" in many Native American tribes and "the evil eye" in Mediterranean cultures. The diagnosis of schizophrenia includes a warning that "in some cultures, visual or auditory hallucinations with a religious content may be a normal part of religious experience (e.g., seeing the Virgin Mary or hearing God's voice)" (American Psychiatric Association, 1994, p. 847), and should not automatically be treated as symptoms.

ETHICS AND PSYCHOLOGY

Almost all psychological research involves people—often college students—or live animals. What responsibilities do psychologists have toward their human and nonhuman animal research subjects?

Ethics in Research on Humans

If the school you attend has a research facility, it is likely that you will have a chance to become a subject in an experiment in your psychology department. You will probably be offered a small sum of money or class credit to participate. But you may not learn the true purpose of the experiment until after it's over. Is this deception necessary to the success of psychology experiments? And what if the experiment causes you discomfort? Before

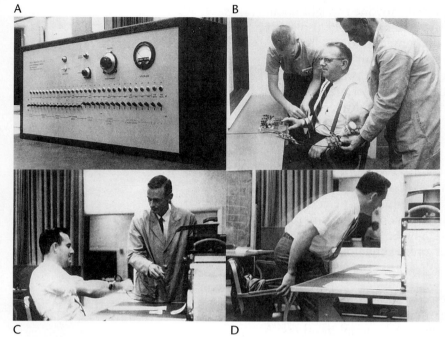

A

B

C

D

Stanley Milgram's Obedience Experiment. (A) The shock generator used in the experiment. (B) With electrodes attached to his wrists, the learner provides answers by pressing switches that light up on an answer box. (C) The subject administers a shock to the learner. (D) The subject breaks off the experiment. Milgram's study yielded interesting results, but it also raised serious questions about the ethics of such experimentation.

answering, consider the ethical debate that flared up in 1963 when Stanley Milgram published the results of several experiments he had conducted.

Milgram hired people to participate in what he said was a learning experiment. When a subject arrived at the laboratory, he was met by a stern-faced researcher in a lab coat; another man in street clothes was sitting in the waiting room. The researcher explained that he was studying the effects of punishment on learning. When the two men drew slips out of the hat, the subject's slips said "teacher." The teacher watched as the "learner" was strapped into a chair and an electrode attached to his wrist. Then the teacher was taken into an adjacent room and seated at an impressive looking "shock generator" with switches from 15 to 450 volts, labeled "Slight Shock," "Very Strong Shock" up to "Danger: Severe Shock" and finally "**XXX**." The teacher's job was to read a list of paired words, which the learner would attempt to memorize and repeat. The teacher was instructed to deliver a shock whenever the learner gave a wrong answer and to increase the intensity of the shock each time the learner made a mistake. At 90 volts, the learner began to grunt; at 120 volts, he shouted "Hey, this really hurts!"; at 150 volts he demanded to be released; at 270 volts his protests became screams of agony. Beyond 330 volts, the learner appeared to pass out. If the teacher became concerned and asked if he could stop, the experimenter politely but firmly replied that he was expected to continue, that this experiment was being conducted in the interests of science.

In reality, Milgram was studying obedience, not learning. He wanted to find out whether ordinary people would obey orders to cause another person pain. As part of his research, Milgram (1974) described the experiment to 110 psychiatrists, college students, and middle-class adults and asked them at what point they thought subjects would stop. Members of all three groups guessed that most people would refuse to continue beyond 130 volts, and no one would go beyond 300 volts. The psychiatrists estimated that only one in a thousand people would continue to the **XXX** shock panel. Astonishingly, 65 percent of Milgram's subjects administered the highest level of shock, even though many worried aloud that the shocks might be causing the learners serious damage.

To find out what he wanted to know, Milgram had to deceive his subjects. The stated purpose of the experiment—to test learning—was a lie. The "learners" were Milgram's accomplices, who had been trained to act as though they were being hurt; the machines were fake; and the learners received no shocks at all (Milgram, 1963). But, critics argued, the "teachers"—the real subjects of the study—were hurt. Most not only voiced concern, but showed clear signs of stress: they sweated, bit their lips, trembled, stuttered, or in a few cases broke into uncontrollable nervous laughter. Critics also worried about the effect of the experiment on the subjects' self-esteem. How would you like to be compared to the people who ran the death camps in Nazi Germany (60 *Minutes*, 1979)?

Although the design of this experiment was not typical of the vast majority of psychological experiments, it sparked such a public uproar that the

American Psychological Association (APA) reassessed its ethical guidelines, first published in 1953 (APA, 1953). A new code of ethics on psychological experimentation was approved. The code is assessed each year and periodically revised to ensure that it adequately protects subjects in research studies. In addition to outlining the ethical principles guiding research and teaching, the code spells out a set of ethical standards for psychologists who offer therapy and other professional services, such as psychological testing (see Chapter 14).

The APA code of ethics requires that researchers obtain informed consent from participants and stipulates that:

Is it ethical for psychologists to use people in psychological experiments without telling them? What about experiments on nonhuman animals?

- 🐾 Subjects must be informed of the nature of research in clearly understandable language.

- 🐾 Informed consent must be documented.

- 🐾 Risks, possible adverse effects, and limitations on confidentiality must be spelled out in advance.

- 🐾 If participation is a condition of course credit, equitable alternative activities must be offered.

- 🐾 Subjects cannot be deceived about aspects of the research that would affect their willingness to participate, such as risks or unpleasant emotional experiences.

- 🐾 Deception about the goals of the research can be used only when absolutely necessary to the integrity of the research.

In addition, psychological researchers are required to follow the government's Code of Federal Regulations, which includes an extensive set of regulations concerning the protection of human subjects in all kinds of research. Failure to abide by these federal regulations may result in the termination of federal funding for the researcher and penalties for the research institution.

Despite these formal ethical and legal guidelines, controversy still rages about the ethics of psychological research on humans. Some people contend that research procedures should never be emotionally or physically distressing (Baumrind, 1985). Others assert that ethical guidelines that are too strict may undermine the scientific value of research or cripple future research (Gergen, 1973; Sears, 1994). Still others maintain that psychology, as a science, should base its ethical code on documented evidence about the effects of research procedures on subjects, not on conjecture about what is "probably" a good way to conduct research (Holmes, 1976b; Trice, 1986). Still another view is that the explanations necessary to produce informed consent may foster a better understanding of the goals and methods of research (Blanck et al., 1992).

The use of animals in laboratory research has become highly controversial.

Ethics in Research on Nonhuman Animals

In the last section we looked at ethical issues related to research involving human beings. In recent years, questions have been raised about the ethics of using nonhuman animals in psychological research (Herzog, 1995; Plous, 1996; Rowan & Shapiro, 1996; Shapiro, 1991).

Psychologists study animal behavior in order to shed light on human behavior. Crowding mice into small cages, for example, has yielded valuable insights into the effects of overcrowding on humans. Animals are used in experiments where it would be clearly unethical to use human subjects, such as studies involving brain lesions (requiring cutting into the brain) or electric stimulation of parts of the brain. In fact, much of what we know about sensation, perception, drugs, emotional attachment, and the neural basis of behavior is derived from animal research (Domjan & Purdy, 1995). Yet animal protectionists and others question whether it is ethical to use nonhuman animals, that cannot give their consent to serve as subjects, in psychological research.

At the heart of this debate is the pain and suffering that some experiments can cause animals. A number of animal-rights groups, including Psychologists for the Ethical Treatment of Animals (PsyETA), are urging legislators to place stricter limits on experimentation with animals on the grounds that it is inhumane (Shapiro, 1991). Their opponents contend that the goals of scientific research—in essence, to reduce or eliminate human suffering—justify the means, even though they agree that animals should be made to suffer as little as possible (Gallistel, 1981; Novak, 1991). They argue that procedures now in place, including the use of anesthesia in many experiments, already minimize animal suffering.

What is the public's attitude toward the use of animals in research? Not surprisingly, vegetarians oppose animal research more strongly than do people who eat meat. People who are highly skeptical toward science are also more likely to oppose animal research than are people who have great faith in science (Skrzycki, 1995). In addition, females tend to oppose animal research more than males do (Broida et al., 1993). How do psychologists themselves feel about this issue? Results from a national survey showed that the majority of psychologists support animal studies involving observation and confinement but generally disapprove of animal studies involving pain or death (Plous, 1996).

The APA has addressed this issue in its ethical guidelines, noting that psychologists using animals in research must ensure "appropriate consideration of [the animal's] comfort, health, and humane treatment." Under these guidelines, animals may not be subjected to "pain, stress, or privation" when an alternative procedure is available (APA, 1992). Significantly, the National Institute of Health (NIH), which opposes animal protectionists' views and funds about 40 percent of biomedical research in the United States, has instituted more stringent policies governing animal research. A project cannot receive NIH funding unless it has been sanctioned by an animal-research committee. This committee must include someone not affiliated with the institution conducting the research, as well as the research institutions' attending veterinarian and a scientist experienced in laboratory animal medicine. Nevertheless, opponents still argue that the only ethical research on nonhuman animals is naturalistic observation such as Jane Goodall's ongoing study of the chimpanzees at Gombe Stream (1986) or Roger Fout's study of communication among chimpanzees who have learned sign language (Fouts, Fouts, & Schoenfeld, 1974).

CAREERS IN PSYCHOLOGY

Some readers may be studying psychology out of general interest; others may be considering careers in psychology. What kinds of careers are open to psychology graduates? People holding bachelor's degrees in psychology may find jobs assisting psychologists in mental-health centers, vocational rehabilitation, and correctional centers. They may also take positions as research assistants, teach psychology in high school, or land jobs as trainees in government or business.

Community college graduates with associates degrees in psychology are well qualified for paraprofessional positions in state hospitals, mental-health centers, and other human-service settings. Job responsibilities may include screening and evaluating new patients, record keeping, and assisting in consultation sessions.

Many careers outside psychology draw on a person's knowledge of psychology without requiring postgraduate study. For example, personnel administrators deal with employee relations; vocational rehabilitation counselors help people with disabilities find employment; directors of volunteer services recruit and train volunteers; probation officers work with parolees; and day-care-center supervisors oversee the care of preschool children of working parents. Indeed, employers in areas such as business and finance seek out psychology majors because of their knowledge of the principles of human behavior and their skills in experimental design and data collection and analysis.

About one-third of psychologists work in colleges and universities. Here, Al Maisto, co-author of this text, talks with a student at the University of North Carolina, Charlotte.

Academic and Applied Psychology

For those who pursue advanced degrees in psychology—a master's degree or doctorate—career opportunities span a wide range. Many doctoral psychologists join the faculties of colleges and universities. Others work in applied settings such as school, health, industrial, commercial, and educational psychology. Nearly half of doctoral psychologists are clinicians or counselors who treat people experiencing mental, emotional, or adaptational problems. Master's graduates in psychology often work as researchers, collecting and analyzing data, at universities, in government, or for private companies. Others work in health, industry, and education. APA standards require that master's graduates who work in clinical, counseling, school, or testing and measurement settings be supervised by a doctoral-level psychologist.

Clinical Settings

Many students who major in psychology want to become therapists. For these students, there are five main career paths. A *psychiatrist* is a medical doctor who, in addition to 4 years of medical training, has completed 3 years of residency training in psychiatry, most of which is spent in supervised clinical practice. Psychiatrists specialize in the diagnosis and treatment of abnormal behavior. They are the only mental health professionals who are licensed to prescribe medications, in addition to providing psychotherapy. A *psychoanalyst* is a psychiatrist (or psychologist) who has received additional specialized training in psychoanalytic theory and practice, usually at a psychoanalytic institute that requires him or her to undergo psychoanalysis before practicing.

Clinical psychologists assess and treat mental, emotional, and behavioral disorders, ranging from short-term crises to chronic disorders such as schizophrenia. They hold advanced degrees in psychology (a Ph.D. or Psy.D.)—the result of a 4 to 6 year graduate program, plus a one-year internship in psychological assessment and psychotherapy and at least one more year of supervised practice. *Counseling psychologists* help people to cope with situational problems such as adjusting to college, vocational guidance, marital problems, or coping with the death of a loved one.

Finally, *social workers* may also offer treatment for psychological problems. Typically they have a master's degree (M.S.W.) or doctorate (D.S.W.). Social workers often work under psychiatrists or clinical psychologists, though in some states they may be licensed to practice independently.

7 What is the difference between a psychologist and a psychiatrist?

Surveys

Survey research generates a large amount of data quickly and inexpensively by asking a standard set of questions of a large number of people. Great care must be taken, however, in how the questions are worded.

Correlational Research

Correlational research is used to investigate the relation, or *correlation*, between two or more variables. Correlational research is useful for clarifying relationships between preexisting variables that can't be examined by other means.

Experimental Research

In the **experimental method** one variable (the **independent variable**) is systematically manipulated and the effects on another variable (the **dependent variable**) are studied, usually using both an **experimental group** of **subjects** (participants) and a **control group** for comparison purposes. By holding all other variables constant, the researcher can draw conclusions about cause and effect. Often a neutral person is used to record data and score results, so **experimenter bias** doesn't distort the findings.

Multimethod Research

Since each research method has benefits as well as limitations, many psychologists use multiple methods to study a single problem. Together they can give much fuller answers to questions.

The Importance of Sampling

Regardless of the particular research method used, psychologists almost always study a small **sample** of subjects and then generalize their results to larger populations. **Random samples,** in which subjects are chosen randomly, and **representative samples,** in which subjects are chosen to reflect the general characteristics of the population as a whole, are two ways of ensuring that results have broader application.

Human Diversity and Research

Because of differences among people based on age, sex, ethnic background, culture, and so forth, findings from studies that use white, male, American college students as subjects cannot always be generalized to other groups. In addition, the gender, race, and ethnic background of a researcher can have a biasing impact on the outcome of his or her research.

ETHICS AND PSYCHOLOGY

The American Psychological Association (APA) has a code of ethics for conducting research involving human or animal subjects. Still, controversy over ethical guidelines continues, with some thinking they are too strict and impede psychological research, and others thinking they are not strict enough to protect subjects from harm.

Ethics in Research on Humans

A key part of the APA code regarding research on humans is the requirement that researchers obtain informed consent from participants in their studies. Subjects must be told in advance about the nature of the research and the possible risks involved. People should not feel pressured to participate if they do not want to.

Ethics in Research on Nonhuman Animals

Although much of what we know about certain areas of psychology has come from animal research, the practice of experimenting on animals has strong opponents. APA and federal guidelines govern the humane treatment of laboratory animals, but animal rights advocates argue that the only ethical research on animals is naturalistic observation.

CAREERS IN PSYCHOLOGY

Psychology is one of the most popular majors in colleges and universities. A background in it is useful in a wide number of fields because so many jobs involve a basic understanding of people.

Academic and Applied Psychology

Careers for those with advanced degrees in psychology include both academic and applied work. They include teaching, research, jobs in government and private business, and a number of occupations in the mental health field.

Clinical Settings

Opportunities in the mental health field depend on one's degree of training. They include the occupations of psychiatrist and psychoanalyst, the job of clinical psychologist, which involves getting a doctoral degree, and the jobs of counseling psychologist and social worker.

REVIEW QUESTIONS

MULTIPLE CHOICE AND SHORT ANSWER

1. Match each of the following subdivisions of psychology with its appropriate description.

_____ Clinical/counseling psychology   a. Studies how people influence one another's thinking and behavior

_____ Social psychology   b. Concerned with such practical issues as selecting and training personnel and improving productivity

_____ Industrial/organizational psychology   c. Concerned with treating psychological disorders and problems of adjustment

_____ Developmental psychology   d. Studies the biological basis of human behavior, thought, and emotion

_____ Physiological psychology   e. Studies the differences among people in traits such as anxiety, sociability, and aggression

_____ Experimental psychology   f. Studies human mental, physical, and social/emotional growth

_____ Personality psychology   g. Conducts research on basic psychological processes such as learning, memory, perception, and emotion

2. Match each of the following enduring issues in psychology with its appropriate description.

_____ Person–Situation   a. How much do we stay the same as we develop and how much do we change?

_____ Heredity–Environment   b. In what ways do people differ in how they think and act?

_____ Stability–Change   c. What is the relationship between our internal experiences and our biological processes?

_____ Diversity   d. Is behavior caused more by inner traits or by external situations?

_____ Mind–Body   e. How do genes and experiences interact to influence people?

3. Indicate which of the following help to make psychology a science.

_____ a. Psychologists collect data through careful, systematic observation.

_____ b. Psychologists try to explain their observations by developing theories.

_____ c. Psychologists form hypotheses or predictions based on theories.

_____ d. Psychologists appeal to common sense in their arguments.

_____ e. Psychologists systematically test hypotheses.

_____ f. Psychologists base their conclusions on widely shared values.

4. It was not until the late _____ that psychology came into its own as a separate discipline.

5. Match each of the following schools of thought in psychology with its appropriate description.

_____ Structuralism   a. Explores the origins of human behavior and establishes links to the behavior of other animals

_____ Functionalism   b. Stresses the whole character of perception

_____ Behaviorism   c. Concerned with alienation in modern life and resulting psychological problems

_____ Psychodynamic psychology   d. Studies only observable and measurable behavior

_____ Existential psychology   e. Stresses the basic elements of experience and how they combine

_____ Humanistic psychology

_____ Gestalt psychology

_____ Cognitive psychology

_____ Evolutionary psychology

f. Emphasizes the realization of one's potential

g. Studies mental processes in the broadest sense

h. Maintains that hidden motives and unconscious desires govern much of our behavior

i. Concerned with how an organism uses its perceptual abilities to function in its environment

6. Match each of the following famous psychologists with the appropriate accomplishment.

_____ Wilhelm Wundt

_____ William James

_____ Sigmund Freud

_____ John B. Watson

_____ B. F. Skinner

a. Developed psychoanalysis and explored unconscious conflicts

b. An early psychologist at Harvard who developed a functionalist theory

c. Established the first psychological laboratory

d. Extensively studied the effects of rewards on behavior

e. Used conditioning principles to instill a fear of rats in "Little Albert"

7. Which of the following are reasons for studying human diversity?

_____ a. Because our society is made up of so many different kinds of people

_____ b. As a way of helping to solve interpersonal tensions based on misunderstandings of others

_____ c. To help define what humans have in common

_____ d. Because diversity psychology is one of the major subdivisions of psychology

8. A subculture is a group within a larger society that shares a certain set of values, beliefs, outlooks, and norms of behavior. T/F

9. Subcultures that contribute to diversity in our own society include:

_____ a. African Americans
_____ b. gay men
_____ c. teenagers
_____ d. blue-eyed blondes
_____ e. the homeless

10. People who have ancestors from the same region of the world and who share a common language, religion, and set of social traditions are said to be part of the same _____ group.

11. Minority groups are seriously underrepresented among psychologists. T/F

12. A method of research known as _____ allows psychologists to study behavior as it occurs in real-life settings.

13. Psychologists use _____ research to examine relationships between two or more variables without manipulating any variable.

14. The experimental method is associated with all of the following except:
   a. hypotheses
   b. variables
   c. experimenter bias
   d. subjects or participants

15. Difficulty generalizing from observations is a major shortcoming of the case study method. T/F

16. The method of research best suited to explaining behavior is _____ research.

17. The _____ variable in an experiment is manipulated to see how it affects a second variable; the _____ variable is the one observed for any possible effects.

18. To ensure that the results of a particular study apply to a larger population, researchers use _____ or _____ samples.

19. Controversy over ethical standards in psychology has almost disappeared. T/F

20. The APA code of ethics used today is unchanged since 1953. T/F

21. Ethical questions in psychological research apply only to laboratory experiments. T/F

22. Getting the informed consent of participants in studies is central to the ethics of doing research on humans. T/F

23. Researchers who fail to follow the Federal Code of Regulations are subject to penalties. T/F

24. Psychologists are much less concerned about ethical guidelines pertaining to animal research. T/F

25. Careers in psychology are largely limited to people with Ph.D.s. T/F

26. Almost all the careers related to a knowledge of psychology are in the mental health field. T/F

27. Which of the following must be medical doctors?
    _____ a. psychiatrists
    _____ b. psychoanalysts
    _____ c. clinical psychologists

28. Psychologists can be found working in which of the following settings?
    _____ a. research laboratories
    _____ b. schools
    _____ c. government
    _____ d. corporations and other businesses
    _____ e. hospitals and clinics

CRITICAL THINKING

1. What is the difference between a science and a pseudoscience?

2. Choose an aspect of human behavior such as kindness, intelligence, or aggressiveness and describe how a contemporary psychologist might use multiple perspectives to understand it.

3. You notice that some students in your psychology class take many more notes than others, and you wonder whether the amount of note-taking ultimately affects grades. What research methods might you use to find out? What would each of these methods tell you about the issue? What are the drawbacks of each? Be specific about your procedures.

4. How do you feel about animal research and experimentation in psychology? When, if ever, do you think that animal research is justified? Do you approve of the current regulations concerning it? Why or why not?

(Answers to the Review Questions appear in the back of the book.)

2 The Biological

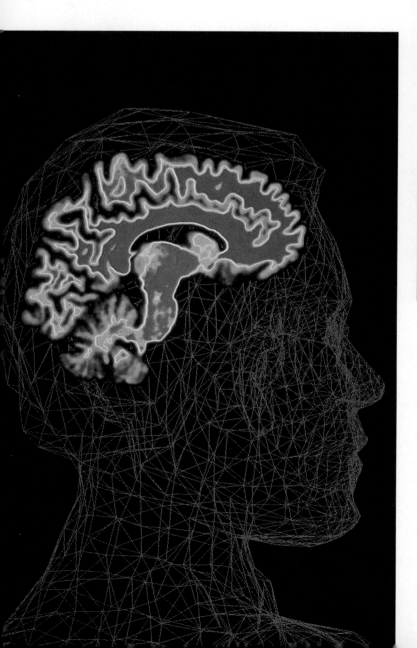

Basis of Behavior

When neurologist Oliver Sacks first met Dr. Carl Bennett, he was astonished that the man could ever be a surgeon (Sacks, 1995). Bennett has a disorder called Tourette's syndrome, characterized by tics, twitches, and gestures, which are punctuated by outbursts of bizarre, involuntary sounds. On a visit to Bennett's home in British Columbia, Bennett met Sacks at the airport, walking rapidly with a jerky skip every fifth step, and periodically lunging toward the floor as if to snatch up a hundred dollar bill he had just spotted. In the car, while driving, he repeatedly tapped both forefingers on the windshield and kept chirping out in a high-pitched voice "Hi Patty! Hi Patty!" even though no one named Patty was there.

Watching Bennett scrub for surgery was a spectacle that filled Sacks with both amusement and dread. Bennett's hands kept darting involuntarily toward unsterile objects (although never quite touching them), while all the time he was hooty-hooing like some huge, green-clad owl. Yet to Sacks's

Think About It!

1. How do drugs like caffeine, marijuana, and LSD affect the behavior of neurons?

2. *True or False:* Injuries to certain parts of the brain can produce blindness, even if the eyes themselves are not damaged.

3. You burn your finger on a match, and you instantly pull your finger away. What kinds of activities occur within your body during this very brief period?

4. What is magnetic resonance imaging?

5. Can we control our own blood pressure and headaches?

6. Can behavioral traits such as shyness and aggressiveness be inherited?

7. Do behaviors that promoted survival in the early evolution of human beings still influence the way people behave today?

Nervous system The brain, the spinal cord, and the network of nerve cells that transmit messages throughout the body.

Endocrine system Internal network of glands that release hormones directly into the bloodstream to regulate body functions.

Neurons Individual cells that are the smallest units of the nervous system.

Dendrites Short fibers that branch out from the cell body and pick up incoming messages.

amazement, when Bennett began the operation, a difficult mastectomy, his Tourette's symptoms vanished! For two and a half hours he worked confidently with a completely steady hand, never showing even a single trace of his disorder. The abnormalities in his brain that so dominated his everyday life miraculously came under control as he concentrated on his painstaking work.

The human brain is a biological system of enormous complexity. For people with tourette's syndrome, something in the brain malfunctions to cause extraordinary behaviors against the person's will. But under circumstances that demand intense concentration the brain can apparently bypass these malfunctioning circuits and produce speech and actions that are perfectly normal. Clearly, a complex interplay exists among the brain, the environment, and behavior. The brain may be the master control center of all we say and do, yet surrounding conditions also "feed back" on the brain, affecting its activities. This intricate feedback and control characterizes all the organs of the human body. It is a fundamental biological process that forms the basis of all our behavior. Our bodies evolved to live in a world of things and events outside us, and all our biological systems are geared to make adjustments which keep us in tune with our surroundings.

In this chapter we will explore the two major systems that integrate and coordinate our behavior, keeping it in constant touch with what is going on "out there." One is the **nervous system,** of which the brain is a part. The other is the **endocrine system,** made up of glands that secrete chemical messages into the blood. We begin by putting under a microscope the nervous system's smallest unit: the nerve cell, or neuron.

NEURONS: THE MESSENGERS

The nervous system is composed of individual parts that work together to form a remarkable communication network. These parts are numerous and complex, and, in some cases, their functions are still a mystery. Before we consider the larger parts of the nervous system, we will examine the system's smallest unit, the individual nerve cell or **neuron,** which underlies the activity of the entire nervous system.

As many as 100 billion nerve cells or neurons may be found in the brain of an average human being. In addition, billions more neurons are in other parts of the nervous system. Like most other cells, each neuron has a cell body. Unlike other cells, however, neurons have tiny fibers extending from the cell body that enable the neuron to receive messages from surrounding cells and pass them on to other cells. Figure 2–1 contains an actual photograph of a neuron as well as a stylized drawing that illustrates the various parts of a typical neuron.

Many small fibers called **dendrites** branch out from the cell body. The dendrites pick up messages coming in from other neurons and transmit them to

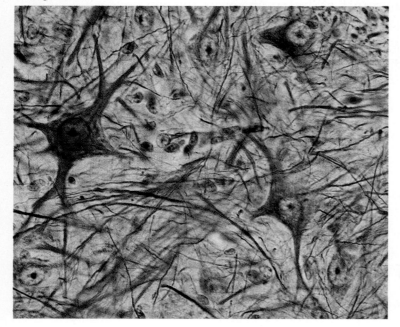

A photomicrograph showing the cell bodies, dendrites, and axons of several neighboring neurons.

the cell body. Also extending from the cell body of the neuron is a single long fiber called an **axon.** The axon is very thin and is usually much longer than the dendrites. For example, in adults, the axons that run from the brain to the base of the spinal cord or from the spinal cord to the tip of the thumb may be as long as 3 feet. Most axons, however, are only 1 or 2 millimeters long. A group of axons bundled together like parallel wires in an electrical cable is called a **nerve** or **tract.** The axon carries outgoing messages from the cell and either relays them to neighboring neurons or directs a muscle or gland to take action. Although there is just one axon per neuron, near its end the axon splits into many terminal branches. Because a single neuron may have hundreds or thousands of dendrites, and because the axon itself may branch out in numerous directions, one neuron can be in touch with hundreds or thousands of others at both its input end (dendrites) and its output end (axon).

Axon Single long fiber extending from the cell body; it carries outgoing messages.

Nerve or **tract** Group of axons bundled together.

**Figure 2–1
A typical myelinated neuron.**

Source: Adapted from *Fundamentals of Human Neuropsychology* (2nd ed.), by Brian Kolb and Ian Q. Whishaw. Copyright © 1980, 1985, by W. H. Freeman and Company. Reprinted with permission.

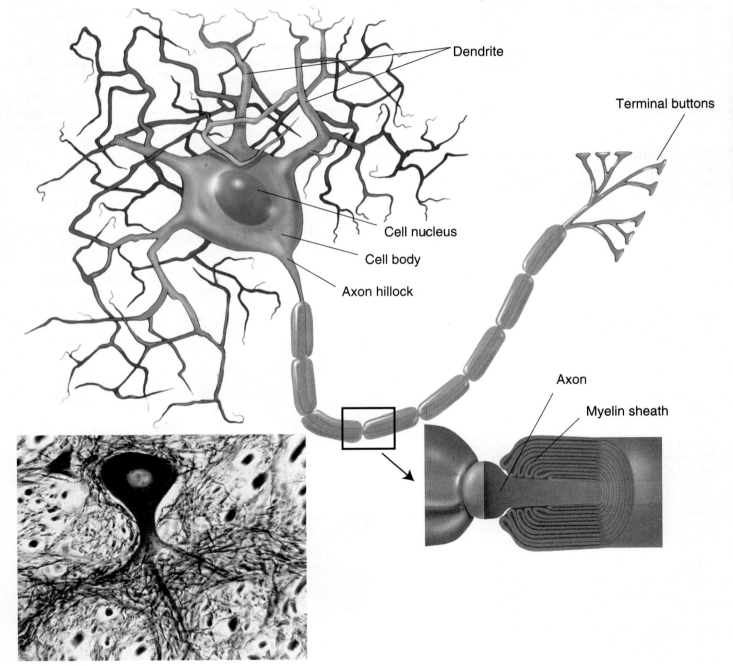

Myelin sheath White fatty covering found on some axons.

Sensory (or afferent) neurons Neurons that carry messages from sense organs to the spinal cord or brain.

Motor (or efferent) neurons Neurons that carry messages from the spinal cord or brain to the muscles and glands.

Interneurons (or association neurons) Neurons that carry messages from one neuron to another.

Glial cells (or glia) Cells that form the myelin sheath; they insulate and support neurons by holding them together, removing waste products, and preventing harmful substances from passing from the bloodstream into the brain.

Ions Electrically charged particles found both inside and outside the neuron.

Resting potential Electrical charge across a neuron membrane due to excess positive ions concentrated on the outside and excess negative ions on the inside.

Examine the neuron in Figure 2–1. Its axon is surrounded by a white fatty covering called a **myelin sheath.** Not all axons are covered by myelin sheaths, but myelinated axons are found throughout the body. The myelin sheath appears pinched at intervals, which makes the axon resemble a string of microscopic sausages. Because of this white covering, tissues made up of lots of myelinated axons are known as "white matter," whereas tissues comprising mostly unmyelinated axons and cell bodies look gray and thus are called "gray matter." The sheaths have two purposes: to help neurons act with greater efficiency and to provide insulation for the neuron.

All neurons relay messages, but the kind of information they collect and the places to which they carry it help us distinguish among different types of neurons. Neurons that collect messages from sense organs and carry those messages to the spinal cord or the brain are called **sensory** (or **afferent**) **neurons.** Neurons that carry messages from the spinal cord or the brain to the muscles and glands are called **motor** (or **efferent**) **neurons.** And neurons that carry messages from one neuron to another are called **interneurons** (or **association neurons**).

The nervous system also contains a vast number of **glial cells,** or glia. Glial cells support neurons in a number of ways. They hold the neurons in the nervous system together; they remove waste products that could interfere with neural functions; and they prevent harmful substances from passing from the bloodstream into the brain. In addition, they form the myelin sheath that insulates and protects neurons. Recent evidence also suggests that glial cells may influence learning and memory (Roitbak, 1993).

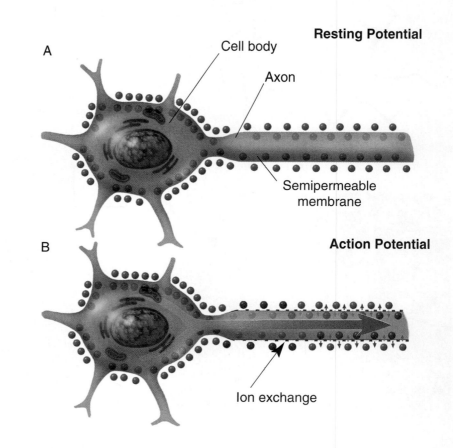

Figure 2–2
The neural impulse—communication within the neuron.
At rest (A), there is an excess of negative ions inside the neuron compared to the outside. When a point on the semipermeable neural membrane is adequately stimulated by an incoming message, the membrane opens at that point, and positively charged ions flow in. (B) This process is repeated along the length of the membrane, creating the neural impulse that travels down the axon, causing the neuron to fire.

Source: Adapted from *Psychology* (2nd ed.), by John G. Seamon and Douglas Kenrick. Copyright © 1994, p. 45. Reprinted by permission of Prentice Hall, Inc.

The Neural Impulse

Several times we have noted that neurons carry messages. How do these messages originate? When a neuron is at rest, the membrane surrounding the cell forms a partial barrier between the fluids that are inside and outside of the neuron. Both solutions contain electrically charged particles, or **ions.** Because there are more negative ions inside the neuron than outside, there is a small electrical charge (called the **resting potential**) across the cell membrane. Thus, the resting neuron is said to be in a state of **polarization.** Figure 2–2A shows a resting neuron in a state of polarization.

In its resting state, a polarized neuron is like a spring that has been compressed or a guitar string that has been pulled but not released. All that is needed to generate a neuron's signal is the release of the tension stored in the polarized state.

When a small area on the cell membrane is adequately stimulated by an incoming message, pores (or channels) in the membrane at the stimulated area allow positively charged sodium ions to move across the cell membrane. When enough sodium ions have entered the neuron to make the inside positively charged relative to the outside—that is, it becomes *depolarized*—those pores close, and no more sodium ions can enter at that time.

The opening of the cell membrane does not occur at just one point. In fact, as soon as the cell membrane allows sodium to enter the cell at one point, the next point on the membrane also opens. More sodium ions flow into the neuron at the second spot and depolarize this part of the neuron, and so on. The process is repeated along the length of the neuron, creating a **neural impulse,** or **action potential,** that travels down the axon, much like a fuse burning from one end to the other (see Figure 2–2B). When this happens, we say that the neuron has fired.

As a general rule, single impulses received from neighboring neurons do not make a neuron fire. Incoming impulse messages cause temporary small shifts in the electrical charge in areas of the neuron that receive the impulse. These **graded potentials** are transmitted along the cell membrane and may simply fade away, leaving the neuron in its normal polarized state. However, if the graded potentials caused by impulses from many neighboring neurons—or even from one other neuron firing repeatedly—combine to exceed a certain minimum **threshold of excitation,** the neuron will fire. Just as a light switch requires a minimum amount of pressure to be activated, an incoming message must be above the minimum threshold to make a neuron fire.

Immediately after firing, during the **absolute refractory period,** the neuron will not fire again no matter how strong the incoming messages may be. In the **relative refractory period,** when the cell is returning to the resting state, the neuron will fire, but only if the incoming message is considerably stronger than is normally necessary to make it fire. Finally, the neuron is returned to its resting state, ready to fire again, as shown in Figure 2–3.

Although individual action potentials occur very quickly, the speed with which individual neurons conduct impulses varies. In some of the largest myelinated axons, the fastest impulses may travel at speeds of nearly 400 feet per second. Axons with myelin sheaths can conduct impulses very rapidly because the impulses leapfrog along the string of pinched intervals, or nodes, that lie along the sheaths. Neurons without myelin sheaths tend to conduct impulses more slowly, in a steady flow like a fuse. Impulses in the slowest of these unmyelinated neurons poke along at little more than 3 feet per second.

At any instant, a neuron may be in any number of states determined by the overall pattern of graded potentials. For example, it may be engaged

---

Polarization The condition of a neuron when the inside is negatively charged relative to the outside; for example, when the neuron is at rest.

Neural impulse (or action potential) The firing of a nerve cell.

Graded potential A shift in the electrical charge in a tiny area of a neuron.

Threshold of excitation The level an impulse must exceed to cause a neuron to fire.

Absolute refractory period A period after firing when a neuron will not fire again no matter how strong the incoming messages may be.

Relative refractory period A period after firing when a neuron is returning to its normal polarized state and will fire again only if the incoming message is much stronger than usual.

Figure 2–3
Electrical changes during the action potential.
The incoming message must be above a certain threshold to cause a neuron to fire. After it fires, the neuron is returned to its resting state. This process happens very quickly, and within a few thousandths of a second the neuron is ready to fire again.

Source: Adapted from *Physiology of Behavior,* 5/E by Neil R. Carlson. Copyright © 1994 by Allyn & Bacon. Reprinted by permission.

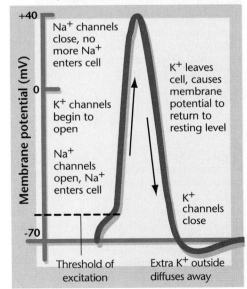

All-or-none law Principle that the action potential in a neuron does not vary in strength; the neuron either fires at full strength or it does not fire at all.

Terminal button (or synaptic knob) Structure at the end of an axon terminal branch.

Synaptic space (or synaptic cleft) Tiny gap between the axon terminal of one neuron and the dendrites or cell body of the next neuron.

Synapse Area composed of the axon terminal of one neuron, the synaptic space, and the dendrite or cell body of the next neuron.

in an action potential, it may be moving toward an action potential, or it may even be moving below a resting potential. Although we are just beginning to study the messages in graded potential activities of neurons, we can, to some extent, interpret the messages transmitted in action potentials.

Strong incoming signals do not cause stronger action potentials in a neuron. Neurons either fire or they do not, and every firing of a particular neuron produces an impulse of the same strength. This is called the **all-or-none law.** However, the neuron is likely to fire *more often* when stimulated by a strong signal. The result is rapid neural firing that communicates the message "There's a very strong stimulus out here."

The Synapse

We have been probing the operation of a single neuron. But the billions of neurons in the nervous system work together to coordinate the body's activities. How do they interact? How does a message get from one neuron to another?

Imagine a single neuron that receives its messages from just one other neuron and transmits messages to just one neuron. The dendrites or cell body of the neuron pick up a signal. Then, as we have seen, if the signal is strong enough, the neuron fires, and an impulse starts down the axon and travels to the end of the terminal branches. At the end of each branch is a tiny knob called a **terminal button** or **synaptic knob.** In most cases, a tiny gap, called a **synaptic space** or **synaptic cleft,** exists between this knob and the next neuron. The entire area composed of the axon terminal of one neuron, the synaptic space, and the dendrite or cell body of the next neuron is called the **synapse** (see Figure 2–4).

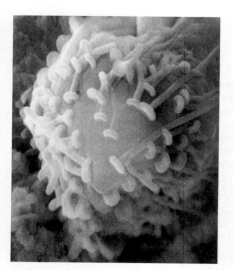

A photograph taken with a scanning electron microscope, showing the synaptic knobs at the ends of axons. Inside the knobs are the vesicles that contain neurotransmitters.

Figure 2–4
Synaptic transmission—communication between neurons.
When a neural impulse reaches the end of an axon, tiny oval sacs, called synaptic vesicles, at the end of most axons release varying amounts of chemical substances called neurotransmitters. These substances travel across the synaptic space and affect the next neuron.

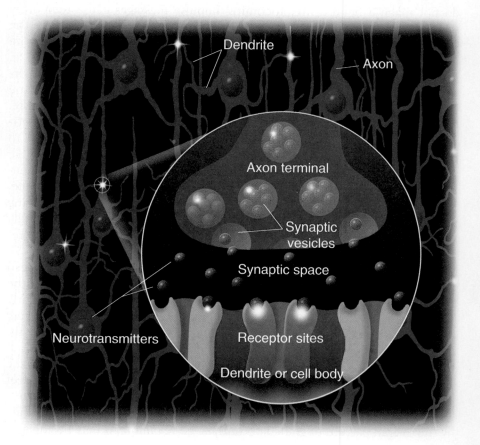

MAJOR NEUROTRANSMITTERS AND THEIR EFFECTS

Acetylcholine (ACh)	Generally excitatory	Affects arousal, attention, memory, motivation, movement. Too much: spasms, tremors. Too little: paralysis, torpor.
Dopamine	Inhibitory	Inhibits wide range of behavior and emotions, including pleasure. Implicated in schizophrenia and Parkinson's disease.
Serotonin	Inhibitory	Inhibits virtually all activities. Important for sleep onset, mood, eating behavior.
Norepinephrine	Generally excitatory	Affects arousal, wakefulness, learning, memory, mood.
Endorphins	Inhibitory	Inhibit transmission of pain messages.

Synaptic vesicles Tiny sacs in a terminal button that release chemicals into the synapse.

Neurotransmitters Chemicals released by the synaptic vesicles that travel across the synaptic space and affect adjacent neurons.

Receptor site A location on a receptor neuron into which a specific neurotransmitter fits like a key into a lock.

If the neural impulse is to move on to the next neuron, it must somehow cross the synaptic space. It is tempting to imagine that the neural impulse simply leaps across the gap like an electrical spark, but in reality the transfer is made by chemicals. What happens is this: Most axon terminals contain a number of tiny oval sacs called **synaptic vesicles** (see Figure 2–4). When the neural impulse reaches the end of the axon, it causes these vesicles to release varying amounts of chemicals called **neurotransmitters.** The neurotransmitters diffuse randomly into the synaptic space, where they can affect the next neuron.

There are many different neurotransmitters, and their functions are still being studied. Each of these substances has matching **receptor sites** on the other side of the synaptic space. Each neurotransmitter fits into its corresponding receptor sites just as a key fits into a lock. Some neurotransmitters "excite" the next neuron, making it more likely to fire. For example, *acetylcholine* (ACh) acts as an excitatory transmitter where neurons meet skeletal muscles. It also appears to play a critical role in such psychological processes as arousal, attention, memory, and motivation (Panksepp, 1986). Alzheimer's disease, which involves loss of memory and severe language problems, is thought to be due to a reduction in ACh and a decrease in the number of brain cells that respond to ACh.

Other transmitter substances "inhibit" the next neuron, making it less likely to fire. *Dopamine* is one prevalent inhibitory transmitter that seems to figure prominently in schizophrenia and the motor disorder known as Parkinson's disease. *Serotonin,* another inhibitory neurotransmitter, affects emotions, arousal, and sleep. *Norepinephrine* similarly influences wakefulness and arousal, as well as learning, memory, and emotional mood. (See the Summary Table above for a more detailed list of major neurotransmitters and their effects.)

Some transmitter substances have widespread effects on the nervous system. They seem to regulate or adjust the sensitivity of large numbers

Endorphins, which are released into the brain and body during exercise, are neurotransmitters that act as natural painkillers.

of synapses, in effect "turning up" or "turning down" the activity level of whole portions of the nervous system. This process is especially clear in substances that are involved in the body's relief of pain. *Endorphins* appear to reduce pain by inhibiting, or "turning down," the neurons that transmit pain messages in the brain. Endorphins are chains of amino acids that act like neurotransmitters. One endorphin was found to be 48 times more potent than morphine when injected into the brain and 3 times more potent when injected into the bloodstream (Snyder, 1977).

Once a chemical transmitter has been released into the synaptic space and has performed its job, what happens to it? If it remains loose or if it continues to occupy receptor sites, it will continue to affect other neurons indefinitely, long after the initial message or signal is over. The action of most neurotransmitters is terminated in two ways. First, some neurotransmitters are broken down by other chemicals. In some cases, the by-products are recycled to make new neurotransmitters; in other cases, they are treated as wastes and are removed from the body. Second, many neurotransmitters are simply reabsorbed into axon terminals to be used again. In either case, the synapse is cleared up and returned to its normal state.

Synapses and Drugs

How do drugs like caffeine, marijuana, and LSD affect the behavior of neurons?

Most drugs and toxins that affect psychological functions alter the transmission of chemicals across synapses. Some substances impede the release of transmitter chemicals from neurons into the synaptic space. For example, the toxin produced by the microorganism that causes botulism prevents the release of ACh. The result is paralysis and sometimes rapid death. Drugs such as reserpine cause transmitter chemicals to leak out of the synaptic vesicles and be rapidly broken down, creating a shortage of transmitters and decreased activity at the synapse. Reserpine is often prescribed to reduce blood pressure because it decreases the activity of neurons that excite the circulatory system.

In contrast to toxins or drugs that reduce the quantity of neurotransmitters, some drugs speed up the release of transmitter chemicals into the synaptic space. For example, the poison of the black widow spider causes ACh to spew into the synapses of the nervous system. As a result, neurons fire repeatedly, causing spasms and tremors. Caffeine increases release of excitatory, arousing neurotransmitters by blocking the action of adenosine, a transmitter substance that *inhibits* the release of these substances (Nehlig, Daval, & Debry, 1992). In fact, two or three cups of coffee contain enough caffeine to block half the adenosine receptors for several hours, producing a high state of arousal in the nervous system. In some cases, the arousal is so intense we say the person is suffering from "coffee nerves."

To summarize, some chemicals produce their effects by increasing or decreasing the quantity of neurotransmitters in the synapse. Other substances work directly on the receptor sites at the other side of the synaptic gap. Lysergic acid diethylamide (LSD), for example, attaches to receptor sites on neurons that receive serotonin, inhibiting the activity of those neurons. LSD may also affect levels of dopamine, although scientists do not know exactly how. You may be wondering how suppressing of the activity of serotonin-releasing neurons could produce the bizarre sensations of an LSD "trip." Some psychologists have speculated that, while we are awake, a number of these neurons suppress dreaming. When LSD inhibits or interferes with those neurons, a kind of dreaming occurs, even though the user is actually awake (Carlson, 1994). Other investigators warn, however, that the process might be more complex than this theory indicates (Cooper, Bloom, & Roth, 1991; Shepherd, 1994).

Some drugs act by blocking receptors so that neurotransmitters can neither excite nor inhibit their targets. For example, atropine, a poison derived from belladonna and other plants, blocks receptor sites for ACh in the brain, often disrupting memory functions. Curare, the poison with which some native peoples of South America traditionally have tipped their arrows, blocks the ACh receptors that control skeletal muscle function and rapidly produces paralysis.

Still other drugs interfere with the removal of neurotransmitters from the synapse after they have done their job. Recall that once transmitter chemicals have bonded to receptor sites and have stimulated or inhibited the neuron, they are normally either removed from the body or returned to the axon terminals from which they came. A number of stimulant drugs interfere with this process. Cocaine, for example, prevents dopamine from being reabsorbed. As a result, excess amounts of dopamine accumulate in the synapses, producing heightened arousal of the entire nervous system.

Sometimes our investigations of drug effects lead to surprising discoveries about the brain and its neurotransmitters. For example, in attempting to explain the effects of *opiates*—painkilling drugs like morphine and heroin that are derived from the opium plant—Candace Pert and Solomon Snyder discovered that the central nervous system contained receptor sites for these substances (Pert & Snyder, 1973). They reasoned that such receptor sites would not exist unless the body somehow was able to produce its own natural painkillers. Not long after, researchers discovered that our brains actually do produce such substances—the endorphins discussed earlier. It turns out that morphine and other narcotics lock into the receptors for endorphins and have the same painkilling effects. Similarly, people researching the effects of marijuana found brain receptors for a chemical called tetrahydrocannabinal (THC), the active ingredient in marijuana (Herkenham et al., 1990; Howlett, Evans, & Houston, 1992; Matsuda et al., 1990; Restak, 1993). They, too, reasoned that there should be a natural substance in the body that would fit into these receptor sites. Sure enough, researchers later discovered a natural transmitter substance produced by the brain, called *anandamide*, that binds to those same receptors (Devane et al., 1992). Although its natural functions are not yet known, anandamide should have at least some of the effects of marijuana, because it locks into the same receptors as THC.

Another fascinating discovery is that imbalances in some neurotransmitters may contribute to certain kinds of mental illness. Schizophrenia, for example, seems to be associated with an overabundance of dopamine. Some drugs that have been developed to treat schizophrenia seem to reduce the symptoms of this disorder by blocking dopamine receptors. Similarly, some theories link depression to reduced serotonin activity. Antidepressant drugs such as Prozac (the chemical fluoxetine) alleviate the symptoms of depression by blocking reabsorption of serotonin, thus increasing the overall level of serotonin in the synapses of the nervous system. We will explore these intriguing discoveries more fully in the chapters on psychological disorders (Chapter 13) and therapies (Chapter 14).

Plasticity The ability of the brain to change in response to experience.

Central nervous system (CNS) Division of the nervous system that consists of the brain and spinal cord.

Peripheral nervous system Division of the nervous system that connects the central nervous system to the rest of the body.

Long-term potentiation (LTP) A long-lasting change in the structure or function of a synapse that increases the efficiency of neural transmission.

Experience and Neurons

That drugs can change the way neurons and synapses behave is probably something you would expect. But researchers studying the physiology of neurons have, over the past few decades, made some discoveries that are quite surprising. Neuroscientists performing a laboratory experiment observed that changing a rat's *surroundings* also caused changes in the animal's brain (Rosenzweig, 1984). The brain's ability to be physically and chemically altered by experience is called **plasticity.** The brain's plasticity has many important implications, which we'll turn to later in the chapter. In the accompanying *Highlights* we focus on the pioneering work of M. R. Rosenzweig and several other teams of neuroscientists.

THE CENTRAL NERVOUS SYSTEM

If the brain alone has as many as 100 billion neurons, and if each neuron can be "in touch" with thousands of other neurons, then our bodies must contain trillions of synapses through which each neuron is indirectly linked to every other neuron in the nervous system. We turn now to the overall structure of this immense system of interconnected neurons. As we noted earlier in this chapter, the **central nervous system (CNS)** consists of the brain and spinal cord. The **peripheral nervous system** connects the brain and spinal cord to everything else in the body: sense organs, muscles, glands, and so on (see Figure 2–5).

The Brain

Containing more than 90 percent of the body's neurons, the brain is the seat of awareness and reason, the place where learning, memory, and emotions are centered. It is the part of us that decides what to do and whether that decision was right or wrong, and it imagines how things might have turned out if we had acted differently. As soon as the brain begins to take shape in the human embryo, we can detect three distinct parts: the hindbrain, the midbrain, and the forebrain. These three parts are still present in the fully developed adult brain, although they are not so easily distinguished from one another (see Figure 2–7). We will use these three basic divisions to describe the parts of the brain, what they do, and how they interact to influence our behavior.

**Figure 2–5
A schematic diagram of the divisions of the nervous system and their various subparts.**

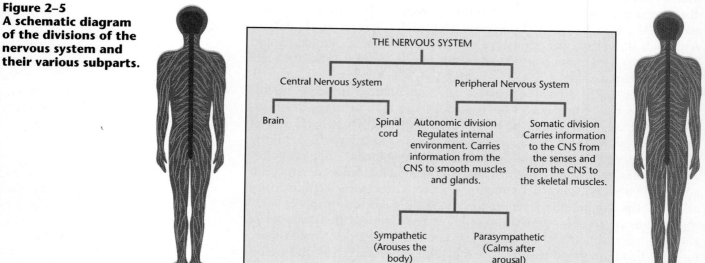

HIGHLIGHTS
NEW CONNECTIONS FOR OLD NEURONS: EXPERIENCE AND PLASTICITY

Among the neural investigators to observe changes in response to experience (*plasticity*) was M. R. Rosenzweig (1984) who examined the brains of young rats raised in either "impoverished" or "enriched" environments. The enriched environments contained small objects for manipulation and provided a variety of opportunities for exploration. In the impoverished environments, the rats had little opportunity for either exploration or manipulation. Rats raised in the enriched environments were found to have larger neurons with more synaptic connections than rats reared in the impoverished environments (Figure 2–6). More recent experiments by Rosenzweig (1996) have shown that these changes can be produced in rats of any age if they are placed in an enriched environment.

In humans, experience also has been found to alter the brain. One study found that when the left hands of string musicians and non-musicians were stimulated, a corresponding increase in neural activity occurred in the area of the brain responsible for those functions (Elbert et al., 1995). In another study, psychotherapy aimed at treating patients with obsessive-compulsive behavior was also shown to produce changes in brain function (Schwartz et al., 1996).

Experience can cause changes in the brain's neurons.

Other investigators have examined how experience causes changes in synapses. For example, British scientist Timothy Bliss and his colleagues, used a single electrical pulse to stimulate nerves in the hippocampus—a structure in the brain involved in memory formation—and then measured the resulting current in the nerves. Although the current they measured was initially very weak, subsequent stimulation of the same pathway with a series of high-frequency pulses caused the nerve to respond vigorously. Weeks later it still retained this ability (Bliss & Collingridge, 1993). This long-term effect on synaptic transmission, known as **long-term potentiation (LTP),** apparently enables the brain to store information about new experiences (Martinex & Derrick, 1996).

As we will see in later chapters, research on nervous system plasticity has important implications for memory, intelligence, early childhood education, as well as for designing programs to overcome the effects of poverty and abuse.

Figure 2–6
Brain growth and experience.
In Rosenzweig's experiment, young rats lived in two kinds of cages: "impoverished," with nothing to manipulate or explore, or "enriched," with a variety of objects. When Rosenzweig examined their brains, he found that the enriched group had larger neurons with more synaptic connections (shown as dendrites in the drawing) than the rats who lived in the bare cages. Experience, then, can actually affect the structure of the brain.

Source: From "Brain changes in response to experience" by M. R. Rosenzweig, E. L. Bennett, and M. C. Diamond. Copyright © 1972, Scientific American, Inc. All rights reserved.

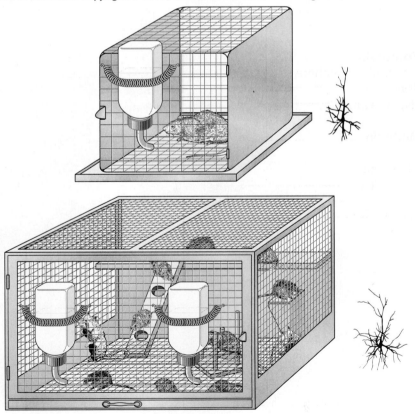

Hindbrain Area containing the medulla, pons, and cerebellum.

Medulla Part of the hindbrain that controls such functions as breathing, heart rate, and blood pressure.

Pons Part of the hindbrain that connects the cerebral cortex at the top of the brain to the cerebellum.

Cerebellum Structure in the hindbrain that control certain reflexes and coordinate the body's movements.

Brain stem The top of the spinal column; it widens out to form the hindbrain and midbrain.

Midbrain Region between the hindbrain and the forebrain; it is important for hearing and sight, and it is one of several places in the brain where pain is registered.

Forebrain Top part of the brain, including the thalamus, hypothalamus, and cerebral cortex.

Thalamus Forebrain region that relays and translates incoming messages from the sense receptors, except those for smell.

Because the **hindbrain** is found in even the most primitive vertebrates, it is believed to have been the earliest part of the brain to evolve. The part of the hindbrain nearest to the spinal cord is the **medulla,** a narrow structure about 1.5 inches long. The medulla controls such bodily functions as breathing, heart rate, and blood pressure. The medulla is also the point at which many of the nerves from the body cross over on their way to and from the higher brain centers; axons from neurons on the left part of the body cross to the right side of the brain and vice versa.

Above the medulla lies the **pons,** which connects upper portions of the brain to the section of the hindbrain called the **cerebellum.** Chemicals produced in the pons help maintain our sleep-wake cycle (discussed in Chapter 4, States of Consciousness). The cerebellum performs a wide range of functions. It handles certain reflexes, especially those that have to do with balance, and it coordinates the body's actions to ensure that movements go together in efficient sequences. Damage to the cerebellum causes severe problems in movement, such as jerky motions, loss of balance, and lack of coordination.

Above the pons and cerebellum, the **brain stem** widens to form the **midbrain.** As its name implies, the midbrain is in the middle of the brain, between the hindbrain at the base and the forebrain at the top. The midbrain is especially important for hearing and sight. It is also one of several places in the brain where pain is registered.

Supported by the brain stem, budding out above it and drooping over somewhat to fit into the skull, is the **forebrain.** In the center of the forebrain, and more or less directly over the brain stem, are the two egg-shaped structures that make up the **thalamus.** The thalamus relays and translates incoming messages from sense receptors (except those for smell) throughout the body. Some of the neurons in the thalamus seem to be important for reg-

Figure 2–7
A cross section of the brain.
This diagram shows the areas that make up the hindbrain, the midbrain, and the forebrain.

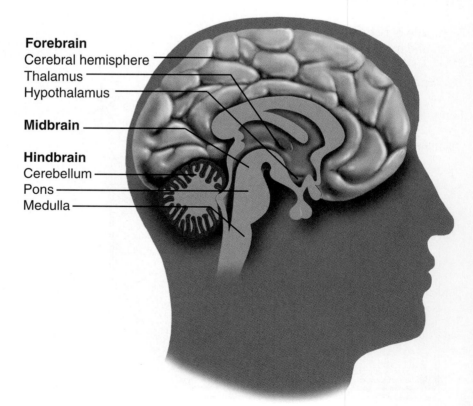

Forebrain
Cerebral hemisphere
Thalamus
Hypothalamus

Midbrain

Hindbrain
Cerebellum
Pons
Medulla

ulating the activity of brain centers in the cortex. Others control the activities of those parts of the nervous system outside the brain and spinal cord.

Located directly below the thalamus is a smaller structure called the **hypothalamus.** This part of the forebrain exerts an enormous influence on many kinds of motivation. Portions of the hypothalamus govern eating, drinking, sexual behavior, sleeping, and temperature control (Winn, 1995). The hypothalamus is directly involved in emotional behavior such as rage, terror, and pleasure, and it appears to play a central role in times of stress, coordinating and integrating the activity of the nervous system.

Above the brain stem, thalamus, and hypothalamus are the two *cerebral hemispheres*, the outer surface of which is called the **cerebral cortex.** These are what most people think of first when they talk about "the brain," though, as we've seen, the "brain" actually consists of the forebrain, midbrain, and hindbrain taken together. As you can see in Figures 2–8 and 2–9, the two cerebral hemispheres take up most of the room inside the skull. They balloon out over the brain stem, fold down over it, and actually hide most of it from view. The cerebral hemispheres are the most recently evolved part of the nervous system, and they are more highly developed in humans than in any other animal. They account for about 80 percent of the weight of the human brain, and they contain about 70 percent of the neurons in the central nervous system. If they were spread out, they would cover 2 to 3 square feet and would be about as thick as an uppercase letter on a typed page. An intricate pattern of folds, hills, and valleys, called

Hypothalamus Forebrain region that governs motivation and emotional responses.

Cerebral cortex The outer surface of the two cerebral hemispheres that regulate most complex behavior.

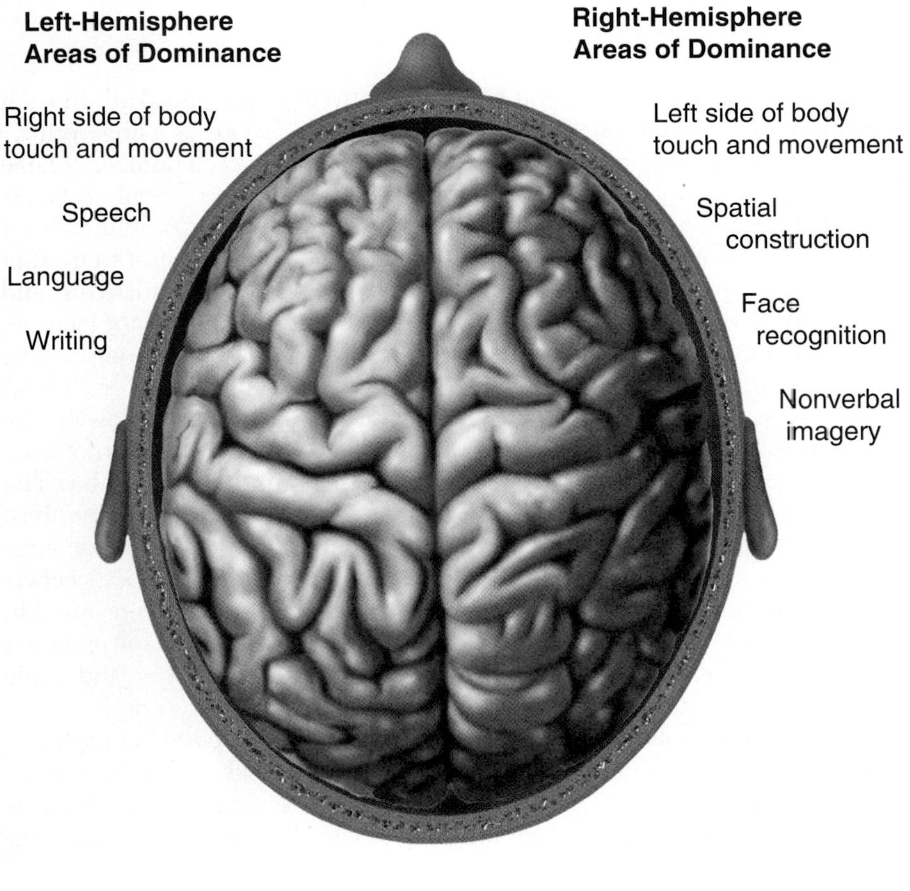

Left-Hemisphere Areas of Dominance

Right side of body touch and movement

Speech

Language

Writing

Right-Hemisphere Areas of Dominance

Left side of body touch and movement

Spatial construction

Face recognition

Nonverbal imagery

Figure 2–8
The two cerebral hemispheres.
The left hemisphere controls touch and movement of the right side of the body; the right hemisphere controls the left side of the body. The left hemisphere is usually dominant in verbal tasks, whereas the right hemisphere is typically superior at nonverbal, visual, and spatial tasks.

Association areas Areas of the cerebral cortex where incoming messages from the separate senses are combined into meaningful impressions and outgoing messages from the motor areas are integrated.

Occipital lobe Part of the cerebral hemisphere that receives and interprets visual information.

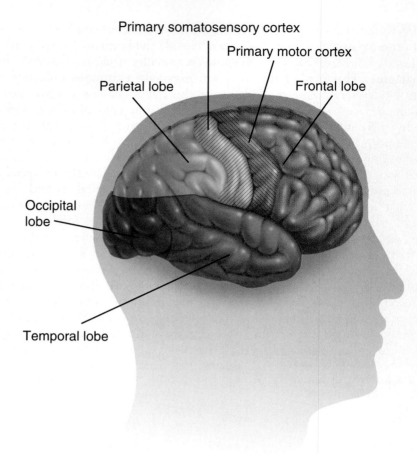

Figure 2–9
The four lobes of the cerebral cortex.
Deep fissures in the cortex separate these areas or lobes. Also shown are the primary sensory and motor areas.

convolutions, enable the cerebral hemispheres to fit inside the skull. In each person, these convolutions form a pattern that is as unique as a fingerprint.

Despite each cerebral hemisphere's unique appearance, a number of large landmarks on the cortex allow us to identify common functional areas. As seen in Figure 2–9, the cerebral cortex is divided approximately into front and rear halves by a vertical "valley" or "crack." Cortical areas just in front of this dividing line (motor areas) are devoted to the planning, sequencing, and execution of body movement. Areas to the rear of this boundary (sensory areas) are involved in processing and combining inputs from our senses. The cerebral hemispheres can each be divided into four large parts, or "lobes," which are separated from one another by the deep *fissures* or cracks on the cortex (see Figure 2–9). Three of these lobes are in the rear portion of each hemisphere, the portion that primarily processes sensory information. The remaining lobe in each hemisphere lies in the front half, which is involved primarily with integration of movement and emotions. Also, there are large areas on the cortex of all four lobes called **association areas.** Experts generally believe that information from diverse parts of the cortex is integrated in the association areas and that these areas are the sites of mental processes such as learning, thinking, remembering, and comprehending and using language.

The **occipital lobe,** located at the very back of the cerebral hemispheres, receives and processes visual information. It is in the occipital lobe that we actually experience shapes, color, and motion in the environment. Damage to the occipital lobe can produce blindness, even though the eyes and their

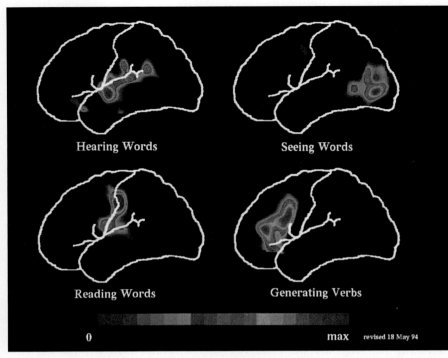

Hearing Words

Seeing Words

Reading Words

Generating Verbs

0   **max**   revised 18 May 94

PET scans of the human brain as it processes language. These scans actually spotlight the areas of the brain most active in hearing, seeing, thinking, and speaking.

Temporal lobe Part of the cerebral hemisphere that helps regulate hearing, balance and equilibrium, and certain emotions and motivations.

Parietal lobe Part of the cerebral cortex that receives sensory information from throughout the body.

Primary somatosensory cortex Area of the parietal lobe where messages from the sense receptors are registered.

Frontal lobe Part of the cerebral cortex that is responsible for voluntary movement; it is also important for attention, goal-directed behavior, and appropriate emotional experiences.

Motor projection areas Areas of the cerebral cortex where response messages from the brain to the muscles and glands begin.

True or False: Injuries to certain parts of the brain can produce blindness, even if the eyes themselves are not damaged.

neural connections to the brain are perfectly healthy and intact. The **temporal lobe,** located in front of the occipital lobe, roughly behind the temples, plays an important role in complex visual tasks such as recognizing faces. The temporal lobe also receives and processes information from the ears, contributes to balance and equilibrium, and regulates emotions and motivations such as anxiety, pleasure, and anger. In addition, the ability to understand and comprehend language is thought to be concentrated primarily in the rear portion of the temporal lobes, though recent research indicates that some language comprehension may also occur in the parietal lobe and the frontal lobe (Ojemann et al., 1989).

The **parietal lobe** sits on top of the temporal and occipital lobes and occupies the top back half of each hemisphere. This lobe receives sensory information from all over the body—from sense receptors in the skin, muscles, and joints. Messages from these sense receptors are registered in areas called the **primary somatosensory cortex.** The parietal lobe also seems to oversee spatial abilities, such as the ability to follow a map or to tell someone how to get from one place to another (Cohen & Raffal, 1991).

The **frontal lobe,** located just behind the forehead, accounts for about half the volume of the human brain. Response messages from the brain start their return trip in the **primary motor cortex** of the frontal lobe, and from there they go to the various muscles and glands in the body. Scientists are still uncertain of all the functions performed by the frontal lobes. In part, this is because much of our knowledge about brain function comes from research on animals, whose frontal lobes are relatively undeveloped, or from studying the rare cases of people with some kind of frontal lobe damage. One such famous case became public in 1848. It involved a bizarre accident that happened to a man named Phineas Gage.

Gage, who was the foreman of a railroad construction gang, made a careless mistake while using some blasting powder and a tamping iron. As a

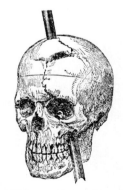

The skull of Phineas Gage, showing where the tamping iron passed through it, severely damaging his frontal lobes.

Corpus callosum A thick band of nerve fibers connecting the left and right cerebral cortex.

result, the tamping iron tore through his cheek and severely damaged his frontal lobes. Gage remained conscious, walked part of the way to a doctor, and, to the amazement of those who witnessed the accident, suffered few major aftereffects. No physical impairment followed the accident, and Gage's memory and skills seemed to be as good as ever. He did, however, undergo major personality changes. Once a steady worker, he lost interest in work and drifted from job to job. Other personality changes were so radical that, in the view of his friends, Gage was no longer the same man.

Since Gage's time, careful research has refined these early impressions of the functions of the frontal lobe. This part of the brain seems to permit and anticipate goal-directed behavior. People with damage to the frontal lobe have trouble following complex directions or performing tasks in which the directions change during the course of the job. Low levels of activity in portions of the frontal lobe are associated with hyperactivity and attention deficits in some people (Zametkin et al., 1990), and abnormalities in frontal lobes are often observed in people with schizophrenia (Raine et al., 1992).

The frontal lobe also figures prominently in the ability to lead a normal, mature emotional life. People whose frontal lobes have been severed often seem apathetic and capable of only shallow emotions, although this apathy may be interrupted by periods of boastfulness and silliness. Moreover, some people with injuries to the frontal lobe experience explosive anger: They react with inappropriate, purposeless, and instantaneous rage to the slightest provocation and often feel embarrassed about their behavior afterward (Damasio, Tranel, & Damasio, 1990b). And some research indicates that the frontal lobe is linked to emotional temperament (being cheerful and optimistic or melancholy and alarmist) (Tomarken, Davidson, & Henriques, 1990). The frontal lobe also receives and coordinates messages from the other three lobes of the cortex. And it seems to play a role in the ability to keep track of previous and future movements of the body. Much more research needs to be done before psychologists can understand how this part of the cortex contributes to such a wide and subtle range of mental activities. (See the Summary Table for a summary of parts of the brain and their individual functions.)

Hemispheric Specialization

As we saw earlier, most of what we normally consider "the brain" consists of two separate cerebral hemispheres. In a sense, humans have a "right half-brain" and a "left half-brain." The two hemispheres are connected at several locations, but the primary connection between the left and right cortex is a thick, ribbonlike band of nerve fibers under the cortex called the **corpus callosum,** which is illustrated in Figure 2–13 on page 67.

Under normal conditions, the left and right cerebral hemispheres are in close communication through the corpus callosum, and they work together as a coordinated unit (Hellige, 1993; Hoptman & Davidson, 1994; Semrud-Clikeman & Hynd, 1990). Nonetheless, some evidence suggests that the cerebral hemispheres are not really equivalent (see Figure 2–9). For example, damage to the left hemisphere often results in severe language problems, whereas similar damage to the right hemisphere seldom has that effect. More dramatic evidence comes from research carried out on people with epilepsy in the early 1960s at the California Institute of Technology. In some cases of severe epilepsy, surgeons cut the corpus callosum in an effort to stop the spread of epileptic seizures from the cortex of one hemisphere to the other. But this operation also cuts the only direct communication link between the two hemispheres, enabling researchers to watch each hemisphere work on its own (Sperry, 1964, 1968, 1970). The results proved startling.

PARTS OF THE BRAIN AND THEIR FUNCTIONS

Hindbrain	Medulla	Sensory and motor nerves crossover
	Pons	Regulation of sleep-wake cycle
	Cerebellum	Reflexes (e.g., balance) Coordinates movement
Midbrain		Hearing, vision relay point Pain registered
Forebrain	Thalamus	Major message relay center Regulates higher brain centers and peripheral nervous system
	Hypothalamus	Motivation Emotion Stress reactions
	Cerebral Hemispheres	
	Occipital lobe	Receives and processes visual information
	Temporal lobe	Complex vision Smell Hearing Balance and equilibrium Emotions and motivations Some language comprehension
	Parietal lobe	Sensory projection and association areas Visual/spatial abilities
	Frontal lobe	Goal-directed behavior, concentration Emotional control and temperament Motor projection and association areas Coordinate messages from other lobes

When such "split-brain patients" are asked to stare at a spot on a projection screen while pictures of various objects are projected to the *right* of that spot, they can name the objects. And, with their right hands they can pick them out of a group of hidden objects (see Figure 2–10). However, when pictures of objects are shown on the *left* side of the screen, something changes. Subjects can still pick out the objects by feeling them with their left hands, but they can't say what the objects are! In fact, most often when objects are projected on the left side of the screen, split-brain patients say that they see "nothing" on the screen, even though they can accurately identify the objects when given a chance to touch and feel them with their left hands (see Figure 2–11).

The explanation for these startling results is to be found in the way each hemisphere of the brain operates. The left cerebral hemisphere receives information only from the right side of the body and from the right half of the visual field. So, it can match an object shown in the right visual field with

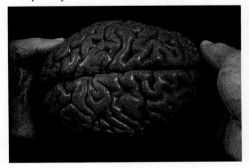

The human brain, viewed from the top. Its relatively small size belies its enormous complexity.

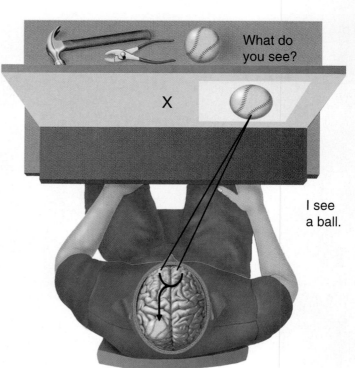

Figure 2–10
When split-brain patients stare at the "X" in the center of the screen, visual information projected on the *right* side of the screen goes to the patient's *left* hemisphere, which controls language. When asked what they see, patients can reply correctly.

Source: Adapted from Carol Ward, © *Discover Magazine,* 1987.

Figure 2–11
When split-brain patients stare at the "X" in the center of the screen, visual information projected on the *left* side of the screen goes to the patient's *right* hemisphere, which does not control language. When asked what they see, patients cannot name the object but can pick it out by touch with the *left* hand.

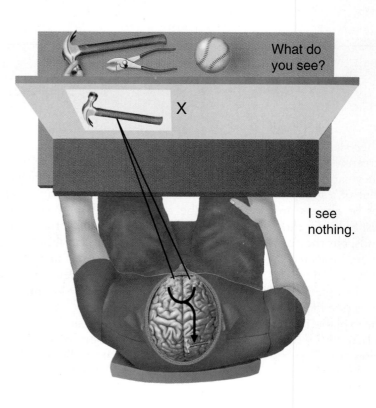

information received by touch from the right hand. However, in split-brain patients the left hemisphere is unaware of (and therefore unable to identify) objects shown in the left visual field or touched by the left hand. Conversely, the right hemisphere of the brain receives information only from the left side of the visual field and the left side of the body. So, the right hemisphere can match an object shown in the left visual field with information received by touch from the left hand, but in split-brain patients it is unaware of any objects shown in the right visual field or touched with the right hand.

This description of the two hemispheres explains all of Sperry's findings except one: When an object is shown in the left visual field, why can't split-brain patients name the object? The answer seems to be that, for the great majority of people, language ability is concentrated primarily in the left cortex of the brain (Hellige, 1990, 1993). In most split-brain patients, the right hemisphere of the brain cannot verbally identify the object that it is "seeing" in the left visual field, even though the object can be picked out by touch using the left hand. When the person is asked, "What do you see?" the left hemisphere (which monitors the right visual field) correctly reports, "Nothing."

These results indicate that the two cerebral hemispheres not only are connected to opposite sides of the body, but also appear to excel at different functions. In most people, the left hemisphere is dominant in verbal tasks, such as identifying spoken and printed words and speaking (Figure 2–9) (Hellige, 1990, 1993; Semrud-Clikeman & Hynd, 1990; Springer & Deutsch, 1989). The left hemisphere may also operate more analytically, logically, rationally, and sequentially (Kingstone et al., 1995) than the right hemisphere, though clearly demonstrating such differences is difficult, if not impossible (Hellige, 1990, 1993). By contrast, research reveals that the right hemisphere excels at visual and spatial tasks, nonverbal imagery (such as visual images, music, and environmental noises), face recognition, and the perception and expression of emotion (Hellige, 1990, 1993; Metcalfe, Funnell & Gazzaniga, 1995; Semrud-Clikeman & Hynd, 1990).

A common misconception about hemispheric specialization holds that it is related to handedness. Many people believe that the pattern of hemispheric asymmetry described above is reversed for left-handed people. That is, in left-handed people the right hemisphere governs language, analytic, and sequential tasks, whereas the left hemisphere dominates in visual, spatial, and nonverbal tasks. However, research on the relationship between handedness and hemispheric specialization demonstrates that speech is most often localized in the left hemisphere for *both* right- and left-handed people, though left-handed individuals are somewhat more likely than right-handed people to have their language functions centered in their right hemisphere (Hellige, 1993, 1994).

One intriguing line of contemporary research suggests that the left and right frontal lobes may influence emotional reactivity and temperament in distinctive ways. Using a wide variety of research techniques, Richard Davidson and his colleagues at the University of Wisconsin have discovered that people whose left frontal lobe is more active than the right tend to be more cheerful, sociable, ebullient, and self-confident; they also respond more positively to events around them, take delight in other people and novel situations, and are less upset by unpleasant events. By contrast, people with more right frontal lobe activity are more easily stressed, frightened, and upset and threatened by unpleasant events around them; they (not surprisingly) tend to shrink from encounters with other people and novel situations. They also tend to be more suspicious and depressed than people with predominantly

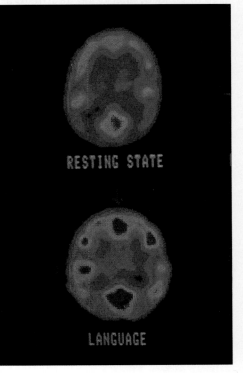

PET scans of a person at rest (top) and using language (bottom). The "hot" colors (red and yellow) indicate greater brain activity. These scans show that language activity is located primarily, but not exclusively, in the brain's left hemisphere.

RESTING STATE

LANGUAGE

Reticular formation (RF) Network of neurons in the hindbrain, the midbrain, and part of the forebrain whose primary function is to alert and arouse the higher parts of the brain.

Limbic system Ring of structures that play a role in learning and emotional behavior.

Severing the spinal cord at the neck typically causes paralysis of everything below the head because nerves connecting to the body's muscles no longer have a cable to the brain. Actor Christopher Reeves suffered this tragedy after being thrown from a horse. He and others may someday benefit from recent research into the possibility of regenerating neurons across damaged areas.

left frontal lobe activity (Henriques & Davidson, 1990; Tomarken et al., 1990). Rather dramatic supporting evidence comes from studies of patients suffering from seizure disorders. Patients whose right hemisphere is anesthetized frequently laugh and express positive emotions. Conversely, anesthetizing the left hemisphere often produces crying (Lee et al., 1993).

Not everyone shows the same pattern of differences between the left and right hemispheres; in particular, some evidence suggests that the differences between the hemispheres may be greater in men than in women (Hellige, 1993; Seamon & Kenrick, 1992; Semrud-Clikeman & Hynd, 1990). (See *Controversies*.) Moreover, even though the differences between the two hemispheres are provocative, we must remember that under normal conditions, the right and left halves of the brain are in close communication through the corpus callosum and thus work together in a coordinated, integrated way (Hoptman & Davidson, 1994). Nevertheless, in recent years, a good deal of popular literature has seized on the highly publicized split-brain research and drawn all kinds of unwarranted conclusions about human behavior. In particular, some authors have inaugurated what is sometimes called a "right-brain movement" to promote the uses and virtues of such supposedly right-brain skills as intuition and creativity. In response, Michael Gazzaniga, one of the pioneers in split-brain research, simply points out: "You don't have to invoke one cent's worth of experimental psychological data or neuroscience to make the observation that there are some people in this world who are terribly intuitive and creative, and some who aren't" (McKean, 1985, p 34).

Split-brain patients, a tiny fraction of people whose cases appear in the annals of odd medical treatments, may shed light on the different abilities of the two sides of the brain, but serious injuries to the brain and spinal cord restrict the mobility and lifestyle of thousands of people each year. Some new research is now offering hope of actually regenerating damaged nerves in people who have been paralyzed through accidents or those severely impaired by degenerative diseases (see *Highlights*).

The Reticular Formation

We separated the brain into hindbrain, midbrain, and forebrain to simplify our discussion. But in the brain different parts often work together to perform certain functions.

The **reticular formation (RF)** is a netlike bundle of neurons running through the hindbrain, the midbrain, and part of the forebrain. Its main job seems to be to send "Alert!" signals to the higher parts of the brain in response to incoming messages. The RF can be subdued, however. An anesthetic, for example, works largely by shutting down this system. Permanent damage to the RF can induce a coma.

The Limbic System

Another example of the interconnected "wiring" of the central nervous system is the **limbic system** (see Figure 2–13). Two of the structures—the

CONTROVERSIES
DO MEN AND WOMEN SPEAK DIFFERENT LANGUAGES?

The notion that human language is controlled primarily by the left cerebral cortex was first set forth in the 1860s by a French physician named Paul Broca. Broca's ideas were modified a decade later by the scientist Karl Wernicke. Thus, it should come as no surprise that the two major language areas in the brain have traditionally been called Broca's area and Wernicke's area (see Figure 2–12).

Wernicke's area lies toward the back of the temporal lobe. This area is crucial in processing and understanding what others are saying. By contrast, Broca's area, found in the frontal lobe, is considered to be essential to our ability to talk. To oversimplify a bit, Wernicke's area seems to be important for listening, and Broca's area seems to be important for talking. Support for these distinctions comes from patients who have suffered left-hemisphere strokes and resulting brain damage. Such strokes often produce language problems, called aphasias, that can be quite predictable. If the brain damage primarily affects Broca's area, the aphasia tends to be "expressive." That is, the patients' language difficulties lie predominantly in sequencing and producing language (talking). If the damage primarily affects Wernicke's area, the aphasia tends to be "receptive," and patients generally have profound difficulties understanding language (listening).

Do the physical differences in men's and women's brains cause any behavioral differences?

Recent research reveals, however, that this model of the brain may apply only to males. Doreen Kimura of the University of Western Ontario has shown that women who have brain damage near Wernicke's area rarely, if ever, experience language difficulties (E. Hampson & Kimura, 1992 Kimura, 1985). Kimura suggests that, in women, an area in the frontal lobe quite close to Broca's area actually combines the functions of both Broca's area and Wer-

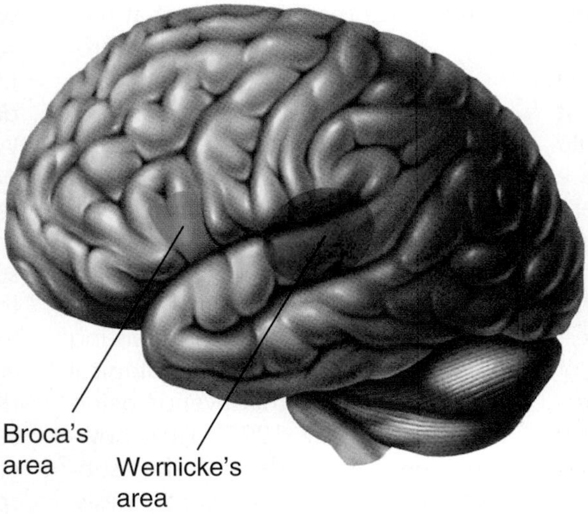

Figure 2–12
Broca's area and Wernicke's area.

Source: Adapted from *Physiology and Behavior* (5th ed.), by Neil R. Carlson. Copyright © 1994 by Allyn & Bacon. Reprinted by permission.

nicke's area. Other brain-mapping studies have lent support to this view (Mateer, Polen, & Ojemann, 1982; Vignolo, Boccardi, & Caverni, 1986).

Along a similar line, Sally Shaywitz of the Yale University School of Medicine discovered that, while reading, men use a portion of the brain near Broca's area, whereas women use both this area and a similar region on the right side of the brain (Shaywitz et al. 1995). This study provides direct evidence that men and women use different areas of the brain for language. Women's use of the right hemisphere for some language functions may also help to explain why women, more often than men, recover their language abilities after strokes involving the left side of the brain.

These data, along with reports that men's and women's brains differ in other ways as well (see Breedlove, 1994), raise a number of questions. Do all males have separate Broca and Wernicke areas for language, and do all females have the more economical, single frontal language area described by Kimura? If so, can we distinguish between male and female ways of understanding and producing language? More generally, are the sexes "hard-wired" in their very brain structures to think differently? Do experience and culture shape specific "male" and "female" ways of thinking and speaking? Or are our patterns of thought and speech based on individual, rather than gender, differences? Scientists know that male and female brains differ in certain demonstrable ways. Whether these physical differences necessarily underlie behavioral differences is a question that requires continuing research.

Questions

1. Can you think of ways in which men and women understand or use language differently?

2. What might be the advantages or disadvantages of having language structures on both sides of the brain?

HIGHLIGHTS
GROWING BRAIN CELLS: NEUROGENESIS

Each year thousands of people suffer injuries to the brain and spinal cord. Traditionally, such injuries have been considered permanent and treatment options were limited to rehabilitation. However, recent research may offer several new options for treating injuries to the central nervous system (CNS) as well as for degenerative disorders such as Parkinson's disease and Alzheimer's disease.

Before birth, human fetuses have a large supply of cells known as *precursor cells* that are capable of becoming neurons in a process known as *neurogenesis*. For many years it was thought that new neurons could not form in adult brains because there were no precursor cells left. Studies with birds, however, gave researchers the first clues into the process of neurogenesis in adults. Scientists discovered that in canaries, new neurons grow in the regions of the brain associated with song learning (Goldman & Nottebohm, 1983). They also found that in black-capped chickadees, neurons die off and are replaced each October when the birds face environmental changes requiring increased learning and memory (Nottebohm & Barnea, 1994). In other studies, researchers learned that new neurons in adult birds arise from precursor cells (Lois & Alvarez-Buylla, 1993, 1994; B. A. Weiss & Reynolds, 1992). Would the same process occur in adult human brains? The question led researchers to obtain tissue from the brains of patients undergoing surgery for severe epilepsy (Altman, 1995). When the brain tissue from these patients was placed in a supportive environment, it produced functioning neurons, demonstrating that adult cells can indeed undergo neurogenesis. More recently, researchers have isolated precursor cells in the spinal cords of adults as well (Wilcox et al., 1997).

These findings hold promise for the development of new methods of treating brain and spinal-cord injuries. Once the substances that regulate neurogenesis are more fully understood, it may be possible to increase the amounts of those substances in areas of the central nervous system where neural growth needs to occur. Growing neurons in the laboratory and transplanting them into patients with neurological damage is yet another avenue being explored (McKay, 1997). First, however, we must identify the substances that control neurogenesis, then grow the millions of neurons required for transplantation, and, finally, figure out a way to place them in the appropriate areas of the nervous system.

Research may offer several new options for treating injuries to the CNS

Other promising research involves the use of fetal brain tissue. For reasons that are still unknown, fetal nerve tissue is not rejected by the brain into which it is implanted. When it is implanted into injured areas of adult brains, fetal brain tissue readily establishes new connections in the recipient brains, replacing damaged or missing tissue. Fetal tissue implants offer hope for arresting or slowing the course of Parkinson's disease and may even be useful in treating Alzheimer's disease. The use of fetal tissues for these purposes raises many ethical issues, however, and therefore remains highly controversial. Eventually, neurogenesis may yield an alternative source of nerve tissue.

Research into repairing neurons within the spinal cord may also allow surgeons to reverse or even prevent the paralysis that now results from damage to the nerves of the spine. When the spinal cord is injured, the body produces cells that block the regrowth of damaged nerves and cause a deterioration of the tissue surrounding the injury. X-rays timed to destroy these cells have been found to prevent some of the damage and allow partial recovery (Kalderon & Fuks, 1996). Microsurgery to guide growth of nerve cells across damaged areas of the spinal cord has also been successful in restoring function in rats that had sections of their spines completely removed (Olson, Cheng, & Cao, 1996). Recently, researchers discovered precursor cells in the spinal cords of adult rats (Wilcox et al., 1997). Because precursor cells have also been found in the spinal cords of human adults (Wilcox et al., 1997), this raises the exciting possibility that future treatments may reverse the paralysis in people with injured spines.

amygdala and the *hippocampus*—play an essential role in the formation of new memories. People with severe damage in these regions cannot form new memories, though they can still remember names, faces, and events that they embedded in memory before they were injured. Animals with damage

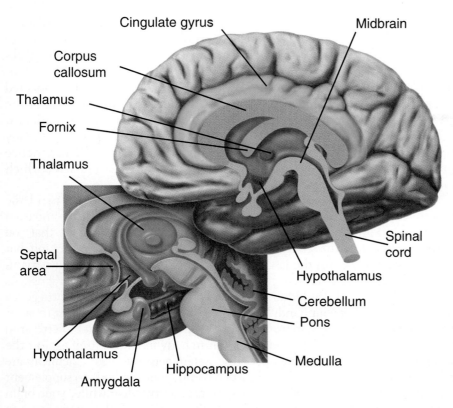

Cingulate gyrus

Corpus callosum

Thalamus

Fornix

Thalamus

Septal area

Hypothalamus

Amygdala

Hippocampus

Midbrain

Spinal cord

Hypothalamus

Cerebellum

Pons

Medulla

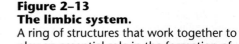

Spinal cord Complex cable of neurons that runs down the spine, connecting the brain to most of the rest of the body.

Figure 2–13
The limbic system.
A ring of structures that work together to play an essential role in the formation of new memories as well as influencing motivation and emotion.

in these areas fail to recognize where they have just been; as a result, they explore the same small part of their environment over and over again, as if it were constantly new to them.

The limbic system influences emotion and motivation (topics we will examine more fully in Chapter 9, Motivation and Emotion). The amygdala and the hippocampus govern emotions related to self-preservation (MacLean, 1970). When portions of these structures are damaged or removed, hostile animals, for example, become tame and docile; by contrast, when portions of these two structures are electrically stimulated, animals show signs of fear and panic, whereas stimulation of other portions of these same structures triggers attack behavior. Two other limbic structures, the *cingulate gyrus* and the *septum*, heighten the experience of pleasure and inhibit aggression. Destruction of areas in these two structures can prompt high levels of aggression. Electrical stimulation of portions of the septum, especially, results in intense pleasure: Animals that are given the opportunity to electrically stimulate themselves in these areas will do so endlessly, even to the point of ignoring all food and water. Evidence suggests that humans also experience pleasure when some areas of the septum are electrically stimulated, though apparently it is not as intense an experience as it is for nonhumans. The limbic system is also closely connected to the *hypothalamus*, which, as we saw earlier in this chapter, plays a central role in a wide variety of motivational and emotional activities such as hunger, thirst, sexual motivation, fear, and anger (Kupfermann, 1991; Olds & Forbes, 1981).

The Spinal Cord

The complex cable of axons that connects the brain to most of the rest of the body is known as the **spinal cord.** We talk of the brain and the spinal cord as two distinct structures, but there is no clear boundary between them because, at its upper end, the spinal cord enlarges and merges into the hindbrain and midbrain. And although the spinal cord tends to receive less attention than the brain, without it we would be severely limited. People who have accidentally severed their spinal cords by breaking their necks provide tragic evidence of how pivotal the spinal cord is to normal functioning. When the cord is severed, parts of the body are literally disconnected from the brain. Accident victims lose all sensations from the parts of the body that can no longer send information to higher brain areas. Similarly, they can no longer control the movements of those body parts, and many times the result is total paralysis. Some with spinal injuries also experience problems with bowel and bladder control or low blood pressure, which makes it difficult to maintain a comfortable body temperature.

The spinal cord is made up of bundles of long axons and has two basic functions: to permit some reflex movements and to carry messages to and from the brain. To understand how intricate these activities are, imagine that you burn your finger on the stove. You pull your hand away without thinking, but that quick response was the last event in a series of reactions in your nervous system. First, special sensory cells pick up the message that your finger is burned. They pass this information along to the spinal cord, which triggers a quick withdrawal of your hand. Meanwhile, the message is being sent to other parts of your nervous system. Your body goes on "emergency alert": You breathe faster, your heart pounds, your entire body mobilizes itself against the wound. At the same time, the endocrine system gets involved: Chemicals are released into the bloodstream and carried throughout the body to supplement and reinforce the effects of nervous system activity. Meanwhile, your brain continues to interpret the messages being sent to it: You feel pain, you look at the burn, you run cold water over your hand. A simple, small burn, then, triggered a complex, coordinated sequence of activities involving the body's nervous system working hand in hand with the endocrine system. A similar reaction occurs when the doctor taps your knee with a rubber mallet (see Figure 2–14). Most spinal reflexes are protective: They enable the body to avoid serious damage and maintain muscle tone and proper position.

3 You burn your finger on a match, and you instantly pull your finger away. What kinds of activities occur within your body during this very brief period?

Figure 2–14
The spinal cord and reflex action.
Simple reflexes are controlled by the spinal cord. The message travels from the sense receptors near the skin through the afferent nerve fibers to the spinal cord. In the spinal cord, the messages are relayed through association neurons to the efferent nerve fibers, which carry them to the muscle cells that cause the reflex movement.

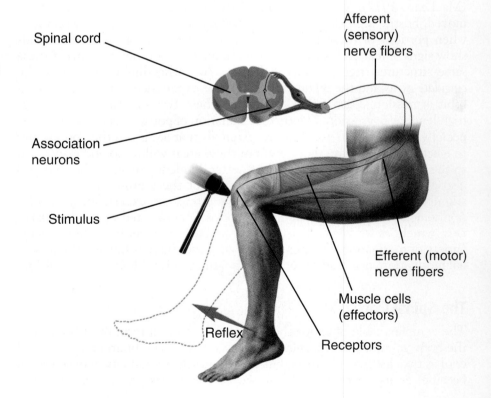

Spinal cord

Association neurons

Stimulus

Afferent (sensory) nerve fibers

Efferent (motor) nerve fibers

Muscle cells (effectors)

Receptors

Reflex

Tools for Studying the Nervous System

Much of what we know about the structure and functioning of the brain was generated by increasingly sophisticated technology. For centuries, our understanding of the brain depended entirely on observing patients who had suffered brain injury or from examining the brains of cadavers. Then, in 1929, Hans Berger developed the *electroencephalograph* (EEG), which provided insight into the living, fully functioning brain. Since that time, there has been a virtual explosion of techniques for studying the nervous system. These techniques include microelectrode, macroelectrode, structural imaging, and functional imaging techniques.

MICROELECTRODE TECHNIQUES *Microelectrode recording techniques* are used to study the functions of single neurons. A microelectrode is a tiny glass or quartz pipette (smaller in diameter than a human hair) that is filled with a conducting liquid. When technicians place the tip of this electrode inside a neuron, they can study changes in the electrical conditions of that neuron. Microelectrode techniques have been used to understand the dynamics of action potentials, the effects of drugs or toxins on neurons, and even processes that occur in the neural membrane.

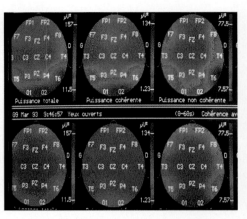

An EEG recording of one person's alpha brain waves. Red and violet colors indicate greater alpha-wave activity.

MACROELECTRODE TECHNIQUES Berger's EEG is an example of how a *macroelectrode* technique is used to study the brain. Macroelectrode techniques require large recording devices to be placed directly on the surface of the scalp, where they can detect the collective electrical activity of millions of neurons in the underlying cortex. These so-called brain waves provide an index of both the size and rhythm of neural activity. The shape and pattern of these waves vary depending on what you happen to be doing at the time. *Alpha waves* are commonly found when you are relaxing with your eyes closed. Alphas change to higher-frequency *beta waves* when you are awake and still but your eyes are open. At the other extreme are the low-frequency *delta waves*, which occur during deepest sleep. As we will see in Chapter 4, States of Consciousness, the changes that occur in brain waves during sleep have given researchers valuable insights into sleep and dreaming.

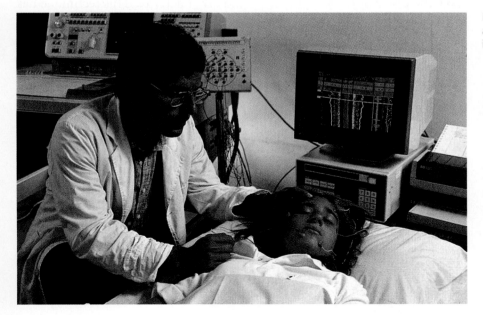

In an EEG, electrodes attached to the scalp are used to create a picture of neural activity in the brain.

An EEG presents a continuous picture of the brain over an extended period. Sometimes, however, technicians want to see what the brain is doing when it is responding to a specific stimulus. To accomplish this, they take a series of EEG traces during the stimulus event. These traces are then analyzed by computer to produce an *event-related potential* (ERP) or *evoked potential* (EP), a pattern representing a specific cortical response to the stimulus. Researchers have discovered that certain components of the ERP appear in the interval between some type of warning signal and response, such as pressing a button. This seems to suggest that brain waves can reflect subtle psychological processes, such as a state of expectancy (Rosenzweig & Leiman, 1982). Because of this, the waves can be "read" as indicators of a person's psychophysiological state; however, they do not reveal information about actual thoughts (Donchin, 1987).

4 What is magnetic resonance imaging?

STRUCTURAL IMAGING   *Computerized axial tomography* (CAT or CT) *scanning* allows scientists to create three-dimensional images of a human brain without performing surgery. To create a CAT scan, an X-ray photography unit rotates around the patient, moving from the top of the head to the bottom; a computer then combines the resulting images. Even more successful at producing pictures of the inner regions of the brain—its ridges, folds, and fissures—is an imaging technique called *magnetic resonance imaging* (MRI). Here the patient's head is placed in a magnetic field, and the brain is exposed to radio waves which causes hydrogen atoms in the brain to release energy. The energy released by different structures in the brain generates an image that appears on a computer screen.

FUNCTIONAL IMAGING   Both CAT scanning and MRI permit unparalleled mapping of the brain's *structures* in living human beings. Neither technique, however, can provide a picture of the brain's *activity* as it actually reacts to sensory stimuli such as pain, tones, and words. This is the goal of several functional imaging methods. In one technique, called *EEG imaging*, measurements of the actual functioning of the brain are made "on a millisecond-by-millisecond basis" (Fischman, 1985, p. 18). In this technique, more than two dozen electrodes are placed at important locations on the scalp. These electrodes record brain activities, which are then converted by a computer into colored images on a television screen. These images show the distribution of alpha, beta, and other activity. This technique has been extremely useful in detecting abnormal cortical activity such as that observed during an epileptic seizure.

Two related techniques, called *magnetoencephalography* (MEG) and *magnetic source imaging* (MSI), take the procedure a step further. In standard EEG, electrical signals are distorted as they pass through the skull, and their exact origin is difficult to determine. However, those same electrical signals create magnetic fields that are unaffected by bone. Both MEG and MSI actually measure the strength of the magnetic field and identify its source with considerable accuracy. Using these procedures, biopsychologists have begun to determine exactly which parts of the brain actually do most of the work in such psychological processes as memory (Gabrieli et al., 1996), language processing (Tulving et al., 1994), and reading. In turn, this research is beginning to shed new light on such disorders as amnesia and dyslexia (a reading disorder). Through these new functional imaging techniques, researchers also hope to pinpoint the areas of the brain affected by particular drugs, such as those used to treat severe psychological disorders like schizophrenia. With this knowledge in hand, they hope to one day eliminate the deleterious side effects these drugs sometimes produce.

MRI image of the human head.

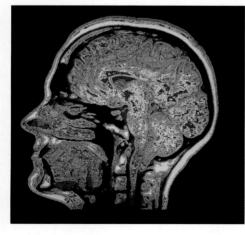

Another family of functional imaging techniques—*positron emission tomography* (PET) *scanning, radioactive PET,* and *single photon emission computed tomography* (SPECT)—uses radioactive energy to map brain activity. In all these techniques, a person first receives an injection of a radioactive substance. Brain structures that are especially active immediately after the injection absorb most of the substance. When the substance starts to decay, it releases subatomic particles. By studying where most of the particles come from, physicians can determine exactly which portions of the brain are most active. Some of the findings produced by these techniques have been surprising. For example, preliminary data indicates that, in general, the brains of people with higher IQ scores are actually *less* active than those of people with lower IQ scores, perhaps because they process information more efficiently (Haier, 1988). Progress has also been made in locating the damaged brain region in which reduced levels of the neurotransmitter dopamine contribute to Parkinson's disease. These techniques also increase our knowledge of the effects of psychoactive drugs such as tranquilizers.

Even more recent techniques measure the movement of blood molecules and water molecules as neurons work. Because these methods enable us to collect images rapidly, and because they do not require radioactive chemicals, they are especially promising as new research tools.

By combining these various techniques, neuroscientists can simultaneously observe anatomical structures (from CAT and MRI), sites of energy use (PET, SPECT, MEG), blood and water movement, and areas of electrical activity in the brain (EEG and ERP). As a result, scientists have begun to study, with unprecedented success, the impact of drugs on the brain, the formation of memories, and the sites of many other mental activities (Sarter, Berntson, & Cacioppo, 1996).

Somatic nervous system The part of the peripheral nervous system that carries messages from the senses to the central nervous system and between the central nervous system and the skeletal muscles.

Autonomic nervous system The part of the peripheral nervous system that carries messages between the central nervous system and the internal organs.

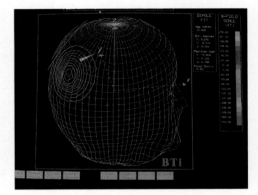
A computer printout of an MEG.

THE PERIPHERAL NERVOUS SYSTEM

Recall from Figure 2–5 that the nervous system is made up of two major parts: the central nervous system (the brain and spinal cord) and the peripheral nervous system. Up to now, we have touched on how the peripheral nervous system transmits messages to and from the central nervous system. In this section, we will examine in greater detail the two branches of the peripheral nervous system: the somatic and the autonomic nervous systems.

The Somatic Nervous System

The **somatic nervous system** is composed of all the *afferent*, or sensory, neurons that carry information to the central nervous system and all the *efferent*, or motor, neurons that carry messages from the central nervous system to the skeletal muscles of the body. All the things that we can sense—sights, sounds, smells, temperature, pressure, and so on—have their origins in the somatic part of the peripheral nervous system. In later chapters, we will see how the somatic nervous system affects our experience of the world both inside and outside our bodies.

The Autonomic Nervous System

The **autonomic nervous system** comprises all the neurons that carry messages between the central nervous system and the internal organs of the body (the glands and the smooth muscles such as the heart and digestive system). The autonomic nervous system is crucial to such body functions as breathing

Sympathetic division Branch of the autonomic nervous system; it prepares the body for quick action in an emergency.

Parasympathetic division Branch of the autonomic nervous system; it calms and relaxes the body.

and ensuring a proper flow of blood. But it also figures in the experience of various emotions—a fact that makes it of special interest to psychologists.

To understand the autonomic nervous system, we must make one more distinction. The autonomic nervous system consists of two branches: the *sympathetic* and *parasympathetic* divisions (see Figure 2–15). Both branches control and integrate the actions of the glands and the smooth muscles within the body.

The axons of the **sympathetic division** are busiest when you are frightened or angry. They carry messages that tell the body to prepare for an emergency and to get ready to act quickly or strenuously. In response to messages from the sympathetic division, your heart pounds, you breathe faster, your pupils enlarge, and your digestion stops. As we will see shortly, the sympathetic nervous system also tells the endocrine system to start pumping chemicals into the bloodstream to further strengthen these reactions. Sympathetic nerve fibers connect to every internal organ in the body—a fact that explains why the body's reaction to sudden stress is so widespread. However, the sympathetic division can also act selectively on a single organ.

Parasympathetic nerve fibers connect to the same organs as the sympathetic nerve fibers, but they cause just the opposite effects. The **parasympathetic division** says, in effect, "Okay, the heat's off, back to normal." The heart then goes back to beating at its normal rate, the stomach muscles

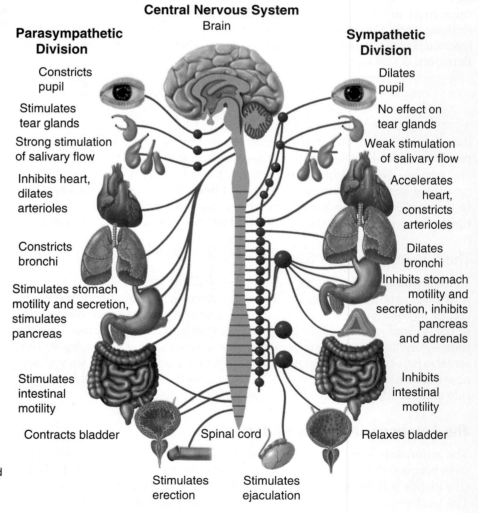

Central Nervous System
Brain

Parasympathetic Division

Constricts pupil

Stimulates tear glands

Strong stimulation of salivary flow

Inhibits heart, dilates arterioles

Constricts bronchi

Stimulates stomach motility and secretion, stimulates pancreas

Stimulates intestinal motility

Contracts bladder

Stimulates erection

Sympathetic Division

Dilates pupil

No effect on tear glands

Weak stimulation of salivary flow

Accelerates heart, constricts arterioles

Dilates bronchi

Inhibits stomach motility and secretion, inhibits pancreas and adrenals

Inhibits intestinal motility

Relaxes bladder

Stimulates ejaculation

Spinal cord

Figure 2–15
The sympathetic and parasympathetic divisions of the autonomic nervous system.
The sympathetic division generally acts to arouse the body, preparing it for "fight or flight." The parasympathetic follows with messages to relax.

Source: Adapted from *General Biology,* revised edition, by Willis Johnson, Richard A. Laubengayer, and Louis E. Delanney, Copyright © 1961 by Holt, Rinehart, and Winston, Inc., and renewed 1989 by Willis H. Johnson and Louis E. Delanney. Reproduced by permission.

relax, digestion resumes, breathing slows down, and the pupils of the eyes contract. So the sympathetic division arouses the body in response to stress; then the parasympathetic division quiets down the system once danger has passed.

To illustrate how these two systems work in an emergency situation, imagine that you are walking through the woods when you suddenly hear a growl. When you turn around, you see a large bear staring right at you. If you are like most people, you become overwhelmed with fear, which is reflected in immediate sympathetic nervous system arousal. Your heart begins to pound rapidly, your respiration increases, and chemicals are released into your bloodstream to sustain this response. The sudden activation of the sympathetic nervous system at a time like this has an obvious adaptive value—it prepares you for "fight or flight." Moreover, the body's quick response to danger is often sustained or prolonged for quite some time after the danger itself has receded, perhaps because menaces in the wild, where humans evolved, may come back. Therefore there is an advantage to being "on alert" for a bit longer than may seem necessary. After a few seconds the bear turns and wanders harmlessly back into the woods, but it will probably take a while for the parasympathetic nervous system to return your body to its normal level of functioning—your heart will continue to race and your respiration will remain rapid long after the threat has passed.

Although an event exactly like the one described above may never happen to you in today's world, our ability to react quickly with a sustained "fight or flight" response—organized in rapid-fire sequence by the sympathetic nervous system—played a significant role in the survival of our ancestors. When they were threatened, the sympathetic nervous system would go into high gear so they could react quickly and have the strength, energy, and stamina to run away, or stand and fight. Today, many of the dangers we face are only momentary and unlikely to return; nonetheless, our bodies continue to produce a sustained sympathetic nervous system response to danger even though there is little or no adaptive value in doing so. For example, although avoiding an automobile collision generally involves a quick response (such as stepping on the brake), a sustained response is not called for. But, because of the widespread way the sympathetic nervous system normally operates, your heart and respiration rate still remain in a heightened state of alert when faced with a near collision because you sense danger. Though both these responses have lost some of their adaptive value—at least in this situation, when merely stepping on the brake will keep us from danger—they are part of our evolutionary heritage, an issue we will take up later in this chapter.

As noted in the example above, these two systems often work in tandem: After the sympathetic division has aroused the body, the parasympathetic division follows with messages to relax. In many people, however, one division or the other may dominate. In general, people who have an overactive parasympathetic division tend to salivate heavily, their hearts beat rather slowly, and their digestive systems are often overactive. People whose sympathetic division dominates show the opposite symptoms: Their mouths are dry, their palms moist, and their hearts beat quickly even when they are resting. Moreover, recent findings indicate that the sympathetic and parasympathetic divisions do not always act in opposition to each other: Sometimes they can act independently of each other, and at other times they can even act simultaneously (Berntson, Cacioppo, & Quigley, 1993).

The autonomic nervous system was traditionally regarded as the "automatic" part of the body's response mechanism. You could not, it was believed, tell your own autonomic nervous system when to speed up or slow down your heartbeat or when to stop or start your digestive processes.

Can we control our own blood pressure and headaches?

Hormones Chemical substances released by the endocrine glands; they help regulate bodily activities.

Endocrine glands Glands of the endocrine system that release hormones into the bloodstream.

Thyroid gland Endocrine gland located below the voice box; it produces the hormone thyroxin.

Evidence suggests, however, that we have more control over the autonomic nervous system than previously thought. According to a number of studies, people (and animals) can indeed manipulate this so-called automatic facet of the nervous system. For example, people can be taught to moderate the severity of high blood pressure or migraine headaches. Some have even learned to regulate their own heart rate and brain waves. These are all cases in which the autonomic nervous system is brought under deliberate control. We will look more closely at these possibilities when we discuss biofeedback in Chapter 5, Learning.

THE ENDOCRINE SYSTEM

The nervous system is not the only mechanism that regulates the functioning of our bodies. Let's return once more to our earlier example. When you burn your finger on a match, you quickly withdraw your finger from the heat. But your response to the burn does not end with the nervous system. Chemical substances called **hormones** are also released into your bloodstream by your **endocrine glands.** These hormones are carried throughout your body, where they have widespread effects on a variety of organs. Hormones interest psychologists for two reasons. First, at certain stages of our development, hormones *organize* the nervous system and body tissues. Consider, for example, the dramatic hormone-induced changes that occur at puberty and at menopause. Second, hormones *activate* behaviors. They affect such things as alertness or sleepiness, excitability, sexual behavior, the ability to concentrate, aggressiveness, reactions to stress, even the desire for companionship. Hormones can also have dramatic effects on mood, emotional reactivity, the ability to learn, and the ability to resist disease. Radical changes in some hormones may also contribute to serious psychological disorders such as depression.

The locations of the endocrine glands are shown in Figure 2–16. We focus below on those glands whose functions are best understood and those whose effects are most closely related to the way we behave.

The Thyroid Gland

The **thyroid gland** is located just below the larynx, or voice box. It produces one primary hormone, *thyroxin*, which regulates the body's rate of metabolism; that is, it determines how fast or how slowly the foods we eat are transformed into the energy we need to function normally. Differences in metabolic rate determine how alert and energetic people are and how fat or thin they tend to be.

An overactive thyroid can produce a great variety of symptoms: overexcitability, insomnia, reduced attention span, fatigue, agitation, acting out of character, and making snap decisions, as well as reduced concentration and difficulty focusing on a task. Little wonder, then, that there was considerable concern in the spring of 1991 when it was discovered that President George Bush was suffering from an

**Figure 2–16
The glands of the endocrine system.**

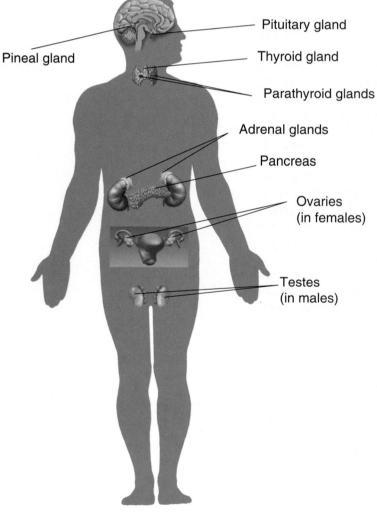

Pineal gland

Pituitary gland

Thyroid gland

Parathyroid glands

Adrenal glands

Pancreas

Ovaries
(in females)

Testes
(in males)

overactive thyroid. Too little thyroxin leads to the other extreme: You will want to sleep and sleep and will still feel constantly tired. Without enough thyroxin, your body is unable to maintain normal temperature, muscle tone is reduced, and metabolism is sluggish.

The Parathyroid Glands

Embedded in the thyroid gland are the **parathyroids**—four tiny, pea-shaped organs. They secrete the hormone *parathormone*, which controls and balances the levels of calcium and phosphate in the blood and tissue fluids. The level of calcium in the blood has a direct effect on the excitability of the nervous system. A person with too little parathormone will be hypersensitive and may suffer from twitches or muscle spasms. Too much parathormone, on the other hand, can lead to lethargy and poor physical coordination.

The Pineal Gland

The **pineal gland** is a pea-sized gland that apparently regulates activity levels over the course of a day. Increased levels of light in the morning stimulate the pineal gland, which, in turn, reduces the amount of the hormone *melatonin* it releases into the bloodstream. As a result, body temperature rises, and the organism becomes more active—it "wakes up" and prepares for a new day. At the end of the day, as light levels decrease, the pineal gland releases more melatonin, which lowers body temperature and reduces the organism's overall level of activity in preparation for sleep. These effects (which we will study in greater detail in Chapter 4, States of Consciousness) are most evident in lower animals such as birds and rats; in fact, in birds, sunlight can shine right through the skull onto the pineal gland (Levinthal, 1990). The pineal gland may have similar effects on humans, though research evidence is sketchy on this point. There is some speculation that people who suffer from *seasonal affective disorder*—becoming depressed during the dark winter months—may be suffering from too much melatonin released by the pineal gland in response to the reduced hours of daylight in that season, though research on this hypothesis is only in the early stages.

The Pancreas

The **pancreas** lies in a curve between the stomach and the small intestine. The pancreas controls the level of sugar in the blood by secreting two regulating hormones: *insulin* and *glucagon*. These two hormones work against each other to keep the blood-sugar level properly balanced.

When the pancreas secretes too little insulin, making for too much sugar in the blood, the kidneys attempt to get rid of the excess sugar by excreting a great deal more water than usual. Body tissues become dehydrated and poisonous wastes accumulate in the blood. These symptoms are characteristic of *diabetes mellitus*. People with diabetes must take insulin and maintain a special diet to keep their blood-sugar levels normal. Oversecretion of insulin leads to the chronic fatigue of *hypoglycemia*, a condition in which there is too little sugar in the blood.

The Pituitary Gland

The endocrine gland that produces the largest number of different hormones, and thus has the widest range of effects on the body's functions, is the **pituitary gland.** This gland is located on the underside of the brain and is connected to the hypothalamus. The pituitary gland has two parts that function separately.

Parathyroids Four tiny glands embedded in the thyroid; they secrete parathormone.

Pineal gland A gland located roughly in the center of the brain that appears to regulate activity levels over the course of a day.

Pancreas Organ lying between the stomach and small intestine; it secretes insulin and glucagon to regulate blood-sugar levels.

Pituitary gland Gland located on the underside of the brain; it produces the largest number of the body's hormones.

Production of too much growth hormone by the pituitary results in giantism; too little hormone results in dwarfism.

The **posterior pituitary,** so called because it is located toward the back of the pituitary gland, is controlled by the nervous system. It secretes two hormones. One, *vasopressin*, causes blood pressure to rise and regulates the amount of water in the body's cells. Too little vasopressin results in extreme thirst. The other, *oxytocin*, has long been known to cause the uterus to contract during childbirth and the mammary glands to start producing milk. But scientists have noted a puzzling fact: Males also have significant levels of oxytocin, suggesting that this hormone may have functions beyond childbirth and nursing. Research now indicates that oxytocin has a powerful effect on sexual behavior, grooming, maternal and paternal behavior, and social companionship: Animals with higher levels of oxytocin or increased numbers of receptors for oxytocin in the brain are more sexually active, they engage in much more grooming, they pay greater attention to their young, and they seem to crave companionship from other animals (Caldwell et al., 1989; Insel & Harbaugh, 1989; Jirikowski et al., 1989; Witt & Insel, 1991). Whether oxytocin plays a similar role in humans is still under investigation, but we do know that during sexual intercourse oxytocin levels in men are three to five times higher than normal and that people who have lost interest in sex can regain that interest when the level of oxytocin in the body is increased.

The **anterior pituitary,** located toward the front of the pituitary gland, is controlled by chemical messages from the bloodstream and is often called the "master gland." It produces numerous hormones that trigger the action of other endocrine glands. Among the functions of the anterior pituitary is the production of the body's growth hormone, through which it controls the amount and timing of body growth. Dwarfism and giantism are the result of too little and too much growth hormone, respectively.

The functioning of the anterior pituitary provides a good example of the interaction between the endocrine system and the nervous system. The operation of the anterior pituitary is partly controlled by hormones released by the hypothalamus—part of the nervous system (Schally, Kastin, & Arimura, 1977). Hormones released from the anterior pituitary cause the reproductive glands to produce still other hormones, which, in turn, affect the hypothalamus, producing changes in behavior or feeling. Thus, the hypothalamus triggers action by the anterior pituitary, which indirectly affects the hypothalamus. This circular route is typical of the kind of two-way interaction that often takes place between the body's nervous system and endocrine system.

The Gonads

The **gonads**—the *testes* in males and the *ovaries* in females and, to a lesser extent, the adrenal glands—secrete hormones that have traditionally been classified as masculine and feminine. These are the *androgens* and *estrogens*, respectively. Although both sexes produce both types of hormone, androgens predominate in males, whereas estrogens predominate in females. These hormones play a number of important organizing roles in human development. For example, in humans, if the hormone *testosterone* is present during the third and fourth month after conception, the fetus will develop as a male; otherwise it will develop as a female (Kalat, 1988). Testosterone and other androgens are also linked to sexual interest and behavior in adults of both sexes.

Testosterone has long been thought to play a role in aggressive behavior. Violence is greatest among males between 15 and 25 years of age, the years when testosterone levels are at their highest. Both male and female prisoners with high levels of testosterone are likely to have committed crimes at an earlier age and to have committed more violent crimes (Dabbs et al., 1995; Dabbs & Morris, 1990). Even in a noncriminal population, men with higher levels of testosterone "more often reported having trouble with parents, teachers, and classmates . . ." (Dabbs & Morris, 1990, p. 209).

Recent evidence, however, seems to point to an excess of estrogen, rather than testosterone, as a source of aggressive behavior. In both sexes the brain has receptors for testosterone as well as estrogen. Male mice that are genetically engineered to lack estrogen receptors are much less aggressive than normal male mice (Ogawa et al., 1997). In humans, men who have lower levels of testosterone report feeling more aggressive and irritable before they receive replacement testosterone (Angier, 1995; Wang, 1995). A similar study found that when testosterone levels are experimentally lowered in normal males, they feel more aggressive. Taken together, these results indicate that aggression has a source other than testosterone. Indeed, when boys and girls have delayed onset of puberty and are therapeutically treated with hormones, girls actually become more aggressive under the influence of estrogen than the boys given testosterone (Angier, 1995).

Although estrogen is related to testosterone, the precise way it influences sexual behavior is still unclear. Most female mammals, including humans, are more sexually receptive during the ovulatory phase of their estrous (nonhuman) or menstrual (human) cycles, when estrogen levels are highest (D. B. Adams, Gold, & Burt, 1978). However, when the ovaries have been surgically removed, which dramatically lowers levels of estrogen, human female sexual activity and interest do not diminish significantly. Thus researchers have concluded that estrogen does not affect sexual drive or behavior directly (Dennerstein & Burrows, 1982; Martin, Roberts, & Clayton, 1980).

Interestingly, estrogen seems to boost cognitive abilities. It has been associated with increased performance on certain tests of manual dexterity, verbal skills, and perceptual speed. Thus, women do better at these sorts of cognitive tasks during the ovulatory phase of their menstrual cycles. In addition, postmenopausal women show improvement in these tasks when they undergo estrogen replacement therapy (E. Hampson & Kimura, 1992; Kimura & Hampson, 1994). Beyond the cognitive effects of estrogen, the rate of strokes and heart attacks in premenopausal women is generally lower than that in men, but after menopause, when estrogen levels decline, strokes and heart attacks increase in women. These findings suggest that estrogen may serve some "protective" function in women but not in men.

The Adrenal Glands

The two **adrenal glands** are located just above the kidneys. Each adrenal gland has two parts: an outer covering, called the **adrenal cortex,** and an inner core, called the **adrenal medulla.** Both the adrenal cortex and the adrenal medulla affect the body's reaction to stress. Imagine that you are walking down the street when you see a professor to whom you owe an overdue paper. As you approach the professor, you realize that there is no graceful escape. You begin to experience stress. The hypothalamus secretes a hormone that causes the anterior pituitary gland to release two more hormones. One is **beta endorphin,** one of the body's natural painkillers. The other is *ACTH*, a messenger hormone that goes to the adrenal cortex. Alerted by ACTH from the pituitary, the adrenal cortex, in turn, secretes hormones that increase the level of blood sugar, help to break down proteins, and help the body respond to injury. Meanwhile, the adrenal medulla is stimulated by the autonomic nervous system so that it also pours several hormones into the bloodstream: *Epinephrine* activates the sympathetic nervous system,

Adrenal glands Two endocrine glands located just above the kidneys.

Adrenal cortex Outer covering of the two adrenal glands; the adrenal cortex releases hormones important for dealing with stress.

Adrenal medulla Inner core of the adrenal glands that also releases hormones to deal with stress.

Beta endorphin One of the endorphins, a natural painkiller released by the body.

Nature versus nurture A debate surrounding the relative importance of heredity (nature) and environment (nurture) in determining behavior.

Behavior genetics Study of the relationship between heredity and behavior.

Evolutionary psychology A subfield of psychology concerned with the origins of behaviors and mental processes, their adaptive value, and the purposes they continue to serve.

making the heart beat faster, stopping digestion, enlarging the pupils of the eyes, sending more sugar into the bloodstream, and preparing the blood to clot fast, if necessary. Another hormone, *norepinephrine* (previously noted as a neurotransmitter), not only raises the blood pressure by causing the blood vessels to become constricted but is also carried by the bloodstream to the anterior pituitary, where it triggers the release of still more ACTH, thus prolonging the response to stress. The result: Your body is well prepared to deal with the stress. It may even mobilize you to finish and submit that overdue paper.

Rather than dwelling on the complicated details of all these hormonal processes, all we need to understand is that the endocrine system plays a key role in helping to coordinate and integrate complex psychological reactions. In fact, as we've noted throughout this chapter, the nervous system and the endocrine system work together in a constant chemical conversation. We will see other examples of this interaction in Chapter 9, Motivation and Emotion.

BEHAVIOR GENETICS AND OUR HUMAN HERITAGE

At the moment that a sperm from your father united with an egg from your mother, the first cell that was to grow into you was created. In its nucleus was packed a set of chemically encoded messages, called *genes*, that would help to guide the development and functioning of your body. Most important to psychologists, these genes have influenced the workings of your nervous and endocrine systems, which in turn have affected how you tend to think and act. Genes, in other words, are at least partly responsible for some of your behavior.

Although the idea of genes influencing human behavior seems simple enough, in the past it has sparked much controversy. The impact of genes on behavior represents one side of the **nature versus nurture** debate. The question of nature versus nurture, in its *purest* form, is concerned with identifying the factors that cause us all to develop, think, and behave differently from one another. Supporters of the nature side of the debate argue that hereditary factors play the major role in determining such characteristics as our intelligence, personality, and temperament. Advocates of the nurture side would argue that the environment including our daily experiences, upbringing, and education are the major determinants of these characteristics. Today, no psychologist would take either a pure nature or pure nurture position. Contemporary psychologists recognize the influence of *both* genetics and environment in shaping human behavior. Researchers have made enormous strides in understanding how these two forces interact. For example, recall the experiments described in *Highlights*, p. 55. There, we saw that the environment can actually cause chemical and structural changes in the brain. Nonetheless, strong disagreement still exists regarding the relative importance of heredity and environment and their influence on our thoughts, abilities, personalities, and behaviors.

Two different, but related fields address the influence of heredity on human behavior—behavior genetics and evolutionary psychology. **Behavior genetics** is concerned with how specific traits are transmitted from parents to their children. **Evolutionary psychology,** as the name suggests, emphasizes the evolutionary mechanisms that may account for the origins of various behaviors and mental processes. In the remainder of this chapter we will discuss both of these perspectives and see how research in these areas has contributed to contemporary psychology.

Genetics

Genetics is the study of how plants, animals, and people pass on traits from one generation to the next. A **trait** is any characteristic that differs from one organism to another: hair texture, eye color, intelligence, aggressiveness, even an allergy to poison ivy. The transmission of traits from one generation to the next is **heredity.**

Gregor Mendel, an Austrian monk, pioneered the study of modern genetics in 1867 when he reported the results of his research on many years of systematically breeding peas. Mendel believed that every trait was controlled by elements that were transmitted from one generation to the next. He called these elements **genes.**

Much more is known today about genes and how they work. We know, for example, that within a cell nucleus genes are lined up on tiny threadlike bodies called **chromosomes,** which are visible under an electron microscope. The chromosomes are arranged in pairs, and each species has a constant number of pairs. Mice have 20 pairs, monkeys have 27, peas have 7. Human beings have 23 pairs of chromosomes in every normal cell.

The main ingredient of chromosomes and genes is **deoxyribonucleic acid (DNA),** a complex organic molecule that looks like two chains twisted around each other in a double helix pattern. The order of this twisting DNA forms a code that carries our genetic information. The individual genes, which are the smallest units the DNA, carry instructions for a particular process or trait. We now know that the nucleus of every cell contains DNA with enough genetic coding to direct the development of that single cell into a fully grown adult with billions of cells!

Each pair of chromosomes carries a complete set of genes. Because each pair provides the coding for the same kinds of traits, a gene for a given trait may exist in two alternate forms. We can think of a gene for eye color, for example, as having one form, B, which will result in brown eyes, and another form, b, which will result in blue eyes. If a girl receives b genes from both parents, her eyes will be blue. But if she inherits a b gene from one parent and a B gene from the other, her eyes will be brown (see Figure 2–17).

The B form is thus said to be the **dominant gene,** whereas the b form is the **recessive gene.** Although the girl with one B gene and one b gene has brown eyes, the recessive b gene is still present in her and can be passed on

Genetics Study of how traits are transmitted from one generation to the next.

Traits Characteristics on which organisms differ.

Heredity The transmission of traits from one generation to the next.

Genes Elements that control the transmission of traits; they are found on the chromosomes.

Chromosomes Pairs of threadlike bodies within the cell nucleus that contain the genes.

Deoxyribonucleic acid (DNA) Complex molecule in a double-helix configuration that is the main ingredient of chromosomes and genes and forms the code for all genetic information.

Dominant gene Member of a gene pair that controls the appearance of a certain trait.

Recessive gene Member of a gene pair that can control the appearance of a certain trait only if it is paired with another recessive gene.

The 23 pairs of chromosomes found in every normal human cell. The two members of twenty-two of these pairs look exactly alike. The two members of the 23rd pair, the sex chromosomes, may or may not look alike. Females have equivalent X chromosomes, while males have one X and one Y, which look very different. Shown in the inset is the chromosome pattern that causes Down syndrome—the presence of three chromosomes number 21.

The twisted chain of the long DNA molecule contains the genetic code.

Polygenic inheritance Process by which several genes interact to produce a certain trait; responsible for our most important traits.

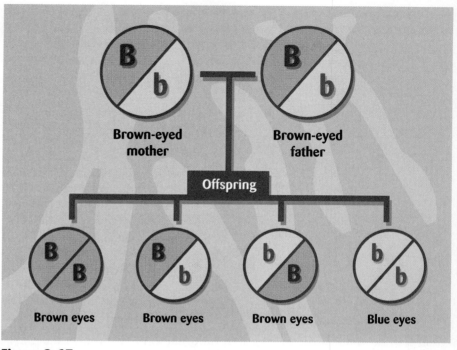

Figure 2–17
Transmission of eye color by dominant (B) and recessive (b) genes.
This figure represents the four possible combinations of eye-color genes in these parents' offspring. Because three out of the four combinations result in brown-eyed children, the chance that any child will have brown eyes is 75 percent.

to her offspring, thus producing a blue-eyed child, if it is paired with a recessive *b* gene from the male parent.

We have been talking about characteristics such as eye color that are controlled by single genes. In fact, however, most of our important traits, such as intelligence, height, and weight, *cannot* be traced back to a single gene. Rather, a number of genes make a small or moderate contribution to the trait in question in a process known as **polygenic inheritance.** For instance, imagine the number of genes that must be involved in determining the potential structure and number of synapses in the human brain and how they ultimately affect such traits as intelligence and personality. Just as each of the instruments in a symphony orchestra contributes separate notes to the sound that reaches the audience, each of the genes in a polygenic system contributes separately to the total effect (McClearn et al., 1991).

The effects of heredity need not be immediately or fully apparent. In some cases, expression of a trait is delayed until later in life. For example, many men inherit "male-pattern baldness" that does not show up until middle age. Moreover, quite often genes may predispose a person to developing a particular trait, but environmental factors alter or suppress the expression of that trait. Having the proper genes provides a person with the potential for a trait, but that trait may not come to the fore unless the environment cooperates. That is, both nature and nurture are required for the expression of most traits. For example, people with an inherited tendency to gain weight may or may not become obese depending on their diet, exercise program, and overall health. With these general principles in mind, let's look at how psychologists study the relationship between genetics and behavior and see what they have learned so far.

Genetics and Behavior

We have been examining the role of genetics in determining differences among people in various *physical* characteristics, such as eye color, height, and weight. But there is increasing evidence that heredity also has a significant impact on a wide range of behavior and conditions, including hypertension, epilepsy, hyperactivity, some forms of mental retardation, emotionality and responsiveness to stress, nervousness, shyness, aggressiveness, intelligence, some forms of mental illness, and alcohol dependence and other drug addictions (Brunner et al., 1993; Johnson, 1990; Loehlin, Willerman, & Horn, 1988; Plomin, DeFries, & McClearn, 1990; Plomin & Rende, 1991). Of course, genes do not directly cause behavior. Rather, they affect both the development and operation of the nervous system and the endocrine system, which, in turn, influence the likelihood that a certain behavior will occur under the proper circumstances.

In the remainder of this chapter, we will look at some of the methods used by behavior geneticists as well as some of their more interesting discoveries. We will start with methods appropriate for animal studies and then examine the techniques used to study behavior genetics in humans.

ANIMAL BEHAVIOR GENETICS Psychologists have devised several ways to determine the extent to which particular behavioral traits are passed on from one generation to the next (Plomin, DeFries, & McClearn, 1990). **Strain studies** are often used with animals to determine the heritability of traits. Close relatives, such as siblings, are intensively inbred over many generations to create strains of animals that are genetically similar to one another and different from other strains. Mice are often used because they breed quickly and yet have relatively complex behavior patterns. When animals from different strains are raised together in the same environment, differences between them largely reflect genetic differences in the strains. Using this method, it has been shown that differences between mice with respect to such traits as sense of smell, susceptibility to seizures, and performance on a number of learning tasks are all affected by heredity.

Selection studies can also be used with animals to assess heritability. If a trait is closely regulated by genes, then when animals having the trait are bred with one another, more of their offspring should have the trait than one would normally find in the general population. By measuring changes in the proportion of successive generations that have the trait, scientists can estimate the heritability of that trait.

Artificial selection has been used for thousands of years to create breeds of dogs and many other animals that have desirable traits. Terriers, for example, were originally bred to crawl into burrows and chase out small animals living there. In France, dogs have been bred for specialized aspects of farmwork; in the United Kingdom, dogs have been bred for centuries to point to hidden prey or to retrieve downed birds. Taking note that dog breeds differ greatly in many respects, including the development of social relationships, excitability, and trainability, scientists conclude that variations in these psychological characteristics are, at least to some extent, governed by genetics (Plomin, DeFries, & McClearn, 1990).

HUMAN BEHAVIOR GENETICS Both strain and selection studies are out of the question for studying the genetic basis of human behavior. However, scientists have developed a number of new molecular genetics techniques that are making it possible to study, and even change, the human genetic code directly. The so-called Human Genome Project has set out to map all 23 pairs of human chromosomes (the entire human genome) and to determine

Strain studies Studies of the heritability of behavioral traits using animals that have been inbred to produce strains that are genetically similar to one another.

Selection studies Studies that estimate the heritability of a trait by breeding animals with other animals that have the same trait.

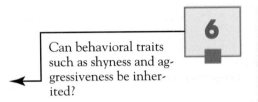

6

Can behavioral traits such as shyness and aggressiveness be inherited?

People clearly do inherit physical traits from their parents. Whether—and to what extent—they also inherit behavioral traits remains uncertain.

Family studies Studies of heritability in humans based on the assumption that if genes influence a certain trait, close relatives should be more similar on that trait than distant relatives.

Twin studies Studies of identical and fraternal twins to determine the relative influence of heredity and environment on human behavior.

Identical twins Twins developed from a single fertilized ovum and therefore identical in genetic makeup at the time of conception.

Fraternal twins Twins developed from two separate fertilized ova and therefore different in genetic makeup.

Identical twins develop from a single ovum and consequently start out with the same genetic material. Fraternal twins develop from two different fertilized ova and so are as different in genetic makeup as any two children of the same parents.

which genes influence which characteristics (Johnson, 1990; Plomin & Rende, 1991). For example, researchers have already identified an individual gene on chromosome 19 that is associated with some forms of Alzheimer's disease (Corder et al., 1993), and other specific chromosome sites have been implicated in alcoholism (Uhl et al., 1993) and intelligence (Plomin et al., 1994). By using these genetic markers, researchers expect that eventually we will be able to understand the role of heredity in even the most complex behaviors (Plomin, DeFries, & McClearn, 1990).

Although the results of those studies lie in the future, a good deal has already been learned indirectly about human behavior genetics by analyzing the behavioral similarities of members of the same family. **Family studies** are based on the assumption that if genes influence a trait, close relatives should share that trait more often than distant relatives because close relatives have more genes in common. So far, family studies have uncovered strong evidence that heredity plays a role in some forms of mental illness. Siblings of people with schizophrenia, for example, are about eight times more likely to develop schizophrenia than someone chosen randomly from the general population. And children of schizophrenic parents are about ten times more likely to develop schizophrenia than are other children. Moreover, a recent controversial study in the Netherlands (Brunner et al., 1993) found what appears to be a genetic link in one family between aggressive and violent tendencies on the one hand and mutations in a gene responsible for one of the enzymes that deactivate dopamine, norepinephrine, and serotonin on the other. Although findings such as these may lead to greater understanding of some types of behavior, no one is claiming that a genetic flaw lies at the base of every case of schizophrenia or all human violence. Moreover, such findings do not completely rule out the influence of environment. Growing up in a household in which both parents have schizophrenia might cause a child to develop the disorder even if that child does not have a genetic predisposition for the illness (Plomin, DeFries, & McClearn, 1990). Similarly, we cannot rule out the behavioral effects of growing up in a family in which violence is commonplace.

In an effort to separate more clearly the influences of heredity from that of environment on human behavior, psychologists often use **twin studies.** Twins can be either identical or fraternal. **Identical twins** develop from a single fertilized ovum, and at the moment of conception they are therefore identical in genetic makeup. Any differences between them should be due to environmental differences. **Fraternal twins,** however, develop from two separate fertilized egg cells and are no more similar genetically than are other brothers and sisters. The differences between fraternal twins thus stem from both heredity and environment. Assuming that the various pairs of twins studied grow up in similar environments, if identical twins share no more similarities on particular characteristics than fraternal twins do, then heredity cannot be very important for that trait.

Twin studies have bolstered evidence for the heritability of a number of behaviors. Let's return to the example of schizophrenia. Overall, schizophrenia occurs in only 1 to 2 percent of the general population (Robins, 1991). When one identical twin develops schizophrenia, however, the other twin will develop the disorder about 50 percent of the time. For fraternal twins, the chances are about 15 percent that the second twin will develop the disorder (Gottesman, 1991). The much higher rate exhibited by twins, particularly identical twins, suggests that heredity plays a crucial role in schizophrenia.

Mental abilities are also affected by heredity. Numerous studies reveal that genetics figures strongly in general intelligence (Loehlin & Nichols, 1976; Wilson, 1983). We will examine this relationship more closely in Chapter 8, Intelligence and Mental Abilities. Genetics influences specific cognitive abilities, too, such as verbal and spatial skills, and memory. Twin studies also substantiate genetic influences on temperament and personality, ranging from mannerisms such as the strength of a handshake to smoking and drinking habits, and even tastes in food (Farber, 1981).

Similarities between twins, even identical twins, cannot automatically be attributed to genetics, however. Twins generally are reared in the same environment; thus, similarities in their behavior may reflect the fact that they are often treated alike. It would be easier to separate the effects of heredity from those of the environment if we could study identical twins who were separated at birth or in very early childhood and then raised in different homes. A University of Minnesota research team led by Thomas Bouchard has done just that for more than 10 years (Bouchard, 1984; 1996; Bouchard et al., 1990). The Minnesota team has confirmed that genetics plays a major role in such things as mental retardation, schizophrenia, depression, and intelligence. Bouchard and his colleagues have also found that complex personality traits, interests, and talents, and even the structure of brain waves are guided by genetics. Studies of twins reared apart became a source of heated debate, however, when researchers reported some genetic basis for such things as the ability to tell a good story, preference in dogs and cigarette brands, use of specific aftershaves, choice of hobbies, preference for particular automobile brands, attraction to tattoos, and even preferred names for children.

Critics of twin studies are numerous (see, for example, Ford, 1993; Wyatt, 1993), and their criticisms have some merit. For example, even identical twins reared apart are likely to grow up in similar environments because adoption agencies usually try to place siblings in similar homes. If these twins turn out to share particular traits, how do we know whether the similarity is due to genetics or to the similarities of the homes in which they were reared? Moreover, people with a certain characteristic (such as intelligence or attractiveness) are likely to be treated in similar ways by other people. How can we tell with confidence whether their similarities are due to genetics or to the ways that others have reacted to them during the course of their lives? Do studies of twins raised separately really eliminate environmental variables and focus exclusively on heredity? Or do they instead demonstrate the extent to which similar environments and life experiences interact with similar genetic codes to produce similar traits and behaviors?

Recently, researchers have become interested in **adoption studies.** Adoption studies focus on children who were adopted at birth and brought up by parents not genetically related to them. Adoption studies provide additional evidence for the heritability of intelligence and some forms of mental illness (Horn, 1983; Scarr & Weinberg, 1983). For example, one study located 47 people who had mothers with schizophrenia but who had been adopted at birth and reared by normal parents. Of these 47 people, 5 subsequently suffered from schizophrenia. In another group of people who had been adopted at birth but whose parents did not have schizophrenia, there was not a single case of schizophrenia (Heston, 1966). By combining the results of *twin, adoption,* and *family* studies, psychologists have obtained an even clearer picture of the role of heredity in schizophrenia. As shown in Figure 2–18, the average risk of schizophrenia steadily increases in direct relation to the closeness of one's biological relationship to an individual with the disorder.

Adoption studies Research carried out on children, adopted at birth by parents not related to them, to determine the relative influence of heredity and environment on human behavior.

Natural selection The mechanism proposed by Darwin in his theory of evolution, which states that organisms best adapted to their environment tend to survive, transmitting their genetic characteristics to succeeding generations, whereas organisms with less adaptive characteristics tend to vanish from the earth.

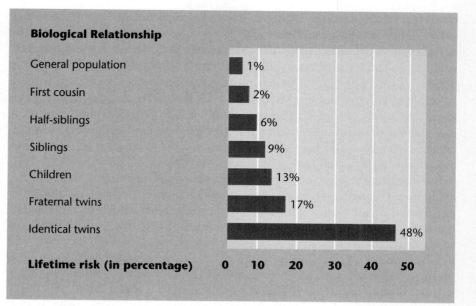

Biological Relationship

General population — 1%
First cousin — 2%
Half-siblings — 6%
Siblings — 9%
Children — 13%
Fraternal twins — 17%
Identical twins — 48%

Lifetime risk (in percentage)   0   10   20   30   40   50

Figure 2-18
Average risk of schizophrenia among biological relatives of people with schizophrenia.

Source: Adapted from Gottesman, *Schizophrenia genesis: The origins of madness,* New York: Freeman, 1991, p. 96.

In the past few years, researchers from the field of behavior genetics have begun to probe a wide array of human behaviors once thought to be solely determined by environmental factors. This research has revealed that traits as diverse as sexual orientation (Bailey & Bell, 1993; Bailey & Benishay, 1993; King & McDonald, 1992; Whitam, Diamond, & Martin, 1993) and smoking (Boomsma et al., 1994; Heath & Martin, 1993) are influenced by heredity. Other studies of biological and adoptive families have noted that chronic alcoholism (Heath et al., 1994) and even suicide—two phenomena that would at first appear to be tightly tied to environmental influences—may have a strong genetic basis. This might help explain why most people who drink do not develop chronic alcoholism, and why only a fraction of the population resorts to suicide when they despair (Kety, 1979).

In the preceding section we saw how heredity, as studied by behavior geneticists, helps psychologists explain some of the *differences* in human behavior. Now we'll examine how the related field of evolutionary psychology uses the principles of heredity to help psychologists understand some of the *commonalities* in human behavior.

Evolution

Although Charles Darwin was not the first person to propose a theory of evolution to account for the origin and diversity of life, his theory of **natural selection,** put forth in the book *On the Origin of Species* in 1859, was the first to offer a credible mechanism to explain *how* evolution occurs.

Darwin's theory of natural selection rests on the following observations:

1. *Variations exist between the individual members of a species.* (For example, although all giraffes have long necks, some have longer necks than others.)

2. *These characteristics may, in turn, be inherited by their offspring.* (Giraffes with the longest necks tend to have offspring with longer necks than other giraffes.)

3. *Individuals with characteristics that give them an advantage over others in surviving and reproducing will leave more offspring.* (If giraffes with the

longest necks have access to a more abundant food supply in higher trees, they will be more likely to survive and produce more baby giraffes than giraffes with shorter necks.)

4. *The advantaged offspring are also more likely to survive and reproduce, resulting in an increase in individuals with those characteristics.* (Giraffes with the longest necks will increase in number.)

Natural selection therefore promotes the survival and reproduction of individuals that are adapted to their particular environment. If the environment changes, or the individual moves into a new environment, the survival and reproductive value of inherited characteristics may also change.

Darwin proposed his theory of evolution before the mechanism of heredity through genes was discovered. Today we know that genes are the unit of selection and that it is the change in the frequencies of genes within populations that leads to evolution. In modern terms, we can restate Darwin's theory as follows:

1. *Individual members of any given species vary in the genes they carry.*

2. *These genes may, in turn, be inherited by an individual's offspring.*

3. *Individuals with genes that give them an advantage over others in surviving and reproducing will leave more offspring.*

4. *The advantaged offspring are also more likely to survive and reproduce, resulting in an increase in the frequency of those genes within a population.*

Even though the principles of evolution and natural selection were described by Darwin over 100 years ago, they still serve today as a cornerstone of all contemporary life sciences. Darwin's principles also unify theories in biology, geology, geography, and anthropology. Some psychologists too, are applying the principles of evolution and natural selection to human emotions, thoughts, and behaviors.

Evolutionary Psychology

As described in Chapter 1, evolutionary psychology spotlights the evolutionary origins of behaviors and mental processes, emphasizing the adaptive or survival value of such traits. Rather than focusing on the *structural changes* in organisms, as biologists do in their application of evolutionary theory, evolutionary psychologists concern themselves with the role natural selection may have played in selecting for adaptive *behaviors*.

Evolutionary psychologists are especially interested in social behaviors such as aggression, jealousy, number of sexual partners, and criteria for choosing a mate—behaviors that may have been adaptive and thus perpetuated the genes of individuals displaying those behaviors. For example, in selecting a mate, the different behaviors exhibited by males and females can be explained by examining the different adaptive strategies that may have been naturally selected for in males and females. Consider the greater investment in reproduction that a female makes compared to a male in terms of producing an egg, going through pregnancy, and caring and providing nourishment for the offspring. It would seem to be most adaptive for females to look for males who will provide the best genes, resources, and long-term parental care. Males, on the other hand, are limited only by the number of prospective mates they can attract because sperm are plentiful and quickly replaced. It may be that it is most adaptive for males to seek to mate with as many females as they can and to compete with other males for access to females.

7

Do behaviors that promoted survival in the early evolution of human beings still influence the way people behave today?

Amniocentesis Technique that involves collecting cells cast off by the fetus into the fluid of the womb and testing them for genetic abnormalities.

Studies analyzing human behaviors associated with sexual selection have found that men and women do indeed take different approaches to sexuality, mate choice, and aggression, as predicted by evolutionary psychology. For example, Buss (1989; 1992) surveyed over 10,000 people from 37 cultures to determine what they considered to be desirable characteristics of potential mates. In every culture, the men who were surveyed put greater emphasis on youth and attractiveness than did the women. In addition, in almost every culture women found men with higher earning capacity to be more desirable. Women in most cultures also considered ambitiousness and industriousness in men to be more important traits than did the men in those same cultures. In comparing the evolutionary psychology explanation with the more traditional social learning explanation of the origins of sex differences in social behavior, another researcher concluded that evolutionary psychology accounted much better for the overall pattern of results (Archer, 1996).

Evolutionary psychology, however, has its critics. Some opponents argue that evolutionary psychology uses science to justify perpetuating unjust social policies. These critics claim that simply by saying a trait is adaptive implies that it is both genetically determined and good. In the past, they note, racists and fascists have misused biological theories to promote social injustices. In Nazi Germany, for example, Jews were considered genetically inferior, a view that was used to justify the Holocaust. The example in the last paragraph, too, could be interpreted to endorse male (but not female) sexual promiscuity and aggression, claiming that because these traits are adaptive, they are, therefore, just. But evolutionary psychologists are quick to point out that their aim is not to shape social policy but to understand the origins of human behavior. They would argue further that behaviors that may have contributed to our adaptive success during the early years of human evolution may no longer be adaptive in our current environment and should not be viewed as *just* simply because *at one time* they may have served an important adaptive function.

Other critics chide evolutionary psychologists for too hastily explaining behaviors from an evolutionary perspective rather than investigating other plausible origins of them. Just because a behavior occurs to some degree across a wide variety of cultures does not necessarily mean that it is not a learned behavior.

A relatively new approach in psychology, the evolutionary perspective has yet to take its place among psychology's most respected theoretical paradigms. Only the results of empirical research, which compares it with competing theoretical explanations of behavior, will determine the fate of this provocative and intriguing new perspective in psychology.

Social Implications

Science is not simply a process that takes place in a laboratory; its influence on all of our lives is enormous. To the extent that we can trace such human traits as intelligence, temperament, and mental illness to their origins in chromosomes and genes, we increase the extent to which we can control human lives. And because this control permits choices that were previously unavailable, we face new ethical dilemmas.

Advances in genetics, for example, have improved our ability to predict birth defects in babies not yet conceived. Using family histories, genetic counselors can spell out the likelihood that the children of a given marriage will inherit genetic problems. Before deciding to have a child, therefore, a high-risk couple must weigh some serious ethical questions.

Once conception has occurred, several tests can detect certain specific genetic abnormalities before the baby is born. **Amniocentesis** involves col-

In 1997, the first successful cloning of a mammal was announced. A female sheep named Dolly was grown from an egg cell whose chromosomes had been replaced with the complete DNA of another sheep. Should society allow the similar cloning of human beings?

lecting some of the cells that the fetus casts off into the fluid surrounding it in the womb and testing them for chromosomal or genetic defects. However, amniocentesis usually cannot be performed until the 11th week of pregnancy and generally requires 2 to 3 weeks more to obtain results. A newer procedure called **chorionic villus sampling** is similar to amniocentesis except the cells for analysis in this procedure are drawn from the membranes surrounding the fetus. Chorionic villus sampling can be performed between the 6th and 12th week of pregnancy (considerably earlier than amniocentesis), and the results are available immediately, although it does carry a slightly greater risk of miscarriage than does amniocentesis. Using procedures like these, genetic problems are detected in about 2 percent of pregnancies. Does the child nonetheless have a right to life? Do the parents have a right to abort the fetus? Should society protect all life, no matter how imperfect it is in the eyes of some? If not, which defects are so unacceptable that abortion is justified? Most of these questions have a long history, but recent progress in behavior genetics and medicine has given them a special urgency.

The study of behavior genetics and evolutionary psychology make many people uneasy. Some fear that it may lead to the conclusion that who we are is written in some kind of permanent ink before we are born. Some people also fear that research in these fields could be used to undermine movements toward social equality. But far from finding human behavior to be genetically predetermined, the recent work of behavior geneticists actually shows just how important the environment is in determining which genetic predispositions come to be expressed and which do not (Rutter, 1997). In other words, we may inherit predispositions, but we do not inherit destinies. The emerging picture confirms that both heredity and environment (nature *and* nurture) together shape most significant behaviors and traits.

Chorionic villus sampling A procedure that involves collecting cells from the membranes surrounding the fetus and testing them for genetic abnormalities.

SUMMARY

This chapter presents the basic biological processes that are at the root of our thoughts, feelings, and actions. The body possesses two systems for coordinating and integrating behavior: the **nervous system** and the **endocrine system.**

NEURONS, THE MESSENGERS

The billions of **neurons,** or nerve cells, that underlie all the activity of the nervous system form a communication network that coordinates all the systems of the body and enables them to function. Neurons usually receive messages from other neurons through short fibers, called **dendrites,** that pick up messages and carry them to the neuron's cell body. The **axon** carries outgoing messages from the cell. A group of axons bundled together makes up a **nerve.** Some axons are covered with a **myelin sheath,** made up of **glial cells.** The myelin sheath increases neuron efficiency and provides insulation.

The Neural Impulse

Neurons that carry messages from the sense organs to the brain or spinal cord are called **sensory (afferent)**
neurons. Neurons that carry messages from the brain or spinal cord to the muscles and glands are called **motor (efferent) neurons. Interneurons (association neurons)** carry messages from one neuron to another. When the neuron is at rest, or at its **resting potential,** a slightly higher concentration of negative **ions** exists inside the membrane surrounding the cell body than outside, so there is a negative electrical charge inside relative to outside. At rest, a neuron is in a state of **polarization.** When an incoming message is strong enough, the electrical charge is changed, an **action potential (neural impulse)** is generated, and the neuron is depolarized. Incoming messages cause **graded potentials,** which, when combined, may exceed the minimum **threshold of excitation** and make the neuron fire. After firing, the neuron goes through the **absolute refractory period,** when it will not fire again, and then enters the **relative refractory period,** when firing will only occur if the incoming message is much stronger than usual. However, according to the **all-or-none law,** the impulse sent by a neuron does not vary in strength.

The Synapse

Neurotransmitter molecules, released by **synaptic vesicles,** cross the tiny **synaptic space** (or **cleft**) between the **axon terminal** (or **synaptic knob**) of the sending neuron and the dendrite of the receiving neuron, where they latch on to a **receptor site,** much the way a key fits into a lock. This is how they pass on their excitatory or inhibitory messages.

Synapses and Drugs

Certain drugs produce psychological effects by increasing or decreasing the quantity of neurotransmitters at the **synapse.** Other drugs work at the receptor sites, blocking the receptors or interfering with the removal or reabsorption of the neurotransmitters. Drugs that block the dopamine receptors, for example, reduce the symptoms of schizophrenia.

Experience and Neurons

The brain has **plasticity,** that is, it can be physically and chemically altered by experience. In a pioneering study of the influence of the environment on the brain, researchers found that rats that had been raised in a stimulating environment had more synaptic connections than rats that had been raised in cages that offered them no opportunities to explore or to manipulate objects.

THE CENTRAL NERVOUS SYSTEM

The billions of neurons in the brain are connected to neurons throughout the body by trillions of synapses. The nervous system is organized into two parts: the **central nervous system,** which consists of the brain and the spinal cord, and the **peripheral nervous system,** which connects the central nervous system to the rest of the body.

The Brain

The brain contains more than 90 percent of the body's neurons. Physically, the brain has three more or less distinct areas: the hindbrain, the midbrain, and the forebrain.

The **hindbrain** is found in even the most primitive vertebrates. It is made up of the cerebellum, the pons, and the medulla. The **medulla** is a narrow structure nearest the spinal cord; it is the point at which many of the nerves from the left part of the body cross to the right side of the brain and vice versa. The medulla controls such functions as breathing, heart rate, and blood pressure. The **pons,** located just above the medulla, connects the top of the brain to the cerebellum. Chemicals produced in the pons help maintain our sleep-wake cycle. The **cerebellum** is divided into two hemispheres and handles certain reflexes, especially those that have to do with balance. It also coordinates the body's actions.

The **midbrain** lies between the hindbrain and forebrain and is crucial for hearing and sight.

The **forebrain** is supported by the **brain stem** and buds out above it, drooping somewhat to fit inside the skull. It consists of the thalamus, the hypothalamus, and the cerebral cortex. The **thalamus** relays and translates incoming messages from the sense receptors—except those for smell. The **hypothalamus** governs motivation and emotion and appears to play a role in coordinating the responses of the nervous system in times of stress.

The cerebral hemispheres, located above the thalamus and hypothalamus, take up most of the room inside the skull. The outer covering of the cerebral hemispheres is known as the **cerebral cortex.** The cerebral hemispheres are what most people think of when they think of the brain. They are the most recently evolved portion of the brain, and they regulate the most complex behavior. Each cerebral hemisphere is divided into four lobes, delineated by deep fissures on the surface of the brain. The **occipital lobe** of the cortex, located at the back of the head, receives and processes visual information. The **temporal lobe,** located roughly behind the temples, is important to the sense of smell; it also helps us perform complex visual tasks, such as recognizing faces. The **parietal lobe,** which sits on top of the temporal and occipital lobes, receives sensory information, in the **sensory projection areas,** from all over the body and figures in spatial abilities. The ability to comprehend language is concentrated in two areas in the parietal and temporal lobes. The **frontal lobe** is the part of the cerebral cortex responsible for voluntary movement and attention as well as goal-directed behavior. The brain starts response messages in the **motor projection areas,** from which they proceed to the muscles and glands. The frontal lobe may also be linked to emotional temperament.

These four lobes are both physically and functionally distinct. Each lobe contains areas for specific motor sensory function as well as **association areas.** The association areas—areas that are free to process all kinds of information—make up most of the cerebral cortex and enable the brain to produce behaviors requiring the coordination of many brain areas.

Hemispheric Specialization

The two hemispheres of the cerebral cortex are linked by the **corpus callosum,** through which they communicate and coordinate. Nevertheless, they appear to have some separate functions. The right hemisphere of the cortex excels at nonverbal and spatial tasks, whereas the left hemisphere is usually more dominant in verbal tasks such as speaking and writing. The right hemisphere controls the left side of the body, and the left hemisphere controls the right side.

The Reticular Formation

The **reticular formation** is a network of neurons running through the hindbrain, midbrain, and forebrain that serves to arouse the higher parts of the brain.

The Limbic System

The **limbic system** encompasses structures that are critical for forming memories and experiencing pleasure, as well as for various motivational and emotional activities.

The Spinal Cord

The **spinal cord** is a complex cable of nerves that connects the brain to most of the rest of the body. It is made up of bundles of long nerve fibers and has two basic functions: to permit some reflex movements and to carry messages to and from the brain.

Tools for Studying the Nervous System

In recent decades science has developed increasingly sophisticated techniques for investigating the brain and nervous system. Among the most important tools are microelectrode techniques; macroelectrode techniques (ERP); structural imaging (CAT scanning, MRI); functional imaging (EEG imaging, MEG, MSI), and tools such as PET scanning that use radioactive energy to map brain activity. Scientists often combine these techniques to study brain activity in unprecedented detail.

THE PERIPHERAL NERVOUS SYSTEM

The second major division of the nervous system, the peripheral nervous system, carries messages to and from the central nervous system. It comprises two parts: the somatic and the autonomic nervous systems.

The Somatic Nervous System

The **somatic nervous system** is composed of the sensory (afferent) neurons that carry messages to the central nervous system and the motor (efferent) neurons that carry messages from the central nervous system to the skeletal muscles of the body.

The Autonomic Nervous System

The **autonomic nervous system** carries messages between the central nervous system and the internal organs. It is broken into two parts: the **sympathetic** and **parasympathetic** divisions. The first acts primarily to arouse the body; the second, to relax and restore the body to normal levels of arousal.

THE ENDOCRINE SYSTEM

The endocrine system—the other communication system in the body—is made up of **endocrine glands** that produce **hormones,** chemical substances released into the bloodstream to guide such processes as metabolism, growth, and sexual development. Hormones are also involved in regulating emotional life.

The Thyroid Gland

The **thyroid gland** secretes thyroxin, a hormone that can reduce concentration and lead to irritability when the thyroid is overactive, and cause drowsiness and a sluggish metabolism when the thyroid is underactive.

The Parathyroid Glands

Within the thyroid are four tiny pea-shaped organs, the **parathyroids,** that secrete parathormone to control and balance the levels of calcium and phosphate in the blood and tissue fluids. This, in turn, affects the excitability of the nervous system.

The Pineal Gland

The **pineal gland** is a pea-sized gland that apparently responds to exposure to light and regulates activity levels over the course of the day.

The Pancreas

The **pancreas** lies in a curve between the stomach and the small intestine and controls the level of sugar in the blood by secreting insulin and glucagon.

The Pituitary Gland

The **pituitary gland** produces the largest number of different hormones and therefore has the widest range of effects on the body's functions. The **posterior pituitary** is controlled by the nervous system. It produces two hormones: vasopressin, which causes blood pressure to rise and regulates the amount of water in the body's cells, and oxytocin, which causes the uterus to contract during childbirth and lactation to begin. The **anterior pituitary,** often called the "master gland," responds to chemical messages from the bloodstream to produce numerous hormones that trigger the action of other endocrine glands.

The Gonads

These reproductive glands—the testes in males and the ovaries in females, and, to a lesser extent, the adrenal glands—secrete androgens (including testosterone) and estrogens.

The Adrenal Glands

The two **adrenal glands** are located above the kidneys. Each has two parts: an outer covering, the **adrenal cortex,** and an inner core, the **adrenal medulla.** Both influence the body's responses to stress. For example, in response to a stressful situation, the pituitary gland may release **beta endorphin** and ACTH, which, in turn, prompt the adrenal cortex to release hormones. Meanwhile, the autonomic nervous system stimulates the adrenal medulla to secrete hormones such as epinephrine into the bloodstream.

BEHAVIOR GENETICS AND OUR HUMAN HERITAGE

The **nature versus nurture** question refers to the interactive role that heredity (nature) and environment (nurture) play in human behavior. Although no contemporary psychologist would take either a pure nature or a pure nurture view of human behavior, the extent to which many traits are influenced by genetics and environment is still debated. The related fields of **behavior genetics** and **evolutionary psychology** help psychologists explore the influence of heredity on human behavior.

Genetics

Genetics is the study of how plants, animals, and people pass on **traits** from one generation to the next through **genes.** The transmission of traits is referred to as **heredity.** Each gene is lined up on tiny threadlike bodies called **chromosomes,** which are made up predominantly of **deoxyribonucleic acid (DNA).** Members of a gene pair can be either **dominant** or **recessive genes.** In **polygenic inheritance,** several genes interact to produce a certain trait.

Genetics and Behavior

Psychologists use a variety of methods to study the relationships between genes and various behaviors. **Strain studies** help to determine the heritability of certain traits in inbred animals; **selection studies** estimate the heritability of a trait by breeding animals with other animals that have the same trait. Through **family studies,** scientists examine genetic influences on human behavior, whereas **twin studies** probe **identical twins** who share identical genetic makeup, as opposed to **fraternal twins** who are only as genetically similar as regular siblings. **Adoption studies** are useful in determining the influence of heredity and environment on human behavior.

Evolution

In 1859 Charles Darwin proposed the theory of natural selection to account for evolution—the idea that groups of organisms change over time. In modern terms, the theory of **natural selection** states that organisms best adapted to their environment tend to survive, transmitting their genetic characteristics to succeeding generations, whereas organisms with less adaptive characteristics tend to disappear.

Evolutionary Psychology

Evolutionary psychology analyzes human thoughts, traits, and behaviors by examining their adaptive value from an evolutionary perspective. It has proved useful in explaining many cross-cultural commonalities in human behavior.

Social Implications

The study of behavior genetics and evolutionary psychology makes many people uneasy. With the development of **amniocentesis** and **chorionic villus sampling,** prospective parents can often detect genetic abnormalities in a fetus, leading to questions about the rights of a child versus those of the parents. Some fear that research in evolutionary psychology will undermine movements toward social equality by attempting to justify the adaptive value of certain forms of social injustice. Others fear that it will make people feel that genetics is destiny—that who we are is written in some kind of permanent ink before we are born.

REVIEW QUESTIONS

MULTIPLE CHOICE AND SHORT ANSWER

1. Match the following terms with the correct definition.
   - —————— neuron
   - —————— nerve
   - —————— axon
   - —————— dendrite
   a. group of axons bundled together
   b. receives incoming messages from surrounding neurons
   c. carries outgoing messages away from the nerve cell
   d. single nerve cell

2. When a neuron is in a polarized state, there are mostly _____ ions on the outside of the cell membrane and mostly _____ ions on the inside.

3. During the _____ period, the neuron will fire only if the incoming message is considerably stronger than usual:

   a. absolute refractory
   b. relative refractory

4. A very strong incoming signal will cause a neuron to fire more strongly than before and in turn cause neighboring neurons to fire more strongly. T / F

5. When a neural impulse reaches the end of the axon, it is transferred to the next neuron chemically through the release of _____.

6. Match the following drugs with the ways they affect neurotransmission.
   ———— Amphetamines
   ———— Curare, LSD, and Atropine
   ———— Antidepressants

   a. occupy or block receptor sites
   b. increase release of neurotransmitter
   c. interfere with the reabsorption of neurotransmitter

7. The ————— nervous system connects the central nervous system to all parts of the body beyond the brain and spinal cord.

8. Which brain structure is a vital center for such important biological functions as temperature control, eating, drinking, and sexual behavior?
   a. cerebral cortex
   b. cerebellum
   c. pons
   d. hypothalamus

9. Which brain structure is a "relay station" for sensory systems?
   a. thalamus
   b. corpus callosum
   c. hypothalamus
   d. pons

10. In the cerebral cortex the ————— lobe receives sensory information from all over the body, and the ————— lobe sends messages to various muscles and glands in the body.

11. Which of the following is not part of the brain's structure?
    a. hypothalamus
    b. limbic system
    c. corpus callosum
    d. parathyroid

12. Although the left and right hemispheres of the brain are specialized, they are normally in close communication through the
    a. midbrain
    b. corpus callosum
    c. temporal lobe
    d. cerebellum

13. In the great majority of humans, the ————— side of the cortex is specialized for language.

14. Communication in the endocrine system is dependent on —————, chemicals secreted directly into the bloodstream.

15. Depression, schizophrenia, intelligence, and general emotional reactivity may all be influenced by genes.
    T / F

CRITICAL THINKING AND APPLICATIONS

1. In the previous chapter we examined various schools of psychology, including behaviorism, psychoanalytic psychology, and cognitive psychology. Which school or schools did you find most convincing before you read this chapter? Now that you have been exposed to the physiological and hereditary bases of behavior, have you changed your opinion? If so, how and why?

2. What are some of the most current methods for studying the brain and nervous system? What can they teach us? When do you think they should be used?

3. In this chapter we noted possible biological and hereditary bases for schizophrenia. Do you think scientists will eventually find biological causes for some—or most—mental illnesses? If so, is the use of drugs to treat these disorders appropriate? Why or why not?

4. What do behavior scientists mean when they state that certain behaviors have a genetic component?

ENDURING ISSUES

Heredity–Environment
In this chapter you read a great deal about the effects of genetics (heredity) on people. What psychological characteristics are most heavily influenced by heredity, and which are least influenced?

Mind–Body
After reading this chapter, how would you describe the relationship between our thoughts and feelings and activity in the nervous and endocrine systems? Are your thoughts simply the result of physical processes in the brain?

(Answers to the Review Questions can be found in the back of the text.)

3 Sensation and

Perception

Suppose you wanted to figure out how far away a thunderstorm was. How would you get the necessary information? If you lived on a prairie, you could simply look at the sky to pick up relevant information, though at night you would have to rely more on your sense of hearing. Some people claim that they can smell a storm coming or that they experience a tingling sensation on their skin as a storm is rolling in. But sensation alone is not enough to give us a good grasp of the external world. Sounds, colors, tastes, and smells are just random sensory impressions until we interpret them in some meaningful way. Our perceptual processes are the tools

Think About It!

1. How far away can you see a candle flame on a clear, dark night?
2. Can advertisers persuade you to buy products by placing hidden messages in their ads?
3. Why does the rate of automobile accidents go up at night?
4. How many different colors can we distinguish?
5. Does listening to loud music really damage the ears?
6. Which sense is more sensitive—taste or smell?
7. What causes motion sickness?
8. What kinds of visual cues do we use to judge distance and depth?

we use to understand and make sense of the countless sensations that we are continually experiencing; without these perceptual processes, even the most mundane tasks would become impossible. Take driving a car, for example. As you negotiate traffic, you focus on visual cues about your surroundings. From a complicated array of colors, shapes, and patterns, you must be able to distinguish a road sign that tells you how to get to your destination from one that tells you to stop. You depend on visual cues to judge the distances of other cars, bicycles, and pedestrians. If you see a motorist trying to enter the flow of traffic from a

Sensation The experience of sensory stimulation.

Perception The process of creating meaningful patterns from raw sensory information.

Receptor cell A specialized cell that responds to a particular type of energy.

driveway just ahead of you, you must be able to determine whether that car and yours are on a collision course. And, as you drive, if you hear a siren, you must determine quickly where it is coming from and how close it is so that you can yield the right of way, if necessary. In all these cases, you have to make sense out of raw sensory information and act accordingly.

In this chapter, we will explore how we interpret the raw data picked up by our senses from the outside world. First, we will discuss **sensation**—the basic experience of stimulation of the body's senses: sight, hearing, smell, taste, balance, touch, and pain. We will examine each of the body's senses and learn how each one converts physical energy—light or sound waves, for example—into nerve impulses. Then, by exploring how our perceptual processes organize and interpret elementary sensations, we will see how we arrive at our **perception** of meaningful events. In the process, we will discover how we perceive patterns, distance, and movement, and how we are able to identify an object despite changing or even contradictory information. And finally, we will look at how our personal characteristics influence the way we perceive the world.

THE NATURE OF SENSORY PROCESSES

The Character of Sensation

Described in general terms, the sequence of events that produces a sensation seems quite simple. Initially, some form of energy, either from an external source or from inside the body, stimulates a **receptor cell** in one of the sense organs, such as the eye or the ear. A receptor cell is designed to respond to one particular form of energy—light waves, in the case of vision, or vibration, in the case of hearing. The energy must be sufficiently intense for the receptor cell to react to it. But given sufficient energy, the receptor responds to the energy by sending to the brain a coded electrochemical signal, which varies according to the characteristics of the stimulus. For instance, a very bright light might be coded by the rapid firing of a set of nerve cells, whereas a dim light would set off a much slower firing sequence. As the neural signal passes along the sensory nerves of the central nervous system, it is coded still further, so that by the time it reaches the brain, the message is precise and detailed. Thus, the coded signal that the brain receives from a flashing red light differs significantly from the message signaling a soft yellow haze. And both these signals are coded in a much different way than a loud, piercing noise.

Our sensory experiences, then, are the result of patterns of neural signals. In a way, every sensory experience is an illusion created in the brain. The brain sits within the skull, isolated from external events; yet, bombarded by the "clicking" of coded neural signals coming in over millions of nerve fibers, this nerve center creates images. The clicks on the optic nerve are no more "visual" than the clicks on an auditory nerve. But clicks on the optic nerve reliably produce an experience we call vision, just as clicks moving along an auditory nerve produce the experience we call hearing. Even if the clicks on the optic nerve are caused by something other than light, the result is still a visual experience. Gentle pressure on an eye, for instance, results in signals from the optic nerve that the brain interprets as visual patterns. In the same way, both a symphonic recording and a stream of water trickling into the ear stimulate the auditory nerve, and both cause us to hear something. In 1842, Johannes Müller, an influential German physiologist, discovered this one-to-one relationship between stimulation of a specific nerve and the resulting type of sensory experience, a concept now known as the *doctrine of specific nerve energies*.

Sensory Thresholds

Earlier we noted that the energy reaching a receptor must be sufficiently intense for it to have a noticeable effect. The minimum intensity of physical energy required to produce any sensation at all in a person is called the **absolute threshold.** Any stimulation below the absolute threshold will not be experienced.

How much sensory stimulation is needed to produce a sensation? How loud does a sound have to be, for example, for a person to hear it? How bright does a "blip" on a radar screen have to be for the operator to see it? To answer these kinds of questions, psychologists present a stimulus at different intensities and ask people whether they sense anything. You might expect that there would come a point where people would suddenly say, "Now I see the flash" or "Now I hear a sound." But actually there is a range of intensities over which a person sometimes, but not always, can sense a stimulus. For a variety of reasons, psychologists have agreed to set the absolute threshold at the point where a person can detect the stimulus 50 percent of the time that it is presented (see Figure 3–1).

Although there are differences among people, and even differences from moment to moment for the same person, the absolute threshold for each of our senses is remarkably low. According to McBurney and Collings (1984), the approximate absolute thresholds are as follows:

Absolute threshold The least amount of energy that can be detected as a stimulation 50 percent of the time.

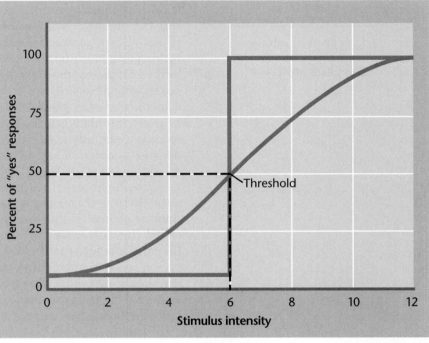

Figure 3–1
Determining a sensory threshold.
The red line represents an ideal case: At all intensities below the threshold, the person reports no sensation or no change in intensity; at all intensities above the threshold, the person reports a sensation or a change in intensity. In actual practice, however, we never come close to the ideal of the red line. The blue line shows the actual responses of a typical person. The threshold is taken as the point where the person reports a sensation or a change in intensity 50 percent of the time.

- *Taste:* 1 gram (.0356 ounce) of table salt in 500 liters (529 quarts) of water.
- *Smell:* 1 drop of perfume diffused throughout a three-room apartment.
- *Touch:* The wing of a bee falling on your cheek from a height of 1 centimeter (.39 inch).
- *Hearing:* The tick of a watch from 6 meters (20 feet) in very quiet conditions.
- *Vision:* A candle flame seen from 50 kilometers (30 miles) on a clear, dark night.

Of course these figures apply only under ideal circumstances—in extremely quiet or dark or "taste-free" or "smell-free" conditions. Under more normal

Adaptation An adjustment of the senses to the level of stimulation they are receiving.

Difference threshold or **just noticeable difference (jnd)** The smallest change in stimulation that can be detected 50 percent of the time.

Weber's law The principle that the jnd for any given sense is a constant fraction or proportion of the stimulation being judged.

How far away can you see a candle flame on a clear, dark night?

conditions, absolute thresholds vary depending on the level and nature of ongoing sensory stimulation. For example, your threshold for the taste of salt would be considerably higher after you had eaten salted peanuts or potato chips; it would take much more than just 1 gram of salt in 500 liters of water for you to notice the salty taste. In the same way, your vision threshold would be much higher in the middle of a bright, sunny day than at midnight on a moonless night; you certainly wouldn't see a candle flame 30 miles away during the daytime! In both these cases, the absolute threshold would rise because of sensory **adaptation.** Our senses automatically adjust to the overall, average level of stimulation in a particular setting. When confronted by a great deal of stimulation, they become much less sensitive than when the overall level of stimulation is low. By the same token, when the level of stimulation drops, our sensory apparatus becomes much more sensitive than under conditions of high stimulation. This process of adaptation allows all our senses to be keenly attuned to environmental conditions, picking up a multitude of cues without getting overloaded. When we enter a hushed room, we are able to hear the faint tick of a wristwatch. But when we go out onto a busy city street at rush hour, the noise of street traffic would be deafening or even painful unless our ears adapted and became less sensitive to noise. Similarly, through visual adaptation, we can move from a dark room into the bright sunshine without experiencing great pain or damaging our visual system. Later in this chapter we will examine various kinds of adaptation in more detail.

Imagine now that you can hear a particular sound. How much stronger must the sound become before you notice that it has grown louder? The smallest change in stimulation that you can detect 50 percent of the time is called the **difference threshold,** or the **just noticeable difference (jnd).** Like the absolute threshold, the difference threshold varies from person to person and from moment to moment for the same person. And like absolute thresholds, difference thresholds tell us something about the flexibility of sensory systems. For example, adding 2 pounds to a 10-pound load will certainly be noticed, so we might assume that the difference threshold must be considerably *less* than 2 pounds. Yet adding 2 pounds to a 100-pound load probably would not make much of a difference, so we might conclude that the difference threshold must be considerably *more* than 2 pounds. But how can the difference threshold (jnd) be both less than and greater than 2 pounds? It turns out that the difference threshold varies according to the strength or intensity of the original stimulus. The greater the stimulus, the greater the change necessary to produce a jnd. In the 1830s, Ernst Weber concluded that the difference threshold is a constant *fraction* or *proportion* of the specific stimulus. The theory that the jnd is a constant fraction of the original stimulus is known as **Weber's law.** The values of these fractions vary significantly for the different senses. Hearing, for example, is very sensitive: We can detect a change in sound of 0.3 percent (1⁄3 of 1 percent). By contrast, producing a jnd in taste requires a 20 percent (1⁄5) change. To return to our earlier example of weight, a change in weight of 2 percent (1⁄50) is necessary to produce a jnd. Thus, adding 1 pound to a 50-pound load would produce a noticeable difference 50 percent of the time; adding 1 pound to a 100-pound load would not.

Subliminal Perception

The idea of a threshold implies that certain events in the real world occur below our level of conscious experience. But does stimulation below the sensory threshold influence behavior in some way? According to a 1991 survey, nearly two-thirds of Americans believe that advertisers put hidden messages and images in their advertisements to increase sales of their products (Lev, 1991). Such messages are called *subliminal* because they occur below the threshold of awareness. Are subliminal messages actually used in advertisements and in motivational products such as self-help tapes? If so, do they have the power to change people's behavior?

In a classic example of subliminal advertising, a movie theater in Fort Lee, New Jersey, allegedly flashed messages such as "Drink Coca-Cola" and "Eat Popcorn" between frames of the 1950s movie *Picnic*. Although the messages flashed too quickly for moviegoers to notice them consciously, legend has it that soft drink and popcorn sales increased dramatically at that theater. In fact, there was no change in refreshment sales, but the story has circulated for decades nonetheless.

More recently, the sale of audiotapes with subliminal self-help messages has become a big business, constituting anywhere from a quarter to a third of spoken-word audiocassette sales. Rather than manipulating behavior in some sinister way, however, the tapes are designed to improve it. These tapes claim to incorporate *affirmations*, messages that are not perceptible to the ear but that nonetheless affect behavior. A weight-loss tape might carry the subliminal message "Eat less," and a tape geared toward improving self-esteem might subliminally convey the message "I am capable."

Can people be influenced by information of which they are not consciously aware? The answer is a qualified yes: Under carefully controlled conditions, individuals have responded briefly to sights and sounds outside their conscious awareness. For example, in one study one group of people was shown a list of words related to competition, and a second group was exposed to a list of neutral words (Nuberg, 1988). In both cases, the words were flashed so rapidly that the subjects could not identify them. Later, when the subjects were playing a game, researchers found that the subjects who had been shown the subliminal list of words with competitive overtones became especially competitive. In another study, one group of subjects was subliminally exposed to words conveying honesty (a positive trait), whereas other subjects were subliminally exposed to words conveying meanness (a negative trait). Subsequently, all the subjects read a description of a woman whose behavior could be viewed as either honest or mean. When asked to assess various personality characteristics of the woman, the subjects who had been subliminally exposed to "honest" words rated her as the more honest, and those who had been subliminally exposed to "mean" words judged her as being more mean (Erdley & D'Agostino, 1988). Thus, people's behaviors and judgments seem to be affected by subliminal exposure to lists of words.

Another line of evidence for subliminal perception comes from research in which a message intended to elicit feelings of security and safety (such as "Mommy and I Are One") is projected on a screen too quickly for subjects to report seeing anything other than a flash of light. In a review of more than 50 studies of this sort, one researcher concluded that subliminal presentations of this phrase (and others similar to it) tended to reduce feelings of anxiety, hostility, and threat, and to promote recall of more positive memories (Hardaway, 1991).

Finally, a group of students at the University of Michigan was shown a series of geometric figures so rapidly—one every 0.001 second—that the subjects reported seeing only a pulse of light (Kunst-Wilson & Zajonc, 1980). Later, however, these students expressed a preference for the figures they had been exposed to subliminally compared to ones they were seeing for the first time.

These studies, and others like them, indicate that in a controlled laboratory setting people can process and respond to information of which they are

2

Can advertisers persuade you to buy products by placing hidden messages in their ads?

not consciously aware. It does not follow, however, that advertisers using such techniques will influence consumer behavior or that subliminal phrases embedded in self-help tapes will succeed in changing behavior. So far, no independent scientific evidence exists that subliminal messages in advertising or self-help tapes have any appreciable effect (Beatty & Hawkins, 1989; Greenwald et al., 1991; Smith & Rogers, 1994; T. G. Russell, Rowe, & Smouse, 1991; Underwood, 1994). For example, in one representative study, half the subjects saw an advertisement that had no sexual images, whereas the other half viewed the identical advertisement with a subliminal sexual image incorporated. The addition of the sexual imagery made no difference in people's preference ratings of the product (Gable et al., 1987). Along a similar line, a study that examined the influence of backward speech played during rock music found it had no effect on the listeners nor could the content of the message be interpreted by the listeners (Begg, Needham, & Bookbinder, 1993).

In another series of studies, volunteers used self-improvement tapes with subliminal messages for several weeks; about half said they felt better about themselves and had improved as a result of listening to the tapes. However, objective tests detected no measurable change. Moreover, the perceived improvement seemed to have more to do with the label on the tape than its subliminal content: About half the people who received a tape labeled "Improve Memory" said their memory had improved, even though many of them had actually received a tape intended to boost self-esteem; and about one-third of the people who listened to tapes labeled "Increase Self-Esteem" said their self-esteem had gone up, though many of them had actually been listening to tapes designed to improve memory (Greenwald et al., 1991).

In response to research like this, the National Academy of Science issued a report in 1991 concluding that there is no evidence that self-help tapes are useful for their stated purposes (Druckman & Bjork, 1991). Moreover, officers of the Institute of Canadian Advertisers and the American Association of Advertising Agencies (AAAA) have consistently denied that subliminal messages figure in any advertising campaign, adding that such messages are not effective. The president of the AAAA recently concluded, "There is no such thing [as subliminal advertising]. In 36 years of advertising, I've never heard the issue seriously discussed" (Lev, 1991). Psychologists also disagree about the existence of special powers of perception (see *Controversies*).

So far, we have been talking about the general characteristics of sensation, but each of the body's sensory systems works a little differently. These individual sensory systems contain receptor cells that specialize in converting a particular kind of energy into neural signals. The threshold at which this conversion occurs varies from system to system. So do the mechanisms by which sensory data are processed and coded and sent to the brain for additional processing. We now turn to the unique features of each of the sensory systems.

VISION

Different animal species depend more on some senses than on others. Dogs rely heavily on the sense of smell, bats on hearing, some fish on taste. But for humans, vision ranks as the most important sense; as a result, it has received the most attention from psychologists. To understand vision, we need to look first at the parts of the visual system, beginning with the structure of the eye.

The Visual System

The structure of the human eye, including the cellular path to the brain, is shown in Figure 3–2. Light enters the eye through the **cornea,** the transparent protective coating over the front part of the eye. It then passes through the **pupil,** the opening in the center of the **iris,** the colored part of the eye. In very bright light, the muscles in the iris contract to make the pupil

Cornea The transparent protective coating over the front part of the eye.

Pupil A small opening in the iris through which light enters the eye.

Iris The colored part of the eye.

CONTROVERSIES
EXTRASENSORY PERCEPTION: REAL OR IMAGINED?

Some people claim to have an extra power of perception, one beyond those of the normal senses. This unusual power, known as *extrasensory perception,* or *ESP,* has been defined as "a response to an unknown event not presented to any known sense" (McConnell, 1969). ESP re-fers to a variety of phenomena, including *clairvoyance*—awareness of an unknown object or event; *telepathy*—knowledge of someone else's thoughts or feelings; and *precognition*—foreknowledge of future events. The operation of ESP and other psychic phenomena is the focus of a field of study called *parapsychology.*

Much of the research into ESP has been criticized for poor experimental design, dishonesty, selective reporting of results, or results that cannot be replicated (Cornell, 1984; Hansel, 1969). But a recent research paper has added new fuel to the controversy because it cannot be challenged on those grounds (Bem & Honorton, 1994). Daryl Bem, a research psychologist and an ESP skeptic, visited the New Jersey laboratory of the late Charles Honorton, a researcher and advocate of the reality of psychic phenomena, to examine his claims of improved controls and procedures. Bem was so impressed with Honorton's approach to ESP research that he

agreed to conduct some joint experiments with him.

In their procedure, a "sender," isolated in a soundproof room, concentrates on a picture or video segment randomly selected (by a computer) from a set of 80 photos or 80 videotape segments. A "receiver" is placed alone in another soundproof room. The receiver engages in deep relaxation while wearing a half Ping-Pong ball over each eye and headphones playing a hissing sound (to provide uniform visual and auditory stimulation). The receiver then tries to mentally pick up any message or image coming from the sender. The experiment concludes with a test in which a computer displays four photos or videotape segments to the receiver, who rates them for similarity to impressions or images received during the sending phase of the experiment. Although receivers did not identify all the actual photos and videos that the senders were looking at, they performed significantly better than chance alone would predict.

Although Bem and Honorton's studies are intriguing, Ray Hyman, a

> *Much of the research into ESP has been criticized for poor experimental design, dishonesty, selective reporting of results, or results that cannot be replicated. But a recent research paper has added new fuel to the controversy. . . .*

leading skeptic of psychic research, has criticized them on the grounds that items were not appropriately randomized during the test phase of the experiment and that the authors failed to control for the tendency of receivers to pick certain images—for example, the first or last one—regardless of a match between the test item and a mental image (Hyman, 1994).

According to surveys, psychologists and other scientists do not discount ESP entirely. In fact, one survey indicated that 34 percent of psychologists accepted ESP as either an established fact or a likely possibility (Wagner & Monnet, 1979). Even many of those who remain skeptical do not dismiss ESP out of hand but rather point out that experimentation has not yet lent scientific credence to these phenomena.

Questions

1. Have you had experiences that seemed to involve some kind of extrasensory perception? Did you rule out the possibility that your experience was just a coincidence, and if so, on what did you base your decision?

2. What percentage of your fellow students accept ESP as either an established fact or a likely possibility?

Lens The transparent part of the eye inside the pupil that focuses light onto the retina.

Retina The lining of the eye containing receptor cells that are sensitive to light.

Fovea The area of the retina that is the center of the visual field.

Light The small segment of the electromagnetic spectrum to which our eyes are sensitive.

Wavelengths The different energies represented in the electromagnetic spectrum.

Rods Receptor cells in the retina responsible for night vision and perception of brightness.

Cones Receptor cells in the retina responsible for color vision.

Bipolar cells Neurons that have only one axon and one dendrite; in the eye, these neurons connect the receptors on the retina to the ganglion cells.

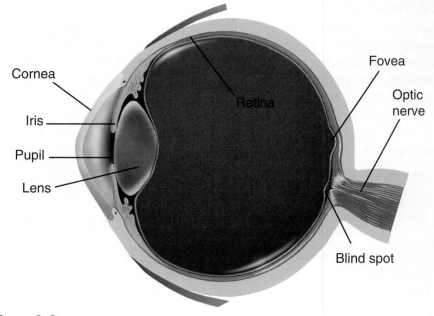

Figure 3–2
A cross section of the human eye.
Light enters the eye through the cornea, passes through the pupil, and is focused by the lens onto the retina.

Source: Adapted from Hubel, 1963.

Figure 3–3
The retina.
A view of the retina through an ophthalmoscope, an instrument used to inspect blood vessels in the eye. The small dark spot is the *fovea.* The yellow circle marks the *blind spot,* where the optic nerve leaves the eye.

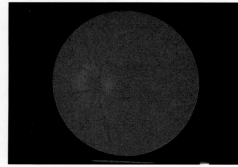

smaller and thus protect the eye from damage. This contraction also helps us see better in bright light. In dim light, the muscles relax to open the pupil wider and let in as much light as possible.

Inside the pupil, light moves through the **lens,** which focuses it onto the **retina,** the light-sensitive inner lining of the back of the eyeball. The lens changes shape to focus on objects that are closer or farther away. Normally the lens is focused on a middle distance, at a point neither very near nor very far away. To focus on an object that is very close to the eyes, tiny muscles around the lens contract and make the lens rounder. To focus on something far away, the muscles work to flatten the lens.

On the retina and directly behind the lens lies a depressed spot called the **fovea** (see Figure 3–3). The fovea occupies the center of the visual field, and images that pass through the lens are in sharpest focus here. Thus, the words that you are now reading are hitting the fovea, and the rest of what you see—a desk, walls, or whatever—is striking other areas of the retina.

THE RECEPTOR CELLS   The retina of each eye contains the *receptor cells* responsible for vision. These cells are sensitive to only a fraction of the spectrum of electromagnetic energy, which includes **light** along with other energies (see Figure 3–4). We generally refer to energies in the electromagnetic spectrum by their **wavelength.** The shortest wavelengths that we can see are experienced as violet-blue colors; the longest appear as reds.

The retina contains two kinds of receptor cells—**rods** and **cones**—named for their characteristic shapes (see Figure 3–5). About 120 million rods and 8 million cones are present in the retina of each eye. Rods respond only to varying degrees or intensities of light and dark, not to colors. They are chiefly responsible for *night vision.* Cones, on the other hand, allow us to see light and dark as well as colors. Operating chiefly in daylight, cones are

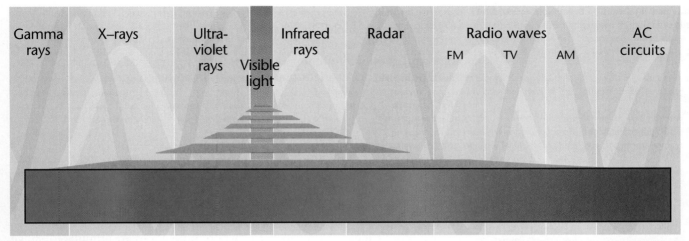

Figure 3–4
The electromagnetic spectrum.
The eye is sensitive to only a very small segment of the spectrum, known as *visible light*.

less sensitive to light than rods are (MacLeod, 1978). In this regard, cones, like color film, work best in relatively bright light. The more sensitive rods, like black-and-white film, respond to much lower levels of illumination.

Rods and cones differ in other ways as well. Cones are found mainly, but not exclusively, in the fovea, which contains no rods. The greatest density of cones is in the very center of the fovea, which, as you recall, is where images are projected onto the retina in sharpest focus. Rods predominate just outside the fovea. As we move outward from the fovea toward the edges of the retina, both rods and cones get sparser, and almost no cones and only a few rods can be found at the extreme edges of the retina.

Rods and cones also differ in the way they connect to the nerve cells leading to the brain. Both rods and cones connect to specialized neurons called **bipolar cells,** which have only one axon and one dendrite (see Figure 3–6). In the fovea, cones generally connect with only one bipolar cell—a

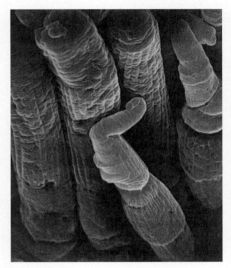

Figure 3–5
Rods and cones.
As you can see from this photomicrograph, the rods and cones are named for their shapes.

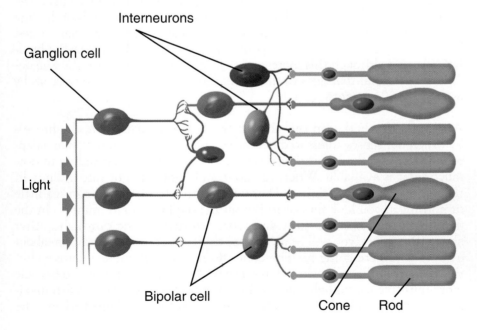

Figure 3–6
A close-up of the layers of the retina.
Light must pass between the *ganglion cells* and the *bipolar cells* to reach the rods and cones. The sensory messages then travel back out from the receptor cells, through the bipolar cells, to the ganglion cells. The axons of the ganglion cells gather together to form the *optic nerve*, which carries the messages from both eyes to the brain (see Figure 3–2).

Visual acuity The ability to distinguish fine details visually.

sort of "private line" arrangement. Rods are usually on a "party line"—several may share a single bipolar cell.

Knowing these facts about rods and cones can help you understand some of the more common experiences in seeing. For example, you may have noticed that at night you can see a dimly lit object better if you look slightly to one side of it rather than directly at it. This has to do with the location of the rods and cones. When you look directly at an object, its image falls on the fovea, which consists only of relatively light-insensitive cones. However, when you look slightly to one side of the object, its image falls next to the fovea and onto the highly light-sensitive rods. Moreover, a weak stimulus will prompt only a weak response in the cones, and this probably will not be sufficient to fire their bipolar cells. But because many rods converge on a single bipolar cell, that neuron is much more likely to fire and thereby initiate a sensory message to the brain in dim light.

At other times, vision gets better when more cones are stimulated. Have you ever tried to examine something and been unable to make out the details? You probably found that by increasing the amount of light on the object—perhaps by moving it into direct sunlight or under a lamp—you could see it better. That's because the stronger the illumination, the greater the number of cones stimulated; the greater the numbers of cones stimulated, the more likely they are to stimulate the bipolar cells, initiating a message to the brain. Our ability to see improves as light intensity increases. So for "close" activities such as reading, sewing, and writing, the more light the better.

For related reasons, vision is sharpest—even in normal light—whenever you look directly at an object and its image falls on the fovea. In the fovea, the one-to-one connection between cones and bipolar cells allows for maximum **visual acuity**—the ability to visually distinguish fine details. You can easily see how acuity works by conducting the following experiment: Hold the book about 18 inches from your eyes and look at the "X" in the center of the line below. Notice how your vision drops off for words and letters toward the left or right end of the line.

This is a test to show how visual**X**acuity varies across the retina.

Your fovea picks up the "X" and about four letters to either side. This is the area of greatest visual acuity. The letters at the left and right ends of the line fall well outside the fovea, where there are many more rods than cones. Rods, as you remember, tend to "pool" their signals on the way to the bipolar cells; and although this increases sensitivity, it cuts down on the fine details in the signal that goes to the brain. Outside the fovea, acuity drops by as much as 50 percent!

ADAPTATION   Earlier in this chapter we discussed adaptation, the process by which our senses adjust to different levels of stimulation. In vision, adaptation occurs as the sensitivity of rods and cones changes according to how much light is available. When you go from bright sunlight into a dimly lit theater, your cones are initially fairly insensitive to light: You can see little or nothing as you look for a seat. But during the first 5 or 10 minutes in the dark, the cones become more and more sensitive to the dim light. After about 10 minutes, you will be able to see things directly in front of you about as well as you are going to: The cones do not get any more sensitive after this point. But the rods, which have also been adapting, continue to become more sensitive to the light for another 20 minutes or so. They reach maximum sensitivity about 30 minutes after you enter a darkened room. The process by which rods and cones become more sensitive to light in response to lowered levels of illumination is called **dark adaptation.** But even with dark adaptation, there is not enough energy in very dim light to stimulate the cones to respond to colors. This is why even when your eyes are adapted to the dark, you see only a black-and-white-and-gray world of different brightnesses.

Problems with dark adaptation account in part for the much greater incidence of highway accidents at night (Leibowitz & Owens, 1977). When people drive at night, not all their visual abilities degrade equally. The eyes shift from the darkened interior of the car to the road area illuminated by the headlights to the darker areas at the side of the road. Unlike the situation in a darkened movie theater, these changing night-driving conditions do not allow for complete adaptation of either rods or cones; so neither system is operating at maximum efficiency. Thus, people may be able to focus on the location of an object, such as a pedestrian, fairly well: They can see that the pedestrian is in the middle of the road. However, they are not able to determine who the pedestrian is, how far away the pedestrian is, or how fast the pedestrian is moving. As a result, drivers may overestimate their ability to stop in time. Because most drivers are generally unaware of the deterioration of their vision at night, they may drive with an exaggerated confidence in their visual abilities.

In the reverse process, **light adaptation,** the rods and cones become less sensitive to light. By the time you leave a movie theater, your rods and cones have grown very sensitive, and the bright outdoor light sometimes hurts as a result. In the bright light, all the neurons fire at once, overwhelming you. You squint and shield your eyes, and each iris contracts, all of which reduces the amount of light entering your pupils and striking each retina. As light adaptation proceeds, the rods and cones become less sensitive to stimulation by light, and within about a minute, both rods and cones are fully adapted to the light. At this point, you no longer need to squint and shield your eyes.

You can observe the effects of dark and light adaptation by staring continuously at the dot in the center of the upper square in Figure 3–7 for about 20 seconds. Then shift your gaze to the dot in the lower square. A gray-and-white pattern should appear in the lower square (when looking at the lower square, if you blink your eyes or shade the book from bright light, the illusion will be even stronger). When you look at the lower square, the striped areas that were black in the upper square will now seem to be white, and the areas that were white in the upper square will now appear gray. The **afterimage** appeared because the part of the retina that was exposed to the dark stripes of the upper square became more sensitive (it dark-adapted), and the area exposed to the white part of the upper square became less sensitive (it light-adapted). When you shifted your eyes to the lower square, the less sensitive parts of the retina produced the sensation of gray rather than white. This afterimage fades within a minute as the retina adapts again, this time to the solid white square.

These examples show that visual adaptation is a partial, back-and-forth kind of process. The eyes adjust—from no stimulation to stimulation, from less stimulation to more, and vice versa—but they never adapt completely. If stimulation somehow remained constant and the eyes adapted completely, all the receptors would gradually become totally insensitive and we would be unable to see anything at all. If you want to see a normal occurrence of full adaptation, go into a dark room with a penlight and shine the light into one of your eyes from above and to the side of your head. You will see something that looks like the branches of a tree. These are the blood vessels that run across your retina in front of the rods and cones. Normally, these vessels are

Dark adaptation Increased sensitivity of rods and cones in darkness.

Light adaptation Decreased sensitivity of rods and cones in bright light.

Afterimage Sense experience that occurs after a visual stimulus has been removed.

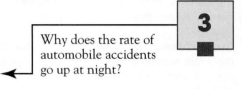

3

Why does the rate of automobile accidents go up at night?

**Figure 3–7
An afterimage.**
First stare continuously at the center of the upper square for about 20 seconds, then look at the dot in the lower square. Within a moment, a gray-and-white afterimage should appear inside the lower square.

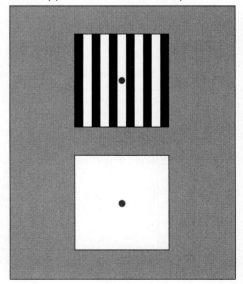

Ganglion cells Neurons that connect the bipolar cells in the eyes to the brain.

Optic nerve The bundle of axons of ganglion cells that carries neural messages from each eye to the brain.

Blind spot The place on the retina where the axons of all the ganglion cells leave the eye and where there are no receptors.

Optic chiasm The point near the base of the brain where some fibers in the optic nerve from each eye cross to the other side of the brain.

invisible because their shadows are held perfectly still on the retina where they fall on the same rods and cones. However, when you shine the light from a very unusual direction, as suggested here, the shadows stimulate different rods and cones, and you are thus allowed to see the vessels.

Clearly, it is crucial that our eyes not adapt this way when we are trying to see objects in the real world. And they usually don't, because light stimulation is rarely focused on the same receptor cells long enough for them to become completely insensitive. This is because small, involuntary eye movements cause the image on the retina to drift slightly and then snap back in place again very quickly. At the same time, the eyes continually exhibit a slight, extremely rapid tremor—a tremor so minute that it goes completely unnoticed. All these movements together keep the image moving slightly on the retina, so the receptor cells never have time to adapt completely.

FROM EYE TO BRAIN   Up to now, we have directed our attention to the eye itself and the origins of visual processing in the retina. But messages from the eye must eventually reach the brain for a visual experience to occur. As you can imagine from Figure 3–6, the series of connections between eye and brain is quite intricate. To begin with, rods and cones are connected to bipolar cells in many different numbers and combinations. In addition, sets of neurons, called *interneurons*, link receptor cells to one another and bipolar cells to one another. Eventually these bipolar cells hook up with the **ganglion cells,** leading out of the eye. The axons of the ganglion cells join to form the **optic nerve,** which carries messages from each eye to the brain.

Although each retina has about 100 million rods and cones, the optic nerve has only about 1 million ganglion cells. Clearly the information collected by the 100 million receptor cells must be combined and reduced in some fashion to fit the mere 1 million "wires" that lead from each eye to the brain. Research indicates that most of this reduction takes place as a result of the abundant interconnections between the ganglion cells and the receptor cells (Hubel & Livingstone, 1990; Livingstone & Hubel, 1988b). Although it may be a bit of an oversimplification, it appears that a single ganglion cell, connected to a large number of receptor cells, summarizes or reduces the information collected by those receptor cells. Thus, the message, which is ultimately transferred to the brain by a single ganglion cell, represents the input from a large number of individual receptor cells.

The place on the retina where the axons of all the ganglion cells join to leave the eye is called the **blind spot.** This area contains no receptor cells. Even when light from a small object is focused directly on the blind spot, the object will not be seen (see Figure 3–8). After they leave the eyes, these fibers, which make up the optic nerves, separate, and some of them cross to the other side of the head at the **optic chiasm** (see Figure 3–9). The nerve fibers from the right side of each eye travel to the right hemisphere of the

Figure 3–8
Finding your blind spot.
To locate your blind spot, hold the book about a foot away from your eyes. Then close your right eye, stare at the "X," and slowly move the book toward you and away from you until the red dot disappears.

brain; those from the left side of each eye travel to the left hemisphere. Thus, as shown in Figure 3–9, visual information about any object in *the left visual field*, the area to the left of the viewer, will go to the right hemisphere (the pathway traced by the red line in Figure 3–9). Similarly, information about any object in the *right visual field*, the area to the right of the viewer, will go to the left hemisphere (the pathway traced by the blue line). You may refer back to Figures 2–10 and 2–11 in Chapter 2 (The Biological Basis of Behavior) to recall how researchers took advantage of the split-processing of the two visual fields to study split-brain patients.

The optic nerves carry their messages to various parts of the brain. Some messages reach the segment of the brain that controls the reflex movements that adjust the size of the pupil. Others find their way to the area of the brain that directs the eye muscles to change the shape of the lens. But the main destinations for messages from the retina are the visual projection areas of the cerebral cortex, where the complex coded messages from the retina are registered and interpreted.

Several kinds of evidence show that the sensory messages entering the brain are routed along multiple pathways for simultaneous processing in a number of different areas. For example, stroke victims who suffer from a disorder called *prosopagonsia* cannot recognize faces but otherwise can still see as well as any normal person. All but the most severely brain-damaged are able to tell whether faces in photographs are happy, sad, surprised, disgusted, fearful, or angry; they can also estimate age as accurately as anyone else can (Damasio, Tranel, & Damasio, 1990a; Tranel, Damasio, & Damasio, 1988). This suggests that sensory information goes to at least two areas in the brain: one that allows us to recognize faces, and one that enables us to assess whether faces appear happy or sad, male or female, old or young, and so on.

Another way researchers have determined that sensory messages follow several pathways is through studies of patients with severe damage to the *visual cortex*, the area of the cortex responsible for vision. These "cortically

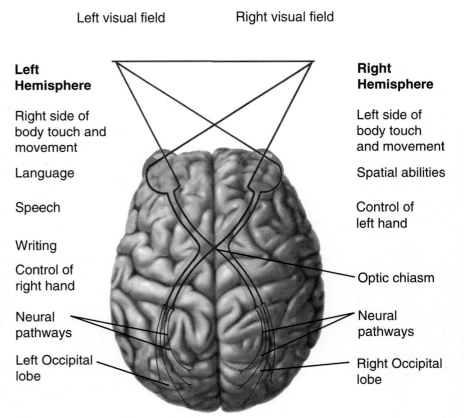

Figure 3–9
The neural connections of the visual system.
Messages about the red-colored area in the left visual field of each eye travel to the right occipital lobe; information about the blue area in the right visual field of each eye goes to the left occipital lobe. The crossover point is the *optic chiasm*.

Source: Adapted from "The Split Brain of Man," by Michael S. Gazzaniga. Copyright © 1967 by Scientific American, Inc.

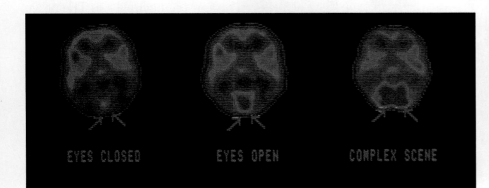

Nerve fibers from each eye cross to opposite sides of the brain, enabling the optic nerves to carry visual information to different parts of the brain. As these PET scans show, the more complex the scene, the more the visual areas of the brain (primarily the occipital lobes to the rear of both hemispheres, as shown by the arrows) are engaged in active processing. (High levels of brain activity are shown as yellow and red; low levels of activity are shown as green and blue.)

blind" patients may have healthy retinas and optic nerves, but they report partial or total blindness. A few of these patients demonstrate an odd phenomenon called *blindsight:* They behave as if they can see forms, colors, and motion—even though they claim that they cannot see at all (Barbur, Harlow, & Weiskrantz, 1994; Gazzaniga, Fendrich, & Wessiner, 1994; Weiskrantz, Barbur, & Sahraie, 1995). Some researchers have speculated that these patients' ability to see stems from lower brain centers, rather than the visual cortex, leading scientists to conclude that parts of the brain other than the cortex receive and help process visual messages (Gazzaniga et al., 1994; Weiskrantz, 1995; Zeki, 1992, 1993).

Finally, studies of monkeys show that information from the retina about movement and depth goes to one area of the visual cortex, whereas detailed information about color and shape goes to nearby, but different areas of the visual cortex (Hubel & Livingstone, 1987; Livingstone & Hubel, 1988a; Zeki, 1992, 1993). As a result, researchers contend that certain parts of the visual cortex specialize in color vision, other parts are used in detecting motion, and still others recognize specific forms in motion. If the color area is damaged, patients develop a special type of colorblindness called *achromatopsia,* in which they can neither see color nor remember color experience they had before the injury. In all other ways, however, they can see as well as anybody else—further evidence that many different areas in the brain process visual information.

Knowledge about the way visual information is coded and relayed to the brain has valuable, practical applications. For example, in a condition known as *glaucoma,* fluid pressure inside the eye builds up and can cause permanent damage to the optic nerve and consequent loss of vision. Recent research indicates that people in the early stages of glaucoma tend to lose their dim-light vision before any permanent damage is done to the optic nerve or to daylight vision. Thus, researchers are hopeful that loss of dim-light vision can be used as an early warning sign of glaucoma, prompting physicians to initiate treatment long before there is any permanent damage to daylight vision (Dadona, Hendrickson, & Quigley, 1991).

Color Vision

Like most mammals, humans can see a range of colors. In the following pages, we will first explore characteristics of color vision and then consider how the eyes convert light energy into sensations of color.

Figure 3–10
The color solid.
In the center portion of the figure, known as a color solid, the dimension of *hue* is represented around the circumference. *Saturation* ranges along the radius from the inside to the outside of the solid. *Brightness* varies along the vertical axis. The drawing (at left) illustrates this schematically. The illustration at right shows changes in saturation and brightness for the same hue.

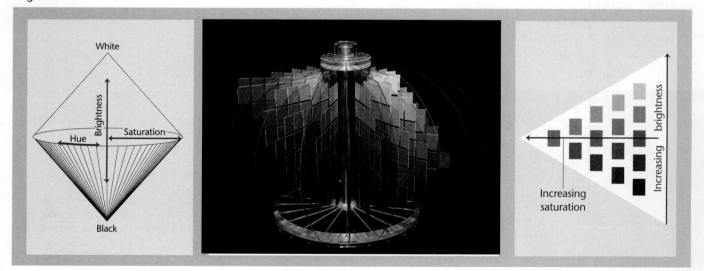

PROPERTIES OF COLOR Look at the color solid (the central portion) in Figure 3–10. What do you see? Most people say they see a number of different colors: some oranges, some yellows, some reds, and so forth. Psychologists call these different colors **hues,** and to a great extent, what hues you see depend on the wavelength of the light reaching your eyes (see Figure 3–4).

Now look at the triangle of green colors on the right side of Figure 3–10. Although each color patch on the triangle is the same hue, the green color is deepest or richest toward the left side of the triangle. Psychologists refer to the vividness or richness of a hue as its **saturation.**

Finally, notice that the colors near the top of the triangle are almost white, whereas those close to the bottom are almost black. This is the dimension of **brightness,** which varies to a great extent based on the strength of the light entering your eyes. If you squint your eyes and look at the color solid, you will reduce the apparent brightness of all the colors in the solid, and many of them will appear to become black.

Hue, saturation, and brightness are three separate aspects of our experience of color. Although people can distinguish only about 150 hues (Coren, Porac, & Ward, 1984), gradations of saturation and brightness within those 150 hues allow us to see more than 300,000 different colors (Hochberg, 1978; Kaufman, 1979). Some of this variety is captured in Figure 3–10.

THEORIES OF COLOR VISION Think for a moment about what you already know about color vision. You know that roughly 8 million cones in the retina are responsible for color vision. You also know that we can distinguish approximately 300,000 different kinds of colors. But in the fovea there are only about 150,000 cones. So there are not enough cones in the fovea to have even one cone for every color! Somehow a relatively few cones must be able to combine their messages in a way that provides both the full range of color and the clear, sharp images we perceive when we look directly at objects. How does this occur?

For centuries scientists have known that it is possible to produce all 150 basic hues by mixing together only a few lights of different colors (see Figure 3–11). Specifically, red, green, and blue lights, the *primary colors* for light mixtures, can be blended to create any hue. For example, red and green lights combine to make yellow; red and blue lights together yield magenta. Combining red, green, and blue lights in equal intensities produces white. Television picture tubes use this principle to provide a full range of colors: If you look closely at the screen, you will see that the picture is actually made up of tiny red, green, and blue dots that blend together to give all possible hues. The process of mixing lights of different wavelengths is called **additive color mixing,** because each light *adds* additional wavelengths to the overall mix.

The rules for mixing paints (or pigments) differ from those for lights (see Figure 3–12). For example, mixing red and blue paints will give you violet not magenta. That is because the red paint absorbs light from the blue end of the spectrum and reflects light from the red end of the spectrum, whereas blue paint absorbs light from the red end of the spectrum and reflects the light from the blue end of the

Hue The aspect of color that corresponds to names such as red, green, and blue.

Saturation The vividness or richness of a hue.

Brightness The nearness of a color to white as opposed to black.

Additive color mixing The process of mixing lights of different wavelengths to create new hues.

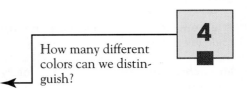

How many different colors can we distinguish?

Figure 3–11
Additive color mixing.
Mixing light waves is an *additive process.* When red and green lights are combined, the resulting hue is yellow. Adding blue light to the other two yields white light.

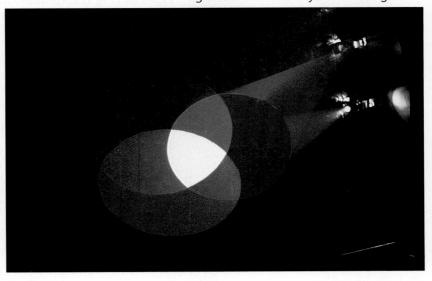

Subtractive color mixing The process of mixing pigments, each of which absorbs some wavelengths of light and reflects others.

Trichromatic theory The theory of color vision that holds that all color perception derives from three different color receptors in the retina (usually red, green, and blue receptors).

Colorblindness Partial or total inability to perceive hues.

Trichromats People who have normal color vision.

Monochromats People who are totally colorblind.

Dichromats People who are blind to either red-green or yellow-blue.

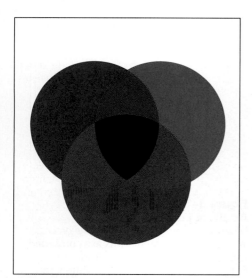

Figure 3–12
Subtractive color mixing.
The process of mixing paint pigments rather than lights is a *subtractive process,* because the pigments absorb some wavelengths and reflect others. A mixture of the three primary pigments (red, yellow, and blue) absorbs all wavelengths, producing black.

spectrum (see Figure 3–4). Together, they reflect only the red and blue wavelengths that combine to result in the experience of violet. This is called **subtractive color mixing,** because each paint *subtracts* or absorbs light from various portions of the spectrum. For paint pigments, the primary colors are red, yellow, and blue.

In the 1800s, the German physiologist Hermann von Helmholtz drew on his knowledge of additive color mixing to propose that the eye contains some cones that are sensitive to red, others that pick up greens, and still others that respond most strongly to blue-violet. According to this view, color experiences in the brain come from mixing the signals from the three receptors. For example, yellow light would stimulate the red and green cones fairly strongly and the blue cones minimally, resulting in a pattern of receptor firing that would be experienced as yellow. Helmholtz's explanation of color vision is known as **trichromatic theory.**

Trichromatic theory explains how three primary colors can be combined to produce any other hue. It also accounts for some kinds of **colorblindness**—the partial or total inability to perceive hues. People with normal color vision are called **trichromats.** Trichromats perceive all hues by combining the three primary colors. However, approximately 10 percent of men and 1 percent of women display some form of colorblindness. Those suffering from the most severe type of colorblindness, called **monochromats,** are rare people who see no color at all but respond only to shades of light and dark. Considerably more common than monochromats are **dichromats**—people who are blind either to red-green or blue-yellow (see Figure 3–13). For dichromats with red-green colorblindness, both red and green appear as a desaturated yellow; thus, their entire color experience consists of varying shades of yellow and blue. For dichromats with yellow-blue colorblindness, yellows and blues appear greenish, and their entire world of color appears in shades of red and green.

Unfortunately, trichromatic theory does not adequately explain all color experiences. For example, it isn't clear why people with normal color vision never see a light or a pigment that can be described as "reddish-green" or "yellowish-blue." Moreover, trichromatic theory cannot account for color afterimages. If you look at the flag in Figure 3–14

Figure 3–13
Experiencing colorblindness.
Perceiving the numbers 8 and 96 embedded in the mass of green circles is easy, except for people who have red-green colorblindness.

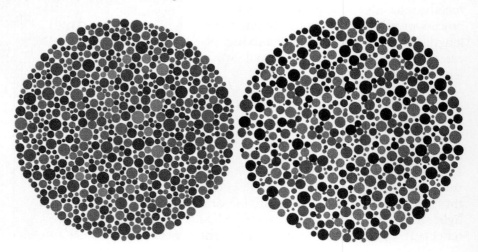

for about 30 seconds and then look at a sheet of white paper, you will see an afterimage. Where the picture is green, you will see a red afterimage; where the picture is yellow, you will see a bright blue afterimage; and where the picture is black, you will see a white afterimage. Why we experience color afterimages such as this cannot be explained by trichromatic theory.

To account for color afterimages, and other phenomena not adequately explained by trichromatic theory, another German scientist, Edward Hering ,proposed an alternative theory of colorblindness in 1878. Hering posited the existence of three pairs of color receptors: a yellow-blue pair and a red-green pair that determine the hue you see; and a black-white pair that determines the brightness of the colors you see. The members of each pair work in opposition to each other. The yellow-blue pair cannot relay messages about yellow and blue light at the same time, nor can the red-green pair send both red and green messages at the same time. This explains why we never see yellowish-blue or reddish-green. Hering's theory is now known as the **opponent-process theory.**

Hering's theory does a good job of explaining afterimages: They appear because the receptor pairs he identified have adapted to the stimulation. While you were looking at the green bars in the flag in Figure 3–14, the red-green receptors were sending "green" messages to your brain; but they were also adapting to the stimulation by becoming less sensitive to green light. When you later looked at the white page (made up of light from all parts of the spectrum), the red-green receptors responded vigorously to wavelengths in the red portion of the spectrum, and so you saw a red bar. Take a look at Figure 3–15 and you will see a corresponding afterimage that involves the yellow-blue receptors. Hering's opponent-process theory also explains the color experiences of dichromats. If the red-green system fails, then all that is left is the yellow-blue system. Similarly, if the yellow-blue system fails, the red-green system will generally remain unaffected.

Today we believe that both the trichromatic and opponent-process theories are valid—although at two different stages in the visual process. We now know for certain that there are usually three kinds of cones for color, as trichromatic theory asserts (although, according to Neitz, Neitz, and Jacobs, 1993, some individuals may, in fact, have four). One set of receptors is most sensitive to violet-blue light, another set to green light, and the third set to yellow light. However, all the receptors are at least somewhat responsive to a broad range of colors. Contrary to Helmholtz's original theory, there is no "red" receptor in the retina, but the yellow cones respond to red more than the other two types of cones do. Thus, trichromatic theory corresponds fairly closely to the types of color receptors that actually do exist in the retina.

Neurons higher up in the visual pathway appear to code color in the manner suggested by the opponent-process theory. Some neurons respond only to brightness, not to color: As the intensity of light increases, so does the rate at which these neurons fire (DeValois & DeValois, 1975). These neurons correspond to Hering's black-white pairs. A second set of neurons increases its rate of firing when red light strikes the cones and decreases it when a green light strikes them. A third set of neurons increases its firing rate in response to blue light and reduces its rate of firing when a yellow light strikes the cones. All three sets are paired with cells that react in exactly the opposite way. Thus the opponent-process theory closely reflects

Opponent-process theory Theory of color vision that holds that three sets of color receptors (yellow-blue, red-green, black-white) respond to determine the color you experience.

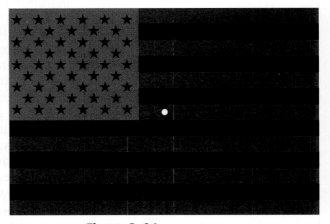

Figure 3–14
Afterimage.
Stare at the white spot in the center of the flag for about 30 seconds. Then look at a blank piece of white paper and you will see an *afterimage* in complementary colors.

Figure 3–15
Complementary afterimages.
An afterimage always appears in complementary colors. After staring at the center of the top square for about 30 seconds and then looking at the center dot of the bottom square, you will see complementary afterimages. The small yellow squares will appear as blue, and the blue squares will appear as yellow.

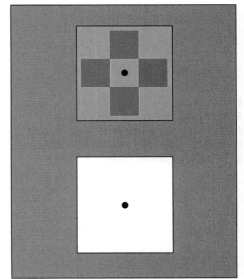

Timbre The quality of texture of sound; caused by overtones.

Hammer, anvil, stirrup The three small bones in the middle ear that relay vibrations of the eardrum to the inner ear.

vibrates as a whole, but also vibrates in halves, thirds, quarters, and so on, all at the same time. Because of physical differences in their construction, a violin and a piano playing the same note will be "in tune" but produce different overtones. Thus, the two instruments can play the same melody, yet retain their distinctive sounds. Similarly, two vocalists may sing the same note, but because of the way their voices resonate in response to their different vocal cords and body shapes, their voices sound different. This complex pattern of overtones determines the **timbre,** or "texture," of the sound. Music synthesizers can mimic different instruments electronically because they produce not only pure tones, but also the overtones that signal the timbre of different musical instruments.

Like our other senses, hearing undergoes adaptation so it can function optimally under a wide variety of conditions. Many a city resident enjoying a weekend in the country is struck at first by how quiet everything seems. After a couple of days, however, the country starts to sound very noisy. Hearing, which had adapted to the high level of noise in the city, has adapted again, this time to the relatively low level of sound in the country. Our sense of hearing adapts to tone as well. If you have difficulty hearing the difference between two tones, for example, listening repeatedly to only one of the tones will cause adaptation for that tone, and you will then find it much easier to detect the difference between that tone and the other.

The Ear

Hearing begins when sound waves strike the eardrum (see Figure 3–18) and cause it to vibrate. The quivering of the eardrum prompts three tiny bones in the middle ear—called the **hammer,** the **anvil,** and the **stirrup**—to hit

Figure 3–18
How we hear.
The first stage of the hearing process is a series of vibrations: (A) Sound waves enter the outer ear and travel to the eardrum, causing it to vibrate. The vibrating eardrum causes the bones of the middle ear (B) (the hammer, anvil, and stirrup) to hit each other, amplifying and carrying the vibrations to the oval window and on to the fluid in the coiled cochlea of the inner ear (C). Now, the moving fluid sets the basilar membrane, inside the cochlea, moving. The organ of Corti, on top of the basilar membrane, moves too. Inside the organ of Corti, thousands of tiny receptor cells are topped by a bundle of hair-like fibers. As the basilar membrane vibrates, the fibers bend, stimulating the receptor cells to send a signal through afferent nerve endings which join to form the auditory nerve to the brain. There the impulses are interpreted as sounds.

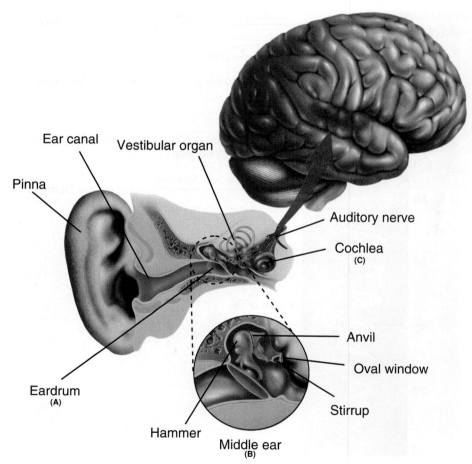

each other in sequence and to carry the vibrations to the inner ear. The last of these three bones, the stirrup, is attached to a membrane called the **oval window.** Just below the oval window is another membrane, known as the **round window,** which equalizes the pressure in the inner ear when the stirrup strikes the oval window.

The air waves are magnified during their trip through the middle ear. Thus, when the oval window starts to vibrate in response to the stirrup, it has a powerful effect on the inner ear. There the vibrations are transmitted to the fluid inside a snail-shaped structure called the **cochlea.** The cochlea is divided lengthwise by the **basilar membrane** (see Figure 3–19). The basilar membrane is stiffer near the oval and round windows and gets gradually more flexible toward its other end. When the fluid in the cochlea begins to move, the basilar membrane is pushed up and down, rippling in response to the movement of the cochlear fluid.

Lying on top of the basilar membrane, and moving in sync with it, is the **organ of Corti.** Here the messages from the sound waves finally reach the receptor cells for the sense of hearing: thousands of tiny hair cells that are embedded in the organ of Corti (Spoendlin & Schrott, 1989). As you can see in Figure 3–19, each hair cell is topped by a bundle of fibers. These fibers are pushed and pulled by the vibrations of the basilar membrane. If the fibers bend by so much as 100 trillionths of a meter, the receptor cell sends a signal to be transmitted through the **auditory nerve** to the brain. The brain pools the information from thousands of these cells to perceive sounds. Scientists now know that each hair cell not only sends messages to the brain but also receives messages from the brain. The brain apparently can send the hair cells signals that reduce their sensitivity to sound in general or to sound waves of particular frequencies. The brain can, in effect, "shut down" the ears somewhat, but for what purpose remains one of the mysteries of research on hearing (Hudspeth, 1983; Kim, 1985).

NEURAL CONNECTIONS   The sense of hearing is truly bilateral. Each ear sends messages to both cerebral hemispheres. The switching station where the nerve fibers from the ears cross over is in the medulla, part of the hindbrain (see Figure 2–7). From the medulla, other nerve fibers carry the messages from the ears to the higher parts of the brain. Some messages go to the brain centers that coordinate the movements of the eyes, head, and ears. Others travel through the reticular formation (examined in the previous chapter), which probably tacks on a few special "wake-up" or "ho-hum" postscripts to the sound messages. The primary destinations for these auditory messages are the auditory areas in the temporal lobes of the two cerebral hemispheres.

En route to the temporal lobes, auditory messages pass through at least four lower brain centers—a much less direct route than visual messages follow. At each stage, auditory information becomes more precisely coded. In some animals, hearing is one of the most acute senses. Bats, for example, hear by sending out a number of different sounds while they are flying. Neurons in their auditory systems extract an extraordinary amount of information from the echoes of those sounds as they bounce off nearby objects. Remarkably, if a flying insect is nearby, the bat can determine exactly where it is, how far away it is, how fast it is flying, its size, characteristics of its wing beats, and its general features. Each of those coded messages goes to a different area of the bat's brain. Equally sophisticated coding most likely occurs in the human auditory system as auditory messages make their way through the brain (Suga, 1990).

Oval window Membrane across the opening between the middle ear and inner ear that conducts vibrations to the cochlea.

Round window Membrane between the middle ear and inner ear that equalizes pressure in the inner ear.

Cochlea Part of the inner ear containing fluid that vibrates, which in turn causes the basilar membrane to vibrate.

Basilar membrane Vibrating membrane in the cochlea of the inner ear; it contains sense receptors for sound.

Organ of Corti Structure on the surface of the basilar membrane that contains the receptor cells for hearing.

Auditory nerve The bundle of axons that carries signals from each ear to the brain.

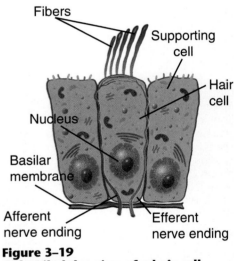

Figure 3–19
A detailed drawing of a hair cell located in the organ of Corti.
At the top of each hair cell is a bundle of fibers. If the fibers bend so much as 100 trillionths of a meter, the receptor cells transmit a sensory message to the brain.

Source: Adapted from "The Hair Cells of the Inner Ear," by A. J. Hudspeth, © 1983 by Scientific American, Inc. All rights reserved.

Place theory Theory that pitch is determined by the location of greatest vibration on the basilar membrane.

Frequency theory Theory that pitch is determined by the frequency with which hair cells in the cochlea fire.

Volley principle Refinement of frequency theory; it suggests that receptors in the ear fire in sequence, with one group responding, then a second, then a third, and so on, so that the complete pattern of firing corresponds to the frequency of the sound wave.

Theories of Hearing

The thousands of tiny hair cells in the organ of Corti send messages about the infinite variations in the frequency, amplitude, and overtones of sound waves. But how are the different sound-wave patterns coded into neural messages? One aspect of sound—loudness—seems to depend on how many neurons are activated—the more cells that fire, the louder the sound seems to be. The coding of messages about pitch is more complicated. There are two basic views of pitch discrimination: place theory and frequency theory. According to **place theory,** the brain determines pitch by noting the *place* on the basilar membrane at which the message is strongest. This theory asserts that any given sound wave has a point on the basilar membrane at which vibrations are most intense. Thus, high-frequency sounds cause the greatest vibration at the stiff base of the basilar membrane; low-frequency sounds resonate most strongly at the opposite end (Zwislocki, 1981). The brain detects the location of the most intense nerve-cell activity and uses this to determine the pitch of a sound.

The **frequency theory** of pitch discrimination holds that the *frequency* of vibrations of the basilar membrane as a *whole*, not just *parts* of it, is translated into an equivalent frequency of nerve impulses. Thus, if a hair bundle is pulled or pushed rapidly, its hair cell sends a high-frequency message to the brain. However, because neurons cannot fire as rapidly as the frequency of the highest-pitched sound that can be heard, theorists have modified the frequency theory to include a **volley principle.** According to this view, auditory neurons can fire in sequence: One neuron fires, then a second one, then a third. By then, the first neuron has had time to recover and can fire again. In this way, several neurons together, firing in a volley, can send a more rapid series of impulses to the brain than any single neuron could send by itself.

Because neither place theory nor frequency theory alone fully explain pitch discrimination, some combination of the two is needed. Frequency theory appears to account for the ear's responses to frequencies up to about 4,000 Hz; above that, place theory provides a better explanation of what is happening.

HEARING DISORDERS Because the mechanisms that allow us to hear are so subtle and complicated, the number of possible problems that can compromise our hearing is extensive. Deafness is one of the most common concerns. Some instances of deafness result from defects in the outer or middle ear—for instance, the eardrum may be damaged, or the small bones of the middle ear may not work properly. Other cases of deafness occur because the basilar membrane in the cochlea or the auditory nerve itself has been damaged. Disease, infections, and even long-term exposure to loud noise can harm the ear and cause partial or complete deafness. In fact, of the estimated 28 million Americans with some loss of hearing, approximately 10 million are the victims of protracted loud noise on the job or at home, with the chief culprits being leaf blowers, chain saws, snowmobiles, and personal stereo systems (Leary, 1990). Even high-impact aerobics has been shown to contribute to hearing loss (Weintraub, 1990).

For some people with a hearing loss, hearing aids provide an effective remedy by simply amplifying incoming sound. For patients with a *conductive hearing loss,* surgery is often recommended. A conductive hearing loss is due to a stiffening of the connections between the bones (hammer, anvil, and stirrup) of the middle ear so that vibrations are not transmitted effectively from the eardrum to the oval window. To correct a hearing loss of this type,

5

Does listening to loud music really damage the ears?

surgeons generally break, loosen, or replace the bones, enabling better transmission across the middle ear.

Cochlear implants offer some hope to people who suffer from deafness due to cochlear damage. One or more platinum electrodes are inserted into the cochlea of one ear. The electrodes bypass the damaged hair cells and convey electrical signals directly to the auditory nerve. However, cochlear implants, hearing aids, or middle-ear surgery will not work for people who have auditory nerve damage. Moreover, even in cases where the auditory nerve is healthy, the effectiveness of cochlear implants varies greatly. In some people who were totally deaf, however, these implants have produced as much as 70 percent correct word recognition (Erickson, 1990; Loeb, 1985).

Another technique involving ultra-high-frequency sounds delivered directly to the bones of the skull, has shown promise with profoundly deaf patients who have not been helped by other means (Lenhardt et al., 1991). Exactly why sounds delivered directly to the bones of the skull help deaf people to hear is not yet known; apparently there is some other organ besides the cochlea that is capable of picking up and deciphering sounds (one promising candidate, the saccule, is part of the vestibular system, which we will discuss shortly).

Far from not hearing enough sound, some people hear too much of the wrong kind of sound and suffer greatly because of it. Almost everybody has at some time heard a steady, high-pitched hum that persists even in the quietest room. This sound seems to come from inside the head. In about 1 percent of the population, this tone, called a *tinnitus*, becomes unbearably loud—like the screeching of subway brakes—and does not go away (Dunkle, 1982). In a few cases, tinnitus is caused by blood flowing through vessels near the inner ear. In most cases, however, it is due to irritation or damage to the hair cells. Prolonged exposure to loud sound or toxins, even some antibiotics, can cause permanent damage to the hair cells.

THE OTHER SENSES

Psychologists and other scientists have focused most of their attention on the senses of vision and hearing because humans rely primarily on these two senses to gather information about their environment. However, we also use other senses, such as smell, taste, balance, motion, pressure, temperature, and pain. Let's look briefly at each of these senses, starting with the chemical senses—smell and taste.

Smell

The sense of smell in humans is extremely sensitive. According to one estimate, it is about 10,000 times as sensitive as that of taste (Moncrieff, 1951). Only a few molecules of a substance reaching the smell receptors are necessary to cause humans to perceive an odor. Certain substances, such as decayed cabbage, lemons, and rotten eggs, can be detected in minute amounts. As another example, mercaptan, a foul-smelling substance added to natural gas, can be smelled in concentrations as small as 1 part per 50 billion parts of air.

Despite this great sensitivity, the sense of smell undergoes adaptation much like the other senses. The perfume that was so pleasant to its wearer early in the evening seems to have "worn off" after a few hours. Others continue to notice it, however. Similarly, the enticing aroma that led you to a restaurant seems to have disappeared by the time your meal begins. However, it continues to draw other patrons to the restaurant. Fortunately, the ability to smell some substances—like the mercaptan added to natural gas—adapts more slowly than our ability to smell other substances.

Which sense is more sensitive—taste or smell?

Olfactory epithelium Nasal membranes containing receptor cells sensitive to odors.

Olfactory bulb The smell center in the brain.

Certain animal species rely more on their sense of smell than humans do. This dog has been trained to use its keen sense of smell to detect bombs hidden in luggage.

Most mammals, including humans, have two different sensory systems devoted to the sense of smell. The first allows us to detect and discriminate among common odors. This branch of our olfactory (smell) system helps us to tell the difference between the citrus scents of lemon and orange and the sour smell of spoiled milk. The second branch of the smell sense is used in communicating sexual, aggressive, or territorial scent signals. As we will see, even though humans have this system, it is much more important to nonhuman animals.

DETECTING COMMON ODORS Our sense of smell is activated by a complex protein produced in a nasal gland. As we breathe, a fine mist of this protein, called *odorant binding protein (OBP)*, is sprayed through a duct in the tip of the nose. The protein binds with airborne molecules that then activate the receptors for this sense, located high in each nasal cavity in a patch of tissue called the **olfactory epithelium** (see Figure 3–20). The olfactory epithelium is only about half the size of a postage stamp, but it is packed with millions of receptor cells. Interestingly, these nerve cells die and are replaced by new ones every few weeks (Graziadei, Levine, & Graziadei, 1979)—the only neurons known to be replaced naturally in the human body. The axons from these millions of receptors go directly to the **olfactory bulb,** where some recoding takes place. From the olfactory bulb, messages are routed to the temporal lobes of the brain, resulting in our awareness of the smells. But messages are also routed to lower brain centers such as the amygdala and the hippocampus, which, as we saw in the previous chapter, figure prominently in emotion and memory.

Researchers have uncovered some intriguing facts about smell. First, although people can discriminate among a large number of odors, they find it much more difficult to identify the sources of many familiar odors. For example, more than 90 percent of people can correctly identify the smell of coffee, but only 80 percent can identify leather, only about 70 percent can identify bubble gum or mustard, and just 60 percent can identify bologna.

Figure 3–20
The human olfactory system.
The sense of smell is triggered when odor molecules in the air reach the olfactory receptors located inside the top of the nose. Inhaling and exhaling odor molecules from food does much to give food its flavorful "taste."

Source: From Human Anatomy and Physiology by Anthony J. Gaudin and Kenneth C. Jones. Copyright © 1989 by Holt, Rinehart, and Winston, Inc. Reprinted by permission.

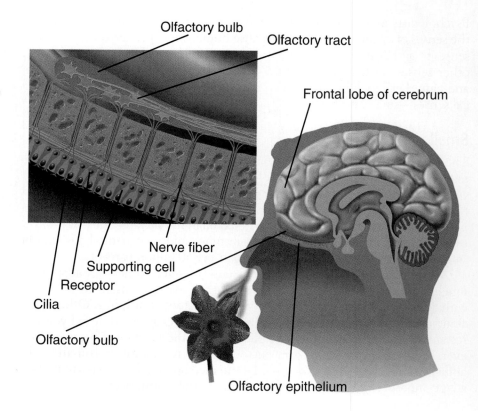

Olfactory bulb

Olfactory tract

Frontal lobe of cerebrum

Nerve fiber

Supporting cell

Receptor

Cilia

Olfactory bulb

Olfactory epithelium

Less than 50 percent of people can correctly identify turpentine, vinegar, honey, and vanilla extract (Cain, 1982; Engen, 1982).

Odor sensitivity also appears to be related to gender. Numerous studies confirm that women generally have a better sense of smell than men do (Cain, 1982; Doty, 1984; Doty et al., 1985).

Age also makes a difference in the ability to detect and identify odors (Doty, 1989). Generally, the ability to smell is sharpest during the early adult years (ages 20 to 40) (Doty et al., 1984). Of the people tested by Doty and his colleagues, one-quarter of those over the age of 65 and half of those over the age of 80 had completely lost their ability to smell. The complete loss of smell, known as *anosmia*, can be devastating. In almost all cases, it causes people to lose interest in food; in some cases, it can even reduce the desire for sexual activity. And it can also be dangerous: People who are unable to smell are unable to detect such things as escaped natural gas, spilled gasoline, spoiled food, and smoke.

PHEROMONE COMMUNICATION Some animals use smells as a means of communication. Certain chemicals, called **pheromones,** can have quite specific and powerful effects on behavior. For example, ants use pheromones to mark trails, and queen bees have a distinctive smell that sets them apart from all other bees. Many animals, including domestic dogs and wolves, also use pheromones to mark their territory. In male fruit flies, it has even been demonstrated that bisexual behavior may result when the areas of their brains responsive to pheromones are altered (Ferveur et al., 1995). Moreover, pheromones signal sexual receptivity in female mice, rats, cattle, and pigs. Research indicates that pheromones are sensed by receptors in the **vomeronasal organ (VNO),** located in the roof of the nasal cavity. The VNO sends messages to a second olfactory bulb specially designed to interpret pheromonal communications (Bartoshuk & Beauchamp, 1994; Wysocki & Meredith, 1987).

Humans, like other mammals, have a VNO (Takami et al., 1993), but so far no one has conclusively established what role (if any) pheromones play in human interaction. For example, no clear evidence suggests that pheromones affect human sexual response (Quadagno, 1987). However, we do know that women who live together tend to synchronize their menstrual cycles over time (McClintock, 1971), and there is considerable experimental evidence from studies involving both humans and nonhumans that menstrual synchronicity occurs as a result of some kind of pheromone communication (McClintock, 1978, 1984; Preti et al., 1986; M. J. Russell, Switz, & Thompson, 1980).

Human evolutionary history may have been influenced by pheromone communication. In a recent study that examined the role male body odor may play in female mate choice, volunteers were asked to smell T-shirts previously worn by males and to rate the smells for pleasantness and sexiness (Wedeking et al., 1995). The participants were then sorted into categories based on characteristics of their immune systems. Interestingly, females preferred the odors of men who had immune systems most different from their own. One possible explanation for this otherwise puzzling finding is that offspring resulting from a union of parents with different immune systems will possess a broader immune response (and thus be more likely to survive) than the offspring of parents with similar immune systems (Mirsky, 1995). Thus, evolution might favor females who are most attracted to males with very different immune systems.

We also know that humans are capable of some other remarkable feats involving the sense of smell, although we do not yet know which of the two

Pheromone Chemical that communicates information to other organisms through smell.

Vomeronasal organ (VNO) Location of receptors for pheromones in the roof of the nasal cavity.

Taste buds Structures on the tongue that contain the receptor cells for taste.

Papillae Small bumps on the tongue that contain taste buds.

olfactory systems is at work here. For example, mothers can identify their babies by smell after only a few hours of contact (Porter, Cernich, & McLaughlin, 1983). In turn, newborn infants can discriminate between their mothers' body odors and the odors of other mothers (Schaal, 1986), and they will even turn their heads toward the scent of a perfume that has been worn by their mothers while ignoring a different perfume (Schleidt & Genzel, 1990). Scent recognition may even bind families throughout life: Adults can recognize clothing worn by their relatives, even after they have been separated for several years (Porter et al., 1986).

Taste

To understand taste, we must first distinguish it from *flavor*. The flavor of food arises from a complex combination of taste and smell. If you hold your nose when you eat, most of the food's flavor will disappear, even though you will still experience sensations of *bitterness, saltiness, sourness,* or *sweetness*. In other words, you will get the taste, but not the flavor. To demonstrate the impact of flavor on our sense of taste, one group of researchers first asked subjects to taste and smell substances dropped on their tongues: More than half were able to correctly identify coffee, cherry, garlic, root beer, and chocolate. But when they were prevented from smelling the substances, only 1 to 3 percent of the subjects could identify those same substances. The effect was much less pronounced for strong-tasting substances such a vinegar, whiskey, and lemon; more than 35 percent of subjects could still correctly identify those substances without using the sense of smell (Mozel et al., 1969).

We experience only four primary taste qualities: sweet, sour, salty, and bitter. All other tastes derive from combinations of these four. The tip of the tongue is most sensitive to sweetness and saltiness, the back to bitterness, and the sides to sourness. But recent studies have shown that each area can distinguish all four qualities to some degree (Bartoshuk & Beauchamp, 1994).

The receptor cells for the sense of taste are housed in the **taste buds,** most of which are found on the tip, sides, and back of the tongue. An adult has about 10,000 taste buds (Bartoshuk, 1993). The number of taste buds decreases with age, a fact that partly explains why older people often lose interest in food—they simply cannot taste it as well as they used to.

The taste buds are embedded in the tongue's **papillae,** bumps that you can see if you look at your tongue in the mirror. Each taste bud contains a cluster of taste receptors or taste cells (see Figure 3–21), which die and are replaced about every 7 days. The chemical substances in the foods we eat dissolve in saliva and fall into the crevices between the papillae of the tongue, where they come into contact with the taste receptors. The chemical interaction between food substances and the taste cells causes adjacent neurons to fire, sending a nerve impulse to the parietal lobe of the brain and to the limbic system. This happens very fast: People can accurately identify a taste within one-tenth of a second after something salty or sweet has touched the tongue (Cain, 1981). Interestingly, the same nerves that carry messages about taste also conduct information about chewing, swallowing, and the temperature and texture of food.

Taste, like the other senses, also displays adaptation. You might have noticed that when you first start eating salted peanuts, the saltiness is quite strong, but after a while it becomes less noticeable. Furthermore, exposure to one quality of taste can modify other taste sensations in a process called cross-adaptation (Bartoshuk, 1974). For example, many people find

Figure 3–21
The structure of a taste bud.
The sensory receptors for taste are found primarily on the tongue. Taste cells can detect only sweet, sour, salty, and bitter qualities. All other tastes result from different combinations of these taste sensations.

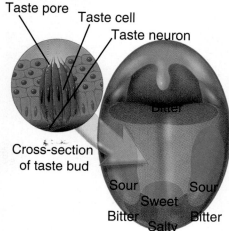

Taste pore

Taste cell

Taste neuron

Cross-section of taste bud

Bitter

Sour

Sour

Sweet

Bitter

Bitter

Salty

that after eating fresh artichokes, other foods, as well as plain water, tend to have a sweet taste. Conversely, after brushing your teeth in the morning, you may notice that your orange juice has lost its sweetness. That's partly because toothpaste contains an ingredient that reduces our sensitivity to sweetness and heightens our sensitivity to the sourness of the juice's citric acid.

Kinesthetic and Vestibular Senses

The **kinesthetic senses** provide information about the speed and direction of our movement in space. More specifically, they relay information concerning muscle movement, changes in posture, and strain on muscles and joints. Specialized nerve endings, called **stretch receptors,** are attached to muscle fibers, and different nerve endings, known as **Golgi tendon organs,** are attached to the tendons, which connect muscle to bones. Together, these two types of receptors provide constant feedback from the stretching and contraction of individual muscles. The information from these receptors travels via the spinal cord to the brain, where it is ultimately represented on the cortex of the parietal lobes, the same area of the cortex that perceives the sense of touch.

The **vestibular senses** give us clues about our orientation or position in space (R. J. Leigh, 1994). We use this information to determine which way is up and which way is down. Birds and fish also rely on these senses to determine in which direction they are heading when they cannot see well. Like hearing, the vestibular senses originate in the inner ear, where hair cells serve as the sense organs. There are actually two kinds of vestibular sensation. The first one, which relays messages about the speed and direction of body rotation, arises in the three **semicircular canals** of the inner ear. Like the cochlea, each canal is filled with fluid that shifts hair bundles, which, in turn, stimulate hair cells, sending a message to the brain about the speed and direction of body rotation.

The second vestibular sense gives us information about *gravitation* and *movement* forward and backward, up and down. This sense arises from the two **vestibular sacs** that lie between the semicircular canals and the cochlea. Both sacs are filled with a jellylike fluid that contains millions of tiny crystals. When the body moves horizontally or vertically, the crystals bend hair bundles, prompting a sensory message.

The nerve impulses from both vestibular organs travel to the brain along the auditory nerve, but their ultimate destinations in the brain are still something of a mystery. Certain messages from the vestibular system go to the cerebellum, which controls many of the reflexes involved in coordinated movement. Others reach the areas that regulate the internal body organs, and some find their way to the parietal lobe of the cerebral cortex for analysis and response.

Sensations of Motion

Motion sickness arises in the vestibular organs. Certain kinds of motion, such as riding in ships, cars, airplanes, even on camels and elephants, trigger strong reactions in some people (Stern & Koch, 1996). Two-thirds of astronauts experience motion sickness during their first flights (Davis et al., 1988), and this phenomenon has even been observed under laboratory conditions in animals such as monkeys, cats, and dogs (Daunton, 1990). Susceptibility to motion sickness appears to be related to both race and genetics (Muth et al., 1994), with people of Asian ancestry displaying the highest frequency of the disorder.

Kinesthetic senses Senses of muscle movement, posture, and strain on muscles and joints.

Stretch receptors Receptors that sense muscle stretch and contraction.

Golgi tendon organs Receptors that sense movement of the tendons, which connect muscle to bone.

Vestibular senses The senses of equilibrium and body position in space.

Semicircular canals Structures in the inner ear particularly sensitive to body rotation.

Vestibular sacs Sacs in the inner ear that sense gravitation and forward, backward, and vertical movement.

This Olympic gymnast is utilizing information provided by both her kinesthetic and her vestibular senses. Her kinesthetic senses are relaying messages pertaining to muscle strain and movements; her vestibular senses are supplying feedback about her body position in space.

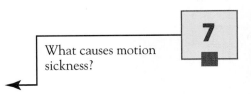

7

What causes motion sickness?

According to one theory, motion sickness stems from discrepancies between visual information and vestibular sensations (Stern & Koch, 1996). To experience this conflict between visual and vestibular information, try reading a book while your body is being jolted up and down in a bus. Occasionally the vestibular sense can be completely overwhelmed by visual information. This is what happens when we watch an automobile chase scene that was filmed from inside a moving car. We feel a sensation of movement because our eyes are telling our brain that we are moving, even though the organs in our inner ear insist that we are sitting still. In fact, the sense of motion can be so strong that some people experience motion sickness while sitting absolutely still as they watch a movie filmed from an airplane or a boat! This visual trick has an advantage: People who have had one or even both vestibular organs removed can function normally as long as they have visual cues on which to rely.

The Skin Senses

Our skin is actually our largest sense organ (see *Highlights*). A person 6 feet tall has about 21 square feet of skin. Aside from protecting us from the environment, holding in body fluids, and regulating our internal temperature, the skin is a sense organ with numerous nerve receptors distributed in varying concentrations throughout its surface. The nerve fibers from all these receptors travel to the brain by two routes. Some information goes through the medulla and the thalamus and from there to the sensory cortex in the parietal lobe of the brain—which is presumably where our experiences of touch, pressure, and so on arise. Other information goes through the thalamus and then on to the reticular formation, which, as we saw in the previous chapter, is responsible for arousing the nervous system or quieting it down.

The various skin receptors give rise to what are called the *cutaneous sensations* of pressure, temperature, and pain. But the relationship between these receptors and our sensory experiences is a subtle one. Researchers believe that our brains draw on complex information about the *patterns* of activity received from many different receptors to detect and discriminate among skin sensations. For example, there are cold fibers that speed their firing rate as the skin cools down and slow down their firing when the skin heats up. Conversely, there are warm fibers that accelerate their firing rate when the skin gets warm and slow down when the skin cools. The brain may use the combined information from these two sets of fibers as the basis for determining skin temperature. If both sets are activated at once, the brain may read their combined pattern of firings as "hot" (Craig & Bushnell, 1994). Thus, you might sometimes think that you are touching something hot when you are really touching something warm and something cool at the same time. This phenomenon is known as *paradoxical heat* (see Figure 3–22).

The skin senses are remarkably sensitive: Skin displacement of as little as .00004 inch can result in a sensation of pressure. Moreover, various parts of the body differ greatly in their sensitivity to pressure: Your face and fingertips are extremely sensitive, whereas your legs, feet, and back are much less so (Weinstein, 1968). It is no wonder, then, that when we examine things with our hands, we tend to do so with our fingertips. It is this remarkable sensitivity in our fingertips that makes possible Braille touch reading, which requires identifying patterns of tiny raised dots distributed over a very small area.

Like other senses, the skin senses undergo sensory adaptation. When we first sit in a hot bath, it may be too hot to tolerate, but in a few minutes, we adapt to the heat, just as our eyes adapt to darkness. Similarly, when we put

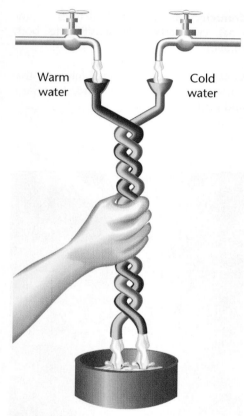

Figure 3–22
Paradoxical heat.
Touching a warm pipe and a cold pipe at the same time causes two sets of skin receptors to signal at once to the brain. The brain reads their combined pattern of firings as "hot," a phenomenon known as *paradoxical heat.*

Warm water

Cold water

HIGHLIGHTS
TOUCH: THE COMFORT SENSE

Of all our senses, touch may be the most comforting. By touching and being touched by others, we bridge, at least momentarily, our isolation and our loneliness by giving and receiving tenderness and care. This explains to some extent why in most societies hellos and goodbyes are accompanied by gestures involving touch—shaking hands, brushing lips against cheeks, or hugging—and why lovers express their affection by kissing, holding hands, and caressing.

Indeed, research such as psychologist Harry Harlow's work with monkeys has affirmed the vital importance of touch in human development. In a series of classic experiments, Harlow (1958; Harlow & Zimmerman, 1959) showed that infant primates deprived of maternal contact suffered psychologically and physically (this research is explored in greater detail in Chapter 9, Motivation and Emotion). More recent research that examines the neurochemical effects of skin-to-skin contact suggests that the experience of being touched may play a crucial role in human development: It may directly affect the growth of an infant's mind and body. In one study, premature infants who were massaged three times a day for 15 minutes at a time gained weight much more quickly than did a control group that was left untouched (Field, 1986). The massaged babies were subsequently more responsive to faces and rattles and were generally more active than the other babies. Because of their comparatively rapid growth, the massaged infants were discharged from the hospital an average of 6 days earlier than the nonmassaged infants were. And 8 months later, the massaged infants

maintained their weight advantage and performed better on tests of motor and mental ability. Significantly, the massaged infants did not eat more than the others: Their accelerated weight gain appears to be due solely to the effect of physical touch on their metabolism.

This new research has significant implications for hospital care of premature infants. Traditionally, these babies have been placed in incubators, fed intravenously, and touched only minimally, because when approached or handled, premature babies often become agitated, which can put a life-threatening strain on their lungs. But Field found that gentle massage of the babies immediately restored their calm.

Why does touch produce such beneficial effects? Studies of rats, whose basic neural and tactile (touch) systems are similar to those of humans, indicate that a specific pattern of touch by the mother rat—especially licking—inhibits the baby's manufacture of beta endorphin, a chemical that reduces levels of growth hormone (Schanberg & Field, 1987). In response to maternal licking, the infant rats' level of beta endorphin decreased, and levels of growth hormone increased. If the rat pups were separated from their mothers, levels of beta endorphins increased, growth hormones decreased, and the baby rats' growth was stunted. When the pups were reunited with their mothers and maternal licking resumed, beta endorphin levels decreased once again, and growth speeded up.

In related studies, when infant rats and monkeys were separated from their mothers, they showed a stress response that disappeared when maternal contact resumed

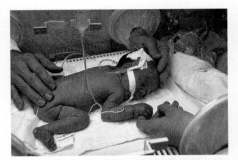

The human response to touch may sometimes be therapeutic. Gentle massage tends to calm agitated premature babies, and by regularly massaging them their growth rate can be increased. These findings agree with the common belief that touch is among our most comforting senses.

(S. Levine, Johnson, & Gonzales, 1985). According to the researchers, skin-to-skin contact may reduce the level of stress hormones, soothing all infants, not just premature babies. It may be that both the mental and physical development of all infants could be enhanced if they were touched more (Jacobsen, Edelstein, & Hofmann, 1994; Wachs & Smitherman, 1985).

Each of us, of course, is comfortable with a different degree of physical contact. The uniqueness of our nervous systems may account for some of this difference, but our past experiences with touch undoubtedly play a role as well. In one study, the nerve cells in the area of the cortex that controls touch sensations were better developed in rats that had experienced more physical contact than in rats that had less contact (Rosenzweig, Bennett, & Diamond, 1972). Researchers suspect that those who have had little physical contact may become hypersensitive to touch, so much so that they find the experience of touching physically uncomfortable.

Gate control theory The theory that a "neurological gate" in the spinal cord controls the transmission of pain messages to the brain.

on an article of clothing that is a bit tight, we may feel uncomfortable at first but not even notice it later on. How soon this adaptation occurs, or whether it occurs at all, appears to depend on how large an area of the skin is being stimulated and the intensity of the pressure (Geldard, 1972): The larger the area and the more intense the pressure, the longer it takes for us to adapt.

Pain

The sensation of pain is an extraordinarily complex sensory event. For example, it seems reasonable to assume that body damage causes pain, yet in many cases physical injury is not accompanied by pain. And conversely, people may feel pain even though they have not suffered any physical injury.

We might also assume that pain occurs when some kind of pain receptor is stimulated. But there is no simple relationship between pain receptors and the experience of pain. In fact, scientists have had great difficulty even locating pain receptors. The most likely candidate for a pain receptor is the simple free nerve ending, but this receptor also contributes to our sense of touch or pressure. Perhaps chemicals released from damaged tissues somehow convert free nerve endings from touch and pressure sensors into pain sensors.

Pain also differs from the other senses in the ways in which people react to it. As a result, some psychologists question whether pain should even be considered a basic sensation like pressure and temperature (Melzack, 1992).

Glowing coals smolder under the feet of these participants in an annual ritual at Mt. Takao, Japan. How do they do it? Is it mind over matter—the human ability to sometimes "turn off" pain sensations? The secret in this case may actually lie more in the coals than in the men. Because wood is a poor conductor of heat, walking over wood coals quickly may not be that painful after all.

INDIVIDUAL DIFFERENCES   People perceive and react to pain in strikingly different ways. Some of us appear to be completely insensitive to pain (Manfredi et al., 1981). In one famous case, a young Canadian girl reported feeling nothing when she inadvertently bit off part of her tongue and suffered third-degree burns as a result of kneeling on a hot radiator (Baxter & Olszewski, 1960; McMurray, 1950). If you burn your hand, you might calmly run cold water over it; someone else might scream. Our beliefs about pain can also affect our experience of it. For example, hospital patients who believed that a particular medical procedure was not painful actually reported experiencing less pain than people who had not been given that information (DiMatteo & Friedman, 1982). Emotional or motivational conditions have an impact on our perception of pain as well. One researcher noted that only 25 percent of soldiers wounded during battle requested pain medication, whereas more than 80 percent of surgical patients asked for painkillers for comparable "wounds" (Beecher, 1972). Athletes injured during a game often feel no pain until the excitement of competition has passed.

Culture and belief systems dramatically influence our response to injury (Bates & Rankin-Hill, 1994). For instance, in a religious ceremony practiced in parts of India, a young man swings from a ceremonial platform, supported by hooks embedded in his back, seemingly without pain (Melzack, 1973). It should not be surprising, then, that in cases of serious injury the perception of pain is not related to the amount of tissue damage sustained (Schiffman, 1982). Because of the great variability in the ways that people experience pain, scientists encounter difficulty in measuring typical pain thresholds and studying how individuals adapt to pain (Irwin & Whitehead, 1991).

EXPLAINING DIFFERENCES   How do psychologists explain our varying sensitivities to pain? One commonly accepted view is the **gate control theory** of pain which suggests that a "neurological gate" in the spinal cord controls the transmission of pain impulses to the brain. If the gate is open, we experience more pain than we do if it is closed. Whether the gate is closed or open depends on a complex competition between two different types of sensory nerve fibers. On the one hand, there are large fibers that tend to "close the gate" when they are stimulated, thus preventing pain impulses from reaching the brain. But there are also small fibers that "open the gate" when they are stimulated, allowing pain messages to get through to the brain. Moreover, certain areas of the brain stem can also close the gate from above, so to speak, by sending down signals to fibers in the spinal cord to close the gate. Finally, by focusing our attention away from pain (as in certain forms of meditation), we may also experience greatly diminished feelings of pain. All these mechanisms may be at work when, in the same circumstances, one person experiences excruciating pain while another feels no pain at all (Melzack, 1980; Wall & Melzack, 1989). We cannot pinpoint why some individuals experience pain differently than others. From the perspective of gate control theory, these differences might be due to the numbers of small fibers or large fibers that a person has, or varying levels of control exerted on the gate mechanism from higher brain areas. It may also turn out that some people have faulty gates.

Despite its complexities, gate control theory is already being used to develop new techniques for the control of pain (Aronoff, 1993). For example, some dentists are experimenting with devices that electrically stimulate large nerve fibers and block the action of small fibers, thus closing the gate on pain. Patients can adjust the amount of stimulation based on their own needs.

Studies of pain relief suggest that there are two other pain-controlling systems that may be independent of or in some way related to the spinal pain gate. In the first case, if you give pain sufferers a chemically neutral pill, or *placebo*, but tell them that it is an effective pain reducer, they will often experience less pain after taking it. No doubt many home remedies and secret cures rely on the **placebo effect.** In addition, traditional Chinese and Korean medicine has demonstrated that acupuncture treatments, involving the insertion of thin needles into parts of the body, can reduce or eliminate pain. Research indicates that both placebos and acupuncture work through the release of endorphins, the pain-blocking neurotransmitters that we examined in the previous chapter. A number of drugs block the effects of endorphins, and if these blockers are given before administering placebos or acupuncture, these pain reducers are far less effective. As a result, scientists assert that endorphins somehow contribute to the pain relief provided by placebos and acupuncture (Coren, Ward, & Enns, 1994; He, 1987).

However, some other pain-reduction techniques have nothing to do with endorphins. For example, pain can be reduced through hypnosis or related concentration exercises (as in the Lamaze birth technique). These concentration techniques are just as effective when endorphin blockers are administered, indicating that there is a second pain-control system that works independently of the brain's chemical painkillers (Akil & Watson, 1980; D. J. Mayer & Watkins, 1984). Pain researchers suspect that these concentration techniques act to close the spinal pain gate, but nobody knows how.

PERCEPTION

As we noted in the introduction, our senses bring us raw data about the environment, but unless we interpret this raw information, the world would be nothing more than what William James (1890) called "a booming, buzzing confusion." The eye records patterns of light and dark, but it does not "see" a bird flittering from branch to branch. The eardrum vibrates in a particular fashion, but it does not "hear" a symphony. Deciphering *meaningful* patterns in the jumble of sensory information is what we mean by *perception*.

Placebo effect Pain relief that occurs when a person believes a pill or procedure will reduce pain. The actual cause of the relief seems to come from endorphins.

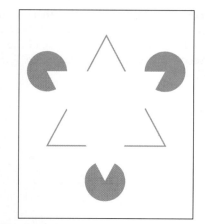

Figure 3–23
An illusory triangle.
When sensory information is incomplete, we tend to create a complete perception by supplying the missing details. In this figure, we fill in the lines that let us perceive a white triangle in the center of the pattern.

Figure 3–24
Perceiving a pattern.
Knowing beforehand that the black blotches in this figure represent a person riding a horse changes our perception of it.

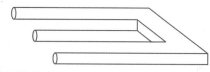

Figure 3–25
An optical illusion.
In the case of the trident, we go beyond what is sensed (blue lines on flat white paper) to perceive a three-dimensional object that isn't really there.

Ultimately, it is the brain that interprets the complex flow of information from the various senses. Using sensory information as raw material, the brain creates perceptual experiences that go beyond what is sensed directly. For example, looking at Figure 3–23, we tend to perceive a white triangle in the center of the pattern, although the sensory input consists only of three circles from which "pie slices" have been cut and three 60-degree angles. In Figure 3–24, you probably see only an assortment of black blotches at first, but if you are told that the blotches represent a person riding a horse, suddenly your perceptual experience changes. What was meaningless sensory information now takes shape as a horse and rider.

Sometimes, as in certain optical illusions, you perceive things that could not possibly exist. The trident shown in Figure 3–25 exemplifies such an "impossible" figure; on closer inspection, you discover that the object that you "recognized" is not really there. In all these cases, the brain actively creates and organizes perceptual experiences out of raw sensory data—sometimes even from data we are not aware of receiving. Below we discuss how perceptual processes organize sensory experience.

Perceptual Organization

Early in this century, a group of German psychologists, calling themselves *Gestalt psychologists*, set out to discover the principles through which we interpret sensory information. The German word *Gestalt* has no exact English equivalent, but essentially it means "whole," "form," or "pattern." The Gestalt psychologists believed that the brain creates a coherent perceptual experience, which is more than simply the sum of the available sensory information, and that it does so in predictable ways.

Figure 3–26
Random dots or something more?
This pattern does not give us enough cues to allow us to easily distinguish the *figure* of the Dalmatian dog from the *ground* behind it.

Source: Gregory, 1970.

In one important facet of the perceptual process, we distinguish **figures** from the **ground** against which they appear. A colorfully upholstered chair stands out from the bare walls of a room. A marble statue is perceived as a whole figure separate from the red brick wall behind it. The illusory trident in Figure 3–25 stands out from the white page. In all these cases, we perceive some objects as "figures" and other sensory information as "background."

The figure-ground distinction pertains to all our senses, not just vision. We can distinguish a violin solo against the ground of a symphony orchestra, a single voice amid cocktail party chatter, and the smell of roses in a florist's shop. In all these instances, we perceive a figure apart from the ground around it.

Sometimes, however, there are not enough cues in a pattern to permit us to easily distinguish a figure from its ground. The horse and rider in Figure 3–24 illustrate this problem, as does Figure 3–26, which shows a spotted dog investigating shadowy surroundings. It is hard to distinguish the dog because it has few visible contours of its own and, as a result, it seems to have no more form than the background. This is the principle behind camouflage—to make a figure blend into its background (see Figure 3–27).

Sometimes a figure with clear contours can be perceived in two very different ways because it is unclear which part of the stimulus is the figure and which the ground. Examples of such reversible figures are shown in Figures 3–28 and 3–29. At first glance, you perceive figures against a specific background, but as you stare at the illustrations, you will discover that the figures

Figure Entity perceived to stand apart from the background.

Ground Background against which a figure appears.

Figure 3–27
Camouflage.
Predators may have difficulty seeing the figure of the walking stick against the background of its natural environment.

Figure 3–28
The reversible figure and ground in this M. C. Escher woodcut cause us to see first black devils and then white angels in each of the rings.

Figure 3–29
Figure-ground relationship . . . How do you perceive this figure?
Do you see a vase or the silhouettes of a man and a woman? Both interpretations are possible, but not at the same time. Reversible figures like this work because it is unclear which part of the stimulus is the figure and which is the neutral ground against which the figure is perceived.

eventually dissolve into the ground, making for two very different perceptions of the same illustration.

Figure 3–30 demonstrates some other important principles of perceptual organization. In every case, our perceptual experience makes a leap beyond the raw sensory information available to us. In other words, we use sensory information to create a perception that is more than just the sum of the parts. Although this can sometimes cause problems, this perceptual tendency to "fill in the blanks" usually broadens our understanding of the world. As creatures searching for meaning, we tend to fill in the missing information, to group various objects together, to see whole objects and hear meaningful sounds rather than just random bits and pieces of raw sensory data (see *Controversies*).

CORTICAL CODING AND PERCEPTION   Important research undertaken decades after the original work of the Gestalt psychologists has begun to shed light on how neurons in the brain organize perceptual experiences. One pivotal study was conducted by David H. Hubel and Torsten N. Wiesel (1959, 1979), who received the Nobel Prize for their work. Hubel and Wiesel inserted an electrode into the visual areas of the brain of an anesthetized cat.

Figure 3–30
Gestalt principles of perceptual organization.

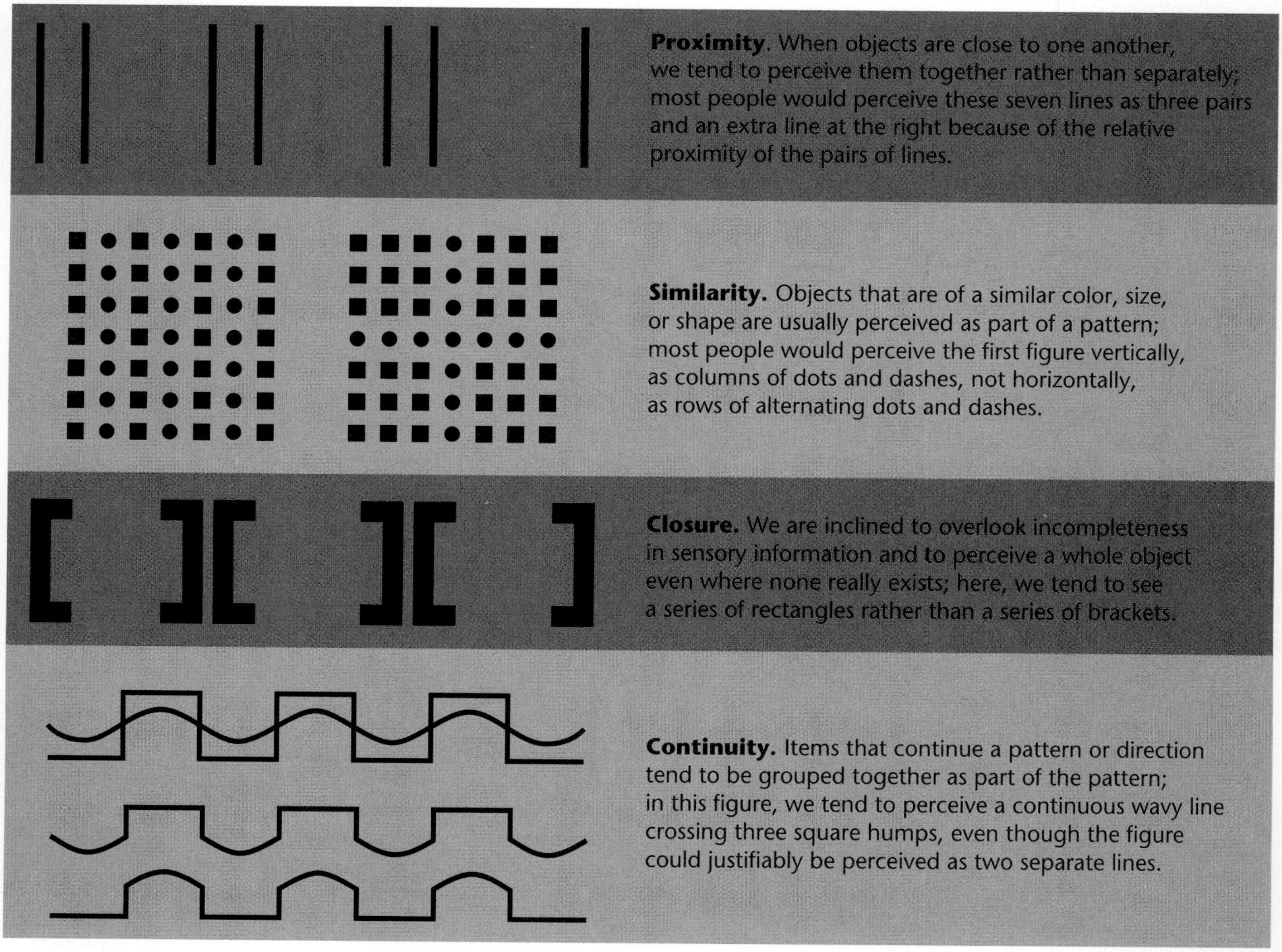

Proximity. When objects are close to one another, we tend to perceive them together rather than separately; most people would perceive these seven lines as three pairs and an extra line at the right because of the relative proximity of the pairs of lines.

Similarity. Objects that are of a similar color, size, or shape are usually perceived as part of a pattern; most people would perceive the first figure vertically, as columns of dots and dashes, not horizontally, as rows of alternating dots and dashes.

Closure. We are inclined to overlook incompleteness in sensory information and to perceive a whole object even where none really exists; here, we tend to see a series of rectangles rather than a series of brackets.

Continuity. Items that continue a pattern or direction tend to be grouped together as part of the pattern; in this figure, we tend to perceive a continuous wavy line crossing three square humps, even though the figure could justifiably be perceived as two separate lines.

Stop reading and just look at your open psychology text. Almost without thinking, you see a book. Your perception of the book is extraordinarily reliable. The book remains a book if you view it from different angles, if the lighting in the room changes, if you move it closer, if it's open or closed. You can close your eyes and come up with a fairly accurate mental image of the book; you can imagine viewing the book from several angles, in different lighting, and in motion. Not even the most sophisticated computer can do these things, yet we do them effortlessly. What have psychologists learned about the processes that enable us to create complex and meaningful perceptual experiences from sensory information?

First, psychologists assume that perception begins with some real-world object with real-world properties "out there." Psychologists call that object, along with its important perceptual properties, the *distal stimulus*. We never experience the distal stimulus directly, however. Energy from it (or in the case of our chemical senses, molecules from it) must activate our sensory system. We call the information that reaches our sensory receptors the *proximal stimulus*. Strangely enough, even though the distal stimulus and the proximal stimulus are never the same thing, our perception of the distal stimulus is usually very accurate. So, as we view the book on the desk, how does the pattern on the retina (the proximal stimulus) become an integrated perception of the book (the distal stimulus)—one that captures all the important aspects of "bookness"?

The discovery of detector cells by David H. Hubel and Torsten N. Wiesel (1959, 1979) moved us a step closer to answering that ques-

tion. But these detector cells provide only fundamental information about lines, positions, angles, motion, and so on. Somehow we take the very basic information provided by detector cells and use it to create coherent perceptual experiences. Scientists have advanced a number of theories to explain how this process works.

According to some theorists, at least a two-stage process occurs in which the image on the retina is literally decomposed and then reassembled in the brain. Anne Treisman believes that an automatic "preattentive" stage of processing first breaks a proximal stimulus into independent, fundamental properties such as color, curves, positions, and motion. Then "focused attention" is required to reassemble the image by combining the independent parts (Treisman, 1986; Treisman et al., 1990). In a similar way, Irving Biederman asserts that three-dimensional objects can be broken down into 36 basic geometric shapes (cylinders, blocks, pyramidal shapes, and so on) that can be combined to represent thousands of real-world objects. Biederman contends that if we can visually recognize the basic shapes of an object, then we can completely and correctly recognize the object itself (Biederman, 1987; Hummel & Biederman, 1992).

In contrast to the "take it apart and then put it back together" schemes of Treisman and Biederman, other theorists assert that perception occurs via *parallel distributed processing networks* or *neural networks* (Rummelhart & McClelland, 1986). Rather than looking at the raw data taken from the retinal image, these theories posit that thousands or even millions of neurons in the brain act in coordinated ways through a weblike mechanism, in which some parts of

the web represent the color, other parts the curves, and yet others the positions, shapes, or other fundamental information in a stimulus. Whereas Treisman and Biederman argue that the various parts of a stimulus are analyzed separately and then reassembled, the neural-networks approach maintains that the parts are processed simultaneously, or in parallel. Thus, because these parts are never separated, they need not come back together. All the important features of a stimulus are simultaneously represented in the network, and the entire web of neural activity constitutes the perceptual image.

Theories like those advanced by Treisman and Biederman envision only one large perceptual system that is used to perceive everything from faces to landmarks. Other theories, however, propose that multiple, specialized subsystems figure in object perception. For example, Stephen Kosslyn suggests that the brain has one system for "what" and another system for "where." That is, one specialized system recognizes the kind or category of thing that we see, whereas the other reads information about its spatial position and spatial relationships. He further maintains that the two systems operate differently in each of the cerebral hemispheres (Kosslyn, 1980, 1987).

What have psychologists learned about the processes that enable us to create complex and meaningful perceptual experiences from sensory information?

An entirely different approach to understanding form vision is called *computational neuroscience*. One of the more influential researchers in this area, the late David Marr (1982), advanced the theory that visual perception emerges from the brain's complex mathematical analysis of patterns of light and dark areas, edges, ends of segments, and positions. Through sophisticated, high-speed calculations, this analysis produces a finished visual image. Marr's perspective has been influential in shaping more recent theories of how we create meaningful perceptual experiences (see Kosslyn, 1994; Kosslyn & Koenig, 1992).

No one can say with certainty which of these approaches sheds the most light on form perception. Perhaps still other approaches that have not yet been developed will do an even better job of explaining our perception of forms. We do know that the brain accomplishes a remarkable feat when it creates a clear and cohesive world of objects and shapes simply from the information it receives from the eyes.

Questions

1. Is a lemon or a tomato red? If you shine blue light on a lemon, it appears black; similarly if you shine a green light on a tomato, it appears black. Have the lemon and tomato now become black, or are they still yellow and red?

2. It has been said that "The world as we experience it is never simply a copy of what is on our retina." Look at an object near you. In what ways does your perception of the object differ from the image of that object on your retina?

Feature detectors Specialized brain cells that only respond to particular elements in the visual field such as movement or lines of specific orientation.

Perceptual constancy A tendency to perceive objects as stable and unchanging despite changes in sensory stimulation.

They were then able to record the activity of individual neurons when certain stimuli—such as a vertical or horizontal line—were projected onto a screen in front of the cat's eye. They found that certain cells, dubbed *simple cells*, would respond to a line presented only at a certain angle or orientation. For example, some cells fired only when the line was tilted 45 degrees from the vertical. When the line was displayed vertically, for example, simple cells specialized for that orientation started to respond. Cells that respond to orientation are just one of a variety of cells called **feature detectors,** which are highly specialized to respond to particular elements in the visual field. For example, some feature detectors are sensitive to movement: Frogs have "bug detector" cells that are especially well suited for picking out small, dark, moving objects. In addition to simple feature detectors, *complex cells* appear to coordinate information drawn from a number of simple cells—for example, some complex cells respond only to a 45-degree line moving from left to right. Furthermore, *hypercomplex cells* are believed to coordinate information at a still higher level of complexity, such as two different lines forming an angle (Maunsell, 1995).

Researchers have not confirmed the existence of cells specialized to respond to such aspects of Gestalt organization as closure and proximity. But some psychologists believe that just as the frog has its "bug detector" cells, humans and other higher animals must have neural structures sensitive to the complex patterns that these species must perceive in order to survive. Through evolution, we may be prewired to perceive many of the complex shapes and movements that appear in our natural environment. For example, as we will see in Chapter 10, Life Span Development, newborns, given the choice, will spend significantly more time gazing at sketches of human faces than at other types of patterns or figures. Yet, because we could not possibly be born with an innate grasp of all the different objects that we encounter in the world around us, learning and experience clearly play an important part in the way we organize perception. Perceptual constancies, to which we turn next, serve as one illustration of the role of experience in perception.

Perceptual Constancies

Perceptual constancy refers to the tendency to perceive objects as relatively stable and unchanging despite changing sensory information. Without this ability, we would find the world very confusing. Once we have formed a sta-

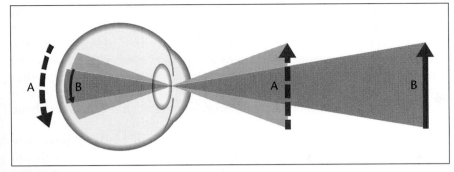

Figure 3–31
The relationship between distance and the size of the retinal image.
Object A and object B are the same size, but A, being much closer to the eye, casts a much larger image on the retina.

Figure 3–32
Perceptual constancy.
Look at the picture and then turn the book upside down so that the picture is rightside up. Based on experience, you use certain perceptual cues to recognize facial expressions, so the upside-down picture looks fairly normal. Those same cues make the rightside-up picture look grossly distorted.

Figure 3–33
Look again!
Context, hair style, and head shape lead us to believe that this is a picture of President Clinton and Vice President Gore when, in reality, President Clinton's face is superimposed over the face of Vice President Gore.

Source: APA Monitor, March, 1997.

ble perception of an object, we can recognize it from almost any position, at almost any distance, under almost any illumination. A white house looks like a white house by day or by night and from any angle. We see it as the same house. The sensory information may change as illumination and perspective change, but the object is perceived as constant.

We also tend to perceive objects at their true size regardless of the size of the image that they cast on the retina. As Figure 3–31 shows, the farther away an object is from the lens of the eye, the smaller the retinal image it casts. For example, a 6-foot-tall man standing 20 feet away casts a retinal image that is only 50 percent of the size of the retinal image he casts at a distance of 10 feet. Yet he is not perceived as having shrunk to 3 feet.

Memory and experience play important roles in perceptual constancy. For example, look at Figure 3–32, a slightly altered photograph of former British Prime Minister Margaret Thatcher. Before reading further, turn the book upside down, and look at the picture again. An essentially normal face now looks gruesome. Your experience in recognizing people and interpreting their facial expressions has accustomed you to focus on certain perceptual cues (particularly eyes and mouths). When you look at the upside-down picture, the eyes and mouth are normal, so you perceive the entire face as normal. In other words, you use your experience in perceiving normal human faces to perceive this (very unusual) face and, as a result, you do not perceive it as grossly distorted until you look at it rightside up.

For another dramatic example of how memory and experience influence perceptual constancy, look at Figure 3–33. If you see President Clinton and Vice President Gore in this photograph, look again! Actually, Clinton's face has been superimposed over the face of Gore. In this case, our memory and experience cause us to focus on the perceptual cues of head shape, hair style, and context. As a result, we perceive the more likely image of the president and vice president standing together (Sinha, 1996).

Size constancy, too, depends partly on experience—information about the relative sizes of objects is stored in memory—and partly on distance cues. When there are no distance cues, size constancy has to rely solely on what we have learned from our previous experience with an object. Naturally, more errors occur when there are no distance cues, but fewer than we might expect in view of the radical changes in the size of the retinal image. We might guess that a woman some distance away is 5 feet 4 inches tall when she is really 5 feet 8 inches, but hardly anyone would perceive her as being 3 feet tall, no matter how far away she is. We know from experience that adults are seldom that short.

Shape constancy A tendency to see an object as the same shape no matter what angle it is viewed from.

Brightness constancy The perception of brightness as the same, even though the amount of light reaching the retina changes.

Color constancy An inclination to perceive familiar objects as retaining their color despite changes in sensory information.

Familiar objects also tend to be seen as having a constant shape, even though the retinal images they cast change as they are viewed from different angles. A dinner plate is perceived as a circle even when it is tilted and the retinal image is oval. A rectangular door will project a rectangular image on the retina only when it is viewed directly from the front. From any other angle, it casts a trapezoidal image on the retina, but it is not perceived as having suddenly become a trapezoidal door. These are all examples of **shape constancy** (see Figure 3–34).

Two other important perceptual constancies are **brightness constancy** and **color constancy.** The former principle means that even though the amount of light available to our eyes varies greatly over the course of a day, the perceived brightness of familiar objects hardly varies at all. We perceive a sheet of white paper as brighter than a piece of coal whether we see these objects in candlelight or under bright sunlight. This may seem obvious, but bear in mind that coal in sunlight reflects more light than white paper in the candlelight, yet we always perceive white paper as being brighter. Brightness constancy occurs because a white object—or a black or gray one—will reflect the same percentage of the light falling on it whether that light is from a candle, a fluorescent lamp, or the sun. Rather than basing our judgment of brightness on the *absolute* amount of light that the object reflects, we assess how the relative *reflection* compares to the surrounding objects.

Similarly, we tend to perceive familiar objects as keeping their colors, regardless of information that reaches the eye. If you own a red automobile, you will see it as red whether it is on a brightly lit street or in a dark garage, where the small amount of light may send your eye a message that the color is closer to brown or black than red. But color constancy does not always hold true. When objects are unfamiliar or there are no customary color cues to guide us, color constancy may be distorted—as when we buy a pair of paints in a brightly lit store, only to discover that in ordinary daylight they are not the shade we thought they were.

In exploring these various principles, we have noted that perceptual experiences often go far beyond the available sensory information. Indeed, our perceptual experiences rarely, if ever, correspond exactly to the information that we receive through our senses.

Observer Characteristics: Individual Differences and Culture

We have seen how neural structures organize sensory information. Other kinds of individual variables also influence and organize sensation. Our own motivations, values, expectations cognitive style, and preconceptions grounded in our culture can strongly influence what we *think* we are seeing and feeling.

Figure 3–34
Examples of shape constancy.
Even though the image of the door on the retina changes greatly as the door opens, we still perceive the door as being rectangular.

Source: Boring, Langfeld, & Weld, 1976.

MOTIVATION   Our desires and needs strongly shape our perceptions. People in need are more likely to perceive something that they think will satisfy that need. For example, several interesting experiments have tested the influence of hunger on perception. If people are deprived of food for some time and are then shown vague or ambiguous pictures, they are apt to perceive the pictures as being related to food (Sanford, 1937). Similarly, blurred pictures were shown to people who had not eaten for varying lengths of time. Some had eaten 1 hour before; others had gone as long as 16 hours without food. Those who had not eaten for 16 hours perceived the blurred images as pictures of food more often than those who had eaten just 1 hour before (McClelland & Atkinson, 1948).

VALUES   In an experiment that revealed how strongly perceptions can be affected by a person's values, nursery-school children were shown a poker chip. Each child was asked to compare the size of the chip to the size of an adjustable circle of light until the child said the chip and the circle of light were the same size. The children were then brought to a machine with a crank that, when turned, produced a poker chip that could be exchanged for candy. Thus, the children were taught to value the poker chips more highly than they had before. After the children had been rewarded with the candy for the poker chips, they were again asked to compare the size of the chips to a circle of light. This time, the chips seemed larger to the children (Lambert, Solomon, & Watson, 1949).

EXPECTATIONS   Preconceptions about what we are supposed to perceive may also influence perception by causing us to *delete, insert, transpose,* or otherwise *modify* what we see (Lachman, 1996). For example, in a well-known children's game, a piece of cardboard with a red stop sign is flashed in front of you. What did the sign say? Nearly everyone will say that the sign read "stop." In fact, however, the sign is misprinted "stopp." Because we are accustomed to seeing stop signs reading "stop," we tend to perceive the familiar symbol rather than the misprint. Lachman (1984) demonstrated this phenomenon by asking people to copy a group of stimuli similar to this one:

PARIS
IN THE
THE SPRING

When the expressions were flashed briefly on a screen, the vast majority of subjects tended to omit the "extra" words and to report seeing more familiar (and more normal) expressions, such as PARIS IN THE SPRING. This phenomenon of *perceptual familiarization* or *perceptual generalization* reflects a strong tendency to see what we expect to see even if our expectation conflicts with external reality.

COGNITIVE STYLE   As we mature, we develop a cognitive style—our own way of dealing with the environment—and this also affects how we see the world. Some psychologists distinguish between two general approaches that people use in perceiving the world (Witkin et al., 1962). People taking the *field-dependent approach* tend to perceive the environment as a whole and do not clearly delineate in their minds the shape, color, size, or other qualities of individual items. If field-dependent people are asked to draw a human figure, they generally draw it so that it blends into the background. By contrast, people who are *field independent* are more likely to perceive the elements of the environment as separate and distinct from one another and to draw each element as standing out from the background.

Cognitive styles can also be viewed from the perspective of "levelers" and "sharpeners"—those who level out the distinctions among objects and those who magnify them. To investigate the differences between these two cognitive styles, G. S. Klein (1951) showed people sets of squares of varying sizes and asked them to estimate the size of each one. One group, the "levelers," failed to perceive any differences in the size of the squares. The "sharpeners," however, picked up the differences in the size of the squares and made their size estimates accordingly.

EXPERIENCE AND CULTURE   Cultural background also influences people's perceptions. As we will see in Chapter 7, Cognition and Language, the language people speak affects the ways in which they perceive their surroundings. Cultural differences in people's experiences can also determine how they use perceptual cues. Historically, for example, the Mbuti pygmies of Zaire seldom left the Ituri rain forest and rarely encountered objects that were more than a few feet away. On one occasion, anthropologist Colin Turnbull (1961) took a pygmy guide named Kenge on a trip onto the African plains. When Kenge looked across the plain and saw a herd of buffalo, he asked what kind of insects they were. He refused to believe that the tiny black spots he saw were buffalo. As he and Turnbull drove toward the herd, Kenge believed that magic was making the animals grow larger. Because he had no experience of distant objects, he could not perceive the buffalo as having constant size.

PERSONALITY   A number of researchers have shown that our individual personalities influence our perceptions (for a review of the research, see Greenwald, 1992). For example, normal college students were compared to depressed or moderately anorexic students in terms of their ability to identify words related to depression and food (von Hippel, Hawkins, & Narayan, 1994). All the words in this study were flashed on a screen very quickly (generally less than one-tenth of a second). In general, anorexic people were faster at identifying the words that referred to foods they commonly thought about than they were at identifying foods they rarely thought about. Simi-

Figure 3–35
Superposition.
(left panel) Because the king of clubs appears to have been superimposed on the blank card, we perceive it as being closer to us than the king of spades (right panel). When the cards are spaced out, however, we can see that the king of spades is actually no farther away than the king of clubs. It appears to be farther away because the other two cards seem to be superimposed on it.

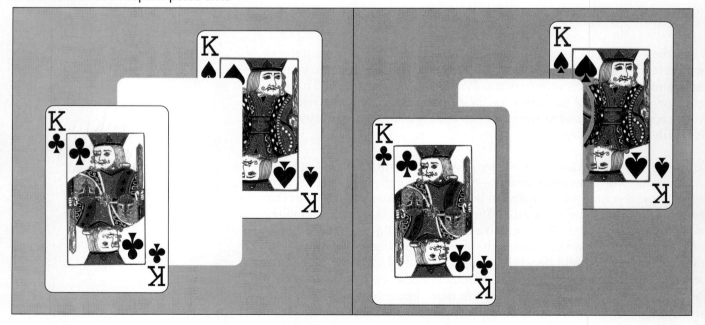

larly, depressed people were faster at identifying adjectives describing personality traits they commonly thought about (such as *quiet, withdrawn, hesitant,* and *timid*) than they were at identifying adjectives relating to traits they rarely thought about (such as *extrovert, lively,* and *bold*). Interestingly, these findings suggest that not only personality, but possibly the presence of a personality disorder, may influence perception.

Next, we will look at a basic perceptual phenomenon—distance and depth—to see how we use both stimulus information and past experience to create perceptual experiences.

Perceiving Distance and Depth

We are constantly judging the distance between ourselves and other objects. When we walk through a room, our perception of distance helps us avoid bumping into the furniture. If we reach out to pick up a pencil, we automatically judge how far to extend our arms. And as a matter of course, we also assess the depth of objects—how much total space they occupy. We use many cues to determine the distance and the depth of objects. Some of these cues depend on visual messages that one eye alone can transmit; these are called **monocular cues.** Others, known as **binocular cues,** require the use of both eyes. Having two eyes allows us to make more accurate judgments about distance and depth, particularly when objects are relatively close. But monocular cues alone are often all we need to judge distance and depth quite accurately.

MONOCULAR CUES   One important distance cue, used to determine the relative position of objects, is called **superposition.** Superposition occurs when one object partly blocks a second object. The first object is perceived as being closer, the second as more distant (see Figure 3–35).

As all students of art know, there are several ways in which perspective can help in estimating distance and depth. Two parallel lines that extend into the distance seem to come together at some point on the horizon. This cue to distance and depth is known as **linear perspective.** In **aerial perspective,** distant objects have a hazy appearance and a somewhat blurred outline.

Monocular cues Visual cues requiring the use of one eye.

Binocular cues Visual cues requiring the use of both eyes.

Superposition Monocular distance cue in which one object, by partly blocking a second object, is perceived as being closer.

Linear perspective Monocular cue to distance and depth based on the fact that two parallel lines seem to come together at the horizon.

Aerial perspective Monocular cue to distance and depth based on the fact that more distant objects are likely to appear hazy and blurred.

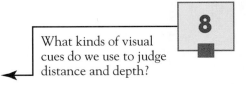

8

What kinds of visual cues do we use to judge distance and depth?

The artist who painted this mural on a building used monocular cues to create a visual illusion of depth on a flat surface. Contrast this with the sixteenth century painting, which does not utilize such cues.

Elevation Monocular cue to distance and depth based on the fact that the higher on the horizontal plane an object is, the farther away it appears.

Texture gradient Monocular cue to distance and depth based on the fact that objects seen at greater distances appear to be smoother and less textured.

Shadowing Monocular cue to distance and depth based on the fact that shadows often appear on the parts of objects that are more distant.

Figure 3–36
Elevation as a visual cue.
Because of the higher elevation and the suggestion of depth provided by the road, the tree on the right is perceived as being more distant and about the same size as thetree at lower left. Actually, it is appreciably smaller, as you can see if you measure the heights of the two drawings.

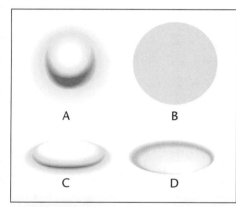

Figure 3–37
Shadowing.
Shadowing on the outer edges of a spherical object, such as a ball or globe, gives it a three-dimensional quality (A). Without shadowing (B), it might be perceived as a flat disk. Shadowing can also affect our perception of the direction of depth. In the absence of other cues, we tend to assume overhead lighting, so figure (C) appears to be a bump because its top edge is lit, whereas (D) appears to be a dent. If you turn the book upside down, the direction of depth is reversed.

On a clear day, mountains often seem to be much closer than on a hazy day, when their outlines become indistinct. The **elevation** of an object also serves as a perspective cue to depth. An object that is on a higher horizontal plane seems to be farther away than one on a lower plane (see Figure 3–36).

Still another useful monocular cue to distance and depth is **texture gradient.** An object that is close seems to have a rough or detailed texture. As distance increases, the texture becomes finer until, finally, the original texture cannot be distinguished clearly, if at all. A man standing on a pebbly beach, for example, can distinguish among the gray stones and gravel in front of his feet. As he looks down the beach, however, the stones appear to become smaller and finer until eventually he cannot make out individual stones at all.

Shadowing provides another important cue to distance, depth, and solidity of an object. Because shadows normally appear on the parts of objects that are more distant, the shadowing of the outer edges of a spherical object, such as a ball or a globe, gives it a three-dimensional quality (see Figure 3–37). Without this shadowing, the object might be perceived as a flat disk. In addition to serving as cues of three-dimensionality, shadows give us cues to the direction of depth—whether an object rises above or rests below the surface. We tend to assume that light comes from overhead, so when we look at Figure 3–37C, we see a bump because the top edge is lighter, the way a bump lit from above would be. By contrast, Figure 3–37D appears as a dent because of the shadowing along the top edge. Looking at the image upside down reverses the effect. The shadow that an object casts behind itself also gives a cue to its depth. The presence of shadows either in front of or behind objects indicates how far away they are.

People traveling on buses or trains often notice that the tree or telephone poles close to the road or the railroad track seem to flash past the windows quickly, whereas buildings and other objects farther away seem to move slowly. These differences in the speeds of *movement* of images across the retina as you move give you an important cue to distance and depth. You can observe the same effect if you stand still and move your head from side to side as you focus your gaze on something in the middle distance: Objects close to you seem to move in the direction opposite from the way in which your head is moving, whereas objects far away seem to move in the same direction as your head. This distance cue is known as **motion parallax.**

BINOCULAR CUES   All the visual cues examined so far depend on the action of only one eye. Many animals, such as horses, deer, and fish, rely entirely on monocular cues. Although they have two eyes, the two visual fields do not overlap because their eyes are located on the sides of the head rather than in front. Humans, apes, and many predatory animals—such as lions, tigers, and wolves—have a distinct physical advantage over these animals. Because both eyes are set in the front of the head, the visual fields overlap. The **stereoscopic vision** derived from combining the two retinal images makes the perception of depth and distance more accurate.

Because our eyes are set approximately 2-1/2 inches apart, each one has a slightly different view of things. The difference between the two images that the eyes receive is known as **retinal disparity.** The left eye receives more information about the left side of an object, and the right eye receives more information about the right side. You can easily prove that each of your eyes receives a different image. Close one eye and line up a finger with some vertical line, such as the edge of a door. Then open that eye and close the other one. Your finger will appear to have moved a great distance. When you look at the finger with both eyes, however, the two different images become one.

One binocular cue to distance comes from the muscles that control the **convergence** of the eyes. When we look at objects that are fairly close to us, our eyes tend to converge—to turn slightly inward toward each other. The sensations from the muscles that control the movement of the eyes thus provide another cue to distance. If the object is very close, such as at the end of the nose, the eyes cannot converge, and two separate images are perceived. If the object is more than a few yards (meters) away, the sight lines of the eyes are more or less parallel, and there is no convergence.

LOCATING SOUNDS   Just as we use monocular and binocular cues to determine visual depth and distance, we draw on **monaural** (single-ear) and **binaural** (two-ear) **cues** to locate the source of sounds (see Figure 3–38). In one monaural cue, loud sounds are perceived as closer than faint sounds, with changes in loudness translating into changes in distance. Binaural cues work on the principle that because sounds off to one side of the head reach one ear slightly ahead of the other (in the range of a thousandth of a second), the time difference between sound waves reaching the two ears registers in the brain and helps us to make accurate judgments of location.

In a second binaural cue, sound signals arriving from a source off to one side of you are slightly louder in the nearer ear than in the ear farther from the source. The slight difference occurs because your head itself, in effect, blocks the sound from one side, muting the intensity of the sound in the opposite ear. This relative loudness difference between signals heard separately by the two ears is enough for the brain to locate the sound source and to judge its distance. When sound engineers record your favorite musical group, they may place microphones at many different locations. On playback, the two speakers or headphones project sounds at slightly different instants to mimic the sound patterns that you would pick up if you were actually listening to the group perform right in front of you.

Most of us rely so heavily on visual cues that we seldom pay much attention to the rich array of auditory information available in the world around

Motion parallax Monocular distance cue in which objects closer than the point of visual focus seem to move in the direction opposite to the viewer's moving head, and objects beyond the focus point appear to move in the same direction as the viewer's head.

Stereoscopic vision Combination of two retinal images to give a three-dimensional perceptual experience.

Retinal disparity Binocular distance cue based on the difference between the images cast on the two retinas when both eyes are focused on the same object.

Convergence A visual depth cue that comes from muscles controlling eye movement as the eyes turn inward to view a nearby stimulus.

Monaural cue Cue to sound location that requires just one ear.

Binaural cue Cue to sound location that involves both ears working together.

Figure 3–38
Cues used in sound localization.
Sound waves coming from source (B) will reach both ears simultaneously. A sound wave from source (A) reaches the left ear first, where it is also louder. The head casts a "shadow" over the other ear, thus reducing the intensity of the delayed sound in that ear.

Source: Langfeld & Weld, 1976.

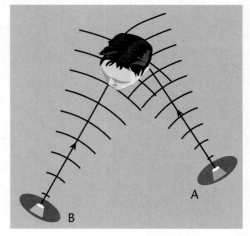

During a stereo recording session, microphones are generally placed at many different locations. On playback, the twin speakers or headphones project sounds picked up by the microphones at different instants, mimicking what would occur if you were hearing a live performance.

us. Blind people, who often compensate for their lack of vision by sharpening their ability to perceive sounds (Arias et al., 1993), can figure out where obstacles lie in their paths by listening to the echoes from a cane, their own footsteps, and their own voices. In one notable case, a blind boy had grown so adept at avoiding obstacles by sound that he could safely ride a bicycle in public places. Many blind people can judge the size and distance of one object in relation to another using nothing more than sound cues. They can also discriminate between contrasting surfaces, such as glass and fabric, by listening to the difference in the echo produced when sound strikes them.

Perceiving Movement

The perception of movement is a complicated process involving both visual information from the retina and messages from the muscles around the eyes as they follow an object. On occasion, our perceptual processes play tricks on us, and we think we perceive movement when the objects we are looking at are, in fact, stationary. We must distinguish, therefore, between real and apparent movement.

Real movement refers to the physical displacement of an object from one position to another. The perception of real movement depends only in part on the movement of images across the retina of the eye. If you stand still and move your head to look around you, the images of all the objects in the room will pass across your retina. Yet you will probably perceive all the objects as stationary. Even if you hold your head still and move only your eyes, the images will continue to pass across your retina. But the messages from the eye muscles seem to counteract those from the retina, so the objects in the room will be perceived as motionless.

The perception of real movement seems to be determined less by images moving across the retina than by how the position of objects changes in relation to a background that is perceived as stationary. When we perceive a car moving along a street, for example, we see the street, the buildings, and the sidewalk as a stationary background and the car as a moving object. Remarkably, the brain can distinguish these retinal images of an object moving against an immobile background from all the other moving images of the retina.

The perception of real movement is highly accurate. Imagine that you are watching a videotape of someone lifting a box of unknown weight. Research indicates that you would probably be able to predict the weight of the box fairly accurately, and you would probably also be able to tell if the person lifting the box was simply pretending it was heavier than it was (Runeson & Frykholm, 1983). Moreover, there is some evidence that we may be specially equipped to detect *biological movement*, the movement of another human body. To demonstrate this, one researcher attached lights to various parts of a person's body and then filmed movement of the lights in an extremely dark room. People watching the film were immediately able to tell that the lights in motion were really a human body in motion, even though they saw part of the film for only a fraction of a second (Johansson, 1975; Johansson, von Hofsten, & Jansson, 1980). Human infants, given a choice of watching random movement of dots of light versus dots of light in biological motion, prefer to watch biological motion (Bertenthal, 1992).

Apparent movement occurs when we see movement in objects that are actually standing still. One form of apparent movement is referred to as the **autokinetic illusion**—the perceived motion created by a single stationary object. If you stand in a room that is absolutely dark except for one tiny spot of light and stare at the light for a few seconds, you will begin to see the light drift. In the darkened room, your eyes have no visible framework; there are no cues telling you that the light is really stationary. The slight movements of the eye muscles, which go unnoticed most of the time, make the light appear to move.

Another form of illusory movement is **stroboscopic motion**—the apparent motion created by a rapid series of still images (see Figure 3–39). This form of apparent movement is illustrated best by a motion picture—which is not in motion at all. The film consists of a series of still pictures showing people and objects in slightly different positions. When the separate images are projected sequentially onto a screen at a specific rate of speed, the people and objects seem to be moving because of the rapid change from one still picture to the next.

Another common perceptual illusion, known as the **phi phenomenon,** occurs as a result of stroboscopic motion. When a light is flashed on at a certain point in a darkened room, then flashed off, and a second light is flashed on a split second later at a point a short distance away, most people will perceive these two separate lights as a single spot of light moving from one point to another. Of course, the distance between the two points, the intensity of the two lights, and the time interval between the two flashes must be carefully controlled for the illusion to succeed. This perceptual process causes us to see motion in neon signs or theater marquees, where words appear to move from one side to the other as different combinations of stationary lights are flashed on and off.

Visual Illusions

Visual illusions graphically demonstrate the ways in which we use a variety of sensory cues to create perceptual experiences that may (or may not) correspond to what is out there in the real world. By understanding how we are fooled into "seeing" something that isn't there, psychologists can figure out how perceptual processes work in the everyday world and under normal circumstances.

Psychologists generally distinguish between *physical* and *perceptual* illusions. One example of a **physical illusion** is the bent appearance of a

Autokinetic illusion The perception that a stationary object is actually moving.

Stroboscopic motion Apparent movement that results from flashing a series of still pictures in rapid succession, as in a motion picture.

Phi phenomenon Apparent movement caused by flashing lights in sequence, as on theater marquees.

Physical illusion Illusion due to distortion of information reaching receptor cells.

Figure 3–39
Stroboscopic motion.
If after just the right delay (50 to 100 msec), form 1 is replaced by form 2 in A, B, or C, *stroboscopic motion* will be perceived as indicated by the dotted line. In A, this will be a horizontal motion of the bulb from left to right. In B, it will be a tipping of the bar from vertical to horizontal. In C, the top angular bar will appear to flip over. In all these cases, you perceive the most "reasonable" pattern of movement.

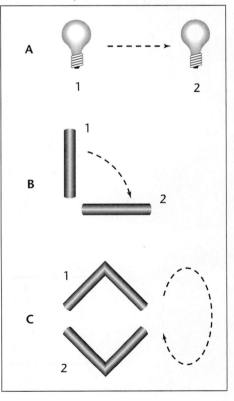

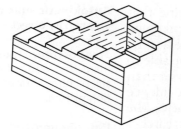
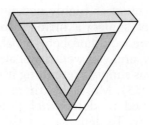

Figure 3–40
Visual illusions using misleading depth cues.
These visual illusions trick us through deceptive *depth cues.* For example, the odd triangle is drawn so that a false depth cue signals a three-dimensional object that cannot exist.

Source: Adapted from Gregory, 1978.

Figure 3–41
Reversible figures and misleading depth cues.
A, B, and C are examples of reversible figures—drawings that we can perceive two different ways, but not at the same time. D, E, and F show how, through the use of misleading *depth cues,* we misjudge the size of objects. The middle circles in D are exactly the same size, as are the lines in E and the monsters in F.

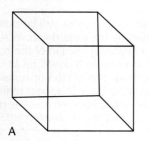

A

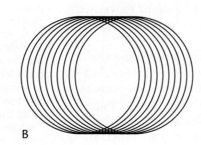

B

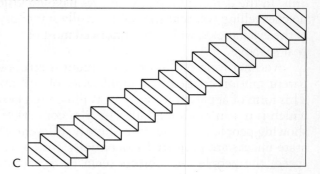

C

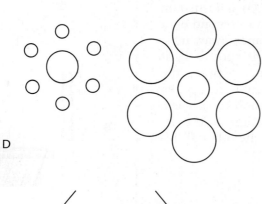

D

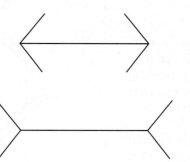

E

F

stick when it is placed in water—an illusion easily understood because the water acts like a prism, bending the light waves before they reach our eyes.

Other illusions depend primarily on our own perceptual processes, of which we are not ordinarily aware; as a result, these illusions can be quite startling. **Perceptual illusions** occur because the stimulus contains misleading cues that give rise to inaccurate or impossible perceptions.

In Figure 3–40, for example, a false and misleading depth cue makes us perceive the strange triangle as a three-dimensional figure that clearly cannot exist. Another graphic that fools us by presenting false depth cues is Figure 3–41E, in which the top line is perceived as shorter than the bottom, when, in reality, both lines are the same length. Our experience tells us that objects appear smaller when they are far away. In Figure 3–41F, both monsters cast the same-size image on the retina in our eyes. But the depth cues in the tunnel suggest that we are looking at a three-dimensional scene and that therefore the top monster is much farther away. In the real world, this would mean that the top monster is actually much larger than the bottom monster. Therefore, we "correct" for the distance and actually perceive the top monster as larger. We do this despite other cues to the contrary: We know that the image is actually two-dimensional, but we still respond to it as if it were three-dimensional.

There are also "real-world" illusions that illustrate how perceptual processes work, such as the illusion of *induced movement*. When you are sitting in a stationary train and the train next to you begins to move forward, you seem to be moving backward. Because you have no reference point by which to tell if you are standing still, you are confused as to which train is actually moving. However, if you look at the ground, you can establish an unambiguous frame of reference and make the situation clear to yourself.

Artists rely on many of these perceptual phenomena both to represent reality accurately and to distort it deliberately. In paintings and sketches drawn on a two-dimensional surface, it is almost always necessary to distort objects for them to be perceived correctly by viewers. For example, in representational art, railroad tracks, sidewalks, and tunnels are always drawn closer together in the distance. Figure 3–42 illustrates how an artist can use distance cues not only to give realistic depth to a picture but also to create perceptual experiences that don't correspond to anything in the real world. Three-dimensional movies also work on the principle that the brain can be deceived into seeing three dimensions if slightly different images are presented to the left and right eyes (working on the principle of retinal disparity). Thus, our understanding of perceptual illusion enables us to manipulate images for deliberate effect—and to delight in the results.

Perceptual illusion Illusion due to misleading cues in stimuli that give rise to inaccurate or impossible perceptions.

Figure 3–42
Perceptual illusion.
How has the artist, M. C. Escher, manipulated distance cues to create the perceptual illusion of water traveling uphill?

SUMMARY

This chapter examines sensation and perception, the processes that enable us to gather and understand information from numerous sources. **Sensation** refers to the raw sensory data from the senses of sight, hearing, smell, taste, balance, touch, and pain. **Perception** is the process of creating meaningful patterns from that raw sensory data.

THE NATURE OF SENSORY PROCESSES

The Character of Sensation

In all sensory processes, some form of energy stimulates a **receptor cell** in one of the sense organs. The receptor cell converts that energy into a neural signal, which is further coded as it travels along sensory nerves. By the time it reaches the brain, the message is quite precise.

Sensory Thresholds

The energy reaching a receptor must be sufficiently intense to produce a noticeable effect. The least amount of energy needed to generate any sensation at all in a person 50 percent of the time is called the **absolute threshold.** The **difference threshold** or the **just noticeable difference (jnd)** is the smallest change in stimulation that is detectable 50 percent of the time. Generally speaking, the stronger the stimulation, the bigger the change must be to be sensed. According to **Weber's law,** the jnd for a given sense is a constant fraction of the original stimulus. In most cases, our senses adjust to the level of stimulation they are experiencing, a process known as **adaptation.**

Subliminal Perception

Subliminal messages are messages that fall below the threshold of conscious perception and are therefore assumed to be perceived subconsciously. Some studies have indicated that, in a controlled laboratory setting, people can be influenced briefly by sensory messages that are outside their conscious awareness. No scientific studies support the claims, however, that subliminal messages in advertising influence consumer choices or that subliminal phrases in self-help tapes significantly change a person's behavior.

VISION

Unlike most animals, humans rely most heavily on their sense of vision to perceive the world.

The Visual System

In the process leading to vision, **light** enters the eye through the **cornea,** then passes through the **pupil** (in the center of the **iris**) and the **lens,** which focuses it onto the **retina.** The lens changes its shape to allow light to be focused sharply on the retina. Directly behind the lens and on the retina is a depressed spot called the **fovea,** which lies at the center of the visual field.

The retina of each eye contains the two kinds of receptor cells responsible for vision: **rods** and **cones.** Rods, chiefly responsible for night vision, respond to varying degrees of light and dark but not to color. Cones respond to light and dark as well as to color or different **wavelengths** of light, and operate mainly in daytime. Only cones are present in the fovea.

Rods and cones connect to nerve cells, called **bipolar cells,** leading to the brain. In the fovea, a single cone generally connects with one bipolar cell. Rods, on the other hand, share bipolar cells. The one-to-one connection between cones and bipolar cells in the fovea allows for maximum **visual acuity,** the ability to distinguish fine details. Vision is thus sharpest whenever the image of an object falls directly on the fovea; outside the fovea, acuity drops dramatically.

The sensitivity of rods and cones changes according to the amount of available light. **Light adaptation** helps our eyes adjust to bright light; **dark adaptation** allows us to see, at least partially, in conditions of darkness. An **afterimage** can appear until the retina adapts after a visual stimulus has been removed.

Neural messages originating in the retina must eventually reach the brain for a visual sensation to occur. The bipolar cells connect to **ganglion cells,** whose axons converge to form the **optic nerve** that carries messages to the brain. The place on the retina where the axons of the ganglion cells join to leave the eye is the **blind spot.**

At the base of the brain is the **optic chiasm,** where some of the optic nerve fibers cross to the other side of the brain.

Color Vision

The human vision system allows us to see an extensive range of colors. **Hue, saturation,** and **brightness** are three separate aspects of our experience of color. Hue refers to colors (red, green, blue, etc.), saturation indicates the vividness or richness of the hues, and brightness signals the intensity of the hues. Humans can distinguish only about 150 hues but, through gradations of saturation and brightness, we can perceive about 300,000 colors.

Theories of color vision attempt to explain how the cones, which number only about 150,000 in the fovea, are able to distinguish some 300,000 different colors. One clue lies in color mixing: **Additive color mixing** is the process of mixing only a few *lights* of different wavelengths to create many new colors; **subtractive color mixing** refers to mixing a few *pigments* to come up with a whole palette of new colors.

Based on the principles of additive color mixing, the **trichromatic theory** of color vision holds that the eye contains three kinds of color receptors that are most responsive to either red, green, or blue light. By combining signals from these three basic receptors, the brain can detect any color and even subtle differences among nearly identical colors. This theory accounts for some kinds of **colorblindness.** People referred to as **dichromats** have a deficiency in either red-green or blue-yellow vision; **monochromats** see no color at all. People with normal color vision are referred to as **trichromats.** By contrast, the **opponent-process theory** maintains that receptors are specialized to respond to either member of the three basic color pairs: red-green, yellow-blue, and black-white (dark and light).

Drawing on elements of the two theories, current knowledge holds that while there are three kinds of receptors for colors in the retina (for violet-blue, green, and yellow light), the messages they transmit are coded by other neurons in the visual system into opponent-process form.

Color Vision in Other Species
In addition to humans, many other primates, including tree shrews, monkeys, and apes, also distinguish colors quite well. In contrast to humans, however, most are dichromats—experiencing the whole world only in terms of reds and greens or blues and yellows. Rodents, such as hamsters, rats, and squirrels, appear to be completely colorblind. Some reptiles, fish, insects, birds, and shellfish can distinguish color, but differ in which colors they can see; for example, bees can see ultraviolet light but not red. Knowing an animal is sensitive to light of a certain wavelength does not mean we know how that animal actually *experiences* color.

HEARING
Sounds we hear are psychological experiences created by the brain in response to stimulation.

Sound
The physical stimuli for the sense of hearing are **sound waves,** which produce vibration in the eardrum. **Frequency** is the number of cycles per second in a wave, expressed in a unit called **hertz.** Frequency is the primary determinant of **pitch**—how high or low the tone seems to be. **Amplitude** is the magnitude of a wave; it largely determines the loudness of a sound. Loudness is measured in **decibels.** The complex pattern of **overtones** determines the **timbre** of a sound.

The Ear
Hearing begins when sound waves strike the eardrum and cause it to vibrate. This vibration, in turn, makes three bones in the middle ear—the **hammer,** the **anvil,** and the **stirrup**—vibrate in sequence. These vibrations are magnified in their passage through the middle ear deep into the inner ear. The **oval window,** which is attached to the stirrup, and the **round window** are membranes between the middle and inner ear. In the inner ear, the vibrations cause the fluid inside the **cochlea** to vibrate, pushing the **basilar membrane** and the **organ of Corti** up and down.

Inside the organ of Corti are tiny hair cells that act as sensory receptors for hearing. Stimulation of these receptors produces auditory signals that are transmitted to brain through the **auditory nerve.** The brain pools the information from thousands of these cells to create the perception of sounds.

Theories of Hearing
There are two basic views that explain how different sound-wave patterns are coded into neural messages. **Place theory** states that the brain determines pitch by noting the place on the basilar membrane where the message is strongest. **Frequency theory** holds that the frequency of vibrations of the basilar membrane as a whole is translated into an equivalent frequency of nerve impulses. Neurons, however, cannot fire as rapidly as the frequency of the highest-pitched sound. This suggests a **volley principle,** whereby nerve cells fire in sequence to send a rapid series of impulses to the brain.

THE OTHER SENSES

Smell
The sense of smell is activated by substances carried by airborne molecules into the nasal cavities, where the substances activate highly specialized receptors for smell, located in the **olfactory epithelium.** From there messages are carried directly to the **olfactory bulb** in the brain, where they are sent to the brain's temporal lobe, resulting in our awareness of smells. **Pheromones** are sensed by receptors in the **vomeronasal organ (VNO),** which sends messages to a specialized olfactory bulb.

Taste
The receptor cells for the sense of taste are housed in the **taste buds** on the tongue, which, in turn, are found in the **papillae,** the small bumps on the surface of the tongue. Each taste bud contains a cluster of taste receptors, or taste cells, that cause their adjacent neurons to fire when they become activated by the chemical substances in food, sending a nerve impulse to the brain.

We experience only four primary taste qualities: sweet, sour, salty, and bitter. All other tastes derive from combinations of these four. Flavor is a complex blend of taste and smell.

Kinesthetic and Vestibular Senses

The **kinesthetic senses** relay specific information about muscle movement, changes in posture, and strain on muscles and joints. They rely on feedback from two sets of specialized nerve endings: **stretch receptors,** which are attached to muscle fibers, and **Golgi tendon organs,** which are attached to the tendons.

The **vestibular senses** control equilibrium and create an awareness of body position. The receptors for these senses are located in the vestibular organs in the inner ear. The sensation of body rotation stems from the three **semicircular canals** of the inner ear. The sensation of gravitation and movement forward and backward, as well as up and down, arises in the two **vestibular sacs** that lie between the semicircular canals and the cochlea.

Sensations of Motion

The vestibular organs are also responsible for motion sickness, which triggers strong reactions in some people. Motion sickness may be caused by discrepancies between visual information and vestibular sensation.

The Skin Senses

The skin is the largest sense organ, with numerous nerve receptors distributed in varying concentrations throughout its surface. The nerve fibers from these receptors travel to the brain.

Skin receptors give rise to what are known as the *cutaneous sensations* of pressure, temperature, and pain. Research has not established a simple connection between the various types of receptors and these separate sensations. Because the brain uses complex information about the patterns of activity on many different receptors to detect and discriminate among skin sensations, a direct connection between receptors and sensations has so far eluded researchers.

Pain

People have varying degrees of sensitivity to pain. The most commonly accepted explanation of pain is the **gate control theory,** which holds that a "neurological gate" in the spinal cord controls the transmission of pain impulses to the brain. Studies of pain relief suggest the existence of the **placebo effect,** which occurs when a pain sufferer feels relief from pain when given a chemically neutral pill but told that it is an effective pain reliever.

PERCEPTION

There are several ways in which the brain interprets the complex flow of information from the various senses and creates perceptual experiences that go far beyond what is sensed directly.

Perceptual Organization

One important way our perceptual processes work is through distinguishing **figures** from the **ground** against which they appear. The figure-ground distinction, first noted by Gestalt psychologists, pertains to all our senses, not just vision. For instance, a violin solo stands out against the "ground" of a symphony orchestra. When we use sensory information to create perceptions, we fill in the missing information, group various objects together, see whole objects, and hear meaningful sounds. Visual information in the brain is coded by cells called **feature detectors,** which respond to particular elements of the visual field.

Perceptual Constancies

Perceptual constancy is our tendency to perceive objects as unchanging in the face of changes in sensory stimulation. Once we have formed a stable perception of an object, we can recognize it from almost any angle. Thus, **size, shape, brightness,** and **color constancies** help us understand and relate to the world better. Memory and experience play an important part in perceptual constancy, compensating for confusing stimuli.

Observer Characteristics: Individual Differences and Culture

In addition to past experience and learning, several personal factors color our perception. For example, our familiarity with a symbol or object affects our expectation of how the object should look, even if we observe subtle changes in its appearance. Our perceptions are also influenced by our individual ways of dealing with the environment and by our cultural background, values, motivation, personality, and cognitive style.

Perceiving Distance and Depth

We can perceive distance and depth through **monocular cues,** from one eye, or **binocular cues,** which depend on the interaction of both eyes.

Superposition is a monocular distance cue in which one object, by partly blocking a second, appears closer. **Linear perspective** is another monocular cue to distance and depth based on the fact that two parallel lines seem to come together at the horizon. Other monocular cues include **aerial perspective, elevation, texture gradient, shadowing,** and **motion parallax.**

With binocular cues, the **stereoscopic vision** derived from combining the two retinal images makes perceptions of depth and distance clearer. **Retinal disparity** accounts for the different images each eye receives. **Convergence** is another binocular cue. Humans, apes, and some predatory animals with the ability to use binocular cues have a distinct advantage over animals whose vision is limited to monocular cues.

Sounds, too, add to our sense of space. **Monaural cues,** such as loudness and distance, require only one ear. On the other hand, **binaural cues,** such as discrepancies in the arrival time of sound waves and their volume, help us to locate the source of a sound. Binaural cues depend on the collaboration of both ears.

Perceiving Movement

Perception of movement is a complicated process involving both the visual messages from the retina and messages from the muscles around the eyes as they shift to follow a moving object. At times our perceptual processes trick us into believing that an object is moving when, in fact, it is stationary. Thus, there is a difference between *real* movement and *apparent* movement.

Autokinetic illusion, the perceived motion created by a single stationary object, **stroboscopic motion,** resulting from the flashing of a series of still pictures in rapid succession, and the **phi phenomenon,** which occurs when lights flashed in sequence are perceived as moving, are all examples of apparent movement.

Visual Illusions

Visual illusions occur when we use a variety of sensory cues to create perceptual experiences that do not actually exist.

More easily understood are **physical illusions,** an example of which is the bent appearance of a stick when placed in water. **Perceptual illusions** depend primarily on our own perceptual processes and occur because the stimulus contains misleading cues.

REVIEW QUESTIONS

MULTIPLE CHOICE AND SHORT ANSWER

1. The process that involves converting physical energy into nerve impulses is referred to as _____.

2. The _____ threshold is the smallest change in stimulation that can be detected 50 percent of the time.
   a. absolute
   b. difference
   c. jnd
   d. relative

3. Match the following terms with their definitions:

   _____ cornea   a. colored part of the eye
   _____ pupil   b. center of the visual field
   _____ iris   c. receptor cell responsible for color vision
   _____ lens   d. protective layer over front part of the eye
   _____ fovea   e. contains the receptor cells that respond to light
   _____ retina   f. focuses light onto the retina
   _____ rod   g. receptor cell responsible for night vision
   _____ cone   h. opening in the iris through which light enters

4. The process whereby the rods and cones adjust to become more sensitive to lowered levels of illumination is known as _____.
   a. dark adaptation
   b. light adaptation

5. The place on the retina where the axons of all the ganglion cells come together to leave the eye is called the _____.
   a. fovea
   b. blind spot
   c. optic chiasm
   d. visual cortex

6. _____, _____, and _____ are three separate aspects of our experience of color.

7. The process of mixing pigments is known as _____ color mixing.
   a. additive
   b. subtractive

8. Trichromats can mix _____, _____, and _____ lights to perceive virtually any hue.

9. The theory of color that best explains color afterimages is _____.
   a. the volley theory
   b. trichromatic theory
   c. opponent-process theory
   d. subtractive color theory

10. As a sound wave moves from the outer ear to the inner ear, number the following in the order that it would reach them:
    _____ oval window
    _____ anvil
    _____ cochlea
    _____ auditory nerve
    _____ round window

11. Match the following theories with their definitions:
    _____ frequency theory   a. groups of cells fire in sequence, not each individually

    _____ volley principle   b. rate at which hair cells in the cochlea fire determines pitch

    _____ place theory   c. different parts of basilar membrane respond to different frequencies

12. Placebos and acupuncture may affect the sensation of pain by _____.
    a. closing the pain gate
    b. releasing endorphins
    c. blocking pain receptors in the skin

13. The process by which we create meaningful experiences out of the jumble of sensory information is called _____.

14. In the case of reversible figures, we have difficulty distinguishing the _____ from the _____ behind it.

15. Match the following principles of perception with their definitions:
    _____ similarity   a. tendency to perceive a whole object even where none exists

    _____ continuity   b. elements that continue a pattern are likely to be seen as part of the pattern

    _____ proximity   c. objects that are like one another tend to be grouped together

    _____ closure   d. elements found close together tend to be perceived as a unit

16. Next to each depth cue, put *B* if it is a binocular cue and *M* if it is a monocular cue.
    _____ retinal disparity
    _____ texture gradient
    _____ convergence
    _____ stereoscopic vision
    _____ linear perspective
    _____ superposition

17. The perception of loud sounds as being closer than faint sounds is a common _____ cue to sound localization.
    a. monaural
    b. binaural

CRITICAL THINKING AND APPLICATIONS

1. When we look directly at an object, the image is focused on each eye's fovea. Why is this advantageous?

2. When we are reading or studying, we often seem to be aware of movement off to our sides. Why is it so easy to sense these events?

3. What is the difference between a vestibular sense and a kinesthetic sense? What kinds of activities require both?

4. Adults seem to enjoy the flavors of many foods that children find disgusting. What might contribute to changes in taste preference throughout the life span?

5. "Flavor" is thought of as the combination of senses of taste and smell. How could you demonstrate the difference between flavor and taste? Between flavor and smell?

6. Examine a few passages of your favorite song. Explain how the Gestalt principles of organization (proximity, similarity, closure, etc.) operate in the perception of music.

ENDURING ISSUES

Person–Situation
To what extent are our perceptual experiences determined by objects and events in the real world, and to what extent are they shaped by our thoughts, emotions, motives, attitudes, values, personalities, etc.?

Diversity
After reading this chapter, to what extent do you think that people's sensory and perceptual experiences differ depending on their race or culture or gender?

(Answers to the Review Questions appear in the back of the book.)

4 States of

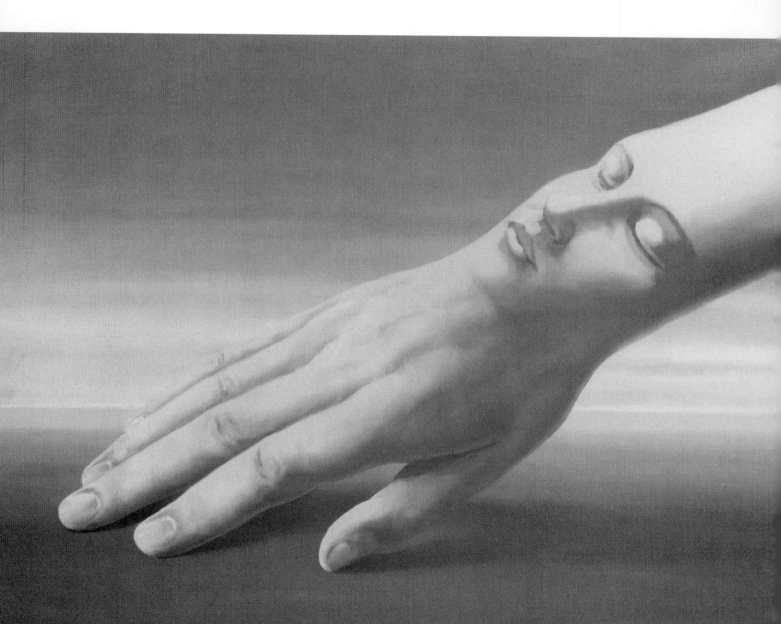

OVERVIEW

Natural Variations in Consciousness
Daydreaming and Fantasy
Sleep and Dreaming

Artificial Alterations in Consciousness
Sensory Deprivation
Meditation
Hypnosis

Drug-Altered Consciousness
Substance Use, Abuse, and Dependence
Depressants: Alcohol, Barbiturates, the Opiates
Stimulants: Caffeine, Nicotine, Amphetamines, and Cocaine
Hallucinogens and Marijuana

Consciousness

Consider the following scenario. You wake up and start your day by deciding what to eat for breakfast and what to wear. After breakfast, you sit down to study for an upcoming history exam, but you soon find yourself daydreaming. You try to refocus your attention on history. During lunch, you drink a cup of coffee or tea to stay alert. After lunch, you spend some time reflecting on bigger questions, such as what subject to major in or what direction you want your life to take. You meditate to ease your anxiety over the upcoming test. Later you decide to go out for dinner, and you have a glass of wine or beer with your meal. Fi-nally, at the end of the day, you fall asleep and, shortly thereafter, experience the first of several dreams you will have before morning.

Think About It!

1. What do we mean by *consciousness*, and why is it of interest to psychologists?
2. Does daydreaming serve any useful purpose?
3. Do people actually have "biological clocks"?
4. Is going without sleep harmful?
5. Does everyone dream and, if so, how often?
6. Can hypnosis really change behavior?
7. How and why does alcohol affect our behavior?
8. Does caffeine use have any negative effects?

Making decisions, remembering, daydreaming, concentrating, reflecting, sleeping, and dreaming are but a few of the mental processes we commonly experience. Our awareness of these various mental processes is called **consciousness.**

Consciousness Our awareness of various cognitive processes, such as sleeping, dreaming, concentrating, and making decisions.

Waking consciousness Mental state that encompasses the thoughts, feelings, and perceptions that occur when we are awake and reasonably alert.

Altered state of consciousness (ASC) Mental state that differs noticeably from normal waking consciousness.

1

What do we mean by *consciousness*, and why is it of interest to psychologists?

From an evolutionary standpoint, consciousness has had important survival value. Slow and weak compared to many other animals, the mental skills that enable us to think, reason, remember, plan, and predict were highly adaptive for survival.

Throughout human history, philosophers, theologians, artists, and, most recently, scientists have all tried to grasp the elusive nature of consciousness. From William James's early characterization of consciousness as a kaleidoscopic flow or "stream" mingling internal and external information to behaviorists John B. Watson and B. F. Skinner's outright rejection of consciousness as a legitimate subject of scientific inquiry, contemporary scientific psychology has settled on a middle ground of sorts. Pioneering techniques such as electroencephalography (EEG), positron emission tomography (PET), computerized axial tomography (CAT), magnetic resonance imaging (MRI), and magnetoencephalography (MEG) cast new light on brain activity during various states of consciousness, allowing us to study these states with an unprecedented measure of precision. By linking data from these techniques with subjective reports of conscious processes, scientists have made tremendous strides in understanding human consciousness.

Psychologists generally divide consciousness into two broad areas. **Waking consciousness**—or conscious awareness—includes all the thoughts, feelings, and perceptions that occur when we are awake and reasonably alert. Such waking consciousness encompasses sensation and perception, learning, memory, thinking, problem solving, decision making, intelligence, and creativity—all processes so pivotal in contemporary psychology that whole chapters are devoted to them in this book.

But there are times when we experience **altered states of consciousness (ASC);** then our mental state differs markedly from normal waking consciousness. Some altered states (such as daydreaming, sleep, and dreaming) occur routinely, even spontaneously. Other ASCs (such as hypnosis, meditation, and intoxication) are brought on by deliberate attempts to alter normal consciousness. In this chapter we will begin by examining natural variations in consciousness. Then we will turn to strategies people use to deliberately alter normal states of consciousness.

NATURAL VARIATIONS IN CONSCIOUSNESS

Even when we are fully awake and alert, we are usually conscious of only a small portion of what is going on around us. At any given moment, we are exposed to a great variety of sounds, sights, and smells from the outside world. At the same time, we experience all sorts of internal sensations (such as heat and cold, touch, pressure, pain, equilibrium) as well as an array of thoughts, memories, emotions, and needs. Normally, however, we are not aware of all these competing stimuli; after all, to survive and make sense of our environment, we are forced to select only the most important information to attend to and then filter out everything else. At times we pay such

HIGHLIGHTS
GOING WITH THE FLOW

Most of us have experienced moments of total absorption when we are so focused on what we are doing that time seems to pass unnoticed and we are filled with happiness. Research suggests that such wholehearted absorption—whether in reading a book, skiing, building something, or playing an instrument—leads to an altered state of consciousness in which our minds function at peak effectiveness and we experience a feeling of effortless engagement.

Mike Csikszentmihalyi, a psychologist at the University of Chicago, refers to these moments of absorption as "flow states," periods when everything falls into place perfectly and you feel most alive and fully intent on what you're doing. In one study, Csikszentmihalyi and his colleagues at Chicago and at the Milan Medical School found that people enter the flow state when the demands on them are a little higher than usual, so they are not bored, but not so great that they become anxious (Massimini, Csikszentmihalyi, & Della Fave, 1988). Certain techniques promote the flow state. One method is to make a task more challenging. For example, an assembly-line worker whose job is tightening screws escaped the boredom inherent in the daily repetition by experimenting with ways to cut a few seconds from the time it took to complete the task. Another method is to pay strict attention to a task; initially, this is a struggle, but then the person relaxes into an effortless flow state.

Flow researchers distinguish between strained and effortless attention. Findings by scientists at the National Institute of Mental Health indicate that these two kinds of attention correspond to opposing patterns of brain function (J. A. Hamilton, Haier, & Buchsbaum, 1984). Strained concentration is accompanied by increased cortical arousal, whereas the effortless concentration typical of flow is associated with decreased arousal.

The deep concentration of the flow state bears a striking similarity to the altered state of hypnosis. Research shows that people who enjoy fantasizing or who easily become absorbed in a painting are more readily hypnotized than other people (Pekala & Kumar, 1984). Once hypnotized, such individuals frequently report feelings mirroring those in flow states—joy, a sense of deep meaningfulness coupled with rich imagery, a distorted sense of time, and profound attentiveness (Pekala & Kumar, 1986).

close attention to what we are doing that we are wholly absorbed in it and oblivious to what is going on around us (see *Highlights*). Indeed, the hallmark of normal waking consciousness is the highly selective nature of attention. (We return to attention in Chapter 6, Memory.)

We are subject to numerous cognitive processes, undergo all sorts of experiences, and perform numerous tasks without being consciously aware of them. For example, we are rarely attuned to such vital bodily processes as blood pressure and respiration. And most of us can walk down the street or ride a bicycle without consciously thinking about every movement we are making. In fact, we perform certain tasks better when we are not consciously aware of doing them. You probably sign your name several times in a day automatically when asked to do so. But if you think carefully about each movement you are making with your pen or pencil, you will find that signing your name so that it looks normal becomes very difficult.

Many psychologists believe that certain key mental processes, such as recognizing a word or a friend's face, also go on outside of normal waking consciousness. As we saw in the first chapter, Sigmund Freud thought that many of the most important influences on our behavior—such as erotic feelings for our parents—are screened from our consciousness even though they underlie much of our behavior. According to Freud, the conscious part of the mind is only the tip of the iceberg. The real driving forces

Daydreaming Alteration in consciousness that occurs seemingly without effort, typically when we want to momentarily escape the demands of the real world.

behind human actions are sexual and aggressive instincts that remain largely hidden, though they may come to the fore in such altered states of consciousness as hypnosis and dreaming. We will explore the notion of nonconscious mental processes as we consider various ASCs in this chapter, and when we examine behavior disorders in Chapter 13, Psychological Disorders.

Daydreaming and Fantasy

It takes deliberate effort to enter an ASC via hypnosis, drugs, or meditation, but **daydreaming** is an ASC that occurs seemingly without effort. For example, while sitting in a class, you may suddenly find yourself thinking about things that have nothing to do with the subject of the lecture.

Typically, we daydream when we would rather be somewhere else or be doing something else—it is a momentary escape. Your daydreams give you the chance to write, star in, and stage-manage a private drama for which you are the only audience.

Are daydreams random paths your mind travels? Not at all. Psychologists have discovered that people's daydreams fall into several distinct categories and that different people prefer particular kinds of daydreams (Singer, 1975). People who score high on measures of anxiety often have fleeting, loosely connected daydreams related to worrying, which give them little pleasure. By contrast, people who are achievement oriented tend to replay in their daydreams recurring themes of achievement, guilt, fear of failure, and hostility, reflecting the self-doubt and competitive envy that accompanies great ambition. Still other people derive considerable enjoyment from their daydreams and use them to solve problems, think ahead, or distract themselves. These "happy daydreamers" stage for themselves pleasant fantasies uncomplicated by guilt or worry. Finally, people with unusual curiosity about their environment, who also place a premium on objective thinking, experience daydreams filled with scenes from the objective world and marked by controlled lines of thought.

2

Does daydreaming serve any useful purpose?

Does daydreaming, which is nearly universal, serve any useful purpose? Some psychologists argue that daydreams have little or no positive or practical value. They regard daydreaming as nothing more than a retreat from the real world, especially when that world is not meeting our needs. One study, for example, found that television viewing stimulates spontaneous daydreaming, but decreases the purposeful use of creative imagination (Valkenburg & van der Voort, 1994).

Other psychologists stress the positive value of daydreaming and fantasy (Klinger, 1990). According to Freudian theorists, daydreams allow us to express and deal with desires—generally relating to sex or hostility—that would otherwise make us feel guilty or anxious (Giambra, 1974). And some speculate that daydreaming builds cognitive skills and creativity (Pulaski, 1974). Daydreaming helps people endure difficult situations as well: Prisoners of war have used it to survive torture and deprivation. Daydreaming and fantasy, then, may provide welcome relief from everyday—often unpleasant—reality and reduce internal tension and external aggression.

Sleep and Dreaming

We spend about one-third of our lives in the altered state of consciousness known as sleep. Throughout history, cultures have paid varying degrees of respect to sleep and the dreams that inhabit it. In some societies people believe that universal truths are revealed in dreams; members of other societies view sleep as a nonproductive, though essential, activity. Only recently have sleep researchers started to analyze the fascinating complexity of sleep, its functions, and its psychological and biological value.

CIRCADIAN CYCLES: THE BIOLOGICAL CLOCK   Like many other biological functions, sleep and waking follow a daily, or *circadian*, cycle (from the Latin expression *circa diem*, meaning "about a day") (Moore-Ede, Czeisler, & Richardson, 1983). The time we spend asleep and awake follows a 24-hour cycle influenced by the sun. Sleep-wake cycles change as the days grow longer or shorter with the seasons. Metabolism, stomach acidity, alertness, body temperature, blood pressure, and the level of most hormones also vary predictably over the course of a day. Together, these rhythms are often referred to as our *biological clock*. Not all body cycles follow the same pattern. For example, the level of the hormone epinephrine (which causes the body to go on alert) reaches a peak in the late morning hours and then steadily declines until around midnight, when it suddenly drops to a very low level and remains there until morning. By contrast, levels of melatonin (involved in the onset of sleep) surge at night and drop off during the day.

Normally, the rhythms and chemistry of all these different cycles interact smoothly, so that a shift in one brings about a corresponding shift in others (Moore-Ede et al., 1983). In fact, we rarely notice these circadian rhythms until they are disturbed. Jet lag is a familiar example: You might take a 6-hour flight departing from New York at 7 P.M. New York time and arriving at 7 A.M. London time. While Londoners are starting their day, according to your biological clock it's really 2 A.M. Shift work serves as another example: Workers who are transferred from the day shift to the midnight shift often experience weight loss and suffer from irritability, health problems, insomnia, and extreme drowsiness around the clock for a very long time (Richardson, Miner, & Czeisler, 1989–1990). These disruptions of the biological clock pose a threat to safety in the case of pilots or workers operating dangerous equipment.

Even the change from standard time to daylight savings time and back again creates temporary problems of adjustment for most people. The everyday use of artificial lights in our homes and offices suppresses our otherwise natural response to seasonal changes in the light cycle (Wehr et al., 1995). To illustrate this point, a controlled laboratory study examined the impact of *moderate* changes in the timing of the sleep-wake cycle on a group of healthy young college students (Boivin et al., 1997). In this study a group of male and female students were put on a 28-hour sleep-wake schedule (compared to the normal 24-hour cycle), for 33 to 36 days. Surprisingly, even this relatively small change in the timing of the sleep-wake cycle produced profound effects on the subsequent mood of the participants.

Recent evidence suggests that researchers may have found a way to adjust our biological clocks. It seems that light inhibits the production of melatonin, which goes up as the sun goes down. A small dose of melatonin taken in the morning (the time when the hormone is usually tapering off) sets back or slows down the biological clock. Taken in the evening, melatonin speeds up the biological clock, making the person fall asleep earlier than usual (Lewy, 1992). A team of investigators applied this reasoning to treat a child with severe insomnia brought on by a tumor of the pineal gland, which suppressed the gland's output of melatonin. Following a 2-week period, when melatonin was artificially supplied to the child, a normal sleep-wakefulness cycle was restored (Etzioni et al., 1996). Results like these suggest that someday a melatonin pill, perhaps used in conjunction with timed exposure to sunlight or darkness, may help people adjust their circadian rhythms at will.

3

Do people actually have "biological clocks"?

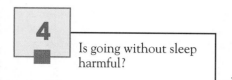

SLEEP Nobody who has tried to stay awake longer than 20 hours at a time could doubt the necessity of sleep. Some people claim they never sleep, but, when observed under laboratory conditions, they actually sleep soundly without being aware of it; others engage in short periods of "microsleep," dozing for a second or two at a time. Merely resting doesn't satisfy us. When an organism is sleep-deprived, it craves sleep just as strongly as it would food or water after a period of deprivation.

A recent study suggests that the naturally occurring chemical adenosine may play a pivotal role in the need for sleep (Porkka-Heiskanen et al., 1997). In this study, cats kept awake an abnormally long time were found to have elevated levels of adenosine in their brains during wakefulness. When the cats were finally permitted to sleep, the adenosine levels dropped. To determine whether the adenosine buildup actually caused the sleepiness, the investigators injected it into well-rested cats—who immediately became sleepy and began to exhibit the EEG patterns typical of drowsiness. Exactly why the level of adenosine appears to trigger sleepiness is not known, but additional research along this line may soon provide us with a better understanding of the neurological processes underlying the need for sleep.

Working from an evolutionary perspective, some psychologists see sleep as an adaptive mechanism that evolved to encourage organisms to remain inactive and conserve energy during times of the day when their food supplies were low or their predators were especially numerous. In support of this theory, researchers have shown that less energy is used when we're asleep than when we're awake (Madsen, 1993). In addition, the manner in which many organisms sleep appears to be adapted to their specific needs and environment. For instance, dolphins, which are required to come to the surface to breathe, sleep with only one hemisphere of their brain at a time (Borbely, 1986), whereas lions, which have few predators, sleep undisturbed for many hours of the day.

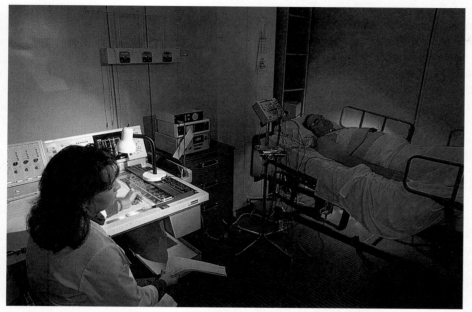

Sleep researchers monitor volunteers' brain waves, muscle tension, and other physiological changes during a night's sleep.

Although still uncertain about the function of sleep, scientists have learned a great deal about the rhythms of sleep. To study sleep, researchers typically recruit volunteers who spend one or more nights in a "sleep lab." With electrodes painlessly attached to their skulls, the volunteers sleep comfortably as their brain waves, eye movements, muscle tension, and other physiological functions are monitored. Data from such studies show that although there are significant individual differences in sleep behavior, almost everyone goes through several stages of sleep (Anch et al., 1988). Each stage is marked by characteristic patterns of brain waves, muscular activity, blood pressure, and body temperature. Figure 4–1 illustrates the electrical activity related to the brain, heart, and facial muscles at each stage.

"Going to sleep" means losing awareness and failing to respond to a stimulus that would produce a response in the waking state. As measured by an EEG, brain waves during this "twilight" state are characterized by irregular, low-voltage *alpha waves*. This brain-wave pattern mirrors the sense of relaxed wakefulness that we experience while lying on a beach or in a hammock or when resting after a big meal. In this twilight state with the eyes closed, people often report seeing flashing lights and colors, geometric patterns, and visions of landscapes. Sometimes they also experience a floating or falling sensation, followed by a quick jolt back to consciousness.

After this initial twilight phase, the sleeper enters Stage 1 of sleep. Stage 1 brain waves are "tight" and of very low amplitude, resembling those recorded when a person is alert or excited. But, in contrast to normal waking consciousness, Stage 1 of the sleep cycle is marked by a slowing of the pulse, muscle relaxation, and side-to-side rolling movements of the eyes—the last being the most reliable indication of this first stage of sleep (Dement, 1974). Stage 1 usually lasts only a few moments. The sleeper is easily aroused at this stage and, once awake, may be unaware of having slept at all.

Stages 2 and 3 are characterized by progressively deeper sleep. Brain waves increase in amplitude and become slower. At these stages, the sleeper is hard to awaken and does not respond to stimuli such as noises or lights. Heart rate, blood pressure, and temperature continue to drop.

In Stage 4 sleep, the brain emits very slow *delta waves*. Heart rate, breathing rate, blood pressure and body temperature are as low as they will get during the night. In young adults, delta sleep occurs in 15- to 20-minute segments—interspersed with lighter sleep—mostly during the first half of the night. Delta sleep time lessens with age but continues to be the first sleep to be made up after sleep has been lost.

About an hour after falling asleep, the sleeper begins to ascend from Stage 4 sleep to Stage 3, Stage 2, and back to Stage 1—a process that takes about 40 minutes. The brain waves return to the low-amplitude, saw-toothed shape characteristic of Stage 1 sleep and waking alertness. Heart rate and blood pressure also increase, yet the muscles are more relaxed than at any other point in the sleep cycle, and the person is very difficult to awaken. The eyes move rapidly under closed eyelids. This **rapid eye movement (REM) sleep** stage is distinguished from all other stages of sleep (called **non-REM** or **NREM**) that precede and follow it.

REM sleep is also called **paradoxical sleep,** because although measures of brain activity, heart rate, blood pressure, and other physiological functions closely resemble those recorded during waking consciousness, the person in this stage appears to be deeply asleep and is incapable of moving; the body's voluntary muscles are essentially paralyzed. This is also the stage when most vivid dreaming occurs. When researchers made lesions on the brain stems of cats to prevent this paralysis from occurring, the results were spectacular.

REM (paradoxical) sleep Sleep stage characterized by rapid eye movement; it is during this stage that most vivid dreaming occurs.

Non-REM (NREM) sleep Non-rapid-eye-movement stages of sleep that alternate with REM stages during the sleep cycle.

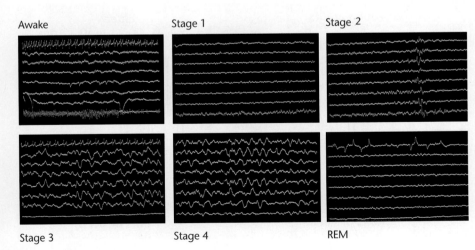

Awake   Stage 1   Stage 2

Stage 3   Stage 4   REM

Figure 4–1
Waves of sleep.
This series of printouts illustrates electrical activity in the brain, heart, and facial muscles during the various stages of sleep. Note the characteristic delta waves that begin to appear during Stage 3 and become more pronounced during Stage 4.

After they entered the REM stage, although otherwise sound asleep, the cats raised their heads, tried to stand up, and in some cases even searched for and attacked prey (Morrison, 1983). Obviously, the normal inhibition of this kind of movement through muscle paralysis makes REM sleep safer for all of us.

The first Stage 1-REM period lasts about 10 minutes and is followed by Stages 2, 3, and 4 of NREM sleep. This sequence of sleep stages repeats itself all night, averaging 90 minutes from Stage 1-REM to Stage 4 and back again. Normally, a night's sleep consists of four to five sleep cycles of this sort. But the pattern of sleep changes as the night progresses. At first Stages 3 and 4 dominate; but as time passes, the Stage 1-REM periods gradually become longer and Stages 3 and 4 become shorter, eventually disappearing altogether. Over the course of a night, then, about 45 to 50 percent of the sleeper's time is spent in Stage 2, whereas REM sleep takes up another 20-25 percent of the total.

Sleep requirements and patterns vary considerably from person to person, though. Some adults need hardly any sleep. Researchers have documented the case of a Stanford University professor who slept for only 3 to 4 hours a night over the course of 50 years and that of a woman who lived a healthy life on only 1 hour of sleep per night (Rosenzweig & Leiman, 1982). Sleep patterns also change with age (see Figure 4–2). Infants sleep much longer than adults—13 to 16 hours during the first year—and much more of their sleep is REM sleep (see Figure 4–3). Unlike adults, infants enter the REM stage immediately after falling asleep and change sleep stages often. The elderly, on the other hand, tend to sleep less than younger adults, wake up more often during the night, and spend much less time in the deep sleep of Stages 3 and 4. Finally, men generally sleep less well than women do: During early adulthood, they awaken more often and sleep less restfully; after age 60, their sleep patterns are more disturbed and they engage in less Stage 3 and 4 sleep than women do (Paulson, 1990).

If a tape recorder plays back information while you sleep, will you effortlessly learn? Unfortunately, no. Even experiments designed to teach sleepers simple pairs of words have failed. Very rudimentary forms of learning may be possible, however. The first time a stimulus such as a loud noise is presented to a sleeper, it produces signs of arousal. Repetition of the stimulus causes less and less arousal, suggesting that the sleeper has learned that the stimulus is not a cause for alarm.

Figure 4–2
A night's sleep across the life span.
Sleep patterns change from childhood to young adulthood to old age. The red areas represent REM sleep, the stage of sleep that varies most dramatically across age groups.

Source: Adapted by permission of *The New England Journal of Medicine, 290, 487, 1974.*

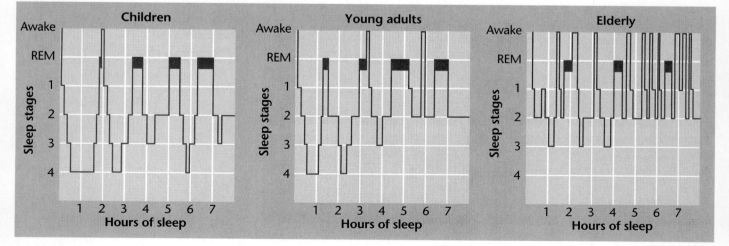

DREAMS We typically have four or five dreams a night, accounting for about 1-2 hours of our total time spent sleeping. **Dreams** are vivid visual and auditory experiences that our minds create primarily during REM periods. People awakened during REM sleep report graphic dreams about 80 to 85 percent of the time (R. J. Berger, 1969). Less striking experiences that resemble the thinking done during normal wakeful consciousness tend to occur during NREM sleep.

At times, REM dreams can be so vivid that it is hard to distinguish them from reality. In some cultures, in fact, dreams are considered to be real experiences of a world that is inaccessible to us in our waking lives. Similarly, most young children have great difficulty distinguishing between dreams and waking experiences. REM dreams seem so real to the dreamer because the state of brain arousal during REM sleep mirrors that of normal waking consciousness. But during REM sleep, the brain is relatively insensitive to outside sensory input. Thus, during REM sleep, the brain is alert and excited, but its only input is internal images from memory (Koulack & Goodenough, 1976).

Psychologists have long been fascinated by dream activity and the contents of dreams. Sigmund Freud (1900), whose theories are explored more comprehensively in Chapter 11, Personality, called dreams the "royal road to the unconscious." Believing that dreams represent wishes that have not been fulfilled in reality, he asserted that people's dreams reflect the motives guiding their behavior—motives of which they may not be consciously aware. Freud

Dreams Vivid visual and auditory experiences that occur primarily during REM periods of sleep.

Does everyone dream and, if so, how often?

Figure 4–3
Changes in REM and NREM sleep.
The amount of REM sleep people need declines sharply during the first few years of life. Newborns spend about 8 hours, or almost half of their total sleep time in REM sleep, whereas older children and adults spend just 1-2 hours or about 20-25 percent of their total sleep time in REM sleep.

Source: Adapted from H. P. Roffwarg, "Ontogenetic Development of the Human Sleep-Dream Cycle," *Science, 152*, p. 60. Copyright © 1966 by the American Association for the Advancement of Science. Reprinted with permission.

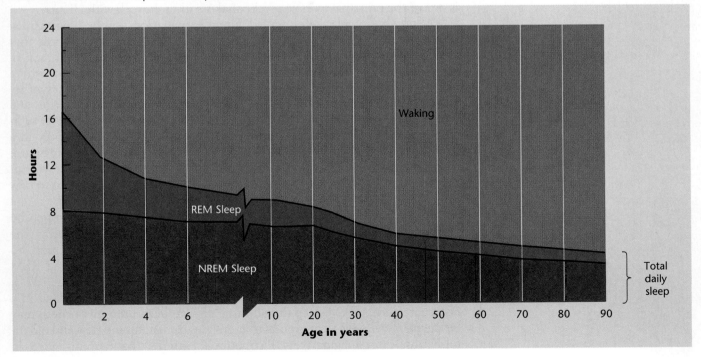

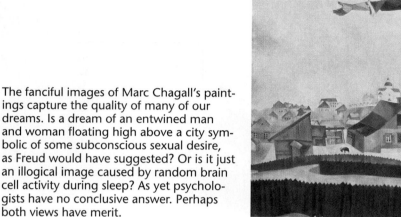

The fanciful images of Marc Chagall's paintings capture the quality of many of our dreams. Is a dream of an entwined man and woman floating high above a city symbolic of some subconscious sexual desire, as Freud would have suggested? Or is it just an illogical image caused by random brain cell activity during sleep? As yet psychologists have no conclusive answer. Perhaps both views have merit.

distinguished the *manifest*, or surface, *content* of dreams from their *latent content*—the hidden, unconscious thoughts or desires that he believed were expressed indirectly through dreams. In dreams, according to Freud, people permit themselves to express primitive desires that are relatively free of moral controls. For example, someone who is not consciously aware of hostile feelings toward a sister may dream about murdering her. However, even in a dream, such hostile feelings may be censored and transformed into a highly symbolic form. For example, the desire to do away with one's sister (the dream's latent content) may be recast into the dream image of seeing her off at a train "terminal" (the dream's manifest content). According to Freud, this process of censorship and symbolic transformation accounts for the highly illogical nature of many dreams. Deciphering the disguised meanings of dreams is one of the principal tasks of psychoanalysts in their work with clients.

Neurophysiologists offer quite different explanations for the illogical, disjointed nature of so many dreams. Two prominent researchers propose that dreams are generated by random outbursts of nerve-cell activity (Hobson & McCarley, 1977). In responding to these internal stimuli—many of which involve brain cells used in vision and hearing—the brain attempts to synthesize or make sense of them by drawing on memory to create the images and scenes we experience as dreams. The brain of a dreaming person is sufficiently aroused to sketch a narrative of events, but it can do this only in a primitive, concrete fashion. Other researchers have suggested that the bizarre content of dreams reflects the brain's effort to free itself of irrelevant, repetitious thoughts or associations during sleep so that it will be more open to new information during waking consciousness (Crick & Mitchison, 1983).

Another neurophysiological hypothesis, however, comes to the opposite conclusion: that in dreams we reprocess information, gathered during the day, as a way of strengthening the memory of information that is crucial to our survival. How does this work? At the neurophysiological level, REM sleep may be related to brain "restoration" and growth (Oswald, 1973, 1974), and researchers have indeed confirmed that protein synthesis proceeds at a faster rate during REM sleep than during NREM sleep. Protein synthesis may be the neurophysiological process that enables us to combine new and old information into imaginatively restructured patterns that are inscribed in memory. Other research has demonstrated not only that both human and nonhuman subjects spend more time in REM sleep after learning difficult material but also that interfering with REM sleep in the days immediately after subjects initially learn something severely disrupts their memory for the newly learned material (C. T. Smith, 1985; C. T. Smith & Lapp, 1986; C. T. Smith & Kelly, 1988). Thus, if you study hard during the week and then stay up all night on Friday and Saturday, you are likely to forget up to one-third of the material you would have remembered had you had a more restful weekend.

Whatever the ultimate explanation for dream content, we do know that it is related to several factors. For example, when you are closest to waking, your dreams are apt to center on recent events. Because the last dream that you have before waking is the one you are most likely to remember, it follows that most of the dreams you remember deal with recent events. In the middle of the night, however, dreams generally focus on childhood or past events.

Dream content also appears to be modified by presleep events. In one study, volunteers who had engaged in 6 hours of strenuous exercise before sleep tended to have dreams marked by relatively little physical activity (Hauri, 1970). The researcher concluded from that finding that, to some extent, dream content complements and compensates for waking experiences. Another study found that people who had experienced a day of social isolation had dreams filled with social interaction (P. B. Wood, 1962). Still another study showed the volunteers who had been water-deprived during the day dreamed of drinking (Bokert, 1970). These compensatory effects may be short-lived, however; long-term deprivation seems to bring on a reduction in related dream content. For example, recently paralyzed individuals reported more physical activity in their dreams than did people paralyzed for a long time, indicating that compensatory dreams die out when they are not nourished by reality (Newton, 1970).

Most dreams last about as long as the events would in real life; they do not flash on your mental screen just before waking, as was once believed. Generally, dreams consist of a sequential story or a series of stories. Stimuli, both external (such as a train whistle or a low-flying airplane) and internal (say, hunger pangs), may modify an ongoing dream, but they do not initiate dreams.

Are all the dreams dreamt in a single night related to one another? Typically, experimenters encounter a methodological problem when they try to answer this question: Each time the subject is awakened to be asked about a dream, the natural course of the dream is interrupted and is usually lost forever. If someone is preoccupied with a problem or event, however, it will often recur in dreams throughout the night (Dement, 1974).

Do we need to dream? In Freud's view, dreams serve as a psychic safety valve. That is, they allow us to give harmless expression to otherwise disturbing thoughts—sometimes so disturbing that they must be transformed into highly symbolic forms even in dreams. If this theory is correct, depriving people of the opportunity to dream should have significant effects on their waking lives. To some extent, research has proved Freud right. Experiments have shown that people deprived of REM sleep become anxious, testy, and hungry, have difficulty concentrating, and even hallucinate in their waking hours—deleterious effects that disappear as soon as they are permitted to experience REM sleep again (Dement, 1965; May & Kline, 1987). Furthermore when people deprived of REM sleep are finally allowed to sleep undisturbed, the amount of REM sleep nearly doubles—a phenomenon called REM rebound. However, people with schizophrenia show little or no REM rebound, and people who tend to daydream experience less REM rebound than the norm (D. B. Cohen, 1976). These findings indicate that we can make up for the loss of REM sleep either in NREM sleep or in dreamlike fantasies during waking life (Dement et al., 1970). REM rebound may be one reason some people have difficulty breaking the habit of using sleeping pills or a "nightcap" to fall asleep. Alcohol and most sleep medications are central nervous system depressants that reduce the amount of REM sleep and dreaming in users. The sharp increase in bizarre dreams—the rebound effect that occurs when these drugs are discontinued—is so disturbing to many people that they are driven back to the drugs in an attempt to avoid dreaming. The hallucinations that sometimes accompany alcohol withdrawal, may, in fact be a kind of REM rebound during waking life (Greenberg & Pearlman, 1967).

Dreams typically reflect the personality, interests, concerns, and emotional experiences of the dreamer. Some people seem able to use them to solve intricate work problems. For instance, the chemist Friedrich August von Kekule figured out the structure of the benzene molecule after he dreamt about a snake that grabbed its own tail: He awoke with the inspiration that the molecule must be configured in the shape of a ring, an insight that proved to be true. Dreams may also help us process emotional information. In dreams, emotionally significant events may be assimilated with previous experiences (Farthing, 1992). For example, children's first experience of a carnival or amusement park is usually a blend of terror and excitement. Later in life, whenever they undergo experiences that are exciting but also somewhat frightening, carnival rides or images may dominate their dreams.

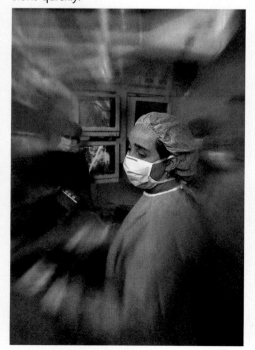

Sleep deprivation impairs cognitive skills to a greater extent than many people realize. When deprived of sleep we react more slowly, have more trouble focusing attention, and are more prone to making errors in judgment. Emergency room doctors often lose sleep because of the unpredictable and demanding nature of their work. This can be a serious problem when they are called upon to make critical decisions quickly.

SLEEPTALKING AND SLEEPWALKING We often associate *sleeptalking* and *sleepwalking* with dreaming, but actually only 20 percent of sleeptalking and sleepwalking occur during REM sleep. In fact, most episodes of sleeptalking and sleepwalking take place during delta sleep (Stage 4). Both sleepwalking and sleeptalking are more common among children than adults, with approximately 20 percent of children experiencing at least one episode of either sleepwalking or sleeptalking before adolescence. Boys are more likely to walk in their sleep than girls. Waking a sleepwalker is not dangerous, but it is difficult, because sleepwalking commonly occurs during a very deep stage of sleep (Hobson, 1994).

SLEEP DEPRIVATION Americans get too little sleep. Between one-third and one-half of adults in the United States are regularly sleep deprived, and the problem is getting worse: Americans were sleeping an average of 8 to 12 hours a night in the 1950s, but by 1990, they were down to only 7 hours a night. Similarly, in the 1930s only 17.9 percent of men reported feeling unrested in the morning, compared to 26.3 percent in the 1980s (Bliwise, 1996). Moreover, the number of accredited sleep-disorder clinics in the United States rose from 25 in 1980 to over 337 in 1997, with still more on the way (Grady, 1997).

When people chronically lose an hour or two of sleep every night, they have difficulty paying attention (especially to monotonous tasks) and remembering. Reaction time slows, behavior becomes unpredictable, accidents and errors in judgment increase, and productivity and the ability to make decisions decline (Babkoff et al., 1991; Webb & Levy, 1984).

These research findings have important implications. Sleep loss is a contributing factor in 200,000 to 400,000 car accidents each year and in 15 to 20 percent of deaths from car accidents, making it the most common contributing factor after alcohol (Brody, 1994; Richardson et al., 1989, 1990; Wald, 1995). Sleep deprivation may also routinely affect the performance of those in high-risk positions, such as pilots, hospital staff, and nuclear-power-plant operators, who often have to make critical decisions on short notice. A dramatic example of the effects of sleep deprivation on decision-making ability is the 1979 accident at the nuclear power plant at Three Mile Island in Pennsylvania. The three control-room operators on duty the morning of the accident were working a "slow-shift rotation": They were working during the daytime for one week, then evenings for a week, and then late nights for a third week. According to biologists, such a work schedule may result in the worst possible human performance because it severely disrupts the body's biological clock and sleep cycle.

During the first 100 minutes of the accident, the operators made an unusual number of errors. Fourteen seconds after the trouble began, one of them failed to notice two warning lights. A few seconds later, none of the operators realized that a valve that should have closed was open. The presidential commission that investigated the Three Mile Island incident concluded that human error had transformed a minor mishap into a major nuclear accident.

Awareness of the relationship between sleep deprivation and accidents has led to several changes in the working patterns of people whose jobs can have life-and-death consequences. Shifts of medical residents, for example, have been shortened in several states to prevent errors in judgment caused by sleep deprivation.

SLEEP DISORDERS The scientific study of typical sleep patterns has also yielded insights into sleep disorders such as **insomnia,** which afflicts as many as 35 million Americans. Most episodes of insomnia grow out of stressful events and are temporary (see *Applying Psychology*). But for some sufferers, insomnia is a persistent disruption. Treatments can create problems as well. Halcion, one of the most widely prescribed remedies for insomnia, frequently causes anxiety, memory loss, hallucinations, and violent behavior.

Insomnia Sleep disorder characterized by difficulty in falling asleep or remaining asleep throughout the night.

APPLYING PSYCHOLOGY
COPING WITH OCCASIONAL INSOMNIA

Even occasional insomnia can interfere with your alertness and ability to function during the day. What can you do if you sometimes find yourself awake long after going to bed? Sleep researchers recommend the following strategies.

Often a simple alteration in routine, such as changing the temperature of the bedroom or avoiding certain foods before bedtime, markedly improves the quality of sleep for many people who suffer from occasional insomnia. Among the keys: maintaining regular bedtime hours and not sleeping late on weekends,

abstaining from drugs (including alcohol, caffeine and nicotine, and the routine use of sleeping pills), avoiding anxious thoughts while in bed, and not fighting insomnia when it occurs. Sleep researchers also advise getting out of bed and doing something for an hour or so until you feel sleepy again. Establish a regular exercise program during the day, but never exercise within several hours of bedtime. Make it a habit to have a regular bedtime routine that you follow each night before retiring, such as a warm bath, followed by a little reading or writing a letter. Another

gambit for people who suffer from insomnia is to set aside regular times during the day—well before bedtime—to mull over their worries. This technique may be supplemented by relaxation training, using such methods as biofeedback, self-hypnosis, or meditation (Morin et al., 1994). Finally, tryptophan, a substance that promotes sleep, may be taken as a sleep aid in the form of warm milk, confirming a folk remedy for sleeplessness.

To learn more about sleep, visit our website at **www.prenhall.com/ morris**

Apnea Sleep disorder characterized by breathing difficulty during the night and feelings of exhaustion during the day.

Narcolepsy Hereditary sleep disorder characterized by sudden nodding off during the day and sudden loss of muscle tone following moments of emotional excitement.

For some people, insomnia is part of a larger psychological problem, such as depression, so its cure requires treating the underlying disorder. For others, insomnia results from an overaroused biological system. A biological predisposition to insomnia may combine with distress over chronic sleeplessness to create a cycle in which biological and emotional factors reinforce one another. People may worry so much about not sleeping that their bedtime rituals, such as brushing teeth and getting dressed for bed, "become harbingers of frustration, rather than stimuli for relaxation" (Hauri, 1982). Furthermore, bad sleep habits—such as varying bedtimes—and distracting sleep settings may aggravate or even cause insomnia.

Neurophysiological researchers looking to treat insomnia have been probing the mechanisms that enable us to switch between periods of wakefulness and sleep. One recent investigation using rats identified a specific area of the hypothalamus known as the *ventrolateral preoptic nucleus (VPN)* that appears to play an important role in switching the brain between sleep and wakefulness and vice versa (Sherin et al., 1996). By way of its connections to other brain centers involved in sleep, the VPN seems to inhibit the neurotransmitters involved in wakefulness, arousal, and consciousness throughout the brain—in effect, causing us to switch from wakefulness to sleep. If these findings are confirmed, future research along this line may ultimately lead to a safe and effective treatment for insomnia.

Another sleep disorder, **apnea,** affects 2 to 4 percent of the population. This condition is associated with breathing difficulties at night: In severe cases, the victim actually stops breathing after falling asleep. When the level of carbon dioxide in the blood rises to a certain point, apnea sufferers are spurred to a state of arousal just short of waking consciousness. Because this may happen hundreds of times a night, apnea patients typically feel exhausted and fall asleep repeatedly the next day.

Too much sleep has serious repercussions as well. **Narcolepsy** is a hereditary disorder whose victims nod off without warning in the middle of a conversation or other alert activity. People with narcolepsy often experience a sudden loss of muscle tone upon expression of any sort of emotion. A joke, anger, sexual stimulation—all bring on a feeling of weakness. Another symptom of the disorder is immediate entry into REM sleep, which produces frightening hallucinations that are, in fact, dreams the person is experiencing while still partly awake. Narcolepsy is believed to arise from a defect in the central nervous system (Bassetti & Aldrich, 1996).

Night terrors, or *sleep terrors,* is a disorder affecting 1 to 6 percent of children between 4 and 12 years old (Thorpy & Glovinsky, 1987). A child experiencing a night terror suddenly sits up in bed, screaming. Sleep terrors are very different from *nightmares.* Children generally cannot be awakened from night terrors and will push away anyone trying to comfort them. Unlike nightmares, too, sleep terrors are not remembered in the morning. They occur more often if the child is very tired. Night terrors usually do not continue into adulthood; adults who have them are likely to suffer from a personality disorder or to abuse drugs or alcohol (Kales et al., 1980). Brain injuries associated with epilepsy may also contribute to night terrors in adults.

Neither nightmares nor night terrors alone are evidence of psychological problems. Anxious people have no more nightmares than other people do. And like night terrors, nightmares become less frequent with age (J. M. Wood & Bootzin, 1990). People whose nightmares stem from a traumatic experience, however, may be plagued by these terrifying nighttime episodes for years.

ARTIFICIAL ALTERATIONS IN CONSCIOUSNESS

Daydreams and dreams are the most common alterations of normal consciousness, and both occur naturally under normal conditions. Moreover, people often start daydreaming or falling asleep when sensory stimulation is reduced (for example, when the eyes are closed and/or the environment is quiet). This raises an intriguing question for scientists: What would happen if we were deprived of *all* sensory stimulation? Would we just feel deeply rested? Or would sensory deprivation affect our consciousness in more profound ways?

Sensory Deprivation

In the 1950s and 1960s, experimenters explored the effects of **sensory deprivation**—the radical reduction of sensory stimuli—on human subjects. In the initial study, done at McGill University in Montreal in the late 1950s, student volunteers spent days at a time in special sensory deprivation chambers where they were masked and bandaged to severely restrict their visual, auditory, and tactile stimulation. They were released from these constraints only for three meals a day and for trips to the bathroom. The results were dramatic. The volunteers were increasingly unable to do the mental tasks that they had set for themselves, such as reviewing their studies or thinking about papers they had to write. They grew more and more irritable and eventually began to hallucinate. When they were freed from their cubicles, they performed poorly on a number of tests in comparison with a control group given the same tests (Heron, 1957).

Subsequent research modified the techniques for studying sensory deprivation used in the McGill study (Suedfeld & Borrie, 1978). But no matter how deprivation was induced, its effects were similar. The volunteers hallucinated; they experienced altered perceptions; and they dreamed, daydreamed, and fantasized. Within a few hours of entering the sensory deprivation chamber, most of the volunteers began to pass through alternating states of drowsiness, sleep, and wakefulness. Because the distinctions among wakefulness, drowsiness, and sleep became blurred in the chamber, the volunteers found it difficult to distinguish between waking hallucinations and dreams (Suedfeld, 1975). They reported seeing flashes of light, geometrical forms, and complex images of objects or living beings, as well as hearing various noises. Some of the participants also described smelling nonexistent odors, such as tobacco smoke, and feeling that the room or they themselves were moving. When the people emerged from solitary confinement to face a battery of perceptual tests, they showed impaired color perception and reaction time. However, their visual acuity and perception of brightness remained relatively unimpaired, and some faculties, such as pain and taste sensitivity, had actually been heightened by the experience. Some of the effects described lasted for up to a day after the end of the experiment.

Meditation

For centuries, people have used various forms of **meditation** to experience an alteration in consciousness (Benson, 1975). Each form of meditation focuses the meditator's attention in a slightly different way. *Zen meditation* concentrates on respiration, for example, whereas *Sufism* relies on frenzied dancing and prayer (G. E. Schwartz, 1974). In *transcendental meditation (TM)*, practitioners intone a *mantra*, which is a sound, specially selected for a student by the teacher of TM, to keep all other images and problems at bay and allow the meditator to relax more deeply (Deikman, 1973; Schwartz, 1974).

Sensory deprivation Extreme reduction of sensory stimuli.

Meditation Any of the various methods of concentration, reflection, or focusing of thoughts undertaken to suppress the activity of the sympathetic nervous system.

Although it may at first seem like a restful escape from the demands of the everyday world, being confined to a sensory deprivation chamber for a prolonged period of time can impair cognitive functioning and cause hallucinations. This volunteer is alternating between wakefulness, drowsiness, and sleep, as is common during sensory deprivation. It is often hard to tell the difference between waking hallucinations and dreams.

Hypnosis Trancelike state in which a person responds readily to suggestions.

Meditation can help relieve anxiety and promote peace of mind and a sense of well-being.

Although hypnosis is often applied in clinical situations, psychologists disagree about whether it is really an altered state of consciousness.

In all its diverse forms, meditation suppresses the activity of the sympathetic nervous system, the part of the nervous system that prepares the body for strenuous activity during an emergency (see Chapter 2, The Biological Basis of Behavior). Meditation also lowers the rate of metabolism and reduces heart and respiratory rates. Alpha brain waves (which accompany relaxed wakefulness) increase noticeably during meditation, and there is a decrease in blood lactate, a chemical linked to stress.

Meditation has been used to treat certain medical problems, including drug abuse. Some studies have found that a high percentage of people who used drugs stopped using them after taking up meditation (Benson & Wallace, 1972).

Besides physiological benefits, people who regularly practice some form of meditation may gain emotional and even spiritual advantages: They often report increased sensory awareness, a sense of timelessness, well-being, and total relaxation (Deikman, 1973; S. R. Dean, 1970).

Hypnosis

Hypnosis, while sharing some attributes with other ASCs, has a distinct history dating back to mid-eighteenth-century Europe, where Anton Mesmer, a Viennese physician, fascinated audiences by putting patients into trances to cure their illnesses. Hence, the term *mesmerism* was first used to describe the phenomenon, though *hypnosis* has since become the preferred term (Hypnos was the Greek god of sleep). Mesmer's abilities were initially discredited by a French commission chaired by Benjamin Franklin; but in the nineteenth century, some respectable physicians revived interest in hypnosis when they discovered it could be used to treat certain forms of mental illness. Even today, however, considerable disagreement persists about how to define hypnosis and even about whether it constitutes a valid ASC.

One of the reasons for the controversy is that, from a behavioral standpoint, there is no simple definition of what it means to be hypnotized. Different individuals believed to have undergone hypnosis describe their experiences in strikingly different ways. The following quotations (Farthing, 1992, p. 349) from hypnotized subjects illustrate some of these disparities:

> "I felt as if I were 'inside' myself; none of my body was touching anything . . . "

> "I was very much aware of the split in my consciousness. One part of me was analytic and listening to you (the hypnotist). The other part was feeling the things that the analytic part decided I should have."

HYPNOTIC SUGGESTIONS   Although consciousness may be altered by hypnosis, the exact means by which this occurs and the ways in which it is felt vary from one individual to another. Some people who are told they cannot move their arms or that their pain has vanished do, in fact, experience paralysis or anesthesia; if told they are hearing a certain piece of music or are unable to hear anything, they may hallucinate or become deaf temporarily. Other hypnotized people remember events from their early childhood and say they feel as though they are experiencing those events all over again, as when a hypnotist tells a 40-year-old person that she is 6 years old. Finally, some people experience amnesia, which lingers even after they are no longer hypnotized, through instructions such as "You will remember nothing that happened under hypnosis until I tell you." In still other cases, instructions received while under hypnosis can temporarily diminish the person's desire to smoke or overeat.

CLINICAL APPLICATIONS OF HYPNOSIS   Because hypnotic susceptibility varies significantly from one person to another, its value in clinical and therapeutic settings is difficult to assess. Nevertheless, hypnosis is used in a variety of medical and counseling situations (Rhue, Lynn, & Kirsch, 1993). Although some research indicates that the use of hypnosis in conjunction with traditional forms of psychotherapy enhances the efficacy of the psychotherapeutic experience (Kirsch, Montgomery, & Sapirstein, 1995), psychologists have by no means reached agreement on this issue. Hypnosis has been found to be more effective as an anesthetic than morphine in controlling certain types of pain. Dentists have been using it as an anesthetic for years. Hypnosis has also been used to alleviate pain in children with leukemia who have to undergo repeated bone-marrow biopsies: Those who are able to imagine themselves living temporarily in a world outside their bodies can learn to tolerate this extremely painful procedure quite well (Hilgard, Hilgard, & Kaufmann, 1983).

Can hypnosis make someone change or eliminate bad habits? The jury is still out on this question. Critics point out that if people really want to change a behavior, they are likely to do so without hypnosis. Hypnosis may shore up their will, but so might joining a support group such as Weight Watchers. In other words, posthypnotic suggestions may be no more effective than other kinds of supportive help.

Psychoactive drugs Chemical substances that change moods and perceptions.

Can hypnosis really change behavior?

DRUG-ALTERED CONSCIOUSNESS

So far, our discussion has focused on ASCs produced without using drugs. Meditation, hypnosis, daydreams, sleep, and dreaming can all occur without chemical intervention. In this final section of this chapter, we will examine ASCs that are induced by **psychoactive drugs,** chemical substances that change moods and perceptions.

Since ancient times, people have used drugs to alter their consciousness for social, religious, and personal reasons. Wine is mentioned often in the Bible and plays a sacramental role in several major religions. Marijuana is alluded to in the herbal recipe book of a Chinese emperor in 2737 B.C.; and the Jivaro Indians of Ecuador, who consider the world of the senses an illusion, habitually use drugs to contact the "real world" of supernatural forces. In our own culture, the use of some substances to alter mood or behavior is, under certain circumstances, regarded as normal behavior. This includes moderate intake of alcohol and of the caffeine in coffee, tea, or cola. In some circles, illegal substances such as marijuana, cocaine, and amphetamines are used on a regular basis as well.

The problems associated with the abuse of drugs have also been recognized since ancient times. The Greeks advocated moderation in all things, including the drinking of wine, and the Bible preaches against the sin of alcohol abuse. One national survey showed that more than 60 percent of adult Americans believe that all mind-altering drug use is immoral and should be illegal ("61% of Americans," 1990). These concerns about drug abuse are not without foundation. For example, substance abuse among employees costs U.S. businesses more than $100 billion a year through absenteeism from work, lost productivity, and medical expenditures (Freudenheim, 1988). More than 15,000 Americans die every year, and more than a million more are injured, in alcohol-related car accidents. Smoking is at least partly responsible for the deaths of over a quarter of a million people each year—more than one out of every six deaths in the United States.

Substance abuse A pattern of drug use that diminishes the ability to fulfill responsibilities at home or at work or school, that results in repeated use of a drug in dangerous situations, or that leads to legal difficulties related to drug use.

Substance dependence A pattern of compulsive drug taking that results in tolerance, withdrawal symptoms, or other specific symptoms for at least a year.

Tolerance Phenomenon whereby higher doses of a drug are required to produce its original effects or to prevent withdrawal symptoms.

Withdrawal symptoms Unpleasant physical or psychological effects that follow the discontinuance of a dependence-producing substance.

Substance Use, Abuse, and Dependence

Substance abuse refers to a pattern of drug use that diminishes one's ability to fulfill responsibilities at home, at work, or at school; that results in repeated use of a drug in dangerous situations; or that leads to legal difficulties related to drug use (Oltmanns & Emery, 1995). For example, people who regularly go on drinking binges severe enough to impair their health and cause problems in their families or on the job are abusing alcohol.

The ongoing abuse of many drugs, including alcohol, may lead to compulsive use of the substance, or **substance dependence** (also known as *addiction*). Although not everyone who abuses a psychoactive substance develops dependence, dependence usually follows a period of abuse. Dependence often leads to **tolerance,** the phenomenon whereby higher doses of the drug are required to produce its original effects or to prevent **withdrawal symptoms,** the unpleasant physical or psychological effects following discontinued use of the substance.

The most recent clinical definition of dependence (APA, 1994) describes a broad pattern of drug-related behaviors characterized by at least three of the following seven symptoms over a 12-month period:

1. Developing tolerance: needing increasing amounts of the substance to gain the desired effect *or* experiencing a diminished effect when using the same amount of the substance. For example, the person might have to drink an entire six-pack to get the same effect formerly experienced after drinking just one or two beers.

2. Experiencing withdrawal symptoms—physical and psychological problems that occur if the person tries to stop using the substance. Withdrawal symptoms range from anxiety and nausea to convulsions and hallucinations.

3. Using the substance for a longer period or in greater quantities than intended.

4. Having a persistent desire or making repeated efforts to cut back on the use of the substance.

5. Devoting a great deal of time to obtaining or using the substance.

6. Giving up or reducing social, occupational, or recreational activities as a result of drug use.

7. Continuing to use the substance even in the face of ongoing or recurring physical or psychological problems likely to be caused or made worse by the use of the substance.

The causes of substance abuse and dependence are complex and generally are rooted in some combination of biological, psychological, and social factors that vary for each person and for each substance. Also keep in mind that the development of substance dependence does not follow an established timetable. One person might drink socially for years before abusing alcohol, whereas someone else might become addicted to crack (a crystalline form of cocaine) in a matter of weeks.

HOW DRUG EFFECTS ARE STUDIED   The effects of particular drugs are usually studied under carefully controlled scientific conditions. In most cases, researchers compare people's behavior before the administration of the drug to their behavior afterward, taking special precautions to ensure that any observed changes in behavior are due to the drug alone. Sometimes, simply *expecting* that a drug will yield a particular effect is enough to produce that effect. If, for example, the active ingredient is removed from marijuana or the caffeine is removed from coffee, participants in a study of those drugs will act just as though they had actually ingested marijuana or caffeine! Similarly, if experimenters expect that alcohol will slow down behavior, they are more likely to look for and observe that phenomenon in research participants who consume alcohol.

To eliminate sources of research error, most drug researchers use the *double-blind procedure*, in which some research participants receive the active drug, and others take an inactive substance called a *placebo*. In the double-blind procedure neither the researcher *nor* the participants know which people take the active drug and which get the placebo. After data are collected, the researcher compares the behavior of those who unknowingly took the placebo. Then, if the groups differ in their behavior, the cause is likely to be the active ingredient in the drug.

Studying drug-altered consciousness is complicated as well because most drugs not only affect different people in different ways but also produce different effects in the same person from one occasion to another or from one setting to another. For example, some people are powerfully affected by even small amounts of alcohol, whereas others are not. And drinking alcohol in a social setting usually produces somewhat different effects than does consuming alcohol under the watchful eye of a scientist! Researchers must carefully control all these variables to ensure that the observed drug effects reflect only those of the chemical under scrutiny.

Recently, sophisticated neuroimaging procedures have also proved useful in the study of drug effects. Techniques such as PET imaging have enabled researchers to isolate specific differences between the brains of addicted and nonaddicted people. For example, one researcher found that the "addicted brain" is qualitatively different from the nonaddicted brain in a variety of ways, including metabolism and responsiveness to environmental cues (Leshner, 1996). Other investigators have focused on the role played by neurotransmitters in the addictive process, noting that every addictive drug causes dopamine levels in the brain to increase (Glassman & Koob, 1996). Results like these will undoubtedly one day provide not only a better understanding of the biological basis of addiction, but suggest more effective treatments for dealing with it.

In assessing the effects of particular drugs, it is convenient to group them into the categories of *depressants*, *stimulants*, and *hallucinogens*. Even though these are not rigid categories, this division helps organize our knowledge about drugs.

Depressants: Alcohol, Barbiturates, the Opiates

Depressants are chemicals that retard behavior and thinking by either speeding up or slowing down nerve impulses. Generally speaking, alcohol, barbiturates, and the opiates have depressant effects.

ALCOHOL   Our society recognizes many appropriate occasions for the consumption of alcohol: to celebrate milestone events, to break down social isolation and inhibitions, and to promote group harmony. Perhaps because of its social acceptability and legality, **alcohol** is widely used in our society. Much of this drinking is done by American youth, despite age restrictions on the purchase and consumption of alcohol (see Figure 4–4).

Depressants Chemicals that slow down behavior or cognitive processes.

Alcohol Depressant that is the intoxicating ingredient in whiskey, beer, wine, and other fermented or distilled liquors.

Since ancient times people have recognized the problems associated with alcohol abuse. Excessive drinking and public drunkenness have been widely frowned upon in many cultures. In this etching, Gin Lane, by the eighteenth-century English artist William Hogarth, a baby slips carelessly from the arms of a drunken mother.

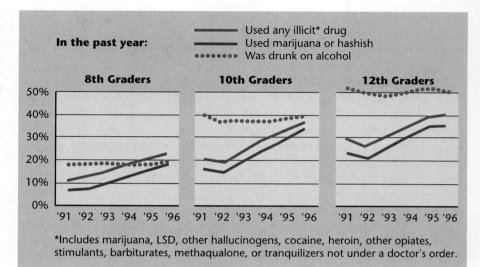

Figure 4–4
Teenage drug use.
A national survey conducted in 1996 found that the use of illegal drugs and alcohol by American teenagers continues to grow. Among high school seniors, 40 percent reported that they used an illegal drug in the previous year. Over 20 percent of 8th graders admitted to drug use, up from 10 percent just 5 years earlier. In this group, 20 percent reported getting drunk during the past year. Among 12th graders, that number rises to 50 percent.

Source: Adapted from a study conducted by the University of Michigan and reported in *The New York Times,* December 20, 1996, p. A8.

The social costs of abusing alcohol are high. Alcohol is implicated in more than two-thirds of all fatal automobile accidents, two-thirds of all murders, two-thirds of all spouse beatings, and more than half of all cases of violent child abuse. Moreover, the use of alcohol during pregnancy has been linked to a variety of birth defects, the most notable being *fetal alcohol syndrome*, which will be addressed more fully in Chapter 10, Life Span Development. Alcohol abuse costs society more than $100 billion a year through lost productivity, crime, accidents, and medical treatment (Steele & Josephs, 1990). A study conducted by the National Institute on Alcohol Abuse and Alcoholism (NIAAA) found that more than 40 percent of all "heavy drinkers" die before the age of 65 (compared to less than 20 percent of nondrinkers), and that even light to moderate drinking is associated with shorter life spans ("Study Links," 1990). In addition, there is the untold cost in psychological trauma suffered by the nearly 30 million children of alcohol abusers.

Its dangers notwithstanding, alcohol continues to be a popular drug because of its short-term effects. As a depressant, it calms down the nervous system very much like a general anesthetic (McKim, 1997). Thus, some people consume alcohol to relax, to enhance their mood, to put them at ease in social situations, and to relieve the stress and anxiety of everyday living (Steele & Josephs, 1990). Paradoxically, although it is a depressant, alcohol is often experienced subjectively as a stimulant because it inhibits centers in the brain that govern critical judgment and impulsive behavior. To drinkers, the long-term negative consequences of alcoholism pale beside the short-term positive consequences, such as the sense that alcohol makes them feel more courageous, less inhibited, and more spontaneous (Steele & Josephs, 1990).

A study by Muriel Vogel-Sprott (1967) demonstrated the strength of these short-term effects of alcohol. Vogel-Sprott conducted an experiment in which the participants received both painful shocks and money for engaging in certain behaviors. Some of the participants were given alcohol before the experiment began; others received a placebo. The people who received a placebo sharply reduced the behaviors that caused them to receive shocks—the money just wasn't worth the pain. But the people under the influence of alcohol showed no such inhibition—they weathered the shocks to get the money. Apparently, the negative consequences of their behavior (the shocks) did not dissuade them from pursuing the painful course of action. The term *alcohol myopia* was coined to refer to the alcohol-induced shortsightedness that makes drinkers oblivious to many behavioral cues in the environment and less able to make sense of those cues they do perceive (Steele & Josephs, 1990).

Several dozen research studies have clearly demonstrated that alcohol use is correlated with an increase in aggression, hostility, violence, and abusive behavior (Bushman, 1993; Bushman & Cooper, 1990; Ito, Miller, & Pollock, 1996). In all these studies, alcohol dulled the effects of environmental cues to proper behavior and made the users less aware of and less concerned about the negative consequences of their actions.

Physiologically, alcohol first affects the frontal lobes of the brain (Adams & Johnson-Greene, 1995), which figure prominently in inhibitions, impulse control, reasoning, and judgment. As consumption continues, alcohol impairs functions of the cerebellum, the center of motor control and balance (Johnson-Greene et al., 1997). Eventually, alcohol consumption affects the spinal cord and medulla, which regulate such involuntary functions as breathing, body temperature, and heart rate. A blood-alcohol level of 0.25 percent or more may cause this part of the nervous system to shut down and severely impairs functioning; slightly higher levels can cause death from alcohol poisoning (see Table 4–1).

Alcohol compromises perception, motor processes, and memory. It diminishes visual acuity, depth perception, and the perception of the differences

Statistics show that alcohol use is a major cause of car accidents. It was implicated in the fatal crash of the car carrying Princess Diana.

TABLE 4-1	
THE BEHAVIORAL EFFECTS OF BLOOD-ALCOHOL LEVELS	
Levels of Alcohol in the Blood	**Behavioral Effects**
0.05%	Feels good; less alert
0.10%	Slower to react; less cautious
0.15%	Reaction time much slower
0.20%	Sensory-motor abilities suppressed
0.25%	Staggering (motor abilities severely impaired); perception is limited as well
0.30%	Semistupor
0.35%	Level for anesthesia; death is possible
0.40%	Death is likely (usually as a result of respiratory failure)

Source: Data from *Drugs, Society, and Human Behavior* (3 ed.) by Oakey Ray, 1983, St. Louis: The C. V. Mosby Co.

between bright lights and colors; interestingly, it seems to improve the ability to perceive dim lights. Alcohol also impairs spatial-cognitive functioning—clearly necessary for the safe navigation and operation of an automobile (Matthews et al., 1996). Some aspects of hearing, such as the perception of loudness, are not affected by alcohol consumption, but the ability to discriminate between different rhythms and pitches is impaired by just a single dose of the drug. Smell and taste perception are uniformly diminished, and the perception of time also becomes distorted. Most people report that time seems to pass more quickly when they are "under the influence" (National Commission on Marijuana and Drug Abuse [NCMDA], 1973b).

Alcohol interferes with memory storage: People find it difficult to recall what happened after having only two or three drinks (E. S. Parker, Birnbaum, & Noble, 1976). Prolonged drinking impairs retrieval of memories—that is, heavy drinkers have difficulty recalling memories they once could retrieve easily. In heavy drinkers, alcohol may also produce *blackouts*, which make them unable to remember any of the events that occurred when they were drinking.

Does alcohol have a stronger impact on women than on men? Yes, partly because the same quantity of alcohol will have more wide-ranging consequences for a lighter person than for a heavier person. Because women generally weigh less than men, the same dose of alcohol has a stronger effect on the average woman than on the average man (York & Welte, 1994). But research has shown that even when the element of weight is canceled out, a given dose of alcohol has a more pronounced effect on women than on men. Why? It turns out that the amount of alcohol reaching the bloodstream is regulated by an enzyme in the stomach. The more of this enzyme the body contains, the smaller the quantity of alcohol that passes through the stomach into the bloodstream, where it spreads throughout the body. Most women have less of this stomach enzyme than men do, so more alcohol reaches their bloodstream. (In similar fashion, drinking alcohol on an empty stomach has more pronounced effects because less of this enzyme is present in an empty stomach [Frezza et al., 1990].) Putting these facts together, we can conclude that one drink is likely to have the same biological and psychological effects on the average woman as two drinks on the average man.

Despite its social and legal acceptance, alcohol is a highly addictive drug with potentially devastating long-term effects. Approximately 13 percent of U.S. adults (about 20 million people) either abuse alcohol or are dependent on it, making alcohol abuse and dependence the most serious substance-abuse problem in the United States (see *Applying Psychology*). One study found the rate of alcohol dependence among men between the ages of 18 and 44 to be 27 percent. Long-term abuse of alcohol can cause memory loss, decreased sexual drive or impotence, menstrual problems, liver and kidney damage, damage to the stomach and intestine, cancers of the mouth and esophagus, anxiety, insomnia, and brain damage. Long-term heavy use may also bring on a form of mental illness known as Korsakoff's syndrome, which is characterized by hallucinations, confusion, and severe memory problems (Bowden, 1990; see a more in-depth discussion of this topic in Chapter 7, Memory). Ultimately, chronic abuse of alcohol may lead to death: Approximately 100,000 Americans die each year as a result of using alcohol with other drugs or from alcohol-related breathing difficulties, heart failure, pneumonia, automobile accidents, and suicide (Van Natta et al., 1985).

Are some people especially prone to alcohol abuse? To fully understand the causes of alcoholism and other drug addictions, we need to take account of a wide variety of factors: heredity, personality, social setting, and culture (Zucker & Gomberg, 1990). Children whose parents do not use alcohol tend to abstain or to drink only moderately; to a lesser extent, children

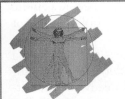

APPLYING PSYCHOLOGY
WHAT ARE THE SIGNS OF ALCOHOLISM?

The following test, excerpted from a self-test published by the National Council on Alcoholism, points out many of the common symptoms of alcoholism. It will help you determine whether you or someone you know needs to find out more about alcoholism, but it should not be used to establish a diagnosis of alcoholism.

1. Do you ever drink heavily when you are disappointed, under pressure, or have had a quarrel with someone?
2. Can you handle more alcohol now than when you first started to drink?
3. Have you ever been unable to remember part of an evening when you were drinking, even though your friends say you didn't pass out?
4. When drinking with other people, do you try to put away a few extra drinks the others won't know about?
5. Has a family member or close friend ever expressed concern or complained about your drinking?
6. Have you been having more memory "blackouts" recently?
7. Do you often want to continue drinking after your friends say they've had enough?
8. Do you usually have a reason for the occasions when you drink heavily?
9. When you're sober, do you sometimes regret things you did or said while drinking?
10. Have you tried switching brands or drinks, or following different plans to control your drinking?
11. Have you sometimes failed to keep promises you made to yourself about controlling or cutting down on your drinking?

If your answer to any of these questions is "yes," you may be at risk for alcoholism. More than one affirmative answer may signal an alcohol-related problem and the need to consult with an alcoholism counselor. To find out more, contact the National Council on Alcoholism and Drug Dependence in your area.

To learn more about drug addiction or for help in dealing with an addiction, call or e-mail the following organizations:

National Council on Alcoholism
(800) 622-2255

Alcoholics Anonymous
http://www.alcoholics-anonymous.org/

National Institute of Drug Abuse
(800) COCAINE
http://www.nida.nih.gov

American Cancer Society (nicotine)
(800) 227-2345
http://www.cancer.org/smoking.html

Additional resources can be found on our website,
www.prenhall.com/morris

whose parents abuse alcohol tend to drink heavily (Gordis, 1996; Harburg, DiFranceisco et al., 1990; Harburg, Gleiberman et al., 1990). These findings could point to either cultural or hereditary factors, but there is some direct evidence of a genetic basis for alcohol abuse. Identical twins are far more likely to have similar drinking patterns than are fraternal twins. Moreover, people whose biological parents have alcohol-abuse problems are likely to abuse alcohol even if they are adopted and raised by people who do not abuse alcohol (Gordis, 1996; McGue, 1993).

Psychologists have reached no consensus on the exact role heredity plays in the propensity for alcoholism. Some point to hereditary differences in levels of the stomach enzyme mentioned earlier, deducing that people born with higher levels of the enzyme have to drink more alcohol to achieve the same psychological effects as those with lower levels of the enzyme. People also appear to differ genetically in their tolerance for alcohol in the

Barbiturates Potentially deadly depressants, first used for their sedative and anticonvulsant properties, now used only to treat such conditions as epilepsy and arthritis.

Opiates Drugs, such as opium and heroin, derived from the opium poppy, that dull the senses and induce feelings of euphoria, well-being, and relaxation. Synthetic drugs resembling opium derivatives are also classified as opiates.

Nineteenth-century immigrants to the United States are shown gambling and smoking opium pipes at a clubhouse in New York's Chinatown. Problems associated with abuse of this drug led to it being banned for nonmedical use early in the twentieth century.

blood and in the ways they react to alcohol, although the specific genetic mechanism that may put people at risk for developing alcoholism has not been identified (Bolos et al., 1990; Gordis, 1996).

Other researchers cite nonbiological factors as the keys in determining who is likely to abuse alcohol. Some researchers have identified an "alcoholic personality," one that is emotionally immature and needy, low in self-esteem, and unable to tolerate frustration well (Coleman et al., 1984). But this personality profile falls short of fully accounting for alcoholism because many people who have these characteristics do not abuse alcohol. Another line of research holds that specific psychological disorders underlie the propensity for addiction to alcohol and other drugs. According to this view, people who are so cut off from their own feelings that they are unable to form relationships with others are likely to be attracted to alcohol because it helps them experience and express affection, aggression, and closeness. By contrast, people who are depressed or hyperactive are more likely to be drawn to stimulants such as amphetamines, and people who have difficulty controlling their anger and hostility favor the opiates (Khantzian, 1990).

Culture, too, may steer people toward or away from alcoholism. Parents and spouses may introduce people to a pattern of heavy drinking. Alcohol is also more acceptable in some cultures than in others. For example, Orthodox Jews, who frown on the use of alcohol, and Muslims, who prohibit it, have low rates of alcoholism.

BARBITURATES Commonly known as "downers," **barbiturates** include such medications as Amytal, Nembutal, and Seconal. Developed about a century ago, this class of depressants was first prescribed for its sedative and anticonvulsant qualities. But when researchers realized that barbiturates had potentially deadly effects—particularly in combination with alcohol—their use declined in the 1950s. At the same time, pharmaceutical companies introduced a new group of sedatives—the "minor tranquilizers," which include the widely prescribed drug Valium. Nonetheless, barbiturates are sometimes used today to treat such diverse conditions as insomnia, anxiety, epilepsy, arthritis, and bedwetting (Reinisch & Sanders, 1982).

The effects of barbiturates bear striking similarities to those of alcohol: Taken on an empty stomach, 150 mg will cause lightheadedness, silliness, and poor motor coordination (McKim, 1997). Larger doses—400 mg to 700 mg—may bring on such effects as slurred speech, loss of inhibition, and increases in aggressive behavior (Aston, 1972). As with alcohol, the effect of the drug varies from one setting to another: A dose that prompts aggressive behavior at a party may cause only drowsiness when taken at home. Like alcohol, barbiturates can cause birth defects when taken during pregnancy (Wilder & Bruni, 1981).

Though often prescribed to help people sleep, barbiturates actually disrupt the body's natural sleep patterns and cause dependence when used for long periods. Frequently prescribed for elderly people, who tend to take them chronically along with their other medications, barbiturates may produce significant negative side effects such as confusion and anxiety (Celis, 1994).

THE OPIATES Although heroin is the best known of the **opiates**—a group of substances derived from the opium poppy or synthetic substances resembling it—it is a relative newcomer on the scene. A Sumerian tablet from 4,000 B.C. refers to a "joy plant" that is thought to have been the poppy plant, from which the drug opium is derived. Ancient Greek and Roman physicians prescribed opium for a number of conditions. Among royalty, it was a popular poison for killing rivals. The use of opium spread from the Middle East into China, where for centuries its uses were primarily medicinal. However, in 1644, when tobacco smoking was banned by the Chinese emperor, smokers replaced the tobacco in their pipes with opium, and the use of the drug to produce an altered state of consciousness was firmly established.

In the United States, during most of the nineteenth century and into the early part of the twentieth century, opium was a widely used ingredient in a variety of over-the-counter (patent) medicines. Chiefly in the form of *laudanum*—opium dissolved in alcohol—the drug was used to treat a variety of ailments and was marketed under such innocuous names as "Mrs. Winslow's Soothing Syrup" and "Street's Infant Quietness." In this same period, the drug morphine (named after Morpheus, the Greek god of dreams) was chemically isolated from opium, and it, too, was relatively easy to obtain (although a prescription was required). By the latter part of the nineteenth century, people had recognized that opiates were highly addictive. Ironically, heroin—a further refinement of opium developed in 1898—was originally proposed as a cure for morphine addiction. Although the nonmedicinal distribution of opiates was banned early in this century, opiate dependence remained a social problem and appears to be on the rise today (Kantrowitz et al., 1993).

Initially, the opiates produce subjective feelings of euphoria, well-being, and relaxation. However, controlled studies reveal that these pleasant effects are short-lived and are quickly replaced by undesirable changes in mood and behavior (Meyer & Mirin, 1979).

Extremely unpleasant withdrawal symptoms follow discontinuance of heroin. The first symptom of withdrawal is restlessness, accompanied by fits of yawning, chills, and hot flashes. The skin often breaks out into goose bumps resembling the texture of a plucked turkey (hence the term "cold turkey"). This is generally followed by periods of prolonged sleep lasting up to 12 hours. When awake, the addict experiences severe cramps, vomiting, and diarrhea, along with convulsive shaking and kicking. All this is accompanied by profuse sweating. In about a week's time, the withdrawal symptoms diminish and then disappear.

Heroin addicts must take larger and larger doses to obtain the same positive mood-altering effects they did when they first used the drug. Lesser doses simply provide some limited relief from the terrible pains of withdrawal. In advanced stages of addiction, heroin becomes less a means to alter consciousness than a painkiller to stave off withdrawal symptoms. Because heroin is illegal and expensive, addicts must spend a great deal of time—often engaged in criminal activities—obtaining the wherewithal to buy it. These factors underlie policy makers' concerns about heroin as a social problem.

Stimulants: Caffeine, Nicotine, Amphetamines, and Cocaine

The drugs classified as **stimulants**—caffeine, nicotine, amphetamines, and cocaine—have legitimate uses, but because they produce feelings of optimism and boundless energy, the potential for abuse is high. Coffee and cigarettes contain powerful mind-altering drugs. Aside from their harmful physical effects, they share many characteristics of the "more serious" drugs we have been examining. Caffeine, which occurs naturally in coffee, tea, and cocoa, belongs to a class of drugs known as *xanthine stimulants*. Nicotine, which occurs naturally only in tobacco, also has stimulant effects, although, paradoxically, at higher doses it acts as a depressant.

Stimulants Drugs, including amphetamines and cocaine, that stimulate the sympathetic nervous system and produce feelings of optimism and boundless energy.

CAFFEINE Although caffeine is popularly believed to maintain wakefulness and alertness, many of its stimulant effects are illusory. In one study, the participants were asked to perform a series of motor and perceptual tasks after taking a dose of caffeine. All thought they were doing better when they were on caffeine, but their actual performance was no better than it had been without caffeine. The primary ingredient in over-the-counter stimulants, caffeine reduces the total number of sleep minutes and increases the time it takes to fall asleep. Interestingly, it is the only stimulant that does not appear to alter sleep stages or cause REM rebound, making it much safer than amphetamines.

Caffeine is generally considered a benign drug, although large doses— more than 600 mg a day (see Figure 4–5), the equivalent of five or six cups of coffee—may cause *caffeinism,* or "coffee nerves." Symptoms include anxiety, headaches, heart palpitations, insomnia, and diarrhea. Because caffeine works in part by suppressing the transmission of naturally occurring chemicals that have calming effects, it also interferes with the action of prescribed medications such as tranquilizers and sedatives. Moreover, caffeine appears to aggravate the symptoms of many psychiatric disorders. Without the knowledge of either patients or staff, researchers switched patients on a psychiatric ward to decaffeinated coffee (DeFreitas & Schwartz, 1979). Following the switch, they observed a decrease in symptoms such as anxiety and an increase in socially appropriate behavior. These effects were reversed when regular coffee was served once again. Many coffee drinkers are dependent on caffeine and experience headaches, lethargy, and depression if they stop consuming it.

NICOTINE Nicotine is far more dangerous than caffeine. Besides immediate effects of increased heart rate and constricted blood cells, which cause smokers to lose skin color and to have cold hands, it accelerates the process of wrinkling and aging (Daniell, 1971). Its long-term physical effects include placing users at increased risk for lung cancer and other cancers as well as for cardiovascular disease and blindness (Seddon et al., 1996). Nicotine increases levels of endorphins, norepinephrine, and acetylcholine in the nervous system (see Chapter 2, The Biological Basis of Behavior); it also

Figure 4–5
The amount of caffeine in some common preparations.
Caffeine occurs in varying amounts in coffee, tea, soft drinks, and many nonprescription medications. Americans consume about 200 mg of caffeine each day.

Source: Copyright © 1991 by the New York Times Company. Reprinted by permission.

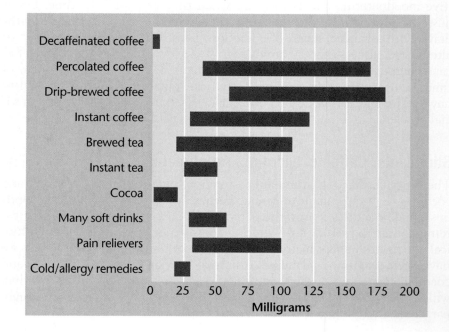

raises levels of dopamine in the areas of the brain affecting mood (Brandon, 1994). Furthermore, recent studies probing the neurochemical properties of nicotine determined that its addictiveness probably stems from its neurobiological similarity to such drugs as cocaine, amphetamines, and morphine—all of which have strong additive properties (Glassman & Koob, 1996; Pontieri et al., 1996). When ingested through smoking, nicotine tends to arrive at the brain all at once following each puff. This rush, which is similar to the "high" experienced by heroin users, makes the brain crave even more nicotine.

Users tend to become highly dependent on nicotine. In one study, smokers were required to pull a plunger a number of times in order to take a puff of a cigarette. When the number of pulls required to get a puff was gradually increased, most of the participants simply inhaled more during each puff. One subject pulled the plunger 14,000 times over 45 minutes to get just two puffs of tobacco (T. Adler, 1993a).

This research shows how strong the craving for nicotine is and how difficult it is to quit. The withdrawal symptoms for nicotine users include nervousness, insomnia and drowsiness, head-aches, irritability, and an intense craving for nicotine (Brandon, 1994). Research on treatment outcomes indicates that as few as 15 percent of smokers manage to quit permanently.

AMPHETAMINES   Although reports of amphetamine-like substances date back more than 5,000 years, researchers did not discover the medicinal value of amphetamines until the early part of the twentieth century. At the chemical level, **amphetamines** resemble epinephrine, a neurotransmitter that stimulates the sympathetic nervous system (see Chapter 2, The Biological Basis of Behavior). Because of this chemical similarity, amphetamines have been used to treat asthma: They open respiratory passages and ease breathing. Amphetamines have also been prescribed for narcolepsy because of their stimulant qualities. The popularity of amphetamines stems from their wide use by the military during World War II. Truck drivers and students also came to rely on amphetamines to stay awake and alert. And because amphetamines tend to suppress the appetite, they were widely used for a time as "diet pills."

However, these drugs have a tremendous potential for abuse because of their effects on consciousness and behavior. One of their side effects is the ability to make people feel happy. Higher doses increase this effect, and when injected, users report "rushes" of euphoria. But after the drug's initial effects wear off, users may experience a "crash" and subsequent severe depression (Gunne & Anggard, 1972). To avoid this unpleasant experience, users tend to take more amphetamines, leading to a condition called *amphetamine psychosis*, similar to paranoid schizophrenia and characterized by delusions, hallucinations, and paranoia. Habitual amphetamine use can also lead to aggressive and violent behavior, caused not so much by the drug itself as by the profound personality changes—particularly paranoia—that accompany excessive use (Leccese, 1991).

Recently, the illegal use of *methamphetamines*—one of the amphetamine derivatives known on the street as *MDMA* or *Ecstasy*—has increased among college students. The people who take methamphetamines report an extraordinary loss of inhibition in addition to the euphoria and increased energy associated with amphetamine use. Unfortunately, evidence suggests that even short-term excessive use of the methamphetamines may have *long-term* harmful consequences, affecting sleep, mood, appetite, and impulsiveness by damaging the neuroconnections between lower brain centers and the cortex (McCann, Slate, & Ricaurte, 1996).

Amphetamines Stimulant drugs that initially produce "rushes" of euphoria often followed by sudden "crashes" and, sometimes, severe depression.

Cocaine Drug derived from the coca plant that, while producing a sense of euphoria by stimulating the sympathetic nervous system, also leads to anxiety, depression, and addictive cravings.

The label "dope fiend" more accurately describes the behavior of amphetamine addicts than that of heroin addicts. Because of the addictive potential of amphetamines, their medicinal use is now restricted to the treatment of narcolepsy and hyperactivity in children.

COCAINE   Cocaine is also a stimulant and, like the amphetamines, can bring on euphoric moods. Cocaine is extracted from the leaves of the coca bush, which is native to the Andes Mountains in South America. The original method for ingesting this drug, which is still practiced today in South America, involves chewing the leaves of the coca bush. The Spanish conquistadors used coca to pay laborers on plantations and in gold and silver mines because they found they could extract more labor from workers under the stimulant effects of the drug. At the same time, they could cut down on food rations, because the drug suppresses the appetite (McKim, 1997).

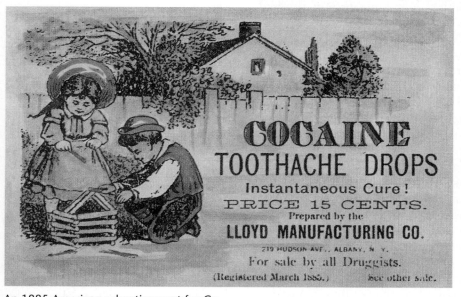

An 1885 American advertisement for Cocaine Toothache Drops, obviously intended for young children as well as adults. The addition of cocaine to everyday products, including Coca-Cola, was quite common in the nineteenth century.

Among Europeans, the drug remained largely unknown until the mid-nineteenth century when it became popular to blend coca with wine and other drinks. The Coca-Cola Company used chemically active coca leaves in its original formula. To this day, Coca-Cola—and other colas—are blended with coca leaves from which the active ingredient has been removed. Among the more famous users of cocaine was Sigmund Freud, who had very positive personal experiences with the drug and recommended its use to his friends and relatives. He also promoted it as a cure for alcoholism and morphine addiction. Eventually, Freud became disillusioned with the drug, but one of his colleagues developed what is still the only legitimate medical use for cocaine—as a local anesthetic (Novocain is the familiar form).

The use of cocaine as a recreational drug gradually declined in the first half of the twentieth century, partly because cocaine was associated in the popular culture with the opiates, even though it is chemically quite distinct from them. In recent decades, however, cocaine use became more widespread, particularly in its crystalline form, known as "crack," which can be smoked easily in a pipe or cigarette. What makes crack such a serious problem is that many users report becoming dependent on the drug almost immediately; in addition, because of how the drug acts on the brain, the craving for it is difficult to break.

The effects of cocaine mirror those of the amphetamines, although they are shorter in duration. The effects of crack, however, are even faster and more intense than those produced by amphetamines. Along with the feelings of euphoria, increased energy, and perceived clarity of thought, physiological effects include stimulation of the sympathetic nervous system, an increase in heart rate and blood pressure, and constriction of the blood vessels. Large doses also raise the body temperature and dilate the pupils. After relatively large doses wear off, some users experience a "crash" characterized by anxiety, depression, and a strong craving for more cocaine. In one survey of habitual users, one-third to one-half reported experiencing such mood and behavioral symptoms as paranoia, visual hallucinations, cravings for the drug, and attention and concentration problems (R. K. Siegel, 1982). When smoked as crack, molecules of cocaine reach the brain in less than 10 seconds, producing a high that lasts from 5 to 20 minutes and is followed by a swift and equally intense depression. Crack and cocaine stimulate a pleasure center in the base of the brain—an area that, as we will see in Chapter 9 (Motivation and Emotion), governs our emotions. As the levels of cocaine in the brain drop, users begin to feel depressed and anxious. With crack, this pleasureless state begins to set in within 30 minutes. Because cocaine interferes with the chemistry of this pleasure center in the brain, and subsequently with the brain's ability to reestablish emotional balance, the craving for the drug is doubly painful and difficult to overcome. The compulsion to take more and more of this expensive drug may impoverish even wealthy users.

Cocaine use creates problems not only for users but also for their unborn children. Women addicted to crack and cocaine often give birth to premature, low-birth-weight babies.

Hallucinogens and Marijuana

The hallucinogens include lysergic acid diethylamide (LSD, also known as "acid"), mescaline, peyote, psilocybin, and phencyclidine (PCP, or "angel dust"). Marijuana is sometimes included in this group, although its effects are normally less powerful. Even in very small doses, these drugs often produce striking visual effects that resemble hallucinations, giving rise to the term *hallucinogen*. Although many other drugs will, in large enough doses, also bring on hallucinatory or delusional experiences, mimicking those that occur in severe mental illnesses, hallucinogens do so in far less than toxic quantities.

HALLUCINOGENS   Many of the **hallucinogens** occur in natural forms such as mushrooms and other fungi. In natural form, they share with other consciousness-altering drugs an ancient history. Mescaline, for example, occurs in the peyote cactus, and historians believe that it has been used for at least 8,000 years by Native Americans.

By contrast, the story of **lysergic acid diethylamide (LSD),** the drug that triggered the current interest in the hallucinogens, begins in the 20th century. In 1943, an American pharmacologist synthesized LSD, and after ingesting it, he reported experiencing "an uninterrupted stream of fantastic pictures and extraordinary shapes with an intense, kaleidoscopic play of colors." His report led others to experiment with LSD as a means of altering normal consciousness. In the 1960s, the development of LSD as a street drug was prompted in large part by Timothy Leary, a Harvard psychologist who, after trying the chemically related drug psilocybin, began spreading what became the gospel of the 1960s hippie movement—"Turn On, Tune In, Drop Out." After a steady decline in use since the 1970s, LSD and marijuana have recently become popular once again with high school and college students (Janofsky, 1994).

The use of LSD changes auditory perceptions in a variety of ways. Some people report hearing imaginary conversations, fully orchestrated original symphonies, or foreign languages previously unknown to them. Auditory acuity may be increased, making the person keenly aware of low sounds like breathing, heartbeat, and the light rustle of leaves in the wind.

Unlike depressants and stimulants, LSD and the other hallucinogens appear to produce no withdrawal effects in the user. On the other hand, tolerance builds up quite rapidly: If LSD is taken repeatedly, after a few days no amount of the drug will produce its usual effects until administration is halted for about a week (McKim, 1997). This rapid development of tolerance is a built-in deterrent to continuous use—a fact that helps explain why

Hallucinogens Any of a number of drugs, such as LSD and mescaline, that distort visual and auditory perception.

Lysergic acid diethylamide (LSD) Hallucinogenic or "psychedelic" drug that produces hallucinations and delusions similar to those occurring in a psychotic state.

These Native-American women in Mexico are grinding dry peyote that will be mixed with water and drunk during an upcoming festival. Many Native-American peoples have traditionally included peyote in their religious ceremonies.

Marijuana A mild hallucinogen that produces a "high" often characterized by feelings of euphoria, a sense of well-being, and swings in mood from gaiety to relaxation; may also cause feelings of anxiety and paranoia.

LSD is generally taken episodically rather than habitually. After a time, users seem to get tired of the experience and decrease or discontinue their use of the drug, at least for a period of time.

One strong negative effect of some hallucinogens is "bad trips," or unpleasant experiences that may be set off by a change in dosage or an alteration in setting or mood. During a bad trip, the user may not realize that the experiences are being caused by the drug, and panic may set in. More serious are the stories of users who kill themselves because the drug makes them think they can fly out a window or who commit murders while under the influence of the drug. *Flashbacks*, or recurrences of hallucinations that occur weeks after ingesting LSD, are also relatively common. Other consequences include memory loss, paranoia, panic attacks, nightmares, and aggression (Seligmann et al., 1992).

MARIJUANA **Marijuana,** a drug produced from the *cannabis* plant, was cultivated as far back as 5,000 years ago in China. The ancient Greeks also were aware of its existence, and it has been used in India for centuries because of its intoxicating effects. Only in this century did it become popular in the United States. Currently, marijuana is the fourth most popular drug among students, after alcohol, caffeine, and nicotine (Treaster, 1994). Figure 4–4 shows the increase in marijuana use by adolescents in recent years.

Although the active ingredient in marijuana, *tetrahydrocannabinol (THC)*, shares some chemical properties with hallucinogens like LSD, it is far less potent and affects consciousness much less profoundly. The marijuana "high" is often marked by euphoric feelings and a sense of well-being accompanied by swings from gaiety to relaxation. But some people experience feelings of anxiety and paranoia. Whether the user is suffused with happiness or filled with anxiety and paranoia depends in large part on the overall setting and the mood of others in that setting. Indeed, one team of researchers notes that the experience a person initially has with marijuana is predictive of their continued use (E. S. Davidson & Schenk, 1994). These researchers found that college students who reported a positive first experience with the drug were more likely to use it sooner on a second occasion, and more likely to begin using it regularly sooner than those who had a less positive initial experience.

Marijuana induces a number of physiological effects. It dilates the blood vessels in the eyes, making the eyes appear bloodshot. Because it is generally smoked, users frequently experience a dry mouth and coughing, as well as increased thirst and hunger and mild muscular weakness, often in the form of drooping eyelids (Donatelle & Davis, 1993). Among the drug's psychological effects is a distortion of time, which has been confirmed under experimental conditions (Chait & Pierri, 1992). In addition, marijuana may produce alterations in attention and memory, including an inability to concentrate on many types of tasks—an observation that contributes to concern about people's ability to drive a car under the influence of marijuana (Chait & Pierri, 1992). One-third of car-accident victims admitted to the trauma unit of one hospital had noticeable levels of THC in their blood (Donatelle & Davis, 1993).

Marijuana use has also been shown to interfere with short-term memory. Oftentimes users cannot retain information for later use (Hollister, 1986), which triggers anxiety and even panic (Leccese, 1991). While under the influence of marijuana, people often lose the ability to remember and coordinate information, a phenomenon known as *temporal disintegration*. For instance, it would not be uncommon for people who had just smoked marijuana to forget what they were talking about in mid-sentence.

DRUGS: CHARACTERISTICS AND EFFECTS

	Typical Effects	Effects of Overdose	Tolerance/Dependence
Depressants			
Alcohol	Biphasic; tension-reduction "high," followed by depressed physical and psychological functioning.	Disorientation, loss of consciousness, death at extremely high blood-alcohol levels.	Tolerance; physical and psychological dependence; withdrawal symptoms.
Barbiturates Tranquilizers	Depressed reflexes and impaired motor functioning, tension reduction.	Shallow respiration, clammy skin, dilated pupils, weak and rapid pulse, coma, possible death.	Tolerance; high psychological and physical dependence on barbiturates, low to moderate physical dependence on such tranquilizers as Valium, although high psychological dependence; withdrawal symptoms.
Opiates	Euphoria, drowsiness, "rush" of pleasure, little impairment of psychological functions.	Slow shallow breathing, clammy skin, nausea, vomiting, pinpoint pupils, convulsions, coma, possible death.	High tolerance; physical and psychological dependence; severe withdrawal symptoms.
Stimulants			
Amphetamines Cocaine Caffeine Nicotine	Increased alertness, excitation, euphoria, increased pulse rate and blood pressure, sleeplessness.	For amphetamines and cocaine: agitation and, with chronic high doses, hallucinations (e.g., "cocaine bugs"), paranoid delusions, convulsions, death. For caffeine and nicotine: restlessness, insomnia, rambling thoughts, heart arrhythmia, possible circulatory failure. For nicotine: increased blood pressure.	For amphetamines, cocaine and nicotine: tolerance, psychological and physical dependence. For caffeine: physical and psychological dependence; withdrawal symptoms.
Hallucinogens			
LSD	Illusions, hallucinations, distortions in time perception, loss of contact with reality.	Psychotic reactions.	No physical dependence for LSD; degree of psychological dependence unknown for LSD.
Marijuana	Euphoria, relaxed inhibitions, increased appetite, possible disorientation.	Fatigue, disoriented behavior, possible psychosis.	Psychological dependence.

One recent study found that heavy marijuana use—defined as smoking marijuana at least two out of every three days—continued to affect performance even after the immediate effects of the drug had worn off (Block, 1996). This study, which compared the performance of college students a full day after going without the drug, found that heavy users performed significantly worse than their nonusing counterparts on tasks that involved sustaining and shifting attention.

The major negative physiological effects of marijuana are potential respiratory and cardiovascular damage (Sridhar, Ruab, & Weatherby, 1994); these effects are found in smokers of any substance. However, some studies have observed "apathy, loss of effectiveness, and diminished capacity to carry out complex, long-term plans, endure frustration, concentrate for long periods, follow routines, or successfully master new material" in marijuana users (McGothlin & West, 1968). It is difficult to determine from such reports whether these changes are produced by marijuana in normal people or whether people who are predisposed toward apathy are more likely to choose to use marijuana for a long period of time.

SUMMARY

Consciousness is our awareness of the various cognitive processes that operate in our daily lives: making decisions, remembering, daydreaming, concentrating, reflecting, sleeping, and dreaming, among others. Psychologists divide consciousness into two broad areas: **waking consciousness,** which includes the thoughts, feelings, and perceptions that arise when we are awake and reasonably alert; and **altered states of consciousness (ASC),** during which our mental state differs noticeably from normal waking consciousness.

NATURAL VARIATIONS IN CONSCIOUSNESS

To make sense of our complex environment, we choose what to absorb from the myriad happenings around us and filter out the rest. This applies to both external stimuli such as sounds, sights, and smells, and internal sensations such as heat, cold, pressure, and pain. Even our thoughts, memories, emotions, and needs are subjected to this selective process. We also perform familiar tasks, such as signing our names, without deliberate attention. Many psychologists believe that important mental processes go on outside of normal waking consciousness, perhaps as a form of automatic processing.

Daydreaming and Fantasy

Daydreaming occurs without effort, often when we seek to escape the demands of the real world briefly. Some psychologists see no positive or practical value in daydreaming. Others contend that daydreams and fantasies allow us to express and deal with hidden desires without guilt or anxiety. Still others believe that daydreams build cognitive and creative skills that help us survive difficult situations—that they serve as a useful substitute for reality or a beneficial way of relieving tension. Finally there are those who view daydreaming as a mechanism for processing the vast array of information we take in during the day, enabling us to retrieve thoughts put aside for later review and to transform them into new and more useful forms.

Sleep and Dreaming

Research into sleep patterns shows that normal sleep consists of several stages. Following the initial "twilight" state, which is characterized by irregular, low-voltage alpha waves and a state of relaxed wakefulness, the sleeper enters Stage 1 of sleep. This stage, which is marked by a slowing of the pulse, muscle relaxation, and side-to-side rolling movements of the eyes, lasts only a few moments. The sleeper is easily awakened from Stage 1 sleep.

Stages 2 and 3 are characterized by progressively deeper sleep. In these stages, the sleeper is hard to awaken and does not respond to noise or light. Heart rate, blood pressure, and temperature continue to drop.

During Stage 4 sleep, when the brain emits very slow delta waves, heart and breathing rates, blood pressure, and body temperature are as low as they will get during the night. About an hour after first falling asleep, the sleeper begins to ascend through the stages back to Stage 1—a process that takes about 40 minutes. At this stage in the sleep cycle, heart rate and blood pressure increase, the muscles become more relaxed than at any other time in the cycle, and the eyes move rapidly under closed eyelids. It is this rapid eye movement (REM) that gives this stage of sleep its name.

REM sleep is also called **paradoxical sleep** because while brain activity and other physiological symptoms resemble those recorded during waking consciousness, the sleeper appears to be deeply asleep and is incapable of moving because of paralysis of the body's voluntary muscles. **Non-REM,** or **NREM sleep,** refers to the non-rapid-eye-movement stages of sleep that alternate with REM stages during the sleep cycle.

Dreams are visual or auditory experiences that occur primarily during REM periods of sleep. Less vivid experiences that resemble conscious thinking tend to occur during NREM sleep. One theory to explain why REM dreams are so vivid cites the level of brain arousal during

REM sleep. The brain's activity closely resembles that of normal waking consciousness, but because of its relative insensitivity to outside sensory input, it draws on nothing but internal images from memory.

Several theories have been developed to explain the nature and content of dreams. According to Freud, dreams have two kinds of contents: manifest (the surface content of the dream itself) and latent (the disguised, unconscious meaning of the dream). One recent hypothesis suggests that dreams arise out of the mind's reprocessing of information absorbed during the day—information that is important to the survival of the organism. Thus, dreaming strengthens our memories of important information. At the neurophysiological level, REM sleep may be related to brain "restoration" and growth. If people are deprived of REM sleep, they often become anxious, irritable, and testy, and, when they are permitted to have REM sleep again, the amount of REM they experience almost doubles—an effect referred to as REM *rebound*.

Other phenomena associated with sleep and dreaming include *sleepwalking, sleeptalking, sleep terrors, nightmares,* and *sleep learning*. Most episodes of sleeptalking and sleepwalking occur during delta sleep. Unlike nightmares, sleep terrors, which are more common among children than adults, prove difficult to be awakened from, and are rarely remembered the next morning. The learning of complex material during sleep has never been scientifically confirmed.

Sleep deprivation is a major problem in the United States. Inadequate sleep has been shown to adversely affect attention, memory, reaction time, judgment, and job performance. Moreover it is implicated as one of the major causes of automobile accidents.

Many people are afflicted by sleep disorders. **Insomnia** is characterized by difficulty in falling asleep or remaining asleep throughout the night. **Apnea** is marked by breathing difficulties during the night and feelings of exhaustion during the day. **Narcolepsy** is a hereditary sleep disorder characterized by sudden nodding off during the day and sudden loss of muscle tone following moments of emotional excitement.

ARTIFICIAL ALTERATIONS IN CONSCIOUSNESS

Sensory Deprivation
Sensory deprivation is the extreme reduction of sensory stimuli. Research indicates that it can cause such symptoms as altered perceptions, hallucinations, dreaming, daydreaming, and fantasizing.

Meditation
Meditation refers to any of several methods of concentration, reflection, or focusing of thoughts intended to suppress the activity of the sympathetic nervous system.

Meditation not only lowers the rate of metabolism but also reduces heart and respiratory rates. Brain activity during meditation resembles that experienced during relaxed wakefulness, and the accompanying decrease in blood lactate reduces stress.

Hypnosis
Hypnosis is a trancelike state in which the person responds readily to suggestions. People's susceptibility to hypnosis depends on how suggestible they are. Hypnosis has several practical applications; for instance, it eases the pain of certain medical conditions and can help people stop smoking and break other habits.

DRUG-ALTERED CONSCIOUSNESS
Some ASCs are induced with the help of **psychoactive drugs.**

Substance Use, Abuse, and Dependence
It is important to distinguish between substance use and substance abuse. *Substance use* may be essential for medical reasons and it may also be culturally approved and valued. By contrast, **substance abuse** is a pattern of drug use that diminishes the person's ability to fulfill responsibilities at home or at work or school, that results in repeated use of a drug in dangerous situations, or that leads to legal difficulties related to drug use.

Continued abuse over time can lead to **substance dependence,** a pattern of compulsive drug taking that is much more serious than substance abuse. It is often marked by **tolerance,** the need to take higher doses of a drug to produce its original effects or to prevent withdrawal symptoms. **Withdrawal symptoms** are the unpleasant physical or psychological effects that follow discontinuance of the psychoactive substance.

To study the effects of drugs scientifically, most researchers use the *double-blind procedure* to eliminate biases that might arise out of the experimenter's or the participant's prior knowledge or expectations about a drug.

Consciousness-altering drugs are grouped into three broad categories: depressants, stimulants, and hallucinogens.

Depressants: Alcohol, Barbiturates, the Opiates
Depressants are chemicals that slow down behavior or cognitive processes. **Alcohol,** a depressant, is the intoxicating ingredient in whiskey, beer, wine, and other fermented or distilled liquors. It is responsible for tens of thousands of deaths each year and contributes to a great deal of crime and domestic violence. Its dangers notwithstanding, alcohol continues to be a popular drug because of its short-term effects. As a depressant, it calms down the nervous system working like a general anesthetic. It is often experienced subjectively as a

stimulant because it inhibits centers in the brain that govern critical judgment and impulsive behavior.

Barbiturates, popularly known as "downers," are potentially deadly depressants. They were first used for their sedative and anticonvulsant properties, but today their use is limited to the treatment of such conditions as epilepsy and arthritis.

The **opiates** are highly addictive drugs such as opium, morphine, and heroin that dull the senses and induce feelings of euphoria, well-being, and relaxation. Morphine and heroin are derivatives of opium.

Stimulants: Caffeine, Nicotine, Amphetamines, and Cocaine

Stimulants are drugs such as caffeine, nicotine, amphetamines, and cocaine that stimulate the sympathetic nervous system and produce feelings of optimism and boundless energy, making the potential for their abuse significant.

Caffeine occurs naturally in coffee, tea, and cocoa; nicotine occurs naturally only in tobacco. Caffeine is considered to be a benign drug, but in large doses it can cause anxiety, insomnia, and other unpleasant conditions. Although nicotine is a stimulant, it acts like a depressant when taken in large doses.

Amphetamines are stimulants that initially produce "rushes" of euphoria often followed by sudden "crashes"

and, sometimes, depression. **Cocaine** brings on a sense of euphoria by stimulating the sympathetic nervous system, but is can also cause anxiety, depression, and addictive cravings. Its crystalline form—crack—is highly addictive.

Hallucinogens and Marijuana

Hallucinogens are any of a number of drugs, such as LSD, phencyclidine (PCP, or "angel dust"), and mescaline, that distort visual and auditory perception.

Many of the hallucinogens occur naturally in mushrooms or other fungi. In these forms, they share an ancient history with other consciousness-altering drugs of natural origin. By contrast, **lysergic acid diethylamide (LSD)** is an artificial hallucinogen, synthesized in the laboratory, that produces hallucinations and delusions similar to those that occur in a psychotic state.

Marijuana is a mild hallucinogen that is capable of producing feelings of euphoria, a sense of well-being, and swings in mood from gaiety to relaxation to paranoia. Currently, marijuana is the fourth most popular drug among students, following alcohol, caffeine, and nicotine. Though similar to hallucinogens in certain respects, marijuana is far less potent and its effects on consciousness are far less profound.

REVIEW QUESTIONS

MULTIPLE CHOICE AND SHORT ANSWER

1. We experience _____ consciousness when our mental state differs noticeably from the state we experience when we are awake and alert.

2. The hallmark of normal waking consciousness is highly selective _____ .

3. According to Freud, the real driving forces behind human actions are _____ instincts that are hidden but brought into consciousness through such states as dreaming and hypnosis.

4. True or false: Psychologists have a clear understanding of the biological and psychological necessity for sleep.

5. REM sleep is usually called _____ sleep, because in this phase of sleep such physical functions as heart rate closely resemble those of waking consciousness, even though the sleeper's voluntary muscles appear to be paralyzed.

6. The increase in dreaming that occurs after the cessation of dream deprivation is known as _____ _____ .

7. Match the sleep disorder with the symptoms:
   _____ insomnia   a. excessive, unpredictable sleeping sessions
   _____ apnea   b. breathing difficulties and day-after exhaustion
   _____ narcolepsy   c. acute or chronic inability to sleep

8. Sensory deprivation results in a state in which most people cannot distinguish between dreams and waking _____ .

9. In all its diverse forms, meditation reduces the activity of the _____ system.

10. Many psychologists believe that the effects of hypnosis can be accounted for by the variable of _____ .

11. Although alcohol is a _____, it is sometimes experienced subjectively as a _____.

12. _____ are commonly known as "downers."

13. The crystalline form of cocaine is called:
   a. LSD
   b. angel dust
   c. crack
   d. opium

CRITICAL THINKING AND APPLICATIONS

1. Should psychologists study consciousness? Is it a valid subject for scientific research? Why or why not?

2. A close friend informs you that she has been having a number of unusual dreams in recent weeks. What would you advise her to do? Do you believe that dreams offer insights into our innermost thoughts and feelings? Should psychologists study dreams or discuss the content of dreams with their patients? Why or why not?

3. What, in your opinion, are the major causes of substance abuse and dependence? How should society deal with these problems?

ENDURING ISSUES

Diversity
To what extent does culture affect the ways in which people use various drugs and their reactions to those drugs?

Mind–Body
To what extent do people have similar/different reactions to mind altering drugs?

After reading about how drugs can profoundly influence psychological processes, have you changed your opinions about the relationship between mind and body (the extent to which our thoughts and feelings are dependent on biological processes)?

(Answers to the Review Questions can be found in the back of the text.)

5 Learning

As unlikely as it may seem, the following situations have something in common:

🔸 On completion of a training course at the National Zoo, the star students demonstrate their newly acquired behaviors: Junior, a young orangutan, cleans up his cage for the chance to blow a whistle; a pair of 18-inch-long lizards jump 2 feet in the air to snatch insects from the tip of a forceps; a chinchilla weighs itself by hopping into a basket on top of a scale; and Peela the tiger retrieves a floating keg from the moat in his exhibition area.

🔸 While driving along a congested boulevard, a middle-aged man glances at a park bench and, for a moment, his heart pounds as he experiences a warm feeling throughout his body. At first, he can't understand why passing this spot has evoked such a strong emotion. Then he remembers: It was the meeting place he once shared with his high school sweetheart over 20 years ago.

Think About It!

1. How can a household pet learn to identify the sound of a can opener?
2. What do we mean by reinforcement of behaviors?
3. How do we learn superstitions? Do animals other than humans exhibit superstitious behaviors?
4. Why is money a secondary reinforcer?
5. *True or False*: Punishing a child for aggressive behavior by slapping or spanking can teach the child to act more violently.
6. Are humans the only species that can cognitively process information?

Unconditioned stimulus (US) A stimulus that invariably causes an organism to respond in a specific way.

Unconditioned response (UR) A response that takes place in an organism whenever an unconditioned stimulus occurs.

Conditioned stimulus (CS) An originally neutral stimulus that is paired with an unconditioned stimulus and eventually produces the desired response in an organism when presented alone.

Conditioned response (CR) After conditioning, the response an organism produces when only a conditioned stimulus is presented.

Pavlov, in which the bell has been replaced by a tactile (touch) stimulus, applied to the dog's leg, just before food is presented.

Elements of Classical Conditioning

Generally speaking, classical conditioning involves pairing a response that is usually evoked by one stimulus with a different, previously neutral stimulus. Pavlov's experiment illustrates the four basic elements of classical conditioning. The first is an **unconditioned stimulus (US),** like food, which invariably prompts a certain reaction—salivation, in this case. That reaction—the **unconditioned response (UR)**—is the second element and always results from the unconditioned stimulus: Whenever the dog is given food (US), its mouth waters (UR). The third element is the neutral stimulus—the ringing bell—which is called the **conditioned stimulus (CS).** At first, the conditioned stimulus is said to be "neutral" with respect to the desired response (salivation), because dogs do not salivate at the sound of a bell unless they have been conditioned to react in this way by repeatedly presenting the CS and US together. Frequent pairing of the CS and US produces the fourth element in the classical conditioning process: the **conditioned response (CR).** The conditioned response is the behavior that the animal has learned in response to the conditioned stimulus. Usually, the unconditioned response and the conditioned response are slightly different versions of the same response—salivation, in our example (see Figure 5–2).

Figure 5–1
Pavlov's apparatus for classically conditioning a dog to salivate.
The experimenter sits behind a one-way mirror and controls the presentation of the conditioned stimulus (touch applied to the leg) and the unconditioned stimulus (food). A tube runs from the dog's salivary glands to a vial, where the drops of saliva are collected as a way of measuring the strength of the dog's response.

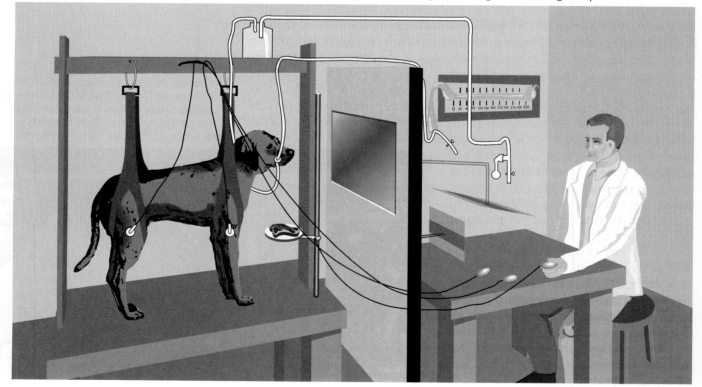

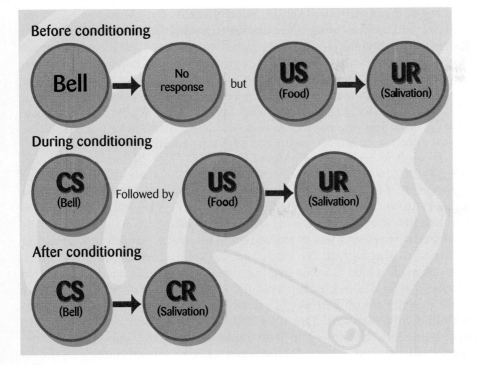

Before conditioning

Bell → No response

but

US (Food) → UR (Salivation)

During conditioning

CS (Bell)

Followed by

US (Food) → UR (Salivation)

After conditioning

CS (Bell) → CR (Salivation)

**Figure 5–2
A paradigm of the classical conditioning process.**

Without planning to do so, you may have conditioned your own pet the same way that Pavlov trained his dogs. Your cat may begin to purr when it hears the sound of a can being opened in the kitchen. The taste and smell of food are unconditioned stimuli (USs) that cause, among other responses, purring (the UR). Based on experience, your cat associates the sound of the can opener (the CS) with the food; over time, the CS by itself causes your cat to purr even before food is presented (the CR). Dog owners who have used physical punishment with their pet may notice that the dog cringes or trembles when they speak in a loud and angry voice. In the past, physical pain (US)—which causes a number of responses, including cowering and trembling (URs)—may have been paired with shouting (a CS). Now, merely the sound of a loud voice can evoke a fear response (the CR).

Changes in behavior brought about by classical conditioning are not limited to dogs, cats, and humans. Classical conditioning has been demonstrated in virtually every form of animal including cephalopod mollusks (octopi and squid) and arthropods (insects and spiders). Indeed, learning by classical conditioning plays a significant role in the lives of most animals (Krasne & Glanzman, 1995).

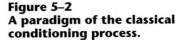

1

How can a household pet learn to identify the sound of a can opener?

Classical Conditioning in Humans

You might wonder what Pavlov's dogs and reflexive responses have to do with human learning. Quite simply, human beings also learn behaviors through classical conditioning. Consider, for example, the positive thoughts and feelings that we associate with the smell of a fresh-baked bread or cake.

As another example of classical conditioning in humans, let's think for a moment about phobias—irrational fears of particular things, activities, or situations, such as cats, spiders, or snakes, or high places (acrophobia), closed places (claustrophobia), or busy public places (agoraphobia). Many of us approach a visit to the dentist or the prospect of making a speech with fear, but for some people, these situations can provoke a major panic attack, which leaves sufferers unable to catch their breath, perspiring profusely, or

Desensitization therapy A conditioning technique designed to gradually reduce anxiety about a particular object or situation.

Desensitization therapy is based on the belief that we can overcome fears by learning to remain calm in the face of increasingly fear-arousing situations. Here people being desensitized for a fear of heights are able to swing high above the ground without panicking.

shaking from uncontrollable chills. Some victims of phobias even have convulsions and pass out when seized by an irrational fear. Sigmund Freud, the father of psychoanalysis, explained phobias in terms of unresolved inner conflicts in which the phobic object (the thing that is feared) represents some other problem or situation that troubles the patient. As we will see, however, phobias may also be acquired through observational learning (Cook et al., 1985). Another view, advanced by Wolpe and Rachman (1960), considers phobias an instance of classical conditioning: An object comes to be feared after being linked with a frightening stimulus.

To see how phobias might develop through classical conditioning, consider a classic experiment conducted by John Watson and Rosalie Rayner (Watson & Rayner, 1920). In this famous study, an 11-month-old boy, named "Little Albert," was taught to fear a harmless laboratory rat. The experimenters started by showing Albert a white rat. At first the child displayed no apparent fear of the rodent. The infant crawled toward the rat and tried to play with it. But every time he approached the rat, the experimenters made a loud noise by striking a steel bar. Because nearly all children are afraid of loud noises, Albert's natural reaction was fear. After just a few of these experiences, Albert would cry whenever he saw the rat and quickly withdraw from it in fear. This is a simple case of classical conditioning. An unconditioned stimulus—the loud noise—caused the unconditioned response of fear. Next, the loud noise was associated several times with the rat (conditioned stimulus). Soon the rat alone caused Albert to behave as if he were afraid (conditioned response).

Several years later, psychologist Mary Cover Jones demonstrated a method by which children's fears can be unlearned by means of classical conditioning (Jones, 1924). Her subject was a 3-year-old boy named Peter who, like Albert, had a fear of white rats. Jones paired the sight of a rat with a pleasant experience—eating candy. While Peter sat alone in a room, a caged white rat was brought in and placed far enough away so that the youngster would not be frightened. At this point, Peter was given plenty of candy to eat. On each successive day of the experiment, the cage was moved closer and was followed by the presentation of candy until, eventually, Peter showed no fear of the rat. In this case, eating candy (US) elicited a pleasant response (UR). By pairing the candy with the sight of the rat (CS), Jones was able to teach Peter to respond with pleasure (CR) when the rat appeared.

Many years later, psychiatrist Joseph Wolpe adapted Jones's method to the treatment of certain kinds of anxiety (Wolpe, 1973, 1982). Wolpe reasoned that because irrational fears and anxieties are learned or conditioned, they could also be unlearned through conditioning. He noted that people cannot be both fearful and relaxed at the same time; therefore, if people could be taught to relax in fearful or anxious situations, their anxiety should disappear. His **desensitization therapy** begins by teaching the person a series of deep-muscle relaxation techniques. Then the therapist helps the person construct a list of situations that prompt various degrees of fear or anxiety. These situations are then rated on a scale from zero (the person would feel absolutely calm and relaxed) to 100 (the person would be terrified). For example, people who are afraid of heights might rate "standing on top of the Empire State Building" near the top of the scale, whereas "standing on the first rung of a ladder" might be rated near the bottom. Then they enter a state of deep relaxation during which they imagine the least distressing situation on the list. When they succeed in remaining relaxed while imagining that situation, they progress to the next one, and so on until they experience no anxiety even when imagining the most frightening situation on the list. We will examine desensitization therapy in greater detail in Chapter 14, Therapies but, for now, let's just note that it is one way in which classical conditioning can be used to change human behavior.

In another example of classical conditioning in humans, researchers have devised a novel way to treat a group of diseases, called *autoimmune disorders*, which cause the immune system to attack healthy organs or tissues. Although powerful drugs can be used to suppress the immune system and thus reduce the impact of the autoimmune disorder, these drugs often have serious side effects: They may produce nausea and headaches and may actually damage organs such as the pancreas and liver, so they must be administered sparingly. The challenge, then, was to find a treatment that could suppress the immune system without damaging vital organs. Researchers working on the treatment of such autoimmune disorders as lupus discovered that, through classical conditioning techniques, they could use formerly neutral stimuli either to elevate or to suppress the activity of the immune system (Markovic, Dimitrijevic, & Jankovic, 1993). Here's how it works: The researchers use immune-suppressing drugs as USs and pair them with a specific CS, such as a distinctive smell or taste. After only a few pairings of the drug (US) with the smell or taste (CS), the CS alone suppresses the immune system (the CR) without any dangerous side effects!

Classical Conditioning Is Selective

Think back to the examples of phobias learned through classical conditioning. If any object can come to be feared after being linked with a frightening or anxiety-arousing stimulus, why don't people have phobias about almost everything? As M. E. P. Seligman notes, "Only rarely, if ever, do we have pajama phobias, grass phobias, electric-outlet phobias, hammer phobias, even though these things are likely to be associated with trauma in our world" (1972, p. 455). Why should this be?

To Seligman, the answer lies in *preparedness* and *contrapreparedness*. Some stimuli serve readily as CSs for certain kinds of responses (preparedness), and other stimuli do not (contrapreparedness). All the common objects of phobias—heights, snakes, cats, the dark, and so on—are "related to the survival of the human species through the long course of evolution" (Seligman, 1972, p. 455). Thus, humans may be prepared to develop fear responses and phobias about these things but we are very unlikely to acquire phobias about flowers.

Recent studies of preparedness both confirm and moderate Seligman's views. For example, some stimuli unrelated to human survival through evolution, but which we have learned to associate with danger, can serve as CSs for fear responses. Pictures of handguns and butcher knives, for example, are as effective as pictures of snakes and spiders in conditioning fear in some people (Lovibond, Siddle, & Bond, 1993). Other studies have shown that people who do not suffer from phobias can rather quickly unlearn fear responses to spiders and snakes if those stimuli appear repeatedly without painful or threatening USs (Honeybourne, Matchett, & Davey, 1993). These studies suggest that preparedness may be the result of learning rather than evolution. However, Seligman's basic claim still stands: Our evolutionary history and our personal learning histories interact to increase the likelihood of certain kinds of conditioning while making other kinds of conditioning less likely to occur.

Preparedness also underlies **conditioned food** or **taste aversion.** Classical conditioning generally requires many presentations of the CS and US

Conditioned food (or **taste**) **aversion** Conditioned avoidance of certain foods even if there is only one pairing of conditioned and unconditioned stimuli.

with a short interval between the appearance of the two. Conditioned food aversion is a notable exception to these rules. Animals rarely require more than one occasion of being poisoned to learn not to eat a particular food. This phenomenon was discovered by accident by John Garcia in the midst of experiments on the effects of exposure to radiation (Garcia et al., 1956). Garcia was exposing rats in a special chamber to high doses of radiation that made them sick. He noticed that the rats were drinking less and less water when in the radiation chamber, although they drank normally in their "home" cages. Garcia realized that the water bottles in the radiation chamber were plastic, perhaps giving the water a different taste from the water contained in glass bottles in the home cages. He theorized that the taste of the water from the plastic bottles had served as a conditioned stimulus (CS) that the rats associated with radiation (US); as a result of this conditioning, the plastic-tasting water by itself made the rats feel ill (CR).

Because conditioned taste aversion has been demonstrated in a wide variety of animals by Garcia and a number of other researchers, we have learned a great deal about this phenomenon (Braveman & Bronstein, 1985). For example, we now know that conditioned food aversion can take place only after one bad experience; in addition, the interval between eating the food (the CS) and falling ill (the US) can be quite long—up to 12 hours among rats.

Why do taste-illness combinations produce such rapid and long-lasting learning? Garcia traces the answer to evolution: Rapid learning of taste-illness combinations increases some animals' chances of survival. Rats, for example, are scavengers: They will nibble at almost anything, so they are quite likely to come into contact with potentially toxic foods. It makes sense that over thousands of generations rats would have evolved a nervous system that is especially good at remembering taste-illness combinations (Gar-

A bird's nervous system is adapted to remember sight-illness combinations, such as the distinctive color of a certain berry and subsequent food poisoning. In mammals it is generally taste-illness combinations that are quickly and powerfully learned.

cia & Keolling, 1966). By contrast, birds depend on vision to find and identify their food; it follows that birds should have evolved a nervous system that is especially good at remembering sight-illness combinations—and this turns out to be the case. In one study, both rats and quail were fed water that was flavored with salt, colored blue, and contaminated with a chemical that would make both animals ill. Later they were offered a choice between water just colored blue and water just flavored with salt. The rats chose the blue water and avoided the salty water; the quails did just the reverse. The rats seemed to have associated the salty flavor cues with their illness, whereas the birds associated the blue visual cue with their illness (Wilcoxin, Dragoin, & Kral, 1971). In other words, each species seems to have been prepared or preprogrammed for certain types of learning that are critical to its own survival.

Of course, the learning of food aversions is not limited to nonhumans. People develop food aversions based on a variety of cues, including taste, appearance, and smell. For example, if you become ill after trying a new salad dressing, you will probably develop a strong aversion to that dressing, no matter how much you enjoyed it. One study found that over half the college students surveyed had at least one conditioned taste aversion (Logue, Ophir, & Strauss, 1981). The conditioned aversion response is so ingrained that even when we know a particular food did not make us sick, we still tend to form an aversion to the food we ate before we became ill. One psychologist described a dinner party at which he and several other guests all picked up an intestinal virus that left many of them with an aversion to tarragon chicken (the main dish) or any food with tarragon spicing (Mazur, 1994). Even though they knew that the tarragon chicken was not the source of their illness, they were unable to overcome the powerful conditioned response. Similarly, patients undergoing treatment for cancer frequently develop taste aversions. Because the drugs used in chemotherapy can cause nausea, patients commonly develop strong taste aversions for foods eaten both before and after injections of these chemicals, even though they know that the foods do not bring on their nausea (Jacobsen et al., 1994).

OPERANT CONDITIONING

Classical conditioning is concerned with behavior that invariably follows a particular event: the salivation that automatically occurs when food is placed in the mouth, the blink of an eye that always results when a puff of air strikes the eye. In classical conditioning, we usually learn to transfer this reaction to another stimulus that would not normally produce it: salivating at the sound of a bell, blinking to a tone. In a sense, classical conditioning is passive. The behavior is initially elicited by the unconditional stimulus.

But most of our behavior is voluntary rather than triggered by outside events. You wave your hand in a particular way to signal a taxi or bus to stop for you. Children pick up their toys either to avoid punishment or to gain some reward from their parents. We put money into machines and pull on levers or push buttons to obtain soft drinks, food, entertainment, or a chance to win money. These and similar actions can be classified as **operant behavior.** They are learned behaviors that are designed to operate on the environment in a way that will gain something desired or avoid something unpleasant; they are not automatic reflexes caused by biologically important stimuli. This kind of learning is called *operant* or *instrumental conditioning*. We now turn to the basic principles of operant conditioning.

Operant behavior Behavior designed to operate on the environment in a way that will gain something desired or avoid something unpleasant.

Reinforcer A stimulus that follows a behavior and increases the likelihood that the behavior will be repeated.

Punisher A stimulus that follows a behavior and decreases the likelihood that the behavior will be repeated.

Law of Effect Thorndike's theory that behavior consistently rewarded will be "stamped in" as learned behavior, and behavior that brings about discomfort will be "stamped out" (also known as the principle of reinforcement).

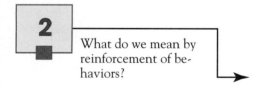

2 What do we mean by reinforcement of behaviors?

Figure 5–3
A cat in a Thorndike "puzzle box."
The cat can escape and be rewarded with food by tripping the bolt on the door. As the graph shows, Thorndike's cats learned to make the necessary response more rapidly after an increasing number of trials.

Thorndike's Conditioning Experiments

Around the turn of the twentieth century, while Pavlov was busy with his dogs, Edward Lee Thorndike, an American psychologist and educator, was using a "puzzle box," or simple wooden cage, to determine how cats learn (Thorndike, 1898). As illustrated in Figure 5–3, Thorndike placed a hungry cat in the close quarters of the puzzle box, with food just outside the cage where the cat could see and smell it. To get to the food, the cat had to figure out how to open the latch on the cage door, a process Thorndike timed. In the beginning, it took the cats quite a while to discover how to open the door. But each time a cat was put back into the puzzle box, it took less time to open the door, until the cat eventually could escape from the box in almost no time.

Elements of Operant Conditioning

Thorndike's experiments illustrate two factors that are essential in operant or instrumental conditioning. The first is the operant response. In analyzing operant learning—whether we're using conditioning principles to acquire good work habits or avoiding the street where we once received a speeding ticket—we realize that operant conditioning occurs when we choose a particular response, called the *operant response*, from a wide variety of behaviors and then focus on observing and changing that response.

The second essential element in operant conditioning is the *consequence* that follows the behavior. Thorndike's cats gained either freedom or a piece of fish for escaping from their constraining puzzle boxes; a dog gets a biscuit for sitting on command; and a child may receive praise or a chance to play a computer game for helping to clear the table. Consequences like these that increase the likelihood that the behavior will be repeated are called **reinforcers.** By contrast, consequences that decrease the chances that a behavior will be repeated are called **punishers.** Imagine how Thorndike's cats might have performed had they been greeted by a large, snarling dog when they escaped from their puzzle boxes, or what might happen if a dog that sits on command is scolded for doing so or if a child who has helped to clear the table is sent to sit in a "time-out" corner. Thorndike's understanding of the importance of reinforcement is reflected in his **law of effect:** "Responses which are accompanied or closely followed by satisfaction to the animal will, other things being equal, be . . . more likely to recur; those which are

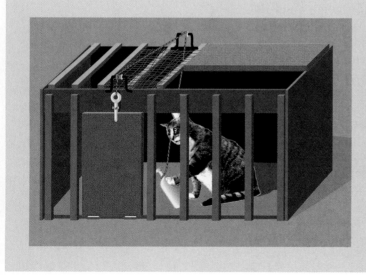

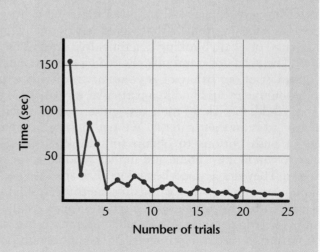

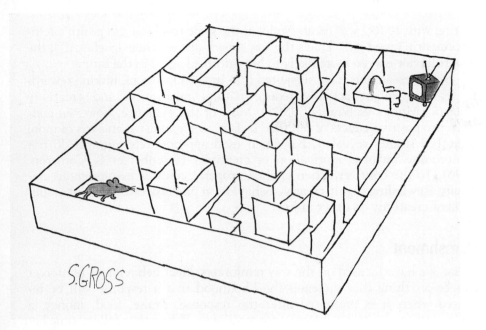

S. GROSS

Positive reinforcer Any event whose presence increases the likelihood that ongoing behavior will recur.

Negative reinforcer Any event whose reduction or termination increases the likelihood that ongoing behavior will recur.

accompanied or closely followed by discomfort to the animal will, other things being equal, . . . be less likely to occur" (Thorndike, 1911, p. 244). In a given stimulus situation, a response that consistently brings about a satisfying effect (reinforcement) will be stamped in, and responses that bring about discomfort (punishment) will be stamped out. Contemporary psychologists often refer to the *principle of reinforcement* rather than the law of effect, but the two terms refer to the same phenomenon.

Types of Reinforcement

POSITIVE AND NEGATIVE REINFORCEMENT Psychologists distinguish among several kinds of reinforcers. **Positive reinforcers,** such as food or pleasant music, add something rewarding to a situation. By contrast, **negative reinforcers** subtract something unpleasant from a situation by removing a noxious or unpleasant stimulus. You might find it helpful to use the plus symbol (+) to refer to a positive (+) reinforcer that *adds* (+) something rewarding to the environment and the minus sign (−) to refer to a negative (−) reinforcer that *subtracts* (−) something negative or unpleasant from the environment. Animals will learn to press bars and open doors not only to obtain food and water (positive reinforcement) but also to avoid electric shocks or loud noises (negative reinforcement).

Both positive and negative reinforcement result in the learning of new behaviors or the strengthening of existing behaviors. Remember, in everyday conversation when we say that we have "reinforced" something, we mean we have strengthened it. "Reinforced concrete" is strengthened by the addition of steel rods or steel mesh; generals "send reinforcements" to strengthen a military force; people "reinforce" their arguments by marshaling facts that strengthen them. Similarly, in operant conditioning, all reinforcements—whether positive or negative—strengthen behavior. A boy might practice the piano to receive praise (positive reinforcement) or to avoid doing tedious homework for a while (negative reinforcement). If a girl is scolded for eating spaghetti with her fingers and the scolding stops when she picks up a fork and uses it, she is more likely to use a fork in the future. This is an example of a negative reinforcer, because reducing or terminating unpleasant events (such as a scolding) increases the likelihood that the behavior going on at the time

Punishment Any event whose presence decreases the likelihood that ongoing behavior will recur.

A punishment is any consequence which decreases the chances that a particular behavior will be repeated. This man being carried to the pillory in colonial New England will probably think twice before repeating whatever misdeed he committed because public humiliation is a powerful form of punishment.

(eating with a fork) will recur. And if at the same time you add positive reinforcement ("Good girl! That's the way grown-ups eat their spaghetti!"), the new behavior is even more likely to be performed again in the future.

Some researchers have suggested that in the classroom, linking rewards to learning might actually reduce natural motivation and creativity (Tagano, Moran, & Sawyers, 1991). Most of the evidence, however, confirms the positive effects of rewards. In fact, one extensive analysis of more than 100 studies revealed that when used appropriately, rewards do not compromise intrinsic motivation or creativity (Eisenberger & Cameron, 1996). To the contrary, when applied properly, rewards may promote creativity. Rewarding highly creative behavior on one task often enhances subsequent creativity on other tasks.

Punishment

So far, we have focused on the way reinforcers affect behavior. A reinforcer can be anything that increases the likelihood that a response will be repeated when it is presented after the response. Praise, food, money, a smile—all are positive reinforcers for most of us. When they follow some behavior, we are more likely to behave the same way in the future.

But behavior can also be controlled by **punishment.** For most of us, receiving a fine for speeding or littering reduces the likelihood that we will speed or litter in the future. Being rudely turned down when we ask someone for a favor makes it less likely that we will ask that person for a favor again. In both these cases, the unpleasant aftereffect reduces the likelihood that we will repeat that behavior. Be sure you understand the difference between punishment and negative reinforcement: Reinforcement of whatever kind *strengthens* (reinforces) behavior; negative reinforcement strengthens behavior by removing something unpleasant from the environment. By contrast, punishment adds something unpleasant to the environment, and as a result it tends to *weaken* behavior. Turning off a loud, unpleasant sound is likely to be reinforcing (you are more likely to turn off future unpleasant sounds as a result of the reinforcement you received); accidentally turning on a loud, unpleasant sound is likely to be punishing (as a result, you are less likely to make the same mistake again).

Although the examples listed above suggest that punishment works, we can all think of situations in which punishment clearly does not work. Children often continue to misbehave even after they have been punished repeatedly for that misbehavior. Some drivers persist in driving recklessly despite repeated fines. The family dog may sleep on the couch at night despite being punished for this behavior every morning. And criminals continue to commit crimes when facing both threatened and real punishment. So an important question comes to mind: Under what conditions does punishment work?

For punishment to be effective, it must be imposed properly. First, punishment should be *swift*. Children who misbehave should be punished right away so they know that what they have done is wrong. If punishment comes too long after the offensive action, it may not be clear to children why they are being punished. Punishment should also be *sufficient* without being cruel. If a parent merely warned a child not to bully other children, the effect might be less pronounced than if the warning were accompanied by the threat of being "grounded" for a day. Moreover, the common practice of making the punishment for each successive misdeed more severe than the last is not as effective as maintaining a constant level of punishment. Effective punishment, then, is also consistent, or *certain*. Parents should try to punish children each and every time they misbehave. Otherwise the misbehavior may persist.

The proper application of punishment can change behavior quickly, which is critical in certain cases. A child who likes to play in the street or who enjoys poking things into electric outlets must be stopped quickly and, in these instances, punishment may be the best course of action. Similarly, some severely disturbed children repeatedly injure themselves by banging their heads against the wall or by hitting themselves in the face with their fists. Punishment may stop this self-destructive behavior so that other forms of therapy can proceed. But even in situations like these, punishment has significant drawbacks (Skinner, 1953). First, punishment only suppresses behavior: It doesn't teach a more desirable behavior. If the punisher or the threat of punishment is removed, the negative behavior is likely to recur. Drivers who are speeding on a highway generally slow down when they see a radar-equipped police car on the side of the road because the police car introduces the threat of punishment. But as soon as the threat is past, they tend to speed up again. Thus, punishment rarely works when long-term changes in behavior are sought. Second, punishment often stirs up unpleasant emotions that can impede learning of the behavior we want to teach in place of the punished behavior. For example, when children are learning to read and a teacher or parent scolds them every time they mispronounce a word, they may become frightened and confused. As they become more frightened and confused, they mispronounce more words and get scolded more often. In time, they may become so overwhelmed with fear that they do not want to read at all. Third, punishment may convey the notion that inflicting pain on others is justified, thereby inadvertently teaching undesirable aggressive behavior. In laboratory studies, monkeys that are punished tend to attack other monkeys; likewise, pigeons other pigeons, and so on (B. Schwartz, 1989). In addition, punishment often makes people angry, and angry people frequently become more aggressive and hostile.

If punishment must be used to suppress undesirable behavior, it should be terminated when more desirable behavior occurs (to negatively reinforce that behavior). Positive reinforcement (praise, rewards) should also be used to strengthen the desired behavior. This approach is more productive than punishment alone, because it teaches an alternative behavior to replace the actions that prompted the punishment. Positive reinforcement also makes the learning environment less threatening overall.

As a method for controlling behavior, punishment is one of the least pleasant options because it is often ineffective, and it can have negative side effects. Most of us would prefer to avoid using punishment at all, relying instead on the threat of punishment when behavior is getting out of control. If the threat of punishment induces a change to more desirable behavior, punishment need not be imposed at all. Psychologists call this **avoidance training.**

Avoidance training with animals in a laboratory usually includes some sort of warning devices, such as a light or a buzzer. For example, an animal might be placed in a box with a wire floor that can deliver a mild shock. The experimenter first sounds a buzzer and then a few seconds later turns on the shock. If the animal presses a bar after hearing the buzzer, no shock will be

Avoidance training Learning a desirable behavior to prevent the occurrence of something unpleasant such as punishment.

delivered. Pressing the bar after the shock has already started will have no effect. The animal must learn to press the bar after hearing the buzzer, but before the shock starts, to prevent the shock from occurring. At first this usually happens accidentally. But once the animal learns that pressing the bar prevents the shock, it will run to the bar whenever it hears the buzzer, thus avoiding the shock altogether.

We, too, derive lessons from avoidance training, as when we learn to carry an umbrella when it looks like rain or not to touch a hot iron. But sometimes avoidance learning outlives its usefulness. Children taught not to go into deep water may avoid deep water even after they have learned how to swim. In other cases, avoidance behavior may persist long after the fear has been removed. So while fear is essential for *learning* the avoidance response, it is not always necessary for *sustaining* the learned response.

Remember that we do not know whether a particular entity is reinforcing or punishing until we see whether it increases or decreases the occurrence of a response. We might assume that candy, for example, is a reinforcer for children, but some children don't like candy. In addition, an event or object might not be consistently rewarding or punishing over time. So even if candy is initially reinforcing for some children, if they eat large amounts of it, it can become neutral or even punishing. We must therefore be very careful in labeling items or events as reinforcers or punishers.

Operant Conditioning Is Selective

In our discussion of preparedness in classical conditioning, we saw that some stimuli serve readily as CSs for certain kinds of responses whereas other stimuli do not. Classical conditioning is more likely to occur when a natural fit exists between the stimulus and the response—for example, a fear response to snakes or an aversive response to an unpleasant odor. Similarly, in operant conditioning, some behaviors are easier to train than others. In general, the behaviors that are easiest to condition are those that animals typically would perform in the training situation. For example, Shettleworth (1975) used food pellets to teach food-deprived hamsters to spend more time doing a variety of things: washing their faces, digging, scent marking, scratching, rearing up on their hind legs, and scraping a wall with their paws. The hamsters quickly learned to spend much more time rearing up on their hind legs, scraping walls, and digging, but there was only a slight increase in the amount of time they spent washing their faces, scratching, and scent marking. The first three behaviors are responses that hamsters typically make when they are hungry, whereas the last three behaviors usually occur less often when a hamster is hungry. Thus, learning was most successful for those responses that are most likely to occur naturally in the training situation. Other examples of preparedness in operant conditioning come from Breland and Breland (1972), a husband-and-wife team who trained animals to perform in shows. They tried to condition a bantam chicken to stand still on a platform for 12 to 15 seconds as part of a complex stunt, but the chicken insisted on scratching. The Brelands finally gave up and billed their bantam as a "dancing chicken." A raccoon was trained to insert a coin into a container for food but then reverted to its natural "washing" response. The animal was content to rub the coins together and handle them, and it refused to give them up to the food dispenser.

These cases illustrate the remarkable differences among species concerning which behaviors they can learn and the circumstances under which learning will occur. These species' differences put significant constraints on both classical and operant conditioning.

A chicken can easily be trained to "dance," like this one shown hopping from one foot to the other, but it is hard to teach a chicken to lie down and roll over. This illustrates the importance of preparedness in operant conditioning: Learning is less likely for any behavior that an animal isn't likely to perform naturally.

Superstitious Behavior

Whenever something we do is followed closely by a reinforcer, we will tend to repeat the action—even if the reinforcement is not produced directly by what we have done. In an experiment by the American psychologist B. F. Skinner (1948), a pigeon was placed in a cage that contained only a food hopper. There was nothing the bird could do directly to get food, but at random intervals Skinner dropped a few grains of food into the hopper. He found that the pigeon began to repeat whatever it had been doing just before it was given food: standing on one foot, hopping around, or strutting around with its neck stretched out. None of these actions had anything to do with getting the food—it was pure coincidence that the food appeared when the bird was standing on one foot, for example, but that action would usually be repeated. Skinner labeled the bird's behavior *superstitious*.

Humans can learn superstitions in the same way. If we happen to be wearing a particular piece of jewelry or a certain pair of socks when something good happens to us, we may come to believe that these incidental factors caused the positive incident, or reinforcement. We may even develop elaborate cognitive explanations for accidental or randomly occurring reinforcements.

3

How do we learn superstitions? Do animals other than humans exhibit superstitious behaviors?

Learned Helplessness

In the preceding section, we saw that the random delivery of reinforcements (beyond an organism's control) may result in superstitious behavior. But what happens if an animal experiences random exposure to painful or aversive stimuli over which they have no control? This question was addressed in a classic two-part experiment by Maier, Seligman, and Soloman (1969) (see Figure 5–4). In the first part of the experiment, two groups of dogs were placed in an experimental chamber that delivered an identical series of electric shocks to their feet at random intervals. The dogs in the control group could turn off (or escape) the shock by pushing a panel with their noses. The dogs in the experimental group, however, could not turn off the shock—they were, in effect, helpless. In the second part of the experiment, both the

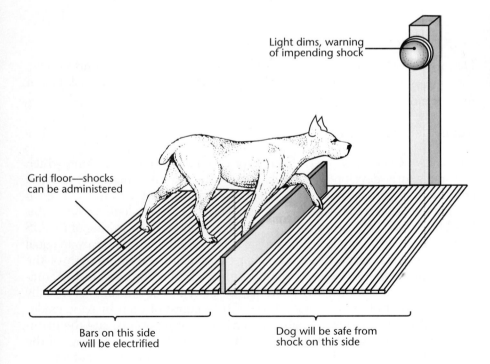

Light dims, warning of impending shock

Grid floor—shocks can be administered

Bars on this side will be electrified

Dog will be safe from shock on this side

Figure 5–4
Learned helplessness.
Dogs who had previously been able to avoid being shocked quickly learned to avoid shocks by jumping over a hurdle when a warning light came on. Other dogs, who had not been able to avoid the original series of shocks, did not learn to jump the hurdle in response to the light.

Learned helplessness Failure to take steps to avoid or escape from an unpleasant or aversive stimulus that occurs as a result of previous exposure to unavoidable painful stimuli.

Response acquisition The "building phase" of conditioning during which the likelihood or strength of the desired response increases.

experimental and control animals were placed in a different situation in which both groups could escape shock by jumping over a hurdle. In this phase of the experiment, at random intervals, a 10-second warning light would come on, followed by an electric shock that lasted for 50 seconds. The dogs in the control group quickly learned to avoid the shock by jumping over the hurdle when the warning light came on. However, the dogs in the experimental group (which had previously experienced unavoidable shocks) failed to learn either to avoid (jumping in response to the warning light) or to escape (jumping after the shock started) the shock. Moreover, Seligman observed that many of the animals that experienced the inescapable shocks became less active, experienced a loss of appetite, and displayed many of the symptoms associated with depression in humans. This failure to avoid or escape from an unpleasant or aversive stimulus that occurs as a result of previous exposure to unavoidable painful stimuli is referred to as **learned helplessness.**

Seligman and his colleagues have since conducted numerous experiments in learned helplessness and have produced similar results in both animals and humans (Maier & Seligman, 1976). On the basis of their research it appears that, once established, learned helplessness generalizes to new situations and decreases the motivation of both people and animals to try different responses that might bring relief from an unpleasant situation (Peterson, Maier, & Seligman, 1993). Indeed, even if a response does bring relief, people often have difficulty recognizing that their response had anything to do with the relief. For example, when faced with a series of unsolvable problems, a college student may eventually give up and make only half-hearted attempts to solve new problems, even when the new problems are easily solvable. Moreover, success in solving new problems has little effect on their behavior—they continue to make only half-hearted attempts, as if they had never had *any* success at all. Similarly, children raised in an abusive family where punishment is unrelated to a child's behavior, often develop feelings of powerlessness. Such children, even when placed in relatively normal environments outside their home, often appear listless, passive, and indifferent. They make little attempt to either seek rewards or avoid discomfort.

COMPARING CLASSICAL AND OPERANT CONDITIONING

Despite the clear differences between classical and operant conditioning, the two forms of learning are similar in a number of ways. We look first at how responses are acquired.

Response Acquisition

CLASSICAL CONDITIONING   Except for conditioned food aversions, which can apparently develop as a result of just one fearful experience, classical conditioning generally requires repeated pairing of the CS and US. Each pairing builds on the learner's previous experience. Psychologists refer to this "building phase" of learning as **response acquisition;** each pairing of the US and CS is called a trial. Learning does not increase indefinitely or by an equal amount on each successive trial. At first the likelihood or strength of the conditioned response increases significantly each time the conditioned stimulus and the unconditioned stimulus are paired. But learning eventually reaches a point of diminishing returns: The amount of each increase gradually becomes smaller until, finally, no further learning occurs, and the likelihood or strength of the CR remains constant despite further pairings of the US and CS. For example, imagine that we first direct a mild puff of air into the subject's eye (the US); the resulting reflexive eye blink is the UR. Then we sound an annoying "buzz" (the CS) just before the puff of air hits the eye. After only 10 trials, we test for conditioning by presenting the "buzz" (CS) alone. In all likelihood, some of the participants in our experiment will blink when they hear the buzzing sound, others may only partially blink, and still others may not blink at all. But after 50 pairings, most or all of the people in the experiment will respond to the buzz with a full and forceful eye blink. At that point, if we continue to pair the US (air puff) and CS (buzz), we will probably see little or no evidence of additional learning. Thus, in general, classical conditioning is a cumulative process with an end point at which no new learning occurs.

Barry Schwartz (1989) has pointed out that the cumulative nature of most classical conditioning works to our benefit. There are always lots of different environmental stimuli present when we experience pain, for example, yet most of those stimuli are irrelevant to the pain. If conditioning occurred on the basis of single events, then these irrelevant stimuli would all generate some type of CR, and we would soon become overwhelmed by the amount of learning—most of it inappropriate or unnecessary—that would take place. Because a number of pairings are usually required to produce a CR, however, in most cases only the relevant cues consistently produce this reaction. We have seen that, up to a point, the more often the US and CS are paired, the stronger the learning. It turns out that the spacing of trials—that is, the time between one pairing and the next—is at least as important as their number. If the trials follow one another rapidly, or if they are very far apart, the subject may need many trials to achieve the expected response strength. If the trials are spaced evenly—neither too far apart nor too close together—learning will occur after fewer trials. It is also important to ensure that the CS and US rarely, if ever, occur alone (not paired). Pairing the CS and US on only some of the learning trials and presenting them separately on other trials is called **intermittent pairing,** a procedure that reduces both the rate of learning and the final level of learning achieved.

OPERANT CONDITIONING   Response acquisition in operant conditioning is somewhat more difficult than in classical conditioning. In classical conditioning, the US invariably elicits the UR, which is the behavior we want to link to the CS. But in operant conditioning, the behavior we want to teach is usually *voluntary* and is not inevitably triggered by outside events. As a result, ensuring that the behavior occurs at all often poses a significant challenge. Sometimes you simply have to wait for the subject to hit on the correct response. In the case of Thorndike's cats, for example, which had only a limited range of action in the puzzle box, Thorndike simply waited for them to trip the latch to open the cage and then reinforced that behavior. Similarly, most babies on their own will eventually make a sound like "mama" in the course of their babbling. If parents just wait long enough, the sound will occur spontaneously, and then they can reinforce the baby with smiles and hugs to increase the likelihood that the baby will say "mama" again in the future.

Waiting for the correct response to occur spontaneously can be a slow and tedious process, however. If you were an animal tamer for a circus, imagine how long you would have to wait for a tiger to decide to jump through a flaming hoop so that you could reinforce that behavior! There are several ways to speed up the process and make it more likely that the desired response will occur so that it can then be reinforced. One possibility is to increase motivation: A hungry laboratory rat is more active and thus more likely to give the response you're looking for than is a well-fed rat. Similarly, an alert and motivated child is more likely to perform some desired behavior than is a passive, unmotivated child.

Intermittent pairing Pairing the conditioned stimulus and the unconditioned stimulus on only a portion of the learning trials.

Skinner box A box often used in operant conditioning of animals, which limits the available response and thus increases the likelihood that the desired response will occur.

Shaping Reinforcing successive approximations to a desired behavior.

Figure 5–5
A rat in a Skinner box.
By pressing the bar, the rat releases food pellets into the box, which reinforces its bar-pressing behavior.

Another way to speed up the process of operant learning is to reduce or eliminate the opportunities for making irrelevant responses, thereby boosting the chances that the correct response will occur. Many researchers interested in operant conditioning make extensive use of the **Skinner box,** a device named after B. F. Skinner, who pioneered the study of operant conditioning. A Skinner box for rats is small, with solid walls. It is relatively bare except for a bar with a cup underneath it (see Figure 5–5). In this simple environment, it doesn't take long for an active, hungry rat to happen to step on the bar, thereby releasing food pellets into the cup, which reinforces the rat's bar-pressing behavior. A Skinner box for pigeons is also bare except for a round disk on one wall and a cup underneath the disk. When a pigeon, exercising its natural food-finding behavior, eventually pecks at the disk, food is released into a cup, and the pecking behavior is reinforced.

Yet another way to speed up response acquisition during operant conditioning is to reinforce *successive approximations* to the desired response. This approach is called **shaping.** In a Skinner box, for example, we might first reward a rat for turning toward the response bar. Once the rat has learned this behavior, we might withhold reinforcement until the rat moves toward the bar. Later, we might reward it only for sniffing the bar or touching it with its nose or paw, and so on. In this way, by reinforcing successive approximations to the desired behavior, we gradually shape the bar-pressing response without waiting passively for the response to occur on its own.

The circus is a wonderful place to see the results of shaping. To teach a tiger to jump through a flaming hoop, the trainer might first reinforce the animal for simply jumping up on a certain pedestal. After that behavior has been learned, the tiger might be reinforced only for leaping from that pedestal to another. Next, the tiger might be required to jump through a hoop between the pedestals to gain its reward. Finally, the hoop might be set on fire and the tiger required to leap through the burning hoop to be rewarded.

How does an animal trainer get a tiger to jump through a flaming hoop so that behavior can be rewarded? The answer is usually through shaping. The trainer reinforces closer and closer approximations of the desired response, until eventually the tiger leaps through the hoop on command.

Shaping can also be used for some types of human learning. A diver's movements are developed and perfected through a series of successive approximations.

Extinction and Spontaneous Recovery

CLASSICAL CONDITIONING Once a behavior is conditioned, does learning last forever, even if the US or the reinforcement is stopped? Let's go back to Pavlov's dogs, which had learned to salivate upon hearing a bell. What would you predict happened over time when the dogs heard the bell (CS) but no food (US) appeared? The conditioned response to the bell—the amount of salivation—gradually decreased until eventually it stopped altogether: The dogs no longer salivated when they heard the bell. This process is called **extinction.** If the conditioned stimulus (the bell) appears alone so often that the learner no longer associates it with the unconditioned stimulus (the food) and stops making the conditioned response (salivation), extinction has taken place. If the sound of a can being opened or a cupboard door opening (CS) is no longer associated with the sight or smell of food (US), your cat may no longer purr (CR) when it hears the CS. If scary music in films (CS) is not associated with frightening events on screen (US), you will eventually stop becoming tense and anxious (CR) when you hear that kind of music. These are all examples of extinction of classically conditioned responses.

Once such a response has been extinguished, is the learning gone forever? Pavlov trained his dogs to salivate when they heard a bell, then extinguished the learning. A few days later, the same dogs were again taken to the laboratory. As soon as they heard the bell, their mouths began to water. The response that had been learned and then extinguished reappeared on its own, with no retraining. This phenomenon is known as **spontaneous recovery.** The dogs' response was only about half as strong as it had been before extinction, but the fact that the response occurred at all indicated that the original learning was not completely lost during extinction (see Figure 5–6). Similarly, if your cat is away for a while and then returns home, it may run to the kitchen and start purring the first few times it hears cans or cupboard doors being opened. And if you stop going to the movies for some time, you may find, the next time you go, that scary music once again makes you tense or anxious. In both cases, responses that were once extinguished have returned spontaneously after the passage of time. Note, however, that responses reappearing during spontaneous recovery do not return at full strength and that generally they extinguish very quickly.

How can extinguished behavior disappear, then reappear again at some later time? According to Mark Bouton (1993, 1994), extinction does not

Extinction A decrease in the strength or frequency of a learned response because of failure to continue pairing the US and CS (classical conditioning) or withholding of reinforcement (operant conditioning).

Spontaneous recovery The reappearance of an extinguished response after the passage of time, without further training.

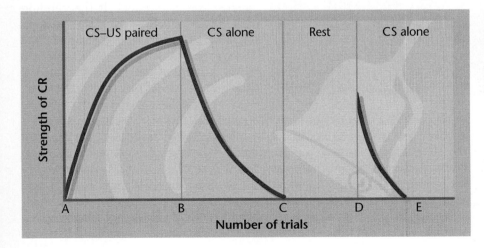

Figure 5–6
Response acquisition and extinction in classical conditioning.
From point *A* to point *B*, the conditioned stimulus and the unconditioned stimulus were paired, and learning increased steadily. From *B* to *C*, however, the conditioned stimulus was presented alone. By point *C*, the response had been extinguished. After a rest period from *C* to *D*, spontaneous recovery occurred—the learned response reappeared at about half the strength that it had at point *B*. When the conditioned stimulus was again presented alone, the response extinguished rapidly (point *E*).

erase conditioned responses. Rather, extinction occurs because *new* learning during extinction interferes with the previously learned response. That is, stimuli that were paired with conditioned responses come to elicit responses different from, and sometimes incompatible with, those original conditioned responses. A buzzer paired with electric shock initially means "Pain is coming!" and comes to elicit a number of responses—changes in heart rate and blood pressure, for example—that accompany painful stimulation. During extinction, the association between the buzzer and pain disappears, and the buzzer therefore elicits another set of responses, which may be entirely different from the originally learned responses. In fact, these new responses may even antagonize or oppose those original responses. For example, if one response during training was an increased heart rate but the new response during extinction is a decreased heart rate, the two clearly cannot happen at the same time. The result is interference, and spontaneous recovery consists of overcoming this interference. According to Bouton, we overcome this interference in one of two ways. The first is called the *renewal effect*. Imagine that you are conditioned in one setting (for example, a dim and dark laboratory), and then your conditioned response is extinguished in a very different setting (for example, a bright and cheerful room). Even with total extinction in the new setting, if you return to the original laboratory room, your conditioned response will immediately return. This occurs because the new, interfering responses learned during extinction are associated with stimuli in the new setting and not with stimuli in the original lab room. The originally learned stimulus-response connections, then, are still intact.

OPERANT CONDITIONING   Extinction and spontaneous recovery also occur in operant conditioning. In operant conditioning, extinction happens as a result of withholding reinforcement. Yet withholding reinforcement does not usually lead to an immediate decrease in the frequency of the response; in fact, when reinforcement is first discontinued, there is often a brief increase in responding before the strength or frequency of the response declines. The behavior itself also changes at the start of extinction: It becomes more variable and often more forceful. For instance, if you put coins in a vending machine and it fails to deliver the goods, you may pull the lever more violently or slam your fist against the glass panel. If the vending machine still fails to produce the item for which you paid, your attempts to get it to work will decrease, and you will finally stop trying altogether.

When reinforcement has been frequent a learned behavior tends to be retained even after reinforcement is reduced. A dog "shaking hands" is an excellent example. Many previous pats on the head for this response tend to keep the dog offering people its paw even when no reward follows.

Just as in classical conditioning, however, extinction does not erase a response forever. Spontaneous recovery may occur if a period of time passes after initial extinction. And once again, both extinction and spontaneous recovery may be understood in terms of interference from new behaviors. If a rat is no longer reinforced for pressing a lever, it will start to engage in other behaviors—turning away from the lever, biting at the corners of the operant chamber, attempting to escape, and so on—and these new behaviors will interfere with the operant response of lever pressing, causing extinction. Spontaneous recovery is a brief victory of original training over these interfering responses.

How easy is it to extinguish behaviors learned through operant conditioning? The stronger the original learning, the longer it takes to stop the action from being performed. That is, in general, the more reinforcement a learner has received, the longer it takes for the response to be extinguished. If you spend many hours training a puppy to sit on command, you will not need to reinforce this behavior very often once the dog grows up. Also, the greater the variety of settings in which learning takes place, the harder it is to extinguish it. Rats trained to run in a single straight alley for food will stop running sooner than rats trained in several different alleys that vary in width, brightness, floor texture, and other features. Complex behavior is also much more difficult to extinguish than simple behavior: Because complex behavior consists of many actions, every action contributing to the total behavior must be extinguished. The pattern of reinforcement used during operant conditioning strongly affects the extinction process as well. Responses that are reinforced only occasionally during acquisition usually resist extinction more strongly than responses that are reinforced every time they occur.

Finally, behaviors learned through punishment rather than reinforcement are especially hard to extinguish. If you have been repeatedly chased by a barking dog when jogging down a particular street, you may change your route. Months later, you don't know if the dog is still around, but your learning may never extinguish: You may never return to running the original route.

One way to speed up the extinction of any kind of learning is to put the learner in a situation that is different from the one in which the response was learned. The response is likely to be weaker in the new situation, and therefore it will disappear more quickly. When the learner is returned to the original setting after extinction has occurred elsewhere, however, the response may return spontaneously, just as in classical conditioning; but it is likely to be weaker than it was initially, and it should be relatively easy to extinguish once and for all.

Generalization and Discrimination

CLASSICAL CONDITIONING   Recall the case of Little Albert and his conditioned fear of white rats. When the experimenters later showed Albert a white rabbit, Albert cried and tried to crawl away, even though he had not been taught to fear rabbits. Similarly, Pavlov noticed that after his dogs had been conditioned to salivate when they heard a bell, their mouths would often water when they heard a buzzer or the ticking of a metronome, even though they had not been taught to salivate to buzzers or ticking sounds. Often in classical conditioning we see that a response learned to one CS also occurs in the presence of other, similar objects or situations. Reacting to a stimulus that is similar to the one to which you have learned to respond is called **stimulus generalization.** In Pavlov's case, the conditioned response generalized from the ringing of a bell to other unusual noises in the testing room. Albert's learned fear of white, furry rats generalized not only to white, furry rabbits but also to all kinds of white, furry objects—he came to fear cotton balls, a fur coat, and even a white-bearded Santa Claus mask.

Wolpe's desensitization therapy, mentioned earlier, provides another illustration of stimulus generalization. In the example we used previously, people who most feared great heights (such as standing on top of a tall building), had generalized the fear response to a wide variety of more or less similar situations: flying in an airplane, standing on a ladder, perhaps watching a high-wire performer in a circus. Photos shot from the tops of tall buildings

Stimulus generalization The transfer of a learned response to different but similar stimuli.

Stimulus discrimination Learning to respond to only one stimulus and to inhibit the response to all other stimuli.

Response generalization Giving a response that is somewhat different from the response originally learned to that stimulus.

Discrimination is an important part of learning, as any wild mushroom fancier knows. A dog or a human who can't distinguish between an edible mushroom and a poisonous one is at a real disadvantage in the hunt for this food.

may even trigger fear in these people while they're sitting safely at home looking at the two-dimensional images.

Stimulus generalization is not inevitable. In a process called **stimulus discrimination,** we can train animals and people not to generalize but rather to make a learned response only to a single specific object or event. If we present several similar objects, only one of which is followed by the unconditioned stimulus, the subject will learn over time to respond only to that stimulus and to inhibit the response in the presence of all other stimuli. If Albert has been presented with a rat and a rabbit and cotton balls and other white, furry objects, but the loud noise (US) had occurred only when the rat appeared, he would have learned to discriminate the white rat from the other objects, and the fear response would not have generalized as it did.

Learning to discriminate is essential in everyday life. As we noted earlier, most children fear loud noises. Because thunder cannot harm a child, however, it would be helpful if children learned not to be afraid when they heard it. Similarly, not all mushrooms are good to eat, and not all strangers are unfriendly. Thus, discrimination is crucial to learning.

OPERANT CONDITIONING   Stimulus generalization can also occur in operant conditioning. For example, a baby who is hugged and kissed for saying "Mama" when he sees his mother may begin to call everyone "Mama"— males and females alike. Although the person whom the baby sees—the stimulus—changes, he responds with the same word. In the same way, the skills you learn when playing tennis may be generalized to badminton, Ping-Pong, and squash.

We often encounter situations in which the same stimulus triggers responses that are different from, but similar to, the one that was taught. In operant conditioning, this process is called **response generalization.** For example, the baby who calls everyone "Mama" may also call his mother "Gaga" or "Baba"—the learning has generalized to other sounds that are similar to the correct response, "Mama." Note that in classical conditioning, response generalization does not occur. If a dog is taught to salivate when it sees an orange light, it will salivate less when it sees a reddish or orange-yellow light, but the response is still salivation rather than some other response.

Discrimination in operant conditioning is accomplished by reinforcing *only* the specific, desired response, and then *only* in the presence of specific stimuli. In this way, pigeons have been trained to peck at a red disk but not at a green one. First, the pigeon is taught to peck at a disk. Then it is presented with two disks, one red and one green. The bird gets food when it pecks at the red one but not when it pecks at the green one. Eventually, it learns to discriminate between the two and will peck only at the red disk. And if it is reinforced only for pecking, and not for other behaviors, it will learn that pecking is the only correct response in this situation. Similarly, babies can learn to say "Mama" only for their own mothers if they are reinforced for using "Mama" correctly and not reinforced when they use the term for other people. In the same way, if they are reinforced only when they say "Mama" and not when they say "Gaga" or "Baba," they will learn that those responses are not appropriate.

NEW LEARNING BASED ON ORIGINAL LEARNING

Learning would be severely limited if learned responses were elicited (or emitted, in operant conditioning) only in the presence of the specific stimuli that are present during training. We have already seen how learning can be expanded to different situations. Here, we see how original learning can be the basis for new learning. We will see that in classical conditioning a conditioned response to one US can be transferred to a different US. Similarly, in operant conditioning, objects that have no intrinsic value can nevertheless become reinforcers because of their association with other, more basic reinforcers.

Higher-Order Conditioning in Classical Conditioning

In classical conditioning, once subjects have learned a conditioned response in the presence of a conditioned stimulus, they can build on that learning to acquire new kinds of learning. For example, after Pavlov's dogs had learned to salivate when they heard a bell, Pavlov was able to use the bell (without food) to teach the dogs to salivate at the sight of a black square. Instead of showing them the square and following it with food, he showed them the square and followed it with the bell until the dogs learned to salivate when they saw the square. In effect, the bell served as a substitute unconditioned stimulus and the black square became a new conditioned stimulus. This procedure is known as **higher-order conditioning,** not because it is more complex or because it incorporates any new principles, but simply because it is conditioning based on previous conditioning.

Higher-order conditioning is difficult to achieve because it races against extinction. The original US, the foundation of the original conditioning, is no longer presented along with the CS and, as we saw earlier, that is precisely the way to extinguish a classically conditioned response. During higher-order conditioning, Pavlov's dogs were exposed to the square and the bell, but no food was presented. In fact, the square became a signal that the bell would *not* be followed by food, so the dogs soon stopped salivating to the square/bell pairing. For higher-order conditioning to succeed, then, the US has to be reintroduced occasionally: Food must be given to the dogs once in a while at the sound of the bell, so that they will continue to salivate when they hear the bell.

Secondary Reinforcers in Operant Conditioning

You have probably noticed that classical conditioning and operant conditioning can act in concert. Specifically, we can use classical conditioning principles to explain why operant learning, particularly human operant learning, is not restricted to food reinforcers and painful punishers.

Some reinforcers, such as food, water, and sex, are intrinsically rewarding in and of themselves. These are called **primary reinforcers.** No prior learning is required to make them reinforcing. Other reinforcers have no intrinsic value, but they acquire value or a sense of reward through association with primary reinforcers. These are called **secondary reinforcers** not because they are less important, but because prior learning or conditioning is required before they will function as reinforcers. Much like conditioned stimuli, secondary reinforcers acquire reinforcing properties because they have been paired with primary reinforcers. A rat learns to get food by pressing a bar; then a buzzer is sounded every time food drops into the dish. Even if the rat stops getting the food, it will continue to press the bar for a while just to hear the buzzer. Although the buzzer by itself has no intrinsic value to the rat, it has become a secondary reinforcer through association with food, a primary reinforcer.

Money is one of the best examples of a secondary reinforcer. Although money is just paper or metal, through its exchange value for food, clothing, and other primary reinforcers, it becomes a powerful reinforcer. Children come to value money only after they learn that it will buy such things as

Higher-order conditioning Conditioning based on previous learning; the conditioned stimulus serves as an unconditioned stimulus for further training.

Primary reinforcer A reinforcer that is rewarding in itself, such as food, water, and sex.

Secondary reinforcer A reinforcer whose value is acquired through association with other primary or secondary reinforcers.

Why is money a secondary reinforcer?

Contingency A reliable "if-then" relationship between two events such as a CS and a US.

candy (a primary reinforcer). Then the money becomes a secondary reinforcer. And through the principles of higher-order conditioning, stimuli paired with a secondary reinforcer can acquire reinforcing properties. Checks and credit cards, for example, are one step removed from money, but can also be highly reinforcing.

CONTINGENCIES

Contingencies in Classical Conditioning

Pavlov's analysis of classical conditioning emphasized that the CS and US must occur closely together in time for classical conditioning to take place. More recent research, however, has shown that a brief time lapse between CS and US is not sufficient; rather, the CS must also precede and provide predictive information about the US. Robert Rescorla (1966, 1967, 1988) refers to this *informative* relationship between CS and US as a **contingency.** Imagine an experiment in which animals are exposed to a tone (CS) and a mild electrical shock (US). One group always hears the tone a fraction of a second before it experiences the shock. Another group sometimes experiences that same tone-shock sequence; at other times the tone sounds a fraction of a second *after* the shock; on still other occasions the tone and shock occur simultaneously. We would expect animals in the first group to show a well-developed startle or fear response when they hear the tone alone; that is just straightforward classical conditioning of a fear response. You might expect the second group also to show a startle or fear response, because the US and CS always occurred closely together in time. In fact, however, the second group will show little, if any, conditioning. Rescorla attributes the superior learning in the first group to the contingency between CS and US: When the tone (CS) always precedes the shock (US), the tone always means that a shock is coming. Not surprisingly, the animals learn to fear the sound of the tone. In the second group, however, the tone says little or nothing about the shock: Sometimes it means that a shock is coming, sometimes it means that the shock is here, and sometimes it means that the shock is over and "the coast is clear." Because the meaning of the tone is ambiguous for this second group, there is little or no conditioning of a fear response.

Although scientists once believed that conditioning was impossible if the CS followed the US, Rescorla's work demonstrates that this is not the case. Imagine a situation in which the tone (the CS) always follows the shock (the US), a so-called *backward conditioning* experiment. After many conditioning trials, we play the tone alone. It's true that we will not see a conditioned startle or fear response; after all, the tone does not predict that a shock is about to occur. But that does not mean that no conditioning has occurred. In fact, the tone predicts that the shock is all over and will not occur again for some time. Thus, the tone comes to produce a conditioned relaxation response rather than a fear response!

The idea that a CS must provide information about the US for conditioning to occur was confirmed when Leon Kamin (1969) discovered that the rat experiencing a noise (CS) followed by a brief shock (US) would indeed quickly learn to react with fear to the onset of the noise. Then, he added a second CS—a light—along with the noise. Contrary to what you might expect, the rats showed no conditioned fear when only the light was presented; it was as if they did not realize that the light was also a signal that a shock was forthcoming. Kamin concluded that the original learning had a

blocking effect on new learning. Once the rats learned that noise signaled the onset of shock, adding yet another cue (a light) provided no new information about the likelihood of shock, so no new learning took place. According to Kamin, then, classical conditioning occurs only when a CS tells the learner something *new* or *additional* about the likelihood that the US will be forthcoming.

Contingencies in Operant Conditioning

Contingencies also figure prominently in operant conditioning. Seldom, either in life or in the laboratory, are we rewarded every time we do something. And this is just as well. Experiments demonstrate that *partial* or *intermittent reinforcement* results in behavior that will persist longer than behavior learned by *continuous reinforcement*. When they receive only occasional reinforcement, subjects learn not to expect reinforcement with every response, so they continue responding in the absence of reinforcement in hopes that they will eventually gain the desired reward. Vending machines and slot machines illustrate the effects of continuous and partial reinforcement on extinction. Each time you put the correct change into a vending machine, you get something such as food in return (reinforcement); if a vending machine is broken and you receive nothing for your coins, you are unlikely to drop additional coins into it! By contrast, casino slot machines pay off only occasionally; therefore, you might continue putting coins into a slot machine for a long time even though you are not receiving anything in return.

Whenever partial reinforcement is given, the rule for determining when and how often reinforcers will be delivered is called the **schedule of reinforcement**. Schedules are either fixed or variable, and may be based on either the number of correct responses or the elapsed time between correct responses. The most common reinforcement schedules are fixed-interval and variable-interval schedules, which are based on time, and fixed-ratio and variable-ratio schedules, which are based on the number of correct responses. Table 5–1 describes some everyday examples of reinforcement schedules.

Blocking A process whereby prior conditioning prevents conditioning to a second stimulus even when the two stimuli are presented simultaneously.

Schedule of reinforcement In operant conditioning, the rule for determining when and how often reinforcers will be delivered.

The slot machine is a classic example of a variable-ratio schedule of reinforcement. The machine eventually pays off, but always after a variable number of plays. Because people keep hoping that the next play will be rewarded, they maintain a high rate of response over a long period of time.

Fixed-interval schedule A reinforcement schedule in which the correct response is reinforced after a fixed length of time since the last reinforcement.

Variable-interval schedule A reinforcement schedule in which the correct response is reinforced after varying lengths of time following the last reinforcement.

Fixed-ratio schedule A reinforcement schedule in which the correct response is reinforced after a fixed number of correct responses.

On a **fixed-interval schedule,** subjects are reinforced for the first correct response only after a certain time has passed following the previous correct response; that is, they have to wait for a set period before they can be reinforced again. With fixed-interval schedules, performance tends to fall off immediately after each reinforcement and then to pick up again as the time for the next reinforcement draws near. For example, when exams are given at fixed intervals—like midterms and finals—students tend to increase the intensity of their studying just before an exam and then decrease it sharply right after the exam until shortly before the next one (see Figure 5–7).

A **variable-interval schedule** reinforces correct responses after varying lengths of time following the last reinforcement. One reinforcement might be given after 6 minutes, the next after 4 minutes, the next after 5 minutes, the next after 3 minutes. Subjects learn to give a slow, steady pattern of responses, being careful not to be so slow as to miss all the rewards. Thus, if several exams are given during a semester at unpredictable intervals, students have to keep studying at a steady rate all the time, because on any given day there might be an exam.

On a **fixed-ratio schedule,** a certain number of correct responses must occur before reinforcement is provided. This results in a high response rate because making many responses in a short time yields more rewards. Being paid on a piecework basis is an example of a fixed-ratio schedule. Farmwork-

---

TABLE 5-1

EXAMPLES OF REINFORCEMENT IN EVERYDAY LIFE

Continuous reinforcement (reinforcement every time the response is made)	Putting money in the parking meter to avoid a ticket. Putting coins in a vending machine to get candy or soda.
Fixed-ratio schedule (reinforcement after a fixed number of responses)	Being paid on a piecework basis—in the garment industry, workers may be paid a fee per 100 dresses sewn. Taking a multi-item test. This is an example of negative reinforcement—as soon as you finish those items on the test, you can leave!
Variable-ratio schedule (reinforcement after a varying number of responses)	Playing a slot machine—the machine is programmed to pay off after a certain number of responses have been made, but that number keeps changing. This type of schedule creates a steady rate of responding, because players know if they play long enough, they will win. Sales commissions—you have to talk to many customers before you make a sale, and you never know whether the next one will buy. Again, the number of sales calls you make, not how much time passes, will determine when you are reinforced by a sale. And the number of sales calls will vary.
Fixed-interval schedule (reinforcement after a fixed amount of time has passed)	You have an exam coming up, and as time goes by and you haven't studied, you have to make up for it all by a certain time, and that means cramming. Picking up a salary check, which occurs every week or every 2 weeks.
Variable-interval schedule (reinforcement of first response after varying amounts of time)	Surprise quizzes in a course cause a steady rate of studying because you never know when they'll occur, and so you have to be prepared all the time. Watching a football game, waiting for a touchdown. It could happen anytime—if you leave the room, you may miss it, so you have to keep watching continuously.

Source: From Landy, 1987, p. 212. Adapted by permission.

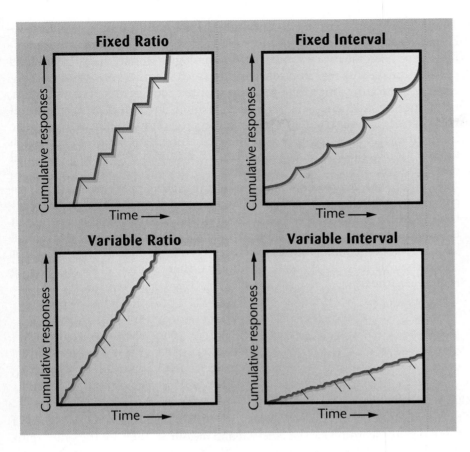

Fixed Ratio

Cumulative responses

Time →

Fixed Interval

Cumulative responses

Time →

Variable Ratio

Cumulative responses

Time →

Variable Interval

Cumulative responses

Time →

Figure 5–7
Response patterns to schedules of reinforcement.
The *fixed-ratio* schedule is characterized by a high rate of response and a pause after each reinforcement. On a *fixed-interval* schedule, as the time for reinforcement approaches, the number of responses increases, and the slope becomes steeper. A *variable-ratio* schedule produces a high rate of response with little or no pause after each reinforcement. On a *variable-interval* schedule, the response rate is moderate and relatively constant. Notice that each tick mark on the graph represents one reinforcement.

ers might get $3 for every 10 baskets of cherries they pick. The more they pick, the more money they make. Under a fixed-ratio schedule, a brief pause after reinforcement is followed by a rapid and steady response rate until the next reinforcement.

On a **variable-ratio schedule,** the number of correct responses necessary to gain reinforcement is not constant. The casino slot machine is a good example of a variable-ratio schedule: It may pay off, but you have no idea when. And because there is always a chance of hitting the jackpot, the temptation to keep playing is great. Subjects on a variable-ratio schedule tend not to pause after reinforcement and have a high rate of response over a long period of time. Because they never know when reinforcement may come, they keep on trying. Similarly, salespeople working on commission know that every attempt will not produce a sale, but it is certain that the more customers they approach, the more sales they will make.

A REVIEW OF CLASSICAL CONDITIONING AND OPERANT CONDITIONING

Classical and operant conditioning both focus on building associations between stimuli and responses. Both are subject to extinction and spontaneous recovery as well as to generalization and discrimination. The main difference between the two is that in classical conditioning, the learner is passive and the desired behavior is usually involuntary, whereas in operant conditioning, the learner is active and the desired behavior is usually voluntary.

However, some psychologists play down these differences, suggesting that classical and operant conditioning are simply two different ways of bringing about the same kind of learning. For example, classical conditioning can be used to shape voluntary movements (P. L. Brown & Jenkins,

Biofeedback A technique that uses monitoring devices to provide precise information about internal physiological processes, such as heart rate or blood pressure, to teach people to gain voluntary control over these functions.

Cognitive learning Learning that depends on mental processes that are not directly observable.

Latent learning Learning that is not immediately reflected in a behavior change.

1968). Moreover, operant conditioning of involuntary processes has occurred in automatic conditioning studies in which both humans and animals have been taught to control certain biological functions, such as blood pressure, heart rate, and skin temperature (see *Controversies*). Finally, in operant conditioning, once the operant response becomes linked to a stimulus, the response looks and acts very much like an unconditioned response. If you have been reinforced repeatedly for stepping on the brake when a traffic light turns red, the red light comes to elicit braking behavior just as an unconditioned stimulus elicits an unconditioned response in classical conditioning.

If, then, classical and operant conditioning are simply two different procedures for achieving the same end (Hearst, 1975), we need to pay more attention to the similarities between the two. But the nature of learning itself is still open to new theories. Classical and operant conditioning concern the learning of observable, external, objectively measurable responses. But it seems that, at least in the case of humans, there's often more to learning than meets the eye.

COGNITIVE LEARNING

Classical and operant conditioning both depend on direct experience and stimulus control. Classical conditioning requires that a learner be exposed to a CS and a US. Similarly, operant conditioning requires that a response be followed by a consequence. Without a reinforcer or punisher, operant conditioning cannot occur. Some psychologists insist that because the elements of these types of learning can be *observed* and *measured*, they are the only legitimate kinds of learning to study scientifically. Other psychologists, however, point up the importance of mental activities such as attention, expectation, thinking, and remembering as crucial to the process of learning. We learn how to find our way around a building or neighborhood, we learn what to expect from a given situation, we learn abstract concepts, and we can even learn about situations that we have never experienced firsthand. These kinds of **cognitive learning** are impossible to observe and measure directly, but they can be *inferred* from behavior; thus, they, too, are legitimate subjects for scientific inquiry. In fact, much of the recent research in the area of learning concerns cognitive learning: What goes on *inside* us when we learn.

Latent Learning and Cognitive Maps

Interest in cognitive learning actually began shortly after the earliest work in both classical and operant conditioning. Edward Chace Tolman, one of the pioneers in the study of cognitive learning, acknowledged in his presidential address to the American Psychological Association (1938) that the psychology of learning "has been and still is primarily a matter of agreeing or disagreeing with Thorndike, or trying in minor ways to improve upon him." For his part, Tolman disagreed with Thorndike on two key points. First, Tolman felt that Thorndike's law of effect neglected the inner drives or motives that made learners pursue the "satisfying state," and he felt that the concept of response needed to include a range of behaviors—a "performance" that would allow learners to reach their goal. Second, Tolman felt that learning occurs even before the subject reaches the goal and with or without reinforcement. Tolman called this process **latent learning** and demonstrated it in a famous experiment with C. H. Honzik in 1930.

Two groups of hungry rats were placed in a maze and required to find their way from a start box to an end box. The first group found food pellets

CONTROVERSIES
SHAPING BETTER HEALTH THROUGH BIOFEEDBACK

For 20 of her 29 years, Janet B. had suffered from tension headaches. The dull aching would begin in the morning and last all day. Her doctor referred her to a psychologist who traced the headaches to excessive contraction of the frontalis muscle, the main muscle in the forehead. He then set about teaching Janet to relax this muscle through biofeedback. Electrodes attached to Janet's forehead measured the degree of contraction in the frontalis muscle. The machine also registered the contraction with an audible tone—the less the contraction, the lower the pitch of the tone. Janet worked to relax the muscle more and more, using the dropping pitch of the tone as her guide. Over the course of several dozen 30-minute training sessions Janet became increasingly adept at controlling frontalis contraction. Three months after therapy had begun, she reported virtually no further tension headaches (Budzynski, Stoyva, & Adler, 1970).

Biofeedback training is an operant conditioning technique in which instruments are used to give learners information about the strength of a biological response over which they seek to gain control. A biofeedback device records information about a particular biological response—muscle contractions, blood pressure, heart rate—which normally proceeds outside our conscious awareness. Variations in the strength of the response are reflected in the form of a light, a tone, or some other signal that varies according to the measured level of the response. Through the feedback information—the tone or light—the response is learned little by little, as with other shaping techniques.

Biofeedback training has been used for a wide variety of disorders. More recently, researchers have drawn on biofeedback techniques to treat a painful bowel condition in infants (Cox et al., 1994), incontinence in adults (Keck et al., 1994), as well as migraine (Wauquier et al., 1995) and post-traumatic headaches (Ham & Packard, 1996).

Biofeedback has become a well-established treatment for a number of medical problems, including tension headaches and migraine head-aches as well as asthma and peptic ulcers. Biofeedback has also been used by athletes, musicians, and other performers to control the anxiety that can interfere with their performance. Marathon runners use it to help overcome the tight shoulders and shallow breathing that can prevent them from finishing races. Although most reports of the effectiveness of biofeedback in sports come from personal accounts, rather than controlled studies, this anecdotal evidence strongly suggests that bio-feedback offers real benefits (Peper, 1990). It has even been used in space. NASA combined a program of biofeedback with cognitive therapy (such as mental messages) to reduce the motion sickness astronauts experience at zero gravity (Cowlings, 1989).

Biofeedback has become a well-established treatment for a number of medical problems, but some still reject it as quackery.

Biofeedback treatment does have some drawbacks. Learning the technique takes considerable time, effort, patience, and discipline. But it gives control of treatment to the patient, a major advantage over other types of treatment, and it has achieved impressive results in alleviating certain medical problems (Olton & Noonberg, 1980).

Despite its successes, some still reject biofeedback as quackery (National Institute of Health Consensus Development Conference, 1996). Critics challenge the scientific rigor of studies that have evaluated biofeedback and the professional caliber of the technicians who operate the various biofeedback instruments (Middaugh, 1990). In addition, some conditions, such as high blood pressure, do not always respond well to biofeedback training (McGrady, 1996; Weaver & McGrady, 1995). Further research may reveal other conditions for which this type of treatment is not appropriate. Advocates of the technique argue that when biofeedback is viewed properly—as a way to learn self-regulation of biological processes rather than as a therapy—and when it's evaluated on those terms, it can stand up to the most rigorous scientific scrutiny (P. A. Norris, 1986).

Questions

1. Have you, or anyone you know, ever used biofeedback procedures for self-regulation of biological processes? If so, what kind of feedback information did you use (tone, light, etc.), how well were you able to learn to control the biological process, and what reinforcers did you use (if any) other than the feedback information itself?

2. Based on what you have read, would you recommend biofeedback to someone who suffers from motion sickness or headaches? Why or why not?

Cognitive map A learned mental image of a spatial environment that may be called on to solve problems when stimuli in the environment change.

(a reward) in the end box; the second group found nothing there. According to the principles of operant conditioning, the first group would learn the maze better than the second group—which was, indeed, what happened. But when Tolman took some of the rats from the second, unreinforced group and gave them food at the goal box, almost immediately they started running the maze as well as the rats in the first group (see Figure 5–8). He explained these dramatic findings by noting that the unrewarded rats had actually learned a great deal about the maze as they wandered around inside it. In fact, they may actually have learned *more* about the maze than had the rats that had been trained with food reinforcement, but their learning was *latent*—stored internally in some way but not yet reflected in their behavior. When they were given a good reason (a food reward) to run the maze quickly, they put their latent learning to use.

Since Tolman's time, a great deal of work has been done on the nature of latent learning. From their studies of how animals or humans find their way around a maze, a building, or a neighborhood with many available routes, psychologists have proposed that latent learning is stored in the form of a mental image, or **cognitive map**, of the whole area. When the proper time comes, the learner can call up the stored image or map and put it to use.

In response to Tolman's theory of latent learning, Thorndike proposed an experiment to test whether a rat could learn to run a maze and store a cognitive image of the maze without experiencing a maze firsthand. His experimental design envisioned researchers carrying each rat through the maze in a small wiremesh container and then rewarding the rat at the end of each trail as if it had run the maze itself. He predicted that the rat would show little or no evidence of learning compared to rats that had learned the same maze on their own through trial and error. Neither he nor Tolman ever conducted the experiment.

Two decades later, however, researchers at the University of Kansas picked up on Thorndike's idea (McNamara, Long, & Wike, 1956). But instead of taking the passive rats through the "correct" path in a simple maze, they carried each passenger rat over the same path that a free-running part-

Figure 5–8
Maze used to study latent learning in rats.
The results of the classic Tolman-Honzik study are revealed in the graph. Group A never received a food reward; Group B was rewarded each day. Group C was not rewarded until the eleventh day, but note the significant change in the rats' behavior on Day 12. The results suggest that Group C had been learning all along, although this learning was not reflected in their performance until they were rewarded with food for demonstrating the desired behaviors.

Source: From Tolman and Honzik, 1930.

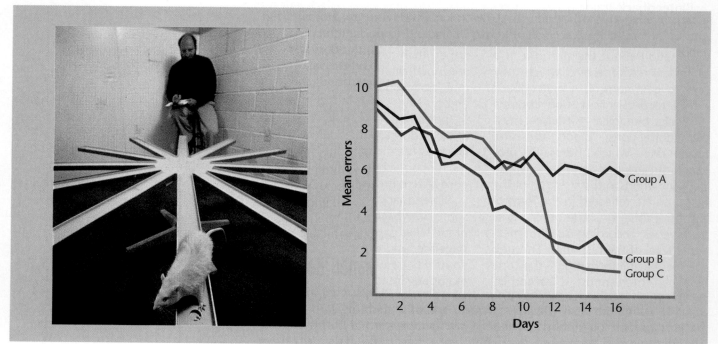

ner rat had taken on the same trail. Contrary to Thorndike's prediction, the passenger rats learned the maze just as well as their active counterparts. In a second version of the experiment, the experimenters covered windows and masked the lights in the room so that the passenger rats would have only the directional cues to orient them to the maze. Under these conditions, the passenger rats seemed not to have learned to run the maze at all, performing only as well as they might by chance.

The first experiment seems to confirm Tolman's view of latent learning of cognitive maps. The second experiment suggests that rats use information from their surroundings as an important part of their cognitive maps. More recent research reconfirms this picture of cognitive spatial learning in animals. It appears that animals demonstrate a great deal more flexibility when it comes to solving problems and making choices than can be explained by simple conditioning (Domjan, 1987). In a series of experiments with rats in a radial maze, the rats consistently recalled which arms they had previously traveled down and which they hadn't, even when scent cues were removed and all arms contained a bait reward. Researchers concluded that these rats had developed a cognitive map or spatial memory of their experiences in the maze (Olton & Samuelson, 1976). The key point is that, even in rats, learning involves more than a change in observable behavior. It also appears to involve changes in unobservable mental processes that may (or may not) be reflected at some future time in the subject's behavior.

Insight Learning that occurs rapidly as a result of understanding all the elements of a problem.

Insight and Learning Sets

Another phenomenon that highlights the importance of cognitive processing in learning is **insight,** the sudden "coming together" of the elements of a situation so that the most efficient path is instantly clear or the solution to a problem suddenly strikes the learner. In this case, learning does not progress slowly and gradually on a smooth curve as a result of practice but suddenly shoots up from unsuccessful trial and error to instant success.

During World War I, the German Gestalt psychologist Wolfgang Köhler conducted a series of experiments on insightful learning. He placed a chimpanzee in a cage with a banana on the ground just outside the cage, but not within reach. When the animal realized that it couldn't reach the banana by stretching out its arms, it initially reacted with frustration. After a while, the chimp started looking at what was in the cage, including a stick left there by the experimenters. Sometimes quite suddenly, the chimp would grab the stick, poke it through the bars of the cage, and drag the banana within reach. The same kind of sudden insight occurred when the banana was hung from the roof of the cage, just out of the chimp's grasp. This time, inside the cage were some boxes, which the chimp quickly learned to move to the spot under the banana and stack up high enough so it could climb up to snatch the food.

Are the complex cognitive processes that produce insight limited to higher animals such as apes and humans? In 1984, four Harvard University psychologists presented the banana-and-box problem to a small group of pigeons to see if they, too, were capable of insight learning (R. Epstein

Learning set The ability to become increasingly more effective in solving problems as more problems are solved.

Köhler's experiments with chimpanzees illustrate learning through insight. In this photo one of the chimps has arranged a stack of boxes to reach bananas hanging from the ceiling. Insights gained in this problem-solving situation may transfer to similar ones.

et al., 1984). Because moving boxes around is not as natural a behavior for pigeons as it is for chimps, the researchers first conditioned the pigeons, through standard shaping procedures, to push a box toward a particular target—a green spot on the wall of the training cage. On separate occasions, the pigeons were also taught to climb onto a box that was stuck to the floor and to peck at a small picture of a banana to receive a food reward. The question then was: Could the pigeons put the two new behaviors together to solve the problem of the banana and the box? When the pigeons were presented with an out-of-reach hanging picture of a banana and with a box, Epstein and his coworkers reported that each pigeon initially showed confusion and, just like Köhler's chimps, looked for a while from the hanging picture to the box. Then, fairly suddenly, each pigeon began to push the box toward the picture, stopping now and then to sight the picture and to check the direction in which to push the box. When they had the box underneath the picture of the banana, each of the pigeons then climbed on top and pecked at the picture to receive its reward.

Epstein and his coworkers felt that the main reason pigeons couldn't solve the problem without preliminary training is that pigeons (unlike chimps) don't already know how boxes can be pushed around and used in various ways, nor do they normally value bananas. When pigeons are given the right tools and are taught how to use them, however, they show that they can solve quite complex cognitive problems. In other words, in this view, Köhler's chimps quickly learned how to reach the banana because they already knew how to use sticks and boxes to get at objects and because they valued bananas.

Previous learning can also be used to speed up new learning, a process demonstrated clearly in a series of studies by Harry Harlow with rhesus monkeys (Harlow, 1949). Harlow presented each monkey with two boxes—say, a round green box on the left side of a tray and a square red box on the right side. A morsel of food was put under one of the boxes. The monkey was permitted to lift just one box; if it chose the correct box, it got the food. On the next trial, the food was put under the same box (which had been moved to a new position), and the monkey again got to choose just one box. Each monkey had six trials to figure out which box covered the food no matter where that box was located. Then the monkeys were given a new set of choices—say, between a blue triangular box and an orange pentagonal one—and another six trials, and so on with other shapes and colors of boxes.

How long did it take for the monkeys to figure out that in any set of six trials, food was always under the same box? Initially, the monkeys chose boxes randomly, by trial and error; sometimes they would find food, but just as often they would not. However, after a while their behavior changed: In just one or two trials, they would find the correct box, which they chose consistently thereafter until the experimenter supplied new boxes. They seemed to have learned the underlying principle—that the food would always be under the same box—and they used that learning to solve almost instantly each new set of choices presented by the experimenter.

Harlow concluded that the monkeys had "learned how to learn" or that they had established **learning sets:** Within the limited range of choices available, they had discovered how to tell which box would give them what they wanted. By extension, Köhler's chimps could be said to have established learning sets for various ways of obtaining food that was just out of reach. When presented with the familiar problem of reaching the banana, the chimps simply called up the appropriate learning sets and solved the problem. By contrast, Epstein's pigeons first had to be taught the appropriate learning sets, and then they, too, were able to solve the problem. In all these cases, the animals seemed to have learned more than just specific behaviors—they apparently learned how to learn. Whether this means that animals can think is an issue that is still being studied and debated. We will explore the question of cognitive learning in animals later in this chapter; then, in Chapter 7, Cognition and Language, we will look more closely at the question of whether animals can think.

Learning by Observing

Another group of psychologists, *social learning theorists*, also challenge the idea that most or all human learning stems from classical or operant conditioning. **Social learning theory** focuses on the extent to which we learn not just from firsthand experience, the kind of learning explained by classical and operant conditioning, but also from watching what happens to other people or by hearing about something. In fact, we can learn new behaviors without ever actually performing them or being reinforced for them. The first time you drive a car, you tend to drive carefully because you have been told to do so, you have been warned about driving carelessly, you have watched people drive carefully, and you've seen what happens when people drive carelessly. In other words, you learned a great deal about driving before you ever got behind the wheel of a car.

This kind of **observational** or **vicarious learning** is quite common. By watching models, we can learn such things as how to start a lawn mower and how to saw wood. In this way, we also learn how to show love or respect or concern, as well as how to show hostility and aggression. When the Federal Communications Commission (FCC) banned cigarette commercials on TV, the commissioners were acting on the belief that when people saw attractive models smoking, they would be prompted to imitate that behavior. They removed the model to discourage the behavior.

Of course, we do not imitate everything that other people do. Social learning theory accounts for this in several ways (Bandura, 1977, 1986). First, you must not only see but also *pay attention* to what the model does; this is more likely if the model commands attention (as does a famous or attractive person or an expert). Second, you must *remember* what the model did. Third, you have to convert what you learned into action: You may learn a great deal from watching a model but have no particular reason to display what you have learned as behavior. This distinction between *learning* and *performance* is crucial to social learning theorists: They stress that learning can occur without any change in outward or overt behavior. Finally, the extent to which we display behaviors that have been learned through observation can be affected by **vicarious reinforcement** and **vicarious punishment.** That is, our willingness to perform acts that we learn by observation depends in part on what happens to the people we are watching. So, when children watching TV or movies see people using drugs or behaving violently, we have cause for concern about whether the plot punishes the actors for their behavior.

The foremost proponent of social learning theory is Albert Bandura, who refers to his learning theory as a *social cognitive theory* (Bandura, 1986). In a classic experiment, Bandura (1965) demonstrated that people can learn a behavior without being reinforced for doing so and that learning a behavior

Social learning theory A view of learning that emphasizes the ability to learn by observing a model or receiving instructions, without firsthand experience by the learner.

Observational or **vicarious learning** Learning by observing other people's behavior.

Vicarious reinforcement and **vicarious punishment** Reinforcement or punishment experienced by models that affects the willingness of others to perform the behaviors they learned by observing those models.

In observational or vicarious learning, we learn by watching a model perform a particular action and then trying to imitate that action correctly. Some actions would be very difficult to master without observational learning.

and performing it are not the same thing. Bandura randomly divided a group of 66 nursery-school children (33 boys and 33 girls) into three groups of 22 subjects each. Each child individually watched a film in which an adult model walked up to an adult-size plastic doll and ordered it to move out of the way. When the doll failed to obey, the model became aggressive, pushing the doll on its side, punching it in the nose, hitting it with a rubber mallet, kicking it around the room, and throwing rubber balls at it.

The film ended differently for children in each of the three groups, however. Children in the *model-rewarded condition* saw the model showered with candies, soft drinks, and praise by a second adult—an example of vicarious reinforcement. Those in the *model-punished condition* witnessed the second adult shaking a finger at the model, scolding, and spanking him—an example of vicarious punishment. Youngsters in the *no-consequences condition* saw a version of the film that ended with the scene of aggression—no second adult appeared, so there were no consequences for the model.

Immediately after seeing the film, the children were individually escorted into another room where they found a doll, rubber balls, a mallet, and many other toys. As a child played alone for 10 minutes, observers recorded the youngster's behavior from behind a one-way mirror. Every time a child spontaneously repeated any of the aggressive acts seen in the film, that child was coded as *performing* the behavior. After 10 minutes, an experimenter entered the room and offered the child treats in return for imitating or repeating things the model had done or said to the doll. Bandura used the number of successfully imitated behaviors as a measure of how much the child had *learned* by watching the model (see Figure 5–9).

Analysis of the data revealed that (1) children who had observed the model being rewarded were especially likely to perform the model's behavior spontaneously; but (2) children in all three groups had learned to imitate the model's behavior equally well, and quite accurately at that (see Figure 5–10).

Figure 5–9
Bandura's experiment in learned aggressive behavior.
After watching an adult behave aggressively toward an inflated doll, the children in Bandura's study imitated many of the aggressive acts of the adult model.

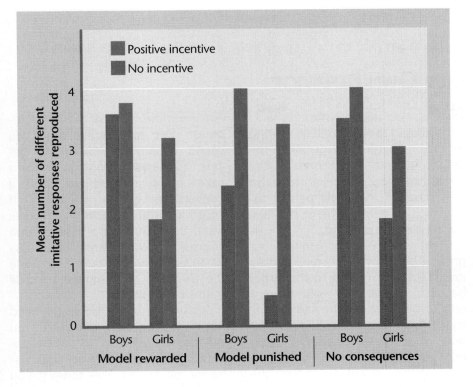

Figure 5–10
As the graph shows, even though all the children in Bandura's study of imitative aggression learned the model's behavior, they *performed* differently depending on whether the model they saw was rewarded or punished.

Source: Bandura, 1965, p. 592. Copyright © 1965 by the American Psychological Association. Reprinted by permission.

The children in this study learned aggressive behavior without being reinforced for it. Although reinforcement of a model is not necessary for vicarious learning to occur, seeing a model reinforced or punished nonetheless provides us with useful information that may then affect our willingness to show or perform what we have learned. Vicarious reinforcement and punishment tell us what the correct or incorrect behavior is and what is likely to happen to us if we imitate the model. Moreover, Bandura stresses that human beings are capable of setting performance standards for themselves and then rewarding (or punishing) themselves for achieving or failing to achieve those standards as a way to regulate their own behavior. (see *Applying Psychology*)

The emphasis that social learning theory places on expectations, insight, information, self-satisfaction, and self-criticism enables us to broaden our understanding of how people learn skills and gain abilities as it helps us grasp how attitudes, values, and ideas pass from person to person. According to this view of learning, human beings use the powers of sight as well as insight, hindsight, and foresight to interpret their own experiences and those of others (Bandura, 1962). By drawing attention to the importance of modeling, social learning theory also points out how not to teach something unintentionally. For example, suppose you want to teach a child not to hit other children. You might think that slapping the child as punishment would change the behavior, while reinforcing more desirable behavior. But social learning theory maintains that slapping the child only demonstrates that hitting is an effective means of getting one's way. You and the child would both be better off if your actions reflected a less aggressive way of dealing with other people (Bandura, 1973, 1977).

COGNITIVE LEARNING IN NONHUMANS

Contemporary approaches to conditioning emphasize that conditioned stimuli, reinforcers, and punishers provide *information* about the environment. According to this view, classical and operant conditioning are not purely

True or False: Punishing a child for aggressive behavior by slapping or spanking can teach the child to act more violently

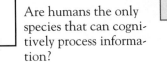

Are humans the only species that can cognitively process information?

APPLYING PSYCHOLOGY
MODIFYING YOUR OWN BEHAVIOR

Can you modify your own behavior? Yes, but first identify the behavior you want to acquire—the "target" behavior. You will be more successful if you focus on acquiring a new behavior rather than on eliminating an existing behavior. For example, instead of setting a target of being less shy, you might define the target behavior as becoming more outgoing or more sociable. Other possible target behaviors might include behaving more assertively, studying more, and getting along better with your roommates. In each case, you have spotlighted the behavior that you want to *acquire* rather than the behavior that you want to reduce or eliminate.

The next step is to *define the target behavior precisely:* What exactly do you mean by "assertive" or "sociable"? Begin by imagining situations in which the target behavior could be performed. Then describe in writing these situations and the way in which you now respond to them. For example, in the case of shyness, you might write: "When I am sitting in the lecture hall, waiting for class to begin, I don't talk to the people around me." Next, write down how you would rather act in that situation: "Ask the person sitting next to me how he or she likes the class or the professor."

Then you need to *monitor* your present behavior by keeping a daily log of activities related to the target behavior to establish your present rate of behavior. At the same time, try to figure out whether your present, undesirable behavior is being reinforced in some way. For example, instead of talking before the class begins, you may be reading the newspaper.

The next step—the basic principle of self-modification—is to provide yourself with a positive reinforcer that is contingent on specific improvements in the target behavior. You may be able to use the same reinforcer that now maintains your undesirable behavior, or you may want to pick a new reinforcer.

For example, if you want to increase the amount of time you spend socializing, you might decide to reward yourself with a token for every time you begin a conversation with a new person. If your favorite pastime is movie watching, you might then charge yourself three tokens for a day when you haven't socialized, while the privilege of going to a movie might cost six.

Remember that behavior need not be learned all in one piece. You can use shaping, or successive approximations, to change your behavior bit by bit over time. If you would like to attempt a program of self-improvement, a book by David Watson and Roland Tharp, titled *Self-Directed Behavior: Self-Modification for Personal Adjustment* (1997), offers step-by-step instructions and exercises.

To learn more about modifying your behavior, visit our website at **www.prenhall.com/morris**

mechanical processes that can proceed without at least some cognitive activity. Thus, because all animals can be conditioned, we might suspect that all animals are capable of at least minimal cognitive processing of information. We have also seen that animals can perform whole patterns of operant behaviors, even when the pattern as a whole has never been reinforced. Moreover, animals are capable of latent learning, learning cognitive maps, and insight, all of which involve cognitive processes. Do nonhuman animals also exhibit other evidence of cognitive learning? The answer seems to be a qualified yes. For example, rats that watch other rats try a novel or unfamiliar food without negative consequences show an increased tendency to eat the new food (Galef, 1993). In a different experiment, one group of rats watched another group experience extinction; as a result, the observer rats themselves extinguished faster than if they had not watched the model rats (Heyes, Jaldow, & Dawson, 1993). Apparently, the observer rats learned something about the absence of reward simply by seeing what happened to the other rats. These surprising results, along with reports that animals as diverse as chickens and octopi learn by watching others, further support the notion that nonhuman animals do indeed learn in ways that reflect the cognitive theory of learning.

SUMMARY

This chapter concentrates on **learning,** the process by which experience or practice produces a relatively permanent change in behavior or potential behavior. The basic form of learning is known as **conditioning.** In **classical (or Pavlovian) conditioning,** a response naturally elicited by one stimulus comes to be elicited by a different, formerly neutral stimulus. In **operant (or instrumental) conditioning,** behaviors are emitted to earn rewards or avoid punishment.

CLASSICAL CONDITIONING

Pavlov's Conditioning Experiments

Russian psychologist Ivan Pavlov hit upon classical (or Pavlovian) conditioning almost by accident when studying digestive processes. He trained a dog to salivate at the sound of a bell by presenting the sound just before food was brought into the room. Eventually the dog began to salivate at the sound of the bell alone.

Elements of Classical Conditioning

Classical conditioning involves pairing a response naturally caused by one stimulus with another, previously neutral stimulus. There are four basic elements to this transfer: The **unconditioned stimulus (US),** often food, invariably causes an organism to respond in a specific way. The **unconditioned response (UR)** is the reaction (such as salivation) that always results from the unconditioned stimulus. The **conditioned stimulus (CS)** is a stimulus (such as a bell) that does not initially bring about the desired response; over the course of conditioning, however, the CS comes to produce the desired response when presented alone. Finally, the **conditioned response (CR)** is the behavior that the organism learns to exhibit in the presence of a conditioned stimulus.

Classical Conditioning in Humans

Humans also learn to associate certain sights or sounds with other stimuli. John Watson and Rosalie Rayner conditioned a little boy, Albert, to fear white rats by making a loud, frightening noise every time the boy was shown a rat. Using much the same principle, Mary Cover Jones developed a method for unlearning fears: She paired the sight of a caged rat, at gradually decreasing distances, with a child's pleasant experience of eating candy. This method evolved into **desensitization therapy,** a conditioning technique designed to gradually reduce anxiety about a particular object or situation. Recently, scientists have discovered that the immune system may respond to classical conditioning techniques, thus allowing doctors to use fewer drugs in treating certain disorders.

Classical Conditioning Is Selective

Some kinds of conditioning are accomplished very easily, whereas other kinds may never occur. Research demonstrating that we develop phobias about snakes and spiders, for example, but almost never about flowers or cooking utensils illustrates Seligman's principles of *preparedness* and *contrapreparedness*, respectively. The ease with which we develop **conditioned food** (or **taste**) **aversions** also illustrates learning preparedness. Conditioned food aversions are exceptions to the general rules about classical conditioning. Animals can learn to avoid poisonous food even if there is a lengthy interval between eating the food and becoming ill. In many cases, only one pairing of conditioned and unconditioned stimuli is necessary for learning to take place.

OPERANT CONDITIONING

Classical conditioning focuses on a behavior that invariably follows a particular event, whereas **operant (or instrumental) conditioning** concerns the learning of behavior that operates on the environment: The person or animal behaves in a particular way to gain something desired or avoid something unpleasant. This behavior is initially emitted rather than elicited—you wave your hand to flag down a taxi, dogs beg at the dinner table to get food.

Thorndike's Conditioning Experiments

Psychologist Edward Lee Thorndike was the first researcher to study **operant behavior** systematically. He used a "puzzle box" to determine how cats learn.

Elements of Operant Conditioning

Thorndike's work still stands as a landmark in our understanding of the effects of both **reinforcers** and **punishers.** In operant conditioning, reinforcement (such as food) is used to increase the probability that a particular response will occur in the future. To decrease the probability that a particular response will recur, punishers (such as scolding) are used. Thorndike proposed the **law of effect,** which states that behavior that is consistently rewarded will become "stamped in" as learned behavior and behavior that is consistently punished will be "stamped out."

Types of Reinforcement

There are several kinds of reinforcers; all of them strengthen behavior just as steel rods reinforce or *strengthen* concrete.

The presence of **positive reinforcers** (such as food) adds to or increases the likelihood that a behavior will recur. **Negative reinforcers** (such as terminating electric shocks) also increase the likelihood that a behavior will recur, but they do so by reducing or eliminating something unpleasant from the environment.

Punishment

Although all reinforcers (both positive and negative) *increase* the likelihood that a behavior will occur again, **punishment** is any event whose presence *decreases* the likelihood that ongoing behavior will recur. Reinforcement always *strengthens* behavior; punishment *weakens* it. **Avoidance training** involves learning a desirable behavior that prevents an unpleasant condition, such as punishment, from occurring.

Operant Conditioning Is Selective

Studies have revealed that in operant conditioning the behaviors that are easiest to condition are those that animals typically would perform in the training situation. These behaviors vary from species to species, and put significant constraints on both classical and operant conditioning.

Superstitious Behavior

When something we do is followed closely by a reinforcer, we tend to repeat that behavior, even if it was not actually responsible for producing the reinforcement. Such behaviors are called *superstitious*. Nonhumans as well as humans exhibit superstitious behaviors.

Learned Helplessness

The failure to avoid or escape from an unpleasant or aversive stimulus that occurs as a result of previous exposure to unavoidable painful stimuli is referred to as **learned helplessness.** Learned helplessness, which has been demonstrated in both animals and humans, is associated with many of the symptoms characteristic of depression.

COMPARING CLASSICAL AND OPERANT CONDITIONING

A number of phenomena characterize both classical conditioning and operant conditioning, and there are several terms and concepts common to both kinds of learning.

Response Acquisition

In classical conditioning, responses occur naturally and automatically in the presence of the unconditioned stimulus. During the phase of the learning process called **response acquisition,** these naturally occurring responses are attached to the conditioned stimulus by pairing that stimulus with the unconditioned stimulus. **Intermittent pairing** reduces both the rate of learning and the final level of learning achieved.

In operant conditioning, response acquisition refers to the phase of the learning process in which desired responses are followed by reinforcers. A **Skinner box** is often used to limit the range of available responses and thus increase the likelihood that the desired response will occur. To speed up this process and make the occurrence of a desired response more likely, motivation may be increased by letting the animal become hungry; the number of potential responses may also be reduced by restricting the animal's environment.

For behaviors outside the laboratory, which cannot be controlled so conveniently, the process of **shaping** is often useful: Reinforcement is given for successive approximations to the desired behavior. However, there are differences among species in what behaviors can be learned and the circumstances under which learning will take hold.

Extinction and Spontaneous Recovery

If the unconditioned stimulus and the conditioned stimulus are no longer paired, **extinction** occurs, meaning the strength and/or frequency of the learned response diminishes. When Pavlov's dogs received no food after repeatedly hearing the bell, they ceased to salivate at the sound of the bell. However, after a while, this extinguished response may reappear without retraining in a process called **spontaneous recovery.** Extinction is complete when the subject no longer produces the conditioned response.

Extinction occurs in operant conditioning when reinforcement is withheld. However, the ease with which a behavior is extinguished varies according to several factors: the strength of the original learning, the variety of settings in which learning takes place, and the schedule of reinforcement used during conditioning. Especially hard to extinguish is behavior learned through punishment rather than reinforcement.

Generalization and Discrimination

In classical conditioning, situations or stimuli may resemble each other enough that the learners will react to one the way they have learned to react to the other through a process called **stimulus generalization.** On the other hand, the process of **stimulus discrimination** enables learners to perceive differences among stimuli so that not all loud sounds, for example, provoke fear.

Just as in classical conditioning, responses learned through operant conditioning can generalize from one stimulus to other, similar stimuli. **Response generalization** occurs when the same stimulus leads to different but similar responses. Discrimination in operant conditioning is taught by reinforcing a response only in the presence of certain stimuli.

NEW LEARNING BASED ON ORIGINAL LEARNING

In both classical and operant conditioning, original learning serves as a building block for new learning.

Higher-Order Conditioning in Classical Conditioning

Higher-order conditioning in classical conditioning uses an earlier conditioned stimulus as an unconditioned stimulus for further training. For example, Pavlov used the bell to condition his dogs to salivate at the sight of a black square. This sort of conditioning is difficult to achieve because of extinction: Unless the first unconditioned stimulus is presented occasionally, the initial conditioned response will be extinguished.

Secondary Reinforcers in Operant Conditioning

In operant conditioning, neutral stimuli can become reinforcers by being paired or associated with other reinforcers. A **primary reinforcer** is one that, like food and water, is rewarding in and of itself. A **secondary reinforcer** is one whose value is learned through its association with primary reinforcers or with other secondary reinforcers. Money is an example of a secondary reinforcer—in and of itself, it is not rewarding; it is valuable only for what it can buy.

CONTINGENCIES

The "if-then" relationship between conditioned stimuli and unconditioned stimuli in classical conditioning or between responses and reinforcers (or punishers) in operant conditioning is called a **contingency.**

Contingencies in Classical Conditioning

Robert Rescorla has demonstrated that classical conditioning requires more than merely presenting an unconditioned stimulus and a conditioned stimulus together in time. His work shows that for conditioning to occur, a conditioned stimulus must provide information about the unconditioned stimulus—that is, there must be a CS–US contingency. **Blocking** can occur when prior conditioning prevents conditioning to a second stimulus, even when the two stimuli are presented simultaneously.

Contingencies in Operant Conditioning

In operant conditioning, response contingencies are usually referred to as **schedules of reinforcement.** We rarely receive reinforcement every time we do something. Interestingly, it turns out that *partial reinforcement*—in which rewards are given for some correct responses but not for every one—results in behavior that persists longer than that learned by continuous reinforcement. The schedule of reinforcement specifies when a reinforcer will be delivered. Reinforcers may be provided on the basis of time since last reinforcement (the *interval* between reinforcements). Or reinforcement may depend on the number of correct responses since the last reinforcement (the *ratio* of reinforcement per correct response).

A **fixed-interval schedule** provides reinforcement of the first correct response after a fixed, unchanging period of time. A **variable-interval schedule** reinforces the learner for the first correct response that occurs after various periods of time, so the subject never knows exactly when a reward is going to be delivered. In a **fixed-ratio schedule,** behavior is rewarded each time a fixed number of correct responses is given; in a **variable-ratio schedule,** reinforcement follows a varying number of correct responses.

A REVIEW OF CLASSICAL CONDITIONING AND OPERANT CONDITIONING

Despite their differences, classical and operant conditioning share many similarities; both involve associations between stimuli and responses; both are subject to extinction and spontaneous recovery as well as generalization and discrimination. In fact, many psychologists now question whether classical and operant conditioning are not simply two ways of bringing about the same kind of learning.

Biofeedback is an operant conditioning technique in which instruments are used to give learners information about the strength of a biological response over which they seek to gain control.

COGNITIVE LEARNING

Both human and nonhuman animals also demonstrate **cognitive learning,** learning that is not tied to immediate experience by stimuli and reinforcers.

Latent Learning and Cognitive Maps

Early experiments by Tolman and other psychologists demonstrated that learning takes place even before the subject reaches the goal and occurs whether or not the learner is reinforced. Tolman proposed the concept of **latent learning,** which maintains that subjects store up knowledge even if this knowledge is not reflected in their current behavior because it is not elicited by reinforcers. Later research suggested that latent learning is stored as a mental image, or **cognitive map.** When the proper time comes, the learner calls up this map and puts it to use.

Insight and Learning Sets

One phenomenon that highlights the importance of cognitive processing in learning is **insight,** in which learning seems to occur in a "flash." Through insight learning, human and some nonhuman animals suddenly discover whole patterns of behavior or solutions to problems. **Learning sets** refer to the increasing effectiveness at problem solving that comes about as more problems are solved.

Learning by Observing

Social learning theory argues that we learn not just from firsthand experience, but also from watching others or by hearing about something. Albert Bandura contends that **observational** (or **vicarious**) **learning** accounts for many aspects of human learning. His highly influential theory of learning holds that although reinforcement is unrelated to learning itself, reinforcement may influence whether learned behavior is actually displayed. Such observational learning stresses the importance of models in our lives. To imitate a model's behavior, we must (1) pay attention to what the model does; (2) remember what the model did; and (3) convert what we learned from the model into action. The extent to which we display behaviors that have been learned through observation can be affected by **vicarious reinforcement** and **vicarious punishment.** Social cognitive theory emphasizes that learning a behavior from observing others does not necessarily lead to performing that behavior. We are more likely to imitate behaviors we have seen rewarded.

Cognitive Learning in Nonhumans

Research has demonstrated that nonhuman animals can be classically conditioned, that they can be taught to perform whole patterns of operant behaviors, and that they are capable of latent learning. All this evidence lends support to the argument that nonhuman animals use cognitive processing in learning.

REVIEW QUESTIONS

MULTIPLE CHOICE AND SHORT ANSWER

1. The simplest type of learning is called _____. It refers to the establishment of fairly predictable behavior in the presence of well-defined stimuli.

2. For the most effective learning in classical conditioning, should the conditioned stimulus (CS) be presented before or after the unconditioned stimulus (US)?

3. To extinguish classical conditioning, you must break the association between which pair?
   a. CS and US
   b. US and UR
   c. US and CR

4. After extinction and a period of rest, a CS may again elicit a CR; this phenomenon is known as _____ _____ .

5. The process by which a learned response to a specific stimulus comes to be associated with different but similar stimuli is known as _____ _____ .

6. A type of learning that essentially involves reinforcing the desired response is known as _____ _____ .

7. In the technique called _____, a new response is acquired by successively reinforcing partial responses.

8. Which kind of conditioning technique is administered when an aversive stimulus is turned off?
   a. positive reinforcement
   b. negative reinforcement
   c. positive punishment
   d. negative punishment

9. Classify the following as (1) primary or (2) secondary reinforcers:
   _____ food _____ diploma
   _____ money _____ sex

10. You offer your two roommates a box of their favorite cookies each time they leave the room clean. What type of conditioning technique are you using?
    a. positive reinforcement
    b. negative reinforcement
    c. stimulus generalization
    d. punishment

11. You like to listen to loud music when you are at your parents' home. If you turn off the music only when your mother or father offers you money to go to the movies, what type of reinforcement are you experiencing?
    a. positive reinforcement
    b. negative reinforcement
    c. stimulus generalization
    d. punishment

12. Identify the following schedules of reinforcement as FI (fixed interval), VI (variable interval), FR (fixed ratio), or VR (variable ratio):
    _____ The subject is reinforced on the first correct response after 2 minutes have passed since the last reinforcement.
    _____ The subject is reinforced on every sixth correct response.
    _____ The subject is reinforced after four correct responses, then after six more correct responses, then after five more correct responses.

_____ The subject is reinforced on the first correct response after 3 minutes have passed since the last reinforcement, then the first correct response 6 minutes since reinforcement, then the first correct response 5 minutes since reinforcement.

13. Unreinforced, or latent, learning may be stored internally. Particularly when this learning concerns spatial relationships, it is stored as a _____ _____.

14. An ape examines a problem and the tools available for solving it. Suddenly, the animal leaps up and quickly executes a successful solution. This is an example of
    a. insight
    b. operant conditioning
    c. trial-and-error learning

15. Which of the following factors have been identified by contingency theorists as necessary for learning?
    a. a CS that provides new information about the likelihood of the US occurring
    b. strong reinforcement
    c. blocking

16. According to social learning theorists, what is the source of reinforcement?
    a. internal standards of behavior
    b. external rewards
    c. both a and b

17. _____ is likely to happen whether we see someone else punished or rewarded for behavior.

18. _____ occurs when we see someone else punished for a behavior.

19. What kinds of evidence indicate that all learning is cognitive?

CRITICAL THINKING AND APPLICATIONS

1. If you imaging biting into a large dill pickle or a slice of lemon, you might notice that your mouth puckers and that you secrete saliva. Use classical conditioning principles to explain this phenomenon.

2. Many people dread going to the dentist. How would classical conditioning explain this?

3. Explain how a sound—a siren, for example—could be a conditioned stimulus for fear on the one hand and for relief on the other.

4. Think about your daily schedule. What kinds of things do you do every day that could be called "operant behaviors"?

5. Imagine that you want to keep your dog from barking and annoying the neighbors. What kind of reinforcement would you use to do this? How would you use the principles of extinction to do this?

6. Describe a cognitive map that you use in your daily activities. Were you reinforced for learning it? For navigating it correctly?

ENDURING ISSUES

Person–Situation
After reading about classical and instrumental conditioning, what do you think about the extent to which our behavior is controlled by external factors such as cues and stimuli as opposed to internal factors such as thoughts and feelings?

Stability–Change
To the extent that people are capable of various kinds of learning, what does that tell us about the extent to which human beings are capable of changing significantly over the course of their lives?

(Answers to the Review Questions appear in the back of the book.)

6 Memory

The world-renowned conductor Arturo Toscanini memorized every single note written for every instrument in some 250 symphonies and all the music and lyrics for more than 100 operas. Once, when he could not locate a score of Joachim Raff's Quartet No. 5, he sat down and reproduced it purely from memory—even though he had not seen or played the score for decades. When a copy of the quartet turned up, people were astonished to discover that with the exception of a single note, Toscanini had reproduced it perfectly (Neisser, 1982).

Think About It!

1. We are constantly bombarded with information from our senses. What mechanisms determine which information is stored and which is replaced or forgotten?

2. Why do we remember things shortly after they occur but forget them over time?

3. What is hysterical amnesia? How does it differ from other types of amnesia?

4. How far back into our childhood can most of us recall events? What kinds of events are we most likely to recall from our earliest years?

5. Why can so many people remember what they were doing when John F. Kennedy was shot or when the space shuttle *Challenger* exploded?

6. How can you improve your memory?

A waiter named John Conrad routinely handled parties of 6 to 8 in a busy Colorado restaurant, remembering every order from soup to salad dressing. He once waited on a party of 19, serving 19 complete dinners to his customers without a single error (Singular, 1982).

Memory The ability to remember the things that we have experienced, imagined, and learned.

Information-processing Model A computerlike model used to describe the way humans encode, store, and retrieve information.

Sensory registers Entry points for raw information from the senses.

Before being stricken with a viral illness, a 29-year-old woman known as MZ told researchers she could remember "the exact day of the week of future or past events of almost anything that touched my life . . . all personal telephone numbers . . . colors of interiors and what people wore . . . pieces of music . . . recalling a picture, as a painting in a museum, was like standing in the museum looking at it again" (Klatzky, 1980).

Accounts of people with extraordinary memories raise many questions about the nature of **memory** itself. Why are some people so much better at remembering things than others? Are they simply born with this ability, or could any of us learn to remember as much as these people do? And why is it that remembering may sometimes be so simple (think how effortlessly baseball fans remember the batting averages of their favorite players) and other times so difficult (as when we grope for answers on an exam)? Why do we find it so hard to remember something that happened only a few months back, yet we can recall in vivid detail some other event that happened 10, 20, even 30 years ago? Just how does memory work, and what makes it fail? Among the first to seek scientific answers to these questions was the nineteenth century German psychologist Hermann Ebbinghaus. Using himself as a subject, Ebbinghaus composed lists of "nonsense syllables," meaningless combinations of letters, such as PIB, WOL, or TEB. He memorized lists of 13 nonsense syllables each. Then, after varying amounts of time, he tried to relearn each list of syllables. He found that the longer he waited after first learning a list, the longer it took to learn the list again. Most of the information was lost in the first few hours. Ebbinghaus's contributions dominated memory research for many years.

Today many psychologists find it useful to think about memory as a series of steps in which we process information, much like a computer stores and retrieves data (Massaro & Cowan, 1993). Together, these steps form what is known as the **information-processing model** of memory. In this chapter, you will find terms like *encoding, storage,* and *retrieval,* convenient ways of comparing human memory to computers. But the social, emotional, and biological factors that make us human also separate our memories from computers, and far more information bombards our senses than we can possibly process. The first stage of information processing, then, involves selecting some of this material to think about and remember.

1

We are constantly bombarded with information from our senses. What mechanisms determine which information is stored and which is replaced or forgotten?

THE SENSORY REGISTERS

Look slowly around the room. Each glance—which may last for only a fraction of a second—takes in an enormous amount of visual information, including colors, shapes, textures, relative brightness, and shadows. At the same time, you pick up sounds, smells, and other kinds of sensory data. All this raw information flows from your senses into what are known as the **sensory regis-**

ters. These registers are like waiting rooms in which information enters and stays for only a short time. Whether we remember any of this information depends on which operations we perform on it, as you will see throughout this chapter. Although all our senses have registers, the visual and auditory registers have been studied most extensively, and therefore we begin with them.

Visual and Auditory Registers

Although the sensory registers have virtually unlimited capacity (Cowan, 1988), information disappears from them quite rapidly. To understand how much visual information we take in, and how quickly it is lost, bring an instant camera into a darkened room and take a photograph using a flash. During the split second that the room is lit up by the flash, your visual register will absorb a surprising amount of information about the room and its contents. Try to hold on to that visual image, or *icon*, as long as you can. You will find that it fades rapidly; in a few seconds it is gone. Then compare your remembered image of the room with what you actually saw at the time, as captured in the photograph. You will notice that your visual register took in far more information than you were able to retain for even a few seconds.

A clever set of experiments by George Sperling (1960) clearly demonstrates the speed with which information disappears from the visual register. Sperling flashed groups of letters, arranged in rows, on a screen for just a fraction of a second. When the letters were gone, he sounded a tone to tell his participants which row of letters to recall: A high-pitched tone indicated that they should try to remember the top row of letters, a low-pitched tone meant that they should recall the bottom row, and a medium-pitched tone signaled them to recall the middle row. Using this *partial-report technique,* Sperling found that if he sounded the tone immediately after the letters were flashed, his participants could usually recall 3 or 4 of the letters in any of the three rows; that is, they seemed to retain at least 9 of the original 12 letters in their visual registers. But if he waited for even 1 second before sounding the tone, his participants were able to recall only 1 or 2 letters from any single row—in just 1 second, then, all but 4 or 5 of the original set of 12 letters had vanished from their visual registers.

Look quickly at this photograph of New York City's Times Square, then try to recall as many details as you can. Your visual register will take in far more information than you can remember from a quick glance.

Attention The selection of some incoming information for further processing.

Visual information may actually disappear from the visual register even more rapidly than Sperling thought (Cowan, 1988). In everyday life, new visual information keeps coming into the register, and this new information replaces the old information almost immediately, a process often called *masking*. This is just as well, because otherwise the visual information would simply pile up in the sensory register and get hopelessly scrambled. Under normal viewing conditions, visual information is erased from the sensory register in about a quarter of a second as it is replaced by new information.

Auditory information fades more slowly than visual information. The auditory equivalent of the icon, the *echo*, tends to last for several seconds, which, given the nature of speech, is certainly fortunate for us. Otherwise, "*You* did it!" would be indistinguishable from "You *did* it!" because we would be unable to remember the emphasis on the first word by the time we registered the last word.

Initial Processing

If information disappears from the sensory registers so rapidly, how do we remember *anything* for more than a second or two? One way is that we select some of the incoming information for further processing by means of **attention** (see Figure 6–1). Attention is the process of selective looking, listening, smelling, tasting, and feeling. At the same time, we give meaning to the information that is coming in. Look at the page in front of you. You will see a series of black lines on a white page. Until you recognize these lines as letters and words, they are just meaningless marks. For you to make sense of this jumble of data, you process the information in the sensory registers for meaning.

How do we select what we are going to pay attention to at any given moment, and how do we give that information meaning? Donald Broadbent (1958) suggested that a filtering process at the entrance to the nervous system allows only those stimuli that meet certain requirements to pass

Figure 6–1
The sequence of information processing.
Raw information flows from the senses into the sensory registers, where it fades away or is processed in terms of existing knowledge and information. Information that is determined to be meaningful is passed on for further processing in short-term memory; the rest is discarded. Once in short-term memory, information is either forgotten or transferred into long-term memory, where it can be stored and retrieved when necessary.

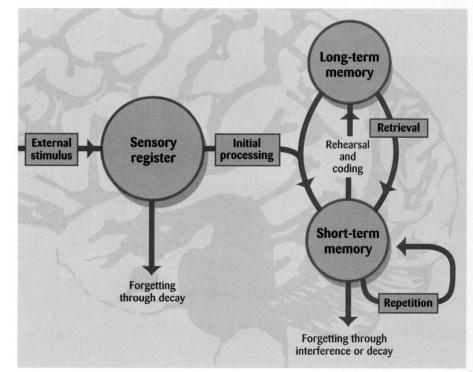

through. Those stimuli that get through the filter are compared with what we already know, so that we can recognize them and figure out what they mean. If you and a friend are sitting in a restaurant talking, you filter out all other conversations taking place around you, a practice known as the *cocktail-party phenomenon* (Cherry, 1966; Wood & Cowan, 1995). Although you might be able to describe certain characteristics of those other conversations, such as whether the people speaking were men or women and whether their voices were loud or soft, you normally would not be able to recount what was being discussed, even at neighboring tables. Because you filtered out those other conversations, processing of that information did not proceed far enough for you to understand the meaning of what you heard.

Now suppose that someone at a neighboring table mentions your name. In all likelihood your attention would shift to that conversation. Anne Treisman (1960, 1964) modified the filter theory to account for phenomena like this. She contended that the filter is not a simple on/off switch but rather a variable control, like the volume control on a radio, that can "turn down" unwanted signals without rejecting them entirely. According to this view, we may be paying attention to only some incoming information, but we monitor the other signals at a low volume. In this way, we can shift our attention if we pick up something particularly meaningful. This automatic processing works even when we are asleep: Parents often wake up immediately when they hear the baby crying, but sleep through other, louder noises.

To summarize, we consciously attend to very little of the information in our sensory registers; instead, we select some information and process those signals further as we work to recognize and understand them. However, unattended information receives at least some initial processing, so that we can shift our attention to focus on any element of our surroundings that strikes us as potentially meaningful.

What happens to the information that we do attend to? It enters our short-term memory.

SHORT-TERM MEMORY

Short-term memory (STM) holds the information we are thinking about or are aware of at any given moment (Stern, 1985). It was originally called primary memory by William James (1890; Waugh & Norman, 1960). When you listen to a conversation or a piece of music, when you watch a ballet or a tennis tournament, when you become aware of a leg cramp or a headache—in all these cases, you are using STM both to hold on to and to think about new information coming in from the sensory registers. STM therefore has two primary tasks: to store new information briefly and to work on that (and other) information. Thus, STM is sometimes called *working memory* to emphasize the active or working component of this memory system (Baddeley & Hitch, 1994).

Capacity of STM

The arcade fanatic absorbed in a video game is oblivious to the outside world. Chess masters at tournaments demand complete silence while they ponder their next move. You shut yourself in a quiet room to study for final exams. As these examples illustrate, STM can handle only so much information at any given moment. Research suggests that STM can hold as much information as can be repeated or rehearsed in 1.5 to 2 seconds (Baddeley, 1986; Schweickert & Boruff, 1986).

Chess players demand complete silence as they consider their next move. This is because there is a definite limit to the amount of information STM can handle at any given moment.

Chunking The grouping of information into meaningful units for easier handling by short-term memory.

To get a better idea of the limits of STM, read the first row of letters in the following list just once. Then close your eyes and try to remember the letters in the correct sequence before going on to the next row:

1. C X W
2. M N K T Y
3. R P J H B Z S
4. G B M P V Q F J D
5. E G Q W J P B R H K A

Like most people, you probably found rows 1 and 2 fairly easy, row 3 a bit harder, row 4 extremely difficult, and row 5 impossible to remember after just one reading. This gives you an idea of the relatively limited capacity of STM.

Now try reading through the following set of 12 letters just once and see whether you can repeat them: TJYFAVMCFKIB. How many letters were you able to recall? In all likelihood, not all 12. But what if you had been asked to remember the following 12 letters instead: TV FBI JFK YMCA. Could you do it? Almost certainly the answer is yes. These are the same 12 letters as before, but here they are grouped into four separate meaningful "words." This way of grouping and organizing information so that it fits into meaningful units is called **chunking.** The 12 letters have been chunked into four meaningful elements that STM can readily handle—they are well below the 5 to 10-item limit of STM, and they can be repeated in less than 2 seconds. Here's another example of chunking. Try to remember this list of numbers:

106619451812

Remembering 12 separate digits is usually very difficult, but try chunking the list into three groups of four:

1066 1945 1812

For those who take an interest in military history, these three chunks will be much easier to remember than 12 unrelated digits.

By chunking words into sentences or sentence fragments, we can process an even greater amount of information in STM (Baddeley, 1994; Aaronson & Scarborough, 1976, 1977). For example, suppose you want to remember the following list of words: *tree, song, hat, sparrow, box, lilac, cat.* One strategy would be to cluster as many of them as possible into phrases or sentences: "The sparrow in the tree sings a song"; "a lilac hat in the box"; "the cat in the hat." But isn't there a limit to this strategy? Would five sentences be as easy to remember for a short time as five single words? Simon (1974) found that as the size of any individual chunk increases, the number of chunks that can be held in STM declines. Thus, STM can easily handle five unrelated letters or words simultaneously, but five unrelated sentences are much harder to remember.

In a dramatic study of the power of chunking, a person, known as "SF" spent more than 250 hours in the laboratory over 2 years, purposefully using chunking to increase his short-term memory for strings of digits (Chase & Ericsson, 1981). At that point the young man could accurately recall strings of more than 80 digits. He accomplished this feat by associating groups of digits with his already vast knowledge of common and record times for running races of particular lengths. The digit string 3492 might be broken out, for instance, as a chunk associated with a near-record time for the mile, 3 minutes, 49.2 seconds. SF, by the way, was no better than average at remembering strings that he could not relate to running, such as strings of letters.

Keep in mind that short-term memory usually has more than one task to perform at once (Baddeley & Hitch, 1994). During the brief time you spent memorizing the rows of letters on page 230, you probably gave them your full attention. But normally, you have to attend to new incoming information while you work on whatever is already present in your short-term memory. Competition between these two tasks for the limited work space in STM means that neither task will be done as well as it could be. Try counting backward from 100 while trying to learn the rows of letters in our earlier example. What happens?

Encoding in STM

We encode verbal information for storage in STM according to how it *sounds* even if we see the word, letter, or number on a page rather than hear it spoken (Baddeley, 1986). Numerous experiments have shown that when people try to retrieve material from STM, they generally mix up items that sound alike (Sperling, 1960). A list of words such as *mad, man, mat, cap* is harder for most people to recall accurately than is a list such as *pit, day, cow, bar* (Baddeley, 1986).

But not all material in short-term memory is stored phonologically. At least some material is stored in visual form, and other information is retained based on its meaning (Cowan, 1988; Matlin, 1989). For example, we don't have to convert visual data like maps, diagrams, and paintings into sound before we can code them into STM and think about them. And, of course, deaf people rely primarily on shapes rather than sounds to retain information in STM (Conrad, 1972; Frumkin & Ainsfield, 1977). In fact, it appears that the capacity for visual encoding in STM actually exceeds that for phonological coding (Reed, 1992).

Retention and Retrieval in STM

Why do we forget material stored in short-term memory? According to the **decay theory,** the mere passing of time causes the strength of memory to decrease, thereby making the material harder to remember. Most of the evidence supporting the decay theory comes from experiments known as *distractor studies*. For example, in one experiment, participants learned a sequence of letters, such as PSQ. Then they were given a 3-digit number, such as 167, and asked to count backwards by threes: 167, 164, 161, and so on, for up to 18 seconds (Peterson & Peterson, 1959). At the end of that period, they were asked to recall the three letters. The results of this test astonished the experimenters. The subjects showed a rapid decline in their ability to remember the letters. Because the researchers assumed that counting backwards would not interfere with remembering, they could only account for the forgotten letters by noting that they had simply faded from short-term memory in a matter of seconds. Decay, then, seems to be at least partly responsible for forgetting in short-term memory.

Subsequent studies found that interference may also lead to forgetting in STM (Shiffrin & Cook, 1978). In contrast to decay theory, **interference theory** holds that information gets mixed up with, or pushed aside by, other information and thus becomes harder to remember. Some of this forgetting may be due simply to the limited capacity of STM, as new information pushes out old. This process is most pronounced, however, when the new information resembles the old in some way. If you are counting items, keeping a running total in your head, or repeating a phone number over and over to

2

Why do we remember things shortly after they occur but forget them over time?

Decay theory A theory that argues that the passage of time causes forgetting.

Interference theory A theory that argues that interference from other information causes forgetting.

Rote rehearsal Retaining information in STM simply by repeating it over and over.

"Hold on a second, Bob. I'm putting you on a stickie."

remember it, you may not lose your train of thought if some friends start talking to you about a movie. But, if someone begins counting another set of items or calls your attention to some other group of numbers, you will quickly become confused about which set of digits was yours.

Now, without looking back, try to recall the five rows of letters you learned on page 230. In all likelihood, you will not be able to remember them. That's because material in short-term memory disappears in 15 to 20 seconds unless it is rehearsed or practiced (Bourne et al., 1986).

It is probably just as well that we lose much of what is initially stored in STM. This process not only provides space in STM for new information, but also keeps us from being overwhelmed with a jumble of irrelevant, trivial, or unrelated data. In this sense, loss of information from STM is usually not a "problem." However, sometimes we want to hold on to some information for a bit longer than 15 or 20 seconds, and at other times we want to remember a new piece of information permanently. How do we guard against forgetting in these cases?

Rote Rehearsal

If you want to hold on to information for just a minute or two, the most effective way to do this is through **rote rehearsal,** also called *maintenance rehearsal* (Greene, 1987): you talk to yourself, repeating information over and over, silently or out loud. Although this is hardly the most efficient way to remember something permanently, it can be quite effective for a short time. In fact, if you repeat something to yourself long enough, but cannot recall it later, you may still recognize the information when you hear or use it again. If you look up a telephone number and then 20 minutes later you are asked, "What was that telephone number?" you are not likely to recall it. But if someone asks instead, "Were you dialing 555-1356?" you might recognize the number if you had repeated it often enough (Glenberg, Smith, & Green, 1977).

Rote rehearsal—simply repeating material over and over—is a very common memory strategy. Millions of students have learned the alphabet

Rote rehearsal—simply repeating material over and over—is a very common memory strategy. Repetition without any intent to learn, however, does not enhance memory.

and multiplication tables by doggedly repeating letters and numbers. Mere repetition without any intent to learn does enhance subsequent recall, but not very much (Greene, 1987). Think of the number of times in your life that you have handled (and presumably recognized) pennies. Stop here and try to draw from memory the front side of a U.S. penny. Now look at Figure 6–2 and pick the illustration that matches your memory of a real penny. For most people, this task is surprisingly difficult: Despite seeing and exchanging tens of thousands of pennies, most people cannot accurately draw one, or even pick one out from among other, similar objects (Nickerson & Adams, 1979).

Laboratory experiments have confirmed that repeating an item more often does not necessarily improve later recall. One study asked experimental participants to keep track of the last word beginning with a given letter in a 21-word list (Craik & Watkins, 1973). If the given letter was G, a typical list might include: *daughter, oil, rifle, garden, grain, table, football, anchor, giraffe,* and so on. Participants would hold *garden* in short-term memory by repeating it silently until *grain* was heard, *grain* until *giraffe* was heard, and so on. As you can see from the list *garden* was held in STM for just an instant, because *grain* followed it immediately. But *grain* was held in STM for quite a while until *giraffe* finally replaced it. Nonetheless, the participants were equally likely to recall that *garden* and *grain* were on the list, despite the difference in rehearsal times for the two words. In other words, it is not so much the amount of rehearsal that increases memory, but rather the type of rehearsal. Rote memorizing is unlikely to be very effective over the long term.

Elaborative Rehearsal

If simple rote repetition is not sufficient, what do we have to do to ensure that information in STM gets stored and remembered for a long time? Most researchers believe that we need to practice **elaborative rehearsal** (Postman, 1975), a method of relating new information to something that we already know. Suppose that you had to remember that the French word *poire* means "pear." You are already familiar with *pear*, both as a word and as a fruit. *Poire*, however, means nothing to you. To remember what it means, you have to connect it to *pear*, either by telling yourself that "*pear* and *poire* both begin with *p*," or by associating *poire* with the familiar taste and image of a *pear*.

Clearly, elaborative rehearsal calls for a deeper and more meaningful processing of new data than does simple rote repetition (Craik & Lockhart, 1972). Unless we rehearse material in this way, we will probably forget it quickly. For example, consider what happens when elaborative rehearsal is either interrupted or prevented. Frequently, people in accidents who suffer concussions cannot recall events just before the injury even though they can remember what happened some time earlier. This condition is known as **retrograde amnesia.** The events right before the accident were at the short-term memory level and had not been rehearsed enough to be remembered for more than a short time. Thus, they were forgotten.

Figure 6–2
A penny for your thoughts.
Which of these accurately illustrates a real U.S. penny? The answer is on page 234.

Long-term memory (LTM) The portion of memory that is more or less permanent, corresponding to everything we "know."

Semantic memory The portion of long-term memory that stores general facts and information.

Episodic memory The portion of long-term memory that stores more specific information that has personal meaning.

Another example of rehearsal failure is probably more familiar to you. Have you ever been in a group where people were taking turns speaking up—perhaps on the first day of class when all present are asked to introduce themselves briefly, or at the beginning of a panel discussion when the speakers are asked to do the same in front of a large audience? Did you notice that you forgot virtually everything that was said by the person who spoke just before you did? According to research, your failure to remember was because you did not elaboratively rehearse what that person was saying (Bond, Pitre, & Van Leeuwen, 1991). That person's comments simply "went in one ear and out the other" while you were preoccupied with thinking about your own remarks.

Elaborative rehearsal is crucial to future recall. But before we delve further into understanding this process, we need to know more about long-term memory. (The accurate illustration of a penny in Figure 6–2 is the third from the left.)

LONG-TERM MEMORY

Everything that we "know" is stored in **long-term memory (LTM):** the words to a popular song; the results of the last election; the meaning of *justice*; the fact that George Washington was the first president of the United States; the meaning of abbreviations such as TV, FBI, JFK, and YMCA; what you ate for dinner last night; the date you were born; and what you are supposed to be doing tomorrow at 4 P.M. Endel Tulving (1972, 1985) of the University of Toronto contends that LTM should be divided into separate memory systems. One system, called **semantic memory,** is much like a dictionary or encyclopedia, filled with general facts and information, such as the first five examples in this paragraph. When you see the words George Washington, you call up all sorts of additional information from LTM: 1776, the first president, Father of Our Country, Mt. Vernon, crossing the Delaware, a holiday in February. This kind of information is stored in semantic memory. Still other information in LTM is more personal and specific. This personal memory system, known as **episodic memory** (Tulving, 1972, 1985), encompasses specific events that have personal meaning for us, such as the last three examples that began this paragraph. If we compare semantic memory to an encyclopedia or dictionary, episodic memory is more like a diary, although it may also include events in which you did not participate but that are still important to you. Episodic memory lets you "go back in time" to a childhood birthday party, to the day you got your driver's license, to the story of how your parents met.

Information in LTM is highly organized and cross-referenced, like a cataloging system in a library. The more carefully we organize information, the more likely we will be to retrieve it later.

Encoding in LTM

Can you picture the shape of Florida? Do you know what a trumpet sounds like? Can you imagine the smell of a rose or the taste of coffee? When you answer the telephone, can you sometimes identify the caller immediately, just from the sound of the voice? Your ability to do most or all these things means that at least some long-term memories are coded in terms of nonverbal images: shapes, sounds, smells, tastes, and so on (Cowan, 1988).

Yet most of the information in LTM seems to be encoded in terms of meaning. If material is especially familiar (the national anthem, say, or the opening of the Gettysburg Address), you may have stored it verbatim in LTM, and you can often retrieve it word for word when you need it. Generally speaking, however, we do not use verbatim storage in LTM. If someone tells you a long, rambling story, complete with flashbacks, you may listen to

"I may want to sit. Just give me a chance to process this."

every word, but you certainly will not try to remember the story verbatim. Instead, you will extract the main points of the story and try to remember those. Even simple sentences are usually encoded in terms of their meaning. Thus, when people are asked to remember that "Tom called John," they often find it impossible to remember later whether they were told "Tom called John" or "John was called by Tom." They usually remember the meaning of the message but not the exact words (Bourne et al., 1986).

Information in STM gets transferred to LTM if it is rehearsed. Through *elaborative* rehearsal, you extract the meaning of the information and then link the new information to as much of the material already in LTM as possible. The more links or associations you can make, the more likely you are to remember the new information later, just as it is easier to find a book in the library if it is catalogued under many headings rather than just one or two. This is one reason we tend to remember semantic material better than episodic material: Episodic material is quickly dated, and we code fewer cross-references for it. For instance, you may remember that you ate a hamburger last night, but normally there is no good reason to relate that piece of information to anything else in LTM, so it is not something you are likely to remember for very long. But if you had been a vegetarian for years and found the very thought of eating beef repulsive, then eating that hamburger was a very meaningful event, and it is probably linked to all kinds of other facts in your LTM. As a result, you are unlikely to forget it for quite some time.

We can rehearse material many different ways. Think for a moment about how you might study for an examination in this course. If you expected a multiple-choice test, the way you would study is likely to be quite different than if you expected essay questions. Research confirms that the way we encode material for storage in LTM affects the ease with which we can retrieve it later on (Flexser & Tulving, 1978; Leonard & Whitten, 1983). We will examine this principle in greater detail later in the chapter when we look at how to improve memory.

Implicit Memory

Most of the memories we've considered so far are things that you intended to remember, at least at one time. Psychologists call such memories **explicit memory.**

Implicit memory Memory for information that either was unintentionally committed to memory or was unintentionally retrieved from memory.

But you also acquire a great deal of information that you never intended to remember. For example, have you ever misplaced something like a pair of eyeglasses and then retraced your steps in an effort to find it? "Let's see, I came in the door, put down my keys, then I went to the kitchen, where I put down the packages. . . ." And then you go to the kitchen and find your glasses, although you may not actually recall having left them there. Or perhaps you have had the experience of recalling exactly where on a page a particular piece of information appeared, even though you did not try to remember the item or its placement. If you think about it, such memories are really quite remarkable. You made no deliberate effort to remember either of these things, yet in each case memories were apparently formed outside your awareness and without any conscious elaborative processing on your part (Cowan, 1988; T. Adler, 1990). Similarly, memories are sometimes called up spontaneously (Roediger, 1990). The smell of a particular perfume or the taste of a distinctive cake may bring back a flood of memories. In these cases, too, you first stored and then retrieved information without any conscious intention to do so. Moreover, the recall of stored information does not include any conscious awareness of the occasion when it was acquired. Psychologists call such unintentional memories **implicit memory** (Graf & Schacter, 1985; Jacoby & Witherspoon, 1982; Squire, Knowlton, & Musen, 1993; Tulving & Schacter, 1990).

The importance of implicit memory might become clearer if you think about the following experiment (Schab, 1990). A group of people were given a list of 40 adjectives and asked to write down the opposite of each word. The experimenter informed them that the next day he would ask them to recall the words they had written. The smell of chocolate permeated the air surrounding one group of students while they were writing their list of words. The next day, adding a chocolate smell to the air significantly increased the number of words these students recalled from the previous day. In other words, the smell of chocolate somehow became linked to the words they wrote, and the smell then became an effective cue or "hint" that helped them find and recall the correct words. Although this may seem odd, it happens all the time: Whenever we try (explicitly) to commit something to memory, we are also unintentionally (implicitly) picking up facts about the context in which the learning is taking place. Those facts, lodged in implicit memory, become useful retrieval cues when we later try to retrieve the corresponding information from explicit memory.

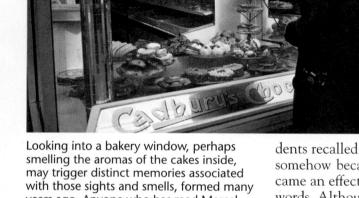

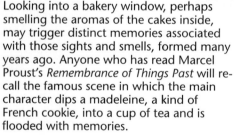

Looking into a bakery window, perhaps smelling the aromas of the cakes inside, may trigger distinct memories associated with those sights and smells, formed many years ago. Anyone who has read Marcel Proust's *Remembrance of Things Past* will recall the famous scene in which the main character dips a madeleine, a kind of French cookie, into a cup of tea and is flooded with memories.

Interestingly, people suffering from some forms of amnesia (which is a failure of explicit memory) have nothing wrong with their implicit memory (Graf, Shimamura, & Squire, 1985; Graf, Squire, & Mandler, 1984). For example, one study gave several people with amnesia a list of words to remember. When these people were asked to recall the words or pick them out of longer lists, they performed poorly, as one might expect. But when the experimenters showed the amnesia sufferers fragments of the words or just the first three letters and asked them simply to guess what the word might be or to say the first thing that popped into their heads, they "remembered" just as many of the words on the list as did the control group, made up of people not suffering from amnesia (Warrington & Weiskrantz, 1970). The researchers' conclusion: The amnesia victims had perfectly good (implicit) memories for words that they did not (explicitly) know they had heard!

TYPES OF MEMORY

Type of Memory	Definition	Example
Semantic memory	Portion of long-term memory that stores general facts and information	Recalling the capital of Ohio
Episodic memory	Portion of long-term memory that stores specific information that has personal meaning	Recalling where you went on your first date
Implicit memory	Memory for information that either was not intentionally committed to memory or that is retrieved unintentionally from memory	Suddenly thinking of a friend's name without knowing why

Understanding the workings of implicit memory has concrete implications for everyday memory. Say you are having difficulty remembering something. If possible, return to the setting in which you first learned it; otherwise, try to recreate the setting vividly in your mind in as much detail as possible, including the thoughts and feelings you were having at the time. Your implicit memory of the setting should help trigger your memory of the fact you are trying to recall.

Storage and Retrieval in LTM

We saw earlier that information in short-term memory disappears in less than 20 seconds unless it is rehearsed. But under the proper circumstances, we can often recall an astonishing amount of information from LTM. In one study, for example, adults who had graduated from high school more than 40 years earlier were still able to recognize the names of 75 percent of their classmates (Bahrick, Bahrick, & Wittlinger, 1974). Not everything stored in LTM can be remembered when we need it, however. A classic example of this is the *tip-of-the-tongue phenomenon,* or *TOT* (Brown & McNeil, 1966). Everyone has had the experience of knowing a word but not quite being able to recall it. We say that such a word is "right on the tip of my tongue." If you want to experience TOT yourself, try naming the Seven Dwarfs (Meyer & Hilterbrand, 1984).

The TOT phenomenon has several intriguing characteristics (Brown & McNeil, 1966; Brown, 1991). Although everyone experiences TOTs, these experiences become more frequent during stressful situations and as people get older. Moreover, the other words—with a sound or meaning similar to the word you are seeking—occur to you while you are in the TOT state. These words interfere with and sabotage your attempt to recall the desired word. The harder you try, the worse the TOT state gets. The best way to recall a blocked word, then, is to stop trying to recall it! The word you were searching for may just pop into your head minutes, or even hours, after you stopped consciously searching for it (Norman & Bobrow, 1976).

The TOT phenomenon occurs most often with words that are seldom used. Researchers believe that it is the infrequent use of these words that weakens the link between their meaning and their pronunciation (Burke et al., 1991). When you try to remember one of these words, lots of other words that sound like them or mean roughly the same thing come to mind

7 Cognition and

Language

Perhaps you know the following riddle. "A man married 20 different women in the same small town. All of these women are still alive, and he never divorced a single one of them. How did this happen?" The solution to the riddle is that the man was a clergyman. When you hear the answer for the first time, you are liable to groan because the solution is so obvious once you know it. In this chapter, we will consider those processes that enable us to solve little problems, such as riddles, as well as bigger, more important problems.

Psychologists use the term **cognition** to refer to all the processes whereby we acquire and use information. We have already considered several cognitive processes, including perception, learning, and memory. In later chapters, we examine cognition's crucial relation to intelligence, coping and adjustment, abnormal behavior, and interpersonal relations. In this chapter, we will focus on a family of cognitive processes, all of which illustrate types of thinking: These include language, imagery, conceptualization, evaluation or interpretation, problem solving, and decision making.

Think About It!

1. Is trial and error an effective way to solve problems?
2. In what ways can previous experiences interfere with your ability to solve problems?
3. What do psychologists mean by a compensatory model of decision making?
4. *True or False*: People often make decisions based on whatever information is most readily available, even if that information is not accurate.
5. What is the relationship between language and thinking?
6. Can animals think and use language?

Cognition The processes whereby we acquire and use knowledge.

Language A flexible system of communication that uses sounds, rules, gestures, or symbols to convey information.

We will first review the emergence of the study of cognition in contemporary psychology. Then we turn to the building blocks of thought—the tools we think with—and the ways in which we use these building blocks to solve problems and make decisions. Finally, we will explore the relation between human language and thought and consider the possibility that animals also think and use language.

THE DEVELOPMENT OF COGNITIVE PSYCHOLOGY

If you were taking this course a generation ago, you probably would not have studied most of the topics in this chapter. The study of such processes as imagery, language, problem solving, and decision making has grown as a result of the popularity of cognitive psychology. We saw in Chapter 1 that cognitive psychology is a relatively recent perspective that focuses on mental processes. It developed in part as a reaction to the behaviorists, who believed that unobservable mental processes could not be the subject of scientific study. Among the first and most influential cognitive psychologists were George Miller (Miller, Galanter, & Pribram, 1962) and Ulric Neisser (1967). Their books drew attention to the similarity between cognitive processes and computer programs. They pointed out that a good way to create a theory of mental processes is to write a computer program that will mimic those processes, an activity they called *computer simulation*. If the computer program behaves in the same way as a person, then the program can be a useful model of mental processes.

In addition to using computer programs as models of human cognition, cognitive psychologists employ the same experimental and research procedures found in other areas of psychology. Work by cognitive psychologists over the past few decades has helped us realize the extent to which cognition affects virtually all facets of our behavior (Holyoak & Spellman, 1993). The information-processing approach to memory we considered in the last chapter is an example of the application of cognitive psychology to the study of memory. Cognitive psychologists have also explored higher mental processes. For example, research on *language* has shown that the way in which we *think* about a topic influences the way we *talk* about it, and that, in turn, the way in which we *speak* about a topic affects the way we *think* about it. Research on *imagery* has demonstrated the importance of being able to manipulate our mental images to represent situations from different perspectives. Research on *concepts* has shown that rather than putting people and events in rigid established categories, we often create new categories to adapt to changing circumstances. When we think, we make use of language, imagery, and concepts.

When we think we use language, images, and concepts—the building blocks of thought. To think about a friend, for instance, we might wonder in words how she is doing, picture her in our mind's eye with images, and associate with her concepts, such as *kind, friendly,* and *smart*. These building blocks of thinking help us organize our thoughts.

THE BUILDING BLOCKS OF THOUGHT

Language, images, and concepts are the three most important building blocks of thought. Say that you are thinking about a close friend. You may have in mind statements such as "I would like to talk to her sometime soon" or "I wish I could be more like her." You may also have an image of her—probably her face, but perhaps also the sound of her voice. Or you may think of your friend by using various concepts or categories such as *woman, kind, funny, strong, caring, dynamic, gentle*. We consider now the role that language and images play in thinking. Then we turn to concepts and their relationship to thought.

Language

Human **language** is a flexible system of symbols that enables us to communicate our ideas, thoughts, and feelings. Spoken language is based on universal sound units called **phonemes.** The sounds of *t*, *th*, and *k*, for instance, are phonemes. There are about 45 phonemes in English, and as many as 85 in some languages (Bourne et al., 1986). By themselves, phonemes are meaningless and therefore seldom play an important role in helping us think. The sound *b*, for example, has no inherent meaning. But phonemes can be grouped together to form words, prefixes (*un-*, *pre-*), and suffixes (*-ed*, *-ing*). These are called **morphemes,** which are the smallest meaningful units in a language. Morphemes play an extremely important role in human cognition. By themselves, they can represent ideas such as "red" or "calm" or "hot." The suffix *-ed* signifies "in the past" (as in *walked* or *liked* or *cared*). The prefix *pre-* reflects the idea of "before" or "prior to" (as in *preview* or *predetermined*).

Some psychologists who study sign language now believe that it has components that perform the same functions as phonemes (e.g., Emmorey, 1994). For example, specific shapes and positions of the hand function like particular sounds in a language. Thus, the hand in sign language works like the tongue in spoken language. Also, sign languages, like spoken languages, have rules for combining these basic units to form meaningful units such as verbs and nouns.

We can combine morphemes to make up complex words that represent quite complex ideas, such as *pre-exist-ing, un-excell-ed, psycho-logy*. In turn, words can be combined to form phrases and sentences, which can represent even more complex thoughts. When we are thinking about something—say, the ocean or a sunset—our ideas about it rarely reflect the single thoughts expressed by such morphemes as red or calm. Instead, our ideas usually consist of phrases and sentences, such as "The ocean is unusually calm tonight."

Sentences have both a **surface structure**—the particular words and phrases—and a **deep structure**—the underlying meaning. The same deep structure can be conveyed by various different surface structures:

The ocean is unusually calm tonight.

Tonight the ocean is particularly calm.

Compared to most nights, tonight the ocean is calm.

When you wish to communicate an idea, you start with a thought, then choose words and phrases that will express the idea, and finally produce the speech sounds that make up those words and phrases. This is sometimes called *top-down processing*, and you can see from the left arrow in Figure 7–1 that the movement is indeed from top to bottom. When you want to understand a sentence, your task is reversed. You must start with speech sounds and work your way up to the meaning of those sounds. This is sometimes called *bottom-up processing*, as shown by the right arrow in Figure 7–1.

Just as there are rules for combining phonemes and morphemes, there are also rules for structuring sentences and their meanings. Such rules exist for both spoken and sign languages, although we will focus here on spoken language. These rules are what linguists call a **grammar.** The work of

Phonemes The basic sounds that make up any language.

Morphemes The smallest meaningful units of speech, such as simple words, prefixes, and suffixes.

Surface structure The particular words and phrases used to make up a sentence.

Deep structure The underlying meaning of a sentence.

Grammar The language rules that determine how sounds and words can be combined and used to communicate meaning within a language.

Figure 7–1
The direction of movement in speech production and comprehension.
Producing a sentence involves movement from thoughts and ideas to basic sounds; comprehending a sentence requires movement from basic sounds back to the underlying thoughts and ideas.

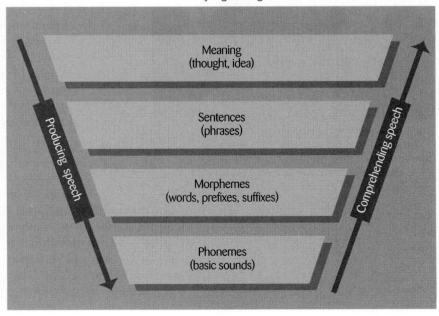

Meaning
(thought, idea)

Sentences
(phrases)

Morphemes
(words, prefixes, suffixes)

Phonemes
(basic sounds)

Producing speech

Comprehending speech

the linguist Noam Chomsky (1957) has greatly influenced our understanding of the way grammar works. The rules of grammar enable speakers and listeners to perform what Chomsky calls the *transformations* that allow a person to go from surface to deep structure.

The two major components of a grammar are semantics and syntax. **Semantics** describes how we assign meaning to the morphemes we use. Some rules describe how a word may refer to an object—for example, that a large striped cat is a *tiger*. Other semantic rules explain how different combinations of morphemes affect meaning, such as adding the suffix *-ed* to a verb like *play* to put the action in the past, or adding the prefix *un-* to *necessary* to reverse its meaning. **Syntax** is the system of rules that governs how we combine words to form meaningful grammatical sentences. After all, a random jumble of individually meaningful words doesn't communicate very much. In English, for example, a rule specifies that adjectives come before nouns. In other languages, such as Spanish and French, adjectives follow nouns.

Later in this chapter (and again in Chapter 10, Life Span Development), we will explore how we learn language and how we use it to think and to communicate. Knowing more than one language may actually contribute to a person's ability to think in general (see the *Controversies* box). Words, phrases, and sentences are among the building blocks of thought. Images are another.

Images

Think for a moment about Abraham Lincoln. Then think about being outside in a summer thunderstorm. Your thoughts of Lincoln may have included such phrases as "wrote the Gettysburg Address," "president during the Civil War," and "assassinated by John Wilkes Booth." But you probably also had some mental images concerning Lincoln: bearded face, lanky body, a log cabin. When you thought about the thunderstorm, you probably formed mental images of wind, rain, and lightning. An **image** is a mental representation of a sensory experience; it can be used to think about things. We can visualize the Statue of Liberty or people we know; we can smell Thanksgiving dinner; we can hear Martin Luther King, Jr., saying "I have a dream!" In short, we can think by using sensory images.

Researchers have confirmed that we not only visualize things in order to think about them, but also manipulate these mental images. Shepard and Metzler (1971), for example, presented people with pairs of geometrical patterns (see Figure 7–2). In some cases, the two pictures were of the same pattern rotated to provide different views; see Figures 7–2(A) and 7–2(B). In other cases, the two pictures were of different patterns; see Figure 7–2(C). The participants were asked to determine whether each pair of patterns was the same or different. (The computer game Tetris simulates this task.) The researchers discovered that the participants invariably rotated the image of one pattern in their minds until they could see both patterns from the same perspective. Then they tried to see whether the mental image of one pattern matched the other pattern. The more one pattern had to be rotated, the more time it took to match it to the other. In other words, a pattern that had to be mentally rotated 180 degrees would take longer to compare than one that had to be rotated 90 degrees. Subsequent studies have supported these findings (e.g., Kosslyn & Sussman, 1995). In addition, experiments using neuroimaging procedures have shown that when we manipulate images, we often use the same brain centers that are involved in visual perception (Moscovitch, Behrmannn, & Winocur, 1994). We can and do manipulate mental images to help us think about things.

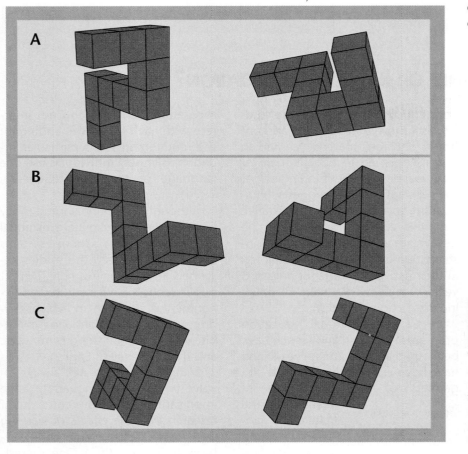

Concept A mental category for classifying objects, people, or experiences.

Figure 7–2
Examples of the pairs of geometrical patterns used in Shepard and Metzler's (1971) experiment.
The researchers found that participants first rotated an image of one pattern in their minds until they could see both patterns from the same perspective. They then matched the mental images of the pairs of patterns to decide whether they were the same (A and B) or different (C).

Images allow us to think about things in nonverbal ways. Albert Einstein relied heavily on his powers of visualization to understand phenomena that would later be described by complex mathematical formulas. Einstein believed that his extraordinary genius resulted in part from his skill in visualizing the possibilities of abstract conceptions (Shepard, 1978). Although few of us can match Einstein's brilliance, we all use imagery to think about and solve problems. We've all seen a teacher clarify a difficult idea by drawing a simple sketch on a blackboard. Many times, when words make a tangled knot of an issue, a graphic image resolves the confusion.

Images also allow us to use concrete forms to represent complex and abstract ideas. For example, Figure 7–3 uses a pie chart to illustrate the composition of households in the United States, based on data from the 1990 census. Each type of household is represented by a wedge, the size of which varies according to its percentage of the total number of households. You can mentally compare the sizes of each wedge and imagine how the pie would look if a particular item received a larger or smaller wedge. Thus, images are an important part of thinking and cognition. We turn now to concepts, another important building block of thought.

Figure 7–3
The composition of U.S. households in 1990.
How might the sizes of the wedges have differed 30 years ago? What are the advantages of presenting numerical data in this visual form?

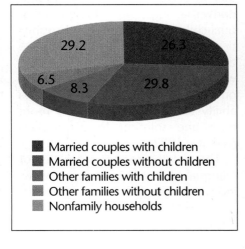

- Married couples with children
- Married couples without children
- Other families with children
- Other families without children
- Nonfamily households

Concepts

Concepts are mental categories for classifying specific people, things, or events (Komatsu, 1992). *Dogs, books,* and *cars* are all concepts that let us categorize objects in the world around us. *Fast, strong,* and *interesting* are also concepts that we can use to categorize objects. When you think about something, say, a leopard, you usually think of the concepts that apply to it, such

CONTROVERSIES
ENGLISH ONLY OR BILINGUAL EDUCATION?

By the year 2000, it is estimated that approximately 5 million students in the United States will come from homes in which a language other than English is spoken. Which language is best to use when teaching such children? On one side of this debate are those educators who believe that nonnative speakers will be assimilated into U.S. culture more easily if they are placed in English-only classes. Some educators supporting this position also point to studies showing that bilingual education confuses the children, causing them to fall behind academically (Gerardi, 1996; Tobias, 1994). On the other side of the debate are those who argue that nonnative speakers should be taught in both English and their native language in order to preserve their culture.

Some research evidence bolsters the argument for bilingual education by showing that being bilingual has cognitive advantages. For example, a study of Latino children in New Haven showed a positive correlation between bilingualism and superior cognitive abilities (Hakuta, 1987). The more a child used both Spanish and English, the researcher observed, the greater his or her intellectual advantage in the skills necessary to perform well in reading and nonverbal logic. In addition, bilingual children showed a more sophisticated understanding of language than children whose only language was English, and they scored higher on tests of mental flexibility—the ability to consider objectively more than one solution to a problem (Hakuta, 1987).

The greater cognitive abilities of bilingual children, in Hakuta's view, indicate that a wide range of experi-

ence enriches the mind. These studies also show that rather than confusing children, material learned in Spanish seemed to benefit their intellectual development in English. At the very least, Hakuta suggests, bilingualism apparently has no negative cognitive effects. Consequently, he believes that U.S. schools should instruct non-English-speaking children in their native language for at least 3 years, while only gradually introducing instruction in English.

In Canada, bilingual education programs in English and French have been in place for many years and have been extensively evaluated. Regardless of whether English or French is the native language, training in a second language does not impair the normal development of the first language. Moreover, bilingual education seems to enhance overall academic achievement. Indeed, some Canadian researchers have referred to this phenomenon as the "bilingual advantage," because, in general, children provided with a bilingual education score higher in tests of general intelligence, cognitive flexibility, and math, and also show an enhanced appreciation for cultural diversity (Lambert et al., 1993).

Some educators . . . point to studies showing that bilingual education confuses children. . . . [Others] argue that nonnative speakers should be taught in both English and their native language in order to preserve their culture.

Another study found that bilingual students do not appear to be confused by having two languages from which to choose, because both languages apparently exist as

separate systems that do not interfere with each other. Depending on the requirements of a particular situation, bilingual individuals use one language or the other (Genesee, 1994).

Although the national trend today is for schools to eliminate bilingual programs, some school systems have begun to heed the studies described above. For example, Detroit public schools have instituted an experimental program in which children whose native language is Arabic are taught half the day in Arabic and the other half in English.

Bilingualism need not always involve two spoken languages. Some important findings have come out of research into the effects of learning sign language in childhood (Mayberry & Eichen, 1991). One interesting contrast is between (1) children who learned a spoken language before they became deaf and subsequently learned sign language in adolescence, and (2) children who were born deaf but who also acquired sign language in adolescence. In spite of the fact that both groups learned sign language at the same time, the first group learned it more easily. This shows the positive effect that learning one language in childhood can have on learning a second language later on.

Questions

1. After reading about this controversy, what is your position on the question of whether bilingual children should be placed in classes where only English is taught?

2. How would you justify your position on this issue?

as *fast*, *sleek*, *spotted*, and *cat*. Similarly, concepts can also be used to create and organize hierarchies or groups of subordinate categories. For example, the general concept of *plants* can be broken down into the subordinate categories of *trees*, *bushes*, and *grasses*, just as the subordinate concept of *trees* can be further subdivided into *oaks*, *maples*, *pines*, and so forth (Reed, 1996). Without the ability to form concepts, we would need a different name for every individual object. Thus, concepts help us think more efficiently about things and how they relate to one another.

Concepts also give meaning to new experiences. We do not form a new concept for every new experience we have; instead, we draw on concepts that we have already formed and place the new object or event into the appropriate categories. In the process, we may modify some of our concepts to better match our experience. Consider, for example, the concept of *professor*. You probably had some concept of *professor* before you ever attended any college classes. Your concept probably changed somewhat after you actually met some professors and took your first college courses. Perhaps your concept became more accurate: You might realize now that professors are not all absentminded, that some professors are even under 30 years old—in fact, most professors are not very different from all the other people whom you have come to know. Your concept will become fuller as you add new information about professors based on your experiences at college. In the future, because you have formed a concept of *professor*, you will not have to respond to each new professor as a totally new experience; you will know what to expect and how you are expected to behave. Conceptualizing *professor* (or anything else) is a way of grouping or categorizing experiences so that every new experience need not be a surprise. We know, to some extent, what to think about it.

Interestingly, some research suggests that humans may not be unique in their ability to form concepts (Depy, Fagot, & Vauclair, 1997). For example, Edward Wasserman and his colleagues at the University of Iowa trained pigeons to peck different buttons when shown pictures of cats, people, flowers, cars, and chairs (Bhatt et al., 1988; Wasserman, Kledinger, & Bhatt, 1988). Once the pigeons mastered the task, they were shown a new set of pictures of cats, flowers, and so on. Remarkably, the pigeons were able to correctly categorize the new pictures about 70 percent of the time. It seems that they had learned the essential features that distinguish, say, cats from other objects, and they were able to apply that learning to pictures they had never seen before.

PROTOTYPES   We may be tempted to think of concepts as simple and clear-cut. But, as Eleanor Rosch (1973, 1978) discovered, most of the concepts that people use in thinking are neither simple nor unambiguous. Rather, they are "fuzzy": They overlap one another and are often poorly defined. For example, most people can tell a mouse from a rat, but we would be hard-pressed to come up with an accurate list of the critical differences between mice and rats.

If we cannot explain the difference between mouse and rat, how can we use these *fuzzy concepts* in our thinking? One possibility that Rosch proposed is that we construct a model, or **prototype,** of a representative mouse and one of a representative rat; we then use those prototypes in our thinking. Our concept of bird, for example, does not consist of a list of key attributes such as "feathered," "winged," "two feet," and "lives in trees." Instead, most of us have a model bird, or prototype, in mind—such as a robin or a sparrow—that captures for us the essence of *bird*. When we encounter new objects, we compare them to this prototype to determine whether they are,

Prototype According to Rosch, a mental model containing the most typical features of a concept.

When you think about the concept *bird*, you don't think about every different kind of bird you know, nor do you imagine a list of features that all birds share (wings, feathers, beak, two feet, egg-laying). Instead you think of a prototype of a "typical" bird, which probably looks much like this bluebird. A penguin doesn't match this prototype very well, but you can still tell it is a bird by its degree of category membership.

Idealized cognitive model (ICM) Our conception of events as we expect to typically find them.

in fact, birds. And when we think about birds, we usually think about our prototypical bird.

Most people would agree that a robin somehow expresses "birdness" more than a penguin does—it more nearly fits our prototypical image of a bird. But prototypes are seldom perfect models. Robins do not contain every single feature that can be possessed by birds. For example, they do not have the talons of an eagle. Because natural categories are fuzzy, prototypes are only the best and most suitable models of a concept, not perfect and exclusive representations of it. As P. H. Lindsay and Norman (1977) point out, "The typical dog barks, has four legs, and eats meat. We expect all actual dogs to be the same. Despite this, we would not be too surprised to come across a dog that did not bark, had only three legs, or refused to eat meat." We would still be able to recognize such an animal as a dog.

How, then, do we know which objects belong to a concept? For instance, how do we know that a lion is not a bird but that a penguin is a bird? The answer is that we decide what is most probable or most sensible, given the facts at hand. This is what Rosch calls relying on the *degree of category membership*. For example, a lion and a bird both have two eyes. But the lion does not have wings, it does not have feathers, and it has four feet and a mouth full of teeth, all of which indicate that it is quite unlike our prototype for a bird. Thus, we are able to eliminate lions from the general category of birds. Penguins, on the other hand, share many features that belong to our prototype for a bird. As a result, we recognize these Arctic creatures as members of the bird family even though they don't fly.

George Lakoff (1987) has extended Rosch's prototype theory by observing that most of our concepts fit together to form **idealized cognitive models,** or **ICMs.** ICMs constitute our conception of events as we typically expect to find them. ICMs are similar to, but more complex than, schemata, which we considered in the previous chapter. In fact, ICMs enable us to combine and make use of schemata to meet the demands of particular situations. Our ICMs do not fit the events we experience precisely, and we are continually tinkering with them so that they work for us in a constantly changing environment.

ICMs allow us to theorize about the ways in which the world works. We can construct prototypes of the things and events about which we think. Lakoff uses the example of a *week* to illustrate how ICMs work. In our culture, a week is a length of time that has 7 parts, or *days*. The ICM of a week allows us to imagine a prototypical day, which is, in turn, made of parts, such as *morning* and *afternoon*. Notice that our ICM of a week allows us to generate different kinds of prototypical days, such as *workdays* and *weekend* days. But ICMs are at least somewhat arbitrary, as demonstrated by the fact that different cultures have different kinds of weeks. Some cultures have weeks that are 5 days long, for example (see the *Highlights* box).

"Well, you don't look like an experimental psychologist to me."

HIGHLIGHTS
HOW DO CONCEPTS DIFFER ACROSS CULTURES?

All known cultures use categories to help form concepts (Kluckhohn, 1954), but what information gets included in a given category, and how the categories are shaped by experience, can differ substantially from one culture to another (Rogoff & Chavajay, 1995). Cross-cultural psychologist David Matsumoto provides an amusing example of how cultural differences can affect perception, cognition, and behavior:

> We have probably all seen imported, handmade, brass pitchers of various designs and sizes. Once, after dinner with a Persian friend at an American's home, we all gathered in the living room. After a moment, our Persian friend turned red, giggled, and looked embarrassed, but didn't say anything. When the host left the room a few minutes later, the Persian pointed out a large ornate brass pitcher with a long spout that was sitting on a coffee table as a decoration. It had been made in the Middle East where toilet paper is scarce and people clean themselves after going to the bathroom by using such pitchers to pour water on themselves. So what was a prized decoration to our host was an embarrassment to my friend. (Matsumoto, 1995, p. 52)

As this example illustrates, two people perceiving the same object may assign it to very different categories!

Cultures differ even in the extent to which they categorize basic information, such as colors or shapes. We all know that a circle, an oval, and an ellipse belong together, whereas a triangle is not part of that group. However, what we "all know" may not be universal. For example, the Dani, a people who live in the highlands of New Guinea, do not have names for geometric shapes. Nonetheless, cognitive psychologist Eleanor Rosch (1973) found that the Dani learned geometric categories more easily when presented with a prototypical example (such as a square) than when presented with a less prototypical example (a crudely drawn irregular square). Similarly, the Dani use only two color terms, which correspond roughly to "light" and "dark." When Rosch presented them with prototypical colors (such as a pure red), the Dani were able to learn the color categories more readily than when presented with nonprototypical colors (a reddish brown).

These findings indicate that people learn category concepts based on prototypes quickly, even when the categories are not part of their culture or language. In addition, Berlin and Kay (1969) found another regularity in the use of color terms. If a culture's language has only two color names, these names will refer to black and white. If the language has three terms, the third always refers to red, and if it has a fourth term, it will refer to either yellow or green. More complex languages add blue and then brown, and if a language has more than seven color terms, it will include names for pink, purple, orange, and gray.

Taken together, these findings support two basic principles. First, some aspects of categorization are universal. Members of all cultures, for example, either have or can easily learn categories for basic colors, shapes, and other icons. These are areas in which we all are likely to have had similar experiences, no matter what our culture (Matsumoto, 1995). Second, where cultural experiences differ, there are likely to be differences in categorization. This diversity is partly responsible for the different worldviews of various cultures. If members of different cultures use different concepts and categories as a result of their different experiences, then they will probably think about the world and organize experiences in different ways, which can, in turn, lead to significant differences in behavior.

If members of different cultures use different concepts and categories as a result of their different experiences, then they will probably think about the world and organize experiences in different ways . . .

Another of Lakoff's examples of the use of ICMs is the flexible way in which we construct the concept *mother*. This concept has undergone many changes as the nature of the family has changed in modern life. Once the ICM of a family that gave meaning to the concept mother would have been very simple, but now there are many different models of the family that can yield different concepts of motherhood to be used on specific occasions. To illustrate the wide range of meanings of mother, Lakoff (1987, p. 74) lists the following:

The birth model: The person who gives birth is the mother.

The genetic model: The female who contributes the genetic material is the mother.

The nurturance model: The female adult who nurtures and raises a child is the mother.

The marital model: The wife of the father is the mother.

The genealogical model: The closest female ancestor is the mother.

Lakoff observes that each of us may want to regard one of the models as more real than the others, but conceptually they are all more or less equally realistic. Thus, you may use ICMs to generate different concepts of motherhood. You can conceive of a wide variety of mothers, such as stepmothers, adoptive mothers, and natural mothers. Someone will be regarded as a prototypical mother to the extent that she combines all the possible ways of being a *mother*, but nobody is likely to be able to embody *all* of the possibilities.

Obviously our ICMs allow us to construct other concepts, such as *father*, *brother*, and *sister*. A useful exercise would be for you to work out the different ways in which someone can be a father, brother, or sister.

So far, we have seen that words, images, and concepts form the building blocks of thought. But human cognition involves more than just passively thinking about things. It also involves actively using words, images, and concepts to solve problems and to make decisions. In the next two sections of the chapter, we will see how this is done.

PROBLEM SOLVING

Consider the following problems:

PROBLEM I   Three five-handed extraterrestrial monsters are holding three crystal globes (see Figure 7–4). Because of the peculiarities of their planet, both monsters and globes come in exactly three sizes: small, medium, and

Figure 7–4

large. The medium-sized monster is holding the small globe, the small monster is holding the large globe, and the large monster is holding the medium-sized globe. Because this situation offends their keenly developed sense of symmetry, they proceed to transfer globes from one monster to another so that each monster has a globe proportionate to its own size. By what sequence of transfers could the monsters solve this problem? (Adapted from J. R. Hayes & Simon, 1976)

PROBLEM 2 You have three measuring spoons (see Figure 7–5). One is filled with 8 teaspoons of salt; the other two are empty but have a capacity of 2 teaspoons each. Divide the salt among the spoons so that only 4 teaspoons of salt remain in the largest spoon.

PROBLEM 3 You have a 5-minute hourglass and a 9-minute hourglass (see Figure 7–6). How can you use them to time a 14-minute barbecue? (Adapted from Sternberg, 1986)

Most people find these problems easy to solve. (The answers to these problems appear at the end of the chapter.) But now consider more elaborate versions of the same three problems:

PROBLEM 4 Three five-handed extraterrestrial monsters are holding three crystal globes. Because of the peculiarities of their planet, both monsters and globes come in exactly three sizes: small, medium, and large. The medium-sized monster is holding the small globe; the small monster is holding the large globe; and the large monster is holding the medium-sized globe. Because this situation offends their keenly developed sense of symmetry, they proceed to transfer globes from one monster to another so that each monster has a globe proportionate to its own size. However, monster etiquette complicates the solution of the problem because it requires: (a) that only one globe be transferred at a time; (b) that a monster can hold no more than two globes, and only the larger of the two may be transferred; and (c) that a globe may not be transferred to a monster who is holding a larger globe. By what sequence of transfers could the monsters solve this problem? (Adapted from J. R. Hayes & Simon, 1976)

PROBLEM 5 You have three measuring spoons (see Figure 7–7). One (spoon A) is filled with 8 teaspoons of salt. The second and third spoons are both empty; the second spoon (spoon B) can hold 5 teaspoons, and the third (spoon C) can hold 3 teaspoons. Divide the salt among the spoons so that spoon A and spoon B each have exactly 4 teaspoons of salt and spoon C is empty.

PROBLEM 6 You have a 5-minute hourglass and a 9-minute hourglass. How can you use them to time a 13-minute barbecue? (Adapted from Sternberg, 1986)

Most people find the last three problems much more difficult to solve than the first three. (Solutions to these last three problems can also be found at the end of the chapter.) Why should this be so? In part, it is because the solutions to Problems 4, 5, and 6 simply take longer to work out than the solutions to the first three problems. But there is more to it than that. The first three problems are considered trivial because what you are asked to do is obvious; the strategy for solving them is simple and easily identified, and it is easy to verify that each step is moving you closer to a solution. The last

Figure 7–5

5 min.   9 min.

Figure 7–6

A

B

C

Figure 7–7

three problems, however, require some interpretation, the strategy for solving them is not at all obvious, and it is much harder to know whether any given step has actually helped move you closer to a solution.

Let's examine each of these aspects of the problem-solving process. After we have looked at the principles of solving a problem and the steps and strategies involved in the process, we will turn to common obstacles that people face when they tackle a problem.

The Interpretation of Problems

The first step in solving a problem is called **problem representation,** which means interpreting or defining the problem. You may be tempted to leap ahead and try to solve a problem just as it is presented, but this impulse often leads to poor solutions. For example, if your business is losing money, you might sit down to figure out how to cut costs. But by defining the solution narrowly as cost cutting, you have ruled out the possibility that the best way to stop losing money might be to figure out how to increase income rather than to cut costs. A better representation of this problem would be to discover ways to cut costs or increase income or both.

Now consider these problems:

PROBLEM 7   You have four pieces of chain, each of which is made up of three links (see Figure 7–8). All links are closed. It costs 2 cents to open a link and 3 cents to close a link. How can you join all 12 links together into a single, continuous circle without paying more than 15 cents?

PROBLEM 8   Arrange six kitchen matches into four equilateral triangles (see Figure 7–9). Each side of every triangle must be only one match length. Before going on, stop and try to work out solutions to Problems 7 and 8.

These two problems are difficult because they are represented in a way that makes them seem impossible to solve. For example, in Problem 7, most people assume that the best way to proceed is to open and close the end links on the various pieces of chain. As long as they persist with this "conceptual block," they will be unable to solve the problem. If the problem is represented differently, the solution is almost immediately obvious. Similarly, for the kitchen match problem, most people assume that they can work only in two dimensions—that is, that the triangles must lie flat on a surface—or that one match cannot serve as the side of two triangles. When

Figure 7–8

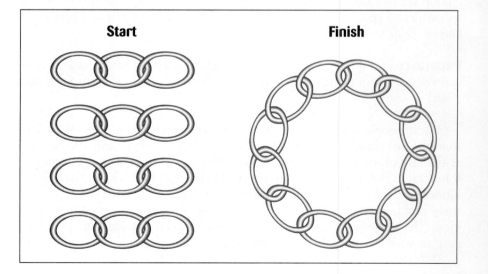

the problem is presented differently, the solution becomes much easier. (The solutions to both of these problems appear at the end of the chapter.) In each case, a narrow definition of the problem sets up conceptual blocks that make the solution of the problem impossible.

Let's turn to a more difficult example. J. M. Carroll, Thomas, and Malhotra (1980) asked two groups of participants to work on two different problems. One group was given a problem that dealt with time: organizing seven stages of a manufacturing process, taking into account specific guidelines or constraints. The other group received a problem that dealt with space: organizing the location of seven business offices on a corridor, again taking into account specific constraints. Although the two problems appeared to be quite different, they were actually the same: They had the same number of variables and constraints, and they had the same solution. Nonetheless, the people who worked on the spatial problem were far more successful than those who worked on the time problem. Why should this be so? The answer seems to be that the participants who received the space problem automatically represented or interpreted the problem in visual terms. They all drew diagrams that showed how the offices could be arranged. This approach made this particular problem easy to solve. Most of the people working on the time problem, however, did not interpret it visually. They used no charts, maps, or other visual images. After many attempts, they became tangled in a complex maze of language and logic. When the researchers repeated the experiment but instructed all participants to use a graphic approach to solving the problem, the two problems turned out to be equally easy to solve.

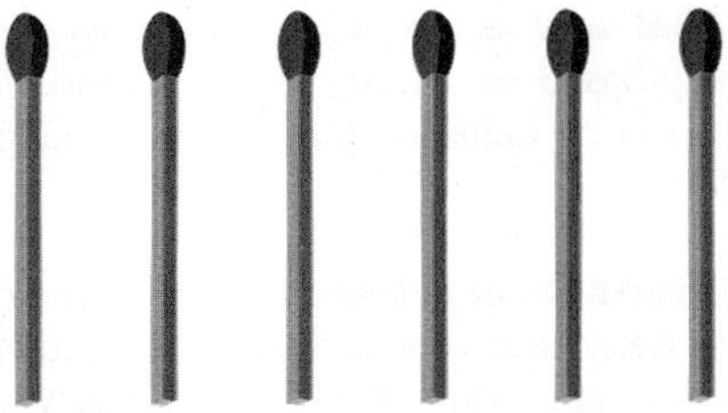

PROBLEM 9   A monk wishes to get to a retreat at the top of a mountain. He starts climbing the mountain at sunrise and arrives at the top of the mountain at sunset of the same day. During the course of his ascent, he travels at variable speeds and stops often to rest and eat the food he has brought with him. He spends the night engaged in meditation. The next day he starts his descent at sunrise, following the same narrow path that he used to climb the mountain. As before, he travels at various speeds and stops often to rest and to eat. Because he takes great care not to fall on the way down, the trip down takes as long as the trip up, and he does not arrive at the bottom until sunset. Prove that there is one place on the path that the monk passes at exactly the same time of day on the trip up and on the trip down.

This problem is extremely difficult to solve if it is represented verbally or mathematically. It is considerably easier to solve if it is represented visually, as you can see from the explanation that appears at the end of the chapter.

Another aspect of problem interpretation is deciding which class or category of problem the problem belongs to. Properly categorizing a problem can provide clues about how to solve it. In fact, once a simple problem has been properly categorized, its solution may be as easy as painting by numbers. For example, many people find the following problem difficult to solve:

> A farmer is counting the hens and rabbits in his barnyard. He counts a total of 50 heads and 140 feet. How many hens and how many rabbits does the farmer have? (S. K. Reed, 1988, p. 277)

This problem becomes much easier to solve when you realize it belongs to the same category as the following, more familiar problem:

> Bill has a collection of 20 coins that consists entirely of dimes and quarters. If the collection is worth $4.10, how many of each kind of coin are in the collection? (S. K. Reed, 1988, p. 277)

Figure 7–9
The six-match problem.
Arrange the six matches so that they form four equilateral triangles. The solution is given in Figure 7–15.

Trial and error A problem-solving strategy based on the successive elimination of incorrect solutions until the correct one is found.

Information retrieval A problem-solving strategy that requires only the recovery of information from long-term memory.

Algorithm A step-by-step method of problem solving that guarantees a correct solution.

Quite often, people who seem to have a knack for solving problems are actually just very skilled at interpreting and representing them in effective ways. Star chess players, for example, can readily categorize a new game situation by comparing it to various standard situations stored in their long-term memories. This strategy helps them interpret the current pattern of chess pieces with greater speed and precision than the novice chess player. A seasoned football coach may quickly recognize that a certain situation on the gridiron calls for a particular kind of defense. He has interpreted the game in terms of familiar categories. To a great extent, gaining expertise in any field, from football to physics, consists of increasing your ability to represent and categorize problems in such a way that they may be solved more quickly and effectively (Haberlandt, 1997).

Producing and Evaluating Solutions

Once you have properly interpreted a problem, the next step is to select a solution strategy that best suits the problem. When casting about for the right strategy, you must choose from a rich assortment of possibilities. In the following pages, we will examine some of the strategies that are often available.

TRIAL AND ERROR One possibility is simple **trial and error.** This strategy works best when choices are limited. For example, if you had only three or four keys to choose from, trial and error would be the best way to find out which one unlocked your uncle's garage door. In most cases, however, trial and error usually wastes many hours because it may take a very long time for the solution to appear. Moreover, many problems can never be solved strictly through this scattershot approach. How many guesses would it take, for example, to come up with the name of the seventh caliph of the Islamic Abbasid dynasty? Or, how soon could you guess the square root of the product of two sides of a given triangle? You could probably go on guessing for the rest of your life and never come up with the correct answer.

To solve most problems, you have to choose some strategy other than trial and error. The particular strategy you use should be based on an accurate categorization and representation of the problem. But it should also take into account the limits of short-term memory. We have to be able to retrieve information and work on it without overcrowding the limited work space of short-term memory. With this in mind, let's look at some of the alternative problem-solving strategies that are available.

INFORMATION RETRIEVAL In some cases, the solution to a problem may be as simple as retrieving information from long-term memory. **Information retrieval** is an important option when a solution must be found quickly. For example, a pilot is expected to memorize the slowest speed at which she can fly a particular airplane before it stalls and heads for the ground. When she needs this information, she has no time to sit back and calculate the correct answer. Because time is of the essence, she simply refers to her long-term memory for an immediate answer.

ALGORITHMS More complex problems require more complex methods. In some cases, you may be able to use an **algorithm.** Algorithms are problem-solving methods that guarantee a solution if they are appropriate for the problem and are properly carried out. For example, an algorithm for solving an anagram (a group of letters that can be rearranged to form a word) entails trying every possible combination of letters until we come up with the hidden word. Suppose we are given the letters *acb*. We try *abc, bac, bca, cba,* and finally come up with *cab*, whereby the problem is solved. To calculate the

Is trial and error an effective way to solve problems?

product of 323 and 546, we multiply them according to the rules of multiplication (the algorithm). If we do it accurately, we are guaranteed to get the right answer. To convert temperatures from Fahrenheit to Celsius, we use the formula C = 5/9(F–32). This formula, like all formulas, is an algorithm.

HEURISTICS   Many of the problems that we encounter in everyday life, however, cannot be solved by using algorithms. In these cases, we often turn to heuristics. **Heuristics** are rules of thumb that help us simplify problems. They do not guarantee a solution, but they may bring it within reach. Some heuristic methods work better in some situations than in others. Some heuristics have special purposes only, such as those applied to chess or word puzzles. But other general heuristics can be applied to a wide range of human problems. Part of problem solving is to decide which heuristic is most appropriate for a given problem (Bourne et al., 1986).

A very simple heuristic method is **hill climbing.** In this process, we try to move continually closer to our final goal without ever digressing or going backward. At each step, we evaluate how far "up the hill" we have come, how far we still have to go, and precisely what the next step should be to bring us closer to the goal. On a multiple-choice test, for example, one useful strategy in answering each question is to eliminate the alternatives that are obviously incorrect. Even if this does not leave you with the one correct answer, you are closer to a solution. In trying to balance a budget, each reduction in expenses brings you closer to the goal and leaves you with a smaller deficit with which to deal.

For other problems, however, the hill-climbing heuristic is not optimal. Problems 4 and 5 on p. 269 are of this sort. In each case, there comes a point where you must digress, or actually move backward, to make ultimate progress toward your goal.

Let's consider some other examples for which the hill-climbing strategy is inappropriate. You have probably played checkers at one time or another. At a decisive moment you may have had to "give up" a piece to maneuver toward a more strategic position on the board. Although losing that one piece seemed to push you further from victory, the move in fact nudged you closer to your goal. In baseball, a pitcher can prevent a good hitter from batting in runs at a critical time by giving him or her an "intentional walk." This tactic puts an extra player on base and seems to work against the goal of keeping runners off the bases. But the shrewd pitcher knows that by conceding a walk to a strong batter, he or she will get to pitch to the next batter, a weaker hitter who is less likely to drive in runs.

Another problem-solving heuristic is to create **subgoals.** By setting subgoals, we can often break a problem into smaller, more manageable pieces, each of which is easier to solve than the problem as a whole (Reed, 1996). Consider the problem of the Hobbits and the Orcs:

PROBLEM 10   Three Hobbits and three Orcs are on the bank of a river. They all want to get to the other side of the river, but their boat will carry only two creatures at a time. Moreover, if at any time the Orcs outnumber the Hobbits, the Orcs will attack the Hobbits. How can all the creatures get across the river without danger to the Hobbits? The solution to this problem may be found by thinking of it in terms of a series of subgoals. Consider what has to be done to get just one or two creatures across the river at a time—leaving aside, temporarily, the main goal of getting everyone across. We could first send two of the Orcs across and have one of them return. That gets one Orc across the river. Now we can think about the next trip. It's clear that we can't then send a single Hobbit across with an Orc because the Hobbit would be outnumbered as soon as the boat landed on the opposite shore. So that means we have to send

Heuristics Rules of thumb that help in simplifying and solving problems, although they do not guarantee a correct solution.

Hill climbing A heuristic problem-solving strategy in which each step moves you progressively closer to the final goal.

Subgoals Intermediate, more manageable goals used in one heuristic strategy to make it easier to reach the final goal.

If you were facing a hitter like Ken Griffey, Jr., you might decide to walk him intentionally. Although this wouldn't accomplish your subgoal of keeping runners off the bases, it might ultimately help you to win the game, and so can be a smart choice. Means-end analysis is a problem-solving heuristic that involves this kind of flexible thinking.

Means-end analysis A heuristic strategy that aims to reduce the discrepancy between the current situation and the desired goal at a number of intermediate points.

either two Hobbits or two Orcs. By working on the problem in this fashion—concentrating on subgoals—we can eventually get everyone across safely.

Once you have mastered Problem 10, you might want to try Problem 11, which is considerably more difficult (the answers to both problems are at the end of the chapter):

PROBLEM 11 This problem is identical to Problem 10, except that there are five Hobbits and five Orcs, and the boat can carry three creatures at a time across the river.

Subgoals are often helpful in solving a variety of everyday problems. For example, a student whose goal is to write a term paper might set subgoals by breaking the project into a series of separate tasks: choosing a topic, doing research and taking notes, preparing an outline, writing the first draft, editing, rewriting, and so on. Even the subgoals can sometimes be broken down into separate tasks. For example, writing the first draft of the paper might break down into subgoals such as writing the introduction, describing the position to be taken, supporting the position with evidence, drawing conclusions, writing a summary, and writing a bibliography. In this case, the subgoals need not be reached in any particular order: It might be easier to start writing out the evidence in support of a position, then back up and write down a detailed description of the position to be taken, and only then write the introduction and summary to the paper. This strategy is often extremely helpful for writers who find themselves struggling with the opening paragraphs of a paper. Go on and write some other section of the paper, and come back to the introduction later when you may have a better idea of what you need to say and how best to say it. In any situation, subgoals make problem solving more manageable because they free us from the burden of having to "get to the other side of the river" all at once. This tactic allows us to set our sights on closer, more manageable goals. Of course, the overall purpose of setting subgoals is still to reach the ultimate goal—the solution to the problem.

One of the most frequently used heuristics, called means-end analysis, combines hill climbing and subgoals. **Means-end analysis** is not as shortsighted as hill climbing. Like hill climbing, means-end analysis involves analyzing the difference between the current situation and the desired end, and then doing something to reduce that difference. However, as we saw earlier, hill climbing does not allow the person to take detours or to move away from the final goal in order to solve the problem. By contrast, means-end analysis takes into account the entire problem situation, and it formulates subgoals in such a way as to allow us temporarily to move away from the final goal so that we can reach it in the end. Means-end analysis begins by setting up a series of choices about how to proceed. We then assess each choice to see which will ultimately lead us to our goal. At each point, we make the most likely choice and continue to the next point. For example, a person driving toward a clear landmark—a mountain range—with no specific directions for guidance will probably choose roads that appear, from his or her present position, to be headed in that direction. If the road then curves and leads in a different direction than was expected, the person will realize that such a detour may still ultimately lead to the mountain and might decide, "I'll go another mile, and if I'm not any closer by then, I'll turn around and go back" (Wickelgren, 1979).

Although means-end analysis focuses on achieving the final goal, it allows us to pursue subgoals that may require digressions or temporary steps backward that are absolutely necessary for the solution of a problem. One potential danger with this approach, of course, is that if we stray too far from the end goal, it may vanish from sight altogether. One way of minimizing the chances that this will happen is to use the heuristic method of **working backward** (Bourne et al., 1986). With this strategy, the search for a solution begins at the goal and works backward toward the "givens." This method is often used when the goal has more information than the givens and when the operations can work both forward and backward. If, for example, we wanted to spend exactly $100 on clothing, it would be difficult to reach that goal by simply buying some items and hoping that they totaled exactly $100. A better strategy would be to purchase one item, subtract its cost from $100 to determine how much money we have left, then purchase another item, subtract its cost, and so on, until we have spent $100. Another good example of working backward is when a person solves a paper-and-pencil maze by starting at the end and working backwards to the beginning.

Up to this point, we have seen how various strategies can be used to solve problems. Yet in real life, problem solving often bogs down, and we find ourselves either unable to arrive at a solution or faced with a solution that is not effective. In the next section, we will examine various obstacles to problem solving.

Obstacles to Solving Problems

Many factors other than those we have already discussed affect success in solving problems. One such factor is level of motivation, or emotional

HIGHLIGHTS
COMPUTER SIMULATION OF PROBLEM SOLVING

We can program computers to solve problems using many of the problem-solving techniques you've been reading about. Because computers are so fast, they can often use simple trial and error to solve even fairly complex problems: The computer program simply tries one solution after another until it finds one that works. However, for more complicated problems, computers—like humans—need to use heuristics. As a result, scientists have devised computer systems based on our understanding of how the human brain works (Buonomano & Merzenich, 1995; also see Haberlandt, 1997). Computer systems that mimic the way the human brain solves problems using heuristics are called *neural networks*.

One of the earliest and most famous computer problem-solving programs was created by Allan Newell and Nobel Prize winner Herbert A. Simon of Carnegie Mellon University (Newell & Simon, 1972; Simon, 1979). At every step in the problem solution, their General Problem Solver (GPS) tries to reduce the difference between its current state and the goal of the problem, using all the heuristic techniques we discussed above. Thus, GPS is capable of a full-blown means-end analysis, using subgoals, and working backward.

[F]or more complicated problems, computers—like humans—need to use heuristics. As a result, scientists have devised computer systems based on our understanding of how the human brain works.

Computer programs, then, can use many of the same problem-solving techniques that humans use. In fact, it was not until the creation of the computer programs that researchers fully realized the important role that subgoals and hill climbing play in human problem solving. However, the success of the computer simulation of human problem solving does not mean that humans and computers work in the same ways. In some cases, a computer may achieve the same goal as a human, but by very different means. Moreover, some aspects of problem solving may be well suited to computer simulation, but other aspects may be difficult to simulate. Can you imagine a computer having insight, for example?

Set The tendency to perceive and to approach problems in certain ways.

Functional fixedness The tendency to perceive only a limited number of uses for an object, thus interfering with the process of problem solving.

2

In what ways can previous experiences interfere with your ability to solve problems?

arousal. In Chapter 9, Motivation and Emotion, we see that the "peak," or optimal state of performance, in problem solving is achieved at intermediate levels of excitement or arousal. Moreover, the more complex the problem-solving task, the lower the level of emotion that can be tolerated without interfering with performance. Generally speaking, we must generate a certain surge of excitement to motivate ourselves adequately to solve a problem, but too much arousal can hamper our ability to find a solution.

Another factor that can either help or hinder problem solving is **set,** which refers to our tendency to perceive and to approach problems in certain ways. Our set determines which information we will be able to retrieve from memory in a given situation. Set can be helpful if we have learned certain operations and perceptions in the past that we can apply to the present. For example, people tend to do better when they solve problems for the second or third time, because they have learned more effective strategies for choosing moves and because they understand the problem better (Haberlandt, 1997). Much of our education involves learning sets and ways to solve problems (i.e., heuristics and algorithms), even though it may seem that we are learning only specific information. We are taught to integrate new information into forms that we already know or to use methods that have proved effective in the past. In fact, the strategies that we use in problem solving are themselves a set. We have learned that approaching a problem in a certain logical order is the best way to solve it.

But sets do not always help solve problems. If a problem requires you to apply your previous experience in a new and different way, a strong set could become a serious obstacle. People who are most successful in solving problems often are those who have many different sets at their disposal and can judge when to change sets or when to give up a set entirely. Great ideas and inventions come out of such a balance. For example, the famous astronomer Copernicus was familiar with the sets of his time, but he had the flexibility to see that they might not be relevant to his work. Only by putting aside these sets could he discover that the earth revolves around the sun, rather than the other way around, as was popularly believed.

The point is to use a set when it is appropriate but not to let the set use you. In other words, sets are useful as long as they do not obscure novel approaches to solving problems. In one study, for example, researchers discovered that fifth- and sixth-graders who were doing poorly in math did not realize that they should use different strategies for familiar as opposed to unfamiliar problems (Hasselbring, Goin, & Bransford, 1985). For the most part, the children made few attempts to distinguish between the problems they knew (and could solve from memory) and the problems they did not know and that required a different problem-solving strategy. With specific instruction, however, the children learned that some problem-solving situations require a change in strategies, and they were then better able to draw on a wide range of relevant strategies to improve their performance. Similar approaches have been used in situations as different as military training (Halff, Hollan, & Hutchins, 1986) and expository writing (Hayes & Flower, 1986).

One characteristic of sets that can seriously hinder problem solving is called **functional fixedness.** Consider Figure 7–10. Do you see a way to mount the candle on the wall? The more you use an object in one way, the harder it is to see new uses for it. When you get used to seeing or using something in only one way, you have assigned a fixed function to it. To some extent, of course, part of the learning process is to assign correct functions to objects. We teach a child that the "proper" function of a spoon is stirring, not pounding. Much of how we form concepts involves learning the "right"

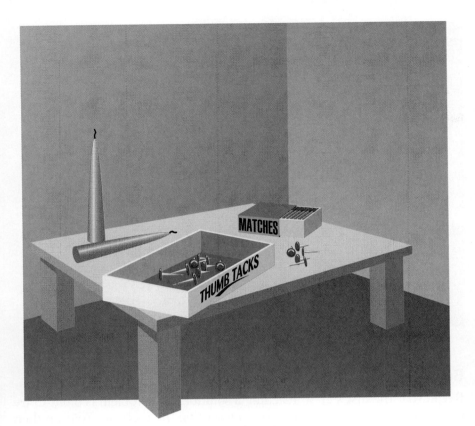

Figure 7–10
To test the effects of functional fixedness, participants might be given the items shown on the table and asked to mount a candle on the wall. See Figure 7–18 for a solution.

functions of objects. But it is important to remain open enough to see that an object can be used for an entirely different function if need be. (The solution to this problem is given at the end of the chapter.)

Another illustration of functional fixedness is shown in Figure 7–11. This classic problem was invented by N. R. F. Maier (1931) and was used by Birch and Rabinowitz (1951) in their study of the effect of sets on productive thinking. Here is the problem: Two strings are hanging from the ceiling far enough apart that one cannot be reached without letting go of the other. A toolbox with tools is on a nearby table. The task is to get hold of both strings simultaneously. For most people, functional fixedness is a major obstacle to solving this problem. (The solution to this problem appears at the end of the chapter.)

We have been talking about functional fixedness in terms of objects, but the idea can also be applied to problems with people. For example, the problem of the elderly has received much attention recently. Older people who are put into institutions often feel useless and depressed. Unwanted children who live in institutions also do not always receive the time and care they need. Instead of seeing the elderly as people who are no longer productive and need to be looked after, someone came up with the idea that they might serve as foster grandparents to the children in institutions. This was a case of suspending the fixed function of both groups. The "grandparents" gave the children love and attention, and the children gave the older people the feeling of being useful. Two human problems were addressed with one wise, new, and compassionate solution.

Despite the pitfalls that we may encounter when trying to solve problems, many techniques are available to us for sharpening our performance on such tasks. Let's take a look at some of the ways in which we can become better and more efficient problem solvers.

Tactic of elimination A problem-solving strategy in which possible solutions are evaluated according to appropriate criteria and discarded as they fail to contribute to a solution.

Visualizing A problem-solving strategy in which principles or concepts are drawn, diagrammed, or charted so that they can be better understood.

Figure 7–11
Maier's two-string problem.
In another test of functional fixedness, participants were asked to solve the problem of how to grasp both strings at the same time. The solution appears in Figure 7–19.

Visualizing the requirements of a problem can be very helpful. For a novice, drawing the problem on paper may be the best tactic, but for an expert the visualization can often be "in the head." The ability to mentally visualize complex new plays is one of many factors that gives expert basketball players an edge over beginners.

Becoming Better at Problem Solving

Recall that the first step in reaching a solution to a problem is often to try out various ways of interpreting or representing the problem. You can then experiment with a number of solution strategies, shifting your perspective of the problem from one angle to another. Let's look more closely at how some of these strategies work.

TACTIC OF ELIMINATION   If in a given problem you are more sure of what you do not want than of what you do want, the **tactic of elimination** can be very helpful. The best approach is first to create a list of all the possible solutions that you can think of. Then you discard all the solutions that take you where you definitely do not want to go. That leaves a smaller number of potential solutions that you can examine more closely. This strategy will only work if your list of possible solutions contains at least one good solution to the problem. Otherwise you'll end up eliminating all the possible solutions on your list, and you'll have to start over. Also, you have to be careful not to throw out a solution that seems on the surface to lead to an undesirable outcome but, on closer examination, might turn out to be an excellent solution to the problem.

VISUALIZING   Other useful tactic is **visualizing,** diagramming, and charting various courses of action (J. L. Adams, 1980). For example, in the Hobbit and Orc problem, it might help to draw a picture of the river and show the Hobbits and Orcs at each stage of the problem as they are ferried back and forth. By drawing a diagram of a problem, or even constructing a simple model of it, you may find it easier to grasp the principle of the problem and to avoid irrelevant or distracting details. Some chess masters, for example, can visualize chess games in their heads; as a result, they are able to play blindfolded as many as 50 simultaneous games! Similarly, members of the Canadian National Women's Basketball Team could learn the patterns of new plays more effectively than a group of psychology graduate students could. The basketball players were able to visualize the new plays based on their wide basketball experience. The psychology students had to learn the plays step-by-step.

Divergent thinking Thinking that meets the criteria of originality, inventiveness, and flexibility.

Convergent thinking Thinking that is directed toward one correct solution to a problem.

THE DEVELOPMENT OF EXPERTISE   The examples of skilled chess and basketball players point out not only the usefulness of visualizing but also the importance of acquiring relevant knowledge. Visualization, for example, is a good skill to have when working in particle physics, but it is highly unlikely to help a person solve physics problems unless he or she has a working knowledge of physics. Many occupations require training that involves learning specific knowledge and skills particularly related to a given area. An experimental physicist needs to learn both theory and how to operate various types of apparatus. Experience also allows an auto mechanic to know that a particular color of exhaust smoke indicates that an engine may be burning oil. An expert mechanic develops a number of such rules, as well as a mental map of the internal combustion engine. This type of knowledge allows an expert to work efficiently on problems without the elaborate preparation that a new problem would require of a beginner (Haberlandt, 1997).

Research shows that experts not only know more about a particular domain but also organize it in larger units or "chunks" that are extensively interconnected, much like a cross-referencing system in a library (Bédard & Chi, 1992). This practice enables experts to approach a problem with many more potentially relevant ideas than a novice would. For example, research shows that the most important difference between chess masters and novices is not that the masters can conceive a greater number of moves; rather, the chess masters' years of experience enable them to recognize more quickly and accurately the significance of various board positions. In turn, this ability to recognize a situation as resembling one with which they are already familiar enables them to generate a good next move more quickly (Klein et al., 1995). Chess masters also can remember the positions from chess games better than novices can (Chase & Simon, 1973). This is probably because the relations between the pieces are meaningful to chess experts but have little or no meaning to novices (Bédard & Chi, 1992).

Expertise has its limits, however. Under some circumstances, it may even be detrimental (Bédard & Chi, 1992). For example, expertise in one area (e.g., medicine) often does not transfer very well to another domain (e.g., interpersonal skills). Moreover, expertise may lead to a rigid way of handling problems, and a novice may outperform an expert if a novel or creative response is required. We will now look more closely at creative problem solving.

CREATIVE PROBLEM SOLVING   Many problems, of course, do not lend themselves to straightforward strategies but rely more on the use of flexible and original thinking. For example, how many unusual uses can you think of for a brick? It's easy to think of a few good uses but quite another task to come up with 50 or 60 distinct ones. Psychologists sometimes refer to this type of thinking as **divergent thinking,** in contrast to **convergent thinking** (Guilford, 1967). A problem requiring convergent thinking has only one solution or a very few—for example, a math problem. We use convergent thinking when a problem has a known solution. By contrast, problems that have no single correct solution and that require a flexible, inventive approach call for divergent thinking. In recent years, schools of business and engineering have begun to stress the development of divergent thinking skills in their classes to encourage their students to use more creative and inventive problem-solving strategies (Kaplan & Simon, 1990).

Because creative problem solving requires thinking up new and original ideas, the process is not always aided by planning and the deliberate use of problem-solving strategies. Solutions to many problems rely on *insight*, a seemingly arbitrary flash "out of the blue" that solves a problem. (You may

The Guggenheim Museum in Bilbao, Spain, is a feat of creative problem solving. The architect, Frank Gehry, gave the outside a dramatic shimmering effect by using a skin of titanium. The originality of the design is further heightened by its unusual juxtaposition of shapes. Flexible thinking underlies creative ideas like these.

recall that insight was discussed in Chapter 5, Learning.) Many of us have had the experience of suddenly seeing our way to a solution that previously had seemed all but impossible. Henri Poincaré, the French mathematician, has written about his own experiences with this phenomenon:

> One evening, contrary to my custom, I drank black coffee and could not sleep. Ideas rose in crowds; I felt them collide until pairs interlocked, so to speak, making a stable combination. By the next morning I had established the existence of a new class of Fuschian functions. (Poincaré, 1924)

Many people have provided strikingly similar accounts of their own processes of creative thinking. Drawing on heuristics, algorithms, and expertise, they simply cannot come up with the solution to their problem. Then, as if by magic, the solution suddenly "pops into their heads," often after they've stopped working on the problem for a while. Therefore, if you simply cannot arrive at a solution to a problem after careful preparation and step-by-step efforts at problem solving, try to stop thinking about the problem for a while and return to it later, approaching it from a new angle (H. G. Murray & Denny, 1969). Sometimes you get so enmeshed in the details of a problem that you lose sight of the obvious. Taking a rest from a problem may allow you to discover a fresh approach. Psychologists have only recently begun to investigate these seemingly nonconscious problem-solving phenomena such as insight and intuition (Bechara et al., 1997; see also Underwood, 1996).

Another creative strategy is to *redefine* the problem. It is easy to look at problems just as they are presented to us—to assume, for example, that we cannot work in more than two dimensions when solving the kitchen match problem. Recall also the example of the business that was losing money, the only solution to which seemed to be cost cutting. Once we expanded the range of solutions to include increasing income, we presented the business with a new set of possibilities.

These examples demonstrate the importance of developing a questioning attitude toward problems. Ask yourself, "What is the real problem here? Can the problem be interpreted in other ways?" By redefining the problem, you may find that you have opened up new avenues to creative solutions. And try to maintain an uncritical attitude toward potential solutions: Don't reject a potential solution because at first it seems not to be ideal for that problem. On closer examination, the solution may turn out to be effective, or it may suggest similar solutions that would work. This is the rationale behind the technique called **brainstorming:** When solving a problem, generate lots of ideas without evaluating them prematurely. Only after lots of ideas have been collected should you review and evaluate them (Haefele, 1962).

Finally, some evidence suggests that people become more creative when they are exposed to creative peers and teachers who can serve as role models (Amabile, 1983). Although some creative people work well in isolation, many others find it stimulating to work in teams with other creative people.

Different cultures approach creative thinking in different ways. For example, Howard Gardner, professor of education at Harvard University, claims to have learned one of his most important lessons about the differences between Chinese and American approaches to creative thinking while observing Chinese hotel attendants help his 18-month-old son Benjamin place a room key into a box (Gardner, 1990). The key was attached to a large plastic block and had to be aligned just right to go into the box. The little boy was too young to understand what he needed to do to get the key into the box. Besides, he lacked the manual dexterity for lining the key up correctly. Although he rarely accomplished the task, he enjoyed playing with the key and trying to get it into the slot. His American parents allowed him to entertain himself this way without interfering. He was happy exploring the possibilities of the key and the box. But hotel attendants who saw the little boy playing this way frequently took hold of the child's hand, lined up the key for him, and made sure that the key dropped into the box.

Gardner points out that this small incident demonstrates a basic difference between the two cultures' approaches to creative thinking. Americans stress self-reliance in problem solving, allowing children to explore a situation and deemphasizing successful accomplishment of a particular task. The idea behind this approach is that it will foster independence and originality, two qualities valued in our culture. The Chinese approach is to assist the child gently but firmly in successfully completing the task, eliminating possible frustration while paving the way to learning more complex tasks later on. The American approach to creativity is to encourage early experimentation on the assumption that there will be plenty of time later on to master skills. The Chinese believe that skills must be acquired early and do not make a priority of fostering creativity.

DECISION MAKING

Decision making is a special kind of problem solving in which we already know all the possible solutions or choices. The task is not to come up with new solutions, but rather to identify the best available solution or choice using a predetermined set of criteria. This might sound like a fairly simple process, but sometimes we have to juggle a large and complex set of criteria as well as a large number of possible choices. As the number of criteria and choices grows, so does the difficulty of making a good decision. For example, suppose that you are looking for an apartment. There are hundreds of apartments to choose from. And while the amount of rent is important, so are the neighbors, location, level of noise, and cleanliness. If you find a noisy

Brainstorming A problem-solving strategy in which an individual or a group produces numerous ideas and evaluates them only after all ideas have been collected.

Compensatory model A rational decision-making model in which choices are systematically evaluated on various criteria.

Noncompensatory model A decision-making model in which weaknesses in one or more criteria are not offset by strengths in other criteria.

3 What do psychologists mean by a compensatory model of decision making?

apartment with undesirable neighbors but a bargain-basement rent, should you take it? Is it a better choice than the apartment in a more desirable location with less noise but with a higher rent? How can you weigh the various characteristics to ensure that you make the best possible choice among the hundreds of available apartments?

The logical way to proceed in making any decision is to rate each of the available choices on all the criteria and to arrive at some overall measure of the extent to which each choice matches your criteria. For each choice the attractive features can offset or compensate for the unattractive features; thus, this approach to decision making is called a **compensatory model.** For example, if you are buying a house, one criterion might be that you prefer a brick house. You might, however, buy a wooden house if it is located in a good school district, has a pleasing floor plan, and is reasonably priced. In this case, the attractive features offset, or compensate for, the lack of a brick exterior.

Table 7–1 illustrates one of the most useful compensatory models. The various criteria are listed, and each one is assigned a weight according to its importance. Here the decision involves the purchase of a new car, and only three criteria are considered: price (which is not weighted heavily) and gas mileage and service record (which are weighted more heavily). Each car is then rated from 1 (poor) to 5 (excellent) on each of the criteria. You can see that Car 1 has an excellent price (5) but relatively poor gas mileage (2) and service record (1); Car 2 has a less desirable price but a fairly good mileage and service record. Each rating is then multiplied by the weight for that criterion (e.g., for Car 1, the price rating of 5 is multiplied by the weight of 4, and the result is put in parentheses next to the rating). Then the numbers in parentheses are added to give a total for each car. Clearly Car 2 is the better choice: It has a less desirable price, but that is offset by the fact that its mileage and service record are better, and these two criteria are more important than price to this particular buyer.

Using a table like this one allows you to evaluate a large number of choices on a large number of criteria. It can be extremely helpful in making choices such as which college to attend, which job offer to accept, which career to pursue, and where to take a vacation. If you have properly weighted the various criteria and correctly rated each alternative in terms of each criterion, then you can be sure that the alternative with the highest total score is, in fact, the most rational choice, given the information available to you.

Most people, however, do not follow such a precise system of making decisions. Rather, they use various **noncompensatory models** in which shortcomings on one criterion are not offset by strengths on other criteria. Especially

---

TABLE 7-1			
COMPENSATORY DECISION TABLE FOR PURCHASING A NEW CAR			
	Price (weight = 4)	Gas Mileage (weight = 8)	Service Record (weight = 10)	Weighted Total
Car 1	5(20)	2(16)	1(10)	(46)
Car 2	1(4)	4(32)	4(40)	(76)
Ratings:	5 = Excellent 1 = Poor			

popular is the *elimination-by-aspects* tactic (S. K. Reed, 1988). In this case, we toss out specific choices if they do not meet one or two of our requirements, regardless of how good they are on other criteria. For example, we might eliminate Car 2, regardless of all its advantages, because "it costs more." As you might guess, noncompensatory models tend to be shortsighted. They do not help us weigh the values of particular features, nor do they invite us to compare all the alternatives. As a result, such a decision-making model can lead to a decision that is merely adequate, but not the best.

Sometimes compensatory and noncompensatory strategies can be mixed to arrive at a decision. When there are many alternatives and many criteria, we could use a noncompensatory approach to eliminate any choices that are especially weak on one or more key criteria, even though they may be strong on other criteria. When the field has been narrowed to a few alternatives, all of which are at least average on the various criteria, then we might adopt some form of compensatory decision model to identify the best choice from the remaining alternatives. For example, in purchasing a car, we might first eliminate all the choices that clearly are too expensive or all those with especially poor service records (noncompensatory strategy). We can then evaluate and choose from the remaining choices based on a number of weighted criteria (compensatory strategy).

Choosing an appropriate decision-making model often depends on how much is at stake. We are more likely to use a compensatory model when the stakes are high: buying a home or choosing a college. When the stakes are low, the noncompensatory model usually helps us decide quickly such casual matters as which shoes to wear or who might win an Academy Award.

In important matters, however, making rational decisions is more complicated. Sometimes, for example, information about an alternative is incomplete or uncertain. In the case of the two cars, we may not know the repair record of either car, perhaps because both are new models. In this case, we have to make some estimates based on information about past repair records, which then help us predict the repair records of these new models. In the absence of any reliable information at all, we may have to guess about some of the facts that we need to make a decision, and research indicates that in many cases our guesses are incorrect (Gilovich, 1991).

The heuristic of **representativeness** is widely used in making judgments and reaching decisions. We use representativeness whenever we make a decision on the basis of certain information that matches our model of the typical member of a category. Representativeness can help simplify the decision-making process. For example, if every time you went shopping you bought the least expensive items, and if all of these items turned out to be poorly made, you might eventually decide not to buy anything that seems typical of the category "very cheap."

One potential shortcoming of representativeness is the tendency to *stereotype*; that is, to attribute certain characteristics to all members of a particular group. For example, many people discriminate against all elderly people in filling a job without considering a particular individual's ability to do the job. They have a stereotype of the elderly being incapable of certain tasks, and they judge *all* elderly individuals as being representative of the general model. (Stereotypes are discussed in more detail in Chapter 15, Social Psychology.) A good illustration of representativeness is a study conducted by Tversky and Kahneman (1973) in which students at a particular university were asked to choose whether a student who was described as "neat and tidy," "dull and mechanical," and a "poor writer" was a computer science major or a humanities major. More than 95 percent chose computer science as the student's major. Even after they were told that more than 80 percent of the students at their school were majoring in humanities, the

Representativeness A heuristic by which a new situation is judged on the basis of its resemblance to a stereotypical model.

Availability A heuristic by which a judgment or decision is based on information that is most easily retrieved from memory.

Confirmation bias The tendency to look for evidence in support of a belief and to ignore evidence that would disprove a belief.

4

True or False: People often make decisions based on whatever information is most readily available, even if that information is not accurate.

estimates remained virtually unchanged. Thus, although representativeness enables us to make decisions quickly, it will also lead us to make mistakes in some situations.

The faulty application of the heuristic of representativeness is closely related to our tendency to see *patterns* or *connections* where none exist (Kahneman & Tversky, 1996; Rottenstreich & Tversky, 1997). For example, some historians still report that President William Henry Harrison caught a case of fatal pneumonia on the day of his inaugural speech because he delivered it in a freezing rain. The implication is that pneumonia is caused by exposure to cold weather, when in fact a virus, not exposure to inclement weather, causes pneumonia. (The same myth underlies the belief that a person can catch a cold by going out in the winter with wet hair, or by being caught in a downpour without an umbrella.) Many people still believe that chocolate causes acne to flare up in susceptible teen-agers, yet this myth was completely disproved by Dr. Albert M. Kligman, a dermatologist, almost a half a century ago (Kolata, 1996). Similarly, many parents strongly believe that sugar may cause hyperactivity in children—despite the scientific evidence to the contrary. Another study found no evidence to support the generally accepted idea that changing weather conditions influence arthritis (Redelmeier & Tversky, 1996). In all these cases, people believe they see patterns where in fact none exist.

Another common heuristic is **availability.** In the absence of full and accurate information, we often make decisions based on whatever information we can most easily retrieve from memory, even though this information may not be accurate. In one experiment, the participants were asked whether the letter *r* appears more frequently as the first or third letter in English words. Most people said first, but the correct answer is third. Their estimates were incorrect because they relied on the most readily available information in their memories, and it is easier to recall words that *begin* with *r* than words that have *r* as their third letter.

Everyday examples of the availability heuristic in action are not hard to find (Gilovich, 1991). For example, consider the so-called subway effect: It seems to be a law of nature that if you are waiting at a subway station, one train after another will come along headed in the opposite direction from the direction you want to go. Similarly, if you need a taxi, it seems inevitable that there will be an unusually long string of occupied or off-duty taxis. The problem here is that once a subway train or a taxi does come along, we leave the scene, so we never get to see the opposite situation: several subway trains going in our direction before one comes the other way or a long string of empty taxis. As a result, we tend to assume that those situations seldom or never occur! Consider another example: If you are driving at the speed limit, you naturally conclude that you are virtually the only person driving at that speed and that almost everyone on the road is driving either faster or slower than you are. Why? Because even if there are hundreds of cars going just as fast as you are, you will see very few of them: You'll never pass them, and they'll never pass you. Thus, most of the cars that you notice are those that are going faster or slower than you are and that either pass you or are passed by you. The natural conclusion, based on the limited evidence available to you, is that nearly everyone is going faster or slower than you are.

Another faulty heuristic closely related to availability is **confirmation bias**—the tendency to seek evidence in support of our beliefs and to ignore evidence that contradicts them (Myers, 1996). Confirmation bias is one of the processes that enables people to maintain stereotypes in the face of disconfirming evidence. Using an example from earlier in the chapter, suppose that you consider elderly people to be infirm and mentally slow. Every time you see an elderly person in need of care or assistance, you take it as evidence for your belief. However, you are likely to ignore the many cases of elderly people who are active, healthy, and leading very productive lives. As long as you ignore disconfirming evidence, your stereotype of the elderly is likely to remain unchanged.

Despite the commonness of faulty heuristics, for the most part people manage to make reasonably satisfactory decisions in the real world (Kleinmuntz, 1991). In part, this is because it is often possible to revise decisions if it appears that an initial choice is not optimal. Moreover, real-world decisions often don't have to be ideal or optimal, as long as the results are acceptable. A financial investment that returns a 20 percent profit in one year is still a fine investment, despite the fact that another investment might have returned 25 percent or 30 percent. Einhorn (1980) discusses a similar case regarding strategies for accepting people into a professional school. The admissions officers may adopt a strategy that leads to an 80 percent success rate among those applicants accepted. They would conclude that they had a good admissions model, even if the reality is that 80 percent of the rejected applicants also would have been successful students. Furthermore, there is some evidence that when making personal decisions such as choosing a car, it may be better to rely on intuition or "gut instinct" rather than to analyze the decision in too much detail (T. D. Wilson & Schooler, 1991). The reason appears to be that in personal matters, feelings are important guides about the best alternative. For example, using a rational, compensatory decision model, you might identify a car that is an outstanding choice on all your criteria but that just doesn't "feel right" to you and that you would feel uncomfortable driving. In this case, some other car would probably be a better choice for you.

In certain situations, however, "close is not good enough." For example, Spettle and Liebert (1986) studied the potential for error in decision making among operators at nuclear power plants. They found that in addition to the kinds of heuristic errors that we have been discussing, the stress of an emergency situation causes decision making to deteriorate further. Great stress may even erode performance to the point of panic. Spettle and Liebert suggest that training that simulates actual emergency conditions can prepare people to use efficient and effective decision-making strategies not only in those situations but also in novel situations where quick and accurate decisions are crucial. Preparatory training is also central to the Outward Bound program. This program was originally developed because British sailors whose boats were torpedoed panicked and died when calm decision making would have ensured their survival. (Do not confuse the Outward Bound program with Upward Bound, an American educational program.) The Outward Bound program puts people in a variety of stressful wilderness situations in the belief that they will learn effective personal strategies that can be transferred to a wide variety of everyday situations. A review of the research literature confirms that trained experts performing familiar tasks are less likely to be swayed by judgmental biases then is the average person faced with an unfamiliar task (Smith & Kida, 1991).

CULTURE AND DECISION MAKING Psychologists have only recently begun to explore the cross-cultural aspects of decision making (Radford, 1996). Although little is known about precisely how culture affects the decision process, researchers have shown that cultural differences do indeed exist. For example, a study that compared university students from Australia, China, and Japan found that when coping with the pressure of making a difficult decision, Japanese students experienced more *decisional stress* than Australian students (Radford et al., 1990). In addition, the Japanese participants in this study emphasized the importance of involving the members of an entire team

If you believe that most elderly people suffer declining health and cognitive abilities, you are likely to ignore evidence showing how active and mentally capable they can be. At the same time, you are apt to focus on evidence that confirms your existing stereotypes. When you make decisions about the elderly based on these skewed perceptions, those decisions are said to be influenced by the confirmation bias.

in a decision-making process, whereas the Australian students tended to be more self-reliant and focus on their own personal ability. As the world's cultures become increasingly interdependent in the 21st century, and projects that involve international cooperation such as the Mir Space Station become more commonplace, it will be increasingly necessary for psychologists to explore the influence culture has on the decision-making process.

So far in this chapter, we have examined language, images, and concepts, and the ways in which these three building blocks of thought can be used in problem solving and decision making. In the next section, we will examine the relationship between language and thought. We will then look at the question of whether nonhuman animals are also capable of using language and the implications of this for understanding the nature of thought in lower animals.

LANGUAGE AND THOUGHT

5

What is the relationship between language and thinking?

We have seen that language is closely tied to the expression and understanding of thoughts. Many words in our language—such as *friend, family, airplane, love*—correspond to concepts that are among the building blocks of thought. By combining words into sentences, we can link concepts to other concepts, forming complex thoughts and ideas. Because our language determines not only the words we use but also the way in which we combine those words into sentences, can language also determine how we think and what we can think about?

Some theorists believe that it does indeed. Recall that in Chapter 6, Memory, we noted that language affects long-term memory. In a study of this effect, experimental participants looked at color patches and assigned each one a name (Brown & Lenneberg, 1954). Colors that were quickly and easily named (such as blue) were more readily coded and retrieved than were those that took longer to name and were given less common labels (such as sky blue or pale blue). This indicates that the ease with which we remember an experience is closely related to the ease and speed with which we name and encode that experience. As Lindsay and Norman (1977) point out, "memory for single perceptual experiences is directly related to the ease with which language can communicate that experience" (p. 483).

If language affects our ability to store and retrieve information, it should also affect our ability to think about things. Benjamin Whorf (1956) was the strongest spokesperson for this position. According to Whorf's **linguistic relativity hypothesis,** the language that a person speaks determines the pattern of that person's thinking and his or her view of the world. For Whorf, if a language lacks a particular expression, the thought to which the expression corresponds will probably not occur to the people who speak that language. Whorf noted, for example, that the Hopi, a Native American people of the southwestern United States, have only two nouns for everything that flies. One noun refers to birds; the other is used for everything else, whether airplanes, kites, or dragonflies. Thus, according to Whorf, the Hopi would interpret all flying things in terms of either of these two nouns—something in the air would be either a bird or a nonbird.

Think for a moment about how linguistic relativity might apply to what you are learning in this course. Such phrases as *linguistic relativity hypothesis* and *surface* and *deep structure* capture very complex ideas. To the extent that you understand those terms, you probably find it easier to think about the relationship between language and thought, or between words and sentences and their underlying meaning. The technical vocabulary of any field of study permits people to think and communicate more easily, more precisely, and in more complex ways about the content of that field. In this way, language can help us organize our thoughts into concepts that serve as a kind of shorthand for a whole array of meanings. But this example also illustrates some of the criticisms of Whorf's hypothesis. The *idea* of deep structure had to occur before someone thought up that particular phrase. Similarly, you were able to identify and think about basic speech sounds before you learned that they are called *phonemes*. And you certainly recognize the difference between what someone says and what that person means without having to know that these are called *surface structure* and *deep structure*, respectively.

In the same vein, some critics of the linguistic relativity hypothesis suggest that it is more likely that the need to think about things differently changes a language than that a language changes how we think. For example, if the Hopi had been subjected to air raids, they would probably have created a word to distinguish a butterfly from a bomber! In fact, the more complex a society is, the more terms its language contains (Berlin & Kay, 1969). As a society becomes more complex, its people apparently have no trouble adding the necessary words to accommodate their expanded concepts. For example, most English-speaking people know only one word for snow. But skiers, realizing that different textures of snow can affect their downhill run, have coined such specific words for snow as powder, corn, and ice. So, to some extent at least, experience shapes language: People create new words when they need them.

Moreover, although language efficiently organizes human thought, both common sense and research evidence indicate that language does not necessarily capture all the experiences of the people who speak it. For example, although nonskiers may call all types of snow simply "snow," they can nonetheless think about the differences among icy snow, powdery snow, and slush. As we have seen, the Dani of New Guinea have no words for colors— everything is either dark/cool or light/ warm. Nonetheless, they remember basic colors like red, green, and yellow. Furthermore, when taught the names of these basic colors, they learn them faster than they learn the names of other colors. In addition, the Dani judge the similarity of colors much as English-speaking people do (Heider, 1972; Heider & Oliver, 1972; Rosch, 1973). Thus, people from different cultures with very different languages can think about some things, such as color, in very similar ways, even if their language contains no words for those things.

In summary, language, culture, and thought are intertwined (Matsumoto, 1996). People create words to capture important aspects of their experiences, and in turn, words may indeed shape how people think and what they think about. Experience shapes language, and language, in turn, affects subsequent experience. But people also can think about things for which they have no words, so thinking is not limited to the words in one's language. (See the *Controversies* box.)

Figurative language Expressive or nonliteral language such as metaphor and irony.

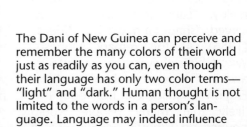

The Dani of New Guinea can perceive and remember the many colors of their world just as readily as you can, even though their language has only two color terms— "light" and "dark." Human thought is not limited to the words in a person's language. Language may indeed influence thought, but it doesn't seem to restrict thought to the extent that Whorf believed.

FIGURATIVE LANGUAGE   People are also very good at using language in creative ways to express their ideas. Recently, a great deal of research has been done on **figurative language:** expressive or nonliteral language such as

CONTROVERSIES
IS OUR LANGUAGE MALE-DOMINATED?

In describing his influential linguistic relativity hypothesis, linguist Benjamin Whorf argued that different languages impose different ideas of reality. "Language itself," he observed, "shapes a man's basic ideas" (1956). As this remark suggests, Whorf himself was only imperfectly aware of how male-dominated the English language can be. Today it is likely that many people would pounce on Whorf's generic use of *man* as evidence of how our language often excludes women. This example illustrates the ways in which the language we use can affect the way we think about certain issues.

The English language has traditionally used masculine terms such as *man* and *he* to refer to all people, female as well as male. Don't people know that these terms include females? One study found that people do not necessarily make this assumption (Hyde, 1984a). Hyde asked children to complete stories after she gave them a first line such as, "When a kid goes to school, _____ often feels excited on the first day." When Hyde filled in the blank with *he,* the children nearly always composed stories about boys. When she used *he or she* in the blank, a third of the children made up stories about girls.

In another illuminating study of the impact of male and female pronouns, Hyde (1984b) discovered that the use of *he* or *she* to describe a factory worker who made "wudges" (imaginary plastic parts for video games) affected how children thought male and female wudgemakers would perform their jobs. Those children who heard wudgemakers described by the masculine pronoun *he* rated women wudgemakers poorly; children who heard wudgemakers identified by the pronoun *she* judged female wudge-makers most positively; and the ratings of children who heard gender-neutral descriptions of wudgemakers as *they* or *he or she* fell in between those of the two other groups. All the groups of children, however, viewed male wudgemakers equally positively.

[R]ecent research has focused on the unconscious, automatic nature of gender stereotyping and language

More recent research has focused on the unconscious, automatic nature of gender stereotyping and language (Greenwald & Banaji, 1995). In an experiment that required men and women to respond rapidly to gender-neutral and gender-specific pronouns, both sexes responded more quickly to stimuli that contained traditional gender stereotypes (e.g., nurse/she) than to stimuli that contained nontraditional gender stereotypes (e.g., nurse/he). This oc-

curred even among participants who were explicitly opposed to gender stereotyping (Banaji & Hardin, 1996).

We still tend to refer to doctors, college professors, bankers, and executives by the generic *he,* contributing to the gender stereotyping of these respected occupations as appropriate for men but not for women. In contrast, secretaries and housekeepers still tend to be referred to as *she,* reinforcing the stereotype that those lower-level occupations are appropriate occupations for women, not men.

Questions

1. How does language shape or influence the way you think? Have you personally been affected by gender stereotypes in language? Are you surprised when a nurse is identified as "he" or a physician is identified as "she"?

2. Some languages have many gender-neutral terms, whereas others tend to identify almost everything as either male or female. Do you think that this makes a significant difference in the way people think about the world around them? Would it be a good idea to create some gender-neutral pronouns for the English language that could be used in place of "he/she" or "him/her"? Why, or why not?

metaphor and irony (Roberts & Kreuz, 1994). As you probably know, metaphor is a nonliteral description. For example, saying of someone that "He was a lion in combat" does not mean that he was literally a lion; rather, it draws attention to features of his behavior such as courage and ferocity. Irony involves saying one thing but meaning the opposite, as in "What a great day!" when it is pouring rain. In both these cases, and in others like them, language expresses an idea that is different from what the literal words would suggest. One interesting finding is that people appear to be able to comprehend figurative language as quickly as they comprehend literal language (e.g., Gibbs, 1986). This suggests that people are very good at using figurative language to express ideas that would be difficult to communicate using only literal language. Researchers asked undergraduate students why people might use figurative language (Roberts & Kreuz, 1994). To a surprising degree, the students agreed that irony is useful as a way to express negative emotions or to add interest or to provoke thought. They also generally agreed that metaphor is especially useful for clarifying a topic or being eloquent. Thus, figurative language is just one more example of the flexible relationship that exists between language and thought.

We have seen that the linguistic relativity hypothesis somewhat overstates the relationship between language and thought. Nonetheless, we have also seen that language is closely related to the expression and understanding of thoughts: Language reflects and organizes our thoughts, it changes as our way of thinking changes, and, to a limited extent, it affects what we think about and remember most effectively. Moreover, people are very good at exploiting figurative language to express an incredible range of ideas and emotions. By all accounts, then, language plays an important role in our thinking. In the next section of the chapter we will examine the question of whether nonhuman animals can think and use language.

Can animals think and use language?

NONHUMAN THOUGHT AND LANGUAGE

Are human beings the only organisms that can think? If not, what are the similarities and differences between human and nonhuman thought? Those of us who have lived with pets sometimes feel as though they can anticipate our every move, particularly when it involves feeding them or taking them outside. Moreover, dogs and cats seem to know how to go from one window to another to watch something going on outside the house; they seem to understand that each window offers a different view of the outside world, and they seem to know which window to go to next in order to follow what is going on outside. They also seem to be able to work out even very complex paths or routes between where they are and where they want to go. And they seem to miss us when we are gone and be happy when we return. Does such behavior mean that animals can think? Or are these animal behaviors simply conditioned responses such as those we discussed in Chapter 5, Learning?

We are tempted to believe that pets can think because we are able to put ourselves in their place and imagine what we would be thinking in a similar situation. Projecting human characteristics onto nonhuman creatures is called *anthropomorphism*. Although anthropomorphism is an understandable human tendency, it is not good science (see Mitchell, Thompson, & Miles, 1997, for a thorough discussion of anthropomorphism and science). Just because we can imagine what a cat might be thinking does not mean that the cat is really thinking. Just because we would use thought to work out a complex path from one place to another doesn't mean that our pet dog has also used thought to follow that same route. To determine whether nonhuman animals can actually think, we need to resort to the scientific method.

Laboratory experiments suggest that animals may indeed have some cognitive capacities. For example, after extensive training, pigeons and monkeys are able to sort photographs into categories—grouping, for example, all pictures containing trees, all pictures containing people, or all pictures containing automobiles (D'Amato & Van Sant, 1988; Wasserman et al., 1988; also see Thompson, 1995). From our discussion earlier in this chapter, you will recognize that this evidence suggests that pigeons and monkeys can form concepts, one of the building blocks of thought. Moreover, dolphins are able to select which of two objects detected by either sight or echolocation (using sound waves to determine the position of an object) is identical to a sample object (Harley, Roitblat, & Nachtigall, 1996; Roitblatt, Penner, & Nachtigall, 1990). And chimpanzees and dolphins are able to respond to a sequence of symbols that represent objects or actions. For example, a dolphin will respond to a set of symbols that instruct it to bring a Frisbee to a surfboard (Herman, Richards, & Wolz, 1984; Rumbaugh, 1990).

The most impressive cognitive abilities show up in chimpanzees, who appear to be able to solve analogies (e.g., symbol A is to symbol B as symbol C is to what symbol?) (Cook, 1991). As you know, analogies of that sort are often included on college entrance tests. Chimps also are capable of deceiving other chimpanzees as to the location of food (Goodall, 1971; Menzel, 1974); and it seems that bonobos (pygmy chimpanzees) can learn the meaning and uses of symbols simply by watching others use them (Savage-Rumbaugh, 1990). On the surface, then, the research evidence seems to support the notion that nonhuman animals can think. The performance of chimpanzees, in particular, certainly seems to approach primitive thinking. But is this really thinking? Do the chimps and dolphins and pigeons know what they know? Do they have some kind of consciousness?

The issue of consciousness in animals is very difficult to address scientifically (Blumberg & Wasserman, 1995), but one procedure has proved to be especially useful as a test for self-awareness in animals. This procedure involves self-recognition in a mirror. If an animal uses a mirror in its cage to examine body parts not normally visible without the aid of a mirror, then it would seem reasonable to conclude that at some level the animal understands that the image in the mirror is a reflection of its own body. Now let's say that after the animal has had access to the mirror for several days, we paint a bright mark above its eyebrows while it is asleep. When it awakes, if it spends much more time examining its forehead the next time it goes to the mirror, it seems reasonable to conclude that the animal has an image of its own body (including body parts that are not visible without a mirror) and can recognize from the mirror image that a part of its body has been changed. The criterion of self-awareness is that the animal realizes that it is looking at itself in the mirror.

This mirror test has been used with hundreds of animals and many different species. Only two species other than humans show signs of self-awareness—chimpanzees and orangutans. Other seemingly intelligent animals such as monkeys and elephants show no signs of self-awareness, even after extended exposure to the mirrors (Gallup, 1985; also see Vauclair, 1996). That is, the animal looks in the mirror without showing any sign that it realizes that a part of its own body has been changed. Perhaps you have noticed the reaction of cats to being held in front of a mirror. They typically show no sign of self-recognition.

Nonhuman Language?

So far we have examined evidence indicating that some nonhuman animals apparently are capable of concept formation and imagery (including self-awareness). Moreover, we have seen that some nonhuman animals are capable of representational thought: They can relate a symbol of an object to the object itself. And we know from other research that species communicate in various ways. For example, dolphins successfully match objects in a matching-to-sample task after listening to (or eavesdropping on) another dolphin solving the problem using echolocation (Xitco & Herbert, 1996).

Do these abilities—symbolic representation and communication—indicate that nonhuman animals can represent their world through language? Are nonhuman animals also capable of using language, the third building block of thought?

We have long regarded language as a uniquely human capability that sets us apart from all other animals (Savage-Rumbaugh & Brakke, 1996). But some research on animal behaviors has challenged this assumption. For example, honeybees go through an intricate dance to inform their hive mates of the location and distance of a pollen source (von Frisch, 1974). Many observers have argued that bee communication is somewhat inflexible, unlike human language, and may even be inaccurate if the bee has to fly upwind back to the hive. However, recent research (Kirchner & Towne, 1994) has shown that bee language is more intricate than had earlier been believed. For example, the bee conducts its dance in the darkness of the beehive. If the other bees cannot see the dance, how do they pick up information from it? It now appears that bees make use of sound to convey information when they dance in the dark. These sounds are correlated with the dancing movements and constitute a sophisticated system of communication. Nevertheless, few observes would argue that bee language approaches the ability of human language to adapt flexibly to changes in the environment (McNeill, 1972).

Researchers have been fascinated by the beeps and clicks that dolphins use to communicate with each other. Do they use these sounds in a way that is comparable to human language? Are dolphins capable of using a primitive form of language to help represent their world?

Perhaps the most intriguing and controversial studies of nonhuman language have been conducted with the great apes: chimpanzees, gorillas, orangutans, and gibbons (Rumbaugh, Savage-Rumbaugh, & Sevcik, 1994). Along with humans, these species are classified as primates and are, loosely speaking, cousins to one another. In some of the early experiments with primates, researchers' attempts to teach chimpanzees to speak met with little success. In 1933, W. A. and L. N. Kellogg raised a chimpanzee named Gua with their own son, Donald. Although Gua showed good problem-solving abilities, learned socialized actions like kissing for forgiveness, and was able to respond to verbal commands, the chimpanzee demonstrated no ability to approximate human vocalizations. C. Hayes and Hayes (1951) also raised a chimpanzee in their home, combining a homelike atmosphere with operant conditioning. Even with strong reinforcement, their chimpanzee, Viki, could approximate the human vocalizations of only four words: mama, papa, cup, and up.

Physical limitations on the chimpanzee's vocal apparatus may have played a major role in the relative failure of the early chimpanzee language experiments (Kellogg, 1968). This raises the question of whether chimpanzees could acquire the ability to communicate in a language that does not require speech. R. A. Gardner and Gardner attempted to teach American Sign Language (ASL) to a chimpanzee named Washoe (1969, 1975, 1977). Washoe was raised in an environment where she never heard oral speech but was communicated with only by signing. The Gardners' method relied on the well-known ability of chimpanzees to imitate gestures, and appropriate responses were reinforced by operant conditioning.

Washoe had learned 38 signs by age 2, 85 by age 4, and 160 by age 5. She also learned to make combinations of one-word signs into simple

Telegraphic speech An early speech stage of one- and two-year-olds that omits words that are not essential to the meaning of a phrase.

two-word sentences, such as "more milk." Notably, Washoe's two-word combinations were very similar to the **telegraphic speech** that characterizes the early utterances of one- and two-year-old human infants. Apparently, she invented these new combinations on her own. Another feature of Washoe's development that paralleled development in children was her ability to generalize signs so that they applied to a variety of objects. For example, she was able to sign "dog," not only for an actual dog, but for a picture of a dog as well. And she was able to adapt her use of signs to novel situations. For example, after seeing a swan, she signed "water bird," even though the sign had never been modeled for her. Other chimpanzees have duplicated this behavior; a chimpanzee named Lucy even created the sign "drink fruit" for a watermelon (Fouts, 1973).

Another researcher used a slightly different method to study language acquisition in chimpanzees (Premack, 1971, 1976). With the aid of reinforcements, Premack taught a chimpanzee named Sarah to communicate by arranging plastic chips on a magnetic board. Each chip stood for a different word, and the order in which the chips could be arranged on the board could also convey meaning. Sarah, like Washoe, learned a large number of signs. She, too, could arrange the chips to form telegraphic sentences like "Place orange dish." Sarah even learned how to construct sentences that involve conditional relationships ("If Sara take apple, then Mary give Sarah chocolate. If Sarah take banana, then Mary no give Sarah chocolate").

Another group of researchers (Rumbaugh, 1977; Rumbaugh & Savage-Rumbaugh, 1978; Rumbaugh et al., 1974) worked with a chimpanzee named Lana, who learned to type messages on a geometric keyboard connected to a computer. Reportedly, Lana was able to comprehend complex human sentences. For example, she was able to respond correctly to such questions as "What is the name of the object that is green?" Moreover, Lana also demonstrated the ability to create orig-

Psychologist Herbert Terrace spent nearly four years teaching sign language to a chimpanzee named Nim Chimpsky (after the linguist Noam Chomsky). Here a researcher is signing with Nim. Terrace questions whether Nim, and other apes taught to sign, can use language to produce complex sentences they have never "heard" before.

inal messages, such as "apple which is orange" for an orange. These researchers (Greenfield & Savage-Rumbaugh, 1984) have also reported that apes, like human children, will use their newly developed language to comment on their environment. And recent research by Greenfield and Savage-Rumbaugh using the geometric keyboard indicates that at least one chimpanzee (named Kanzi) has not only learned grammatical rules but also invented new rules that it did not learn from its human trainers (McDonald, 1990). For example, Kanzi spontaneously combined the geometric symbol for "dog" with its own gesture for "go" before going to play with some dogs.

Finally, some researchers extended these studies beyond chimps by training a gorilla named Koko to use sign language (Patterson, 1978, 1980, 1981; Patterson & Cohn, 1990). Koko, too, could arrange signs in new combinations, such as "white tiger" for zebra. Patterson observed that Koko would sign to her dolls when she was alone, and she seemed to express a sense of self-awareness when she referred to herself as "a fine animal gorilla." She was observed signing back and forth with another gorilla and has been known to express emotions such as happiness and to swear, joke, and lie.

Despite these accomplishments, Koko's vocabulary remained much smaller than that of children of the same age. For example, by age 5, children have a vocabulary of between 1,000 and 5,000 words, whereas Koko had a vocabulary of 500 to 600 signs (Patterson & Cohn, 1990). However, Koko's vocabulary at age 5 was not that different from that of a typical 5-year-old deaf child who uses sign language. Patterson suggests that Koko's level of language skill is lower than that of a normal human child's because she has far fewer opportunities to socialize with other language users. Another possible reason for Koko's deficit is the fact that signing is less natural for apes, who walk on all fours, than it is for humans.

Do these studies establish that other species share with humans the ability to acquire and use language? There is a great deal of controversy about the answer to this question, and the findings, although intriguing, remain inconclusive (Blumberg & Wasserman, 1995). For example, pigeons can be taught to peck a sequence of keys to get grain by the use of operant conditioning, but no one would claim that this is evidence that pigeons are capable of developing language (Straub et al., 1979). And apes require a tremendous amount of intensive reinforcement to develop their very limited linguistic skills (Limber, 1977). Human children learn language effortlessly and swiftly, without the necessity of deliberate, intensive adult instruction. Finally, apes fail to develop language that is truly flexible, rule-driven, and capable of expressing abstract concepts (Terrace, 1979, 1985). The "linguistic" apes, according to Terrace, have not developed a syntactical use of language—the ability that allows humans to understand and produce complex sentences that have never been heard or uttered before.

Given this controversy, it is still not possible to arrive at a consensus about the linguistic behavior of apes (Premack, 1986). Still, the well-established ability of some primates to use a sign to refer to an object is an impressive cognitive achievement, even if it does not constitute language (Terrace, 1985). Moreover, language training has the side effect of improving apes' abilities to perform various reasoning tasks (Premack, 1983). And some work with pygmy chimps seems to show that chimps can pick up language spontaneously (Savage-Rumbaugh et al., 1986). At the very least, continued investigation of the possibility of nonhuman language should shed light on the evolutionary origins of human language (Savage-Rumbaugh, 1993; Wasserman, 1993). Whatever the eventual outcome of the nonhuman language debate, humans have already benefited from the research on apes. For instance, a computer-based language originally designed to instruct chimpanzees has been successfully applied to the teaching of children with severe mental retardation. Using this technique, these children are able to communicate their needs and wants to others, and in many cases their behavior no longer reflects the frustration that can result from an isolating communication disorder.

ANSWERS TO PROBLEMS IN THE CHAPTER

PROBLEM 1   The small monster gives the large globe to the large monster. The large monster gives the medium-sized globe to the medium-sized monster. The medium-sized monster gives the small globe to the small monster.

PROBLEM 2   Fill each of the smaller spoons with salt from the larger spoon. That will require 4 teaspoons of salt, leaving exactly 4 teaspoons of salt in the larger spoon.

PROBLEM 3 Turn the 5-minute hourglass over; when it runs out, turn over the 9-minute hourglass. When it, too, runs out, 14 minutes have passed.

PROBLEM 4 The small monster passes the large globe to the large monster (see Figure 7–12). The medium-sized monster passes the small globe to the small monster. The large monster passes the large globe back to the small monster and then passes the medium-sized globe to the medium-sized monster. The small monster returns the large globe to the large monster.

PROBLEM 5 As shown in Figure 7–13, fill spoon C with salt from spoon A (now A has 5 teaspoons of salt and C has 3). Pour the salt from spoon C into spoon B (now A has 5 teaspoons of salt and B has 3). Again fill spoon C with salt from spoon A (leaving A with only 2 teaspoons of salt, while B and C each have 3). Fill spoon B with salt from spoon C (this leaves 1 teaspoon of salt in spoon C while B has 5 teaspoons and A has only 2). Pour all the salt from spoon B into spoon A (now A has 7 teaspoons of salt and C has 1). Pour all the salt from spoon C into spoon B, and then fill spoon C from spoon A (this leaves 4 teaspoons of salt in A, 1 teaspoon in B, and 3 teaspoons in C). Finally, pour all the salt from spoon C into spoon B (this leaves 4 teaspoons of salt in spoons A and B, which is the solution).

PROBLEM 6 Start both hourglasses. When the 5-minute hourglass runs out, turn it over to start it again. When the 9-minute hourglass runs out, turn over the 5-minute hourglass. Because there is 1 minute left in the 5-minute hourglass when you turn it over, it will run for only 4 minutes. Those 4 minutes, together with the original 9 minutes, give the required 13 minutes for the barbecue.

Figure 7–12

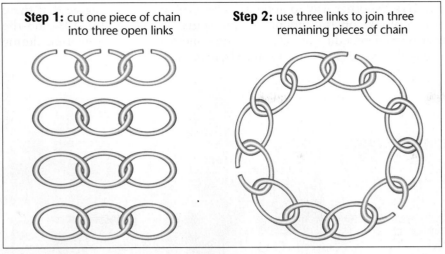

Step 1: cut one piece of chain into three open links

Step 2: use three links to join three remaining pieces of chain

Figure 7–14

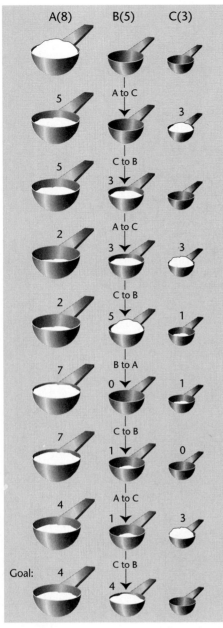

A(8)	B(5)	C(3)

A to C
C to B
A to C
C to B
B to A
C to B
A to C
C to B

Goal:

Figure 7–13

PROBLEM 7 Take one of the short pieces of chain shown in Figure 7–14 and open all three links (this costs 6 cents). Use those three links to connect the remaining three pieces of chain (closing the three links costs 9 cents).

PROBLEM 8 Join the matches to form a pyramid as shown in Figure 7–15.

PROBLEM 9 One way to solve this problem is to draw a diagram of the ascent and the descent as in Figure 7–16. From this drawing, you can see that indeed there is a point that the monk passes at exactly the same time on

Figure 7–16

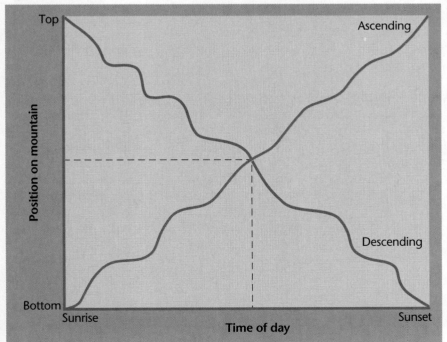

Figure 7–15

both days. Another way to approach this problem is to imagine that there are two monks on the mountain; one starts ascending at 7 A.M. and the other starts descending at 7 A.M. on the same day. Clearly, sometime during the day the monks must meet somewhere along the route.

Figure 7–17

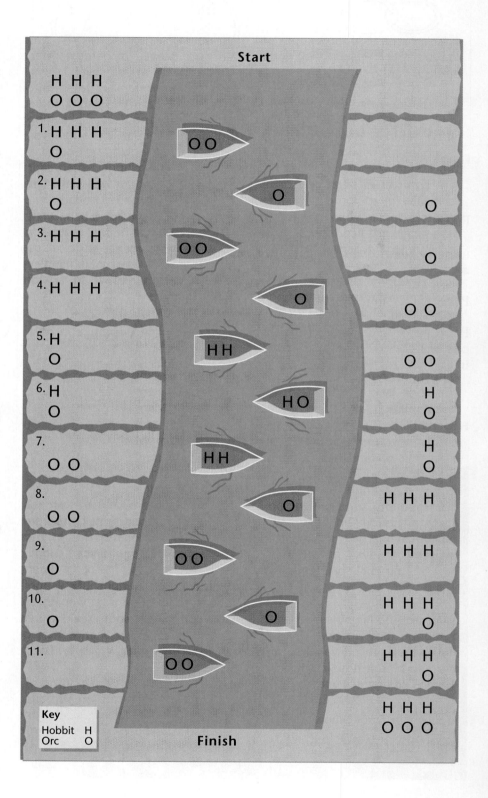

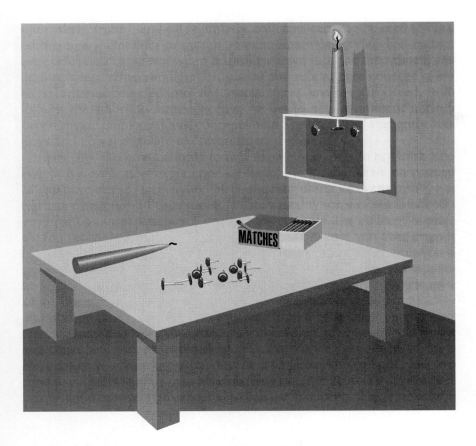

Figure 7–18

PROBLEM 10   This problem has four possible solutions, one of which is shown in Figure 7–17 (the other three solutions differ only slightly from this one).

PROBLEM 11   This problem has 15 possible solutions, of which this is one: One Hobbit and one Orc cross the river in the boat; the Orc remains on the opposite side while the Hobbit rows back. Next, three Orcs cross the river; two of those Orcs remain on the other side (making a total of three Orcs on the opposite bank) while one Orc rows back. Now three Hobbits cross the river; two stay on the opposite side with two Orcs while one Hobbit and one Orc row the boat back. Again, three Hobbits row across the river, at which point all five Hobbits are on the opposite bank with only two Orcs. One of the Orcs then rows back and forth across the river twice to transport the remaining Orcs to the opposite side.

SOLUTION TO FIGURE 7–10   In solving the problem given in Figure 7–10, many people have trouble realizing that the box of tacks can also be used as a candleholder, as shown in Figure 7–18.

SOLUTION TO FIGURE 7–11   The solution is difficult as long as you continue to think of the normal functions of tools. But once you realize that a heavy tool (such as a hammer or a pair of pliers or a wrench) can be attached to a string and used as a pendulum, the solution to the problem becomes clearer (see Figure 7–19).

Figure 7–19

SUMMARY

This chapter discusses **cognition,** or the process of thinking, and its role in problem solving and decision making. Thinking involves language, imagery, reflection, conceptualization, evaluation, and insight, among other functions. Thus, in addition to the retrieval and processing of information from memory, cognition requires the manipulation of information in various ways.

THE DEVELOPMENT OF COGNITIVE PSYCHOLOGY

Psychologists such as George Miller and Ulric Neisser were among the first cognitive psychologists. Their use of computer programs that mimic cognitive processes is called computer simulation.

THE BUILDING BLOCKS OF THOUGHT

The basic building blocks of thought are language, images, and concepts. When we think about an object or a person, we think in terms of verbal statements, an image, or a concept consisting of certain attributes of the object or person.

Language

Language is a flexible system of symbols used for communication. Spoken language is based on **phonemes,** the basic sounds that make up a language. Phonemes group together to form **morphemes,** the smallest meaningful units of speech, such as simple words, prefixes, and suf-

fixes. When we wish to communicate an idea, we start with a thought, then choose words and phrases that will express the idea, and produce the speech sounds of those words and phrases. To understand speech, the task is reversed. Sentences have both a **surface structure** (particular words and phrases) and a **deep structure** (the underlying meaning).

The rules that determine the meaning and form of words and sentences are called **grammar.** Semantics and syntax are the two major components of grammar. **Semantics** refers to how we assign meaning to the morphemes we use. **Syntax** is the system of rules for the structure of word forms and sentences.

Images

An **image** is a mental representation or recollection of a sensory experience. Using images and manipulating them help us think about and solve problems. Images also give us the power of visualization.

Concepts

A **concept** is a mental category for classifying objects, people, and experiences based on their common features. Concepts help us think more efficiently about things and to categorize new experiences.

Some concepts are "fuzzy," lacking clear-cut boundaries. Therefore, we often use **prototypes,** mental models of the most typical examples of a concept, to classify new objects. George Lakoff has extended the prototype model by observing that most of our concepts fit together to form **idealized cognitive models (ICMs),** which are our theories of events as we typically expect to find them.

PROBLEM SOLVING

In addition to thinking about things, human cognition involves the active use of language, images, and concepts—the building blocks of thought—to solve problems and make decisions.

The Interpretation of Problems

Problem representation, defining or interpreting the problem, is the first step in problem solving. We must decide whether to view the problem verbally, mathematically, or visually and how to categorize the problem. Expertise in a field increases a person's ability to interpret a particular problem.

Producing and Evaluating Solutions

Selection of an optimum strategy for solving a problem follows problem interpretation.

Trial and error is a problem-solving strategy based on the successive elimination of incorrect solutions until the correct one is found. But trial and error is time-consuming, and its scattershot approach is unsuitable to many problem situations. **Information retrieval** requires only the recovery of information from long-term memory, a strategy useful when a factual solution must be found quickly. An **algorithm** is a prescribed method of problem solving that guarantees a correct solution if the method suits the problem and if it is carried out properly. Solving a mathematical problem by use of a formula is an example of the use of an algorithm.

Heuristics are rules of thumb that help to simplify and solve problems, though they do not guarantee a correct solution. **Hill climbing** is a heuristic in which each step moves the problem solver closer to the final goal. Another heuristic is the creation of **subgoals**—intermediate, more manageable goals that may make it easier to reach the final goal. **Means-end analysis,** a heuristic that combines hill climbing and subgoals, aims to reduce the discrepancy between the current situation and the desired goal at a number of intermediate points. It allows us to take digressions or temporary steps backward that may be essential to solving the problem. **Working backward** involves working from the desired goal back to the given conditions. This method is useful when the goal offers more information than the givens and the operation can work both forward and backward.

Obstacles to Solving Problems

Effective problem solving is tied to many factors, including the right level of motivation or emotional arousal. Too little emotion does not motivate, and too much may hinder the process of solution. Another factor that can help or hinder problem solving is **set,** the tendency to perceive and to approach problems in certain ways. Sets enable us to draw on past experience to solve a present problem, but a strong set can also interfere with ability to use new and different approaches to solving a problem. One set that can seriously hamper problem solving is **functional fixedness,** the tendency to perceive only a limited number of uses for an object.

Becoming Better at Problem Solving

Several strategies help us analyze and solve problems by shifting our perspective of the problem from one angle to another.

The **tactic of elimination** calls for discarding possible solutions that clearly will not work, an approach that is suitable if we are more sure of what we do not want than of what we do want. In **visualizing,** various possible courses of action are drawn, diagrammed, or charted so that they can be better understood. Expertise in a field is an asset in solving problems; experts do not need the elaborate preparations required of a beginner. **Convergent thinking** is appropriate for problems that have just one correct solution, whereas problems that have no single correct solution call for creativity—**divergent thinking,** thinking that is original, inventive, and flexible. On occasion, taking a rest from a problem may allow you to discover a fresh approach through *insight, a* "bolt from the blue." The technique of **brainstorming** requires an individual or group to collect numerous ideas and to evaluate them only after all possible ideas have been collected. In this way, no potential solution is rejected prematurely.

DECISION MAKING

Unlike other kinds of problem solving, decision making starts off with a knowledge of all the possible solutions or choices. The task is to select the best alternative by using a predetermined set of criteria.

In the **compensatory model,** we systematically evaluate choices on various criteria and then examine how the attractive features of each choice might compensate for the unattractive ones. A less precise alternative is the **noncompensatory model,** which does not try to systematically weigh comparisons among alternatives. When we use the elimination-by-aspects tactic, for example, we toss out choices that do not meet one or two of our requirements even though they may be excellent choices on other grounds.

Often we lack complete or accurate information about one or more alternatives. In such a case, we may end up judging a new situation in terms of its resemblance to a more familiar model—the **representativeness** heuristic. This runs the risk of causing us to fall back on stereotypes or to see connections where none exist. Another common heuristic is **availability,** in which we base a judgment or decision on information that is most easily retrieved from memory, whether or not that information is accurate. **Confirmation bias** is another faulty heuristic that involves the tendency to seek evidence in support of our beliefs and to ignore evidence that does not support them.

In the real world, the use of faulty heuristics does not always spell disaster. This is partly because such decisions are often not final, and partly because we often do not need to make an absolutely perfect decision so long as the results are satisfactory.

LANGUAGE AND THOUGHT

Language is crucial to the expression and understanding of thought. According to Benjamin Whorf, patterns of thinking are, in fact, determined by the language one speaks. His theory, called the **linguistic relativity hypothesis,** states that if a language lacks a particular expression, the thought to which the expression corresponds probably never occurs to the people who speak the language. Some critics of this theory maintain that an idea can occur to a person before the corresponding word or phrase is learned. Others point out that it is more likely that the need to think about things changes a language rather than vice versa. However, it may still be the case that once different phrases for an object come into use, we are then able to think about the object differently.

The flexible relationship between language and thought is demonstrated by the use of **figurative language.** Figurative language is expressive or nonliteral language such as metaphor or irony.

NONHUMAN THOUGHT AND LANGUAGE

Research suggests that animals may have cognitive capacities, such as conceptualization, communication skills, and even self-awareness, especially in the case of the higher apes.

Nonhuman Language?

Primates are more capable of acquiring communication skills (simple words and sign language) than are other types of animals. In fact, chimpanzees and gorillas have even been taught to type simple messages on a geometric keyboard connected to a computer. Similar to young children, chimpanzees have been observed using two-word combinations called **telegraphic speech** during early language acquisition. Nonetheless, the extent to which animals have the ability to acquire and use true language is still not clear. For example, apes do not demonstrate a syntactical use of language—the ability that allows humans to understand and create complex sentences.

REVIEW QUESTIONS

MULTIPLE CHOICE AND SHORT ANSWER

1. The term that psychologists use to refer to all the processes whereby we gather and use information is _____.

2. _____, _____, and _____ are the three most important building blocks of thought.

3. Categories for classifying specific people, things, or events are
   a. concepts   b. images
   c. phonemes   d. morphemes

4. Images help us think about things because images are more concrete than words. T/F

5. People decide which objects belong to a concept by comparing the facts to a model or prototype. T/F

6. Match each problem-solving strategy with its definition:
   _____ algorithm
   _____ heuristics
   _____ hill climbing
   _____ means-end analysis
   _____ working backward

   a. rules of thumb that help to simplify and solve problems, although they do not guarantee a correct solution
   b. strategy in which each step moves you progressively closer to a solution
   c. step-by-step method that guarantees a solution
   d. strategy in which one moves from the goal to the starting point
   e. strategy that aims to reduce the discrepancy between the current situation and the desire goal at a number of intermediate points

7. All of the following are potential obstacles to problem solving except
   a. sets
   b. excitement
   c. functional fixedness
   d. hill climbing

8. Bill is trying to decide between taking a ski vacation in Vermont and a beach vacation in the Caribbean. To make the choice, he sets up some criteria for a good vacation and then rates the two alternatives on each criterion to see how they stack up against each other. Bill is using a _____ model of decision making.

9. Our tendency to perceive and to approach problems in certain ways is termed a _____.

10. The tendency to perceive only a limited number of uses for an object, a tendency that interferes with the process of problem solving, is known as _____ _____.

11. Decision-making models that do not try to systematically weigh comparisons among alternatives are _____ models.

12. People are most likely to use a compensatory model when
    a. the stakes are low
    b. the stakes are high
    c. others are observing them
    d. the problem is simple

13. In language, universal sounds, called _____, are combined to form the smallest meaningful units, which are called _____. These meaningful units can then be combined to create words, which, in turn, can be used to build phrases and whole _____.

14. We use _____ to link concepts with other concepts and thus form more complex thoughts.

15. According to Whorf's _____ hypothesis, the language that one speaks determines the pattern of one's thinking and one's view of the world.

16. According to Chomsky, language users employ rules or _____ to allow them to go from the surface to the deep structure of language.

17. Models of the way in which we typically expect to find events are called _____ models.

18. Computer programs that mimic the behavior of a person in a particular situation are called _____.

19. The tendency to look for confirming rather than disconfirming evidence for our beliefs is called _____.

CRITICAL THINKING AND APPLICATIONS

1. You must decide between an inexpensive, noisy apartment with neighbors who are a nuisance, and a quieter, more expensive apartment with nice neighbors. How would you go about making your decision using a compensatory model?

2. Based on what you have read in this chapter, do you feel that nonhuman animals can think and use language? Can we learn anything about ourselves by studying these processes in other species?

3. Think for a moment of the last time you were confronted with a difficult problem. What types of thinking or reasoning did you use to deal with that problem? Now that you have read this chapter, would you respond differently if you were faced with a similar problem?

4. You are headed for Mount Rushmore, and you can see it from a distance. You have no map. What is the best problem-solving strategy you can use to get there, and why?

ENDURING ISSUES

Stability–Change
After reading this chapter, to what extent do you think that it is possible to teach people to think, solve problems, and make decisions in new ways? If you have taken a critical thinking course, has it significantly changed the way that you think? Has this course in psychology changed the way you think?

Diversity
Do you think that our discussion of cognition applies equally well to every human being? Does it perhaps apply better to men than women (or vice versa), or to particular racial or ethnic groups, or particular societies? Are there particular topics in the chapter that you think are more universally applicable than others? If so, which topics are those?

(Answers to the Review Questions appear in the back of the book.)

8 Intelligence and

Mental Abilities

In Chapter 7, Cognition and Language, we focused on the ways in which people solve problems and make decisions. But people clearly differ in their abilities to think intelligently and creatively. Before we explore this often controversial issue, take a few minutes to answer the following questions:

1. Describe the difference between *laziness* and *idleness.*

2. Which direction would you have to face so your right hand would be facing the north?

3. What does *obliterate* mean?

4. In what way are an *hour* and a *week* alike?

5. Choose the set of words that, when inserted in the sentence, best fits in with the meaning of the sentence as a whole: From the first, the islanders, despite an outward _____, did what they could to _____ the ruthless occupying power.

   (a) harmony . . . assist   (b) enmity . . . embarrass   (c) rebellion . . . foil

   (d) resistance . . . destroy   (e) acquiescence . . . thwart

Think About It!

1. How do psychologists define intelligence? Do psychologists and laypersons define intelligence in the same way?
2. What is an IQ? How is it measured? Is IQ the same as intelligence?
3. What are some of the most common criticisms of IQ tests?
4. Can intervention programs like Head Start improve people's mental abilities?
5. What does research tell us about the mathematical skills of men and women?
6. In what ways is academic achievement related to culture?
7. Are very creative people more intelligent than less creative people?

6. Choose the lettered block that best completes the pattern in the figure below.

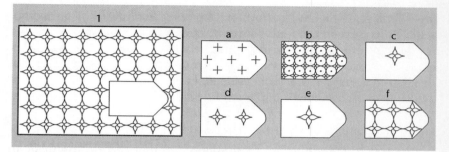

7. The opposite of *hate* is:
   (a) enemy (b) fear (c) love (d) friend (e) joy

8. If three pencils cost 25 cents, how many pencils can be bought for 75 cents?

9. Choose the word that is most nearly *opposite* in meaning to the word in capital letters:
   SCHISM: (a) majority (b) union (c) uniformity
   (d) conference (e) construction

10. Select the item that completes the following series of four figures:

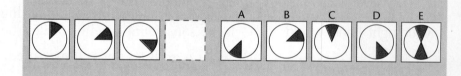

11. Select the lettered pair that best expresses a relationship similar to that expressed in the original pair:
   CRUTCH: LOCOMOTION: (a) paddle: canoe
   (b) hero: worship (c) horse: carriage (d) spectacles: vision
   (e) statement: contention

12. The first three figures are alike in some way. Find the figure at the right that goes with the first three.

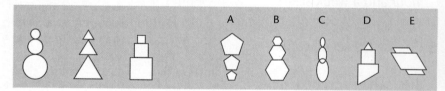

13. Decide how the first two figures are related to each other. Then find the one figure at the right that goes with the third figure in the same way that the second figure goes with the first.

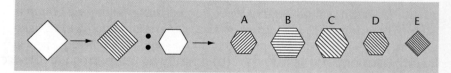

14. For each figure, decide whether it can be completely covered by using some or all of the given pieces without overlapping any.

Given pieces

Complete pieces

1   2   3   4   5

Intelligence tests Tests designed to measure a person's general mental abilities.

Intelligence A general term referring to the ability or abilities involved in learning and adaptive behavior.

These questions are drawn from various **intelligence tests** designed to measure general mental abilities (the answers appear at the end of the chapter). What do these tests actually tell us? Do they reflect all the abilities that make up **intelligence?** Because we cannot see the complex mental processes that underlie intelligence, we have to approach the subject indirectly—by watching what people do in various situations. But what exactly is intelligence? How is it related to creativity? Do tests such as the Scholastic Aptitude Test (SAT) measure all the aspects of intelligence needed for success in school? Do such tests predict your success on the job or in your personal life?

Before we explore the answers to these questions, let's consider the way psychologists use the words *intelligence, ability,* and *aptitude.* This is not a simple matter, because psychologists have not always used these words consistently. The distinction between abilities and aptitudes is the most straightforward. An ability refers to a skill that people actually have and for which they need no additional training. An aptitude is a *potential* ability. For example, someone may have an aptitude for playing the violin but not yet possess the ability to play the instrument. If a test is designed to *predict* an individual's future achievement in a specific area, it is usually called an aptitude test (Anastasi & Urbina, 1997). The Scholastic Aptitude Test is an example of such a test; its purpose is to predict how well a person will perform in college. Intelligence refers to a person's general intellectual ability, whether actual or potential, so intelligence tests are usually designed to test general mental ability. People who do well on intelligence tests are also likely to do well in school. Therefore, we should not be surprised to discover that scholastic aptitude tests and intelligence tests often ask similar types of questions.

Now that we have reviewed the basic vocabulary of intelligence, ask yourself what intelligence actually is. The concept is notoriously difficult to define. Before reading further, write down some behaviors that you believe reflect intelligence. How are they different from behaviors that reflect a lack of intelligence?

Most people agree that intelligence refers to a collection of mental abilities, but there is some disagreement about which abilities should

How do psychologists define intelligence? Do psychologists and laypersons define intelligence in the same way?

be included as part of overall intelligence. For example, Robert Sternberg and his associates (Sternberg, 1982; Sternberg et al., 1981) discovered that laypersons with no expertise in psychology generally think of intelligence as a mix of practical problem-solving ability, verbal ability, and social competence (see Table 8–1). Practical problem-solving ability includes using logic, connecting ideas, and viewing a problem in its entirety. Verbal ability encompasses using and understanding both written and spoken language in well-developed ways. Social competence refers to interacting well with others—being open-minded about different kinds of people and showing interest in a variety of topics. Psychologists who specialize in the area of intelligence generally agree with laypersons that overall intelligence includes verbal intelligence and problem-solving ability, but they do not agree that it includes social competence. Instead, they think that practical intelligence is an important component. A majority of experts now list creativity and the ability to adapt to the environment as crucial components of intelligence as well (Snyderman & Rothman, 1987).

Compare your own description of intelligent behaviors with those listed in Table 8–1. Was your description closer to that of the laypersons

---

TABLE 8–1

SOME CHARACTERISTICS OF INTELLIGENCE AS SEEN BY LAYPERSONS AND EXPERTS

LAYPERSONS

I. Practical problem-solving ability: reasons logically, makes connections among ideas, can see all sides of a problem, keeps an open mind, responds thoughtfully to the ideas of others, good at sizing up situations, interprets information accurately, makes good decisions, goes to original source for basic information, good source of ideas, perceives implied assumptions, deals with problems in a resourceful way.

II. *Verbal ability:* speaks articulately, converses well, is knowledgeable about a particular field, studies hard, reads widely, writes without difficulty, has a good vocabulary, tries new things.

III. *Social competence:* accepts others as they are, admits mistakes, shows interest in the world at large, arrives on time for appointments, has social conscience, thinks before speaking and acting, shows curiosity, avoids snap judgments, makes fair judgments, assesses the relevance of information to the problem at hand, is sensitive to others, is frank and honest with self and others, shows interest in the immediate environment.

EXPERTS

IV. *Practical intelligence:* sizes up situations well, determines how best to achieve goals, shows awareness of world around him or her, shows interest in the world at large, uses self-knowledge of own motives to select the tasks that will best accomplish own goals.

V. *Verbal intelligence:* has a good vocabulary, reads with high comprehension, is intellectually curious, sees all sides of a problem, learns rapidly, shows alertness, thinks deeply, shows creativity, converses easily on a wide range of subjects, reads widely, sees connections among ideas.

IV. *Problem-solving ability:* makes good decisions, displays common sense, shows objectivity, is good at solving problems, plans ahead, has good intuition, gets to the heart of problems, appreciates truth, considers the results of actions, approaches problems thoughtfully.

Source: Sternberg, 1982; Wagner & Sternberg, 1986.

or the experts? Which of the characteristics of intelligence do you think is most important? Why do you think so?

In the next section, we will look more closely at the ways in which psychologists think about intelligence and then we will see how those formal theories of intelligence affect the content of intelligence tests.

THEORIES OF INTELLIGENCE

For more than a century, psychologists have pondered and argued about what constitutes general intelligence—or even if this notion has any validity at all. One of the most basic questions facing anyone who tries to understand intelligence is whether intelligence is a singular, general aptitude or ability or whether it is composed of many separate and distinct aptitudes or abilities.

Early Theories: Spearman and Thurstone

Charles Spearman, an early twentieth-century British psychologist, maintained that intelligence is quite general—a kind of well, or spring, of mental energy that flows through every action. Spearman noted that people who are bright in one area are often bright in other areas as well. The intelligent person understands things quickly, makes sound decisions, carries on interesting conversations, and tends to behave intelligently in a variety of situations. Although it's true that each of us is quicker in some areas than in others, Spearman saw these differences simply as ways in which the same underlying general intelligence is revealed in different activities. To return to the image of a well or spring, according to Spearman, general intelligence is the fountain from which specific abilities flow like streams of water in many different directions.

The American psychologist L. L. Thurstone disagreed with Spearman. Thurstone argued that intelligence comprises seven distinct mental abilities (Thurstone, 1938):

S—Spatial ability[*]	M—Memory
P—Perceptual speed	W—Word fluency
N—Numerical ability	R—Reasoning
V—Verbal meaning	

Unlike Spearman, he believed that these abilities are relatively independent of one another. Thus, a person with exceptional spatial ability might lack word fluency. To Thurstone, these seven primary mental abilities, taken together, make up general intelligence.

In contrast to Thurstone, psychologist R. B. Cattell (1971) identifies just two clusters of mental abilities. The first cluster—what Cattell calls *crystallized intelligence*—includes abilities such as reasoning and verbal and numerical skills. Because these are the kinds of abilities stressed in school, Cattell believes the scores on tests of crystallized intelligence are greatly affected by experience and formal education. The second cluster of abilities makes up what Cattell calls *fluid intelligence*, or skills such as spatial and visual imagery, the ability to notice visual details, and rote memory. Scores on tests of fluid intelligence are influenced much less by experience and education.

Spatial ability is the ability to perceive distance, recognize shapes, and so on.

Triarchic theory of intelligence Sternberg's theory that intelligence involves mental skills (componential aspect), insight and creative adaptability (experiential aspect), and environmental responsiveness (contextual aspect).

Componential intelligence According to Sternberg, the ability to acquire new knowledge, to solve problems effectively.

Experiential intelligence Sternberg's term for the ability to adapt creatively in new situations, to use insight.

Contextual intelligence According to Sternberg, the ability to select contexts in which you can excel, to shape the environment to fit your strengths.

Theory of multiple intelligences Howard Gardner's theory that there is not one intelligence, but rather many intelligences, each of which is relatively independent of the others.

Contemporary Theories: Sternberg and Gardner

More recently, Robert Sternberg (1985a, 1986) has proposed a **triarchic theory of intelligence.** Sternberg argues that human intelligence encompasses a broad variety of skills. Among them are skills that influence our effectiveness in many areas of life. These, says Sternberg, are just as important as the more limited skills assessed by traditional intelligence tests. Sternberg illustrates his theory by comparing three graduate students he worked with at Yale, whom he calls Alice, Barbara, and Celia. Alice fit the standard definition of intelligence perfectly. She scored high on tests of intelligence and achieved nearly a 4.0 average as an undergraduate. Her analytical abilities were excellent. Alice excelled in her first year of graduate work, but in the second year, she was having trouble developing her own research ideas and had dropped from the top of the class to the lower half. By contrast, Barbara's undergraduate record was far from exemplary, and her admission test scores were well below Yale's standards. Nevertheless, professors who had worked with her as an undergraduate described Barbara as highly creative and able to do good research. Barbara proved to be the associate Sternberg had hoped for. In fact, he believes that some of his most important work has been done in collaboration with her. The third graduate student, Celia, was somewhere between the other two: She had good recommendations and fairly good admission test scores. Celia did good (but not great) research work, yet she turned out to have the easiest time finding a good job after graduate school.

These three students seemed to have different kinds of intelligence, leading them to excel in different ways. Alice, Barbara, and Celia each represent one of the three aspects of Sternberg's triarchic theory. Alice was high in **componential intelligence,** which refers to the mental processes emphasized by most theories of intelligence, such as the ability to learn how to do things or acquire new knowledge and carry out tasks effectively. Barbara was particularly strong in what Sternberg calls **experiential intelligence**—the ability to adjust to new tasks, to use new concepts, to respond effectively in new situations, to gain insight, and to adapt creatively. Celia had the easiest time finding a job because of her strong **contextual intelligence** skills. According to Sternberg, people scoring high in contextual intelligence are very good at capitalizing on their strengths and compensating for their weaknesses. They make the most of their talents by seeking out situations that match their skills, by shaping those situations so they can make optimal use of their skills, and by knowing when to change situations to better fit their talents.

For Sternberg, intelligence is tied to a broad range of skills needed to function effectively in the real world. In this sense, Sternberg's theory of intelligence mirrors the informal view that most laypersons hold of intelligence (see Table 8–1). Sample questions that test experiential and contextual aspects of intelligence appear in the *Highlights* box.

Another influential theory of intelligence is the **theory of multiple intelligences** advanced by Howard Gardner and his associates at Harvard (Gardner, 1983a, 1993). Gardner's theory resembles Thurstone's theory of intelligence in one key respect: Gardner believes that intelligence is made up of many separate abilities or multiple intelligences, each of which is relatively independent of the others. It is difficult to determine precisely how many separate intelligences might exist, but Gardner (1993) lists seven: *logical-mathematical intelligence, linguistic intelligence, spatial intelligence, musical intelligence, bodily-kinesthetic intelligence, interpersonal intelligence,* and *intrapersonal intelligence.* The first two should be familiar to you because they are included in the other theories of intelligence already noted. Spatial

HIGHLIGHTS
TYPES OF INTELLIGENCE

The questions that introduced this chapter represent *componential intelligence*—for Sternberg, the problem-solving type of intelligence measured by traditional IQ tests (1985a, 1986).

Experiential intelligence depends heavily on insight—being able to distinguish relevant from irrelevant information, to combine information in novel ways, and to relate new information to old information in nonobvious ways (Sternberg, 1986). For example:

1. A man who lived in a small town married 20 different women in that same town. All of them are still living, and he never divorced any of them. Yet he broke no laws. How could he do this? (Sternberg, 1986, p. 214)

2. Susan gets in her car in Boston and drives toward New York City, averaging 50 miles per hour. Twenty minutes later, Ellen gets in her car in New York City and starts driving toward Boston, averaging 60 miles per hour. Both women take the same route, which extends a total of 220 miles between the two cities. Which car is nearer to Boston when they meet? (Sternberg, 1986, p . 215)

3. Identify which of the four facts (a–d) are relevant to answering the question (more than one fact may be relevant):

   "Why is it necessary to add detergent to water in order to wash clothes?"

   (a) The combination of detergent and water allows the detergent to penetrate between the clothes and the dirt.

   (b) One hundred pounds of domestic washing is soiled with between two and four pounds of dirt.

   (c) Most dirt cannot be dissolved by water alone.

   (d) One hundred pounds of domestic washing usually has 0.9 pounds of protein-free organic matter (waxes, alcohol), 0.3 pounds of protein (hair, skin), 0.15 pounds of grease and sweat, as well as sand and dust. (Sternberg, 1986, p. 217)

4. A boy and a girl are talking. "I'm a boy," said person A. "I'm a girl," said person B. If at least one of them is lying, which is the boy and which is the girl? (Sternberg, 1986, p. 224)

5. In the following analogy, assume for the moment that *radishes are candies*. Given that "fact," work out the following analogy:

   PRETZEL is to SALTY as RADISH is to:

   | BITTER | CHOCOLATE |
   | SALAD | SWEET |

   (Sternberg, 1986, p. 236)

Contextual intelligence requires people to select situations that maximize their strengths and minimize their weaknesses, to shape situations so that they more closely match those strengths, and to adapt effectively to unsatisfactory situations that can neither be avoided nor reshaped to their advantage. There can be no single correct answer to questions that tap this ability—the best answer depends on the person's individual strengths and weaknesses in relation to the specific situation. Consider the following questions, for example:

6. The cafeteria at your place of work serves virtually inedible food. Everyone in the company agrees that the food is horrible, but nobody can agree on a solution. Do you:

   (a) buy their fruit and yogurt, which are rather difficult to ruin?

   (b) petition for a new, improved food service?

   (c) eat at the diner down the street?" (Sternberg, 1986, p. 318)

7. Your son gets his birthday wish: a cute cocker spaniel puppy. Eight months later, the dog is untrained, unruly, and a general nuisance. Do you:

   (a) tell your son he had better do something about the dog, and fast?

   (b) proceed to train the dog yourself?

   (c) sell the dog? (Sternberg, 1986, p. 319)

Contextual intelligence also requires what Sternberg calls "tacit knowledge," information that we pick up from experience without its having to be taught to us explicitly. In the following questions, rate each alternative on a scale of 1 to 7 according to how important you think it is, where (7) corresponds to "extremely important" and (1) corresponds to "not important":

8. Rate the following strategies of working according to how important you believe them to be for doing well at the day-to-day work of a business manager:

   _____ a. Think in terms of tasks accomplished rather than hours spent working.

intelligence, referring to the ability to imagine the relative location of objects in space, is prominent in people with artistic ability. Exceptional musical intelligence is demonstrated by people with an outstanding gift for music, such as musical prodigies. Exceptional athletes and dancers show strong bodily kinesthetic abilities. People who are extraordinarily talented at understanding and communicating with others, such as exceptional teachers and parents, have strong interpersonal intelligence. Intrapersonal intelligence reflects the ancient adage "Know thyself." People who understand themselves and who use this knowledge effectively to attain their goals would rank high in intrapersonal intelligence.

Gardner cites a number of well-known people who possessed one of these intelligences to an extreme degree. You can probably think of many other examples.

Author Toni Morrison, whose vivid, compelling prose has been likened to poetry, possesses an abundance of what Howard Gardner calls linguistic intelligence. In recognition of her exceptional talent, she was awarded a Nobel Prize in literature.

- Logical-mathematical intelligence: Albert Einstein; Nobel Prize–winning microbiologist Barbara McClintock

- Linguistic intelligence: Toni Morrison, whose ability to manipulate language won her a Nobel Prize in literature

- Spatial intelligence: Nadia, an autistic child whose drawings reminded some observers of those of Leonardo da Vinci

- Musical intelligence: violinist Yehudi Menuhin, who was internationally renowned by the age of 10

- Bodily-kinesthetic intelligence: Babe Ruth; Nadia Comaneci (Romanian gymnast who won three gold medals and achieved seven perfect Olympic scores)

- Interpersonal intelligence: Anne Sullivan (Helen Keller's teacher)

- Intrapersonal intelligence: Novelist Virginia Woolf, who could describe her inner life so vividly that it came alive for other people

Gardner's approach has become quite influential, largely because he emphasizes the unique abilities that each person possesses. Because we have unique patterns of strengths and weaknesses in separate abilities, Gardner believes that education should be designed to suit the profile of abilities demonstrated by each child.

COMPARING THE THEORIES   How do these formal theories of intelligence compare with each other? Spearman had the simplest view: He believed that people had different amounts of the "mental energy" he called general intelligence. Thurstone and Cattell attempted to identify the structure of mental abilities in more detail. The two most influential contemporary theorists are Sternberg and Gardner. Their theories both emphasize practical abilities, but the two theories differ in some basic ways. Sternberg has shown great ingenuity in designing mental tests to measure different aspects of intelligence (Sternberg, 1993) as well as in proposing educational interventions to help students develop their intelligence (Sternberg, 1997). Gardner, by contrast, has relied more on a case-history method that explores the development of a specific intelligence in a particular person. It is entirely possible that future work will lead to a synthesis of these two approaches (Gardner, 1993, p. 40).

Formal theories of intelligence shape the content of intelligence tests and other measures of mental abilities. These tests are used to help evaluate the abilities of millions of people. We look now at how these tests are developed and administered, whether they accurately measure intelligence, and how they should be used.

INTELLIGENCE TESTS

The Stanford-Binet Intelligence Scale

The first "intelligence test" was designed for the French public school system by Alfred Binet, director of the psychological laboratory at the Sorbonne, and his colleague, Theodore Simon. Binet and Simon developed a number of questions and tested them on schoolchildren in Paris to identify those who might have difficulty in school.

The first **Binet-Simon Scale** was issued in 1905. It consisted of 30 tests arranged in order of increasing difficulty. With each child, the examiner started at the top of the list and worked down until the child could no longer answer questions. By 1908, enough children had been tested to predict how the average child would perform at each age level. From these scores Binet developed the concept of *mental age*. A child who scores as well as an average 4-year-old has a mental age of 4; a child who scores as well as an average 12-year-old has a mental age of 12.

During the decade following the debut of the Binet-Simon Scale, numerous Binet adaptations were issued, the best known of which was prepared at Stanford University by L. M. Terman and published in 1916. Terman introduced the now-famous term **intelligence quotient,** or **IQ,** to establish a numerical value of intelligence, setting the score of 100 for a person of average intelligence. Figure 8–1 shows an approximate distribution of IQ scores in the population.

For several reasons, the **Stanford-Binet Intelligence Scale** has been revised four times since 1916. First, any test must be updated as the meaning and usage of words change. Second, Terman and his colleagues found that some questions were easier for people from one part of the country than for those from another, that some were harder for boys than for girls (and vice versa), and that some failed to discriminate among age levels because nearly everyone tested could answer them correctly. Such questions were replaced.

In 1972, the norms for scoring the test were restandardized and included scores of nonwhites for the first time. The test items themselves were not changed. The latest version of the Stanford-Binet was released in 1986. Items that were determined to be biased against ethnic groups or against

Binet-Simon Scale The first test of intelligence, developed for testing children.

Intelligence quotient (IQ) A numerical value given to intelligence that is determined from the scores on an intelligence test; based on a score of 100 for average intelligence.

Stanford-Binet Intelligence Scale Terman's adaptation of the Binet-Simon Scale.

2

What is an IQ? How is it measured? Is IQ the same as intelligence?

Alfred Binet, along with his associate Theodore Simon, developed the first intelligence test in France at the turn of the twentieth century. It was created for the very practical purpose of identifying children who needed special help in school.

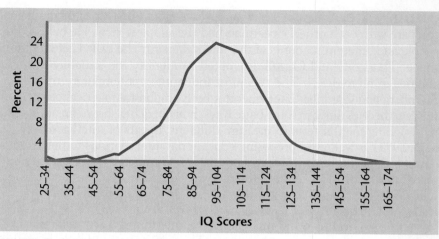

Figure 8–1
The approximate distribution of IQ scores in the population.
Note that the greatest percentage of scores fall around 100. Very low percentages of people score at the two extremes of the curve.

males or females were replaced with neutral items. In addition, new items were added that permitted testers to identify people with mental retardation and the intellectually gifted, as well as people with specific learning disabilities (Sattler, 1992). Questions 1 and 2 at the opening of this chapter were drawn from an early version of the Stanford-Binet.

The current version of the Stanford-Binet Intelligence Scale comprises 15 different subtests designed to measure four kinds of mental abilities that are almost universally considered to be characteristics of intelligence: *verbal reasoning, abstract/visual reasoning, quantitative reasoning,* and *short-term memory*. Scores on these subtests can be used to estimate general intelligence (Sattler, 1992). Test items vary according to the person's age. For example, a 3-year-old might be asked to describe the purpose of a cup and to name objects such as chair and key. A 6-year-old might be asked to define words such as orange and envelope and to complete a sentence such as "An inch is short; a mile is _____." A 12-year-old might be asked to define *skill* and *juggler* and to complete the sentence: "The streams are dry _____ there has been little rain" (Cronbach, 1990).

The Stanford-Binet test is given individually by a trained examiner. It resembles an interview and takes about 30 minutes for young children and up to an hour and a half for older ones. Testing usually begins just below the expected mental age of the subject. If the person fails that test, he or she is then tested at the next lowest level, and so on, until he or she can pass the test. This level is then established as the subject's *basal age*. Once the basal age is determined, the examiner continues testing at higher and higher levels until the person fails all the tests. Then the tests stop. After scoring the tests, the examiner figures the subject's mental age by adding to the basal age credits for each test passed above that age level. Notice that the ages in Table 8-2 go up only to 26 years. Although the Stanford-Binet has been used with older people, it is best suited for children, adolescents, and very young adults.

The Wechsler Intelligence Scales

The most commonly used individual test of intelligence for adults is the **Wechsler Adult Intelligence Scale-Third Edition (WAIS-III).** The original WAIS was developed in 1939 by David Wechsler, a psychologist at

TABLE 8-2

AREAS, SUBSETS, AND AGE SPANS FOR STANFORD-BINET: FOURTH EDITION

Designated Area	Subtest	Age Span
Verbal reasoning	Vocabulary	2–23
	Comprehension	2–23
	Absurdities	2–14
	Verbal relations	12–23
Abstract/visual reasoning	Pattern analysis	2–23
	Copying	2–13
	Matrices	7–23
	Paper folding and cutting	12–23
Quantitative reasoning	Quantitative	2–23
	Number series	7–23
	Education Building	12–26
Short-term memory	Bead memory	2–23
	Memory for sentences	2–23
	Memory for digits	7–23
	Memory for objects	7–23

Bellevue Hospital in New York City. Wechsler objected to using the Stanford-Binet for adults on three grounds. First, the problems had been designed for children and seemed juvenile to adults. Second, the mental-age norms of the Stanford-Binet did not apply to adults. Finally, whereas the Stanford-Binet emphasizes verbal skills, Wechsler felt that adult intelligence consists more in the ability to handle life situations than in solving verbal and abstract problems.

The WAIS-III is divided into two parts. One part stresses verbal skills, the other performance skills. The verbal scale includes tests of information

The Wechsler Intelligence Scales, developed by David Wechsler, are individual intelligence tests administered to one person at a time. There are versions of the Wechsler Scales for both adults and children. Here a child and an adult are being asked to copy a pattern using blocks.

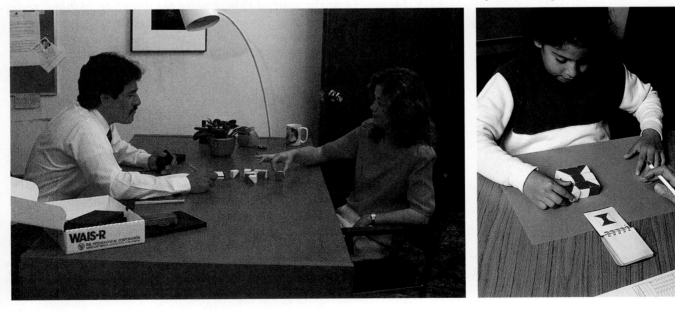

Wechsler Intelligence Scale for Children-Third Edition (WISC-III) An individual intelligence test developed especially for school-aged children; measures verbal and performance abilities and also yields an overall IQ score.

Group tests Written intelligence tests administered by one examiner to many people at one time.

("Who wrote *Paradise Lost?*"), tests of simple arithmetic ("Sam had three pieces of candy, and Joe gave him four more. How many pieces of candy did Sam have then?"), and tests of comprehension ("What should you do if you see someone forget a book on a bus?"). All these tests require a verbal or written response. The performance scale also measures routine tasks. People are asked to "find the missing part"—buttonholes in a coat, for example; to copy patterns; and to arrange three to five pictures so that they tell a story. Questions 3 and 4 at the start of this chapter resemble questions on the WAIS-III.

Although the content of the WAIS-III is somewhat more sophisticated than that of the Stanford-Binet, Wechsler's chief innovation was in scoring: His test offers separate verbal and performance scores as well as an overall IQ score. Second, on some items, one or two extra points can be earned depending on the complexity of the answer given. This unique scoring system gives credit for the reflective qualities that we expect to find in intelligent adults. Third, on some questions, both speed and accuracy affect the score.

Wechsler also developed a similar intelligence test for use with school-aged children. Like the WAIS-III, the 1991 version of the **Wechsler Intelligence Scale for Children-Third Edition (WISC-III)** yields separate verbal and performance scores as well as an overall IQ score.

Group Tests

The Stanford-Binet, the WAIS-III, and the WISC-III are individual tests. The examiner takes the person to an isolated room, spreads the materials on a table, and spends from 30 to 90 minutes administering the test. The examiner may then take another hour or so to score the test according to detailed instructions in the manual. So this is a time-consuming, costly operation. Moreover, the examiner's behavior may greatly influence the score.

For these reasons, test makers have devised **group tests.** These are written tests of mental abilities that a single examiner can administer to a large group of people at the same time. Instead of sitting across the table from a person who asks you questions, you receive a test booklet that contains questions for you to answer within a certain amount of time. Questions 5 through 14 at the start of this chapter are drawn from group tests. There are group tests not only for intelligence but also for aptitudes and other mental abilities.

When most people talk about "intelligence" tests, they are usually referring to group tests, because this is generally the means by which they were themselves tested in school. Schools are among the biggest users of group tests. From fourth grade through high school, tests such as the *School and College Ability Tests (SCAT)* and the *California Test of Mental Maturity (CTMM)* are used to measure students' specific abilities. The *SAT*—questions 9 through 11 at the start of this chapter—and the *American College Testing Program (ACTP)* are designed to measure a student's ability to do college-level work. The *Graduate Record Examination (GRE)* performs the same function on the graduate level. Group tests are also widely used in different industries, the civil service, and the military.

Group tests have some distinct advantages over individualized tests. They eliminate bias on the part of the examiner. Answer sheets can be scored quickly and objectively. And because more people can be tested in this way, more useful norms can be established. But there are also some distinct disadvantages to group tests. The examiner is less likely to notice whether a person is tired, ill, or confused by the directions. People who are not used to being tested tend to do less well on group tests than on individual tests. Finally, emotionally disturbed children seem to do better on individual tests than on group tests (Anastasi & Urbina, 1997).

Performance and Culture-Fair Tests

The intelligence tests we have discussed thus far share one common element: To perform well, people must be able to read, speak, and understand English. In many situations, however, people might experience language problems that are not necessarily related to intelligence. For example, infants and preschool children are too young to understand directions or answer questions. Hearing-impaired children often take longer to learn words than do children without a hearing impairment. Immigrants trained as lawyers or teachers in their native countries may need time to learn English. Immigrant children with above-average intelligence have been placed in classes for children with mental retardation simply because they do not know English well enough to perform at the level of their true ability. In such cases, standard intelligence tests simply cannot accurately assess people's cognitive abilities. How, then, can we test these people? Psychologists have designed two general forms of tests for such situations: performance tests and culture-fair tests.

Performance tests consist of problems that minimize or eliminate the use of words. One of the earliest performance tests, the *Seguin Form Board*, was devised in 1866 to test people with mental retardation. The form board is essentially a puzzle. The examiner removes specifically designed cutouts, stacks them in a predetermined order, and asks the person to replace them as quickly as possible. A more recent performance test, the *Porteus Maze*, consists of a series of increasingly difficult printed mazes. Subjects trace their way through the maze without lifting the pencil from the paper. Such tests require the test taker to pay close attention to a task for an extended period and to continuously plan ahead in order to make the correct choices that solve the maze.

One of the most effective tests used for very young children is the *Bayley Scales of Infant Development*, now in its second edition (Bayley-II; Bayley, 1993). The Bayley Scales are used to evaluate the developmental abilities of children from 1 month to 3 1/2 years of age. The Bayley-II has three scales: One scale tests perception, memory, and the beginning of verbal communication; a second measures sitting, standing, walking, and manual dexterity; the third is designed to assess emotional, social, and personality development. The Bayley Scales can detect early signs of sensory and neurological deficits, emotional difficulties, and troubles in a child's home environment (J. R. Graham & Lilly, 1984; Maisto & German, 1986).

Culture-fair tests are designed to measure the intelligence of people who are outside the culture in which the test was devised. Like performance tests, culture-fair tests minimize or eliminate the use of language. Culture-fair tests also try to downplay skills and values—such as the need for speed—that vary from culture to culture. A good example of this is the *Goodenough-Harris Drawing Test*. Subjects are asked to draw the best picture of a person that they can. Drawings are scored for proportions, correct and complete representation of the parts of the body, detail in clothing, and so on. They are not rated on artistic talent.

Cattell's *Culture-Fair Intelligence Test* combines some questions that demand verbal comprehension and specific cultural knowledge with other

Performance tests Intelligence tests that minimize the use of language.

Culture-fair tests Intelligence tests designed to eliminate cultural bias by minimizing skills and values that vary from one culture to another.

The Bayley Scales are a performance test used to assess the development of very young children. Such performance tests are essential to gauge developmental progress when children are too young to answer questions.

Reliability Ability of a test to produce consistent and stable scores.

Split-half reliability A method of determining test reliability by dividing the test into two parts and checking the agreement of scores on both parts.

Correlation coefficients Statistical measures of the degree of association between two variables.

culture-fair questions. By comparing scores on the two kinds of questions, cultural factors can be isolated from general intelligence. An example of a culture-fair item from the Cattell test is question 5 at the beginning of this chapter.

Another culture-fair test is the *Progressive Matrices* (question 6 at the start of this chapter). This test consists of 60 designs, each with a missing part. The person is given six to eight possible choices to replace the part. The test involves various logical relationships, requires discrimination, and can be given to one person or to a group.

WHAT MAKES A GOOD TEST?

All the tests we have looked at so far claim to measure a broad range of mental abilities, or "intelligence." How can we tell whether they really do measure what they claim to be measuring? And how do we determine whether one test is better than another? Psychologists address these questions by referring to a test's reliability and validity. As you read the following sections, keep in mind that the issues of reliability and validity apply equally to all psychological tests, not just to tests of mental abilities.

Reliability

By **reliability** psychologists mean the dependability and consistency of the scores yielded by a given test. If your alarm clock is set for 8:15 A.M. and goes off at that time every morning, it is reliable. But if it is set for 8:15 and rings at 8:00 one morning and 8:40 the next, you cannot depend on it; it is unreliable. Similarly, a test is reliable when it yields consistent results. If you score 90 on a verbal aptitude test one week and 60 on the same or an equivalent test a week later, something is wrong.

How do we know whether a test is reliable? The simplest way to find out is to give the test to a group and then, after a short time, give the same people the same test again. If they score the same each time, the test is reliable. For example, look at Table 8–3, which shows the IQ scores of eight people tested one year apart using the same test. This is a very reliable test. Although the scores did change slightly, none changed by more than 6 points.

This way of determining reliability poses a serious problem, however: Because the exact same test was used on both occasions, people might simply have remembered the answers from the first testing and repeated them the second time around. To avoid this, alternate forms of the test are often used. In this method, two equivalent tests are designed to measure the same ability. If a person gets the same score on both forms, the tests are considered reliable. One way to create alternate forms is to split a single test into two parts—for example, to assign odd-numbered items to one part and even-numbered items to the other. If scores on the two halves agree, the test is said to have **split-half reliability.** Most intelligence tests do, in fact, have alternate equivalent forms, just as each college admission test often has many versions.

These methods of testing reliability can be very effective. But is there some way of being more precise than simply calling a test "very reliable" or "fairly reliable"? Psychologists express reliability in terms of **correlation coefficients**, which measure the relationship between two sets of scores. If test scores on one occasion are absolutely consistent with those on another occasion, the correlation coefficient is 1.0. If there is no relationship between the scores, the correlation coefficient is zero. In Table 8–2, where there is a very close, but not perfect, relationship between the two sets of scores, the coefficient is .96.

TABLE 8-3		
IQ SCORES ON THE SAME TEST GIVEN 1 YEAR APART		
Person	First Testing	Second Testing
A	130	127
B	123	127
C	121	119
D	116	122
E	109	108
F	107	112
G	95	93
H	89	94

*For more information on correlation coefficients, consult the appendix on measurement and statistical methods at the end of this book.

How reliable are intelligence tests? In general, the reliability coefficients are around .90; that is, people's IQ scores on most intelligence tests are about as stable as the scores in Table 8–2. Performance and culture-fair tests are somewhat less reliable. However, scores on even the best tests vary somewhat from one day to another. Therefore, many testing services now report a person's score along with a range of scores that allows for variations due to chance, for example, a score of 105 could have a range of 95–115. This implies that the true score almost certainly lies somewhere between 95 and 115 but is most likely within a few points of 105. Even with the best intelligence tests though, differences of a few points mean little and should not be the basis for placing a child in an accelerated or remedial program.

We turn now to another question. Do intelligence tests really measure intelligence? We know that test scores are fairly consistent from day to day, but how do we know that the consistency is due to intelligence and not to something else? When psychologists ask these questions, they are concerned with test validity.

Validity

Validity refers to a test's ability to measure what it has been designed to measure. How can we determine whether a given test actually measures what it claims to measure?

CONTENT VALIDITY One measure of validity is known as **content validity**—whether the test adequately assesses the skills or knowledge that it is supposed to measure.

Do the results of IQ tests truly reflect the kinds of mental abilities that they set out to assess? The answer is somewhat mixed. Alfred Binet specifically designed his test to measure such qualities as judgment, comprehension, and reasoning; as a result, his test was more heavily focused on verbal skills than on perceptual or sensory abilities. As we saw earlier, Binet's original test has been revised and updated several times. At the earliest age levels, the test now measures eye-hand coordination, discrimination, and the ability to follow directions. Children build with blocks, string beads, match lengths, and so on. Older children are tested on skills that they learn in school, such as reading and math. The tests still focus heavily on verbal content: vocabulary, sentence completion, and interpreting proverbs, for instance. Even the tests that are not strictly verbal often require test takers to understand fairly complex verbal instructions.

Most people would agree that the content of the Stanford-Binet reflects at least part of what we commonly consider "intelligence," so we can conclude that the Stanford-Binet has some content validity. But because of its heavy emphasis on verbal skills, the test may not adequately sample all aspects of intelligence equally well.

As we saw earlier, it was partly the Stanford-Binet's stress on verbal skills that prompted Wechsler to devise the WAIS and the WISC. Wechsler believes that, taken together, his subtests adequately measure what we call "intelligence," which he defines as "the aggregate or global capacity of the individual to act purposefully, to think rationally, and to deal effectively with his environment." In fact, the WAIS-III and WISC-III appear to cover many of the primary abilities that Thurstone included under the heading of "intelligence" and that Cattell grouped under the headings of "fluid" and "crystallized" intelligence. Thus, the WAIS-III and WISC-III also appear to have some content validity as intelligence tests. Most group intelligence tests, such as those from which questions 5 through 14 at the beginning of

Validity Ability of a test to measure what it has been designed to measure.

Content validity Refers to a test's having an adequate sample of questions measuring the skills or knowledge it is supposed to measure.

Criterion-related validity Validity of a test as measured by a comparison of the test score and independent measures of what the test is designed to measure.

this chapter were taken, also seem to measure at least some of the mental abilities that make up intelligence.

In general, then, most intelligence tests assess many of the abilities that most people consider to be components of intelligence. These abilities include concentration, planning, memory, understanding language, and writing (Carroll & Horn, 1981). Yet intelligence tests do not measure every type of mental ability. Some tests focus on skills that other tests leave out, and each intelligence test emphasizes the abilities that it measures in a slightly different way.

CRITERION-RELATED VALIDITY   Is test content the only way to determine whether an intelligence test is valid? Fortunately, it is not. For example, if both the Stanford-Binet and the WISC-III measure intelligence in children, high scorers on one should be high scorers on the other. Think of two rulers, one that measures in inches and one that measures in centimeters. The measurements obtained by one ruler should correspond with those obtained by the other because both rulers are measuring the same thing—length. Similarly, two different measures of intelligence should be correlated with each other, because they should both be measuring the same thing. In fact, various intelligence tests do relate well with one another despite the differences in their content: People who score high on one test tend to score high on the others. Again, we can use the correlation coefficient to describe the strength of the relationship. The Stanford-Binet and Wechsler Scales correlate around .80. The SAT and Wechsler Scales correlate about .60 to .80. The Progressive Matrices and the Porteus Maze Test correlate .40 to .80 with other intelligence tests. The Goodenough-Harris Drawing Test correlates about .50 or better with other tests. Thus, despite their differences in surface content, most intelligence tests do seem to be measuring similar things.

However, the fact that intelligence tests tend to correlate with one another is not a sufficient criterion of their validity, for it is conceivable that the tests could be measuring the same things but that these things do not constitute intelligence. To demonstrate that the tests are valid, we need an independent measure of intelligence against which to compare intelligence test scores. The most common independent measure used for this purpose is academic achievement (Anastasi & Urbina, 1997). Ever since Binet invented the intelligence test, these tests have been used to predict school achievement. The underlying idea is that individual differences in school grades must reflect individual differences in intelligence, at least to some extent. Therefore, students with good grades should get high scores on the Stanford-Binet and other intelligence tests, and students with poor grades should do less well on such tests. Using such a procedure to determine the validity of a test is called **criterion-related validity.**

Do IQ tests accurately predict academic achievement? Even the strongest critics agree that this is one thing that IQ tests do well (Aiken, 1988). The Stanford-Binet was designed specifically to predict school performance, and it typically performs this function quite well. Correlations between grades and IQ of .50 to .75 are quite common. The Wechsler Scales also correlate highly with school grades, especially the verbal IQ score (Parker, Hanson, & Hunsley, 1988). The SAT and ACT college admission tests correlate around .40 with college grades, and the GRE is a good predictor of performance in graduate school. Evidence on the various performance and culture-fair tests is scanty but suggests that these tests do not predict school grades as well as other intelligence tests do (Blum, 1979).

We know that intelligence tests are quite reliable: Scores on these tests are consistent from day to day. These tests also seem to assess many of the qualities that psychologists define as components of intelligence. And intelligence test scores seem to agree with one another and with other indicators of intelligence, such as school grades. Nonetheless, in recent decades, intelligence tests have come under severe criticism.

Criticisms of IQ Tests

What are some of the most common criticisms of IQ tests?

TEST CONTENT AND SCORES   One major criticism of IQ tests concerns their content. Many critics believe that intelligence tests assess only a very narrow set of skills: passive verbal understanding; the ability to follow instructions; common sense; and, at best, scholastic aptitude (Ginsberg, 1972; Sattler, 1992). For example, one critic observes, "Intelligence tests measure how quickly people can solve relatively unimportant problems making as few errors as possible, rather than measuring how people grapple with relatively important problems, making as many productive errors as necessary with no time factor" (Blum, 1979, p. 83).

These critics pointedly observe that if there is one thing that all intelligence tests measure, it is the ability to take tests. This would explain why people who do well on one IQ test also tend to do well on others. And it would also explain why intelligence test scores correlate so closely with school performance: Academic grades also depend heavily on test scores. Notice that this criticism of intelligence tests challenges the assumption that academic achievement depends on intelligence. Rather, it proposes that neither academic achievement nor intelligence tests measure the capacity to successfully handle real-life situations requiring intellectual activity. Not surprising, then, is the tendency to "abandon the term IQ and replace it with a more accurate descriptor, such as school ability or academic aptitude" (Reschly, 1981, p. 1097). However, recent reviews of the evidence have reasserted the claim that both school grades and intelligence tests are good predictors of occupational success (Barret & Depinet, 1991). Thus, this particular criticism of intelligence tests may have to be reconsidered.

Still other critics maintain that the content and administration of IQ tests discriminate against minorities. High scores on most IQ tests require considerable mastery of standard English, which biases the tests in favor of middle- and upper-class white people (Blum, 1979). Moreover, white middle-class examiners may not be familiar with the speech patterns of lower-income black children or children from homes where English is not the primary language, a complication that may hamper good test performance (Sattler, 1992). In addition, certain questions may have very different meanings for children of different social classes. The Stanford-Binet, for instance, asks, "What are you supposed to do if a child younger than you hits you?" The "correct" answer is, "Walk away." But for a child who lives in an environment where survival depends on being tough, the "correct" answer might be, "Hit him back." This answer, however, receives zero credit on the Stanford-Binet.

Even presumably culture-fair tests may accentuate the very cultural differences that they were designed to minimize (Linn, 1982), to the detriment of test takers. For example, when given a picture of a head with the mouth missing, one group of Asian-American children responded by saying that the body was missing, thus receiving no credit. To them, the absence of a body under the head was more remarkable than the absence of the mouth (Ortar, 1963).

Although some investigators believe that the most widely used and thoroughly studied tests are not biased against minorities (Bersoff, 1981; Cole, 1981; Herrnstein & Murray, 1994; Reschly, 1981), this conclusion is very controversial. Janet Helms (1992) of the University of Maryland

Some people argue that intelligence tests largely measure test-taking skills, not a person's underlying mental capabilities. Others contend that the content of these tests and the ways they are administered discriminate against minorities.

argues that a proper study of cultural equivalence in testing has yet to be made. By cultural equivalence, Helms means that items on a test have the same meaning in different cultures and subcultures. She outlines several characteristics of tests and test procedures that should be scrutinized to determine whether a test is biased because it includes items that have different meanings to different groups. These characteristics include sampling equivalence (e.g., Were samples of each racial and ethnic group used to develop and validate the test items?); equivalence of testing condition (e.g., Was the examiner of the same race as the subject?); and contextual equivalence (e.g., Are the abilities being tested evaluated in the same way in different cultures?). Examination of these sources of potential bias may explain why individuals from different cultures and subcultures give different answers to test items than people brought up in the cultural mainstream (Helms, 1992, p. 1092).

The issue of whether tests are unfair to minorities will be with us for some time. If IQ tests were used only for obscure research purposes, their results would not matter much, but because they are used for so many significant purposes, it is critical that we understand their strengths and their weaknesses.

USE OF IQ SCORES   Recall that Alfred Binet developed the first IQ test to help the French public school system identify students who needed to be put in special classes. In fact, Binet believed that courses of "mental orthopedics" could be used to help those with low IQ scores. But the practice of using IQ tests to put a person into a "track" or "slot" in school may backfire. To the extent that children get low scores on IQ tests because of test bias, language handicap, or their own lack of interest in test taking, the administrative decision to label these children as "slow" or "retarded" and put them into special classes apart from "normal" students can have a disastrous effect—one that may get worse, not better, with time. Of course, such tracking may also have the opposite effect, especially with those identified early on as having high IQ scores. In a self-fulfilling prophecy, such children may come to believe that they will be high achievers, and this expectation may figure prominently in their subsequent success (Dahlström, 1993). Thus, IQ test scores may not simply predict future achievement or the lack of it; they may also be partly responsible for it.

Although IQ tests are useful for predicting academic performance, they do not measure other elements that may underlie academic achievement—motivation, emotion, and attitudes, for example. Yet in many instances, these characteristics may have more to do with an individual's success and effectiveness than IQ does. Let's look briefly at the relationship between IQ scores and success.

IQ AND SUCCESS   Despite their limitations, IQ tests do a good job of predicting future school performance. What does this fact mean, and how important is it?

IQ scores should correlate well with academic performance because both involve some intellectual activity and both stress verbal ability. Moreover, both academic achievement and high IQ scores require similar kinds of motivation, attention, and perseverance. And as we noted earlier, because academic success depends largely on test-taking ability, the correlation is not surprising. But critics suggest that there may be another, less savory, reason for the relationship between school performance and IQ test scores. If teachers expect particular students to do well in school on the basis of their IQ scores, they may encourage those students. By the same token, if teachers expect students with low IQ scores not to perform well, they may neglect those students.

Whatever the reason, IQ scores do predict success in school with some accuracy. Moreover, people with high IQ scores tend to enter high-status occupations: Physicians and lawyers tend to have higher IQs, whereas truck drivers and janitors tend not to. However, this pattern can be explained in various ways. For one thing, because people with higher IQs tend to do better in school, they stay in school longer and earn advanced degrees, which, in turn, opens the door to high-status jobs. Moreover, children from wealthy families are more likely to have the money needed for graduate school and advanced occupational training. They also tend to have helpful family connections. Perhaps most important, they grow up in environments that encourage academic success and reward good performance on tests (Blum, 1979).

Although research confirms that people with high IQ scores are more successful in school and tend to get higher-status jobs, are these people also more likely to succeed in their careers? In a classic paper, David C. McClelland (1973), of Harvard University, argued that IQ scores and grades in college have very little to do with later occupational success. His review of the research evidence seemed to indicate that when education and social class are held constant, on a wide range of jobs people with high IQs do not perform better than people with lower IQs. However, a more recent survey of the relevant research contradicts McClelland's conclusion. Barret and Depinet (1991) found considerable evidence that grades and results on tests of intellectual ability *do* predict occupational success. They concluded that "test results were not an artifact of social status, nor were they unfair to minorities" (p. 1021). Similarly, Ree and Earles (1992) present evidence that measures of general intelligence are excellent predictors of job performance. They concluded that "if an employer were to use only intelligence tests and select the highest-scoring applicant for each job, training results would be predicted well regardless of the job, and overall performance from the employees selected would be maximized" (p. 88).

In response to such statements McClelland (1993) has reiterated his earlier views, charging that these recent investigations fail to allow for the influence of such variables as family advantage and achievement motivation. Robert J. Sternberg, some of whose work we considered earlier, and his colleague, Richard K. Wagner (1993), have proposed that new tests be developed specifically to measure skills relevant to job performance. Such tests might emphasize what Sternberg and Wagner call **tacit knowledge,** which they define as the kind of practical knowledge people need to perform their jobs effectively, even though they may not be able to state this knowledge explicitly. For example, one test item designed to assess tacit knowledge could require people to evaluate different strategies for maximizing sales of photocopiers. Although people may not be able to answer direct questions about what they know in this area, they may still be exceedingly knowledgeable about selling these high-priced machines. Just as you may be able to ride a bicycle quite well but be unable to explain exactly how to perform this operation to someone else, so may good mechanics have skills that they cannot describe but can nonetheless put to use effectively.

In this section, we have reviewed several criticisms that have been leveled at IQ tests and their use. But not all critics of IQ tests want to see them eliminated. Many simply want to make IQ tests more useful. For example, Jane Mercer has developed a *System of Multicultural Pluralistic Assessment (SOMPA)*, designed for children between the ages of 5 and 11. SOMPA involves collecting a wide range of data on a child, including information

Tacit knowledge Knowledge one needs for success in completing particular practical tasks; this knowledge may not be explicit.

about health and socioeconomic status, that provides a context within which IQ test scores can be interpreted. SOMPA takes into account both the dominant school culture and the child's family background, and then adjusts the child's IQ score (based on the Wechsler Scales) accordingly (Rice, 1979). And, as we have seen, Sternberg is developing new intelligence test items that will tap a much broader set of skills that may underlie intelligence.

In any event, an IQ score is not the same as intelligence. Tests measure our ability level at a certain point in time and in relation to the norms for our age group. IQ scores do not tell us why someone performs poorly or well. Moreover, as we have seen, most psychologists today believe that "intelligence" is not a single entity but, rather, a combination of abilities and aptitudes required for adaptation to, and effective behavior in, the real world (Anastasi & Urbina, 1997; Frederickson, 1986; Sternberg, 1985a, 1986). Clearly, these abilities will vary to some extent from culture to culture and with the age of the person (Berry et al., 1992). For instance, optimal environments for school achievement, creativity, or music ability may differ between cultures. Abilities considered most important in one culture will tend to be brought to the fore in that culture; those that are downplayed will tend to fade from the scene (McAndrew, 1993). Finally, an IQ score is a very simplistic way of summing up an extremely complex set of abilities. Maloney and Ward (1976) point out that we do not describe a person's personality with a 2- or 3-digit number. Why, then, they ask, should we try to sum up something as complex as intelligence by labeling someone "90" or "110"? As Sternberg (1992) points out, we have come to rely too much on single tests yielding a single score. What is required are more differentiated measures of different types or aspects of intelligence, especially in the area of practical intelligence.

WHAT DETERMINES INTELLIGENCE?

Heredity

Robert C. Tryon (1901–1967) of the University of California, Berkeley, was a pioneer in behavior genetics. More than 50 years ago, he began investigating whether the ability to run mazes could be bred into rats. Horse breeders and cattle farmers have long known that selective breeding—for example, crossing a fast horse with a strong one—can change the physical characteristics of animals. Could the same technique alter mental abilities? Tryon isolated eligible pairs of "maze-bright" rats in one pen and "maze-dull" rats in another. The animals were left free to breed. Within a few generations, the difference between the two groups was astounding: The maze-dull rats made many more mistakes learning a maze than their bright counterparts (Tryon, 1940; see Figure 8–2).

It is difficult to explain how maze ability is transmitted. Perhaps the brighter rats inherited better eyesight, larger brains, quicker reflexes, greater motivation, or a combination of these advantages. Regardless of how it works, Tryon did demonstrate that a specific ability can be passed down from one generation of rats to another.

Obviously, performing laboratory experiments in the selective breeding of humans is unethical. However, as we saw in Chapter 2, The Biological Basis of Behavior, scientists can use studies of identical twins to measure the effects of heredity in humans. Twin studies of intelligence begin by comparing the IQ scores of identical twins who have been raised together.

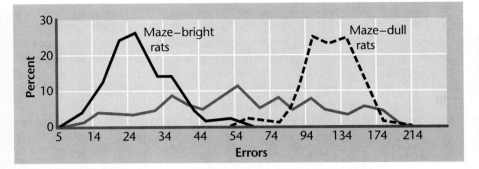

Figure 8–2
Errors made by Tryon's maze-bright and maze-dull rats in learning a maze.
The colored line shows what percentage of the parent group made equal numbers of errors. The black lines show the errors of the eighth generation of rats. Notice that almost all the maze-dull rats made more errors than the maze-bright rats.

As Figure 8–3 shows, the correlation between their IQ scores is very high. These twins grew up in very similar environments: They shared parents, home, teachers, vacations, and probably friends and clothes, too. These common experiences could explain their similar IQ scores. To check this possibility, researchers have tested identical twins who were separated early in life—generally before they were 6 months old—and raised in different families. As Figure 8–3 shows, even when identical twins are raised in different families, they tend to have very similar IQ scores; in fact, the similarity is much greater than that between siblings who grow up in the *same* environment.

So far, the case for heredity seems to be ironclad: Identical twins have very similar IQ scores even when they have not been raised together. For several reasons, however, twin studies do not constitute "final proof" of this assertion. First, finding identical twins who were separated at birth is very difficult; therefore, very few such pairs have been studied. Assessing the influence of heredity given such a small sample of subjects is extremely

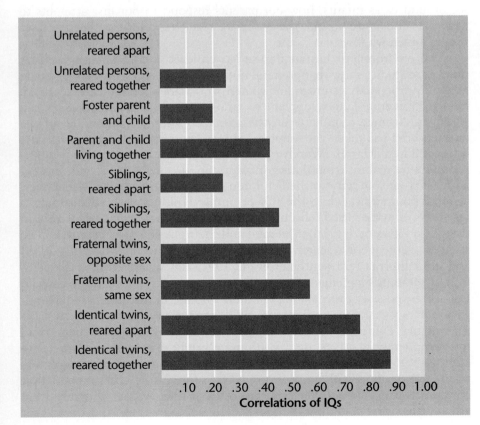

Figure 8–3
Correlations of IQ scores and familial relationships.
Identical twins who grow up in the same household have IQ scores that are almost identical to each other. Even when they are reared apart, their scores are highly correlated.

Source: Adapted from "Genetics and Intelligence: A Review," by L. Erlenmeyer-Kimling and L. F. Jarvik 1963, *Science, 142,* pp. 1477–1479. Copyright © 1963 by the American Association for the Advancement of Science.

difficult (Loehlin, 1989). Second, adoption agencies try to match natural and adoptive parents. If twins are born to educated middle-class parents, the adopted twin will most likely be placed with educated middle-class adoptive parents. Thus, twins reared apart will often share somewhat similar environments. Finally, even if twins grow up in radically different environments, they lived for 9 very critical months inside the same mother: Their prenatal experiences were virtually identical, and it is difficult to determine the extent to which those shared experiences might contribute to their similarities. Therefore, even among identical twins, at least some of their similarity may actually be due to similarity of environment.

Other adoption studies have also shown the influence of heredity on IQ. Adopted children who are not related have been found to have IQs that are more similar to their *biological* mothers than to the mothers who are raising them (Loehlin, Horn, & Willerman, 1997). Researcher John Loehlin finds these results particularly interesting because "[they] reflect genetic resemblance in the absence of shared environment: These birth mothers had no contact with their children after the first few days of life . . ." (Loehlin et al., 1997, p. 113).

What, then, is the case for the influence of the environment? We turn now to that question.

Environment

Proponents of the environment's influence on intelligence do not deny that, to some degree, intelligence is inherited, but they feel this is only the beginning. Each of us inherits a certain body build from our parents, but our actual weight is primarily determined by what we eat and how much we exercise. Similarly, although we inherit certain mental capacities, the development of those inherited intellectual abilities depends on what we see around us as infants, how our parents respond to our first attempts to talk, the schools we attend, the books we read, the television programs we watch—even what we eat.

The environment has an impact on children before birth as well: A number of studies show that prenatal nutrition affects IQ scores (Hack et al., 1991). In one study of pregnant women who were economically deprived, half were given a dietary supplement, and half were given placebos. When given intelligence tests between the ages of 3 and 4, the children of the mothers who had taken the supplement scored significantly higher than the other children (Harrell, Woodyard, & Gates, 1955).

Extreme malnutrition during infancy can also lower IQ scores. For example, severely undernourished children in South Africa had IQs that averaged 20 points lower than the IQs of similar children with adequate diets (Stock & Smythe, 1963). If children do not get an adequate diet early in their development, both their mental and their physiological growth will be stunted. Subsequent research in Great Britain (Benton & Roberts, 1988) and in California (Schoenthaler et al., 1991) has suggested that the addition of vitamin supplements to the diet of young children can increase IQ test scores, possibly even among children who are not experiencing malnutrition. However, these findings are still controversial.

Further evidence for the importance of environment comes from follow-up experiments using Tryon's maze-bright and maze-dull rats. Psychologists raised one group of mixed bright and dull rats in absolutely plain surroundings and another group in a stimulating environment that contained toys, an activity wheel, and a ladder. When the rats were grown, they were tested on the mazes. The experimenters discovered that

Compared with women who eat poor diets during pregnancy, those who eat nutritious ones tend to have larger, healthier newborns who go on to become preschoolers with higher IQ scores than peers who were not well nourished prenatally. Prenatal environments apparently matter as much as postnatal ones.

there was no longer much difference between genetically bright and dull rats: In the restricted environment, the inherited abilities of the bright rats apparently failed to develop, and all the rats acted like maze-dull rats. In the stimulating environment, the genetically maze-dull rats apparently made up through experience what they lacked in heredity and, as a result, all the rats in this environment acted like maze-bright rats (R. Cooper & Zubek, 1958). In subsequent experiments, Rosenzweig and Bennett (1976) found that enriched environments improved rats' ability to learn (see Chapter 2).

Quite by chance, psychologist H. M. Skeels found evidence in the 1930s that IQ scores among children also depend on environmental stimulation. While investigating orphanages for the state of Iowa, Skeels noticed that the wards where the children lived were very overcrowded and that the few adults charged with caring for the children had almost no time to play with them, talk to them, or read them stories. Many of these children were classified as "subnormal" in intelligence. Skeels followed the cases of two girls who, after 18 months in an orphanage, were sent to a ward for women with severe retardation. Originally, the girls's IQs were in the range of retardation, but after a year on the adult ward, as if by magic, their IQs had risen to normal (Skeels, 1938). He repeated the experiment by placing 13 slow children as house guests in adult wards (Skeels, 1942). Within 18 months, the mean IQ of these children had risen from 64 to 92 (within the normal range)—all because they had had someone (even someone of below-normal intelligence) to play with them, to read to them, to cheer them when they took their first steps, and to encourage them to talk. During the same period, the mean IQ of a group of children who had been left in orphanages dropped from 86 to 61. Thirty years later, Skeels found that all 13 of the children raised on adult wards were self-supporting, their occupations ranging from waiting on tables to real-estate sales. Of the contrasting group, half were unemployed, 4 were still in institutions, and all those who had jobs were dishwashers (Skeels, 1966).

Another more recent study conducted in France by Capron and Duyme (1989) also provides strong support for the influence of the environment on

Individual differences in intelligence can be partly explained by differences in environmental stimulation and encouragement. The specific forms of stimulation given vary from culture to culture. Because our culture assigns importance to developing academic skills, the stimulation of reading and exploring information in books can give children an IQ edge over those who are not so encouraged.

intelligence. Half the children in this study had been born to parents of high socioeconomic status (SES), and half had been born to parents of low SES. Half the children born to high-SES parents were adopted and raised by parents of similar status, and half were adopted and raised by low-SES parents. Similarly, half the children born to low-SES parents were adopted and raised by high-SES parents, and half were adopted and raised by other low-SES parents. The results showed that the socioeconomic status of the adoptive parents had an effect on their adopted children's IQs. Regardless of the socioeconomic status of the child's biological parents, those children adopted by high-SES parents had higher IQs than did those children adopted by low-SES parents. Why? High-SES families tend to provide children with better nutrition and heightened stimulation; thus, these results are consistent with earlier studies showing the importance of an adequate diet and intellectually stimulating surroundings. In the accompanying *Applying Psychology* box, we look at the results of several studies aimed at enhancing the environments of children from lower-SES families.

The IQ Debate: A Continuing Controversy

We have seen evidence that both heredity and environment have important effects on mental abilities. Is one of them more important than the other? As Turkheimer (1991) observes, the question of whether mental abilities are determined primarily by nature (genes) or nurture (environment) is almost as old as psychology itself, and it is still being hotly debated (e.g., Herrnstein & Murray, 1994).

When IQ test scores of U.S. soldiers in World War I were collected and analyzed, psychologists discovered large differences in test scores among various ethnic groups (C. C. Brigham, 1923; Yerkes, 1921, 1948). For example, men who were originally from northern European countries such as England and Germany scored higher than men originally from southern European countries including Greece and Italy. Some psychologists believed strongly that these differences arose because of environment: Some ethnic groups had lived in the United States longer than others and thus were more familiar with the cultural norms reflected in the tests. Other psychologists argued vehemently that differences among ethnic groups could only be explained by genetics.

4

Can intervention programs like Head Start improve people's mental abilities?

APPLYING PSYCHOLOGY
INTERVENTION PROGRAMS: HOW MUCH CAN WE BOOST IQ?

In 1961 the so-called Milwaukee Project was launched. Its purpose was to learn whether intervening in a child's family life could offset the negative effects of cultural and socioeconomic deprivation on IQ scores. Rick Heber and his associates at the University of Wisconsin Infant Center worked with 40 poor pregnant women in the Milwaukee area (Garber & Heber, 1982; Heber et al., 1972). On average, the women initially scored less than 75 on the Wechsler intelligence scales. They were then split into two groups. One group was given job training and sent to school. As they found jobs, they were also instructed in child care, household management, and personal relationships. The other group received no special education or job training.

After all 40 women had their babies, the research team began to concentrate on the children. Starting when they were 3 months old and continuing for the next 6 years, the children of the mothers who were being given special training spent the better part of each day in an infant education center, where they received nourishing meals and participated in an educational program that included a wide range of educational toys. They were cared for by paraprofessionals who behaved like nonworking mothers in affluent families. The other group of children, whose mothers were not receiving any special training, had no access to the education center.

All the children were periodically tested for IQ. The children in the experimental group, whose mothers received special training and who themselves had access to the education center, achieved an average IQ score of 126—51 points higher than their mothers' average scores. By contrast, the children in the control group, whose mothers did not re-

ceive special training and who did not have access to the education center, scored an average IQ of 94—not as high as the experimental group, but still much higher than their mothers' average scores, perhaps in part because they had become accustomed to taking tests, an experience their mothers had never had.

Head Start, the nation's largest intervention program, began in 1965 and today provides "comprehensive services for 721,000 children lasting at least a half a day for 128 days a year" (Kassebaum, 1994). Head Start focuses on preschoolers between the ages of 3 and 5 who live in low-income families. It has two key goals: to provide the children with some educational and social skills before they get to school and to provide information about nutrition and health to the children and their families. Head Start involves parents in all its aspects, from daily activities to administration of the program itself, and some evidence suggests that the involvement of parents in the Head Start program has been crucial to its success (Cronan, Walen, & Cruz, 1994).

Several studies evaluating the long-term effects of Head Start concluded that the program had improved children's cognitive abilities (Brown & Grotberg, 1981). Today, however, some experts are concerned that these improvements may not be lasting. For example, some evidence suggests that boosts in IQ tend to be modest or short term. Nevertheless, there seems to be no question that children leaving Head Start are in a better position to profit from schooling than they would be otherwise (Zigler & Styfco, 1994). Researchers who followed Head Start graduates until age 27 found several benefits, including higher academic achievement. The

Head Start is a program designed to do just what its name implies: to give children from disadvantaged environments a head start in acquiring the skills and attitudes needed for success in school. Although researchers debate whether Head Start produces significant and lasting boosts in IQ, it does have many school-related benefits for those who participate in it.

Head Start graduates tended to stay in school longer and were more likely to graduate from college (Schweinhart, Barnes, & Weikart, 1993). Thus, even if the IQ gains due to Head Start are not long lasting, the program still seems to provide long-term, practical benefits.

Overall, the effectiveness of early intervention appears to depend on the quality of the particular program (Collins, 1993; Zigler & Muenchow, 1992; Zigler & Styfco, 1993). Intervention programs whose goals are clearly defined and that take into account the broad context of human development including health care and other social services achieve the most significant and long-lasting results. Also, interventions that begin in the preschool years and include a high degree of parental involvement (to ensure continuity after the official program ends) are generally more successful (Cronan et al., 1994; Hart & Risley, 1995; Jaynes & Wlodkowski, 1990).

To learn more about this and related topics, visit our website at **www.prenhall.com/morris**

In the years following World War I, the intensity of the debate declined. Decades later, however, the controversy reached a fever pitch after the publication of an article by psychologist Arthur Jensen (1969). In his article, Jensen argued that heredity accounts for about 80 percent of the variation in IQ test scores among various racial groups. Predictably, Jensen's article generated a furious controversy among educators and social scientists over the validity of IQ testing, the heritability of intelligence, and the relationship between race and intelligence. Between 1969 and 1973 alone, 117 articles were published in response to Jensen's article.

Over the next 2 decades the controversy subsided, but it did not go away. Then, in 1994, the issue resurfaced with the publication of *The Bell Curve: Intelligence and Class Structure in American Life* by Richard Herrnstein and Charles Murray. Herrnstein and Murray argued that intelligence is largely inherited, that different people inherit different levels of intellectual ability, and that levels of intelligence vary among ethnic and racial groups. They further maintained that U.S. society has become increasingly dominated by an elite group with greater cognitive abilities.

Conflicting data and claims still surround Herrnstein and Murray's conclusions (Lynn, 1997; Neisser, 1997; Rushton, 1995; 1997; Scarr, 1995), but one point emerges clearly: Most of the participants in the debate, including Jensen, Herrnstein, and Murray, agree that both heredity and environment affect IQ scores. Indeed, Robert Plomin, one very influential researcher in the field, concludes, "the world's literature suggests that about half of the total variance in IQ scores can be accounted for by genetic variance . . . " (Plomin, 1997, p. 89).

GENES AND ENVIRONMENT   A useful way to think about heredity, environment, and intelligence comes from plants (Turkheimer, 1991). Suppose you take groups of the same type of plant. You grow one group in enriched soil and the other in poor soil. The enriched group will grow to be higher and stronger than the nonenriched group; the difference between the two groups in this case is due entirely to differences in their environment. However, *within* each group of plants, differences among individual plants are likely to be due primarily to genetics, because all plants in the same group share essentially the same environment. Nevertheless, the height and strength of any single plant will reflect both heredity and environment. Similarly, group differences in IQ scores might be due to environmental factors, differences among people *within* racial groups could be due primarily to genetics, and the IQ score of particular people would reflect the effects of both heredity and environment.

Of course, this example assumes that the plants have been distributed randomly between the two groups; thus, general differences between the groups are due entirely to the environment. It is possible, however, to select plants with specific genetic characteristics for each group; for example, tall plants in one group and short plants in another. In this case, differences between the two groups would be the products of both environment and heredity. Just as plant development reflects both genetic and environmental influences that are often difficult to isolate, human IQ scores, too, have both genetic and environmental sources. Scientists are likely to debate this issue for years to come (see, for example, Humphreys, 1992, pp. 272–273).

An interesting side note to the IQ debate is that IQ scores have *gone up* in the population as a whole (Humphreys, 1992; Jensen, 1992; Neisser et al., 1996). They cite evidence gathered by Flynn (1984, 1987) showing that between 1932 and 1978 IQ scores rose about 3 points per decade. There are many explanations for this finding. Perhaps people are simply getting better at taking tests. Another possibility is that environmental factors, such as improved nutrition and health care, account for the improvement. Yet another possibility is that our culture is now richer and more stimulating than it ever was before.

MENTAL ABILITIES AND HUMAN DIVERSITY

Are there differences in mental abilities between males and females or among people from different cultures? Many people assume that males and females differ significantly in verbal and mathematical abilities, for example. Others believe that the sexes are basically alike in mental abilities. Similarly, how do we account for the superior academic performance by students in certain cultures whereas those in other cultures lag behind? Some researchers stress innate ability; others focus on cultural and educational factors. Considerable research offers some interesting insights into these controversial issues.

Gender

Many occupations are dominated by one gender or the other. Engineering, for example, has traditionally been almost exclusively a male domain. Is it possible that this occupational difference and others like it reflect underlying gender differences in intellectual or mental abilities?

In 1974 psychologists Eleanor Maccoby and Carol Jacklin published a review of psychological research on gender differences. They found no differences at all between males and females in most of the studies they examined. However, a few differences did appear in cognitive abilities: Girls tended to display greater verbal ability and boys tended to exhibit stronger spatial and mathematical abilities. Largely as a result of this research, gender differences in verbal, spatial, and mathematical abilities became so widely accepted that they were often cited as one of the established facts of psychological research (Hyde, Fennema, & Lamon, 1990; Hyde & Linn, 1988).

Yet a closer examination of the research literature, including more recent work, indicates that gender differences in math and verbal ability may be virtually nonexistent. For example, Janet Shibley Hyde and her colleagues analyzed 165 research studies, involving more than a million people, in which gender differences in verbal ability were examined. They concluded that "there are no gender differences in verbal ability, at least at this time, in American culture, in the standard ways that verbal ability has been measured" (Hyde & Linn, 1988, p. 62). In a similar analysis of studies examining mathematical ability, Hyde and her colleagues concluded that "females outperformed males by only a negligible amount . . . Females are superior in computation, there are no gender differences in understanding of mathematical concepts, and gender differences favoring males do not emerge until the high school years" (Hyde et al., 1990, pp. 139, 151).

Males apparently do have an advantage over females in spatial ability, however (Halpern, 1992; Voyer, Voyer, & Bryden, 1995). Spatial tasks include mentally rotating an object and mentally estimating horizontal and vertical dimensions (see the figures on pages 304–305). These skills are particularly useful in solving certain engineering, architecture, and geometry problems. They are also handy in deciding how to arrange furniture in your new apartment or how to fit all those suitcases into the trunk of your car!

Although the average male and female IQ is about the same, there does appear to be a higher proportion of men with both mental retardation and superior IQs than women. In one review of several large studies, Hedges and Nowell (1995) found that males accounted for 7 out of 8 people with extremely high IQs (top 1 percent). These authors also reported that males

5

What does research tell us about the mathematical skills of men and women?

represented an almost equally large proportion of the IQ scores within the range of mental retardation.

What should we conclude from these findings? First, the cognitive differences between males and females appear to be restricted to specific cognitive skills. Scores on tests such as the Stanford-Binet or the WAIS reveal no gender differences in general intelligence (Halpern, 1992). Second, gender differences in specific cognitive abilities typically are small and in some cases appear to be diminishing—even when studied cross-culturally (Skaalvik & Rankin, 1994). Finally, we do not know whether the origins of the differences that do exist are a result of biological or cultural factors. Considerable research has identified several factors that discourage females from pursuing careers in mathematics and science. For example, one study found that women avoid careers in math and science partly because of *mathematics anxiety*. Girls and college women are more likely than males to agree with the statement "I dread mathematics class." (Chipman, Krantz, & Silver, 1992). Findings like these suggest that occupational and career differences may simply be an outgrowth of the distinctive socialization of boys and girls. See the *Controversies* box on reporting sex differences for another perspective on this issue.

Academic Performance: The Influence of Culture

U.S. educators, policymakers, and parents are concerned that American students are falling behind students in other countries. Is this concern valid? And if it is, how can we explain it?

In a series of comprehensive studies, a team of researchers led by Harold Stevenson investigated differences in academic performance among members of various cultures (Stevenson, 1992, 1993; Stevenson, Chen, & Lee, 1993). In 1980, he and his colleagues began their research by examining the performance of first- and fifth-grade children in American, Chinese, and Japanese elementary schools (Stevenson, Lee, & Stigler, 1986). At that time, the Japanese and Chinese students at both grade levels far surpassed the American pupils in mathematics, and the Chinese were also more proficient readers. A decade later, when the study was repeated with a new group of fifth-graders, the researchers discovered an even larger difference in mathematical proficiency when the American students were compared to their Asian counterparts. The vocabulary scores of the three groups also showed changes. In 1980, Chinese fifth-graders scored the highest on vocabulary, whereas Japanese students scored the lowest. By 1990, however, Japanese fifth-graders performed the best, and American students had dropped to the lowest position. In 1990, the research team also studied the original first-graders from all three cultures, now in the eleventh grade. The result? The American students retained their low standing in mathematics compared to the Asian students.

Having established that the performance of the children from these three cultures was, in fact, different, the next questions was why. One explanation advanced by Stevenson's team suggested that cultural attitudes toward ability and effort may, in part, be responsible. To test this hypothesis, Stevenson and his colleagues (1993) asked students, their parents, and their teachers in all three countries whether they thought effort or ability had a greater impact on academic performance. From first through eleventh grade, American students disagreed with the statement that "everyone in my class has about the same natural ability in math." "Studying hard," the Americans thought, has little to do with performance. Their responses appear to reflect a belief that mathematical skill is primarily a function of innate ability. American mothers expressed a similar view. Moreover, 41 percent of the

6 In what ways is academic achievement related to culture?

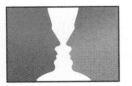

CONTROVERSIES
SHOULD WE REPORT SEX DIFFERENCES IN BEHAVIOR?

Whenever psychologists conduct research, they need to consider how their research findings should be framed, whether all conclusions should be given equal weight, and how many details should be included in the research report. But recently a new issue has been raised: When should psychologists report evidence of gender differences?

Some argue that unexamined assumptions about the sexes contaminate psychological research by influencing the way theories are developed, how some research questions are approached, and the manner in which findings regarding the behavior of males and females are reported (McHugh, Koeske, and Frieze, 1986). For example, some early theories of intelligence (e.g., Thorndike, 1903) held that women's intellectual skills differed substantially from men's. For a long time, such theories were used to justify keeping women out of colleges and universities, or treating them differently if they were admitted (see the *Highlights* box, Missing: Women in Psychology, in Chapter 1).

To ensure fairness and accuracy in psychological research involving sex differences, McHugh et al. (1986) propose several guidelines that psychologists should follow when interpreting and reporting their findings. They recommend that "sex-related differences that have not been replicated or have not been predicted by

... a theoretical model may not be appropriate . . . for published research" (p. 883). This implies that only predicted, well-confirmed sex differences should be published.

By contrast, Alice Eagly (1987a) of Purdue University proposes another strategy. Rather than reporting only well-confirmed sex differences, she urges psychologists to report research results indicating differences between the sexes but to use the same precision and caution they exercise in reporting other types of research. She warns that if psychologists begin to censor themselves by reporting only those gender differences that flow from an established theory, many potentially important findings that don't accord with current theories may go unrecognized. In addition, if only well-established sex differences were reported, there would be less chance of replicating newer findings because researchers would be unable to compare their results to results that have not been reported. Finally, if published reports were limited to sex differences the researchers had predicted ahead of time, many findings of *no differences* between the sexes would be unreported (Eagly, 1995).

Roy Baumeister (1988) of Case Western Reserve University proposes an alternative strategy: By not re-

> *Does reporting on differences between the sexes only perpetuate those differences?*

porting or focusing on sex differences at all, we can disarm political and social factions who use information about differences to perpetuate gender stereotypes and myths. If psychologists don't accentuate differences between the sexes, he believes, the general public may stop believing that the sexes differ markedly. Baumeister also points out that media reports of scientific findings often exaggerate the size or importance of a reported sex difference. A small difference between the sexes can be blown out of proportion. He urges psychologists to strive for a "sex neutral psychology of people" (p. 1094). In response, Eagly (1990) argues that *any* scientific finding runs the risk of being misinterpreted in the popular media. In addition, until the advent of the women's movement, psychologists spent little time investigating or reporting sex differences, yet gender stereotypes still flourished among the general public.

No consensus has been reached on this issue.

Questions

1. How do you think we should treat findings that the sexes differ behaviorally in some respects?

2. In your opinion, does acknowledging these differences in a research report do more harm than good?

American eleventh-grade teachers thought "innate intelligence" is the most important factor in mathematics performance. By contrast, Asian students, parents, and teachers believed that effort and "studying hard" determined success in math.

Asians and Americans clearly hold different opinions concerning the origins of academic performance, and these culturally influenced views of

Mental retardation Condition of significantly subaverage intelligence combined with deficiencies in adaptive behavior.

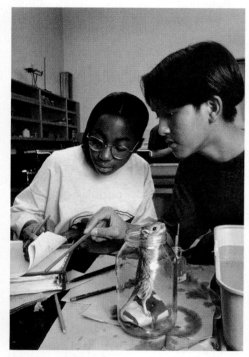

Why do more males than females pursue careers in science? The reason is not that males have more innate aptitude for mathematics, because gender differences in math ability are negliglible during childhood. The answer probably has more to do with cultural stereotypes about what girls are "good at" and what they are not.

the relative importance of effort and innate ability may have profound consequences on the way children and their parents approach the task of learning. Students who believe that learning is based on natural ability will see little value in working hard to learn a difficult subject. By contrast, students who believe that academic success comes from studying are more likely to work hard. Indeed, even the brightest students will not get far without making an effort to develop, refine, and direct their intellectual abilities. Although many Americans no doubt believe in the value of effort and hard work, our widespread perception that ability is the key to success may be affecting the performance of U.S. students.

But are differing cultural attitudes alone responsible for the differences in academic performance in these cultures? Evidence suggests that the nature of the educational system in the three cultures may also play a crucial role. First, when the eleventh-grade American, Japanese, and Chinese schoolchildren were tested on general information that they could have learned outside of school, all three groups earned nearly identical scores. This suggests that American students are just as competent as their Asian counterparts at learning information that does not originate in the school curriculum. Second, when the students' mothers were polled, 79 percent of the American mothers thought the schools were doing a "good" or "excellent" job of educating their children. Asian mothers were more critical of their schools' performance. Third, American mothers and students were generally satisfied with students' academic performance, even though it was comparatively low. Stevenson has proposed that the structure of the school day and the role of the teacher might contribute to cultural differences in student performance as well (1992, 1993). Asian students spend more time in school each day than do American students. However, much of this additional time is taken up by longer lunch periods, more frequent recesses, and after-school clubs and activities. Contrast this with the typical American school day, in which the student arrives, begins classes, has a single recess and a short lunch, then leaves soon after the last class ends. In Stevenson's view, the diversity of activities in Asian schools contributes to students' liking and wanting to attend school each day and, therefore, indirectly contributes to academic achievement. Moreover, teachers in Asian schools typically are better trained in educational methods, have more time to spend with students, and are required to do fewer course preparations than American teachers. As a result, Chinese and Japanese teachers have more time, energy, and skills to work closely and actively with their pupils.

We have been discussing various factors that influence intelligence and achievement. But we have focused only on people within the "normal" range of intellectual functioning. We look now at the extremes of the intellectual continuum.

EXTREMES OF INTELLIGENCE

In general, the average IQ score on intelligence tests is 100. Nearly 70 percent of all people have IQs between 85 and 115, and all but 5 percent of the population have IQs that fall between 70 and 130. In this section, we will focus on individuals who score at the two extremes of intelligence—people with mental retardation and those who are intellectually gifted.

Mental Retardation

Mental retardation encompasses a vast array of mental deficits with a wide variety of causes, treatments, and outcomes. The American Psychological Association (1994) defines mental retardation as "significantly subaverage general intellectual functioning . . . that is accompanied by significant limitations in adaptive functioning" (p. 39); in addition, the condition must appear before the individual is 18 years old. This definition has several important points. First, people with mental retardation are well below normal in intelligence. Mild retardation corresponds to Stanford-Binet IQ scores ranging from a high of about 70 to a low near 50. Moderate retardation corresponds to IQ scores ranging from the low 50s to the mid 30s. People with IQ scores between the mid 30s and 20 are considered severely retarded, and the profoundly retarded are those whose scores are below 20 (see Table 8–4).

But a low IQ score is not in itself sufficient for diagnosing mental retardation. The person must also be unable to perform the kinds of daily living skills everyone needs to function independently (Wielkiewicz & Calvert, 1989). Therefore, evaluations of people with mental retardation usually include tests of motor development and social adaptation as well as tests of intelligence. One widely used group of motor-development tests is the *Oseretsky Tests of Motor Proficiency*. These tests measure control of facial muscles, hand and finger coordination, and posture. Two measures of social adaptation are the *Adaptive Behavior Scale (ABS)* and the *Vineland Adaptive Behavior Scale*. Both are based on observations of the individual's behavior in everyday situations. The ABS has two versions, one designed primarily for use with adults (Nihira, Leland, & Lambert, 1993), and one aimed at the assessment of children's adaptive behavior (Lambert, Nihira, & Leland, 1993). In the ABS, individuals are scored in such areas of adaptation as language development, understanding and use of number and time concepts, domestic activity, responsibility, and social action. Another portion of the ABS focuses on the individual's maladaptive behaviors, such as withdrawal, hyperactivity, and disturbing interpersonal behaviors.

What causes mental retardation, and what can be done to overcome it? In most cases, the causes are simply not known (Beirne-Smith, Patton, & Ittenbach, 1994). This is especially true in cases of mild retardation, which account for nearly 90 percent of all retardation. Where causes can be

---

TABLE 8-4

LEVELS OF MENTAL RETARDATION

TYPE OF RETARDATION	IQ RANGE	LEVEL OF FUNCTIONING
Mild retardation	Low 50s–70s	The individual may be able to function adequately in society. The individual is "educable": He or she can learn academic skills comparable to those of a sixth-grader and can be minimally self-supporting, although requiring special help at times of unusual stress.
Moderate retardation	Mid 30s–low 50s	These people profit from vocational training and may be able to travel alone. They can learn on a second-grade level and perform skilled work in a sheltered workshop if provided with supervision and guidance.
Severe retardation	Low 20s–mid 30s	Such people do not learn to talk or to practice basic hygiene until after age six. Although they cannot learn vocational skills, simple tasks can be carried out with supervision.
Profound retardation	Below 20 or 25	Constant care is needed. Usually, people in this group have a diagnosed neurological disorder.

Source: Based on APA, DSM-IV, 1994.

Down syndrome is a common biological cause of mental retardation, affecting 1 in 600 newborns. The prognosis for Down syndrome children today is much better than it was in the past. With adequate support, many children with Down syndrome can participate in regular classrooms and other childhood activities.

identified, most often they stem from a wide variety of environmental, social, nutritional, and other risk factors (Scott & Carran, 1987).

About 25 percent of cases, especially the more severe forms of retardation, appear to involve genetic or biological disorders. Recently, more than 100 single genetic traits that can result in mental retardation have been identified (Plomin, 1997). One such cause is the genetically based disease *phenylketonuria,* or *PKU.* In people suffering from PKU, the liver fails to produce an enzyme necessary for early brain development. PKU occurs in about 1 out of 25,000 people (Minton & Schneider, 1980). Fortunately, early dietary intervention—which involves removing *phenylalanine* from the diet—can prevent the symptoms of mental retardation from developing. Another cause of severe mental retardation is chromosomal abnormality. For example, babies with *Down syndrome,* which affects 1 in 600 newborns, are born with defects on part of chromosome 21 (see the photo on page 79). Down syndrome is named for the nineteenth-century British physician Langdon Down, who first described the symptoms. It is marked by moderate to severe mental retardation and also by a characteristic pattern of physical deformities, including skinfolds on the hands, feet, and eyelids. Research evidence indicates that in the great majority of cases of Down syndrome, the egg from which the baby developed either was defective at the time of the mother's birth or developed defects during ovulation. In about 5 percent of the cases, the defect seems to originate with the father's sperm (Antonarakis, 1991). Another common type of mental retardation is *fragile-X syndrome.* This disorder, which affects about 1 in every 1,250 males and 1 in every 2,500 females, is hereditary (Plomin, 1997): A defect in the X chromosome is passed on from one generation to the next. Researchers have identified the specific gene believed to cause fragile-X syndrome (Hoffman, 1991).

Although little can be done to reverse the biological conditions that cause many cases of severe mental retardation, the effects of retardation can be moderated through education and training. For people with no physical impairment but with a history of social and educational deprivation, education and social contact may have a dramatic impact. Today the majority of students with physical disabilities are educated in local school systems (Lipsky & Gartner, 1996; Schroeder, Schroeder, & Landesman, 1987), through a process called *mainstreaming,* which helps these students to socialize with their nondisabled peers. The principle of mainstreaming, also known as *inclusion,* has also been applied to programs for adults with mental retardation, by taking them out of large, impersonal institutions and placing them in smaller community homes that offer a greater opportunity for normal life experiences and personal growth (Conroy, 1996; Landesman & Butterfield, 1987 Maisto & Hughes, 1995; Stancliffe, 1997). Although benefits of mainstreaming are debatable, most psychologists and educators support the effort (Zigler & Hodapp, 1991).

ASSESSMENT To fully assess individuals and to place them in appropriate treatment and educational programs, mental health professionals need information on emotional adjustment, physical health, and social adjustment. Federal legislation, passed in 1975, requires four procedures. First, handicapped children must be tested to identify their disabilities. Second, a team of specialists must determine each child's educational needs. Third, an educational program that meets those needs must be provided. Finally, children are to be periodically retested to determine whether the educational program is adequate.

In the assessment phase, special attention must be paid to possible biases in measuring instruments. Like intelligence, mental retardation is a highly complex phenomenon. Just as intelligence tests do not measure certain abilities, such as artistic talent, people with mental retardation sometimes display exceptional skills in areas other than general intelligence. Probably the most dramatic and intriguing examples involve *savant performance*, in which people with mental retardation or who suffer from mental handicaps or brain injuries exhibit remarkable abilities in highly specialized areas, such as numerical computation, memory, art, or music (O'Connor & Hermelin, 1987). Savant performances include mentally calculating large numbers almost instantly; determining the day of the week for any date over many centuries; and playing back a long musical composition after hearing it played only once. Whatever its origins, savant performance constitutes an intriguing mixture of retardation and of giftedness, the topic to which we now turn.

Giftedness

At the other extreme of the intelligence scale are "the gifted"—those with exceptional mental abilities as measured by scores on standard intelligence tests. As with mental retardation, the causes of **giftedness** are largely unknown.

The first and now-classic study of giftedness was begun by Lewis Terman and his colleagues in the early 1920s. Terman's (1925) was the first major research study in which giftedness was defined in terms of academic talent and measured by an IQ score in the top 2 percentile. More recently, some experts have sought to broaden the definition of giftedness beyond that of simply high IQ (Csikszentmihalyi, Rathunde, & Whalen, 1993; Subotnik & Arnold, 1994). Renzulli (1978), for instance, proposes thinking of giftedness as the interaction of above-average general ability, exceptional creativity, and high levels of commitment. Sternberg and Davidson (1985) define giftedness as especially effective use of what we earlier called componential aspects of intelligence: planning, allocating resources, acquiring new knowledge, and carrying out tasks effectively.

People have used various criteria to identify gifted students, including scores on intelligence tests, teacher recommendations, and achievement-test results. Most school systems also use diagnostic testing, interviews, and evaluation of academic and creative work (Sattler, 1992). These selection methods can identify students with a broad range of talent, but they can miss students with specific abilities, such as a talent for mathematics or music.

Giftedness Refers to superior IQ combined with demonstrated or potential ability in such areas as academic aptitude, creativity, and leadership.

Definitions of giftedness have recently broadened beyond high scores on IQ tests. These young people at the Moscow School of Music, for example, have demonstrated exceptional musical abilities. They are considered gifted in their own country, as they would be in ours.

Unfortunately, there has been little systematic study of programs for the gifted, making it difficult to document their effectiveness (Reis, 1989). Without such data, many critics have challenged some of the fundamental assumptions about gifted children. For example do gifted people constitute a distinct group, superior to other people in all areas of intelligence and creativity? Critics argue that people gifted in one area are not necessarily gifted in others. On tests of moral and social reasoning, for example, gifted children performed no better than other bright children (Gardner, 1983b). Additionally, current tests may miss gifted students in minority populations (Baldwin, 1985). To address this concern, experts have devised alternative tests for minority students (Bruch, 1971; Mercer & Lewis, 1978). Many schools also use several screening methods to increase the participation of minority students in special programs.

Yet another reservation about programs for gifted children involves how students themselves feel about being labeled as exceptional. Some children are uneasy being thought of as "brains," and others may resent the pressure to perform. Finally, the relationship of creativity and giftedness remains unclear (Isaksen et al., 1993). Some children who score only moderately high on intelligence, but high on creative measures, are capable of exceptional achievement (Getzels & Jackson, 1962). We look now at the relationship between creativity and intelligence.

CREATIVITY

Creativity is the ability to produce novel and socially valued ideas or objects ranging from philosophy to painting, from music to mousetraps (Mumford & Gustafson, 1988; Sternberg, 1996).

Some researchers believe that creative ability is simply one aspect of intelligence. For example, the study by Sternberg and his associates (1981), noted earlier in the chapter, found that experts on intelligence generally placed creativity under the heading of verbal intelligence (see Table 8–1). Sternberg also included creativity and insight as important elements in the experiential component of human intelligence.

Although some psychologists believe that creativity is one aspect of intelligence, most IQ tests do not measure creativity, and many researchers in the area of cognitive abilities would argue that intelligence and creativity are not the same thing. What, then, is the relationship between intelligence and creativity? Are people who score high on IQ tests likely to be more creative than those who score low?

Early studies typically found little or no relationship between creativity and intelligence (e.g., Getzels & Jackson, 1962; Wing, 1969). Critics pointed out, however, that these early studies examined only bright students. For example, the average IQ score of the students tested by Getzels and Jackson was 132. Perhaps creativity and intelligence are linked until IQ reaches a certain level, or threshold, after which there is little or no relationship between them. This is called the *threshold theory* of creativity and intelligence and, in fact, there is considerable evidence that this theory may be correct. For example, one study found that intelligence and creativity correlated .88 for people with IQs below 90, .69 for those with IQs ranging from 90 to 110, –.30 for those with IQs between 110 and 130, and –.09 for those with IQs above 130. That is, below an IQ of 110, higher IQ scores were accompanied by higher creativity, but above this threshold there was little or no relationship between IQ and creativity. Other studies have borne out these findings (Barron, 1963; Yamamoto & Chimbidis, 1966). However, all these studies relied heavily on tests of creativity. Thus, any conclusions drawn from them must assume that scores on creativity tests reflect real-life creativity, an assumption

7 Are very creative people more intelligent than less creative people?

that many people question. But other studies of people who have demonstrated outstanding creativity in their lives also seem to support the threshold theory of creativity and intelligence. These studies (e.g., Bachtold & Werner, 1973; Barron, 1963; R. B. Cattell, 1971; Helson, 1971) show that creative people tend to be highly intelligent; that is, highly creative artists, writers, scientists, and mathematicians tend, as a group, to score high on intelligence tests. But for individuals in this special group, there is little relationship between IQ scores and levels of creative achievement, just as the threshold theory would predict. Thus, for creativity to be displayed, intelligence appears to be a necessary, but not sufficient, contributing element (Amabile, 1983).

Interestingly, creative people are often *perceived* as being more intelligent than less creative people who have equivalent IQ scores. Perhaps some characteristic that creative people share—possibly "effectiveness" or some quality of social competence—conveys the impression of intelligence even though it is not measured by intelligence tests (Barron & Harrington, 1981).

In general, creative people are *problem finders* as well as problem solvers (Getzels, 1975; Mackworth, 1965). The more creative people are, the more they like to work on problems they have set for themselves. Thus, creative scientists, such as Charles Darwin or Albert Einstein, often work for years on a problem that has sprung from their own curiosity. Great artists, scientists, and writers have more than simple "talent" or "genius." They have intense dedication, ambition, and perseverance.

The highly imaginative costuming and staging of the Broadway musical *The Lion King* is one example of creativity: the ability to produce novel and socially valued ideas. Is a person who is extremely creative also more intelligent than most other people? Researchers are still exploring the relationship between creativity and intelligence. But it seems as if a certain threshold level of intelligence is needed for high creativity to develop.

Creativity Tests

Although many psychologists consider creativity an aspect of intelligence, opinions differ over the best way to test creativity. Because creativity involves original responses to situations, questions that can be answered only true or false, *a* or *b* are not a good measure. More open-ended tests are better: Instead of asking for one predetermined answer to a problem, the examiner asks the test taker to think of as many answers as possible. Scores are based on the number and originality of the person's answers.

In one such test, the *Torrance Test of Creative Thinking*, people are asked to explain what is happening in a picture, how the scene came about, and what its consequences are likely to be. The *Christensen-Guilford Test* asks the people to list as many words containing a given letter as possible; to name things belonging to a particular category—such as liquids that will burn; and to write four-word sentences beginning with the letters RDLS—"Rainy days look sad, Red dogs like soup, Renaissance dramas lack symmetry," and so on.

One of the most widely used creativity tests, S. A. Mednick's (1962) *Remote Associates Test (RAT)*, asks people to give a single verbal response that relates to a set of three apparently unrelated words. For example, the three stimulus words might be poke, go, and molasses. A desirable response—although not the only possible one—relates them through the word *slow*: slowpoke, go slow, slow as molasses. Arriving at such responses is not easy, especially because the stimulus words have no apparent connection to one another.

The newer *Wallach and Kogan Creative Battery* focuses on having the person form associative elements into new combinations that meet specific requirements. Children are asked to "name all the round things you can think of" and to find similarities between objects—for example, a potato and a carrot. Although people who do not have high IQs can score well on the Wallach and Kogan test, the Torrance test seems to require a reasonably high IQ for adequate performance. Current tests of creativity do not show a high degree of validity (Feldhusen & Goh, 1995), so measurements derived from them must be interpreted with caution.

ANSWERS TO CHAPTER OPENING QUESTIONS

1. *Idleness* generally means the state of being inactive, not busy, unoccupied; *laziness* generally means an unwillingness or reluctance to work. Laziness is one possible cause of idleness, but not the only cause.

2. If you face west, your right hand will be toward the north.

3. *Obliterate* means to erase or destroy something completely, without a trace.

4. Both an hour and a week are measures of time.

5. Alternative (d) is correct. Each sector starts where the previous sector left off and extends 45 degrees clockwise around the circle.

6. Alternative (f) is the correct pattern.

7. The opposite of hate is love (c).

8. 75 cents will buy nine pencils.

9. Union (b) is most nearly opposite in meaning to schism. Union means a uniting or joining of several parts into a whole; schism means a splitting apart or dividing of something that was previously united.

10. Alternative (e) makes the most sense. The phrase "despite an outward" implies that the words in the blanks should form a contrast of some sort. Acquiescence (agreeing, consenting without protest) certainly contrasts with thwarting (opposing, hindering, obstructing).

11. Alternative (d) is correct. A crutch is used to help someone who has difficulty with locomotion; spectacles are used to help someone who has difficulty with vision.

12. Alternative (b) is correct. In each case, the figure is made up of three shapes that are identical except for their size; the largest shape goes on the bottom and the smallest on top, with no overlapping between the shapes.

13. Alternative (d) is correct. The second figure is the same shape and size but with diagonal cross-hatching from upper left to lower right.

14. Figures 3, 4, and 5 can all be completely covered by using some or all of the given pieces.

ANSWERS TO QUESTIONS ON P. 309

1. The man is a minister. The key to solving this problem is the realization that to "marry" someone does not always mean "become married to" someone.

2. Neither car is closer to Boston. When the cars pass, they are next to each other and thus they are both the same distance from Boston.

3. Facts (a) and (c) are relevant to answering the question.

4. Person A is the girl and person B is the boy. Because there is one girl and one boy, if "at least one of them is lying" then they must both be lying.

5. If indeed radishes were candies, then it would follow that PRETZEL is to SALTY as RADISH is to SWEET. In each case, the connection is to the way the object tastes.

6. (c) might be a good strategy if you are not comfortable starting a petition and if you do not like fruit or yogurt; (b) might be a good strategy if neither of the other alternatives works for you and if you are comfortable organizing a petition campaign; (a) might be a good strategy if you are not satisfied with either of the other alternatives.

7. (a) might be a good choice if neither of the other alternatives appeals to you and if you think your son can, in fact, train the dog if he decides to do so; (b) might be the best choice if your son cannot train the dog, provided you feel competent to do so and selling the dog is not a realistic possibility; (c) might be the best choice if neither you nor your son is likely to be able to train the dog.

8. Successful people in business management tended to rate (a), (b), and (c) as quite important, whereas they rated (d) and (e) as relatively unimportant.

9. Successful academic psychologists tended to rate (a), (b), (e), and (f) as quite important and the other characteristics as relatively unimportant.

SUMMARY

This chapter examines **intelligence** and mental abilities, which are cognitive abilities that promote learning and adaptive behavior. The complex processes underlying mental abilities cannot be studied directly; instead, they must be inferred from a person's actions in situations requiring their use. **Intelligence tests** are designed to measure a person's general mental abilities.

Recent research indicates that experts do not yet agree on a single definition of "intelligence." Moreover, "intelligence" apparently means somewhat different things to experts and to nonexperts. In the early 1980s, Sternberg and his associates discovered that both experts and nonexperts described an intelligent person as someone with practical problem-solving ability and verbal ability. But laypersons included social competence in their concepts of intelligence, whereas experts put more emphasis on motivation.

THEORIES OF INTELLIGENCE

Intelligence theorists fall into two categories. In one group are those who argue for a "general intelligence" that characterizes a person's actions and thinking in all areas. Their critics believe that intelligence is composed of many separate types of aptitudes and abilities, and that a person who excels in one area will not necessarily excel in all areas.

Early Theories: Spearman and Thurstone

Spearman believed that intelligence is general: People who are bright in one area are bright in other areas as well. Thurstone disagreed: He believed that intelligence encompasses seven mental abilities that are relatively independent of one another.

In contrast, Cattell divided mental abilities into two clusters. The first is *crystallized intelligence*, or abilities such as reasoning and the verbal and numerical skills that are stressed in school. The second is *fluid intelligence,* or skills such as spatial and visual imagery, the ability to notice visual details, and rote memory.

Contemporary Theories: Sternberg and Gardner

In the mid-1980s, Yale psychologist Robert Sternberg proposed a **triarchic theory of intelligence** that includes a much broader range of skills and abilities. According to this theory, intelligence consists of three overarching aspects: **componential intelligence,** the traditional mental processes or skills emphasized by earlier theories of intelligence, such as the ability to acquire new knowledge and perform tasks efficiently; **experiential intelligence,** characterized by insight and creative adaptability as well as efficient and quick processing of information without conscious thought; and **contextual intelligence,** marked by responsiveness to the environment. Intelligent people, according to Sternberg, are adept at making the most of their strengths and compensating for their weaknesses.

Howard Gardner has proposed his **theory of multiple intelligences,** which asserts that what we refer to as intelligence actually consists of many separate abilities, each of which is relatively independent of the others.

Formal theories of intelligence serve as the foundation for the design and administration of intelligence tests. And because experts do not view intelligence in exactly the same way that nonexperts do, it is understandable that most tests of intelligence do not include items that many nonexperts think of as part of intelligence.

INTELLIGENCE TESTS

The Stanford-Binet Intelligence Scale

The **Binet-Simon Scale,** the first test of intelligence, was developed in France by Alfred Binet and Theodore Simon for testing children. Originally issued in 1905, it consisted of 30 tests arranged in order of increasing difficulty. From the average scores of children, Binet developed the concept of mental age.

The best-known Binet adaptation, created by Stanford University's L. M. Terman in 1916, is the **Stanford-Binet Intelligence Scale.** Terman introduced the term **intelligence quotient (IQ),** which is a numerical value given to scores on an intelligence test (a score of 100 corresponds to average intelligence).

The Stanford-Binet is designed to measure skills in four areas: verbal reasoning, abstract/visual reasoning, quantitative reasoning, and short-term memory.

The Wechsler Intelligence Scales

The **Wechsler Adult Intelligence Scale-Third Edition (WAIS-III)** was developed by David Wechsler especially for adults. The test measures both verbal and performance abilities. Wechsler also created the **Wechsler In-**telligence Scale for Children-Third Edition **(WISC-III),** which is meant to be used with school-aged children. It measures verbal and performance abilities separately, though it also yields an overall IQ score.

Group Tests

Group tests are administered by one examiner to many people at one time. Group tests are most commonly used by schools. The California Test of Mental Maturity (CTMM) and the SAT are group tests.

Group tests aim to overcome the problems of time and expense associated with individual tests and to eliminate bias on the part of the examiner. However, in a group setting the examiner is less likely to notice whether an individual test taker is tired, ill, or confused by the directions. Emotionally disturbed children and people who have less experience taking tests usually do better on individual tests than on group tests.

Performance and Culture-Fair Tests

Some intelligence tests may discriminate against members of certain cultural or ethnic groups. **Performance tests** are intelligence tests that do not involve language, so they can be useful for testing people who lack a strong command of English. The *Seguin Form Board,* the *Porteus Maze,* and the *Bayley Scale of Infant Development* are performance tests.

Culture-fair tests are designed to eliminate cultural bias by minimizing skills and values that vary from one culture to another. The *Goodenough-Harris Drawing Test* and the *Progressive Matrices* are examples of culture-fair tests.

WHAT MAKES A GOOD TEST?

Psychologists use reliability and validity as measures of a test's quality, and for purposes of comparing different tests.

Reliability

Reliability is the ability of a test to produce consistent and stable scores. The simplest way to determine a test's reliability is to give the test to a group and then, after a short time, give it again to the same group. If the group scores the same each time, the test is reliable. The problem with this way of determining reliability is that the group may have remembered the answers from the first testing. One method of eliminating this problem is to divide the test into two parts and check the consistency of people's scores on both parts. If the scores generally agree, the test is said to have **split-half reliability.** Psychologists express reliability in terms of **correlation coefficients,** the statistical measure of the degree of linear association between two variables. Correlation coefficients can vary from -1.0 to $+1.0$. The reliability of intelligence tests is about .90; that is, scores remain fairly stable across repeated testing.

Validity

Validity is the ability of a test to measure what it has been designed to measure. **Content validity** exists if a test contains an adequate sample of questions relating to the skills or knowledge it is supposed to measure. In general, most intelligence tests assess many of the abilities considered to be components of intelligence: concentration, planning, memory, language comprehension, and writing. However, a single test may not cover all the areas of intelligence, and tests differ in their emphasis on the abilities they do measure.

Criterion-related validity refers to the relationship between test scores and independent measures of whatever the test is designed to measure. In the case of intelligence, the most common independent measure is academic achievement. Despite their differences in surface content, most intelligence tests are good predictors of academic success. Based on this criterion, these tests seem to have adequate criterion-related validity.

Criticisms of IQ Tests

Much of the criticism of intelligence tests has focused on their content. Critics point out that most intelligence tests are concerned with only a narrow set of skills and may, in fact, measure nothing more than the ability to take tests. Critics also maintain that the content and administration of IQ tests are shaped by the values of Western middle-class society and that, as a result, they may discriminate against minorities. IQ tests are also criticized because the results are often used to label some students as slow learners. Finally, IQ tests do not offer information on motivation, emotion, attitudes, and other similar factors that may have a strong bearing on a person's success in school and in life.

Other critics hold that intelligence is far too complex to be precisely measured by tests. IQ tests are also criticized for neglecting to account for social influences on a person's performance. According to recent reviews of the evidence, intelligence tests are good predictors of success on the job. However, because so many variables figure in occupational success, psychologists continue to debate this issue. Robert Sternberg and Richard Wagner have called for a test to be developed specifically to measure skills related to job performance. They refer to the knowledge that people need to perform their jobs effectively as **tacit knowledge.**

WHAT DETERMINES INTELLIGENCE

Heredity

Historically, research on the determinants of intelligence has focused on identical twins—some reared together; others reared apart in separate households. The correlation between the IQs of all identical twins is usually very high, indicating that their identical genetic inheritance is a more powerful determinant of intelligence than their ex-periences. But critics of this research make several strong points: (1) It is difficult to find identical twins who have been separated at birth, so that there are only a few such studies; (2) identical twins tend to be placed in households similar in socioeconomic background to those of their biological parents; and (3) even twins separated at birth have had nearly identical prenatal experiences.

Environment

Research on rats as well as on humans strengthens the case for environment as a factor in the development of superior intellectual ability. Thus, even though certain mental abilities are inherited, without the necessary stimulation a child's intelligence will not develop. This finding is important because lower-income families don't have access to the kinds of resources that other families do. Significantly, when they are placed in more stimulating environments, economically deprived children show an improvement in their level of intelligence. For example, lower-income children raised in middle-class homes display significant gains in IQ compared with their counterparts growing up in low-income households. Similarly, children who participate in intervention programs such as Head Start frequently exhibit improvements in cognitive abilities, although the long-terms effects of such programs have yet to be confirmed.

The IQ Debate: A Continuing Controversy

Accounting for group differences in IQ poses a vexing problem in psychology. A milestone in this debate was the 1969 publication of an article by psychologist Arthur Jensen, claiming that overall differences in IQ scores between the races are largely inherited. Jensen's article raised a storm of controversy, which swelled up again in 1994 with the publication of a book on this topic by Richard Herrnstein and Charles Murray. Significantly, most participants in this debate agree that both heredity and environment affect IQ scores.

MENTAL ABILITIES AND HUMAN DIVERSITY

Gender

Overall, women and men do not differ significantly in general intelligence as measured by scores on standardized tests. Women may show a slight advantage in mathematical computation skills and men a slight advantage in spatial ability.

Academic Performance: The Influence of Culture

Differences in academic performance between American and Asian students are found from first grade through high school in mathematics and reading. Extensive research by Stevenson suggests that at least some of these differences may be related to (1) the educational curricula and (2) American students' tendency to attribute academic success more to innate ability than Asian students, who believe it stems more from individual effort and hard work.

EXTREMES OF INTELLIGENCE

The IQs of nearly 70 percent of the general population fall between 85 and 115, and all but 5 percent of the population have IQs between 70 and 130. Individuals with mental retardation and those who are gifted score at the two extremes of intelligence.

Mental Retardation

Mental retardation is a condition of significantly subaverage intelligence combined with deficiencies in adaptive behavior. The condition includes a range of mental deficits with a wide array of causes, treatments, and outcomes. There are varying degrees of mental retardation, from moderately retarded to profoundly retarded. In addition to having a low IQ, to be considered mentally handicapped a person must also lack skills essential for independent daily living.

In most cases, the causes of mental retardation are not known. Where causes can be identified, the majority of cases involve a variety of environmental, social, nutritional, and other risk factors. About 25 percent of mental retardation cases can be traced to biological causes, including *PKU, Down syndrome*, and *fragile-X syndrome*.

Giftedness

Giftedness refers to superior IQ combined with demonstrated or potential ability in academic aptitude, creativity, leadership, and fine arts. The recent movement to identify and assist gifted children in schools has come under criticism, as have the assumptions underlying notions of giftedness. Critics say, among other things, that gifted people may not be a distinct group superior to the general population in all areas, but rather people who excel only in some areas. Critics also contend that it is erroneous to assume that career success automatically comes to people who are gifted.

CREATIVITY

Creativity—the ability to produce novel and socially valued ideas or objects—is regarded by some psychologists as one aspect of intelligence. But there is some disagreement about the link between creativity and intelligence. The *threshold theory* of the relation between intelligence and creativity states that although creativity requires a certain amount of intelligence, once intelligence rises above the threshold level, creativity and intelligence are related only moderately, if at all.

Creativity Tests

Because creativity involves original responses to situations, it is helpful to measure it with tests composed of open-ended questions. Mednick's *Remote Associates Test (RAT)* and the *Wallach and Kogan Creative Battery* are two examples of creativity tests.

REVIEW QUESTIONS

MULTIPLE CHOICE AND SHORT ANSWER

1. Match each of the following with his concept of intelligence:

   _____ Cattell   a. proposed a triarchic theory of intelligence

   _____ Spearman   b. identified seven somewhat independent mental abilities

   _____ Sternberg   c. argued that intelligence is general

   _____ Thurstone   d. specified two clusters of mental abilities

   _____ Gardner   e. advanced a theory of multiple intelligences

2. According to Sternberg, the three complex aspects of intelligence are the _____ aspect, which includes the acquisition of new knowledge; the _____ aspect, which includes the ability to understand new concepts; and the _____ aspect, which includes the ability to adapt to or reshape the environment.

3. In 1916, the Stanford psychologist L. M. Terman introduced the term _____ and set the score of _____ for a person of average intelligence. His test was based on the first intelligence test, the _____ _____, designed by Alfred Binet.

4. The IQ test that L. M. Terman constructed is called the Stanford-Binet Intelligence Scale. T/F

5. The individual IQ test most often given to adults is the _____ _____ _____ _____.

6. Written tests of intelligence designed to be administered by a single examiner to many people at one time are called _____ _____. Which of the following is *not* such a test?
   a. GRE   c. Wechsler Adult Intelligence Scale
   b. SAT   d. SCAT

7. _____ tests eliminate or minimize the use of words. They are designed for people who cannot speak English and for preschoolers and people with disabilities. Like these tests, _____ _____ tests minimize the use of language, but they also include questions that downplay the use of skills and values that vary across cultures.

8. Which of the following makes a good test?
   a. high reliability   c. correlation coefficients
   b. high validity   d. a and b

9. If you take a test several times and score about the same each time you take it, your results suggest that the test is _____.

10. Which of the following is a measure of reliability?
    a. correlation coefficient   c. criterion validity
    b. median   d. average

11. _____ is a test's ability to measure what it has been designed to measure.

12. IQ scores predict success in _____ pretty well.

13. Tryon's experiments with rats demonstrated the role of the _____ in intelligence.

14. The ability to produce novel and unique ideas or objects, ranging from philosophy to painting, from music to mousetraps, is known as:
    a. creativity   c. fluid intelligence
    b. IQ   d. wit

15. Two important features of creative people are:
    a. They take risks and like to work on problems they invent themselves.
    b. They are perceived as less intelligent and more irresponsible than other people.
    c. They excel at art, but are poor at science.

CRITICAL THINKING AND APPLICATIONS

1. Outline Howard Gardner's theory of multiple intelligences, paying particular attention to his criteria for an intelligence.

2. Are people with high IQ scores necessarily more successful in their jobs and careers? Explain your answer.

3. You attend a lecture in which the speaker states, "Because a performance test does not rely on language skills, it is necessarily culture-fair." Is this statement accurate?

4. Is intelligence one thing or many things? Explain your position.

5. Why has intelligence testing had such a profound impact on our lives? Do you think this impact has been predominantly positive or negative? What could be done to make intelligence tests fairer and better able to reflect all sorts of intelligence?

ENDURES ISSUES

Diversity
To what extent do men and women differ in the ways that they think and in their mental abilities? Are there significant racial or cultural differences in thinking and mental abilities?

Heredity–Environment
To what extent are our mental abilities the result of heredity (nature) and to what extent do they reflect our experiences (nurture)?

(Answers to the Review Questions appear in the back of the book.)

9 Motivation

and Emotion

Classic detective stories are usually studies of motivation and emotion. At the beginning, all we know is that a murder has been committed: After eating dinner with her family, sweet old Amanda Jones collapses and dies of strychnine poisoning. "Now, why would anyone do a thing like that?" everybody wonders. The police ask the same question, in different terms: "Who had a motive for killing Miss Jones?" In a good mystery, the answer is: "Practically everybody."

The younger sister—now 75 years old—still bristles when she thinks of that tragic day 50 years ago when Amanda stole her sweetheart. The next-door neighbor, a frequent dinner guest, has been heard to say

Think About It!
1. Is human behavior based on instincts?
2. How does your body signal when you are hungry?
3. Why do many people have so much trouble losing weight beyond a certain point?
4. Do most psychologists feel that aggression is basically learned behavior or an inborn drive?
5. *True or False*: Different peoples throughout the world categorize emotions in essentially the same way.
6. What do psychologists mean by "body language"?
7. Is it true that men generally feel less emotion than women?

that if Miss Jones's poodle tramples his peonies one more time, he intends to. . . . The nephew, who stands to inherit a fortune from the deceased, is deeply in debt. The parlor maid has a guilty secret that Miss Jones knew. All four people were in the house on the night that Amanda Jones was poisoned. All four had easy access to strychnine, which was used to kill rats in the basement. All four had strong emotional reactions to Amanda Jones—envy, anger, shame, guilt. All of them had a motive for killing her.

Motive Specific need, desire, or want, such as hunger, thirst, or achievement, that prompts goal-oriented behavior.

Emotion Feeling, such as fear, joy, or surprise, that underlies behavior.

Motivation and emotion also play a role in some of the less dramatic events in the story. Motivated by hunger, the family sits down together to eat a meal. The poodle, motivated by curiosity or the call of nature, is attracted on repeated occasions to the neighbor's peonies. The next-door neighbor visits because he is lonely and longs for company. The parlor maid's guilt stems from activities that satisfy sexual urges. The tragedy of Amanda Jones's death brings the four suspects closer together out of a need for affiliation, but the fear generated by the murder prompts the self-preservation drive to kick in, making each of the suspects suspicious of the others.

In this story, motivation and emotion are so closely intertwined that it is difficult to draw distinctions between them. A **motive** is an inner directing force—a specific need or want—that arouses the organism and directs its behavior toward a goal. All motives are triggered by some kind of stimulus: a bodily need, such as hunger or thirst; a cue in the environment, such as the peonies in the garden; or a feeling, such as loneliness, guilt, or anger. When one or more stimuli create a motive, the result is goal-directed behavior (see Figure 9–1). **Emotion** refers to the experience of such feelings as fear, joy, surprise, or anger. Like motives, emotions also activate and affect behavior, but it is more difficult to predict the *kind* of behavior that a particular emotion will prompt. If a man is hungry, we can be reasonably sure that he will seek food. If, however, this same man experiences a feeling of joy or surprise, we cannot know with certainty how he will act.

The important thing to remember about both motives and emotions is that they push us to take some kind of action—from an act as drastic as murder to a habit as mundane as drumming our fingers on a table when we are nervous. Motivation occurs whether we are aware of it or not. We do not need to think about feeling hungry to make a beeline for the refrigerator or focus on our need for achievement to study for an exam. We do not have to consciously recognize that we are afraid to step back from a growling dog or know that we are angry before raising our voice at someone. Moreover, the same motivation or emotion may produce different behaviors in different people. Ambition might motivate one person to go to law school and another to join a crime ring. Feeling sad might lead one person to cry alone and another to seek out a friend. On the other hand, the same behavior might arise from different motives or emotions: You may buy liver because you like

Figure 9–1
How motivation works.
A *motive* is triggered by some kind of *stimulus*—a bodily need or a cue in the environment. A motive, in turn, activates and directs *behavior*.

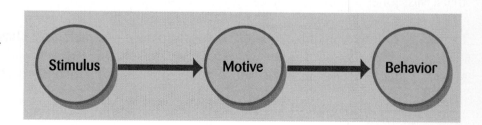

it, because it is inexpensive, or because you know that your body needs the iron it contains. You may go to a movie because you are happy, bored, or lonely. The workings of motives and emotions are very complex.

In this chapter, we will first look at specific motives that play an important role in human behavior. Then we will turn our attention to emotions and the various ways they are expressed.

PERSPECTIVES ON MOTIVATION

Early in the twentieth century, psychologists were inclined to attribute behavior to **instincts**—specific, inborn behavior patterns characteristic of an entire species. Inborn animal instincts motivate salmon to swim upstream to spawn and spiders to spin webs. In 1890, William James proposed such diverse human instincts as hunting, rivalry, fear, curiosity, shyness, love, shame, and resentment. But by the 1920s, instinct theory began to fall out of favor as an explanation of human behavior for two reasons: (1) Most significant human behavior is not inborn but learned through experience; and (2) human behavior is rarely rigid, inflexible, unchanging, and characteristic of the species. In addition, ascribing every conceivable human behavior to a corresponding instinct really explains nothing (calling a person's propensity to be alone an "antisocial instinct," for example, merely describes the behavior without pinpointing its origins). So after World War I, psychologists started looking for more credible explanations of human behavior.

One alternative view of motivation holds that bodily needs (such as the need for food or the need for water) create a state of tension or arousal called a **drive** (such as hunger or thirst). According to **drive-reduction theory,** motivated behavior is an attempt to reduce this unpleasant state of tension in the body and to return the body to a state of **homeostasis,** or balance. When we are hungry, we look for food to reduce the hunger drive. When we are tired, we go to sleep. When we are thirsty, we find something to drink. In each of these cases, behavior is directed toward reducing a state of bodily tension or arousal.

Drive reduction doesn't explain all motivated behavior, however. When we are bored, for instance, we may actually seek out activities that *heighten* tension and arousal. Some people go to horror movies, take up skydiving, or climb steep peaks just to raise their level of arousal. As we can see from these examples, human beings strive to maintain an optimal state of arousal: If arousal is too high, we will make efforts to reduce it; if arousal is too low, we will take steps to increase it.

To complicate matters further, some behavior isn't triggered by internal states at all. For example, bakery aromas may prompt us to eat, even if we have just finished a satisfying meal; a sample copy of a new magazine, a demonstration of a new product, or a store window display may lead us to buy something we would not have otherwise bought. In other words, objects in the environment—called **incentives**—can also motivate behavior Bolles, 1972; Rescorla & Solomon, 1967). Advertisers are well aware of the lure of incentives. Some psychologists believe that much of our behavior is motivated by *unconscious* drives. A middle-aged man may buy a new sports car, claiming that the car is fun to drive and well designed. But the purchase may also reflect his concerns about growing older, insecurity about his attractiveness, or an aggressive desire to be behind the wheel of the fastest car on the road.

Instinct Inborn, inflexible, goal-directed behavior that is characteristic of an entire species.

Drive State of tension or arousal brought on by biological needs.

Drive-reduction theory Theory that motivated behavior is aimed at reducing a state of bodily tension or arousal and returning the organism to homeostasis.

Homeostasis State of balance and stability in which the organism functions effectively.

Incentive External stimulus that prompts goal-directed behavior.

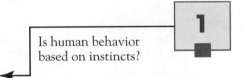

Is human behavior based on instincts?

Salmon swimming upstream to spawn provide an example of instinctive behavior. All salmon innately engage in this behavior without having to learn it from other salmon. Psychologists question whether human behavior can be explained in terms of instincts.

Intrinsic motivation A desire to perform a behavior that originates within the individual.

Extrinsic motivation A desire to perform a behavior to obtain an external reward or avoid punishment.

Primary drive Physiologically based unlearned motive, such as hunger.

Thrill-seeking behaviors cannot be explained by drive-reduction theory, because thrill-seekers are trying to *increase* arousal, not reduce it. Everyone sometimes seeks to increase arousal, but thrill-seekers seem to desire higher levels of arousal than most people do.

Along a similar line, psychologists sometimes refer to behavior as arising from either **intrinsic** or **extrinsic motivation.** Intrinsic motivation comes from *within* the individual. For example, when a little girl spontaneously picks up a pencil and paper and composes a letter to her grandparents, we would refer to her behavior as being intrinsically motivated. Children who climb trees and finger paint often are intrinsically motivated—just as adults who do crossword puzzles and tinker in a workshop may be. In contrast, when a child writes a letter to her grandparents in the hope that she will receive some reward (such as a gift from the grandparent) or as a requirement to receive her allowance, we would refer to her behavior as being extrinsically motivated—the child performs this behavior to receive some *external* reward or avoid some threat of punishment. Whether behavior is intrinsically or extrinsically motivated can have important consequences as the following statement from a report by the National Advisory Mental Health Council (1995) makes clear:

> When people pursue activities for their intrinsic interest they are especially likely to become and remain fascinated and absorbed by them and feel happy. Conversely, when people concentrate on the external rewards of particular tasks, they experience decreased emotional involvement and negative feelings. Studies have also revealed that higher intrinsic motivation is linked to higher school achievement and psychological adjustment in children, adolescents and college students. (p. 843)

The motivation section of this chapter begins with a look at hunger—a motive we are generally conscious of and that is primarily guided by internal biological states. From there we will turn to sexual behavior, which is responsive to both internal states and external incentives. We then examine several motives, such as curiosity and manipulation, that depend heavily on external environmental cues. Finally, we describe several additional motives that figure prominently in human social relationships.

PRIMARY DRIVES

Biological needs that trigger a corresponding state of psychological arousal or tension (a drive) are called **primary drives.** The unlearned drives—principally hunger, thirst, and sex—are common to all animals, including humans. Primary drives are strongly influenced by stimuli within the body that are part of the biological programming for survival of the organism (or, in the case of sex, with the survival of the species).

Hunger

When you are hungry, you eat. If you don't, your need for food will continue to increase. But your appetite, your feeling of hunger, will not necessarily increase. Suppose you decide to skip lunch to study at the library. Your need for food will not go away; in fact, it will increase throughout the day. But your hunger will come and go. You will probably be hungry around lunchtime; then your hunger will likely abate while you are at the library. But by dinnertime, no concern will seem as pressing as eating. The psychological state of hunger, then, is not the same as the biological need for food, although that need often sets the psychological state in motion.

Two centers in the brain are pivotal in our experience of and response to hunger. One, the hunger center, stimulates eating; the other, the satiety center ("satiety" means being full to satisfaction), reduces the feeling of hunger. Both centers are located in the hypothalamus. When the neurons in one of these centers are stimulated, the neurons in the other center fire less often. Thus, if your hunger center "tells" you that you are hungry, you will pick up few signals from the satiety center to contradict this message (see Figure 9.2). Scientists have also discovered that the sensation of hunger comes from more than just these two centers alone. Neurons that pass through the hunger and satiety centers on their way to other parts of the brain also appear to help regulate hunger. So do other areas of the hypothalamus (such as the *paraventricular nucleus*) as well as another part of the brain near the hypothalamus, called the *amygdala*, though its exact role has not been defined.

How do areas of the brain "know" when to signal hunger? Scientists believe that the brain monitors the level in the blood of a simple sugar called **glucose.** A fall in the glucose level stimulates neurons in the hunger center and inhibits neurons in the satiety center. Researchers see the same effect when the level of fats in the blood increases as the body draws down reserve energy supplies.

The brain also monitors the amount and kind of food that you have eaten, with some help from the stomach. Receptors in the stomach sense not only how much food the stomach is holding but also how many calories that food contains. (A stomach full of salad is far less satisfying to most people than a stomach full of turkey with all the trimmings.) Signals from these receptors go to the brain, where they stimulate the satiety center and make you feel less hungry.

These hunger mechanisms regulate our day-to-day intake of food. But there appears to be yet another hunger regulator, one that operates on a long-term basis to regulate the body's weight. Have you ever noticed that very few animals besides humans and some domesticated animals become grossly overweight? The body seems to have a way of monitoring its own fat stores and regulating the intake of food to provide just enough energy to maintain normal activities without storing excessive fat deposits.

Why can't humans do this? Their hunger does not always stem from a biological need for food. They are vulnerable to external cues, such as the smell of a cake baking in the oven, which may trigger the desire to eat at almost any hour of the day. Sometimes just looking at the clock and realizing that it is dinnertime may make us feel hungry. One intriguing line of research suggests that such external cues set off internal biological processes that mimic real internal needs. For example, Rodin (1985) found that the mere sight, smell, or thought of food causes an increase in insulin

Glucose Simple sugar that is the main source of body energy.

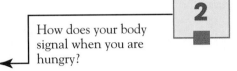

How does your body signal when you are hungry?

We do not know the precise role that the brain plays in hunger, but after lesions were made in the hypothalamus of this rat, it ate so much that its body weight tripled.

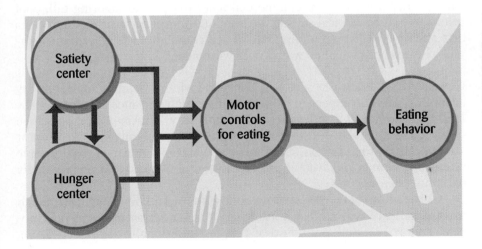

Figure 9–2
A diagram of the dual mechanisms in the brain that control hunger and eating.
The *hunger center* signals when you are hungry and stimulates eating. The *satiety center* reduces the feeling of hunger and the desire to eat.

Satiety center

Motor controls for eating

Eating behavior

Hunger center

production, which, in turn, lowers glucose levels in the body's cells, mirroring the body's response to a physical need for food. So the aroma from a nearby restaurant may serve as more than an incentive to eat; it may actually arouse the primary drive of hunger.

Recently, researchers have identified a mechanism in the brain that may be responsible for obesity (Chua et al., 1996; Leroy et al., 1996; Vaisse et al., 1996). According to this theory, fat cells within our body produce a hormone called *leptin*, which travels in the bloodstream and is sensed by the hypothalamus. High levels of leptin signal the brain to reduce appetite, or to increase the rate at which fat is burned. Research with mice suggests that a defective gene may fail to regulate the level of leptin in the brain and at least be partly responsible for obesity. Replacing this hormone in obese animals results in a rapid loss of body fat. Because leptin also appears to be involved in the human response to hunger (Ravussin et al., 1997), this finding may someday lead to safe and effective treatments for obesity in humans.

Emotions may also affect the hunger drive. Suppose you are very hungry, but in the midst of preparing dinner, you have a serious argument with your boyfriend or girlfriend. You may not want to eat for hours. Or imagine that you are sitting down to dinner when you receive a phone call notifying you that one of your favorite relatives has just died. You probably would not have much appetite after hearing that news. On the other hand, some people become hungry whenever they are anxious or nervous.

Social influences also affect our motivation to eat. Say you are at an important business lunch where you need to impress a prospective client. You may not feel very hungry, even though this lunch is taking place an hour past your usual lunchtime. Conversely, social situations may prompt you to eat even when you are *not* hungry. Imagine that on a day when you have slept late and eaten a large breakfast, you visit your grandparents. When you arrive, you discover, much to your dismay, that a wonderful home-cooked meal is being served in a few minutes. Although you are not at all hungry, you may decide to eat merely out of courtesy toward your grandparents.

Like hunger, thirst is stimulated by both internal and external cues. Internally, thirst is controlled by two regulators that interact and complement each other. One monitors the level of fluids inside the cells of the body, prompting activation of the thirst drive when the cells become dehydrated. The other thirst regulator monitors the amount of fluid outside the cells. When the level of extracellular fluid drops, less blood flows to the kidneys, which, in turn, releases a substance into the bloodstream that triggers the thirst drive (Epstein, Fitzsimmons, & Simmons, 1969).

Just as we become hungry in response to external cues, we sometimes get thirsty when we see a TV commercial featuring people savoring tall, cool drinks in a lush, tropical setting. Seasonal customs and weather conditions also affect our thirst-quenching habits: Ice-cold lemonade is a summer staple, whereas hot chocolate warms cold winter nights.

CULTURAL DIFFERENCES How you respond when you are hungry will vary according to your experiences with food, which are mostly governed by learning and social conditioning. The majority of Americans eat three meals a day at regular intervals. A typical American family eats breakfast at 7 A.M., lunch around noon, and dinner about 6 P.M. But in Europe, people often have dinner much later in the evening. Italians, for example, rarely eat dinner before 9 P.M.

Culture also influences what we choose to eat and how much. Although most Americans will not eat horse meat, it is very popular in several European countries. Some preindustrial peoples traditionally ate insect larvae,

How and when you satisfy hunger and thirst depends on social, psychological, environmental, and cultural influences as well as on physiological needs. For example, the Japanese tea ceremony is concerned more with restoring inner harmony than with satisfying thirst. Do you think the office worker in the top photo is drinking coffee because she is thirsty?

the thought of which would disgust most Americans. Yet many Americans consume pork, which violates both Islamic and Jewish dietary laws (Scupin, 1995). Just as in humans, the environment influences what animals eat as well. For example, rats and chimpanzees both prefer to consume foods that they have seen eaten by other members of their species. So although hunger is basically a biological drive, it is not merely an internal state that we satisfy when our body tells us to. Both the motivation to eat and overeating behavior are guided by psychological, cultural, and environmental considerations in addition to biological factors.

WEIGHT LOSS   Based on what we know about the hunger drive and the relationship between eating and body weight, how should someone go about losing excess weight? First, it is important to realize that the body interprets weight loss as a danger signal and takes a number of countermeasures to protect against further loss. So if you significantly reduce the number of calories in your diet, your weight will probably start to decline, but in response your body will lower your metabolism so that you need fewer calories to maintain your weight! This explains why some dieters, after losing 10 or 15 pounds, reach a plateau where further weight loss is more difficult to achieve. How does this process occur?

According to one theory, a homeostatic mechanism in the body known as the **set point** regulates metabolism, fat storage, and food intake (Bennett & Gurin, 1982). Set-point theory argues that the body is preprogrammed for

Set point A homeostatic mechanism in the body that regulates metabolism, fat storage, and food intake so as to maintain a preprogrammed weight.

Why do many people have so much trouble losing weight beyond a certain point?

APPLYING PSYCHOLOGY
LOSING WEIGHT INVOLVES MORE THAN JUST DIETING

To be successful, a program of weight control has to be long-term and work with, rather than against, the normal tendency of the body to maintain weight. That means finding a way to increase the body's metabolism. The most effective metabolism raiser is a regular program of exercise—20 to 30 minutes of moderate activity several times a week in which only 200 to 300 calories are burned off during each session (Craighead, 1990; Pi-Sunyer, 1987). Coupled with such an exercise program, dietary changes do reduce weight. A moderate reduction in calories is beneficial, but even more important is reducing the consumption of fats (particularly saturated fats) and substances (such as table sug-

ars and syrups) that trigger an increase in the body's level of insulin. High levels of fat and insulin in the blood stimulate the hunger center, and dietary fats are more easily stored by the body as fat than as muscle.

Dieters should also consider reducing, as much as possible, external cues that trigger hunger or encourage the eating of undesirable foods. The mere sight or smell of food can increase the amount of insulin in the body, thus triggering the hunger drive. If possible, keep foods high in calories or fat out of the house, or at least out of sight. Many people find that if they do their food shopping on a full stomach, they are less tempted to buy foods high in calories and fat.

Finally, set realistic goals for weight loss and focus at least as much on *maintaining* the lower weight that you reach as on losing more weight. If you need to lose weight, try to shed just 1 pound a week for 2 or 3 months, and then concentrate on maintaining that new, lower weight for the rest of the year before moving on to further weight loss. And most important, reward yourself—in ways unrelated to food—for small improvements. Use some of the behavior-modification techniques described in Chapter 5, Learning: Reward yourself not only for each pound of weight loss, but also for each day or week that you maintain that weight loss.

To learn more about weight and dieting, visit our website at **www.prenhall.com/morris**

Anorexia nervosa A serious eating disorder that is associated with an intense fear of weight gain and a distorted body image.

certain weight. If you regularly weigh about 150 pounds and gain 10 pounds on vacation, you will be able to lose the additional pounds relatively easily because you will be returning to a weight that is consistent with your body's set point. Set-point theory helps explain plateauing and backsliding among dieters, as well as why a thin person can consume the same number of calories as an overweight person and stay thin. It may also offer insights into how genes influence weight.

Set-point theory challenges the notion that there is one *ideal* body type. Indeed, achieving an ideal body has become an unhealthy obsession for many Americans that can lead to serious—sometimes life-threatening—eating disorders. Even when the drive to lose weight and become "fit" is not so extreme, it may reflect a lack of self-esteem more than a real need to lose weight. Researchers point out the need to separate overweight people who are close to their set-point weight from those who are unhealthily overweight or obese (more than 20 percent overweight). For people in the first group, acceptance of their body may contribute more to overall health than losing weight (Brownell & Rodin, 1994).

Set-point theory and the finding that there may be a genetic basis for body weight should not discourage those who are considerably overweight from trying to lose weight, because obesity may lead to serious health risks (Bray, 1986) as well as depression. Research has shown that even small weight losses in people who are obese can bring about significant improvements in blood pressure and blood sugar levels (Brownell & Rodin, 1994).

EATING DISORDERS "When people told me I looked like someone from Auschwitz [the Nazi concentration camp], I thought that was the highest compliment anyone could give me." This confession comes from a young woman who as a teenager suffered from a serious eating disorder known as **anorexia nervosa.** She was 18 years old, 5 feet 3 inches tall, and weighed 68 pounds. This young woman was lucky. She managed to overcome the disorder and has since maintained normal body weight. Others are less fortunate. In 1983, the singer Karen Carpenter died of cardiac arrest following a long battle with anorexia. More recently, the world-class gymnast Christy Henrich succumbed to the disease, weighing just 61 pounds at her death (Pace, 1994).

People with anorexia nervosa perceive themselves as overweight and strive to lose weight, usually by severely limiting their intake of food. Even after they become very thin, they constantly worry about weight gain. The following four symptoms are used in the diagnosis of anorexia nervosa (APA, 1994):

1. Intense fear of becoming obese, which does not diminish as weight loss progresses.

2. Disturbance of body image (for example, claiming to "feel fat" even when emaciated).

3. Refusal to maintain body weight at or above a minimal normal weight for age and height.

4. In females, the absence of at least three consecutive menstrual cycles.

Approximately 1 percent of all adolescents suffer from anorexia nervosa; about 90 percent of these are white upper- or middle-class females (Brumberg, 1988; Gilbert & DeBlassie, 1984; Romeo, 1984). Before the development of more successful treatment methods in recent years, perhaps as many as 6 percent of people with anorexia died from the disorder (Agras & Kraemer, 1983). Generally, people suffering from anorexia enjoy an other-

This photo of gymnast Christy Henrich was taken about a year before her death in June 1994. Henrich suffered from the eating disorder known as *anorexia nervosa,* as her gaunt appearance shows.

wise normal childhood and adolescence. They are usually successful students and cooperative, well-behaved children. They have an intense interest in food but view eating with disgust. They also have a very distorted view of their own body.

Anorexia is frequently compounded by another eating disorder known as **bulimia** (Fairburn & Wilson, 1993; Yanovski, 1993). The following criteria are used for the diagnosis of bulimia (APA, 1994):

1. Recurrent episodes of binge eating (rapid consumption of a large amount of food in a discrete period of time, usually less than 2 hours).

2. Recurrent inappropriate behaviors to try to prevent weight gain, such as self-induced vomiting.

3. The binge eating and compensatory behaviors must occur at least twice a week for 3 months.

4. Body shape and weight excessively influence the person's self-image.

5. These behaviors do not occur only during episodes of anorexia.

It is estimated that 4 to 8 percent of all adolescent females and up to 2 percent of adolescent males suffer from bulimia (Gwirtsman, 1984; Heatherton & Baumeister, 1991; Johnson et al., 1984).

The binge-eating behavior usually begins at about age 18, when adolescents are facing the challenge of new life situations. Not surprisingly, residence on a college campus is associated with a higher incidence of bulimia (Squire, 1983). The socioeconomic group at high risk for bulimia—again, primarily upper-middle- and upper-class women—is highly represented on college campuses. Also, college campuses foster social as well as academic competition. Some evidence suggests that bulimia is more prevalent on campuses where dating is emphasized than on those where it is not (Rodin, Striegel-Moore, & Silberstein, 1985).

Although anorexia and bulimia are apparently much more prevalent among females than males (Turnbull et al., 1996), many more men are affected by these disorders than was once suspected (Anderson, 1990; Tanofsky et al., 1997). For example, in a 1992 survey of people who had graduated from Harvard University in 1982, reported cases of eating disorders had dropped by half for women over the decade but had doubled for men (Seligman, Rogers, & Annin, 1994).

Because studies of eating disorders have focused almost entirely on females, we know very little about what might predispose an adolescent male to develop such a disorder. Among adolescent women, several factors appear likely (Brooks-Gunn, 1993). The media promote the idea that a woman must be thin to be attractive (Crandall, 1994). How often have you seen a fashion magazine cover feature a well-proportioned woman of normal weight for her height? Interestingly, an analysis of height-to-weight ratios of Playboy centerfolds and Miss America pageant contestants shows that the trend toward taller and thinner models of feminine beauty parallels the rise of eating disorders in the population at large (Agras, 1987). Perhaps because of this media emphasis on weight, American women are prone to overestimate their body size (Bruch, 1980; Fallon & Rozin, 1985). One study found that over 95 percent of the female subjects believed they were about one-fourth larger than they actually were in the waist, thighs, and hips (Thompson et al., 1986).

Psychological factors also contribute to the risk of eating disorders (Walters & Kendler, 1995). An individual with an obsessive-compulsive disorder (see Chapter 13, Psychological Disorders) who feels personally

Bulimia An eating disorder characterized by binges of eating followed by self-induced vomiting.

Testosterone The primary male sex hormone.

Pheromones Substance secreted by some animals; when scented they enhance the sexual readiness of the opposite sex.

ineffective and depends on others fits the portrait of an adolescent with an eating disorder (Phelps & Bajorek, 1991). Women with bulimia commonly have a lowered self-esteem and have experienced some form of clinical depression prior to the development of the eating disorder (Klingenspor, 1994). Feelings of vulnerability and helplessness apparently dispose people to adopt inappropriate ways of controlling the world around them.

Eating disorders are notoriously hard to treat, and there is considerable disagreement on the most effective approach to therapy (Garfinkel & Garner, 1982). In fact, some psychologists doubt that we can ever eliminate eating disorders in a culture bombarded with the message that "thin is in." Regrettably, in many developing countries such as Taiwan, Singapore, and China, where dieting is becoming a fad, eating disorders, once little known, are now becoming a serious problem (Hsu, 1996).

Sex

Sex is the primary drive that motivates reproductive behavior. Like the other primary drives, it can be turned on and off by biological conditions in the body and by environmental cues. But it differs from them in one important way: Hunger and thirst are vital to the survival of the individual, but sex is vital only to the survival of the species.

Describing the physiology of sexual behavior, sex researchers William Masters and Virginia Johnson identified a *sexual response cycle* that consists of four phases: excitement, plateau, orgasm, and resolution (Masters & Johnson, 1966). In the *excitement phase*, the man's penis becomes engorged with blood and erect, and the woman's breasts and clitoris swell. This engorgement of the sexual organs continues into the *plateau phase*, in which sexual tension levels off as breathing becomes more rapid and genital secretions and muscle tension increase. During *orgasm*, the male ejaculates and the woman's uterus contracts, as both men and women experience a loss of muscle control. The *resolution phase* is one of relaxation in which muscle tension decreases and the engorged penis and clitoris return to normal. Heart rate, breathing, and blood pressure also return to normal.

BIOLOGICAL FACTORS IN SEXUAL BEHAVIOR At one time it was thought that fluctuations in the level of hormones like **testosterone**—the male sex hormone—*determined* sex drive. Today we realize that hormonal influences on human sexual behavior are considerably more complex. Testosterone plays a role in early sexual development (such as the onset of puberty), the differentiation of male and female sex organs, and to some extent in establishing characteristic patterns of adult sexual behavior (Kalat, 1988). But moment-to-moment fluctuations in testosterone levels are not necessarily linked to sex drive. In fact, adult males who have been castrated (resulting in a significant decrease in testosterone levels) often report little decrease in sex drive (Persky, 1983). Unlike lower animals whose sexual activity is largely controlled by hormones and is tied to the female's reproductive cycle, humans are capable of sexual arousal at any time.

Scientists suspect that, as in other animals, subtle smells may affect the sex drive in humans. Many animals secrete substances called **pheromones** that, when smelled by the opposite sex, promote sexual readiness (see Chapter 3). Some indirect evidence suggests that humans, too, secrete pheromones, in the sweat glands of the armpits and in the genitals (Michael, Bonsall, & Warner, 1974). The perception of these odors may influence human sexual attraction as well (Wedekind et al., 1995).

The brain exerts a powerful influence on the sex drive, too. In particular, the limbic system, located deep within the brain, is involved in sexual excitement (see Chapter 2, Biological Basis of Behavior). When experimenters implanted electrodes into the limbic system of male monkeys, they located three areas that, when stimulated, caused erections (Hyde, 1982). Two human subjects, who had electrodes placed in their limbic systems for therapeutic reasons, reported sexual pleasure when the electrodes were electrically stimulated (Heath, 1972).

PSYCHOLOGICAL AND CULTURAL INFLUENCES ON SEXUAL MOTIVATION

Although hormones and the nervous system do figure in the sex drive, human sexual motivation, especially in the early stages of excitement and arousal, is much more dependent on experience and learning than on biology.

What kind of stimuli activate the sex drive in humans? It need not be anything as immediate as a sexual partner. Erotic fantasies (Laan et al., 1995), the sight of one's lover, the smell of perfume or after-shave lotion—all of these can stimulate sexual excitement. As with the other drives, experience shapes human responses to the sexual drive. Soft lights and music often have an aphrodisiac effect. One person may be unmoved by an explicit pornographic movie but aroused by a romantic love story, whereas another may respond in just the opposite way. The human sexual response is also affected by social experience, sexual experience, nutrition, emotions—particularly feelings about one's sex partner—and age. In fact, just thinking about sex can arouse the sex drive in humans (Leitenberg & Henning, 1995). Ideas about what is moral, appropriate, and pleasurable also influence our sexual behavior.

Men and women tend to be sexually aroused in different ways. In general, men are more aroused by visual cues, whereas women respond more to touch (Schulz, 1984). A man may be aroused to erection simply by watching his partner undress, but a woman may need to have her body caressed to achieve the same state of arousal. In addition, although descriptions or scenes of sexual activity are arousing to both men and women, the rate of arousal in women is slow compared with the instantaneous response that often occurs in males (Christensen, 1986). The focus of interest also differs for males and females: Men tend to favor viewing close-ups of sexual acts, whereas women respond more to style, setting, and mood (Masters, Johnson, & Kolodny, 1982).

Men and women also differ somewhat in sexual experiences, though these differences are less pronounced than we might expect. According to one survey by the National Opinion Research Center (NORC), women are more likely to have had only one sexual partner since age 18 (31 percent of women as compared with only 20 percent of men), yet roughly the same proportion of women (22 percent) and men (23 percent) reported having from five to ten sexual partners since age 18. However, women were somewhat less likely than men to be satisfied sexually. The survey found that 95 percent of men, single or married, said they usually or always had an orgasm, compared with 75 percent of married women and 62 percent of single women. When it came to thinking about sex, more than half of the men surveyed said that they thought about sex every day or several times a day, whereas only 19 percent of women reported thinking about sex so often (Lewin, 1994b).

Just as society dictates standards for sexual conduct, culture guides our views of sexual attractiveness. Culture and experience may influence the extent to which we find particular articles of clothing or body shapes sexually arousing. In some cultures, most men prefer women with very large breasts, but in other cultures small delicate breasts are preferred. Among some

Do his elongated ear lobes and other bodily adornments enhance this young man's sexual attractiveness? It all depends on your cultural point of view. In the Samburu society of Kenya in which he lives, these particular adornments are considered highly attractive.

African cultures, elongated earlobes are considered very attractive. In our own culture, what we find attractive often depends on the styles of the time.

As creatures grounded in individual societies and cultures, our primary biological drives, including sex, are strongly guided by environmental cues. By the same token, sexual dysfunctions—including diminished or nonexistent sexual drive—may be traced to both biological and psychological factors. We will examine sexual dysfunctions in depth in Chapter 13, Psychological Disorders.

SEXUAL ORIENTATION   As described in Chapter 1, *sexual orientation* refers to the direction of an individual's sexual interest. A person with a *heterosexual orientation* is sexually attracted to members of the opposite sex. People with a *homosexual orientation* are sexually attracted to members of their own sex, whereas *bisexuals* are attracted toward members of both sexes. Early surveys (Kinsey et al., 1948, 1953) estimated that approximately 10 percent of the population was homosexual. More recent statistics, however, indicate that only about 2.8 percent of males and 1.4 percent of females have a homosexual orientation (Laumann et al., 1994; Sell, Wells, & Wypij, 1995).

Why people display different sexual orientations, and in particular homosexuality, has been argued for decades in the form of the classic nature versus nurture debate. Those on the nature side hold that sexual orientation has its roots in biology and is primarily influenced by genetics. They point out that homosexual men and women generally knew before puberty that they were "different" and often remained "in the closet" regarding their sexual orientation for fear of recrimination. They cite evidence from family and twin studies that show a higher incidence of homosexuality in families with other gay men, and a higher rate of homosexuality among men with a homosexual twin (even when the twins were raised separately) (LeVay & Hamer, 1994). The nature position also derives support from studies that have shown the sizes of specific brain structures may differ between homosexual and heterosexual men (Allen & Gorski, 1992; LeVay, 1991; Swaab & Hoffman, 1995).

On the nurture side are those who hold that sexual orientation is primarily a learned behavior, influenced by early experience and largely under voluntary control. They criticize research supporting the biological position as methodologically flawed—sometimes confusing what causes homosexuality with what results from homosexuality (Byne, 1994). They contend that early socialization determines sexual orientation. Moreover, they find support for their position from cross-cultural studies that show a difference in the frequency of different sexual orientations between cultures.

To date, neither the biological theories (nature) nor the socialization theories (nurture) have provided a completely satisfactory explanation for the origin of sexual orientation. As with most complex behaviors, a more likely explanation probably involves a combination of these two positions rather than either taken in isolation (Kelley & Dawson, 1994).

In our discussion so far, we have moved from motives that heavily depend on biological needs (hunger and thirst) to a motive that (in humans, at least) is considerably more sensitive to external cues (sex). In the next section, we will continue this progression by examining some motives that are even more responsive to environmental cues.

STIMULUS MOTIVES

Like the primary drives, **stimulus motives** are largely unlearned, but in all species, these motives are more dependent than primary drives on external stimuli—things in the world around us. Whereas primary drives are associated with the survival of the organism or the species, stimulus motives are associated with obtaining information about the environment. Motives such as *curiosity*, *exploration*, *manipulation*, and *contact* push us to investigate, and often to change, our environment.

Exploration and Curiosity

Where does that road go? What is in that dark little shop? How does a television set work? How will a real-life mystery be solved? What is the answer to the question about Hobbits and Orcs on page 273? Answering these questions has no obvious benefit: You do not expect the road to take you anywhere you need to go or the shop to contain anything you really want. You are not about to start a TV repair service or use an unknown tool. You just want to know. Exploration and curiosity are motives sparked by the new and unknown and directed toward no more specific goal than "finding out." The family dog will run around a new house, sniffing and checking things out, before it settles down to eat its dinner. Even rats, when given a choice, will opt to explore an unknown maze rather than run through a familiar one (see Figure 9–3).

Psychologists disagree about the nature and causes of curiosity (Loewenstein, 1994). William James viewed it as an emotion; Freud considered it as a socially acceptable expression of the sex drive. Others have seen it as a response to the unexpected and as evidence of a human need to make sense of or find meaning in life. We might assume that curiosity is a key component of intelligence, but studies attempting to establish a positive correlation between the two have been inconclusive. However, curiosity has been linked to creativity (Loewenstein, 1994).

Curiosity can also vary according to our familiarity with events and circumstances. As we continually explore and learn from our environment, we raise our threshold for the new and complex, and in turn our explorations and our curiosity become much more ambitious. In this respect, curiosity is linked to cognition. A gap in our understanding may stimulate our curiosity. But as our curiosity is satisfied and the unfamiliar becomes familiar, we tend to become bored. This, in turn, prompts us to explore our surroundings further (Loewenstein, 1994).

Manipulation and Contact

Why do you suppose that museums have *Do Not Touch* signs everywhere? It is because the staff knows from experience that the urge to touch is

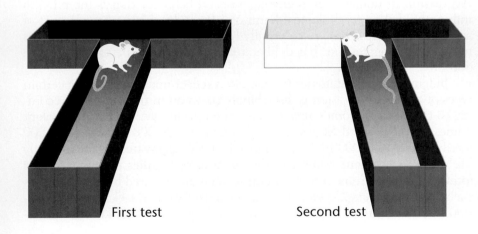

First test   Second test

Figure 9–3
Curiosity at work.
On a first trial, a rat will explore either one of the black arms of the maze at random. On a second trial, however, given a choice between a black arm and a white one, a rat will consistently choose the unfamiliar one.

Social motive Learned motive associated with relationships among people, such as the needs for affiliation, achievement, and power.

Aggression Behavior aimed at doing harm to others; also the motive to behave aggressively.

An infant monkey with Harlow's surrogate "mothers"—one made of bare wire, the other covered with soft terrycloth. The baby monkey clings to the terrycloth "mother," even though the wire "mother" is heated and dispenses food. Apparently, there is contact comfort in the cuddly terrycloth that the bare wire "mother" can't provide.

irresistible. Unlike curiosity and exploration, manipulation focuses on a specific object that must be touched, handled, played with, and felt before we are satisfied. Manipulation is a motive limited to primates, which have agile fingers and toes.

People also want to touch other people. The need for *contact* is more universal than the need for manipulation. Furthermore, it is not limited to touching with the fingers—it may involve the whole body. Manipulation is an active process, but contact may be passive.

In a classic series of experiments, Harry Harlow demonstrated how important our need for contact is (Harlow, 1958; Harlow & Zimmerman, 1959). Newborn baby monkeys were separated from their mothers and given two "surrogate mothers." Both "mothers" were the same shape, but one was made of wire mesh and had no soft surfaces. The other was cuddly—layered with foam rubber and covered with terry cloth. Both "mothers" were warmed by means of an electric light placed inside them, but only the wire-mesh "mother" was equipped with a nursing bottle. Thus the wire-mesh "mother" fulfilled two physiological needs for the infant monkeys: the need for food and the need for warmth. But baby monkeys most often gravitated to the terry-cloth "mother," which did not provide food: When they were frightened, they would run and cling to it as they would to a real mother. Because both mothers were warm, the researchers concluded that the need for affection, cuddling, and closeness goes deeper than a need for mere warmth. More recently, the importance of contact has been demonstrated with premature infants. Low-birth-weight babies who were held and massaged gained weight faster and were calmer than those who were touched only minimally (Field, 1986).

OTHER IMPORTANT MOTIVES

We are not born with all our motives intact. In fact, as we have already seen, some motives that appear to be innate—such as hunger, thirst, and sex—are actually partly learned. As we develop, new motives that are even more strongly influenced by learning govern our behavior. Some of these motives, such as aggression, may exert just as much influence over our behavior as primarily unlearned drives and motives do. We will first look at aggression, a complex motive shaped both by biological and environmental factors. Then we will consider some of the most crucial **social motives**—achievement, power, and affiliation—which center on our relationships with other people.

Aggression

Aggression in human beings encompasses all behavior that is intended to inflict physical or psychological harm on others. Intent is a key element of aggression (Beck, 1983). Accidentally hitting a pedestrian with your car is not an act of aggression, but deliberately gunning for a person whom you don't like is aggressive.

Judging from the statistics (which often reflect underreporting of certain types of crimes), aggression is disturbingly common in this country. According to the *FBI's Uniform Crime Reports*, there were over 1.9 million violent crimes in the United States in 1992, including 24,000 murders, 110,000 forcible rapes, 672,000 robberies, and 1,100,000 aggravated assaults. Family life also has a violent underside: One-quarter of families experience some form of violence. Some 3 to 4 million women are battered by their partners each year; more than 25 percent of these battered women seek medical attention for their injuries. In addition, over 1 million cases of child abuse are re-

A scene from a shelter for battered women. In the United States, women are frequent targets of aggression by men.

ported each year (National Research Council Panel on Child Abuse and Neglect, 1993), and more than 1,000 children die annually as a result of abuse.

Why is aggression so widespread? According to one view, it is a vestige of our evolutionary past that is triggered by pain or frustration (Lorenz, 1968). Some evidence suggests that pain and frustration may prompt aggressive behavior. In one experiment, a pair of rats received painful electric shocks through a grid in the floor of their cage; frustrated in their efforts to escape, they started to fight each other. As the frequency and intensity of the shocks increased, so did the fighting (Ulrich & Azrin, 1962). Frustration plays a role in human aggression as well. One experiment divided subjects into two groups who were both told they could earn money by soliciting charitable donations over the telephone (Kulik & Brown, 1979). One group was informed that previous callers had been quite successful in eliciting pledges; the other group was led to expect only scant success. Each group was given a list of prospective donors, all of whom had instructions to refuse to pledge any money. The subjects who had been led to believe that success would come easy tended to argue with uncooperative respondents and even slam down the phone. They expressed considerably more frustration than the other group.

Although studies like this one reveal a link between frustration and aggression, frustration does not always produce aggression. In fact, individuals have very different responses to frustration: Some seek help and support, others withdraw from the source of frustration, and some choose to escape into drugs or alcohol. Frustration seems to generate aggression only in people who have learned to be aggressive as a means of coping with unpleasant situations in general (Bandura, 1973).

Freud considered aggression an innate drive, similar to the hunger and thirst drives, that builds up until it is released. In his view, one important function of society is to channel the aggressive drive into constructive and socially acceptable avenues, such as sports, debating, and other forms of competition. If Freud's analysis is correct, then expressing aggression should reduce the aggressive drive. Yet this does not always hold true. Sometimes angry people who are encouraged to express their aggression find their anger dissipating, but nonangry people prodded to express aggression may actually become more aggressive (Doob & Wood, 1972).

MOTIVATION AND EMOTION   359

Yerkes-Dodson law States that there is an optimal level of arousal for the best performance of any task; the more complex the task, the lower the level of arousal that can be tolerated before performance deteriorates.

B. I *hate* thunderstorms—I always have. Don't you think we ought to shut off all the lights so we won't attract the lightning? My grandmother used to hide in a closet till a thunderstorm was over, and I don't blame her.

C. (*Going to the window*): Look at it! It's fantastic—the way the blue flashes light up everything! It makes the whole world different. I've always loved thunderstorms—they're so wild and happy. They make me feel so alive!

A is frustrated and angry: This category of emotions moves us to *approach* something, but in an aggressive or hostile way. B is fearful and anxious: These emotions make us want to *avoid* something. C is happy and exhilarated, experiencing a sense of release and joy: These emotions prompt us to *approach* something in a positive way.

But emotions, like motives, may trigger a chain of complex behavior that goes far beyond simple approach or avoidance reactions. For example, if we are anxious about something, we may collect information about it, ask questions, and then decide whether to approach it, flee from it, or stay and fight it. Imagine a family faced with an anxiety-provoking situation: The husband and wife have both been temporarily laid off from their jobs; several months of severe economic hardship lie ahead, and they are anxious. Where should supplementary income be found? How should family goals be adjusted? Will it be possible for the family to survive the crisis without suffering too seriously? Faced with these uncertainties and the anxiety they create, the family decides to tackle the problem through a series of positive strategies. The husband, who is knowledgeable about cars, goes to work for his neighbor, who owns an automobile repair shop. The wife takes advantage of her former employer's offer to return to a part-time position. Their daughter attends a local campus of the state university instead of a more expensive private college. In short, the emotional anxiety brought on by this situation has focused the family members on the crisis at hand and triggered a complex sequence of goal-directed behavior in much the same way that motives do.

Of course, our emotions sometimes overwhelm our good sense. Most of us have found ourselves in situations in which we desperately wanted to think rationally but could not because our emotions were getting in the way of our concentration. Under what circumstances does emotion hinder what we do, and when does it help? Psychologists agree that there is no single simple answer. Rather, it is largely a question of degree—of both the strength of the emotion and the difficulty of the task. The **Yerkes-Dodson law** puts it this way: The more complex the task, the lower the level of arousal that can be tolerated without interfering with performance. You may feel very angry while boiling an egg, without it making much difference in how well you perform that task, but the same degree of emotional arousal may interfere with your ability to drive safely. Although a certain minimal level of arousal is necessary for good performance, a very high level may hamper your performance (see Figure 9–5).

Basic Emotional Experiences

Emotions, then, may be broadly grouped according to how they affect our behavior—whether they motivate us to approach or to avoid something. But within these broad groups, how many different emotions are there?

Many people have attempted to identify and describe the basic emotions experienced by humans (Ekman, 1980; Plutchik, 1980; also see Cor-

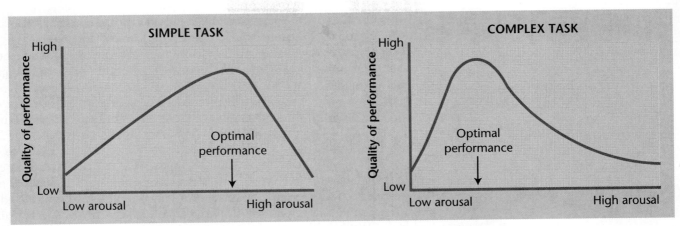

Figure 9–5
Graphs illustrating the Yerkes-Dodson law.
A certain amount of arousal is needed to perform most tasks, but a very high level of arousal interferes with the performance of complicated activities. That is, the level of arousal that can be tolerated is higher for a simple task than for a complex one.

Source: After Hebb, 1955.

nelius, 1996). Robert Plutchik (1980), for example, proposes that animals and human beings experience eight basic categories of emotions that motivate various kinds of adaptive behavior: *fear, surprise, sadness, disgust, anger, anticipation, joy,* and *acceptance.* Each of these emotions helps us adjust to the demands of our environment, although in different ways. Fear, for example, underlies flight, which helps protect animals from their enemies; anger propels animals to attack or destroy.

Emotions adjacent to each other on Plutchik's emotion "circle" (see Figure 9–6) are more alike than those situated opposite each other or that are farther away from each other. Surprise is more closely related to fear than to anger; joy and acceptance are more similar to each other than either is to disgust. Moreover, according to Plutchik's model, different emotions may combine to produce an even wider and richer spectrum of experience. Occurring together, anticipation and joy, for example, yield optimism; joy and acceptance fuse into love; surprise and sadness make for disappointment.

Within any of Plutchik's eight categories, emotions vary in intensity, represented by the vertical dimensions of the model in Figure 9–7. At the top of the figure lie rage, vigilance, ecstasy, adoration, terror, amazement, grief, and loathing—the most intense forms of his eight basic emotions. As we move toward the bottom, each emotion becomes less intense, and the distinctions among the emotions become less sharp. Anger, for example, is

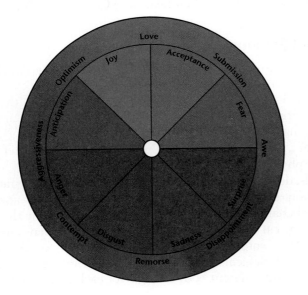

Figure 9–6
Plutchik's eight basic categories of emotion.
Emotions adjacent to each other on Plutchik's emotion "circle" are more alike than those that lie opposite each other or are farther apart. When adjacent emotions are combined, they yield new but related emotions. For example, sadness mixed with surprise leads to disappointment.

Source: Plutchik, 1980.

James-Lange theory States that stimuli cause physiological changes in our bodies, and emotions result from those physiological changes.

5

True or False: Different peoples throughout the world categorize emotions in essentially the same way.

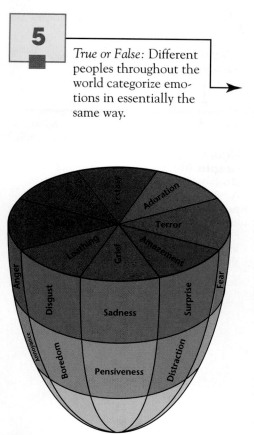

Figure 9–7
Plutchik's three-dimensional model of the eight basic emotions.
Within any of the categories, emotions vary in intensity. Intensity is represented on the vertical dimension of the model, ranging from maximum intensity at the top to a state of deep sleep at the bottom. The model tapers inward at the bottom to indicate that emotions are less clearly distinguishable from one another at low intensities. Note that the eight basic emotions are a more moderate expression of the most intense emotions.

Source: Plutchik, 1980.

less intense than rage, and annoyance is even less intense than anger. But all three emotions—annoyance, anger, and rage—are closely related.

Some scientists challenge the *universality* of Plutchik's model, noting that it may apply only to the emotional experience of English-speaking people. Anthropologists report enormous differences in the ways that other cultures view and categorize emotions. Some languages, in fact, do not even have a word for "emotion" (J. A. Russell, 1991). Languages also differ in the number of words they have to name emotions. English includes over 2,000 words to describe emotional experiences, but Taiwanese Chinese has only 750 such descriptive words. One tribal language has only 7 words that could be translated into categories of emotion. Interestingly, words used to name or describe an emotion may influence how that emotion is experienced. For example, the Tahitian language has no direct translation for the concept of sadness. Instead, Tahitians experience sadness in terms of physical illness. The sadness we feel over the departure of a close friend would be experienced by a Tahitian as, say, exhaustion. Some cultures lack words for anxiety or depression or guilt. Samoans have one word encompassing love, sympathy, pity, and liking—all distinct emotions in our own culture (J. A. Russell, 1991).

More recent attempts to classify the richness and varieties of the human emotional experience have generally used cross-cultural methodologies (Ekman et al., 1987; Izard, 1994). For example, one group of researchers asked participants from 10 countries to interpret photographs depicting various facial expressions of emotions (Ekman et al., 1987). (We will look at facial expressions of emotion in more detail later in this chapter.) The percentage of participants from each country who correctly identified the emotions ranged from 60 to 98 percent, and there was a high level of agreement across the 10 cultures. The researchers use this and other evidence to argue for the *universality* of these six emotions—*happiness, surprise, sadness, fear, disgust,* and *anger* (see also Cornelius, 1996). You might note that love is not included in this list. Although Ekman did not find a universally recognized facial expression for love, many psychologists nevertheless hold that love does represent a basic human emotion (Hazan & Shaver, 1987). Its outward expression, however, may owe much to the stereotypes promoted by a culture's media (Fehr, 1994). In one study in which American college students were asked to display a facial expression for love, the participants mimicked the conventional "Hollywood" prototypes such as sighing deeply, gazing skyward, and holding their hand over their heart (see Cornelius, 1996).

Theories of Emotion

Why do we feel on top of the world one minute and down in the dumps the next? What causes emotional experiences?

The American psychologist William James formulated the first modern theory of emotion in the 1880s; at almost the same time, a Danish psychologist, Carl Lange, reached the same conclusions. According to the **James-Lange theory,** stimuli in the environment (say, seeing a ferocious grizzly bear) cause physiological changes in our bodies (accelerated heart rate, enlarged pupils, deeper or shallower breathing, increased perspiration, a gooseflesh sensation as body hairs stand on end), and emotions arise from those physiological changes. The emotion of fear, then, is simply the awareness of these physiological changes. All of this, of course, happens almost instantaneously and in an automatic way.

If these physiological changes alone *cause* specific emotions, we should be able to pinpoint different body changes for each emotion. Perhaps butterflies in the stomach make us afraid and blushing causes shame or guilt. And, indeed, some evidence shows that the physiological changes associated with fear and anxiety are somewhat different from those that accompany anger and aggression (McGeer & McGeer, 1980). Similarly, fear and anger appear to be distinguishable from happiness by subtle changes in heart rate acceleration (Levenson, 1992). We also may process different emotions on different sides of the brain. Positive emotions are accompanied by an increase in the electrical activity on the left side of the brain, whereas negative emotions result in more activity on the right side (Davidson, 1992). But beyond this, psychologists have not found distinct bodily states that account for all our various emotions. Moreover, as we saw in Chapter 2, sensory information about bodily changes flows to the brain through the spinal cord. If bodily changes are the source of emotions, then people with severe spinal cord injuries should experience fewer and less intense emotions. Research, however, has demonstrated that this is not so (Chwalisz, Diener, & Gallagher, 1988). Thus, bodily changes do not cause specific emotions and may not even be necessary for emotional experience.

An alternative theory of emotions, the **Cannon-Bard theory,** dating back nearly 70 years, holds that processing of emotions and bodily responses occur simultaneously, not one after another. Thus, when you see the bear, you feel afraid *and* you start running—neither of these precedes the other.

Recently, cognitive psychologists have developed and extended this idea by contending that our perception or judgment of situations (cognition) is absolutely essential to our emotional experience of those situations (Lazarus, 1982, 1991a, 1991b, 1991c). All emotional states involve arousal of the nervous system, but, according to the **cognitive theory** of emotion, the situation that we are in when we are aroused—the environment—gives us clues as to how we should respond to this general state of arousal. Thus, our cognitions tell us how to label our diffuse feelings in a way that suits our current thoughts and ideas about our surroundings. (See Figure 9–8 for a comparison of these three theories of emotion.)

In a fascinating test of the cognitive theory of emotion (Spiesman, 1965), people were shown a violent, stress-inducing film that aroused strong emotional responses. But the researcher was able to manipulate people's emotional responses to the film by varying the sound track. Those who heard a sound track that narrated what was happening in the film responded with more emotion than those who saw the film with no accompanying narration. But those who heard a sound track that described the events in a detached and clinical way and those who heard a sound track that glossed over, denied, or spoke in glowing terms about what was depicted experienced much less emotion than either of the first two groups. These results show that our emotional responses are directly and sharply affected by how we interpret a situation, or how it is interpreted for us.

Later attempts to repeat these experiments, however, have not always produced the same results (Hogan & Schroeder, 1981). Interpreting emotional states may be a two-part process: People respond to emotional arousal with a quick appraisal of their feelings, and then they search for environmental cues to back up their assessment. In the process, they pay greater attention to internal cues that agree with external cues; thus, they tend to experience the kind of emotion they expect to experience (Pennebaker & Skelton, 1981).

Although a cognitive theory of emotion makes a great deal of sense, some critics reject the idea that feelings always stem from cognitions. Quoting the poet e. e. Cummings, Zajonc argues that "feelings come first." Human infants, he points out, can imitate emotional expressions at 12 days

Cannon-Bard theory States that the experience of emotion occurs simultaneously with biological changes.

Cognitive theory States that emotional experience depends on one's perception or judgment of the situation one is in.

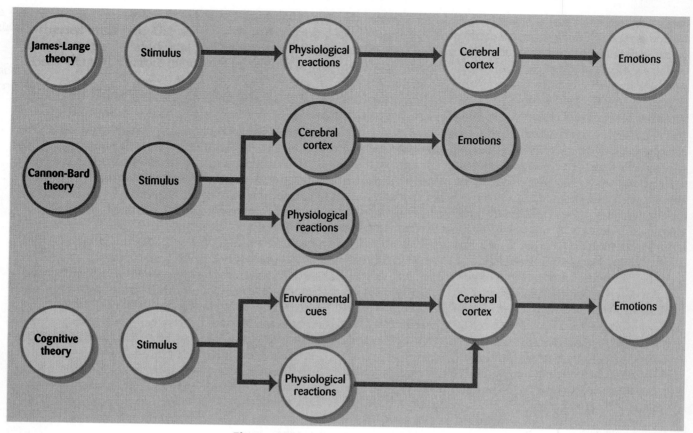

Figure 9–8
The three major theories of emotion.
According to the *James-Lange theory,* the body first responds physiologically to a stimulus, and then the cerebral cortex determines which emotion is being experienced. The *Cannon-Bard theory* holds that impulses are sent simultaneously to the cerebral cortex and the peripheral nervous system; thus, the response to the stimulus and the processing of the emotion are experienced at the same time, but independently. *Cognitive theorists* assert that the cerebral cortex interprets physiological changes in the light of information about the situation to determine which emotions we feel.

of age, well before they acquire language. Animals rely on their sense of danger to survive: A rabbit doesn't evaluate the possibilities that might account for a rustle in the bushes before it runs away (Zajonc, 1980). Zajonc notes that the affective (emotional) system has the ability to respond instantaneously to the situations in which we find ourselves, without taking time to interpret and evaluate those situations. But some affective reaction is fairly diffuse and difficult to explain. When we feel sort of jittery, a cross between nervous and excited, we ask ourselves, "What's going on?" Zajonc (1984) believes that we invent explanations to label feelings: Cognition thus comes *after* emotion.

Another direct challenge to the cognitive theory claims that emotions can be experienced without the intervention of cognition (Izard, 1971). According to this view, a situation such as separation or pain provokes a unique pattern of unlearned facial movements and body postures that may be completely independent of conscious thought (Trotter, 1983). When information about our facial expressions and posture reaches the brain, we automatically experience the corresponding emotion. According to Izard, then, the James-Lange theory was essentially right in suggesting that emotional experience arises from bodily reactions. But Izard's theory stresses facial expression and body posture as crucial to the experience of emotion, whereas the James-Lange theory emphasized muscles, skin, and internal organs.

Considerable evidence supports the contention that facial expressions do influence emotions (Adelmann & Zajonc, 1989; Cappella, 1993; Ekman & Davidson, 1993; Zajonc, Murphy, & Inglehart, 1989). If further research bolsters Izard's theory, we will be able to say with certainty that a key element in determining our emotional experience is our own expressive behavior, the next topic in this chapter.

THE EXPRESSION OF EMOTION

Sometimes you are vaguely aware that a person makes you feel uncomfortable. When pressed to be more precise, you might say: "You never know what she is thinking." But you do not mean that you never know her opinion of a film or what she thought about the last election. It would probably be more accurate to say that you do not know what she is *feeling*. Almost all of us conceal our emotions to some extent to protect our self-image or to conform to social conventions. But usually we give off some clues to help others determine what we are feeling.

Verbal Communication

If your roommate finishes washing the dishes and says acidly, "I hope you are enjoying your novel," the literal meaning of his words is quite clear, but you know very well that he is not expressing pleasure at your choice of reading material. If he were to say, "I am furious that you did not offer to help clean up after dinner," he would be giving you an accurate report of his emotions at that moment.

For many reasons, we may be unable or unwilling to report our emotions accurately. In some situations, people simply cannot pinpoint what they are feeling. A father who abuses his child may sincerely profess affection for the child, yet act in ways that reflect emotions far removed from tender affection—feelings that are hidden from his own awareness. Even when we are aware of our emotions, we sometimes minimize the degree of emotion that we are feeling: We may say we are "a little worried" about an upcoming exam when in fact we are terrified. Or we may deny the emotion entirely, especially if it is negative (hatred toward a parent or sibling, for example). So often what people say does not mirror what they are feeling. Thus, we must frequently turn to other cues to emotion if we are to understand them fully.

Nonverbal Communication

"Actions speak louder than words," the saying goes, and people are often more eloquent with their bodies than they realize or intend. We transmit a good deal of information to others through our facial expressions, body postures, and physical distance—in fact, our bodies often send emotional messages that contradict our words.

Here's an example of this process at work. A pickpocket goes to work at a football game. Standing behind someone, the nimble-fingered thief prepares to relieve the person of his wallet. Slowly, the thief's hand moves toward the victim's back pocket and is almost touching the wallet, when suddenly the thief pulls his hand back empty. The pickpocket moves casually through the crowd, whistling. What went wrong? What gave the thief a clue that his intended victim might have been about to reach for his wallet? A pickpocket skillful enough to stay out of jail learns to heed all kinds of signs:

The hairs on the back of the victim's neck might have bristled slightly; there might have been an almost imperceptible stiffening of the back, a twitch in a neck muscle, a subtle change in skin color, a trickle of sweat. The victim might not yet have been consciously aware that his pocket was about to be picked, but these signals showed that he was physiologically aware something was afoot. These kinds of physiological changes are not normally under our control. They tend to function independently of our will—indeed, often against it. (See the *Controversies* box.)

CONTROVERSIES
TRUTH IS MORE THAN SKIN DEEP: THE LIE DETECTOR

Lie detectors do not register lies. What the peaks and valleys on a polygraph actually reflect are the emotional conflicts that lead to specific physiological changes. When people lie, they usually experience uncontrollable changes in blood pressure, in breathing, and in the resistance of the skin to electrical current, known as galvanic skin response. However, no set of responses definitively indicates that a person has been lying; the pattern of responses varies from person to person (Saxe, 1994).

In the typical lie detector situation, failing the test has serious consequences. Thus, subjects generally become quite nervous and fearful as the blood pressure cuff is strapped to their arm, sensors designed to measure breathing are attached to their chest and stomach, and electrodes are placed on their fingertips to measure galvanic skin response. Because the blood pressure cuff soon starts cutting off circulation, the examination must be completed within 3 to 4 minutes.

Not surprisingly, then, lie detectors are far from perfect in identifying liars. Figures vary widely, but according to one estimate, polygraphs correctly identify only about 75 percent of those who are lying. About 49 percent of people telling the truth are falsely branded as liars (Horvath,

1977). One major source of error: Galvanic skin response changes in reaction to all kinds of emotions, not just those associated with deception (Lykken, 1975). When someone is asked if he committed a murder, the lie detector is likely to surge. Although this reaction may reflect guilt, it may also signal anxiety, fear, or loathing—all possible reactions to being suspected of murder. If the subject were questioned about marital problems, relationships with parents, or even attitudes toward work, the polygraph might register a similar sharp peak, indicating emotional response (Stern et al., 1981). Subjects' feelings about the accuracy of the test also have an impact on the strength of their physiological reactions. The more accurate subjects believe the polygraph to be, the more arousal they are likely to experience when responding deceptively (Saxe, 1994).

Personal and social factors may affect the physiological signs monitored by the machine. The galvanic skin response of some people changes quickly and spontaneously, making it more likely that their truthful answers will appear to be lies. The degree to which examiner and subject are matched in terms of

About 49 percent of people telling the truth are falsely branded as liars.

sex, age, race, and ethnicity may have an impact on polygraph results. In one study, the lie detector failed most often when examiner and subjects shared the same ethnicity, possibly because the subjects felt most at ease in this situation (Waid & Orne, 1981).

Complicating this issue even more is that preconceptions based on individual or social biases may color how officials interpret the results of a lie detector test. In each case, someone must decide whether to trust the results. Uncertainty about lie detector results encourages a great deal of subjectivity in deciding whether to accept them—and such decisions can have very serious consequences. Who makes those decisions? On what basis? To what degree are such decisions affected by people's preconceptions? Those who feel the polygraph's unreliability is a serious drawback are convinced that polygraph examinations pose more risks than benefits for society.

Questions

1. How can decisions about the results of a polygraph test be affected by prejudice?

2. Should life or death decisions about guilt or innocence be influenced by polygraph tests?

Facial expressions are the most obvious emotional indicators. We saw earlier that facial expressions may actually cause some emotional experiences. Facial expressions are also good indicators of the emotions a person is experiencing, from whatever source. We can tell a good deal about a person's emotional state by observing whether that person is laughing, crying, smiling, or frowning. Many facial expressions are innate, not learned (Ekman, 1994). Children who are born deaf and blind use the same facial expressions as other children do to express the same emotions. Charles Darwin first advanced the idea that most animals share a common pattern of muscular facial movements. For example, dogs, tigers, and humans all bare their teeth in rage. Darwin also observed that expressive behaviors serve a basic biological as well as social function. Darwin's notion that emotions have an evolutionary history and can be traced across cultures as part of our biological heritage laid the groundwork for many modern investigations of emotional expression (Izard, 1992; Izard, 1994). Today, psychologists who take an evolutionary approach believe facial expressions served an adaptive function, enabling our ancestors to compete successfully for status, to win mates, and to defend themselves (Ekman, 1992; Tooby & Cosmides, 1990).

Body language is another way we communicate messages nonverbally. When we are relaxed, we tend to stretch back into a chair; when we are tense, we sit more stiffly with our feet together. Slumping and straightness of the back supply clues about which emotion someone is feeling. Beier (1974) videotaped subjects acting out six emotions: anger, fear, seductiveness, indifference, happiness, and sadness. Although most subjects could accurately portray two out of the six emotions, the rest of their portrayals did not reflect their intentions. Indeed, one young woman appeared angry no matter which emotion she tried to project; another was invariably seductive.

What do psychologists mean by "body language"?

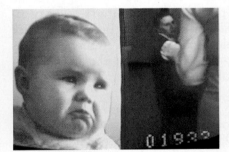

Sadness: Brows' inner corners raised, mouth drawn out and down.

Interest: Brows raised or knit, mouth softly rounded, lips pursed.

Distress: eyes tightly closed; mouth as in anger, squared and angular.

Joy: Mouth forms smile, cheeks lifted, twinkle in eyes.

Working from Charles Darwin's theory that certain emotional and facial expressions have an evolutionary basis, psychologist Caroll Izard believes he has isolated ten universal emotions that can be seen in the facial expressions of infants. Four are illustrated here.

When having a conversation, most Arabs stand closer to one another than most Americans do. In our society, two men would not usually stand as closely together as these two Arabs unless they were very aggressively arguing with each other (a baseball player heatedly arguing with an umpire, for example).

Body communication is also reflected in personal distance. The normal conversing distance between people differs from culture to culture. Two Swedes conversing would ordinarily stand much farther apart than would two Arabs or Greeks. If someone within your own culture is standing closer than usual to you, it may indicate aggressiveness or seductiveness; if farther away than usual, it may indicate withdrawal or repugnance.

Explicit *acts*, of course, can also serve as nonverbal clues. When we receive a telephone call at 2 A.M., we expect that the caller has something urgent to say. A slammed door tells us that the person who just left the room is angry. If friends drop in for a visit and you invite them into your living room, you are probably less at ease with them than with friends who generally sit down with you at the kitchen table. Gestures, such as a slap on the back or an embrace, can also indicate feelings. Whether people shake your hand briefly or for a long time, firmly or limply, tells you something about how they feel about you.

A word of caution is needed here. Although overt behavior may offer a clue to a person's feelings, it is not an *infallible* clue. Laughing and crying sound alike, for example, and we bare our teeth in smiles as well as in snarls. Crying may signify sorrow, joy, anger, nostalgia—or that you are slicing an onion. Moreover, as with verbal reports, someone may be projecting false clues. We all have done something thoughtlessly—turned our backs, frowned when thinking about something else, laughed at the wrong time—that has given offense because these acts were misinterpreted as an expression of an emotion that we were not, in fact, feeling at the time. In all these cases, nonverbal cues do not correspond well to the actual emotions being felt.

We not only sometimes send out complex and contradictory emotional messages by nonverbal cues, but also sometimes misread such messages. In fact, most people overestimate their ability to interpret nonverbal cues. For example, in one study of several hundred "professional lie catchers," including members of the Secret Service, government lie detector experts, judges, police officers, and psychiatrists, every group (except for the psychiatrists) rated themselves above average in their ability to tell whether another person was lying. The subjects then viewed a set of 10 videotapes: Some showed a person lying; others showed a person telling the truth. In every instance when the person was lying, telltale changes in that person's behavior showed up on the videotape. Nonetheless, only the Secret Service agents managed to identify the liars at a better-than-chance rate (Ekman & O'Sullivan, 1991). Similar results have been obtained with other groups of people (e.g., DePaulo & Pfeifer, 1986).

Closely related to the ability to read other people's emotions is *empathy*—the arousal of emotion in an observer who responds vicariously to another's situation (Parke & Asher, 1983). Empathy depends not only on our ability to identify someone else's emotions but also on our capacity to put ourselves in the other person's place and to experience an appropriate emotional response. Just as sensitivity to nonverbal cues increases with age, so does empathy: The cognitive and perceptual abilities required for empathy develop only as a child matures.

7 Is it true that men generally feel less emotion than women?

GENDER AND EMOTION

Experience tells us that males and females differ considerably in how they express emotion and the emotions they choose to express. For example, men are often perceived as being less emotional than women. But is it that men feel less emotion, or are they simply less likely to *express* the emotions they feel? And are there some emotions that men are more likely to express than women?

Recent research sheds some light on these issues. In one study, when men and women saw depictions of people in distress, the men showed little emotion but the women expressed feelings of concern for those in distress (Eisenberg & Lennon, 1983). However, physiological measures of emotional arousal (such as heart rate and blood pressure) showed that the men in the study were actually just as affected as the women were. The men simply inhibited the expression of their emotions, whereas the women were more open about their feelings. Emotions such as sympathy, sadness, empathy, and distress are often considered to be "unmanly," and boys are trained from an early age to suppress those emotions in public (O'Leary & Smith, 1988).

In other circumstances, men and women react with very different emotions to the same situation. For example, in one study subjects responded to hypothetical situations in which they were betrayed or criticized by another person (Brody, 1985). Males usually said that they would feel angry; females were likely to report that they would feel hurt, sad, or disappointed.

When men get angry, they tend to interpret the source of their anger as something or someone in the environment around them, and they generally turn their anger outward, against other people and against the situation in which they find themselves. Women, as a rule, are more likely to see themselves as the source of the problem and turn their anger inward, against themselves. Given these gender-specific reactions, it is not surprising that men are four times more likely than women to become violent in the face of life crises, whereas women are much more likely than men to become depressed.

Men, in general, often have less skill than women at decoding the emotional expressions of others. One reason may be that men aren't usually the primary caregivers of children who are too young to speak, and so they get less practice "reading" emotion in the face and body. As traditional sex roles in our society change and fathers take a larger role in the care of very young children, many men may become more attuned to the subtleties of emotional expression.

Some women do allow themselves to feel anger and hostility. But if they don't allow themselves to *express* their anger, they are at a very serious health risk (Julius et al., 1986). Tracking a group of women over 18 years, the study found that those who scored high on hostility were three times more likely to die during the course of the study than those who scored low. However, this higher level of risk applied only to subjects who said they got angry in many situations but did not vent their anger. Other subjects who reported frequent bouts of anger, which they expressed, were in the same low-risk group as those who said they rarely or never felt angry.

At the most basic level there are two aspects to communicating emotion: (1) sending an emotional message (through facial expressions, tone of voice, posture, and so on); and (2) perceiving the emotional content of a message sent by someone else. According to the stereotype, women are more expressive than men, which suggests that they should be better "senders" of emotional information. Furthermore, the popular notion of "women's intuition" suggests that women should be better than men at perceiving or "decoding" the emotional expressions of others.

Research indicates that these stereotypes have a kernel of truth. A meta-analysis of studies in this area (Hall, 1984) concluded that women are more skilled than men at decoding the facial expressions, body cues, and tones of voice of others. Several explanations could account for these gender differences (Taylor, Peplau, & Sears, 1994). One is that because many women are the primary caregivers for preverbal infants, they need to become more attuned than men to the subtleties of emotional expressions. Consistent with an evolutionary perspective, some have even suggested that this skill may be genetically programmed into females. Another explanation is based on the social power held by women and men. Because women historically have occupied less powerful positions in society, they may have felt the need to become acutely attuned to the emotional displays of others, particularly those in more powerful positions (namely, men). Indeed, one researcher found that regardless of gender, followers are more sensitive to the emotions of leaders than vice versa (Snodgrass, 1992).

The fact that men are more likely than women to hold positions of power may affect emotional experience in other ways as well. In the types of jobs traditionally held by women, workers are often called on to regulate, manage, or otherwise alter their emotional expression. Sociologist Arlie Hochschild (1983) described this process as *emotional labor*. In a study of flight attendants, the majority of whom were women, Hochschild found clear guidelines regarding which emotions were to be displayed, to whom, by whom, and how often. Most of the flight attendants felt they were being robbed of genuine emotional experiences on the job: ". . . [I]n the flight attendant's work, smiling is separated from its usual function, which is to express a personal feeling, and attached to another one—expressing a company feeling" (p. 127). Hochschild also noted that jobs that are high in emotional labor—such as secretaries, registered nurses, cashiers, social workers, and bank tellers—tend to be filled by women.

CULTURE AND EMOTION

Emotional experiences across cultures are similar in certain ways and very different in others. The death of a loved one, for example, is sure to produce feelings of grief and sadness in all cultures. Similarly, being unexpectedly attacked will produce fear and surprise in anyone. In contrast, the feelings experienced after a job promotion are likely to differ depending on one's cultural values and the meaning one attaches to personal success. If you perceive your work as an individual effort, you will no doubt feel proud, happy, and perhaps boastful when you are promoted. If, however, you see your success as reflecting the efforts of your group, you will still be happy, but you will probably be more humble about taking individual credit for the success, perhaps even ashamed.

For psychologists, the key issue is how the larger defining elements of cultures help shape emotional experiences. One defining element is whether a culture is individualist or collectivist, a distinction we mentioned earlier. For example, the English language has many terms for self-focused emotions (anger, sadness), whereas the Japanese language has many terms for other-focused emotions (sympathy, empathy) (Markus & Kitayama, 1991). This difference parallels the predominantly individualist orientation of most English-speaking cultures and the collectivist orientation of Japanese culture. The emotions of people in collectivist cultures also tend to be shorter in duration than those of individualists (Markus & Kitayama, 1991). American college students, for example, reported experiencing emotions that lasted longer, were more intense, and were accompanied by more bodily symptoms than emotions reported by Japanese students (Matsumoto et al., 1988). Matsumoto and his colleagues suggest that, in general, "collective cultures will foster emotional displays of their members that maintain and facilitate group cohesion, harmony, or cooperation to a greater degree than individualistic cultures" (p. 132).

How a cultural dimension like individualism/collectivism might explain these differences is just now being investigated (Scherer & Wallbott, 1994), largely because research on how various cultures define, acknowledge, and experience emotions is relatively recent. Most of the well-established findings in the psychology of emotions come from studies of emotional expression within a single culture.

Culture and the Facial Expression of Emotion

Among nonverbal channels of communication, facial expressions seem to communicate the most specific information. Hand gestures or posture can communicate general emotional states (e.g., feeling bad), but the complexity of the muscles in the face allows facial expressions to communicate very specific feelings (e.g., feeling sad, angry, or fearful). That is why researchers studying cultural differences in emotional communication have focused on facial expressions.

Some researchers have argued that across cultures, peoples, and societies, the face looks the same whenever certain emotions are expressed; this is known as the *universalist* position. Charles Darwin subscribed to this view, arguing that part of our common evolutionary heritage was to use the same expressions to convey the same emotions. In contrast, other researchers support the *culture-learning* position, which holds that facial expressions of emotion are learned within a given culture and therefore may differ greatly from one culture to the next. Which view is more accurate?

We have a wealth of information regarding how emotions are expressed and understood in a cultural context (Ekman, 1993; Ekman & Friesen, 1986; Ekman et al., 1987). As we saw earlier in the chapter, Ekman and his colleagues have concluded from cross-cultural studies that at least six primary emotions are accompanied by universal facial expressions: happiness, sadness, anger, surprise, fear, and disgust. Carroll Izard (1980) conducted similar studies in England, Germany, Switzerland, France, Sweden, Greece, and Japan with similar results. These studies seem to support the universalist position: Regardless of culture, people tended to agree on which emotions others were expressing facially. However, this research does not completely rule out the culture-learning view. Because the participants were all members of developed countries that likely had been exposed to one another through movies, magazines, and tourism, they might simply have become familiar with the facial expressions seen in other cultures. A stronger test was needed that reduced or eliminated this possibility.

This test was made possible by the discovery of several contemporary cultures that had been totally isolated from Western culture for most of their existence. Members of the Fore and the Dani cultures of New Guinea, for example, had their first contact with anthropologists only a few years before Ekman's research took place. They provided a nearly perfect opportunity to test the universalist/culture-learning debate. If members of these cultures gave the same interpretation of facial expressions and produced the same expressions on their own faces as people in Western cultures, there would be much stronger evidence for the universality of facial expressions of emotion. Ekman and his colleagues (Ekman & Friesen, 1971; Ekman, Sorenson, & Friesen, 1969) presented members of the Fore culture with three photographs of people from outside their culture and asked them to point to the picture that represented how they would feel in a certain situation. For example, if a participant was told "Your child has died and you feel very sad," he or she would have the opportunity to choose which of the three pictures most closely corresponded to sadness. The results indicated very high rates of agreement on facial expressions of emotions. Moreover, when photographs of the Fore and Dani posing the primary emotions were shown to college students in the United States, the same high agreement was found

Display rules Culture-specific rules that govern how, when, and why facial expressions of emotion are displayed.

(Ekman & Friesen, 1975). In summary, it appears that facial expressions of primary emotions are indeed universal.

If this is true, why are people so often confused about the emotions being expressed by people in other cultures? For example, an American student living with a Japanese family might sense her hosts were disappointed about some decision she had made, yet they continued to smile. If facial expressions reliably convey emotional states, why did her Japanese hosts appear to be pleased at her mistakes?

The answer lies in a principle called **display rules** (Ekman & Friesen, 1975). Display rules refer to the circumstances under which it is appropriate for people to show emotion on their faces. In essence, display rules help govern which emotions get displayed, by whom, to whom, and under what conditions. Some common display rules intensify, deintensify, mask, or neutralize one's expression. You practice *intensification* when you exaggerate your facial expression and *deintensification* when you mute your facial expression. For example, when showing greater joy than you are actually experiencing at a surprise party your friends have thrown for you, you are following the intensification display rule that dictates "Look happy and thrilled when people unexpectedly do nice things for you." *Masking* is a quite different display rule: Here you are feeling one emotion but showing a completely different one. Smiling when you are feeling sad is an example. Finally, *neutralizing* means keeping a "poker face," or showing a blank expression, regardless of what you are feeling. Following this rule might be appropriate in situations that require you to be "strong and silent."

Although facial expressions of primary emotions have a universal quality, display rules differ substantially from culture to culture. In a study of Japanese and American college students (Ekman, Friesen, & Ellsworth, 1972), the subjects watched graphic films of surgical procedures, either by themselves or in the presence of an experimenter. The students' facial expressions were secretly videotaped as they viewed the films. The results showed that when the students were by themselves, both the Japanese and the Americans showed facial expressions of disgust (precisely the emotion the films were intended to elicit). This supports the universality of facial expressions: Members of two very different cultures showed virtually the same facial expression in response to the same emotional event. But when the subjects watched the film in the presence of an experimenter, the two groups displayed different responses. American students continued to show disgust on their faces, but the Japanese students showed facial expressions that were more neutral, even somewhat pleasant.

Why the sudden switch? The answer lies in the different use of display rules by members of the two cultures. The Japanese norm says "Don't display strong negative emotion in the presence of a respected elder" (in this case, the experimenter). Americans typically don't honor this display rule; hence, they expressed their true emotions whether they were alone or with someone else. Similarly, the student's Japanese hosts undoubtedly were displeased with some of her decisions, but they displayed positive emotions out of respect for their guest. To interpret what others are feeling, we need to understand both the universal expression of emotions *and* the particular rules operating in a culture.

Unlike facial expressions of primary emotions which have a universal quality, other forms of nonverbal communication vary from one culture to another. This is especially true of *emblems*, or hand gestures that have a specific meaning (Johnson, Ekman, & Friesen, 1975). Giving someone the "thumbs up," for example, or circling your thumb and index finger in an "OK" sign, or flashing a friend two fingers in a "V" shape all have well-

Figure 9–9
People throughout the world use the "brow-raise" greeting when a friend approaches.

Source: Eibl-Eibesfeldt, I (1972). *Love and Hate.* New York: Holt, Rinehart, Winston.

defined meanings within U.S. culture. Outside this cultural context, however, these emblems may either be meaningless or take on very different meanings.

Cultures also differ in the amount of touch that takes place among people, the distance between people who are interacting, and the amount of eye contact that is appropriate between friends, business partners, loved ones, and strangers. One form of eye contact, however, is almost universal: the "brow-raise" greeting used when a friend approaches (Figure 9–9) (Eibl-Eibesfeldt, 1972). The next time a friend approaches you, watch to see whether he or she uses this greeting.

SUMMARY

Motivation and emotion help guide our behavior. **Motives** are specific inner needs or wants that arouse an organism and direct its behavior toward a goal. **Emotions** are experiences of feelings such as fear, joy, or surprise, which also underlie behavior.

PERSPECTIVES ON MOTIVATION
At the turn of the twentieth century, psychologists believed that motivated behavior was caused by **instincts,** specific, inborn behavior patterns characteristic of a species. **Drive-reduction theory** viewed motivated behavior as a strategy to ease an unpleasant state of tension or arousal (a **drive**) and return the body to a state of **homeostasis,** or balance. Today scientists assert that an organism seeks to maintain an optimum state of arousal. External stimuli called **incentives** also prompt goal-oriented behavior. Finally, motivation can be **intrinsic** (coming from within the individual) or **extrinsic** (for external reward or avoidance of punishment).

PRIMARY DRIVES
In some instances, a biological need triggers a corresponding state of psychological arousal or tension. This unlearned drive is called a **primary drive.** Hunger, thirst, and sex are the principal primary drives.

Hunger
Hunger is primarily regulated by two centers in the brain: the hunger center, which stimulates eating, and the satiety center, which reduces the feeling of hunger. Whenever the level of the simple sugar **glucose** in the blood falls to a certain point, neurons in the hunger center are stimulated. Receptors in the stomach and a hormone released by the small intestine also send signals to the brain. Another hunger regulator monitors long-term body weight. Both the motivation to eat and overeating are influenced by biological, psychological, cultural, and environmental factors.

Thirst parallels hunger in that both internal and external cues can trigger the thirst drive. Dehydration both inside and outside the cells prompts activation of the thirst drive; so do weather conditions as well as social, psychological, and cultural influences, and other external stimuli.

Weight loss is difficult to achieve and maintain for many obese people because the body appears to have a homeostatic mechanism, known as the **set point,** that regulates metabolism, fat storage, and food intake so as to maintain a preprogrammed weight. Genetic factors also play a major role in determining who is thin and who is overweight.

Anorexia nervosa is a serious eating disorder associated with an intense fear of weight gain and a distorted body image. Another eating disorder known as **bulimia** is characterized by binges of eating followed by self-induced vomiting. Eating disorders are notoriously difficult to treat, especially in a culture obsessed with dieting.

Sex

Sex is a primary drive that gives rise to reproductive behavior essential for the survival of the species. The sexual response cycle in humans progresses through four phases: excitement, plateau, orgasm (climax), and resolution.

Biological factors have a complex effect on sexual response. The male sex hormone **testosterone** influences early development, male/female differentiation, and to some extent characteristic patterns of adult sexual behavior. It is also possible that scents, called **pheromones,** secreted by one sex promote sexual readiness in the other sex.

Psychological influences are at least as important as biological influences in stimulating sexual arousal. People have individual preferences for certain fantasies, pictures, words, music, and so on. Men tend to be aroused by visual cues; women respond more to touch. What we find attractive is also influenced by our culture.

Sexual orientation refers to the direction of an individual's sexual interest—heterosexuals are sexually attracted to members of the opposite sex, homosexuals to members of their own sex, and bisexuals toward members of both sexes. As with most complex behaviors, the origins of sexual orientation appear to involve both biological and environmental factors.

STIMULUS MOTIVES

Like primary drives, **stimulus motives** are largely unlearned. Stimulus motives place a premium on obtaining information about the environment and depend more on external stimuli than on internal states.

Exploration and Curiosity

Exploration and curiosity are motives activated by the unfamiliar and are directed toward the goal of discovering how the world works. Psychologists disagree on the nature and causes of curiosity, but it has been linked to creativity.

Manipulation and Contact

Humans and primates need to manipulate objects to gain both tactile information and a sense of comfort.

Contact, the need for affection and closeness, is another important stimulus motive. Although manipulation requires active "hands-on" exploration, contact may be passive.

OTHER IMPORTANT MOTIVES

As we develop, our behavior is governed by a number of new motives strongly influenced by learning: aggression and the **social motives**—achievement, power, and affiliation—which center on our relationships with others.

Aggression

Any behavior that is intended to inflict physical or psychological harm on others is an act of **aggression.** Some psychologists consider aggression part of an unlearned instinct that is triggered by pain and frustration; others see it as an innate drive that must be channeled into constructive avenues. Many contemporary psychologists believe aggression is a learned response, modeled after the aggressive behavior of others.

Cultural differences in aggressiveness are reflected in statistics on violent crimes. Individualist cultures, which value personal independence, tend to be high in crime, whereas collectivist cultures, emphasizing interdependence and group cohesion, tend to be lower. Research has also linked the dimension of individualism/collectivism to how various cultures interpret aggressive behavior.

Across cultures and at every age, males are more likely than females to behave aggressively both in verbal and physical ways. Both biological and social factors appear to contribute to these gender differences.

Achievement

The **achievement motive,** a learned social motive, underlies the desire to excel, to overcome obstacles, and to strive to do something difficult as well as possible. The need for achievement, which varies among individuals, has been measured using the Thematic Apperception Test (interpretations of drawings) and the Work and Family Orientation scale, a questionnaire that measures work orientation, mastery, and competitiveness. It has been found that a high degree of competitiveness may actually interfere with achievement.

Power

The **power motive** is defined as the need to win recognition or to influence or control other people or groups. College students who score high in the need for power tend to hold important positions on campus and pursue careers in teaching, psychology, and business.

Affiliation

The **affiliation motive,** the need to be with other people, is especially pronounced when people feel threatened. But we may also choose to get together with others to obtain positive feedback or to give us the physical contact we crave. Our need for affiliation may have an evolutionary basis stemming from the survival value associated with maintaining formal social relationships.

A HIERARCHY OF MOTIVES

Abraham Maslow suggested that the various motives—learned and unlearned, social and primary drives—can be arranged in a hierarchy. The lower motives spring from bodily needs that must be satisfied for survival; the higher motives, such as the striving to belong or to achieve self-esteem, do not emerge until the more basic motives have largely been satisfied. Recent research challenges this view by indicating that in some societies difficulty in meeting lower needs can actually foster the satisfaction of higher needs.

EMOTIONS

Emotions, like motives, both arouse and direct our behavior. They tend to prompt us to move toward or away from an object. However, also like motives, emotions may trigger a complex chain of behavior that may promote or interfere with the accomplishment of our goals. According to the **Yerkes-Dodson law,** the more complex the task, the lower the level of emotional arousal that can be tolerated without interfering with performance.

Basic Emotional Experiences

Robert Plutchik's classification system for emotions uses a "circle" to position eight basic categories of emotions that motivate various kinds of adaptive behavior. However, not all cultures view or categorize emotions this way; some do not even have a word for emotion. Others describe feelings by their physical sensations.

A cross-cultural analysis of emotional expression has led Paul Ekman and his colleagues to argue for the universality of at least six emotions—*happiness, surprise, sadness, fear, disgust,* and *anger.* Many psychologists also add love to this list of basic emotions.

Theories of Emotion

According to the **James-Lange theory,** environmental stimuli bring on physiological changes in our bodies and emotions then arise from those physical changes. The **Cannon-Bard theory** states that the processing of emotions and bodily responses occurs simultaneously rather than one after the other. The **cognitive theory** of emo-

tion holds that the situation that we are in when we are aroused—the overall environment—gives us clues that help us interpret this general state of arousal. According to recent research, facial expression may influence emotions apart from cognition.

THE EXPRESSION OF EMOTION

Verbal Communication

What people say about what they are feeling often doesn't accurately reflect their emotions. In some cases, they may not know or be aware of what they are feeling; in others, they may choose to minimize or conceal their feelings.

Nonverbal Communication

Facial expressions are the most obvious nonverbal emotional indicators. It seems there are certain inborn or universal facial expressions that serve an adaptive function. Body language—our posture, the way we move, our preferred personal distance from others when talking to them—also expresses emotion. Explicit acts, such as slamming a door, are another clue to someone's emotional state. People vary in their sensitivity to nonverbal cues.

GENDER AND EMOTION

When confronted with a person in distress, women are more likely than men to express emotion about the situation, even though the levels of physiological arousal for the two sexes are the same. In some stressful situations men and women label what they are feeling differently. Women also tend to be better at decoding emotional expression and tend to regulate their own expression more than men.

CULTURE AND EMOTION

The individualism/collectivism dimension helps to explain the diversity across cultures in the experience of emotions. Members of collectivist cultures, for example, tend to have many terms for other-focused emotions, have emotions of shorter duration, and promote emotional displays that are designed to maintain group cohesion.

Culture and the Facial Expression of Emotion

Facial expressions of the primary emotions appear to have a universal quality: The face shows a similar expression for a given emotion regardless of the cultural background of the expressor. These cross-cultural findings run counter to the culture-learning view, which suggests that facial expressions of emotion are learned within a particular culture.

Overlaying the universal expression of emotion are **display rules,** which govern when it is appropriate to show emotion: to whom, by whom, and under what circumstances. These do tend to differ from culture to culture. Common display rules include intensification, deintensification, masking, and neutralizing.

Other forms of nonverbal communication vary more from culture to culture than facial expressions do. Understanding the way emotion is communicated in a cultural context requires knowing both the universal aspects of such communication and the cultural rules that govern in the specific communication setting.

REVIEW QUESTIONS

MULTIPLE CHOICE AND SHORT ANSWER

1. Both _____ and _____ direct our behavior and can activate behavior even without our awareness.

2. Motivation begins with which of the following?
   a. emotion
   b. drive
   c. stimulus
   d. arousal

3. According to drive-reduction theory, the state of balance toward which motivated behavior is directed is called _____.

4. True or False: Primary motives are not at all affected by learning or experience.

5. In the brain, signals from the _____ center stimulate eating, whereas those from the _____ center reduce the desire to eat.

6. A category of wants or needs that is activated by external stimuli and pushes us to investigate our environment is called _____ motives.

7. A person who is willing to contend with the high risks of a career in sales is probably motivated by a high _____ motive.

8. The _____ motive is sometimes aroused when a person needs to be consoled or supported by a group of peers.

9. True or False: According to Maslow, humans are motivated to realize their highest potential.

10. According to the _____-_____ law, there is a relationship between the complexity of a task and the level of emotional arousal that can be tolerated while performing the task.

11. Robert Plutchik asserts that emotions vary in _____, a fact that accounts in part for the great range of emotions we experience.

12. True or False: Cultural differences, particularly language, influence how we experience emotion.

13. Match the following theories of emotion with their definitions:

    _____ Cannon-Bard   a. States that physical reactions come before experienced emotions

    _____ Cognitive theory   b. Contends that emotions and bodily responses occur simultaneously

    _____ James-Lange   c. Says that emotional experience depends on the perception of a given situation

14. Izard's theory of emotion stresses the importance of
    a. cognition
    b. expressive behavior

15. Two important nonverbal clues to emotion are _____ _____ and _____ _____.

CRITICAL THINKING AND APPLICATIONS

1. Recent research confirms that obesity has a much larger genetic component than scientists previously thought. Will this finding change our society's attitudes toward people who are overweight? If so, how? Will it prompt people to think differently about their own weight problems? If so, how?

2. We often view people who get low grades in school or do poorly on the job as lacking motivation. What are some other possible explanations for their substandard performance?

3. Some research reveals that boredom inspires curiosity; other studies show that curiosity is piqued by the new and unknown. Explain why these findings do not contradict each other. How would you apply these concepts in an elementary-school classroom?

4. Think about how you experience and handle feelings of love, anger, and sadness. Do you express all these emotions with equal ease? Do any of these emotions make you uncomfortable? Are your responses to these feelings typical of your gender and culture? In what ways?

ENDURING ISSUES

Diversity
After reading this chapter, to what extent do you think that people's emotions and motivations differ depending on their race or culture or gender? Are there sex differences in the ability to control emotions?

Person–Situation
To what extent are emotions and motives triggered by and under the control of external events? To what extent do you think people can exercise control over their emotions and motivations?

Mind–Body
Are "happiness" or "sadness" simply the result of complex biological processes, or are they at least in part separate from biological processes?

(Answers to the Review Questions appear in the back of the book.)

10 Life Span

Development

Kay's was a very unusual childhood. Born the fourth of five children in a very wealthy family, she grew up in palatial houses tended by large staffs of servants. Yet oddly enough, she had no sense of being wealthy. Money was never talked about in her home, and she and her brother and sisters were never showered with expensive toys. From her earliest days she saw herself as shy, passive, and lacking self-assurance, dowdy and never quite "measuring up." She envied her second sister's rebellious nature, but didn't have the courage to be rebellious herself. Her mother did nothing to nurture greater self-confidence. She set such high expectations for her children that

Think About It!

1. How do psychologists study changes across the life span?
2. How and why can drug use by a pregnant woman affect her child?
3. Does the behavior of an infant or a young child provide any clues as to how that person will behave as an adult?
4. How do young children learn languages?
5. Does television watching influence children's behavior?
6. *True or False*: Most psychologists consider adolescence to be an exceptionally stressful time of life.
7. What is Alzheimer's disease? Can it be treated?
8. *True or False*: Elderly people are much less afraid of death than are younger people.

reaching those heights seemed an impossible goal. The man Kay married was brilliant, witty, charming, and extremely successful. He dominated all the decisions in their family life. He was the creative thinker, she the implementer. He was the provider of excitement and zest, she the dutiful follower. And yet, after quietly suffering her husband's bouts of heavy drinking, his unpredictable anger, his long

Biographical (or **retrospective**) **study** A method of studying developmental changes by reconstructing subjects' past through interviews and investigating the effects of past events on current behaviors.

Prenatal development Development from conception to birth.

To avoid the huge expense of such a long study, researchers have devised a third way of studying adulthood: the **biographical** or **retrospective study.** Whereas a longitudinal study might start with some 20-year-olds and follow them as they grow older, a biographical approach might start with some 70-year-olds and pursue their lives backward. That is, the researchers would try to reconstruct their subjects' past by interviewing them and by consulting various other sources, much as a biographer does when writing someone's life. Biographical data are less trustworthy than either longitudinal or cross-sectional data, however, because people's recollections of the past are not always accurate.

Each of these three kinds of studies has both advantages and disadvantages, which are summarized in Table 10-1. You will come across examples of all three methods in this chapter.

PRENATAL DEVELOPMENT

During the earliest period of **prenatal development**—the stage of development from conception to birth—the fertilized egg divides, embarking on the process that will transform it, in just 9 months, from a one-celled organism

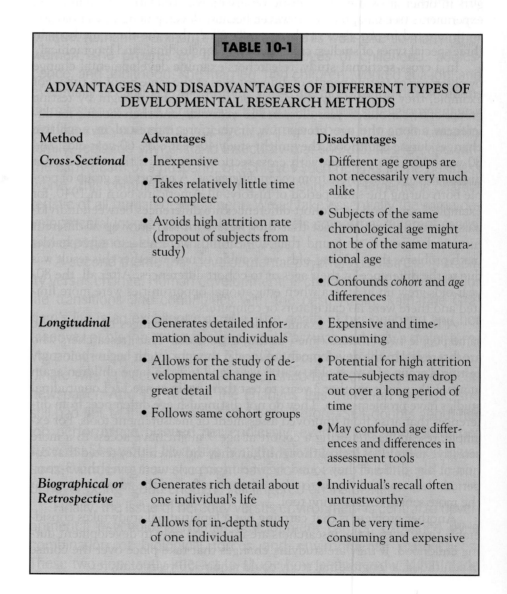

TABLE 10-1

ADVANTAGES AND DISADVANTAGES OF DIFFERENT TYPES OF DEVELOPMENTAL RESEARCH METHODS

Method	Advantages	Disadvantages
Cross-Sectional	• Inexpensive • Takes relatively little time to complete • Avoids high attrition rate (dropout of subjects from study)	• Different age groups are not necessarily very much alike • Subjects of the same chronological age might not be of the same maturational age • Confounds *cohort* and *age* differences
Longitudinal	• Generates detailed information about individuals • Allows for the study of developmental change in great detail • Follows same cohort groups	• Expensive and time-consuming • Potential for high attrition rate—subjects may drop out over a long period of time • May confound age differences and differences in assessment tools
Biographical or Retrospective	• Generates rich detail about one individual's life • Allows for in-depth study of one individual	• Individual's recall often untrustworthy • Can be very time-consuming and expensive

into a complex human being. The dividing cells form a hollow ball, which implants itself in the wall of the uterus. Two weeks after conception, the cells begin to specialize: Some will form the baby's internal organs, others will form muscles and bones, and still others will form the skin and the nervous system. No longer an undifferentiated mass of cells, the developing organism is now called an **embryo.**

The embryo stage ends 3 months after conception, when the stage of the **fetus** begins. At this point, although it is only 1 inch long, the fetus roughly resembles a human being, with arms and legs, a large head, and a heart that has begun to beat. Although it can already move various parts of its body, another month is likely to pass before the mother feels those movements.

An organ called the **placenta** nourishes the embryo and the fetus. Within the placenta, the mother's blood vessels transmit nutritive substances to the embryo or fetus and carry waste products away from it. Although the mother's blood never actually mingles with that of her unborn child, almost anything she eats, drinks, or inhales is capable of being transmitted through the placenta. If she develops an infection such as syphilis, rubella ("German measles"), or AIDS, the microorganisms that cause these diseases can cross the placenta and infect the fetus, often with disastrous results. If she inhales nicotine, drinks alcohol, or uses other drugs during pregnancy, these too can cross the placenta, compromising the baby's development (Harris & Liebert, 1991).

Many potentially harmful substances have a **critical period** when they are most likely to have a major effect on the fetus. At other times, the same substance may have no effect at all. For example, if a woman contracts rubella during the first 3 months of pregnancy, the effects can range from death of the fetus to a child who is born deaf. However, rubella contracted during the final 3 months of pregnancy is unlikely to cause severe damage to the fetus because the critical period for the formation of major body parts has passed.

Pregnancy is most likely to have a favorable outcome when the mother gets good nutrition and good medical care, and when she avoids exposure to substances that could be harmful to her baby, including alcohol. Alcohol is the drug most often abused by pregnant women, and with devastating consequences (Steinhausen, Willms, & Spohr, 1993). Pregnant women who consume large amounts of alcohol risk giving birth to a child with *fetal alcohol syndrome (FAS)*, a condition characterized by facial deformities, heart defects, stunted growth, and cognitive impairments. Even smaller amounts of alcohol can cause neurological problems (Hunt et al., 1995; Shriver & Piersel, 1994). This is why doctors recommend that pregnant women and those who are trying to become pregnant abstain from drinking alcohol altogether.

Pregnant woman are also wise not to smoke. Smoking restricts the oxygen supply to the fetus, slows its breathing, and speeds up its heartbeat. These changes are associated with a significantly increased risk of miscarriage. In this country alone, smoking may cause over 100,000 miscarriages a year. Babies of mothers who smoke are also more apt to suffer low birth weight, which puts the child at risk for other developmental problems (DiFranza & Lew, 1995; Feng, 1993). If a pregnant woman is unwilling to give up smoking for her own health, she should do so for the health of her child.

Differences in access to good nutrition and health care help explain why the infant death rate in this country is over twice as high for African Americans as it is for whites (see Figure 10–1) (Singh & Yu, 1995). A much

Embryo A developing human between 2 weeks and 3 months after conception.

Fetus A developing human between 3 months after conception and birth.

Placenta The organ by which an embryo or fetus is attached to its mother's uterus and that nourishes it during prenatal development.

Critical period The time when certain internal and external influences have a major effect on development; at other periods, the same influences will have little or no effect.

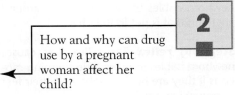

How and why can drug use by a pregnant woman affect her child?

2

The human fetus can be affected by anything its mother eats, drinks, or inhales.

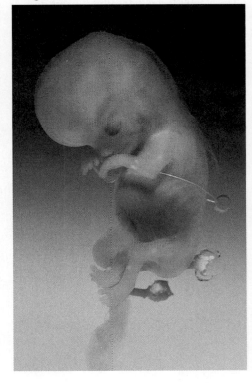

Neonates Newborn babies.

Rooting reflex The reflex that causes a newborn baby to turn its head toward something touching its cheek and to grope around with its mouth.

Sucking reflex The reflex that causes the newborn baby to suck on objects placed in its mouth.

Swallowing reflex The reflex that enables the newborn baby to swallow liquids without choking.

Grasping reflex The reflex that causes newborn babies to close their fists around anything that is put in their hands.

Stepping reflex The reflex that causes newborn babies to make little stepping motions if they are held upright with their feet just touching a surface.

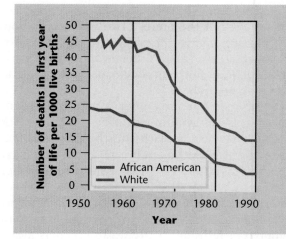

Figure 10–1
Mortality rates for white and African American infants.

Source: National Center for Health Statistics, 1995.

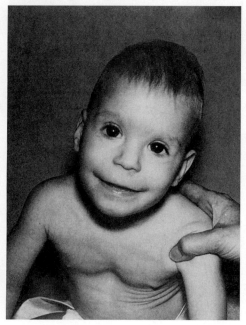

Children born with fetal alcohol syndrome often exhibit facial deformities, heart defects, stunted growth, and cognitive impairments that can last throughout life. The syndrome is entirely preventable.

higher percentage of African Americans live in poverty, and it is much harder for the poor to eat a healthy diet and see a doctor regularly during pregnancy (Aved et al., 1993).

THE NEWBORN BABY

Research has disproved the old idea that **neonates,** or newborn babies, do nothing but eat, sleep, and cry, while remaining oblivious to the world. True, newborns can sleep up to 16 or 20 hours a day (depending on the baby), but when awake they are much more aware and competent than they may seem at first glance.

For one thing, newborns come equipped with a number of useful reflexes. Many of these reflexes, such as those that control breathing, are essential to life outside the uterus. Some enable babies to nurse. The **rooting reflex** causes them to turn the head toward the touch of a nipple on the cheek and grope around with the mouth. The **sucking reflex** causes them to suck on anything that enters the mouth, and the **swallowing reflex** enables them to swallow milk and other liquids without choking.

Other reflexes have purposes that are less obvious. The **grasping reflex** causes newborns to cling vigorously to an adult's finger or to any object placed in their hands. The **stepping reflex** causes very young babies to take what looks like walking steps if they are held upright with their feet just touching a flat surface. These two reflexes normally disappear after 2 or 3 months, reemerging later as voluntary grasping (at around 5 months of age) and real walking (at the end of the first year).

Very young babies are also capable of a surprisingly complex kind of behavior: imitating the facial expressions of adults. If an adult opens his or her mouth or sticks out his or her tongue, newborn babies often respond by opening their mouths or sticking out their tongues (McCall, 1979; Meltzoff & Moore, 1985). When this ability to imitate was first noted in newborns, psychologists could hardly believe it. How could babies carry out such complex responses at an age when they can have no idea how their own face looks, much less how to make specific facial expressions? It now appears that this early imitation is only a primitive reflex, like the grasping and stepping reflexes. The behavior disappears after a few weeks, and then reemerges in a more complex form many months later (Bjorklund, 1989; Wyrwicka, 1988).

Almost all newborns respond to the human face, the human voice, and the human touch. This improves their chances of survival. After all, babies are totally dependent on the people who take care of them, so it is essential that their social relationships get off to a good start. From the very beginning, they have a means of communicating their needs to those they live with: They can cry. And very soon—in only about 6 weeks—they have an even better method of communication, one that serves as a thank-you to the people who are working so hard to keep them happy: They can smile.

Temperament

We may be tempted to talk about babies as if they are all the same, but babies display individual differences in **temperament** (Goldsmith & Harman, 1994; Piontelli, 1989). Some cry much more than others; some are much more active. Some babies love to be cuddled; others seem to wriggle uncomfortably when held. Some are highly reactive to stimuli around them, whereas others are quite placid no matter what they see or hear.

In a classic study of infant temperament, Alexander Thomas and Stella Chess (1977) identified three types of babies: "easy," "difficult," and "slow-to-warm-up." "Easy" babies are good-natured and adaptable, easy to care for and please. "Difficult" babies are moody and intense, reacting to new people and new situations both negatively and strongly. "Slow-to-warm-up" babies are relatively inactive and slow to respond to new things, and when they do react, their reactions are mild. To these three types, Jerome Kagan and his associates (Kagan et al., 1988; Kagan & Snidman, 1991) have added a fourth: the "shy child." Shy children are timid and inhibited, fearful of anything new or strange. Their nervous systems react to stimuli in a characteristically hypersensitive way (Kagan, 1994). Kagan found interesting differences in the frequency with which various behaviors related to temperament appear in babies from different cultures. He and his colleagues have speculated that such differences may be due in large part to the effects of different gene pools and genetic predispositions (Kagan et al., 1993).

Regardless of what initially causes a baby's temperament, it often remains quite stable over time. In one study that asked mothers to describe their children's temperaments, characteristics such as degree of irritability, flexibility, and persistence were all relatively stable from infancy through age 8 (Pedlow et al., 1993). Other studies have found that fussy or difficult infants are likely to become "problem children" who are aggressive and have difficulties in school (Guérin, 1994; Patterson & Bank, 1989; Persson-Blennow & McNeil, 1988). A longitudinal study of shy children and some of their less inhibited peers showed that most shy infants continue to be relatively shy and inhibited in middle childhood, just as most uninhibited infants remained relatively outgoing and bold (Kagan & Snidman, 1991).

A combination of biological and environmental factors generally contribute to this stability in behavior. For instance, if a newborn has an innate predisposition to cry often and react negatively to things, the parents may

Temperament A term used by psychologists to describe the physical/emotional characteristics of the newborn child and young infant; also referred to as personality.

If they are raised in a compatible environment, easy, uninhibited babies will most likely grow to be outgoing children and adults.

3

Does the behavior of an infant or a young child provide any clues as to how that person will behave as an adult?

find themselves tired, frustrated, and often angry. These reactions in the parents may serve to reinforce the baby's difficult behaviors, and so they tend to endure. Even if children are born with a particular temperament, then, they need not have that temperament for life. Each child's predispositions interact with his or her experiences, and how the child turns out is the result of that interaction (Kagan, 1989, 1994; Kagan, Snidman, & Arcus, 1992).

The Perceptual Abilities of Infants

Newborns can see, hear, and understand far more than previous generations gave them credit for. Their senses work fairly well at birth and rapidly improve to near-adult levels. Neonates begin to absorb and process information from the outside world as soon as they enter it—or, in some cases, even before.

VISION   Unlike puppies and kittens, human babies are born with their eyes open and functioning, even though the world looks a bit fuzzy to them at first. They see most clearly when faces or objects are only 8 to 10 inches away from them. Visual acuity (the clarity of vision) improves rapidly, however, and so does the ability to focus on objects at different distances. By 6 or 8 months of age, babies can see almost as well as the average college student, though their visual system takes another 3 or 4 years to develop fully (Maurer & Maurer, 1988).

Even very young babies already have visual preferences. They would rather look at a new picture or pattern than one they have seen many times before. If given a choice between two pictures or patterns, both of which are new to them, they generally prefer the one with the clearest contrasts. This is why they choose to look at a black-and-white pattern more than a colored one, even though they are able to distinguish primary colors from gray. For a young baby, however, the pattern shouldn't be too complex: A large black-and-white checkerboard pattern is preferred to one with smaller squares because the smaller squares tend to blur in the baby's vision. As babies get older and their vision improves, they prefer more and more complex patterns, perhaps reflecting their need for an increasingly complex environment (Acredolo & Hake, 1982; Fantz, Fagan, & Miranda, 1975).

Newborns also prefer to look at their own mother rather than at a stranger (Walton, Bower, & Bower, 1992). How do they manage to recognize their mother at such a young age? Walton and Bower (1993) suggest that infants form a prototypical schema, or collection of mental images that represent "mom." This is not to say that they "know" their mother in the way they will as an older baby. It is simply that, because they see the mother so often, they acquire sets of different images of her (from various angles and so on). This visual familiarity makes the mother preferred.

DEPTH PERCEPTION   Depth perception is the ability to see the world in three dimensions, with some objects nearer, others farther away. Although researchers have been unable to find evidence of depth perception in babies younger than 4 months (Aslin & Smith, 1988), the ability to see the world in three dimensions is well developed by the time a baby learns to crawl, between 6 and 12 months of age.

This was demonstrated in a classic experiment using a device called a *visual cliff* (Walk & Gibson, 1961). Researchers divided a table into three parts. The center was a solid runway, raised above the rest of the table by about an inch. On one side of this runway was a solid surface decorated in a checkerboard pattern and covered with a sheet of clear glass. The other side was also covered with a thick sheet of clear glass, but on this side—the visual cliff—the checkerboard surface was not directly under the glass, but 40 inches below it. An infant of crawling age was placed on the center runway, and the mother stood on one side or the other, encouraging the baby to crawl toward her across the glass. All of the 6- to 14-month-old infants tested refused to crawl across the visual cliff, even though they were perfectly willing to cross the "shallow" side of the table. When the "deep" side separated the baby from the mother, some of the infants cried; others peered down at the surface below the glass or patted the glass with their hands. Their behaviors clearly showed that they could perceive depth.

But what about younger babies? Because most infants younger than 6 months cannot crawl, they cannot be tested in the standard way using the visual cliff. In one study, they were simply placed face-down on the two sides of the table, and their pulse rates were measured in both positions. When the infants were moved from the shallow to the deep side, their heart rates slowed down, a reaction typical of both infants and adults who stop to orient themselves in new situations (Campos, Langer, & Krowitz, 1970). Thus, although they did not yet show apprehension toward the cliff, babies younger than 6 months did seem to realize that something was different about the deep side. Apparently, the emergence of apprehension toward heights depends on experience with self-produced movement, such as crawling (Bertenthal, Campos, & Kermoian, 1994).

OTHER SENSES Even before babies are born, their ears are in working order. Fetuses in the uterus can hear sounds and will startle at a sudden, loud noise in the mother's environment. After birth, babies may even show signs that they remember sounds they heard in the womb. In one study, babies modified their rate of sucking on a pacifier in order to hear a recording of the children's book *The Cat in the Hat*, which their mothers had read aloud twice a day in their last 6 weeks of pregnancy. The babies made no such effort to hear a recording of another children's story, to which they had never been exposed (DeCasper & Spence, 1986).

When placed on the visual cliff, babies of crawling age (about 6 to 14 months) will not cross the deep side, even to reach their mothers. This class experiment tells us that by the time they can crawl, babies can also perceive depth.

Babies also are born with the sensory capacity to tell the direction of a sound. They show this simply by turning their heads toward the source of a sound (Muir, 1985). By 4 months, they can even locate the source of a sound in the dark, where there are no visual cues (Hillier, Hewitt, & Morrongiello, 1992).

Infants are particularly tuned in to the sounds of human speech. One-month-olds can distinguish among similar speech sounds such as "pa-pa-pa" and "ba-ba-ba" (Eimas & Tartter, 1979). In some ways, young infants are even better at distinguishing speech sounds than older children and adults are. As children grow older, they often lose their ability to hear the difference between two very similar speech sounds that are not distinguished in their native language (Werker & Desjardins, 1995). For example, young Japanese infants have no trouble hearing the difference between "ra" and "la," sounds that are not distinguished in the Japanese language. By the time they are 1 year old, however, Japanese infants can no longer tell these two sounds apart (Werker, 1989).

With regard to taste and smell, newborns have clear-cut likes and dislikes. They like sweet flavors, a preference that persists through childhood. Babies only a few hours old will show pleasure at the taste of sweetened water but will screw up their faces in disgust at the taste of lemon juice (Steiner, 1979).

As infants grow older, their perceptions of the world become keener and more meaningful. Two factors are important in this development. One is physical maturation of the sense organs and the nervous system; the other is

Developmental norms Ages by which an average child achieves various developmental milestones.

gaining experience in the world. Babies learn about the people and objects in their environment and experience a variety of sights, sounds, textures, smells, and tastes. As a result, a growing fund of memories and understanding increasingly enriches their perceptions.

INFANCY AND CHILDHOOD

During the first dozen or so years of life, a helpless baby becomes a competent member of society. Many important kinds of developments occur during these early years. Here we discuss physical and motor changes as well as cognitive and social ones.

Physical Development

In the first year of life, the average baby grows 10 inches and gains 15 pounds. By 4 months, birth weight has doubled, and by the first birthday, birth weight has tripled. During the second year, physical growth slows considerably. Rapid increases in height and weight will not occur again until early adolescence.

An infant's growth does not occur in the smooth, continuous fashion depicted by growth charts. Rather, growth takes place in fits and starts (Lampl, Veidhuis, & Johnson, 1992). When babies are measured daily over their first 21 months, most show no growth 90 percent of the time, but when they do grow, they do so rapidly—sometimes startlingly so. Incredible though it may sound, some children gain as much as 1 inch in height overnight!

Marked changes in body proportions accompany changes in a baby's size. During the first 2 years after birth, children have heads that are large relative to their bodies as the brain undergoes rapid growth. A child's brain reaches three-quarters of its adult size by about the age of 2, at which point head growth slows down and the body does most of the growing. Head growth is virtually complete by age 10, but the body continues to grow for several more years (see Figure 10–2).

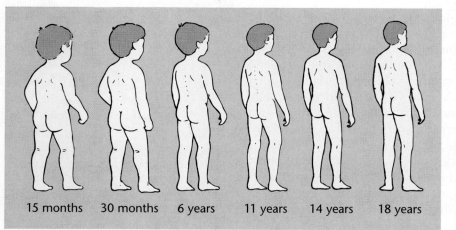

15 months   30 months   6 years   11 years   14 years   18 years

Figure 10–2
Body proportions at various ages.
Young children are top heavy: They have large heads and small bodies. As they get older, the body and legs become longer, and the head is proportionately smaller.

Source: Adapted from Bayley, 1956. Reprinted with the permission of the Society for Research in Child Development, Inc.

Motor Development

Motor development refers to the acquisition of skills involving movement, such as grasping, crawling, and walking. The *average* ages at which such skills are achieved are called **developmental norms.** By about 9 months, for example, the average infant can stand up while holding onto something. Crawling occurs, on average, at 10 months, and walking at about 1 year. However, some normal infants develop much faster than average, whereas others develop more slowly. A baby who is 3 or 4 months behind schedule may be perfectly normal, and one who is 3 or 4 months ahead is not necessarily destined to become a star athlete. To some extent, parents can accelerate the acquisition of motor skills in children by providing them with ample training, encouragement, and practice. Differences in these factors seem to largely account for cross-cultural differences in the average age at which children reach certain milestones in motor development (Hopkins & Westra, 1989, 1990).

Much early motor development consists of substituting voluntary actions for reflexes (Clark, 1994). The newborn grasping and stepping reflexes, for instance, give way to voluntary grasping and walking in the older baby. Motor development proceeds in a *proximodistal* fashion—that is, from nearest the center of the body (proximal) to farthest from the center (distal). For example, the infant initially has much greater control over gross arm movements than over movements of the fingers. Babies start batting at nearby objects as early as 1 month, but they cannot reach accurately until they are about 4 months old. It takes them another month or two before they are consistently successful in grasping objects they reach for (von Hofsten & Fazel-Zandy, 1984). At first, they grasp with the whole hand, but by the end of the first year, they can pick up a tiny object with the thumb and forefinger.

Maturation refers to biological processes that unfold as a person grows older and contribute to orderly sequences of developmental changes, such as the progression from crawling to toddling to walking. Psychologists used to believe that maturation of the central nervous system largely accounted for many of the changes in early motor skills—that environment and experience played only a minor part in their emergence. But in recent years this view has been changing (Thelen, 1994, 1995). Many researchers now see early motor development as arising from a combination of factors both within and outside the child. The child plays an active part in the process by exploring, discovering, and selecting solutions to the demands of new tasks. A baby who is learning to crawl, for example, must figure out how to position the body with belly off the ground and coordinate arm and leg movements to maintain balance while managing to proceed forward (Bertenthal et al., 1994). What doesn't work must be discarded or adapted; what does

Maturation An automatic biological unfolding of development in an organism as a function of the passage of time.

The normal sequence of motor development. At about 2 months, babies can lift their head and shoulders. They can sit up by themselves at about 6 1/2 months, and can stand (while holding on to something) at about 9 months. Crawling begins, on average, at 10 months, and walking at 1 year.

Sensory-motor stage In Piaget's theory, the stage of cognitive development between birth and 2 years of age in which the individual develops object permanence and acquires the ability to form mental representations.

Object permanence The concept that things continue to exist even when they are out of sight.

Mental representations Mental images or symbols (such as words) used to think about or remember an object, a person, or an event.

Jean Piaget

work must be remembered and called on for future use. This is a far cry from seeing the baby as one day starting to crawl simply because he or she has reached the point of maturational "readiness."

As children's coordination improves, they learn to run, skip, and climb. At 3 and 4, they begin to use their hands for increasingly complex tasks, learning how to put on mittens and shoes, then grappling with buttons, zippers, shoelaces, and pencils. Gradually, through a combination of practice and the physical maturation of the body and the brain, they acquire increasingly complex motor abilities, such as bike riding, roller blading, and swimming. By the age of about 11 some begin to be highly skilled at such tasks (Clark, 1994).

Cognitive Development

Early cognitive development consists partly of changes in how children think about the world. The most influential theorist in this area was the Swiss psychologist Jean Piaget (1896–1980). Piaget's early training as a biologist had an important influence on his views. He became interested in cognitive development while working as a research assistant in the laboratory of Alfred Binet and Theodore Simon, creators of the first standardized intelligence test for children. Piaget became intrigued by the reasons young children gave for answering certain questions incorrectly (Brainerd, 1996). Later, he observed and studied other children, including his own three. He watched them play games, solve problems, and perform everyday tasks, and he asked them questions and devised tests to learn how they thought.

Piaget believed cognitive development is a way of adapting to the environment. Unlike other animals, human children do not have many built-in responses. This gives them more flexibility to adapt their thinking and behavior to "fit" the world as they experience it at a particular age. In Piaget's view, children are intrinsically motivated to explore and understand things. They are active participants in creating their own understandings of the world. This view is one of Piaget's major contributions (Fischer & Hencke, 1996; Flavell, 1996). Another contribution is his proposal of four basic stages of cognitive development.

SENSORY-MOTOR STAGE (BIRTH TO 2 YEARS) According to Piaget, babies spend the first 2 years of life in the **sensory-motor stage** of development. They start out by simply applying the skills they are born with—primarily sucking and grasping—to a broad range of activities. Young babies delight in taking things into their mouths—their mother's breast, their own thumb, or anything else within reach. Gradually, they divide the world into what they can suck on and what they cannot. Similarly, young babies will grasp a rattle reflexively. When they eventually realize that the noise comes from the rattle, they begin to shake everything they can get hold of in an effort to reproduce the sound. Eventually, they distinguish between things that make noise and things that do not. In this way, infants begin to organize their experiences, fitting them into rudimentary categories such as "suckable" and "not suckable," "noise making" and "not noise making."

Another important outcome of the sensory-motor stage, according to Piaget, is the development of **object permanence,** an awareness that objects continue to exist even when out of sight. For a newborn child, objects that disappear simply cease to exist—"out of sight, out of mind." But as children gain experience with the world, they develop a sense of object permanence. By the time they are 18 to 24 months old, they can even imagine the movement of an object that they do not actually see move. This last skill depends on the ability to form **mental representations** of objects and to manipulate those representations in their heads. This is a major achievement of the late sensory-motor stage.

By the end of the sensory-motor stage, toddlers have also developed a capacity for self-recognition—that is, they are able to recognize the child in the mirror as "myself." In one famous study, mothers put a dab of red paint on their child's nose while pretending to wipe the child's face. Then each child was placed in front of a mirror. Babies under 1 year of age stared in fascination at the red-nosed baby in the mirror; some of them even reached out to touch the nose's reflection. But babies between 21 and 24 months reached up and touched their *own* reddened noses, showing that they know the red-nosed baby in the mirror was "me" (Brooks-Gunn & Lewis, 1984).

PREOPERATIONAL STAGE (2 TO 7 YEARS)   When children enter the **preoperational stage** of cognitive development, their thought is still tightly bound to their physical and perceptual experiences. But their increasing ability to use mental representations lays the groundwork for the development of language—using words as symbols to represent events and to describe, remember, and reason about experiences. (We will say much more about language development shortly.) Representational thought also lays the groundwork for two other hallmarks of this stage—engaging in *fantasy play* (a cardboard box becomes a castle) and using *symbolic gestures* (slashing the air with an imaginary sword to slay an imaginary dragon).

Although children this age have made advances over sensory-motor thought, in many ways they don't yet think like older children and adults. For example, preschool children are **egocentric.** They have difficulty seeing things from another person's point of view or putting themselves in someone else's place. In one classic study, preschoolers were allowed to walk around a large papier-mache model of a mountain range. Then they faced one side of the model while a doll faced the opposite side. When asked to select a picture that showed the doll's view of the mountains, they repeatedly chose a picture that showed their *own* point of view (Piaget & Inhelder, 1956).

Children this age also find it hard to distinguish between things as they appear to be and things as they really are (Flavell, 1986). They are easily misled by appearances and tend to concentrate on the most outstanding aspect of a display or event, ignoring everything else. In a famous experiment, Piaget showed preoperational children two identical glasses, filled to the same level with juice (see photo). The children were asked which glass held more juice, and they replied (correctly) that both had the same amount. Then Piaget poured the juice from one glass into a taller, narrower glass. Again the children were asked which glass held more juice. They looked at the two glasses, saw that the level of the juice in the tall, narrow one was much higher, and replied that the narrow glass had more. According to Piaget, children at this stage cannot consider the past (Piaget simply poured all the juice from one container into another) or the future (if he poured it back again, the levels of juice would be identical). Nor can they consider a container's height and width at the same time. Thus, they can't understand how an increase in one dimension (height) might be offset by a decrease in another dimension (width).

CONCRETE OPERATIONS (7 TO 11 YEARS)   During the **concrete-operational stage,** children become more flexible in their thinking. They

Preoperational stage In Piaget's theory, the stage of cognitive development between 2 and 7 years of age in which the individual becomes able to use mental representations and language to describe, remember, and reason about the world, though only in an egocentric fashion.

Egocentric Unable to see things from another's point of view.

Concrete-operational stage In Piaget's theory, the stage of cognitive development between 7 and 11 years of age in which the individual can attend to more than one thing at a time and understand someone else's point of view, though thinking is limited to concrete matters.

In Piaget's famous experiment, the child has to judge which glass holds more liquid: the tall, thin one or the short, wide one. Although both glasses hold the same amount, children in the preoperational stage say that the taller glass holds more, because they focus their attention on only one thing—the height of the column of liquid.

Principles of conservation The concept that basic amounts remain constant despite superficial changes in appearance, such as the idea that the volume of a liquid stays the same regardless of the size and shape of the container into which it is poured.

Formal-operational stage In Piaget's theory, the stage of cognitive development between 11 and 15 years of age in which the individual becomes capable of abstract thought.

learn to consider more than one dimension of a problem at a time and to look at a situation from someone else's viewpoint. This is the age at which they become able to grasp **principles of conservation,** such as the idea that the volume of a liquid stays the same regardless of the size and shape of the container into which it is poured. Other related conservation concepts have to do with number, length, area, and mass. All involve an understanding that basic amounts remain constant despite superficial changes in appearance, which can always be reversed.

Another accomplishment of this stage is the ability to grasp complex classification schemes such as those involving superordinate and subordinate classes. For instance, if you show a preschooler four toy dogs and two toy cats and ask whether there are more dogs present or more animals, the child will almost always answer "more dogs." It is not until age 7 or 8 that children are able to think about objects as being simultaneously members of *two* classes, one more inclusive than the other. Yet even well into the elementary school years children's thinking is still very much stuck in the "here and now." Often they are unable to solve problems without concrete reference points that they can handle or imagine handling.

FORMAL OPERATIONS (11 TO 15 YEARS)   This limitation is overcome in the **formal-operational stage** of cognitive development, often reached during adolescence. Youngsters at this stage can think in abstract terms. They can formulate hypotheses, test them mentally, and accept or reject them according to the outcome of these mental experiments. Therefore, they are capable of going beyond the here and now to understand things in terms of cause and effect, to consider possibilities as well as realities, and to develop and use general rules, principles, and theories.

To illustrate formal-operational thinking, Piaget and his associate Bärbel Inhelder gave children of various ages a number of different objects and asked them to separate the objects into two piles: things that would float and things that would sink. The objects included blocks made of different materials, sheets of paper, nails, pebbles, and a lid. After the children finished sorting, the researchers had them test their predictions by putting the objects into a pail of water and then asked them to explain why some things floated and others sank (Inhelder & Piaget, 1958). The younger children, who were still in the concrete-operational stage, were neither good at predicting which objects would float nor able to explain why. The older children, who had reached the formal-operational stage, were better at predicting. And when asked for an explanation, they would make comparisons, gradually concluding that neither weight nor size alone was the determining factor, but rather the relation between the two.

CRITICISMS OF PIAGET'S THEORY   Piaget's work has produced a great deal of controversy. Many question his assumption that there are distinct stages in cognitive development that always progress in an orderly, sequential way, and that a child must pass through one stage before entering the next (Brainerd, 1978; Siegel, 1993). Some see cognitive development as a more gradual process, resulting from the slow acquisition of experience and practice rather than the abrupt emergence of distinctly higher levels of ability (Paris & Weissberg, 1986).

Piaget's theory has also sparked criticism for assuming that young infants understand very little about the world, such as the permanence of objects in it. When young babies are allowed to reveal their understanding of object permanence without being required to conduct a search for a missing object, they often seem to know perfectly well that objects continue to exist when hidden by other objects (Baillargeon, 1994). They also show other quite sophisticated knowledge of the world that Piaget thought they lacked, such as a rudimentary grasp of number (Wynn, 1995). At older ages, too, milestone cognitive achievements seem to be reached much sooner than Piaget believed (Gopnik, 1996).

Other critics have argued that Piaget underplayed the importance of social interaction in cognitive development. For instance, the influential Russian psychologist Lev Vygotsky contended that people who are more advanced in their thinking provide opportunities for cognitive growth for children they interact with (Vygotsky, 1978). These learning experiences greatly depend on a society's culture, another factor that Piaget ignored (Daehler, 1994).

Finally, although Piaget's theory gives a schematic road map of cognitive development, the interests and experiences of a particular child may influence the development of cognitive abilities in ways not accounted for in the theory. Piaget's theory, in other words, does not adequately address human diversity.

Moral Development

One of the important changes in thinking that occurs during childhood and adolescence is the development of moral reasoning. Lawrence Kohlberg (1979, 1981) studied this kind of development by telling his subjects stories that illustrate complex moral issues. The "Heinz dilemma" is the best-known of these stories:

> In Europe, a woman was near death from cancer. One drug might save her, a form of radium that a druggist in the same town had recently discovered. The druggist was charging $2,000, ten times what the drug cost him to make. The sick woman's husband, Heinz, went to everyone he knew to borrow the money, but he could only get together about half of what it cost. He told the druggist that his wife was dying and asked him to sell it cheaper or let him pay later. But the druggist said, "No." The husband got desperate and broke into the man's store to steal the drug for his wife. (Kohlberg, 1969, p. 379)

The children and adolescents who heard this story were asked, "Should the husband have done that? Why?"

On the basis of his subjects' replies to these questions (particularly the second one, "Why?"), Kohlberg theorized that moral reasoning develops in stages, much like Piaget's account of cognitive development. Preadolescent children are at what Kohlberg called the *preconventional level* of moral reasoning: They tend to interpret behavior in terms of its concrete consequences. Younger children at this level base their judgments of "right" and "wrong" behavior on whether it is rewarded or punished. Somewhat older children, still at this level, guide their moral choices on the basis of what satisfies needs, particularly their own.

With the arrival of adolescence and the shift to formal-operational thought, the stage is set for progression to the second level of moral reasoning, the *conventional level*. At this level, the adolescent at first defines right behavior as that which pleases or helps others and is approved by them. Around midadolescence, there is a further shift toward considering various abstract social virtues, such as being a "good citizen" and respecting authority. Both forms of conventional moral reasoning require an ability to think about such abstract values as "duty" and "social order," to consider the intentions that lie behind behavior, and to put oneself in the "other person's shoes."

Babbling A baby's language that consists of repetition of consonant-vowel combinations.

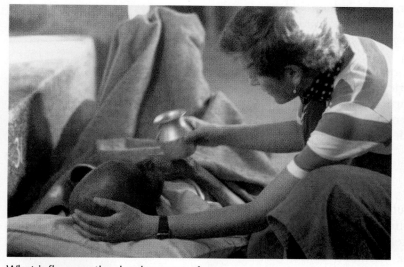

What influences the development of compassionate behavior? Researchers in moral development want to understand why people make the moral choices they do. This young woman has volunteered to work in the Mother Teresa Home for the Dying in India.

4 How do young children learn languages?

The third level of moral reasoning, the *postconventional level*, requires a still more abstract form of thought. This level is marked by an emphasis on abstract principles such as justice, liberty, and equality. Personal and strongly felt moral standards become the guideposts for deciding what is right and wrong. Whether these decisions correspond to the rules and laws of a particular society at a particular time is irrelevant. For the first time, people may become aware of discrepancies between what they judge to be moral and what society has determined to be legal.

Kohlberg's views have been criticized on several counts. First, research indicates that many people in our society, adults as well as adolescents, never progress beyond the conventional level of moral reasoning (Conger & Petersen, 1991). Does this mean that these people are morally "underdeveloped," as Kohlberg's theory implies?

Second, Kohlberg's theory does not take account of cultural differences in moral values. Kohlberg put considerations of "justice" at the highest level of moral reasoning. In Nepal, however, researchers discovered that a group of adolescent Buddhist monks placed the highest moral value on alleviating suffering and showing compassion, concepts that have no place in Kohlberg's scheme of moral development (Huebner, Garrod, & Snarey, 1990).

Third, Kohlberg's theory has been criticized as sexist. Kohlberg found that boys usually scored higher than girls on his test of moral development. According to Carol Gilligan (1982, 1992), this was because boys are more inclined to base their moral judgments on the abstract concept of justice, whereas girls tend to base theirs more on the criteria of caring about other people and the importance of maintaining personal relationships. In Gilligan's view, there is no valid reason to assume that one of these perspectives is morally superior to the other. Although subsequent research has found that gender differences in moral thinking tend to diminish in adulthood (Cohn, 1991), concerns about gender bias in Kohlberg's theory still remain.

More recent research on moral development has moved in the direction of broadening Kohlberg's focus on changes in moral reasoning. These researchers are interested in the factors that influence moral choices in everyday life, and the extent to which those choices are actually put into action. In other words, they want to understand moral behavior as much as moral thinking (Power, 1994).

Language Development

The development of language follows a predictable pattern. At about 2 months of age, an infant begins to coo (a nondescript word for nondescript sounds). In another month or two, the infant enters the **babbling** stage and starts to repeat sounds such as *da* or even meaningless sounds that developmental psychologists refer to as "grunts"; these sounds are the building blocks for later language development (Dill, 1994). A few months later, the infant may string together the same sound, as in *dadadada*. Finally, the baby will form combinations of different sounds, as in *dabamaga* (Ferguson & Macken, 1983).

Even deaf babies with deaf parents who communicate with sign language engage in a form of babbling (Pettito & Marentette, 1991). Like hearing infants, these babies begin to babble before they are 10 months old—but they babble with their hands! Just as hearing infants utter sounds over and over, deaf babies make repetitive movements of their hands, like those of sign language.

Gradually, an infant's babbling takes on certain features of adult language. At about age 4 to 6 months, the infant's vocalizations begin to show signs of *intonation*, the rising and lowering of pitch that allows adults to distinguish, for example, between questions ("You're tired?") and statements ("You're tired."). Also around this time babies learn the basic sounds of their native language. This sound learning occurs well before babies actually comprehend words, even though they may recognize commonly used words, such as their own names (Kuhl, Williams, & Lacerda, 1992; Mandel, Jusczyk, & Pisoni, 1995).

By around their first birthday, babies begin to use intonation to indicate commands and questions (Greenfield & Smith, 1976). At about the same age, they show signs of understanding what is said to them, and they begin not only to imitate what others say but also to use sounds to get attention. Vocalization also becomes more and more communicative and socially directed. Parents facilitate this process by speaking to their babies in what is called *motherese*. This "mother talk" is spoken slowly, and uses simple sentences, a higher-pitched voice, repetition, and exaggerated intonations—all of which engage babies' attention and help them to distinguish the sounds of their language (J. Hampson & Nelson, 1993).

The culmination of all this preparation is the utterance of the first word, usually *dada*, at about 12 months. During the next 6 to 8 months, children build a vocabulary of one-word sentences called **holophrases**: "Up!"; "Out!"; "More!" At first, they use these words to describe their own behavior, but later they use the words to describe the actions of others (Huttenlocher, Smiley, & Charney, 1983). Children may also use compound words such as *awgone* [all gone]. To these holophrases they add words used to address people—*Bye-bye* is a favorite—and a few exclamations, such as *Ouch!*

In the second year of life, children begin to distinguish between themselves and others. Possessive words become a big part of the vocabulary: [The shoes are] "Daddy's." But the overwhelming passion of children from 12 to 24 months old is naming. With little or no prompting, they will name virtually everything they see, though not always correctly! Children at this age are fascinated by objects. If they don't know the name of an object, they will simply invent one or use another word that is almost right. Feedback from parents ("No, that's not a dog, it's a cow") enhances vocabulary and helps children understand what names can and cannot be assigned to classes of things ("dog" is not used for big four-legged animals that live on farms and moo rather than bark).

During the third year of life, children begin to form two- and three-word sentences such as "See daddy," "Baby cry," "My ball," and "Dog go woof-woof." Recordings of mother-child conversations show that children from 24 to 36 months old noticeably omit auxiliary verbs and verb endings ([Can] "I have that?"; "I [am] eat[ing] it up"), as well as prepositions and articles ("It [is] time [for] Sarah [to] take [a] nap") (Bloom, 1970). Apparently, children this age seize on the most important parts of speech, those that contain the most meaning.

Holophrases One-word sentences, commonly used by children under 2 years of age.

From 12 to 24 months babies typically point at and name, although not always correctly, whatever object interests them.

Imprinting A form of primitive bonding seen in some species of animals; the new-

relationships have usually expanded to include siblings, playmates, and other children and adults outside the family. Their social world more and more...

being female, thinking about suicide, having a mental disorder (such as depression), and having a poorly educated father who is absent from the home.

But it is hard to tell which adolescents at higher-than-average risk will actually attempt suicide. For example, depression in and of itself rarely leads to suicide: Although 3 percent of adolescents suffer severe depression at any one time, the suicide rate among adolescents is only .01 percent (Connelly et al., 1993). Apparently, a combination of depression and other risk factors makes suicide more likely, but exactly which factors are most important and what kinds of intervention might reduce adolescent suicides are still unclear.

ADULTHOOD

Compared with adolescent development, development during adulthood is much less predictable, much more a function of the individual's decisions, circumstances, and even luck. In adulthood, unlike in childhood and adolescence, developmental milestones do not occur at a particular age. Still, certain experiences and changes take place sooner or later in nearly everyone's life and nearly every adult tries to fulfill certain needs, including nurturing partnerships and satisfying work.

Love, Partnerships, and Parenting

Nearly all adults form a long-term, loving partnership with another adult at some point in their lives. This can happen at any stage in the life course, but it is especially common in young adulthood. According to Erik Erikson, the major challenge of young adulthood is *intimacy versus isolation*. Failure to form an intimate partnership with someone else can cause a young adult to feel painfully lonely and incomplete. Erikson believed that a person is not ready to commit to an intimate relationship until he or she has developed a firm sense of personal identity, the task of the preceding stage of life.

FORMING PARTNERSHIPS More than 90 percent of Americans eventually get married (Doherty & Jacobson, 1982), but those who marry are waiting longer to do so. In 1970, only 15 percent of men and women aged 25 to 29 had never married; by 1988, the percentage had increased to 36 percent (U.S. Bureau of the Census, 1990). This postponement of marriage is even greater among African Americans than among whites (Balaguer & Markman, 1994).

Most people marry someone of similar age, race, religion, education, and background (Gagnon et al., 1994). This is because people with similar characteristics and backgrounds are more likely to meet, and once they meet, they are more likely to discover shared interests and compatibility (Murstein, 1986). Choice of a partner for cohabitation (living together) seems to proceed in much the same way. Often there is a spoken or unspoken assumption among couples that "if things work out, then we'll marry." Interestingly, couples who live together before marriage are generally *less* satisfied with their marriages and more likely to divorce later than couples who married without first living together (DeMaris & Rao, 1992). One reason may be that many of those who decide to live together first are more tentative about their relationships than those who proceed directly to marriage (Balaguer & Markman, 1994).

Although heterosexual marriage is still the statistical norm in our society, other types of partnerships are increasingly meeting the needs of a diverse population. Long-term cohabiting relationships are one example.

Most people marry someone of similar race, religion, education, and social background. The couple shown here are marrying in an Eastern Orthodox wedding ceremony.

Contrary to popular belief, the greatest recent increase in cohabiting couples is not among the very young, but rather among people over age 35 (Steinhauer, 1997). Among elderly widows and widowers, cohabitation is increasingly seen as a way of enjoying a life together without financial complications and tax penalties.

Homosexual couples are another example of intimate partnerships outside the tradition of heterosexual marriage. Studies show that most gays and lesbians seek the same loving, committed, and meaningful partnerships as most heterosexuals do (Peplau & Cochran, 1990). Moreover, successful relationships among them have the same characteristics as successful relationships in the heterosexual world: high levels of mutual trust, respect, and appreciation, shared decision making, good communication, and good skills at resolving conflicts (Birchler & Fals-Stewart, 1994; Edwards, 1995; Kurdek, 1991, 1992).

Forming and maintaining any kind of close relationship is important to living a long and happy life. In one 6-year study of men aged 24 to 60, those who had good social support networks outlived those who lacked such support (Kaplan & Novorr, 1994). People who didn't join social organizations were twice as likely to die during the same period as those who did join such groups. And those who were dissatisfied with the quality of their interpersonal relationships were twice as likely to die as those who were satisfied with them. See *Applying Psychology* for some useful information about resolving conflicts in intimate relationships.

PARENTHOOD   For most parents, loving and being loved by their children is an unparalleled source of fulfillment. As they watch their children grow, they experience a sense of achievement and pride. However, the birth of the

APPLYING PSYCHOLOGY
RESOLVING CONFLICTS IN INTIMATE RELATIONSHIPS

Even the closest, most loving couples have disagreements. People, after all, are different. They have different desires, different approaches, different priorities, different points of view. This makes conflict inevitable in every intimate relationship. But conflict does not have to be destructive. It can be resolved in constructive ways that don't tear a couple apart. Constructive fighting can actually bring people closer together in search of mutually satisfactory solutions.

Psychologists who have studied intimate relationships often suggest a number of steps to constructive conflict resolution:

1. *Carefully choose the time and place for an argument.* People who start airing a grievance at some inappropriate time shouldn't be surprised when the outcome is unsatisfactory. Try not to begin a major disagreement while your partner is in the middle of completing some important task, or ready to fall asleep after a long, tiring day. Bring up the subject when there is ample time to discuss it fully.

2. *Be a good listener.* Don't go on the defensive as soon as your partner brings up a concern or complaint. Listen carefully without interrupting. Try to understand what your partner is saying from his or her point of view. Listening calmly, without anger will help get the discussion off to a good start. Don't let your body give nonverbal cues that contradict good listening. For instance, don't continue to do chores or watch TV while your partner is speaking. Don't shrug your shoulders or roll your eyes as if discounting your partner's view.

3. *Give feedback regarding your understanding of the other person's grievance.* Restate what your partner has told you in your own words. Ask questions about anything you're not sure of. For instance, if a wife says she is fed up with the amount of time her husband spends watching TV sports, he might respond by saying: "I know you don't like me watching sports a lot, but do you expect me to stop entirely?" Such feedback helps to clarify and avoid misunderstandings.

4. *Be candid.* Level with your partner about your feelings. Say what you really think. If you are angry, don't make your partner guess your feelings by giving the "silent treatment" or showing anger in indirect ways. Of course, being candid does not mean being tactless or hurtful. Don't engage in name-calling, sarcasm, mockery, or insults. Such tactics are counterproductive.

5. *Use "I" rather than "you" statements.* For instance, if you're angry with your partner for being late, say: "I've been really worried and upset for the last hour" rather than "You're a whole hour late! Why couldn't you get here on time?" "You" statements sound like accusations and tend to put people on the defensive. "I" statements sound more like efforts to communicate feelings in nonjudgmental ways.

6. *Focus on behavior, not on the person.* For example, focus on your partner's lateness as a problem. Don't accuse your partner of being thoughtless and self-centered. People respond defensively to broadside attacks on their character. Such attacks threaten their self-esteem.

7. *Don't overstate the frequency of a problem or over-generalize about it.* Don't tell your partner that he's *always* late, or that she's *exactly* like her mother. Such exaggerations are annoying and tend to sidetrack discussions away from legitimate complaints.

8. *Focus on a limited number of specific issues.* Don't overwhelm your partner with a barrage of grievances. Stick to current concerns of high priority. Don't get distracted by trivial matters that waste emotional energy. Don't dredge up long lists of complaints from the past.

9. *Don't find scapegoats for every grievance against you.* We all tend to explain away our shortcomings by blaming them on circumstances, or sometimes on other people. Resist the temptation to offer excuses designed to get you "off the hook." Take responsibility for your actions and encourage your partner to do the same.

10. *Suggest specific, relevant changes to solve a problem.* Both participants in the conflict should propose at least one possible solution. A proposed solution should be reasonable and take into account the other person's viewpoint as well as your own.

11. **Be open to compromise.** Settling disputes successfully often involves negotiation. Both people must be willing to give in a little. Don't back your partner into a corner by giving an ultimatum: "Do what I want, *or else!*" Partners need to be willing to change themselves to some extent in response to each other's feelings. This is the essence of being in an intimate relationship. Being loved by your partner doesn't necessarily mean being accepted *exactly* as you are.

12. **Don't think in terms of winner and loser.** Popular books have been written on how always to *win* arguments. This competitive approach to conflict resolution is unfortunate in intimate relationships. If one partner is repeatedly the winner and the other repeatedly the loser, their relationship inevitably suffers. Strive for solutions that are satisfactory to both parties. Think of each other as allies attacking a mutual problem. In this way your relationship will strengthen.

To learn more about resolving interpersonal conflicts, visit our website at **www.prenhall.com/morris**

first child is also a major turning point in a couple's relationship, one that requires many adjustments. Romance and fun often give way to duty and obligations. Young children demand a lot of time and energy, which may leave parents with little time or energy for each other. New parents in particular may worry about the mixed emotions they sometimes feel toward their baby.

Parenthood may also heighten conflicts between pursuit of careers and responsibilities at home. This is especially likely among women who have had an active career outside the home. They may be torn between feelings of loss and resentment at the prospect of leaving their job, and anxiety or guilt over the idea of continuing to work. This conflict is added to the usual worries about being an adequate wife and mother (Warr & Perry, 1982). No wonder women feel the need for their partner's cooperation more strongly during this period of life than men do (Belsky, Lang, & Rovine, 1985). Today's fathers spend more time with their children than their fathers did, but mothers still bear the greater responsibility for both child rearing and housework. Although homosexual couples as a group believe more strongly in equally dividing household duties than heterosexual couples do, homosexuals tend to make an exception when it comes to child rearing. After the arrival of a child (through adoption or artificial insemination), child-care responsibilities tend to fall more heavily on one member of a homosexual couple, whereas the other spends more time in paid employment (Patterson, 1994, 1995).

Given the demands of child rearing, it isn't surprising that marital satisfaction tends to decline after the arrival of the first child (Ruble et al., 1988). But once children leave home, many parents experience renewed satisfaction in their relationship as a couple. Rather than lamenting over their "empty nests," most women breathe a sigh of relief (Rovner, 1990). For the first time in years, the husband and wife can be alone together and enjoy one another's company (Orbuch, Houser, Mero, & Webster, 1996). (see *Highlights*.)

Parenthood can bring deep fulfillment and pride, but it also requires major adjustments by both partners.

ENDING A RELATIONSHIP   Intimate relationships frequently break up. Although this is true for all types of couples—married and unmarried, heterosexual and homosexual—most of the research on ending relationships has focused on divorced couples. The U.S. divorce rate has risen substantially since the 1960s, as it has in many other developed nations (Lewin, 1995). Although the divorce rate appears to have stabilized, it has stabilized at quite a high level. Almost half of American marriages eventually end in divorce (Darnton, 1992).

HIGHLIGHTS
ADULT SEXUAL BEHAVIOR

Until a few years ago, the only comprehensive studies done on the sexual behavior of adults were the Kinsey Report, completed back in 1948, and the work of Masters and Johnson in the 1960s. Both these studies involved a generally nonrandom and therefore unrepresentative sample of all adults. This (plus the age of the studies) makes them questionable sources for drawing reliable conclusions about adult sexual behavior today, or for formulating important public policies concerning AIDS and other sexually transmitted diseases.

Now we have a report (Gagnon et al., 1994) based on 3,432 randomly selected men and women, aged 18 to 59, who were interviewed at length about their sexual behaviors. Some of the results obtained from this more representative study are surprising. For example, contrary to the popular view, extramarital affairs and casual sex are not the norm in contemporary America. Eighty-five percent of the married women and 74 percent of the married men reported being faithful to their spouses. And contrary to the common belief that many single people have very active and exciting sex lives, only 23 percent of single persons reported having sex two or more times weekly. Roughly equal percentages reported rates of a few times monthly, a few times yearly, or not at all. In contrast, 41 percent of all married couples said they had sex two or more times weekly, as did 56 percent of unmarried cohabiting couples.

Eighty-five percent of the married women and 74 percent of the married men reported being faithful to their spouses.

Some other findings from the study point to relatively tame sex lives among many Americans. For instance:

- More than 80 percent of the sample said they had had only one sexual partner over the last year. What's more, 44 percent of the men and 70 percent of the women reported four or fewer lovers since the age of 18.

- Nearly half the married people (47 percent) reported that they had not had sex with their partner until a year after first meeting.

Despite these indications of fairly subdued sexual action, sex remains on the minds of many Americans, at least American men. More than half of the men interviewed (compared with 19 percent of the women) said they thought about sex at least once a day. This is not surprising in a culture such as ours where sexual themes and images are so abundant.

Rarely is the decision to separate a mutual one. Most often, one partner takes the initiative in ending the relationship after a long period of slowly increasing unhappiness. Making the decision does not necessarily bring relief. In the short term, it often brings turmoil, animosity, and apprehension. However, in the longer term, most divorced adults report that the divorce was a positive step that eventually resulted in greater personal contentment and healthier psychological functioning, although a substantial minority seem to suffer long-term negative effects (Kelly, 1982; Stack, 1994).

Divorce can have serious and far-reaching effects on children—especially on their school performance, self-esteem, gender-role development, emotional adjustment, relationships with others, and attitudes toward marriage (Barber & Eccles, 1992; Vaughn, 1993). Children adapt more successfully to divorce when they have good support systems, when the divorcing parents maintain a good relationship, and when sufficient financial resources are made available to them (Miller, Kliewer, & Burkeman, 1993; Davies & Cummings, 1994; Ahrons, 1994; Edwards, 1995).

The World of Work

Three or four generations ago, choosing a career was not an issue for most young adults. Men followed in their fathers' footsteps or took whatever apprenticeships were available in their communities. Women were occupied in child care, housework, and helping with the family farm or business, or they pursued such "female" careers as secretarial work, nursing, and teaching. Today career choices are far more numerous for both men and women. In 1990, for example, women were 25 percent of full-time employed physicians, 27 percent of lawyers, and 30 percent of college professors. All told, women accounted for about 39 percent of the labor force (Gilbert, 1994). However, on average, women get paid 30 percent less than men for doing the same job. Moreover, many women experience discrimination or sexual harassment at work. And women typically have fewer opportunities to change jobs or receive a promotion, two ways by which men tend to get out of an unsatisfactory job (Aranya, Kushnir, & Valency, 1986).

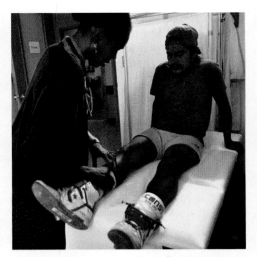

In her mother's generation, discrimination by professional schools and the attitudes of society in general might have kept this woman from becoming a physician. Today, over one-quarter of full-time employed physicians are women.

DUAL-CAREER FAMILIES Over the last 50 years, the number of married women in the paid labor force has increased dramatically: 71 percent of married women with school-aged children and 60 percent of women with children under 6 now have jobs outside the home (Gilbert, 1994; Harris & Liebert, 1991). The two-paycheck family is not always a matter of choice. With increasingly unstable economic conditions and the rising costs of essentials such as health care and education, it is not unusual for both adults in a family to have to work simply to make ends meet. This increasing role of women as economic providers is a worldwide trend (Lewin, 1995).

Balancing the demands of career and family is a problem in many families, especially for women. Even when the wife has a full-time job outside the home, she is likely to end up doing far more than half of the housework and child care. She is also likely to be aware of this imbalance and to resent it (Benin & Agostinelli, 1988). The "double shift"—one at paid work outside the home and another at unpaid household labor—is the common experience of millions of women throughout the world (Mednick, 1993). True equality—the hopeful goal of the dual-career movement—has yet to be achieved (Gilbert, 1994).

Despite the pressures associated with the "double shift," most women report increases in self-esteem when they have a paid job (Baruch & Barnett, 1986). They also tend to experience less anxiety and depression than childless working women do (Barnett, 1994). The vast majority say they would continue to work even if they didn't need the money (Schwartz, 1994). Those women most apt to feel stressed by a "double shift" are those who do not find satisfaction in their various roles (Barnett, 1994).

CHILDREN IN DUAL-CAREER FAMILIES Most dual-career families must entrust their young children to the care of someone else for a sizable percentage of the children's waking hours. About 5 million American children under the age of 5 are cared for in day-care centers, preschools, or a relative's home (Hofferth, 1991). Is it a good idea to leave infants and very young children with substitute caregivers?

Some research shows clear benefits for the children of mothers who work, even if the children are still very young (Greenstein, 1993). For example, the children of employed mothers tend to be more independent and self-confident and to have less stereotyped views of males and females (Harris & Liebert, 1991). Nonetheless, there has been concern that being entrusted to caregivers outside the immediate family may interfere with the development of secure attachments and put children at greater risk for emotional maladjustment (Barglow, Vaughn, & Molitor, 1987; Belsky & Rovine, 1988). But according to the findings of a recent large-scale longitudinal study (NICHD, 1996), placing a baby in full-time day care even in the first few months of life doesn't in itself undermine attachment. Working

Midlife crisis A time when adults discover they no longer feel fulfilled in their jobs or personal lives and attempt to make a decisive shift in career or lifestyle.

parents and their babies still have ample opportunity to engage in the daily give-and-take of positive feelings on which secure attachments are built. When a mother provides generally insensitive and unresponsive care, however, her baby is even *more* likely to develop an insecure attachment to her if the child also experiences extensive day care, especially poor quality care or changing day-care arrangements. One conclusion, then, is that quality care counts. A secure, affectionate, stimulating environment is likely to produce children who are healthy, outgoing, and ready to learn, just as an environment that encourages fears and doubts is likely to stunt development.

Cognitive Changes

Only recently have researchers begun to explore the ways in which an adult's thinking differs from that of an adolescent. Although adolescents are able to test alternatives and to arrive at what they see as the "correct" solution to a problem, adults gradually come to realize that there isn't a single correct solution to every problem—there may, in fact, be no correct solution, or there may be several. Adolescents rely on authorities to tell them what is "true," but adults realize that "truth" often varies according to the situation and one's viewpoint. Adults are also more practical: They know that a solution to a problem must be realistic as well as reasonable (Cavanaugh, 1990). No doubt these changes in adult thinking derive from greater experience of the world. Dealing with the kinds of complex problems that arise in adult life requires moving away from the literal, formal, and somewhat rigid thinking of adolescence and young adulthood (Labouvie-Vief, 1986).

Just as physical exercise is necessary for optimal physical development, so mental exercise is necessary for optimal cognitive development. Research has verified the benefits of regular cognitive exercise. For example, adults who received training in spatial orientation skills improved their performance by 40 percent. Thus, although some decline in cognitive skills is inevitable as people age, the decline can be minimized if people stay mentally active (Schaie, 1994).

Personality Changes

Research shows certain broad patterns of personality change through adulthood. Both men and women tend to become less self-centered and develop better coping skills with age (Neugarten, 1977). One longitudinal study found that people are more sympathetic, giving, productive, and dependable at 45 than they were at 20 (Block, 1971). Another found that people in their middle years feel an increasing commitment to and responsibility for others, develop new ways of adapting, and are more comfortable in interpersonal relationships (Vaillant, 1977). Such finding suggest that the majority of people are successfully meeting what Erik Erikson saw as the major challenge of middle adulthood: *generativity versus stagnation*. Generativity refers to the ability to continue being productive and creative, especially in ways that guide and encourage future generations. For those who fail to achieve this state, life becomes a drab and meaningless routine, and the person feels stagnant and bored.

Feelings of boredom and stagnation in middle adulthood may be part of what is called a **midlife crisis.** The person in midlife crisis feels painfully unfulfilled, ready for a radical, abrupt shift in career, personal relationships, or lifestyle. Research shows, however, that the midlife crisis is not typical; most people do not make sudden dramatic changes in their lives in midadulthood (Martino, 1995). In fact, many use this time to renew their commitments to marriage, work, and family (Newman, 1982).

Daniel Levinson, who has studied personality development in men and women throughout adulthood (Levinson, 1978, 1986, 1987), prefers the term **midlife transition** for the period when people tend to take stock of their lives. Many of the men and women in his studies, confronted with the first signs of aging, began to think about the finite nature of life. They realized that they may never accomplish all that they had hoped to do, and they questioned the value of some of the things they had accomplished so far, wondering how meaningful they were. As a result, some gradually reset their life priorities, establishing new goals based on their new insights. Levinson's view of the tasks that men must master within each stage of adulthood is summarized in Table 10-3.

The "Change of Life"

A decline in the function of the reproductive organs occurs during middle age. In women, the amount of estrogen (the principal female hormone) produced by the ovaries drops sharply at around age 45, although the exact age varies considerably from woman to woman. Breasts, genital tissues, and the uterus begin to shrink, and menstrual periods become irregular and then cease altogether at around age 50. The cessation of menstruation is called **menopause.**

Midlife transition According to Levinson, a process whereby adults assess the past and formulate new goals for the future.

Menopause The time in a woman's life when menstruation ceases.

TABLE 10-3

LEVINSON'S MODEL OF THE DEVELOPMENTAL SEQUENCES OF ADULT LIFE

Stage	Task
Entering the adult world (22–28)	Resolution of the conflict between exploring available options and establishing a stable life structure—"I will keep my options open."
Age 30 . . . transition (28–33)	Tentative commitments and life goals reexamined and questioned—"Did I make the right choices?"
Settling dow and becoming one's own man (33–40)	Achieving stability, security, and comfort—actively carving out niche in society—"I want to make my place in this world."
Midlife transition (40–45)	Assessment of accomplishments and evolvement of another life structure—"What is it I really want?"
Midlife (45–50)	Accepting one's fate—"What I have achieved is OK."
Age 50 . . . transition and midlife culmination (50–60)	Finding security and self-acceptance—"What I have become is OK."
Late adult transition (60+)	Achieving a satisfactory life outlook—"My life has been OK and will continue to be OK."

Source: Adapted from *The Season's of a Man's Life* by Daniel L. Levinson, 1978. Copyright © 1978 by Daniel J. Levinson. Reprinted by permission of Sterling Lord Literstic, Inc., and Alfred A. Knopf, Inc.

The hormonal changes that accompany menopause often cause certain physical symptoms; the most noticeable are "hot flashes." In some women, menopause also leads to a serious thinning of the bones, making them more vulnerable to fractures. Both of these symptoms can be prevented by estrogen replacement therapy (a pill or a skin patch that must be prescribed by a physician). Although this therapy may slightly increase a woman's risk for breast and uterine cancer (Steinberg et al., 1991), it appears to significantly decrease her risk for heart disease (Barrett-Connor & Bush, 1991). Some women are apprehensive about the "change of life," but others revel in their newfound freedom from fear of pregnancy.

Experts disagree about whether a "male menopause" exists. Men never experience as severe a drop in testosterone (the principal male hormone) as women do in estrogen. Instead, studies have found a more gradual decline— perhaps 30 to 40 percent—in testosterone in men between 48 and 70 (Angier, 1992). In any case, there is much disagreement about whether older men should be treated with hormones, as menopausal women commonly are. Some are concerned that hormone therapy could increase men's risk of prostate cancer and heart disease.

LATE ADULTHOOD

Older adults constitute the fastest-growing and one of the most politically powerful segments of the U.S. population. At present, 3.5 million Americans are over age 65; by the year 2030, there may be more than 70 million in this age group (Kolata, 1992). This dramatic rise stems from the aging of the large baby boom generation, coupled with increases in life expectancy due primarily to better health care and nutrition (Downs, 1994).

However, a sizable gender gap exists in life expectancy. The average woman today enjoys a life span that is 7 years longer than that of the average male. The reasons for this gender gap are still unclear, but likely factors include differences in hormones, exposure to stress, health-related behaviors, and genetic makeup. There is also a gap in life expectancy between whites and African Americans in this country. The average white American child is likely to live to age 76, whereas the average African American child is apt to live only to age 71. This difference stems largely from disparities in socioeconomic well-being.

Because older adults are becoming an increasingly visible part of American society, it is important to understand their development. Unfortunately, our views of older adults are often heavily colored by myths. For example, many people believe that most older adults are lonely, poor, and troubled by ill health. Even health-care professionals sometimes assume that it is natural for elderly people to feel ill. As a result, symptoms that would indicate a treatable medical problem in younger people are taken as inevitable signs of decay in the elderly and frequently go untreated. The false belief that "senility" is inevitable in old age is another damaging myth, as is the belief that most older adults are helpless and dependent on their families for care and financial support. All the research on late adulthood contradicts these stereotypes. Increasingly, people age 65 and over are healthy, productive, and able (Kolata, 1996).

Physical Changes

Aging brings with it inevitable physical signs. Beginning in middle adulthood and continuing through late adulthood, physical appearance and the functioning of every organ change. The hair thins and turns white or gray. The skin wrinkles. Bones become fragile and more easily broken. Muscles

Late adulthood can be a successful and productive time of life. Pianist Eubie Blake, for example, continued to perform well into his 90s.

lose power, and joints stiffen or wear out. Circulation slows, blood pressure rises, and because the lungs hold less oxygen, the older adult has less energy. Body shape and posture change, and the reproductive organs atrophy. Difficulties in falling asleep and staying asleep become more common, and reaction times are slower. Vision, hearing, and the sense of smell all become less acute (Cavanaugh, 1990; LaRue & Jarvik, 1982). Most people are at first unaware of these change, because they occur gradually. But the decline eventually becomes undeniable.

We do not yet know why physical aging happens (DiGiovanna, 1994). One explanation is that genes may program our cells to eventually deteriorate and die. This programming might occur through "death genes" that guide the onset, speed, and course of the body's decline. Alternatively, the genetic instructions for running the body may be capable of being read only a limited number of times before they begin to degrade and instructional errors (aging) result. Eventually, the genetic instructions become so illegible and confused that the body can no longer live. Another explanation for aging is that the parts of the body simply wear out through repeated use, much as the parts of a car ultimately wear out after so many miles. Contributing to this wearing out process may be toxins that the body is exposed to, both external toxins in the environment (radiation, chemicals, viruses, and so forth) and toxins that accumulate as inevitable by-products of the body's own activities.

Still, the physical changes of aging need not be incapacitating for most or even all of late adulthood. In fact, older people can to some extent control the speed at which these changes unfold. In contrast to the physical changes that occurred in adolescence, the changes of middle and late adulthood are only loosely controlled by a person's biological clock. Many factors affect the physical well-being of older adults, some of which they can influence, such as diet (including type and amount of food), exercise, health care, smoking, drug use, and overexposure to sun (Levenson & Aldwin, 1994). Attitude and interests also matter. People who have a continuing sense of usefulness, who maintain old ties, investigate new ideas, and take up new activities, and who feel in control of their lives have the lowest rates of disease and the highest survival rates (Butler & Lewis, 1982; Caspi & Elder, 1986). So there's a good deal of truth in the saying "You're only as old as you feel." In fact, psychologists are starting to use functional or psychological age, instead of chronological age, to predict an older adult's adaptability to life's demands.

Although physical changes are inevitable during late adulthood, how people respond to these changes has a major effect on their quality of life.

Social Development

Far from being weak and dependent, most men and women over 65 live autonomous lives apart from their children and outside of nursing homes, and most are very satisfied with their lifestyles. In one survey of people 65 years and older, more than half reported being just as happy as they were when younger. Three-quarters said they were involved in activities that were as interesting to them as any they had engaged in during their younger years (Birren, 1983). Political interest certainly does not decline with age: Almost 90 percent of older adults are registered to vote, and two-thirds vote regularly—the greatest percentage turnout of any age group. The American Association of Retired People (AARP) has more than 8 million active members and uses its political force to ensure that entitlement programs for older adults, such as Social Security, are maintained (Butler & Lewis, 1982).

Still, gradual social changes do take place in late adulthood. These changes have been described as occurring in three stages (Cumming & Henry, 1961). The first stage is shrinkage of life space: The older person starts to interact with fewer people and perform fewer social roles. The second stage is increased individuality: Behavior becomes less influenced by social rules and expectations than it was earlier in life. The third and final stage involves acceptance of the changes in the first two stages: The person steps back and assesses life, realizes there is a limit to the capacity for social involvement, and learns to live comfortably with those restrictions. This process does not necessarily entail a psychological "disengagement" with the social world, as some researchers have contended. Instead, older people may simply be making sensible choices that suit their more limited time frames and physical capabilities (Carstensen, 1995).

RETIREMENT Another major change that most people experience in late adulthood is retiring from paid employment. People's reactions to retirement differ greatly, partly because society has no clear idea of what retirees are supposed to do. Should they sit in a rocking chair and watch life go by, or should they play golf, become foster grandparents, and study Greek? The advantage to this lack of clear social expectations is that older adults have the flexibility to structure their retirement as they please.

Of course, the nature and quality of retired life depend in part on financial status. If retirement means a major decline in a person's standard of living, that person will be less eager to retire and will lead a more limited life after retirement. Another factor in people's attitudes toward retirement is their feelings about work. People who are fulfilled by their jobs are usually less interested in retiring than people whose jobs are unrewarding (Atchley, 1982). Similarly, people who have very ambitious, hard-driving personalities tend to want to stay at work longer than those who are more relaxed. The feeling of being forced to retire before you are ready can be a source of real stress. In general, involuntary retirees suffer more depression, ill health, and poor adjustment than do people who choose to retire.

SEXUAL BEHAVIOR A common misconception about the aged is that they have outlived their sexuality. This myth reflects our stereotypes. To the extent that we see the elderly as physically unattractive and frail, we find it difficult to believe that they are sexually active. True, older people respond more slowly and are less sexually active than younger people, but the majority of older adults can enjoy sex and have orgasms. One survey revealed that 37 percent of married people over 60 have sex at least once a week, 20 percent have sex outdoors, and 17 percent swim in the nude (Woodward & Springen, 1992). Another study of people ages 65 to 97 found that about half the men still viewed sex as important, and slightly over half of those in committed relationships were satisfied with the quality of their sex lives (Mark Clements Research, 1995).

Cognitive Changes

Healthy people who remain intellectually involved maintain a high level of mental functioning in old age (Schaie, 1984; Shimamura et al., 1995). Far from the common myth that the brain cells of elderly people are rapidly dying off, the brain of the average person shrinks only about 10 percent in size between the ages of 20 and 70 (Goleman, 1996). This means that, for a sizable number of older adults, cognitive abilities remain largely intact. For instance, interviews with men, now in their 70s, who are part of a long-running longitudinal study of "gifted children," found that those who had remained mentally active and healthy showed no noticeable declines in intellect or vocabulary (Shneidman, 1989). True, the aging mind works a little more slowly (Birren & Fisher, 1995; Salthouse, 1991), and certain types of memories are a little more difficult to store and retrieve (Craik, 1994), but these changes are not serious enough to interfere with the ability to enjoy an active, independent life. Furthermore, training and practice can greatly reduce the decline in cognitive performance in later adulthood (Willis, 1985; Willis & Schaie, 1986).

The psychologist K. Warner Schaie (1994) has spent his entire career studying adult intellectual development. He has collected longitudinal data on 5,000 adults, looking for patterns of changes and the factors that might cause them. Although he has observed a general decline in intellectual abilities over a lengthy portion of the life span (more than 50 years), different abilities decline at different rates. For example, the sharpest decline is in mathematics: At age 74, men tested about one-third lower than they had in their 50s. The smallest decline is in spatial ability (for example, reading a map): At age 80, men tested only about one-eighth lower than they had at age 50.

ALZHEIMER'S DISEASE Unfortunately, some people in late adulthood are not functioning so well. They forget the names of their children or are unable to find their way home from the store. Some even fail to recognize their husband or wife. These people are not suffering from the normal consequences of aging, but rather are victims of **Alzheimer's disease,** named for the German neurologist Alois Alzheimer. Alzheimer's most famous case involved a woman who died in her 50s after suffering a progressive loss of the ability to communicate and reason. When Alzheimer performed an autopsy on her brain, he observed abnormalities: Some neurons had clumped together in tangles, whereas others were shrunken or dead. These are characteristic changes of Alzheimer's disease (Glenner, 1994).

For many years, Alzheimer's disease was considered rare, and it was diagnosed only in people under 60 who developed symptoms of memory loss and confusion. But now Alzheimer's is recognized as a common disorder in older people who used to be called "senile." According to current estimates, 5 to 7 percent of adults over 65 (some 4 million people) and at least 20 percent of adults 85 or older suffer from Alzheimer's disease (Anthony & Aboraya, 1992). Factors that put people at risk for developing the disorder are having a family history of *dementia* (a general decline in physical and cognitive abilities), having Down syndrome or Parkinson's disease, being born to a woman over the age of 40, suffering a head trauma (especially one that caused unconsciousness), and being heterozygous for a certain gene located on chromosome 19 (Kokmen, 1991; Myers, 1996).

Alzheimer's usually begins with minor memory losses, such as difficulty in recalling words and names or in remembering where one put something. As it progresses—and this may take anywhere from 2 to 20 years—personality changes are also likely. First, people may become emotionally withdrawn or flat. Later, they may suffer from delusions, such as thinking that relatives are stealing from them. These people become confused, and may not know where they are or what time of day it is. Eventually, they lose the ability to speak, to care for themselves, and to recognize family members. If they do not die of other causes, Alzheimer's will eventually prove fatal, as the body "forgets" how to swallow and how to breath.

At present there is no known cure for Alzheimer's, but breakthroughs in research are now occurring so fast that a drug to slow the progress of the disorder may be developed in the near future (Henry, 1996).

Facing the End of Life

Fear of death is seldom a central concern for people in later adulthood. In fact, such fear seems to be a greater problem in young adulthood or in middle age, when the first awareness of mortality coincides with a greater interest in living (Kimmel, 1974). One study of attitudes toward death found that 19 percent of

Alzheimer's disease A disorder of common in late adulthood that is characterized by progressive losses in memory and cognition and changes in personality and that is believed to be caused by a deterioration of the brain's structure and function.

7

What is Alzheimer's disease? Can it be treated?

Because people with Alzheimer's disease suffer memory loss, signs can remind them to perform ordinary activities.

8

True or False: Elderly people are much less afraid of death than are younger people.

young adults were afraid of dying, compared with less than 2 percent of people over age 65 (Rogers, 1980). Older people spend more time taking stock of past accomplishments than worrying about death (Butler, 1963). This does not mean that the elderly are constantly brooding about the past. Rather, review of one's life goes on alongside concerns about the present.

But the elderly do have some major fears associated with dying. They fear the pain, indignity, and depersonalization they might experience during a terminal illness, as well as the possibility of dying alone. They also worry about burdening their relatives with the expenses of their hospitalization or nursing care. As for their relatives, they have their own fears about dying, and these fears, combined with the psychological pain they feel watching a loved one die, sometimes makes them depersonalize the loved one just at the time when that person most needs comfort and compassion (Kübler-Ross, 1975).

STAGES OF DYING   Psychiatrist Elisabeth Kübler-Ross (1969) interviewed more than 200 dying people of all ages to try to understand the psychological aspects of dying. From these interviews, she described a sequence of five stages that she believed people pass through as they react to their own impending death.

- *Denial:* The person denies the diagnosis, refuses to believe that death is approaching, insists that an error has been made, and seeks other, more acceptable opinions or alternatives.

- *Anger:* The person now accepts the reality of the situation, but expresses envy and resentment toward those who will live to fulfill a plan or dream. The question becomes "Why me?" Anger may be directed at the doctor or randomly in all directions. The patience and understanding of other people are particularly important at this stage.

- *Bargaining:* The person desperately tries to buy time, negotiating with doctors, family members, clergy, and God in a healthy attempt to cope with the realization of death.

- *Depression.* As bargaining fails and time is running out, the person may succumb to depression, lamenting failures and mistakes that can no longer be corrected.

- *Acceptance:* Tired and weak, the person at last enters a state of "quiet expectation," submitting to fate.

According to Kübler-Ross, Americans have a greater problem coping with death than people in some other cultures because we fear and deny it. She observes that while some cultures are *death affirming,* American culture is *death denying:* "We are reluctant to reveal our age; we spend fortunes to hide our wrinkles; we prefer to send our old people to nursing homes" (1975, p. 28). We also shelter children from knowledge of death and dying. By trying to protect them from these unpleasant realities, however, we may actually make them more fearful of death.

Some observers have found fault with Kübler-Ross's model of dying. Most of the criticisms have focused on her methodology. She studied only a relatively small sample of people and provided little information about how they were selected and how often they were interviewed. Also, all her patients were suffering from cancer. Does her model apply as well to people dying from other causes? Finally, some critics question the universality of her model. Death itself is universal, but reactions to dying may differ greatly from one culture to another.

Despite these legitimate questions, there is nearly universal agreement that Kübler-Ross deserves credit for pioneering the study of the transitions people undergo during the dying process. She was the first to investigate an area long considered taboo, and her research has made dying a more "understandable" experience, perhaps one that is easier to deal with.

WIDOWHOOD   The death of one's spouse may be the most severe challenge people face during late adulthood. Especially if it was unexpected, people respond to such a loss with initial disbelief, followed by numbness. Only later is the full impact of the loss felt, and that can be severe. The incidence of depression rises significantly following the death of a spouse (Norris & Murrell, 1990). Moreover, a long-term study of several thousand widowers 55 years of age and older revealed that nearly 5 percent of them died in the 6-month period following their wife's death, a figure that is well above the expected death rate for men that age. Thereafter, the mortality rate of these men fell gradually to a more normal level (Butler & Lewis, 1982).

Perhaps because they are not as used to taking care of themselves, men seem to suffer more than women from the loss of a mate. But because women have a longer life expectancy, there are many more widows than widowers. Thus, men have a better chance of remarrying. More than half the women over 65 are widowed, and half of them will live another 15 years without remarrying. For somewhat different reasons, then, the burden of widowhood is heavy for both men and women (Feinson, 1986).

SUMMARY

This chapter deals with **developmental psychology,** the study of the changes that occur in people from birth through old age.

METHODS IN DEVELOPMENTAL PSYCHOLOGY

To examine changes that take place over time, developmental psychologists use three different methods. In **cross-sectional studies,** researchers test groups of subjects of different ages. In **longitudinal studies,** researchers test the same subjects—usually a **cohort,** or group of people born during the same historical period—as they grow older. For studying adulthood, researchers sometimes use **biographical** or **retrospective studies,** in which subjects' lives are examined *backward* through interviews. Each of these methods has certain advantages and disadvantages.

PRENATAL DEVELOPMENT

The period from conception to birth is called **prenatal development.** Two weeks after conception, the fertilized egg has become an **embryo;** 3 months after conception, the developing organism is called a **fetus.** The fetus is nourished by an organ called the **placenta.** Disease-producing organisms and substances the mother eats, drinks, or inhales can pass through the placenta and, at **critical periods,** do major harm to the fetus.

THE NEWBORN BABY

Neonates (newborn babies) come equipped with a number of reflexes, such as those that help them breathe and nurse. The **rooting reflex** causes a newborn, when touched on the cheek, to turn its head in that direction and grope around with its mouth. The **sucking reflex** causes the newborn to suck on anything that is placed in its mouth, and the **swallowing reflex** enables it to swallow liquids without choking. The **grasping reflex** causes a newborn to close its fist around anything that is put in its hand. The **stepping reflex** causes the newborn to make little stepping motions if held upright with its feet just touching a surface.

Temperament

Babies are born with personalities that differ in **temperament.** The pioneering work of Thomas and Chess identified three basic types of temperament in newborns— easy, difficult, and slow-to-warm-up. A great deal of research has examined the differences among them.

The Perceptual Abilities of Infants

Infants can see as soon as they are born. Vision is fuzzy at first, but visual acuity improves rapidly. Newborns prefer patterns with clear contrasts, so they like looking at black-and-white patterns better than at colored ones. As they grow older they prefer more complex patterns. They also prefer to look at their mother rather than a stranger. A classic experiment using a device called the *visual cliff* showed that infants of crawling age can perceive depth.

Fetuses can hear sounds in the uterus, and newborns can tell the direction of a sound. Infants can distinguish between some speech sounds that are indistinguishable to an adult. Infants also have clear-cut preferences in taste and smell.

INFANCY AND CHILDHOOD
Physical Development
Growth of the body is most rapid during the first year, when it can occur in startling spurts. It then slows down until early adolescence. During the prenatal period and the first 2 years of life, the head grows rapidly. The body does most of the growing from then on.

Motor Development
Motor development refers to the acquisition of abilities such as grasping and walking. **Developmental norms** indicate the ages at which the average child achieves certain developmental milestones. During early motor development, the reflexes of the newborn give way to voluntary action. **Maturation**—the biological processes that unfold as we grow older—interacts with environmental factors in promoting developmental changes in our early motor skills.

Cognitive Development
Cognitive development refers to changes in the way children think about the world. The Swiss psychologist Jean Piaget saw cognitive development as a way of adapting to the environment and theorized that it proceeds in a series of distinct stages.

During the **sensory-motor stage** (birth to age 2), infants develop **object permanence,** the concept that things continue to exist even when they are out of sight. At birth, there is no sign of object permanence, but the concept is fully developed by 18 to 24 months, when the child acquires the ability to form **mental representations**—mental images or symbols (such as words) used in thinking and remembering. The development of self-recognition also occurs during the sensory-motor stage.

In the **preoperational stage** (ages 2 through 7), children are able to use mental representations and language assumes an important role in describing, remembering, and reasoning about the world. But preoperational thought is **egocentric:** Children of this age are unable to see things from another person's point of view. They are also easily misled by appearances and tend to focus on the most striking aspect of an object or event.

Children in the **concrete-operational stage** (7 to 11) can pay attention to more than one thing at a time and are able to understand someone else's point of view. They grasp the **principles of conservation**—that basic amounts remain constant despite changes in appearance—and they can understand classification schemes.

When they enter the **formal-operational stage** (between 11 and 15), adolescents can think in abstract terms and test their ideas internally, using logic. Thus, they can grasp theoretical cause-and-effect relationships and consider possibilities as well as realities.

Piaget's theory has been criticized for the content of the stages as well as for his assumption that all children proceed through the stages in the same order. Critics also fault Piaget for not taking human diversity into consideration.

Moral Development
Like Piaget, Lawrence Kohlberg developed a stage theory, although his involves moral development. Kohlberg's stages—preconventional, conventional, and postconventional—hinge on the different ways the developing child views morality. The preconventional child sees doing right and wrong as a function of physical consequences; the conventional child sees it as a function of what others think; and the postconventional individual sees right behavior as based on a system of values and justice.

Language Development
Language begins with cooing and progresses to **babbling,** the repetition of speechlike sounds. The first word is usually uttered at about 12 months; at the same age, infants show signs of understanding what is said to them. In the next 6 to 8 months, children build a vocabulary of one-word sentences, called **holophrases.** Between 2 and 3, children begin to put words together into simple sentences, though they leave out unimportant parts of speech such as auxiliary verbs. Between 3 and 4, children fill out their sentences and are able to use past and present tenses. By 5 or 6, most children have a vocabulary of over 2,500 words and can create sentences of 6 to 8 words.

There are two different theories of language development. Skinner proposed that parents listen to their infant's babbling and reinforce (reward) the infant for making sounds that most resemble adult speech. Chomsky, on the other hand, maintained that children are born with a **language acquisition device,** an innate mechanism that enables them to understand the rules of grammar, make sense of the speech they hear, and form intelligible sentences themselves. Most researchers agree with Chomsky's view.

The critical period hypothesis postulates that there is a critical time for the acquisition of language. If language is not acquired during that time, it will be very difficult for the child to master it later.

Social Development
A baby duck or goose follows its mother because of a phenomenon called **imprinting,** a primitive form of bonding. Bonding in humans is a more complex emotional process called **attachment.** The first attachment is likely to be to the infant's primary caregiver, usually the mother. It develops during the first year of life, usually along with a wariness of strangers.

Infants who are securely attached to their mothers are better able to develop **autonomy,** a sense of independence. Children who are insecurely attached to others are less likely to explore an unfamiliar environment.

At about 2 years of age, the child's desire for autonomy clashes with the parents' need for peace and order. These conflicts are a necessary first step in **socialization,** the process by which children learn the behaviors and attitudes appropriate to their family and culture. Parenting style affects children's behavior and self-image. The most successful parenting style is authoritative, in which parents provide firm guidance but are willing to listen to the child's opinions. However, parents do not act the same way toward every child in the family because children are different from each other and elicit different parental responses.

The earliest kind of play is **solitary play**—children engaging in some activity all by themselves. The earliest kind of social interaction is **parallel play,** in which two toddlers play side by side at the same activity but largely ignore each other. By 3 or 3½, they are engaging in **cooperative play** involving group imagination. As children get older, they develop a deeper understanding of the meaning of friendship and come under the influence of a **peer group**.

By age 3, a child has developed a **gender identity,** a girl's knowledge that she is a girl and boy's knowledge that he is a boy. But children that age have little idea of what it means. By 4 or 5, most children develop **gender constancy,** the realization that gender depends on what kind of genitals one has and cannot be changed.

Gender-role awareness—the knowledge of what behavior is appropriate for each gender—develops as children interact with their society. As a result they develop **gender stereotypes,** oversimplified beliefs about "typical" males and females. From an early age, children show **sex-typed behavior**—behavior that is typical of females (for example, playing with dolls) or of males (for example, playing with trucks).

Television and Children

American children spend more time watching television than engaging in any other activity except sleeping. If TV viewing involves constant exposure to scenes of violence, the evidence suggests that children become more aggressive in their behavior. The most convincing theoretical argument linking violent behavior with TV watching is based on social learning theory. Viewing behaviors on television that are violent and characters who are reinforced for such violence leads children to imitate that behavior. Some evidence suggests TV can be an effective teaching tool.

ADOLESCENCE

Adolescence is the period of life when the individual is transformed from a child to an adult between age 10 and 20.

Physical Changes

The **growth spurt** is a rapid increase in height and weight that begins, on the average, at about age 10½ in girls and 12½ in boys, and reaches its peak at age 12 in girls and 14 in boys. Growth is essentially complete about 6 years after the start of the growth spurt. During this period, changes occur in body shape and proportions as well as in size.

Signs of **puberty**—the onset of sexual maturation—begin around 11½ in boys. In girls, the growth spurt typically precedes the approaching puberty. **Menarche,** the first menstrual period, occurs between 12½ and 13 for the average American girl. But individuals vary widely in when they go through puberty.

Teen pregnancy is a serious problem in the United States, with more than 1 million births per year to teenagers, 80 percent of whom are unmarried.

Cognitive Changes

The cognitive abilities of adolescents undergo an important transition to formal-operational thought, allowing them to manipulate abstract concepts, reason hypothetically, and speculate about alternatives. These new mental abilities often make them overconfident and overimpressed with their own importance. Elkind described two patterns of thought characteristic of this age: the **imaginary audience,** which makes teenagers feel they are constantly being watched and judged; and the **personal fable,** which gives young people the sense that they are unique and invulnerable and encourages them to take needless risks.

Personality and Social Development

The classical view of adolescence as a period of "storm and stress" fraught with conflict, anxiety, and tension is not borne out in most teenagers' lives, although there is inevitably some stress to handle.

Identity formation is the process by which a person develops a stable sense of self. According to Marcia, identity formation takes place during an intense period of self-exploration called an **identity crisis.**

Most adolescents rely on a peer group for social and emotional support. They often rigidly conform to the values of their friends. From small unisex **cliques** in early adolescence, friendship groups change to mixed-sex groups in which short-lived romantic interests are common. Later stable dating patterns emerge.

Parent-child relationships are difficult during adolescence. Teenagers become aware of their parents' faults and question every parental role. Conflicts are most common during early adolescence, though only in a minority of families does the parent-child relationship show a severe deterioration.

Some Problems of Adolescence

Dissatisfaction with one's body image and one's academic performance can lower an adolescent's self-esteem. A sizable number of adolescents thinks about committing suicide; a much smaller proportion attempt it. Depression, drug abuse, and disruptive behaviors are linked to suicidal thoughts.

ADULTHOOD

Unlike childhood and adolescence, adulthood is not marked by clear, predictable milestones. Still, there are certain experiences and changes that nearly everyone goes through and certain needs that nearly everyone tries to fulfill.

Love, Partnerships, and Parenting

Almost every adult forms a long-term loving partnership with at least one other adult at some point during his or her life. More than 90 percent of all Americans eventually get married, although they are waiting longer to do so. Most people select a marriage or cohabitation partner of similar race, religion, education, and background. Heterosexual marriage is the norm, but other relationships include long-term cohabitation and homosexual partnerships.

Parenthood entails new responsibilities and adjustments. It often heightens conflicts between career and domestic concerns. Once children leave home, parents often renew their relationship as a couple.

Almost half of American marriages end in divorce, which has far-reaching effects on children.

The World of Work

Most people desire satisfaction from their jobs. But a married woman who works outside the home is likely to be burdened with child care and housework as well as a job; moreover, her job is likely to be less prestigious than her husband's. The emergence of the dual-career family has also raised many questions concerning the availability of quality child care.

Cognitive Changes

An adult's thinking is more flexible and practical than an adolescent's. Whereas adolescents search for the one "correct" solution to a problem, adults realize that there may be several "right" solutions or none at all.

One model of cognitive change maintains that cognitive exercises can minimize the inevitable decline in cognitive functioning as people age.

Personality Changes

Adults become less self-centered and develop better coping skills with age. Some people may experience a **midlife crisis,** when they feel unfulfilled and ready for a decisive shift in career or lifestyle. More commonly, people go through a **midlife transition,** a period of taking stock of one's life and formulating new goals.

The "Change of Life"

Middle adulthood brings a decline in the functioning of the reproductive organs. Women go through **menopause,** the cessation of menstruation accompanied by a sharp drop in estrogen. Men experience a slower decline in testosterone.

LATE ADULTHOOD

Older adults are the fastest-growing segment of the U.S. population. Our stereotypes of "elderly" people are contradicted by research showing people 65 and older are increasingly healthy, productive, and able.

Physical Changes

The physical changes of late adulthood affect outward appearance and the functioning of every organ. Although aging is inevitable, heredity and lifestyle play a role in the timing of this process.

Social Development

Most older adults have an independent and satisfactory lifestyle and engage in social activities that interest them. But they gradually go through a process of disengagement and life assessment and accept necessary limitations on their social involvement.

People's reactions to leaving the world of paid employment differ, depending on their financial status and their feelings about work.

Sexual responses are slower in older adults, but most recent information indicates that people continue to enjoy sex.

Cognitive Changes

Cognitive abilities remain largely intact for a sizable number of older adults. Older adults who engage in intellectually stimulating activities remain mentally alert.

Old people who used to be called "senile" are now recognized as having a specific disorder called **Alzheimer's disease,** which causes progressive losses in memory and cognition and changes in personality. However, it is important to distinguish Alzheimer's disease from other causes of mental impairment that may be treatable.

Facing the End of Life

Elderly people fear death less than younger people. What they do fear are the pain, indignity, depersonalization, and loneliness associated with a terminal illness. They also worry about being a financial burden to their families.

Kübler-Ross described a sequence of five stages that people go through when they are dying: denial, anger, bargaining, depression, and acceptance.

Widowhood may be the most severe challenge people face as older adults. Loss of a spouse may bring on depression. Men seem to suffer more from loss of a mate but have a better chance of remarrying.

REVIEW QUESTIONS

MULTIPLE CHOICE AND SHORT ANSWER

1. In a _____ study the researcher studies a group of subjects two or more times as they grow older.

2. Neonates are only capable of simple reflexes and are relatively unresponsive to the outside world. T/F

3. Newborn babies will sometimes imitate the facial expressions of adults. T/F

4. Very young infants prefer a black-and-white pattern to a colored one. T/F

5. Put Piaget's stages of cognitive development in the right order and describe how thinking changes at each stage.
   Formal-operational stage
   Preoperational stage
   Sensory-motor stage
   Concrete-operational stage

6. What makes a duckling follow its mother? Why is this an important activity for ducklings?

7. What makes a human baby 12 months old cling to his or her mother when frightened or hurt?

8. The process by which children learn the behaviors and attitudes appropriate to their family and their culture is called _____.

9. The growth spurt begins at an average age of _____ in girls and _____ in boys.

10. An important milestone for a girl is _____, her first menstrual period.

11. In the conventional level of moral reasoning, adolescents judge "right" and "wrong" in terms of whether they are rewarded or punished for their actions. T/F

12. The most important milestone in the transition to adulthood is _____.

CRITICAL THINKING AND APPLICATIONS

1. Serena, a pregnant woman, says that the fetus inside her is safe and oblivious to what is happening, either to itself or to Serena. She says that the baby will "wake up" when he or she is born. Briefly respond to these statements.

2. With the expansion of dual-income families, what kinds of child-care arrangements have been developed in U.S. society? Do you think they help or hurt children?

3. Rick and Ann's adult children blush at the suggestion that their 65-year-old parents still have sex together. What evidence could you present to convince them that it's likely Rick and Ann are not only sexually active but very much enjoy making love to each other?

ENDURING ISSUES

Stability–Change

To what extent do mental abilities (intelligence, ability to remember, cognitive skills) change over the life span? If someone is unusually good at these kinds of things early in life, is he or she likely also to be unusually good at them later in life?

Heredity–Environment

After reading this chapter, to what extent do you think that people are shaped by heredity (nature) and to what extent shaped by their environment and their experiences (nurture)?

(Answers to the Review Questions appear in the back of the book.)

11 Personality

The Case of Jaylene Smith   Thirty-year-old Jaylene Smith is a talented physician who visits a psychologist because she is troubled by certain aspects of her social life. Acquaintances describe Jay in glowing terms—highly motivated, intelligent, attractive, and charming. But Jay feels terribly insecure and anxious. When asked by a psychologist to pick out some self-descriptive adjectives, she selected "introverted," "shy," "inadequate," and "unhappy."

Jay was the first-born in a family of two boys and one girl. Her father is a quiet and gentle medical researcher. His work often allowed him to

Think About It!

1. What do psychologists mean by "personality"?
2. According to Freud, how do unconscious desires and processes affect our behavior?
3. What do psychologists mean by "humanistic personality theories"?
4. Is human behavior consistent across time and situations, or does it vary with circumstances?
5. What is a Rorschach test, and what can it tell us about personality?

study at home, so he had extensive contact with his children when they were young. He loved all his children but clearly favored Jay. His ambitions and goals for her were extremely high, and as she matured, he responded to her every need and demand almost immediately and with full conviction. Their relationship remains as close today as it was during Jay's childhood.

Jay's mother worked long hours away from home as a store manager and consequently saw her children primarily at night and on an occasional free weekend. When she came home, Mrs. Smith was tired and had little energy for "nonessential" interactions with her children. She had always been career oriented, but she experienced considerable conflict and frustration trying to reconcile her roles as mother, housekeeper, and financial provider. Mrs. Smith was usually amiable toward all her children but tended to argue more with Jay, until the bickering subsided when Jay was about 6 or 7 years of age. Today their relationship is cordial but lacks the closeness apparent between Jay and Dr. Smith. Interactions between Dr. and Mrs. Smith were sometimes marred by stormy outbursts over seemingly trivial matters. These episodes were always followed by periods of mutual silence lasting for days.

Jay was very jealous of her first brother, born when she was 2 years old. Her parents recall that Jay sometimes staged temper tantrums when the new infant demanded and received a lot of attention (especially from Mrs. Smith). The temper tantrums intensified when Jay's second brother was born, just one year later. As time went on, the brothers formed an alliance to try to undermine Jay's supreme position with their father. Jay only became closer to her father, and her relationships with her brothers were marked by greater-than-average jealousy and rivalry from early childhood to the present.

Throughout elementary, junior high, and high school, Jay was popular and did well academically. Early on she decided on a career in medicine. Yet off and on between the ages of 8 and 17, she had strong feelings of loneliness, depression, insecurity, and confusion—feelings common enough during this age period, but stronger than in most youngsters and very distressing to Jay.

Jay's college days were a period of great personal growth, but several unsuccessful romantic involvements caused her much pain. The failure to achieve a stable and long-lasting relationship persisted after college and troubled Jay greatly. Although even-tempered in most circumstances, Jay often had an explosive fit of anger that ended each important romantic relationship she had. "What is wrong with me?" she would ask herself. "Why do I find it impossible to maintain a serious relationship for any length of time?"

In medical school, her conflicts crept into her consciousness periodically: "I don't deserve to be a doctor"; "I won't pass my exams"; "Who am I, and what do I want from life?"

How can we describe and understand Jaylene Smith's personality? How did she become who she is? Why does she feel insecure and uncertain despite her obvious success? Why do her friends see her as charming and attractive, though she describes herself as introverted and inadequate? These are the kinds of questions that personality psychologists are likely to ask about Jay—and the kinds of questions we will try to answer in this chapter.

Psychologists typically define **personality** as an individual's unique pattern of thoughts, feelings, and behaviors that persists over time and across situations. Notice that this definition has two important parts. First, personality refers to a *unique pattern,* those aspects of a person that distinguish him or her from everybody else. Second,

1 What do psychologists mean by "personality"?

this pattern persists through time and across situations—that is, personality is relatively *stable* and *enduring.* Perhaps you have had the chance to view yourself at various ages in home movies or videos. At each age some of the same characteristics are evident—maybe you are a natural performer, always showing off for the camera, or it could be you are a director type, telling the camera operator what to do at 4 years of age as well as at 14. We expect people's personalities to be relatively consistent from day to day and from one situation to another; in fact, when that is not so, we generally suspect that something is wrong with the person.

Psychologists approach the study of personality in a number of ways. Some try to identify the most important characteristics of personality. Others seek to understand why personalities differ. Among the latter group, some psychologists identify the family as the most important factor in the development of the individual's personality, whereas others emphasize environmental influences outside the family, and still others see personality as the result of how we learn to think about ourselves and our experiences. Out of these various approaches have come four major categories of personality theories:

- *Psychodynamic theories* place the origins of personality in unconscious, often sexual, motivations and conflicts.
- *Humanistic theories* spotlight positive growth motives and the realization of potential in shaping personality.
- *Trait theories* categorize and describe the ways in which people's personalities differ.
- *Cognitive–social learning theories* find the roots of personality in the ways people think about, act on, and respond to their environment.

To varying degrees, each of these theoretical approaches contributes to our overall understanding of personality.

In this chapter, we will examine some representative theories each approach has produced. We will also see how each theory can help us to shed light on and understand the personality of Jaylene Smith.

PSYCHODYNAMIC THEORIES

Psychodynamic theories see behavior as the end product of psychological dynamics that interact within the individual, often outside conscious awareness. Freud drew on the physics of his day to coin the term *psychodynamics*: As thermodynamics is the study of heat and mechanical energy and how one may be transformed into the other, psychodynamics is the study of psychic energy and how it is transformed and expressed in behavior. Psychodynamic theorists disagreed among themselves about the exact nature of this psychic energy. Some, like Freud, traced it to sexual and aggressive urges; others, like Karen Horney, saw it as rooted in the individual's struggle to deal with dependency. But all psychodynamic theorists share the sense that unconscious processes primarily determine personality and can best be understood within the context of life-span development.

Unconscious In Freud's theory, all the ideas, thoughts, and feelings of which we are not and normally cannot become aware.

Psychoanalysis The theory of personality Freud developed as well as the form of therapy he invented.

Id In Freud's theory of personality, the collection of unconscious urges and desires that continually seek expression.

Pleasure principle According to Freud, the way in which the id seeks immediate gratification of an instinct.

2 According to Freud, how do unconscious desires and processes affect our behavior?

Sigmund Freud

To this day, Sigmund Freud (1856–1939) is the best-known and most influential of the psychodynamic theorists. Freud created an entirely new perspective on the study of human behavior. Up to his time, psychology had focused on consciousness—that is, on those thoughts and feelings of which we are aware. Freud, however, stressed the **unconscious**—all the ideas, thoughts, and feelings of which we are not normally aware. Freud's ideas form the basis of **psychoanalysis,** a term that encompasses both his theory of personality and the form of therapy that he invented.

According to Freud, human behavior is based on unconscious instincts, or drives. Some instincts are aggressive and destructive; others, such as hunger, thirst, self-preservation, and sex, are necessary to the survival of the individual and the species. Freud used the term *sexual instincts* to refer not just to erotic sexuality but also to the desire for virtually any form of pleasure. In this broad sense, Freud regarded the sexual instinct as the most critical factor in the development of personality.

HOW PERSONALITY IS STRUCTURED Freud theorized that personality is formed around three structures: the *id*, the *ego*, and the *superego*. The **id** is the only structure present at birth and is completely unconscious (see Figure 11–1). In Freud's view, the id consists of unconscious urges and desires that continually seek expression. It operates according to the **pleasure principle**—that is, it tries to obtain immediate pleasure and avoid pain. As soon as an instinct arises, the id seeks to gratify it. Because the id is not in contact with the real world, however, it has only two ways of obtaining gratification. One is by reflex actions, such as coughing, which relieve unpleasant sensations at once. Another is through fantasy, or what Freud referred to as *wish fulfillment*: A person forms a mental image of an object or situation that partially satisfies the instinct and relieves the uncomfortable feeling. This kind of thought occurs most often in dreams and daydreams, but it may

Figure 11–1
The structural relationship formed by the id, ego, and superego.
Freud's conception of personality is often depicted as an iceberg to illustrate how the vast workings of the mind occur beneath its surface. Notice how the ego is partly conscious, partly unconscious, and partly preconscious; it derives knowledge of the external world through the senses. The superego also works at all three levels. But the id is an entirely unconscious structure.

Source: Adapted from *New Introductory Lectures on Psychoanalysis* by Sigmund Freud, 1933, New York: Carlton House.

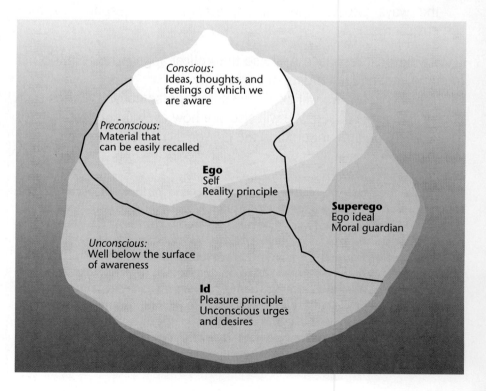

take other forms. For instance, if someone enrages you and you spend the next half hour imagining all the brilliant things you might say or do to get even with that person, you are engaging in a form of wish fulfillment.

Mental images of this kind provide fleeting relief, but they cannot fully satisfy most needs. Just thinking about being with someone you love may be gratifying, but it is a poor substitute for actually being with that person. Therefore, the id by itself is not very effective at gratifying instincts. It must link up with reality if it is to relieve its discomfort. The id's link to reality is the ego.

Freud conceived of the **ego** as the psychic mechanism that controls all thinking and reasoning activities. The ego operates partly consciously, partly *preconsciously*, and partly unconsciously. ("Preconscious" refers to material that is not currently in awareness but can easily be recalled.) The ego learns about the external world through the senses and sees to the satisfaction of the id's drives in the external word. But instead of acting on the pleasure principle, the ego operates by the **reality principle:** By means of intelligent reasoning, the ego tries to delay satisfying the id's desires until it can do so safely and successfully. For example, if you are thirsty, your ego will attempt to determine how best to obtain something to quench your thirst effectively and safely.

A personality that consisted only of ego and id would be completely selfish. It would behave effectively but unsociably. Fully adult behavior is governed not only by reality but also by morality—that is, by the individual's conscience, or the moral standards the individual develops through interaction with parents and society. Freud called this moral watchdog the **superego.**

The superego is not present at birth. In fact, as young children, we are amoral and do whatever is pleasurable. As we mature, however, we assimilate, or adopt as our own, the judgments of our parents about what is "good" and "bad." In time, the external restraint applied by our parents gives way to our own internal self-restraint. The superego, eventually acting as conscience, takes over the task of observing and guiding the ego, just as the parents once observed and guided the child. Like the ego, it works at the conscious, preconscious and unconscious levels.

According to Freud, the superego also compares the ego's actions with an **ego ideal** of perfection and then rewards or punishes the ego accordingly. Unfortunately, the superego is sometiems too harsh in its judgments. An artist dominated by such a punishing superego, for example, may realize the impossibility of ever equaling Rembrandt and give up painting in despair.

Ideally, our id, ego, and superego work in harmony, the ego satisfying the demands of the id in a reasonable, moral manner approved by the superego. We are then free to love and hate and to express our emotions sensibly and without guilt. When our id is dominant, our instincts are unbridled, and we are apt to endanger both ourselves and society. When our superego dominates, our behavior is checked too tightly, and we are inclined to judge ourselves too harshly or too quickly, impairing our ability to act on our own behalf and enjoy ourselves.

HOW PERSONALITY DEVELOPS   Freud's theory of personality development focuses on the way in which we satisfy the sexual instinct during the course of life. Freud thought of the sexual instinct broadly, as a craving for sensual pleasure of all kinds. He called the energy generated by the sexual instinct **libido.** As infants mature, their libido becomes focused on different sensitive parts of the body. During the first 18 months of life, the dominant source of sensual pleasure is the mouth. At about 18 months, sensuality shifts to the

Ego Freud's term for the part of the personality that mediates between environmental demands (reality), conscience (superego), and instinctual needs (id); now often used as a synonym for "self."

Reality principle According to Freud, the way in which the ego seeks to satisfy instinctual demands safely and effectively in the real world.

Superego According to Freud, the social and parental standards the individual has internalized; the conscience and the ego ideal.

Ego ideal The part of the superego that consists of standards of what one would like to be.

Libido According to Freud, the energy generated by the sexual instinct.

Fixation According to Freud, a partial or complete halt at some point in the individual's psychosexual development.

Oral stage First stage in Freud's theory of personality development, in which the infant's erotic feelings center on the mouth, lips, and tongue.

Anal stage Second stage in Freud's theory of personality development, in which a child's erotic feelings center on the anus and on elimination.

Phallic stage Third stage in Freud's theory of personality development, in which erotic feelings center on the genitals.

Oedipus complex and **Electra complex** According to Freud, a child's sexual attachment to the parent of the opposite sex and jealousy toward the parent of the same sex; generally occurs in the phallic stage.

Latency period In Freud's theory of personality, a period in which the child appears to have no interest in the other sex; occurs after the phallic stage.

Genital stage In Freud's theory of personality development, the final stage of normal adult sexual development, which is usually marked by mature sexuality.

Freud believed that during the oral stage, when babies are dependent on others to fulfill their needs, they derive pleasure from the mouth, lips, and tongue. Lack of confidence is among the traits he attributed to fixation at this stage.

anus; and at about age 3, it shifts again, this time to the genitals. According to Freud, children's experiences at each of these stages stamp their personality with tendencies that endure into adulthood. If a child is deprived of pleasure (or allowed too much gratification) from the part of the body that dominates a certain stage, some sexual energy may remain permanently tied to that part of the body, instead of moving on in normal sequence to give the individual a fully integrated personality. This is called **fixation,** and as we shall see, Freud believed that it leads to immature forms of sexuality and to certain characteristic personality traits. Let's look more closely at the psychosexual stages that Freud identified and their presumed relationship to personality development.

In the **oral stage** (birth to 18 months), infants, who depend completely on other people to satisfy their needs, relieve sexual tension by sucking and swallowing; when their baby teeth come in, they obtain oral pleasure from chewing and biting. According to Freud, infants who receive too much oral gratification at this stage grow into overly optimistic and dependent adults; those who receive too little may turn into pessimistic and hostile people later in life. Fixation at this stage is linked to such personality characteristics as lack of confidence, gullibility, sarcasm, and argumentativeness.

During the **anal stage** (roughly 18 months to $3^1/_2$years) the primary source of sexual pleasure shifts from the mouth to the anus. Just about the time children begin to derive pleasure from holding in and excreting feces, toilet training takes place, and they must learn to regulate this new pleasure. In Freud's view, if parents are too strict in toilet training, some children throw temper tantrums and may live in self-destructive ways as adults. Others become obstinate, stingy, and excessively orderly.

When children reach the **phallic stage** (after age 3), they discover their genitals and develop a marked attachment to the parent of the opposite sex while becoming jealous of the same-sex parent. Freud called this the **Oedipus complex,** after the character in Greek mythology who killed his father and married his mother. Girls go through a corresponding **Electra complex,** involving possessive love for their fathers and jealousy toward their mothers. Most children eventually resolve these conflicts by identifying with the parent of the same sex. However, Freud contended that fixation at this stage leads to vanity and egotism in adult life, with men boasting of their sexual prowess and treating women with contempt, and women becoming flirtatious and promiscuous. Phallic fixation may also prompt feelings of low self-esteem, shyness, and worthlessness.

At the end of the phallic period, Freud believed, children lose interest in sexual behavior and enter a **latency period.** During this period, which begins around the age of 5 or 6 and lasts until age 12 or 13, boys play with boys, girls play with girls, and neither sex takes much interest in the other.

At puberty, the individual enters the last psychosexual stage, which Freud called the **genital stage.** At this time, sexual impulses reawaken. In lovemaking, the adolescent and the adult are able to satisfy unfulfilled desires from infancy and childhood. Ideally, immediate gratification of these desires yields to mature sexuality, in which postponed gratification, a sense of responsibility, and caring for others all play a part.

Feminists have assailed Freud's male-centered, phallic view of personality development, especially because he also hypothesized that all little girls feel inferior because they do not have a penis. Many people now see penis envy as much less central to female personality development than Freud thought it was (Gelman, 1990). In fact, the whole notion that male and female personality development proceeds along similar lines is being challenged. For example, if the developmental tasks facing boys and girls are quite different, then the unique developmental tasks encountered by girls may leave them with important skills and abilities that Freud overlooked or minimized.

Freud's beliefs, particularly his emphasis on sexuality, were not completely endorsed even by members of his own psychoanalytic school. Carl Jung and Alfred Adler, two early associates of Freud, eventually broke with him and formulated their own psychodynamic theories of personality. Jung accepted Freud's stress on unconscious motivation but expanded the scope of the unconscious well beyond the selfish satisfactions of the id. Adler believed that human beings have positive—and conscious—goals that guide their behavior. Other psychodynamic theorists put greater emphasis on the ego and its attempts to gain mastery over the world. These neo-Freudians, principally Karen Horney and Erik Erikson, also focused more on the influence of social interaction on personality.

Carl Jung

Carl Jung (1875–1961) embraced many of Freud's tenets; however, his beliefs differed from Freud's in many novel ways. Jung contended that libido, or psychic energy, represents *all* the life forces, not just the sexual ones. Both Freud and Jung emphasized the role of the unconscious in determining human behavior. But, where Freud viewed the id as a "cauldron of seething excitations" that the ego has to control, Jung saw the unconscious as the ego's source of strength and vitality. He also believed that the unconscious breaks down into the personal unconscious and the collective unconscious. Within the realm of the **personal unconscious** fall our repressed thoughts, forgotten experiences, and undeveloped ideas, which may rise to consciousness if an incident or sensation triggers their recall.

The **collective unconscious,** Jung's most original concept, comprises the memories and behavior patterns inherited from past generations. Just as the human body is the product of millions of years of evolution, so too, according to Jung, is the human mind. Over millennia it has developed "thought forms," or collective memories, of experiences that people have had in common since prehistoric times. He called these thought forms **archetypes.** Archetypes appear in our thoughts as typical mental images or

Personal unconscious In Jung's theory of personality, one of the two levels of the unconscious; it contains the individual's repressed thoughts, forgotten experiences, and undeveloped ideas.

Collective unconscious In Jung's theory of personality, the level of the unconscious that is inherited and common to all members of a species.

Archetypes In Jung's theory of personality, thought forms common to all human beings, stored in the collective unconscious.

Carl Jung

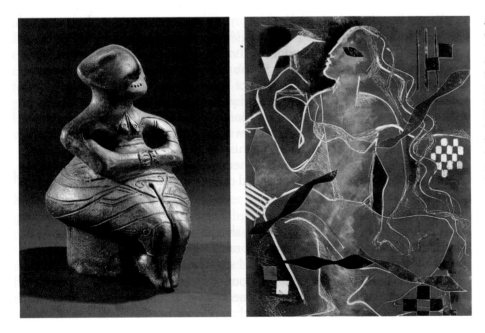

According to Carl Jung, we all inherit from our ancestors collective memories or "thought forms" that people have had in common since the dawn of human evolution. The image of a mother-like figure with protective, embracing arms is one such primordial thought form that stems from the important, nurturing role of women throughout human history. This thought form is depicted here in this Bulgarian clay figure of a goddess that dates back some six or seven thousand years. It is also captured in this contemporary painting, *In Communication,* by the artist Bharati Chaudhuri.

view themselves and others. Freud's ideas have also had a lasting impact on history, literature, and the arts. Yet Freud was a product of his time and place. Critics of his theories have pointed out that he was apparently unable to imagine a connection between his female patients' sense of inferiority and their subordinate position in society. In addition, when patients allegedly told him of sexual abuse they had endured at the hands of family members, Freud initially took these stories at face value but later reversed himself and saw them as fantasies, supporting his theory of the Oedipus and Electra complexes.

Frued's reversal has been challenged on two fronts. First, given our heightened awareness of the high rates of sexual abuse of children, some critics claim that the stories were probably true, and Freud's about-face amounted to caving in to the social disapproval of his hypotheses regarding childhood sexuality (Masson, 1984). More disturbingly, there is growing evidence that Freud's patients may never have actually reported instances of sexual abuse to him; rather, it appears that Freud may have *inferred* sexual abuse in their childhoods from their adult symptoms (Cioffi, 1974; Esterson, 1993; Schatzman, 1992).

Psychodynamic views have also been criticized because they are based largely on retrospective (backward-looking) accounts of individuals who have sought treatment rather than on experimental research with individuals who have not sought treatment. Yet it is often difficult to translate psychodynamic personality theories into hypotheses that can be tested experimentally (Cloninger, 1993).

Still, Freud's theory has received some limited confirmation from experimental research. For example, people who eat and drink too much tend to mention oral images when interpreting inkblot tests (Bertrand & Masling, 1969; Masling, Rabie, & Blondheim, 1967). Orally fixated people also seem to depend heavily on others, as Freud predicted (Fisher & Greenberg, 1985). In addition, some research indicates that a few characteristics of anally fixated people do tend to appear together; for instance, individuals who are stingy are indeed also likely to be neat (Fisher & Greenberg, 1985). However, research has not confirmed that these various personality characteristics stem from the kinds of early-childhood experiences described by Freud. More recent research that uses stimuli designed to activate or "trigger" particular unconscious processes lends some support to Freud's theory (Cloninger, 1993). The effectiveness of psychoanalysis as a therapy has also been cited as evidence in support of Freud's theories. Still, as we shall see in Chapter 14, Therapies, however, psychoanalysis does not seem to be any more or less effective than therapies based on other theories (Stiles, Shapiro, & Elliott, 1986).

Erikson's theory of stages of identity has also prompted a good deal of research, particularly the concept of identity resolution. It has been found, for example, that people who successfully handled the crises of the first four stages were, in fact, more likely to achieve a stable source of identity in the fifth stage (Waterman, Beubel, & Waterman, 1970). Research has also shown that forging a strong identity is necessary for achieving intimacy. College men who were the least isolated socially were also those with the clearest sense of self (Orlofsky, Marcia, & Lesser, 1973). In a follow-up study of the same group of college men, identity continued to be related to intimacy (Marcia, 1976). Yet another study found the same connection between identity and intimacy for both sexes. Men and women both believe that a positive sense of identity is crucial to achieving satisfactory relationships (Orlofsky, 1978).

Freud's theories have clearly expanded our understanding of personality, or they would not still be so vigorously debated today, 100 years after he proposed them. Whatever their merit as science, psychodynamic theories attempt to explain the root causes of all human behavior. The sheer magnitude of this undertaking helps to account for their lasting attractiveness.

HUMANISTIC PERSONALITY THEORIES

Freud believed that personality grows out of the resolution of unconscious conflicts and developmental crises. Many of his followers—including some who modified his theory and others who broke away from his circle—also embraced this basic viewpoint. The theory of Alfred Adler presents a very different view of human nature. Adler focused on forces that contribute to positive growth and a move toward personal perfection. For these reasons, Adler is sometimes called the first humanistic personality theorist.

Humanistic personality theory emphasizes that we are positively motivated and progress toward higher levels of functioning—in other words, that there is more to human existence than dealing with hidden conflicts. Humanistic psychologists believe that life is a process of opening ourselves to the world around us and experiencing joy in living. Humanists stress people's potential for growth and change as well as the ways they subjectively experience their lives right now, rather than dwelling on how they felt or acted in the past. This approach holds all of us personally responsible for our lives and their outcome. Finally, humanists also believe that given reasonable life conditions, people will develop in desirable directions (Cloninger, 1993). Adler's concept of striving for perfection laid the groundwork for later humanistic personality theorists such as Abraham Maslow and Carl Rogers. We discussed Maslow's theory of the hierarchy of needs leading to self-actualization in Chapter 9, Motivation and Emotion. We now turn to Rogers's theory of self-actualization.

Carl Rogers

One of the most prominent humanistic theorists, Carl Rogers (1902–1987) contended that men and women develop their personalities in the service of positive goals. According to Rogers, every organism is born with certain innate capacities, capabilities, or potentialities—"a sort of genetic blueprint, to which substance is added as life progresses" (Maddi, 1989, p. 102). The goal of life, Rogers believed, is to fulfill this genetic blueprint, to become the best of whatever each of us is inherently capable of becoming. Rogers called this biological push toward fulfillment the **actualizing tendency.** Although Rogers maintained that the actualizing tendency characterizes all organisms—plants, animals, and humans—he noted that human beings also form images of themselves, or *self-concepts.* Just as we try to fulfill our inborn biological potential, so, too, we attempt to fulfill our self-concept, our conscious sense of who we are and what we want to do with our lives. Rogers called this striving the **self-actualizing tendency.** If you think of yourself as "intelligent" and "athletic," for example, you will strive to live up to those images of yourself.

When our self-concept is closely matched with our inborn capacities, we are likely to become what Rogers called a **fully functioning person.** Such people are self-directed: They decide for themselves what it is they wish to do and to become, even though their choices may not always be sound ones. They are not unduly swayed by other people's expectations for

Humanistic personality theory Any personality theory that asserts the fundamental goodness of people and their striving toward higher levels of functioning.

Actualizing tendency According to Rogers, the drive of every organism to fulfill its biological potential and become what it is inherently capable of becoming.

Self-actualizing tendency According to Rogers, the drive of human beings to fulfill their self-concepts, or the images they have of themselves.

Fully functioning person According to Rogers, an individual whose self-concept closely resembles his or her inborn capacities or potentials.

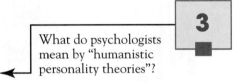

3 What do psychologists mean by "humanistic personality theories"?

Carl Rogers believed that the goal of life is to fulfill our innate potential, which ideally comes to be reflected in the image we have of ourselves. This young woman's work painting houses for the poor suggests that she sees herself as kind and caring and is striving to reflect that image in her actions. In Rogers's view she would be on the way to becoming a self-actualized person.

Unconditional positive regard In Rogers's theory, the full acceptance and love of another person regardless of that person's behavior.

Conditional positive regard In Rogers's theory, acceptance and love that are dependent on behaving in certain ways and fulfilling certain conditions.

them. Fully functioning people are also open to experience—to their own feelings as well as to the world and other people around them—and thus find themselves "increasingly willing to be, with greater accuracy and depth, that self which [they] most truly [are]" (Rogers, 1961, pp. 175–176).

According to Rogers, people tend to become more fully functioning if they are brought up with **unconditional positive regard,** or the experience of being treated with warmth, respect, acceptance, and love regardless of their own feelings, attitudes, and behaviors.

But often parents and other adults offer children what Rogers called **conditional positive regard:** They value and accept only certain aspects of the child. The acceptance, warmth, and love the child receives from others then depends on the child's behaving in certain ways and fulfilling certain conditions. The condition may be expressed explicitly, such as "Daddy won't love you if . . ." or "Mommy doesn't love girls who . . ." But it may also come through subtly, as in statements like "That's a nice idea, but wouldn't you rather do . . . ?" The message here is twofold: The other person finds your feelings or behavior questionable and proposes alternatives that are allegedly better for you. Not surprisingly, one response to conditional positive regard is a tendency to change your self-concept to include those things that you "ought to be," to become more like the person you are expected to be to win the caregiver's love. In the process, your self-concept comes to resemble your inborn capacity less and less, and your life deviates from the genetic blueprint.

When people lose sight of their inborn potential, they become constricted, rigid, and defensive. They feel threatened and anxious and experience considerable discomfort and uneasiness. Because their lives are directed toward what other people want and value, they are unlikely to experience much real satisfaction in life. At some point, they may realize that they don't really know who they are or what they want.

"Do you mind if I say something helpful about your personality?"

Copyright © 1995 Mike Twohy from The Cartoon Bank.

A Humanistic View of Jaylene Smith

Humanistic personality theory would focus on the discrepancy between Jay's self-concept and her inborn capacities. For example, Rogers would point out that Jay is intelligent and achievement-oriented but nevertheless feels that she doesn't "deserve to be a doctor," worries about whether she will ever be "truly happy," and remembers that when she was 13, she never was able to be herself and really express her feelings, even with a good friend. Her unhappiness, fearfulness, loneliness, insecurity, and other dissatisfactions similarly stem from Jay's inability to become what she "most truly is." Rogers would suspect that other people in Jay's life conditioned acceptance and love on her living up to their ideas of what she should become. We know that for most of her life, Jay's father was her primary source of positive regard. Very possibly he conditioned his love for Jay on her living up to his goals for her.

Evaluating Humanistic Theories

The central tenet of most humanistic personality theories—that the overriding purpose of the human condition is to realize one's potential—is difficult if not impossible to verify scientifically. The resulting lack of scientific evidence and rigor is one of the major criticisms of these theories. In addition, some critics claim that humanistic theories present an overly optimistic view of human beings and fail to take into account the evil in human nature. Others contend that the humanistic view fosters self-centeredness and narcissism, and reflects Western values of individual achievement rather than universal human potential.

Nonetheless, Maslow and, especially, Rogers did attempt to test some aspects of their theories scientifically. For example, Rogers studied the discrepancy between the way people perceived themselves and the way they ideally wanted to be. He presented subjects with statements such as "I often feel resentful" and "I feel relaxed and nothing really bothers me." They were asked to sort the statements into several piles indicating how well the statements described their real selves. Then they were asked to sort them again, this time according to how well they described their *ideal* selves. In this way, Rogers discovered that people whose real selves differed considerably from their ideal selves were more likely to be unhappy and dissatisfied. A subsequent study showed that Rogers's client-centered approach to therapy (see Chapter 14) helps to close the gap between a person's *real* and *ideal selves*, leading to greater self-acceptance and an ideal self that includes qualities the person already possesses (Butler & Haigh, 1954).

TRAIT THEORIES

The personality theories we have examined all emphasize the importance of early-childhood experiences in personality development. Other personality theorists take a different approach. They focus on the present, describing the ways in which already-developed adult personalities differ from one another. These *trait theorists*, as they are known, assert that people differ according to the degree to which they possess certain **personality traits,** such as dependency, anxiety, aggressiveness, and sociability.

We infer a trait from how a person behaves. If someone consistently throws parties, goes to great lengths to make friends, and travels in groups, we might safely conclude that this person possesses a high degree of sociability. Our language has many words that describe personality traits. Gordon Allport, along with his colleague H. S. Odbert (1936), went through the dictionary and found nearly 18,000 words that might refer to personality traits. For Allport, traits—or "dispositions," as he called them—are literally encoded in the nervous system as structures that guide consistent behavior across a wide variety of situations. Allport also believed that while traits describe behaviors that are common to many people, each individual personality comprises a unique constellation of traits.

Only about 2,800 of the words on Allport and Odbert's list concern the kinds of stable or enduring characteristics that most psychologists would call personality traits, and when synonyms and near-synonyms are removed, the number of possible personality traits drops to around 200—which is still a formidable list. Psychologist Raymond Cattell (1965), using a statistical technique called **factor analysis,** rated people on 200 personality characteristics. He found that traits tend to cluster in groups. Thus, a person who is

Personality traits Dimensions or characteristics on which people differ in distinctive ways.

Factor analysis A statistical technique that identifies groups of related objects; used by Cattell to identify trait clusters.

According to trait theorists this woman would probably rate high on the traits of cheerfulness, extroversion, friendliness, and sociability. Trait theorists seek to identify sets of human characteristics on the basis of which personality can be assessed.

described as persevering or determined is also likely to be thought of as responsible, ordered, attentive, and stable and probably would not be described as frivolous, neglectful, and changeable. On the basis of extensive research, Cattell originally concluded that just 16 traits account for the complexity of human personality; later he suggested that it might be necessary to add another 7 traits to the list (Cattell & Kline, 1977). According to Cattell, each individual personality consists of a relatively unique constellation of those basic traits.

Other theorists thought that Cattell used too many traits to describe personality. For example, Eysenck (1976) argued that personality could be reduced to three basic dimensions: *emotional stability*, *introversion-extroversion*, and *psychoticism*. According to Eysenck, the basic dimension of *emotional stability* refers to how well people control their emotions. Individuals at one end of this trait would be seen as poised, calm, and composed, whereas people at the other end might be described as anxious, nervous, and excitable. Eysenck's second dimension, *introversion-extroversion*, refers to the degree that a person is inwardly or outwardly oriented. At one end of this dimension would be socially outgoing, talkative, and affectionate people known as *extroverts*. *Introverts*, generally described as reserved, silent, shy, and socially withdrawn, would represent the other extreme. Eysenck used the term *psychoticism* to describe people characterized by insensitivity and uncooperativeness at one end and warmth, tenderness, and helpfulness at the other end. Figure 11–3 shows how Eysenck's first two dimensions of emotional stability and introversion-extroversion can be combined to produce a variety of different individual characteristics.

The Big Five

Although many contemporary trait theorists recognize the importance of Eysenck's early work in reducing the number of traits used to describe per-

Figure 11–3
Eysenck's personality dimensions.
In Eysenck's view, people display varying degrees of *introversion-extroversion* and *emotional stability-instability.* The combination of varying degrees of these two basic traits results in a variety of individual characteristics.

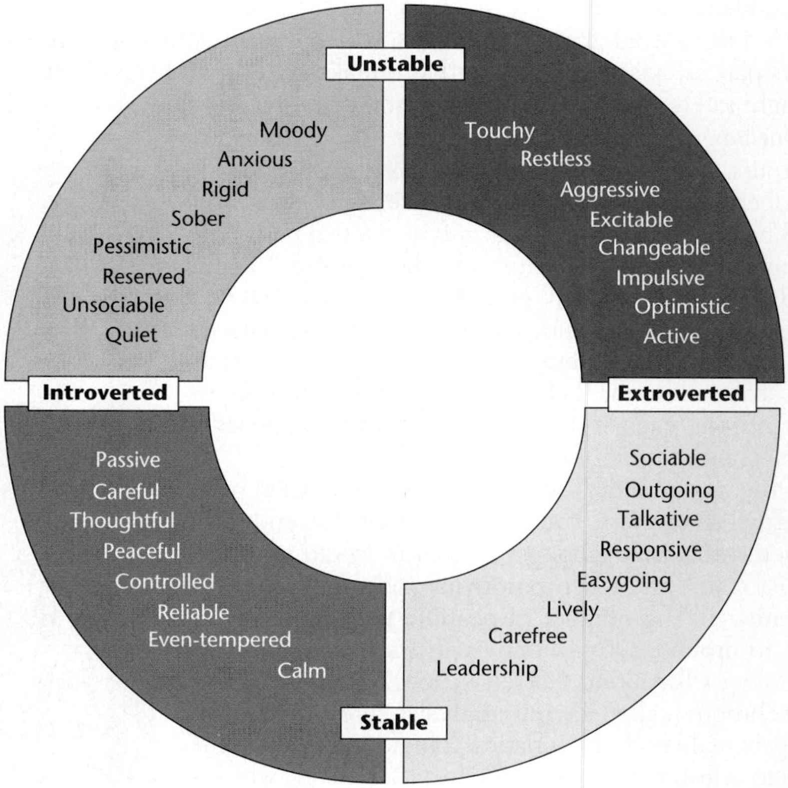

sonality, other studies have indicated that a few additional traits are probably necessary. One early study had boiled personality traits down to five basic dimensions: *extroversion, agreeableness, conscientiousness, emotional stability,* and *culture* (Tupes & Christal, 1961). Subsequent research has repeatedly confirmed this finding (see Table 11–1) (Botwin & Buss, 1989; Goldberg, 1993; Wiggins, 1996), although there is some disagreement about whether the fifth dimension should be called "culture" or "openness to experience" (McCrae & Costa, 1985, 1987, 1989) or "intellect" (Digman & Takemoto-Chock, 1981; Peabody & Goldberg, 1989). At any rate, there is a growing consensus today that the **Big Five** personality dimensions, also known as the *five-factor model,* indeed capture the most salient dimensions of human personality (Funder, 1991; McCrae & Costa, 1996; Wiggins, 1996).

Cross-cultural studies suggest the Big Five may represent universal dimensions of personality. Studies that have looked at the basic dimensions of personality in people from other cultures find that the Big Five model of personality generally applies across a wide variety of Western and non-Western cultures (de Raad & Szirmak, 1994; Narayanan, Menon, & Levin, 1995; Noller, Law, & Comrey, 1987).

The idea that basic personality traits may be universal also draws support from studies showing that at least some traits may, in part, have a genetic basis (Zuckerman, 1995; also see Mayer & Sutton, 1996). Although some early theorists (Eysenck, 1947) suggested that physiological mechanisms underlay basic personality

Big Five Five traits or basic dimensions currently thought to be of central importance in describing personality.

Peter was a born worrier . . .

Source: Drawing by Chas. Addams; © 1984 The New Yorker Magazine, Inc.

TABLE 11–1

THE "BIG FIVE" DIMENSIONS OF PERSONALITY

Extroversion	High scorers: enthusiastic, gregarious, playful, expressive, happy-go-lucky, impetuous, energetic, talkative, assertive, demonstrative, daring, confident, frank, witty, enterprising, optimistic
	Low scorers: unsociable, untalkative, detached, timid, restrained, unadventurous, submissive, lethargic, moody
Agreeableness	High scorers: accommodating, genial, understanding, lenient, courteous, generous, flexible, unassuming, principled, affectionate, down-to-earth, natural
	Low scorers: antagonistic, unsympathetic, demanding, impolite, cruel, condescending, irritable, conceited, stubborn, distrustful, selfish, insensitive, surly, devious, prejudiced, unfriendly, volatile, stingy, deceitful, thoughtless
Conscientiousness/ Dependability	High scorers: organized, efficient, reliable, meticulous, persistent, cautious, punctual, decisive, dignified, consistent, thrifty, conventional, analytical
	Low scorers: disorganized, careless, inconsistent, forgetful, rash, aimless, lazy, indecisive, impractical, nonconforming
Emotional Stability	High scorers: unexcitable, unemotional, autonomous, individualistic
	Low scorers: insecure, anxious, touchy, emotional, envious, gullible, meddlesome
Culture/ Intellect/Openness	High scorers: introspective, deep, insightful, intelligent, creative, curious, sophisticated
	Low scorers: shallow, unimaginative, unobservant, ignorant

traits, only recently has solid evidence from twin studies begun to support this idea (Eaves et al., 1994; Heath, Cloninger, & Martin, 1994; Plomin, 1994). The precise role that genes play in personality is still far from clear, but most contemporary psychologists would agree that both biological and environmental factors contribute to the development of personality (see the *Highlights* box).

One recent survey of the literature found that the Big Five dimensions of personality may also have some important real-world applications—particularly as they relate to employment decisions (Hogan, Hogan, & Roberts, 1996). For example, one study (Ones, Viswesvaran, & Schmidt, 1993) found that the dimensions of conscientiousness and emotional stability were reliable predictors of job performance in a wide variety of occupational settings. In another study the measures of agreeableness and emotional stability

HIGHLIGHTS
How the Home Environment Shapes Personality: An Unexpected Finding

How much of your personality can be attributed to your genes, and how much to your early childhood environment? While there is no exact answer to this question, studies suggest they are approximately equal in importance (Plomin & Rende, 1991; Rutter, 1997). Researchers have found that identical twins raised in the same home are no more alike in personality than identical twins separated during infancy and reared in different homes (Bouchard et al., 1990). This finding makes it appear that environment has no effect on personality. And yet developmental psychologists have always believed that environment *is* important—and they still believe it. How can we reconcile this apparent contradiction?

Recently, psychologists have come up with an unexpected finding: The aspects of the environment that they have traditionally focused on are *not* the ones that seem to have the most impact on a child's personality. The home and family you grew up in, the parents who reared you, the schools you attended, the books and toys in

The aspects of the environment that have the power to shape children's personalities now appear to be those that they do not share with their siblings.

your house, the discussions at the dinner table—none of these seem to have a strong, long-term effect on personality. How do we know this? Because two children who grow up in the same home in these same circumstances do not turn out to be very much alike. In fact, adopted children reared as siblings in the same family have no more similarity in personality as adults than any two people taken at random from a crowd. Genetically related siblings are somewhat similar in personality, but they owe their similarity to their shared genes, not to their shared environment.

The aspects of the environment that have the power to shape children's personalities now appear to be those that they do not share with their siblings. Researchers are becoming more and more convinced that each child in the family grows up in a different environment—an

environment that is unique to that particular child. For example, consider a child who was an "easy" baby and is now a "good girl," who is not very pretty, and who has a younger brother who is always getting into trouble. She gets along well with her mother, who relies on her help and cooperation, but her father wishes he had a prettier daughter. Compare this child's environment to that of her brother, who was a "difficult" baby (and has been typecast as the "bad one" ever since) but who gets along well with his father because the father admires the boy's energy, athletic talent, and good looks. These children are growing up in the same home, with the same parents, but their human relationships and day-to-day experiences are very different.

"The message is not that family experiences are unimportant," concludes one review. But the environmental influences that shape personality development "are specific to each child, rather than general to an entire family" (Plomin & Rende, 1991, p. 180).

predicted performance for employees in customer service positions (Mc-Daniel & Frei, 1994). Thus, the Big Five dimensions of personality may show promise as reliable predictors of job performance.

A Trait View of Jaylene Smith

A psychologist working from the trait perspective would infer certain traits from Jay's behavior. When we observe that Jay chose at an early age to become a doctor, did well academically year after year, and graduated first in her medical-school class, it seems reasonable to infer a trait of "determination" or "persistence" to account for her behavior. Similarly, we might reasonably conclude from her description that she also has traits of sincerity, motivation, and intelligence, as well as insecurity, introversion, shyness, and anxiety. These relatively few traits account for a great deal of Jay's behavior, and they also provide a thumbnail sketch of "what Jay is like."

Evaluating Trait Theories

Traits are the language that we commonly use to describe other people (e.g., as "shy" or "insecure" or "arrogant"). Thus, the trait view of personality has considerable commonsense appeal. Moreover, although psychologists disagree as to the exact number of traits, it is easier to scientifically study personality traits than to study such things as "self-actualization" and "unconscious motives." But trait theories have several shortcomings (Eysenck, 1993; Kroger & Wood, 1993).

First, they are primarily descriptive: They seek to delineate the basic dimensions of personality but generally do not try to explain causes (Funder, 1991). As you can see from the trait view of Jaylene Smith, trait theory tells us little about why she is the way she is. Thus, the five-factor theory of personality helps us much the way north-south and east-west axes do in map making (Goldberg, 1993a, cited in Ozer & Reise, 1994)—that is, it helps us to locate personality more precisely. But like a point on a map, it gives us no information about what kind of terrain is there and how it got to be that way.

In addition, some critics argue that the dangers in reducing the diversity and complexity of human nature to just a few traits are greater than the usefulness that traits offer in terms of description and classification (Mischel & Shoda, 1995). Moreover, psychologists disagree about whether three traits, five traits, or even eight traits are sufficient to capture the complexity of human personality (Almagor, Tellegen, & Waller, 1995; Eysenck, 1992; Mershon & Gorsuch, 1988). Finally, some psychologists question whether traits can really describe and predict behavior. Are "agreeable" people always agreeable? Are they agreeable in all situations? Of course not. But then, how useful is the trait designation of "agreeable" to begin with? The issue of consistency in human behavior has intrigued personality theorists, particularly Walter Mischel.

WALTER MISCHEL: HOW CONSISTENT ARE WE? For Walter Mischel, the answer was, not very. In his early research, Mischel argued that human behavior is more inconsistent than consistent. People act, he reported, in very different ways in different situations (Mischel, 1968). But later research confirmed that at least some behaviors are relatively stable over long periods of time and in different situations (Mischel, 1977; Mischel & Peake, 1982). And, in fact, the big five dimensions of personality show some continuity during early childhood and appear to be "essentially fixed by age 30" (McCrae & Costa, 1994, p. 173). Nonetheless, much human behavior is quite

4

Is human behavior consistent across time and situations, or does it vary with circumstances?

Cognitive–social learning theories Personality theories that view behavior as the product of the interaction of cognitions, learning and past experiences, and the immediate environment.

Expectancies In Bandura's view, what a person anticipates in a situation or as a result of behaving in certain ways.

Locus of control According to Rotter, an expectancy about whether reinforcement is under internal or external control.

inconsistent across situations and over time. This raises two questions: Why does behavior usually *appear* to be more consistent than it actually is? And how can personality theories explain *inconsistency* in behavior?

Mischel argues that behavior seems to be consistent because we see a person only in those situations that tend to elicit the same behavior. Moreover, Mischel believes people need to find consistency and stability even in the face of inconsistency and unpredictability. We therefore see consistency in the behavior of others even when there is none (Hayden & Mischel, 1976).

Other theorists have brought a different perspective to the question of consistency and differences in personality. For this group, behavior is a product of the person and the situation. At any time, our actions are influenced by the people around us, by the way we think we are supposed to behave in a given situation. That interaction, the blending of the self and the social, is the focus of cognitive–social learning theorists.

COGNITIVE–SOCIAL LEARNING THEORIES

Cognitive–social learning theories hold that people internally organize their expectancies and values to guide their own behavior. This set of personal standards is unique to each one of us, growing out of our own life history. Our behavior is the product of the interaction of cognitions (how we think about a situation and how we view our behavior in that situation), learning and past experiences (including reinforcement, punishment, and modeling), and the immediate environment. For example, Albert Bandura (1977, 1986) asserts that people evaluate a situation according to certain internal **expectancies,** such as personal preferences, and this evaluation affects their behavior. Environmental feedback that follows the actual behavior, in turn, influences future expectancies. In this way, expectancies guide behavior in a given situation, and the results of the behavior in that situation shape expectancies in future situations. For example, two young women trying a video game for the first time may experience the situation quite differently, even if their scores are similarly low. One may find the experience fun and be eager to gain the skills necessary to go on to the next level of games, whereas the other may be disheartened by getting a low score, assume she will never be any good at video games, and never play again. Similarly, a person who interprets math problems as a challenge to succeed will approach the math SAT with a different expectancy than someone who sees math problems as opportunities to fail.

To Rotter (1954), **locus of control** is a prevalent expectancy, or cognitive strategy, by which people evaluate situations. People with an *internal locus* of control are convinced they can control their own fate. They believe that

An individual's behavior often appears quite consistent across both time and situations. We are not surprised when the child who spent hours studying his shell collection becomes a doctor who thoughtfully ponders sets of x-rays. But how consistent is behavior really? Some psychologists believe that the consistencies we perceive may be as much the result of our own selective attention as of reality.

through hard work, skill, and training, they can find reinforcements and avoid punishments. People with an *external locus* of control do not believe they control their fate. Instead, they are convinced that chance, luck, and the behavior of others determine their destiny and that they are helpless to change the course of their lives (Strickland, 1989). Some evidence suggests that drug use, inactivity among people suffering from depression, and school truancy are linked to an external locus of control (Lefcourt, 1992). In all these cases, people do not believe that making an effort to be active or productive will bring about any positive consequences.

Both Bandura and Rotter have tried to combine personal variables (such as expectancies) with situational variables in an effort to understand the complexities of human behavior. Both theorists believe that expectancies become part of a person's *explanatory style*, which, in turn, greatly influences behavior. Explanatory style, for example, separates optimists from pessimists. It is what causes two beginners who get the same score on a video game to respond so differently.

Some research shows that children as young as 8 years old have already developed a habitual explanatory style (Nolen-Hoeksema, Girgus, & Seligman, 1986). Third-graders were asked to read descriptions of 12 good and 12 bad events and then come up with reasons the events happened. Their scores reflected their degree of pessimism or optimism. Pessimists tended to believe that negative events were due to personal characteristics they could not change; optimists viewed negative events as unfortunate incidents they could remedy. Children with a more pessimistic style were found to be more prone to depression and to do worse on achievement tests.

General expectancies or explanatory styles such as optimism or pessimism can have a significant effect on behavior. In a now-famous study, researchers tracked 99 students from the Harvard graduation classes of 1939 to 1944 (Peterson, Vaillant, & Seligman, 1988). The men were interviewed about their experiences and underwent physical checkups every 5 years. When the researchers analyzed the men's interviews for signs of pessimism or optimism, they found that the explanatory style demonstrated in those interviews predicted the state of an individual's health decades later. Those men who were optimists at age 25 tended to be healthier at age 65, whereas the health of the pessimists had begun to deteriorate at about age 45. Although the reasons for these findings are not yet clear, a separate investigation that used a checklist about health habits found that the pessimists in this study were less careful about their health than were optimists. They tended to smoke and drink more and reported twice as many colds and visits to doctors. Another study looked at insurance agents in their first 2 years on the job (Seligman & Schulman, 1986). Explanatory style predicted which agents would become excellent agents and which would quit the company (three-fourths of all agents quit within 3 years). Optimists sold 37 percent more insurance than pessimists in the first 2 years and persisted through the difficulties of the job.

Explanatory style dovetails with **self-efficacy,** Bandura's way of describing the degree to which we feel we can meet our personal goals. Suppose a math professor has a son and a daughter. Say the son's mathematical aptitude is low, whereas the daughter is especially gifted in math. Imagine further that both children develop an expectation, a **performance standard,** to do well in mathematics. The son will probably feel incapable of meeting his standard, whereas the daughter will almost certainly feel confident about meeting hers. In Bandura's terms, the son will probably develop a low sense of self-efficacy; he will feel incapable of meeting his life goals. The daughter will likely develop a strong sense of self-efficacy. In turn, these explanatory

Self-efficacy According to Bandura, the expectancy that one's efforts will be successful.

Performance standards In Bandura's theory, standards that people develop to rate the adequacy of their own behavior in a variety of situations.

styles will have a profound effect on their behavior. But, Bandura (1986) also emphasizes that people have the power of self-determination. The son who is poor at math might excel at languages, or he may develop an interest in music.

Personality, situations, and behaviors constantly interact. Certain people may be prone to be aggressive, but whether they will actually act aggressively depends on their perception of a given situation. They may ask themselves if they are prepared to cope with aggressive behavior in return. Furthermore, the results of their aggression will affect their behavior in similar situations in the future. They learn where and when it is rewarding to be aggressive. According to Bandura, each of us develops a personality out of a unique blend of personal standards (learned by observation and reinforcement), situations, and the consequences of our own behaviors.

A Cognitive–Social Learning View of Jaylene Smith

Jaylene may have *learned* to be shy and introverted because she was rewarded for spending much time by herself studying. Her father probably encouraged her devotion to her studies; certainly, she earned the respect of her teachers. Moreover, long hours of studying helped her avoid the somewhat uncomfortable feelings that she experienced when she was around other people for long periods.

Reinforcement may have shaped other facets of Jay's personality as well. No doubt her father and her teachers reinforced her self-discipline and her need to achieve academically. Even her aggression toward men may have been learned in childhood as a successful coping mechanism. If her hostility put an end to her brothers' taunts and was also rewarded by her father's affection, she may have learned to react with aggression to perceived threats from males in general.

In addition, at least some aspects of Jaylene's personality were formed by watching her parents and brothers and learning subtle lessons from these family interactions. Her aggressive behavior with boyfriends, for example, may have grown out of seeing her parents fight. As a young child, she may have observed that some people deal with conflict by means of outbursts. Moreover, as Bandura's concept of self-efficacy would predict, Jay surely noticed that her father enjoyed both his family life and his career as medical researcher, whereas her mother's two jobs as housewife and store manager left her somewhat frustrated and overtired. This contrast may have contributed to Jay's own interest in medicine and to her mixed feelings about establishing a close relationship that might lead to marriage.

Evaluating Cognitive–Social Learning Theories

Cognitive–social learning theories of personality seem to have great potential. They put mental processes back at the center of personality. We can define and scientifically study the key concepts of these theories, such as self-efficacy and locus of control, which is not true of the key concepts of psychodynamic and humanistic theories. Moreover, cognitive–social learning theories help explain why people behave inconsistently, an area in which trait approaches fall short. Cognitive–social learning theories of personality have also spawned useful therapies that help people recognize and change a negative sense of self-efficacy or explanatory style. In particular, as we will see in Chapter 14, these therapies have helped people overcome depression.

However, it is still too early to say how well cognitive–social learning theories account for the complexity of human personality. Some critics

THEORIES OF PERSONALITY

Theory	Roots of Personality	Methods of Assessing
Psychodynamic	Unconscious thoughts, feelings, motives, and conflicts; repressed problems from early childhood.	Projective tests, personal interviews.
Humanistic	A drive toward personal growth and higher levels of functioning.	Objective tests and personal interviews.
Trait	Relatively permanent dispositions within the individual that cause the person to think, feel, and act in characteristic ways.	Objective tests.
Social Learning	Determined by past reinforcement and punishment as well as by observing what happens to other people.	Interviews, objective tests, observations.

point out that the benefit of hindsight allows us to explain any behavior as the product of certain cognitions, but that doesn't mean those cognitions were the *causes*—or at least the sole causes—of the behavior.

Just as there is great diversity in the way psychologists view personality, psychologists also disagree on the best way to measure or assess personality, the topic we turn to next.

PERSONALITY ASSESSMENT

In some ways, testing personality is much like testing intelligence (see Chapter 8). In both cases, we are trying to measure something intangible and invisible. And in both cases, a "good test" is one that is both reliable and valid: It gives dependable and consistent results, and it measures what it claims to measure. But there are special difficulties in measuring personality.

Personality, as you know, reflects *characteristic* behavior. In assessing personality, then, we are not interested in someone's *best* behavior. We are interested in *typical* behavior—how a person usually behaves in ordinary situations. Further complicating the measurement process, such factors as fatigue, the desire to impress the examiner, and the fear of being tested can profoundly affect a person's behavior in a personality-assessment situation.

In the intricate task of measuring personality, psychologists use four basic tools: (1) the personal interview; (2) direct observation of behavior; (3) objective tests; and (4) projective tests.

The Personal Interview

An interview is a conversation with a purpose: to obtain information from the person being interviewed. Interviews are often used in clinical settings to find out, for example, why someone is seeking treatment and to help diagnose the person's problem. Such interviews are generally *unstructured*—that is, the interviewer asks the client questions about any material that comes up and asks follow-up questions whenever appropriate. The most effective interviewers are warm, interested in what the respondent has to say, calm, relaxed, and confident (Feshbach & Weiner, 1982).

Objective tests Personality tests that are administered and scored in a standard way.

The personal interview is a basic tool of personality assessment. The structured interview follows a fixed order and content of questioning.

When conducting systematic research on personality, investigators more often rely on the *structured* interview. Here the order and content of the questions are fixed and the interviewer adheres to the set format. Although less personal, this kind of interview allows the interviewer to obtain comparable information from everyone interviewed. Generally speaking, structured interviews draw out information about sensitive topics that might not come up in an unstructured interview.

Observation

Another way to find out how a person usually behaves is to *observe* that person's actions in everyday situations over a long period. Behaviorists and social learning theorists prefer this method of assessing personality because it allows them to see how situation and environment influence behavior and note the range of behaviors the person is capable of exhibiting. Because most people are self-conscious when they suspect they are being watched, observation works best with young children. But this technique can be used successfully with people of almost any age and in many settings—a company cafeteria, an assembly line, wherever people work or socialize together.

One way to ensure that people will "be themselves" when psychologists are observing them is to conduct the observations surreptitiously. Here a one-way window allows two researchers to watch some kindergarten children while the children cannot see them.

In *direct observation*, observers watch people's behavior firsthand. Ideally, their unbiased accounts of the subjects' behavior paint an accurate picture of that behavior, but an observer runs the risk of misinterpreting the true meaning of an act. For example, the observer may think that children are being hostile when they are merely protecting themselves from the class bully. An expensive and time-consuming method of research, direct observation may also yield faulty results if, as noted earlier, the presence of the observer affects the subjects' behavior.

Whatever the method used, systematic observation allows psychologists to look at aspects of personality (e.g., traits, moods, or motives) as they are expressed in real life (Ozer & Reise, 1994).

Objective Tests

To avoid depending on the skills of an interviewer or the interpretive abilities of an observer in assessing personality, psychologists devised **objective tests,** or personality inventories. Generally, these are written tests that are administered and scored according to a standard procedure. The tests are usually constructed so that the person merely chooses a "yes" or "no" response or selects one answer among many choices. Objective tests are the most widely used tools for assessing personality, but they have two serious drawbacks. First, they rely entirely on self-report. If people do not know themselves well, or cannot be entirely objective about themselves, or want to paint a particular picture of themselves, self-report questionnaire results have limited usefulness (Funder, 1991). In fact, some research indicates that peers who know you well often do a better job characterizing you than you do yourself (Funder, 1995). Second, if subjects have taken other personality questionnaires, their familiarity with the test format may affect their responses to the present questionnaire. This is a particular problem on college campuses, where students are likely to participate in multiple research studies, many of which rely on some kind of personality inventory (Council, 1993).

Because of their interest in accurately measuring personality traits, trait theorists favor objective tests. Cattell, for example, developed a 374-question personality test called the **Sixteen Personality Factor Questionnaire.** Not surprisingly, the 16PF (as it is usually called) provides scores on each of the 16 traits originally identified by Cattell. The 16PF has proved useful in studies aimed at understanding the role personality factors play in cancer (Nair, Deb, & Mandal, 1993), heart disease (Pruneti, L'Abbate, & Steptoe, 1993), alcoholism (Rodriguez, 1994), and war-related stress (Poikolainen, 1993). More recently, objective tests such as the NEO-PI-R have been developed to assess the "Big Five" major personality traits described earlier in this chapter (Costa & McCrae, 1992, 1995).

The most widely used and thoroughly researched objective personality test, however, is the **Minnesota Multiphasic Personality Inventory** (MMPI); (Butcher & Rouse, 1996). The MMPI was originally developed as an aid in diagnosing psychiatric disorders (Hathaway & McKinley, 1942). The person taking the test is asked to answer "true," "false," or "cannot say" to such questions as "Once in a while I put off until tomorrow what I ought to do today," "At times I feel like swearing," and "There are persons who are trying to steal my thoughts and ideas." Some of the items repeat very similar thoughts in different words: for example, "I tire easily" and "I feel weak all over much of the time." This redundancy provides a check on the possibility of false or inconsistent answers.

The MMPI also includes several scales that check the validity of the responses. For example, if a person has answered too many items "cannot say," the test is considered invalid. The L, or lie, scale is scored on 15 items scattered throughout the test. Sample items rated on this scale are "I do not always tell the truth" and "I gossip a little at times." Most of us would have to admit that our answers to these two questions would be "true." People who mark these and many other similar items "false" are probably consciously or unconsciously distorting the truth to present themselves in a more favorable light.

By analyzing people's answers, researchers have extracted a number of personality scales from this test, rating people in terms of masculinity-femininity, depression, and hypochondriasis. These elements make the MMPI useful as a tool for differentiating among psychiatric populations (Anastasi & Urbina, 1997). The MMPI is also used to differentiate among more normal personality dimensions, such as extroversion-introversion and assertiveness, but with less success.

To accommodate social changes over the last 50 years, the MMPI was revised and updated in the 1980s. The MMPI-2 reworded outdated or sexist items ("Sometimes at elections I vote for men about whom I know very

Sixteen Personality Factor Questionnaire Objective personality test created by Cattell that provides scores on the 16 traits he identified.

Minnesota Multiphasic Pesonality Inventory (MMPI) The most widely used objective personality test, originally intended for psychiatric diagnosis.

Projective tests Personality tests, such as the Rorschach inkblot test, consisting of ambiguous or unstructured material.

Rorschach test A projective test composed of ambiguous inkblots; the way people interpret the blots is thought to reveal aspects of their personality.

Thematic Apperception Test (TAT) A projective test composed of ambiguous pictures about which a person is asked to write a complete story.

little") and added new items to assess such disorders as Type A behavior, suicidal tendencies, and anorexia nervosa (Butcher et al., 1989). Now there are two versions of the test: The full-length, adult form of the MMPI-2 has 704 items, and the adolescent form has 654 items. Both include 550 items from the original MMPI to ensure that clinical information from the new test does not differ too much from that on the original. Table 11–2 shows the 10 clinical scales that are assessed by the MMPI-2.

Projective Tests

Psychodynamic theorists, who believe that people are often unaware of the determinants of their behavior, put very little faith in objective personality tests that rely on self-reports. Instead, they prefer to use **projective tests** of personality. Most projective tests consist of simple ambiguous stimuli that can elicit an unlimited number of responses. People may be shown some essentially meaningless material or a vague picture and be asked to explain what the material means to them. Or they may be given a sentence fragment, such as "When I see myself in the mirror, I . . ." and be asked to complete the statement. They get no clues regarding the "best way" to interpret the material or complete the sentence.

Projective tests have several advantages for testing personality. Because these tests are flexible and can even be treated as games or puzzles, people can take them in a relaxed atmosphere, without the tension and self-consciousness that sometimes accompany objective tests. Often the person being examined doesn't even know the true purpose of the test, so responses are less likely to be faked. Some psychologists believe that the projective test can uncover unconscious thoughts and fantasies, such as

---

TABLE 11–2

THE 10 CLINICAL SCALES OF THE MMPI-2

Clinical Scale	Description of High Scorers
Hypochondriasis	Excessive concern with physical health and bodily function, somatic complaints, chronic weakness
Depression	Unhappy, pessimistic, hopeless; lack of self-confidence, loss of energy, feeling of futility
Hysteria	Reacts to stress with physical symptoms such as blindness or paralysis; lacks insights about motives and feelings
Psychopathic deviation	Disregard for rules, laws, ethics, and moral conduct; impulsive; rebellious toward authority figures; may engage in lying, stealing, and cheating
Masculinity-femininity	Adheres to nontraditional gender traits, or rejects the typical gender role
Paranoia	Suspicious, particularly in the area of interpersonal relations; guarded, moralistic, and rigid; overly responsive to criticism
Psychasthenia	Obsessive and compulsive; unreasonably fearful; anxious, tense, and highly strung
Schizophrenia	Experiences detachment from reality, often accompanied by hallucinations and delusions and bizarre thought processes; often confused, disorganized
Hypomania	Elevated mood, accelerated speech, flight of ideas; overactive, energetic, and talkative
Social introversion	Shy, insecure, and uncomfortable in social situations; timid; reserved; often described by others as cold and distant

latent sexual or family problems. In any event, the accuracy and usefulness of projective tests depend largely on the skill of the examiner in eliciting and interpreting responses.

The **Rorschach test** is the best known and one of the most frequently used projective personality tests (Ball, Archer, & Imhof, 1994; Watkins et al., 1995). It is named for Hermann Rorschach, a Swiss psychiatrist who in 1921 published the results of his research on interpreting inkblots as a key to personality (see Figure 11–4). Each inkblot design is printed on a separate card and is unique in form, color, shading, and white space. People are asked to specify what they see in each blot. Test instructions are kept to a minimum so people's responses will be completely their own. After interpreting all the blots, the person goes over the cards again with the examiner and explains which part of each blot prompted each response.

Somewhat more demanding is the **Thematic Apperception Test (TAT),** developed at Harvard by H. A. Murray and his associates. It consists of 20 cards picturing one or more human figures in deliberately ambiguous situations (see Figure 11–5). A person is shown the cards one by one and asked to write a complete story about each picture, including what led up to the scene depicted, what the characters are doing at that moment, what their thoughts and feelings are, and what the outcome will be.

Although various scoring systems have been devised for the TAT (Hibbard et al., 1994), examiners usually interpret the stories in the light of their personal knowledge of the subjects. One key in evaluating the TAT is whether the subject identifies with the hero or heroine of the story or with one of the minor characters. Then the examiner determines what the attitudes and feelings of the character reveal about the storyteller. The examiner also assesses each story for content, language, originality, organization, and consistency. Certain themes, such as the need for affection, repeated failure, or parental domination, may recur in several plots.

Both the Rorschach and the TAT may open up a conversation between a clinician and a person who is reluctant or unable to talk about personal problems. Both may also provide useful information about motives, events, or feelings of which the person is unaware. However, because projective tests are often not administered in a standard fashion, their validity and reliability have been called into question (Dawes, 1994; Wierzbicki, 1993). As a result, their use has declined since the 1970s. Still, when interpreted by a skilled examiner, these tests can offer insight into a person's attitudes and feelings.

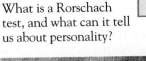
5 What is a Rorschach test, and what can it tell us about personality?

Figure 11–5
A sample item from the Thematic Apperception Test (TAT).
In the photo the subject is making up a story to explain the scene. The examiner then interprets and evaluates the subject's story for what it reveals about her personality.

Figure 11–4
Inkblots used in the Rorschach projective test.

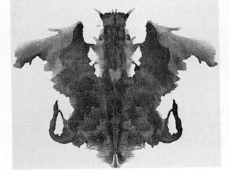

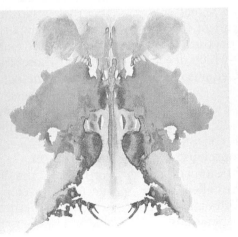

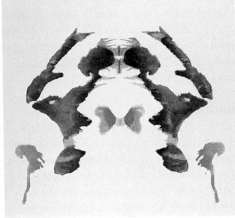

SUMMARY

Ever since the discipline of psychology began, psychologists have been attempting to define those characteristic thoughts, feelings, and behaviors that persist over time and that distinguish one person from another. **Personality** is a person's unique psychological signature; it characterizes the person's unique pattern of thoughts, feelings, and behaviors.

PSYCHODYNAMIC THEORIES

Psychodynamic theories of personality consider behavior to be the result of psychological dynamics within the individual. Often these processes go on outside of awareness.

Sigmund Freud

For Freud, the founder of **psychoanalysis,** our personality is rooted in the dynamics of our **unconscious**—all the ideas, thoughts, and feelings of which we are normally unaware. Freud identified sexual and aggressive instincts as the primary unconscious drives that determine human behavior.

According to Freud personality is made of three structures. The **id,** the only personality structure present at birth, operates in the unconscious according to the **pleasure principle,** meaning it tries to obtain immediate pleasure and avoid pain. The **ego,** the id's link to the real world, controls all conscious thinking and reasoning activities and operates according to the **reality principle.** It tries to delay satisfying the id's desires until it can do so safely and effectively in the real world. The **superego** acts as the person's moral guardian or conscience and helps the person function in society. It also compares the ego's actions with an **ego ideal** of perfection.

Freud called energy generated by the sexual instinct **libido.** As an infant matures, his or her libido becomes focused on different sensitive parts of the body. A **fixation** occurs if a child is deprived of pleasure or allowed too much pleasure from the part of the body that dominates one of the five developmental stages—**oral, anal, phallic, latency,** and **genital**—and some sexual energy may remain permanently tied to that part of the body. Strong attachment to the parent of the opposite sex and jealousy of the parent of the same sex—which develops during the phallic stage—is called the **Oedipus** or **Electra complex.**

Carl Jung

Carl Jung believed that the unconscious consists of two distinct components: the **personal unconscious,** which contains an individual's repressed thoughts, forgotten experiences, and undeveloped ideas; and the **collective unconscious,** a subterranean river of memories and behavior patterns flowing to us from previous generations.

Over the millennia, the human mind has developed certain thought forms, called **archetypes,** which give rise to mental images or mythological representations. The **persona,** one of the many archetypes Jung described, is that part of our personality by which we are known to other people, like a mask we put on to go out in public. Two other important archetypes are the **anima,** the expression of female traits in a man, and the **animus,** the expression of male traits in a woman.

Jung also believed that people generally exhibit one of two attitudes toward the world: **Extroverts** are interested in other people and the world at large, whereas **introverts** are more concerned with their own private worlds. Jung further divided people into **rational individuals,** who regulate their behavior by thinking and feeling, and **irrational individuals,** who base their actions on perceptions, whether sensual or intuitive.

Alfred Adler

Adler believed that people possess innate positive motives and strive toward personal and social perfection. He originally proposed that the main shaper of personality is **compensation,** the individual's attempt to overcome actual physical weakness. He later modified his theory to stress the importance of feelings of inferiority. When people become so fixated on their feelings of inferiority that they become paralyzed by them, they are said to have an **inferiority complex.** Later still, Adler concluded that strivings for superiority and perfection, both in one's own life and in the society in which one lives, are crucial to personality development.

Karen Horney

For Horney, a person's reaction to real or imagined dangers or threats, which she defined as **anxiety,** is a stronger motivating force than the sexual drive, or libido. She believed that there are several **neurotic trends** or strategies that people use to cope with emotional problems, and that these strategies are reflected in personality type: the compliant type of personality, whose strategy is to move toward others (submission); the aggressive type of personality, whose strategy is to move against others (aggression); and the detached type, whose strategy is to move away from others (detachment). Horney emphasized that culture and not anatomy determines many of the personality traits that differentiate women from men.

Erik Erikson

For Erikson, the quality of the parent-child relationship affects the development of the personality in that it helps determine whether the child feels competent and valuable and is able to form a secure sense of identity. Erikson believed that the personality develops over a lifetime. He outlined eight life stages—*trust versus mistrust, autonomy versus shame and doubt, initiative versus guilt, industry versus inferiority, identity versus role confusion, intimacy versus isolation, generativity versus stagnation,* and *integrity versus despair.* Success in each stage depends on whether adjustments in previous stages were successful.

Evaluating Psychodynamic Theories

Psychodynamic theories have had a profound impact on the way we view ourselves and others as well as on the arts. However, some of Freud's theories have been criticized as unscientific and culture-bound, especially penis envy in women and the Oedipus and Electra complexes. Some experimental evidence supports the existence of the unconscious, but this research does not show a clear link between unconscious processes and personality. As a therapy, psychoanalysis has been shown to be beneficial in some cases, but no more so than other therapies.

HUMANISTIC PERSONALITY THEORIES

Adler's notion of the individual's perpetual striving for perfection laid the groundwork for **humanistic personality theory.**

Carl Rogers

For Rogers, people develop their personalities in the service of positive goals. The biological push to become whatever it is that we are capable of becoming is called the **actualizing tendency.** In addition to trying to realize our biological potential, we attempt to fulfill our conscious sense of who we are, which Rogers called the **self-actualizing tendency.** A **fully functioning person** is someone whose self-concept closely matches his or her inborn capabilities. Fully functioning people were usually raised with **unconditional positive regard,** or the experience of being valued by other people regardless of their emotions, attitudes, and behaviors. Often children are brought up with **conditional positive regard**—that is, with parents and others who accept and value only certain aspects of their individuality. These people tend to deviate from their inborn capacities to construct a personality more in line with how other people see them.

Evaluating Humanistic Theories

There is a lack of scientifically derived evidence for humanistic theories of personality. In addition, they are criticized as taking too rosy a view of human nature and as promoting a view of the self that fosters self-centeredness. However, research on humanist therapies, particularly Rogers's client-centered therapy, has shown they do promote self-acceptance.

TRAIT THEORIES

Trait theorists insist that each person possesses a unique constellation of fundamental **personality traits** that can be inferred from how the person behaves.

Psychologists disagree about the number of different personality traits. Gordon Allport argued that possibly several thousand words could be used to describe human personality traits. Raymond Cattell identified 16 basic traits using a statistical technique called **factor analysis.** Eysenck argued that personality could be reduced to three basic dimensions: *emotional stability, introversion-extroversion,* and *psychoticism.*

The Big Five

Recently, considerable research has focused on the importance of five basic personality traits. Included in the **Big Five** are *extroversion, agreeableness, conscientiousness, emotional stability,* and *culture* or *openness.* The big five traits appear to be universal across cultures, and some evidence suggests they may have, in part, a physiological basis.

Evaluating Trait Theories

Trait theories are primarily descriptive. They provide a way of classifying personalities, but they do not explain why a person's personality is what it is. But trait theories do have the advantage of being rather easy to test experimentally, and research does support the value of the five-factor model in pinpointing personality.

According to Walter Mischel, we tend to overestimate the consistency of another person's actions both because we see that person in only a limited number of situations that elicit similar behavioral responses and because we disregard any behavior that does not fit with our preexisting image of that person.

COGNITIVE–SOCIAL LEARNING THEORIES

Cognitive–social learning theories view behavior as the product of the interaction of cognitions, learning and past experiences, and the immediate environment. Albert Bandura suggests that certain internal **expectancies** determine how a person evaluates a situation and that this evaluation has an effect on the person's behavior. **Locus of control** is one prominent expectancy. People with an internal locus of control believe they can control their own fate through their actions, whereas people with an external locus of control believe their fate rests with chance and the behavior of others. Expectancies lead people to conduct themselves according to unique **performance standards,** individually determined measures of excellence by which they judge their behavior. Those who succeed in meeting their own internal performance standards develop an attitude that Bandura calls **self-efficacy.**

Evaluating Cognitive–Social Learning Theories

Cognitive–social learning theories avoid the narrowness of trait and behavioral theories, as well as the reliance on case studies and anecdotal evidence that weakens psychodynamic and humanistic theories. Expectancies and locus of control can be tested scientifically, and they have proved to be useful concepts for predicting health and depression. However, such correlations do not provide evidence for causes of behavior.

PERSONALITY ASSESSMENT

Psychologists use four different methods to assess personality: the personal interview, direct observation of behavior, objective tests, and projective tests.

The Personal Interview

There are two types of personal interviews. During an unstructured interview, the interviewer asks questions about any material that comes up during the course of the conversation as well as follow-up questions where appropriate. In a structured interview, the order and the content of the questions are fixed and the interviewer does not deviate from the format.

Observation

Behavioral and social learning theorists prefer the technique of direct observation of a person over time to determine the environmental influence on that person's behavior. This method of personality assessment doesn't rely on self-reports and it gives a good idea of the range of a person's behaviors, but it is expensive and time-consuming and open to misinterpretation.

Objective Tests

Objective tests of personality, such as the **Sixteen Personality Factor Questionnaire** and the **Minnesota Multiphasic Personality Inventory (MMPI),** are given and scored according to standardized procedures. These tests are inexpensive to use and easy to score, but rely on people's self-report of their behavior.

Projective Tests

Psychodynamic theorists are more likely to use **projective tests,** which consist of ambiguous stimuli that can draw out an unlimited number of responses and are thought to tap the unconscious. The **Rorschach test** has 10 inkblots that the subject interprets. The **Thematic Apperception Test (TAT)** asks subjects to make up stories about 20 pictures.

REVIEW QUESTIONS

MULTIPLE CHOICE AND SHORT ANSWER

1. Personality is the pattern of thoughts, feelings, and behaviors that persists over _____ and _____ and that distinguishes one person from another.

2. Match the following of Freud's terms with their appropriate definitions:
   _____ Unconscious
   _____ Superego
   _____ Id
   _____ Ego
   _____ Ego ideal
   _____ Libido

   a. Energy that comes from the sexual instinct
   b. Mediator between reality, the superego, and the id
   c. Unconscious urges seeking expression
   d. That part of the superego concerned with standards
   e. Ideas and feelings of which we are normally not aware
   f. Moral guardian of the ego

3. According to Freud, the _____ operates according to the reality principle, whereas the _____ acts according to the pleasure principle.

4. According to Freud, _____ _____ is the means by which the id partially relieves the discomfort of instinctual drives through mental images.

5. Match the following of Jung's terms with their appropriate definitions:
   _____ Persona
   _____ Animus
   _____ Collective unconscious
   _____ Archetype

   a. Typical mental image or mythical representation
   b. Memories and behavior patterns inherited from past generations
   c. Aspect of the personality by which one is known to other people
   d. Expression of male traits in females

6. Match the following of Adler's terms with their appropriate definitions:
   _____ Style of life
   _____ Inferiority complex
   _____ Compensation

   a. Fixation on or belief in a negative characteristic
   b. Individual's effort to overcome weaknesses
   c. Individual's particular set of meanings and beliefs

7. Horney believed that _____ is a more powerful motivational force than sexual urges.

8. Match Erikson's eight stages of personality development with their appropriate descriptions:

_____ Industry versus inferiority	a. The infant appreciates the predictability of the environment and learns optimism about the future.
_____ Trust versus mistrust	b. The child's independence and contact with the environment increase.
_____ Generativity versus stagnation	c. Children become increasingly active, undertake new projects, and manipulate things in the environment.
_____ Intimacy versus isolation	d. Children encounter new expectations and begin learning adult skills.
_____ Identity versus role confusion	e. Childhood ends and the responsibilities of adulthood loom large.
_____ Autonomy versus shame and doubt	f. The question of becoming intimate with the opposite sex arises.
_____ Initiative versus guilt	g. The adult faces the challenge of remaining productive and creative.
_____ Integrity versus despair	h. Individuals assess life roles and face death.

9. Rogers believed that a person strives to live up to and fulfill a self-image; he called this a person's _____ tendency.

10. In Bandura's view, what a person anticipates in a situation or as a result of behaving certain ways is known as _____.

11. Cognitive–social learning theorists believe that locus of control is a cognitive strategy by which people _____ situations.

12. _____ tests require people to fill out questionnaires, which are then scored according to a standardized procedure.

13. In _____ tests of personality, people are shown ambiguous stimuli and asked to describe them or make up a story about them.

CRITICAL THINKING AND APPLICATIONS

1. One of the key issues addressed by personality theorists is consistency: Does a person behave the same way across different situations, or does behavior vary with circumstances? What are your feelings on this issue?

2. Explain how Jung, Adler, Horney, and Erikson modified Freud's psychodynamic theory of personality.

3. What are the major forms of personality assessment? Which do you consider the most valuable? The least valuable? Why?

4. Look back at the case study of Jaylene Smith. Which theory or theories do you think best explain her behavior? Why do you feel this way?

ENDURING ISSUES

Stability–Change

Do people's personalities change significantly over the life span? If someone is introverted or dependable at age 30, are they likely to be introverted or dependable at age 60 and age 90 as well? How do you explain your answer?

Diversity

Can one's sex, race, or culture cause significant differences in personality? Are people in certain cultures more likely to be extroverted, for example, or conscientious?

(Answers to the Review Questions appear in the back of the book.)

12 Stress and

Health Psychology

In 1979, Iranian militants stormed the U.S. embassy in Teheran and took more than 50 Americans hostage. For 444 days, the hostages lived in fear for their lives and endured the humiliations of captivity. To feel less like a prisoner and more like a person in charge of his life, one hostage saved food from meals brought to him by his captors and then played gracious host by offering the saved food to other hostages who visited him in his cell. A diary kept by one prisoner records some other prisoners' coping strategies: "Al's working on his painting . . . . Dick's walking his daily three miles back and forth across the room, and Jerry's lying on his mattress reading."

When Eric de Wilde, an orphan, found a bag of jewels worth $350,000 on a Florida railroad track, he thought it was a fairy tale come true. But reporters hounded him, and schoolmates and others

---

Think About It!

1. *True or False*: Stress is always a response to negative events in our lives.
2. *True or False*: Stressful events almost inevitably involve changes in our lives.
3. What kinds of factors influence whether we find a particular situation stressful?
4. What is meant by "defense mechanisms"? What are some common types of defense mechanisms?
5. Do men generally handle stress better than women do?
6. How can stress lead to physical illness?
7. What is post-traumatic stress disorder? What kinds of events are most likely to trigger this disorder?

Stress Any environmental demand that creates a state of tension or threat and requires change or adaptation.

Adjustment Any effort to cope with stress.

Health psychology A subfield of psychology concerned with the relationship between psychological factors and physical health and illness.

kept calling him up with demands and threats. "Life is very difficult for the young man—a lot of things have happened to him in a hurry," said the lawyer whom de Wilde was forced to retain. But when the boy arrived in New York to sell his jewels at a public auction, he conducted himself with such dignified restraint that he managed to maintain his privacy and self-possession.

When Janet Garcia had her first baby at age 34, she was filled with special joy because she had feared she would never become pregnant. But she found taking care of the baby, on top of all her other responsibilities, exhausting. Her husband, Michael, resented her constant fatigue and the fact that he didn't come first in her life anymore. To alleviate the situation, Janet and Michael drew on their savings to pay for household help and Michael took a more active role in looking after the baby. These measures relieved some of Janet's burden, leaving her with more time and energy for her other responsibilities and for her life with Michael.

These three stories sound quite different, but they have several things in common. First, all involved some degree of **stress**—that is, the people in the stories encountered significant new demands from their environments that gave rise to a state of tension or threat. Second, the people under stress had to find ways to *cope* with these new events. Finally, in all three situations, the people *adjusted* about as well as could be expected under the circumstances.

Most people must adjust to a life that is less than perfect, a life in which bad events happen and even pleasures come with built-in complications. We need to adapt to stress, not just the stress of crises or unexpected strokes of good fortune, but also the stress of everyday minor demands.

Every **adjustment** is an attempt—successful or not—to balance our desires against the demands of the environment, to weigh our needs against realistic possibilities, and to cope as well as we can within the limits of our situation. The student who fails to get the lead in the school play may quit the production in a huff, accept a smaller role, serve as theater critic for the school paper, or join the debating team. Each response is an adjustment to failure, although some of these responses will probably be less constructive in the long run than others.

How we adjust to the stresses—both major and minor—that we encounter is crucial to our health and the quality of our lives. As we shall see in this chapter and the following one on psychological disorders, stress can contribute to both psychological and physical illness. In fact, some medical experts believe that all physical ailments, from colds to ulcers to cancer, have a psychological as well as a physical component. For this reason, stress and its effects on people's lives is a key focus of **health psychology,** a subfield of psychology (see Table 1–1, p. 3) concerned with the relationship between psychological factors and physical health and illness. Health psychologists seek to understand the relationship between stress and illness: Why do some people manage stress well enough to remain healthy? Why do others become ill? Can personality traits influence recovery from serious illness? How can we promote healthy behaviors? To answer these questions, they study the interaction of biological, psychological, and social factors, an approach we follow in this chapter.

SOURCES OF STRESS

Stress refers to any environmental demand that creates a state of tension or threat and requires change or adaptation. Many situations prompt us to change our behavior in some way: We stop our car when a traffic light turns red; we switch television channels to avoid a boring program and find an interesting one to watch; we go inside when it starts to rain. Normally, these situations are not stressful because they are not accompanied by tension or threat. Now imagine that when the light turned red you were rushing to make an important appointment, or that the person watching TV with you

All major life changes—whether positive or negative—involve a certain amount of stress. This is partly because major life changes typically bring strong emotion, and even joy and elation can arouse the body and begin to take a toll on its resources. Major life events can also be stressful because any new experience requires some adjustment.

True or False: Stress is always a response to negative events in our lives.

definitely does not want to switch the channel, or that you are about to host a large outdoor party when it starts to rain. Now these situations can be quite stressful.

Some events, such as wars and natural disasters, are inherently stressful, because the danger is real. But even in inherently stressful situations, the time of greatest stress is not necessarily the time when danger is most imminent. We feel the most stress when we're *anticipating* the danger. Parachutists, for example, report feeling most afraid as the time for the jump approaches. Once they are in line and cannot turn back, they calm down. By the time they reach the most dangerous part of the jump—in free fall and waiting for their chutes to open—their fears have subsided (Epstein, 1962).

Of course, stress is not limited to life-and-death situations, nor even to unpleasant or tension-filled experiences. Even good things can cause stress, because they require us to change or adapt in order to meet our needs (Morris, 1990, p. 72). A wedding is stressful as well as exciting: Most weddings are very complicated affairs to arrange, and marriage marks a profound change in many relationships. Being promoted is gratifying—but it demands that we relate to new people in new ways, learn new skills, perhaps dress differently or work longer hours. We'll look more closely now at some factors that cause stress.

Change

True or False: Stressful events almost inevitably involve changes in our lives.

All of the stressful events we have considered so far involve change. Most people have a strong preference for order, continuity, and predictability in their lives. Therefore, they experience any event, good or bad, that brings about change as stressful. By the same token, the amount of change various situations require denotes how stressful they are. In fact, some questionnaires measure the amount of stress in a person's life by calculating the "life changes" that a person has experienced over a specified period of time. For example, the Social Readjustment Rating Scale (SRRS) devised by T. H. Holmes and R. H. Rahe (1967) consists of several dozen events that are assigned a point value depending on the amount of change they require (see Table 12–1). The stress ratings of events on the SRRS have little to do with whether the events are desirable or undesirable. For example, "Change in responsibilities at work" carries 29 life change units, whether it is due to a promotion to more interesting and rewarding work or to being assigned a much bigger volume of boring work.

Using the SRRS, one simply adds up the stress ratings of all the events that a person has lived through in a given period to determine the amount of stress that he or she has experienced. In general, a score of 150 or less is considered normal; 150 to 190 corresponds to mild stress; 200 to 299 suggests a moderate crisis; and 300 or higher indicates a major life crisis. According to Holmes and Rahe, the likelihood that a person will experience a "stress-induced illness" increases sharply for scores above 300.

Although intuitively appealing, the SRRS has been criticized. Studies have often failed to confirm a relationship between a person's SRRS score and health (see Krantz, Grunberg, & Baum, 1985). Indeed, many people with very high scores on the SRRS do not experience any stress-induced illnesses. Another criticism of the SRRS concerns the failure of the scale to take into account different life situations. For instance, pregnancy probably results in a very different stress response depending on whether it was planned or occurred by accident in an unwed teenager (Oltmanns & Emery, 1998). Nevertheless the SRRS is still widely used, and with modification, appears to have some cross-cultural applications (Yahiro, Inoue, & Nozawa, 1993).

TABLE 12-1

SOCIAL READJUSTMENT RATING SCALE*

Life Event	Life-Change Units
Death of one's spouse	100
Divorce	73
Personal injury or illness	53
Marriage	50
Being fired at work	47
Retirement	45
Pregnancy	40
Gain of a new family member	39
Change in one's financial state	38
Death of a close friend	37
Change to a different line of work	36
Foreclosure of a mortgage or loan	30
Change in responsibilities at work	29
Son or daughter leaving home	29
Outstanding personal achievement	28
Beginning or ending school	26
Change in living conditions	25
Trouble with one's boss	23
Change in residence	20
Change in schools	20
Change in social activities	18
Change in sleeping habits	16
Change in eating habits	15
Vacation	13

*The SRRS assigns "life-change units" to several dozen stressful events. Holmes and R. H. Rashe linked the number of units to risk for medical problems.

Source: "The social readjustment rating scale," by T. H. Holmes and R. H. Rahe, 1967, *Journal of Psychosomatic Research, 11.* Copyright © 1967, Pergamon Press. Reprinted with permission.

Hassles

Holmes and Rahe's SRRS emphasizes the kind of stress that arises from fairly dramatic, one-time life events. But as other psychologists (Lazarus et al., 1985; Ruffin, 1993; Whisman & Kwon, 1993) have pointed out, much stress is generated by "hassles," life's petty annoyances, irritations, and frustrations. Such seemingly minor matters as being stuck in traffic, misplacing car keys, and getting into a trivial argument may be as stressful as the major life

Pressure A feeling that one must speed up, intensify, or change the direction of one's behavior or live up to a higher standard of performance.

Frustration The feeling that occurs when a person is prevented from reaching a goal.

Much of the stress we experience in our lives arises not from major traumas, but rather from small everyday hassles such as traffic jams, petty arguments, and equipment that doesn't work right.

events listed on the Holmes-Rahe scale. Lazarus believes that big events matter so much because they trigger the little hassles that eventually overwhelm us with stress. People who have recently suffered a major traumatic event are more likely to be plagued by minor stressors or hassles than those who have not experienced a recent trauma (Pillow, Zautra, & Sandler, 1996). "It is not the large dramatic events that make the difference," notes Lazarus, "but what happens day in and day out, whether provoked by major events or not" (1981, p. 62).

In short, both major and minor events are stressful because they lead to feelings of pressure, frustration, conflict, and anxiety. We turn now to the ways that these emotional experiences contribute to our overall feeling of stress.

Pressure

Pressure occurs when we feel forced to speed up, intensify, or shift direction in our behavior, or when we feel compelled to meet a higher standard of performance (Morris, 1990). Pressure may come from within—as when we push ourselves to reach personal standards of excellence. This internal pressure may be either constructive or destructive. For instance, it may drive us to learn how to play a musical instrument, which may ultimately bring us great pleasure, or it may erode our self-esteem if we set standards for ourselves that are impossible to achieve. Outside demands also cause pressure: We compete for grades, for popularity, for sexual and marital partners, and for jobs. In addition, we're pressured to live up to the expectations of our family and close friends.

Frustration

Frustration also contributes to stress. **Frustration** occurs when a person is prevented from reaching a goal because something or someone stands in the way. A high school student who does poorly on his college boards does not get into his father's alma mater; a woman looking forward to a well-deserved promotion is denied it for sexist reasons. These people must either give up their goals as unattainable, modify their goals, or find some way to overcome the obstacles blocking their way.

The high school student faces a complex problem. Most likely his first reaction will be to get angry—at himself for not having done better, at his father for pushing him to apply to a college that is difficult to get into, at the admissions board for not taking into account the bad cold he had the day he took the college boards. He may not be able to express his anger directly; he may not even realize or admit to himself how disappointed he is. Nevertheless, he must either find a new way to reach his goal or change it by applying to another school with lower admission standards. The woman denied the promotion has an even more difficult task. She could protest her company's decision by going through a lengthy and potentially even more frustrating appeals process, or she could seek employment at another company that may or may not prove less sexist, or she could start her own firm.

Morris (1990) identifies five common sources of frustration in American life. *Delays* are annoying because our culture puts great stock in the value of time. *Lack of resources* is frustrating to those Americans who cannot afford the new cars or lavish vacations that the mass media tout as every citizen's due. *Losses,* such as the end of a love affair or a cherished friendship, cause frustration because they often make us feel helpless, unimportant, or worthless. *Failure* generates intense frustration—and accompanying guilt—in our competitive society. Because we imagine that if we had done things differently, we might have succeeded, we feel responsible for our own or someone else's pain and disappointment. *Discrimination* also frustrates us: Being denied opportunities or recognition simply because of one's sex, age, religion, or skin color is immensely frustrating.

Conflict

Of all life's troubles, conflict is probably the most common. A student finds that both the required courses she wanted to take this semester are given at the same hours on the same days. We find ourselves in agreement with one political candidate's views on policy, but prefer the personality of the opponent. A boy does not want to go to his aunt's for dinner, but neither does he want to listen to his parents complain about his decision if he stays home.

Conflict arises when we face two or more incompatible demands, opportunities, needs, or goals. We can never resolve conflict completely. We must either give up some of our goals, modify some of them, delay our pursuit of some of them, or resign ourselves to not attaining all of our goals. Whatever we do, we are bound to experience some frustration, which adds to the stressfulness of conflicts.

In the 1930s, Kurt Lewin described two opposite tendencies of conflict: approach and avoidance. When something attracts us, we want to approach it; when something frightens us, we try to avoid it. Lewin (1935) showed how different combinations of these tendencies create three basic types of conflict: approach/approach conflict, avoidance/avoidance conflict, and approach/avoidance conflict.

Approach/approach conflict occurs when a person is simultaneously attracted to two appealing goals. For example, a student who has been accepted at two equally desirable colleges or universities, neither of which has any significant drawbacks, will experience an approach/approach conflict in choosing between these two desirable options.

The reverse of this dilemma is **avoidance/avoidance conflict,** in which a person is confronted with two undesirable or threatening possibilities, neither of which has any positive attributes. When faced with an avoidance/avoidance conflict, people usually try to escape the situation altogether. If escape is impossible, their coping method depends on how threatening each alternative is. Most often they vacillate between choosing one threat or the

Conflict Simultaneous existence of incompatible demands, opportunities, needs, or goals.

Approach/approach conflict According to Lewin, the result of simultaneous attraction to two appealing possibilities, neither of which has any negative qualities.

Avoidance/avoidance conflict According to Lewin, the result of facing a choice between two undesirable possibilities, neither of which has any positive qualities.

Approach/avoidance conflict According to Lewin, the result of being simultaneously attracted to and repelled by the same goal.

A classic example of avoidance/avoidance conflict is a baseball player caught between two bases. Running in either direction is an undesirable option to be avoided.

other, like a baseball runner caught in a rundown between first and second base. The player starts to run toward second, then realizes that he will be tagged and turns around, only to realize that he will be tagged on first if he tries to go back there. In no-exit situations like this, people sometimes simply wait for events to resolve their conflict for them.

In **approach/avoidance conflict,** a person is both attracted to and repelled by the same goal. This is the most common form of conflict, and it, too, is often difficult to resolve. According to Lewin, the closer we come to a goal with good and bad features, the stronger grow our desires both to approach and to avoid, but the tendency to avoid increases more rapidly than the tendency to approach. In an approach/avoidance conflict, therefore, we approach the goal until we reach the point at which the tendency to approach equals the tendency to avoid the goal. Afraid to go any closer, we stop and vacillate, making no choice at all, until the situation changes. In real life, we are often faced simultaneously with two or more goals, each of which is less than ideal but each of which also has enough positive features to attract us. The existence of multiple goals of this sort simply increases our conflict, for on top of the conflict inherent in each goal is piled the conflict of choosing from among the various goals.

Lewin's types of conflict are outlined in the Summary Table.

SUMMARY TABLE

TYPES OF CONFLICT	
Type of Conflict	Nature of Conflict
Approach/Approach	The person is attracted to two incompatible goals at the same time.
Avoidance/Avoidance	Repelled by two undesirable alternatives at the same time, the person is inclined to try to escape, but often other factors prevent such an escape.
Approach/Avoidance	The person is both repelled by, and attracted to, the same goal.

Self-imposed Stress

People sometimes create problems for themselves quite apart from stressful events in their environment. Albert Ellis has proposed that many people carry around a set of irrational, self-defeating beliefs that add unnecessarily to the normal stresses of living (Ellis & Harper, 1975). For example, some people believe "It is essential to be loved or approved by almost everyone for everything I do"; For people who share this belief, any sign of disapproval will be a source of considerable stress. Other people believe "I must be competent, adequate, and successful at everything I do"; Such people take the slightest sign of failure or inadequacy as evidence that they are worthless human beings. Still others believe "It is disastrous if everything doesn't go the way I would like"; When things don't go perfectly, such people feel upset, miserable, and unhappy. As we will see in the next chapter, Aaron Beck (1984) believes that many cases of depression arise from self-defeating thoughts such as these.

Stress and Individual Differences

Why do some people find it easy to cope with major life stresses while others find it hard to deal with even minor problems? The answer seems to lie in individual differences in perceiving and reacting to potentially stressful events.

An obstacle that looks minor to one person looms large to another. One patient facing surgery may feel less anxious than someone else visiting a doctor for a routine physical exam. The person who gets fired from a job and the soldier who gets caught behind enemy lines may feel equally threatened. In short, how much stress we experience depends partly on the way we interpret the situation.

Several factors determine whether we find a particular situation stressful (Kessler, Price, & Wortman, 1985). Confident people who feel capable of coping with life events are likely to feel less stressed by a given situation than someone who lacks self-assurance. For example, students who generally do well on exams tend to be calmer the night before an important test than students who tend to do poorly. People who have handled job changes well in the past are likely to find a new change less stressful than those who have had great difficulty adjusting to previous job changes or have never had to face a change in jobs.

Suzanne Kobasa identified a trait that she called *hardiness* in people who either tolerated stress exceptionally well or seemed to thrive on it (1979). They felt very much in control of their lives, were deeply committed to their work and their own values, and experienced difficult demands from the environment as challenging rather than intimidating. Kobasa's study suggests that people's response to stress depends partly on whether they believe they have some control over events or whether they feel helpless. Conversely, recall from our discussion of *learned helplessness* in Chapter 5 that when people are placed in seemingly hopeless situations long enough they may grow to feel powerless and apathetic (Peterson, Maier, & Seligman, 1993). In such cases, even when the situation changes they may fail to recognize that it is now possible to cope more effectively. They remain passive even when there are opportunities for improving the situation.

Behavior under stress also reflects individual differences. In natural disasters, for example, some people immediately mobilize to save themselves. Others fall apart. Still others are shaken but regain their composure—and ability to respond—almost instantly. And then there are those who refuse to admit that there is any danger.

3

What kinds of factors influence whether we find a particular situation stressful?

Confrontation Acknowledging a stressful situation directly and attempting to find a solution to the problem or attain the difficult goal.

COPING WITH STRESS

Whatever its source, stress calls for adjustment. Psychologists distinguish between two general types of adjustment: direct coping and defensive coping. *Direct coping* refers to any action we take to change an uncomfortable situation. When our needs or desires are frustrated, for example, we attempt to remove the obstacles between ourselves and our goal or we give up. Similarly, when we are threatened, we try to eliminate the source of the threat, either by attacking it or by escaping from it (for a discussion of coping with stress at college, see *Applying Psychology.*)

Defensive coping refers to the ways people convince themselves that they are not really threatened or that they do not really want something they cannot get. A form of self-deception, defensive coping is characteristic of internal, often unconscious conflicts. When we are emotionally unable to bring a problem to the surface of consciousness and deal with it directly because it is too threatening, our only option may be to cope with it defensively.

Direct Coping

When we are threatened, frustrated, or in conflict, we have three basic choices for coping directly: *confrontation, compromise,* or *withdrawal.* We can meet a situation head-on and intensify our efforts to get what we want (confrontation). We can give up some of what we want and perhaps persuade others to give up part of what they want (compromise). Or we can admit defeat and stop fighting (withdrawal).

Take the case of a woman who has worked hard at her job for years but is not promoted. She learns that the reason is her stated unwillingness to move temporarily from the company's main office to a branch office in another part of the country to acquire more experience. Her unwillingness to move stands between her and her goal of advancing in her career. She has several choices.

CONFRONTATION Facing a stressful situation forthrightly, acknowledging to oneself that there is a problem for which a solution must be found, attacking the problem head-on, and pushing resolutely toward one's goals is call **confrontation.** The hallmark of the "confrontational style" (Morris, 1990) is making intense efforts to cope with stress and to accomplish one's aims. This may involve learning skills, enlisting other people's help, or just

Taking a break from studying may help to relieve the stress of working on a difficult assignment.

APPLYING PSYCHOLOGY
COPING WITH STRESS AT COLLEGE

It is two weeks before finals and you have two papers to write and four exams to study for. You are very worried. You are not alone. To help students cope with the pressures of finals week, and indeed, the stress that many students feel throughout the semester, many colleges and universities are offering stress-reduction workshops, aerobics classes, and counseling. At the University of California at Los Angeles, students are taught to visualize themselves calmly answering difficult test questions. Even if you do not attend a special program for reducing stress, you can teach yourself techniques to help cope with the pressures of college life.

1. Plan ahead. Do not procrastinate. Get things done well before deadlines. Start working on large projects well in advance.

2. Exercise. Do whatever activity you enjoy.

3. Listen to your favorite music, watch a TV show, or go to a movie as a study break.

4. Talk to other people.

5. Meditate or use other relaxation techniques. See the paperback *The Relaxation Response* by Herbert Benson.

One technique that is very effective is to make a list of everything you have to do right down to doing the laundry, getting birthday cards for family and friends, etc. Then star the highest priority tasks, the ones that really have to be done first (a looming deadline) or those that will take a long time. Use all available time to work on only those tasks. Free up time by not doing things that are not on the highest priority list. Cross off high-priority tasks as they are done, add new tasks as they arrive, and continually adjust the priorities so the most critical tasks are always starred.

This technique serves various purposes: It removes the fear that you'll forget something important, because everything you can think of is on a single sheet of paper. It helps you realize that things are not as overwhelming as they might otherwise seem (the list is finite and there are probably only a few things that are truly high priority tasks). It lets you focus your energy on the most important tasks and makes it easy to avoid spending time on less important things that might drift into your attention. Finally, it assures you that you are doing everything possible to do the most important things in your life, and if you don't manage to do them all you can truly say "There's no way I could have done any better, it simply wasn't possible in the time available." Actually, that will seldom be the case. Usually, the highest priority tasks get done and the lower priority tasks simply wait, often for weeks or months after which you have to wonder how important they really are if they always come out on the bottom of the totem pole.

To learn more about reducing stress, visit our website at **www.prenhall.com/morris**

trying harder. Or it may require steps to change either oneself or the situation. The woman whom we have been describing might decide that if she wants very much to move up in the company, she will have to agree to relocate. Or she might try to change the situation itself in one of several ways. She could challenge the assumption that working at the branch office would give her the kind of experience her supervisor thinks she needs. She could try to persuade her boss that she is ready to handle a better job in the main office. Or she could remind her supervisor of the company's stated goal of promoting more women to top-level positions.

Confrontation may also include expressions of anger. Anger may be effective, especially if we really have been treated unfairly and if we express our anger with restraint instead of exploding in rage. A national magazine once reported an amusing, and effective, example of controlled anger in response to an annoying little hassle. As a motorist came to an intersection, he had to stop for a frail old lady crossing the street. The driver of the car behind him honked his horn impatiently, whereupon the first driver shut off

Compromise Deciding on a more realistic solution or goal when an ideal solution or goal is not practical.

Withdrawal Avoiding a situation when other forms of coping are not practical.

Defense mechanisms Self-deceptive techniques for reducing stress, including denial, repression, projection, identification, regression, intellectualization, reaction formation, displacement, and sublimation.

his ignition, removed the key, walked back to the other car, and handed the key to the second driver. "Here," he said, "you run over her. I can't do it. She reminds me of my grandmother."

COMPROMISE   One of the most common, and effective, ways of coping directly with conflict or frustration is **compromise.** We often recognize that we cannot have everything we want and that we cannot expect others to do just what we would like them to do. In such cases, we may decide to settle for less than we originally sought. The woman denied a job promotion may agree to take a less desirable position that doesn't require branch office experience, or she may strike a bargain to go to the branch office for a shorter period of time.

WITHDRAWAL   In some circumstances, the most effective way of coping with stress is **withdrawal** from the situation. A person at an amusement park who is overcome by anxiety just looking at a roller coaster may simply move on to a less threatening ride or even leave the park entirely. The woman whose promotion depends on temporarily relocating might just quit her job and join another company.

We often disparage withdrawal as a refusal to face problems. But sometimes withdrawal is a positive and realistic response, such as when we realize that our adversary is more powerful than we are, or that there is no way we can effectively change ourselves, alter the situation, or reach a compromise, and that any form of aggression would be self-destructive. In seemingly hopeless situations, such as submarine and mining disasters, few people panic. Believing there is nothing they can do to save themselves, they give up. If a situation, in fact, is hopeless, resignation may be the most effective way of coping with it.

Perhaps the greatest danger of coping by withdrawal is that we will come to avoid all similar situations. Someone who grew extremely anxious looking at the roller coaster may refuse to go to an amusement park again. The woman who did not want to relocate to her company's branch office may quit her job without even looking for a new one. In such cases, coping by withdrawal becomes maladaptive avoidance. Moreover, people who have given up on a situation can miss out on an effective solution.

Withdrawal, in whatever form, is a mixed blessing. Although it can be an effective method of coping, it has built-in dangers. The same tends to be true of defensive coping.

Defensive Coping

So far, we have focused on stress that arises from recognizable sources, but at times, we either cannot identify or cannot deal directly with the source of our stress. For example, you return to a parking lot to discover that someone has damaged your new car and then left the scene. Or a trip you have planned for months is delayed by an airline strike. Some problems are too emotionally threatening to be faced directly. Perhaps you find out that someone close to you is seriously ill. Or you learn that after 4 years of hard work you have not been admitted to medical school and may have to abandon your plan to become a doctor.

In such situations, many people automatically adopt **defense mechanisms** as a way of coping. Defense mechanisms are techniques for *deceiving* oneself about the causes of a stressful situation in order to reduce pressure, frustration, conflict, and anxiety. The self-deceptive nature of such adjustments led Freud to conclude that they are entirely unconscious. He was par-

4 What is meant by "defense mechanisms"? What are some common types of defense mechanisms?

ticularly interested in distortions of memory and in irrational feelings and behavior, all of which he considered symptoms of a struggle against unconscious impulses. Not all psychologists accept Freud's interpretation of defensive coping as always springing from unconscious conflicts. Often we are aware that we are pushing something out of our memory or otherwise deceiving ourselves. For example, all of us have blown up at one person when we *knew* we were really angry at someone else. Whether defense mechanisms operate consciously or unconsciously, they do provide a means of coping with stress that might otherwise be unbearable. We review the defense mechanisms below.

DENIAL Denial is the refusal to acknowledge a painful or threatening reality. Although denial is a positive response in some situations, in other situations it clearly is not. Students who deny their need to study and instead spend several nights a week at the movies may fail their exams. Similarly, frequent drug users who insist that they are merely experimenting with drugs are also deluding themselves.

REPRESSION The most common mechanism for blocking out painful feelings and memories is repression, a form of forgetting that excludes painful thoughts from consciousness. Soldiers who break down in the field often block out the memory of the experiences that led to their collapse (Grinker & Spiegel, 1945). Repression may indicate that the person is struggling against impulses (such as aggression) that conflict with conscious values. For example, most of us were taught in childhood that violence and aggression are wrong. This conflict between our feelings and our values can create stress, and one way of coping defensively with that stress is to repress our feelings, to block out completely any awareness of our underlying anger and hostility.

Denial and repression are the most basic defense mechanisms. In denial, we block out situations we can't cope with; in repression, we block out unacceptable impulses or thoughts. These psychic strategies form the bases for several other defensive ways of coping, discussed below.

PROJECTION If a problem cannot be denied or completely repressed, we may distort its nature so that we can handle it more easily. One example of this is projection, the attribution of one's own repressed motives, ideas, or feelings to others. We ascribe feelings to someone else that we do not want to acknowledge as our own, locating the source of our conflict outside ourselves. A corporate executive who feels guilty about the way he rose to power may project his own ruthless ambition onto his colleagues. He is simply doing his job, he believes, while his associates are all crassly ambitious and consumed with power.

IDENTIFICATION The reverse of projection is identification. Through projection, we *rid* ourselves of undesirable characteristics that we have repressed by attributing them to someone else. Through identification, we *take on* the characteristics of someone else so that we can vicariously share in that person's triumphs and overcome feeling inadequate. The admired person's actions, that is, become a substitute for our own. A parent with unfulfilled career ambitions may share emotionally in a son's or daughter's professional success. When the child is promoted, the

Denial Refusal to acknowledge a painful or threatening reality.

Repression Excluding uncomfortable thoughts, feelings, and desires from consciousness.

Projection Attributing one's own repressed motives, feelings, or wishes to others.

Identification Taking on the characteristics of someone else to avoid feeling incompetent.

Through identification with an admired person we vicariously take on that other person's highly regarded characteristics. In this way we counteract painful perceptions about our own shortcomings. Parents who themselves have never been stars at anything may identify with their child's outstanding achievements, taking pride in them as if they were their own.

Regression Reverting to childlike behavior and defenses.

Intellectualization Thinking abstractly about stressful problems as a way of detaching oneself from them.

Reaction formation Expression of exaggerated ideas and emotions that are the opposite of one's repressed beliefs or feelings.

Displacement Shifting repressed motives and emotions from an original object to a substitute object.

Sublimation Redirecting repressed motives and feelings into more socially acceptable channels.

parent may feel personally triumphant. Identification is often used as a form of self-defense in situations where a person feels utterly helpless, including being taken as a hostage or being a prisoner. Some prisoners gradually come to identify with their guards as a way of defensively coping with unbearable and inescapable stress.

REGRESSION   People under severe stress may revert to childlike behavior through a process called **regression.** Why do people regress? Some psychologists say that it is because an adult cannot stand feeling helpless. Children, on the other hand, feel helpless and dependent every day, so becoming more childlike can make total dependency or helplessness more bearable.

Regression is sometimes used as a manipulative strategy, too, albeit an immature and inappropriate one. Adults who cry or throw temper tantrums when their arguments fail may expect those around them to react sympathetically, as their parents did when they were children.

INTELLECTUALIZATION   **Intellectualization** is a subtle form of denial in which we detach ourselves from our feelings about our problems by analyzing them intellectually and thinking of them almost as if they concerned other people. Parents who start out intending to discuss their child's difficulties with a teacher, but instead talk to her about educational philosophy, may be intellectualizing a very upsetting situation. They appear to be dealing with their problems, but in fact they are not because they have cut themselves off from their emotions.

REACTION FORMATION   **Reaction formation** is a form of denial in which people express with exaggerated intensity ideas and emotions that are the *opposite* of their own. *Exaggeration* is the clue to this behavior: Someone who extravagantly praises a rival may be covering up jealousy over the opponent's success. Reaction formation may also be a way of convincing oneself that one's motives are pure. The man who feels ambivalent about being a father may devote a disproportionate amount of time to his children in an attempt to prove to *himself* that he is a good father.

DISPLACEMENT   **Displacement** involves the redirection of repressed motives and emotions from their original objects to substitute objects. The woman who has always wanted to be a mother may feel inadequate when she learns that she cannot have children. As a result, she may become extremely attached to a pet or to a niece or nephew. In another example of displacement, the person who must smile and agree with a difficult boss may yell at family members for no reason.

SUBLIMATION   **Sublimation** refers to transforming repressed motives or feelings into more socially acceptable forms. Aggressiveness, for instance, might be channeled into competitiveness in business or sports. A strong and persistent desire for attention might be transformed into an interest in acting or politics. Freud believed that sublimation is not only necessary but desirable. People who can transform their sexual and aggressive drives into more socially acceptable forms are clearly better off, for they are able to at least partially gratify instinctual drives with relatively little anxiety and guilt. Moreover, society benefits from the energy and effort such people channel into the arts, literature, science, and other socially useful activities.

DEFENSE MECHANISMS

Denial	Refusing to acknowledge a painful or threatening reality: Ray, whose parents frequently flew off the handle and hit him, denies this ever happened.
Repression	Excluding uncomfortable thoughts from consciousness: Lisa, whose grandmother died of breast cancer, is at higher-than-average risk for developing breast cancer herself; still she routinely forgets to do a self-exam.
Projection	Attributing one's own repressed motives, feelings, or wishes to others: Marilyn is unfairly passed over for a promotion; she denies that she is angry about this, but is certain that her supervisor is angry with her.
Identification	Taking on the characteristics of someone else to avoid feeling incompetent: Anthony, uncertain of his own attractiveness, takes on the dress and mannerisms of a popular teacher.
Regression	Reverting to childlike behavior and defenses: Angry because his plan to reorganize his division has been rejected, Bob throws a tantrum.
Intellectualization	Thinking abstractly about stressful problems as a way of detaching oneself from them: After learning that she has not been asked to a classmate's costume party, Tina coolly discusses the ways in which social cliques form and how they serve to regulate and control school life.
Reaction formation	Expression of exaggerated ideas and emotions that are the opposite of one's repressed beliefs or feelings: At work, Michael loudly professes that he would never take advantage of a rival employee, though his behavior indicates quite the opposite.
Displacement	Shifting repressed motives from an original object to a substitute object: Angry at his instructor's unreasonable request that he rewrite his term paper, but afraid to confront his instructor, Nelson comes home and yells at his housemates for telling him what to do.
Sublimation	Redirecting repressed motives and feelings into more socially acceptable channels: The child of parents who never paid attention to him, Bill is running for public office.

Does defensive coping mean that a person is immature, unstable, or on the edge of a "breakdown"? Not at all. In some cases of prolonged and severe stress, defensive coping not only contributes to our overall ability to adapt and adjust, but even becomes essential to survival. And even in less extreme situations, people may rely on defense mechanisms to get through everyday problems and stress. As Coleman et al. (1987) point out, defenses are "essential for softening failure, alleviating tension and anxiety, repairing emotional hurt, and maintaining our feelings of adequacy and worth" (p. 190). Only when a defense mechanism interferes with a person's ability to function or creates more problems than it solves is it considered maladaptive.

Socioeconomic and Gender Differences in Coping with Stress

People differ in how they deal with stressful events. In particular, economic and social factors figure not only in the amount of stress that people encounter but also in their ability to cope with that stress. Poor people frequently have to deal with more stress than other people who are better off (Adler et al., 1994; Cohen & Williamson, 1988). They often live in substandard housing in neighborhoods with high rates of crime and violence. They are more likely than others to experience long-term joblessness, and they face greater obstacles in addressing such basic needs as feeding their children adequately, maintaining good health, securing high-quality medical care, and providing a home.

General adaptation syndrome (GAS)
According to Selye, the three stages the body passes through as it adapts to stress: alarm reaction, resistance, and exhaustion.

5 Do men generally handle stress better than women do?

These children in a low-income neighborhood of Chicago probably experience more stress in their lives than their middle- and upper-class peers. They inhabit a world with high rates of crime and violence and their families are often struggling just to meet basic needs. Such stresses can take a harsh toll on the poor when they have few means of coping with them effectively.

Moreover, some data indicate that people in low-income groups cope less effectively with stress; as a result, stressful events have a harsher impact on their emotional lives (Kessler, 1979; Wills & Langer, 1980). Psychologists have offered several possible explanations for these data. It may be that people in lower socioeconomic classes have fewer means for coping with hardship and stress (Pearlin & Schooter, 1978). Low-income people tend to have fewer people to turn to and fewer community resources to draw on for support during stressful times (Liem & Liem, 1978). In addition, people living in poverty may believe to a greater extent than other people that external factors are responsible for what happens to them and that they have little personal control over their lives (see the discussion of locus of control in Chapter 11, Personality). Finally, there is some evidence that members of low-income groups are more likely to have low self-esteem and to doubt their ability to master difficult situations. All these factors help explain why stress often takes a greater toll on people in lower socioeconomic classes.

Gender differences have also been studied in relation to stress and coping. One study of victims of Hurricane Andrew found that although women *reported* experiencing more stress than men, men and women turned out to be affected equally when stress was measured physiologically (Adler, 1993b). In another study of 300 couples in which both spouses worked, women and men felt equally stressed by the state of their marriage and jobs and how well their children were doing. However, the women in this study experienced greater stress than men when problems developed in long-term relationships, largely because they were more committed to their personal and professional relationships than the men were (Barnett, 1993; Gore & Colten, 1991).

HOW STRESS AFFECTS HEALTH

The Canadian physiologist Hans Selye (1907–1982) contended that we react to physical and psychological stress in three stages he collectively called the **general adaptation syndrome (GAS)** (Selye, 1956, 1976). These three stages are alarm reaction, resistance, and exhaustion.

Stage 1, *alarm reaction,* is the first response to stress. It begins when the body recognizes that it must fend off some physical or psychological danger. Emotions run high. Activity of the sympathetic nervous system increases, resulting in the release of hormones from the adrenal gland. We become more sensitive and alert, our respiration and heartbeat quicken, our muscles tense. These and other physiological changes help us to mobilize our coping resources in order to regain self-control. At the alarm stage, we might use either direct or defensive coping strategies. If neither of these approaches reduces the stress, we enter the second stage of adaptation.

During Stage 2, *resistance,* physical symptoms and other signs of strain appear as we struggle against increasing psychological disorganization. We rely more strongly on both direct and defensive coping techniques. If we then feel less stress, we return to a more normal state. But if the stress is extreme or prolonged, we may turn in desperation to inappropriate coping techniques and cling to them rigidly, despite the evidence that they are not working. When that happens, we further deplete our physical and emotional resources, and signs of psychic and physical wear and tear become even more apparent.

In the third stage, *exhaustion,* we draw on increasingly ineffective defense mechanisms in a desperate attempt to bring the stress under control. Some people lose touch with reality and show signs of emotional disorder or mental illness at this stage. Others show signs of "burnout," including inability to concentrate, irritability, procrastination, and a cynical belief that nothing is worthwhile (Maslach & Leiter, 1997). Physical symptoms such as skin or stomach problems may erupt. Some victims of burnout turn to alcohol or drugs to cope with the stress-induced exhaustion. If the stress continues, the person may suffer irreparable physical or psychological damage or even death.

One of the most startling implications of Selye's theory is the possibility that prolonged psychological stress can cause disease, or at least make certain diseases worse. This idea is controversial, but recent studies strongly support the belief that psychological factors lie at the root of some of our worst afflictions, including heart disease and diseases of the immune system.

How exactly does psychological stress lead to physical illness? There are at least two routes. First, when people experience stress, their hearts, lungs, nervous systems, and other physiological systems are forced to work harder. Prolonged exposure to the powerful biological changes that accompany alarm and mobilization is harmful to the body. Second, stress has a powerful negative effect on the body's immune system, and prolonged stress can destroy the body's ability to defend itself against disease.

How can stress lead to physical illness?

Stress and Heart Disease

Stress is a major contributor to coronary heart disease (CHD), the leading cause of death and disability in the United States (McGinnis, 1994). Heredity influences our risk of developing CHD, but even among identical twins, the incidence of CHD is closely linked to attitudes toward work, problems in the home, and the amount of leisure time available (Kringlen, 1981).

Mental stress predisposes a person to CHD. Blood flow to the heart *decreases* dramatically (a condition known as *myocardial ischemia*) immediately following mental stress in people who show signs of cardiac disease (Gullette et al., 1997). Generally, life stress and social isolation are significant predictors of mortality among those who have suffered heart attacks for whatever reason (Ruberman et al., 1984).

Personality also plays an important role in predisposing us to heart disease. For years, researchers have studied people who exhibit the *Type A behavior pattern*—that is, who respond to life events with impatience, hostility, competitiveness, urgency, and constant striving (Friedman & Rosenman, 1959). This pattern of behavior was first identified in the 1950s by cardiologists Meyer Friedman and Ray Rosenman, who devised a structured interview to distinguish Type A people from more easygoing *Type B* people. The interview not only assesses people's own accounts of their achievement and striving but also attempts to provoke interviewees because Friedman and Rosenman were convinced that Type A behavior was most likely to surface in stressful situations.

A number of studies have shown that the Friedman and Rosenman structured interview not only does an excellent job of identifying people with Type A behavior but also predicts CHD (Booth-Kewley & Friedman, 1987; Miller et al., 1991). For example, one study found that when Type A personalities were being evaluated, subjected to harassment or criticism, or playing video games, their heart rate and blood pressure were much higher than those of Type B personalities under the same circumstances (Lyness, 1993). And high heart rate and high blood pressure are known to contribute to CHD.

Other studies maintain that the link between Type A behavior and CHD is less direct—that the tendency toward Type A behavior may influence people to engage in behaviors, such as smoking or overeating, that directly contribute to heart disease (Matthews, 1988). However, the preponderance of evidence suggests that *chronic anger* and *hostility* (both components of Type A behavior) do indeed predict heart disease (Miller et al., 1996). Thus, it is not surprising that Friedman and his colleagues (1996) have reported some success in reducing the incidence of CHD through the use of counseling designed to diminish the intensity of time urgency and hostility in patients with Type A behavior.

Because long-term stress increases the likelihood of developing CHD, reducing stress has become part of the treatment used to slow the progress of the disease known as *atherosclerosis,* or blockage of the arteries, which can lead to a heart attack. A very low fat diet coupled with stress-management techniques such as yoga and deep relaxation can significantly improve blocked arteries in patients with severe heart disease (Ornish, 1990).

Stress and the Immune System

Because so many people come down with colds or flu after a stressful period in their lives, scientists have long suspected that stress also affects the functioning of the immune system. Recall that the immune system is strongly affected by hormones and signals from the brain. Therefore, the nervous and endocrine systems are also involved in the interactions between stress and the immune system. The relatively new field of **psychoneuroimmunology** studies the interaction between stress on the one hand and immune, endocrine, and nervous system activity on the other (Ader & Cohen, 1993; Maier, Watkins, & Fleshner, 1994).

What sort of changes does stress cause in the immune system and how do these changes affect health? The immune system defends the body against invading substances, or *antigens,* such as bacteria, viruses, and other microbes. It does so primarily with the help of white blood cells called *lymphocytes.* To the extent that stress disrupts the functioning of the immune system, it can impair health (Cohen & Herbert, 1996). In fact, stress associated with college exams and with depression has been linked to suppressed functioning of the immune system (O'Leary, 1990; Oltmanns & Emery, 1998). Chronic stress, such as caring for an elderly parent or living in poverty, also compromises the body's defenses. Increased stress may also make us more susceptible to upper respiratory infections such as the common cold (Cohen, 1996).

Prolonged stress may even increase vulnerability to cancer. Stress does not *cause* cancer, but it apparently impairs the immune system so that cancerous cells are better able to establish themselves and spread throughout the body. Animal research has demonstrated this connection between stress and cancer. One study used as subjects mice known to be vulnerable to cancer. One group was kept for 400 days in crowded conditions in which it heard noise made by people and other animals. By the end of this period, 92 percent of the mice had developed cancer. By contrast, only 7 percent of a comparable group of mice kept in quiet, low-stress conditions developed cancer. In other animal experiments, cancer was diagnosed earlier and death occurred sooner in mice that received frequent shocks under conditions that made escape impossible (presumably a stressful situation) than in mice that were allowed to cope with the stress of shocks by escaping (Anderson, 1983).

Studies of humans also show a link between life stress and incidence of cancer. For example, people who developed cancer generally reported a number of stressful life events in the year before diagnosis (O'Leary, 1990). They were also likely to be fatigued and to feel helpless (see the *Controversies* box). Interestingly, these people reported less distress and were less likely to express negative emotions, such as anger, than others who had the same number of

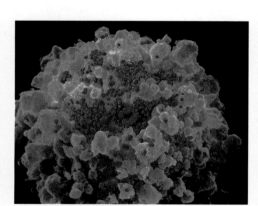

A T-lymphocyte blood cell infected with HIV, the virus that causes AIDS. HIV particles can be seen budding on the cell's lumpy membrane. Eventually the HIV will cripple the cell, making it ineffective in combating the microorganisms that cause diseases.

CONTROVERSIES
CAN ILLUSIONS KEEP YOU HEALTHY?

For most of us, including most psychotherapists, illusion is a bad word. Staying in touch with reality is the hallmark of mental health. But for more than two decades, Shelley E. Taylor (Taylor, 1983; Taylor & Armor, 1996) has taken a strikingly different view: "Far from impeding adjustment," she says, "illusion may be essential for adequate coping" (1983, p. 1171). Taylor initially reached this conclusion after a 2-year study of women with breast cancer. The women who coped best with the stress of disfiguring surgery, painful follow-up treatment, and fear of death proved to be those who constructed comforting illusions about themselves and their illness. Taylor defined illusions as beliefs that were based on an overly optimistic view of the facts or that had no factual basis at all.

In subsequent research, Taylor and Jonathan Brown (1988a, 1988b) expanded on the idea that positive illusions can promote mental and physical health. They found that mentally healthy people distort reality in a way that enhances self-esteem and maintains optimism. In other words, such people tend to overestimate their ability to control or influence chance events and believe—despite contrary evidence—that the future will be better than the present. Taylor and

Brown contend that these people are happier, have more friends, and are usually more persistent, creative, and productive than those laboring under no such positive illusions. Their optimistic outlook draws other people to them and also gives them the confidence to pursue their interests.

Mildly positive illusions may foster behaviors that can improve health.

Still, relying on illusions seems to be a rather risky way of handling stress, for if the illusion is shattered, the person's sense of well-being may collapse as well. Moreover, because illusions are often symptoms of a psychiatric disorder, many psychologists dispute the notion that in certain circumstances they are cornerstones of mental health. When Randall Colvin and Jack Block (1994) reviewed Taylor's studies as well as other studies, they found evidence for the beneficial effect of illusions inconclusive.

In their response to Colvin and Block's criticism, Taylor and Brown (1994) emphasized that they did not contend that mildly positive illusions cure physical illness, but rather that such illusions foster behaviors that can improve health (e.g., eating better and taking better care of oneself). They also noted that not all illusions are good, and that more illusion is not necessarily better than less.

Although more research needs to be done in this area, one explanation for the different viewpoints on illusion may be semantic. It seems, at least in some cases, that what Taylor and others of like mind call "illusions" are just realistic and positive strategies for dealing with certain health problems. Research demonstrates, for example, that maintaining an optimistic attitude can have both psychological and physical health benefits (Scheier & Carver, 1993). At what point, though, does an "optimistic attitude" become an illusion?

Questions

1. Can you think of times in your own life when positive illusions (such as overestimating your ability to control or influence events, or believing that the future will be better than the present) have helped you cope with stress?

2. Were you better off believing in these illusions, however briefly, than if you had not?

3. How did such illusions change the way you behaved in response to the stressful situation?

stressful life events. This suggests that suppressing negative emotions may be more stressful (and less healthful) than expressing them.

Of course, cancer treatments themselves are very stressful. Chemotherapy and radiation treatments can suppress immune function, so patients who are depressed at their diagnosis must then deal with a double blow to the immune system. Some studies indicate that relaxation techniques improve immune functioning, increasing survival rates among cancer patients (Andersen et al., 1994). Cancer therapy now often includes stress-reduction components such as group therapy (see the *Highlights* box).

HIGHLIGHTS
THE BENEFITS OF GROUP THERAPY FOR BREAST CANCER PATIENTS

Faced with the diagnosis of late-stage breast cancer, women understandably experience high levels of depression and mental stress. In turn, the stress and depression often undermine compliance with vitally important medical treatments (Andersen, Kiecolt-Glaser, & Glaser, 1994). Many physicians now routinely recommend their breast cancer patients attend group therapy sessions, which seem to be effective in reducing depression and mental stress (Kissane et al., 1997; Spiegel, 1995).

Interestingly, intensive group therapy on terminally ill breast cancer patients may do more than simply help the women cope with psychological stress—*it may actually increase their survival rate* (Spiegel & Moore, 1997). In a study of 86 women with late-stage breast cancer, women who had received intensive group therapy survived, on average, a year and a half longer than those who did not receive therapy. But was this outcome due to greater compliance with medical services on the part of the women who attended group therapy compared with those who did not? A follow-up study (Kogon et al., 1997) ruled out that possibility. "Whatever it was," according to psychiatrist Dr. David Spiegel, "it wasn't simply that they used their health care services differently. It must have been something else . . . that occurred as a result of the therapy that allowed these women to live longer" (NPR, 1997).

Because stress affects both the immune and endrocine systems, subsequent studies (van der Pompe et al., 1997) have already begun to explore the effect that psychosocial intervention may have on these systems. According to Dr. Robert Carlson, a colleague of Dr. Spiegel: "We know that the immune system has some impact on how individuals handle their cancer. And one of the things we're doing [in our current research] is seeing whether the immune responses are different in the women who are in the psychosocial intervention group compared with those women who are not" (NPR, 1997).

Social Support and Health

A strong network of friends and family who provide *social support* can help to maintain good health (Uchino, Cacioppo, & Kiecolt-Glaser, 1996). Recent research has found that people who attend religious services regularly enjoy better health and markedly lower rates of depression than those who do not (Koenig, 1997). Indeed, one review of the literature concluded that the positive relationship between social support and health is on a par with the negative relationship to the health of such well-established risk factors as physical inactivity, smoking, and high blood pressure (House, Landis, & Umberson, 1988).

Exactly why the presence of a strong social support system is related to health is not fully understood. Clearly, friends and relatives can play an important role by providing strength and encouragement when we face stressful situations (Williams et al., 1992). We often reassess difficulties discussed in a supportive and sensitive environment and find new ways of coping with and reducing the perceived stress. However, some researchers contend that social support may directly affect our response to stress and health by producing physiological changes in endocrine, cardiac, and immune functioning (Uchino et al., 1996). For example, one study found that hostility and negativity in newlyweds was related to suppressed immune system functioning as compared to newlyweds displaying more positive styles of interaction (Kiecolt-Glaser et al., 1993). Similarly, another study found that older adults who regularly attend religious services have healthier immune systems than those who don't attend services (Koenig et al., 1997).

Still many investigators remain skeptical about the effect of social support, suggesting that the association between social support and health is the result of other related factors. They note that people with high levels of social support may simply engage in healthier behaviors such as better diets and more physical exercise—ultimately accounting for their improved health status.

SOURCES OF EXTREME STRESS

Extreme stress has a variety of sources, ranging from unemployment to wartime combat, from violent natural disaster to rape. We look briefly now at some major stressors, the effects they have on people, and the coping mechanisms people use to deal with them.

1. *Unemployment.* Joblessness is a major source of stress. When the jobless rate rises, so do first admissions to psychiatric hospitals, infant mortality, deaths from heart disease, alcohol-related diseases, and suicide (Brenner, 1973, 1979; Rayman & Bluestone, 1982). "Things just fell apart," one worker said after both he and his wife lost their jobs.

   People usually react to the stress of unemployment in several stages (Powell & Driscoll, 1973). First comes a period of relaxation and relief, in which they take a vacation of sorts, confident they will find another job. Stage 2, marked by continued optimism, is a time of concentrated job hunting. In Stage 3, a period of vacillation and doubt, jobless people become moody, their relationships with family and friends deteriorate, and they scarcely bother to look for work. By Stage 4, a period of malaise and cynicism, they have simply given up.

   Although these effects are not universal, they are quite common. Moreover, there are indications that joblessness may not so much create new psychological difficulties as bring previously hidden ones to the surface. Two studies have shown that death rates go up and psychiatric symptoms worsen not just during periods of unemployment but also during short, rapid upturns in the economy (Brenner, 1979; Eyer, 1977). This finding lends support to the observation that change, whether good or bad, causes stress.

2. *Divorce and separation.* As Coleman and colleagues (1988) observe, "the deterioration or ending of an intimate relationship is one of the more potent of stressors and one of the more frequent reasons why people seek psychotherapy" (p. 155). After a breakup, both partners often feel they have failed at one of life's most important endeavors. Strong emotional ties frequently continue to bind the pair. If only one spouse wants to end the marriage, the one initiating the divorce may feel sadness and guilt at hurting a once-loved partner, while the rejected spouse may vacillate between anger, humiliation, and self-recrimination over his or her role in the failure. Even if the decision to separate was mutual, ambivalent feelings of love and hate can make life upsetting and turbulent. Thus, people commonly use defensive coping techniques, particularly denial and projection, to cushion the impact of divorce or separation.

3. *Bereavement.* Following the death of a loved one, people generally experience the strong feelings of grief and loss known as *bereavement*. Most people emerge from this experience without suffering permanent psychological harm, but usually not before they pass through a long process that Freud called the "work of mourning."

Divorce is a major source of extreme stress in people's lives—one that over half of newly married American couples will one day face. Divorce is stressful not only because of the conflict leading up to it, but also because of the anger, guilt, depression, and other negative emotions that often come in its wake.

Janis and his colleagues (1969) have described normal grief as beginning with numbness and progressing through months of distress in which anger, despair, intense grief and yearning, depression, and apathy may all come to the fore. During this phase, people in mourning tend to cope defensively with an inescapable and extremely painful reality. In most cases, denial, displacement, and other defense mechanisms allow the survivor to gather strength for the more direct coping efforts that will be necessary later on—such as, in the case of a spouse's death, selling belongings and moving out of the marital home.

4. *Catastrophes.* Catastrophes include floods, earthquakes, violent storms, fires, and plane crashes. Psychological reactions to all these stressful events have much in common. At first, in the *shock stage*, "the victim is stunned, dazed, and apathetic," and sometimes even "stuporous, disoriented, and amnesic for the traumatic event." Then, in the *suggestible stage*, victims are passive and quite ready to do whatever rescuers tell them to do. In the third phase, the *recovery stage*, victims regain emotional balance, but anxiety often persists, and they may need to recount their experiences over and over again (Morris, 1990). Some investigators report that in later stages survivors may feel irrationally guilty because they lived while others died.

5. *Combat and other threatening personal attacks.* Wartime experiences often cause soldiers intense and disabling combat stress. Similar reactions—including bursting into rage over harmless remarks, sleep disturbances, cringing at sudden loud noises, psychological confusion, uncontrollable crying, and silently staring into space for long periods—are also frequently seen in survivors of serious accidents and violent crimes such as rapes and muggings.

7 What is post-traumatic stress disorder? What kinds of events are most likely to trigger this disorder?

Post-traumatic Stress Disorder

In extreme cases, severely stressful events can cause a psychological disorder known as **post-traumatic stress disorder (PTSD).** Dramatic nightmares in which the victim reexperiences the terrifying event exactly as it happened are common. So are daytime *flashbacks*, in which the victim relives the trauma. Often, victims of PTSD withdraw from social life and from job and family responsibilities.

Post-traumatic stress disorders can set in right after a traumatic event or within a short time. But sometimes, months or years may go by in which the victim seems to have recovered from the experience, and then, without warning, psychological symptoms appear, then may disappear only to recur repeatedly; some people suffer for years (Kessler et al., 1995). Exposure to events reminiscent of the original trauma intensify symptoms of PTSD (Moyers, 1996).

Combat veterans appear to be especially vulnerable to PTSD. More than one-third of men involved in heavy combat in Vietnam showed signs of serious PTSD. Many veterans of World War II, old men now, still have nightmares from which they awake sweating and shaking. The memories of combat continue to torment them after more than half a century (Gelman, 1994).

Yet not everyone who is exposed to severely stressful events such as heavy combat or childhood sexual abuse develops PTSD. Individual characteristics including gender, personality, a family history of mental disorders, substance abuse among relatives, and even preexisting neurological disorders appear to predispose some people to PTSD more than others (Curle & Williams, 1996; Friedman, Schnurr, & McDonagh-Coyle, 1994;

Gurvits et al., 1997). For instance, vulnerability to PTSD in Vietnam veterans was associated with specific personality characteristics that existed before their military experience (Schnurr, Rosenberg, & Friedman, 1993). Recovery from post-traumatic stress disorder is strongly related to the amount of emotional support survivors receive from family, friends, and community.

THE WELL-ADJUSTED PERSON

Adjustment refers to any effort to cope with stress, but psychologists disagree about what constitutes good adjustment. Some think that it means the ability to live according to social norms. Everyone has hostile and selfish wishes; everyone dreams impossible dreams. People who learn to control their forbidden impulses and to limit their goals to those society allows are, by this definition, well adjusted. A woman who grows up in a small town, attends her state university, teaches for a year or two, then settles down to a peaceful family life might be considered well adjusted to the extent that she is living by the predominant values of her community.

Other psychologists disagree strongly with this conformist viewpoint. Barron (1963) argued that "refusal to adjust . . . is very often the mark of a healthy character." Society is not always right. If we accept its standards blindly, we renounce the right to make independent judgments. Barron contends that well-adjusted people enjoy the difficulties and ambiguities of life; they do not sidestep them through unthinking conformity. They accept challenges and are willing to endure the pain and confusion these challenges may bring. Barron has asserted that flexibility, spontaneity, and creativity, rather than simply fitting in, are signs of healthy adjustment.

Still other psychologists maintain that well-adjusted people have learned to balance conformity and nonconformity, self-control and spontaneity—to adapt flexibly as situations change. They can let themselves go at times, but can control themselves in situations where acting on impulse would run counter to their interests or better judgments. They can change themselves at society's urging, but they also work to change society when this strikes them as the better course. Such people know their strengths and admit their weaknesses, and this realistic assessment underlies an approach to life that is in harmony with their inner selves. They do not feel they must act against their values to be successful. Their self-trust enables them to face conflicts and threats without excessive anxiety and, perhaps more important, lets them risk their feelings and self-esteem in intimate relationships.

We may also evaluate adjustment by using specific criteria, such as the following (Morris, 1990), to judge an action:

1. *Does the action realistically meet the demands of the situation, or does it simply postpone resolving the problem?* Various forms of escapism—drugs, alcohol, and even endless fantasizing through books, movies, and television—may divert us from our pain, but they do not address the causes of our difficulties. Too great a reliance on escapism never makes for effective adjustment to a stressful situation.

2. *Does the action meet the individual's needs?* Often we act to reduce external pressures by shortchanging our personal needs. An aspiring actress may abandon her own career goals to further the goals of her spouse. In the short run, she reduces external pressure, but she may be frustrated and disappointed for the rest of her life. A solution that creates such inner conflict is not an effective adjustment.

A devastating trauma like the bombing of the Federal Building in Oklahoma City can trigger post-traumatic stress disorder in its victims. Survivors may suffer terrifying nightmares and vivid daytime flashbacks. Even for trained rescue workers, exposure to the horrors of the trauma can sometimes prompt strong emotional reactions that endure for weeks or even months.

3. *Is the action compatible with the well-being of others?* Some people satisfy their needs in ways that hurt others. A young executive who ruthlessly uses people and manipulates coworkers may "get ahead" through such actions. But even if he does succeed in becoming vice president of his company, he may find himself without friends and may fear that his superiors will treat him as he does his subordinates. Ultimately, this situation can become extremely stressful and frustrating. Good adjustment takes into consideration both individual needs and the well-being of others.

For Abraham Maslow, whose humanistic views of personality and hierarchy of needs we discussed in Chapters 9 and 11, people who are well adjusted seek to "actualize" themselves. That is, they live in a way that enhances their own growth and fulfillment, regardless of what others may think. Well-adjusted individuals, says Maslow, perceive people and events realistically and can accept uncertainty and ambiguity (1954). Though often quite conventional in behavior, they do not think conventionally; rather, they are creative and spontaneous thinkers. At the same time, self-actualizing people set goals for themselves and work, often independently, to achieve them.

Self-actualizing people also tend to form deep, close relationships with a few chosen individuals and are generally indifferent to such characteristics as sex, birth, race, color, and religion in responding to other people. Maslow also noted that people with a sense of humor that is broad and philosophical rather than pointed and hostile stand the best chance of adjusting to stress and achieving the most they can.

There are many standards for judging whether a person is well adjusted. A person deemed well adjusted by one standard may not be adjudged so by other criteria. The same holds true when we try to specify what behaviors are "abnormal"—the topic of the next chapter.

SUMMARY

We experience **stress** when we are faced with a tense or threatening situation that requires us to change or adapt our behavior. **Adjustment** refers to any attempt we make to cope with a stressful situation, balancing our needs and desires against the demands of the environment and the realistic possibilities available to us. How we adjust to the stresses in our lives affects our health; prolonged or severe stress can contribute to physical and psychological disorders. **Health psychology** is a subfield of psychology concerned with the relationship between psychological factors and physical health.

SOURCES OF STRESS

Some life-and-death situations, such as war and natural disasters, are inherently stressful. Even events that are usually viewed as positive, such as a wedding or a job promotion, may be stressful because they require change or adaptation.

Change

Because most people have a strong desire to maintain order in their lives, any event that involves change will be experienced as stressful. The Social Readjustment Rating Scale (SRRS) developed by Holmes and Rahe measures how much stress a person has undergone in any given period by assigning point values to a series of life-changing events.

Hassles

Much stress comes from nonevents or hassles, defined as petty annoyances, irritations, and frustrations. Major events often trigger the little hassles that give rise to stress.

Pressure

Pressure also contributes to stress. Pressure can derive from both internal and external forces; in either case, we feel forced to intensify our efforts or to perform at higher levels.

Frustration

We feel frustrated when someone or something stands between us and our goal. Five basic sources of **frustration** are delays, lack of resources, losses, failure, and discrimination.

Conflict

Conflict arises when we are faced with two or more incompatible demands, opportunities, needs, or goals. Kurt Lewin analyzed conflict in terms of *approach* and *avoidance,* and showed how these tendencies combine to characterize three basic types of conflict. Someone who is simultaneously attracted to two incompatible goals experiences an **approach/approach conflict,** in which the person must either make a choice between the two goals or opportunities or modify them so as to take some advantage of both goals. The reverse of this problem is **avoidance/avoidance conflict,** in which a person confronts two undesirable or threatening possibilities. People usually try to escape this kind of conflict or vacillate between the two possibilities. Also difficult to resolve is an **approach/avoidance conflict,** in which a person is both attracted to and repelled by the same goal or opportunity. People in this dilemma eventually reach a point where the tendency to approach equals the tendency to avoid and they vacillate until they finally make a decision or until the situation changes.

Self-imposed Stress

Sometimes people subject themselves to stress by internalizing a set of irrational, self-defeating beliefs that add unnecessarily to the normal stresses of living.

Stress and Individual Differences

Some people perceive a particular situation as stressful, whereas others are able to take the same situation in stride. Stress-resistant people may share a trait called *hardiness*—a tendency to experience difficult demands as challenging rather than threatening. Those who feel they have some control over an event are far less susceptible to stress than those who feel powerless in the same situation.

COPING WITH STRESS

People generally adjust to stress in one of two ways: *Direct coping* describes any action people take to change an uncomfortable situation; *defensive coping* denotes the various ways people convince themselves—through a form of self-deception—that they are not really threatened or do not really want something they cannot get.

Direct Coping

When we cope directly with a particular threat or conflict, we do it in one of three ways: **confrontation, compromise,** or **withdrawal.** Confronting a stressful situation may lead us to learn new skills, enlist other people's aid, try harder to reach our goal, or express anger. Compromise usually resolves a conflict by forcing us to settle for less than we originally sought. Sometimes the most effective way of coping with a stressful situation is to distance oneself from it, but the danger of withdrawal is that it may become a maladaptive habit.

Defensive Coping

When a stressful situation arises and little can be done to deal with it directly, people often turn to **defense mechanisms** as a way of coping. Defense mechanisms are ways of deceiving ourselves, consciously or unconsciously, about the causes of stressful events, thus reducing conflict, frustration, pressure, and anxiety.

Denial is the refusal to acknowledge a painful or threatening reality. **Repression** is the blocking out of unacceptable thoughts or impulses from consciousness. When we cannot deny or repress a particular problem, we might resort to **projection**—that is, attributing our repressed motives or feelings to others, thereby locating the source of our conflict outside of ourselves. **Identification** is another form of defensive coping in which people take on the characteristics of a powerful person in order to gain a sense of control.

People under severe stress sometimes revert to childlike behavior, a kind of defensive coping called **regression.** **Intellectualization** is a defense mechanism whereby people emotionally distance themselves from a particularly disturbing situation. In **reaction formation,** a form of denial, people express with exaggerated intensity ideas and emotions that are the opposite of their own. Through **displacement,** repressed motives and feelings are redirected from their original objects to substitute objects. **Sublimation** involves transforming repressed emotions into more socially accepted forms.

Socioeconomic and Gender Differences in Coping with Stress

People living in poverty tend to experience greater stress than other people, primarily because the environments in which they live are generally more threatening and they have fewer resources to draw on in coping with that stress. As a result, they experience more health problems than do people in better financial circumstances. Contrary to popular belief, women and men seem to be equally affected by stress, although women are more likely than men to experience stress when their marriage or other long-term relationships are deeply troubled. This appears to be a sign of greater commitment to the relationship rather than an indication of greater vulnerability to stress.

HOW STRESS AFFECTS HEALTH

Physiologist Hans Selye identified three stages of reacting to physical and psychological stress that he called the **general adaptation syndrome (GAS).** In Stage 1, *alarm reaction,* the body recognizes that is must fight off some physical or psychological danger and acts accordingly. If neither direct nor defensive coping mechanisms succeed in reducing the stress, we move to Stage 2 of adaptation. During this *resistance stage*, physical symptoms of strain appear as we intensify our efforts to cope both directly and defensively. If these attempts to regain psychological equilibrium fail, psychological disorganization rages out of control until *exhaustion*, Stage 3 is reached. In this phase, we use increasingly ineffective defense mechanisms to bring the stress under control. Some people lose touch with reality, while others show signs of "burnout."

Stress and Heart Disease

Stress is known to be an important factor in the development of coronary heart disease (CHD). Type A behavior pattern, a set of characteristics that includes hostility, urgency, competitiveness, and striving, has been linked to a greater likelihood of CHD. Stress-reduction programs can slow, and sometimes arrest, the progress of CHD.

Stress and the Immune System

Studies in **psychoneuroimmunology** have shown that stress can suppress the functioning of the immune system, increasing one's susceptibility to the common cold as well as to cancer in situations of prolonged exposure to stress. Stress-reduction techniques can help cancer patients cope.

Social Support and Health

People with strong social support systems enjoy better health and in some cases increased longevity. Some evidence suggests that social support may directly affect immune system functioning. It may be that people with high levels of social support more frequently engage in healthier behaviors, such as better diets and more physical exercise.

SOURCES OF EXTREME STRESS

Extreme stress derives from a number of sources, including unemployment, divorce and separation, bereavement, combat, and natural disasters. People try to cope with these intense, life-altering events in various ways; most resort to defense mechanisms at one or more stages to allow themselves time to gather their energies for more direct coping efforts later on.

Post-traumatic Stress Disorder

Extreme trauma may result in **post-traumatic stress disorder (PTSD)**, a disabling emotional disorder whose symptoms include anxiety, sleeplessness, and nightmares. Combat veterans and people with a history of emotional problems are especially vulnerable to PTSD.

THE WELL-ADJUSTED PERSON

What constitutes good adjustment? Some psychologists believe that well-adjusted people live according to social norms, having learned to control socially forbidden impulses and limit their goals to those that society allows. Barron, on the other hand, argues that the refusal to adjust to social norms is the mark of a healthy character. He suggests that well-adjusted people accept and enjoy challenges because they are confident of their ability to deal with problems in a realistic and mature way. Still other psychologists believe that well-adjusted people are those who have learned to balance conformity and nonconformity, self-control and spontaneity. Finally, some psychologists use specific criteria to evaluate a person's ability to adjust, such as how well the adjustment solves the problem and satisfies both personal needs and the needs of others.

REVIEW QUESTIONS

MULTIPLE CHOICE AND SHORT ANSWER

1. The process by which we respond to events that create a sense of physiological or psychological tension or threat is known as _____.

2. Both pleasant and unpleasant situations can be stressful. T/F

3. _____ occurs when we feel forced to speed up, intensify, or redirect our behavior, or to meet a higher standard of performance.

4. _____ occurs when people are prevented from achieving a goal.

5. Probably the most common problem to which people must adjust is _____.

6. Match each type of conflict with its definition:

   _____ Approach/ approach   a. We must choose between two undesired, yet unavoidable, alternatives.

   _____ Avoidance/ avoidance   b. We are both attracted and repelled by the same goal.

   _____ Approach/ avoidance   c. We are attracted to two goals at the same time.

7. Though living in poverty can lead to an increase in stress, this has no effect on health. T/F

8. There are two general types of coping: _____ and _____.

9. Confronting problems, compromising, or withdrawing from the situation entirely are all forms of _____ coping.

10. _____ coping is a means of dealing with situations that people feel unable to resolve.

11. Match each of the following defense mechanisms with its definition:

    _____ Denial

    _____ Repression

    _____ Projection

    _____ Identification

    _____ Regression

    _____ Intellectualization

    _____ Reaction formation

    _____ Displacement

    _____ Sublimation

    a. A form of forgetting

    b. Detachment from problems through rational analysis

    c. Reversion to less mature, even childlike behavior

    d. Exaggerated expression of emotions or ideas that are the opposite of what we really feel or believe

    e. Redirection of motives or emotions to other objects

    f. Refusal to acknowledge that a painful or threatening situation exists

    g. Attributing one's own motives and feelings to others

    h. Redirection of motives or emotions into more socially acceptable forms

    i. Taking on the characteristics of someone else to share that person's successes and avoid feelings of personal inadequacy

12. The general adaptation syndrome consists of three stages of reaction to stress: _____, _____, and exhaustion.

13. _____ is the term given to the set of characteristics, such as hostility and a sense of urgency, that many people believe make a person more susceptible to coronary heart disease.

14. Research so far has been unable to find a connection between stress and the strength of the body's immune system. T/F

CRITICAL THINKING AND APPLICATIONS

1. Sherry is an air-traffic controller who has recently been coming home from work with terrible headaches. She is a perfectionist and is easily frustrated, but she loves her job and does it well. Recently, she broke up with her boyfriend rather than leave her job and relocate to another city with him. Try to come up with at least two or three hypotheses to explain Sherry's headaches.

2. Are defense mechanisms bad for you, or do they foster good health? Give an example of defensive coping as it applies to a person you know (without using the person's name). Has this defense mechanism helped or hindered the person? Come up with two other strategies—one that seems better and another that seems worse than the one chosen—this person might have used to cope with the stress that prompted these defense mechanisms.

3. Charlie's father was transferred from New Hampshire to North Dakota in the middle of Charlie's senior year in high school, forcing the family to relocate. By the time he comes home from his new school, Charlie can barely keep his eyes open. His parents tell him his exhaustion and depression are "all in his head." Charlie doesn't think so. Cite some evidence from this chapter to support his claim.

ENDURING ISSUES

Stability–Change
Can people change significantly over time in their ability to cope with stress? If someone is easily overwhelmed by stressful events early in life, are they likely to be the same 20 or 40 years later?

Mind–Body
After reading about the relationship between psychological processes and health, have your thoughts changed about the relationship between mind (psychology) and body (physiology)?

(Answers to the Review Questions appear in the back of the book.)

13 Psychological

Disorders

When does behavior become abnormal? The answer to this question is more complicated than it may seem. There is no doubt that the man on the street corner claiming to be Jesus Christ or the woman insisting that aliens from outer space are trying to kill her is behaving abnormally. But what about the members of a religious cult who follow through on a suicide pact? A business executive who happily drinks three martinis every day for lunch? A young woman who feels depressed much of the time but still functions effectively and "keeps up a front"?

Think About It!

1. What types of problems do mental-health professionals define as psychological disorders?

2. *True or False*: In earlier centuries, people often attributed psychological disorders to supernatural forces.

3. What is the systems approach, and how has it contributed to our understanding of psychological disorders?

4. How is clinical depression different from "normal" depression?

5. What is a psychosomatic illness? Is it the same as hypochondriasis?

6. *True or False*: Schizophrenia refers to split personality.

Many physical diseases can be detected by impartial laboratory tests, but the presence or absence of mental illness cannot be determined so objectively. Whether an individual suffers from an emotional disorder is something of a judgment call, and judgments can differ, depending on perspective.

PERSPECTIVES ON PSYCHOLOGICAL DISORDERS

Table 13–1 presents three distinct views of mental health: societal, individual, and mental-health professional. Each uses different standards to judge normal and abnormal behavior: Society's main standard is whether behavior conforms to the existing social order; the individual's primary criterion is his or her own sense of well-being; and the mental-health professional looks chiefly at personality characteristics as well as *personal discomfort* (the person's experience of inner distress) and *life functioning* (the person's success in meeting societal expectations for performance in work or school and in social relationships). Serious personal discomfort and inadequate life functioning often go together, but some emotional disorders are characterized by only one or the other problem. Such circumstances complicate the definition of abnormal behavior. Consider the imbalance between personal discomfort and life functioning in each of the following examples:

- A young executive is in a state of profound euphoria. He feels exhilarated, invulnerable, and all-powerful. He suddenly decides he's been caught up in a "rat race," quits his successful job, withdraws his life savings from the bank, and hands out fistfuls of his money on the street corner, telling startled passersby that "it's only paper."

- A 40-year-old successful computer programmer who lives alone is awkward at relating to others. She makes little eye contact, rarely initiates a conversation, and almost always acts "jittery." Inwardly, she feels so tense and restless that she avoids being around people. Often she finds it difficult to sleep at night.

TABLE 13–1

PERSPECTIVES ON PSYCHOLOGICAL DISORDERS

	Standards/Values	Measures
Society	Orderly world in which people assume responsibility for their assigned social roles (e.g., breadwinner, parent), conform to prevailing mores, and meet situational requirements.	Observations of behavior, extent to which a person fulfills society's expectations and measures up to prevailing standards.
Individual	Happiness, gratification of needs.	Subjective perceptions of self-esteem, acceptance, and well-being.
Mental-health professional	Sound personality structure characterized by growth, development, autonomy, environmental mastery, ability to cope with stress, adaptation.	Clinical judgment, aided by behavioral observations and psychological tests of such variables as self-concept, sense of identity, balance of psychic forces, unified outlook on life, resistance to stress, self-regulation, ability to cope with reality, absence of mental and behavioral symptoms, adequacy in love, work, and play, adequacy in interpersonal relationships.

Source: Adapted from Strupp & Hadley. Copyright © 1977 by the American Psychological Association. Adapted by permission of the authors.

A 14-year-old boy has been uncontrollable at home and disruptive in school since early childhood. He abuses alcohol and other drugs and frequently steals from stores. As part of his initiation into a gang, he fires a semiautomatic pistol into the air while driving through the territory of a rival gang.

Is each of these brief vignettes an example of abnormal behavior? The answer depends, in part, on whose perspective you adopt. The euphoric young executive certainly feels happy, and the adolescent gang member surely does not think of himself as having a psychological problem. Although their actions clearly are abnormal from the perspective of society, from their own perspectives, neither suffers from the sort of personal discomfort that *can* define abnormal behavior. The opposite is true of the computer programmer. Perhaps society would judge her behavior as eccentric, but society is not likely to view her as "abnormal." Her behavior does not violate any essential social rules, and she is functioning adequately. Yet she is clearly experiencing much personal discomfort. From her own perspective, something is seriously wrong.

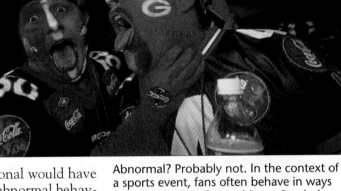

Abnormal? Probably not. In the context of a sports event, fans often behave in ways that they ordinarily would not. Psychologists have developed criteria, such as personal discomfort and inadequate life functioning, to help define abnormal behavior.

Although individual and societal perspectives are in conflict in these cases, a mental-health professional would have little difficulty deciding that all three people are displaying abnormal behavior. Mental-health professionals define abnormal behavior as *either* maladaptive life functioning *or* serious personal discomfort or both. But now imagine that the cases were slightly different. What if the young executive took a trip around the world or gave his savings to a worthy charity instead of handing out money on the street? What if the computer programmer were not quite so anxious and honestly preferred being a "loner"? What if the teenager had been basically a "good kid" until he got involved with the gang members who pressured him to do things he knew were wrong?

The line separating normal from abnormal behavior is somewhat arbitrary, and cases are always much easier to judge when they fall at the extreme end of a dimension than when they fall near the dividing line. Remember, too, that individuals, society, and mental-health professionals do not always view abnormality from the same viewpoint.

1 What types of problems do mental-health professionals define as psychological disorders?

HISTORICAL VIEWS OF PSYCHOLOGICAL DISORDERS

No one knows for sure what was considered abnormal behavior thousands of years ago. However, we can hazard a general description: Mysterious actions were attributed to supernatural powers. Madness was a sign that spirits had possessed a person. Sometimes people who were "possessed" were seen as sacred and their visions considered messages from the gods. At other times, their behavior indicated the presence of evil spirits and their affliction was considered dangerous to the community. It is likely that this *supernatural view* of abnormal behavior dominated all early societies.

The roots of a more *naturalistic view* of abnormal behavior can be traced to ancient Greece. The Greek physician Hippocrates (c. 460–c. 377 B.C.), for example, maintained that madness was like any other sickness—a natural event arising from natural causes. He thought that melancholia

2 *True or False:* In earlier centuries, people often attributed psychological disorders to supernatural forces.

Diathesis-stress model of psychological disorders View that people biologically predisposed to a mental disorder (those with a certain diathesis) will tend to exhibit that disorder when particularly affected by stress.

Diathesis Biological predisposition.

Systems approach to psychological disorders View that biological, psychological, and social risk factors combine to produce psychological disorders. Also known as the biopsychosocial model of psychological disorders.

contingencies) in learned behavior. The cognitive-behavioral model stresses both internal and external learning processes in the development and treatment of psychological disorders. For example, a bright student who considers himself academically inferior to his classmates and who believes that he doesn't have the ability to perform well on a test does not study with much care or confidence. Naturally, he performs poorly, and his poor test score both punishes his minimal efforts and confirms his belief that he is academically inferior. This student is caught up in a vicious circle (Turk & Salovey, 1985). A cognitive-behavior therapist might therefore set out to modify both the young man's dysfunctional studying behavior and his inaccurate and maladaptive cognitive processes.

The cognitive-behavioral model has resulted in innovations in the treatment of psychological disorders. Still, the model can be readily criticized for its limited perspective, especially its extreme emphasis on purely environmental causes and treatments.

The Diathesis-stress Model and Systems Theory

The three major competing theories have each shed some light on certain types of abnormality, and each may continue to do so. However, the most exciting recent developments in abnormal psychology emphasize *integration* of the various theoretical models to discover specific causes and specific treatments for different mental disorders.

The **diathesis-stress model of psychological disorders** is one promising approach to integration. This model suggests that a biological *predisposition* called a **diathesis** must combine with some kind of stressful circumstance before the predisposition to a mental disorder shows up as behavior (Rosenthal, 1970). According to this model, some people are biologically prone to developing a particular disorder under stress, whereas others are not.

The **systems approach to psychological disorders** is an even more promising method of integrating evidence on such behavior (Oltmanns & Emery, 1998). This approach examines how biological, psychological, and social *risk factors* combine to produce psychological disorders; for this reason, it is also known as the *biopsychosocial model*. According to this model, emotional problems are "lifestyle diseases" that, much like heart disease and many other physical illnesses, are caused by a combination of biological risks, psychological stresses, and societal pressures and expectations. We know that heart disease results from a combination of genetic predisposition, stress, characteristic personality styles, poor health behavior, and competitive pressures in our industrialized society. Similarly, according to the systems approach, psychological problems are caused by multiple risk factors that operate together and influence one another. In this chapter, we will follow the systems approach in examining the causes of and treatments for psychological disorders.

3 What is the systems approach, and how has it contributed to our understanding of psychological disorders?

CLASSIFYING PSYCHOLOGICAL DISORDERS

For nearly 40 years, the American Psychiatric Association (APA) has issued an official manual describing and classifying the various kinds of psychological disorders. This publication, the *Diagnostic and Statistical Manual of Mental Disorders (DSM)*, has been revised four times. The fourth edition, DSM-IV, was published in 1994.

The DSM-IV is intended to provide a complete list of mental disorders, with each category painstakingly defined in terms of significant behavior patterns so that diagnoses based on it will be reliable (see Table 13–2). *Reli-*

TABLE 13-2

DIAGNOSTIC CATEGORIES OF DSM-IV

Category	Example
Disorders Usually First Diagnosed in Infancy, Childhood, or Adolescence	Mental retardation, learning disorders, autistic disorder, attention-deficit/hyperactivity disorder.
Delirium, Dementia, and Amnestic and Other Cognitive Disorders	Delirium, dementia of the Alzheimer's type, amnestic disorder.
Mental Disorders Due to a General Medical Condition	Psychotic disorder due to epilepsy.
Substance-related Disorders	Alcohol dependence, cocaine dependence, nicotine dependence.
Schizophrenia and Other Psychotic Disorders	Schizophrenia, schizoaffective disorder, delusional disorder.
Mood Disorders	Major depressive disorder, dysthymic disorder, bipolar disorder.
Anxiety Disorders	Panic disorder with agoraphobia, social phobia, obsessive-compulsive disorder, post-traumatic stress disorder, generalized anxiety disorder.
Somatoform Disorders	Somatization disorder, conversion disorder, hypochondriasis.
Factitious Disorders	Factitious disorder with predominantly physical signs and symptoms.
Dissociative Disorders	Dissociative amnesia, dissociative fugue, dissociative identity disorder, depersonalization disorder.
Sexual and Gender Identity Disorders	Hypoactive sexual desire disorder, male erectile disorder, female orgasmic disorder, vaginismus.
Eating Disorders	Anorexia nervosa, bulimia nervosa.
Sleep Disorders	Primary insomnia, narcolepsy, sleep terror disorder.
Impulse-control Disorders	Kleptomania, pyromania, pathological gambling.
Adjustment Disorders	Adjustment disorder with depressed mood, adjustment disorder with conduct disturbance.
Personality Disorders	Antisocial personality disorder, borderline personality disorder, narcissistic personality disorder, dependent personality disorder.

ability means repeatability, and for the DSM the most important test of reliability is whether different mental health professionals arrive at the same diagnosis for the same individual—that is, do two or more mental-health professionals agree that one person should be diagnosed with schizophrenia, another with depression, and so on?

Although the manual provides careful descriptions of symptoms of different disorders to bolster consistent diagnosis, it is generally silent on cause and treatment. The DSM has gained increasing acceptance because its detailed criteria for diagnosing mental disorders has made diagnosis much more reliable. Today it is the most widely used classification of psychological disorders.

Still, the DSM has its critics. Some charge that the manual is too medically oriented and that it includes too many kinds of behavior that have nothing to do with mental illness. For instance, *premenstrual dysphoric disorder,*

Mood disorders Disturbances in mood or prolonged emotional state.

Depression A mood disorder characterized by overwhelming feelings of sadness, lack of interest in activities, and perhaps excessive guilt or feelings or worthlessness.

Most people feel unhappy and low now and then, but depression goes much deeper than mere unhappiness. Clinically depressed people lose interest in the things that usually give them pleasure. Typically they feel overwhelmed by sadness, loss, and guilt.

4 How is clinical depression different from "normal" depression?

described as an increase in sadness, tension, and irritability that occurs in the week before a woman begins to menstruate, has been denounced as a sexist attempt to label as "illness" what may actually be a normal psychological reaction to significant biological changes (Adler, 1990).

Some of the controversies surrounding the DSM-IV reflect political concerns, whereas others reflect legitimate scientific disagreements about the nature of psychological disorders. These controversies aside, our understanding of the nature, causes, and treatment of some forms of psychological disorders continues to grow.

Throughout this chapter, we will look at a variety of psychological disorders from the integrative systems perspective. As you read, you may occasionally feel an uncomfortable twinge of recognition. This is only natural and nothing to worry about. Much abnormal behavior is simply normal behavior greatly exaggerated or displayed in inappropriate situations.

MOOD DISORDERS

As their name suggests, **mood disorders** are characterized by disturbances in *mood* or prolonged emotional state, sometimes referred to as *affect*. Most people have a wide emotional range—that is, they are capable of being happy or sad, animated or quiet, cheerful or discouraged, overjoyed or miserable, depending on the circumstances. In some people with mood disorders, this range is greatly restricted. They seem stuck at one or the other end of the emotional spectrum—either consistently excited and euphoric or consistently sad—whatever the circumstances of their lives. Other people with a mood disorder alternate between the extremes of euphoria and sadness.

The most common mood disorder is **depression,** a state in which a person feels overwhelmed with sadness, loses interest in activities, and displays other symptoms such as excessive guilt or feelings of worthlessness. People suffering from depression are unable to experience pleasure from activities they once enjoyed. They are tired and apathetic, sometimes to the point of being unable to make the simplest everyday decisions. They may feel as if they have failed utterly in life, and they tend to blame themselves for their problems. Seriously depressed people often have insomnia and lose interest in food and sex. They may have trouble thinking or concentrating—even to the extent of finding it difficult to read a newspaper. In very serious cases, depressed people may be plagued by suicidal thoughts or even attempt suicide (see *Highlights*).

It is important to distinguish between *clinical depression* and the "normal" kind of depression that all people experience from time to time. It is entirely normal to become sad when a loved one has died, when you've come to the end of a romantic relationship, when you have problems on the job or at school—even when the weather's bad or you don't have a date for Saturday night. Most psychologically healthy people also get "the blues" occasionally for no apparent reason. But in all of these instances, the mood disturbance is either a normal reaction to a "real-world" problem (for example, grief) or passes quickly. Only when depression is serious, lasting, and well beyond the typical reaction to a stressful life event is it classified as a mood disorder (APA, 1994).

The DSM-IV distinguishes between two forms of depression. *Major depressive disorder* is an episode of intense sadness that may last for several months; in contrast, *dysthymia* involves less intense sadness (and related symptoms) but persists with little relief for a period of 2 years or more. Some theorists suggest that major depressive disorder is more likely to be caused by

HIGHLIGHTS
SUICIDE

More than 30,000 people in the United States commit suicide each year (Moscicki, 1995). More women than men attempt suicide, but more men actually succeed at it, partly because men more often choose violent and lethal means, such as firearms.

Although the largest number of suicides occur among older white males (see Figure 13–1), there have been disturbing increases in the rate of attempted suicide among adolescents and young adults from the 1960s through the 1990s. Adolescents account for 12 percent of all suicide attempts in this country, and suicide is the second leading cause of death in that age group (Garland & Zigler, 1993). As yet, no convincing explanation has been offered for the increase, though the stresses of leaving home, meeting the demands of college or career, and surviving loneliness or broken romantic attachments seem to be particularly great at this time. External problems such as unemployment, the financial costs of attending college, and the dread that one's future is threatened by economic decline may also add to people's personal problems. Still, suicidal behavior is more common among adolescents who have psychological problems.

There are several dangerous myths concerning suicide. One is the notion that someone who talks of committing suicide will never go through with it. In fact, most people who kill themselves have mentioned their intent beforehand. Such comments should always be taken seriously by the person's friends and family. A related misconception is that someone who

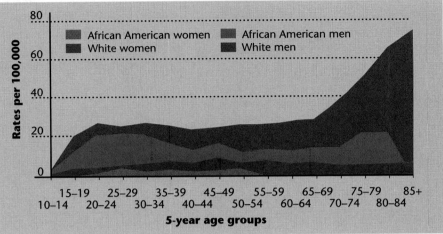

Figure 13–1
Gender and race differences in the suicide rate across the life span.
White males, who commit the largest number of suicides at all ages, show a sharp rise in the rate of suicide beyond the age of 65. In contrast, the suicide rate for African American females, which is the lowest for any group, remains relatively stable throughout the life span.

Source: Moscicki (1995).

has attempted suicide and failed is not serious about it. Often a suicidal person will try again, picking a more deadly method the second or third time around. (And any suicide attempt is a sign that the person is deeply troubled and in desperate need of help.) A third erroneous idea is that those who commit suicide are life's losers—people who have failed vocationally and socially. In fact, many people who kill themselves have prestigious jobs, conventional families, and a good income. Physicians, for example, have a suicide rate several times higher than that for the general population; in this case, the tendency to

Most suicidal people do want help, however much they may despair of obtaining it.

suicide is probably related to their work stresses.

People considering suicide are overwhelmed with hopelessness. They feel that things cannot get better and see no way out of their difficulties. This is depression in the extreme, and it is not a state of mind that someone can easily be talked out of. It does little good to tell a suicidal person that things aren't really so bad; the person will only take this as further evidence that no one understands his or her suffering. But most suicidal people do want help, however much they may despair of obtaining it. A local community mental-health center is a good starting place. Calling one of the national suicide hot lines (see telephone numbers listed in Chapter 14) can be helpful as well.

Psychotic Marked by defective or lost contact with reality.

Mania A mood disorder characterized by euphoric states, extreme physical activity, excessive talkativeness, distractedness, and sometimes grandiosity.

Bipolar disorder A mood disorder in which periods of mania and depression alternate, sometimes with periods of normal mood intervening.

a difficult life event, whereas dysthymia is a biological problem, but this is just speculation at this time. It is true, however, that some depressions can become so intense that people become **psychotic**—that is, they lose touch with reality. Consider the following case:

> A 50-year-old widow was transferred to a medical center from her community mental health center. . . . She believed that her neighbors were against her, had poisoned her coffee, and had bewitched her to punish her because of her wickedness. (Spitzer, et al., 1981, pp. 28–29)

There are other mood disorders besides depression. One that is less common is **mania,** a state in which the person becomes euphoric or "high," extremely active, excessively talkative, and easily distracted. People suffering from mania may become *grandiose*—that is, their self-esteem is greatly inflated. They typically have unlimited hopes and schemes but little interest in realistically carrying them out. People in a manic state sometimes become aggressive and hostile toward others as their self-confidence grows more and more exaggerated. At the extreme, people going through a manic episode may become wild, incomprehensible, or violent until they collapse from exhaustion.

Manic episodes rarely appear by themselves; rather, they usually alternate with depression. Such a mood disorder, in which both mania and depression are present, is known as **bipolar disorder.** In bipolar disorder, periods of mania and depression alternate (each lasting from a few days to a few months), sometimes with periods of normal mood intervening. Occasionally, bipolar disorder is seen in a mild form: The person has alternating moods of unrealistically high spirits followed by moderate depression. Research suggests that bipolar disorder differs in several ways from unipolar depression. Bipolar disorder is much less common and, unlike depression, it is equally prevalent in men and women. Bipolar disorder also seems to have a stronger biological component than depression: It is more strongly linked to heredity and is most often treated by drugs (Gershon, 1990).

Causes of Mood Disorders

Some people insist that mood disorders are caused solely by nature or by nurture. You may have heard, for example, that depression results from "a chemical imbalance in the brain" or "unresolved grief." However, consistent with the biopsychosocial model, most psychologists now believe that mood disorders result from a combination of risk factors. Biological factors seem to be most important in some cases—for example, depression following the experience of a loss (Katz & McGuffin, 1993). Social factors seem to be most important in still other cases—for example, some instances of depression among women. Although we can identify many of the causative factors, we still do not yet know exactly how they interact to cause a mood disorder.

BIOLOGICAL FACTORS   There is consistent evidence that genetic factors play an important role in the development of depression, particularly, as we have noted, in bipolar disorder (Andreasen et al., 1987; Katz & McGuffin, 1993). As we saw in Chapter 2, the strongest evidence for the role of genetic risk factors comes from studies of twins. If one identical twin is clinically depressed, the other twin (who is genetically identical) is relatively likely to be clinically depressed also. Among fraternal twins (who share only about half of the same genes), if one twin is clinically depressed, the likelihood is much less that the second twin will also be clinically depressed (McGuffin et al., 1996).

But just what is it that some people seem to inherit that predisposes them to a mood disorder? Some promising research has linked mood disorders to certain chemical imbalances within the brain—principally to high and low levels of certain neurotransmitters, the chemicals involved in the transmission of nerve impulses from one cell to another (see Chapter 2, "The Biological Basis of Behavior") (Delgado et al., 1992).

Biological research on mood disorders is promising. In fact, as we shall see in the next chapter, several medications have been found to be effective in treating mood disorders. Still, there is no firm evidence linking high or low levels of neurotransmitters to an increased genetic risk for mood disorders. In fact, the so-called chemical imbalance in the brain associated with depression could be caused by stressful life events. Biology affects psychological experience, but psychological experience also alters biological functioning.

PSYCHOLOGICAL FACTORS Although a number of psychological factors are thought to play a role in causing severe depression, in recent years research has focused on the contribution of maladaptive **cognitive distortions.** According to Aaron Beck (1967, 1976, 1984), during childhood and adolescence some people undergo such wrenching experiences as the loss of a parent, severe difficulties in gaining parental or social approval, or humiliating criticism from teachers and other adults. One response to such experience is to develop a negative self-concept—a feeling of incompetence or unworthiness that has little to do with reality but that is maintained by a distorted and illogical interpretation of real events. When a new situation arises that resembles the situation under which the self-concept was learned, these same feelings of worthlessness and incompetence may be activated and result in depression.

Beck describes several kinds of illogical thinking that can contribute to feelings of depression:

1. *Arbitrary inference*. The individual arrives at a sweeping conclusion about himself or herself despite the scarcity or absence of evidence. For example, a man thinks of himself as professionally incompetent because his car won't start on the morning he is scheduled to make an important presentation at work.

2. *Selective abstraction*. The individual arrives at a conclusion based on only one of numerous factors influencing a situation. For example, an athlete blames herself entirely for her team's bad performance although several other members of the team also performed poorly.

3. *Overgeneralization*. The individual arrives at a sweeping conclusion based on a single, sometimes trivial, event. For example, a high school student concludes that he is not worthy of admission to the college of his choice because of his poor performance on a minor quiz for which he was not prepared.

4. *Magnification and minimization*. The individual tends to magnify difficulties and failures while minimizing accomplishments and successes. For example, a man who has been driving for 20 years without an accident minimizes that evidence of skillful motoring and focuses instead on the slight dent he put in his car while trying to back out of a tight parking space.

Cognitive distortions An illogical and maladaptive response to early negative life events that leads to feelings of incompetence and unworthiness that are reactivated whenever a new situation arises that resembles the original events.

Considerable research supports Beck's view of depression. In tests designed to allow respondents to express their immediate thoughts, researchers have found that the thoughts of depressed persons are generally more illogical than the thoughts of people who are not depressed (White, Davison, & White, 1985). When compared to normals, depressed people also seem to perceive and recall information in more negative terms (Roth & Rehm, 1980; Watkins et al., 1996). However, critics of Beck's theories have pointed out that such negative responses may be the *result* of depression instead of the cause (Hammen, 1985). Still, as we shall see in the next chapter, therapy based on Beck's theories has proved quite successful in the treatment of depression.

SOCIAL FACTORS   Many social factors have been linked with mood disorders, particularly difficulties in interpersonal relationships. Freud viewed depression as resulting from excessive and irrational grief over a real or "symbolic" loss. Freud's view of how "unresolved grief" is transformed into depression is complex and not supported by current evidence (Crook & Eliot, 1980). However, the analogy he drew between grief and depression has been fruitfully noted by other theorists, and there is considerable research linking depression with troubled close relationships (Monroe & Simons, 1991). In fact, some theorists have suggested that the link between depression and troubled relationships explains the fact that depression is two to three times more prevalent in women than in men (Simpson, Nee, & Endicott, 1977; Weissman & Olfson, 1995) since women tend to be more relationship-oriented than men are in our society (Gilligan, 1982). Yet not every person who experiences a troubled relationship becomes depressed. As the systems approach would predict, it appears that a genetic predisposition or cognitive distortion is necessary before a distressing close relationship or other significant life stressor will result in a mood disorder.

It is worth making one further point. People with certain depression-prone genetic or cognitive tendencies may be more likely than others to encounter stressful life events by virtue of their personality and behavior. For example, studies show that depressed people tend to evoke anxiety and even hostility in others, partly because they require more emotional support than people feel comfortable giving. As a result, people tend to avoid those who are depressed, and this shunning can intensify the depression. In short, depression-prone and depressed people may become trapped in a vicious circle that is at least partly of their own creation (Coyne & Whiffen, 1995).

ANXIETY DISORDERS

Although all of us are afraid from time to time, we usually know why we are fearful: Our fear is caused by something appropriate and identifiable, and it passes with time. But in the case of **anxiety disorders,** either the person does not know why he or she is afraid or the anxiety is inappropriate to the circumstances. In either case, the person's fear and anxiety don't seem to make sense.

One recent national survey found that anxiety disorders are more common than any other form of mental disorder (Kessler et al., 1994). Anxiety disorders can be subdivided into more specific diagnostic categories. One familiar subtype of anxiety disorder is **specific phobia.** A specific phobia is an intense, paralyzing fear of something that perhaps should be feared, but the fear is excessive and unreasonable. In fact, the fear in a specific phobia is so great that it leads the person to avoid routine or adaptive activities, and thus interferes with life functioning. For example, it is not inappropriate to be a

A phobia causes paralyzing fear in a situation that most people find nonthreatening. Here, a phobia to heights causes extreme discomfort.

Social phobia An anxiety disorder characterized by excessive, inappropriate fears connected with social situations or performances in front of other people.

Agoraphobia An anxiety disorder that involves multiple, intense fear of crowds, public places, and other situations that require separation from a source of security such as the home.

bit fearful as an airplane takes off or lands, but it is inappropriate to be so afraid of flying that you refuse to get on or even go near an airplane—particularly if your career demands frequent travel. Other common phobias focus on animals, heights, closed places, blood, needles, or injury. Some fear of all these objects or situations is normal and common, but excessive, intense, paralyzing fear is a sign of specific phobia. Estimates indicate that about 1 in 10 people in the United States suffers from at least one specific phobia.

Another important subtype of phobia is **social phobia,** which refers to excessive, inappropriate fears connected with social situations or performances in front of other people. Intense fear of public speaking is a common form of social phobia. In other cases simply talking with people or eating in public causes such severe anxiety that the phobic person will go to great lengths to avoid these situations. As with specific phobias, it is normal to experience some mild fear or uncertainty in many social situations. These fears are only considered to be social phobias when they are excessive enough to interfere significantly with life functioning.

Agoraphobia is a much more debilitating type of anxiety disorder than social phobias. *Agoraphobia* is a term formed from Greek and Latin words that literally mean "fear of the marketplace," but the disorder typically involves multiple, intense fears, such as the fear of being alone, of being in public places from which escape might be difficult, of being in crowds, of traveling in an automobile, or of going through tunnels or over bridges. The common element in all these situations seems to be a great dread of being separated from sources of security, such as the home or a loved one with whom the person feels safe.

Agoraphobia can greatly interfere with life functioning: Some sufferers are so fearful that they will venture only a few miles from home, and others will not leave their homes at all. Although agoraphobia is less common than specific or social phobia (it affects about 3 percent of the population), because of the severity of its effects, it is more likely to cause the sufferer to seek treatment (Robins & Regier, 1991). Interestingly, women are far more likely than men to suffer from agoraphobia. One possible explanation is that traditionally it has been more acceptable for a woman to be housebound. It is also possible that women more readily admit to the problem.

Panic disorder An anxiety disorder characterized by recurrent panic attacks in which the person suddenly experiences intense fear or terror without any reasonable cause.

Generalized anxiety disorder An anxiety disorder characterized by prolonged vague but intense fears that are not attached to any particular object or circumstance.

Obsessive-compulsive disorder An anxiety disorder in which a person feels driven to think disturbing thoughts and/or to perform senseless rituals.

In spite of her success, singer Carly Simon feels extremely anxious when appearing before an audience, a condition known as performance anxiety.

Yet another type of anxiety disorder is **panic disorder,** a problem characterized by recurrent panic attacks. A *panic attack* is a sudden, unpredictable, and overwhelming experience of intense fear or terror without any reasonable cause. During a panic attack, a person may have feelings of impending doom, chest pain, dizziness or fainting, sweating, difficulty breathing, and a fear of losing control or dying. A panic attack usually lasts only a few minutes, but such attacks may recur for no apparent reason.

Panic attacks not only cause tremendous fear while they are happening but also leave a dread of having another panic attack that can persist for days or even weeks after the original episode. In some cases, in fact, this dread is so overwhelming that it can lead to the development of agoraphobia: In their efforts to prevent a recurrence, some people avoid any circumstance that might cause anxiety and cling to people or situations that help keep them calm. In other words, their agoraphobia develops out of their attempt to avoid further panic attacks.

In the various phobias and in panic attacks, there is a specific source of anxiety, such as fear of heights, fear of social situations, or fear of being in crowds. In contrast, **generalized anxiety disorder** is defined by prolonged vague but intense fears that are not attached to any particular object or circumstance. Generalized anxiety disorder perhaps comes closest to the everyday meaning attached to the term *neurotic*. Its symptoms include inability to relax, constantly feeling restless or keyed up, muscle tension, rapid heart beat or pounding heart, apprehensiveness about the future, hypervigilance (constant alertness to potential threats), and sleeping difficulties.

A very different form of anxiety disorder is **obsessive-compulsive disorder.** *Obsessions* are involuntary thoughts or ideas that keep recurring despite the person's attempts to stop them, and *compulsions* are repetitive, ritualistic behaviors that a person feels compelled to perform. Obsessive thoughts are often of a horrible and frightening nature. One patient, for example, reported that "when she thought of her boyfriend she wished he were dead; when her mother went down the stairs, she 'wished she'd fall and break her neck'; when her sister spoke of going to the beach with her infant daughter [she] 'hoped that they would both drown'" (Carson & Butcher, 1992, p. 190). Truly compulsive behaviors may be equally dismaying to the person who feels driven to perform them. They often take the form of washing or cleaning, as if the compulsive behavior were the person's attempt to "wash away" the contaminating thoughts. One patient reported that her efforts to keep her clothes and body clean eventually took up 6 hours of her day, and even then, "washing my hands wasn't enough, and I started to use rubbing alcohol" (Spitzer et al., 1981, p. 137).

Another common type of compulsion is checking: repeatedly performing some kind of behavior to make sure that something was or was not done in a certain way. For example, a person might feel compelled to check dozens of times whether the doors are locked before going to bed. In a more unusual case, a man became obsessed with the idea that he had run over someone while driving and spent an entire day driving up and down the same piece of highway trying to find the "body" of the person he was convinced he'd run over (Holzman, 1986).

Anyone can experience mild obsessions or compulsions at times. Most of us have occasionally been unable to get a particular song lyric out of our head or have felt that we had to walk so as to avoid stepping on cracks in the sidewalk. But in an obsessive-compulsive disorder, the obsessive thoughts and compulsive behavior are of a more serious nature. For example, a man who checks his watch every 5 minutes when his wife is late coming home is merely being normally anxious. But a man who feels that he must go through his house every hour checking every clock for accuracy, even though he knows there is no reason to do so, is showing signs of an obsessive-compulsive disorder.

Because people who experience obsessions and compulsions often do not seem particularly anxious, you may wonder why this disorder is considered an anxiety disorder. The answer is that if such people try to *stop* their irrational behavior, or if someone else tries to stop them, they experience severe anxiety. In other words, the obsessive-compulsive behavior seems to have developed to keep anxiety at bay.

Finally, two types of anxiety disorder are clearly caused by some specific highly stressful event. Some people who have lived through fires, floods, tornadoes, or an airplane crash experience repeated episodes of fear and terror after the event itself is over. If the anxious reaction occurs soon after the event, the diagnosis is *acute stress disorder*. If it takes place long after the event is over, the diagnosis is likely to be *post-traumatic stress disorder* (which we discussed in the previous chapter) (Oltmanns & Emery, 1998). Post-traumatic stress disorder is characterized by hyperarousal, avoidance of situations that recall the trauma, and "reexperiencing"—

Extreme stress can cause acute stress disorder. The soldier at left has just learned that his close friend was killed by friendly fire during the Gulf War.

that is, reliving the traumatic event in detail. Two kinds of traumatic experience are particularly likely to lead to acute or post-traumatic stress disorder: military combat exposure among men and rape among women.

Causes of Anxiety Disorders

A starting point in considering the cause of anxiety disorders is to recall our discussion of phobias in Chapter 5, "Learning." We noted that phobias are often learned after only one fearful event and are extremely difficult to shed. We also saw that there is a relatively limited and predictable range of phobic objects: People are more likely to be injured in an automobile accident than by a snake or spider bite, yet snake and spider phobias are far more common than car phobias. Some theorists, therefore, believe phobias are *prepared responses*—that is, responses that evolution has made us biologically predisposed to acquire through learning so that we seem to be "hard-wired" to associate certain stimuli with intense fears (Marks & Nesse, 1994; Öhman, 1996). Consider a young boy who is savagely attacked by a large dog. Because of this experience, he is now terribly afraid of all dogs. Other children who witnessed the attack or just heard about it may also come to fear dogs. Thus are realistic fears or cautions transformed into a phobia.

More generally, and from a more cognitive perspective, research indicates that people who feel they are not in control of stressful events in their lives are more likely to experience anxiety than those who believe they have control over such events. As one real-life example of this, African Americans who live in high-crime areas have a higher incidence of anxiety disorders than other Americans (Neal & Turner, 1991).

Psychologists working from the biological perspective point out, however, that even when there is the same opportunity to learn phobic or obsessive-compulsive behavior, some people develop unrealistic fears and others do not. Thus, there is a distinct possibility that a predisposition to anxiety disorders may be inherited (Eysenck, 1970; Sarason & Sarason,

Psychosomatic disorders Disorders in which there is real physical illness that is largely caused by psychological factors such as stress and anxiety.

Somatoform disorders Disorders in which there is an apparent physical illness for which there is no organic basis.

5 What is a psychosomatic illness? Is it the same as hypochondriasis?

1987). In fact, some evidence suggests that anxiety disorders tend to run in families (Kendler et al., 1992; Torgersen, 1983; Weissman, 1993).

Finally, any comprehensive model of anxiety must account for what would seem to be the vital role of internal psychological conflicts. Most psychoanalytic theorists have focused at length on such conflicts. From the Freudian perspective, unacceptable impulses or thoughts (usually sexual or aggressive in nature) can threaten to overwhelm the ego and break through into full consciousness. The Freudian defense mechanisms protect the conscious mind against such threats, but at a cost in anxiety. For example, according to the psychoanalytic view, phobias are a result of *displacement*, meaning people redirect their strong feelings from whatever originally aroused them toward something else. Thus, a woman who feels unconsciously threatened by unacceptable feelings of fear toward a spouse might redirect her fear toward elevators or spiders. Although we may doubt the validity of specific psychoanalytic interpretations of phobias, inner conflicts—as well as defenses and other internal distortions of these conflicts—certainly seem to play a role in the development of anxiety and its associated disorders.

PSYCHOSOMATIC DISORDERS

To many people, the term *psychosomatic* implies that a condition is not "real," that it exists "only in your head." In fact, **psychosomatic disorders** are *real* physical illnesses that can be indentified with testing. For example, tension headaches are caused by muscle contractions brought on by stress. The headache is real, but it is called "psychosomatic" because psychological factors (such as stress and anxiety) appear to play an important role in causing the symptoms. People suffering from tension headaches are often taught relaxation techniques which relieve stress and reduce muscle tension. The term *psychosomatic* perfectly captures the interplay of psyche (mind) and soma (body) that characterizes these disorders. Scientists used to believe that psychological factors contributed to the development of some physical illnesses, principally headaches, allergies, asthma, and high blood pressure, but not others, such as infectious diseases. Today modern medicine leans toward the idea that *all* physical ailments are to some extent "psychosomatic"—in the sense that stress, anxiety, and various states of emotional arousal alter body chemistry, the functioning of bodily organs, and the body's immune system (which is vital in fighting infections). As we saw in the previous chapter, we now recognize that stress and psychological strains can also alter *health behavior*, which includes positive actions such as eating a balanced diet and exercising as well as such negative activities as cigarette smoking and excessive alcohol consumption. As we noted earlier in the chapter, both physical and mental illnesses are now conceptualized as "lifestyle diseases" that are caused by a combination of biological, psychological, and social factors.

SOMATOFORM DISORDERS

A distinction must be made between psychosomatic disorders, which involve genuine physical illnesses, and **somatoform disorders,** which are characterized by physical symptoms without any identifiable physical cause. Despite reassurances to the contrary from physicians, people suffering from somatoform disorders *believe* they are physically ill and describe symptoms that sound like physical illnesses, yet there is no evidence of physical illness. Their problem is somatic (physical) in appearance only, as indicated by the term *somatoform* (somatic in form or appearance). People who suffer from these disorders do not consciously seek to mislead others about their physical condition. The symptoms are real to them; they are not faked or under voluntary control (APA, 1994).

In one kind of somatoform disorder, **somatization disorder,** the person experiences vague, recurring physical symptoms for which medical attention has been sought repeatedly but no organic cause found. Common complaints are back pains, dizziness, partial paralysis, abdominal pains, and sometimes anxiety and depression. The following case is typical:

> An elderly woman complained of headaches and periods of weakness that lasted for over six months. Her condition had been evaluated by doctors numerous times; she was taking several prescription medications, and she had actually undergone 30 operations for a variety of complaints. She was thin, but examination showed her to be within normal limits in terms of physical health (except for numerous surgical scars). Her medical history spanned half a century, and there can be little doubt that she suffered from somatization disorder. (Quill, 1985)

Another form of somatoform disorder involves complaints of far more bizarre symptoms, such as paralysis, blindness, deafness, seizures, loss of feeling, or false pregnancy. Sufferers from such **conversion disorders** have intact, healthy muscles and nerves, yet their symptoms are very real. For example, a person with such a "paralyzed" limb has no feeling in it, even if stuck with a pin. (The term *conversion disorder* comes from the notion that psychological problems are "converted" into physical illness.) Sometimes it is easy to determine that there is no organic cause for the symptoms of a conversion disorder because the symptoms are anatomically impossible. Take *glove anesthesia,* which is a lack of feeling in the hand from the wrist down. There is no way that damage to the nerves running into the hand could cause such a localized pattern of anesthesia. Another clue that the disorder has psychological causes is that the victim is sometimes quite cheerful about it. Psychologists call this attitude of blithe unconcern about a serious medical condition *la belle indifference* ("beautiful indifference").

Psychologists also look for evidence that the "illness" resolves a difficult conflict or relieves the patient of the need to confront a difficult situation. For example, a housewife reported serious attacks of dizziness, nausea, and visual disturbances that came on in the late afternoon and cleared up at about 8:00 P.M. After ruling out any physical cause for her problems, a therapist discovered that she was married to an extremely tyrannical man who, shortly after coming home from work in the evening, habitually abused her verbally, criticizing her housekeeping, the meal she had prepared, and so on. Her psychological distress was unconsciously converted to physical symptoms that served to remove her from this painful situation (Spitzer et al., 1981).

Yet another somatoform disorder is **hypochondriasis.** Here, the person interprets some small symptom—perhaps a cough, bruise, or perspiration—as a sign of a serious disease. Although the symptom may actually exist, there is no evidence that the serious illness does. Nevertheless, repeated assurances of this sort have little effect, and the person is likely to visit one doctor after another in search of a medical authority who will share his or her conviction.

Body dysmorphic disorder, or imagined ugliness, is a recently diagnosed and poorly understood type of somatoform disorder. Cases of body dysmorphic disorder can be very striking. One man, for example, felt that

Somatization disorder A somatoform disorder characterized by recurrent vague somatic complaints without a physical cause.

Conversion disorders Somatoform disorders in which a dramatic specific disability has no physical cause but instead seems related to psychological problems.

Hypochondriasis A somatoform disorder in which a person interprets insignificant symptoms as signs of serious illness in the absence of any organic evidence of such illness.

Body dysmorphic disorder A somatoform disorder in which a person becomes so preoccupied with his or her imagined ugliness that normal life is impossible.

Dissociative disorders Disorders in which some aspect of the personality seems separated from the rest.

Dissociative amnesia A dissociative disorder characterized by loss of memory for past events without organic cause.

people stared at his "pointed ears" and "large nostrils" so much that he eventually could not face going to work—so he quit his job. Clearly people who become that preoccupied with their appearance cannot lead a normal life. Ironically, most people who suffer body dysmorphic disorder are not ugly. They may be average looking or even attractive, but they are unable to evaluate their looks realistically. When they look in the mirror, all they seem to see is their "defect"—greatly magnified. Many people with the disorder seek physical treatment (such as plastic surgery) rather than psychotherapy. For this reason, it may be some time before we know how widespread the disorder is, why people develop it, and what can be done to treat it.

Somatoform disorders (especially conversion disorders) present a challenge for psychological theorists. They seem to involve some kind of unconscious processes. Freud concluded that the physical symptoms were often related to traumatic experiences buried in a patient's past: A woman who years earlier saw her mother physically abused by her father suddenly loses her sight; a man who was punished for masturbating later loses the use of his hand. By unconsciously developing a handicap, Freud theorized, people accomplish two things. First, they prevent themselves from acting out forbidden desires or repeating forbidden behavior; Freud called this the *primary gain* of the symptom. Second, the symptoms often allow the person to avoid an unpleasant activity, person, or situation; Freud called this *secondary gain*.

Cognitive behavioral theories of somatoform disorders focus on Freud's idea of secondary gain—that is, they look for ways in which the symptomatic behavior is being rewarded. For example, a person may have learned in the past that aches, pains, and so on can be used to avoid unpleasant situations. (Timely headaches and stomachaches have "solved" a lot of problems over the years.) Later in life, this person may use somatic symptoms to avoid facing unpleasant or stressful situations. Moreover, people who are ill often enjoy a good deal of attention, support, and care, which is indirectly rewarding.

Now we turn to the biological perspective. Research has shown that at least some diagnosed somatoform disorders actually were real physical illnesses that were overlooked or misdiagnosed. For example, one set of follow-up studies indicated that some cases of "conversion disorder" eventually proved to be undiagnosed neurological problems such as epilepsy or multiple sclerosis (Shalev & Munitz, 1986). Still, most cases of conversion disorder cannot be explained by current medical science. These cases pose as much of a theoretical challenge today as they did when conversion disorders captured Freud's attention over a century ago.

DISSOCIATIVE DISORDERS

Dissociative disorders are among the most puzzling forms of mental disorders, both to the observer and to the sufferer. *Dissociation* means that part of an individual's personality is separated or dissociated from the rest, and for some reason the person cannot reassemble the pieces. It usually involves memory loss and a complete—though generally temporary—change in identity. More rarely, several distinct personalities are present in one person.

Loss of memory without an organic cause may be a reaction to intolerable experiences. People often block out an event or a period of their lives that has been extremely stressful. During World War II, some hospitalized soldiers could not recall their names, where they lived, where they were born, or how they came to be in battle. But war and its horrors are not the only causes of **dissociative amnesia.** The man who betrays a friend to complete a business deal or the woman who has been raped may also forget—

selectively—what has happened. Sometimes an amnesia victim leaves home and assumes an entirely new identity, although this phenomenon, known as **dissociative fugue,** is highly unusual.

Total amnesia, in which people forget everything, is quite rare, despite its popularity in novels and films. In one unusual case of fugue, the police picked up a 42-year-old man after he became involved in a fight with a customer at the diner where he worked. The man reported that he had no memory of his life before drifting into that town a few weeks earlier. Eventually, the authorities discovered that he matched the description of a missing person who had wandered from his home 200 miles away. Just before he disappeared, he had been passed over for promotion at work and had had a violent argument with his teenage son (Spitzer et al., 1981).

Even more bizarre than amnesia is **dissociative identity disorder**—commonly known as *multiple personality*—in which a person has several distinct personalities that emerge at different times. This dramatic disorder, which has been the subject of popular fiction and films, is thought by most psychologists to be extremely rare. In the true multiple personality, the various personalities are distinct people, with their own names, identities, memories, mannerisms, speaking voices, and even IQs. Sometimes the personalities are so separate that they don't know they inhabit a body with other "people"; at other times, the personalities do know of the existence of other "people" and will even make disparaging remarks about them. Consider the case of Maud and Sara K., two personalities that coexisted in one woman:

> In general demeanor, Maud was quite different from Sara. She walked with a swinging, bouncing gait contrasted to Sara's sedate one. While Sara was depressed, Maud was ebullient and happy. . . . Insofar as she could Maud dressed differently from Sara. . . . Sara used no make-up. Maud used a lot of rouge and lipstick, [and] painted her fingernails and toenails deep red. . . . Sara was a mature, intelligent individual. Her mental age was 19.2 years, IQ, 128. A psychometric done on Maud showed a mental age of 6.6, IQ, 43. (Carson, Butcher, & Coleman, 1988, p. 206)

Actually, this case is typical in that the personalities contrasted sharply with each other. It is as if the two (and sometimes more) personalities represent different aspects of a single person—one the more socially acceptable, "nice" side of the person, the other the darker, more uninhibited or "evil" side.

The origins of dissociative identity disorder have long puzzled researchers and clinicians. One common suggestion is that it develops as a response to childhood abuse. The child learns to cope with abuse by a process of dissociation—by assigning the abuse, in effect, to "someone else," that is, to a personality who is not conscious most of the time (Putnam et al., 1986). The fact that one or more of the multiple personalities in almost every case is a child (even when the patient is an adult) seems to support this idea, and clinicians report a history of child abuse in over three-quarters of their cases of dissociative identity disorder (Ross, Norton, & Wozney, 1989).

Other clinicians suggest that dissociatve identity disorder is not a real disorder at all but an elaborate kind of role playing—feigned in the beginning, and then perhaps genuinely believed in by the patient (Mersky, 1992). However, some intriguing biological data show that in at least some patients with dissociative identity disorder, the various personalities have different blood pressure readings, different responses to medication, different allergies, different vision problems (necessitating several pairs of glasses, one for each personality), and different handedness—all of which would be difficult

Dissociative fugue A dissociative disorder that involves flight from home and the assumption of a new identity, with amnesia for past identity and events.

Dissociative identity disorder A dissociative disorder in which a person has several distinct personalities that emerge at different times.

When she was found by a Florida park ranger, Jane Doe was suffering from amnesia. She could not recall her name, her past, or how to read and write. She never regained her memory of the past.

Depersonalization disorder A dissociative disorder whose essential feature is that the person suddenly feels changed or different in a strange way.

Sexual dysfunction Loss or impairment of the ordinary physical responses of sexual function.

Erectile disorder The inability of a man to achieve or maintain an erection.

Female sexual arousal disorder The inability of a woman to become sexually aroused or to reach orgasm.

to feign. Each personality may also exhibit distinctly different patterns of brain waves (Putnam, 1984).

A far less dramatic (and much more common) dissociative disorder is **depersonalization disorder.** Its essential feature is that the person suddenly feels changed or different in a strange way. Some people feel they have left their bodies, others that their actions have suddenly become mechanical or dreamlike. A sense of losing control over one's own behavior is common, and it is not unusual to imagine changes in one's environment. This kind of feeling is especially common during adolescence and young adulthood, when our sense of ourselves and our interactions with others changes rapidly. Only when the sense of depersonalization becomes a long-term or chronic problem or when the alienation impairs normal social functioning can this be classified as a dissociative disorder (APA, 1994). For example, a 20-year-old college student sought professional help after experiencing episodes of feeling "outside" himself for 2 years. At these times, he felt groggy, dizzy, and preoccupied. Because he had experienced several episodes while driving, he had stopped driving alone. Although he was able to keep up with his studies, his friends began to notice that he seemed "spacey" and preoccupied (Spitzer et al., 1981).

Dissociative disorders, like conversion disorders, seem to involve some kind of unconscious processes. The loss of memory is real in amnesia, fugue, and in many cases of multiple personality disorder as well. The patient often lacks awareness of the memory loss, and memory impairments usually cannot be overcome despite the patient's desire and effort to do so. Biological factors may also play a role in some cases. We know that dissociation and amnesia result from some physical processes: Memory impairments are commonly associated with aging and disorders such as Alzheimer's disease, and dissociative experiences are a common consequence of the ingestion of some drugs such as LSD. Trauma is a psychological factor that is of obvious importance in the onset of amnesia and fugue; it also appears to play a role in the development of dissociative identity disorder (Oltmanns & Emery, 1998). Nonetheless, we must admit that all these observations are only early leads in the fascinating mystery of what causes dissociative disorders.

SEXUAL DISORDERS

Ideas about what is normal and abnormal in sex vary with the times—and the individual. Alfred Kinsey and his associates showed years ago (1948, 1953) that many Americans enjoy a variety of sexual activities, some of which are forbidden by law. As psychologists became more aware of the diversity of "normal" sexual behaviors, they increasingly narrowed their definition of abnormal sexual behavior. Today the DSM-IV recognizes only three main types of sexual disorders: sexual dysfunction, paraphilias, and gender-identity disorders. We will discuss each of these in turn.

Sexual Dysfunction

Sexual dysfunction is the loss or impairment of the ordinary physical responses of sexual function. In men, this usually takes the form of **erectile disorder,** the inability to achieve or keep an erection. In women, it often takes the form of **female sexual arousal disorder,** the inability to become sexually excited or to reach orgasm. (These conditions were once called "impotence" and "frigidity," respectively, but professionals in the field have rejected these terms as too negative and judgmental.) Occasional problems with achieving or maintaining an erection in men or with lubrication or reaching orgasm in women are common. Only when the problem is frequent or constant, and when enjoyment of sexual relationships becomes impaired, should it be considered serious. Most truly dysfunctional men and women, for example, cannot have satisfying sexual relations even after repeated attempts with a partner whom they desire.

Although sexual dysfunction may occur during any of a number of points in the sexual response cycle, some people find it difficult or impossible to experience any desire for sexual activity to begin with. **Sexual desire disorders** involve a lack of interest in sex or perhaps an active distaste for it. Low sexual desire is more common among women than among men and plays a role in perhaps 40 percent of all sexual dysfunctions (Southern & Gayle, 1982). The extent and causes of this disorder in men or women is difficult to analyze, because some people simply have a low motivation for sexual activity; scant interest in sex is normal for them and does not necessarily reflect any sexual disorder (Beck, 1995). Others report no anxiety about or aversion to sex but exhibit physiological indicators of inhibited desire (Wincze, Hoon, & Hoon, 1978). This fact has led some researchers to conclude that the disorder is sometimes caused by a physical abnormality. In those people who report feeling neutral about sex or having an aversion to it, investigators suggest that the problem may have originated in earlier traumatic experiences or unfulfilling relationships.

Other people are able to experience sexual desire but either cannot achieve physical arousal and its accompanying pleasure or cannot sustain arousal until the end of intercourse. This dysfunction is called **sexual arousal disorder.** The DSM-IV has no explicit guidelines as to how often this type of problem must occur to be considered a disorder. Rather, diagnosis is a clinical judgment based on the person's gender, age, and expressed desires. Masters and Johnson (1970) recommended that inhibited sexual excitement be diagnosed in a male only when he fails to attain erection and vaginal entry on 25 percent of his attempts. The causes of sexual arousal disorder include anxiety-provoking attitudes derived from parental or social teaching, fear of pregnancy or inadequate performance, and inexperience on the part of one or both partners. Ackerman and Carey (1995) contend that situational anxiety, including fear of ridicule, inadequate genital size, and (especially) performance failure, also play an important role in sexual arousal disorders. That many dysfunctional men report satisfactory arousal in response to such stimuli as sexually explicit films supports this conclusion.

Still other people are able to experience sexual desire and maintain arousal but are unable to reach **orgasm,** the peaking of sexual pleasure and the release of sexual tension. These people are said to experience **orgasmic disorders.** Male orgasmic disorder—the inability to ejaculate even when fully aroused—is rare but seems to be becoming increasingly common as more men find it desirable to practice the delay of orgasm (Rosen & Rosen, 1981). Masters and Johnson (1970) attribute male orgasmic disorder primarily to such psychological factors as traumatic experiences. The problem also seems to be a side effect of some medications, such as certain antidepressants.

Among the other problems that can occur during the sexual response cycle are **premature ejaculation,** which the DSM-IV defines as the male's inability to inhibit orgasm as long as desired, and **vaginismus,** involuntary muscle spasms in the outer part of a woman's vagina during sexual excitement that make intercourse impossible. Again, the occasional experience of such problems is common; the DSM-IV considers them dysfunctions only if they are "persistent and recurrent."

Paraphilias

A second group of sexual disorders, known as **paraphilias,** involves the use of unconventional sex objects or situations to obtain sexual arousal. Most people have unconventional sexual fantasies at some time, and this kind of

Sexual desire disorders Disorders in which the person lacks sexual interest or has an active distaste for sex.

Sexual arousal disorder Inability to achieve or sustain arousal until the end of intercourse in a person who is capable of experiencing sexual desire.

Orgasm Peaking of sexual pleasure and release of sexual tension.

Orgasmic disorders Inability to reach orgasm in a person able to experience sexual desire and maintain arousal.

Premature ejaculation Inability of man to inhibit orgasm as long as desired.

Vaginismus Involuntary muscle spasms in the outer part of the vagina that make intercourse impossible.

Paraphilias Sexual disorders in which unconventional objects or situations cause sexual arousal.

Fetishism A paraphilia in which a nonhuman object is the preferred or exclusive method of achieving sexual excitement.

Voyeurism Desire to watch others having sexual relations or to spy on nude people.

Exhibitionism Compulsion to expose one's genitals in public to achieve sexual arousal.

Frotteurism Compulsion to achieve sexual arousal by touching or rubbing against a nonconsenting person in public situations.

Transvestic fetishism Wearing the clothes of the opposite sex to achieve sexual gratification.

Sexual sadism Obtaining sexual gratification from humiliating or physically harming a sex partner.

Sexual masochism Inability to enjoy sex without accompanying emotional or physical pain.

Pedophilia Desire to have sexual relations with children as the preferred or exclusive method of achieving sexual excitement.

fantasizing can be a healthy stimulant of normal sexual enjoyment. However, the repeated use of a nonhuman object—a shoe, for instance, or underwear—as the preferred or exclusive method of achieving sexual excitement is considered a sexual disorder known as **fetishism.** Fetishes are typically articles of women's clothing, or items made out of rubber or leather (Junginger, 1997; Mason, 1997). People with fetishisms are almost always male, and the fetish frequently begins during adolescence. At least one theorist has suggested that fetishes derive from unusual learning experiences: As their sexual drive develops during adolescence, some boys learn to associate arousal with inanimate objects, perhaps as a result of early sexual exploration while masturbating or because of difficulties in social relationships (Wilson, 1987).

Other unconventional patterns of sexual behavior are **voyeurism,** watching other people have sex or spying on people who are nude; achieving arousal by **exhibitionism,** the exposure of one's genitals in inappropriate situations, such as to strangers; **frotteurism,** achieving sexual arousal by touching or rubbing against a nonconsenting person in situations like a crowded subway car; and **transvestic fetishism,** wearing clothes of the opposite sex for sexual excitement and gratification Transvestic fetishism seems to be an exclusively male behavior, and its causes are not well understood. There is no evidence of any hormonal or genetic abnormality (Buhrich et al., 1979). One explanation is that childhood experience with cross-dressing may have been associated with sexual play and arousal. Although some gay men dress in women's clothes for their entertainment, this behavior is *not* considered to be transvestic fetishism because their goal is not sexual arousal. In fact, most men with transvestic fetishism are heterosexual. One sample of men with transvestic fetishism found that 78 percent were either married or formerly married (Prince & Bentler, 1972); marital conflict over the disorder is one of the main reasons these men seek therapy.

Sexual sadism ties sexual pleasure to aggression. To attain sexual gratification, sadists humiliate or physically harm sex partners. **Sexual masochism** is the inability to enjoy sex without accompanying emotional or physical pain. Sexual sadists and masochists sometimes engage in mutually consenting sex, but at times sadistic acts are inflicted on unconsenting partners.

One of the most serious paraphilias is **pedophilia,** which is technically defined as "recurrent, intense sexually arousing fantasies, sexual urges, or behaviors involving sexual activity with a prepubescent child" (APA, 1994, p. 528). Child sexual abuse has been found to be shockingly common in the United States. Moreover, evidence indicates that in most cases the person who commits the abuse is someone close to the child, not a stranger. According to one survey, 5 percent of adult women living in the San Francisco area reported that they had been forced into oral, anal, or genital intercourse by their father, stepfather, or brother during their childhood years (Russell, 1986). Other studies suggest that the frequency of sexual abuse of both male and female children is much higher than this (Finkelhor et al., 1990).

Pedophiles are almost invariably men under the age of 40 (Barbaree & Seto, 1997). Although there is no single cause of pedophilia, some of the most common explanations are: Pedophiles cannot adjust to the sexual role of an adult male and have been interested exclusively in children as sex objects since adolescence; they turn to children as sexual objects in response to stress in adult relationships in which they feel inadequate; they have records of unstable social adjustment and generally commit sexual offenses against children in response to a temporary aggressive mood. Studies also indicate that the majority of pedophiles have histories of sexual frustration and failure, tend to perceive themselves as immature, and are rather dependent, unassertive, lonely, and insecure.

Gender-identity Disorders

Gender-identity disorders involve the desire to become—or the insistence that one really is—a member of the other biological sex. Some little boys, for example, want to be girls instead. They may reject boys' clothing, desire to wear their sisters' clothes, and play only with girls and with toys that are considered "girls' toys." In these cases, the diagnosis is **gender-identity disorder in children.** The same is true for girls who wear boys' clothing and play only with boys and "boys' toys." In all these cases, the children are uncomfortable with being a male or a female and are unwilling to accept themselves as such.

Most gender-identity disorders begin in childhood, and although many children with the disorder eventually develop normal gender identities, others carry the disorder into adult life. *Sexual reassignment surgery* (Hage, 1995) is one possible (and controversial) option for adults with gender-identity disorder: Surgical procedures, accompanied by hormonal treatments, are used to remove sex organs and create reasonable facsimiles of the organs of the opposite sex. Generally, people who have undergone sexual reassignment surgery are satisfied with the outcome. In addition, evidence from psychological tests indicate they experience reduced levels of anxiety and depression following the surgery (Bodlund & Kullgren, 1996). One individual who successfully underwent sexual reassignment surgery is the tennis star Renee Richards (formerly Richard Raskin).

The causes of gender-identity disorders are not known. Both animal research and the fact that these disorders are often apparent from early childhood suggest that biological factors, such as prenatal hormonal imbalances, are major contributors. However, family dynamics and learning experiences may also be contributing factors.

PERSONALITY DISORDERS

In Chapter 11, Personality, we saw that personality is the individual's unique and enduring pattern of thoughts, feelings, and behavior. We also saw that, despite having certain characteristic views of the world and ways of doing things, people normally show the ability to adjust their behavior to fit the needs of different situations. But some people, starting at some point early in life, develop inflexible and maladaptive ways of thinking and behaving that are so exaggerated and rigid that they cause serious distress to themselves or problems to others. People with such **personality disorders** range from harmless eccentrics to cold-blooded killers. A personality disorder may also coexist with one of the other problems already discussed in this chapter; that is, someone with a personality disorder may also become depressed, develop sexual problems, and so on.

One group of personality disorders is characterized by odd or eccentric behavior. For example, people who exhibit **schizoid personality disorder** lack the ability or desire to form social relationships and have no warm or tender feelings for others. Such loners cannot express their feelings and are perceived by others as cold, distant, and unfeeling. Moreover, they often appear vague, absentminded, indecisive, or "in a fog." Because their withdrawal is so complete, persons with schizoid personality disorder seldom marry and may have trouble holding jobs that require them to work with or relate to others (APA, 1994). For example:

> A 36-year-old electrical engineer was "dragged" to a marital therapist by his wife because of his unwillingness to join in family activities, failure to take an interest in his children, lack of affection, and disinterest in sex. . . . The patient's history revealed long-standing social indifference, with only an occasional and brief friendship here and there (Spitzer et al., 1981, p. 66)

Gender-identity disorders Disorders that involve the desire to become, or the insistence that one really is, a member of the other biological sex.

Gender-identity disorder in children Rejection of one's biological gender in childhood, along with the clothing and behavior society considers appropriate to that gender.

Personality disorders Disorders in which inflexible and maladaptive ways of thinking and behaving learned early in life cause distress to the person and/or conflicts with others.

Schizoid personality disorder Personality disorder in which a person is withdrawn and lacks feelings for others.

Paranoid personality disorder Personality disorder in which the person is inappropriately suspicious and mistrustful of others.

Dependent personality disorder Personality disorder in which the person is unable to make choices and decisions independently and cannot tolerate being alone.

Avoidant personality disorder Personality disorder in which the person's fears of rejection by others leads to social isolation.

Narcissistic personality disorder Personality disorder in which the person has an exaggerated sense of self-importance and needs constant admiration.

Borderline personality disorder Personality disorder characterized by marked instability in self-image, mood, and interpersonal relationships.

People with **paranoid personality disorder** also appear to be odd. They are suspicious and mistrustful even when there is no reason to be, and they are hypersensitive to any possible threat or trick. They refuse to accept blame or criticism even when it is deserved. They are guarded, secretive, devious, scheming, and argumentative, although they often see themselves as rational and objective. In one case, for example, a construction worker got into disputes with his coworkers because he was afraid they might deliberately let his scaffolding slip to kill or injure him. When he was examined by a psychologist, he thought that his examiner was "taking their side" against him (Spitzer et al., 1981, p. 37).

One cluster of personality disorders is characterized by anxious or fearful behavior. Among these are dependent personality disorder and avoidant personality disorder. People with **dependent personality disorder** are unable to make decisions on their own or to do things independently. They rely on parents, a spouse, friends, or others to make the major choices in their lives and usually are extremely unhappy being alone. Their underlying fear seems to be that they will be rejected or abandoned by important people in their lives. In **avoidant personality disorder,** the person is timid, anxious, and fearful of rejection. Not surprisingly, this social anxiety leads to isolation, but unlike the schizoid type, the person with avoidant personality disorder *wants* to have close relationships with other people.

Another cluster of personality disorders is characterized by dramatic, emotional, or erratic behavior. For example, people with **narcissistic personality disorder** display a grandiose sense of self-importance and a preoccupation with fantasies of unlimited success. (The word *narcissism* comes from a character in Greek mythology named Narcissus who fell in love with his own reflection in a pool and pined away because he could not reach the beautiful face he saw before him.) Such people believe they are extraordinary, need constant attention and admiration, display a sense of entitlement, and tend to exploit others. They are given to envy and arrogance and lack the ability to really care for anyone else (APA, 1994). For example, a male graduate student sought help because he was having difficulty completing his Ph.D. dissertation. He bragged that his dissertation would revolutionize his field and make him famous—but he had not been able to write much of it yet. He blamed his academic adviser for his lack of progress, called his fellow students "drones," and stated that everyone was jealous of his brilliance. He had frequent brief relationships with women but few lasting friendships (Spitzer et al., 1981).

Borderline personality disorder is characterized by marked instability—in self-image, mood, and interpersonal relationships. People with this personality disorder tend to act impulsively and often in self-destructive ways. They feel uncomfortable being alone, and they often manipulate self-destructive impulses in an effort to control or solidify their personal relationships. Such self-destructive behavior includes promiscuity, drug and alcohol abuse, and threats of suicide (Gunderson, 1984, 1994).

Borderline personality disorder is both common and serious. The available evidence indicates that although it runs in families, genetics do not seem to play an important role in its development (Oltmanns & Emery, 1998). Instead, studies of people with borderline personality disorder point to the influence of dysfunctional relationships with their parents, including a pervasive lack of supervision, the frequent exposure to domestic violence, and physical and sexual abuse (Guzder et al., 1996). Moreover, it is often accompanied by mild forms of brain dysfunction (such as attention deficit disorder), schizophrenic-like conditions, and mood disorders, which has led some psychologists to question whether borderline personality disorder should be considered a separate and distinguishable category of personality disorder (Akiskal, 1994; Tyrer, 1994). On the other hand, family studies show that relatives of people diagnosed as borderline individuals are much more likely to be treated for borderline disorder than for other types of personality disorders. This finding supports the position that borderline disorder is a legitimate category of personality disorder.

One of the most widely studied personality disorders is **antisocial personality disorder.** People who exhibit this disorder lie, steal, cheat, and show little or no sense of responsibility, although they often seem intelligent and charming on first acquaintance. The "con man" exemplifies many of the features of the antisocial personality, as does the person who compulsively cheats business partners because he or she knows their weak points. Antisocial personalities rarely show the slightest trace of anxiety or guilt about their behavior. Indeed, they are likely to blame society or their victims for the antisocial actions that they themselves commit. Antisocial personalities are responsible for a good deal of crime and violence, as seen in this case history of a person with antisocial personality disorder:

> Although intelligent, the subject was a poor student and was frequently accused of stealing from his schoolmates. At the age of 14, he stole a car, and at the age of 20, he was imprisoned for burglary. After he was released, he spent another two years in prison for drunk driving and then eleven years for a series of armed robberies. Released from prison yet one more time in 1976, he tried to hold down several jobs but succeeded at none of them. He moved in with a woman whom he had met one day earlier, but he drank heavily (a habit that he had picked up at age 10) and struck her children until she ordered him out of the house at gunpoint. On at least two occasions, he violated his parole but was not turned in by his parole officer. In July of 1976, he robbed a service station and shot the attendant twice in the head. He was apprehended in part because he accidentally shot himself during his escape. "It seems like things have always gone bad for me," he later said. "It seems like I've always done dumb things that just caused trouble for me." (Spitzer et al., 1983, p. 68)

Psychiatric evaluation showed this man to have a superior IQ of 129 and a remarkable store of general knowledge. He slept and ate well and exhibited no significant changes of mood. He admitted to having "made a mess of life" but added that "I never stew about the things I have done."

The subject was named Gary Gilmore, and on January 17, 1977, he became the first person to be executed in the United States in 11 years. While awaiting an execution that was postponed several times, he became the subject of numerous news stories detailing his fight for his announced "right to be executed." He twice attempted suicide.

Approximately 3 percent of American men and less than 1 percent of American women suffer from antisocial personality disorder. Not surprisingly, the prevalence of the disorder is high among prison inmates. One study categorized 50 percent of the populations of two prisons as having antisocial personalities (Hare, 1983). Not all people with antisocial personality disorder are convicted criminals, however. Many skillfully and successfully manipulate others for their own gain while steering clear of the criminal justice system.

Antisocial personality disorder seems to result from a combination of biological predisposition, adverse psychological experiences, and an unhealthy social environment (Moffitt, 1993). Some findings suggest that

People with anti-social personality disorder will lie, cheat, or kill without regret. Ted Bundy, shown here, was a serial killer who expressed no remorse for murdering as many as 50 women.

Schizophrenic disorders Severe disorders in which there are disturbances of thoughts, communications, and emotions, including delusions and hallucinations.

Insanity Legal term for mentally disturbed people who are not considered responsible for their criminal actions.

heredity is a risk factor for the later development of antisocial behavior (Lyons et al., 1995). Impulsive violence and aggression have also been linked with abnormal levels of certain neurotransmitters (Virkkunen, 1983). Although none of this research is definitive, the weight of evidence does suggest that in some people with antisocial personalities the autonomic nervous system is less responsive to stress (Patrick, 1994). Thus, they are more likely to engage in thrill-seeking behaviors, which can be harmful to themselves or others. In addition, because they respond less emotionally to stressful situations, punishment is less effective for them than for other people (Hare, 1993).

Some psychologists feel that emotional deprivation in early childhood predisposes people to antisocial personality disorder. The child for whom no one cares, say psychologists, cares for no one. The child whose problems no one identifies with can identify with no one else's problems. Respect for others is the basis of our social code, but if you cannot see things from the other person's perspective, rules about what you can and cannot do will seem nothing more than an assertion of adult power to be defied as soon as possible.

Family influences may also prevent the normal learning of rules of conduct in the preschool and school years. Theorists reason that a child who has been rejected by one or both parents is not likely to develop adequate social skills and appropriate social behavior. They also point out the high incidence of antisocial behavior in people with an antisocial parent and suggest that antisocial behavior may be partly learned and partly inherited from parents. Once serious misbehavior begins in childhood, there is an almost predictable progression: The child's conduct will result in rejection by peers and failure in school, followed by affiliation with other children who have behavior problems. By late childhood or adolescence, the deviant patterns that will later show up as a full-blown antisocial personality disorder are well established (Patterson, DeBaryshe, & Ramsey, 1989).

Cognitive theorists emphasize that in addition to the failure to learn rules and develop self-control, moral development may be arrested among children who are emotionally rejected and inadequately disciplined. For example, between the ages of about 7 and 11, all children are apt to respond to unjust treatment by behaving unjustly toward someone else who is vulnerable. At about age 13, when they are better able to reason in abstract terms, most children begin to think more in terms of fairness than vindictiveness. This seems to be especially true if new cognitive skills and moral concepts are reinforced by parents and peers (Berkowitz & Gibbs, 1983).

SCHIZOPHRENIC DISORDERS

It is a common misconception that schizophrenia means split personality. This is not the case at all. As we have already seen, split personality (or multiple personality) is actually a dissociative identity disorder. The misunderstanding comes from the fact that the root *schizo* comes from the Greek verb meaning "to split." But what is split in schizophrenia is not so much personality as the connections among thoughts.

Schizophrenic disorders are severe conditions marked by disordered thoughts and communications, inappropriate emotions, and bizarre behavior that lasts for months, even years. People with schizophrenia are out of touch with reality, which is to say they are psychotic. Psychosis is sometimes confused with *insanity*, but the terms are not synonymous. **Insanity** is the legal term for mentally disturbed people who are found not to be responsible for their criminal actions (see *Controversies*).

6

True or False: Schizophrenia refers to split personality.

CONTROVERSIES
THE INSANITY DEFENSE

Particularly horrifying crimes—assassinations of public figures, mass murders, and serial murders, for instance—have often been attributed to mental disturbance because it seems to many people that anyone who could commit such crimes must be crazy. But to the legal system, this presents a problem: If a person is truly "crazy," are we justified in holding him or her responsible for criminal acts? The legal answer to this question is a qualified *yes*. A mentally ill person *is* responsible for his or her crimes unless he or she is determined to be *insane*. What's the difference between being "mentally ill" and being "insane"? Insanity is a legal term, not a psychological one. It is typically applied to defendants who, when they committed the offense with which they are charged, were so mentally disturbed that they either could not distinguish right from wrong or could not control the act—it was an "irresistible impulse."

Actually, when a defendant is suspected of being mentally disturbed, another important question must be answered before that person is brought to trial: Is the person able to understand the charges against him or her and to participate in a defense in court? This issue is known as *competency to stand trial*. The person is examined by a court-appointed expert and, if found to be incompetent, is sent to a mental institution, often for an indefinite period. If judged to be competent, the person is required to stand trial. At this point the defendant may decide to plead not guilty by reason of insanity—which is an assertion that *at the time of the crime* the defendant

lacked substantial capacity to appreciate the criminality of his or her action (know right from wrong) or to conform to the requirements of the law (control his or her behavior).

Despite popular belief to the contrary, the insanity plea is rare, arising in less than 1 percent of serious criminal cases. But it became controversial when it was successfully used by John Hinckley, the man who attempted to assassinate President Ronald Reagan in 1981. Many people were very upset that Hinckley, whose action had been clearly captured on videotape, seemed to escape punishment for his crime by pleading insanity in a jurisdiction (Washington, D.C.) that required the prosecution to prove beyond a reasonable doubt that *he was sane*. (In contrast, most states, as well as the federal courts, place the burden on the defense to prove that the *defendant is insane*.) Since his trial, Hinckley has been confined in a mental hospital.

Is the person able to understand the charges against him or her and to participate in a defense in court?

When a defendant enters an insanity plea, the court system relies heavily on the testimony of forensic psychologists and psychiatrists to determine the mental state of the defendant at the time of the crime. Because most such trials feature well-credentialed experts testifying both for the defense and for the prosecution, the jury is often perplexed about which side to believe. Furthermore, there is much cynicism about "hired-gun" professionals who receive large fees to appear in court and argue that a defendant is or is

not sane. The public, skeptical about professional jargon, often feels that psychological testimony allows dangerous criminals to "get off." Actually, those who successfully plead insanity—like John Hinckley—often are confined longer in mental hospitals than they would have been in prison if convicted of their crimes. Therefore, the insanity plea is not an easy way out of responsibility for a crime.

Theodore J. Kaczynski, the serial terrorist, known as the Unabomber was sought by the FBI for 17 years. Kaczynski pleaded guilty to three killings to avoid a trial in which his lawyers had planned to argue that he was mentally ill.

Questions

1. What is your position on the question of whether insanity should ever be considered a legal defense for criminals?

2. In some states, a person can be found *both* guilty and mentally ill. Such people are sentenced to normal prison terms but must be provided with psychological or psychiatric treatment if they need it. Do you think this is a good alternative to the insanity plea? Why, or why not?

Hallucinations Sensory experiences in the absence of external stimulation.

Delusions False beliefs about reality that have no basis in fact.

Disorganized schizophrenia Schizophrenic disorder in which bizarre and childlike behaviors are common.

Catatonic schizophrenia Schizophrenic disorder in which disturbed motor behavior is prominent.

Paranoid schizophrenia Schizophrenic disorder marked by extreme suspiciousness and complex, bizarre delusions.

People with schizophrenia often suffer from **hallucinations,** false sensory perceptions that usually take the form of hearing voices that are not really there.* They also frequently have **delusions**—false beliefs about reality with no factual basis—that distort their relationships with their surroundings and with other people. Typically, these delusions are *paranoid:* People with schizophrenia believe that someone is out to harm them. They may think that a doctor wishes to kill them or that they are receiving radio messages from aliens invading from outer space. They often regard their own bodies—as well as the outside world—as hostile and alien.

Because their world is utterly different from the one most people live in, people with schizophrenia usually cannot live anything like a normal life unless they are successfully treated with medication (see Chapter 14). Often they are unable to communicate with others, for when they speak, their words are incoherent. The following case illustrates some of the characteristic features of schizophrenia:

> [The patient is a 35-year-old widow.] For many years she has heard voices, which insult her and cast suspicion on her chastity. . . . The voices are very distinct, and in her opinion, they must be carried by a telescope or a machine from her home. Her thoughts are dictated to her; she is obliged to think them, and hears them repeated after her. She . . . has all kinds of uncomfortable sensations in her body, to which something is "done." In particular, her "mother parts" are turned inside out, and people send a pain through her back, lay ice-water on her heart, squeeze her neck, injure her spine, and violate her. There are also hallucinations of sight—black figures and the altered appearance of people—but these are far less frequent. . . . (Spitzer et al., 1981, pp. 308–309)

There are actually several kinds of schizophrenic disorders, which have different characteristic symptoms.

Disorganized schizophrenia includes some of the more bizarre symptoms of schizophrenia, such as giggling, grimacing, and frantic gesturing. People suffering from disorganized schizophrenia show a childish disregard for social conventions and may urinate or defecate at inappropriate times. They are active but aimless, and they are often given to incoherent conversations.

The primary feature of **catatonic schizophrenia** is a severe disturbance of motor activity. People in this state may remain immobile, mute, and impassive. At the opposite extreme, they become excessively excited, talking and shouting continuously. They may behave in a robotlike fashion when ordered to move, and some have even let doctors mold their arms and legs into strange and uncomfortable positions that they then manage to maintain for hours.

Paranoid schizophrenia is marked by extreme suspiciousness and complex delusions. People with paranoid schizophrenia may believe themselves to be Napoleon or the Virgin Mary,

A young schizophrenic patient painted this picture of the monsters he claimed to see in his room.

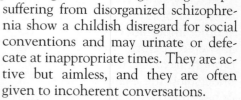

---

*Visual, tactile, or olfactory hallucinations are more likely to indicate substance abuse or organic brain damage than schizophrenia.

or they may insist that Russian spies with laser guns are constantly on their trail because they have learned some great secret. Because they are less likely to be incoherent or to look or act "crazy," these people can appear more "normal" than people with other schizophrenic disorders if their delusions are compatible with everyday life. However, they may become hostile or aggressive toward anyone who questions their thinking or tries to contradict their delusions. Note that this disorder is far more severe than paranoid personality disorder, which does not involve bizarre delusions or loss of touch with reality.

Finally, **undifferentiated schizophrenia** is the classification developed for people who have several of the characteristic symptoms of schizophrenia, such as delusions, hallucinations, or incoherence, yet do not show the typical symptoms of any other subtype of the disorder.

Schizophrenia is a very serious disorder, and considerable research has been directed at trying to discover its causes. As we saw in Chapter 2, The Biological Basis of Behavior, a wide range of studies clearly show that schizophrenia has a genetic component (Gottesman, 1991). People with schizophrenia are more likely than other people to have children with schizophrenia, even when those children have lived with adoptive parents since early in life. And if one identical twin suffers from schizophrenia, the chances are about 50 percent that the other twin will also develop schizophrenia; but if a fraternal twin has schizophrenia, the chances are only about 15 percent that the other twin will also develop schizophrenia (see Figure 2–17).

These studies indicate that a biological predisposition to schizophrenia may be inherited. Recent research suggests that part of the problem may lie in excessive amounts of the neurotransmitter *dopamine* in the central nervous system. Drugs that alleviate schizophrenic symptoms also decrease the amount of dopamine in the brain and block dopamine receptors. On the other hand, amphetamines raise the amount of dopamine in the brain, aggravate schizophrenic symptoms, and, if taken in excess, lead to what is called *amphetamine-psychosis*, which is very similar to schizophrenia.

Some research suggests that pathology in various structures of the brain plays a role in the onset of schizophrenia (Weinberger, 1997). For example, patients with schizophrenia have been shown to have enlarged *ventricles*, which are chambers in the brain that are filled with cerebrospinal fluid (Torrey et al., 1994). Other studies have focused on what appear to be an abnormal pattern of connections between cortical cells in patients with schizophrenia. Because these cortical connections are largely established during the prenatal period, this finding suggests the onset of schizophrenia, which generally takes place in adulthood, may be traceable to some form of early prenatal disturbance (Wolf & Weinberger, 1996). Still, scientists have found only *average* differences in brain structure and chemistry between schizophrenic and healthy people (Noga et al., 1996). As yet, there are no laboratory tests that can be used to diagnose schizophrenia based on brain abnormalities. In fact, studies of identical twins in which only one twin suffers from schizophrenia have sometimes found more evidence of brain abnormalities in the *well* twin than in the sick twin.

This finding brings us back to the research on genetics and schizophrenia. Although this point is often overlooked, studies of identical twins can also be used to identify the importance of *environment* in causing schizophrenia. How? Remember, half of the identical twins of people with schizophrenia do *not* develop schizophrenia themselves. Because identical twins are genetically identical, this means that this severe and puzzling disorder *cannot* be caused by genetic factors alone. Environmental factors—ranging from disturbed family relations to taking drugs to biological damage that may occur at any age, even before birth—must also figure in determining

Undifferentiated schizophrenia Schizophrenic disorder in which there are clear schizophrenic symptoms that don't meet the criteria for another subtype of the disorder.

whether a person will develop schizophrenia. McGuffin, Reveley and Holland (1982) reported on a set of identical triplets, all of whom suffered from chronic psychotic disorders. But while two of the brothers had severe schizophrenic symptoms and were unable to function even between psychotic periods, the third brother was able to function at a higher level and hold down a job between psychotic periods. His IQ was higher than his two brothers, and his relationship with his family was less troubled. As the systems model indicates, environment and experience can increase or decrease the effects of any inherited tendency, with the result that there is often a significant difference between identical twins (or triplets) afflicted with psychological disorders in levels of functioning.

Some psychologists regard family relationships as an important factor in the development of schizophrenia. The evidence regarding this position is mixed. One study found that communication problems between parents was an effective predictor of the development of schizophrenia in their children (Goldstein & Rodnick, 1975). More recent research has discovered that schizophrenic patients whose families display high levels of negative *expressed emotion* are rehospitalized at twice the average rate for people with this disorder (Kavanagh, 1992). Moreover, treatments designed to reduce negative expressed emotion in the families of schizophrenic patients have reduced the rates of rehospitalization. Though it is still not clear how—or if—family variables such as expressed emotion combine with biological predispositions to cause some people to develop schizophrenia, the early research in this area looks promising.

A number of studies have demonstrated a relationship between social class and schizophrenia (Neale & Oltmanns, 1980). The prevalence of schizophrenia is decidedly higher in the lower social classes. One theory holds that lower-class socioeconomic environments—which offer little education, opportunity, or reward and put considerable stress on individuals—are a cause of schizophrenia. Another theory speculates that the symptoms of schizophrenia cause people to drift downward into the lower socioeconomic classes. There appears to be some truth to both theories.

Although obviously quite different in emphasis, the various explanations for schizophrenic disorders are not mutually exclusive. Although genetic factors are universally acknowledged, many theorists believe that it takes a combination of biological, psychological, and social factors to produce schizophrenia (Gottesman, 1991). According to the systems model, genetic factors predispose some people to schizophrenia, and family interaction and life stress activate the predisposition.

CHILDHOOD DISORDERS

Children can suffer from the conditions we have been discussing—depression and anxiety disorders, for example, but other disorders are either characteristic of children or are first evident in childhood. The DSM-IV contains a long list of "disorders usually first diagnosed in infancy, childhood, or adolescence." Two of these disorders are attention-deficit/hyperactivity disorder and autistic disorder.

Attention-deficit/Hyperactivity Disorder (ADHD)

This disorder was once known simply as *hyperactivity*. The new name reflects the fact that children with the disorder typically lack the ability to focus their attention in the sustained way that other children do. Instead, they are easily distracted, often fidgety and impulsive, and almost constantly in motion. Many theorists believe that this disorder—which affects nearly 5 percent of all school-aged children and is much more common in boys than girls—is present at birth but becomes a serious problem only after the child starts school. The class setting demands that children sit quietly, pay attention as instructed, follow directions, and inhibit urges to yell and run around; the child with **ADHD** simply cannot conform to these demands.

The causes of ADHD are not known, but most theorists assume that biological factors such as heredity are very important in its development. Family interaction and other social experiences may be more important in preventing the disorder than in causing it. That is, some exceptionally competent parents and patient, tolerant teachers may be successful in teaching "difficult" children to conform their behavior to the rather stringent demands of schooling. Some psychologists train the parents of ADHD children in these management skills, but the most frequent treatment for these children is a type of drug known as a **psychostimulant.** Psychostimulants do not work by "slowing down" hyperactive children; rather, they appear to increase the children's ability to focus their attention. This enables them to attend to the task at hand, which decreases their hyperactivity (Barkley, 1990). Unfortunately, psychostimulants often produce only short-term benefits.

Autistic Disorder

A very different, and profoundly serious, disorder that is first evident in childhood is **autistic disorder.** Autistic children are usually identified as such in the first few years of life. They fail to form normal attachments to parents, remaining distant and seemingly withdrawn into their own separate worlds. As infants, they may even show distress at being picked up or held. As they grow older, they often do not develop speech, or they develop a peculiar speech pattern called *echolalia,* in which they repeat the words said to them. Autistic children typically show strange motor behavior, such as repeating body movements endlessly or walking constantly on tiptoe. Their play is not like that of normal children. They are not at all social and may use toys in odd ways, such as constantly spinning the wheels on a toy truck or tearing paper into strips. Autistic children are often retarded, but it is hard to test their mental ability because they are frequently nonverbal. This disorder lasts into adulthood in the great majority of cases.

The precise cause of autism is unknown, although most theorists believe that it results almost entirely from biological conditions. Some causes of mental retardation such as fragile X syndrome (see Chapter 8) also seem to increase the risk of autistic disorder. Recent evidence suggests that genetics also plays a strong role in causing the disorder (Bailey et al., 1995).

GENDER DIFFERENCES IN PSYCHOLOGICAL DISORDERS

For the most part, men and women are similar with respect to mental disorders, but differences do exist. Many studies have concluded that women have a higher rate of psychological disorders than men do, but this is an oversimplification. Prevalence rates of mental disorders vary by age, race, ethnicity, marital status, income, and type of disorder (see *Highlights*). Furthermore, how do we determine "rate of psychological disorders"? Do we count only people admitted to mental hospitals? Those who receive a formal diagnosis in an outpatient treatment setting? Or all those persons in the general population who are judged to suffer from mental disorders even if they have not sought treatment and received a formal diagnosis? These

Attention-deficit/hyperactivity disorder (ADHD) A childhood disorder characterized by inattention, impulsiveness, and hyperactivity.

Psychostimulants Drugs that increase ability to focus attention in children with ADHD.

Autistic disorder A childhood disorder characterized by lack of social instincts and strange motor behavior.

HIGHLIGHTS
THE PREVALENCE OF PSYCHOLOGICAL DISORDERS

How common are psychological disorders in the United States? Are they increasing or decreasing over time? Are some population groups more prone to these disorders than other groups? These questions are of interest to psychologists and public-health experts who are concerned with both the prevalence and the incidence of mental-health problems. *Prevalence* refers to the frequency with which a given disorder occurs at a given time. If there were 100 cases of depression in a population of 1,000, the prevalence of depression would be 10 percent. The *incidence* of a disorder refers to the number of new cases of the disorder that arise in a given period. In a population of 1,000, if there were 10 new cases of depression in a year, the incidence rate would be 1 percent per year.

One very large study conducted in the United States has suggested that mental disorders affect a far larger proportion of the population than was once thought. Starting in 1980, the National Institute of Mental Health did an ambitious and wide-ranging study of the prevalence of psychological disorders, which involved interviewing nearly 20,000 people around the country. The results were surprising: Overall, 32 percent of Americans suffer from one or more serious mental disorders during their lifetime, and at any given time, more than 15 percent of the population is experiencing a mental disorder (Robins & Regier, 1991). The most common problem is drug abuse, with abuse of alcohol being more prevalent than abuse of all other drugs combined. More than 13 percent of adults over 18 experience alcoholism at some point in their lives. Anxiety disorders are the next most common psychological disorder. Mood disorders, principally depression, are a problem for almost 8 percent of the population at some point in their lives. In contrast, schizophrenia afflicts only 1.5 percent of the population (but note that this represents more than 3 million people).

Overall, 32 percent of Americans suffer from one or more serious mental disorders during their lifetime, and at any given time, more than 15 percent of the population is experiencing a mental disorder.

Every culture acknowledges some types of mental disorders, although the labels and symptoms may differ. Schizophrenia and depression, for example, are recognized in most cultures, even in those that do not practice psychology as a scientific discipline. A pattern of behavior involving bizarre physical activity, distorted communications, hallucinations, and delusions is understood as "crazy" in cultures as diverse as the Yoruba of West Africa and the Baffin Island Eskimos (Murphy, 1976). Perhaps in future years *epidemiologists*—scientists who study the distribution of health problems—will determine whether our 15 percent prevalence figure for mental disorders is typical of the rest of the world.

---

questions illustrate how hard it is to make a firm generalization about differences between the sexes.

We do know that more women than men are *treated* for mental disorders. Indeed, as one expert observed, "Women have always been the main consumers of psychotherapy from Freud's era onward" (Williams, 1987, p. 465). But this cannot be taken to mean that more women than men have mental disorders, for in our society, it is much more acceptable for women to discuss their emotional difficulties and to seek professional help openly. It may be that mental disorders are equally common among men—or even more common—but that men do not so readily show up in therapists' offices and therefore are not counted in the studies.

All the disorders listed in the DSM-IV (with the exception of a few sexual disorders) affect both men and women. Indeed, those mental disorders for which there seems to be a strong biological component, such as bipolar disorder and schizophrenia, are distributed fairly equally between the sexes. Differences tend to be found for those disorders *without* a strong biological component—that is, disorders in which learning and experience play a more important role. For example, men are more likely than women to suffer from substance abuse and antisocial personality disorder. Women, on the other hand, are more likely to suffer from depression, agoraphobia, simple phobia, obsessive-compulsive disorder, and somatization disorder (Basow, 1986; Douglas et al., 1995; Russo, 1990). These tendencies suggest that socialization plays a part in developing a disorder: When men display abnormal behavior, it is more likely to take the forms of drinking too much and acting aggressively; when women display abnormal behavior, they are more likely to become fearful, passive, hopeless, and "sick" (Basow, 1986).

One commonly reported difference between the sexes concerns marital status. Men who are separated or divorced or who have never married have a higher incidence of mental disorders than do either women of the same marital status or married men. But married women have higher rates than married men. What accounts for the apparent fact that marriage is psychologically less beneficial for women than for men?

Here, too, socialization appears to play a role. For women, marriage, family relationships, and child rearing are likely to be more stressful than they are for men (Basow, 1986). For men, marriage and family provide a haven; for women, they are a demanding job. In addition, women are more likely than men to be the victims of incest, rape, and marital battering. As one researcher has commented, "for women, the U.S. family is a violent institution" (Koss, 1990). For some married women, employment outside the home seems to provide the kind of psychological benefits that marriage apparently provides for many men. Work can supply "stimulation, self-esteem, adult contacts, escape from the repetitive routines of housework and child care, and a buffer against stress from family roles" (Hoffman, 1989, p. 284). However, these benefits are likely to be realized only if the woman freely chooses to work, has a satisfying job, receives support from family and friends, and is able to set up stable child-care arrangements (Basow, 1986; Hoffman, 1989). For women who enter the workforce because they have to rather than because they want to, whose work is routine or demeaning, or who are responsible for all domestic duties as well as their outside jobs, economic pressures and the stress of performing two demanding roles can be additional risk factors for psychological disorder.

We saw in the previous chapter that the effects of stress are greater to the extent that a person feels alienated, powerless, and helpless. Alienation, powerlessness, and helplessness are more prevalent in women that in men. They are especially common factors among minority women, so it is not surprising that the prevalence of psychological disorders is greater among these women than among other women (Russo & Sobel, 1981). And alienation, powerlessness, and helplessness play an especially important role in anxiety disorders and depression—precisely those disorders experienced most often by women (Kessler et al., 1994). A 1990 report by a task force of the American Psychological Association noted that the rate of depression among women is twice that of men and ascribed that difference to the more negative and stressful aspects of women's lives, including lower incomes and the experiences of bias and physical and sexual abuse (APA, 1990).

Once past puberty, therefore, women do seem to have higher rates of anxiety disorders and depression than men do, and they are more likely than men to seek professional help for their problems. However, greater stress, due in part to socialization and lower status rather than psychological weakness, apparently accounts for this statistic. Marriage and family life, associated with lower rates of mental disorders among men, introduce additional stress into the lives of women, particularly young women (25 to 45), and in some instances this added stress translates into a psychological disorder.

SUMMARY

This chapter briefly describes the history of psychological disorders and presents an overview of the major categories of disorders.

PERSPECTIVES ON PSYCHOLOGICAL DISORDERS

Whether an individual suffers from an emotional disorder is, at least in part, a subjective judgment. Mental-health professionals define abnormal behavior as either maladaptive life functioning or serious personal discomfort or both.

HISTORICAL VIEWS OF PSYCHOLOGICAL DISORDERS

In early societies mysterious actions were often attributed to supernatural powers. The roots of a more naturalistic view of psychological disorders can be traced to Hippocrates, who maintained that madness was like any other sickness—a natural event arising from natural causes. This approach to mental illness fell into disfavor in the Middle Ages, and it was not until the nineteenth century that it again received systematic scientific attention.

CONFLICTING THEORIES OF THE NATURE, CAUSES, AND TREATMENT OF PSYCHOLOGICAL DISORDERS

Three influential, conflicting models of psychological disorders emerged during the late 1800s and early 1900s: the biological, psychoanalytic, and cognitive-behavioral models. Each approach has influenced the study and treatment of psychological disorders but none can claim to be the decisively correct theory of abnormal psychology.

The Biological Model

The **biological model of psychological disorders** states that abnormal behavior has a biochemical or physiological basis. Although there is sound evidence that genetic/biochemical factors are involved in mental disorders as diverse as schizophrenia, depression, and anxiety, biology alone cannot account for most mental illnesses.

The Psychoanalytic Model

The **psychoanalytic model of psychological disorders,** proposed by Freud, states that abnormal behavior is a symbolic expression of unconscious mental conflicts that generally can be traced to early childhood or infancy. For all its richly appealing ideas, this approach has produced little scientific evidence to support its theorizing about the causes and effective treatment of mental disorders.

The Cognitive-behavioral Model

The **cognitive-behavioral model of psychological disorders** states that mental disorders are the result of learning maladaptive ways of behaving and proposes that what has been learned can be unlearned. Cognitive-behavioral therapists therefore strive to modify both dysfunctional behavior and inaccurate cognitive processes in their patients. The model has been criticized for its extreme emphasis on environmental causes and treatments.

The Diathesis-stress Model and Systems Theory

The most promising recent development in abnormal psychology is the integration of the major approaches. The **diathesis-stress model of psychological disorders,** for example, states that mental disorders develop when a **diathesis** (biological predisposition to the disorder) is set off by a stressful circumstance. The **systems approach to psychological disorders** states that biological, psychological, and social risk factors combine to produce mental disorders. According to this model, emotional problems are "lifestyle diseases" that are caused by a combination of biological risks, psychological stresses, and societal pressures and expectations.

CLASSIFYING PSYCHOLOGICAL DISORDERS

For nearly 40 years, the American Psychiatric Association has published an official manual describing and classifying the various kinds of psychological disorders. This publication, the *Diagnostic and Statistical Manual of Mental Disorders (DSM)*, has gone through four editions. The current version, known as the DSM-IV, provides careful descriptions of symptoms of different disorders, but includes little on causes and treatments.

MOOD DISORDERS

Mood disorders are characterized by disturbances in mood or prolonged emotional state. The most common mood disorder is **depression,** a state in which a person feels overwhelmed with sadness, loses interest in activities, and displays other symptoms such as excessive guilt or feelings of worthlessness. The DSM-IV distinguishes between two forms of depression. *Major depressive disorder* is an episode of intense sadness that may last for several months; in contrast, *dysthymia* involves less intense sadness but persists with little relief for a period of 2 years or more. Some depressions become so intense that people become **psychotic**—that is, lose contact with reality.

Another, less common mood disorder is **mania.** People suffering from mania become euphoric ("high"), extremely active, excessively talkative, and easily distractible. Manic episodes rarely appear by themselves;

rather, they usually alternate with depression. Such a mood disorder, in which both mania and depression are alternately present, sometimes interrupted by periods of normal mood, is known as **bipolar disorder.**

Causes of Mood Disorders

Most psychologists believe that mood disorders result from a combination of biological, psychological, and social factors. *Biological factors*—including genetics and chemical imbalances within the brain—seem to play an important role in the development of depression and, especially, bipolar disorder. But just as biology affects psychological experience, so does psychological experience alter biological functioning. **Cognitive distortions,** illogical and maladaptive responses to early negative life events, can lead to feelings of incompetence that are reactivated whenever a new situation arises that resembles the original events. This *psychological factor* has been found to operate in many depressed people, though it is uncertain whether the cognitive distortions cause the depression or are caused by it. Finally, *social factors* such as troubled relationships have been linked with mood disorders.

ANXIETY DISORDERS

In **anxiety disorders,** a person's anxiety is inappropriate to the circumstances. Anxiety disorders have been subdivided into many specific diagnostic categories. One familiar subtype is **specific phobia,** an intense, paralyzing fear of something that it is unreasonable to fear so excessively. Another subtype is **social phobia**—excessive, inappropriate fears connected with social situations or performances in front of other people. **Agoraphobia** is a less common and much more debilitating type of anxiety disorder that involves multiple, intense fears such as the fear of being alone or of being in public places or other situations that require separation from a source of security. **Panic disorder** is characterized by recurrent panic attacks, which are sudden, unpredictable, and overwhelming experiences of intense fear or terror without any reasonable cause. **Generalized anxiety disorder** is defined by prolonged vague but intense fears that are not attached to any particular object or circumstance. **Obsessive-compulsive disorder** involves either involuntary thoughts that keep recurring despite the person's attempt to stop them or compulsive rituals that a person feels compelled to perform. Two other types of anxiety disorder are caused by highly stressful events. If the anxious reaction occurs soon after the event, the diagnosis is *acute stress disorder;* if it occurs long after the event is over, the diagnosis is *post-traumatic stress disorder.*

Causes of Anxiety Disorders

Psychologists with an evolutionary perspective believe that we are predisposed by evolution to associate certain stimuli with intense fears and that this is the origin of phobias. Psychologists with a biological perspective propose that a predisposition to anxiety disorders may be inherited because these types of disorders tend to run in families. Cognitive psychologists have suggested that people who believe they have no control over stressful events in their lives are more likely to suffer from anxiety, whereas psychoanalytic theorists have focused on internal psychological conflicts as the source of anxiety disorders.

PSYCHOSOMATIC DISORDERS

Psychosomatic disorders are illnesses that have a valid physical basis but are largely caused by psychological factors such as stress and anxiety. In fact, many physicians now recognize that nearly every physical disease can be linked to psychological stress in the sense that such stress can negatively affect body chemistry, organ functioning, and the immune system.

SOMATOFORM DISORDERS

Somatoform disorders are characterized by physical symptoms without any identifiable physical cause. **Somatization disorder** is defined by vague, recurring, physical symptoms (such as back pains, dizziness, and abdominal pains) for which medical attention has been sought repeatedly but no organic cause found. Sufferers from **conversion disorders** have a dramatic specific disability for which there is no physical cause. In **hypochondriasis,** the person interprets some small symptom as a sign of a serious disease. **Body dysmorphic disorder,** or imagined ugliness, is a type of somatoform disorder characterized by extreme dissatisfaction with some part of one's appearance.

DISSOCIATIVE DISORDERS

In **dissociative disorders,** some part of an individual's personality or memory is separated from the rest. **Dissociative amnesia** involves the loss of at least some significant aspects of memory. When an amnesia victim leaves home and assumes an entirely new identity, the disorder is known as **dissociative fugue.** In **dissociative identity disorder**—commonly known as *multiple personality*—a person has several distinct personalities that emerge at different times. In **depersonalization disorder,** the person suddenly feels changed or different in a strange way.

SEXUAL DISORDERS

The DSM-IV recognizes three main types of sexual disorders: sexual dysfunction, paraphilias, and gender-identity disorders.

Sexual Dysfunction

Sexual dysfunction is the loss or impairment of the ability to function effectively during sex. In men, this may take the form of **erectile disorder,** the inability to achieve or keep an erection; in women, it often takes the form of **female sexual arousal disorder,** the inability to become sexually excited or to reach orgasm. **Sexual desire disorders** are those in which the person either lacks sexual interest or has an active aversion to sex. People with **sexual arousal disorder** experience sexual desire but cannot achieve or maintain physical arousal, whereas those with **orgasmic disorders** experience both desire and arousal but are unable to reach **orgasm.** Other problems that can occur include **premature ejaculation**—the male's inability to inhibit orgasm as long as desired—and **vaginismus**—involuntary muscle spasms in the outer part of a woman's vagina during sexual excitement that make intercourse impossible.

Paraphilias

Paraphilias involve the use of unconventional sex objects or situations. These disorders include **fetishism, voyeurism, exhibitionism, frotteurism, transvestic fetishism, sexual sadism,** and **sexual masochism.** One of the most serious paraphilias is **pedophilia,** the desire to have sexual relations with children.

Gender-identity Disorders

Gender-identity disorders involve the desire to become, or the insistence that one really is, a member of the other sex. **Gender-identity disorder in children** is characterized by rejection of one's biological gender as well as the clothing and behavior society considers appropriate to that gender.

PERSONALITY DISORDERS

Personality disorders are enduring, inflexible, and maladaptive ways of thinking and behaving that are so exaggerated and rigid that they cause serious inner distress and/or conflicts with others. One group of personality disorders is characterized by odd or eccentric behavior. For example, people who exhibit **schizoid personality disorder** lack the ability or desire to form social relationships and have no warm feelings for other people; those with **paranoid personality disorder** are inappropriately suspicious of others. Another cluster of personality disorders is characterized by anxious or fearful behavior. Examples are **dependent personality disorder** (inability to make decisions or do things independently) and **avoidant personality disorder** (social anxiety leading to isolation). A third cluster of personality disorders is characterized by dramatic, emotional, or erratic behavior. For example, people with **narcissistic personality disorder** display a grandiose sense of self-importance. **Borderline personal-**ity disorder is characterized by a marked instability in self-image, mood, and interpersonal relationships. Finally, people with **antisocial personality disorder** lie, steal, cheat, and show little or no sense of responsibility.

SCHIZOPHRENIC DISORDERS

Schizophrenic disorders are severe conditions marked by disordered thoughts and communications, inappropriate emotions, and bizarre behavior that lasts for years. These disorders should not be confused with **insanity,** which is the legal term for mentally disturbed people who are found not to be responsible for their criminal actions. People with schizophrenia are out of touch with reality and usually cannot live anything like a normal life unless they are successfully treated with medication. They often suffer from **hallucinations** (false sensory perceptions) and **delusions** (false beliefs about reality). There are several kinds of schizophrenic disorders, including **disorganized schizophrenia, catatonic schizophrenia, paranoid schizophrenia,** and **undifferentiated schizophrenia.**

CHILDHOOD DISORDERS

The DSM-IV contains a long list of disorders usually first diagnosed in infancy, childhood, or adolescence.

Attention-deficit/Hyperactivity Disorder

One childhood disorder discussed in this chapter is **attention-deficit/hyperactivity disorder (ADHD).** Children with ADHD are highly distractible, often fidgety and impulsive, and almost constantly in motion. The most frequent treatment for children with ADHD are **psychostimulants,** drugs which increase the children's ability to focus their attention.

Autistic Disorder

Autistic disorder, a profound problem identified in the first few years of life, is characterized by a failure to form normal attachments to parents, lack of social instincts, and strange motor behavior.

GENDER DIFFERENCES IN PSYCHOLOGICAL DISORDERS

Studies have concluded that women have a higher rate of psychological disorders than men do, especially for the mood and anxiety disorders. There is controversy about what accounts for these differences, but it seems both socialization and biology play important roles.

REVIEW QUESTIONS

MULTIPLE CHOICE AND SHORT ANSWER

1. Psychologists can readily distinguish abnormal from normal behavior. T/F

2. Match the model of psychological disorders with the appropriate explanation or approach:

_____ biological model	a. Behavior disorders are symbolic expressions of unconscious internal conflicts.
_____ psychoanalytic model	b. Psychological disorders are a product of biological, psychological, and social risk factors.
_____ cognitive-behavioral model	c. Psychological disorders are the result of learning and can be unlearned.
_____ systems approach	d. Psychological disorders are caused by heredity, damage to the nervous system, and/or endocrine dysfunction.

3. The DSM-IV is a classification system for mental disorders that was developed by the
   a. American Psychiatric Association.
   b. American Psychological Association.
   c. National Institutes for Mental Health.

4. Which of the following is *not* an anxiety disorder?
   a. specific phobia
   b. dissociative fugue
   c. obsessive-compulsive disorder
   d. post-traumatic stress disorder

5. Mood disorders include the extremes of
   a. anger and sadness.
   b. mania and depression.
   c. psychosis and neurosis.

6. Psychosomatic disorders involve real physical illness caused by psychological factors. T/F

7. _____ is a form of mood disorder that involves less intense sadness than _____, but the sadness is prolonged for a period of 2 years.

8. Schizophrenic disorders are characterized by _____ symptoms or loss of contact with reality.

9. Lifelong patterns of relatively "normal" but rigid and maladaptive behavior are called
   a. schizophrenic disorders.
   b. personality disorders.
   c. autistic disorders.

10. A paraphilia is
    a. a form of sexual dysfunction.
    b. a sexual attraction to unconventional objects.
    c. a type of sex reassignment surgery.

11. Although the DSM-IV is a system of classification, many theorists believe that differences between normal and abnormal behavior are, in fact, _____.

CRITICAL THINKING AND APPLICATIONS

1. A client comes to you with what he considers to be a weird and inexplicable complaint. One day, while discussing his marriage plans with his parents and siblings, he began to feel as if someone else, not he, were speaking. He could hear himself, at a distance, acquiescing to demands his mother was making and responding to his father's criticisms of his fiancée. However, he felt as if he were hovering above his own body, observing the goings on rather than participating in them. He is afraid that he is losing his mind and wants to know your diagnosis. What name would you give to his experience, and at this point, would you consider it a serious disorder?

2. The mood disorders are among the most common psychological problems, and the symptoms of these problems are at least somewhat familiar to all of us. Use the critical thinking problem above to consider whether abnormal and normal behavior should be viewed in terms of dimensions or categories.

ENDURING ISSUES

Heredity–Environment
To what extent do you think psychological disorders are the result of heredity and to what extent do they stem from experience?

Stability–Change
If someone is prone to anxiety disorders or depression early in life, do you think they will be prone to anxiety or depression throughout their life or can they change significantly?

Diversity
Are there significant sex, race, or cultural differences in people's susceptibility to various behavior disorders?

(Answers to the Review Questions appear in the back of the book.)

14 Therapies

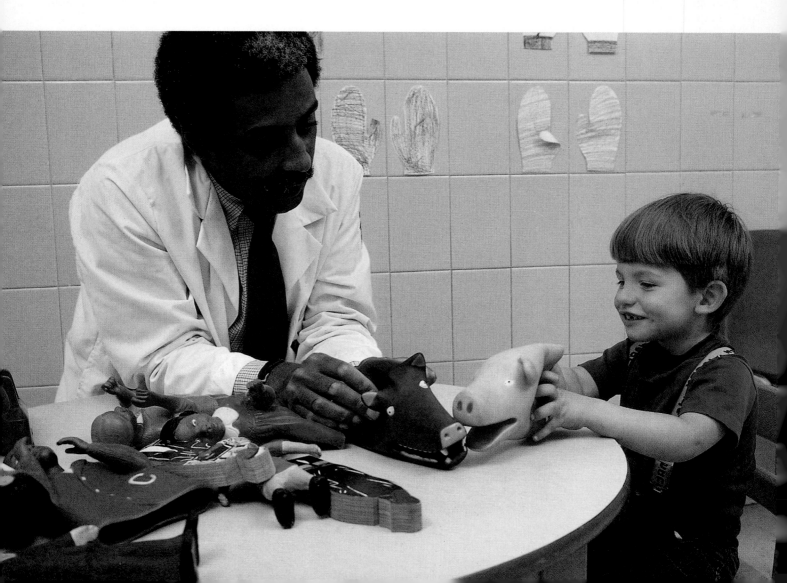

In Chapter 1, we introduced the concept of **psychotherapy,** the use of psychological techniques to treat personality and behavior disorders. To many people, psychotherapy still evokes an image of an analyst sitting silently in a chair while a client, reclining on a nearby couch, recounts traumatic events in his or her life. As the anxious client reveals dreams, fantasies, fears, and obsessions, the therapist nods, scribbles in a notebook, and perhaps asks a question or two. The therapist rarely offers the client advice and never reveals details of his or her own personal life.

This cliché has some truth to it; scenes like this do occur. But

Think About It!

1. How does Freudian psychoanalysis work? How prevalent is this therapy today?

2. How has behaviorism contributed to the development of therapies?

3. Are people who undergo treatment more likely to improve than people who receive no treatment at all?

4. When are drugs used to treat mental illness? Which drugs are effective for which disorders?

5. Is electroconvulsive therapy (ECT) still used to treat patients with mental illness?

6. Why did the movement toward deinstitutionalization emerge? What have been the consequences for mental patients and for society at large?

psychotherapy takes many forms—literally hundreds of variations practiced by several different types of mental-health professionals. In contrast to the image of the clinical, detached analyst, most psychotherapists are warm, understanding, and willing to offer at least some direct information and advice. In some forms of psychotherapy, therapists are very directive, even confrontational, in exploring their clients'

Psychotherapy The use of psychological techniques to treat personality and behavior disorders.

Insight therapies A variety of individual psychotherapies designed to give people a better awareness and understanding of their feelings, motivations, and actions in the hope that this will help them adjust.

Free association A psychoanalytic technique that encourages the patient to talk without inhibition about whatever thoughts or fantasies come to mind.

thoughts and feelings. Some types of psychotherapy occur outside the therapist's office, as clients confront their fears in real life. Other psychotherapies treat couples or entire families, and still others treat groups of people with similar problems or goals. Later in this chapter we will take a close look at the major types of therapy.

Many people tend to be confused about the effectiveness of psychotherapy. Some people who have gone through therapy claim that it changed their lives; others complain that it made little difference. The public's perception of the effectiveness of psychotherapy is particularly important now that health-care costs have escalated and treatments of psychological disorders are being monitored more closely in terms of their costs and outcomes.

The future of psychotherapy rests in demonstrating the effectiveness of different treatments for different problems. In this chapter, we survey the major types of therapies used to treat psychological disorders. Included among these treatments are individual psychotherapies employed by clinical psychologists and psychiatrists in private practice and in institutions, as well as group therapies. We also examine research comparing the effectiveness of different forms of psychotherapies and consider the role of medication and other biological therapies. Finally, we discuss the important issues of institutionalization, deinstitutionalization, and prevention.

Our review of individual psychotherapies follows the sequence of their historical development. Insight therapies were developed early in the twentieth century, followed by behavior therapies in the 1960s and 1970s, and more recently by cognitive therapies.

INSIGHT THERAPIES

Several of the individual psychotherapies used in both private practice and institutions fall under the heading of **insight therapies.** While differing in their details, the common goal of various insight therapies is to give people a better awareness and understanding of their feelings, motivations, and actions, in the hope that this will lead to better adjustment. In this section, we consider three major insight therapies as well as some recent developments in the area.

Psychoanalysis

1

How does Freudian psychoanalysis work? How prevalent is this therapy today?

Psychoanalysis, developed by Sigmund Freud, is based on the belief that anxiety and other problems are symptoms of inner conflicts dating back to childhood. Usually, these problems concern aggressive or sexual drives whose expression was dangerous or forbidden to the child. According to Freud, the impulses repressed by the child lurk in the adult's unconscious mind, where they can give rise to various psychological disorders. Psychoanalysis is designed to bring these hidden feelings to conscious awareness so the person can deal with them more effectively.

In Freudian psychoanalysis, the patient is instructed to talk about whatever comes to mind, with as little editing as possible and without inhibiting or controlling thoughts and fantasies. This process is called **free association.** Freud believed that the resulting "stream of consciousness" would provide insight into the patient's unconscious mind. During the early stages of psychoanalysis, the analyst remains impassive, mostly silent, and out of the patient's sight. In classical psychoanalysis, the patient lies on a couch, while the neutral analyst sits behind him or her. The analyst's silence is a kind of "blank screen" onto which the patient eventually projects unconscious thoughts and feelings.

The interview that follows is characteristic of the early stages of psychoanalysis and demonstrates free association. The analyst remains fairly quiet while the patient, a 32-year-old male teacher with recurring headaches, talks about whatever occurs to him:

Patient: This is like my last resort. I've been to so many doctors for this headache. But I tell you . . . I don't want . . . I know that there's something wrong with me though. I've known it since I was a kid. Like I

started to tell you, when I was 17, I knew there was something wrong with me, that . . . and I told my father that I needed to see a doctor, and he laughed at me and said it was just foolishness, but he agreed to take me to his doctor, Dr. ———— on 125th Street, and I never went in; I chickened out.

Therapist: You chickened out, then. How'd you feel about that chickening out?

Patient: I don't know. I don't feel *proud* that I wasn't able to talk over these . . . this feeling I had. . . . I wouldn't have wanted my father to know about my . . . some of my problems. 'Cause my father, he just . . . you know, I told him, my father, that there was something wrong, that I needed help, and he'd laugh at me and, you know, just to pacify me, you know, he took me to Dr. ————, but I didn't know Dr. ————. He was a friend of my father's, yeah, I don't know if. . . . I don't remember thinking about it, but if I had talked to Dr. ———— about my problems like the problems I talk about in here, and my father found out, he might get pretty mad. Yeah.

Therapist: Well, this would be insulting to him? He'd feel it would be a bad reflection on his upbringing of you, if you went to a doctor like this? Would this humiliate him?

Patient: Yeah. I've got. . . . My father and I didn't get along too well, and to tell the truth, I was ashamed of my father. He was born in Poland, and he was a self-made man. He went to the University of Warsaw and then Fordham. He was a pharmacist, but he was . . . he didn't care how he dressed. He was all sloppy and dirty, and he was short. He's about five foot one and stoop-shouldered. . . . We used to go to restaurants, my mother and him and me, and he would never leave a tip, never leave a tip, never leave a tip. I used to sneak back and I'd throw a few cents that I might have on the table, but he was so stingy, so tight. When we went on a train, when we went somewhere, I would try to pretend I wasn't with them. I'd want. . . . I'd go in another. . . . I

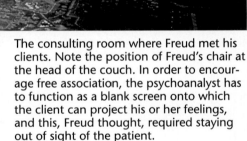

The consulting room where Freud met his clients. Note the position of Freud's chair at the head of the couch. In order to encourage free association, the psychoanalyst has to function as a blank screen onto which the client can project his or her feelings, and this, Freud thought, required staying out of sight of the patient.

Transference The patient's carrying over to the analyst feelings held toward childhood authority figures.

Insight Awareness of previously unconscious feelings and memories and how they influence present feelings and behavior.

do need some help, and I know I've got to do the talking. That's the hardest part for me, that you won't give me any guidelines, that I have to do everything myself, and you'll analyze me. . . . I didn't ever think I'd. . . . I didn't want to think I was gonna end up here. I hate to think that this is the problem, but. . . . (Hersher, 1970, pp. 135–139)

Analysis typically proceeds very slowly. After the initial awkwardness wears off, many people enjoy having the chance to talk without interruption and appreciate having someone interested in their problems. Eventually, they may test their analyst by talking about desires and fantasies they have never revealed to anyone else. But the analyst maintains neutrality throughout the process, showing little of his or her own feelings and personality. When patients discover that their analyst is not shocked or disgusted by their revelations, they are reassured and project on their analyst feelings they have toward authority figures from their childhood—a process known as **transference.** When the patient feels good about the analyst, the process is called *positive transference*.

As patients continue to expose their innermost feelings, they begin to feel increasingly vulnerable. They want reassurance and affection, but their analyst remains silent. Their anxiety builds. Threatened by their analyst's silence and by their own thoughts, patients may feel cheated and perhaps accuse their analyst of being a money-grabber. Or they may suspect that their analyst is really disgusted by their disclosures or is laughing about them behind their backs. This *negative transference* is thought to be a crucial step in psychoanalysis, for it presumably reveals patients' negative feelings toward authority figures and their resistance to uncovering their repressed emotions.

As therapy progresses, the analyst takes a more active role and begins to *interpret* or suggest alternative meanings for patients' feelings, memories, and actions. The goal of interpretation is to help patients gain **insight**—to become aware of what was formerly outside of their awareness. As what was unconscious becomes conscious, patients may come to see how their childhood experiences have determined how they feel and act now. Analysts encourage patients to confront childhood events and recall them fully. As patients relive their childhood traumas, they become able to resolve conflicts they could not resolve in the past. *Working through* old conflicts is thought to provide people with the chance to review and revise the feelings and beliefs that underlie their problems.

The somewhat more active role of the analyst in the later stages of therapy is demonstrated in the following excerpt (from a session with a different patient):

> *Therapist: (summarizing and restating)* It sounds as if you would like to let loose with me, but you are afraid of what my response would be.
>
> *Patient:* I get so excited by what is happening here. I feel I'm being held back by needing to be nice. I'd like to blast loose sometimes, but I don't dare.
>
> *Therapist:* Because you fear my reaction?
>
> *Patient:* The worst thing would be that you wouldn't like me. You wouldn't speak to me friendly; you wouldn't smile; you'd feel you can't treat me and discharge me from treatment. But I know this isn't so; I know it.
>
> *Therapist:* Where do you think these attitudes come from?

Patient: When I was 9 years old, I read a lot about great men in history. I'd quote them and be dramatic, I'd want a sword at my side; I'd dress like an Indian. Mother would scold me: Don't frown; don't talk so much. Sit on your hands, over and over again. I did all kinds of things. I was a naughty child. She told me I'd be hurt. Then, at 14, I fell off a horse and broke my back. I had to be in bed. Mother then told me on the day I went riding not to, I'd get hurt because the ground was frozen. I was a stubborn, self-willed child. Then I went against her will and suffered an accident that changed my life, a fractured back. Her attitude was, "I told you so." I was put in a cast and kept in bed for months.

Therapist: You were punished, so to speak, by this accident.

Patient: But I gained attention and love from Mother for the first time. I felt so good. I'm ashamed to tell you this: Before I healed, I opened the cast and tried to walk, to make myself sick again so I could stay in bed longer.

Therapist: How does that connect up with your impulse to be sick now and stay in bed so much? (*The patient has these tendencies, of which she is ashamed.*)

Patient: Oh. . . . (*pause*)

Therapist: What do you think?

Patient: Oh, my God, how infantile, how ungrownup (*pause*). It must be so. I want people to love me and be sorry for me. Oh, my God. How completely childish. It is, *is* that. My mother must have ignored me when I was little, and I wanted so to be loved.

Therapist: So that it may have been threatening to go back to being self-willed and unloved after you got out of the cast (*interpretation*).

Patient: It did. My life changed. I became meek and controlled. I couldn't get angry or stubborn afterward.

Therapist: Perhaps if you go back to being stubborn with me, you would be returning to how you were before, that is, active, stubborn, but unloved.

Patient: (*excitedly*) And, therefore, losing your love. I need you, but after all, you aren't going to reject me. But the pattern is so established now that the threat of the loss of love is too overwhelming with everybody, and I've got to keep myself from acting selfish or angry. (Wolberg, 1977, pp. 560–561)

Our description up to this point applies to traditional, or orthodox, psychoanalysis. But only a handful of people who seek therapy go into traditional analysis. As Freud himself recognized, analysis requires great motivation to change and an ability to deal rationally with whatever the analysis uncovers. Moreover, orthodox analysis may take 5 years or longer, and most traditional analysts feel that at least three, and sometimes five, sessions a week are essential. Few people can afford this lengthy treatment. Another disadvantage of this therapy is that it does not give immediate help for immediate problems. Finally, psychoanalysis is not effective with severely disturbed patients.

Client-centered Therapy

Carl Rogers, the founder of **client-centered** (or **person-centered**) **therapy,** took bits and pieces of the neo-Freudians' views and revised and rearranged

Client-centered (or **person-centered**) **therapy** Nondirectional form of therapy developed by Carl Rogers that calls for unconditional positive regard of the client by the therapist with the goal of helping the client become fully functioning.

Carl Rogers, far right, leading a group therapy session. Rogers was the founder of client-centered therapy.

them into a radically different approach to therapy. According to Rogers, the goal of therapy is to help people become fully functioning, to open them up to all of their experiences and to all of themselves. Such inner awareness is a form of insight, but for Rogers, it was more important to gain insight into current feelings than into unconscious wishes with roots in the distant past. Rogers called his approach to therapy *client-centered* because he placed the responsibility for change on the person with the problem. The image of a patient seeking advice from an expert, the doctor, contradicted Rogers's view of therapeutic change. He intentionally used the term *client* rather than *patient* to highlight the more active and equal role he assigned to the person who sought therapy.

Rogers's ideas about therapy are quite specific. As we saw in Chapter 11, Personality, Rogers believed that people's defensiveness, rigidity, anxiety, and other signs of discomfort stem from their experiences of *conditional positive regard*. They have learned that love and acceptance are contingent on conforming to what other people want them to be. Therefore, the cardinal rule in person-centered therapy is for the therapist to express *unconditional positive regard*—that is, to show true acceptance of clients no matter what they may say or do. Rogers felt that this was a crucial first step toward getting clients to accept themselves.

Rather than taking an objective approach, Rogerian therapists try to understand things from the clients' point of view. They are also emphatically *nondirective*. They do not suggest reasons why clients feel as they do or how they might better handle a difficult situation. Instead, they try to reflect clients' statements, sometimes asking questions and sometimes hinting at feelings that clients have not put into words. Rogers felt that when therapists provide an atmosphere of openness and genuine respect, clients can find themselves.

The following excerpt conveys the nondirective approach of client-centered therapy. The therapist is far more active and understanding than the traditional analyst, but always follows the client's lead in therapy.

> *Client:* I guess I do have problems at school. . . . You see, I'm chairman of the Science Department, so you can imagine what kind of a department it is.
>
> *Therapist:* You sort of feel that if you're in something that it can't be too good. Is that. . . .
>
> *Client:* Well, it's not that I. . . . It's just that I'm. . . . I don't think that I could run it.
>
> *Therapist:* You don't have any confidence in yourself?
>
> *Client:* No confidence, no confidence in myself. I never had any confidence in myself. I–like I told you–like when even when I was a kid I

didn't feel I was capable and I always wanted to get back with the intellectual group.

Therapist: This has been a long-term thing, then, it's gone on a long time.

Client: Yeah, the *feeling* is—even though I know it isn't, it's the feeling that I have that—that I haven't got it, that—that—that——people will find out that I'm dumb or—or. . . .

Therapist: Masquerade. . . .

Client: Superficial, I'm just superficial. There's nothing below the surface. Just superficial generalities, that. . . .

Therapist: There's nothing really deep and meaningful to you.

Client: No—they don't know it, and. . . .

Therapist: And you're terrified they're going to find out.

Client: My wife has a friend, and—and she and the friend got together so we could go out together with her and my wife and her husband. . . . And the guy, he's an engineer and he's you know–he's got it, you know; and I don't want to go, I don't want to go because—because if—if we get together he's liable to start to—to talk about something I don't know, and I'll—I won't know about that.

Therapist: You'll show up very poorly in this kind of situation.

Client: That I—I'll show up poorly, that I'll—that I'll just clam up, that I'll . . .

Therapist: You're terribly frightened in this sort of thing.

Client: I—I'm afraid to be around people who—who I feel are my peers. Even in pool—now I—I play pool very well and—if I'm playing with some guy that I—I know I can beat, *psychologically*, I can run 50, but—but if I start playing with somebody that's my level, I'm done. I'm done. I—I—I'll miss a ball every time.

Therapist: So the . . . the fear of what's going on just immobilizes you, keeps you from doing a good job. (Hersher, 1970, pp. 29–32)

Rogers was not interested in comparing his therapy to others, nor was he concerned simply with statistics on outcomes (such as the percent of clients who recovered). Rather, he wanted to discover what processes or events in client-centered therapy were associated with positive outcomes. Rogers's interest in the *process* of therapy resulted in important and lasting contributions to the field. For example, it has been found that a therapist's warmth and understanding increase success, no matter what therapeutic approach is used (Frank & Frank, 1991).

Gestalt Therapy

Gestalt therapy is largely an outgrowth of the work of Frederick (Fritz) Perls at the Esalen Institute in California. Perls began his career as a psychoanalyst but later turned vehemently against Freud and psychoanalytic techniques. He felt that "Freud invented the couch because he could not look people in the eye" (Perls, 1969, p. 118). Gestalt therapy emphasizes the here-and-now and encourages face-to-face confrontations.

Gestalt therapy An insight therapy that emphasizes the wholeness of the personality and attempts to reawaken people to their emotions and sensations in the here-and-now.

Gestalt therapy is designed to help people become more genuine or "real" in their day-to-day interactions. It may be conducted with individuals or with groups ("encounter groups"). The therapist is active and directive, and the emphasis in Gestalt therapy is on the *whole* person, the Gestalt (see Chapter 3, Sensation and Perception). The therapist's role, as Perls describes it, is to "fill in the holes in the personality to make the person whole and complete again" (Perls, 1969, p. 2).

Gestalt therapists try to make people aware of their feelings and to awaken them to sensory information they have been ignoring. They use many techniques to accomplish this. For example, people may be told to "own their feelings" by talking in an active rather than a passive way ("I feel angry when he's around" instead of "He makes me feel angry when he's around"). In this way, Gestalt therapists remind clients that they alone are responsible for their feelings and, ultimately, for their lives. Another method commonly used in Gestalt therapy is the *empty chair technique*. Clients are asked to speak to a part of themselves they imagine to be sitting next to them in an empty chair. The objective is to get clients to become more aware of their conflicting inner feelings and, with this insight, to become more genuine. The empty chair technique and other Gestalt methods are illustrated in the following excerpt.

> *Therapist:* Try to describe just what you are aware of at each moment as fully as possible. For instance, what are you aware of now?
>
> *Client:* I'm aware of wanting to tell you about my problem, and also a sense of shame—yes, I feel very ashamed right now.
>
> *Therapist:* Okay. I would like you to develop a dialogue with your feeling of shame. Put your shame in the empty chair over here (*indicates chair*), and talk to it.
>
> *Client:* Are you serious? I haven't even told you about my problem yet.
>
> *Therapist:* That can wait—I'm perfectly serious, and I want to know what you have to say to your shame.
>
> *Client:* (*awkward and hesitant at first, but then becoming looser and more involved*) Shame, I hate you. I wish you would leave me—you drive me crazy, always reminding me that I have a problem, that I'm perverse, different, shameful—even ugly. Why don't you leave me alone?
>
> *Therapist:* Okay, now go to the empty chair, take the role of shame, and answer yourself back.
>
> *Client:* (*moves to the empty chair*) I am your constant companion—and I don't *want* to leave you. I would feel lonely without you, and I don't hate you. I pity you, and I pity your attempts to shake me loose, because you are doomed to failure.
>
> *Therapist:* Okay, now go back to your original chair and answer back.
>
> *Client:* (*once again as himself*) How do you know I'm doomed to failure? (*Spontaneously shifts chairs now, no longer needing direction from the therapist; answers himself back, once again in the role of shame.*) I know that you're doomed to failure because *I* want you to fail and because I control your life. You can't make a single move without me. For all you know, you were *born* with me. You can hardly remember a single moment when you were without me, totally unafraid that I would spring up and suddenly remind you of your loathsomeness.
>
> *Client:* You're right; so far you *have* controlled my life—I feel constantly embarrassed and awkward. (*His voice grows stronger.*) But that doesn't mean that you'll continue to control my life. That's why I've

come here—to find some way of destroying you. *(Shifts to the "shame" chair.)* Do you think *he* can help you? *(As shame, points to the therapist.)* What can he do? He hardly knows you as I know you. Besides, he's only going to see you once or twice each week. I am with you every single moment of every day!

Therapist: Bill, look how one hand keeps rubbing the other when you speak for shame. Could you exaggerate that motion? Who does that remind you of?

Client: (rubbing his hands together harder and harder) My mother would do this—yes, whenever she was nervous she would rub her hands harder and harder.

Therapist: Okay, now speak for your mother. (Shaffer, 1978, pp. 92–93)

Recent Developments

Although Freud, Rogers, and Perls originated the three major forms of insight therapy, other therapists have developed hundreds of variations on those themes. As we noted earlier in this chapter, even among mainstream psychoanalysts, there has been considerable divergence from the traditional form of "couch" psychotherapy. Most present-day insight-oriented therapists are far more active and emotionally engaged with their clients than traditional orthodox psychoanalysts thought fit.

Another general trend in recent years is toward shorter-term "dynamic therapy" for most people—usually occurring once a week for a fixed period of time. In fact, **short-term psychodynamic psychotherapy** is increasingly popular among both patients and mental-health professionals. Insight remains the goal, but the treatment is usually time-limited—for example, to 25 sessions. Regardless of the form of therapy, improvement seems to occur fairly quickly in most people. A review of more than 30 years of research on various kinds of therapy with more than 2,400 patients (Howard et al., 1986) found that about half the patients showed improvement after only 8 sessions and that about three-quarters improved within 26 sessions. However, as we will see later in this chapter, recent evidence (Seligman, 1995) suggests that patients who undergo a longer term of treatment often report more satisfaction and improvement as a result of therapy.

With the trend to a time-limited framework, insight therapies have become more problem- or symptom-oriented. Instead of slowly and patiently trying to construct a "narrative of the psyche"—the aim of traditional Freudian analysis—most contemporary therapists try to help their clients correct the immediate problems in their lives. They see the individual as less at the mercy of early childhood events than the Freudians did. Although they do not discount the impact of early childhood experiences, the focus is on the client's current life situation and relationships. In addition, most contemporary therapists give clients more direct guidance and feedback, commenting on what they are told rather than just listening to their clients in a neutral manner.

Even more notable than the trend toward shorter-term therapy has been the proliferation of behavior therapies in the past few decades. In the next section of the chapter, we examine several types of behavior therapy.

BEHAVIOR THERAPIES

Behavior therapies sharply contrast with insight-oriented approaches: (1) Behavior therapists are more active than psychodynamic therapists; (2) they

Short-term psychodynamic psychotherapy Insight therapy that is time-limited and focused on trying to help clients correct the immediate problems in their lives.

Behavior therapies Therapeutic approaches that are based on the belief that all behavior, normal and abnormal, is learned, and that the objective of therapy is to teach people new, more satisfying ways of behaving.

2

How has behaviorism contributed to the development of therapies?

Systematic desensitization A behavioral technique for reducing a person's fear and anxiety by gradually associating a new response (relaxation) with stimuli that have been causing the fear and anxiety.

concentrate on changing people's *behavior* rather than on increasing their insight into their thoughts and feelings; and (3) they operate within a briefer framework (O'Leary & Wilson, 1987).

As we have noted repeatedly throughout this book, behaviorists believe psychology should focus on observable, measurable behavior rather than on thoughts, feelings, and unconscious processes. Insight-oriented therapists regard personality disorders as the symptoms of unconscious forces or the products of insufficient awareness or insight, but behavior therapists argue that the disorder *is* the problem. They believe that if they can teach people to behave in more appropriate ways, they have cured the problem.

Behavior therapies, then, are based on the belief that all behavior, both normal and abnormal, is learned. Hypochondriacs *learn* that they get attention when they are sick; paranoid personalities *learn* to be suspicious of others. The therapist does not need to know exactly how or why people learned to behave abnormally in the first place. The job of the therapist is simply to teach people new, more satisfying ways of behaving.

Behavior therapies also differ from insight therapies in that they attempt to apply basic findings from psychological science, particularly research on learning processes (see Chapter 5, Learning), to the treatment of clinical problems. Thus, many behavior therapy techniques are simply applications of behavioral concepts discussed in earlier chapters of this text.

Classical Conditioning

As we saw in the chapter on learning, *classical conditioning* involves the pairing of a conditioned stimulus repeatedly with an unconditioned stimulus. If the conditions are right, the conditioned stimulus will eventually produce a conditioned response on its own. Several variations on the classical conditioning approach have been used to treat psychological problems.

DESENSITIZATION, EXTINCTION, AND FLOODING   Systematic desensitization, a method for gradually reducing fear and anxiety, is one of the oldest behavior therapy techniques (Wolpe, 1990). The method works by gradu-

The clients in these photographs are overcoming a simple phobia: fear of snakes. After practicing a technique of deep relaxation, clients in desensitization therapy work from the bottom of their hierarchy of fears up to the situation that provokes the greatest fear or anxiety. Here, clients progress from handling rubber snakes (top left) to viewing live snakes through a window (top center) and finally to handling live snakes. This procedure can also be conducted vicariously in the therapist's office, where clients combine relaxation techniques with imagining anxiety-provoking scenes.

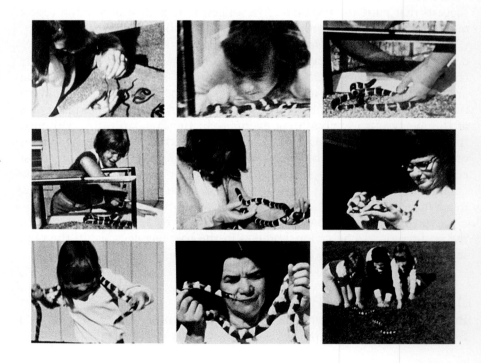

ally associating a new response (relaxation) with stimuli that have been causing anxiety. For example, an aspiring politician might seek therapy because he is very anxious about speaking to crowds. The therapist looks for more details, asking whether the man feels more threatened by an audience of 500 than by an audience of 50, more tense when addressing men than when speaking to both men and women, more anxious when talking to friends or to strangers, and so on. Through such explorations, the therapist develops a *hierarchy of fears* for this individual—a list of situations from the least to the most anxiety-provoking.

After establishing a client's hierarchy of fears, the therapist teaches the client how to relax: to clear his or her mind, to release tense muscles, and to be able to produce this relaxation response readily. In some cases, drugs or mild hypnosis aids relaxation. Once a client has mastered the technique of deep relaxation, he or she begins work at the bottom of the hierarchy of fears. The client is told to imagine the least threatening situation on the list and to signal when feeling the least bit tense. At the signal, the therapist tells the client to forget the scene and to concentrate on relaxing. After a short time, the therapist instructs the client to imagine the scene again. This process is repeated until the client feels completely relaxed when imagining that scene. Then the therapist moves on to the next situation in the client's hierarchy of fears and trains the client to be completely relaxed when imagining that situation as well. Therapist and client advance up the hierarchy this way until finally the client can imagine the most fearful situation at the top of the hierarchy without experiencing any anxiety whatsoever.

Numerous studies indicate that systematic desensitization helps many people overcome their fears and phobias (Wolpe, 1990). Research suggests, however, that the key to desensitization's success may not be the learning of a new conditioned relaxation response but rather the *extinction* of the old fear response through mere exposure. Recall from Chapter 5 that in classical conditioning extinction occurs when the learned, conditioned stimulus is repeatedly presented without the unconditioned stimulus being present. Thus, if a person repeatedly imagines a frightening situation without actually encountering danger, the fear or anxiety associated with that situation should gradually decline.

For some problems, extinction works best if exposure occurs soon, at full intensity, and for a prolonged period of time (O'Leary & Wilson, 1987; Wolpe, 1990). This is the technique of *flooding*, a less familiar, and more frightening, method of desensitization through exposure. Someone with an obsessive-compulsive disorder may be repeatedly forced to encounter and deal directly with the source of his or her irrational fear. Someone with a powerful fear of snakes might be forced immediately to handle dozens of snakes; or someone with an overwhelming fear of spiders might be forced to stroke a tarantula and allow it to crawl up his or her arm. If you think that flooding is an unnecessarily harsh method, it is worth recalling the severity and life impairment that can be caused by untreated anxiety disorders.

AVERSIVE CONDITIONING Another classical conditioning technique aimed at eliminating undesirable behavior patterns is **aversive conditioning,** in which therapists teach clients to associate pain and discomfort with the behavior that they want to unlearn. This form of therapy has been used with limited success to treat alcoholism, obesity, and smoking.

At times the therapist uses real physical pain. Some clinics, for example, treat alcoholism by pairing the taste and smell of alcohol with drug-induced nausea and vomiting. Before long, patients feel sick just seeing a bottle of liquor. A follow-up study of nearly 800 patients who completed

Aversive conditioning Behavioral therapy techniques aimed at eliminating undesirable behavior patterns by teaching the person to associate them with pain and discomfort.

Ads such as this use classical conditioning to link unpleasant stimuli with undesirable behavior. Such ads can help make people aware of positive associations they may have for behavior that is fundamentally undesirable.

Behavior contracting Form of operant conditioning therapy in which the client and therapist set behavioral goals and agree on reinforcements the client will receive upon reaching those goals.

Token economy An operant conditioning therapy in which patients earn tokens (reinforcers) for desired behaviors and exchange them for desired items or privileges.

Modeling A behavior therapy in which the person learns desired behaviors by watching others perform those behaviors.

alcohol-aversion treatment at one clinic in 1978 and 1979 found that 63 percent had maintained continuous abstinence for at least 12 months after treatment (Wiens & Menustik, 1983). Still, the use of aversive conditioning has declined in recent years because of questions about its long-term effectiveness. Although it can create avoidance in the presence of the certainty of punishment, unwanted behaviors often continue in real-life situations when no such threat exists. Moreover, aversive conditioning is a controversial technique because of its unpleasant nature.

Operant Conditioning

As we also saw in Chapter 5, Learning, *operant conditioning* techniques are based on the idea that a person learns to behave in different ways when new behaviors are reinforced and old ones ignored or punished. In one form of operant conditioning called **behavior contracting,** the therapist and the client agree on behavioral goals and on the reinforcement that the client will receive when the goals are reached. This agreement often takes the form of a written contract that binds both the client and the therapist as if by a legal document. The contract specifies the behaviors to be followed, the penalties for not following them, and any privileges to be earned. One such contract might be: "For each day that I smoke fewer than 20 cigarettes, I will earn 30 minutes of time to go bowling. For each day that I exceed the goal, I will lose 30 minutes from the time that I have accumulated."

Another form of operant conditioning is called the **token economy.** As we mentioned in the chapter on learning, token economies are usually employed in institutions like schools and hospitals, where controlled conditions are most feasible (O'Leary & Wilson, 1987). Subjects earn tokens or points for behaviors that are considered appropriate and adaptive; in turn, the tokens or points can be exchanged for desired items and privileges. On the ward of a mental hospital, for example, improved grooming habits might earn points that can be used to purchase special foodstuffs or weekend passes. Token economies have proved effective in modifying the behavior of patients who are resistant to other forms of treatment, such as people with chronic schizophrenia (Paul, 1982; Paul & Lentz, 1977). Although token economies can work in institutions, the positive changes do not always generalize to everyday life outside the hospital or clinic, where adaptive behavior is not always reinforced with tokens and maladaptive behavior is not always ignored or punished.

Modeling

The behavior therapies we have discussed so far rely on classical and operant conditioning principles to change behavior. But as we saw in Chapter 5, Learning, much human behavior is learned by **modeling**—the process of learning a behavior by watching someone else perform it. Modeling can also be used to treat problem behaviors. One experiment tried to help people overcome snake phobia by having them view films in which models confronted snakes and gradually moved closer and closer to them (Bandura, Blanchard, & Ritter, 1969). The researchers reported a notable reduction in the observers' fear of snakes. Similar techniques have succeeded in reducing such common phobias as fear of dental work (Melamed et al., 1975). Moreover, a combination of modeling and positive reinforcement was successful in helping schizophrenic patients learn and use appropriate behavior both inside and outside the hospital (Bellack, Hersen, & Turner, 1976). Modeling has also been used to teach people with mental retardation job skills and appropriate responses to problems encountered at work (LaGreca, Stone, & Bell, 1983).

COGNITIVE THERAPIES

In modeling, people learn a behavior simply by watching others perform it. Thus, the people with snake phobia learned how to confront snakes by watching a film of others moving closer and closer to the snakes. Cognitive psychologists would point out that in addition to learning a *behavior*, these people also learned from watching the film that snakes are not necessarily dangerous and that one can endure contact with them without suffering ill effects. It might be said that in addition to changing their behavior, these people *changed their way of thinking* about snakes, and that their new way of thinking should lead to more adaptive behavior in the future. It is this simple idea—people's ideas about the world can be changed, which will have a beneficial effect on their subsequent behavior—that is at the heart of the **cognitive therapies.**

Cognitive therapists believe that their clients suffer from misconceptions about themselves and the world; it is these misconceptions that cause them psychological problems. The task facing cognitive therapists is to identify the erroneous ways of thinking and to correct them. This focus on learning new ways of thinking shares many similarities with behavior therapy; in fact, many professionals consider themselves to be *cognitive behavior therapists,* therapists who combine both cognitive and behavior therapies (Brewin, 1996). Let's examine some of the more popular forms of cognitive therapy.

Stress-inoculation Therapy

As we go about our lives, we talk to ourselves constantly—we propose courses of action to ourselves, comment on our performance, express wishes, and so on. **Stress-inoculation therapy** is a type of cognitive therapy that makes use of this self-talk process to help clients cope with stressful situations (Meichenbaum & Cameron, 1982). Once the stressful situation is identified, the client is taught to suppress any negative, anxiety-evoking thoughts and to replace them with positive, "coping" thoughts. Take a student with exam anxiety who faces every test telling herself: "Oh, another test. I'm so nervous and I'm sure I won't be able to think calmly enough to remember the answers. If only I'd studied more! If I don't get through this course, I'll never graduate!" This pattern of thought is highly dysfunctional because it will only make her anxiety worse. With the help of a cognitive therapist, the student learns a new pattern of self-talk: "I studied hard for this exam and I know the material well. I looked at the textbook last night and reviewed my notes. I should be able to do well. If some questions are hard, they won't all be, and even if it's tough, my whole grade doesn't depend on just one test." Then the client tries out the new strategy in a real situation, ideally one of only moderate stress (like a short quiz). Finally, the client is ready to use the strategy in a more stressful situation (like a final exam). Stress-inoculation therapy works by turning the client's own thought patterns into a kind of vaccine against stress-induced anxiety. This technique, as you might guess, is particularly effective with anxiety disorders.

Rational-emotive Therapy

Another type of cognitive therapy, one that includes a more elaborate set of assumptions, is known as **rational-emotive therapy (RET).** According to Albert Ellis (1973), the founder of RET, most people in need of therapy hold a set of irrational and self-defeating beliefs. These include such notions as: they should be competent at everything and liked by everyone; life should

Cognitive therapies Psychotherapies that emphasize changing clients' perceptions of their life situation as a way of modifying their behavior.

Stress-inoculation therapy A type of cognitive therapy that trains clients to cope with stressful situations by learning a more useful pattern of self-talk.

Rational-emotive therapy (RET) A directive cognitive therapy based on the idea that clients' psychological distress is caused by irrational and self-defeating beliefs and that the therapist's job is to challenge such dysfunctional beliefs.

Cognitive therapy Therapy that depends on identifying and changing inappropriately negative and self-critical patterns of thought.

Group therapy Type of psychotherapy in which clients meet regularly to interact and help one another achieve insight into their feelings and behavior.

always be fair; quick solutions to problems should be available; and their lives should turn out a certain way. The core problem with such beliefs is that they involve absolutes—"musts" and "shoulds" that allow for no exceptions, no room for making mistakes. When people with such irrational beliefs come up against real-life struggles, they often experience excessive psychological distress. For example, when a college student who believes he must be liked by everyone isn't invited to join a fraternity, he may view the rejection as a catastrophe and become deeply depressed, rather than feeling simply sad and disappointed.

In rational-emotive therapy, therapists confront such dysfunctional beliefs vigorously, using a variety of techniques, including persuasion, challenge, commands, and theoretical arguments. Studies have shown that RET techniques often do enable people to *reinterpret* their negative beliefs and experiences in a more positive light, decreasing the likelihood of becoming depressed (Blatt et al., 1996; Bruder et al., 1997).

Beck's Cognitive Therapy

One of the most important and promising forms of cognitive therapy was developed by Aaron Beck (1967) for the treatment of depression. It is usually known simply as **cognitive therapy,** but is sometimes referred to as "Beck's cognitive therapy" to avoid confusion with the broader category of cognitive therapies.

Beck believes that depression results from negative patterns of thought that people develop about themselves. Principally, depressed people interpret events in a distorted way, one that is strongly and inappropriately self-critical. Such people have unrealistic expectations, magnify their failures, make sweeping negative generalizations about themselves from little evidence, notice only negative feedback from the outside world, and interpret anything less than total success as failure. Take the case of a salesman who reacts to losing an important account with severe, disabling depression. Why? Because the account loss set off a pattern of negative thoughts in his mind: He is not really a good salesman, he will never find any customers as good as the one he just lost, and he will probably now go bankrupt from lack of income. From there his negative thoughts continue to spiral into more general areas of his life, and he may conclude that his life is worthless. According to Beck, this downward spiral of negative thoughts and cognitive distortions is at the heart of depression.

Beck's assumptions about the cause of depression are very similar to the assumptions underlying RET, but the style of treatment differs considerably. Cognitive therapists are much less challenging and confrontational than rational-emotive therapists. Instead, they try to help clients examine each dysfunctional thought in a supportive but objectively scientific manner ("Are you *sure* you'll never find any more good customers? What is your evidence for that?"). Like RET, Beck's cognitive therapy aims to lead the client to more realistic and flexible ways of thinking.

GROUP THERAPIES

The therapies we have been discussing thus far involve only two people, a client and a therapist. Some psychologists think that this sort of therapy is less than ideal, for many of the problems that cause people to go into therapy are interpersonal. They believe that the treatment of several clients simultaneously, or **group therapy,** is preferable to individual therapy. Group therapy allows both client and therapist to see how the client acts around others. If a client is painfully anxious and tongue-tied, or chronically self-critical and self-denigrating, or hostile and aggressive toward the opposite sex, these tendencies will show up quickly in a group setting.

Groups have other advantages. A good group offers a client social support, a feeling that he or she is not the only person in the world with emotional problems. The group can also help the client learn useful new behaviors (how to express feelings, how to disagree without antagonizing others). Interactions with other group members may push the client toward insights into his or her own behavior (seeing how annoying another person's constant complaints are, or how helpful his or her words of encouragement are, can lead the client toward useful behavior change). Finally, group therapy is less expensive for each participant than is individual therapy (Yalom, 1995).

Group therapy can help to identify problems that a client has interacting with other people. The group also offers social support, helping clients to feel less alone with their problems.

There are many kinds of group therapy. Some groups follow the general outlines of the therapies we've already mentioned. Others are oriented toward a specific goal, such as stopping smoking, drinking, or overeating. And some have more open-ended goals—for example, a happier marriage.

SELF-HELP GROUPS   This chapter emphasizes the kinds of therapy provided by trained professionals. But there are not enough mental-health professionals to treat everyone who needs or wants therapy. At any given time, about 40 million Americans suffer from some form of psychological disorder. Mental-health professionals can serve only a fraction of those people.

Because of this gap in the mental-health system (as well as the high cost of many forms of professional treatment), more and more people faced with life crises are turning to low-cost self-help groups for support and help.

What are self-help groups and how do they work? Most such groups are small, local gatherings of people who share a common problem or predicament and who provide mutual assistance at a very low cost. Alcoholics Anonymous is perhaps the best-known self-help group, but similar types of groups serve people suffering from anorexia, arthritis, cancer, divorce, and drug abuse; parents whose children have died or are chronically ill or handicapped; adolescents, retirees, overeaters, compulsive gamblers, AIDS victims, former mental patients, and people suffering from depression or anxiety. In short, self-help groups are available for virtually every conceivable life problem.

Do these self-help groups work? In many cases, apparently they do. Alcoholics Anonymous has developed an enviable reputation for helping people cope with alcoholism. Research confirms that most group members express strong support for their groups (Riordan & Beggs, 1987), and studies that have directly measured the effectiveness of self-help groups have demonstrated that they can indeed be effective (Galanter, 1984; Pisani et al., 1993).

Such groups help to prevent psychological disorders by reaching out to people near the limits of their ability to cope with life stresses. The social support they provide is particularly important in an age when divorce, geographic mobility, and other factors have reduced the ability of the family to comfort people. By increasing their members' coping skills through information and advice, self-help groups may significantly reduce the likelihood that people will develop more serious psychological problems and require professional treatment.

Family Therapy

Family therapy A form of group therapy that sees the family as at least partly responsible for the individual's problems and that seeks to change all family members' behaviors to the benefit of the family unit as well as the troubled individual.

Couple therapy A form of group therapy intended to help troubled partners improve their problems of communication and interaction.

Family Therapy

Family therapy is one form of group therapy (Lebow & Gurman, 1995; Molineux, 1985). Family therapists believe that it is a mistake to treat a client in a vacuum, making no attempt to meet the client's parents, spouse, and children, for if one person in the family is having problems, it is often a signal that the entire family needs assistance. The primary goals of family therapy are improving family communication, encouraging family members to become more empathetic, getting members to share responsibilities, and reducing intrafamily conflict. To achieve these goals, all family members must see that they will benefit from changes in their behavior. Family therapists concentrate on changing the ways in which family members satisfy their needs rather than on trying to change those needs or the individual members' personalities (Gurman & Kniskern, 1991).

Family therapy is especially appropriate when there are problems between husband and wife, parents and children, or other family members. It is also called for when a client's progress in individual therapy is slowed by the family for some reason (often because other family members have trouble adjusting to a client's improvement). Unfortunately, not all families benefit from family therapy. Sometimes the problems are too entrenched; in other cases, important family members may be absent or unwilling to cooperate; in still others, one family member monopolizes the sessions. In all these cases, a different therapeutic approach is warranted.

Couple Therapy

Another form of group therapy is **couple therapy,** which is designed to assist partners who are having difficulties with their relationship. In the past, this therapy was generally called *marital therapy*, but the term *couple therapy* is considered more appropriate today because it captures the broad range of partners who may seek help together (Oltmanns & Emery, 1998).

Most couple therapists concentrate on improving the patterns of communication and mutual expectations between the participants. In *empathy training*, for example, each member of the couple is taught to share inner feelings and to listen to and understand the partner's feelings before responding to them. The empathy technique focuses the couple's attention on feelings and requires that they spend more time listening and less time in rebuttal.

Other couple therapists employ behavioral techniques. For example, a couple might be helped to develop a schedule for exchanging specific caring actions, on the theory that scheduled exchanges of benefits can result in the learning of behavior that benefits both partners. It isn't terribly romantic, but its supporters point out that any strategy that breaks the cycle of dissatisfaction and hostility in a relationship is an important step in the right direction (Margolin, 1987).

Cognitive marital therapy can also help partners recognize the ways they have been misinterpreting each other's communications (Beck, 1989). For example, when one partner says "How's your work going?" the other partner may take this to mean "I wish you would get a better job" or "I hate the way you're always working late at the office." Or an innocent question about helping around the house can be taken as criticism by the other partner. Misinterpretations like these can turn harmless or friendly remarks into criticism or nagging, and evoke unnecessary conflict. Cognitive therapy in the family setting aims at uncovering and undoing such destructive cognitive distortions.

Whatever form of therapy a couple chooses, research indicates that couple therapy for both partners is generally more effective than therapy for only one of them (Dunn & Schwebel, 1995). One study, for example, found that when two married partners underwent therapy together, 56 percent were still married 5 years later; among those couples who underwent therapy separately, only 29 percent remained married (Cookerly, 1980).

Couple and family therapy are being increasingly used when only one family member has a clear psychological disorder, such as schizophrenia, agoraphobia, or, in some cases, depression (Lebow & Gurman, 1996). The goal of treatment in these circumstances is to help the mentally healthy members of the family cope more effectively with the effects of the disorder on the family unit. The improved coping of the well-adjusted family members may, in turn, help the troubled person compensate for or overcome his or her problems.

EFFECTIVENESS OF PSYCHOTHERAPY

The various therapies we have discussed so far all share one characteristic: All are *psycho*therapies—that is, they use psychological methods to treat disorders. But is psychotherapy *effective?* Is it any better than no treatment at all? And if it is, how *much* better is it?

One of the first investigators to raise questions about the effectiveness of psychotherapy was the British psychologist Hans Eysenck (1952). After surveying 19 published reports covering more than 7,000 cases, Eysenck concluded that therapy significantly helped about two out of every three people. However, he also concluded that "Roughly two-thirds of a group of neurotic patients will recover or improve to a marked extent within about two years of the onset of their illness whether they are treated by means of psychotherapy or not" (p. 322). Eysenck's conclusion that individual psychotherapy was no more effective in treating neurotic disorders than no therapy at all caused a storm of controversy in the psychological community and stimulated considerable research.

Ironically, an important but often overlooked aspect of the subsequent debate has little to do with the effectiveness of therapy but rather with the effectiveness of no therapy. Many researchers then and today agree with Eysenck that therapy helps about two-thirds of the people who undergo it. More controversial is the question of what happens to people with psychological problems who do *not* receive formal therapy—is it really true that two-thirds will improve anyway? Bergin and Lambert (1978) questioned the "spontaneous recovery" rate of the control subjects in the studies Eysenck surveyed. They concluded that only about *one* out of every three people improves without treatment (not the two out of three cited by Eysenck). Since twice as many people improve with formal therapy, therapy *is* indeed more effective than no treatment at all (Borkovec & Costello, 1993; Lambert, Shapiro, & Bergin, 1986). Furthermore, these researchers noted that many people who do not receive formal therapy get real therapeutic help from friends, clergy, physicians, and teachers; thus, it is possible that the recovery rate for people who receive *no* therapeutic help at all is even less than one-third.

Other attempts to study the effectiveness of psychotherapy have averaged the results of a large number of individual studies. The general consensus among these studies is also that psychotherapy is effective (Lipsey & Wilson, 1993; Shapiro & Shapiro, 1982; Smith & Glass, 1977), although its

3

Are people who undergo treatment more likely to improve than people who receive no treatment at all?

value appears to be related to a number of other factors. For instance, psychotherapy works best for relatively mild compared to more severe disorders (Kopta et al., 1994) and seems to provide the greatest benefits to people who really *want* to change (Orlinsky & Howard, 1994).

Finally, one very extensive study designed to evaluate the effectiveness of psychotherapy was reported by *Consumer Reports* (1995). Largely under the direction of psychologist Martin E. P. Seligman, this investigation surveyed 180,000 *Consumer Reports* subscribers on everything from automobiles to mental health. Approximately 7,000 people from the total sample responded to the mental health section of the questionnaire that assessed satisfaction and improvement in people who had received psychotherapy.

In reviewing the results of this study, Seligman (1995) summarized a few of its most important findings. First, the vast majority of respondents reported significant overall improvement following therapy. Approximately 90 percent of the people who reported feeling *very poor* or *fairly poor* prior to therapy reported feeling *very good, good,* or *so-so* following therapy. Second, there was no difference in the overall improvement score for people who had received therapy alone and those who had combined psychotherapy with medication. Third, no differences were found between the various forms of psychotherapy. Fourth, no differences in effectiveness were indicated between psychologists, psychiatrists, and social workers, although marriage counselors were seen as less effective. And fifth, patients who had received long-term therapy reported more improvement than those who had received short-term therapy. This last result, one of the most striking findings of the study, is illustrated in Figure 14–1.

Figure 14–1
Duration of therapy and improvement.
One of the most dramatic results of the *Consumer Reports* (1995) study on the effectiveness of psychotherapy was the strong relationship between reported improvement and the duration of therapy.

Source: Adapted from Seligman, M. E. P. (1995). The effectiveness of psychotherapy: The *Consumer Reports* study. *American Psychologist, 50, 965–974.*

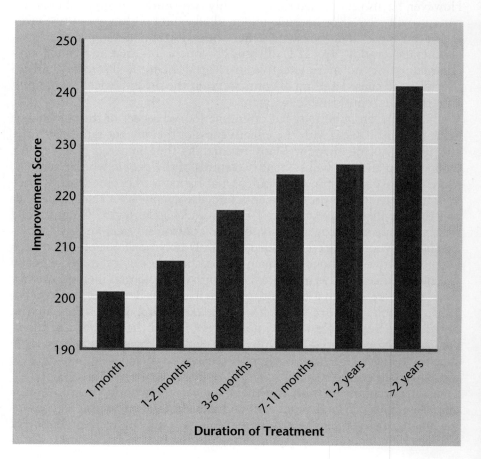

The *Consumer Reports* study lacked the scientific rigor of more traditional investigations designed to assess psychotherapeutic efficacy (Jacobson & Christensen, 1996; Seligman, 1995, 1996). For example, it did not use a control group to assess change in people who did not receive therapy. Nevertheless, it provides broad support for the idea that psychotherapy does work. Exactly why no differences were found between the various forms of psychotherapy is the topic of the next section.

Effectiveness of Various Forms of Psychotherapy

We have seen that researchers generally agree that psychotherapy is usually effective. This raises a second question: Is any particular form of psychotherapy more effective than the others? Is behavior therapy, for example, more effective than insight therapy? In general, the answer seems to be "not much." Most of the benefit of treatment seems to come from being in *some* kind of therapy, regardless of the particular type (Garfield, 1983; Michelson, 1985; Smith, Glass, & Miller, 1980).

But, as we saw at the beginning of the chapter, some kinds of psychotherapy seem to be particularly appropriate for certain people and problems. Insight therapy, for example, seems to be best suited to people seeking profound self-understanding, relief of inner conflict and anxiety, or better relationships with others. Behavior therapy is apparently most appropriate for treating specific anxieties or other well-defined behavioral problems such as sexual dysfunctions. Cognitive therapies have been shown to be effective treatments for depression (Elkin et al., 1989; Robinson, Berman, & Neimeyer, 1990) and seem to be promising treatments for anxiety disorders as well. As you will see later in this chapter, the race, culture, ethnic background, and gender of both client and therapist can also influence which therapy is effective.

Clearly, the trend in psychotherapy is toward **eclecticism**—that is, toward a recognition of the value of a broad treatment package rather than commitment to a single form of therapy (Norcross, Alford, & DeMichele, 1994). The eclectic model doesn't guarantee greater effectiveness—unless carefully thought out, it can result in an inconsistent hodgepodge of concepts and techniques that merely confuses clients. Still, the majority of therapists now claim to use an eclectic approach. Eclectic psychologists rely heavily on scientific research to help determine the best treatment for a particular problem. (See *Applying Psychology* for suggestions on seeking psychological help.)

BIOLOGICAL TREATMENTS

Biological treatments—a group of approaches including medication, electroconvulsive therapy, and psychosurgery—may be used to treat psychological disorders in addition to, or instead of, psychotherapy. Patients and/or therapists select biological treatments for several reasons. First, therapists sometimes find that they cannot help clients with any of the psychotherapies because the clients are extremely agitated, disoriented, or totally unresponsive. In these cases, therapists may decide to use some kind of biological treatment to change clients' behavior so they can benefit from therapy. Second, biological treatment is virtually always used for disorders that have a strong biological component. Schizophrenia and bipolar disorder, for example, cannot be effectively treated with psychotherapy, but often do respond to medication. For other disorders such as depression, psychotherapy can be effective, but the patient may prefer to take medication because it costs less, is more convenient, and allows them to avoid the stigma of seeing a psychotherapist. Third, biological treatment is often used for clients who are

Eclecticism Psychotherapeutic approach that recognizes the value of a broad treatment package over a rigid commitment to one particular form of therapy.

Biological treatments A group of approaches, including medication, electroconvulsive therapy, and psychosurgery, that are sometimes used to treat psychological disorders in conjunction with, or instead of, psychotherapy.

When are drugs used to treat mental illness? Which drugs are effective for which disorders?

The notion that seeking help for your problems is a sign of weakness or mental illness is hard to dispel. But the fact is that tens of thousands of people are helped by psychological counseling and therapy every year. These people include business executives, artists, sports heroes, celebrities—and students. Therapy is a common, useful aid in coping with daily living.

College is a time of stress and anxiety for many people. The pressure of work, the competition for grades, the exposure to many different kinds of people with unfamiliar views, the tension of relating to peers—all these factors can add up to considerable emotional and physical stress, especially for students away from home for the first time. Most colleges and universities have their own counseling services, and many of them are as sophisticated as the best clinics in the country. Most communities also have mental-health programs. As an aid to a potential search for the right counseling service, we include here a list of some of the other available resources for people who would like the advice of a mental-health professional. Many of these services have national offices that will provide you with local branches and the appropriate people to contact in your area.

For Aid in Locating an Appropriate Self-help Group Near You

National Self-Help Clearinghouse
25 W. 43rd St., Room 620
New York, NY 10036
(212) 642-2944
http://www.social.com/health/nhic/data/hr0700/hr0713.html

For Alcohol and Drug Abuse

Alcohol and Drug Problems Association of North America
444 N. Capitol St. NW, Suite 706
Washington, DC 20001

National Clearinghouse for Alcohol and Drug Information
P.O. Box 2345
Rockville, MD 20847-2345
(301) 468-2600
(800) 729-6686
email: info@health.org
http://www.health.org/index.htm

General Service Board
Alcoholics Anonymous, Inc.
P.O. Box 459,
Grand Central Station
New York, NY 10163
(212) 870-3400
http://www.alcoholics-anonymous.org/index

Online Intergroup of Alcoholics Anonymous
http://aa-intergroup.org/

24-Hour Alcohol/Drug Help Line
(800) 562-1240
(206) 722-3700
http://www.adhl.org/

For Those with a Friend or Relative Who Has an Alcohol Problem

National Association for Children of Alcoholics
11426 Rockville Pike
Rockville, MD 20852
(301) 468-0985

For Smoking and Eating Abusers

Smokenders
725 Independence Avenue
Washington, DC 20003
(800) 828-HELP
email: info@smokenders.com
http://www.smokenders.com/

Stop Teen-Age Addiction to Tobacco
511 East Columbus
Springfield, MA 01105
(413) 732-STAT

Weight and Smoking Counseling Service
(212) 755-4363

Overeaters Anonymous
World Service Office
6075 Zenith Ct. NE
Rancho, NM 87124
(505) 891-2664
fax: (505) 891-4320
http://www.overeatersanonymous.org/v20.htm

For Depression and Suicide

American Association of Suicidology
4201 Connecticut Avenue NW,
Suite 310
Washington, DC 20008
(202) 237-2280
fax: (202) 237-2282

Helpful Organizations
http://www.siec.ca/helpful.htm

Mental Health Counseling Hotline
33 East End Ave.
New York, NY 10028
(212) 734-5876

International Association for Suicide Prevention
Suicide Prevention Center
626 South Kingsley Drive
Los Angeles, CA 90005
(213) 381-5111
email: IASP@aol.com

Payne-Whitney Suicide Prevention Program
425 E. 61st Street
New York, NY 10021
(212) 821-0700

Suicide Awareness Voices of Education (SAVE)
P.O. Box 24507
Minneapolis, MN 55424-0507
(612) 946-7998
http://www.save.org/

Depression Awareness, Recognition and Treatment (D/ART) Program
National Institute of Mental Health
(800) 421-4211
(301) 443-4140

Boys Town Suicide Hotline
(800) 448-3000

For Sexual and Sex-related Problems

Sex Information and Educational Council of the United States (SIECUS)
130 W. 42nd St., Suite 350
New York, NY 10036-7802
(212) 819-9770
email: SIECUS@SIECUS.org
http://www.siecus.org

National Organization for Women
Legislative Office
1000 16th St. NW
Washington, DC 20036
http://www.now.org/

National Clearinghouse on Marital and Date Rape
2325 Oak St.
Berkeley, CA 94708-1697
(510) 524-1582 (fee required)
email: ncmdr@aol.com
http://members.aol.com/ncmdr/index.html

Sexual Assault Information Page
http://www.cs.utk.edu/~bartley/saInfoPage.html

Victims of Crime Compensation Board
Rape Crisis Centers
(800) 242-0804 (24-hour Hotline)
http://www.state.nj.us/victims/vccbdir.htm

For Physical Abuse

Child Abuse Listening and Mediation (CALM)
P.O. Box 90754
Santa Barbara, CA 93190-0754
(805) 965-2376
(805) 687-7912 (24-hour listening service)
email: CALM4KIDS@aol.com

For Stress

The International Society for Traumatic Stress Studies
http://www.istss.com/

Stress Free NET
http://www.stressfree.com/index.html

Stress Busters
http://www.stressrelease.com/strssbus.html

Anxiety Disorders Association of America
6000 Executive Blvd., Suite 513
Rockville, MD 20852-3801
(301) 231-8368

For Help Selecting a Therapist

Depressives Anonymous:
Recovery from Depression
329 E. 62nd St.
New York, NY 10021
(212) 689-2600

National Mental Health Consumer Self-help Clearinghouse
1211 Chestnut St.
Philadelphia, PA 19107
(800) 553-4KEY
(215) 751-1810
fax: (215) 636-6310
email: THEKEY@delphi.com
http://libertynet.org/~mha/cl_house.html

Psychiatric Service Section
American Hospital Association
1 North Franklin St.
Chicago, IL 60606
(312) 422-3000
email: rc@aha.org
http://www.aha.org

Mental Health Help Line
(212) 222-7666

For General Information on Mental Health and Counseling

The National Alliance for the Mentally Ill
200 N. Glebe Road, Suite 1015
Arlington, VA 22204
(703) 524-7600
(800) 950-NAMI (help-line)
http://www.nami.org/noframes.htm

The National Mental Health Association
1201 Prince St.
Alexandria, VA 22314-2971
(703) 684-7722

The American Psychiatric Association
1400 K St. NW
Washington, DC 20005
(202) 682-6220

The American Psychological Association
750 1st St. NE
Washington, DC 20002
(202) 336-5500
http://www.apa.org/

The National Institute of Mental Health
5600 Fishers Lane, Rm 15C05
Rockville, MD 20857
(301) 443-4513
http://www.nimh.nih.gov/

Mental Health Info
http://onlinepsych.com/mh/

Psychotherapeutic Drugs
http://www.onlinepsych.com/treat/drugs/htm

Association for Children's Mental Health
(800) 782-0883

National Clearinghouse on Family Support and Children's Mental Health
(800) 628-1696

National Resource Center on Homelessness and Mental Illness
(800) 639-7462

dangerous to themselves and to others, especially if they are residing in institutions where only a few therapists serve many patients.

Three points deserve mention before we go on. First, psychiatrists (who are physicians) currently are the only mental-health professionals licensed to offer biological treatments. Therapists who are not medical doctors often work with doctors who prescribe medication for their patients. Second, in many cases where biological treatments are used, psychotherapy is also recommended. For example, family therapy combined with medicating the patient greatly reduces the need for hospitalization (Kavanagh, 1992). Third, scientists have developed many new medications to treat psychological disorders, and there are many ways of combining biological treatments with psychotherapy. We will highlight a few of the most widely used biological treatments.

Drug Therapies

Medication is frequently and effectively used to treat a number of different psychological problems (see Table 14–1). In fact, Prozac, a drug used to treat depression, is today the best-selling of all prescribed medications—including all drugs used to treat *physical* disorders (such as antibiotics).

Two major reasons for the widespread use of drug therapy are the recent development of several effective drugs and the fact that drug therapies cost less than psychotherapy. But critics have suggested there is another reason for the widespread use of drug therapy: our society's "pill mentality" (take a medicine to fix any problem). The medications used to treat psychological disorders are often prescribed by psychiatrists, but more commonly primary-care physicians such as family practitioners, pediatricians, and gynecologists prescribe them.

TABLE 14-1

MAJOR TYPES OF PSYCHOACTIVE MEDICATIONS

Therapeutic Use	Chemical Structure[*]	Trade Name[*]
Antipsychotics	Phenothiazines	Thorazine
Antidepressants	Tricyclics	Elavil
	MAO inhibitors	Nardil
	SSRIs	Prozac
Psychostimulants	Amphetamines	Dexedrine
	Other	Ritalin
Antimanic	(not applicable)	Tegretol
Antianxiety	Benzodiazepines	Valium
Sedatives	Barbiturates	
Antipanic	Tricyclics	Tofranil
Antiobsessional	Tricyclics	Anafranil

[*]The chemical structures and especially the trade names listed in this table are often just one example of the many kinds of medications available for the specific therapeutic use.

Source: Klerman et al., 1994.

Antipsychotic drugs Drugs used to treat very severe psychological disorders, particularly schizophrenia.

ANTIPSYCHOTIC DRUGS Before the mid-1950s, drugs were not used widely in therapy for psychological disorders because the only available sedatives induced sleep as well as calm. Then the major tranquilizers *reserpine* and the *phenothiazines* were introduced. In addition to alleviating anxiety and aggressive behavior, both drugs reduce psychotic symptoms, such as hallucinations and delusions. Thus they are called **antipsychotic drugs.** Antipsychotic drugs are used primarily in very severe psychological disorders, particularly schizophrenia. They are very effective for treating the "positive symptoms" (such as hallucinations) of this incapacitating disorder, but they are less effective with the "negative symptoms" (such as social withdrawal).

How do antipsychotic drugs work? Research with animals indicates that they block dopamine receptors in the brain. *Dopamine*, you will recall, is a neurotransmitter; the research on antipsychotic drugs is one of the most important pieces of evidence supporting the hypothesis that schizophrenia is linked in some way to an excess of this neurotransmitter (see Chapter 13). In fact, the effectiveness of antipsychotic medications is directly proportional to their ability to block dopamine receptors (Oltmanns & Emery, 1998).

As the following case study shows, the antipsychotics can sometimes have dramatic effects (Grinspoon, Ewalt, & Shader, 1972):

> Ms. W. was a 19-year-old, white, married woman who was admitted to the treatment unit as a result of gradually increasing agitation and hallucinations over a three-month period. Her symptoms had markedly intensified during the four days prior to admission. . . . She had had a deprived childhood, but had managed to function reasonably well up to the point of her breakdown.
>
> At the outset of her hospitalization, Ms. W. continued to have auditory and visual hallucinations and appeared frightened, angry, and confused. . . . Her condition continued to deteriorate for more than two weeks, at which point medication was begun. . . .
>
> She responded [to thioridazine (Mellaril)] quite dramatically during the first week of treatment. Her behavior became, for the most part, quiet and appropriate, and she made some attempts at socialization. She continued to improve, but by the fourth week of treatment began to show signs of mild depression. Her medication was increased, and she resumed her favorable course. By the sixth week she was dealing with various reality issues in her life in a reasonably effective manner, and by the ninth week she was spending considerable time at home, returning to the hospital in a pleasant and cheerful mood. She was discharged exactly 100 days after her admission, being then completely free of symptoms.

Although their benefits can be dramatic, antipsychotic drugs can also produce a number of undesirable physical side effects (Kane & Lieberman, 1992). Another problem is that while antipsychotic drugs allow many schizophrenic patients to leave the hospital, the drugs by themselves are of little value in treating the social incapacity and other difficulties these people encounter when trying to adjust to life outside the institution. And because many discharged patients fail to take their medications, relapse is common. (The relapse rate can be reduced if drug therapy is effectively combined with psychotherapy.)

ANTIDEPRESSANT DRUGS A second group of drugs, known as antidepressants, are used to combat depression. Until the end of the 1980s, there were

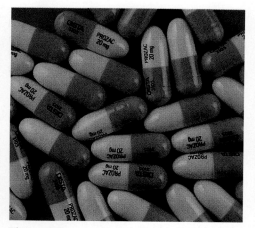

The antidepressant drug Prozac is now the best-selling medication in the United States.

only two main types of antidepressant drugs: *monoamine oxidase inhibitors (MAO inhibitors)* and *tricyclics* (named for their chemical properties). Both drugs work by increasing the concentration of the neurotransmitters serotonin and norepinephrine in the brain (McKim, 1997). Both are effective for most patients with serious depression, but both produce a number of serious and troublesome side effects. The MAO inhibitors require careful dietary restriction, because they can be lethal in combination with some foods. The tricyclics often cause blurred vision, dry mouth, dizziness, low blood pressure, constipation, and other problems. Because of the seriousness of these side effects, the search has continued for better antidepressant drugs.

In 1988, Prozac came onto the market. This drug works by reducing the uptake of serotonin in the nervous system, thus increasing the amount of serotonin active in the brain at any given moment. Prozac has fewer side effects than MAO inhibitors or tricyclics, and has been heralded in the popular media as a "wonder drug" for the treatment of depression. However, there was an early backlash against the medication. Some reports attributed dramatic suicidal or violent actions in people on Prozac, but those stories have since been discredited (Thompson, 1993).

A more pressing question is "How effective is Prozac?" As we have noted, Prozac is now the best selling of all prescribed medications, and its widespread use is considered testimony to its effectiveness in alleviating depression. We must view this development with some caution, however. Prozac undoubtedly has helped many depressed people, but often because of its placebo effect—that is, Prozac frequently works because people believe it will work. This fact underscores the very important point that the success of an antidepressant medication does not mean that depression is caused by a "chemical imbalance in the brain." Aspirin relieves headaches, but this does not mean that a lack of the ingredients in aspirin causes headaches. Although antidepressants clearly have an important role in the treatment of depression, some therapists are concerned that too many people are trying to solve their emotional or life problems with a pill rather than through their own efforts.

LITHIUM   Bipolar disorder or manic depression is frequently treated with lithium carbonate. Lithium is not a drug but a naturally occurring salt that helps level out the wild and unpredictable mood swings of manic depression. Although it is effective in approximately 75 percent of cases, lithium is often prescribed along with antidepressants because it is slow to take effect (Solomon et al., 1995). We do not know exactly how lithium works, but it appears to affect the levels of serotonin and epinephrine in the brain (Oltmanns & Emery, 1998).

OTHER MEDICATIONS   Several other medications can be used to alleviate the symptoms of various psychological problems (see Table 14–1). *Psychostimulants* heighten alertness and arousal. They are also commonly used to treat children with attention-deficit/hyperactivity disorder; strangely, in these cases, they have a calming rather than a stimulating effect. As with the antidepressants, some professionals worry that the psychostimulants are being overused. *Antianxiety medications* (for example, Valium) quickly produce a sense of calm and mild euphoria; they are often used to reduce general tension and anxiety, though their addictive potential limits their current use. *Sedatives* produce both calm and drowsiness; they are used to treat agitation or to induce sleep. These drugs, too, can become addictive. Finally, recent evidence indicates that certain types of antidepressant medications are effective in reducing episodes of panic and alleviating obsessive-compulsive symptoms (Klerman et al., 1994).

Electroconvulsive Therapy

Electroconvulsive therapy (ECT) is most often used for cases of prolonged and severe depression that do not respond to other forms of therapy. The technique of ECT remained largely unchanged for many years: One electrode was placed on each side of the patient's head, and a mild current was turned on for a very short time (about 1.5 seconds). The electrical current passed from one side of the patient's brain to the other, producing a brief convulsion, followed by a temporary loss of consciousness. Muscle relaxants administered in advance prevented dangerously violent contractions. When patients awoke several minutes later, they normally had amnesia for the period immediately before the procedure and remained confused for the next hour or so. With repeated treatments, people often became disoriented, but this condition usually cleared after treatment concluded. Treatment normally consisted of ten or fewer sessions of ECT.

Electroconvulsive therapy (ECT) Biological therapy in which a mild electrical current is passed through the brain for a short period, often producing convulsions and temporary coma; used to treat severe, prolonged depression.

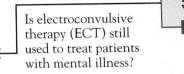

5

Is electroconvulsive therapy (ECT) still used to treat patients with mental illness?

SUMMARY TABLE

MAJOR PERSPECTIVES ON THERAPY

Type of Therapy	Cause of Disorder	Goal	Techniques
Insight Therapies Psychoanalysis	Unconscious conflicts and motives; repressed problems from childhood.	To bring unconscious thoughts and feelings to consciousness; to gain insight.	Free association, dream analysis, interpretation, transference.
Client-centered Therapy	Experiences of conditional positive regard.	To help people become fully functioning by opening them up to all of their experiences.	Regarding clients with unconditional positive regard.
Gestalt Therapy	Lack of wholeness in the personality.	To get people to "own their feelings" and to awaken to sensory experience in order to become whole.	Active rather than passive talk; empty chair techniques; encounter groups.
Behavior Therapies	Reinforcement for maladaptive behavior.	To learn new and more adaptive behavior patterns.	Classical conditioning (systematic desensitization, extinction, flooding); aversive conditioning; operant conditioning (behavior contracting, token economies); modeling.
Cognitive Therapies	Misconceptions; negative, self-defeating thinking.	To identify erroneous ways of thinking and to correct them.	Rational-emotive therapy (rationally examining negative thought patterns); stress-inoculation therapy (consciously replacing negative thoughts with positive, coping thoughts); Beck's cognitive therapy.
Group Therapies	Personal problems are often interpersonal problems.	To develop insight into one's personality and behavior by interacting with others in the group.	Group interaction and mutual support; family therapy; couple therapy; self-help groups.
Biological Treatments	Physiological imbalance or malfunction.	Eliminate symptoms; prevent recurrence.	Electroconvulsive therapy, drugs, psychosurgery.

Psychosurgery Brain surgery performed to change a person's behavior and emotional state; a biological therapy rarely used today.

Recently, an important modification was made to traditional ECT. In this new procedure, called *unilateral ECT*, the electrical current is passed through only one side of the brain. Evidence suggests that unilateral ECT produces fewer side effects, such as memory impairment and confusion, and is only slightly less effective than the traditional method (Diaz, 1997; Khan, 1993). In another modification of the traditional method, some therapists use less powerful electric currents, which also seems to lessen the severity of side effects, and reduce the duration of each stimulation to only one-twenty-fifth of a second.

No one knows exactly why ECT works, but evidence clearly demonstrates its effectiveness. In addition, the fatality rate for ECT is markedly lower than for patients taking antidepressant drugs (Henry, Alexander, & Sener, 1995). Still, ECT has many critics and its use remains controversial. The procedure often produces memory loss, and it is certainly capable of damaging the brain. For these reasons, ECT is best considered a "last resort" treatment when all other methods have failed.

Psychosurgery

Psychosurgery refers to brain surgery performed to change a person's behavior and emotional state. This is a drastic step, especially because it is irreversible and its effects are difficult to predict. In a *prefrontal lobotomy*, the frontal lobes of the brain are severed from the deeper centers beneath them. The assumption is that in extremely disturbed patients the frontal lobes intensify emotional impulses from the lower brain centers (chiefly the thalamus and hypothalamus). Unfortunately, lobotomies can work with one person and fail completely with another—possibly producing permanent undesirable side effects, such as inability to inhibit impulses or a near-total absence of feeling.

Prefrontal lobotomies are rarely performed today. In fact, very few psychosurgical procedures are done nowadays except as desperate measures to control such conditions as intractable psychoses, epilepsy that does not respond to other treatments, severe obsessive-compulsive disorders (Baer et al., 1995), and pain in a terminal illness.

INSTITUTIONALIZATION AND ITS ALTERNATIVES

For the severely mentally ill, hospitalization has been the treatment of choice in the United States for the past 150 years. Several different kinds of hospitals offer care to the mentally ill. General hospitals admit many people suffering from mental disorders, usually for short-term stays until they can be released to their families or to other institutional care. Private hospitals—some nonprofit and some for-profit—offer services to patients with adequate insurance. And for veterans with psychological disorders, there are Veterans Administration hospitals.

When most people think of "mental hospitals," however, it is the large state institutions that come to mind. These public hospitals, many with beds for thousands of patients, were often built in rural areas in the nineteenth century, the idea being that a country setting would calm patients and help restore their mental health. Whatever the good intentions behind the establishment of these hospitals, for most of their history they have not provided adequate care or therapy for their residents. Perpetually underfunded and understaffed, state hospitals have often been little more than warehouses for victims of serious mental illness who were unwanted by their families. Except for new arrivals, who were often intensively treated in the hope of quickly discharging them, patients received little therapy besides drugs, and most spent their days watching television or staring into space. Under these conditions, many patients became completely apathetic and accepted a permanent "sick role."

The development of effective drug therapies starting in the 1950s led to a number of changes in state hospitals. For one thing, patients who were agitated (engaging in violent behavior, for example) could now be sedated with drugs. Although the drugs often produced lethargy, this was considered an improvement over the use of physical restraints. The second major, and more lasting, result of the new drug therapies was wholesale discharge of patients. As we shall see, however, this movement toward deinstitutionalization created new problems, both for individual patients and for society.

Deinstitutionalization

The advent of antipsychotic drugs in the 1950s created a favorable climate for the policy of **deinstitutionalization**—releasing patients with severe psychological disorders back into the community. The idea of deinstitutionalization gained strength in 1963, when Congress passed legislation establishing a network of community mental-health centers around the nation. The practice of placing patients in smaller, more humane facilities or returning them under medication to care within the community intensified during the 1960s and 1970s. By 1975, there were 600 regional mental-health centers accounting for 1.6 million cases of outpatient care.

In recent years, however, deinstitutionalization has created serious problems. Discharged patients today often find poorly funded community mental-health centers—or none at all. Many of these ex-patients are poorly prepared to live in the community, and they receive little guidance in coping with the mechanics of daily life. Those who return home can become a burden to their families, especially when they don't get adequate follow-up care. Residential centers, such as halfway houses, vary in quality, but many provide poor medical and psychological care and minimal contact with the outside world. In any case, there is not enough sheltered housing, forcing many former patients into nonpsychiatric facilities—often rooming houses located in dirty, unsafe, isolated neighborhoods. Perhaps the largest single obstacle to their rehabilitation is the social stigma attached to mental illness. Moreover, although outpatient care is presumed to be a well-established national policy objective in mental health, Medicare, Medicaid, Blue Cross–Blue Shield, and other large insurers typically cover inpatient care completely (or nearly so) but discourage outpatient care by requiring substantial copayments and limiting the number of treatment visits.

The full effects of the deinstitutionalization of recent decades are not yet known. Few follow-up studies have been done on discharged patients, who are difficult to keep track of for long periods. Still, it is obvious that, though a worthy ideal, deinstitutionalization in practice has had dire effects on patients and society. Many released patients, unable to obtain follow-up care or to find housing, and incapable of looking after their own needs, have ended up on the streets. Without supervision, they have stopped taking the drugs that made their release possible in the first place and have again become psychotic. Every major U.S. city now has a population of homeless mentally ill men and women living in makeshift shelters or sleeping in doorways, bus stations, parks, and other public spaces. Estimates of the percentage of homeless people who are mentally ill run

Deinstitutionalization Policy of treating people with severe psychological disorders in the larger community, or in small residential centers such as halfway houses, rather than in large public hospitals.

Why did the movement toward deinstitutionalization emerge? What have been the consequences for mental patients and for society at large?

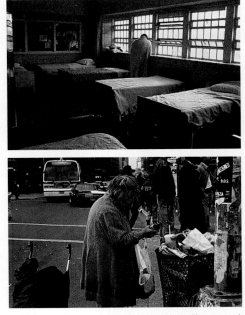

Lacking adequate funding and staff, mental hospitals frequently failed to provide adequate treatment to their residents. Beginning in the 1950s and 1960s, the policy of deinstitutionalization led to the release of many individuals, who, without proper follow-up care, ended up living on the streets. Although not all homeless people are mentally ill, estimates suggest that between 10 and 47 percent of homeless persons suffer from some type of mental disorder.

Prevention Reducing the incidence of emotional disturbance by eliminating conditions that cause or contribute to mental disorders and substituting conditions that foster mental well-being.

Primary prevention Techniques and programs to improve the social environment so that new cases of mental disorders do not develop.

from 10 percent to 47 percent of the total homeless population, which is gauged to be about 600,000 on any given night (Levine & Rog, 1990).

This situation is tragic for the mentally ill homeless, who, often incoherent, are easy prey for criminals. It is also contributing to the coarsening of our society, as the general public, finding the constant presence of "crazies" among them unpleasant, has begun to lose compassion for both the homeless and the mentally ill and to pressure public officials to "get them off the street." Most mental-health professionals now agree that many chronically ill patients should not be released to live "in the community" without better planning, more funding, more community support, and readily available short-term rehospitalization for those who require it.

Alternative Forms of Treatment

Deinstitutionalization assumes that institutionalization occurs in the first place. But for the last two decades Charles Kiesler has argued for a shift from the focus on institutionalization to forms of treatment that avoid hospitalization altogether (Kiesler & Simpkins, 1993). Kiesler (1982) examined ten controlled studies in which seriously disturbed patients were randomly assigned either to hospitals or to an alternative program. The alternative programs took many forms: patients living at home who were trained to cope with daily activities; a small homelike facility in which staff and residents shared responsibility for residential life; hostels offering therapy and crisis intervention; family crisis therapy; day-care treatment; visits from public-health nurses combined with medication; and intensive outpatient counseling combined with medication. All these alternatives involved daily professional contact and skillful preparation of the community to receive the patients. Even though the hospitals to which some people in these studies were assigned provided very good patient care—probably substantially above average for institutions in the United States—nine out of the ten studies found that the outcome was more positive for alternative treatments than for hospitalization. (It is worth noting that hospitalization costs 40 percent more than the alternative programs.) Moreover, the patients who received alternative care were less likely to undergo hospitalization later—which suggests that hospitalizing mental patients is a self-perpetuating process. Many such people "could be treated in alternative settings more effectively and less expensively," Kiesler concludes (1982, p. 358).

Prevention

Yet another approach to mental illness endeavors to prevent its onset in the first place. **Prevention** refers to reducing the incidence of emotional disturbance in society. This requires finding and eliminating the conditions that cause or contribute to mental disorders and substituting conditions that foster well-being. Prevention takes three forms: primary, secondary, and tertiary.

Primary prevention refers to efforts to improve the overall environment so that new cases of mental disorders do not develop. Family planning and genetic counseling are two examples of primary prevention programs. They assist prospective parents to think through such questions as how many children to have and when. They also provide testing to diagnose genetic defects in embryo, and direct parents to treatments, including fetal surgery, that may be able to alleviate defects before the baby is born. Other primary prevention programs aim at increasing personal and social competencies in a wide variety of groups. For example, there are programs designed to help mothers encourage the development of problem-solving skills in their children; other programs have the goal of enhancing competence and adjustment among the elderly. Current campaigns to educate young people about the consequences of drugs, violence, and date rape are other examples of primary prevention (Avery-Leaf et al., 1995).

Secondary prevention requires the identification of groups that are at high risk for mental disorders—for example, abused children, people who have recently divorced, and those who have been laid off from their jobs. The main thrust of secondary prevention is *intervention* with such high-risk groups—that is, detecting maladaptive behavior early and treating it promptly. One form of intervention is *crisis intervention*, which includes such programs as suicide hot lines. Another is the establishment of short-term crisis facilities at which a therapist can provide face-to-face counseling and support for high-risk individuals and families.

The main objective of **tertiary prevention** is to help people adjust to community life after release from a mental hospital. For example, hospitals often grant passes to encourage patients to leave the institution for short periods of time prior to their release. Other tertiary prevention measures are halfway houses, where patients find support and skills training during the period of transition between hospitalization and full integration into the larger community, and nighttime and outpatient programs that provide supportive therapy while patients live at home and hold down a full-time job. Tertiary prevention also includes efforts to educate the community the patient will reenter.

To illustrate how preventive measures work, let's look at the aftermath of the Hyatt Regency Hotel disaster in Kansas City in 1981. Two aerial walkways in the midst of a crowded "tea dance" suddenly collapsed one Friday evening, killing 111 people and injuring more than 200. The disaster had a major emotional impact on both rescuers and survivors, as well as on hotel and media employees, medical personnel, hotel guests, and families and friends of the dead and injured (Gist & Stolz, 1982). An estimated 5,000 people were deeply affected by this disaster. Indeed, because virtually all the victims were local, an entire community felt its psychological impact.

By Monday, all the community mental-health centers in the area had organized support group activities. Professionals and natural caregivers, such as clergy, were trained to respond to Hyatt-related emotional problems. In addition, a major campaign publicized the availability of psychological services as a way to "legitimize the expression and acceptance of psychological reactions to the disaster" (Gist & Stolz, 1982, p. 1137). Press releases delivered a consistent message to the community, describing the reactions that were to be expected after such a disaster, emphasizing that they were normal responses that needed to be shared and accepted, and reminding people that help was available.

This example not only illustrates the potential of prevention, but also highlights the difficulty and limitations of prevention efforts. How do we know whether the beneficial effects of such an intervention program would not otherwise have occurred over the long term? How realistic are preventive efforts of this sort in more ordinary circumstances? And how can government agencies justify spending taxpayers' dollars on programs that claim to head off problems that may never have actually materialized without the programs? These questions all need to be addressed in the years to come (Reiss & Price, 1996; Heller, 1996).

Secondary prevention Programs to identify groups that are at high risk for mental disorders and to detect maladaptive behavior in these groups and treat it promptly.

Tertiary prevention Programs to help people adjust to community life after release from a mental hospital.

Suicide hot lines and other crisis intervention programs are secondary prevention measures designed to serve individuals and groups at high risk for mental disorders.

In sum, prevention is clearly cost-effective compared to therapy, but preventive efforts are constrained by several factors: It is very difficult to bring about social change; our scientific knowledge about the causes of psychological disorders is far from complete; it is very hard to prove conclusively that prevention works; and there are legitimate concerns about forcing people to accept treatments before their problems are manifest.

GENDER DIFFERENCES IN TREATMENTS

Many female clients believe that female therapists are more sensitive to their needs and goals than male therapists are.

In the previous chapter, we saw that there are some significant gender differences in the prevalence of many psychological disorders. Are there significant differences in treatment as well? First, women are more likely than men to be in psychotherapy. In part, this is because women are more willing than men to admit they have psychological problems and need help to solve them. Moreover, psychotherapy is more socially accepted for women than for men (Williams, 1987). Regardless of the reasons for the difference, one national survey found that 60 percent of those seeing psychologists and psychiatrists were women (Williams, 1987).

The treatment given women, in most respects, is the same as that given men. This fact has become somewhat controversial in recent years (Enns, 1993). Because most therapists are male, and most vocational and rehabilitation programs are male-oriented, some critics of "equal treatment" have claimed that women in therapy are often encouraged to adopt traditional, male-oriented views of what is "normal" or "appropriate"; that male therapists tend to urge women to adapt, adjust, or conform to their surroundings passively; and that male therapists are insufficiently sensitive to the fact that much of the stress women experience comes from trying to cope with a world in which they are *not* treated equally (Brown & Ballou, 1992). For all these reasons, there has been an increase recently in the number of "feminist therapists," who attempt to help their female clients become aware of the extent to which their problems derive from external controls and inappropriate sex roles, become more conscious of and attentive to their own needs and goals, and develop a sense of pride in their womanhood rather than passively accepting or identifying with the status quo.

We noted that in *most* respects women receive the same kinds of treatment men receive. There is, however, one very important difference: Traditionally, women have received a disproportionate share of drugs prescribed for psychological disorders (Basow, 1986; Russo, 1985). For example, women receive 70 to 80 percent of all antidepression medications, even though they make up only two-thirds of all cases of depressive disorders. Researchers have not yet identified the reasons for this sex bias in drug prescriptions, but it has become a source of considerable concern. Professionals' willingness to prescribe drugs to women may encourage women to see their problems as having physical causes. Moreover, the readiness to prescribe drugs for women at least partly accounts for women's tendency to abuse prescription drugs more often than men do (Russo, 1985).

CULTURAL DIFFERENCES IN TREATMENTS

Imagine the following scenario: As a Native American client is interviewed by a psychologist, he stares at the floor. He answers questions politely, but during the entire consultation looks away continually, never meeting the doctor's eye. This body language might lead the psychologist to suppose that the man is depressed or has low self-esteem. Unless, that is, the psychologist knows that in the client's culture not making eye contact is a sign of respect.

This example shows how culture-bound are our ideas of what constitutes normal behavior. When psychotherapist and client come from very different cultures, misunderstandings of speech, body language, and customs are almost inevitable. Even when client and doctor are of the same nationality and speak the same language, there can be striking differences if they belong to different racial and ethnic groups (Casas, 1995). Some black clients, for example, are wary of confiding in a white therapist—so much so that their wariness is sometimes mistaken for paranoia. For this reason, many black clients seek out a black therapist, a tendency that is becoming more common as larger members of black middle-class people enter therapy (Williams, 1989).

One of the challenges for U.S. therapists in recent years has been to treat refugees from foreign countries, many of whom have fled such horrifying circumstances at home that they arrive in the United States exhibiting post-traumatic stress disorder. Not only must these refugees overcome the effects of trauma and flight from it, but they also face the new stresses of settling in a strange country, which often include separation from their families, ignorance of the English language, and inability to practice their traditional occupations. Therapists in such circumstances must learn something of their clients' culture. Often they have to conduct interviews through an interpreter—hardly an ideal circumstance for therapy.

These therapists also need to recognize that some disorders that afflict people from other cultures may not exist in Western culture at all. For example, Taijin Kyofusho (roughly translated as "fear of people") involves a morbid fear that one's body or actions may be offensive to others. Because this disorder is rarely seen outside of Japan, American therapists require specialized training to identify it.

In August 1990, the American Psychological Association approved a document titled "Guidelines for Psychological Practice with Ethnic and Culturally Diverse Populations." In it, the APA reminds practitioners that different groups may perform differently on psychological tests, express symptoms in different ways, and relate differently to family members and outsiders than members of the dominant population (Moses, 1990). In 1991, following practitioners' observations that in other countries the "standard" dosages of medication are quite different than in the United States, the National Institutes of Health began a study that attempts to measure the responses of different ethnic groups to several psychiatric medications (DeAngelis, 1991b).

Ultimately, however, the best solution to the difficulties of serving a multicultural population is to train therapists of many different backgrounds so that members of ethnic, cultural, and racial minorities can choose therapists of their own group if they wish to do so (Bernal & Castro, 1994). Indeed, research has shown that psychotherapy is more likely to be effective when the client and the therapist share a similar cultural background (Sue et al., 1994).

SUMMARY

This chapter presents some of the main types of **psychotherapy,** the treatment of personality and behavior disorders by psychological means. It also discusses biological treatments as well as institutionalization and its alternatives.

INSIGHT THERAPIES

The main goal of **insight therapies** is to give clients a better understanding and awareness of their feelings, motivations, and actions in the hope that this will lead to better adjustment.

Psychoanalysis

Psychoanalysis is a therapy based on the belief that psychological problems stem from feelings and conflicts repressed during childhood. One way to uncover what has been repressed is through **free association,** a process in which the client discloses whatever thoughts or fantasies come to mind without editing or otherwise inhibiting them. In classical psychoanalysis, the patient comes to transfer feelings held toward authority figures from childhood to the analyst, a process known as **transference.** The goal of psychoanalysis is **insight,** or awareness of feelings, memories, and actions from the past that were unconscious but were exerting a strong influence on the patient's present feelings and behavior.

Client-centered Therapy

Client-centered (or person-centered) therapy, founded by Carl Rogers, is built on the idea that therapy should be based on the client's view of the world rather than the therapist's and on the client's responsibility for change. The therapist's most important task is to provide unconditional positive regard for clients so that they will learn to accept themselves.

Gestalt Therapy

Gestalt therapy grew out of the work of Fritz Perls and is designed to help people become more aware of their feelings and more genuine in their day-to-day interactions. The emphasis in therapy is on making the person whole and complete.

Recent Developments

Contemporary insight therapists are more active than traditional psychoanalysts, giving clients direct guidance and feedback. They are also more focused on clients' immediate problems than on their childhood traumas. An especially significant development is the trend to **short-term psychodynamic psychotherapy,** which recognizes that most people can be successfully treated within a time-limited framework.

BEHAVIOR THERAPIES

Behavior therapies are based on the belief that all behavior, normal and abnormal, is learned, and that the objective of therapy is to teach people more satisfying ways of behaving.

Classical Conditioning

Classical conditioning therapies attempt to evoke a new conditioned response to old stimuli. For example, **systematic desensitization** is a method for gradually reducing irrational fears by imagining—or confronting in real life—increasingly fearful situations while maintaining a relaxed state. Eventually, relaxation replaces fear as a response, perhaps as a result of extinction. Flooding, which subjects the person to feared situations at full intensity and for a prolonged time, is a somewhat harsh but highly effective method of desensitization. **Aversive conditioning** has the opposite goal: it conditions a negative rather than a positive response to a stimulus such as the sight or taste of alcohol. Its purpose is to eliminate undesirable behaviors by associating them with pain and discomfort.

Operant Conditioning

Operant conditioning techniques work by reinforcing new behaviors and ignoring or punishing old ones. In one such technique, called **behavior contracting,** client and therapist agree on certain behavioral goals and on the reinforcement the client will receive upon reaching those goals. In another technique, called the **token economy,** tokens that can be cashed in for "rewards" are used to positively reinforce many different kinds of desired behavior.

Modeling

In **modeling,** a person learns new behaviors by watching others perform those behaviors.

COGNITIVE THERAPIES

Cognitive therapies aim at changing clients' maladaptive ways of thinking about themselves and the world.

Stress-inoculation Therapy

Stress-inoculation therapy teaches clients new and positive patterns of self-talk they can use to support themselves through stressful situations.

Rational-emotive Therapy

Rational-emotive therapy (RET) is based on the idea that people's emotional problems derive from a set of irrational and self-defeating beliefs they hold about themselves and the world. The therapist vigorously challenges these beliefs until the client comes to see just how irrational and dysfunctional they are.

Beck's Cognitive Therapy

Aaron Beck believes that depression results from negative patterns of thought that are strongly and inappropriately self-critical. His **cognitive therapy** tries to help clients think more positively about themselves and the world.

GROUP THERAPIES

Group therapy is based on the idea that psychological problems are at least partly interpersonal problems and are therefore best approached in an interpersonal setting. Group therapy provides social support and is less costly than individual therapy.

Family Therapy

Family therapy is based on the idea that an individual's psychological problems are to some extent family problems. Therefore, the therapist treats the family unit rather than the isolated individual, with the goal of improving communication and empathy among family members and reducing intrafamily conflict.

Couple Therapy

Couple therapy concentrates on improving patterns of communication and interaction between couples.

EFFECTIVENESS OF PSYCHOTHERAPY

Most researchers agree that psychotherapy helps about two-thirds of the people treated.

Effectiveness of Various Forms of Psychotherapy

Most kinds of therapy are more effective than no treatment at all, but researchers have found few major differences in the effectiveness of various forms of therapy. The general trend in psychotherapy is toward **eclecticism,** the use of a broad treatment package rather than one single form of therapy.

BIOLOGICAL TREATMENTS

Biological treatments, including medication, electroconvulsive therapy, and psychosurgery, are sometimes used when psychotherapy does not work or when a client has a disorder for which biological treatment is known to be safe and effective. Medication, especially, is very often used in conjunction with psychotherapy.

Drug Therapies

Drugs are the most common biological therapies. **Antipsychotic drugs** are valuable in the treatment of schizophrenia; they do not cure the disorder, but they do reduce its symptoms. Side effects can be severe, however.

Antidepressant drugs alleviate depression, though some have serious side effects. Often the effectiveness of antidepressants such as Prozac seems to be due to the patient's belief that the drug will work (the placebo effect).

Many other types of medication are used to treat psychological disorders, including antianxiety drugs, sedatives, and psychostimulants for children with attention-deficit/hyperactivity disorder.

Electroconvulsive Therapy

Electroconvulsive therapy (ECT) is used for cases of severe depression that do not respond to other treatments. An electric current briefly passed through the brain of the patient produces convulsions and temporary coma.

Psychosurgery

Psychosurgery is brain surgery performed to change a person's behavior and emotional state. It is rarely done today, and then only as a last desperate measure on patients with intractable psychoses.

INSTITUTIONALIZATION AND ITS ALTERNATIVES

Large mental hospitals offer people with severe mental disorders shelter and a degree of care, but a number of problems are linked with institutionalization, including inadequate care and the tendency of patients to become lethargic and accept a permanent "sick role."

Deinstitutionalization

With the advent of antipsychotic drugs in the 1950s, many patients were released from large public hospitals to be cared for in a community setting, in the policy of **deinstitutionalization.** But community mental-health centers and other support services proved inadequate to the task. As a result, many former patients stopped taking their medication, became homeless, and ended up suffering from psychosis and living on the street.

Alternative Forms of Treatment

Alternatives to hospitalization range from living in the family home, with training to cope with daily activities for the mentally ill individual and crisis therapy for the family, to small homelike facilities in which residents and staff share responsibilities. Most alternative treatments involve some medication of the troubled individual and skillful preparation of the family/community. The majority of studies have found more positive outcomes for alternative treatments than for hospitalization.

Prevention

Prevention refers to efforts to reduce the incidence of mental illness. **Primary prevention** refers to improving the social environment through assistance to parents, education, and family planning. **Secondary prevention** refers to identifying high-risk groups and directing service to them. The object of **tertiary prevention** is to help hospitalized patients return to the community.

GENDER DIFFERENCES IN TREATMENTS

Women are more likely than men to be in psychotherapy; they are also more likely to be given psychoactive medication. Traditional male-oriented therapy often requires women to conform to gender stereotypes in order to be pronounced "well," so many women have turned to "feminist therapists." The American Psychological Association has issued guidelines to ensure that women receive treatment that is not tied to traditional ideas about appropriate behavior for the sexes.

CULTURAL DIFFERENCES IN TREATMENTS

When client and therapist come from different cultural backgrounds or belong to different racial or ethnic groups, misunderstandings can arise in therapy. The APA has issued guidelines to help psychologists deal more effectively with our ethnically and culturally diverse population.

REVIEW QUESTIONS

MULTIPLE CHOICE AND SHORT ANSWER

1. Which of the following is the goal of working through problems in psychoanalysis?
   a. free association
   b. positive transference
   c. countertransference
   d. insight

2. Match the terms with the appropriate descriptions:
   _____ Psychoanalysis
   _____ Client-centered therapy
   _____ Cognitive behavior therapy
   _____ Rational-emotive therapy

   a. Aimed at teaching clients to stop misinterpreting events and to see themselves more rationally.
   b. Based on the idea that anxiety stems from repressed problems from childhood.
   c. Goal is to help clients become more fully functioning.
   d. Seeks to relieve clients of their misconceptions about themselves and their relationship to their environment.

3. Rogerian therapists show that they value and accept their clients by providing _____ _____ regard.

4. In contrast with _____ therapies, which seek to increase clients' self-awareness, _____ therapies try to teach people more appropriate ways of acting.

5. A client begins therapy to get rid of an irrational fear of elevators. A technique that the therapist is likely to employ is:
   a. desensitization
   b. behavior contracting

6. The behavior therapy known as _____ _____ discourages undesired behaviors by associating them with pain and discomfort.

7. Family therapists concentrate on changing the needs and personalities of individual family members. T / F

8. Behavior therapy has generally been found to be more effective than insight therapy for most types of problems. T / F

9. Drugs that help to control schizophrenia are called:
   a. barbiturates   c. lithium
   b. tricyclics   d. antipsychotics

10. The practice of treating severely mentally ill people in large, state-run facilities is known as _____ .

11. Mentally ill people who receive alternative care are less likely to undergo hospitalization later on. T / F

12. The establishment of halfway houses and similar facilities within the community is an example of the movement toward _____ .

13. Crisis intervention and hot lines are two examples of _____ , that is, coping with mental illness before it occurs.

CRITICAL THINKING AND APPLICATIONS

1. What is the role of insight in traditional psychoanalysis?

2. What are some of the major differences between insight and behavior therapies in the treatment of psychological disorders?

3. What are some of the major differences between behavior and cognitive therapies?

4. Why is it wrong to conclude that depression is caused by a "chemical imbalance in the brain" when antidepressant drugs are known to be effective?

ENDURING ISSUES

Mind–Body
After reading about the effectiveness of various drug therapies, have your thoughts changed about the relationship between mind (psychology) and body (physiology)?

Heredity–Environment
To the extent that the various psychotherapies can cure behavior disorders, what does that say about the extent to which we are the result of our heredity (nature) as opposed to our experiences (nurture)?

(Answers to the Review Questions appear in the back of the book.)

15 Social

Psychology

In 1939, when the Germans occupied Warsaw, Poland, the Nazi army segregated the city's Jews in a ghetto surrounded by barbed wire. Deeply concerned about the fate of her Jewish friends, a 16-year-old Catholic girl name Stefania Podgórska made secret expeditions into the ghetto with gifts of food, clothing, and medicine. When the Jewish son of her former landlord made a desperate flight from the ghetto to avoid being deported to a concentration camp, Stefania agreed to hide him in her apartment. At one point, Stefania and her sister sheltered 13 Jews in their attic at the same time that two German soldiers were bivouacked in their small apartment.

Think About It!

1. Do psychologists agree that in human relationships, opposites attract?
2. What is the relationship between attitudes and behavior?
3. What is the difference between prejudice and discrimination? Do the two always occur together?
4. How do advertisers try to influence your behavior?
5. What do social scientists mean by culture?
6. How do social scientists explain mob behavior?

In May 1991, the "hidden children" of the Holocaust gathered with their friends and relatives to pay tribute to 22 Christian rescuers who literally saved their lives during World War II.

🐾 Gustave Collet, one of the people honored, was a Belgian soldier during World War II who helped hundreds of Jewish children by hiding them in the sanctuary of a Catholic church. According to Gustave, "We are all the sons of the same Father, and there is no reason there should be differences."

🐾 Gisela Sohnlein, a student during World War II and a member of the Dutch underground, helped save thousands of Jewish children. In 1943 she was arrested by Nazi soldiers and spent 1½ years in a concentration camp. According to Gisela, "We didn't feel like rescuers at all. We were just ordinary students doing what we had to do."

🐾 Wanda Kwiatkowska-Biernacka was 20 when she falsely claimed that a 1-month-old Jewish baby was her illegitimate child. (Lipman, 1991)

Are these people heroes, or as Gisela Sohnlein stated, were they simply doing what had to be done? Why did they do what so many millions of other people failed to do? What caused people to acquiesce in the murder of millions of innocent people? Were they following orders? What brought about such hatred?

Social psychologists address questions like these. **Social psychology** is the scientific study of the ways in which the thoughts, feelings, and behaviors of one individual are influenced by the real, imagined, or inferred behavior or characteristics of other people.

We begin this chapter by exploring how people form impressions of and make judgments about one another, as well as the factors that influence attraction. Next we consider the ways in which others can shape or change our attitudes and behaviors. Finally, we discuss relationships among people in small groups and large organizations. Throughout the chapter we will examine the impact of culture on social behavior.

SOCIAL COGNITION

When we are slated to meet someone for the first time, we may try to find out something about that person so we can adjust our expectations and behavior accordingly. More often, we form our first impressions of people based on only scanty and often inaccurate information.

Impression Formation

How do we form our first impressions of people? What external cues do we use? And how accurate are these first impressions?

SCHEMATA   When we meet someone for the first time, we notice a number of things about that person—clothes, gestures, manner of speaking, tone of voice, appearance, and so on. We then draw on these cues to fit the person into a ready-made *category*. No matter how little information we have or how contradictory it is, no matter how many times in the past our initial impressions of people have been wrong, we still classify and categorize people after meeting them only briefly. Associated with each category is a *schema*, which, as we saw in Chapter 6, Memory, is a set of beliefs or expectations about something (in this case, people) based on past experience and that is presumed to apply to all members of that category (Fiske & Taylor, 1991). Schemata (the plural of schema) can be about objects, people, social roles, ourselves. For example, if a woman is wearing a white coat and has a stethoscope around her neck, we might reasonably categorize her as a doctor. As a result of this categorization, we might conclude that she is a highly trained professional, knowledgeable about diseases and their cures, qualified to prescribe medication, and so on. These various conclusions follow from most people's schema of a *doctor*.

Schemata serve a number of important functions. For one thing, they allow us to make inferences about other people. We assume, for example, that a friendly person is likely to be good-natured, to accept a social invitation from us, or to do us a small favor. We may not know these things for sure, but our schema for *friendly person* leads us to make this inference.

As we also saw in the chapter on memory, schemata play a crucial role in how we interpret and remember information. For example, in one study, some subjects were told that they would be receiving information about friendly, sociable men, whereas other subjects were informed that they would be learning about intellectual men. Both groups were then given the same information about a set of 50 men and asked to say how many of the men were friendly and how many were intellectual. The subjects who had expected to hear about friendly men dramatically overestimated the number of friendly men in the set, and those who had expected to hear about intellectual men vastly overestimated the number of intellectual men in the set. Moreover, each group of subjects forgot many of the details they received about the men that were inconsistent with their expectations (Rothbart, Evans, & Fulero, 1979). In short, the subjects tended to hear and remember what they expected to.

Schemata can also lure us into "remembering" things about people that we never actually observed. Most of us associate the traits of shyness, quietness, and preoccupation with one's own thoughts with the schema *introvert*. If we notice that Melissa is shy, we are likely to categorize her as an introvert. Later, we may "remember" that she also seemed preoccupied with her own thoughts. In other words, thinking of Melissa as an introvert saves us the trouble of taking into account all the subtle shadings of her personality. But this kind of thinking can easily lead to errors if we attribute to Melissa qualities that belong to the schema but not to her.

Because other people are so important to us as actual or potential friends, colleagues, and intimate partners, we measure them against our schemata from the moment we meet them. Drawing on our general schemata, we quickly form a first impression. Over time, as we continue to interact with them, we add new information about them to our mental files. However, our later experiences with people generally do not influence us nearly so much as our earliest impressions. The first research done on this **primacy effect** was conducted by Solomon Asch (1946). Asch gave subjects one of two lists describing a target person's traits. One list began with positive traits (e.g., "industrious") and ended with negative descriptors (e.g., "stubborn"). The other list presented the same traits in reverse sequence. Subjects who read the positive-to-negative sequence formed more favorable impressions of the people described than did those who read the same list in negative-to-positive sequence. Asch concluded that early impressions of a person create the context for evaluating later information about that person. Thus, if you already like a new acquaintance, you may excuse a flaw or vice you discover later on. Conversely, if someone has made an early bad impression on you, you may refuse to believe subsequent evidence of that person's good qualities.

Schematic thinking can explain the primacy effect. Susan Fiske and Shelley Taylor (1991) argued that human thinkers are "cognitive misers."

Primacy effect The theory that early information about someone weighs more heavily than later information in influencing one's impression of that person.

If you were to hail this taxi in New York City, based on your assumptions about cab drivers you might never guess that this man from the Middle East holds an advanced degree in biology and is looking for a job at a university. Schemas can be useful, but they can also keep us from finding out what lies beneath the surface.

Self-fulfilling prophecy The process in which a person's expectation about another elicits behavior from the second person that confirms the expectation.

Stereotype A set of characteristics presumed to be shared by all members of a social category.

Instead of exerting ourselves to interpret every detail we learn about a person, we are stingy with our mental efforts. Once we have formed an impression about someone, we keep it, even if our first impressions were formed by jumping to conclusions or through prejudice.

If people are specifically warned to beware of first impressions, or if they are encouraged to interpret information about others slowly and carefully, the primacy effect can be weakened or even nullified (Luchins, 1957; Stewart, 1965). Generally speaking, however, the first impression is the lasting impression, and it can affect our behavior even when it is inaccurate. In one study, pairs of subjects played a competitive game (Snyder & Swann, 1978). The researchers told one member of each pair that his or her partner was either hostile or friendly. Players who were led to believe their partner was hostile behaved differently toward the partner than players led to believe their partner was friendly. In turn, those treated as hostile actually began to display hostility. In fact, these people continued to show hostility later on, when they were paired with new players who had no expectations about them. The expectation of hostility, it seems, produced actual aggressiveness, and this behavior persisted. When we bring about expected behavior in another person in this way, our impression becomes a **self-fulfilling prophecy** (see *Applying Psychology*).

STEREOTYPES A **stereotype** is a set of characteristics believed to be shared by all members of a social category. A stereotype is a special kind of schema that is based on almost any distinguishing feature, including sex, race, occupation, physical appearance, place of residence, and membership in a group or organization (Hilton & Von Hipple, 1996). When our first impressions of people are governed by a stereotype, we tend to infer things about them solely on the basis of their social category and to ignore facts about individual traits that are inconsistent with the stereotype. As a result, we may remember things about them selectively or inaccurately, thereby perpetuating our initial stereotype. For example, with a quick glance at almost anyone, you can classify that person as male or female. Once you have so categorized the person, you may rely more on your stereotype of that gender than on your own perceptions during further interactions with the person. Women have traditionally been viewed as more emotional, submissive, and gentle than men (Deaux & Kite, 1993; Williams & Best, 1990). Thus, you may *expect* a woman to have these qualities—and feel disappointed when you find she does not—merely because your impression is based on a simplistic stereotype rather than on reliable information about a particular individual.

Stereotypes can easily become the basis for self-fulfilling prophecies. One study paired college-aged men and women who were strangers to each other and arranged for each pair to talk by phone (Snyder, Tanke, & Berscheid, 1976). Before the call, each male was given a snapshot, presumably of the woman whom he was about to call. In fact, however, the snapshot was a randomly selected photo of either an attractive or unattractive woman. Attractiveness carries with it a stereotype that includes sociability and social adeptness. The males in the experiment therefore expected the attractive partners to display these qualities and the unattractive partners to be unsociable, awkward, and serious. These expectations produced radically different behavior in the men. Those who believed they were talking to an attractive woman were warm, friendly, and animated; in response, the women acted in a friendly, animated way. The other men spoke to their partners in a cold, reserved manner. In response, the women reacted in a cool, distant manner. Thus, the stereotype took on a life of its own as the

What is going on here? Would you want to stop and find out? If you held stereotypes about motorcyclists, you would probably want to speed away from this scene. In fact, though, these bikers were preparing for their annual Motorcycle Charity Run, a benefit for a local children's hospital.

APPLYING PSYCHOLOGY
SELF-FULFILLING PROPHECY IN THE CLASSROOM

Do the expectations that teachers hold for their students influence student performance? Thirty years of scientific research and over 400 studies show that teacher expectations *do* influence student performance (Cooper, 1993; Harris & Rosenthal, 1985). This finding has been termed the *Pygmalion effect* after the mythical sculptor who created the statue of a woman and then brought it to life.

Although the research does not suggest that high teacher expectations can turn an "F" student into an "A" student, it does indicate that both high and low expectations can exert a powerful influence on student achievement. How does this happen? Four categories of teacher behavior are important:

1. Climate—teachers tend to create a more supportive climate for high-expectancy students by smiling more often, making more frequent eye contact, and acting in a warm and friendly manner.

2. Feedback—teachers tend to provide more positive feedback to high-expectancy students, whereas they tend to be more critical of low-expectancy students.

3. Input—teachers provide more challenging tasks for high-expectancy students.

4. Output—teachers allow high-expectancy students to demonstrate their ability more often than low-expectancy students.

Through these types of actions, teachers influence the attitudes, behaviors, and ultimately the performance of their students. These effects can be especially harmful for students inaccurately perceived as having low ability.

So what can be done to make the Pygmalion effect work in a positive way? One approach is to make teachers aware of this process and to encourage them to establish high expectations for all of their students. This was the focus of a study of ninth-grade students labeled as "at-risk" and assigned to the lowest-level English classes (Weinstein et al., 1991). In a year-long intervention the researchers aimed at changing the classroom environment by increasing the teacher's expectations for the students. After one year, students in the intervention classrooms had higher English and history grades than comparable students who were not in intervention classrooms. After two years, the experimental students were less likely to drop out of high school.

Results from studies like these are encouraging and suggest that raising teachers' expectations can be an effective technique for improving the educational experience of at-risk students (Weinstein, Madison, & Kuklinski, 1995).

To learn more about the influence of teacher expectations on student performance, visit our website at **www.prenhall.com/morris**

---

perceptions of the men determined their behavior, which in turn subtly forced the women to conform to the stereotype.

So far, we have seen how people form impressions of other people and how those impressions affect their subsequent behavior. But social perception goes beyond simple impression formation. We also try to make sense out of people's behavior, to uncover the reasons they act as they do. This is the subject of the next section.

Attribution

Suppose you run into a friend at the supermarket. You greet him warmly, but he barely acknowledges you, mumbles "Hi," and walks away. You feel snubbed and try to figure out why he acted like that. Did he behave that way because of something in the situation? Perhaps you said something that offended him; perhaps he was having no luck finding the groceries he wanted; or perhaps someone had just blocked his way by leaving a cart in the middle

Attribution theory The theory that addresses the question of how people make judgments about the causes of behavior.

of an aisle. Or did something within him, some personal trait such as moodiness or arrogance, prompt him to behave that way?

EXPLAINING BEHAVIOR   Social interaction is filled with occasions like this one that invite us to make judgments about the causes of behavior. Especially when something unexpected or unpleasant occurs, we wonder about it and try to understand it. Social psychologists have discovered that we go about this process of assessment in predictable ways. Their findings and the principles derived from them form the basis of **attribution theory.**

An early attribution theorist, Fritz Heider (1958) argued that a simple or "naïve" explanation for a given behavior attributes that behavior to either internal or external causes, but not both. Thus, you might say a classmate's lateness was caused by his laziness (a personal factor—an internal attribution) *or* by traffic congestion (a situational factor—an external attribution).

How do we decide whether to attribute a given behavior to causes inside or outside a person? According to another influential attributional theorist, Harold Kelley (1967), we rely on three kinds of information about behavior in determining its cause: distinctiveness, consistency, and consensus. For example, if your instructor asks you to stay briefly after class so she can talk with you, you will probably try to figure out what lies behind her request by asking yourself three questions.

First, how *distinctive* is the instructor's request? Does she often ask other students to stay and talk (low distinctiveness), or is such a request unusual (high distinctiveness)? If she often asks students to speak with her, you will probably conclude that she has personal internal reasons for talking with you. But if her request is highly distinctive, you will probably conclude that something about you, not her, underlies her request.

Second, how *consistent* is the instructor's behavior? Does she regularly ask you to stay and talk (high consistency), or is this a first for you (low consistency)? If she has consistently made this request of you before, you will probably guess that this occasion is like those others. But if her request is inconsistent with past behavior, you will probably wonder whether some passing event—perhaps something you said in class—motivated her to request a private conference.

Finally, what is the *consensus* of others' similar behavior; Do your other instructors ask you to stay and talk with them (high consensus), or is this instructor unique in making such a request (low consensus)? If it is common for your instructors to ask to speak with you, this instructor's request is probably due to some external factor. But if she is the only instructor ever to ask to speak privately with you, it is probably something about this particular person—an internal motive or concern—that accounts for her behavior (Iacobucci & McGill, 1990).

If you conclude that the instructor has her own reasons for wanting to speak with you, you may feel mildly curious for the remainder of class, until you can find out what she wants. But if you think external forces—like your own actions—have prompted her request, you may worry about whether you are in trouble and nervously await the end of class.

BIASES IN ATTRIBUTIONS   When making an attribution, you are guessing about the true causes of a particular action. Research shows that these guesses are often vulnerable to a number of *biases*. For instance, imagine that you are at a party and you see an acquaintance, Ted, walk across the room carrying several plates of food and a drink. As he approaches his chair, Ted spills food on himself. You may attribute the spill to Ted's personal characteristics—he is clumsy. However, Ted is likely to make a very different attribution for the event. He will likely attribute the spill to an external factor—he was carrying too many other things. Your explanation for this behavior reflects the **fundamental attribution error**—the tendency to attribute the behavior of others to causes within themselves (Ross, 1977; Ross & Nisbett, 1991).

More generally, the fundamental attribution error is part of the *actor-observer effect*—the tendency to explain the behavior of others as caused by internal factors and the corresponding tendency to attribute one's own behavior to external forces (Fiske & Taylor, 1991). Thus, Ted, the actor, attributed his own behavior to an external source, whereas you, the observer, attributed the behavior to an internal source. Recall the examples used to introduce this chapter—those who risked their own safety to help others in Nazi Germany. From the perspective of an observer, our tendency is to attribute this behavior to personal qualities. Indeed, Robert Goodkind, chairman of the foundation that honored the rescuers, called for parents to "inculcate in our children the values of altruism and moral courage as exemplified by the rescuers." Clearly Goodkind was making an internal attribution for the heroic behavior. However, the rescuers themselves attribute their actions to external factors: "We were only ordinary students who did what we had to do."

A related class of biases is called **defensive attribution.** These types of attributions occur when we are motivated to present ourselves well, either to impress others or to feel good about ourselves (Agostinelli et al., 1992). One example of a defensive attribution is the *self-serving bias*, which is a tendency to attribute personal failure to external factors and personal success to internal factors. A number of studies have shown that we tend to credit our success to our personal attributes while chalking up failures to forces beyond our control (Schlenker & Weingold, 1992; Schlenker, Weingold, & Hallam, 1990). For example, students tend to regard exams on which they do well as good indicators of their abilities and exams on which they do poorly as bad indicators (Davis & Stephan, 1980). Similarly, teachers are more likely to assume responsibility for students' successes than for their failures (Arkin, Cooper, & Kolditz, 1980).

A second type of defensive attribution comes from thinking that people get what they deserve: Bad things happen to bad people, and good things happen to good people. This is called the **just-world hypothesis** (Lerner, 1980). When misfortune strikes someone, we often jump to the conclusion that the person deserved it, rather than giving full weight to situational factors that may have been responsible. Why do we do this? One reason is that it gives us the comforting illusion that such a thing could never happen to us. By reassigning the blame for a terrible crime from a chance event (something that could happen to us) to the victim's own negligence (a trait that *we*, of course, do not share), we delude ourselves into believing that we could never suffer such a misfortune (Chaiken & Darley, 1973). For instance, rape victims are perceived as having "asked for it" by wearing revealing clothes; AIDS victims are thought to have acquired the disease because of some immoral behavior (Bell, Kuriloff, & Lottes, 1994; Kristiansen & Giulietti, 1990).

ATTRIBUTION ACROSS CULTURES Historically, most of the research on attribution theory has been conducted in Western cultures. Do the basic principles of attribution apply to people in other cultures as well? The answer is *no*. For example, Japanese students studying in the United States usually explained failure as a lack of effort (an internal attribution) and attributed their successes to the assistance they received from others (an

Fundamental attribution error The tendency of people to overemphasize personal causes for other people's behavior and to underemphasize personal causes for their own behavior.

Defensive attribution The tendency to attribute our successes to our own efforts or qualities and our failures to external factors.

Just-world hypothesis Attribution error based on the assumption that bad things happen to bad people and good things happen to good people.

Proximity How close two people live to each other.

external attribution) (Kashima & Triandis, 1986). Research data also suggest that the fundamental attribution error may not be as pervasive as once believed. Researchers are finding that in some other cultures people are much less likely to attribute behavior to internal personal characteristics; they place more emphasis on the role of external, situational factors in explaining both their own behavior and that of others (Cousins, 1989; Markus & Kitayama, 1991). For example, a study comparing the descriptions of others given by Indian and American college students found that the Americans used three times as many trait descriptions (internal attributions) and the Indians used twice as many context-related explanations (Miller, 1984). This suggests that the Indian respondents were not overestimating the role of internal causal factors but were instead giving appropriate weight to the external factors that influence behavior.

Interpersonal Attraction

So far, we have seen how people form impressions of one another and judge the causes of their own and others' behavior. The next question we address is: When people meet, what determines whether they will like each other? This is the subject of much speculation and even mystification, with popular explanations running the gamut from fate to compatible astrological signs. Romantics believe that irresistible forces propel them toward an inevitable meeting with their beloved, but social psychologists take a more hard-headed view of the matter. They have found that attraction and the tendency to like someone else are closely linked to such factors as *proximity*, *physical attractiveness*, *similarity*, *exchange*, and *intimacy*.

PROXIMITY **Proximity** is usually the most important factor in determining attraction. The closer two people live to each other, the more likely they are to interact; the more frequent their interaction, the more they will tend to like each other. Conversely, two people separated by considerable geographic distance are not likely to run into each other, and thus have little chance to develop a mutual attraction. The proximity effect has less to do with simple convenience than with the security and comfort we feel with people and things that have become familiar. Familiar people are predictable and safe—thus more likable (Bornstein, 1989).

PHYSICAL ATTRACTIVENESS Physical attractiveness can powerfully influence the conclusions that we reach about a person's character. We generally give attractive people credit for more than their beauty. We presume them to be more intelligent, interesting, happy, kind, sensitive, moral, and successful than people who are not perceived as attractive. They are also thought to make better spouses and to be more sexually responsive (Dion, 1972; Feingold, 1992; Zuckerman, Miyake, & Elkin, 1995).

Not only do we tend to credit physically attractive people with a wealth of positive qualities, but we also tend to like them more than we do less attractive people. One reason is that physical attractiveness itself is generally considered a positive attribute (Baron & Byrne, 1991). We often perceive beauty as a valuable asset that can be exchanged for other things in social interactions. We may also believe that beauty has a "radiating effect"—that the glow of others' good looks enhances our own public image (Kernis & Wheeler, 1981).

Whatever its origins, our preoccupation with physical attractiveness has material consequences. Attractive people *do* tend to be happier, they make more money, and they are more likely to be treated leniently by teachers

(McCall, 1997). In addition, research has found that mothers of more attractive infants tend to show them more affection and play with them more often than mothers of unattractive infants (Langlois et al., 1995). In general, we tend to give good-looking people the benefit of the doubt: If they don't live up to our expectations during the first encounter, we give them a second chance, ask for or accept a second date, or seek further opportunities for interaction. These reactions can give attractive people substantial advantages in life, becoming a self-fulfilling prophecy. Physically attractive people may come to think of themselves as good or lovable because they are continually treated as if they are. Conversely, unattractive people may begin to see themselves as bad or unlovable because they have always been regarded that way—even as children.

Attraction and liking are closely linked to such factors as proximity, similar interests and attitudes, and rewarding behavior.

SIMILARITY Similarity of attitudes, interests, values, backgrounds, and beliefs underlies much interpersonal attractiveness (Buss, 1985; Tan & Singh, 1995). When we know that someone shares our attitudes and interests, we tend to have more positive feelings toward that person (Byrne, 1961); the higher the proportion of attitudes that two people share, the stronger the attraction between them (Byrne & Nelson, 1965). We value similarity because it is important to us to have others agree with our choices and beliefs. By comparing our opinions with those of other people, we clarify our understanding of and reduce our uncertainty about social situations. Finding that others agree with us strengthens our convictions and boosts our self-esteem (Suls & Fletcher, 1983).

If similarity is such a critical determinant of attraction, what about the notion that opposites attract? Aren't people sometimes attracted to others who are completely different from them? Extensive research has failed to confirm this notion. In long-term relationships, where attraction plays an especially important role, people overwhelmingly prefer to associate with other people who are similar to them (Buss, 1985).

In some cases, when people's attraction seems to be founded on their "differentness," research suggests that their critical qualities are not opposites but complements. *Complementary traits* are needs or skills that complete or balance each other (Dryer & Horowitz, 1997; Hendrick & Hendrick, 1992). For example, a person who likes to care for and fuss over others will be most compatible with a mate who enjoys receiving such attention. These people are not really opposites, but their abilities and desires complement each other to their mutual satisfaction. Complementarity almost always occurs between people who already share similar goals and values and are willing to adapt to each other. True opposites are unlikely even to meet each other, much less interact long enough to achieve such compatibility.

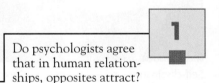

Do psychologists agree that in human relationships, opposites attract?

EXCHANGE According to the *reward theory of attraction*, we tend to like people who make us feel rewarded and appreciated. But the relationship between attraction and rewardingness is subtle and complex. For example, Aronson's (1994) gain-loss theory of attraction suggests that *increases* in rewarding behavior influence attractiveness more than constant rewarding behavior does. Say you were to meet and talk with a young man at three successive parties, and during these conversations that person's behavior toward you changed from polite indifference to overt flattery. You would be inclined to like this person more than if he or she had immediately started to praise you during the first conversation and kept up the stream of praise each time you met. The reverse also holds true: We tend to dislike people whose opinion of us changes from good to bad even more than we dislike those who consistently display a low opinion of us from our first encounter with them.

Exchange The concept that relationships are based on trading rewards among partners.

Equity Fairness of exchange achieved when each partner in the relationship receives the same proportion of outcomes to investments.

Intimacy The quality of genuine closeness and trust achieved in communication with another person.

Attitude Relatively stable organization of beliefs, feelings, and behavior tendencies directed toward something or someone—the attitude object.

Self-disclosure—revealing personal experiences and opinions—is essential to all close relationships.

The reward theory of attraction is based on the concept of **exchange.** In social interactions, two people exchange various goods and resources with each other. For example, you may agree to help a friend paint his apartment in exchange for his preparing dinner for you. Every exchange involves both rewards (you get a free dinner, he gets his apartment painted) and costs (you have to paint first, he has to cook you dinner). As long as both parties find their interactions more rewarding than costly, their exchanges will continue (Clore & Byrne, 1974; Lott & Lott, 1974). People do seem to "keep score" in their interactions, especially in the early stages of relationships (Clark & Mills, 1979).

Such exchanges work only insofar as they are fair or equitable. A relationship is based on **equity** when what one person "gets out of it" is equal to what the other gets (Walster, Walster, & Berscheid, 1978; von Yperen & Buunk, 1990). When exchanges are consistently unfair, the one who reaps fewer rewards feels cheated and the one who gains is apt to feel guilty. As a result, the pain and discomfort may undermine the attraction that once drew the two people together. People may come to like one another because of uncontrollable circumstances like proximity and physical attractiveness, but a relationship will only develop and be maintained through the deliberate efforts of both partners to be fair to each other.

INTIMACY When does liking someone become something more? Social psychologists have found that love depends on several critical processes beyond interpersonal attraction. The process of intimacy has sparked particular interest among relationship theorists. **Intimacy** is the quality of genuine closeness and trust achieved in communication with another person. When people communicate, they do more than just interact—they share their deep-rooted feelings and ideas. When you are first getting to know someone, you communicate about "safe," superficial topics like the weather, sports, or shared activities. As you get to know each other better over time, your conversation progresses to more personal subjects: your personal experiences, memories, hopes and fears, goals and failures (Altman & Taylor, 1973).

Intimate communication is based on *self-disclosure* (Prager, 1995). As you talk with friends, you disclose or reveal personal experiences and opinions that you might conceal from strangers. Because self-disclosure is only possible when you trust the listener, you will seek—and usually receive—a reciprocal disclosure to keep the conversation balanced. For example, after telling your roommate about something that embarrassed you, you may expect him or her to reveal a similar episode; you might even ask directly, "Has anything like that ever happened to you?" Such reciprocal intimacy keeps you "even" and makes your relationship more emotionally satisfying (Collins & Miller, 1994). The pacing of disclosure is important. If you "jump levels" by revealing too much too soon—or to someone who is not ready to make a reciprocal personal response—the other person will retreat and communication will go no further.

ATTITUDES

The phrase "I don't like his attitude" is a telling one. People are often told to "change your attitude" or make an "attitude adjustment." What does this mean? Just what are attitudes? How are they formed? How can they be changed?

The Nature of Attitudes

An **attitude** is a relatively stable organization of beliefs, feelings, and tendencies toward something or someone—the attitude object. Note that an attitude has three major components: *evaluative beliefs* about the object, *feelings* about the object, and *behavior tendencies* toward the object. Beliefs include facts, opinions, and our general knowledge about the object. Feelings encompass love, hate, like, dislike, and similar sentiments. Behavior tendencies refer to our inclinations to act in certain ways toward the object—to approach it, avoid it, and so on. For example, our attitude toward a political candidate includes our beliefs about the candidate's qualifications and positions on crucial issues and our expectations about how the candidate will vote on those issues. We also have feelings about the candidate—like or dislike, trust or mistrust. And because of these beliefs and feelings, we are inclined to behave in certain ways toward the candidate—to vote for or against the candidate, to contribute time or money to the candidate's campaign, to make a point of attending or staying away from rallies for the candidate, and so forth.

As we will see shortly, these three aspects of an attitude are very often consistent with one another. For example, if we have positive feelings toward something, we tend to have positive beliefs about it and to behave positively toward it. This does not mean, however, that our every action will accurately reflect our attitudes. For example, our feelings about going to dentists are all too often negative, yet most of us make an annual visit anyway. Let's look more closely at the relationship between attitudes and behavior.

ATTITUDES AND BEHAVIORS   The relationship between attitudes and behavior is not always straightforward. In a classic study, LaPiere (1934) traveled through the United States with a Chinese couple in the early 1930s—a time when prejudice against the Chinese was running high in the United States. He discovered that they were refused service at only one of the 250 hotels and restaurants they visited. Six months later, LaPiere sent a questionnaire to each of these establishments and asked whether they would serve Chinese people. Most said they would not. LaPiere therefore concluded that attitudes are not reliable predictors of actual behavior.

Subsequent research, however, suggests that attitudes *can* predict behavior—at least in some situations (Eagly, 1992; Kraus, 1995). Variables such as the strength of the attitude, how easily it comes to mind, how salient a particular attitude is in a given situation, and how relevant the attitude is to the behavior help determine whether a person will act in accordance with his or her attitude (Eagly & Chaiken, 1994). For example, LaPiere had measured attitudes toward Chinese people in general and then used that to predict specific behavior. If LaPiere had asked about attitudes toward the particular Chinese people who traveled with him rather than about Chinese people in general, the correlation between attitudes and behavior probably would have been higher.

Personality traits are also important. Some people consistently match their actions to their attitudes (Norman, 1975). Others have a tendency to override their own attitudes in order to behave properly in a given situation. As a result, attitudes predict behavior better for some people than others (Snyder & Tanke, 1976). People who rate highly on **self-monitoring** are especially likely to override their attitudes to behave in accordance with others' expectations. Before speaking or acting, high self-monitors observe the situation for cues about how they should react. Then they try to meet those "demands" rather than behave according to their own beliefs or sentiments. In contrast, low self-monitors express and act on their attitudes with great consistency, showing little regard for situational clues or constraints. Thus, a high self-monitor who disagrees with the politics of a fellow dinner guest may keep her thoughts to herself in an effort to be polite and agreeable, whereas a low self-monitor who disagrees might dispute the speaker openly, even though doing so might disrupt the social occasion (Snyder, 1987).

Self-monitoring The tendency for an individual to observe the situation for cues about how to react.

> **2** What is the relationship between attitudes and behavior?

Prejudice An unfair, intolerant, or unfavorable attitude toward a group of people.

Discrimination An unfair act or series of acts taken toward an entire group of people or individual members of that group.

Attitudes develop early, often through imitation. Can you recall learning positive or negative attitudes by observing or listening to your parents?

3 What is the difference between prejudice and discrimination? Do the two always occur together?

ATTITUDE DEVELOPMENT How do we acquire our attitudes? Where do they come from? Many of our most basic attitudes derive from early, direct personal experience. Children are rewarded with smiles and encouragement when they please their parents, and are punished through disapproval when they displease them. These early experiences give children enduring positive and negative attitudes (Oskamp, 1991). Attitudes are also formed by imitation. Children mimic the behavior of their parents and peers, acquiring attitudes even when no one is deliberately trying to influence their beliefs.

But parents are not the only source of attitudes. Teachers, friends, and even famous people are also important in shaping our attitudes. New fraternity or sorority members, for example, may model their behavior and attitudes on upper-class members. A student who idolizes a teacher may adopt many of the teacher's attitudes toward controversial subjects, even if they run counter to attitudes of parents or friends.

The mass media, particularly television, also have a great impact on the formation of attitudes in our society. Television bombards us with messages—not merely through its news and entertainment programs but also through commercials. Violence is commonplace in life . . . women are dependent on men . . . without possessions your life is empty, and so on. Without experience of their own against which to measure the merit of these messages, children are particularly susceptible to television as an influence on their social attitudes. One study found that white children in England who had little contact with nonwhites tended to associate race relations with conflicts and hostility more often than white children who lived in integrated neighborhoods (Hartmann & Husband, 1971). The only source of information for the first group of children was TV news reports that focused on the problems caused by integration.

Prejudice and Discrimination

Often used interchangeably, the terms *prejudice* and *discrimination* actually refer to different concepts. **Prejudice**—an attitude—is an unfair, intolerant, or unfavorable view of a group of people. **Discrimination**—a behavior—is an unfair act or a series of acts directed against an entire group of people or individual members of that group. To discriminate is to treat an entire class of people in an unfair way.

Prejudice and discrimination do not always occur together. It is possible to be prejudiced against a particular group without openly behaving in a hostile or discriminatory manner toward its members. A racist store owner may smile at a black customer, for example, to disguise opinions that could hurt his business. Likewise, many institutional practices can be discriminatory even though they are not based on prejudice. For example, regulations establishing a minimum height requirement for police officers may discriminate against women and certain ethnic groups whose average height falls below the arbitrary standard, even though the regulations do not stem from sexist or racist attitudes.

PREJUDICE Like attitudes in general, prejudice has three components: beliefs, feelings, and behavior tendencies. Prejudicial beliefs are virtually always stereotypes, and as mentioned earlier, reliance on stereotypes can lead to erroneous thinking about other people. When a prejudiced employer interviews an African American, for example, the employer may attribute to the job candidate all the traits associated with the African American stereotype. To make matters worse, qualities of the individual that do not match the stereotype are likely to be ignored or quickly forgotten (Allport, 1954).

For example, the employer may belittle the candidate's hard-earned college degree by thinking, "I never heard of that college. It must be an easy school if someone like this can get a degree there."

This attributional phenomenon is similar to the fundamental attribution error described earlier in this chapter, and is known as the *ultimate attribution error*. This error refers to the tendency for a person with stereotyped beliefs about a particular group of people to make internal attributions for their shortcomings and external attributions for their successes. Notice that in the example above the employer is making an external attribution (an easy school) for the college success of the African American job seeker. The other side of the ultimate attribution error is to make internal attributions for the failures of people who belong to groups we dislike. For instance, many white Americans believe that differences in income levels between white and black Americans are due to lack of ability or low motivation on the part of blacks (Kluegel, 1990).

Along with stereotyped beliefs, prejudicial attitudes are usually marked by strong emotions, such as dislike, fear, hatred, or loathing. Understandably, such feelings are likely to lead the individual to discriminate against the group in question.

SOURCES OF PREJUDICE   Many theories attempt to sort out the causes and sources of prejudice. According to the **frustration-aggression theory,** prejudice is the result of the frustrations experienced by the prejudiced group (Allport, 1954). As we saw in Chapter 9, Motivation and Emotion, under some circumstances frustration can spill over into anger and hostility. People who feel exploited and oppressed often cannot vent their anger against an identifiable or proper target, so they displace their hostility onto those even "lower" on the social scale than themselves in the form of prejudicial attitudes and discriminatory behavior. The people who are the victims of this displaced aggression become *scapegoats* and are blamed for the problems of the times.

Historically, for example, violence against Jews has often followed periods of economic unrest or natural catastrophe. Research on violence against African Americans in the South between 1882 and 1930 shows a strong relationship between the level of economic prosperity and the number of lynchings (Hepworth & West, 1988; Hovland & Sears, 1940). When cotton prices were low, there were more lynchings than when cotton prices were high. Similarly, African Americans in the United States have been scapegoats for the economic frustrations of some lower-income white Americans who feel powerless to improve their own condition. Latinos, Asian Americans, and women are also scapegoated—at times by African Americans. Like kindness, greed, and all other human qualities, prejudice is not restricted to a particular racial or ethnic group.

Another theory locates the source of prejudice in a bigoted or **authoritarian personality.** Adorno and his colleagues (1950) linked prejudice to a complex cluster of personality traits called *authoritarianism*. Authoritarian individuals tend to be rigidly conventional, favoring following the rules and abiding by tradition, and hostile to those who defy those norms (Stone, Lederer, & Christie, 1993). They respect and submit to authority and are preoccupied with power and toughness. Looking at the world through a lens of rigid categories, they are cynical about human nature, fearing, suspecting, and rejecting all groups other than those to which they belong. Prejudice is only one expression of their suspicious, mistrusting approach to life.

There are also cognitive sources of prejudice. As we saw earlier, people are "cognitive misers" who try to simplify and organize their social thinking

Frustration-aggression theory The theory that under certain circumstances people who are frustrated in their goals turn their anger away from the proper, powerful target toward another, less powerful target it is safer to attack.

Authoritarian personality A personality pattern characterized by rigid conventionality, exaggerated respect for authority, and hostility toward those who defy society's norms.

4. *The social norms should encourage contact.* In many cases, school desegregation took place in a highly charged atmosphere. Busloads of children arrived at their new schools only to face the protests of angry parents. These conditions clearly did not promote contact. In situations where contact is encouraged by the social norms or by those in authority, prejudicial attitudes are less likely to take hold.

In all these suggestions, the primary focus is on changing behavior, not attitudes. But changing behavior is often a fruitful first step toward changing attitudes. Still, attitudes can be difficult to budge because they are often hidden.

Attitude Change

A man watching TV on Sunday afternoon ignores scores of beer commercials but makes a note when a friend recommends a particular imported beer. A political speech convinces one woman to change her vote in favor of the candidate who made it but leaves her next-door neighbor determined to vote against the candidate. Why would a personal recommendation have greater persuasive power than an expensively produced television commercial? How can two people with similar views derive completely different messages from the same speech? What makes one attempt to change attitudes fail and another succeed? More generally, how and why do attitudes change, and how can we successfully resist attitude changes we do not want?

The answers to these questions depend to some extent on the technique used to influence our attitudes. We will look first at attempts to change attitudes through various kinds of persuasive messages.

THE PROCESS OF PERSUASION   To be persuaded, you must first pay attention to the message; then you must comprehend it; finally, you must accept it as convincing. Consider how advertising accomplishes each of these steps.

The first step in persuasion is to seize and retain the audience's attention. An ad must catch your attention, or you will "filter it out" along with all the other stimuli you ignore every hour of the day (Conen & Chakravarti, 1990). As the competition has stiffened, advertisers have become increasingly creative in seizing your attention. For example, ads that arouse emotions, especially feelings you want to act on, can be memorable and thus persuasive (Engel, Black, & Miniard, 1986). Humor, too, is an effective way to keep you watching or reading an entire ad you would otherwise ignore (Scott, Klein, & Bryant, 1990).

Once an ad grabs your attention, other techniques make you comprehend and accept its message. For example, more and more ads "hook" the audience by involving them in a narrative. A commercial might open with a dramatic scene or situation—for example, two people seemingly "meant" for each other but not yet making eye contact—and the viewer stays tuned to find out what happens. Some commercials even feature recurring characters and story lines so that each new commercial in the series is really the latest installment in a soap opera.

What if an ad is annoying? Surprisingly, even an ad that rubs you the wrong way can be effective because your irritation with it makes you remember the name of the product (Aaker & Bruzzone, 1985).

With so many clever strategies focused on seizing and holding your attention, how can you shield yourself from unwanted influences and resist persuasive appeals? One strategy for resisting persuasion is to analyze ads to identify which attention-getting strategies are at work. Make a game of deciphering the advertisers' "code" instead of falling for the ad's appeal. And

4 How do advertisers try to influence your behavior?

For an ad to affect our behavior, it must first attract our attention.

raise your standards for the kinds of messages that are worthy of your attention and commitment.

THE COMMUNICATION MODEL

The second and third steps in persuasion—comprehending and then accepting the message—are influenced by both the message itself and the way it is presented. The *communication model* of persuasion spotlights four key elements to achieve these goals: the source, the message itself, the medium of communication, and characteristics of the audience. Once they have seized your attention, persuaders manipulate each of these factors in the hope of changing your attitudes. Let us take each factor in turn as we consider what is known about effective persuasion.

The effectiveness of a persuasive message first depends on its *source*, the author or communicator who appeals to the audience to accept the message. Here credibility makes a big difference (McGuire, 1985). For example, we are less likely to change our attitude about the oil industry's antipollution efforts if the president of a major refining company tells us about them than if we hear the same information from an impartial commission appointed to study the situation.

Research indicates that the credibility of the source is most important when we are not inclined to pay attention to the message itself (Cooper & Croyle, 1984; Petty & Cacioppo, 1981, 1986a). In cases where we have some interest in the message, it is the message that plays the greater role in determining whether we change our attitudes (Petty & Cacioppo, 1986b). Researchers have discovered that we frequently tune out messages that contradict our own point of view. In addition, the more arguments a message makes in support of a position, the more effective that message is (Calder, Insko, & Yandell, 1974). Novel arguments are more persuasive than rehashes of old standbys, heard many times before.

Research has found that *fear* sometimes works well, especially in convincing people to get tetanus shots (Dabbs & Leventhal, 1966), to drive safely (Leventhal & Niles, 1965), and to take care of their teeth (Evans et al., 1970). But if the message generates too much fear, it will turn off the audience and have little persuasive effect (Worchel, Cooper, & Goethals, 1991).

Messages designed to persuade are more successful when they present both sides of an argument. A two-sided presentation generally makes the speaker seem less biased and thus enhances his or her credibility. We have greater respect and trust for a communicator who acknowledges that there is another side to a controversial issue.

When it comes to a choice of *medium*, writing is best suited to making people understand complex arguments, whereas videotaped or live media presentations are more effective with an audience that already grasps the gist of an argument (Chaiken & Eagly, 1976). Most effective, however, are face-to-face appeals or the lessons of our own experience. Salespeople who sell products door-to-door rely on the power of personal contact.

The most critical factors in changing attitudes—and the most difficult to control—have to do with *audience*. Attitudes are most resistant to change if (1) the audience has a strong commitment to its present attitudes, (2) those attitudes are shared by others, and (3) the attitudes were instilled during early childhood by such pivotal groups as the family.

The *discrepancy* between the contents of the message and the present attitudes of the audience also affects how well the message will be received. Up to a point, the greater the difference between the two, the greater the likelihood of attitude change. However, if the discrepancy is *too* great, the audience may reject the new information altogether. The

Michael Jordan just signed with another team

Michael Jordan knows the value of a good education. That's why he has joined with The College Fund. To give deserving students the chance for an education they otherwise might not receive. Please help the bright and talented students of tomorrow fulfill their dreams of becoming doctors, lawyers, scientists, or anything they want to be. Give to The College Fund. And join Michael Jordan's team for better education.

To support The College Fund,
call 1-800-332-UNCF.

The College Fund/UNCF
A mind is a terrible thing to waste.

This poster gets your attention with a photo of a sports celebrity, Michael Jordan. The message links Jordan to a cause, raising money for the United Negro College Fund.

Cultural truism The belief that most members of a society accept as self-evidently true.

Norm A shared idea or expectation about how to behave.

Cultural norm A behavioral rule shared by an entire society.

more often we learn cultural lessons through modeling and imitation. One result of such learning is the unquestioning acceptance of **cultural truisms**—beliefs that most members of a society accept as self-evidently true (Aronson, 1994).

We also learn cultural lessons through conditioning. We are rewarded (reinforced) for doing as our companions and fellow citizens do in most situations—for going along with the crowd. This social learning process is one of the chief mechanisms by which a culture transmits its central lessons and values. In the course of comparing and adapting our own behavior to that of others, we learn the norms of our culture. A **norm** is a shared idea or expectation about how to behave. Norms are often steeped in tradition and strengthened by habit. For example, it is "normal" in the United States for women to go into professions but not to become construction workers. When visiting a friend in the hospital, you may be surprised and uncomfortable if the nurse in attendance turns out to be a man. Lawmakers and politicians are likewise uncomfortable with images of women flying combat missions into enemy territory.

Cultural Assimilators

Cultures seem strange to us if their norms are very different from our own. It is tempting to conclude that *different* means "wrong," simply because unfamiliar patterns of behavior can make us feel uncomfortable. To transcend our differences and get along better with people from other cultures, we must find ways to overcome such discomfort. Because cultural norms are learned—not inherited—it is possible to *relearn* or otherwise modify our responses to unfamiliar cultures. For example, if you know that the hand gesture that signifies "okay" in our culture (putting the thumb and forefinger together to form a circle) means something offensive or obscene in another person's culture, you can avoid insulting that person simply by refraining from making that gesture.

One technique for understanding other cultures is the *cultural assimilator*, a strategy for perceiving the norms and values of another group (Baron & Graziano, 1991; Brislin et al., 1986). This technique teaches by example, asking students to explain why a member of another cultural or social group has behaved in a particular manner. For example, why do the members of a Japanese grade school class silently follow their teacher single file through a park on a lovely spring day? Are they afraid of being punished for disorderly conduct if they do otherwise? Are they naturally placid and compliant? Once you understand that Japanese children are raised to value the needs and feelings of others over their own selfish concerns, their orderly, obedient behavior seems not mindless but disciplined and considerate.

Cultural assimilators encourage us to remain open-minded about others' norms and values by challenging such cultural truisms as "My country is always the best" or "Our way is the *only* right way."

Conformity

We have been discussing **cultural norms,** the behavioral rules shared by entire societies. Our behavior is also shaped by the norms of smaller organizations, such as families, teams, and communities. Some norms are written into law or official rules; many more are unwritten expectations enforced by teasing, frowns, ostracism, and other informal means of punishment. Without norms, social life would be chaotic. With them, the behavior of other people becomes fairly predictable despite great differences in underlying attitudes and preferences.

Conformity implies a conflict between the individual and the group—a conflict that people resolve by yielding their own preferences or beliefs to the norms or expectations of a larger group. Uniformity should not be confused with conformity. For instance, millions of Americans drink coffee in the morning, but they do not do so as a matter of conforming. They drink coffee because they have learned to like and desire it.

Since the early 1950s, when Solomon Asch conducted the first systematic study of the subject, conformity has been a major topic of research in social psychology. Asch demonstrated in a series of experiments that under some circumstances people will conform to group pressures even if this forces them to deny obvious physical evidence. His studies ostensibly tested visual judgment by asking people to choose from a card with several lines of differing lengths the line most similar to the line on a comparison card (see Figure 15–1). The lines were deliberately drawn so that the comparison was obvious and the correct choice was clear. All but one of the subjects were confederates of the experimenter. On certain trials these confederates deliberately gave the same wrong answer. This put the lone real subject on the spot: Should he conform to what he knew to be a wrong decision and agree with the group, thereby denying the evidence of his own senses, or should he disagree with the group, thereby risking the social consequences of nonconformity?

Overall, subjects conformed on about 35 percent of the trials. There were large individual differences, however, and in subsequent research, experimenters discovered that two sets of factors influence the likelihood that a person will conform: characteristics of the situation and characteristics of the individual.

The *size* of the group is one situational variable that has been studied extensively. Asch (1951) found that the likelihood of conformity increased with expansion of group size until four confederates were present. After that point, the number of others made no difference in the subjects' tendency to ignore the evidence of their own eyes.

Another important situational factor is the degree of *unanimity* in the group. If just one confederate broke the perfect agreement of the majority by giving the correct answer, conformity among subjects in the Asch experiments fell from an average of 35 percent to about 25 percent (Asch, 1956). Apparently, having just one "ally" eases the pressure to conform. The ally does not even have to share the subject's viewpoint—just breaking the unanimity of the majority is enough to reduce conformity (Allen & Levine, 1971).

The *nature of the task* is still another situational variable that affects conformity. For instance, conformity has been shown to vary with the difficulty and the ambiguity of a task. When the task is difficult or poorly defined, conformity tends to be higher (Blake, Helson, & Mouton, 1956). In an ambiguous situation, individuals are less sure of their own opinion and more willing to conform to the majority view.

Personal characteristics also influence conforming behavior. The more an individual is attracted to the group, expects to interact with its members in the future, holds a position of relatively low status in the group, and does not feel completely accepted by the group, the more that person tends to conform. The fear of rejection apparently motivates conformity when a person scores high on one or more of these variables.

Sometimes we can be misled by what we *think* are group norms and conform our behavior to what is not, in fact, a norm. Perception, more than reality, for example, could be influencing the dangerous practice of "binge drinking" (see *Applying Psychology*).

Conformity Voluntarily yielding to social norms, even at the expense of one's own preferences.

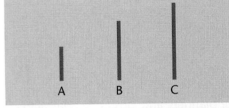

Figure 15–1 Asch's experiment on conformity. In Asch's experiment on *conformity*, subjects were shown a comparison card like the top one and asked to indicate which of the three lines on the bottom card was the most similar.

APPLYING PSYCHOLOGY
BELIEFS AND BINGE DRINKING ON COLLEGE CAMPUSES

Her friends believe that Leslie Baltz, a senior honors student at the University of Virginia, was following a school tradition of the "fourth-year fifth"—drinking a fifth of liquor to celebrate the last home football game. When friends found her that evening unconscious, they rushed her to the hospital. But it was too late. She died the next day, another victim of alcohol poisoning through binge drinking (Winerip, 1998).

Binge drinking, defined as taking five or more alcoholic drinks in a row, has been identified as the number one health hazard for college students (Wechsler et al., 1997). Not only do binge drinkers risk their lives, but their drinking has been linked to higher rates of drinking and driving, unplanned and unsafe sexual activity, physical and sexual assault, unintentional injuries, interpersonal problems, physical or cognitive impairment, and poor academic performance (Wechsler et al., 1994).

So alarming are the consequences of alcohol abuse, the creation of alcohol task forces and education programs has become a growth industry on college campuses. Yet attempts to reduce binge drinking by teaching social skills, increasing awareness of support systems, improving coping skills, and raising self-esteem have met with relatively little success. What more can be done?

It may be as simple as making students aware that most of their peers do *not* indulge in binge drinking and relying on their tendency to conform to social norms. However serious the problem may be, binge drinking is not as prevalent as many students believe it to be. Beliefs about the behavior of others are termed *normative beliefs*. Research shows that those students who believe that binge drinking is common are considerably more likely to try it. And students do

tend to think that "everybody does it"—they have given estimates as high as 70 percent (Gose, 1997). Yet a national survey indicates that the actual figure may be closer to 38 percent (Winerip, 1998). *Normative education* programs can help change student's perceptions about the prevalence of alcohol abuse by their peers. Several recent studies have shown that changing the normative beliefs reduces binge drinking, alcohol use, and other problems associated with substance use (Donaldson et al., 1994; Gose, 1997; Haines & Spears, 1996; Hansen & Graham, 1991; Hansen, 1993). As students' estimates of the numbers who drink decreases, so does the likelihood that they themselves will drink.

To learn more about binge drinking on college campuses, visit our website at **www.prenhall.com/ morris**

Why do Japanese schoolchildren behave in such an orderly way? How does your answer compare with the discussion of cultural influences?

CONFORMITY ACROSS CULTURES A Chinese proverb states that "if one finger is sore, the whole hand will hurt." In a collectivist culture such as China, community and harmony are very important. Although members of all societies show a tendency to conform, one might expect members of collectivist cultures to conform more frequently to the will of a group than members of noncollectivist cultures. Psychologists who have studied this question have utilized tests similar to those conducted by Solomon Asch. Recall that in Asch's study about 35 percent of American male college students agreed with a group's opinion that was obviously wrong. Asch's research was conducted in a relatively individualist culture. What if the same experiment were repeated in a more collectivist culture? (See *Highlights* in Chapter 9.)

Several researchers have performed just such studies. The levels of conformity in collectivist cultures often proved higher than those found by Asch. In collectivist societies as diverse as Fiji, Zaire, Hong Kong, Lebanon, Zimbabwe, Kuwait, Japan, and Brazil, conformity rates ranged from 25 percent among Japanese students to 51 percent among students in Zimbabwe (Smith & Bond, 1994). In a novel extension of this approach, Berry (1967) demonstrated that conformity was greater in farming societies (where members are more dependent on one another for long-term group survival) than in hunting and gathering societies (where people must exercise a good deal of independence to survive).

Not all the research data support the existence of a simple link between collectivism and conformity, however. Although Williams and Sogon (1984) reported that Japanese subjects showed a high tendency to conform when they were among friends, Frager (1970) found evidence of nonconformity among Japanese subjects when the confederates in the Asch situation were strangers. (In fact, in this situation, Japanese participants often deliberately gave the wrong response even when the majority opinion was correct.)

Given these somewhat conflicting data, what conclusion can we reach about the universality of social influence? The fact that rates of conformity in the Asch situation were relatively high across a variety of cultures suggests that there may be some kind of universal conformity norm. But the fact that conformity was especially high within collectivist societies suggests that the tendency toward conformity is heightened or lessened by a specific cultural context. As psychologists gain a better understanding of the differences among cultures, the answers to the questions "What is universal about social influence?" and "What is culturally determined?" should become clearer.

Compliance

Conformity is a response to pressure exerted by norms that are generally left unstated. In contract, **compliance** is a change of behavior in response to an explicit request. The demand may reflect a social norm, as when the doorman at a nightclub informs a jeans-clad prospective customer that proper attire is required. Or the request may be intended to satisfy the needs of the person making it: "Please help me fold the sheets."

Social psychologists have studied several techniques by which people can induce others to comply with their requests. One procedure is based on the so-called *foot-in-the-door effect*. Every salesperson knows that the moment a prospect allows the sales pitch to begin, the chances of making a sale improve greatly. The same effect operates in other areas of life: Once people have granted a small request, they are more likely to comply with a larger one.

In the most famous study of this phenomenon, Freedman and Fraser (1966) approached certain residents of Palo Alto, California, posing as members of a Committee for Safe Driving. They asked residents to place a large ugly sign reading "Drive Carefully" in their front yards. Only 17 percent agreed to do so. Then other residents were asked to sign a petition calling for more safe-driving laws. When these same people were later asked to place the ugly "Drive Carefully" sign in their yards, an amazing 55 percent agreed to do so. Compliance with the first small request more than tripled the rate of compliance with the larger request.

Why does the foot-in-the-door technique work so well? One possible explanation is that agreeing to the token act (signing the petition) realigns the subject's self-perception slightly to that of someone who favors the cause. When presented with the larger request, the subject then feels obligated to comply (Snyder & Cunningham, 1975).

Another strategy commonly used by salespeople is the *lowball procedure* (Cialdini et al., 1978). The first step is to induce a person to agree to do something. The second step is to raise the cost of compliance. Among new-car dealers, lowballing works like this: The dealer persuades the customer to buy a new car by reducing the price well below that offered by competitors.

Compliance Change of behavior in response to an explicit request from another person or group.

Once the customer has agreed to buy the car, however, the terms of the sale shift abruptly (e.g., the trade-in value promised by the used-car manager is cut), so that in the end the car is *more* costly than it would be at other dealerships. Despite the added costs, many customers follow through on their commitment to buy. Although the original inducement was the low price (the "lowball" the salesperson originally pitched), once committed, the buyer remains committed to the now-pricier vehicle.

Under certain circumstances, a person who has refused to comply with one request may be more likely to comply with a second. For example, if saying no to the first request made you feel guilty, you may say yes to something else. This phenomenon has been dubbed the *door-in-the-face effect* (Cialdini et al., 1975). In one study, researchers approached students and asked them to make an unreasonably large commitment: Would they counsel delinquent youths at a detention center for two years? Nearly everyone declined, thus effectively "slamming the door" in the face of the researcher making the request. On then being asked to make a much smaller commitment—supervising children during a trip to the zoo—many of the same students quickly agreed. The door-in-the-face effect may work because subjects interpret the smaller request as a concession by the experimenter, and feel pressured to comply in return.

Obedience

Compliance is agreement to change behavior in response to a request. **Obedience** is compliance with a demand. Like compliance, it is a response to an explicit message; but in this case, the message is a direct order, generally from a person in authority, such as a police officer, principal, or parent, who can back up the command with some sort of force if necessary. Obedience embodies social influence in its most direct and powerful form.

Several studies by Stanley Milgram, discussed in Chapter 1, The Science of Psychology, showed how far many people will go to obey someone in authority (Milgram, 1963). Recall from that chapter that subjects who agreed to participate in what they believed was a learning experiment administered what they thought were severe electrical shocks to the "learners." What factors influence the degree to which people will do what they are told? Studies in which people were asked to put a dime in a parking meter by people wearing uniforms shows that one important factor is the amount of *power* vested in the person giving the orders. People obeyed a guard whose uniform looked like that of a police officer more often than they obeyed a man dressed either as a milkman or as a civilian. Another factor is *surveillance*. If we are ordered to do something and then left alone, we are less likely to obey than if we are being watched. This seems to be true especially when the order involves an unethical act. Most of the subjects still put a dime in the meter when the police impersonator was out of sight, but Milgram found that his "teachers" were less willing to give severe shocks when the experimenter was out of the room.

Milgram's experiments revealed other factors that influence a person's willingness to follow orders. When the victim was in the same room as the "teacher," obedience dropped sharply. When another "teacher" was present who refused to give shocks, obedience also dropped. But when responsibility for an act was shared, so that the person was only one of many doing it, the degree of obedience was much greater.

Why do people willingly obey an authority figure, even if it means violating their own principles? Milgram (1974) thought that people feel obligated to those in power, first, because they respect their credentials and assume that they know what they are doing, and second, because often they have established trust with the people in authority by agreeing to do whatever they ask. Once this happens, participants may feel conflicted over what they are doing, but manage through rationalization to "forget" about it, to push the conflict aside, and thus minimize it. The essence of obedience, says Milgram, is that people come to see themselves as the agents of *another* person's wishes and therefore not responsible for the obedient actions or their consequences. Once this shift in self-perception has occurred, obedience follows, because in their own minds, they have relinquished control of their actions.

Milgram's analysis emphasizes the *power of the situation*: Once participants volunteered to take part in the study, they became caught up in the bizarre circumstances of the experiment and felt compelled to respond to external forces (the experimenter's commands) rather than internal ones (their own moral opposition to harming others). An alternative explanation was offered by Nissani (1990), who argued that obedient participants do not succumb to situational forces but rather fail to *perceive* the situation correctly. Thus, in Milgram's study, the participants began with the belief that the experiment would be safe and the experimenter would be trustworthy. When these assumptions proved false—when the experiment turned out to be dangerous and the experimenter disregarded the victim's obvious suffering—the participant's assumptions were invalidated. But it is hard—sometimes impossible—to change one's beliefs and assumptions quickly, in spite of irrefutable evidence. The real emotional struggle for the obedient participants, Nissani argues, may not have been in deciding whether to obey malevolent orders, but rather in recognizing that a trusted authority figure proved to be treacherous.

SOCIAL ACTION

The various kinds of social influence we have just discussed may take place between two people, in groups of three or more, or even when no one else is physically present. We refrain from playing our stereo at full volume when our neighbors are sleeping, comply with jury notices that we receive in the mail, and obey traffic signals even when no one is on the road to enforce the social norms that dictate these actions. We now turn our attention to processes that *do* depend on the presence of other people. Specifically, we will examine processes that occur when people interact one-on-one and in groups. The social actions we consider next are *deindividuation, helping behavior, group decision making,* and *organizational behavior*.

Deindividuation

We have seen several cases of social influence in which people act differently in the presence of others than they would if they were alone. The most striking and frightening instance of this phenomenon is *mob behavior*. Some well-known violent examples of mob behavior are the beatings and lynchings of African Americans, the looting that sometimes

Mob behavior can be explained in part by *deindividuation:* The more anonymous people feel in a group, the less responsible they feel as individuals.

An example of *altruistic behavior.* Civilians help put out a fire in a California shop without expecting reward or recognition for their action.

and personalities were similar to a victim's, they were more likely to help, even if that meant jeopardizing their own safety (Krebs, 1975).

Mood also makes a difference. A person in a good mood is more likely to help another in need than is someone who is in a neutral or bad mood. Researchers demonstrated this by leaving a dime in the scoop of a pay phone to put the finder in a good mood (Isen & Levin, 1972). Participants finding the dime were much more likely than other participants to help a confederate who dropped a folder full of papers on the sidewalk near the phone booth. Other research indicates that individuals who *fear embarrassment* are less likely to help (McGovern, 1976). Mistakenly offering help to someone who does not really need it can be highly embarrassing. Finally, when others are watching, people who score high on the need for approval are more likely to help than are low scorers (Satow, 1975).

HELPING BEHAVIOR ACROSS CULTURES   People often assume that there is a "helping personality," or a single personality trait that determines who is helpful and who is not. We have seen that this is unlikely; several conditions, both individual and situational, combine to determine when help will be offered. Similarly, it's doubtful that there is such a thing as a "helpful culture"—that is, a society, nation, or group whose members are invariably "more helpful" than those of other groups. Psychologists have instead focused on the cultural factors that make helping more or less likely to take place.

Individualism/collectivism is an important dimension in this area: It seems plausible that members of individualistic cultures feel less obligated to help other people than members of collectivist cultures do. A study using Indian and American subjects investigated this intuitive conclusion (Miller, Bersoff, & Harwood, 1990). Participants were presented with helping scenarios involving either a stranger, a friend, or a close relative whose need was either minor, moderate, or extreme. There were no cultural differences in cases of extreme need; members of both groups reported being equally willing to help. But the two groups did differ in cases of minor need; almost three times as many Indians (collectivist culture) as Americans (individualist culture) felt obligated to help in a scenario involving a close friend or a stranger asking for minor assistance.

Even within collectivist cultures, however, the prediction of when help will be offered can be problematic (Triandis, 1994). Some members of collectivist societies are reluctant to offer help to anyone outside of their ingroup; they are therefore less likely to help strangers. Other cultures treat a stranger as a member of their group until that person's exact status can be determined.

Group Decision Making

Our society tends to turn important decisions over to groups. In the business world, key decisions are often made around a conference table rather than behind one person's desk. In politics, major policy decisions are seldom vested in just one person; groups of advisers, cabinet officers, committee members, or aides meet to deliberate and forge a course of action. In the courts, a defendant may request a trial by jury, and for some serious crimes, a jury trial is required by law. And, of course, the nine-member U.S. Supreme Court renders group decisions on legal issues affecting the entire nation.

GROUP POLARIZATION   Why are so many decisions entrusted to groups rather than to individuals? For one thing, we assume that an individual acting alone is more likely to take risks than a group considering the same issue.

The assumption that groups make more conservative decisions than individuals remained unchallenged until the early 1960s. At that time, James Stoner (1961) designed an experiment to test this idea. He asked subjects individually to counsel imaginary people who had to choose between a risky but potentially rewarding course of action and a conservative and less rewarding alternative. Next, the advisers met in small groups to discuss each decision until they reached unanimous agreement. Stoner and many other social psychologists were surprised to find that the groups consistently proposed a riskier course of action than that counseled by the group members working alone. This phenomenon is known as the **risky shift.**

Subsequent research has shown that the risky shift is simply one aspect of a more general group phenomenon called **polarization**—the tendency for individuals to become more extreme in their attitudes as a result of group discussion. Groups that begin deliberations on a fairly risky note will move further in that direction during discussion than groups inclining to be cautious as they consider an issue (Fraser, 1971).

What causes polarization in decision-making groups? First of all, people discover during discussion that the other group members share their views to a greater degree than they realized. Then, in an effort to be seen in a positive light by the others, at least some group members become strong advocates for what is shaping up to be the dominant sentiment in the group. Arguments leaning toward one extreme or the other not only reassure people that their initial attitudes are correct but also intensify those attitudes so that the group as a whole becomes more extreme in its position. If you refer a problem to a group to ensure that it will be resolved in a cautious, conservative direction, you should make sure that the members of the group hold cautious and conservative views in the first place.

THE EFFECTIVENESS OF THE GROUP Another reason for assigning so many important problems to groups is the assumption that the members of the group will pool their skills and expertise, and therefore solve the problem more effectively than would any individual member working alone. The adage that "Two heads are better than one" reflects this way of thinking.

In fact, groups are more effective than individuals only under specific circumstances. According to Steiner (1972), the effectiveness of a group depends on three factors: (1) the nature of the task, (2) the resources of the group members, and (3) the interaction among group members. There are many different kinds of *tasks*, each of which demands specific kinds of skills. If the requirements of the task match the skills of the group members, the group is likely to be more effective than any single individual.

Even if task and personnel are perfectly matched, however, the ways in which the people *interact* in the group may reduce the group's efficiency. For example, high-status individuals tend to exert more influence in groups, regardless of their problem-solving abilities (Torrance, 1954).

Another factor is group *size*. The larger the group, the more likely it is to include someone who has the skills needed to solve a difficult problem. On the other hand, it is much harder to coordinate the activities of a large group than those of a small group. **Social loafing** refers to the tendency of people to exert less effort on a task when working in a group than when working individually (Karau & Williams, 1993).

Still another variable is the *cohesiveness* of a group. When the people in the group like one another and feel committed to the goals of the group, cohesiveness is high. Under these conditions, members may work hard for

Risky shift Greater willingness to take risks in decision making in a group than independent individuals.

Polarization Shift in attitudes by members of a group toward more extreme positions than the ones held before group discussion.

Social loafing The tendency of people to exert less effort on a task when working in a group than when working individually.

Great person theory The theory that leadership is a result of personal qualities and traits that qualify one to lead others.

the group, spurred on by high morale. But cohesiveness can undermine the quality of group decision making. If the group succumbs to *groupthink*, according to Irvine Janis (1982), strong pressure to conform prevents people in a cohesive group from expressing critical ideas of the emerging consensus. In such a group, amiability and morale supercede judgment. Members with doubts may hesitate to express them. The result may be disastrous decisions—such as the Bay of Pigs invasion, the Watergate cover-up, or the go-ahead for the *Challenger* space flight (Kruglanski, 1986).

LEADERSHIP   Every group has a leader, but how do group leaders come to the fore? For many years the predominant answer to this question was the **great person theory,** which states that leaders are extraordinary people who assume positions of influence and then shape events around them. In this view, individuals like George Washington, Winston Churchill, and Nelson Mandela were "born leaders" who would have led any nation at any time in history.

Most historians and psychologists now regard this theory as naive because it ignores social and economic factors. An alternative theory holds that leadership emerges when the right person is in the right place at the right time. For instance, in the later 1950s and early 1960s, Dr. Martin Luther King, Jr., rose to lead the black civil rights movement. Dr. King was clearly a "great person"—intelligent, dynamic, eloquent, and highly motivated. Yet had the times not been right, according to this theory, it is doubtful that he would have been as successful as he was.

Recently, social scientists have argued that there is more to leadership than either the great person theory or the right-place-at-the-right-time theory implies. According to the *transactional view*, a number of factors interact to determine who becomes the leader of a group. The leader's traits, certain aspects of the situation in which the group finds itself, and the response of the group and the leader to each other are all important considerations. Fred Fiedler's *contingency model* of leader effectiveness is based on such a transactional view of leadership (Fiedler, 1967, 1978, 1993).

According to Fiedler, a number of factors affect the success of a leader. Personal characteristics are important, and Fiedler thinks of them in terms of two contrasting *leadership styles*. One kind of leader is *task-oriented*, concerned with doing the task well even at the expense of worsening relationships among group members. Other leaders are *relationship-oriented*, concerned with maintaining group cohesiveness and harmony. Which style is most effective depends on three sets of factors. One is the nature of the *task*; whether it is clearly structured or ambiguous. The second consideration is the *relationship* between leader and group: whether the leader has good or bad personal relations with the group members. The third consideration is the leader's ability to exercise great or little *power* over the group.

Fiedler has shown that if conditions are either very favorable (good leader-member relations, structured tasks, high leader power) or very unfavorable (poor leader-member relations, unstructured task, low leader power) for the leader, the most effective leader is the one who is task-oriented. However, when conditions within the group are only moderately favorable for the leader, the most effective leader is one who is concerned about maintaining good interpersonal relations.

Fiedler's view of leadership, which has received a great deal of support from research conducted in the laboratory as well as in real-life settings, clearly indicates that there is no such thing as an ideal leader for all situations. "Except perhaps for the unusual case," he states, "it is simply not

One theory of leadership holds that the particularly effective leader is the right person in the right place at the right time. For the American civil rights movement, Martin Luther King, Jr. was such a leader.

meaningful to speak of an effective or of an ineffective leader; we can only speak of a leader who tends to be effective in one situation and ineffective in another" (Fiedler, 1967, p. 261).

LEADERSHIP ACROSS CULTURES We have seen that some leaders are primarily task-oriented, whereas others are more relationship-oriented. This distinction seems to be a main operating principle in most work groups in the United States: Someone explicitly appointed manager, foreperson, or crew chief is charged with making sure the job gets done, whereas someone else usually emerges informally to act as the relationship-oriented specialist who tells jokes, remembers everyone's birthday, smoothes disputes, and generally maintains morale (Bales, 1951). In the Western world, this division of leadership is often the primary operating mode of both formal work groups and less formal social groups. Indeed, it seems sensible, but it is not the only approach to leadership. Consider a collectivist culture that values cooperation and interdependence among group members. In such an environment, it is unlikely that individuals would emerge to serve specific functions within a group. Although one member may be named "the manager," there is less need for individuals to have clearly defined roles as "this type of leader" or "that type of leader" because the emphasis is always on the group's goals and the group's output.

Leadership in American businesses is presently being transformed through the introduction of a management style that has proved successful in Japan and other Eastern collectivist cultures (Dean & Evans, 1994; McFarland, Senn, & Childress, 1993). This approach emphasizes input from all group members regarding decision making, small work teams that promote close cooperation among members, and a style of leadership in which managers receive much the same treatment as any other employee. In the West, it is not uncommon for executives to have their own parking spaces, dining facilities, fitness and social clubs, as well as separate offices and independent schedules. Most Japanese executives consider this privileged style of management very strange. In many Eastern cultures, managers and executives share the same facilities as their workers, hunt for parking spaces like everyone else, and eat and work side by side with their employees. Interestingly, the Japanese model has effectively combined the two leadership approaches—task-oriented and relationship-oriented—into a single overall style. By being a part of the group, the leader can simultaneously work toward and direct the group's goals, while also contributing to the group's morale and social climate. Combining these roles is an effective strategy for Japanese leaders in such diverse workplaces as banks, bus companies, shipyards, coal mines, and government offices (Misumi, 1985).

Organizational Behavior

The places where we work and the various organizations to which we belong shape much of our behavior. **Industrial/organizational (I/O) psychology** spotlights the influence on human interaction of large, complex organizational settings, with special emphasis on behavior in the workplace.

PRODUCTIVITY I/O psychologists focus on practical problems such as how to reduce employee turnover, improve worker morale, and increase productivity. One of the first studies of the relationship between productivity and working conditions was conducted in the late 1920s by Elton Mayo and his colleagues, who gradually increased the lighting in the Western Electric Hawthorne plant in Cicero, Illinois. The researchers were testing the hypothesis that better lighting would boost worker output. But their results showed something else

Industrial/organizational (I/O) psychology The area of psychology concerned with the application of psychological principles to the problems of human organizations, especially work organizations.

Hawthorne effect The principle that people will alter their behavior because of researchers' attention and not necessarily because of any treatment condition.

entirely: Productivity increased with better lighting, too much lighting, and too little lighting. In what has become known as the **Hawthorne effect,** the workers' behavior changed merely because of the researcher's attention, not as a function of any specific manipulations of workplace conditions.

The methods of Mayo's team have since come under criticism (Parsons, 1974; 1992), but their study was one of the first to highlight the importance of psychological and social factors on behavior in the workplace. Since the 1930s, I/O psychologists have attempted to analyze that relationship in more specific terms. For example, workers whose jobs call for a greater variety of skills are more likely to think of their jobs as meaningful and to exhibit increased motivation and satisfaction; and workers whose jobs entail more autonomous activity generally perceive their jobs as responsible and produce work of a higher quality (Melamed et al., 1995). Thus, motivation, satisfaction, and productivity in the workplace can all be improved by making the right changes in job components.

Research by I/O psychologists has also found that small, cohesive work groups are more productive than large, impersonal ones. Putting this idea into practice, managers of assembly-line workers have developed the *autonomous work group*, replacing the massive assembly line with small groups of workers who produce an entire unit (a whole car, for instance) and periodically alternate their tasks. Additional benefits derived from this approach include greater worker satisfaction, higher-quality output, and decreased absenteeism and turnover (Pearson, 1992).

COMMUNICATION AND RESPONSIBILITY The way communications are handled within an organization also has an impact on organizational efficiency and the attitudes of its members. In organizations where members communicate with just one person in authority, for instance, the communications system becomes centralized. This type of communications scheme typically works well in solving simple problems; complex problems, on the other hand, are better handled in a decentralized way, with group members freely communicating with one another (Porter & Roberts, 1976).

I/O psychologists have also examined the issue of assigning responsibility for key decisions to work groups. Although some groups make better decisions than others, it turns out that group decision making in general enhances membership satisfaction (Cotton, 1993). If individuals believe that they had an input into the decision, they are more satisfied with the outcome and their membership in the group. However, the evidence also shows that increasing the number of people who participate in the decision-making process does *not* lead to increased productivity.

SUMMARY

Social psychology is the scientific study of how the thoughts, feelings, and behaviors of one individual are influenced by the real, imagined, or inferred behavior or characteristics of other people. Research in social psychology has concentrated on four topics: social cognition, attitudes, social influence, and social action.

SOCIAL COGNITION

In thinking about others, we organize our thoughts and feelings to enhance our control and effectiveness in social interactions.

Impression Formation

When forming impressions of others, we rely on schemata, sets of expectations and beliefs about different categories of people. Impressions are also affected by the order in which information is acquired. According to the **primacy effect,** first impressions are the strongest. As "cognitive misers," we avoid wasting thought and judge people according to simplistic concepts. One such concept is the **stereotype,** a set of characteristics we presume is shared by all members of a social category or group. Biased treatment of others can bring about the very behavior one expects through the effects of the **self-fulfilling prophecy.**

Attribution

Attribution theory holds that people seek to understand one another by making judgments about the causes of behavior. These attributions can be either internal or external. One theorist maintains that attributions are made by analyzing the distinctiveness, consistency, and consensus of a particular behavior pattern. Biases in perception can lead to the **fundamental attribution error,** in which personal (internal) forces are overemphasized as influences on other people's behavior and situational (external factors) are given far more weight in accounting for our own behavior. Just the opposite goes on when we seek to explain our own behavior. **Defensive attribution** motivates us to explain our own actions in ways that protect our self-esteem: We tend to attribute our successes to internal factors and our failures to external factors. The **just-world hypothesis** may lead us to blame the victim when bad things happen to other people.

Interpersonal Attraction

People are more attracted to each other when **proximity** brings them into frequent contact. We also like people because of physical attractiveness; similarity of attitudes, interests, and values; and rewarding **exchanges** that are based on **equity.** Love is an experience based on such factors as **intimacy** and *trust*.

ATTITUDES

An **attitude** is a relatively stable organization of one's thoughts, feelings, and behavior tendencies toward something or someone—the attitude object.

The Nature of Attitudes

Attitudes can't always predict behavior, especially if one's actions and expressions are influenced by other factors like **self-monitoring.** Attitudes are acquired through learning and developed through experience.

Prejudice and Discrimination

Prejudice is an unfair negative attitude directed against a group and its members; **discrimination** is behavior based on prejudice. Prejudiced beliefs often cause us to make the ultimate attribution error about others, attributing failure to internal factors and success to external factors. Prejudice can be reduced by encouraging contact between groups of equal status, one-on-one contacts, and participation in cooperative enterprises, and by changing social norms. One explanation of the roots of prejudice is the **frustration-aggression theory,** which states that people who feel exploited and oppressed displace their hostility toward the powerful onto people who are "lower" on the social scale than they are. Another theory links prejudice to the **authoritarian personality,** a rigidly conformist and bigoted personality type marked by exaggerated respect for authority and hostility toward those who defy society's norms. A third theory proposes a cognitive source of prejudice—oversimplified thinking about classes of people

and the world. Finally, conformity to the prejudices of one's social group or society explains much individual prejudice. **Racism** is prejudice and discrimination directed at a particular racial group. Although many people believe that racial prejudice is a thing of the past, **modern racism** is reflected by agreement with statements that civil rights groups are too extreme or that African Americans receive more respect and benefits than they deserve. **Institutional racism** is discrimination that occurs because of the overall effect of institutions and policies.

Attitude Change

Attitudes are sometimes changed in response to new experiences and persuasive efforts. The first step in the persuasive process is to get the audience's attention. Then, the task is to get the audience to comprehend and accept the message. According to the communication model, persuasion is a function of the *source*, the *message* itself, the *medium* of communication, and the characteristics of the *audience*. Attitudes may also be changed when new actions contradict preexisting attitudes (**cognitive dissonance**), according to the cognitive dissonance model.

SOCIAL INFLUENCE

Social influence refers to the idea that the presence and actions of others can control our perceptions, attitudes, and actions.

Cultural Influence

The **culture** in which we are immersed—all the tangible products of our society as well as its shared beliefs and values—teaches us what to value and how to behave. Culture dictates differences in beliefs, diet, dress, and personal space. In the course of adapting our behavior to that of others, we learn the **norms** of our culture. We accept **cultural truisms** without questioning their validity.

Cultural Assimilators

Cultures may seem strange to us if their norms are different from ours. Through techniques like the *cultural assimilator*, however, we can learn to understand and accept the perspective of people from different cultures.

Conformity

Besides **cultural norms,** the behavioral rules shared by an entire society, there are norms that pertain to smaller groups within the society, and these, too, shape our behavior. Voluntary yielding of one's own preferences or beliefs to the norms of a larger group is called **conformity.** Research by Solomon Asch and others has shown that characteristics of the situation and characteristics of the individual influence the likelihood of conformity.

Compliance

Compliance is a change in behavior in response to an explicit request from another person or group. Some techniques used to get others to comply are the *foot-in-the-door effect*, the *lowball procedure*, and the *door-in-the-face effect*.

Obedience

Classic work by Stanley Milgram showed that many participants were willing to obey orders to administer harmful shocks to other people. This **obedience,** or compliance to a command, was more in evidence when the authority figure was physically close and apparently legitimate, and when the victim was distant and thus easier to punish. According to Milgram, obedience is brought on by the constraints of the situation, but another interpretation holds that participants fail to perceive the situation correctly.

SOCIAL ACTION

Social actions depend on the presence of other people—as victims, recipients, and sources of influence.

Deindividuation

Immersion in a group may lead to **deindividuation,** the loss of a sense of personal responsibility that makes possible violent, irresponsible behavior. Mob behavior also gains momentum from the snowball effect and from the protection of anonymity in a group.

Helping Behavior

Help without expectation of reward is considered **altruistic behavior.** Helping is constrained by situational factors such as the presence of other passive bystanders, a phenomenon known as the **bystander effect,** and the ambiguity of a situation. Personal characteristics that induce helping are empathy with the victim and good mood.

Group Decision Making

Groups are often entrusted with problem solving in the expectation that they will be more careful and responsible than lone individuals. Research on the **risky shift**

and the broader phenomenon of **polarization** shows that group deliberation actually enhances members' tendencies toward extreme solutions, leaning toward greater risk or caution. Group effectiveness depends on such factors as the nature of the task, the group's resources, and how members interact. The tendency of people to exert less effort when working in a group than when working on their own is known as **social loafing.** Group cohesiveness can lead to *groupthink*, a pattern of thought characterized by self-deception and the manufacture of consent through conformity to group values.

According to the **great person theory,** leadership is a function of personal traits that qualify one to lead others. An alternative theory attributes leadership to being in the right place at the right time. According to the *transactional view*, traits of the leader and traits of the group interact with certain aspects of the situation to determine what kind of leader will come to the fore. Fred Fiedler focused on two contrasting leadership styles (task-oriented and relationship-oriented). The effectiveness of each one depends on the nature of the task, the relationship of the leader with group members, and the leader's power over the group.

Organizational Behavior

Industrial/organizational (I/O) psychology studies behavior in organizational environments like the workplace. Studies of productivity have revealed that worker output increases as a result of researcher's attention, a phenomenon called the **Hawthorne effect.** I/O findings have also led organizations to establish *autonomous work groups* to replace less efficient assembly-line arrangements. Productivity and morale may also be improved by increasing worker responsibility and facilitating communication in the workplace.

REVIEW QUESTIONS

MULTIPLE CHOICE AND SHORT ANSWER

1. The scientific study of how thoughts, feelings, and behavior of one individual are influenced by the real, imagined, or inferred behavior or characteristics of other people is called _____ psychology.

2. When we first meet someone, we use cues to fit that person into preexisting categories called _____. Sometimes we think and behave in accordance with a _____, a set of characteristics thought to be

shared by all the people who belong to a particular social group.

3. The _____ effect exists to the extent that the first information we receive about someone weighs more heavily than later information in the impressions we form.

4. The inferences we make about the causes of people's behavior is addressed by:
   a. psychology   c. attribution theory
   b. social psychology   d. cognitive dissonance

5. Which of the following has *not* been established as a factor that encourages people to like each other?
   a. proximity
   b. attractiveness
   c. complementary attitudes and interests
   d. intimacy

6. A(n) _____ is a fairly stable organization of beliefs, feelings, and behavioral tendencies directed toward some object such as a person or group.

7. True or False: The best way to predict behavior is to measure attitudes.

8. Prejudice and discrimination can be formed and sustained by people's attempts to _____ in society.

9. _____ _____ theory maintains that a state of unpleasant tension arises from the clashing of two incompatible cognitions.

10. When there is a discrepancy between a person's behavior and attitudes, it is often easier for the person to change _____ to reduce the dissonance.
    a. attitudes
    b. behavior
    c. neither attitudes nor behavior
    d. intentions

11. Match each of the following terms with its definition:

    _____ Social influence
    _____ Compliance
    _____ Obedience
    _____ Conformity

    a. Voluntarily yielding to social norms, even at the expense of one's own preferences
    b. A change of behavior in response to a command from another person
    c. A change of behavior in response to an explicit request from another person or from a group
    d. Any actions performed by one or more persons to change the attitudes, behavior, or feelings of others

12. If group members are inclined to take risks, then the group decision is likely to be riskier than one arrived at by individuals acting alone. This phenomenon is known as the _____ _____.

13. A shift in attitudes by members of a group toward more extreme positions than those they held before group discussion is called _____.

14. The effectiveness of a group depends on three factors: (1) the nature of the _____, (2) the resources of the group members, and (3) the _____ among group members.

15. True or False: All groups have a leader, whether a formal one or an informal one.

16. True or False: Worker satisfaction is not related to the position a person occupies within an organization.

CRITICAL THINKING AND APPLICATIONS

1. What is a self-fulfilling prophecy? How does this concept apply to human relationships?

2. What do we mean by internal versus external attribution? Which approach would you be more likely to adopt in trying to explain other people's behavior?

3. What are some of the key factors that determine interpersonal attraction according to social psychologists?

4. Think of an advertisement that influenced your decision to purchase something. What kind of message did the ad convey? How was this message communicated? Why did you respond to it? Were you aware at the time that the ad was designed to elicit this response? Is advertising inherently dishonest and manipulative, or does it sometimes serve a useful purpose?

ENDURING ISSUES

Person–Situation
After reading about social influence, to what extent do you now think that people's behavior is affected by external factors such as other people?

Diversity
Do you think that there are significant sexual, racial, or cultural differences in the extent to which people are affected by social influence? What sexual, racial, or cultural differences exist in what people consider "attractive" in other people?

(Answers to the Review Questions appear in the back of the book.)

APPENDIX A:

MEASUREMENT AND STATISTICAL METHODS

Most of the experiments described in this book involve measuring one or more variables and then analyzing the data statistically. The design and scoring of all the tests we have discussed are also based on statistical methods. **Statistics** is a branch of mathematics. It provides techniques for sorting out quantitative facts and ways of drawing conclusions from them. Statistics let us organize and describe data quickly, guide the conclusions we draw, and help us make inferences.

Statistical analysis is essential to conducting an experiment or designing a test, but statistics can only handle numbers—groups of them. To use statistics, the psychologist first must measure things—count and express them in quantities.

SCALES OF MEASUREMENT

No matter what we are measuring—height, noise, intelligence, attitudes—we have to use a scale. The data we want to collect determine the scale we will use and, in turn, the scale we use helps determine the conclusions we can draw from our data.

NOMINAL SCALES   A nominal scale is a set of arbitrarily named or numbered categories. If we decide to classify a group of people by the color of their eyes, we are using a **nominal scale.** We can count how many people have blue eyes, how many have green eyes, how many have brown eyes, and so on, but we cannot say that one group has more or less eye color than the other. The colors are simply different. Since a nominal scale is more of a way of classifying than of measuring, it is the least informative kind of scale. If we want to compare our data more precisely, we will have to use a scale that tells us more.

Statistics A branch of mathematics that psychologists use to organize and analyze data.

Nominal scale A set of categories for classifying objects.

Ordinal scale Scale indicating order or relative position of items according to some criterion.

Interval scale Scale with equal distances between the points or values, but without a true zero.

Ratio scale Scale with equal distances between the points or values and with a true zero.

Central tendency Tendency of scores to congregate around some middle value.

Mean Arithmetical average calculated by dividing a sum of values by the total number of cases.

ORDINAL SCALES   If we list horses in the order in which they finish a race, we are using an **ordinal scale.** On an ordinal scale, data are ranked from first to last according to some criterion. An ordinal scale tells the order, but nothing about the distances between what is ranked first and second or ninth and tenth. It does not tell us how much faster the winning horse ran than the horses that placed or showed. If a person ranks her preferences for various kinds of soup—pea soup first, then tomato, then onion, and so on— we know what soup she likes most and what soup she likes least, but we have no idea how much better she likes tomato than onion, or if pea soup is far more favored than either one of them.

Since we do not know the distances between the items ranked on an ordinal scale, we cannot add or subtract ordinal data. If mathematical operations are necessary, we need a still more informative scale.

INTERVAL SCALES   An **interval scale** is often compared to a ruler that has been broken off at the bottom—it only goes from, say, 5½ to 12. The intervals between 6 and 7, 7 and 8, 8 and 9, and so forth are equal, but there is no zero. A thermometer is an interval scale—even though a certain degree registered on a Fahrenheit or Centigrade thermometer specifies a certain state of cold or heat, there is no such thing as no temperature at all. One day is never twice as hot as another; it is only so many equal degrees hotter.

An interval scale tells us how many equal-size units one thing lies above or below another thing of the same kind, but it does not tell us how many times bigger, smaller, taller, or fatter one thing is than another. An intelligence test cannot tell us that one person is three times as intelligent as another, only that he or she scored so many points above or below someone else.

RATIO SCALES   We can only say that a measurement is two times as long as another or three times as high when we use a **ratio scale,** one that has a true zero. For instance, if we measure the snowfall in a certain area over several winters, we can say that six times as much snow fell during the winter in which we measured a total of 12 feet as during a winter in which only 2 feet fell. This scale has a zero—there may be no snow.

MEASUREMENTS OF CENTRAL TENDENCY

Usually, when we measure a number of instances of anything—from the popularity of TV shows to the weights of 8-year-old boys to the number of times a person's optic nerve fires in response to electrical stimulation—we get a distribution of measurements that range from smallest to largest or lowest to highest. The measurements will usually cluster around some value near the middle. This value is the **central tendency** of the distribution of the measurements.

Suppose, for example, you want to keep 10 children busy tossing rings around a bottle. You give them three rings to toss each turn, the game has six rounds, and each player scores one point every time he or she gets the ring around the neck of the bottle. The highest possible score is 18. The distribution of scores might end up like this: 11, 8, 13, 6, 12, 10, 16, 9, 12, 3.

What could you quickly say about the ring-tossing talent of the group? First, you could arrange the scores from lowest to highest: 3, 6, 8, 9, 10, 11, 12, 12, 13, 16. In this order, the central tendency of the distribution of scores becomes clear. Many of the scores cluster around the values between 8 and 12. There are three ways to describe the central tendency of a distribution. We usually refer to all three as the *average.*

The arithmetic average is called the **mean**—the sum of all the scores in the group divided by the number of scores. If you add up all the scores and divide by 10, the total number of scores in this group of ring tossers, you find that the mean for the group is 10.

The **median** is the point that divides a distribution in half—50 percent of the scores fall above the median, and 50 percent fall below. In the ring-tossing scores, five scores fall at 10 or below, five at 11 or above. The median is thus halfway between 10 and 11—10.5.

The point at which the largest number of scores occurs is called the **mode.** In our example, the mode is 12. More people scored 12 than any other.

Median Point that divides a set of scores in half.

Mode Point at which the largest number of scores occurs.

Frequency distribution A count of the number of scores that fall within each of a series of intervals.

Differences Between the Mean, Median, and Mode

If we take many measurements of anything, we are likely to get a distribution of scores in which the mean, median, and mode are all about the same—the score that occurs most often (the mode) will also be the point that half the scores are below and half above (the median). And the same point will be the arithmetical average (the mean). This is not always true, of course, and small samples rarely come out so symmetrically. In these cases, we often have to decide which of the three measures of central tendency—the mean, the median, or mode—will tell us what we want to know.

For example, a shopkeeper wants to know the general incomes of passersby so he can stock the right merchandise. He might conduct a rough survey by standing outside his store for a few days from 12:00 to 2:00 and asking every tenth person who walks by to check a card showing the general range of his or her income. Suppose most of the people checked the ranges between $15,000 and $25,000 a year. However, a couple of the people made a lot of money—one checked $100,000–$150,000 and the other checked the $200,000-or-above box. The mean for the set of income figures would be pushed higher by those two large figures and would not really tell the shopkeeper what he wants to know about his potential customers. In this case, he would be wiser to use the median or the mode.

Suppose instead of meeting two people whose incomes were so great, he noticed that people from two distinct income groups walked by his store—several people checked the box for $15,000–$17,000, and several others checked $23,000–$25,000. The shopkeeper would find that his distribution was bimodal. It has two modes—$16,000 and $24,000. This might be more useful to him than the mean, which could lead him to think his customers were a unit with an average income of about $20,000.

Another way of approaching a set of scores is to arrange them into a **frequency distribution**—that is, to select a set of intervals and count how many scores fall into each interval. A frequency distribution is useful for large groups of numbers; it puts the number of individual scores into more manageable groups.

Suppose a psychologist tests memory. She asks 50 college students to learn 18 nonsense syllables, then records how many syllables each student can recall 2 hours later. She arranges her raw scores from lowest to highest in a rank distribution:

2	6	8	10	11	14
3	7	9	10	12	14
4	7	9	10	12	15
4	7	9	10	12	16
5	7	9	10	13	17
5	7	9	11	13	

6	8	9	11	13
6	8	9	11	13
6	8	10	11	13

The scores range from 2 to 17, but 50 individual scores are too cumbersome to work with. So she chooses a set of two-point intervals and tallies the number of scores in each interval:

INTERVAL	TALLY	FREQUENCY
1–2	I	1
3–4	III	3
5–6	JHt I	6
7–8	JHt IIII	9
9–10	JHt JHt III	13
11–12	JHt III	8
13–14	JHt II	7
15–16	II	2
17–18	I	1

Now she can tell at a glance what the results of her experiment were. Most of the students had scores near the middle of the range, and very few had scores in the high or low intervals. She can see these results even better if she uses the frequency distribution to construct a bar graph—a **frequency histogram.** Marking the intervals along the horizontal axis and the frequencies along the vertical axis would give her the graph shown in Figure A-1. Another way is to construct a **frequency polygon,** a line graph. A frequency polygon drawn from the same set of data is shown in Figure A-2. Note that the figure is not a smooth curve, since the points are connected by straight lines. With many scores, however, and with small intervals, the angles would smooth out, and the figure would resemble a rounded curve.

THE NORMAL CURVE

Ordinarily, if we take enough measurements of almost anything, we get a *normal distribution.* Tossing coins is a favorite example of statisticians. If you tossed 10 coins into the air 1,000 times and recorded the heads and tails on each toss, your tabulations would reveal a normal distribution. Five heads and five tails would be the next most frequent, and so on down to the rare all heads or all tails.

Plotting a normal distribution on a graph yields a particular kind of frequency polygon, called a **normal curve.** Figure A-3 shows data on the heights of 1,000 men. Superimposed over the gray bars that reflect the actual data is an "ideal" normal curve for the same data. Note that the curve is absolutely symmetrical—the left slope parallels the right slope exactly. Moreover, the mean, median, and mode all fall on the highest point on the curve.

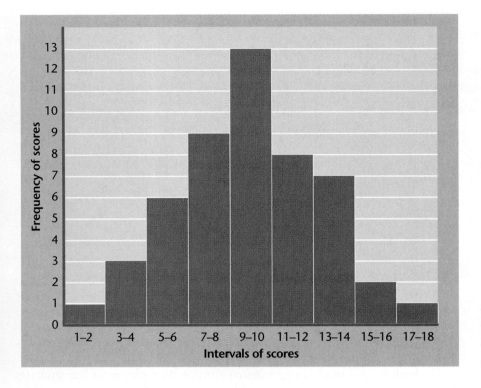

Figure A-1
A frequency histogram for a memory experiment.
The bars indicate the frequency of scores within each interval.

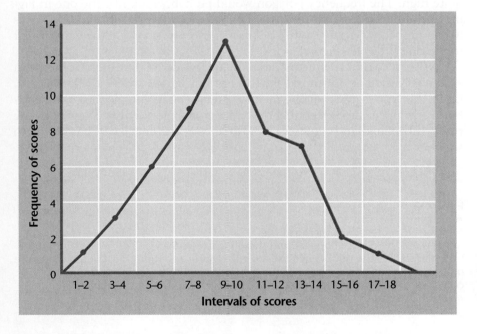

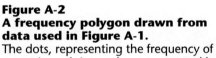

Figure A-2
A frequency polygon drawn from data used in Figure A-1.
The dots, representing the frequency of scores in each interval, are connected by straight lines.

The normal curve is a hypothetical entity. No set of real measurements shows such a smooth gradation from one interval to the next, or so purely symmetrical a shape. But because so many things do approximate the normal curve so closely, the curve is a useful model for much that we measure.

Skewed Distributions

If a frequency distribution is asymmetrical—if most of the scores are gathered at either the high end or the low end—the frequency polygon will be

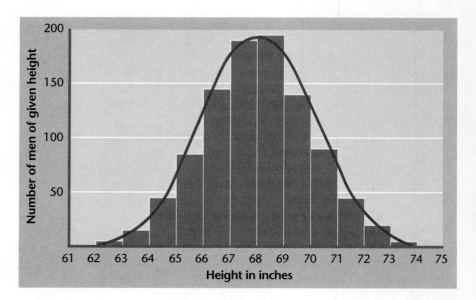

Figure A-3
A normal curve, based on measurements of the heights of 1,000 adult males.

Source: From Hill, 1966.

skewed. The hump will sit to one side or the other, and one of the curve's tails will be disproportionately long.

If a high-school mathematics instructor, for example, gives her students a sixth-grade arithmetic test, we would expect nearly all the scores to be quite high. The frequency polygon would probably look like the one in Figure A-4. But if a sixth-grade class is asked to do advanced algebra, the scores would probably be quite low. The frequency polygon would be very similar to the one shown in Figure A-5.

Note, too, that the mean, median, and mode fall at different points in a skewed distribution, unlike in the normal curve, where they coincide. Usually, if you know that the mean is greater than the median of a distribution, you can predict that the frequency polygon will be skewed to the right. If the median is greater than the mean, the curve will be skewed to the left.

Figure A-4
A skewed distribution.
Most of the scores are gathered at the high end of the distribution, causing the hump to shift to the right. Since the tail on the left is longer, we say that the curve is skewed to the left. Note that the *mean, median,* and *mode* are different.

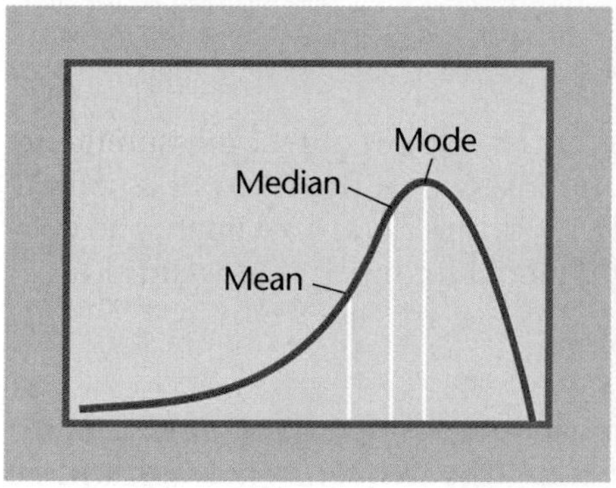

Figure A-5
In this distribution, most of the scores are gathered at the low end, so the curve is skewed to the right. The *mean, median,* and *mode* do not coincide.

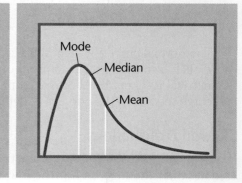

Bimodal Distributions

We have already mentioned a bimodal distribution in our description of the shopkeeper's survey of his customers' incomes. The frequency polygon for a bimodal distribution has two humps—one for each mode. The mean and the median may be the same (Figure A-6) or different (Figure A-7).

MEASURES OF VARIATION

Sometimes it is not enough to know the distribution of a set of data and what their mean, median, and mode are. Suppose an automotive safety expert feels that too much damage occurs in tail-end accidents because automobile bumpers are not all the same height. It is not enough to know what the average height of an automobile bumper is. The safety expert also wants to know about the variation in bumper heights: How much higher is the highest bumper than the mean? How do bumpers of all cars vary from the mean? Are the latest bumpers closer to the same height?

Range

The simplest measure of variation is the **range**—the difference between the largest and smallest measurements. Perhaps the safety expert measured the bumpers of 1,000 cars two years ago and found that the highest bumper was 18 inches from the ground, the lowest only 12 inches from the ground. The range was thus 6 inches—18 minus 12. This year the highest bumper is still 18 inches high, the lowest still 12 inches from the ground. The range is still 6 inches. Moreover, our safety expert finds that the means of the two distributions are the same—15 inches off the ground. But look at the two frequency polygons in Figure A-8—there is still something the expert needs to know, since the measurements cluster around the mean in drastically different ways. To find out how the measurements are distributed around the mean, our safety expert has to turn to a slightly more complicated measure of variation—the standard deviation.

The Standard Deviation

The **standard deviation,** in a single number, tells us much about how the scores in any frequency distribution are dispersed around the mean. Calculating the standard deviation is one of the most useful and widely employed statistical tools.

Range Difference between the largest and smallest measurements in a distribution.

Standard deviation Statistical measure of variability in a group of scores or other values.

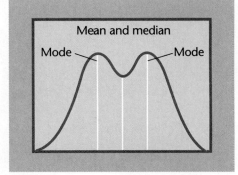

Figure A-6
A bimodal distribution in which the *mean* and the *median* are the same.

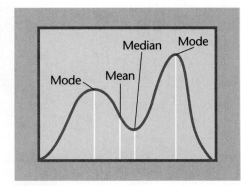

Figure A-7
In this bimodal distribution, the *mean* and the *median* are different.

Figure A-8
Frequency polygons for two sets of measurements of automobile bumper heights.
Both are normal curves, and in each distribution the *mean, median,* and *mode* are 15. But the variation from the mean is different, causing one curve to be flattened and the other to be much more sharply peaked.

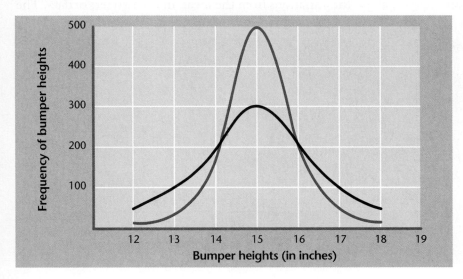

Number of scores = 10		Mean = 7
Scores	Difference from mean	Difference squared
4	$7 - 4 = 3$	$3^2 = 9$
5	$7 - 5 = 2$	$2^2 = 4$
6	$7 - 6 = 1$	$1^2 = 1$
6	$7 - 6 = 1$	$1^2 = 1$
7	$7 - 7 = 0$	$0^2 = 0$
7	$7 - 7 = 0$	$0^2 = 0$
8	$7 - 8 = -1$	$-1^2 = 1$
8	$7 - 8 = -1$	$-1^2 = 1$
9	$7 - 9 = -2$	$-2^2 = 4$
10	$7 - 10 = -3$	$-3^2 = 9$

Sum of squares = 30
÷
Number of scores = 10
Variance = 3
Standard deviation = $\sqrt{3}$ = 1.73

Figure A-9
Step-by-step calculation of the *standard deviation* for a group of 10 scores with a mean of 7.

To find the standard deviation of a set of scores, we first find the mean. Then we take the first score in the distribution, subtract it from the mean, square the difference, and jot it down in a column to be added up later. We do the same for all the scores in the distribution. Then we add up the column of squared differences, divide the total by the number of scores in the distribution, and find the square root of that number. Figure A-9 shows the calculation of the standard deviation for a small distribution of scores.

In a normal distribution, however peaked or flattened the curve, about 68 percent of the scores fall between one standard deviation above the mean and one standard deviation below the mean (see Figure A-10). Another 27 percent fall between one standard deviation and two standard deviations on either side of the mean, and 4 percent more between the second and third standard deviations on either side. Overall, then, more than 99 percent of the scores fall between three standard deviations above and three standard deviations below the mean. This makes the standard deviation useful for comparing two different normal distributions.

Now let us see what the standard deviation can tell our automotive safety expert about the variations from the mean in the two sets of data. The

Figure A-10
A normal curve, divided to show the percentage of scores that fall within each *standard deviation* from the *mean.*

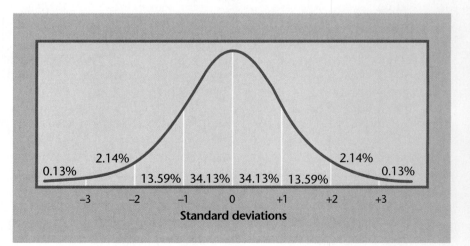

standard deviation for the cars measured 2 years ago is about 1.4. A car with a bumper height of 16.4 is one standard deviation above the mean of 15; one with a bumper height of 13.6 is one standard deviation below the mean. Since the engineer knows that the data fall into a normal distribution, he or she can figure that about 68 percent of the 1,000 cars he measured will fall somewhere between these two heights: 680 cars will have bumpers between 13.6 and 16.4 inches high. For the more recent set of data, the standard deviation is just slightly less than 1. A car with a bumper height of about 14 inches is one standard deviation below the mean; a car with a bumper height of about 16 is one standard deviation above the mean. Thus, in this distribution, 680 cars have bumpers between 14 and 16 inches high. This tells the safety expert that car bumpers are becoming more similar, although the range of heights is still the same (6 inches), and the mean height of bumpers is still 15.

MEASURES OF CORRELATION

Measures of central tendency and measures of variation can be used to describe a single set of measurements—like the children's ring-tossing scores—or to compare two or more sets of measurements—like the two sets of bumper heights. Sometimes, however, we need to know if two sets of measurements are in any way associated with each other—if they are *correlated*. Is parental IQ related to children's IQ? Does the need for achievement relate to the need for power? Is watching violence on TV related to aggressive behavior?

One fast way to determine if two variables are correlated is to draw a **scatter plot.** We assign one variable (X) to the horizontal axis of a graph, the other variable (Y) to the vertical axis. Then we plot a person's score on one characteristic along the horizontal axis and his or her score on the second characteristic along the vertical axis. Where the two scores intersect, we draw a dot. When several scores have been plotted in this way, the pattern of dots tells if the two characteristics are in any way correlated with each other.

If the dots on a scatter plot form a straight line running between the lower left-hand corner and the upper right-hand corner, as they do in Figure A-11a, we have a perfect positive correlation—a high score on one of the characteristics is always associated with a high score on the other one. A straight line running between the upper-left-hand corner and the lower-right-hand corner, as in Figure A-11b, is the sign of a perfect negative correlation—a high score on one of the characteristics is always associated with a low score on the other one. If the pattern formed by the dots is cigar shaped in either of these directions, as in Figure A-11c and d, we have a modest correlation—the two characteristics are related but not highly correlated. If the dots spread out over the whole graph, forming a circle or a random pattern, as they do in Figure A-11e, there is no correlation between the two characteristics.

A scatter plot can give us a general idea if a correlation exists and how strong it is. To describe the relation between two variables more precisely, we need a **correlation coefficient**—a statistical measure of the degree to which two variables are associated. The correlation coefficient tells us the degree of association between two sets of matched scores—that is, to what extent high or low scores on one variable tend to be associated with high or low scores on another variable. It also provides an estimate of how well we can predict from a person's score on one characteristic how high he or she will score on another characteristic. If we know, for example, that a test of

Scatter plot Diagram showing the association between scores on two variables.

Correlation coefficient Statistical measure of the strength of association between two variables.

treats the results of entire studies as its raw data. Meta-analysts begin by collecting all available research reports that are relevant to the question at hand. Next they statistically transform these results into a common scale for comparison. That way differences in sample size (one study might have used 50 participants, another 500), in the magnitude of an effect (one study might have found a small difference, another a more substantial one), and in experimental procedures (which might vary from study to study) can be examined using the same methods. The key element in this process is its statistical basis. Rather than keeping a tally of "yeas" and "nays," meta-analysis allows the reviewer to determine both the strength and the consistency of a research conclusion. For example, instead of simply concluding that there were more studies that found a particular gender difference, the reviewer might determine that the genders differ by six-tenths of a percentage point, or that across all the studies the findings are highly variable.

Meta-analysis has proved to be a valuable tool for psychologists interested in reaching conclusions about a particular research topic. By systematically examining patterns of evidence across individual studies that vary in their conclusions, psychologists are able to gain a clearer understanding of the findings and their implications.

Figure A-12
Meta-analysis. Meta-analysis enables researchers to combine the results of individual studies to reach an overall conclusion.

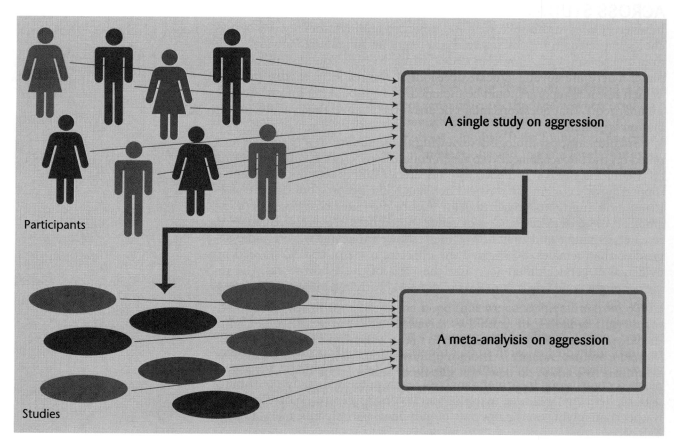

APPENDIX B:
INDUSTRIAL/ORGANIZATIONAL PSYCHOLOGY

Throughout this book, we have seen how psychology can be applied to a variety of settings. The purpose of this appendix is to focus on industrial-organizational psychology, a division of psychology concerned with the application of psychological principles to the problems of human organizations. Of particular concern to organizational psychologists is how organizations can best use and develop the talent, skill, and motivation of their employees.

OVERVIEW OF I/O PSYCHOLOGY

In this appendix, we will first provide an overview of the field and then examine its three main areas: personnel psychology, organizational psychology, and human factors.

Personnel psychology focuses on selecting, training, and evaluating people in an organization. Personnel psychologists are concerned with finding the "right" worker for the job—that is, someone who has both the necessary skills and the personal attributes for the job. To do this, they may develop and administer tests and become involved in the interview process.

Organizational psychology focuses on how workers adapt to the social environment of complex human organizations. This area deals with questions about work motivation, job satisfaction, group issues, and leadership.

Human factors psychology deals with the arrangement and design of work tasks to promote a safer and healthier as well as more efficient work environment. Primary emphasis is given to designing work environments, technology, and equipment to fit the needs and capabilities of workers.

PERSONNEL PSYCHOLOGY

Matching the attributes of workers with the requirements of jobs is the key challenge for the personnel psychologist. In deciding whether an applicant is qualified for a job, employers often consider a variety of factors,

Personnel psychology Area of industrial-organizational psychology that focuses on the selection, training, and evaluation of people in an organization.

Organizational psychology Area of industrial-organizational psychology that focuses on how workers adapt to the social environment of complex human organizations.

Human factors psychology Area of industrial-organizational psychology that deals with the arrangement and design of work tasks to promote a safer, healthier, and more efficient work environment.

There is some risk, however, that a highly structured interview may not turn up some information that would be important in evaluating a particular candidate. For this reason, some organizations have found it useful to combine a structured interview with a more free-wheeling interview later.

Selection Tests

Organizations also use written tests to select people for jobs. During World War I, the army used intelligence tests to screen recruits, and shortly thereafter, employers started using psychological tests and questionnaires to select workers. As we saw in Chapter 8, there has been furious debate over the fair and proper use of intelligence tests. A similar debate surrounds the use of personnel selection tests. In fact, legal rulings have restricted their use.

What makes a good test? As discussed in the chapter on intelligence, a good test is both reliable and valid. *Reliability* means that test scores are stable and consistent. *Validity* means that the test measures what it claims to measure. Thus, a good personnel selection test must measure the knowledge, skills, abilities, and personal attributes necessary for good job performance, and it must do so in a way that provides relatively stable, consistent scores.

How do we know if a test is reliable and valid? The answer is to perform research on the test. Two methods for determining test reliability are *test-retest* and *split-half* (see Chapter 8). The validity of a test can be determined in a variety of ways. For example, let's assume the XYZ company has a new test called the Management Abilities Test (MAT), and it wants to find out if the test is valid—whether it does, in fact, accurately measure management ability. One strategy is to use interviews to hire as many management trainees as are needed and then give the MAT test to all those who have been hired. After a period of time (say 6 to 12 months), their performance can be evaluated and compared with their test scores. If the people who scored high on the MAT turn out to be better managers than those who scored low, this would indicate that the test is a valid predictor of job success.

Another strategy for assessing the validity of the MAT would be to give the test to managers already working in the organization and see if the test discriminates between effective and less effective managers.

A third way to assess the validity of the MAT is to examine the content of the test. If the test requires applicants to perform a wide variety of tasks managers actually do in the job—a so-called *work sample test*—we could have some confidence that the test is measuring some management ability.

Training

Personnel psychologists also spend considerable time training people who are already employed by the company. The objective of training is to raise the workers' level of performance by changing their skills and possibly their attitudes. Today's workplace is placing ever-greater demands on workers to produce quality products and services. Moreover, the rapid pace of technological change requires that workers learn new skills. Training can be an effective way to confront these issues. When training is carefully planned, designed, and evaluated, it gives individuals opportunities to perform new functions, to advance in their careers, and, if their existing job is unsatisfactory, to reenter the job market with needed skills.

Training begins by determining the gap between actual and desired performance—that is, the extent to which knowledge and skill are below expected levels. Information from job analyses and performance evaluations (to be discussed in the next section), as well as requests from managers, are typical ways in which training needs are identified.

The next step is to design the training program. Most training programs use a blend of the learning principles discussed in Chapter 5 and a variety of media, depending on the nature of the training. Today many mechanics are trained using videotaped demonstrations. These are coupled with written training materials that break down the various tasks into carefully defined steps. Afterward the training is evaluated to determine if it has been effective. This feedback is also useful for modifying the training program to make it more effective with future trainees.

Performance Evaluation

Personnel psychologists also work with managers to develop various methods to evaluate employee performance. Here the objective is to determine how well job performance matches performance expectations. Usually, the specific aspects of job performance to be measured and evaluated are identified through a job analysis (Ash et al., 1983).

One procedure is simply to count the number of products of a person's job performance. This approach can work reasonably well in jobs where a quantifiable measure makes sense (e.g., number of cars assembled per day). However, for some jobs it is difficult, if not misleading, to rely on quantity as a measure of success. Consider an employment counselor who helps unemployed people find jobs. How do you measure the counselor's job performance? Should it be based strictly on how many people find jobs? But that measure may not accurately reflect the quality of the counselor's work. For example, the counselor may have helped an individual enroll in a training program that could improve his or her prospects for finding a better-paying job in the future, but that individual would not show up as a "success" on the counselor's record until he or she finds a job. Factors beyond the control of the counselor, such as the state of the economy, may also affect employment opportunities and thus job-placement success rates.

In cases such as this, a more useful procedure is simply to observe the person performing the required job tasks. In many organizations, supervisors are usually the ones who carry out this function. This approach can work if the supervisor has the time to adequately observe the worker over a long enough period to form a true picture of the worker's job performance and if the supervisor observes important, not trivial, aspects of the job.

A third approach is known as the **performance rating system.** Here a supervisor may be asked to consider the behavior of an employee in certain key areas of the job. The supervisor then assigns a numerical rating that represents how well or poorly the employee performs in these areas. This approach can be effective if the supervisor has a clear understanding of the employee's job and has had ample opportunity to observe the employee's work performance. But even under these conditions, supervisory ratings are often imperfect. For example, ratings can be influenced by such factors as the tendency of the supervisor to be lenient and the extent to which the supervisor likes the employee. Another common error is the *halo effect*, which is the tendency of supervisors to allow their overall impressions of an employee to determine how they rate the employee on each of the dimensions of a rating form (Landy & Farr, 1980). Thus, an employee who is liked may receive excellent ratings on every aspect of the job, even though the employee is not doing excellent work in all areas. Some supervisors also have a tendency to cluster their ratings toward the middle of the scale. This, too, limits the usefulness of the evaluation process, particularly with high- and low-performing employees, since everyone ends up with fairly mediocre overall ratings.

Performance rating system A method of performance evaluation in which a numerical rating is given for performance in each key area of the job.

Job enrichment Redesigning jobs to provide workers with more meaningful tasks, increased decision-making authority, and opportunities for feedback.

Autonomous work group A small team of workers that is responsible for an entire product or service.

Self-managed work team An autonomous work group that has the authority to make decisions in such managerial areas as planning, scheduling, and even hiring.

in part because job satisfaction is linked to such practical concerns as absenteeism, turnover, and productivity. For example, studies have shown that job satisfaction and absenteeism are related, although the relationship is not a strong one (Hackett, 1989). Other studies have shown a stronger relationship between job satisfaction and the rate at which people voluntarily quit their jobs to seek employment elsewhere (Cotton & Tuttle, 1986). However, despite the commonsense notion that a happy worker is a productive one, research has shown only a slight connection between satisfaction and job performance (Iaffaldano & Muchinsky, 1985). But job satisfaction does affect an individual's quality of work life and overall health. For example, research studies have shown that job dissatisfaction is related to feelings of stress and poor health among workers (Ivancevichl & Matteson, 1980). One way to increase job satisfaction is **job enrichment.** Basically, a job is redesigned to provide workers with more meaningful tasks, increased decision-making authority, and opportunities for feedback. Some organizations are linking this motivational strategy with new technologies that are changing the way workers do their job, an issue that will be covered in the section on Human Factors Psychology.

Work Teams: An Experiment

Much of the research on groups discussed in Chapter 15 has been useful to industrial/organizational psychologists. For example, the idea of work teams has received a great deal of attention recently. Driven by the need to compete more effectively in the global economy (and to improve the quality of their products and services), organizations have been experimenting with such teams to increase the level of commitment and productivity among their employees. One innovation, mentioned in the chapter on social psychology, is the **autonomous work group** where a small team of workers is responsible for an entire product or service. These teams tend to be cohesive, with members sharing a sense of belonging and unity. As their name implies, autonomous work groups are also designed to give workers significant authority to make decisions in such areas as planning, scheduling, and even hiring. When given this type of managerial authority, they become **self-managed work teams.** In effect, employees in these unique work groups act as their own supervisor.

To date, self-managed teams have not progressed much beyond the experimental stage in the United States. According to one survey, only 7 percent of the largest industrial companies in the United States reported using self-managed work teams. However, half of the firms expected to adopt the technique in the coming years (Dumaine, 1990).

How effective are self-managed teams? A recent review of research showed that self-managed teams have a positive impact on productivity and specific attitudes related to responsibility and control but no significant impact on overall job satisfaction, absenteeism, or turnover (Goodman et al., 1988). Moreover, self-managed teams are not without their problems. Not all workers are capable or willing to be part of a self-managed team—some prefer more traditional work arrangements where managerial and nonmanagerial roles are clearly defined. Moreover, workers need to be adequately trained before they can handle the authority and responsibility that exist in a team setting. For example, members of work teams are often asked to learn not only their own job but also the jobs of other team members. In addition, they may need training in such areas as interpersonal communication skills.

Leadership

Organizational psychologists are also interested in understanding the process of leadership, since leadership is an important ingredient of success in any organization. There have been two major approaches to organizational psychology: studying leadership in the trait or leadership-style approach and the situational approach.

According to the leadership-style approach, most leaders have a typical style of managing people that reflects their unique personality and abilities. They tend to use this style as much as possible because it is comfortable for them. Moreover, leadership styles do not change that easily (Fiedler, 1967). Leadership styles vary along a continuum from task-oriented to relationship-oriented (Fleishman & Harris, 1962). The relationship-oriented style emphasizes trust, respect, two-way communication, and concern for employees' personal needs. The task-oriented leadership style focuses directly on organizational performance goals, with primary emphasis given to planning, organizing, and controlling the work of employees.

The situational approach to leadership emphasizes the need for leaders to be able to modify their behavior to accommodate different situations as well as the different needs of those they manage. For example, an older, more experienced employee is likely to need a different leadership style than a new, younger employee (Hersey & Blanchard, 1988). The situational approach emphasizes that effective leaders must be flexible in order to change their behavior as the situation dictates.

In this and the previous section, we've looked at personnel psychology and organizational psychology. Personnel psychologists are concerned with the selection and evaluation of employees and with developing adequate measures and descriptions of particular jobs. Organizational psychologists are primarily concerned with human relations on the job and the organization's effect on employees. They focus on relations among employees, leadership styles (relations between employees and their supervisors), and ways that organizations can encourage employees' motivation and job satisfaction. In the next section, we turn our attention to a third area of I/O psychology, human factors or engineering psychology.

HUMAN FACTORS PSYCHOLOGY

Technological advances such as computers and robotics are changing the way we work. Human factors psychologists are interested in the relationship between worker and machine. They are also referred to as *human engineering psychologists* because they design work environments and equipment to match the capabilities of the people who use them. Human factors psychologists have been especially involved in two areas: making machines safer to use, and avoiding or reducing the stress that can result among workers when new technologies are introduced.

As we saw in the Highlights box on human factors in Chapter 3, human factors psychology can play a significant role in the prevention of accidents through the design of safer work environments. For example, the way in which dials and controls are displayed in airplanes and nuclear plants can have a significant impact on accident prevention. By designing equipment that yields immediate and clear information that is accessible and compatible with the operator's abilities, the human factors specialist can help minimize the opportunity for human error.

In addition to safety issues, human factors specialists deal with ways of reducing job stress. A key source of job stress is the nature of the job itself:

nitive models; **18.** computer simulations; **19.** confirmation bias; **1.** The compensatory model of decision making analyzes if the attractive features of something you are deciding on can compensate for the unattractive features; **2.** Laboratory experiments suggest that animals may indeed have some cognitive capacities. For example, with training pigeons and monkeys are able to sort photographs into categories. When we study the development of concepts in nonhuman animals we gain insights about the basic building blocks of thought in humans; **3.** (Your personal response.); **4.** You could use "hill climbing" heuristic that moves you closer to your goal with each decision.

CHAPTER 8
1. D Cattell, C Spearman, A Sternberg, B Thurston, E Gardner; **2.** componential–experiential–contextual; **3.** IQ–100–Binet-Simon Scale; **4.** T; **5.** Wechsler Adult Intelligence Scale–Revised (WAIS-R); **6.** group tests, C Wechsler Adult Intelligence Scale; **7.** performance–culture-fair; **8.** D a and b; **9.** reliable; **10.** A correlation coefficient; **11.** validity; **12.** school; **13.** heredity; **14.** A creativity; **15.** A take risks and like working on their own problems; **1.** Gardner believes that intelligence is comprised of many separate abilities, each of which is relatively independent of the others. He lists seven: logical-mathematical, linguistic, spatial, musical, bodily-kinesthetic, interpersonal, and intrapersonal; **2.** Recent reviews of the evidence have reasserted the claim that both school grades and intelligence tests are good predictors of occupational success. This issue is not resolved yet because there are so many variables involved; **3.** The statement is not correct because if the performance skills are used in one culture but not another, it would not be a fair test in the latter culture; **4.** Intelligence appears to be complex and many faceted, but an individual society may place more emphasis on specific components so it is doubtful the controversy will even be resolved; **5.** Intelligence testing has influenced society because decisions regarding schooling and employment are sometimes based on test results. Both positive and negative effects of testing can be cited. Intelligence tests could be improved by being sensitive to cultural context and also to address the many dimensions of intelligence.

CHAPTER 9
1. motives and emotions; **2.** C stimulus; **3.** homeostasis; **4.** F; **5.** hunger–satiety; **6.** stimulus; **7.** achievement; **8.** affiliation; **9.** T; **10.** Yerkes-Dodson; **11.** intensity; **12.** T; **13.** B Cannon-Bard, C cognitive theory, A James-Lange; **14.** B expressive behavior; **15.** facial expressions and body language; **1.** Obesity having a genetic component should lead to less judgmental and discriminatory treatment; however, it is questionable if society will change; **2.** Other possible explanations for low performance levels could be learning disabilities, brain damage, numerous negative past experiences related to performance; **3.** Boredom leads some people to explore their environment; and most people have an innate reaction to novel stimuli. These two ideas represent different components of curiosity. Children need both time and an interesting environment to stimulate their curiosity; **4.** (Your personal response.)

CHAPTER 10
1. longitudinal; **2.** F; **3.** T; **4.** T; **5.** sensory-motor (mainly flex activity), preoperational (can use symbols but are very egocentric), concrete operations (logical but not yet abstract), formal operations (abstract thinking); **6.** Shortly after they are born or hatched, some young animals form a strong bond to the first moving object they see. This is called imprinting, and is important for their survival; **7.** attachment; **8.** socialization; **9.** 10 1/2, 12 1/2; **10.** menarche; **11.** F; **12.** leaving home; **1.** The unborn baby is affected by his or her environment. Everything that Serena ingests is passed on to the fetus. The fetus is very much "awake" already. He or she is physically active and most of his or her senses are already functioning. **2.** Millions of American children under the age of 5 are now being cared for in day-

care centers, in preschools, or in a relative's house. Research indicates that any secure, fun, and stimulating environment is more likely to produce healthy children; **3.** According to a recent survey, 37 percent of married people over 60 have sex at least once a week.

CHAPTER 11
1. time and situations; **2.** E unconscious, C id, F superego, B ego, D ego ideal, A libido; **3.** ego–id; **4.** wish fulfillment; **5.** C persona, D animus, B collective unconscious, A archetype; **6.** C style of life, A inferiority complex, B compensation; **7.** anxiety; **8.** D industry versus inferiority, A trust versus mistrust, G generativity versus stagnation, F intimacy versus isolation, E identify versus role confusion, B autonomy versus shame and doubt, C initiative versus guilt, H integrity versus despair; **9.** self-actualizing; **10.** expectancies; **11.** evaluate; **12.** objective; **13.** projective; **1.** (Your personal feelings); **2.** Jung contended that libido represents all the life forces, not just the sexual ones. He saw the unconscious as the ego's source of strength and vitality. Adler believed that individuals possess innate positive motives and strive toward personal and social perfection. Horney concluded that environmental and social factors are the most important influences in shaping personality. Erikson took a socially oriented view of personality development. He also extended his interest to development throughout the life cycle; **3.** The major forms of personality assessment are observation, objective tests, and projective tests. Behaviorists and social learning theorists prefer observation. Objective tests were devised so as not to be dependent on the skill or interpretation of the psychologist. Psychodynamic theorists put little faith in objective personality tests because they believe in the unconscious determinant of behavior; **4.** (Your personal feelings.)

CHAPTER 12
1. the stress response (or sympathetic nervous system response); **2.** T; **3.** pressure; **4.** frustration; **5.** conflict; **6.** C approach/approach, A avoidance/avoidance, B approach/avoidance; **7.** F; **8.** direct and defensive; **9.** direct; **10.** defensive; **11.** F denial, A repression, G projection, I identification, C regression, B intellectualization, D reaction formation, E displacement, H sublimation; **12.** alarm-resistance; **13.** Type A personality; **14.** F; **1.** Sherry's headaches could be related to the stress experienced by air-traffic controllers, or her perfectionism, or the recent loss of her boyfriend. The problem could also be stress overload by the combination of stresses; **2.** Defense mechanisms are not always bad. Denial can sometimes keep us trying at something when, if we faced the actual odds against us, we might have given up; **3.** The General Adaptation Syndrome theory of a person's response to stress describes the end result of stress as physical exhaustion.

CHAPTER 13
1. F; **2.** D biological model, A psychoanalytic model, C cognitive-behavioral model, B diathesis-stress model; **3.** a. American Psychiatric Association; **4.** b. dissociative fugue; **5.** b. mania and depression; **6.** F; **7.** dysthymia, major depressive disorder; **8.** psychotic; **9.** b. personality disorders; **10.** b. a sexual attraction to unconventional objects; **11.** just a matter of normal behavior greatly exaggerated or displayed in inappropriate situations; **1.** He may be experiencing a dissociative disorder. It becomes serious when he can not control it and it interferes with his life; **2.** Dimension (magnitude) is more important because psychology symptoms are experienced by most people, but these symptoms do not interfere with their lives in any significant way.

CHAPTER 14
1. d–insight; **2.** B psychoanalysis, C client-centered therapy, D cognitive behavior therapy, A rational-emotive therapy; **3.** unconditional positive; **4.** insight–behavior; **5.** A–desensitization; **6.** aversion conditioning; **7.** F; **8.** F; **9.** d–antipsychotics; **10.** institutionalization; **11.** T; **12.** deinstitutionalization; **13.** prevention; **1.** Psychoanalysis focuses on reversing the process of repression so hidden feelings can be dealt with more effectively; **2.** Insight ther-

apy focuses on using free association to uncover inner conflicts dating back to childhood. Behavior therapies are based on the belief that all behavior is learned, and they focus on teaching people, new ways of behaving; **3.** Cognitive therapists believe that in addition to changing behavior, clients also change their way of thinking about themselves and the world; **4.** The chemical imbalance may be a result of another process rather than the cause.

CHAPTER 15

1. social; **2.** schemata—stereotype; **3.** primacy; **4.** c—attribution theory; **5.** c—complementary attitudes and interests; **6.** attitude; **7.** F; **8.** conform; **9.** cognitive dissonance; **10.** a—attitudes; **11.** <u>D</u> social influence, <u>C</u> compliance, <u>B</u> obedience, <u>A</u> conformity; **12.** risky shift; **13.** polarization; **14.** task—interaction; **15.** T; **16.** F; **1.** Self-fulling prophecy is a process in which a person's expectation about another elicits behavior from the second person that confirms the expectation. Our expectations and treatment of others influence our relationships significantly; **2.** Internal versus external attribution refers to how people make judgments about the causes of behavior. Internal is a quality within the person, whereas external refers to an outside circumstance; **3.** Some key factors that determine interpersonal attraction are: proximity, physical attractiveness, similarity, exchange, and intimacy; **4.** Advertising can be useful or it can be dishonest and manipulative, depending on the ethics of the developers.

Barbiturates Potentially deadly depressants, first used for their sedative and anticonvulsant properties, now used only to treat such conditions as epilepsy and arthritis.

Basilar membrane Vibrating membrane in the cochlea of the inner ear; it contains sense receptors for sound.

Behavior contracting Form of operant conditioning therapy in which the client and therapist set behavioral goals and agree on reinforcements the client will receive upon reaching those goals.

Behavior genetics Study of the relationship between heredity and behavior.

Behavior therapies Therapeutic approaches that are based on the belief that all behavior, normal and abnormal, is learned, and that the objective of therapy is to teach people new, more satisfying ways of behaving.

Behaviorism School of psychology that studies only observable and measurable behavior.

Beta endorphin One of the endorphins, a natural painkiller released by the body.

Big Five Five traits or basic dimensions currently thought to be of central importance in describing personality.

Binaural cue Cue to sound location that involves both ears working together.

Binet-Simon scale The first test of intelligence, developed for testing children.

Binocular cues Visual cues requiring the use of both eyes.

Biofeedback A technique that uses monitoring devices to provide precise information about internal physiological processes, such as heart rate or blood pressure, to teach people to gain voluntary control over these functions.

Biographical (or **retrospective**) **study** A method of studying developmental changes by reconstructing subjects' past through interviews and investigating the effects of past events on current behaviors.

Biological model of psychological disorders View that psychological disorders have a biochemical or physiological basis.

Biological treatments A group of approaches, including medication, electro-convulsive therapy, and psychosurgery, that are sometimes used to treat psychological disorders in conjunction with, or instead of, psychotherapy.

Bipolar cells Neurons that have only one axon and one dendrite; in the eye, these neurons connect the receptors on the retina to the ganglion cells.

Bipolar disorder A mood disorder in which periods of mania and depression alternate, sometimes with periods of normal mood intervening.

Blind spot The place on the retina where the axons of all the ganglion cells leave the eye and where there are no receptors.

Blocking A process whereby prior conditioning prevents conditioning to a second stimulus even when the two stimuli are presented simultaneously.

Body dysmorphic disorder A somatoform disorder in which a person becomes so preoccupied with his or her imagined ugliness that normal life is impossible.

Borderline personality disorder Personality disorder characterized by marked instability in self-image, mood, and interpersonal relationships.

Brain stem The top of the spinal column; it widens out to form the hindbrain and midbrain.

Brainstorming A problem-solving strategy in which an individual or a group produces numerous ideas and evaluates them only after all ideas have been collected.

Brightness The nearness of a color to white as opposed to black.

Brightness constancy The perception of brightness as the same, even though the amount of light reaching the retina changes.

Bulimia An eating disorder characterized by binges of eating followed by self-induced vomiting.

Bystander effect The tendency for an individual's helpfulness in an emergency to decrease as the number of bystanders increases.

Cannon-Bard theory States that the experience of emotion occurs simultaneously with biological changes.

Case study Intensive description and analysis of a single individual or just a few individuals.

Catatonic schizophrenia Schizophrenic disorder in which disturbed motor behavior is prominent.

Central nervous system (CNS) Division of the nervous system that consists of the brain and spinal cord.

Central tendency Tendency of scores to congregate around some middle value.

Cerebellum Structure in the hindbrain that controls certain reflexes and coordinates the body's movements.

Cerebral cortex The outer surface of the two cerebral hemispheres that regulates most complex behavior.

Chorionic villus sampling A procedure that involves collecting cells from the membranes surrounding the fetus and testing them for genetic abnormalities.

Chromosomes Pairs of threadlike bodies within the cell nucleus that contain the genes.

Chunking The grouping of information into meaningful units for easier handling by short-term memory.

Classical (or **Pavlovian**) **conditioning** The type of learning in which a response naturally elicited by one stimulus comes to be elicited by a different, formerly neutral stimulus.

Client-centered (or **person-centered**) **therapy** Nondirectional form of therapy developed by Carl Rogers that calls for unconditional positive regard of the client by the therapist with the goal of helping the client become fully functioning.

Cliques Groups of adolescents with similar interests and strong mutual attachment.

Cocaine Drug derived from the coca plant that, while producing a sense of euphoria by stimulating the sympathetic nervous system, also leads to anxiety, depression, and addictive cravings.

Cochlea Part of the inner ear containing fluid that vibrates, which in turn causes the basilar membrane to vibrate.

Cognition The processes whereby we acquire and use knowledge.

Cognitive dissonance Perceived inconsistency between two cognitions.

Cognitive distortions An illogical and maladaptive response to early negative life events that leads to feelings of incompetence and unworthiness that are reactivated whenever a new situation arises that resembles the original events.

Cognitive learning Learning that depends on mental processes that are not directly observable.

Cognitive map A learned mental image of a spatial environment that may be called on to solve problems when stimuli in the environment change.

Cognitive psychology School of psychology devoted to the study of mental processes in the broadest sense.

Cognitive theory States that emotional experience depends on one's perception or judgment of the situation one is in.

Cognitive therapies Psychotherapies that emphasize changing clients' perceptions of their life situation as a way of modifying their behavior.

Cognitive therapy Therapy that depends on identifying and changing inappropriately negative and self-critical patterns of thought.

Cognitive-behavioral model of psychological disorders View that psychological disorders result from learning maladaptive ways of thinking and behaving.

Cognitive–social learning theories Personality theories that view behavior as the product of the interaction of cognitions, learning and past experiences, and the immediate environment.

Cohort A group of people born during the same period in historical time.

Collective unconscious In Jung's theory of personality, the level of the unconscious that is inherited and common to all members of a species.

Color constancy An inclination to perceive familiar objects as retaining their color despite changes in sensory information.

Colorblindness Partial or total inability to perceive hues.

Compensation According to Adler, the person's effort to overcome imagined or real personal weaknesses.

Compensatory model A rational decision-making model in which choices are systematically evaluated on various criteria.

Compliance Change of behavior in response to an explicit request from another person or group.

Componential intelligence According to Sternberg, the ability to acquire new knowledge, to solve problems effectively.

Compromise Deciding on a more realistic solution or goal when an ideal solution or goal is not practical.

Concept A mental category for classifying objects, people, or experiences.

Concrete-operational stage In Piaget's theory, the stage of cognitive development between 7 and 11 years of age in which the individual can attend to more than one thing at a time and understand someone else's point of view, though thinking is limited to concrete matters.

Conditional positive regard In Rogers's theory, acceptance and love that are dependent on behaving in certain ways and fulfilling certain conditions.

Conditioned food (or **taste**) **aversion** Conditioned avoidance of certain foods even if there is only one pairing of conditioned and unconditioned stimuli.

Conditioned response (CR) After conditioning, the response an organism produces when only a conditioned stimulus is presented.

Conditioned stimulus (CS) An originally neutral stimulus that is paired with an unconditioned stimulus and eventually produces the desired response in an organism when presented alone.

Conditioning The acquisition of specific patterns of behavior in the presence of well-defined stimuli.

Cones Receptor cells in the retina responsible for color vision.

Confirmation bias The tendency to look for evidence in support of a belief and to ignore evidence that would disprove a belief.

Conflict Simultaneous existence of incompatible demands, opportunities, needs, or goals.

Conformity Voluntarily yielding to social norms, even at the expense of one's own preferences.

Confrontation Acknowledging a stressful situation directly and attempting to find a solution to the problem or attain the difficult goal.

Consciousness Our awareness of various cognitive processes, such as sleeping, dreaming, concentrating, and making decisions.

Content validity Refers to a test's having an adequate sample of questions measuring the skills or knowledge it is supposed to measure.

Contextual intelligence According to Sternberg, the ability to select contexts in which you can excel, to shape the environment to fit your strengths.

Contingency A reliable "if-then" relationship between two events such as a CS and a US.

Control group In a controlled experiment, the group not subjected to a change in the independent variable; used for comparison with the experimental group.

Convergence A visual depth cue that comes from muscles controlling eye movement as the eyes turn inward to view a nearby stimulus.

Convergent thinking Thinking that is directed toward one correct solution to a problem.

Conversion disorders Somatoform disorders in which a dramatic specific disability has no physical cause but instead seems related to psychological problems.

Cooperative play Two or more children engaged in play that requires interaction.

Cornea The transparent protective coating over the front part of the eye.

Corpus callosum A thick band of nerve fibers connecting the left and right cerebral cortex.

Correlation coefficients Statistical measures of the degree of association between two variables.

Correlational research Research technique based on the naturally occurring relationship between two or more variables.

Couple therapy A form of group therapy intended to help troubled partners improve their problems of communication and interaction.

Creativity The ability to produce novel and socially valued ideas or objects.

Criterion-related validity Validity of a test as measured by a comparison of the test score and independent measures of what the test is designed to measure.

Critical period The time when certain internal and external influences have a major effect on development; at other periods, the same influences will have little or no effect.

Cross-sectional study A method of studying developmental changes by examining groups of subjects who are of different ages.

Cultural norm A behavioral rule shared by an entire society.

Cultural truism The belief that most members of a society accept as self-evidently true.

Culture The tangible goods and the values, attitudes, behaviors, and beliefs that are passed from one generation to another.

Culture-fair tests Intelligence tests designed to eliminate cultural bias by minimizing skills and values that vary from one culture to another.

Dark adaptation Increased sensitivity of rods and cones in darkness.

Daydreaming Alteration in consciousness that occurs seemingly without effort, typically when we want to momentarily escape the demands of the real world.

Decay theory A theory that argues that the passage of time causes forgetting.

Decibel Unit of measurement for the loudness of sounds.

Deep structure The underlying meaning of a sentence.

Defense mechanisms Self-deceptive techniques for reducing stress, including denial, repression, projection, identification, regression, intellectualization, reaction formation, displacement, and sublimation.

Defensive attribution The tendency to attribute our successes to our own efforts or qualities and our failures to external factors.

Deindividuation A loss of personal sense of responsibility in a group.

Deinstitutionalization Policy of treating people with severe psychological disorders in the larger community, or in small residential centers such as halfway houses, rather than in large public hospitals.

Delusions False beliefs about reality that have no basis in fact.

Dendrites Short fibers that branch out from the cell body and pick up incoming messages.

Denial Refusal to acknowledge a painful or threatening reality.

Deoxyribonucleic acid (DNA) Complex molecule in a double-helix configuration that is the main ingredient of chromosomes and genes and forms the code for all genetic information.

Dependent personality disorder Personality disorder in which the person is unable to make choices and decisions independently and cannot tolerate being alone.

Dependent variable In an experiment, the variable that is measured to see how it is changed by manipulations in the independent variable.

Depersonalization disorder A dissociative disorder whose essential feature is that the person suddenly feels changed or different in a strange way.

Depressants Chemicals that slow down behavior or cognitive processes.

Depression A mood disorder characterized by overwhelming feelings of sadness, lack of interest in activities, and perhaps excessive guilt or feelings of worthlessness.

Desensitization therapy A conditioning technique designed to gradually reduce anxiety about a particular object or situation.

Developmental norms Ages by which an average child achieves various developmental milestones.

Developmental psychology The study of the changes that occur in people from birth through old age.

Diathesis Biological predisposition.

Diathesis-stress model of psychological disorders View that people biologically predisposed to a mental disorder (those with a certain diathesis) will tend to exhibit that disorder when particularly affected by stress.

Dichromats People who are blind to either red-green or yellow-blue.

Difference threshold or **just noticeable difference (jnd)** The smallest change in stimulation that can be detected 50 percent of the time.

Discrimination An unfair act or series of acts taken toward an entire group of people or individual members of that group.

Disorganized schizophrenia Schizophrenic disorder in which bizarre and childlike behaviors are common.

Displacement Shifting repressed motives and emotions from an original object to a substitute object.

Display rules Culture-specific rules that govern how, when, and why facial expressions of emotion are displayed.

Dissociative amnesia A dissociative disorder characterized by loss of memory for past events without organic cause.

Idealized cognitive model (ICM) Our conception of events as we expect to typically find them.

Identical twins Twins developed from a single fertilized ovum and therefore identical in genetic makeup at the time of conception.

Identification Taking on the characteristics of someone else to avoid feeling incompetent.

Identity crisis A period of intense self-examination and decision making; part of the process of identity formation.

Identity formation Erickson's term for the development of a stable sense of self necessary to make the transition from dependence on others to dependence on oneself.

Image A mental representation of a sensory experience.

Imaginary audience Elkind's term for adolescents' delusion that they are constantly being observed by others.

Implicit memory Memory for information that either was unintentionally committed to memory or was unintentionally retrieved from memory.

Imprinting A form of primitive bonding seen in some species of animals; the newborn animal has a tendency to follow the first moving thing (usually its mother) it sees after it is born or hatched.

Incentive External stimulus that prompts goal-directed behavior.

Independent variable In an experiment, the variable that is manipulated to test its effects on the other, dependent variables.

Industrial/organizational (I/O) psychology The area of psychology concerned with the application of psychological principles to the problems of human organizations, especially work organizations.

Inferiority complex In Adler's theory, the fixation on feelings of personal inferiority that results in emotional and social paralysis.

Information retrieval A problem-solving strategy that requires only the recovery of information from long-term memory.

Information-processing Model A computerlike model used to describe the way humans encode, store, and retrieve information.

Insanity Legal term for mentally disturbed people who are not considered responsible for their criminal actions.

Insight Learning that occurs rapidly as a result of understanding all the elements of a problem (Chapter 5); awareness of previously unconscious feelings and memories and how they influence present feelings and behavior (Chapter 14).

Insight therapies A variety of individual psychotherapies designed to give people a better awareness and understanding of their feelings, motivations, and actions in the hope that this will help them adjust.

Insomnia Sleep disorder characterized by difficulty in falling asleep or remaining asleep throughout the night.

Instinct Inborn, inflexible, goal-directed behavior that is characteristic of an entire species.

Institutional racism Discrimination that occurs because of the overall effect of institutions and policies.

Intellectualization Thinking abstractly about stressful problems as a way of detaching oneself from them.

Intelligence A general term referring to the ability or abilities involved in learning and adaptive behavior.

Intelligence quotient (IQ) A numerical value given to intelligence that is determined from the scores on an intelligence test; based on a score of 100 for average intelligence.

Intelligence tests Tests designed to measure a person's general mental abilities.

Interference theory A theory that argues that interference from other information causes forgetting.

Intermittent pairing Pairing the conditioned stimulus and the unconditioned stimulus on only a portion of the learning trials.

Interneurons (or association neurons) Neurons that carry messages from one neuron to another.

Interval scale Scale with equal distances between the points or values, but without a true zero.

Intimacy The quality of genuine closeness and trust achieved in communication with another person.

Intrinsic motivation A desire to perform a behavior that originates within the individual.

Introvert According to Jung, a person who usually focuses on his or her own thoughts and feelings.

Ions Electrically charged particles found both inside and outside the neuron.

Iris The colored part of the eye.

Irrational individuals According to Jung, people who base their actions on perceptions, either through the senses (sensation) or through unconscious processes (intuition).

James-Lange theory States that stimuli cause physiological changes in our bodies, and emotions result from those physiological changes.

Job analysis Breaking down a job into its basic components to identify the most important components and thus the most important skills and abilities needed to perform the job.

Job enrichment Redesigning jobs to provide workers with more meaningful tasks, increased decision-making authority, and opportunities for feedback.

Just-world hypothesis Attribution error based on the assumption that bad things happen to bad people and good things happen to good people.

Kinesthetic senses Senses of muscle movement, posture, and strain on muscles and joints.

Language A flexible system of communication that uses sounds, rules, gestures, or symbols to convey information.

Language acquisition device An internal mechanism for processing speech that is "wired into" all humans.

Latency period In Freud's theory of personality, a period in which the child appears to have no interest in the other sex; occurs after the phallic stage.

Latent learning Learning that is not immediately reflected in a behavior change.

Law of Effect Thorndike's theory that behavior consistently rewarded will be "stamped in" as learned behavior, and behavior that brings about discomfort will be "stamped out" (also known as the principle of reinforcement).

Learned helplessness Failure to take steps to avoid or escape from an unpleasant or aversive stimulus that occurs as a result of previous exposure to unavoidable painful stimuli.

Learning The process by which experience or practice results in a relatively permanent change in behavior or potential behavior.

Learning set The ability to become increasingly more effective in solving problems as more problems are solved.

Lens The transparent part of the eye inside the pupil that focuses light onto the retina.

Libido According to Freud, the energy generated by the sexual instinct.

Light The small segment of the electromagnetic spectrum to which our eyes are sensitive.

Light adaptation Decreased sensitivity of rods and cones in bright light.

Limbic system Ring of structures that play a role in learning and emotional behavior.

Linear perspective Monocular cue to distance and depth based on the fact that two parallel lines seem to come together at the horizon.

Linguistic relativity hypothesis Whorf's idea that patterns of thinking are determined by the specific language one speaks.

Locus of control According to Rotter, an expectancy about whether reinforcement is under internal or external control.

Longitudinal study A method of studying developmental changes by examining the same group of subjects two or more times as they grow older.

Long-term memory (LTM) The portion of memory that is more or less permanent, corresponding to everything we "know."

Long-term potentiation (LTP) A long-lasting change in the structure or function of a synapse that increases the efficiency of neural transmission.

Lysergic acid diethylamide (LSD) Hallucinogenic or "psychedelic" drug that produces hallucinations and delusions similar to those occurring in a psychotic state.

Management by objectives (MBO) A goal-setting process that takes place throughout the organization, with goals for each division and individual linked to the overall goals of the organization.

Mania A mood disorder characterized by euphoric states, extreme physical activity, excessive talkativeness, distractedness, and sometimes grandiosity.

Marijuana A mild hallucinogen that produces a "high" often characterized by feelings of euphoria, a sense of well-being, and swings in mood from gaiety to relaxation; may also cause feelings of anxiety and paranoia.

Maturation An automatic biological unfolding of development in an organism as a function of the passage of time.

Mean Arithmetical average calculated by dividing a sum of values by the total number of cases.

Means-end analysis A heuristic strategy that aims to reduce the discrepancy between the current situation and the desired goal at a number of intermediate points.

Median Point that divides a set of scores in half.

Meditation Any of the various methods of concentration, reflection, or focusing of thoughts undertaken to suppress the activity of the sympathetic nervous system.

Medulla Part of the hindbrain that controls such functions as breathing, heart rate, and blood pressure.

Memory The ability to remember the things that we have experienced, imagined, and learned.

Menarche First menstrual period.

Menopause The time in a woman's life when menstruation ceases.

Mental representations Mental images or symbols (such as words) used to think about or remember an object, a person, or an event.

Mental retardation Condition of significantly subaverage intelligence combined with deficiencies in adaptive behavior.

Midbrain Region between the hindbrain and the forebrain; it is important for hearing and sight, and it is one of several places in the brain where pain is registered.

Midlife crisis A time when adults discover they no longer feel fulfilled in their jobs or personal lives and attempt to make a decisive shift in career or lifestyle.

Midlife transition According to Levinson, a process whereby adults assess the past and formulate new goals for the future.

Minnesota Multiphasic Personality Inventory (MMPI) The most widely used objective personality test, originally intended for psychiatric diagnosis.

Mnemonics Techniques that make material easier to remember.

Mnemonist Someone with highly developed memory skills.

Mode Point at which the largest number of scores occurs.

Modeling A behavior therapy in which the person learns desired behaviors by watching others perform those behaviors.

Modern racism A subtle and less extreme form of prejudice reflected by agreement with statements that civil rights groups are too extreme or that African Americans receive more respect and benefits than they deserve.

Monaural cue Cue to sound location that requires just one ear.

Monochromats People who are totally colorblind.

Monocular cues Visual cues requiring the use of one eye.

Mood disorders Disturbances in mood or prolonged emotional state.

Morphemes The smallest meaningful units of speech, such as simple words, prefixes, and suffixes.

Motion parallax Monocular distance cue in which objects closer than the point of visual focus seem to move in the direction opposite to the viewer's moving head, and objects beyond the focus point appear to move in the same direction as the viewer's head.

Motive Specific need, desire, or want, such as hunger, thirst, or achievement, that prompts goal-oriented behavior.

Motor (or efferent) neurons Neurons that carry messages from the spinal cord or brain to the muscles and glands.

Motor projection areas Areas of the cerebral cortex where response messages from the brain to the muscles and glands begin.

Myelin sheath White fatty covering found on some axons.

Narcissistic personality disorder Personality disorder in which the person has an exaggerated sense of self-importance and needs constant admiration.

Narcolepsy Hereditary sleep disorder characterized by sudden nodding off during the day and sudden loss of muscle tone following moments of emotional excitement.

Natural selection The mechanism proposed by Darwin in his theory of evolution, which states that organisms best adapted to their environment tend to survive, transmitting their genetic characteristics to succeeding generations, whereas organisms with less adaptive characteristics tend to vanish from the earth.

Naturalistic observation Research method involving the systematic study of animal or human behavior in natural settings rather than in the laboratory.

Nature versus nurture A debate surrounding the relative importance of heredity (nature) and environment (nurture) in determining behavior.

Negative reinforcer Any event whose reduction or termination increases the likelihood that ongoing behavior will recur.

Neonates Newborn babies.

Nerve or tract Group of axons bundled together.

Nervous system The brain, the spinal cord, and the network of nerve cells that transmit messages throughout the body.

Neural impulse (or action potential) The firing of a nerve cell.

Neurons Individual cells that are the smallest units of the nervous system.

Neurotic trends Horney's term for irrational strategies for coping with emotional problems and minimizing anxiety.

Neurotransmitters Chemicals released by the synaptic vesicles that travel across the synaptic space and affect adjacent neurons.

Nominal scale A set of categories for classifying objects.

Non-REM (NREM) sleep Non-rapid-eye-movement stages of sleep that alternate with REM stages during the sleep cycle.

Noncompensatory model A decision-making model in which weaknesses in one or more criteria are not offset by strengths in other criteria.

Norm A shared idea or expectation about how to behave.

Normal curve Hypothetical bell-shaped distribution curve that occurs when a normal distribution is plotted as a frequency polygon.

Obedience Change of behavior in response to a command from another person, typically an authority figure.

Object permanence The concept that things continue to exist even when they are out of sight.

Objective tests Personality tests that are administered and scored in a standard way.

Observational or vicarious learning Learning by observing other people's behavior.

Observer bias Expectations or biases of the observer that might distort or influence his or her interpretation of what was actually observed.

Obsessive-compulsive disorder An anxiety disorder in which a person feels driven to think disturbing thoughts and/or to perform senseless rituals.

Occipital lobe Part of the cerebral hemisphere that receives and interprets visual information.

Oedipus complex and Electra complex According to Freud, a child's sexual attachment to the parent of the opposite sex and jealousy toward the parent of the same sex; generally occurs in the phallic stage.

Olfactory bulb The smell center in the brain.

Olfactory epithelium Nasal membranes containing receptor cells sensitive to odors.

Operant behavior Behavior designed to operate on the environment in a way that will gain something desired or avoid something unpleasant.

Operant (or instrumental) conditioning The type of learning in which behaviors are emitted (in the presence of specific stimuli) to earn rewards or avoid punishments.

Opiates Drugs, such as opium and heroin, derived from the opium poppy, that dull the senses and induce feelings of euphoria, well-being, and relaxation. Synthetic drugs resembling opium derivatives are also classified as opiates.

Opponent-process theory Theory of color vision that holds that three sets of color receptors (yellow-blue, red-green, black-white) respond to determine the color you experience.

Optic chiasm The point near the base of the brain where some fibers in the optic nerve from each eye cross to the other side of the brain.

Optic nerve The bundle of axons of ganglion cells that carries neural messages from each eye to the brain.

Oral stage First stage in Freud's theory of personality development, in which the infant's erotic feelings center on the mouth, lips, and tongue.

Ordinal scale Scale indicating order or relative position of items according to some criterion.

Organ of Corti Structure on the surface of the basilar membrane that contains the receptor cells for hearing.

Organizational psychology Area of industrial-organizational psychology that focuses on how workers adapt to the social environment of complex human organizations.

Orgasm Peaking of sexual pleasure and release of sexual tension.

Orgasmic disorders Inability to reach orgasm in a person able to experience sexual desire and maintain arousal.

Oval window Membrane across the opening between the middle ear and inner ear that conducts vibrations to the cochlea.

Overtones Tones that result from sound waves that are multiples of the basic tone; primary determinant of timbre.

Pancreas Organ lying between the stomach and small intestine; it secretes insulin and glucagon to regulate blood-sugar levels.

Panic disorder An anxiety disorder characterized by recurrent panic attacks in which the person suddenly experiences intense fear or terror without any reasonable cause.

Papillae Small bumps on the tongue that contain taste buds.

Parallel play Two children playing side by side at the same activities, paying little or no attention to each other; the earliest kind of social interaction between toddlers.

Paranoid personality disorder Personality disorder in which the person is inappropriately suspicious and mistrustful of others.

Paranoid schizophrenia Schizophrenic disorder marked by extreme suspiciousness and complex, bizarre delusions.

Paraphilias Sexual disorders in which unconventional objects or situations cause sexual arousal.

Parasympathetic division Branch of the autonomic nervous system; it calms and relaxes the body.

Parathyroids Four tiny glands embedded in the thyroid; they secrete parathormone.

Parietal lobe Part of the cerebral cortex that receives sensory information from throughout the body.

Pedophilia Desire to have sexual relations with children as the preferred or exclusive method of achieving sexual excitement.

Peer group A network of same-aged friends and acquaintances who give one another emotional and social support.

Perception The process of creating meaningful patterns from raw sensory information.

Perceptual constancy A tendency to perceive objects as stable and unchanging despite changes in sensory stimulation.

Perceptual illusion Illusion due to misleading cues in stimuli that give rise to inaccurate or impossible perceptions.

Performance appraisal interview Meeting between the employee and the supervisor in which they discuss the supervisor's evaluation of the employee's job performance.

Performance rating system A method of performance evaluation in which a numerical rating is given for performance in each key area of the job.

Performance standards In Bandura's theory, standards that people develop to rate the adequacy of their own behavior in a variety of situations.

Performance tests Intelligence tests that minimize the use of language.

Peripheral nervous system Division of the nervous system that connects the central nervous system to the rest of the body.

Persona According to Jung, our public self, the mask we put on to represent ourselves to others.

Personal fable Elkind's term for adolescents' delusion that they are unique, very important, and invulnerable.

Personal unconscious In Jung's theory of personality, one of the two levels of the unconscious; it contains the individual's repressed thoughts, forgotten experiences, and undeveloped ideas.

Personality An individual's unique pattern of thoughts, feelings, and behaviors that persists over time and across situations.

Personality disorders Disorders in which inflexible and maladaptive ways of thinking and behaving learned early in life cause distress to the person and/or conflicts with others.

Personality traits Dimensions or characteristics on which people differ in distinctive ways.

Personnel psychology Area of industrial-organization psychology that focuses on the selection, training, and evaluation of people in an organization.

Phallic stage Third stage in Freud's theory of personality development, in which erotic feelings center on the genitals.

Pheromone Chemical that communicates information to other organisms through smell.

Phi phenomenon Apparent movement caused by flashing lights in sequence, as on theater marquees.

Phonemes The basic sounds that make up any language.

Physical illusion Illusion due to distortion of information reaching receptor cells.

Pineal gland A gland located roughly in the center of the brain that appears to regulate activity levels over the course of a day.

Pitch Auditory experience corresponding primarily to frequency of sound vibrations, resulting in a higher or lower tone.

Pituitary gland Gland located on the underside of the brain; it produces the largest number of the body's hormones.

Place theory Theory that pitch is determined by the location of greatest vibration on the basilar membrane.

Placebo effect Pain relief that occurs when a person believes a pill or procedure will reduce pain. The actual cause of the relief seems to come from endorphins.

Placenta The organ by which an embryo or fetus is attached to its mother's uterus and that nourishes it during prenatal development.

Plasticity The ability of the brain to change in response to experience.

Pleasure principle According to Freud, the way in which the id seeks immediate gratification of an instinct.

Polarization The condition of a neuron when the inside is negatively charged relative to the outside; for example, when the neuron is at rest (Chapter 2); shift in attitudes by members of a group toward more extreme positions than the ones held before group discussion (Chapter 15).

Polygenic inheritance Process by which several genes interact to produce a certain trait; responsible for our most important traits.

Pons Part of the hindbrain that connects the cerebral cortex at the top of the brain to the cerebellum.

Positive reinforcer Any event whose presence increases the likelihood that ongoing behavior will recur.

Posterior pituitary Part of the pituitary that affects thirst, sexual behavior, and perhaps paternal and maternal behavior.

Post-traumatic stress disorder (PTSD) Psychological disorder characterized by episodes of anxiety, sleeplessness, and nightmares resulting from some disturbing event in the past.

Power motive The need to win recognition or to influence or control other people or groups; a social motive.

Prejudice An unfair, intolerant, or unfavorable attitude toward a group of people.

Premature ejaculation Inability of man to inhibit orgasm as long as desired.

Prenatal development Development from conception to birth.

Preoperational stage In Piaget's theory, the stage of cognitive development between 2 and 7 years of age in which the individual becomes able to use mental representations and language to describe, remember, and reason about the world, though only in an egocentric fashion.

Pressure A feeling that one must speed up, intensify, or change the direction of one's behavior or live up to a higher standard of performance.

Prevention Reducing the incidence of emotional disturbance by eliminating conditions that cause or contribute to mental disorders and substituting conditions that foster mental well-being.

Primacy effect The theory that early information about someone weighs more heavily than later information in influencing one's impression of that person.

Primary drive Physiologically based unlearned motive, such as hunger.

Primary prevention Techniques and programs to improve the social environment so that new cases of mental disorders do not develop.

Primary reinforcer A reinforcer that is rewarding in itself, such as food, water, and sex.

Primary somatosensory cortex Area of the parietal lobe where messages from the sense receptors are registered.

Principles of conservation The concept that basic amounts remain constant despite superficial changes in appearance, such as the idea that the volume of a liquid stays the same regardless of the size and shape of the container into which it is poured.

Proactive interference The process by which old material already in memory interferes with new information.

Problem representation The first step in solving a problem; it involves interpreting or defining the problem.

Projection Attributing one's own repressed motives, feelings, or wishes to others.

Projective tests Personality tests, such as the Rorschach inkblot test, consisting of ambiguous or unstructured material.

Prototype According to Rosch, a mental model containing the most typical features of a concept.

Proximity How close two people live to each other.

Pseudoscience A theory or body of knowledge that portrays itself as a science but is not based on empirical observation or is inconsistent with broader scientific theory.

Psychoactive drugs Chemical substances that change moods and perceptions.

Psychoanalysis The theory of personality Freud developed as well as the form of therapy he invented.

Psychoanalytic model of psychological disorders View that psychological disorders result from unconscious internal conflicts.

Psychodynamic theories Personality theories contending that behavior results from psychological dynamics that interact within the individual, often outside conscious awareness.

Psychology The scientific study of behavior and mental processes.

Psychoneuroimmunology A field of medicine that studies the interaction between stress on the one hand and immune, endocrine, and nervous system activity on the other.

Psychosomatic disorders Disorders in which there is real physical illness that is largely caused by psychological factors such as stress and anxiety.

Psychostimulants Drugs that increase ability to focus attention in children with ADHD.

Psychosurgery Brain surgery performed to change a person's behavior and emotional state; a biological therapy rarely used today.

Psychotherapy The use of psychological techniques to treat personality and behavior disorders.

Psychotic Marked by defective or lost contact with reality.

Puberty The onset of sexual maturation, with accompanying physical development.

Punisher A stimulus that follows a behavior and decreases the likelihood that the behavior will be repeated.

Punishment Any event whose presence decreases the likelihood that ongoing behavior will recur.

Pupil A small opening in the iris through which light enters the eye.

Race A subpopulation of a species, defined according to an identifiable characteristic (i.e., geographic location, skin color, hair texture, genes, facial features).

Racism Prejudice and discrimination directed at a particular racial group.

Random sample Sample in which each potential participant has an equal chance of being selected.

Range Difference between the largest and smallest measurements in a distribution.

Ratio scale Scale with equal distances between the points or values and with a true zero.

Rational individuals According to Jung, people who regulate their actions by the psychological functions of thinking and feeling.

Rational-emotive therapy (RET) A directive cognitive therapy based on the idea that clients' psychological distress is caused by irrational and self-defeating beliefs and that the therapist's job is to challenge such dysfunctional beliefs.

Reaction formation Expression of exaggerated ideas and emotions that are the opposite of one's repressed beliefs or feelings.

Realistic job preview A recruitment technique designed to give job applicants a sense of the typical work-day on the job.

Reality principle According to Freud, the way in which the ego seeks to satisfy instinctual demands safely and effectively in the real world.

Receptor cell A specialized cell that responds to a particular type of energy.

Receptor site A location on a receptor neuron into which a specific neurotransmitter fits like a key into a lock.

Recessive gene Member of a gene pair that can control the appearance of a certain trait only if it is paired with another recessive gene.

Regression Reverting to childlike behavior and defenses.

Reinforcer A stimulus that follows a behavior and increases the likelihood that the behavior will be repeated.

Relative refractory period A period after firing when a neuron is returning to its normal polarized state and will fire again only if the incoming message is much stronger than usual.

Reliability Ability of a test to produce consistent and stable scores.

REM (paradoxical) sleep Sleep stage characterized by rapid eye movement; it is during this stage that most vivid dreaming occurs.

Representative sample Sample carefully chosen so that the characteristics of the participants correspond closely to the characteristics of the larger population.

Representativeness A heuristic by which a new situation is judged on the basis of its resemblance to a stereotypical model.

Repression Excluding uncomfortable thoughts, feelings, and desires from consciousness.

Response acquisition The "building phase" of conditioning during which the likelihood or strength of the desired response increases.

Response generalization Giving a response that is somewhat different from the response originally learned to that stimulus.

Resting potential Electrical charge across a neuron membrane due to excess positive ions concentrated on the outside and excess negative ions on the inside.

Reticular formation (RF) Network of neurons in the hindbrain, the midbrain, and part of the forebrain whose primary function is to alert and arouse the higher parts of the brain.

Retina The lining of the eye containing receptor cells that are sensitive to light.

Retinal disparity Binocular distance cue based on the difference between the images cast on the two retinas when both eyes are focused on the same object.

Retroactive interference The process by which new information interferes with old information already in memory.

Retrograde amnesia The inability to recall events immediately preceding an accident or injury, but without loss of earlier memory.

Risky shift Greater willingness to take risks in decision making in a group than independent individuals.

Rods Receptor cells in the retina responsible for night vision and perception of brightness.

Rooting reflex The reflex that causes a newborn baby to turn its head toward something touching its cheek and to grope around with its mouth.

Rorschach test A projective test composed of ambiguous inkblots; the way people interpret the blots is thought to reveal aspects of their personality.

Rote rehearsal Retaining information in STM simply by repeating it over and over.

Round window Membrane between the middle ear and inner ear that equalizes pressure in the inner ear.

Sample Selection of cases from a larger population.

Saturation The vividness or richness of a hue.

Scatter plot Diagram showing the association between scores on two variables.

Schedule of reinforcement In operant conditioning, the rule for determining when and how often reinforcers will be delivered.

Schema (plural: schemata) A set of beliefs or expectations about something that is based on past experience.

Schizoid personality disorder Personality disorder in which a person is withdrawn and lacks feelings for others.

Schizophrenic disorders Severe disorders in which there are disturbances of thoughts, communications, and emotions, including delusions and hallucinations.

Scientific method An approach to knowledge that relies on collecting data, generating a theory to explain the data, producing testable hypotheses based on the theory, and testing those hypotheses empirically.

Secondary prevention Programs to identify groups that are at high risk for mental disorders and to detect maladaptive behavior in these groups and treat it promptly.

Secondary reinforcer A reinforcer whose value is acquired through association with other primary or secondary reinforcers.

Selection studies Studies that estimate the heritability of a trait by breeding animals with other animals that have the same trait.

Self-actualizing tendency According to Rogers, the drive of human beings to fulfill their self-concepts, or the images they have of themselves.

Self-efficacy According to Bandura, the expectancy that one's efforts will be successful.

Self-fulfilling prophecy The process in which a person's expectation about another elicits behavior from the second person that confirms the expectation.

Self-managed work team An autonomous work group that has the authority to make decisions in such managerial areas as planning, scheduling, and even hiring.

Self-monitoring The tendency for an individual to observe the situation for cues about how to react.

Semantic memory The portion of long-term memory that stores general facts and information.

Semantics The criteria for assigning meaning to the morphemes in a language.

Semicircular canals Structures in the inner ear particularly sensitive to body rotation.

Sensation The experience of sensory stimulation.

Sensory deprivation Extreme reduction of sensory stimuli.

Sensory-motor stage In Piaget's theory, the stage of cognitive development between birth and 2 years of age in which the individual develops object permanence and acquires the ability to form mental representations.

Sensory (or afferent) neurons Neurons that carry messages from sense organs to the spinal cord or brain.

Sensory registers Entry points for raw information from the senses.

Set The tendency to perceive and to approach problems in certain ways.

Set point A homeostatic mechanism in the body that regulates metabolism, fat storage, and food intake so as to maintain a preprogrammed weight.

Sex-typed behavior Socially prescribed ways of behaving that differ for boys and girls.

Sexual arousal disorder Inability to achieve or sustain arousal until the end of intercourse in a person who is capable of experiencing sexual desire.

Sexual desire disorders Disorders in which the person lacks sexual interest or has an active distaste for sex.

Sexual dysfunction Loss or impairment of the ordinary physical responses of sexual function.

Sexual masochism Inability to enjoy sex without accompanying emotional or physical pain.

Sexual orientations Refers to the direction of one's sexual interest toward members of the same sex, the other sex, or both sexes.

Sexual sadism Obtaining sexual gratification from humiliating or physically harming a sex partner.

Shadowing Monocular cue to distance and depth based on the fact that shadows often appear on the parts of objects that are more distant.

Shape constancy A tendency to see an object as the same shape no matter what angle it is viewed from.

Shaping Reinforcing successive approximations to a desired behavior.

Short-term memory (STM) Working memory; briefly stores and processes selected information from the sensory registers.

Short-term psychodynamic psychotherapy Insight therapy that is time-limited and focused on trying to help clients correct the immediate problems in their lives.

Significance Probability that results obtained were due to chance.

Sixteen Personality Factor Questionnaire Objective personality test created by Cattell that provides scores on the 16 traits he identified.

Size constancy The perception of an object as the same size regardless of the distance from which it is viewed.

Skinner box A box often used in operant conditioning of animals, which limits the available response and thus increases the likelihood that the desired response will occur.

Social influence The process by which others individually or collectively affect one's perceptions, attitudes, and actions.

Social learning theory A view of learning that emphasizes the ability to learn by observing a model or receiving instructions, without firsthand experience by the learner.

Social loafing The tendency of people to exert less effort on a task when working in a group than when working individually.

Social motive Learned motive associated with relationships among people, such as the needs for affiliation, achievement, and power.

Social phobia An anxiety disorder characterized by excessive, inappropriate fears connected with social situations or performances in front of other people.

Social psychology The scientific study of the ways in which the thoughts, feelings, and behaviors of one individual are influenced by the real, imagined, or inferred behavior or characteristics of other people.

Socialization Process by which children learn the behaviors and attitudes appropriate to their family and their culture.

Solitary play A child engaged in some activity alone; the earliest form of play.

Somatic nervous system The part of the peripheral nervous system that carries messages from the senses to the central nervous system and between the central nervous system and the skeletal muscles.

Somatization disorder A somatoform disorder characterized by recurrent vague somatic complaints without a physical cause.

Somatoform disorders Disorders in which there is an apparent physical illness for which there is no organic basis.

Sound A psychological experience created by the brain in response to changes in air pressure that are received by the auditory system.

Sound waves Changes in pressure caused when molecules of air or fluid collide with one another and then move apart again.

Specific phobia Anxiety disorder characterized by intense, paralyzing fear of something.

Spinal cord Complex cable of neurons that runs down the spine, connecting the brain to most of the rest of the body.

Split-half reliability A method of determining test reliability by dividing the test into two parts and checking the agreement of scores on both parts.

Spontaneous recovery The reappearance of an extinguished response after the passage of time, without further training.

Standard deviation Statistical measure of variability in a group of scores or other values.

Stanford-Binet Intelligence Scale Terman's adaptation of the Binet-Simon Scale.

Statistics A branch of mathematics that psychologists use to organize and analyze data.

Stepping reflex The reflex that causes newborn babies to make little stepping motions if they are held upright with their feet just touching a surface.

Stereoscopic vision Combination of two retinal images to give a three-dimensional perceptual experience.

Stereotype A set of characteristics presumed to be shared by all members of a social category.

Stimulants Drugs, including amphetamines and cocaine, that stimulate the sympathetic nervous system and produce feelings of optimism and boundless energy.

Stimulus discrimination Learning to respond to only one stimulus and to inhibit the response to all other stimuli.

Stimulus generalization The transfer of a learned response to different but similar stimuli.

Stimulus motive Unlearned motive, such as curiosity or contact, that prompts us to explore or change the world around us.

Strain studies Studies of the heritability of behavioral traits using animals that have been inbred to produce strains that are genetically similar to one another.

Stress Any environmental demand that creates a state of tension or threat and requires change or adaptation.

Stress-inoculation therapy A type of cognitive therapy that trains clients to cope with stressful situations by learning a more useful pattern of self-talk.

Stretch receptors Receptors that sense muscle stretch and contraction.

Stroboscopic motion Apparent movement that results from flashing a series of still pictures in rapid succession, as in a motion picture.

Structuralism School of psychology that stresses the basic units of experience and the combinations in which they occur.

Subgoals Intermediate, more manageable goals used in one heuristic strategy to make it easier to reach the final goal.

Subjects or participants Individuals whose reactions or responses are observed in an experiment.

Sublimation Redirecting repressed motives and feelings into more socially acceptable channels.

Substance abuse A pattern of drug use that diminishes the ability to fulfill responsibilities at home or at work or school, that results in repeated use of a drug in dangerous situations, or that leads to legal difficulties related to drug use.

Substance dependence A pattern of compulsive drug taking that results in tolerance, withdrawal symptoms, or other specific symptoms for at least a year.

Subtractive color mixing The process of mixing pigments, each of which absorbs some wavelengths of light and reflects others.

Sucking reflex The reflex that causes the newborn baby to suck on objects placed in its mouth.

Superego According to Freud, the social and parental standards the individual has internalized; the conscience and the ego ideal.

Superposition Monocular distance cue in which one object, by partly blocking a second object, is perceived as being closer.

Surface structure The particular words and phrases used to make up a sentence.

Survey research Research technique in which questionnaires or interviews are administered to a selected group of people.

Swallowing reflex The reflex that enables the newborn baby to swallow liquids without choking.

Sympathetic division Branch of the autonomic nervous system; it prepares the body for quick action in an emergency.

Synapse Area composed of the axon terminal of one neuron, the synaptic space, and the dendrite or cell body of the next neuron.

Synaptic space (or synaptic cleft) Tiny gap between the axon terminal of one neuron and the dendrites or cell body of the next neuron.

Synaptic vesicles Tiny sacs in a terminal button that release chemicals into the synapse.

Syntax The rules for arranging words into grammatical sentences.

Systematic desensitization A behavioral technique for reducing a person's fear and anxiety by gradually associating a new response (relaxation) with stimuli that have been causing the fear and anxiety.

Systems approach to psychological disorders View that biological, psychological, and social risk factors combine to produce psychological disorders. Also known as the biopsychosocial model of psychological disorders.

Tacit knowledge Knowledge one needs for success in completing particular practical tasks; this knowledge may not be explicit.

Tactic of elimination A problem-solving strategy in which possible solutions are evaluated according to appropriate criteria and discarded as they fail to contribute to a solution.

Taste buds Structures on the tongue that contain the receptor cells for taste.

Telegraphic speech An early speech stage of one- and two-year-olds that omits words that are not essential to the meaning of a phrase.

Temperament A term used by psychologists to describe the physical/emotional characteristics of the newborn child and young infant; also referred to as personality.

Temporal lobe Part of the cerebral hemisphere that helps regulate hearing, balance and equilibrium, and certain emotions and motivations.

Terminal button (or synaptic knob) Structure at the end of an axon terminal branch.

Tertiary prevention Programs to help people adjust to community life after release from a mental hospital.

Testosterone The primary male sex hormone.

Texture gradient Monocular cue to distance and depth based on the fact that objects seen at greater distances appear to be smoother and less textured.

Thalamus Forebrain region that relays and translates incoming messages from the sense receptors, except those for smell.

Thematic Apperception Test (TAT) A projective test composed of ambiguous pictures about which a person is asked to write a complete story.

Theory Systematic explanation of a phenomenon; it organizes known facts, allows us to predict new facts, and permits us to exercise a degree of control over the phenomenon.

Theory of multiple intelligences Howard Gardner's theory that there is not one intelligence, but rather many intelligences, each of which is relatively independent of the others.

Threshold of excitation The level an impulse must exceed to cause a neuron to fire.

Thyroid gland Endocrine gland located below the voice box; it produces the hormone thyroxin.

Timbre The quality or texture of sound; caused by overtones.

Token economy An operant conditioning therapy in which patients earn tokens (reinforcers) for desired behaviors and exchange them for desired items or privileges.

Tolerance Phenomenon whereby higher doses of a drug are required to produce its original effects or to prevent withdrawal symptoms.

Traits Characteristics on which organisms differ.

Transference The patient's carrying over to the analyst feelings held toward childhood authority figures.

Transvestic fetishism Wearing the clothes of the opposite sex to achieve sexual gratification.

Trial and error A problem-solving strategy based on the successive elimination of incorrect solutions until the correct one is found.

Triarchic theory of intelligence Sternberg's theory that intelligence involves mental skills (componential aspect), insight and creative adaptability (experiential aspect), and environmental responsiveness (contextual aspect).

Trichromatic theory The theory of color vision that holds that all color perception derives from three different color receptors in the retina (usually red, green, and blue receptors).

Trichromats People who have normal color vision.

Twin studies Studies of identical and fraternal twins to determine the relative influence of heredity and environment on human behavior.

Unconditional positive regard In Rogers's theory, the full acceptance and love of another person regardless of that person's behavior.

Unconditioned response (UR) A response that takes place in an organism whenever an unconditioned stimulus occurs.

Unconditioned stimulus (US) A stimulus that invariably causes an organism to respond in a specific way.

Unconscious In Freud's theory, all the ideas, thoughts, and feelings of which we are not and normally cannot become aware.

Undifferentiated schizophrenia Schizophrenic disorder in which there are clear schizophrenic symptoms that don't meet the criteria for another subtype of the disorder.

Vaginismus Involuntary muscle spasms in the outer part of the vagina that make intercourse impossible.

Validity Ability of a test to measure what it has been designed to measure.

Variable-interval schedule A reinforcement schedule in which the correct response is reinforced after varying lengths of time following the last reinforcement.

Variable-ratio schedule A reinforcement schedule in which a varying number of correct responses must occur before reinforcement is presented.

Vestibular sacs Sacs in the inner ear that sense gravitation and forward, backward, and vertical movement.

Vestibular senses The senses of equilibrium and body position in space.

Vicarious reinforcement and **vicarious punishment** Reinforcement or punishment experienced by models that affects the willingness of others to perform the behaviors they learned by observing those models.

Visual acuity The ability to distinguish fine details visually.

Visualizing A problem-solving strategy in which principles or concepts are drawn, diagrammed, or charted so that they can be better understood.

Volley principle Refinement of frequency theory; it suggests that receptors in the ear fire in sequence, with one group responding, then a second, then a third, and so on, so that the complete pattern of firing corresponds to the frequency of the sound wave.

Vomeronasal organ (VNO) Location of receptors for pheromones in the roof of the nasal cavity.

Voyeurism Desire to watch others having sexual relations or to spy on nude people.

Waking consciousness Mental state that encompasses the thoughts, feelings, and perceptions that occur when we are awake and reasonably alert.

Wavelengths The different energies represented in the electromagnetic spectrum.

Weber's law The principle that the jnd for any given sense is a constant fraction or proportion of the stimulation being judged.

Wechsler Adult Intelligence Scale-Third Edition (WAIS-III) An individual intelligence test developed especially for adults; measures both verbal and performance abilities.

Wechsler Intelligence Scale for Children-Third Edition (WISC-III) An individual intelligence test developed especially for school-aged children; measures verbal and performance abilities and also yields an overall IQ score.

Withdrawal Avoiding a situation when other forms of coping are not practical.

Withdrawal symptoms Unpleasant physical or psychological effects that follow the discontinuance of a dependence-producing substance.

Working backward A heuristic strategy in which one works backward from the desired goal to the given conditions.

Yerkes-Dodson law States that there is an optimal level of arousal for the best performance of any task; the more complex the task, the lower the level of arousal that can be tolerated before performance deteriorates.

REFERENCES

Aaker, D.A., & Bruzzone, D.E. (1985). Causes of irritation in advertising. *Journal of Marketing, 49*, 47–57.

Aaronson, D., & Scarborough, H.S. (1976). Performance theories for sentence coding: Some quantitative evidence. *Journal of Experimental Psychology: Human Perception and Performance, 2*, 56–70.

Aaronson, D., & Scarborough, H.S. (1977). Performance theories for sentence coding: Some quantitative models. *Journal of Verbal Learning and Verbal Behavior, 16*, 277–304.

Abramov, I., & Gordon, J. (1994). Color appearance: On seeing red or yellow, or green, or blue. *Annual Review of Psychology, 45*, 451–485.

Ackerman, M.D., & Carey, M.P. (1995). Psychology's role in the assessment of erectile dysfunction: Historical precedents, current knowledge, and methods. *Journal of Consulting and Clinical Psychology, 63*, 862–876.

Acredolo, L.P., & Hake, J.L. (1982). Infant perception. In B.B. Wolman (Ed.), *Handbook of developmental psychology* (pp. 244–283). Englewood Cliffs, NJ: Prentice Hall.

Adams, D.B., Gold, A.R., & Burt, A.D. (1978). Rise in female-initiated sexual activity at ovulation and its suppression by oral contraceptives. *New England Journal of Medicine, 299*, 1145–1150.

Adams, G.R., & Gullota, T. (1983). *Adolescent life experiences.* Monterey, CA: Brooks/Cole.

Adams, H.E., Wright, L.W., & Lohr, B.A. (1996). Is homophobia associated with homosexual arousal? *Journal of Abnormal Psychology, 105*(3), 440–445.

Adams, J.L. (1980). *Conceptual blockbusting: A guide to better ideas* (2nd ed.). New York: Norton.

Adams, K., & Johnson-Greene, D. (1995). *PET and neuropsychological performance among chronic alcoholics.* Paper presented at the annual meeting of the American Psychological Association, New York.

Adelmann, P.K., & Zajonc, R.B. (1989). Facial efference and the experience of emotion. *Annual Review of Psychology, 40*, 249–280.

Ader, D.N., & Johnson, S.B. (1994). Sample description, reporting, and analysis of sex in psychological research: A look at APA and APA division journals in 1990. *American Psychologist, 49*(3), 216.

Ader, R., & Cohen, N. (1993). Psychoneuroimmunology: Conditioning and stress. *Annual Review of Psychology, 44*, 53–85.

Adler, N., Boyce, T., Chesney, M.A., Cohen, S., Folkman, S., Kahn, R.I., & Syme, S.L. (1994). Socioeconomic status and health. The challenge of the gradient. *American Psychologist, 49*, 15–24.

Adler, T. (1990, January). PMS diagnosis draws fire from researchers. *APA Monitor*, p. 12.

Adler, T. (1993a, May). Raising the cigarette tax can lower smoking rates. *APA Monitor*, p. 15.

Adler, T. (1993b, July). Men and women affected by stress, but differently. *APA Monitor*, pp. 8–9.

Adorno, T.W., Frenkel-Brunswick, E., Levinson, D.J., & Sanford, R.N. (1950). *The authoritarian personality.* New York: Harper & Row.

Agostinelli, G., Sherman, S.J., Presson, C.C., & Chassin, L. (1992). Self-protection and self-enhancement biases in estimates of population prevalence. *Personality and Social Psychology Bulletin, 18*(5), 631–642.

Agras, W.S. (1987). *Eating disorders: Management of obesity, bulimia and anorexia nervosa.* Elmsford, NY: Pergamon.

Agras, W.S., & Kraemer, H. (1983). The treatment of anorexia nervosa. Do different treatments have different outcomes? *Psychiatric Annuals, 13*, 928–935.

Ahrons, C.R., & Miller, R.B. (1993). The effect of the postdivorce relationship on paternal involvement: A longitudinal analysis. *American Journal of Orthopsychiatry, 63*(3), 441–450.

Aiken, L.R. (1988). *Psychological testing and assessment* (6th ed.). Boston: Allyn & Bacon.

Ainslie, G. (1975). Specious reward: A behavioral theory of impulsiveness and impulse control. *Psychological Bulletin, 82*, 463–496.

Ainsworth, M.D. (1989). Attachments beyond infancy. *American Psychologist, 44*, 709–716.

Ainsworth, M.D., Blehar, M.C., Waters, E., & Wall, S. (1978). *Patterns of attachment.* New York: Halstead Press.

Ainsworth, M.D.S. (1977). Attachment theory and its utility in cross-cultural research. In P.H. Leiderman, S.R. Tulkin, & A. Rosenfields (Eds.), *Culture and infancy: Variation in the human experience.* New York: Academic Press.

Ainsworth, M.D.S., & Wittig, B.A. (1969). Attachment and exploratory behavior of one-year olds in a strange situation. In B.M. Foss (Ed.), *Determinants of infant behavior* (Vol. 4., pp. 111–136). London: Methuen.

Akil, H., & Watson, S.J. (1980). The role of endogenous opiates in pain control. In H.W. Kosterlitz & L.Y. Terenius (Eds.), *Pain and society.* Weinheim: Verlag Chemie.

Akiskal, H.S. (1994). The temperamental borders of affective disorders. *Acta Psychiatrica Scandinavica, 89*(Suppl. 379), 32–37.

Alan Guttmacher Institute. (1990). *Adolescent sexuality.* New York: Alan Guttmacher Institute.

Albert, D.J., Walsh, M.L., & Jonik, R.H. (1993). Aggression in humans: What is its biological foundation? *Neuroscience Biobehavior Review, 17*(4), 405–425.

Albus, M. (1989). Cholecystokinin. *Progress in Neuro-Psychopharmacology and Biological Psychiatry, 12*(Suppl.), 5–21.

Allen, L.S., & Gorski, R.A. (1992). Sexual orientation and size of the anterior commissure in the human brain. *Proceedings of the National Academy of Sciences, 89*, 7199–7202.

Allen, V.L., & Levine, J.M. (1971). Social support and conformity: The role of independent assessment of reality. *Journal of Experimental Social Psychology, 7*, 48–58.

Allport, G.W. (1954). *The nature of prejudice.* New York: Anchor.

Allport, G.W., & Odbert, H.S. (1936). Trait-names: A psycholexical study. *Psychological Monographs, 47*(1, Whole No. 211).

Almagor, M., Tellegen, A., & Waller, N.G. (1995). The big seven model: A cross-cultural replication and further explorations of the basic dimensions of natural language descriptors. *Journal of Personality and Social Psychology, 69*, 300–307.

Altabe, M.N., & Thompson, J.K. (1994). Body image. In *Encyclopedia of human behavior* (Vol. 1, pp. 407–414).

Altman, I., & Taylor, D.A. (1973). *Social penetration: The development of interpersonal relationships.* New York: Holt, Rinehart & Winston.

Altman, L.K. (1995, April 18). Research dispels myth that brain in adults is unable to renew itself. *New York Times*, p. B9.

Alvarado, N. (1994). Empirical validity of the Thematic Apperception Test. *Journal of Personality Assessment, 63*, 59–79.

Amabile, T.M. (1983). The social psychology of creativity: A comparative conceptualization. *Journal of Personality and Social Psychology, 45*, 357–376.

Amabile, T.M., (1983). *The social psychology of creativity.* New York: Springer-Verlag.

Amabile, T.M., Hennessey, B.A., & Grossman, B.S. (1986). Social influences on creativity: The effects of contracted-for reward. *Journal of Personality and Social Psychology, 50*, 14–23.

American Psychological Association (APA). (1953). *Ethical standards of psychologists.* Washington, DC: American Psychological Association.

American Psychological Association (APA). (1978). Guidelines for therapy with women. *American Psychologist, 33*, 1122–1123.

American Psychological Association (APA). (1990). *Task force on women's depression* (Final Report). Washington, DC: American Psychological Association.

American Psychological Association (APA). (1992). *Big world, small screen*. Washington, DC: American Psychological Association.

American Psychological Association (APA). (1993). *Violence and youth*. Washington, DC: American Psychological Association.

American Psychological Association (APA). (1994). *Diagnostic and statistical manual of mental disorders* (4th ed.). Washington, DC: American Psychiatric Press.

Anastasi, A., & Urbina, S. (1977). *Psychological testing* (7th ed.). Upper Saddle River, NJ: Prentice Hall.

Anastasi, A., & Urbina, S. (1997). *Psychological testing* (7th ed.). Upper Saddle River, NJ: Prentice Hall.

Anch, A.M., Browman, C.P., Mitler, M.M., & Walsh, J.K. (1988). *Sleep: A scientific perspective*. Englewood Cliffs, NJ: Prentice Hall.

Anderson, A.E. (Ed.). (1990). *Males with eating disorders*. New York: Brunner/Mazel.

Anderson, B.L., Kiecolt-Glaser, J.K., & Glaser, R. (1994). A biobehavioral model of cancer stress and disease course. *American Psychologist, 49*(5), 389–404.

Anderson, R.C., & Pichert, J.W. (1978). Recall of previously unrecallable information following a shift in perspective. *Journal of Verbal Learning and Verbal Behavior, 17*, 1–12.

Andreasen, N.C., Rice, J., Endicott, J., Coyell, W., Grove, W.M., & Reich, T. (1987). Familial rates of affective disorder. *Archives of General Psychiatry, 44*, 451–469.

Andrews, J.A., & Lewinsohn, P.M. (1992). Suicidal attempts among older adolescents: Prevalence and co-occurrence with psychiatric disorders. *Journal of the American Academy of Child and Adolescent Psychiatry, 31*, 655–662.

Angier, N. (1992, May 20). Is there a male menopause? Jury is still out. *New York Times*, p. A1.

Angier, N. (1995, June 20). Does testosterone equal aggression? Maybe not. *New York Times*, p. 1.

Anthony, J.C., & Aboraya, A. (1992). The epidemiology of selected mental disorders in later life. In J.E. Birren, R.B. Sloane, & G.D. Choen (Eds.), *Handbook of mental health and aging* (2nd ed., pp. 3–143). San Diego, CA: Academic Press.

Antonarakis, S.E. (1991). Parental origin of the extra chromosome in trisomy 21 as indicated by analysis of DNA polymorphisms. *New England Journal of Medicine, 324*, 872–876.

Aranya, N., Kushnir, T., & Valency, A. (1986). Organizational commitment in a male dominated profession. *Human Relations, 39*, 433–438.

Archer, J. (1996). Sex differences in social behavior: Are the social role and evolutionary explanations compatible? *American Psychologist, 51*(9), 909–917.

Arias, C., Curet, C.A., Moyano, H.F., Joekes, S., & Blanch, N. (1993). Echolocation: A study of auditory functioning in blind and sighted subjects. *Journal of Visual Impairment and Blindness, 87*, 73–77.

Arkema, P.H. (1981). The borderline personality and transitional relatedness. *American Journal of Psychiatry, 138*, 172–177.

Arkin, R.M., Cooper, H., & Kolditz, T. (1980). A statistical review of literature concerning the self-serving attribution bias in interpersonal influence situations. *Journal of Personality, 48*, 435–448.

Arnett, J. (1991, April). *Sensation seeking and egocentrism as factors in reckless behaviors among a college-age sample*. Paper presented at the meeting of the Society for Research in Child Development, Seattle, WA.

Arnett, J. (1995). The young and the reckless: Adolescent reckless behavior. *American Psychological Society, 4*(3), 67–71.

Aronoff, G.M. (Ed.). (1993). *Evaluation and treatment of chronic pain* (2nd ed.). Baltimore, MD: Williams and Wilkins.

Aronson, E. (1994). *The social animal* (7th ed.). New York: Freeman.

Asch, S.E. (1946). Forming impressions of personality. *Journal of Abnormal and Social Psychology, 41*, 258–290.

Asch, S.E. (1951). Effects of group pressure upon the modification and distortion of judgments. In H. Guetzkow (Ed.), *Groups, leadership, and men*. Pittsburgh: Carnegie Press.

Asch, S.E. (1956). Studies of independence and conformity: I. A minority of one against a unanimous majority. *Psychological Monographs, 70*(9, Whole No. 416).

Aslin, R.N., & Smith, L.B. (1988). Perceptual development. *Annual Review of Psychology, 39*, 435–473.

Aston, R. (1972). Barbiturates, alcohol and tranquilizers. In S.J. Mule & H. Brill (Eds.), *The chemical and biological aspects of drug dependence*. Cleveland, OH: CRC Press.

Atchley, R.C. (1982). Retirement as a social institution. *Annual Review of Sociology, 8*, 263–287.

Atkinson, J.W., & Birch, D. (1970). *The dynamics of action*. New York: Wiley.

Atkinson, J.W., & Raynor, J.O. (1975). *Motivation and achievement*. Washington, DC: Winston.

Aved, B.M., Irwin, M.M., Cummings, L.S., & Findeisen, N. (1993). Barriers to prenatal care for low-income women. *Western Journal of Medicine, 158*(5), 493–498.

Avery-Leaf, S., Cano, A., Cascardi, M., & O'Leary, K.D. (1995). *Evaluation of a dating violence prevention program*. Paper presented at the International Family Violence Research Conference, Durham, New Hampshire.

Awh, E., Jonides, J., Smith, E.H., Schumacher, R.A., Koeppe, R.A., & Katz, S. (1996). Dissociation of storage and rehearsal in verbal working memory: Evidence from positron emission tomography. *Psychological Science, 7*(1), 25–31.

Azzi, R., Fix, D.S.R., Keller, R.S., & Rocha e Silva, M.I. (1964). Exteroceptive control of response under delayed reinforcement. *Journal of the Experimental Analysis of Behavior, 7*, 159–162.

Babkoff, H., Caspy, T., Mikulincer, M., & Sing, H.C. (1991). Monotonic and rhythmic influences: A challenge for sleep deprivation research. *Psychological Bulletin, 109*, 411–428.

Bachtold, L.M., & Werner, E.E. (1973). Personality characteristics of creative women. *Perception and Motor Skills, 36*, 311–319.

Baddeley, A.D. (1986). *Working memory*. Oxford: Clarendon Press.

Baddeley, A.D. (1987). Amnesia. In R.L. Gregory (Ed.), *The Oxford companion to the mind* (pp. 20–22). Oxford: Oxford University Press.

Baddeley, A.D. (1994). The magical number seven: Still magic after all these years? *Psychological Review, 101*, 353–356.

Baddeley, A.D., & Hitch, G. (1974). Working memory. In G.H. Bower (Ed.), *The psychology of learning and motivation* (Vol. 8). New York: Academic Press.

Baddeley, A.D., & Hitch, G.J. (1994). Developments in the concept of working memory. *Neuropsychology, 6*, 485–493.

Baer, L., Rauch, S.L., & Ballantine, T. (1995). Cingulotomy for intractable obsessive-compulsive disorder: Prospective long-term follow-up of 18 patients. *Archives of General Psychiatry, 52*, 384–392.

Bahrick, H.P. (1984). Semantic memory in permastore: Fifty years of memory for Spanish learned in school. *Journal of Experimental Psychology: General, 113*, 1–31.

Bahrick, H.P., & Hall, L.K. (1991). Lifetime maintenance of high school mathematics content. *Journal of Experimental Psychology: General, 120*, 20–33.

Bahrick, H.P., Bahrick, P.O., & Wittlinger, R.P. (1974, December). Those unforgettable high school days. *Psychology Today*, pp. 50–56.

Bailey, A., Le Couteur, A., Gottesman, I., Bolton, P., Simonoff, E., Yuzda, E., & Rutter, M. (1995). Autism as a strongly genetic disorder: Evidence from a British twin study. *Psychological Medicine, 25*(1), 63–77.

Bailey, A., LeCouteur, A., Gottesman, I., Bolton, P., Simonoff, E., Yuzda, E., & Rutter, M. (in press). Autism as a strongly genetic disorder: Evidence from a British twin study. *Psychological Medicine*.

Bailey, J.M., & Bell, A.P. (1993). Familiality of female and male homosexuality. *Behavior Genetics, 23*, 313–322.

Bailey, J.M., & Benishay, D.S. (1993). Familial aggregation of female sexual orientation. *American Journal of Psychiatry, 150*, 272–277.

Baillargeon, R. (1994). How do infants learn about the physical world? *American Psychological Society, 3*(5), 133–140.

Balaguer, A., & Markman, H. (1994). Mate selection. In *Encyclopedia of human behavior* (Vol. 3, pp. 127–135).

Baldwin, A.Y. (1985). Programs for the gifted and talented: Issues concerning minority populations. In F.D. Horowitz & M. O'Brien (Eds.), *The gifted and talented: Developmental perspectives*. Washington, DC: American Psychological Association.

Bales, R.F. (1951). *Interaction Process Analysis: A method for the study of small groups*. Reading, MA: Addison-Wesley.

Ball, J.D., Archer, R.P., & Imhof, E.A. (1994). Time requirements of psychological testing: A survey of practitioners. *Journal of Personality Assessment, 63*, 239–249.

Banaji, M.R., & Hardin, C.D. (1996). Automatic stereotyping. *Psychological Science, 7*(3), 136–141.

Bandura, A. (1962). Social learning through imitation. In M.R. Jones (Ed.), *Nebraska Symposium on Motivation*. Lincoln: University of Nebraska Press.

Bandura, A. (1965). Influence of models' reinforcement contingencies on the acquisition of imitative responses. *Journal of Personality and Social Psychology, 1*, 589–595.

Bandura, A. (1973). *Aggression: A social learning analysis*. Englewood Cliffs, NJ: Prentice Hall.

Bandura, A. (1977). *Social learning theory*. Englewood Cliffs, NJ: Prentice Hall.

Bandura, A. (1986). *Social foundations of thought and action: A social cognitive theory*. Englewood Cliffs, NJ: Prentice Hall.

Bandura, A., Blanchard, E.B., & Ritter, B. (1969). Relative efficacy of desensitization and modeling approaches for inducing behavioral, affective, and attitudinal changes. *Journal of Personality and Social Psychology, 13*, 173–199.

Banyai, E.I., & Hilgard, E.R. (1976). A comparison of active-alert hypnotic induction with traditional relaxation induction. *Journal of Abnormal Psychology, 85*, 218–224.

Barbaree, H.E., & Marshall, W.L. (1991). The role of male sexual arousal in rape: Six models. *Journal of Consulting and Clinical Psychology, 59*, 621–630.

Barbaree, H.E., & Seto, M.C. (1997). Pedophilia: Assessment and treatment. In D.R. Laws & W.T. O'Donohue (Eds.), *Handbook of sexual deviance: Theory and application*. New York: Guilford.

Barber, B.L., & Eccles, J.E. (1992). Long-term influence of divorce and single parenting on adolescent family- and work-related values, behaviors and aspirations. *Psychological Bulletin, 111*, 108–126.

Barber, T.X. (1969). An empirically-based formulation of hypnotism. *American Journal of Clinical Hypnotism, 12*(2), 100–130.

Barbur, J.L., Harlow, A.J., & Weiskrantz, L. (1994). Spatial and temporal response properties of residual vision in a case of hemianopia. *Philosophical Transactions of the Royal Society of London, B, 43*, 157–160.

Barglow, P., Vaughn, B.E., & Molitor, N. (1987). Effects of maternal absence due to employment on the quality of infant-mother attachment in a low-risk sample. *Child Development, 58*, 945–954.

Barkley, R.A. (1990). *Hyperactive children: A handbook for diagnosis and treatment* (2nd ed.). New York: Guilford.

Barnett, R.C., & Brennan, R.T. (1993). *The relationship between job experiences and emotional distress: A structural equation approach*. Wellesley, MA: Center for Research on Women.

Barnett, R.C., Brennan, R.T., & Marshall, N.L. (1994). Gender and the relationship between parent role quality and psychological distress: A study of men and women in dual-earner couples. *Journal of Family Issues, 15*(2), 229–252.

Barnouw, D. (1985). *Culture and personality*. Chicago: Dorsey Press.

Baron, R.A., & Byrne, D. (1991). *Social psychology: Understanding human interaction* (6th ed.). Boston: Allyn & Bacon.

Baron, R.M., Graziano, W.G., & Stangor, C. (1991). *Social psychology*. Fort Worth: Holt, Rinehart & Winston.

Barret, G.V., & Depinet, R.L. (1991). A reconsideration of testing for competence rather than for intelligence. *American Psychologist, 46*, 1012–1024.

Barrett-Connor, E., & Bush, T.L. (1991). Estrogen and coronary heart disease in women. *AMA, Journal of the American Medical Association, 265*(14), 1861–1867.

Barron, F. (1963). *Creativity and psychological health*. Princeton, NJ: Van Nostrand.

Barron, F., & Harrington, D.M. (1981). Creativity, intelligence, and personality. *Annual Review of Psychology, 32*, 439–476.

Bartlett, F.C. (1932). *Remembering: A study in experimental and social psychology*. New York: Macmillan.

Bartoshuk, L.M. (1974). Taste illusions: Some demonstrations. *Annals of the New York Academy of Sciences, 237*, 279–285.

Bartoshuk, L.M. (1993). The biological basis of food perception and acceptance. *Food Quality and Preference, 4*, 21–32.

Bartoshuk, L.M., & Beauchamp, G.K. (1994). Chemical senses. *Annual Review of Psychology, 45*, 419–449.

Baruch, F., & Barnett, R. (1986). Role quality, multiple role involvement, and psychological well-being in mid-life women. *Journal of Personality and Social Psychology, 51*, 578–585.

Basow, S.A. (1986). *Gender stereotypes: Traditions and alternatives* (2nd ed.). Pacific Grove, CA: Brooks/Cole.

Bassetti, C., & Aldrich, M.S. (1996). Narcolepsy. *Neuro Clin, 14*, 545–571.

Bassuk, E.L., & Gerson, S. (1978). Deinstitutionalization and mental health services. *Scientific American, 238*(2), 46–53.

Bates, M.S., & Rankin-Hill, L. (1994). Control, culture, and chronic pain. *Social Science and Medicine, 39*, 629–645.

Bateson, G. (1982). Totemic knowledge in New Guinea. In U. Neisser (Ed.), *Memory observed: Remembering in natural contexts*. San Francisco: Freeman.

Bauer, P.J. (1996). What do infants recall of their lives? Memory for specific events by one- to two-year-olds. *American Psychologist, 51*(1), 29–41.

Baumeister, R.F. (1988). Should we stop studying sex differences altogether? *American Psychologist, 43*, 1092–1095.

Baumeister, R.F., & Leary, M.R. (1995). The need to belong: Desire for interpersonal attachments as a fundamental human motivation. *Psychological Bulletin, 117*(3), 497–529.

Baumrind, D. (1972). Socialization and instrumental competence in young children. In W.W. Hartup (Ed.), *The young child: Reviews of research* (Vol. 2). Washington, DC: National Association for the Education of Young Children.

Baumrind, D. (1985). Research using intentional deception. *American Psychologist, 40*, 165–174.

Baxter, D.W., & Olszewski, J. (1960). Congenital insensitivity to pain. *Brain, 83*, 381.

Bayley, N. (1956). Individual patterns of development. *Child Development, 27*, 45–74.

Bayley, N. (1993) *Bayley Scales of Infant Development Second Edition: Manual*. San Antonio, TX: Psychological Corporation.

Beatty, S.E., & Hawkins, D.I. (1989). Subliminal stimulation: Some new data and interpretation. *Journal of Advertising, 18*, 4–8.

Bechara, A., Damasio, H., Tranel, D., & Damasio, A.R. (1997). Deciding advantageously before knowing the advantageous strategy. *Science, 275*, 1293–1295.

Beck, A.T. (1967). *Depression: Clinical, experimental and theoretical aspects*. New York: Harper (Hoeber).

Beck, A.T. (1976). *Cognitive therapy and emotional disorders*. New York: International Universities Press.

Beck, A.T. (1984). Cognition and therapy. *Archives of General Psychiatry, 41*, 1112–1114.

Beck, A.T. (1989). *Love is never enough*. New York: Harper & Row.

Beck, J.G. (1995). Hypoactive sexual desire disorder: An overview. *Journal of Consulting and Clinical Psychology, 63*, 919–927.

Beck, R. (1983). *Motivation: Theories and principles* (2nd ed.). Englewood Cliffs, NJ: Prentice Hall.

Bédard, J., & Chi, M.T.H. (1992). Expertise. *Current Directions in Psychological Science, 1*, 135–139.

Beecher, H.K. (1972). The placebo effect as a nonspecific force surrounding disease and the treatment of disease. In R. Jansen, W.D. Kerdel, A. Herz, C. Steichele, J.P. Payne, & R.A.P. Burt (Eds.), *Pain, basic principles, pharmacology, and therapy*. Stuttgart: Thieme.

Begg, I.M., Needham, D.R., & Bookbinder, M. (1993). Do backward messages unconsciously affect listeners? No. *Canadian Journal of Experimental Psychology, 47*, 1-14

Beier, E.G. (1974), Octoer), Nonverbal communication: How we send emotional messages. *Psychology Today*, pp. 53–56.

Beirne-Smith, M., Patton, J., & Ittenbach, R. (1994). *Mental retardation* (4th ed.). New York: Macmillan.

Bell, S.T., Kuriloff, P.J., & Lottes, I. (1994). Understanding attributions of blame in stranger rape and date rape situations: An examination of gender, race, identification, and students' social perceptions of rape victims. *Journal of Applied Social Psychology, 24*(19), 1719–1734.

Bellack, A.S., Hersen, M., & Turner, S.M. (1976). Generalization effects of social skills training in chronic schizophrenics: An experimental analysis. *Behavior Research and Therapy, 14*, 391–398.

Belsky, J., & Rovine, M. (1988). Nonmaternal care in the first year of life and infant parent attachment security. *Child Development, 59*, 157–167.

Belsky, J., Lang, M.E., & Rovine, M. (1985). Stability and change in marriage across the transition to parenthood: A second study. *Journal of Marriage and the Family, 97*, 855–865.

Belsky, J., Spritz, B., & Crnic, K. (1996). Infant attachment security and affective-cognitive information processing at age 3. *American Psychological Society, 7*(2), 111–114.

Bem, D.J. (1994). "Anomaly or artifact? Comments on Bem and Honorton": Response to Hyman. *Psychological Bulletin, 115*(1), 25–27.

Bem, D.J., & Honorton, C. (1994). Does psi exist? Replicable evidence for an anomalous process of information transfer. *Psychological Bulletin, 115*(1), 4–18.

Bem, S.L. (1989). Genital knowledge and gender constancy in preschool children. *Child Development, 60*, 649–662.

Benin, M.H., & Agostinelli, J. (1988). Husbands' and wives' satisfaction with the division of labor. *Journal of Marriage and the Family, 50*, 349–361.

Bennett, D.A., & Knopman, D.S. (1994). Alzheimer's disease: A comprehensive approach to patient management. *Geriatrics, 49*(8), 20–26.

Bennett, D.A., & Knopman, D.S. (1994). Alzheimer's disease: A comprehensive approach to patient management. *Geriatrics, 49*(8), 20–26.

Bennett, W., & Gurin, J. (1982). *The dieter's dilemma: Eating less and weighing more*. New York: Basic Books.

Benson, H. (1975). *The relaxation response*. New York: William Morrow.

Benson, H., Alexander, S., & Feldman, E.L. (1975). Decreased premature ventricular contractions through use of the relaxation response in patients with stable ischemic heart disease. *Lancet, 2*, 380–382.

Benson, H., Kotch, J.B., Crassweller, K.D., & Greenwood, M.M. (1979). The relaxation response. In D. Goleman & R. Davidson (Eds.), *Consciousness: Brain, states of awareness and mysticism*. New York: Harper & Row.

Benson, H., Wallace, R.K. (1972). Decreased drug abuse with transcendental meditation—A study of 1,862 subjects. In C.J.D. Zarafonetis (Ed.), *Drug abuse*. Philadelphia: Lea & Febiger.

Benton, D., & Roberts, G. (1988). Effect of vitamin and mineral supplementation on intelligence of a sample of schoolchildren. *Lancet, 1*, 14–144.

Berenbaum, S.A., & Snyder, E. (1995). Early hormonal influences on childhood sex-typed activity and playmate preferences: Implications for the development of sexual orientation. [Special issue: Sexual orientation and human development]. *Developmental Psychology, 31*(1), 31–42.

Berger, R.J. (1969). The sleep and dream cycle. In A. Kales (Ed.), *Sleep: Physiology and pathology*. Philadelphia: Lippincott.

Bergin, A.E., & Lambert, M.J. (1978). The evaluation of therapeutic outcomes. In S.L. Garfield & A.E. Bergin (Eds.), *Handbook of psychotherapy and behavior change: An empirical analysis*. New York: Wiley.

Berkowitz, L. (1983). Aversively stimulated aggression. *American Psychologist, 38*, 1135–1144.

Berkowitz, M.W., & Gibbs, J.C. (1983). Measuring the developmental features of moral discussion. *Merrill-Palmer Quarterly, 29*, 399–410.

Berlin, B., & Kay, P. (1969). *Basic color terms: Their universality and evolution*. Berkeley: University of California Press.

Berliner, L., & Williams, L.M. (1994). Memories of child sexual abuse: A response to Lindsay and Read. [Special issue: Recovery of memories of childhood sexual abuse]. *Applied Cognitive Psychology, 8*(4), 379–387.

Bernal, M.E., & Castro, F.G. (1994). Are clinical psychologists prepared for service and research with ethnic minorities? *American Psychologist, 49*(9), 797–805.

Berntson, G.G., Cacippo, J.T., & Quigley, K.S. (1993). Cardiac psychophysiology and autonomic space in humans: Empirical perspectives and conceptual implications. *Psychological Bulletin, 114*(2) 296–322.

Berry, J.W. (1967). Independence and conformity in subsistence level societies. *Journal of Personality and Social Psychology, 7*, 415–518.

Berry, J.W., Portinga, Y.H., Segall, M.H., & Dasen, P.R. (1992). *Cross-cultural psychology: Research and applications*. New York: Cambridge University Press.

Bersoff, D.N. (1981). Testing and the law. *American Psychologist, 36*, 1047–1056.

Bertenthal, B.I. (1992). Infants' perception of biomechanical motions: Intrinsic image and knowledge based on constraints. In C. Ganrud (Ed.), *Visual perception and cognition in infancy*. Hillsdale, NJ: Erlbaum.

Bertenthal, B.I., Campos, J.J., & Kermoian, R. (1994). An epigenetic perspective on the development of self-produced locomotion and its consequences. *American Psychological Society, 3*(5), 140–145.

Bertrand, S., & Masling, J. (1969). Oral imagery and alcoholism. *Journal of Abnormal Psychology, 74*, 50–53.

Betancourt, H., & López, S.R. (1993). The study of culture, ethnicity, and race in American psychology. *American Psychologist, 48*, 629–637.

Bettencourt, B.A., & Miller, N. (1996). Gender differences in aggression as a function of provocation: A meta-analysis. *Psychological Bulletin, 119*(3), 422–427.

Bhatt, R.S., Wasserman, E.A., Reynolds, W.F., & Knauss, K.S. (1988). Conceptual behavior in pigeons: Categorization of both familiar and novel examples from four classes of natural and artificial stimuli. *Journal of Experimental Psychology: Animal Behavior Processes, 14*, 219–324.

Biederman, I. (1987). Recognition by components: A theory of human image understanding. *Psychological Review, 95*, 115–147.

Birch, H.G., & Rabinowitz, H.S. (1951). The negative effect of previous experience on productive thinking. *Journal of Experimental Psychology, 41*, 121–125.

Birchler, G.R., & Fals-Stewart, W.S. (1994). Marital dysfunction. In *Encyclopedia of human behavior* (Vol. 3, pp. 103–113).

Birren, J.E. (1983). Aging in America: Role for psychology. *American Psychologist, 38*, 298–299.

Birren, J.E., & Fisher, L.M. (1995). Aging and speed of behavior: Possible consequences for psychological functioning. *Annual Review of Psychology, 46*, 329–353.

Bjorklund, D.F. (1989). *Children's thinking, developmental function and individual differences*. Pacific Grove, CA: Brooks/Cole.

Blake, R.R., Helson, H., & Mouton, J. (1956). The generality of conformity behavior as a function of factual anchorage, difficulty of task and amount of social pressure. *Journal of Personality, 25*, 294–305.

Blakeslee, S. (1994, October 5). Yes, people are right. Caffeine is addictive. *New York Times*.

Blanck, D.C., Bellack, A.S., Rosnow, R.L., Rotheram-Borus, M.J., & Schooler, N.R. (1992). Scientific rewards and conflicts of ethical choices in human subjects research. *American Psychologist, 47*, 959–965.

Blatt, S.J., Zuroff, D.C., Quinlan, D.M., & Pilkonis, P. (1996). Interpersonal factors in brief treatment of depression: Further analysis of the NIMH Treatment of Depression Collaborative Research Program. *Journal of Consulting and Clinical Psychology, 64*, 162–171.

Bliss, T.V., & Collingridge, G.L. (1993). A synaptic model of memory: Long-term potentiation in the hippocampus. *Nature, 361*: 31–39.

Bliwise, D. L. (1996). Chronologic age, physiologic age and mortality in sleep apnea. *Sleep, 19,* 277–282.

Block, J. (1971). *Lives through time.* Berkeley, CA: Bancroft.

Block, J., & Robbins, R.W. (1993). A longitudinal study of consistency and change in self-esteem from early adolescence to early adulthood. *Child Development, 64,* 902–923.

Block, R.I. (1996). Does heavy marijuana use impair human cognition and brain function? *Journal of the American Medical Association, 275,* 521–527.

Bloom, L. (1970). *Language development: Form and function in emerging grammar.* Cambridge, MA: MIT Press.

Blum, J.M. (1979). *Pseudoscience and mental ability: The origins and fallacies of the IQ controversy.* New York: Monthly Review Press.

Blumberg, M.S., & Wasserman, E.A. (1995). Animal mind and the argument from design. *American Psychologist, 50,* 133–144.

Blumenthal, S.J. (1990). Youth suicide: The physician's role in suicide prevention. JAMA, *Journal of the American Medical Association, 264*(24), 3194–3196.

Bodlund, O., & Kullgren, G. (1996). Transsexualism–General outcome and prognostic factors: A five-year follow-up study of nineteen transsexuals in the process of changing sex. *Archives of Sexual Behavior, 25,* 303–317.

Boivin, D.B., Czeisler, C.A., Kijk, D.J., Duffy, J.F., Folkard, S., Minors, D.S., Totterdell, P., & Waterhouse, J.M. (1997). Complex interaction of the sleep-wake cycle and circadian phase modulates mood in healthy subjects. *Archives of General Psychiatry, 54,* 145–152.

Bokert, E. (1970). *The effects of thirst and related auditory stimulation on dream reports.* Paper presented to the Association for the Physiological Study of Sleep, Washington, DC.

Bolby, J. (1982). Attachment and loss: Retrospect and prospect. *American Journal of Orthopsychiatry, 52*(4), 664–678.

Bolles, R.C. (1972). Reinforcement, expectancy, and learning. *Psychological Review, 79,* 394–409.

Bolos, A.M., Dean, M., Lucas-Derse, S., Ramsburg, M., Brown, G.L., & Goldman, D. (1990). Population and pedigree studies reveal a lack of association between the dopamine D2 receptor gene and alcoholism. JAMA, *Journal of the American Medical Association, 264,* 3156–3160.

Bond, M.H., Wan, K.C., Leung, K., & Giacolone, R.A. (1985). How are responses to verbal insult related to cultural collectivism and power distance? *Journal of Cross-Cultural Psychology, 16,* 111–127.

Boomsma, D.I., Koopmans, J.R., Van Doornen, L.J.P., & Orlebeke, J.M. (1994). Genetic and social influences on starting to smoke: A study of Dutch adolescent twins and their parents. *Addiction, 89,* 219–226.

Booth-Kewley, S., & Friedman, H.S. (1987). Psychological predictors of heart disease: A quantitative review. *Psychological Bulletin, 101,* 343–362.

Borbely, A. (1986). *Secrets of sleep.* New York: Basic Books.

Borkovec, T.D., & Costello, E. (1993). Efficacy of applied relaxation and cognitive-behavioral therapy in the treatment of generalized anxiety disorder. *Journal of Consulting and Clinical Psychology, 61,* 611–619.

Bornstein, R.F. (1989). Exposure and affect: Overview and meta-analysis of research, 1968–1987. *Psychological Reports, 106,* 265–289.

Botwin, M.D., & Buss, D.M. (1989). The structure of act report data: Is the five factor model of personality recaptured? *Journal of Personality and Social Psychology.*

Bouchard, C., Tremblay, A., Despres, J.P., Nadeau, A., Lupien, P.J., Theriault, G., Dussault, J., Moorjani, S., Pinault, S., & Fournier, G. (1990). The response to long-term overfeeding in identical twins. *New England Journal of Medicine, 322,* 1477–1482.

Bouchard, T.J., Jr. (1984). Twins reared together and apart: What they tell us about human diversity. In S.W. Fox (Ed.), *Individuality and determinism* (pp. 147–178). New York: Plenum.

Bouchard, T.J., Jr. (1996). IQ similarity in twins reared apart: Findings and responses to critics. In R.J. Sternberg & E. Grigorenko (Eds.), *Intelligence: Heredity and environment.* New York: Cambridge University Press.

Bourne, L.E., Dominowski, R.L., Loftus, E.F., & Healy, A.F. (1986). *Cognitive process* (2nd ed.). Englewood Cliffs, NJ: Prentice Hall.

Bouton, M.E. (1993). Context, time and memory retrieval in the interference paradigms of Pavlovian conditioning. *Psychological Bulletin, 114,* 80–99.

Bouton, M.E. (1994). Context, ambiguity and classical conditioning. *Current Directions in Psychological Science, 3,* 49–52.

Bowden, S.C. (1990). Separating cognitive impairment in neurologically asymptomatic alcoholism from Wernicke-Korsakoff's syndrome: Is the neuropsychological distinction justified? *Psychological Bulletin, 107,* 355–366.

Bower, G.H., & Mann, T. (1992). Improving recall by recoding interfering material at the time of recall. *Journal of Experimental Psychology: Learning, Memory, and Cognition, 18,* 1310–1320.

Bowers, K.S. (1973). Situationism in psychology: An analysis and a critique. *Psychological Review, 80*(5), 307–336.

Bowlby, J. (1982). *Attachment and loss* (2nd ed.). New York: Basic Books. (Original work published 1969.)

Brainerd, C.J. (1978). The stage question in cognitive-developmental theory. *Behavioral and Brain Sciences, 2,* 172–213.

Brainerd, C.J. (1996). Piaget: A centennial celebration. *American Psychological Society, 7*(4), 191–225.

Brainerd, C.J., Reyna, V.F., & Brandse, E. (1995). Are children's false memories more persistent than their true memories? *Psychological Science, 6*(6), 359–364.

Brandon, T.H. (1994). Negative affect as motivation to smoke. *Current Directions in Psychological Science, 3,* 33–37.

Braveman, N.S., & Bornstein, P. (Eds.). (1985). *Annals of the New York Academy of Sciences: Vol. 443. Experimental assessments and clinical applications of conditioned food aversions.* New York: New York Academy of Sciences.

Bray, G.A. (1986). Effects of obesity on health and happiness. In K.D. Brownell & J.P. Foreyt (Eds.), *Handbook of eating disorders: Physiology, psychology, and treatment of obesity, anorexia, and bulimia* (pp. 3–44). New York: Basic Books.

Bredemeier, B., & Shields, D. (1985, October). Values and violence in sports today. *Psychology Today,* pp. 23–32.

Breedlove, S.M. (1994). Sexual differentiation of the human nervous system. *American Review of Psychology, 45,* 389–418

Breland, K., & Breland, M. (1972). The misbehavior of organisms. In M.E.P. Seligman & J.L. Hager (Eds.), *Biological boundaries of learning.* Englewood Cliffs, NJ: Prentice Hall.

Brenner, M.H. (1973). *Mental illness and the economy.* Cambridge, MA: Harvard University Press.

Brenner, M.H. (1979). Influence of the social environment on psychopathology: The historic perspective. In J.E. Barrett (Ed.), *Stress and mental disorder.* New York: Raven Press.

Breslau, N., Davis, G.C., & Andreski, P. (1995). Risk factors for PTSD-related traumatic events: A prospective analysis. *American Journal of Psychiatry, 152,* 529–535.

Brewer, W.F., & Nakamura, G.V. (1984). The nature and function of schemas. In R.S. Wyer & T.K. Srull (Eds.), *Handbook of social cognition.* Hillsdale, NJ: Erlbaum.

Brewin, C.R. (1996). Theoretical foundations of cognitive-behavior therapy for anxiety and depression. *Annual Review of Psychology, 47,* 33–57.

Brigham, C.C. (1923). *A study of American intelligence.* Princeton, NJ: Princeton University Press.

Brislin, R.W., Cushner, K., Cherries, C., & Yong, M. (1986). *Intercultural interactions: A practical guide.* Beverly Hills, CA: Sage.

Broadbent, D.E. (1958). *Perception and communication.* New York: Pergamon.

Brody, J.E. (1990, May 10). Personal health: On menopause and the toll that loss of estrogens can take on a woman's sexuality. *New York Times,* Sec. B.

Brody, L. (1985). Gender differences in emotional development: A review of theories and research. In A.J. Stewart & M.B. Lykes (Eds.), *Gender and personality: Current perspectives on theory and research* (pp. 14–61). Durham, NC: Duke University Press.

Broida, J., Tingley, L., Kimball, R., & Miele, J. (1993). Personality differences between pro- and anti-vivisectionists. *Society and Animals, 1,* 129–144.

Bronfenbrenner, U. (1986). Ecology of the family as a context for human development: Research perspectives. *Developmental Psychology, 22,* 723–742.

Brooks-Gunn, J. (1993). *Adolescence.* Paper presented at the meeting of the Society for Research in Child Development, Kansas City, MO.

Brooks-Gunn, J., & Lewis, M. (1984). The development of early visual self-recognition. *Developmental Review, 4,* 215–239.

Brown, A.S. (1991). A review of the tip-of-the-tongue experience. *Psychological Bulletin, 109*(2), 204–223.

Brown, B., & Grotberg, J.J. (1981). Head Start: A successful experiment. *Courrier.* Paris: International Children's Centre.

Brown, L.S., & Ballou, M. (1992). *Personality and psychopathology: Feminists reappraisals.* New York: Guilford.

Brown, P.L., & Jenkins, H.M. (1968). Autoshaping of the pigeon's key peck. *Journal of Experimental and Analytical Behavior, 11,* 1–8.

Brown, R. (1958). *Words and things.* New York: Free Press/Macmillan.

Brown, R., & Kulik, J. (1977). Flashbulb memories. *Cognition, 5,* 73–99.

Brown, R., & McNeill, D. (1966). The "tip of the tongue phenomenon." *Journal of Verbal Learning and Verbal Behavior, 8,* 325–337.

Brown, R.W., & Lenneberg, E.H. (1954). A study in language and cognition. *Journal of Abnormal and Social Psychology, 49,* 454–462.

Browne, A. (1993). Violence against women by male partners. Prevalence, outcomes and policy implications. *American Psychologist, 48,* 1077–1087.

Brownell, K.D., & Rodin, J. (1994). The dieting maelstrom. Is it possible and advisable to lose weight? *American Psychologist, 49,* 781–791.

Bruch, C.B. (1971). Modification of procedures for identification of the disadvantaged gifted. *Gifted Child Quarterly, 15,* 267–272.

Bruch, H. (1980). *The golden cage: The enigma of anorexia nervosa.* New York: Random House.

Bruder, G.E., Stewart, M.W., Mercier, M.A., Agosti, V., Leite, P., Donovan, S., & Quitkin, F.M. (1997). Outcome of cognitive-behavioral therapy for depression: Relation to hemispheric dominance for verbal processing. *Journal of Abnormal Psychology, 106,* 138–144.

Brumberg, J.J. (1988). *Fasting girls: The emergence of anorexia nervosa as a modern disease.* Cambridge, MA: Harvard University Press.

Brunner, H.G., Nelen, M., Breakefield, X.O., Ropers, H.H., & Van Oost, B.A. (1993). Abnormal behavior associated with a point mutation in the structural gene for monoamine oxidase A. *Science, 262,* 578–580.

Brunner, H.G., Nelen, M., Breakfield, X.O., & Ropers, H.H. (1993). Abnormal structures associated with a point mutation in the structural gene for monoamine oxidase A. *Science, 263,* 578–580.

Budzynski, T., Stoyva, J., & Adler, C. (1970). Feedback-induced muscle relaxation: Application to tension headache. *Journal of Behavior Therapy and Experimental Psychiatry, 1,* 205–211.

Buhrich, N., Theile, N., Yaw, A., & Crawford, A. (1979). Plasma testosterone, serum FSH, and serum LH levels in transvestism. *Archives of Sexual Behavior, 8,* 49–54.

Buonomano, D.V., & Merzenich, M.M. (1995). Temporal information transformed into a spatial code by a neural network with realistic properties. *Science, 267,* 1028–1030.

Burke, D.M., McKay, D.G., Worthley, J.S., & Wade, E. (1991). On the tip of the tongue: What causes word finding failures in young and older adults? *Journal of Memory and Language, 30,* 542–579.

Bushman, B.J. (1993). Human aggression while under the influence of alcohol and other drugs: An integrative research review. *Current Directions in Psychological Science, 2,* 148–152.

Bushman, B.J., & Cooper, H.M. (1990). Effects of alcohol on human aggression: An integrative research review. *Psychological Bulletin, 107,* 341–354.

Buss, D.M. (1985). Human mate selection. *American Scientist, 73,* 47–51.

Buss, D.M. (1990). The evolution of anxiety and social exclusion. *Journal of Social and Clinical Psychology, 9,* 196–210.

Buss, D.M. (1991). Evolutionary personality psychology. *Annual Review of Psychology, 42,* 459–491.

Butcher, J.N., & Rouse, S.V. (1996). Personality: Individual differences and clinical assessment. *Annual Review of Psychology, 47,* 87–111.

Butcher, J.N., Dahlstrom, W.G., Graham, J.R., Telegen, A., & Kaemmer, B. (1989). *Minnesota Multiphasic Personality Inventory: II. Manual for administration and scoring.* Minneapolis: University of Minnesota Press.

Butler, R.N. (1963). The life review: An interpretation of reminiscence in the aged. *Psychiatry, 26,* 63–76.

Butler, R.N., & Lewis, M.I. (1982). *Aging and mental health: Positive psychological and biomedical approaches.* St. Louis, MO: Mosby.

Byne, W. (1994, May). The biological evidence challenged. *Scientific American,* 50–55.

Byne, W., & Parsons, B. (1993). Human sexual orientation: The biologic theories reappraised. *Archives of General Psychiatry, 50*(3), 228–239.

Byne, W., & Parsons, B. (1994). Biology and human sexual orientation. *Harvard Mental Health Letter, 10,* 5–7.

Byrd, K.R. (1994). The narrative reconstructions of incest survivors. *American Psychologist, 49,* 439–440.

Byrne, D. (1961). Interpersonal attraction and attitude similarity. *Journal of Abnormal and Social Psychology, 62,* 713–715.

Byrne, D., & Nelson, D. (1965). Attraction as a linear function of properties of positive reinforcements. *Journal of Personality and Social Psychology, 1,* 659–663.

Cain, W.S. (1981, July). Educating your nose. *Psychology Today,* pp. 48–56.

Cain, W.S. (1982). Odor identification by males and females: Predictions versus performance. *Chemical Senses, 7,* 129–142.

Calder, B.J., Insko, C.A., & Yandell, B. (1974). The relation of cognitive and memorial processes to persuasion in simulated jury trial. *Journal of Applied Social Psychology, 4,* 62–92.

Caldwell, J.D., Jirikowski, G.F., Greer, E.R., & Pedersen, C.A. (1989). Medial preoptic area oxytocin and female sexual receptivity. *Behavioral Neuroscience, 103,* 655–662.

Calvert, S., & Cocking, R. (1992). Health promotion through mass media. *Journal of Applied Developmental Psychology, 13,* 143–149.

Campbell, C.P. (1995). *Race, myth and the news.* Thousand Oaks, CA: Sage.

Campos, J.L., Langer, A., & Krowitz, A. (1970). Cardiac responses on the visual cliff in prelocomotor human infants. *Science, 170,* 196–197.

Capaldi, E.J. (1978). Effects of schedule and delay of reinforcement on acquisition speed. *Animal Learning and Behavior, 6,* 330–334.

Cappella, J.N. (1993). The facial feedback hypothesis in human interaction: Review and speculation. *Journal of Language and Social Psychology, 12,* 13–29.

Capron, C., & Duyme, M. (1989). Assessment of effects of socio-economic status on IQ in a full cross-fostering study. *Nature (London), 340,* 552–554.

Carlson, V. (1994). Child abuse. In *Encyclopedia of human behavior* (Vol. 1, pp. 561–578).

Carr, M., Borkowski, J.G., & Maxwell, S.E. (1991). Motivational components of underachievement. *Developmental Psychology, 27,* 108–118.

Carroll, J.B., & Horn, J.L. (1981). On the scientific basis of ability testing. *American Psychologist, 36,* 1012–1020.

Carroll, J.M., Thomas, J.C., & Malhotra, A. (1980). Presentation and representation in design problem solving. *British Journal of Psychology, 71,* 143–153.

Carson, R.C., & Butcher, J.N. (1992). *Abnormal psychology and modern life.* New York: HarperCollins.

Carson, R.C., Butcher, J.N., & Coleman, J.C. (1988). *Abnormal psychology and modern life* (8th ed.). Glenview, IL: Scott, Foresman.

Carstensen, L. (1995). Evidence for a life-span theory of socioemotional selectivity. *American Psychological Society, 4*(5), 151–156.

Carter, B. (1996, February 7). New report becomes a weapon in the debate over TV violence. *New York Times.*

Casas, J.M. (1995). Counseling and psychotherapy with racial/ethnic minority groups in theory and practice. In B. Bongar & L.E. Beutler (Eds.), *Comprehensive handbook of psychotherapy* (pp. 311–335). New York: Oxford University Press.

Caspi, A., & Elder, G.H., Jr. (1986). Life satisfaction in old age: Linking social psychology and history. *Journal of Psychology and Aging, 1*, 18–26.

Cattell, R.B. (1965). *The scientific analysis of personality*. Baltimore: Penguin.

Cattell, R.B. (1971). *Abilities: Their structure, growth, and action*. Boston: Houghton Mifflin.

Cattell, R.B., & Kline, P. (1977). *The specific analysis of personality and motivation*. New York: Academic Press.

Cavanaugh, J.C. (1990). *Adult development and aging*. Belmont, CA: Wadsworth.

Celis, W. (1994, June 8). More college women drinking to get drunk. *New York Times*, p. B8.

Centers for Disease Control. (1991). Attempted suicide among high school students—United States, 1990. JAMA, *Journal of the American Medical Association, 266*(14), 1911.

Chaiken, S., & Eagly, A.H. (1976). Communication modality as a determinant of message persuasiveness and message comprehensibility. *Journal of Personality and Social Psychology, 34*, 605–614.

Chaikin, A.L., & Darley, J.M. (1973). Victim or perpetrator? Defensive attribution of responsibility and the need for order and justice. *Journal of Personality and Social Psychology, 25*, 268–275.

Chait, L.D., & Pierri, J. (1992). Effects of smoked marijuana on human performance: A critical review. In L. Murphy & A. Bartke (Eds.), *Marijuana/cannabinoids: Neurobiology and neurophysiology* (pp. 387–424). Boca Raton, FL: CRC Press.

Chase, W.G., & Ericsson, K.A. (1981). Skilled memory. In J. Anderson (Ed.), *Cognitive skills and their acquisition*. Hillsdale, NJ: Erlbaum.

Chase, W.G., & Simon, H.A. (1973). Perception in chess. *Cognitive Psychology, 4*, 55–81.

Cherry, C. (1966). *On human communication: A review, a survey, and a criticism* (2nd ed.). Cambridge, MA: MIT Press.

Chipman, S.F., Krantz, D.H., & Silver, R. (1992). Mathematics anxiety and science careers among able bodied college women. *Psychological Science, 5*, 292–295.

Chodorow, N.J. (1989). *Feminism and psychoanalytic theory*. New Haven, CT: Yale University Press.

Chomsky, N. (1957). *Syntactic structures*. The Hague: Mouton.

Chomsky, N. (1965). *Aspects of the theory of syntax*. Cambridge, MA: MIT Press.

Christensen, F. (1986). *Pornography: The other side*. Unpublished paper, University of Alberta.

Chua, S.C., Chung, W.K., Wu-Peng, X.S., Zhang, Y., Liu, S.M., Tartaglia, L., & Leibel, R.L. (1996). Phenotypes of mouse diabetes and rat fatty due to mutations in OB (leptin) receptor. *Science, 271*, 994–996.

Church, D.K., Siegel, M.A., & Foster, C.D. (1988). *Growing old in America*. Wylie, TX: Information Aids.

Chwalisz, K., Diener, E., & Gallagher, D. (1988). Autonomic arousal feedback and emotional experience: Evidence from the spinal cord injured. *Journal of Personality and Social Psychology, 54*, 820–828.

Cialdini, R.B., Cacioppo, J.T., Bassett, R., & Miller, J.A. (1978). Lowball procedure for producing compliance: Commitment then cost. *Journal of Personality and Social Psychology, 36*, 463–476.

Cialdini, R.B., Vincent, J.E., Lewis, S.K., Catalan, J., Wheeler, D., & Darby, B.L. (1975). A reciprocal concessions procedure for inducing compliance: The door-in-the-face technique. *Journal of Personality and Social Psychology, 21*, 206–215.

Clark, J.E. (1994). Motor development. In *Encyclopedia of human behavior* (Vol. 3, pp. 245–255).

Clark, M.S., & Mills, J. (1979). Interpersonal attraction in exchange and communal relationships. *Journal of Personality and Social Psychology, 37*, 12–24.

Clark, R.D., & Word, L.E. (1974). Where is the apathetic bystander? Situational characteristics of the emergency. *Journal of Personality and Social Psychology, 29*, 279–287.

Clausen, J.A. (1975). The social meaning of differential physical and sexual maturation. In S.E. Dragastin & G.H. Elder, Jr. (Eds.), *Adolescence in the life cycle: Psychological change and social context* (pp. 25–47). New York: Wiley.

Cloninger, S.C. (1993). *Theories of personality. Understanding persons*. Englewood Cliffs, NJ: Prentice Hall.

Clore, G.L., & Byrne, D. (1974). A reinforcement-affect model of attraction. In T.L. Huston (Ed.), *Foundations of interpersonal attraction* (pp. 143–170). New York: Academic Press.

Cohen, A., & Raffal, R.D. (1991). Attention and feature integration: Illusory conjunctions in a patient with a parietal lobe lesion. *Psychological Science, 2*, 106–110.

Cohen, A.G., & Gutek, B.A. (1991). Differences in the career experiences of members of two APA divisions. *American Psychologist, 46*, 1292–1298.

Cohen, D.B. (1974, May). Repression is not the demon who conceals and hoards our forgotten dreams. *Psychology Today*, pp. 50–54.

Cohen, D.B. (1976). Dreaming: Experimental investigation of representation and adaptive properties. In G. Schwartz & D. Shapiro (Eds.), *Consciousness and self-regulation*. New York: Plenum.

Cohen, E.G. (1984). The desegregated school: Problems in status, power and interethnic climate. In N. Miller & M.B. Brewer (Eds.), *Groups in contact: The psychology of desegregation* (pp. 77–96). New York: Academic Press.

Cohen, J.B., & Chakravarti, D. (1990). Consumer psychology. *Annual Review of Psychology, 41*, 243–288.

Cohen, L.D. (1991). Sex differences in the course of personality development: A meta-analysis. *Psychological Bulletin, 109*(2), 252–266.

Cohen, S. (1996). Psychological stress, immunity, and upper respiratory infections. *Current Directions in Psychological Science, 5*(3), 86–88.

Cohen, S., & Herbert, T.B. (1996). Health psychology: Psychological factors and physical disease from the perspective of human psychoneuroimmunology. *Annual Review of Psychology, 47*, 113–142.

Cohen, S., & Williamson, G.M. (1988). Stress and infectious disease in humans. *Psychological Bulletin, 109*, 5–24.

Cole, N.S. (1981). Bias in testing. *American Psychologist, 36*, 1067–1077.

Colegrove, F.W. (1982). Individual memories. *American Journal of Psychology, 10*, 228–255. (Original work published in 1899). (Reprinted in *Memory observed: Remembering in natural contexts*, by V. Neisser, Ed. San Francisco: Freeman.)

Collaer, M.L., & Hines, M. (1995). Human behavioral sex differences: A role for gonadal hormones during early development? *American Psychological Associations, 118*(1), 55–107.

Collins, N.L., & Miller, L.C. (1994). Self-disclosure and liking: A meta-analytic review. *Psychological Bulletin, 116*, 457–475.

Collins, R.C. (1993). Head Start: Steps toward a two-generation program strategy. *Young Children, 48*(2), 25–73.

Colvin, C.R., & Block, J. (1994). Do positive illusions foster mental health? An examination of the Taylor and Brown formulation. *Psychological Bulletin, 116*, 3–20.

Compas, B.E., Hinden, B.R., & Gerhardt, C.A. (1995). Adolescent development: Pathways and processes of risk and resilience. *Annual Review of Psychology, 46*, 265–293.

Conger, J.J., & Petersen, A.C. (1991). *Adolescence and youth* (4th ed.). New York: HarperCollins.

Connelly, B., Johnston, D., Brown, I.D., Mackay, S., & Blackstock, E.G. (1993). The prevalence of depression in a high school population. *Adolescence, 28*(109), 149–158.

Conrad, R. (1972). Short-term memory in the deaf: A test for speech coding. *British Journal of Psychology, 63*, 173–180.

Conroy, J.W. (1996). The small ICF/MR program: Dimensions of quality and cost. *Mental Retardation, 34*, 13–26.

Conseur, A., Rivara, F.P., Barnoski, R., & Emanuel, I. (1997). Maternal and perinatal risk factors for later delinquency. *Pediatrics, 99*(6), 785–790.

Consumer Reports (1995, November). Mental health: Does therapy help? pp. 734–739.

Contreras, D., Destexhe, A., Sejnowski, T.J., & Steriade, M. (1996). Control of spatiotemporal coherence of a thalamic oscillation by corticothalamic feedback. *Science, 274*(5288), 771–774.

Conway, M.A. (1996). Failures of autobiographical remembering. In D. Hermann, C. McEvoy, C. Hertzog, P. Hertel, & M.K. Johnson (Eds.), *Basic and applied memory research: Theory in context*. Nahwah, NJ: Erlbaum.

Cook, M., Mineka, S., Wolkenstein, B., & Laitsch, K. (1985). Observational conditioning of snake fear in unrelated rhesus monkeys. *Journal of Abnormal Psychology, 94*, 591–610

Cook, R. (1991). *The experimental analysis of cognition in animals*. Paper presented at the meeting of the Psychonomic Society, San Francisco.

Cookerly, J.R. (1980). Does marital therapy do any lasting good? *Journal of Marital and Family Therapy, 6*, 393–397.

Cooper, H. (1993). In search of a social fact. A commentary on the study of interpersonal expectations. In P. Blanck (Ed.), *Interpersonal expectations: Theory, research, and application* (pp. 218–226). Paris, France: Cambridge University Press.

Cooper, J. (1971). Personal responsibility and dissonance. *Journal of Personality and Social Psychology, 18*, 354–363.

Cooper, J., & Croyle, R.T. (1984). Attitudes and attitude change. *Annual Review of Psychology, 35*, 395–426.

Cooper, J.R., Bloom, F.E., & Roth, R.H. (1991). *The biochemical basis of neuropharmacology* (6th ed.). Oxford: Oxford University Press.

Cooper, R., & Zubek, J. (1958). Effects of enriched and restricted early environments on the learning ability of bright and dull rats. *Canadian Journal of Psychology, 12*, 159–164.

Corder, B., Saunders, A.M., Strittmatter, W.J., Schmechel, D.E., Gaskell, P.C., & Small, D.E. (1993). Gene dose of apolipoprotein E type 4 allele and the risk of Alzheimer's disease in late onset families. *Science, 261*, 921–923.

Coren, S., Porac, C., & Ward, L.M. (1984). *Sensation and perception* (2nd ed.). Orlando, FL: Academic Press.

Coren, S., Ward, L.M., & Enns, J.T. (1994). *Sensation and perception* (4th ed.). Orlando, FL: Harcourt Brace.

Cornelius, R.R. (1996). *The science of emotion: Research and tradition in the psychology of emotions*. Upper Saddle River, NJ: Prentice Hall.

Costa, P.T., & McCrae, R.R. (1992). *Revised NEO Personality Inventory (NEO PI-R) and NEO Five-Factor Inventory (NEO-FFI): Professional manual*. Odessa, FL: Psychological Assessment Resources.

Costa, P.T., & McCrae, R.R. (1995). Domains and facets: Hierarchical personality assessment using the Revised NEO Personality Inventory. *Journal of Personality Assessment, 64*, 21–50.

Cotton, J.L. (1993). *Employee involvement: Methods for improving performance and work attitudes*. Newbury Park, CA: Sage.

Council, J.R. (1993). Context effects in personality research. *Current Directions, 2*, 31–34.

Cousins, S. (1989). Culture and self-perception in Japan and in the United States. *Journal of Personality and Social Psychology, 56*, 124–131.

Cowan, N. (1988). Evolving conceptions of memory storage, selective attention, and their mutual constraints within the human information-processing system. *Psychological Bulletin, 104*, 163–191.

Cox, D.J., Sutphen, J., Borowitz, S., & Dickens, M.N. (1994). Simple electromyographic biofeedback treatment for chronic pediatric constipation/encopresis: Preliminary report. *Biofeedback & Self Regulation, 19*(1), 41–50.

Coyle, J.T. (1987). Alzheimer's disease. In G. Adelman (Ed.), *Encyclopedia of neuroscience* (pp. 29–31). Boston: Birkhauser.

Coyne, J.C., & Whiffen, V.E. (1995). Issues in personality as diathesis for depression: The case of sociotropy-dependency and autonomy-self-criticism. *Psychological Bulletin, 118*, 358–378.

Craig, A.D., & Bushnell, M.C. (1994). The thermal grill illusion: Unmasking the burn of cold pain. *Science, 265*, 252–255.

Craighead, L. (1990). Supervised exercise in behavioral treatment for moderate obesity. *Behavior Therapy, 20*, 49–59.

Craik, F.I.M., & Lockhart, R.S. (1972). Levels of processing: A framework for memory research. *Journal of Verbal Learning and Verbal Behavior, 11*, 671–684.

Craik, F.I.M., & Watkins, M.J. (1973). The role of rehearsal in short-term memory. *Journal of Verbal Learning and Verbal Behavior, 12*, 599–607.

Crandall, C.S. (1994). Prejudice against fat people: Ideology and self-interest. *Journal of Personality and Social Psychology, 66*, 882–894.

Crick, F., & Mitchison, G. (1983). The function of dreamsleep. *Nature (London), 304*(5922), 111–114.

Cronan, T.A., Walen, H.R., & Cruz, S.G. (1994). The effects of community-based literacy training on Head Start parents. *Journal of Community Psychology, 22*, 248–258.

Cronbach, L.J. (1990). *Essentials of psychological testing* (5th ed.). New York: HarperCollins.

Crook, T., & Eliot, J. (1980). Parental death during childhood and adult depression: A critical review of the literature. *Psychological Bulletin, 87*, 252–259.

Crovitz, H.F., & Schiffman, H. (1974). Frequency of episodic memories as a function of their age. *Bulletin of the Psychonomic Society, 4*, 517–518.

Crutchfield, R.A. (1955). Conformity and character. *American Psychologist, 10*, 191–198.

Crystal, D.S., Chen, C., Fuligini, A.J., Stevenson, H., Hus, C., Ko, H., Kitamura, S., & Kimura, S. (1994). Psychological maladjustments and academic achievement: A cross-cultural study of Japanese, Chinese, and American high school students. *Child Development, 65*, 738–753.

Csikszentmihalyi, M., Rathunde, K., & Whalen, S. (1993). *Talented teenagers: The roots of success and failure*. New York: Cambridge University Press.

Cumming, E., & Henry, W.E. (1961). *Growing old: The process of disengagement*. New York: Basic Books.

Curle, C.E., & Williams, C. (1996). Post-traumatic stress reactions in children: Gender differences in the incidence of trauma reactions at two years and examination of factors influencing adjustment. *British Journal of Clinical Psychology, 35*, 297–309.

D'Amato, M.R., & Van Sant, P. (1988). The person concept in monkeys (Cebus apella). *Journal of Experimental Psychology: Animal Behavior Processes, 14*, 32–55.

D'Azevedo, W.A. (1982). Tribal history in Liberia. In U. Neisser (Ed.), *Memory observed: Remembering in natural contexts*. San Francisco: Freeman.

Dabbs, J.M., & Leventhal, H. (1966). Effects of varying the recommendations in a fear-arousing communication. *Journal of Personality and Social Psychology, 4*, 525–531.

Dabbs, J.M., Jr., & Morris, R. (1990). Testosterone, social class, and antisocial behavior in a sample of 4,462 men. *Psychological Science, 1*, 209–211.

Dabbs, J.U.M., Jr., Carr, T.S., Frady, R.L., & Riad, J.K. (1995). Testosterone, crime, and misbehavior among 692 male prison inmates. *Personality and Individual Differences, 19*, 627–633.

Dachler, M.W. (1994). Cognitive development. In *Encyclopedia of human behavior* (Vol. 1, pp. 627–637).

Dadona, L., Hendrickson, A., & Quigley, H.A. (1991). Selective effects of experimental glaucoma on axonal transport by retinal ganglion cells to the dorsal lateral geniculate nucleus. *Investigations in Ophthalmology & Visual Science, 32*, 1593–1599.

Dahlström, W.G. (1993). Tests: Small samples, large consequences. *American Psychologist, 48*, 393–399.

Daley, S. (1991, January 9). Girls' self-esteem is lost on way to adolescence, new study finds. *New York Times*, Sec. B.

Daly, M., & Wilson, M. (1988). Evolutionary social psychology and family homicide. *Science, 242*(4878), 519–524.

Daly, M., & Wilson, M.I. (1996). Violence against stepchildren. *American Psychological Society, 5*(3), 77–81.

Damasio, A.R., Tranel, D., & Damasio, H. (1990a). Face agnosia and the neural substrates of memory. *Annual Review of Neuroscience, 13*, 89–109.

Damasio, A.R., Tranel, D., & Damasio, H. (1990b). Individuals with sociopathic behavior caused by frontal damage fail to respond autonomically to social stimuli. *Behavioral Brain Research, 41*, 81–94.

Daniell, H.W. (1971). Smokers' wrinkles: A study in the epidemiology of "Crow's feet." *Annals of Internal Medicine, 75*, 873–880.

Darwin, C.R. (1859). *The origin of species*. London.

658

Darwin, C.R. (1871). *The decent of man*. London.

Daunton, N.G. (1990). Animal models in motion sickness research. In G.H. Crampton (Ed.), *Motion and space sickness* (pp. 87–104). Boca Raton, FL: CRC Press.

Davidson, E.S., & Schenk, S. (1994). Variability in subjective responses to marijuana: Initial experiences of college students. *Addictive Behaviors, 19*, 531–538.

Davidson, R.J. (1992). Emotion and affective style: Hemispheric substrates. *Psychological Science, 3*, 39–43.

Davies, P.T., & Cummings, E.M. (1994). Marital conflict and child adjustment: An emotional security hypothesis. *Psychological Bulletin, 166*(3), 387–411.

Davis, J.R., Vanderploeg, J.M., Santy, P.A., Jennings, R.T., & Stewart, D.F. (1988). Space motion sickness during 24 flights of the space shuttle. *Aviation, Space, and Environmental Medicine, 59*, 1185–1189.

Davis, M.H., & Stephan, W.G. (1980). Attributions for exam performance. *Journal of Applied Social Psychology, 10*, 235–248.

Dawes, R.M. (1994). *House of cards: The collapse of modern psychotherapy*. New York: Free Press.

Dawkins, M.P. (1997). Drug use and violent crime among adolescents. *Adolescence, 32*(126), 395–405.

De Leon, M., Golomb, J., George, A., Convit, A., & Rusinek, H. (1993). Hippocampal formation atrophy: Prognostic significance for Alzheimer's disease. In B. Corain, K. Iqbal, M. Nicolini, B. Winblad, H. Wisniewski, & P. Zatta (Eds.), *Alzheimer's disease: Advances in clinical and brain research*. New York: Wiley.

de Raad, B., & Szirmak, Z. (1994). The search for the "Big Five" in a non-Indo-European language: The Hungarian trait structure and its relationship to the EQP and the PTS. *Revue Européenne de Psychologie Appliqué, 44*, 17–24.

Dean, J.W., Jr., & Evans, J.R. (1994). *Total quality: Management, organization, and strategy*. St. Paul, MN: West.

Dean, S.R. (1970). Is there an ultraconscious? *Canadian Psychiatric Association Journal, 15*, 57–61.

DeAngelis, C. (1993). Hopkins implements innovative medical school curriculum. *Maryland Medical Journal, 42*(5), 461–466.

DeAngelis, T. (1990b, August). NIMH educational effort aimed at panic disorder. *APA Monitor*, p. 13.

DeAngelis, T. (1991a, June). Hearing pinpoints gaps in research on women. *APA Monitor*, p. 8.

DeAngelis, T. (1991b, August). Ethnic groups respond differently to medication. *APA Monitor*, p. 28.

Deaux, K., & Kite, M. (1993). Gender stereotypes. In F.L. Denmark & M.A. Paludi (Eds.), *Psychology of women: A handbook of issues and theories* (pp. 107–139). Westport, CT: Greenwood.

Deaux, K., & Wrightsman, L. (1984). *Social psychology in the 80s* (4th ed.). Monterey, CA: Brooks/Cole.

DeCasper, A.J., & Spence, M.J. (1986). Prenatal maternal speech influences newborns' perception of speech sounds. *Infant Behavior and Development, 9*, 133–150.

DeFreitas, B., & Schwartz, G. (1979). Effects of caffeine in chronic psychiatric patients. *American Journal of Psychiatry, 136*, 1337–1338.

Deikman, A.J. (1973). Deautomatization and the mystic experience. In R.W. Ornstein (Ed.), *The nature of human consciousness*. San Francisco: Freeman.

DeKay, W.T., & Buss, D.M. (1992). Human nature, individual differences and the importance of context: Perspectives from evolutionary psychology. *Current Directions in Psychological Science, 1*, 184–189.

DeMaris, A., & Rao, K.V. (1992). Premarital cohabitation and subsequent marital stability in the United States: A reassessment. *Journal of Marriage and the Family, 54*, 178–190.

Dement, W.C. (1965). An essay on dreams: The role of physiology in understanding their nature. In F. Barron (Ed.), *New directions in psychology* (Vol. 2). New York: Holt, Rinehart & Winston.

Dement, W.C. (1974). *Some must watch while some must sleep*. San Francisco: Freeman.

Dement, W.C., Cohen, H., Ferguson, J., & Zarcone, V. (1970). A sleep researcher's odyssey: The function and clinical significance of REM sleep. In L. Madow & L.H. Snow (Eds.), *The psychodynamic implications of the physiological studies of dreams*. Springfield, IL: Charles C. Thomas.

Denmark, F.L. (1994). Engendering psychology. *American Psychologist, 49*(4), 329–334.

Dennerstein, L., & Burrows, G.D. (1982). Hormone replacement therapy and sexuality in women. *Clinics in Endocrinology and Metabolism, 11*, 661–679.

Denney, N.W. (1984). A model of cognitive development across the life span. *Developmental Review 4*, 171–191.

DePaulo, B.M., & Pfeifer, R.L. (1986). On-the-job experience and skill detecting deception. *Journal of Applied Social Psychology, 16*, 249–267.

Depy, D., Fagot, J., & Vauclair, J. (1997). Categorisation of three-dimensional stimuli by humans and baboons: Search for prototype effects. *Behavioural Processes, 39*(3), 299–306.

Desiher, R.W. (1993). Gay and lesbian youth. In P.H. Tolan & B.J. Cohler (Eds.), *Handbook of clinical research and practice with adolescents* (pp. 249–280). New York: Wiley.

DeValois, R.L., & DeValois, K.K. (1975). Neural coding of color. In E.C. Carterette & M.P. Friedman (Eds.), *Handbook of perception: Seeing* (Vol. 5). New York: Academic Press.

Devane, W.A., Hanus, L., Breuer, A., Pertwee, R.G., Stevenson, L.A., Griffin, G., Gibson, D., Mandelbaum, A., Etinger, A., & Mechoulam, R. (1992). Isolation and structure of a brain constituent that binds to the cannabinoid receptor. *Science, 258*, 1946–1949.

deVeaugh-Geiss, J. (1993). Diagnosis and treatment of obsessive-compulsive disorder. *Annual Review of Medicine, 44*, 53–61.

DeWitt, K. (1991, August 28). Low test scores renew debate on TV. *New York Times*, Sec. B.

DeZazzo, J., & Tully, T. (1995). Dissection of memory formulation from behavioral pharmacology to molecular genetics. *Trends in Neuroscience, 18*, 212–218.

Diamond, J. (1994). Race without color. *Discover, 15*, 82–92.

Diaz, J. (1997). *How drugs influence behavior: Neuro-behavioral approach*. Upper Saddle River, NJ: Prentice Hall.

Dickinson, A., & Mackintosh, N.J. (1978). Classical conditioning in animals. *Annual Review of Psychology, 29*, 587–612.

DiFranza, J.R., & Lew, R.A. (1995). Effect of maternal cigarette smoking on pregnancy complications and sudden infant death syndrome. *Journal of Family Practice, 40*(4), 385–394.

DiGiovanna, A.G. (1994). *Human aging: Biological perspectives*. New York: McGraw-Hill.

Digman, J.M., & Takemoto-Chock, N.K. (1981). Factors in the natural language of personality: Re-analysis, comparison, and interpretation of six major studies. *Multivariate Behavioral Research, 16*, 149–170.

Dill, S. (1994, January 16). Babies' grunts may have meaning. *Associated Press*.

Dilon, S. (1994, October 21). Bilingual education effort is flawed, study indicates. *New York Times*, p. A20.

DiMatteo, M.R., & Friedman, H.S. (1982). *Social psychology and medicine*. Cambridge, MA: Oelgeschlager, Gunn, & Hain.

Dion, K.K. (1972). Physical attractiveness and evaluations of children's transgressions. *Journal of Personality and Social Psychology, 24*, 285–290.

Doherty, W.J., & Jacobson, N.S. (1982). Marriage and the family. In B.B. Wolman (Ed.), *Handbook of developmental psychology* (pp. 667–680). Englewood Cliffs, NJ: Prentice Hall.

Dole, A.A. (1995). Why not drop race as a term? *American Psychologist, 50*, 40.

Domjan, M. (1987). Animal learning comes of age. *American Psychologist, 42*, 556–564.

Domjan, M., & Purdy, J.E. (in press). Animal research in psychology: More than meets the eye of the general psychology student. *American Psychologist*.

Donaldson, S.I., Graham, J.W., Piccinin, A.M., & Hansen, W.B. (1995). Resistance-skills training and onset of alcohol use: Evidence for beneficial and potentially harmful effects in public schools and in private Catholic schools. *Health Psychology, 14*, 291–300.

Donatelle, R.J., & Davis, L.G. (1993). *Access to health* (2nd ed.). Englewood Cliffs, NJ: Prentice Hall.

Donchin, E. (1987). Can the mind be read in the brain waves? In F. Farley & C. Null (Eds.), *Using psychological science: Making the public case* (pp. 25–42). Washington, DC: Federation of Behavioral, Psychological, and Cognitive Sciences.

Doob, A.N., & Wood, L. (1972). Catharsis and aggression: The effects of annoyance and retaliation on aggressive behavior. *Journal of Personality and Social Psychology, 22,* 156–162.

Doty, R.L. (1989). Influence of age and age-related diseases on olfactory function. *Annals of the New York Academy of Sciences, 561,* 76–86.

Doty, R.L., Applebaum, S., Zusho, H., & Settle, R.G. (1985). Sex differences in odor identification ability: A cross-cultural analysis. *Neuropsychologia, 23,* 667–672.

Doty, R.L., Shaman, P., Applebaum, S.L., Giberson, R., Siksorski, L., & Rosenberg, L. (1984). Smell identification ability: Changes with age. *Science, 226,* 1441–1443.

Douglas, H.M., Moffitt, T.E., Dar, R., McGee, R., & Silva, P. (1995). Obsessive-compulsive disorder in a birth cohort of 18-year-olds: Prevalence and predictors. *Journal of the American Academy of Child and Adolescent Psychiatry, 34,* 1424–1429.

Dovidio, J.F., Evans, N., & Tyler, R.B. (1986). Racial stereotypes: The contents of their cognitive representations. *Journal of Experimental Social Psychology, 22,* 22–37.

Dovidio, J.F., Gaertner, S.L., Isen, A.M., & Lawrence, R. (1995). Group representations and intergroup bias: Positive affect, similarity, and group size. *Personality and Social Psychology Bulletin, 21,* 856–865.

Downs, H. (1994, August 21). Must we age? *Parade Magazine,* pp. 3, 5, 7.

Druckman, D., & Bjork, R.A. (Eds.). (1991). *In the mind's eye: Enhancing human performance.* Washington, DC: National Academy Press.

Dryer, D.C., & Horowitz, L.M. (1997). When do opposites attract?: Interpersonal complementarity versus similarity. *Journal of Personality and Social Psychology, 72*(3), 592–603.

Dunkle, T. (1982, April). The sound of silence. *Science,* pp. 30–33.

Dunn, R.L., & Schwebel, A.I. (1995). Meta-analytic review of marital therapy outcome research. *Journal of Family Psychology, 9,* 58–68.

Dyk, P.K. (1993). Anatomy, physiology and gender issues in adolescence. In T.P. Gullota, G.R. Adams, & R. Montemayor (Eds.), *Adolescent sexuality: Advances in adolescent development* (pp. 35–36). Newbury Park, CA: Sage.

Eagly, A.H. (1987a). Reporting sex differences. *American Psychologist, 42,* 756–757.

Eagly, A.H. (1990). On the advantages of reporting sex comparisons. *American Psychologist, 45,* 560–562.

Eagly, A.H. (1992). Uneven progress: Social psychology and the study of attitudes. *Journal of Personality and Social Psychology, 63*(5), 693–710.

Eagly, A.H. (1995). The science and politics of comparing women and men. *American Psychologist, 50*(3), 145–158.

Eagly, A.H., & Carli, L.L. (1981). Sex of researchers and sex-typed communications as determinants of sex differences in influenceability: A meta-analysis of social influence studies. *Psychological Bulletin, 90,* 1–20.

Eagly, A.H., & Steffen, V.J. (1986). Gender and aggressive behavior: A meta-analytic review of the social psychological literature. *Psychological Bulletin, 100,* 309–330.

East, P., & Felice, M.E. (1992). Pregnancy risk among the younger sisters of pregnant and childbearing adolescents. *Developmental and Behavioral Pediatrics, 13,* 128–136.

Eaves, L.J., Heath, A.C., Neale, M.C., Hewitt, J.K., & Martin, N.G. (1993). Sex differences and non-additivity in the effects of genes on personality. Unpublished manuscript, cited in F.S. Mayer & K. Sutton. (1996). *Personality: An integrative approach.* Upper Saddle River, NJ: Prentice Hall.

Eccles, J., Midgley, C., Wigfield, A., Buchanan, C.M., Reuman, D., Flanagan, C., & MacIver, D. (1993). Development during adolescence: The impact of stage-environment fit on young adolescents' experiences in school and families. *American Psychologist, 2,* 90–101.

Eckerman, C.O., Davis, C.C., & Didow, S.M. (1989). Toddlers' emerging ways of achieving social coordinations with a peer. *Child Development, 60,* 440–453.

Edwards, R. (1994). Healthy divorces can lead to well-adjusted children. *The Good Divorce.*

Eibl-Eibesfeldt, I. (1972). *Love and hate.* New York: Holt, Rinehart & Winston.

Eimas, P.D., & Tartter, V.C. (1979). The development of speech perception. In H.W. Reese & L.P. Lipsitt (Eds.), *Advances in child development and behavior* (Vol. 13). New York: Academic Press.

Einhorn, H.J. (1980). Learning from experience and suboptimal rules in decision making. In T.S. Wallsten (Ed.), *Cognitive processes in choice and decision behavior.* Hillsdale, NJ: Erlbaum.

Eisenberg, N., & Lennon, R. (1983). Sex differences in empathy and related capacities. *Psychological Bulletin, 94,* 100–131.

Eisenberger, R., & Cameron, J. (1996). Detrimental effects of reward. *American Psychologist, 51,* 1153–1166.

Eisenman, R. (1994). Birth order, effect on personality and behavior. In *Encyclopedia of human behavior* (Vol. 1, pp. 401–405).

Ekman, P., Sorenson, E.R., & Friesen, W.V. (1969). Pancultural elements in facial displays of emotion. *Science, 164,* 86–88.

Ekman, P. (1976). Movements with precise meanings. *Journal of Communication,* Sum, pp. 14–26.

Ekman, P. (1992). An argument for basic emotions. *Cognition and Emotion, 6,* 169–200.

Ekman, P. (1993). Facial expression and emotion. *American Psychologist, 48*(4), 384–392.

Ekman, P. (1994). Strong evidence for universals in facial expressions: A reply to Russell's mistaken critique. *Psychological Bulletin, 115*(2), 268–287.

Ekman, P., & Davidson, R.J. (1993). Voluntary smiling changes regional brain activity. *Psychological Science, 4,* 342–345.

Ekman, P., & Friesen, W.V. (1971). Constants across cultures in the face and emotion. *Journal of Personality and Social Psychology, 17,* 124–129.

Ekman, P., & Friesen, W.V. (1975). *Unmasking the face.* Englewood Cliffs, NJ: Prentice Hall.

Ekman, P., & Friesen, W.V. (1986). A new pan-cultural facial expression of emotion. *Motivation and Emotion, 10,* 159–168.

Ekman, P., & O'Sullivan, M. (1991). Who can catch a liar? *American Psychologist, 46,* 913–920.

Ekman, P., Freisen, W.V., & Ancoli, S. (1980). Facial signs of emotional experience. *Journal of Personality & Social Psychology, 39*(1-6), 1125–1134.

Ekman, P., Friesen, W.V., & Ellsworth, P. (1972). *Emotion in the human face.* Elmsford, NY: Pergamon.

Ekman, P., Friesen, W.V., O'Sullivan, M., Chan, A., Diacoyanni-Tarlatzis, I., Heider, K., Krause, R., LeCompte, W.A., Pitcairn, T., Ricci-Bitti, P.E., Scherer, K., Tomita, M., & Tzavaras, A. (1987). Universals and cultural differences in the judgments of facial expressions of emotion. *Journal of Personality and Social Psychology, 53,* 712–717.

Elbert, T., Pantev, C., Wienbruch, C., Rockstroh, B., & Taub, E. (1995). Increased cortical representation of the fingers of the left hand in string players. *Science, 270,* 305–307.

Elkin, I., Shea, T., Watkins, J.T., Imber, S.D., Sotsky, S.M., Collins, J.F., Glass, D.R., Pikonis, P.A, Leber, W.R., Docherty, J.P., Fiester, S.J., & Parloff, M.B. (1989). National Institute of Mental Health treatment of depression collaborative research program: General effectiveness of treatments. *Archives of General Psychiatry, 46,* 971–982.

Elkind, D. (1968). Cognitive development in adolescence. In J.F. Adams (Ed.), *Understanding adolescence.* Boston: Allyn & Bacon.

Elkind, D. (1969). Egocentrism in adolescence. In R.W. Grinder (Ed.), *Studies in adolescence* (2nd ed.). New York: Macmillan.

Ellis, A. (1973). *Humanistic psychotherapy: The rational emotive approach.* New York: Julian Press.

Ellis, A., & Harper, R.A. (1975). *A new guide to rational living.* North Hollywood, CA: Wilshire Book Co.

Ellis, L., & Coontz, P.D. (1990). Androgens, brain functioning, and criminality: The neurohormonal foundations of antisociality. In L. Ellis & H. Hoffman (Eds.), *Crime in biological, social, and moral contexts* (pp. 36–49). New York: Praeger Press.

Emmorey, K. (1994). Sign language. In *Encyclopedia of human behavior* (Vol. 4, pp. 193–204). San Diego, CA: Academic Press.

Engel, J.F., Black, R.D., & Miniard, P.C. (1986). *Consumer behavior.* Chicago: Dryden Press.

Engen, T. (1982). *The perception of odors.* New York: Academic Press.

Enns, C.Z. (1993). Twenty years of feminist counseling and therapy: From naming biases to implementing multifaceted practice. *Counseling Psychologist, 21,* 3–87.

Eppley, K.R., Abrams, A.I., & Shear, J. (1989). Differential effects of relaxation techniques on trait anxiety: A meta-analysis. *Journal of Clinical Psychology, 45,* 957–974.

Epstein, A.N., Fitzsimmons, J.T., & Simons, B. (1969). Drinking caused by the intracranial injection of angiotensin into the rat. *Journal of Physiology, 200,* 98–100.

Epstein, R., Kirshnit, C.E., Lanza, R.P., & Rubin, L.C. (1984). "Insight" in the pigeon: Antecedents and determinants of an intelligent performance. *Nature (London), 308,* 61–62.

Epstein, S. (1962). The measurement of drive and conflict in humans: Theory and experiment. In M.R. Jones (Ed.), *Nebraska Symposium on Motivation.* Lincoln: University of Nebraska Press.

Erdley, C.A., & D'Agostino, P.R. (1988). Cognitive and affective components of automatic priming effects. *Journal of Personality and Social Psychology, 54,* 741–747.

Erickson, D. (1990, November). Electronic earful: Cochlear implants sound better all the time. *Scientific American,* pp. 132, 134.

Ericsson, K.A., & Charness, N. (1994). Expert performance. *American Psychologist, 49,* 725–747.

Ericsson, K.A., & Chase, W.G. (1982). Exceptional memory. *American Scientist, 70,* 607–615.

Erikson, E.H. (1963). *Childhood and society* (2nd ed.). New York: Norton.

Erikson, E.H. (1968). *Identity: Youth in crisis.* New York: Norton.

Eron, L.D. (1982). Parent-child interaction, television violence, and aggression of children. *American Psychologist, 37,* 197–211.

Esterson, A. (1993). *Seductive mirage: An exploration of the work of Sigmund Freud.* Chicago: Open Court.

Etzioni, A., Luboshitzky, R., Tiosano, D., Ben-Harush, M., Goldsher, D., & Lavie, P. (1996). Melatonin replacement corrects sleep disturbances in a child with pineal tumor. *Neurology, 46,* 1–4.

Evans, L.I., Rozelle, R.M., Lasater, T.M., Dembroski, R.M., & Allen, B.P. (1970). Fear arousal, persuasion and actual vs. implied behavioral change: New perspective utilizing a real-life dental hygiene program. *Journal of Personality and Social Psychology, 16,* 220–227.

Exner, J.E. (1996). A comment on "the comprehensive system for the Rorschach: A critical examination." *Psychological Science, 7*(1), 11–13.

Eyer, J. (1977). Prosperity as a cause of death. *International Journal of Health Services, 7,* 125–150.

Eysenck, H.J. (1947). *Dimensions of personality.* London: Routledge & Kegan Paul.

Eysenck, H.J. (1952). The effects of psychotherapy: An evaluation. *Journal of Consulting and Clinical Psychology, 16,* 319–324.

Eysenck, H.J. (1970). *The structure of human personality* (3rd ed.). London: Methuen.

Eysenck, H.J. (1976). *The measurement of personality.* Baltimore, MD: University Park Press.

Eysenck, H.J. (1992). Four ways five factors are not basic. *Personality and Individual Differences, 13,* 667–673.

Eysenck, H.J. (1993). Commentary on Goldberg. *American Psychologist, 48,* 1299–1300.

Fagot, B.I. (1994). Parenting. In *Encyclopedia of human behavior* (Vol. 3, pp. 411–419).

Fairburn, C.G., & Wilson, G.T. (Eds.). (1993). *Binge eating: Nature, assessment and treatment.* New York: Guilford Press.

Fallon, A., & Rozin, P. (1985). Sex differences in perceptions of desirable body states. *Journal of Abnormal Psychology, 84,* 102–105.

Fantz, R.L., Fagan, J.F., & Miranda, S.B. (1975). Early visual selectivity. In L.B. Cohen & P. Salapatek (Eds.), *Infant perception: From sensation to cognition* (Vol. 1). New York: Academic Press.

Farber, S. (1981, January). Telltale behavior of twins. *Psychology Today,* pp. 58–62, 79–80.

Farthing, C.W. (1992). *The psychology of consciousness.* Englewood Cliffs, NJ: Prentice Hall.

Fehr, B. (1994). Prototype-based assessment of laypeople's views of love. *Personal Relationships, 1,* 309–331.

Feingold, A. (1992). Good-looking oeioke are not what we think. *Psychological Bulletin, 111,* 304–341.

Feinson, M.C. (1986). Aging widows and widowers: Are there mental health differences? *International Journal of Aging and Human Development, 23,* 244–255.

Feldhusen, J.F., & Goh, B.E. (1995). Assessing and accessing creativity: An integrative review of theory, research, and development. *Creativity Research Journal, 8,* 231–247.

Feldman, R.S., Salzinger, S., Rosario, M., Alvarado, L., Caraballo, L., & Hammer, M. (1995). Parent, teacher, and peer ratings of physically abused and nonmaltreated children's behavior. *Journal of Abnormal Child Psychology, 23*(3), 317–334.

Feldman-Summers, S., & Pope, K.S. (1994). The experience of "forgetting" childhood abuse: A national survey of psychologists. *Journal of Consulting and Clinical Psychology, 62,* 636–639.

Ferguson, C.A., & Macken, M.A. (1983). The role of play in phonological development. In K.E. Nelson (Ed.), *Children's language* (Vol. 4). Hillsdale, NJ: Erlbaum.

Ferveur, J.F., Stortkuhl, K.F., Stocker, R.F., & Greenspan, R.J. (1995). Genetic feminization of brain structures and changed sexual orientation in male Drosophila. *Science, 267,* 902–905.

Feshbach, S., & Weiner, B. (1982). *Personality.* Lexington, MA: D.C. Heath.

Festinger, L. (1957). *A theory of cognitive dissonance.* Evanston, IL: Row, Peterson.

Fibiger, H.C., Murray, C.L., & Phillips, A.G. (1983). Lesions of the nucleus basalis magoncellularis impair long-term memory in rats. *Society for Neuroscience Abstracts, 9,* 332.

Fiedler, F.E. (1967). *A theory of leadership effectiveness.* New York: McGraw-Hill.

Fiedler, F.E. (1978). The contingency model and the dynamics of the leadership process. In L. Berkowitz (Ed.), *Advances in experimental social psychology* (Vol. 11, pp. 59–112). New York: Academic Press.

Fiedler, F.E. (1993). The leadership situation and the black box contingency theories. In M. Chemers & R. Ayman (Eds.), *Leadership theory and research: Perspective and directions* (pp. 1–28). San Diego, CA: Academic Press.

Field, T.M. (1986). Interventions for premature infants. *Journal of Pediatrics, 109,* 183–191.

Finkelhor, D., Hotaling, G., Lewis, I.A., & Smith, C. (1990). Sexual abuse in a national sample of adult men and women: Prevalence, characteristics, and risk factors. *Child Abuse and Neglect, 14,* 19–28.

Fischer, K.W., & Henke, R.W. (1996). Infants' construction of actions in context: Piaget's contribution to research on early development. *Psychological Science, 7*(4), 204–210.

Fischman, J. (1985, September). Mapping the mind. *Psychology Today,* pp. 18–19.

Fisher, S., & Greenberg, R.P. (1985). *The scientific credibility of Freud's theories and therapy.* New York: Columbia University Press.

Fiske, S.T., & Neuberg, S.L. (1990). A continuum of impression formation, from category-based to individuating processes: Influence of information and motivation on attention and interpretation. In M.P. Zanna (Ed.), *Advances in experimental social psychology* (Vol. 23, pp. 399–427). New York: Academic Press.

Fiske, S.T., & Taylor, S.E. (1991). *Social cognition* (2nd ed.). New York: McGraw-Hill.

Fitzgerald, L.F. (1993). Sexual harassment. Violence against women in the workplace. *American Psychologist, 48,* 1070–1076.

Flavell, J.F. (1986). The development of children's knowledge about the appearance-reality distinction. *American Psychologist, 41,* 418–425.

Flavell, J.H. (1996). Piaget's legacy. *Psychological Science, 7*(4), 200–204.

Flexser, A.J., & Tulving, E. (1978). Retrieval independence in recognition and recall. *Psychological Review, 85,* 153–171.

Flynn, J.R. (1984). The mean IQ of Americans: Massive gains 1932 to 1978. *Psychological Bulletin, 95,* 29–51.

Flynn, J.R. (1987). Massive IQ gains in 14 nations: What IQ tests really measure. *Psychological Bulletin, 101,* 171–191.

Fogelman, E., & Wiener, V.L. (1985, August). The few, the brave, the noble. *Psychology Today,* pp. 60–65.

Ford, B.D. (1993, December). Emergenesis: An alternative and a confound. *American Psychologist,* p. 1294.

Fouts, R.S. (1973). Acquisition and testing of gestural signs in four young chimpanzees. *Science, 180,* 978–980.

Frager, R. (1970). Conformity and anticonformity in Japan. *Journal of Personality and Social Psychology, 15,* 203–210.

Frank, J.D., & Frank, J.B. (1991). *Persuasion and healing* (3rd ed.). Baltimore: Johns Hopkins University Press.

Fraser, C. (1971). Group risk-taking and group polarization. *European Journal of Social Psychology, 1,* 7–30.

Frederickson, N. (1986). Toward a broader conception of human intelligence. *American Psychologist, 41,* 445–452.

Freedman, J.L., & Fraser, S.C. (1966). Compliance without pressure: The foot-in-the-door technique. *Journal of Personality and Social Psychology, 4,* 195–202.

Freud, S. (1900). The interpretation of dreams. In J. Strachey (Ed.), *The standard edition of the complete psychological works of Sigmund Freud* (Vol. 5). London: Hogarth Press.

Freud, S. (1909). Analysis of a phobia in a five-year-old boy. In J. Strachey (Ed), *The standard edition of the complete psychological works of Sigmund Freud* (Vol. 10). London: Hogarth Press.

Freud, S. (1933). *New introductory lectures on psychoanalysis.* New York: Carlton House.

Freudenheim, M. (1988, December 12). Workers' substance abuse is increasing, survey says. *New York Times,* Business Sec.

Freyd, J.J. (1996). *Betrayal trauma theory: The logic of forgetting abuse.* Cambridge, MA: Harvard University Press.

Freyd, J.J. (1996). *Betrayal trauma theory: The logic of forgetting abuse.* Cambridge, MA: Harvard University Press.

Frezza, M., di Padova, C., Pozzato, G., Terpin, M., Baraona, E., & Lieber, C.S. (1990). High blood alcohol levels in women: The role of decreased gastric alcohol dehydrogenase activity and first-pass metabolism. *New England Journal of Medicine, 322,* 95–99.

Friedman, E.S., Clark, D.B., & Gershon, S. (1992). Stress, anxiety, and depression: Review of biological, diagnostic, and nosologic issues. *Journal of Anxiety Disorders, 6,* 337–363.

Friedman, M., & Rosenman, R.H. (1959). Association of specific overt behavior patterns with blood and cardiovascular findings: Blood cholesterol level, blood clotting time, incidence of arcus senilis and clinical coronary artery disease. *JAMA, Journal of the American Medical Association, 169,* 1286–1296.

Friedman, M., Breall, W.S., Goodwin, M.L., Sparagon, B.J., Ghandour, G., & Fleischmann, N. (1996). Effect of Type A behavioral counseling on frequency of episodes of silent myocardial ischemia in coronary patients. *American Heart Journal, 132*(5), 933–937.

Friedman, M.J., Schnurr, P.P., & McDonagh-Coyle, A. (1994). Posttraumatic stress disorder in the military veteran. *Psychiatric Clinic of North America, 17*(2), 265–277.

Friedman, S., Paradis, C.M., & Hatch, M. (1994). Characteristics of African-American and white patients with panic disorder and agoraphobia. *Hospital and Community Psychiatry, 45,* 798–803.

Friman, P.C., Allen, K.D., Kerwin, M.L.E., & Larzelere, R. (1993). Changes in modern psychology. *American Psychology, 48,* 658–664.

Frumkin, B., & Ainsfield, M. (1977). Semantic and surface codes in the memory of deaf children. *Cognitive Psychology, 9,* 475–493.

Funder, D.C. (1991). Global traits: A neo-Allportian approach to personality. *Psychological Science, 2,* 31–39.

Funder, D.C. (1995). On the accuracy of personality judgment: A realistic approach. *Psychological Review, 102*(4), 652–670.

Furstenberg, F.F., Jr., Brooks-Gunn, J., & Chase-Lansdale, L. (1989). Teenaged pregnancy and childbearing. *American Psychologist, 44,* 313–320.

Gable, M., Wilkens, H.T., Harris, L., & Feinberg, R. (1987). An evaluation of subliminally embedded sexual stimuli in graphics. *Journal of Advertising, 16,* 25–31.

Gabrieli, J.D., Desmond, J.E., Bemb, J.B., Wagner, A.D., Stone, M.V., Vaidya, C.J. & Glover, G.H. (1996). Functional magnetic resonance imaging of semantic memory processes in the frontal lobes. *Psychological Science, 7,* 278–283.

Gaertner, S.L., & McLaughlin, J.P. (1983). Racial stereotypes: Associations and ascriptions of positive and negative characteristics. *Social Psychology Quarterly, 46,* 23–30.

Gagnon, J.H., Laumanm, E.O., Michael, R.T., & Kolata, G. (1994). *Sex in America: A definitive study.* Boston: Little, Brown.

Galanter, M. (1984). Self-help large-group therapy for alcoholism: A controlled study. *Alcoholism, Clinical and Experimental Research, 8*(1), 16–23.

Galef, B.G. (1993). Functions of social learning about food: A causal analysis of effects of diet novelty on preference transmission. *Animal Behaviour, 46*(2), 257–265.

Gallistel, C.R. (1981). Bell, Magendie, and the proposals to restrict the use of animals in neurobehavioral research. *American Psychologist, 36,* 357–360.

Gallup, G.G., Jr. (1985). Do minds exist in species other than our own? *Neuroscience and Biobehavioral Reviews, 9,* 631–641.

Gannon, L., Luchetta, T., Rhodes, K., Pardie, L., & Segrist, D. (1992). Sex bias in psychological research. *American Psychologist, 47,* 389–396.

Garber, H., & Heber, R. (1982). Modification of predicted cognitive development in high risk children through early intervention. In D.K. Detterman & R.J. Sternberg (Eds.), *How and how much can intelligence be increased?* (pp. 121–137). Norwood, NJ: Ablex.

Garcia, J., & Koelling, R.A. (1966). Relation of cue to consequence in avoidance learning. *Psychonomic Science, 4,* 123–124.

Garcia, J., Hankins, W.G., & Rusiniak, K.W. (1974). Behavioral regulation of the milieu in man and rat. *Science, 185,* 824–831.

Garcia, J., Kimeldorf, D.J., Hunt, E.L., & Davies, B.P. (1956). Food and water consumption of rats during exposure to gamma radiation. *Radiation Research, 4,* 33–41.

Gardner, H. (1982). *Developmental psychology* (2nd ed.). Boston: Little, Brown.

Gardner, H. (1983a). *Frames of mind: The theory of multiple intelligences.* New York: Basic Books.

Gardner, H. (1983b, May). Prodigies' progress. *Psychology Today,* pp. 75–79.

Gardner, H. (1990). *The Chinese experience.* [Videocassette]. Middlesex Community College Professional Development Day.

Gardner, H. (1993). *Multiple intelligences: The theory in practice.* New York: Basic Books.

Gardner, R.A., & Gardner, B.T. (1969). Teaching sign language to a chimpanzee. *Science, 165,* 664–672.

Gardner, R.A., & Gardner, B.T. (1975). Evidence for sentence constituents in the early utterances of child and chimpanzee. *Journal of Experimental Psychology: General, 3,* 244–267.

Gardner, R.A., & Gardner, B.T. (1977). Comparative psychology and language acquisition. In K. Salzinger & R. Denmark (Eds.), *Psychology: The state of the art*. New York: New York Academy of Sciences.

Garfield, S.L. (Ed.). (1983). Special section: Meta-analysis and psychotherapy. *Journal of Consulting and Clinical Psychology, 51*, 3–75.

Garfinkel, P.E., & Garner, D.M. (1982). *Anorexia nervosa: A multidimensional perspective*. New York: Brunner/Mazel.

Garland, A.F., & Zigler, E. (1993). Adolescent suicide prevention. *American Psychologist, 48*, 169–182.

Garry, M., Loftus, E.F., & Brown, S.W. (1994). Memory: A river runs through it. [Special issue: The recovered memory/false memory debate]. *Consciousness & Cognition: An International Journal, 3*(3-4), 438–451.

Gazzaniga, M.S., Fendrich, R., & Wessiner, C.M. (1994). Blindsight reconsidered. *Current Directions in Psychological Science, 3*, 93–96.

Geldard, F.A. (1972). *The human senses* (2nd ed.). New York: Wiley.

Gelman, D. (1990, October 29). A fresh take on Freud. *Newsweek*, pp. 84–86.

Gelman, D. (1994, June 13). Reliving the painful past. *Newsweek*, pp. 20–22.

Genesee, F. (1994). Bilingualism. In V.S. Ramachandran (Ed.), *Encyclopedia of human behavior* (Vol. 1, pp. 383–393). San Diego, CA: Academic Press.

Gentry, J., & Eron, L.D. (1993). American Psychological Association Commission on Violence and Youth. *American Psychologist, 48*, 89.

Gerardi, S. (1996). *The effects of English as a second language on college academic outcomes*. (Research/Technical Report). City University of New York, NYC Technical College.

Gergen, K.J. (1973). The codification of research ethics—views of a Doubting Thomas. *American Psychologist, 28*, 907–912.

Gershon, E.S. (1990). Genetics. In F.K. Goodwin & K.R. Jamison (Eds.), *Manic depressive illness* (pp. 373–401). New York: Oxford University Press.

Getzels, J.W. (1975). Problem finding and the inventiveness of solutions. *Journal of Creative Behavior, 9*, 12–18.

Getzels, J.W., & Jackson, P. (1962). *Creativity and intelligence*. New York: Wiley.

Giambra, L. (1974, December). Daydreams: The backburner of the mind. *Psychology Today*, pp. 66–68.

Gibbs, R. (1986). On the psycholinguistics of sarcasm. *Journal of Experimental Psychology: General, 115*, 3–15.

Gilbert, E.H., & DeBlassie, R.R. (1984). Anorexia nervosa: Adolescent starvation by choice. *Adolescence, 19*, 839–853.

Gilbert, L.A. (1994). Current perspectives on dual-career families. *Current Directions in Psychological Science, 3*, 101–105.

Gilligan, C. (1982). *In a different voice: Psychological theory and women's development*. Cambridge, MA: Harvard University Press.

Gilligan, C. (1992). *Joining the resistance: Girls' development in adolescence*. Paper presented at the meeting of the American Psychological Association, Montreal.

Gilovich, T. (1991). *How we know what isn't so: The fallibility of human reason in everyday life*. New York: Free Press.

Ginsberg, H. (1972). *The myth of the deprived child*. Englewood Cliffs, NJ: Prentice Hall.

Gist, R., & Stolz, S. (1982). Mental health promotion and the media. *American Psychologist, 37*, 1136–1139.

Gladue, B.A. (1994). Sex differences in parent child interaction. In S.U. Philips, S. Steele, & C. Tanz (Eds.), *Language, gender, and sex in comparative perspective*. New York: Cambridge University Press.

Gladue, B.A. (1994). The biopsychology of sexual orientation. *Current Directions in Psychological Science, 3*(5), 150–154.

Glassman, A.H., & Koob, G.F. (1996). Neuropharmacology. Psychoactive smoke. *Nature, 379*, 677–678.

Gleicher, F., & Weary, G. (1991). Effect of depression on quantity and quality of social inferences. *Journal of Personality and Social Psychology, 61*, 105–114.

Glenberg, A., Smith, S.M., & Green, C. (1977). Type I rehearsal: Maintenance and more. *Journal of Verbal Learning and Verbal Behavior, 16*, 339–352.

Glenner, G.G. (1994). Alzheimer's disease. In *Encyclopedia of human behavior* (Vol. 1, pp. 103–111).

Gluck, M.A., & Myers, C.E. (1997). Psychobiological models of hippocampal function in learning and memory. *Annual Review of Psychology, 8*, 481–514.

Goldberg, L.R. (1993). The structure of phenotypic personality traits. *American Psychologist, 48*, 26–34.

Goldman, S.A., & Nottebohm, F. (1983). Neuronal production, migration, and differentiation in a vocal control nucleus of the adult female canary brain. *Proceedings of the National Academy of Sciences of the U.S.A., 80*, 2390–2394.

Goldsmith, H.H., & Harman, C. (1994). Temperament and attachment: Individuals and relationships. *Current Directions in Psychological Sciences*, pp. 53–56.

Goldstein, A.P., & Segall, M.H. (1983). *Aggression in global perspective*. New York: Pergamon.

Goldstein, M., & Rodnick, E. (1975). The family's contribution to the etiology of schizophrenia: Current status. *Schizophrenia Bulletin, 14*, 48–63.

Goleman, D. (1996, February 26). Studies suggest older minds are stronger than expected. *New York Times*.

Golomb, J., Kluger, A., de Leon, M.J., Ferris, S.H., Convit, A., Mittelman, M.S., Cohen, J., Rusinek, H., DeSanti, S., & George, A.E. (1994). Hippocampal formation size in normal human aging: A correlate of delayed secondary memory performance. *Learning & Memory, 1*, 45–54.

Goodall, J. (1971). *In the shadow of man*. New York: Dell.

Goode, E. (1992, December 7). Spiritual questing. *U.S. News & World Report*, pp. 64–71.

Gopnik, A. (1996). The post-Piaget era. *Psychological Science, 7*(4), 221–225.

Gordis, E. (1996). Alcohol research: At the cutting edge. *Archives of General psychiatry, 53*, 199–201.

Gore, S., & Colten, M. (1991). Gender, stress, and distress: Social-relational influences. In J. Eckenrode (Ed.), *The social context of coping*. New York: Plenum.

Gose, B. (1997, October 24). Colleges try to curb excessive drinking by saying moderation is okay. *Chronicle of Higher Education*, pp. A61–A62.

Gottesman, I.I. (1991). *Schizophrenia genesis: The origins of madness*. New York: Freeman.

Grady, D. (1997, March 21). Importance of a sleep disorder is played down in a British study. *New York Times*, p. A15.

Graf, P. (1990). Life-span changes in implicit and explicit memory. (30th Annual Meeting of the Psychonomic Society Symposium: Implicit memory: Multiple perspectives [1989, Atlanta, GA].) *Bulletin of the Psychonomic Society, 28*, 353–358.

Graf, P., & Schacter, D.L. (1985). Implicit and explicit memory for new associations in normal and amnesic subjects. *Journal of Experimental Psychology: Learning, Memory, and Cognition, 11*(3), 501–518.

Graf, P., Shimamura, A.P., & Squire, L.R. (1985). Priming across modalities and priming across category levels: Extending the domain of preserved function in amnesia. *Journal of Experimental Psychology: Learning, Memory, and Cognition, 11*(2), 386–396.

Graf, P., Squire, L.R., & Mandler, G. (1984). The information that amnesic patients do not forget. *Journal of Experimental Psychology: Learning, Memory and Cognition, 10*, 164–178.

Graham, J.R., & Lilly, R.S. (1984). *Psychological testing*. Englewood Cliffs, NJ: Prentice Hall.

Graham, K. (1997). *Personal history*. New York: Knopf.

Graham, S. (1992). Most of the subjects were white and middle class. *American Psychologist, 47*, 629–639.

Graziadei, P.P.C., Levine, R.R., & Graziadei, G.A.M. (1979). Plasticity of connections of the olfactory sensory neuron: Regeneration into the forebrain following bulbectomy in the neonatal mouse. *Neuroscience, 4*, 713–728.

Greaves, G.B. (1980). Psychosocial aspects of amphetamine and related substance abuse. In J. Caldwell (Ed.), *Amphetamines and related stimulants: Chemical, biological, clinical and sociological aspects*. Boca Raton, FL: CRC Press.

Green, L., Fry, A.F., & Myerson, J. (1994). Discounting of delayed rewards: A life-span comparison. 5, 33–36.

Greenberg, R., & Pearlman, C. (1967). Delirium tremens and dreaming. *American Journal of Psychiatry, 124*, 133–142.

Greene, R.L. (1987). Effects of maintenance rehearsal on human memory. *Psychological Bulletin, 102*, 403–413.

Greenfield, P.M., & Savage-Rumbaugh, E.S. (1984). Perceived variability and symbol usage: A common language-cognition interface in children and chimpanzees (Pan Troglodytes). *Journal of Comparative Psychology, 98*, 201–218.

Greenfield, P.M., & Smith, J.H. (1976). *The structure of communication in early language development*. New York: Academic Press.

Greenstein, T.H. (1993). Maternal employment and child behavioral outcomes. *Journal of Family Issues, 14*, 323–354.

Greenwald, A.G. (1992). New Look 3: Unconscious cognition reclaimed. *American Psychologist, 47*, 766–779.

Greenwald, A.G., & Banaji, M.R. (1995). Implicit social cognition: Attitudes, self-esteem, and stereotypes. *Psychological Review, 102*, 4–27.

Greenwald, A.G., Spangenberg, E.R., Pratkanis, A.R., & Eskenazi, J. (1991). Double-blind tests of subliminal self-help audiotapes. *Psychological Science, 2*, 119-122.

Grilo, C.M., & Pogue-Geile, M.F. (1991). The nature of environmental influences on weight and obesity: A behavior genetic analysis. *Psychological Bulletin, 110*, 520–537.

Grinker, R.R., & Spiegel, J.P. (1945). *War neurosis*. Philadelphia: Blakiston.

Grinspoon, L., Ewalt, J.R., & Shader, R.I. (1972). *Schizophrenia: Pharmacotherapy and psychotherapy*. Baltimore: Williams & Wilkins.

Gruber, J.E., & Bjorn, L. (1986). Women's responses to sexual harassment: An analysis of sociocultural, organizational, and personal resource models. *Social Science Quarterly, 67*, 814–826.

Gruetzner, H. (1988). *Alzheimer's: A caregiver's guide and sourcebook*. New York: Wiley.

Guérin, D. (1994). *Fussy infants at risk*. Paper presented at the meeting of the American Psychological Association, Los Angeles.

Guilford, J.P. (1967). *The nature of human intelligence*. New York: McGraw-Hill.

Gullette, E.C., Blumenthal, J.A., Babyak, M., Jiang, W., & Waugh, R.A. (1997). Effects of mental stress on myocardial ischemia during daily life. *Journal of American Medical Association, 277*(19), 1521–1526.

Gunderson, J.G. (1984). *Borderline personality disorder*. Washington, DC: American Psychiatric Press.

Gunderson, J.G. (1994). Building structure for the borderline construct. *Acta Psychiatrica Scandinavica, 89*(Suppl. 379), 12–18.

Gunne, L.M., & Anggard, E. (1972). *Pharmical kinetic studies with amphetamines—relationship to neuropsychiatric disorders*. International Symposium on Pharmical Kinetics, Washington, DC.

Gurman, A.S., Kniskern, D.P., & Pinsof, W.M. (1986). Research on the process and outcome of marital and family therapy. In S.L. Garfield & A.E. Bergin (Eds.), *Handbook of psychotherapy and behavior change* (3rd ed., pp. 565–624). New York: Wiley.

Gurvits, T.V., Gilbertson, M.W., Lasko, N.B., Orr, S.P., & Pitman, R.K. (1997). Neurological status of combat veterans and adult survivors of sexual abuse PTSD. *Annals of the New York Academy of Sciences, 821*, 468–471.

Guzder, J., Paris, J., Zelkowitz, P., & Marchessault, K. (1996). Risk factors for borderline personality in children. *Journal of the American Academy of Child and Adolescent Psychiatry, 35*, 26–33.

Gwirtsman, H.E. (1984). Bulimia in men: Report of three cases with neuroendocrine findings. *Journal of Clinical Psychiatry, 45*, 78–81.

Haber, R.N. (1969, April). Eidetic images. *Scientific American*, pp. 36–44.

Haberlandt, K. (1997). *Cognitive psychology*. Boston: Allyn & Bacon.

Hack, M., Breslau, N., Weissman, B., Aram, D., Klein, N., & Borawski, E. (1991). Effect of very low birth weight and subnormal head size on cognitive abilities at school age. *New England Journal of Medicine, 325*, 231–237.

Haefele, J.W. (1962). *Creativity and innovation*. New York: Reinhold.

Hage, J.J. (1995). Medical requirements and consequences of sex reassignment surgery. *Medicine, Science and the Law, 35*, 17–24.

Haines, M., & Spear, S.F. (1996). Changing the perception of the norm: A strategy to decrease binge drinking among college students. *Journal of American College Health, 45*, 134–140.

Hakuta, K. (1987). Degree of bilingualism and cognitive ability in mainland and Puerto Rican children [Special issue: Schools and development]. *Child Development, 58*, 1372–1388.

Hall, E.T. (1966). *The hidden dimension*. New York: Doubleday.

Hall, G.S. (1904). *Adolescence: Its psychology and its relations to physiology, anthropology, sex, crime, religion and education* (Vol. 1). New York: Appleton-Century-Crofts.

Hall, J.A. (1984). *Nonverbal sex differences: Communication accuracy and expressive style*. Baltimore: Johns Hopkins University Press.

Halpern, D.F. (1992). *Sex differences in cognitive abilities* (2nd ed.). Hillsdale, NJ: Erlbaum.

Ham, L.P., & Packard, R.C. (1996). A retrospective, follow-up study of biofeedback-assisted relaxation therapy in patients with posttraumatic headache. *Biofeedback and Self-Regulation, 21*(2), 93–104.

Hamilton, J.A., Haier, R.J., & Buchsbaum, M.S. (1984). Intrinsic enjoyment and boredom coping scales: Validation with personality evoked potential and attentional measures. *Personality and Individual Differences, 5*(2), 183–393.

Hammen, C.L. (1985). Predicting depression: A cognitive-behavioral perspective. In P. Kendall (Ed.), *Advances in cognitive-behavioral research and therapy* (Vol. 4). New York: Academic Press.

Hampson, E., & Kimura, D. (1992). Sexual differentiation and hormonal influences on cognitive function in humans. In J.B. Becker, S.M. Breedlove, & D. Crews (Eds.), *Behavioral endocrinology*. Cambridge, MA: MIT Press.

Hampson, J., & Nelson, K. (1993). The relation of maternal language to variation in rate and style of language acquisition. *Journal of Child Language, 20*, 313–342.

Hansel, C.E. (1969). ESP: Deficiencies of experimental method. *Nature, 221*(5186), 1171–1172.

Hansen, W.B. (1993). School-based alcohol prevention programs. *Alcohol, Health and Research World, 17*, 54–60.

Hansen, W.B., & Graham, J.W. (1991). Preventing alcohol, marijuana, and cigarette use among adolescents: Peer pressure resistance training versus establishing conservative norms. *Preventive Medicine, 20*, 414–430.

Harburg, E., DiFranceisco, W., Webster, D.W., Gleiberman, L., & Schork, A. (1990). Familial transmission of alcohol use: II. Imitation of and aversion to parent drinking (1960) by adult offspring (1977)—Tecumseh, Michigan. *Journal of Studies on Alcohol, 51*, 245–256.

Harburg, E., Gleiberman, L., DiFranceisco, W., Schork, A. & Weissfeld, L.A. (1990). Familial transmission of alcohol use: III. Impact of imitation/non-imitation of parent alcohol use (1960) on the sensible/problem drinking of their offspring (1977). *British Journal of Addiction, 85*, 1141–1155.

Hardaway, R.A. (1991). Subliminally activated symbiotic fantasies: Facts and artifacts. *Psychological Bulletin, 107*, 177–195.

Hare, R.D. (1983). Diagnosis of antisocial personality disorder in two prison populations. *American Journal of Psychiatry, 140*, 887–890.

Hare, R.D. (1993). *Without conscience: The disturbing world of the psychopaths among us*. New York: Pocket Books.

Harley, H.E., Roitblat, H.L., & Nachtigall, P.E. (1996). Object representation in the bottlenose dolphin (Tursiops truncatus): Integration of visual and echoic information. *Journal of Experimental Psychology and Animal Behavior Process, 22*(2), 164–174.

Harlow, H.F. (1949). The formation of learning sets. *Psychological Review, 56*, 51–65.

Harlow, H.F. (1958). The nature of love. *American Psychologist, 13*, 673–685.

Harlow, H.F., & Zimmerman, R.R. (1959). Affectional responses in the infant monkey. *Science, 130*, 421–432.

Harrell, R.F., Woodyard, E., & Gates, A.I. (1955). *The effect of mother's diet on the intelligence of the offspring.* New York: Teacher's College, Columbia Bureau of Publications.

Harrington, D.M., Block, J.H., & Block, J. (1987). Testing aspects of Carl Rogers's theory of creative environments: Child-rearing antecedents of creative potential in young adolescents. *Journal of Personality and Social Psychology, 52*, 851–856.

Harris, J.R., & Liebert, R.M. (1991). *The child: A contemporary view of development* (3rd ed.). Englewood Cliffs, NJ: Prentice Hall.

Harris, M., & Rosenthal, R. (1985). Mediation of the interpersonal expectancy effect: A taxonomy of expectancy situations. In P. Blanck (Ed.), *Interpersonal expectations: Theory, research, and application* (pp. 350–378). Paris, France: Cambridge University Press.

Hart, B., & Risley, T.R. (1995). *Meaningful differences in the everyday experience of young American children.* Baltimore: Brookes.

Hartmann, P., & Husband, C. (1971). The mass media and racial conflict. *Race, 12*, 267–282.

Hasselmo, M.E., & Bower, J.M. (1993). Acetylcholine and memory. *Trends in Neurosciences, 6*, 218–222.

Hasselmo, M.E., Schnell, E., & Barkai, E. (1995). Dynamics of learning and recall at excitatory recurrent synapses and cholinergic modulation in rat hippocampal region CA3. *Journal of Neuroscience, 15*, 5249–5262.

Hathaway, S.R., & McKinley, J.C. (1942). A multiphasic personality schedule (Minnesota): III. The measurement of symptomatic depression. *Journal of Psychology, 14*, 73–84.

Hauri, P. (1970). Evening activity, sleep mentation, and subjective sleep quality. *Journal of Abnormal Psychology, 76*, 270–275.

Hauri, P. (1982). *Sleep disorders.* Kalamazoo, MI: Upjohn.

Hayden, T., & Mischel, W. (1976). Maintaining trait consistency in the resolution of behavioral inconsistency: The wolf in sheep's clothing? *Journal of Personality, 44*, 109–132.

Hayes, C., & Hayes, K. (1951). The intellectual development of a home-raised chimpanzee. *Proceedings of the American Philosophical Society, 95*, 105–109.

Hayes, J.R., & Simon, H.A. (1976). The understanding process: Problem isomorphs. *Cognitive Psychology, 8*, 165–190.

Hazan, C., & Shaver, P. (1987). Romantic love conceptualized as attachment process. *Journal of Personality and Social Psychology, 52*, 511–524.

He, L. (1987). Involvement of endogenous opioid peptides in acupuncture analgesia. *Pain, 31*, 99–122.

Hearst, E. (1975). The classical-instrumental distinction: Reflexes, voluntary behavior, and categories of associative learning. In W.K. Estes (Ed.), *Handbook of learning and cognitive processes: Vol. 2. Conditioning and behavior theory.* Hillsdale, NJ: Erlbaum.

Heath, A.C., & Martin, N.G. (1993). Genetic models for the natural history of smoking: Evidence for a genetic influence on smoking persistence. *Addictive Behavior, 18*, 19–34.

Heath, A.C., Cloninger, C.R., & Martin, N.G. (1994). Testing a model for the genetic structure of personality: A comparison of the personality systems of Cloninger and Eysenck. *Journal of Personality and Social Psychology, 66*, 762–775.

Heath, A.C., Madden, P.A.F., Bucholz, K.K., Dinwiddie, S.H., & Slutske, W.S. (1994). Genetic contribution to alcoholism risk in women. *Alcohol: Clinical and Experimental Research, 18*, 448 [Abstract].

Heath, R.C. (1972). Pleasure and brain activity in man. *Journal of Nervous and Mental Disease, 154*, 3-18.

Heatherton, T.F., & Baumeister, R.F. (1991). Binge eating as escape from self-awareness. *Psychological Bulletin, 110*, 86–108.

Hebb, D.O. (1955). Drives and the CNS (conceptual nervous system). *Psychological Review, 62*, 243–254.

Heber, R., Garber, H., Harrington, S., & Hoffman, C. (1972). *Rehabilitation of families at risk for mental retardation.* Madison: University of Wisconsin, Rehabilitation Research and Training Center in Mental Retardation.

Hechtman, L. (1989). Teenage mothers and their children: Risks and problems: A review. *Canadian Journal of Psychology, 34*, 569–575.

Hedges, L.V., & Nowell, A. (1995). Sex differences in mental test scores, variability, and numbers of high-scoring individuals. *Science, 269*, 41–45.

Heider, E.R. (1972). Universals in color naming and memory. *Journal of Experimental Psychology, 93*, 10–20.

Heider, E.R., & Oliver, D.C. (1972). The structure of the color space in naming and memory in two languages. *Cognitive Psychology, 3*, 337–354.

Heider, F. (1958). *The psychology of interpersonal relations.* New York: Wiley.

Helgeson, V.S. (1992). Moderators of the relation between perceived control and adjustment to chronic illness. *Journal of Personality and Social Psychology, 63*(4), 656–666.

Heller, K. (1996). Coming of age of prevention science: Comments on the 1994 National Institute of Mental Health–Institute of Medicine prevention reports. *American psychologist, 51*(11), 1123–127.

Hellige, J.B. (1990). Hemispheric asymmetry. *Annual Review of Psychology, 41*, 55–80.

Hellige, J.B. (1993). *Hemispheric asymmetry: What's right and what's left.* Cambridge, MA: Harvard University Press.

Helmreich, R., & Spence, J. (1978). The Work and Family Orientation Questionnaire: An objective instrument to assess components of achievement motivation and scientific attainment. *Personality and Social Psychology Bulletin, 4*, 222–226.

Helms, J.E. (1992). Why is there no study of cultural equivalence in standardized cognitive ability testing? *American Psychologist, 47*, 1083–1101.

Helson, R. (1971). Women mathematicians and the creative personality. *Journal of Consulting and Clinical Psychology, 36*, 210–220.

Hendrick, S., & Hendrick, C. (1992). *Liking, loving and relating* (2nd ed.). Pacific Grove, CA: Brooks/Cole.

Henriques, J.B., & Davidson, R.J. (1990). Regional brain electrical asymmetries discriminate between previously depressed and healthy control subjects. *Journal of Abnormal Psychology, 99*, 22–31.

Henry, J.A., Alexander, C.A., & Sener, E.K. (1995). Relative mortality from overdose of antidepressants. *British Medical Journal, 310*, 221–224.

Henry, S. (1996, March 7). Keep your brain fit for life. *Parade Magazine,* pp. 8–11.

Herdt, G., & Boxer, A. (1993). *Children of horizons.* Boston: Beacon Press.

Hergenhahn, B.R., & Olson, M.H. (1993). *An introduction to theories of learning* (4th ed.). Englewood Cliffs, NJ: Prentice Hall.

Hering, E. (1878). *Zur lehre vom lichtsinne: Sechs mitheilungen an die Kaiserl: Akademie der Wissenschaften im Wien.* Wien: [s.n.].

Herkenham, M., Lynn, A.B., Little, M.D., Johnson, M.R., Melvin, L.S., deCosta, B.R., & Rice, K.C. (1990). Cannabinoid receptor localization in brain. *Proceedings of the National Academy of Sciences of the U.S.A., 87*, 1932–1936.

Herman, C.P., Policy, J., & Silver, R. (1979). Effects of an observer on eating behavior: The induction of sensible eating. *Journal of Personality, 47*, 85-99.

Herman, L.M., Richards, D.G., & Wolz, J.P. (1984). Comprehension of sentences by bottlenosed dolphins. *Cognition, 16*, 1–90.

Heron, W. (1957). The pathology of boredom. *Scientific American, 199*, 52–56.

Herrnstein, R.J., & Mazur, J.E. (1987). Making up our minds: A new model of economic behavior. *The Sciences, 27*, 40–47.

Herrnstein, R.J., & Murray, C. (1994). *The bell curve.* New York: Free Press.

Hersher, L. (Ed.). (1970). *Four psychotherapies.* New York: Appleton-Century-Crofts.

Herzog, H.A. (1995). Has public interest in animal rights peaked? *American Psychologist, 50*, 945–947.

Heston, L.L. (1966). Psychiatric disorders in foster-home-reared children of schizophrenic mothers. *British Journal of Psychiatry, 112*, 819–825.

Hewstone, M., Islam, M.R., & Judd, C.M. (1993). Models of cross categorization and intergroup relations. *Journal of Personality and Social psychology, 64,* 779–793.

Heyes, C.M., Jaldow, E., & Dawson, G.R. (1993). Observational extinction:
Observation of nonreinforced responding reduces resistance to extinction in rats. *Animal Learning & Behavior, 21,* 221–225.

Hibbard, S.R., Farmer, L., Wells, C., Difillipo, E., & Barry, W. (1994). Validation of Cramer's defense mechanism manual for the TAT. *Journal of
Personality Assessment, 63,* 197–210.

Hilgard, E.R. (1965). *Hypnotic susceptibility.* New York: Harcourt Brace Jovanovich.

Hilgard, E.R., Hilgard, J.R., & Kaufmann, W. (1983). *Hypnosis in the relief of
pain* (2nd ed.). Los Altos, CA: Kaufmann.

Hillier, L., Hewitt, K.L., & Morrongiello, B.A. (1992). Infants' perception of
illusions in sound locations: Responding to sounds in the dark. *Journal of
Experimental Child Psychology, 53,* 159–179.

Hilton, J., & von Hipple, W. (1996). Stereotypes. *Annual Review of Psychology, 47,* 237–271.

Hobson, J.A. (1994). *The chemistry of conscious states: How the brain changes
its mind.* Boston: Little, Brown.

Hobson, J.A., & McCarley, R. (1977). The brain as a dream state generator:
An activation–synthesis hypothesis of the dream process. *American Journal of Psychiatry, 134,* 1335–1348.

Hochberg, J. (1978). *Perception* (2nd ed.). Englewood Cliffs, NJ: Prentice
Hall.

Hochschild, A.R. (1983). *The managed heart.* Berkeley: University of California Press.

Hofferth, S.L. (1991). *Family day care in the United States, 1990.* Washington,
DC: Urban Institute.

Hofferth, S.L., Brayfield, A., Beich, S., & Holcomb, P. (1990). *National Child
Care Survey.* Washington, DC: Urban Institute.

Hoffman, H.S., & DePaulo, P. (1977). Behavioral control by an imprinting
stimulus. *American Scientist, 65,* 58–66.

Hoffman, L. (1989). Effects of maternal employment in the two-parent family. *American Psychologist, 44,* 283–292.

Hoffman, M. (1991). Unraveling the genetics of fragile X syndrome. *Science,
252,* 1070.

Hoffman, M.L. (1977). Personality and social development. *Annual Review
of Psychology, 28,* 295–321.

Hogan, R., & Schroeder, D. (1981, July). Seven biases in psychology. *Psychology Today,* pp. 8–14.

Hogan, R., Hogan, J., & Roberts, B.W. (1996). Personality measurement and
employment decisions: Questions and answers. *American Psychologist,
51*(5), 469–477.

Holland, C.A., & Rabbitt, P.M.A. (1990). Aging memory: Use versus impairment. *British Journal of Psychology, 82,* 29–38.

Hollister, L.E. (1986). Health aspects of cannibis. *Pharmacological Reviews,
38,* 1–20.

Holmbeck, G.N. (1994). Adolescence. In *Encyclopedia of human behavior*
(Vol. 1, pp. 17–28).

Holmes, D.S. (1976). Debriefing after psychological experiments. II. Effectiveness of spot experimental desensitizing. *American Psychologist, 31*(12),
868–875.

Holmes, D.S. (1984). Meditation and somatic arousal reduction: A review of
the experimental evidence. *American Psychologist, 39,* 1–12.

Holmes, T.H., & Rahe, R.H. (1967). The social readjustment rating scale.
Journal of Psychosomatic Research, 11, 213.

Holyoak, K.J., & Spellman, B.A. (1993). Thinking. *Annual Review of Psychology, 44,* 265–315.

Holzman, D. (1986, September 15). An obsessive trouble in mind. *Insight,*
p. 62.

Hopkins, B., & Westra, T. (1989). Maternal expectations of their infants' development: Some cultural differences. *Developmental Medicine and Child
Neurology, 31*(3), 384–390.

Hopkins, B., & Westra, T. (1990). Motor development, maternal expectation, and the role of handling. *Infants Behavior and Development, 13,*
117–122.

Hoptman, M.J., & Davidson, R.J. (1994). How and why do the two cerebral
hemispheres interact? *Psychological Bulletin, 116,* 195–219.

Horn, J. (1983). The Texas Adoption Project: Adopted children and their
intellectual resemblance to biological and adoptive parents. *Child Development, 54,* 268–275.

Horney, K. (1937). *The neurotic personality of our time.* New York: Norton.

Horowitz, F.D., & O'Brien, M. (1986). Gifted and talented children: State of
knowledge and directions for research. *American Psychologist, 41,*
1147–1152.

Horowitz, F.D., & O'Brien, M. (Eds.). (1985). *The gifted and talented: Developmental perspectives.* Washington, DC: American Psychological Association.

Horvath, F.S. (1977). The effect of selected variables on interpretation of
polygraph records. *Journal of Applied Psychology, 62,* 127–136.

House, J.S., Landis, K.R., & Umberson, D. (1988). Social relationships and
health. *Science, 241,* 540–545.

Hovland, C.I., & Sears, R.R. (1940). Minor studies in aggression: VI. Correlation of lynchings with economic indices. *Journal of Abnormal and Social
Psychology, 9,* 301–310.

Howard, K.I., Kopta, S.M., Krause, M.S., & Orlinsky, D.E. (1986). The
does-effect relationship in psychotherapy. *American Psychologist, 41,*
159–164.

Howe, M.L., & Courage, M. (1993). On resolving the enigma of infantile
amnesia. *Psychological Bulletin, 113,* 305–326.

Howlett, A.C., Evans, D.M., & Houston, D.B. (1992). The cannabinoid receptor. In L. Murphy & A. Bartke (Eds.), *Marijuana/cannabinoids: Neurobiology and neurophysiology* (pp. 35–72). Boca Raton, FL: CRC Press.

Hoyt, S., & Scherer, D.G. (1998). Female juvenile delinquency: Misunder-
stood by the juvenile justice system, neglected by social science. *Law and
Human Behavior, 22*(1), 81–107.

Hsu, L.K. (1996). Epidemiology of the eating disorder. *Psychiatr Clin North
America, 19*(4), 681–700.

Hubel, D.H., & Livingstone, M.S. (1987). Segregation of form, color, and
stereopsis in primate area 18. *Journal of Neuroscience,* pp. 3378–3415.

Hubel, D.H., & Livingstone, M.S. (1990). Color and contrast sensitivity in
the lateral geniculate body and primary visual cortex of the macaque
monkey. *Journal of Neuroscience, 10,* 2223–2237.

Hubel, D.H., & Wiesel, T.N. (1959). Receptive fields of single neurons in
the cat's striate cortex. *Journal of Physiology (London), 148,* 574–591.

Hubel, D.H., & Wiesel, T.N. (1979). Brain mechanisms of vision. *Scientific
American, 241,* 150–162.

Hudspeth, A.J. (1983). The hair cells of the inner ear. *Scientific American,
248,* 54–64.

Huebner, A.M., Garrod, A., & Snarey, J. (1990). *Moral development in Ti-
betan Buddhist monks: A cross-cultural study of adolescents and young adults
in Nepal.* Paper presented at the meeting of the Society for Research in
Adolescence, Atlanta, GA.

Hummel, J.E., & Biederman, I. (1992). Dynamic binding in a neural network for shape recognition. *Psychological Review, 99,* 480–517.

Humphreys, L.G. (1992). Commentary: What both critics and users of ability tests need to know. *Psychological Science, 3,* 271–274.

Hunt, E., Streissguth, A.P., Kerr, B., & Olson, H.C. (1995). Mothers' alcohol consumption during pregnancy: Effects on spatial-visual reasoning in
14-year-old children. *Psychological Science, 6*(6), 339–342.

Hunt, M. (1974). *Sexual behavior in the 1970s.* Chicago: Playboy Press.

Huston, A.C., Watkins, B.A., & Kunkel, D. (1989). Public policy and children's television. *American Psychologist, 44,* 424–433.

Huttenlocher, J., Smiley, P., & Charney, R. (1983). Emergence of action categories in the child: Evidence from verb meanings. *Psychological Review,
90,* 72–93.

Hyde, J.S. (1982). *Understanding human sexuality* (2nd ed.). New York:
McGraw-Hill.

Hyde, J.S., & Linn, M.C. (1988). Gender differences in verbal ability: A meta-analysis. *Psychological Bulletin, 104,* 53–69.

Hyde, J.S., Fennema, E., & Lamon, S.J. (1990). Gender differences in mathematics performance: A meta-analysis. *Psychological Bulletin, 107,* 139–155.

Hyman, I.E., Jr., & Pentland, J. (1996). The role of mental imagery in the creation of false childhood memories. *Journal of Memory and Language, 35,* 101–117.

Iacobucci, D., & McGill, A.L. (1990). Analysis of attribution data: Theory testing and effects estimation. *Journal of Personality and Social Psychology, 59*(3), 426–441.

Inhelder, B., & Piaget, J. (1958). *The growth of logical thinking from childhood to adolescence* (A. Parson & S. Milgram, Trans.). New York: Basic Books.

Insel, T.R., & Harbaugh, C.R. (1989). Lesions of the hypothalamic paraventricular nucleus disrupt the initiation of maternal behavior. *Physiology & Behavior, 45,* 1033–1041.

Irwin, R.J., & Whitehead, P.R. (1991). Towards an objective psychophysics of pain. *Psychological Science, 2,* 230–235.

Isaksen, S.G., Murdock, M., Firestien, R.L., & Treffinger, D.J. (Eds.). (1993). *Understanding and recognizing creativity: The emergence of a discipline.* Norwood, NJ: Ablex.

Isen, A.M., & Levin, P.F. (1972). The effect of feeling good on helping: Cookies and kindness. *Journal of Personality and Social Psychology, 21,* 384–388.

Isham, W.P., & Kamin, L.J. (1993). Blackness, deafness, IQ, and g. *Intelligence, 17,* 37–46.

Ito, T.A., Miller, N., & Pollock, V. (1996). Alcohol and aggression: A meta-analysis on the moderating effects of inhibitory cues, triggering events, and self-focused attention. *Psychological Bulletin, 120,* 60–82.

Izard, C.E. (1971). *The face of emotion.* New York: Appleton-Century-Crofts.

Izard, C.E. (1980). Cross-cultural perspectives on emotion and emotion communication. In H.C. Triandis & W.J. Lonner (Eds.), *Handbook of cross-cultural psychology* (Vol. 3). Boston: Allyn & Bacon.

Izard, C.E. (1982). The psychology of emotion comes of age on the coattails of Darwin. *Contemporary Psychology, 27,* 426–429.

Izard, C.E. (1994). Innate and universal facial expressions: Evidence from developmental and cross-cultural research. *Psychological Bulletin, 115*(2), 288–299.

Jacobs, G.H. (1993). The distribution and nature of color vision among the mammals. *Biological Review of the Cambridge Philosophical Society, 68,* 413–471.

Jacobs, R.L., & McClelland, D.C. (1994). Moving up the corporate ladder: A longitudinal study of the leadership motive pattern and managerial success in women and men. *Cons. Psychol. J. Pract. Res. 46,* 32–41.

Jacobsen, P.B., Bovbjerg, D.H., Schwartz, M.D., & Andrykowski, M.A. (1994). Formation of food aversions in patients receiving repeated infusions of chemotherapy. *Behaviour Research & Therapy, 38,* 739–748.

Jacobson, N.S., & Christensen, A. (1996). Studying the effectiveness of psychotherapy: How well can clinical trials do the job? *American Psychologist, 51*(10), 1031–1039.

Jamal, M. (1981). Shift work related to job attitudes social participation and withdraw behavior: A study of nurses and industrial workers. *Personnel Psychology, 34,* 535–547.

James, W. (1890). *The principles of psychology.* New York: Holt.

Jamison, K.R. (1989). Mood disorders and patterns of creativity in British writers and artists. *Psychiatry, 52,* 125–134.

Janis, I. (1982). *Groupthink: Psychological studies of policy decisions and fiascoes* (2nd ed.). Boston: Houghton Mifflin.

Janis, I.L., Mahl, G.G., & Holt, R.R. (1969). *Personality: Dynamics, development and assessment.* New York: Harcourt Brace Jovanovich.

Janofsky, M. (1994, December 13). Survey reports more drug use by teenagers. *New York Times,* p. A1.

Jaynes, J.H., & Wlodkowski, R.J. (1990). *Eager to learn: Helping children become motivated and love learning.* San Francisco: Jossey-Bass.

Jensen, A.R. (1969). How much can we boost IQ and scholastic achievement? *Harvard Educational Review, 39,* 1–123

Jensen, A.R. (1992). Commentary: Vehicles of g. *Psychological Science, 3,* 275–278.

Jirikowski, G.F., Caldwell, J.D., Pilgrim, C., Stumpf, W.E., & Pedersen, C.A. (1989). Changes in immunostaining for oxytocin in the forebrain of the female rate during late pregnancy, parturition and early lactation. *Cell Tissue Research, 256,* 411–417.

Jobsen, T., Edelstein, W., & Hofmann, V. (1994). A longitudinal study of the relation between representations of attachment in childhood and cognitive functioning in childhood and adolescence. *Developmental Psychology, 30,* 112–124.

Johansson, G. (1975). Visual motion perception. *Scientific American, 232,* 76–88.

Johansson, G., von Hofsten, C., & Jansson, G. (1980). Event perception. *Annual Review of Psychology, 31,* 27–64.

Johnson, C., Lewis, C., Love, S., & Stuckey, M. (1984). Incidence and correlates of bulimic behavior in a female high school population. *Journal of Youth and Adolescence, 13,* 15–26.

Johnson, D. (1990). Can psychology ever be the same again after the human genome is mapped? *Psychological Science, 1,* 331–332.

Johnson, D.W., Johnson, R.T., & Maruyama, G. (1984). Effects of cooperative learning: A meta-analysis. In N. Miller & M.B. Brewer (Eds.), *Groups in contact: The psychology of desegregation* (pp. 187–212). New York: Academic Press.

Johnson, H.G., Ekman, P., & Friesen, W.V. (1975). Communicative body movements: American emblems. *Semiotica, 15,* 335–353.

Johnson, J.L. (1994). The Thematic Apperception Test and Alzheimer's disease. *Journal of Personality Assessment, 62,* 314–319.

Johnson, M.K., & Raye, C.L. (1981). Reality monitoring. *Psychological Review, 88,* 67–85.

Johnson-Greene, D., Adams, K.M., Gilman, S., Kluin, K.J., Junck, L., Martorello, S., & Heumann, M. (1997). Impaired upper limb coordination in alcoholic cerebellar degeneration. *Archives of Neurology, 54,* 436–439.

Jones, C.P., & Adamson, L.B. (1987). Language use and mother-child-sibling interactions. *Child Development, 58,* 356–366.

Jones, F.D., & Koshes, R.J. (1995). Homosexuality and the military. *American Journal of Psychiatry, 152,* 16–21.

Jones, M.C. (1924). Elimination of children's fears. *Journal of Experimental Psychology, 7,* 381–390.

Julius, M., Harburg, E., Cottington, E.M., & Johnson, E.H. (1986). Anger-coping types, blood pressure, and all-cause mortality: A follow-up in Tecumseh, Michigan (1971–1983). *American Journal of Epidemiology, 124,* 220–233.

Junginger, J. (1997). Fetishism. In D.R. Laws & W.T. O'Donohue (Eds.), *Handbook of sexual deviance: Theory and application.* New York: Guilford.

Kagan, J. (1989). Temperamental contributions to social behavior. *American Psychologist, 44*(4), 668–674.

Kagan, J. (1994, October 5). The realistic view of biology and behavior. *Chronicle of Higher Education.*

Kagan, J., & Snidman, N. (1991). Infant predictors of inhibited and uninhibited profiles. *Psychological Science, 2*(1), 40–44.

Kagan, J., Arcus, D., & Snidman, N. (1993). The idea of temperament: Where do we go from here? In R. Plomin & G.E. McClearn (Eds.), *Nature, nurture, and psychology.* Washington, DC: American Psychological Association.

Kagan, J., Reznick, J.S., Snidman, N., Gibbons, J., & Johnson, M.O. (1988). Childhood derivatives of inhibition and lack of inhibition to the unfamiliar. *Child Development, 59,* 1580–1589.

Kagan, J., Snidman, N., & Arcus, D.M. (1992). Initial reactions to unfamiliarity. *Current Directions, 1*(6), 171–174.

Kahneman, D., & Tversky, A. (1996). On the reality of cognitive illusions. *Psychological Review, 103*(3), 582–591.

Kalat, J.W. (1988). *Biological psychology* (3rd ed.). Belmont, CA: Wadsworth.

Kalderon, N., & Fuks, Z. (1996). Structural recovery in lesioned adult mammalian spinal cord by x-irradiation of the lesion site. *Proceedings of the National Academy of Sciences of the U.S.A., 93,* 11179.

Kales, J.D., Kales, A., Soldatos, C.R., Caldwell, A.B., Charney, D.S., & Martin, E.D. (1980). Night terrors: Clinical characteristics and personality patterns. *Archives of General Psychiatry, 137*, 1413–1417.

Kamin, L.J. (1969). Selective association and conditioning. In N.J. Mackintosh & W.K. Honig (Eds.), *Fundamental issues in associative learning*. Halifax: Dalhousie University Press.

Kane, J., & Lieberman, J. (1992). *Adverse effects of psychotropic drugs*. New York: Guilford Press.

Kantrowitz, B., Rosenberg, D., Rogers, P., Beachy, L., & Holmes, S. (1993, November 1). Heroin makes an ominous comeback. *Newsweek.*

Kaplan, C.A., & Simon, H.A. (1990). In search of insight. *Cognitive Psychology, 22*, 374–419.

Kaplan, W.S., & Novorr, M.J. (1994). Age and season of birth in sudden infant death syndrome in North Carolina, 1982–1987: No interaction. *American Journal of Epidemiology, 140*, 56–58.

Karau, S.J., & Williams, K.D. (1993). Social loafing: A meta-analytic review and theoretical integration. *Journal of Personality and Social psychology, 65*(4), 681–706.

Karon, B.P., & Widener, A.J. (1994). Is there really a schizophrenogenic parent? *Psychoanalytic Psychology, 11*, 47–61.

Kashima, Y., & Triandis, H.C. (1986). The self-serving bias in attributions as a coping strategy: A cross-cultural study. *Journal of Cross-Cultural Psychology, 17*, 83–98.

Kassebaum, N.L. (1994). Head Start: Only the best for America's children. *American Psychologist, 49*, 123–126.

Katz, R., & McGuffin, P. (1993). The genetics of affective disorders. In D. Fowles (Ed.), *Progress in experimental personality and psychopathology research*. New York: Springer.

Katzman, R., & Terry, R.D. (1983). *The neurology of aging*. Philadelphia: F.A. Davis.

Kaufman, L. (1979). *Perception: The world transformed*. New York: Oxford University Press.

Kavanaugh, D.J. (1992). Recent developments in expressed emotion and schizophrenia. *British Journal of Psychiatry, 160*, 601–620.

Keck, J.O., Staniunas, R.J., Coller, J.A., Barrett, R.C., & Oster, M.E. (1994). Biofeedback training is useful in fecal incontinence but disappointing in constipation. *Disorders of the Colon and Rectum, 37*, 1271–1276.

Kehl, L., Fairbanks, C., Laughlin T., & Wilcox, G. (1997). Neurogenesis in postnatal rat spinal cord: A study in primary culture. *Science, 276*, 586–589.

Kelley, H.H. (1967). Attribution theory in social psychology. In D. Levine (Ed.), *Nebraska Symposium on Motivation*. Lincoln: University of Nebraska Press.

Kellogg, W.N. (1968). Communication and language in the home-raised chimpanzee. *Science, 162*, 423–427.

Kelly, I.W., & Saklofske, D.H. (1994). Psychology pseudoscience. *Encyclopedia of human behavior, 3*, 611–618.

Kelly, J.B. (1982). Divorce: The adult perspective. In B.B. Wolman (Ed.), *Handbook of developmental psychology* (pp. 734–750). Englewood Cliffs, NJ: Prentice Hall.

Kelly, K., & Dawson, L. (1994). Sexual orientation. *Encyclopedia of human behavior, 4*, 183–192.

Kelman, H.C. (1974). Attitudes are alive and well and gainfully employed in the sphere of action. *American Psychologist, 230*, 310–324.

Kendler, K.S., Neale, M.C., Kessler, R.C., Heath, A.C., & Eaves, L.J. (1992). Generalized anxiety disorder in women: A population-based twin study. *Archives of General Psychiatry, 49*, 267–272.

Kernis, M.H., & Wheeler, L. (1981). Beautiful friends and ugly strangers: Radiation and contrast effects in perception of same-sex pairs. *Personality and Social Psychology Bulletin, 7*, 617–620.

Kessler, R.C. (1979). Stress, social status, and psychological distress. *Journal of Health and Social Behavior, 20*, 259–272.

Kessler, R.C., McGonagle, K.A., Zhao, S., Nelson, C.R., Highes, M., Eshleman, S., Wittchen, H., & Kendler, K.S. (1994). Lifetime and 12-month prevalence of DSM-III-R psychiatric disorders in the United States: Results from the National Comorbidity Survey. *Archives of General Psychiatry, 51*, 8–19.

Kessler, R.C., Price, R.H., & Wortman, C.B. (1985). Social factors in psychopathology: Stress, social support, and coping processes. *Annual Review of Psychology, 36*, 531–572.

Kessler, R.C., Sonnega, A., Bromet, E., Hughes, M., & Nelson, C.B. (1995). Post-traumatic stress disorder in the national Comorbidity Survey. *Archives of General Psychiatry, 52*, 1057.

Kety, S.S. (1979). Disorders of the human brain. *Scientific American, 241*, 202–214.

Khan, A. (1993). Electroconvulsive therapy: Second edition. *Journal of Nervous and Mental Disease, 181*(9), n.p.

Khantzian, E.J. (1990). Self-regulation and self-medication factors in alcoholism and the addictions: Similarities and differences. *Recent Developments in Alcoholism, 8*, 255–271.

Kiecolt-Glaser, J.K., Malarkey, W.B., Chee, M., Newton, T., & Cacioppo, J.T. (1993). Negative behavior during marital conflict is associated with immunological down-regulation. *Psychosomatic Medicine, 55*, 395–409.

Kiesler, C.A. (1982). Mental hospitals and alternative care: Noninstitutionalization as a potential public policy for mental patients. *American Psychologist, 37*, 349–360.

Kiesler, C.A. (1982). Public and professional myths about mental hospitalization: An empirical reassessment of policy-related beliefs. *American Psychologist, 37*(12), 1323–1339.

Kiesler, C.A., & Simpkins, C.G. (1993). *The unnoticed majority in psychiatric inpatient care*. New York: Plenum.

Kihlström, J.F., & Harackiewicz, J.M. (1982). The earliest recollection: A new survey. *Journal of Personality, 50*, 134–148.

Kihlström, J.F., & McConkey, K.M. (1990). William James and hypnosis: A centennial reflection. *Psychological Science, 1*, 174–178.

Kim, D.O. (1985). Functional roles of the inner and outer-haircell subsystems in the cochlea and brain stem. In C.J. Berlin (Ed.), *Hearing science: Recent advances*. San Diego, CA: College Hill.

Kim, K.H.S., Relkin, N.R., Lee, K., & Hirsch, J. (1997). Distinct cortical areas associated with native and second languages. *Nature, 388*(6638), 171–174.

Kimmel, D.C. (1974). *Adulthood and aging*. New York: Wiley.

Kimura, D. (1985, November). Male brain, female brain: The hidden difference. *Psychology Today*, pp. 50–58.

Kimura, D., & Hampson, E. (1994). Cognitive pattern in men and women is influenced by fluctuations in sex hormones. *Current Directions in Psychological Science*, 57–61.

King, M., & McDonald, E. (1992). Homosexuals who are twins. *British Journal of Psychiatry, 160*, 407–409.

Kingstone, A., Enns, J.T., Mangun, G.R., & Gazzaniga, M.S. (1995). Right-hemisphere memory superiority: Studies of a split-brain patient. *Psychological Science, 6*, 118–121.

Kinsey, A.C., Pomeroy, W.B., & Martin, C.E. (1948). *Sexual behavior in the human male*. Philadelphia: Saunders.

Kinsey, A.C., Pomeroy, W.B., Martin, C.E., & Gebhard, P.H. (1953). *Sexual behavior in the human female*. Philadelphia: Saunders.

Kirchner, W.H., & Towne, W.F. (1994). The sensory basis of the honeybee's dance language. *Scientific American, 270*, 74–80.

Kirsch, I., Montgomery, G., & Saperstein, G. (1995). Hypnosis as an adjunct to cognitive behavioral psychotherapy: A meta analysis. *Journal of Consulting and Clinical Psychology, 63*, 214–220.

Kissane, D.W., Bloch, S., Miach, P., Smith, G.C., Seddon, A., & Keks, N. (1997). Cognitive-existential group therapy for patients with primary breast cancer—techniques and themes. *Psychooncology, 6*(1), 25–33.

Klatzky, R.L. (1980). *Human memory: Structures and processes* (2nd ed.). San Francisco: Freeman.

Klein, G., Wolf, S., Militello, L., & Zsambok, C. (1995). Characteristics of skilled option generation in chess. *Organizational Behavior & Human Decision Processes, 62*(1), 63–69.

Klein, G.S. (1951). The personal world through perception. In R.R. Blake & G.V. Ramsey (Eds.), *Perception: An approach to personality*. New York: Ronald Press.

Kleinmuntz, D.N. (1991). Decision making for professional decision makers. *Psychological Science, 2*, 135, 138–141.

Klerman, G.L., Weissman, M.M., Markowitz, J.C., Glick, I., Wilner, P.J., Mason, B., & Shear, M.K. (1994). Medication and psychotherapy. In A.E. Bergin & S.L. Garfield (Eds.), *Handbook of psychotherapy and behavior change* (4th ed., pp. 734–782). New York: Wiley.

Klingenspor, B. (1994). Gender identity and bulimic eating behavior. *Sex Roles, 31*, 407–432.

Klinger, E. (1990). *Daydreaming: Using waking fantasy and imagery for self-knowledge and creativity*. New York: J.P. Tarcher.

Kluckholn, C. (1954). Culture and behavior. In G. Lindzey (Ed.), *Handbook of social psychology* (Vol. 2, pp. 921–976). Cambridge, MA: Addison-Wesley.

Kluegel, J.R. (1990). Trends in white's explanations of the black-white gap in socioeconomic status, 1977–1989. *American Sociological Review, 55*, 512–525.

Knight, G.P., Fabes, R.A., & Higgins, D.A. (1996). Concerns about drawing causal inferences from meta-analyses: An example in the study of gender differences in aggression. *Psychological Bulletin, 119*(3), 410–421.

Knutson, J.R. (1995). Psychological characteristics of maltreated children: Putative risk factors and consequences. *Annual Review of Psychology, 46*, 401–431.

Kobasa, S.C. (1979). Stressful life events, personality, and health: An inquiry into hardiness. *Journal of Personality and Social Psychology, 37*, 1–11.

Koenig, H.G. (1997). *Is religion good for your health? The effects of religion on physical and mental health*. Binghamton, NY: Haworth Press.

Koenig, H.G., Cohen, H.J., George, L.K., Hays, J.C., Larson, D.B., & Blazer, D.G. (1997). Attendance at religious services, interleukin-6 and other biological parameters of immune function in older adults. *International Journal of Psychiatry in Medicine, 27*(3), 242–256.

Kogon, M.M., Biswas, A., Pearl, D., Carlson, R.W., & Spiegel, D. (1997). The effects of medical and psychotherapeutic treatment on the survival of women with metastatic breast carcinoma. *Cancer, 80*(2), 225–230.

Kohlberg, L. (1969). Stage and sequence: The cognitive–developmental approach to socialization. In D.A. Goslin (Ed.), *Handbook of socialization theory and research*. Chicago: Rand McNally.

Kohlberg, L. (1979). *The meaning and measurement of moral development* (Clark Lectures). Worcester, MA: Clark University.

Kohlberg, L. (1981). *The philosophy of moral development* (Vol. 1). San Francisco: Harper & Row.

Kohn, A. (1993). *Punished by rewards*. Boston: Houghton Mifflin.

Kokmen, E. (1991). The EURODEM collaborative re-analysis of case-control studies of Alzheimer's disease: Implications for clinical research and practice. *International Journal of Epidemiology, 20*(Suppl. 2), S65–S67.

Kolata, G. (1992, November 16). New views on life spans alter forecast on elderly. *New York Times*, p. A1.

Kolata, G. (1996, April 3). Can it be? Weather has no effect on arthritis. *New York Times*, p. B9.

Kolata, G. (1996, February 27). New era of robust elderly belies the fears of scientists. *New York Times*.

Kolbert, E. (1991, October 11). Sexual harassment at work is pervasive, survey suggests. *New York Times*, Sec. A.

Komatsu, L.K. (1992). Recent views of conceptual structure. *Psychological Bulletin, 112*, 500–526.

Kopta, S.M., Howard, K.I., Lowry, J.L., & Beutler, L.E. (1994). Patterns of symptomatic recovery in psychotherapy. *Journal of Consulting and Clinical Psychology, 62*, 1009–1016.

Koss, M.P. (1990). Violence against women. *American Psychologist, 45*, 374–380.

Kosslyn, S.M. (1980). *Image and mind*. Cambridge, MA: Harvard University Press.

Kosslyn, S.M. (1987). Seeing and imaging in the cerebral hemispheres: A computational approach. *Psychological Review, 94*, 148–175.

Kosslyn, S.M. (1994). *Image and brain*. Cambridge, MA: MIT Press.

Kosslyn, S.M., & Koenig, O. (1992). *The wet mind*. New York: Free Press.

Kosslyn, S.M., & Sussman, A.L. (1995). Roles of imagery in perception: Or, there is no such thing as immaculate perception. In Michael S. Gazzaniga (Ed.), *The cognitive neurosciences*. Cambridge, MA: MIT Press.

Koulack, D., & Goodenough, D.R. (1976). Dream recall and dream recall failure: An arousal-retrieval model. *Psychological Bulletin, 83*, 975–984.

Krantz, D. S., Grunberg, N.D., & Baum, A. (1985). Health psychology. *Annual Review of Psychology, 36*, 349–383.

Krasne, F.B., & Glanzman, D.L. (1995). What we can learn from invertebrate learning. *Annual Review of Psychology, 46*, 585–624.

Kraus, S.J. (1995). Attitudes and the prediction of behavior: A meta-analysis of the empirical literature. *Personality and Social Psychology Bulletin, 21*(1), 58–75.

Krebs, D. (1975). Empathy and altruism. *Journal of Personality and Social Psychology, 32*, 1134–1140.

Kringlen, E. (1981). *Stress and coronary heart disease. Twin research 3: Epidemiological and clinical studies*. New York: Alan R. Liss.

Kristiansen, C.M., & Giulietti, R. (1990). Perceptions of wife abuse: Effects of gender, attitudes towards women, and just-world beliefs among college students. *Psychology of Women Quarterly, 14*, 177–189.

Kroger, R.O., & Wood, L.A. (1993). Reification, "faking" and the Big Five. *American Psychologist, 48*, 1297–1298.

Kruglanski, A.W. (1986, August). Freeze-think and the Challenger. *Psychology Today*, pp. 48–49.

Kübler-Ross, E. (1969). *On death and dying*. New York: Macmillan.

Kübler-Ross, E. (1975). *Death: The final stage of growth*. Englewood Cliffs, NJ: Prentice Hall.

Kuhl, P.K., Williams, K.A., & Lacerda, F. (1992). Linguistic experience alters phonetic perception in infants by 6 months of age. *Science, 255*, 606–608.

Kulik, J., & Brown, R. (1979). Frustration, attribution of blame, and aggression. *Journal of Experimental Social Psychology, 15*, 183–194.

Kunst-Wilson, W.R., & Zajonc, R.B. (1980). Affective discrimination of stimuli that cannot be recognized. *Science, 207*(4430), 557–558.

Kupfermann, I. (1991). Hypothalamus and limbic system motivation. In E.R. Kandel, J.H. Schwartz, & T.M. Jessel (Eds.), *Principles of neural science* (3rd ed., pp. 750–760). New York: Elsevier.

Kurdek, L.A. (1991). Correlates of relationship satisfaction in cohabiting gay and lesbian couples: Integration of contextual, investment, and problem-solving models. *Journal of Personality & Social Psychology, 61*(6), 910–922.

Kurdek, L.A. (1992). Assumptions versus standards: The validity of two relationship cognitions in heterosexual and homosexual couples. *Journal of Family Psychology, 6*(2), 164–170.

Laan, E., Everaerd, W., van Berlo, R., & Rijs, L. (1995). Mood and sexual arousal in women. *Behavior Research Therapy, 33*(4), 441–443.

Labouvie-Vief, G. (1986). Modes of knowledge and the organization of development. In M.L. Commons, L. Kohlberg, F.A. Richards, & J. Sinott (Eds.), *Beyond formal operations: 3. Models and methods in the study of adult and adolescent thoughts*. New York: Praeger.

Lachman, S.J. (1984). *Processes in visual misperception: Illusions for highly structured stimulus material*. Paper presented at the 92nd annual convention of the American Psychological Association, Toronto, Canada.

Lachman, S.J. (1996). Processes in perception: Psychological transformations of highly structured stimulus material. *Perceptual and Motor Skills, 83*, 411–418.

LaGreca, A.M., Stone, W.L., & Bell, C.R., III. (1983). Facilitating the vocational-interpersonal skills of mentally retarded individuals. *American Journal of Mental Deficiency, 88*, 270–278.

Lakoff, G. (1987). *Women, fire and dangerous things*. Chicago: University of Chicago Press.

Lambert, M.J., Shapiro, D.A., & Bergin, A.E. (1986). The effectiveness of psychotherapy. In S.L. Garfield & A.E. Bergin (Eds.), *Handbook of psychotherapy and behavior change* (3rd ed., pp. 157–212). New York: Wiley.

Lambert, N., Nihira, K., & Leland, H. (1993). *AAMR Adaptive Behavior Scale–School: Technical manual* (2nd ed.). Austin, TX: PRO-ED.

Lambert, W.E., Genesee, F., Holobow, N., & Chartrand, L. (1993). Bilingual education for majority English-speaking children. *European Journal of Psychology of Education, 8,* 3–22.

Lambert, W.W., Solomon, R.L., & Watson, P.D. (1949). Reinforcement and extinction as factors in size estimation. *Journal of Experimental Psychology, 39,* 637–641.

Lampl, M., Veidhuis, J.D., & Johnson, M.L. (1992). Saltation and stasis: A model of human growth. *Science, 258,* 801–803.

Lande, R. (1993). The video violence debate. *Hospital and Community Psychiatry, 44,* 347–351.

Landesman, S., & Butterfield, E.C. (1987). Normalization and deinstitution of mentally retarded individuals: Controversy and facts. *American Psychologist, 42,* 809–816.

Landy, M.S. (1987). Parallel model of the kinetic depth effect using local computations. *Journal of the Optical Society of America, 4*(5), 864–877.

Langer, E.J., Bashner, R.S., & Chanowitz, B. (1985). Decreasing prejudice by increasing discrimination. *Journal of Personality and Social Psychology, 49,* 113–120.

Langlois, J.H., Ritter, J.M., Casey, R.J., & Sawin, D.B. (1995). Infant attractiveness predicts maternal behaviors and attitudes. *Developmental Psychology, 31,* 464–472.

LaPiere, R.T. (1934). Attitudes versus actions. *Social Forces, 13,* 230–237.

LaRue, A., & Jarvik, L. (1982). Old age and biobehavioral changes. In B.B. Wolman (Ed.), *Handbook of developmental psychology* (pp. 791–806). Englewood Cliffs, NJ: Prentice Hall.

LAS. (no date). Piaget challenged: Babies see world as we do.

Lashley, K.S. (1950). In search of the engram. *Symposia of the Society for Experimental Biology, 4,* 454–482.

Latané, B., & Rodin, J. (1969). A lady in distress: Inhibiting effects of friends and strangers on bystander intervention. *Journal of Experimental Social Psychology, 5,* 189–202.

Laub, J.H., & Lauritsen, J.L. (1993). Violent criminal behavior over the life course: A review of the longitudinal and comparative research. *Violence and Victims, 8,* 235–252.

Laumann, E.O., Gagnon, J.H., Michael, R.T., & Michaels, S. (1994). *The social organization of sexuality: Sexual practices in the United States.* Chicago: University of Chicago Press.

Lazarus, R.S. (1969). *Patterns of adjustment and human effectiveness.* New York: McGraw-Hill.

Lazarus, R.S. (1981, July). Little hassles can be hazardous to health. *Psychology Today,* pp. 58–62.

Lazarus, R.S. (1982). Thoughts on the relations between emotion and cognition. *American Psychologist, 37,* 1019–1024.

Lazarus, R.S. (1991a). Cognition and motivation in emotion. *American Psychologist, 46,* 352–367.

Lazarus, R.S. (1991b). Progress on a cognitive-motivational-relational theory of emotion. *American Psychologist, 46,* 819–834.

Lazarus, R.S. (1991c). *Emotion and adaptation.* New York: Oxford University Press.

Lazarus, R.S., De Longis, A., Folkman, S., & Gruen, R. (1985). Stress and adaptional outcomes. *American Psychologist, 40,* 770–779.

Leary, W.E. (1990, January 25). Risk of hearing loss is growing, panel says. *New York Times,* Sec. B.

Leary, W.E. (1995, April 21). Young who try suicide may succeed more often. *New York Times.*

Lebow, J.L., & Gurman, A.S. (1995). Research assessing couple and family therapy. *Annual Review of Psychology, 46,* 27–57.

Leccese, A.P. (1991). *Drugs and society.* Englewood Cliffs, NJ: Prentice Hall.

Lee, G.P., Loring, D.W., Dahl, J.I., & Meador, K.J. (1993). Hemispheric specialization for emotional expression. *Neuropsychiatry, Neuropsychology, & Behavioral Neurology, 6*(3), 143–148.

Lefcourt, H.M. (1992). Durability and impact of the locus of control construct. *Psychological Bulletin, 112,* 411–414.

Lehman, D.R., Lempert, R.O., Nisbett, R.E. (1988). The effects of graduate training on reasoning: Formal discipline and thinking about everyday-life events. *American Psychologist, 43,* 431–442.

Leibowitz, H.W., & Owens, D.A. (1977). Nighttime driving accidents and selective visual degradation. *Science, 197,* 422–423.

Leigh, R.J. (1994). Human vestibular cortex. *Annals of Neurology, 35,* 383–384.

Leitenberg, H., & Henning, K. (1995). Sexual fantasy. *Psychological Bulletin, 117*(3), 469–496.

Lemish, D., & Rice, M.L. (1986, June). Television as a talking picture book: A prop for language acquisition. *Journal of Child Language, 13,* 251–274.

Lenhardt, M.L., Skellett, R., Wang, P., & Clarke, A.M. (1991, July 5). Human ultrasonic speech perception. *Science,* 82–85.

Leonard, J.M., & Whitten, W.B. (1983). Information stored when expecting recall or recognition. *Journal of Experimental Psychology: Learning, Memory, and Cognition, 9,* 440–455.

Lerner, M.J. (1980). *The belief in a just world: A fundamental delusion.* New York: Plenum.

Leroy, P., Dessolin, S., Villageois, P., Moon, B.C., Friedman, J.M., Ailhaud, G., & Dani, C. (1996). Expression of ob gene in adipose cells. Regulation by insulin. *Journal of Biological Chemistry, 271*(5), 2365–2368.

Leshner, A.I. (1996). Understanding drug addiction: Implications for treatment. *Hospital Practice, 31,* 7–54.

Lev, M. (1991, May). No hidden meaning here: Survey sees subliminal ads. *New York Times,* Sec. C.

LeVay, S. (1991). A difference in hypothalamic structure between heterosexual and homosexual men. *Science, 253,* 1034–1038.

LeVay, S. (1993). *The sexual brain.* Cambridge, MA: MIT Press.

LeVay, S., & Hamer, D.H. (1994, May). Evidence for a biological influence in male homosexuality. *Scientific American,* pp. 44–49.

Levenson, M.R., & Aldwin, C.M. (1994). Aging, personality, and adaptation. In *Encyclopedia of human behavior* (Vol. 1, pp. 47–55).

Levenson, R.W. (1992). Autonomic nervous system differences among emotions. *Psychological Science, 3,* 23–27.

Leventhal, H., & Niles, P. (1965). Persistence of influence for varying duration of exposure to threat stimuli. *Psychological Reports, 16,* 223–233.

Levine, I.S., & Rog, D.J. (1990). Mental health services for homeless mentally ill person: Federal initiatives and current service trends. *American Psychologist, 45,* 963–968.

Levine, S., Johnson, D.F., & Gonzales, C.A. (1985). Behavioral and hormonal responses to separation in infant rhesus monkeys and mothers. *Behavioral Neuroscience, 99,* 399–410.

Levinson, D.J. (1978). *The seasons of a man's life.* New York: Knopf.

Levinson, D.J. (1986). A conception of adult development. *American Psychologist, 41,* 3–13.

Levinson, D.J. (1987). *The seasons of a woman's life.* New York: Knopf.

Levinson, D.J. (1996). *The seasons of a woman's life.* New York: Ballentine Books.

Levinthal, C.F. (1990). *Introduction to physiological psychology.* Englewood Cliffs, NJ: Prentice Hall.

Lewin, K.A. (1935). *A dynamic theory of personality* (K.E. Zener & D.K. Adams, Trans.). New York: McGraw-Hill.

Lewin, T. (1994a, May 18). Boys are more comfortable with sex than girls are, survey finds. *New York Times,* p. A10.

Lewin, T. (1994b, October 7). Sex in America: Faithfulness thrives after all. *New York Times,* p. A1.

Lewin, T. (1995, May 30). The decay of families is global study says. *New York Times,* p. A5.

Lewin, T. (1996, March 27). Americans are firmly attached to traditional roles for sexes, poll finds. *New York Times,* p. 412.

Lewis, M., & Bendersky, M. (1995). *Mothers, babies, and cocaine: The role of toxins in development.* Hillsdale, NJ: Erlbaum.

Lewy, A.J. (1992). (Paper in issue of Chronobiology International in fall of 1992; mentioned by Jane Brody in *New York Times* on 11/3/92; p. B1.)

Liem, R., & Liem, J.V. (1978). Social class and mental illness reconsidered: The role of economic stress and social support. *Journal of Health and Social Behavior, 19*, 139–156.

Limber, J. (1977). Language in child and chimp. *American Psychologist, 32*, 280–295.

Lindsay, D.S. (1993). Eyewitness suggestibility. *Current Directions in Psychological Science, 2*, 86–89.

Lindsay, D.S., & Johnson, M.K. (1989). The eyewitness suggestibility effect and memory for source. *Memory & Cognition, 17*, 349–358.

Lindsay, P.H., & Norman, D.A. (1977). *Human information processing* (2nd ed.). New York: Academic Press.

Linn, R.L. (1982). Admissions testing on trial. *American Psychologist, 37*, 279–291.

Lipman, S. (1991). *Laughter in Hell: The use of humor during the Holocaust.* Northvale, NJ: J. Aronson.

Lipsey, M., & Wilson, D. (1993). The efficacy of psychological, educational, and behavioral treatment: Confirmation from meta-analysis. *American Psychologist, 48*, 1181–1209.

Lipsky, D.K., & Gartner, A. (1996). Inclusive education and school restructuring. In W. Stainback & S. Stainback (Eds.), *Controversial issues confronting special education: Divergent perspectives* (pp. 3–15). Baltimore: Brookes.

Livingstone, M.S., & Hubel, D.H. (1988a). Do the relative mapping densities of the magno- and parvocellular systems vary with eccentricity? *Journal of Neuroscience, 8*, 4334–4339.

Livingstone, M.S., & Hubel, D.H. (1988b). Segregation of form, color, movement, and depth: Anatomy, physiology, and perception. *Science, 340*, 740–749.

Llinás, R. (1996). *The mind-brain continuum.* Proceedings of a meeting held in Madrid, 1995. Cambridge, MA: MIT Press.

Loeb, L.A. (1985). Apurinic sites as mutagenic intermediates. *Cell, 40*(3), 483–484.

Loehlin, J.C. (1989). Partitioning environmental and genetic contributions to behavioral development. *American Psychologist, 44*, 1285–1292.

Loehlin, J.C., & Nichols, R.C. (1976). *Heredity, environment, and personality.* Austin: University of Texas Press.

Loehlin, J.C., Horn, J.M., & Willerman, L. (1997). Heredity, environment, and IQ in the Texas adoption study. In R.J. Sternberg & E. Grigorenko (Eds.), *Intelligence: Heredity and environment.* New York: Cambridge University Press.

Loehlin, J.C., Willerman, L., & Horn, J.M. (1988). Human behavior genetics. *Annual Review of Psychology, 39*, 101–133.

Loewenstein, G. (1994). The psychology of curiosity: A review and reinterpretation. *Psychological Bulletin, 116*, 75–98.

Loftus, E.F. (1983). Silence is not golden. *American Psychologist, 38*, 564–572.

Loftus, E.F. (1993a). The reality of repressed memories. *American Psychologist, 48*, 518–537.

Loftus, E.F. (1993b). Psychologists in the eyewitness world. *American Psychologist, 48*, 550–552.

Loftus, E.F. (1996). Memory distortion and false memory creation. *Bulletin of the American Academy of Psychiatry & The Law, 24*(3), 281–295.

Loftus, E.F. (1997). Repressed memory accusations: Devastated families and devastated patients. *Applied Cognitive Psychology, 11*(1), 25–30.

Loftus, E.F., & Hoffman, H.G. (1989). Misinformation and memory: The creation of new memories. *Journal of Experimental Psychology: General, 118*, 100–114.

Loftus, E.F., & Palmer, J.C. (1974). Reconstruction of automobile destruction: An example of the interaction between language and memory. *Journal of Verbal Learning and Verbal Behavior, 13*, 585–589.

Loftus, E.F., & Pickrell, J.E. (1995). The formation of false memories. *Psychiatric Annals, 25*, 720–725.

Loftus, E.F., Milo, E., & Paddock, J. (1995). The accidental executioner: Why psychotherapy must be informed by science. *Counseling Psychologist, 23*, 30–309.

Logan, C.G., & Grafton, S.T. (1995). Functional anatomy of human eyeblink conditioning determined with regional cerebral glucose metabolism and positron emission tomography. *Proceedings of the National Academy of Science, U.S.A., 92*, 7500–7504.

Logue, A.W., Ophir, I., & Strauss, K.E. (1981). The acquisition of taste aversions in humans. *Behavior Research and Therapy, 19*, 319–333.

Lois, C., & Alvarez-Buylla, A. (1993). Proliferating subventricular zone cells in the adult mammalian forebrain can differentiate into neurons and glia. *Proceedings of the National Academy of Sciences of the U.S.A., 90*, 2074–2077.

Lois, C., & Alvarez-Buylla, A. (1994). Long-distance neuronal migration in the adult mammalian brain. *Science, 264*, 1145–1148.

Lorenz, K. (1935). Der Kumpan inder Umwelt des Vogels. *Journal of Ornithology, 83*, 137–213, 289–413.

Lorenz, K. (1968). *On aggression.* New York: Harcourt.

Lott, A.J., & Lott, B.E. (1974). The role of reward in the formation of positive interpersonal attitudes. In T.L. Huston (Ed.), *Foundations of interpersonal attraction* (pp. 171–192). New York: Academic Press.

Lovibond, P.F., Siddle, D.A., & Bond, N.W. (1993). Resistance to extinction of fear-relevant stimuli: Preparedness or selective sensitization? *Journal of Experimental Psychology: General, 122*, 449–461.

Luchins, A. (1957). Primacy-recency in impression formation. In C. Hovland, W. Mandell, E. Campbell, T. Brock, A. Luchins, A. Cohen, W. McGuire, I. Janis, R. Feierbend, & N. Anderson (Eds.), *The order of presentation in persuasion.* New Haven, CT: Yale University Press.

Luria, A.R. (1968). *The mind of a mnemonist* (L. Solotaroff, Trans.). New York: Basic Books.

Lykken, D.T. (1975, March). Guilty knowledge test: The right way to use a lie detector. *Psychology Today*, pp. 56–60.

Lyness, S.A. (1993). Predictors of differences between Type A and B individuals in heart rate and blood pressure reactivity. *Psychological Bulletin, 114*, 266–295.

Lynn, R. (1997). Direct evidence for a genetic basis for black-white differences in IQ. *American Psychologist, 51*(1), 73–74.

Lynn, S.J., & Rhue, J.W. (1988). Fantasy proneness, hypnosis, developmental antecedents, and psychopathology. *American Psychologist, 43*, 35–44.

Lyons, M.J., True, W.R., Eisen, S.A., Goldberg, J., Meyer, J.M., Faraone, S.V., Eaves, L.J., & Tsuang, M.T. (1995). Differential heritability of adult and juvenile antisocial traits. *Archives of General Psychiatry, 52*, 906–915.

Lytton, H., & Romeny, D.M. (1991). Parents' differential socialization of boys and girls: A meta-analysis. *Psychological Bulletin, 109*(2), 267–296.

Maccoby, E.E. (1990). Gender and relationships: A developmental account. *American Psychologist, 45*, 513–520.

Maccoby, E.E., & Jacklin, C.N. (1974). *The psychology of sex differences.* Stanford, CA: Stanford University Press.

Macionis, J.J. (1993). *Sociology* (4th ed.). Englewood Cliffs, NJ: Prentice Hall.

Mackavey, W.R., Malley, J.E., & Stewart, A.J. (1991). Remembering autobiographically consequential experiences: Content analysis of psychologists' accounts of their lives. *Psychology and Aging, 6*, 50–59.

Mackworth, N. (1965). Originality. *American Psychologist, 20*, 51–66.

MacLean, P.D. (1970). The limbic brain in relation to the psychoses. In P. Black (Ed.), *Physiological correlates of emotion* (pp. 129–146). New York: Academic Press.

MacLeod, D.I.A. (1978). Visual sensitivity. *Annual Review of Psychology, 29*, 613–645.

Maddi, S.R. (1989). *Personality theories: A comparative approach* (5th ed.). Homewood, IL: Dorsey.

Madsen, P.L. (1993). Blood flow and oxygen uptake in the human brain during various states of sleep and wakefulness. *Acta Paediatrica Scandinavica, 148*(Suppl.), 3–27.

Powers, S.I, Hauser, S.T., & Kilner, L.A. (1989). Adolescent mental health. *American Psychologist, 44,* 200–208.

Prager, K.J. (1995). *The psychology of intimacy.* New York: Guilford Press.

Premack, D. (1971). Language in chimpanzees. *Science, 172,* 808–822.

Premack, D. (1976). *Intelligence in ape and man.* Hillsdale, NJ: Erlbaum.

Premack, D. (1983). Animal cognition. *Annual Review of Psychology, 34,* 351–362.

Premack, D. (1986). *Gavagai! Or the future history of the animal language controversy.* Cambridge, MA: MIT Press.

Prentice, A.M. (1991). Can maternal dietary supplements help in preventing infant malnutrition? *Acta Paediatrica Scandinavica, 374*(Suppl.), 67–77.

Prentky, R.A., Knight, R.A., & Rosenberg, R. (1988). Validation analyses on a taxonomic system for rapists: Disconfirmation and reconceptualization. *Annals of the New York Academy of Sciences, 528,* 21–40.

Preti, G., Cutler, W.B., Garcia, C.R., Huggins, G.R., & Lawley, J.J. (1986). Human auxiliary secretions influence women's menstrual cycles: The role of donor extract from females. *Hormones & Behavior, 20,* 474–482.

Prince, V., & Bentler, P.M. (1972). Survey of 504 cases of transvestism. *Psychological Reports, 31,* 903–917.

Prior, M., Smart, D., Sanson, A., & Obeklaid, F. (1993). Sex differences in psychological adjustment from infancy to 8 years. *Journal of the American Academy of Child and Adolescent Psychiatry, 32,* 291–304.

Pruneti, C.A., L'Abbate, A., & Steptoe, A. (1993). Personality and behavioral changes in patients after myocardial infarction. *Res. Comm. Psychol. Psychiatr. Behav., 18,* 37–51.

Puig, C. (1995, February 27). Children say they imitate anti-social behavior on TV: Survey finds shows influence more than two-thirds.

Pulaski, M.A.S. (1974, January). The rich rewards of make believe. *Psychology Today,* pp. 68–74.

Putnam, F.W. (1984). The psychophysiological investigation of multiple personality: A review. *Psychiatric Clinics of North America, 7,* 31–39.

Putnam, F.W., Guroff, J.J., Silberman, E.D., Barban, L., & Post, R.M. (1986). The clinical phenomenology of multiple personality disorder: Review of 100 recent cases. *Journal of Clinical Psychology, 47,* 285–293.

Quadagno, D.M. (1987). Pheromones and human sexuality. *Medical Aspects of Human Sexuality, 21,* 149–154.

Quadrel, M.J., Prouadrel, Fischoff, B., & Davis, W. (1993). Adolescent (In)vulnerability. *American Psychologist, 2,* 102–116.

Quill, T.E. (1985). Somatization disorder: One of medicine's blind spots. *JAMA, Journal of the American Medical Association, 254,* 3075–3079.

Rabinowitz, V.C., & Sechzer, J.A. (1993). Feminist perspectives on research methods. In F.L. Denmark & M.A. Paludi (Eds.), *Psychology of women: A handbook of issues and theories* (pp. 23–66). Westport, CT: Greenwood.

Rachlin, H., Logue, A.W., Gibbon, J., & Frankel, M. (1986). Cognition and behavior in studies of choice. *Psychological Review, 93,* 33–45.

Radford, M. (1996). Culture and its effects on decision making. In W. H. Loke (Ed.), *Perspectives on judgment and decision making.* Lanham, MD: Scarecrow Press.

Radford, M., Mann, L., Ohta, Y., & Nakane, Y. (1990). Differences between Australian and Japanese students in decisional self-esteem, decisional stress and coping styles. Reported in Radford, M. (1996). Culture and its effects on decision making. In W. H. Loke (Ed.), *Perspectives on judgment and decision making.* Lanham, MD: Scarecrow Press.

Raine, A., Lencz, T., Reynolds, G.P., Harrison, G., Sheard, C., Medley, I., Reynolds, L.M., & Cooper, J.E. (1992). An evaluation of structural and functional prefrontal deficits in schizophrenia: MRI and neuropsychological measures. *Psychiatry Research Neuroimaging, 45,* 123–137.

Rastam, M. (1994). Anorexia nervosa: Recent research findings and implications for clinical practice. *European Child and Adolescent Psychiatry, 3,* 197–207.

Ravussin, E., Pratley, R.E., Maffei, M., Wang, H., Friedman, J.M., Bennett, P.H., & Bogardus, C. (1997). Relatively low plasma leptin concentrations precede weight gain in Pima Indians. *Nat. Med., 3*(2), 238–240.

Rayman, P., & Bluestone, B. (1982). *The private and social response to job loss: A metropolitan study.* Final report of research sponsored by the Center for Work and Mental Health, National Institute of Mental Health.

Rebok, G.W., Rasmusson, D.X., & Brandt, J. (1997). Improving memory in community elderly through group-based and individualized memory training. In D.G. Payne & F.G. Conrad (Eds.), *Intersections in basic and applied memory research.* Mahwah, NJ: Erlbaum.

Redelmeier, D.A., & Tversky, A. (1996). On the belief that arthritis pain is related to the weather. *Proceedings of the National Academy of Sciences U.S.A., 93*(7), 2895–2896.

Ree, M.J., & Earles, J.A. (1992). Intelligence is the best predictor of job performance. *Current Directions in Psychological Science, 1,* 86–89.

Reed, S.K. (1988). *Cognition: Theory and applications.* Monterey, CA: Brooks/Cole.

Reed, S.K. (1992). *Cognition: Theory and applications* (3rd ed.). Pacific Grove, CA: Brooks/Cole.

Reed, S.K. (1996). *Cognition: Theory and applications* (4th ed.). Pacific Grove, CA: Brooks/Cole.

Reinisch, J.M., & Sanders, S.A. (1982). Early barbiturate exposure: The brain, sexually dimorphic behavior and learning. *Neuroscience and Biobehavioral Reviews, 6*(3), 311–319.

Reis, S.M. (1989). Reflections on policy affecting the education of gifted and talented students, past and future perspectives. *American Psychologist, 44,* 399–408.

Reiss, D., & Price, R.H. (1996). National research agenda for prevention research: The National Institute of Mental Health report. *American Psychologist, 51*(11), 1109–1115.

Renzulli, J.S. (1978). What makes giftedness? Reexamining a definition. *Phi Delta Kappan, 60,* 180–184, 216.

Reschly, D.J. (1981). Psychology testing in educational classification and placement. *American Psychologist, 36,* 1094–1102.

Rescorla, R.A. (1966). Predictability and number of pairings in Pavlovian fear conditioning. *Psychonomic Science, 4,* 383–384.

Rescorla, R.A. (1967). Pavlovian conditioning and its proper control procedures. *Psychological Review, 74,* 71–80.

Rescorla, R.A. (1988). Pavlovian conditioning: It's not what you think. *American Psychologist, 43,* 151–160.

Rescorla, R.A., & Solomon, R.L. (1967). Two-process learning theory: Relationships between Pavlovian conditioning and instrumental learning. *Psychological Review, 74,* 151–182.

Restak, R. (1993, September/October). Brain by design. *The Sciences,* 27–33.

Reyna, V.F., & Titcomb, A.L. (1997). Constraints on the suggestibility of eyewitness testimony: A fuzzy-trace theory analysis. In D.G. Payne & F.G. Conrad (Eds.), *Intersections in basic and applied memory research.* Mahwah, NJ: Erlbaum.

Reynolds, B. A., & Weiss, S. (1992). Generation of neurons and astrocytes from isolated cells of the adult mammalian central nervous system. *Science, 255,* 1707–1710.

Rhue, J.W., Lynn, S.J., & Kirsch, I. (1993). *Handbook of clinical hypnosis.* Washington, DC: American Psychological Association.

Rice, B. (1979, September). Brave new world of intelligence testing. *Psychology Today,* pp. 27–38.

Richards, R., Kinney, D.K., Lunde, I., & Benet, M. (1988). Creativity in manic-depressives, cyclothymes, their normal relatives, and control subjects. *Journal of Abnormal Psychology, 97,* 281–288.

Richardson, G.S., Miner, J.D., & Czeisler, C.A. (1989–1990). Impaired driving performance in shiftworkers: The role of the circadian system in a multifactional model. *Alcohol, Drugs & Driving, 5*(4), 6(1), 265–273.

Riger, S. (1992). Epistemological debates, feminist voices. *American Psychologist, 47,* 730–740.

Riordan, R.J., & Beggs, M.S. (1987). Counselors and self-help groups. *Journal of Counseling and Development, 65,* 427–429.

Rios, D.M. (1995, January 9). Gay teens struggle to find their sexual identity. *Ann Arbor News.*

Roberts. R.M., & Kreuz, R.J. (1994). Why do people use figurative language? *Psychological Science, 5,* 159–163.

Robins, L.N., & Regier, D.A. (1991). *Psychiatric disorders in America: The Epidemiologic Catchment Area Study.* New York: Free Press.

Robins, L.N., Schoenberg, S.P., Holmes, S.J., Ratcliff, K.S., Benham, A., & Works, J. (1985). Early home environment and retrospective recall: A test for concordance between siblings with and without psychiatric disorders. *American Journal of Orthopsychiatry, 55,* 27–41.

Robinson, L.A., Berman, J.S., & Neimeyer, R.A. (1990). Psychotherapy for the treatment of depression: A comprehensive review of controlled outcome research. *Psychological Bulletin, 108,* 30–49.

Rodin, J. (1981a). Current status of the internal-external hypothesis for obesity. *American Psychologist, 36,* 361–371.

Rodin, J. (1981b). Understanding obesity: Defining the samples. *Personality and Social Psychology Bulletin, 7,* 147–151.

Rodin, J. (1985). Insulin levels, hunger, and food intake: An example of feedback loops in body weight regulation. *Health Psychology, 4,* 1–24.

Rodin, J., Striegel-Moore, R.H., & Silberstein, L.R. (1985, July). *A prospective study of bulimia among college students on three U.S. campuses.* First unpublished progress report, Yale University, New Haven, CT.

Rodriguez, M. (1994). Influence of sex and family history of alcoholism on cognitive functioning in heroin users. *European Journal of Psychology, 8,* 29–36.

Roediger, H.L. (1990). Implicit memory: Retention without remembering. *American Psychologist, 45*(9), 1043–1056.

Rofe, Y. (1984). Stress and affiliation: A utility theory. *Psychological Review, 91,* 251–268.

Rofe, Y., Hoffman, M., & Lewin, I. (1985). Patient affiliation in major illness. *Psychological Medicine, 15,* 895–896.

Rogers, C.R. (1961). *On becoming a person: A therapist's view of psychotherapy.* Boston: Houghton Mifflin.

Rogers, D. (1980). *The adult years: An introduction to aging.* Englewood Cliffs, NJ: Prentice Hall.

Rogoff, B., & Chavajay, P. (1995). What's become of research on the cultural basis of cognitive development. *American Psychologist, 50*(10), 859–877.

Roitbak, A.I. (1993). *Glia and its role in nervous activity.* Saint Petersburg, Russia: Nauka.

Roitblatt, H.L., Penner, R.H., & Nachtigall, P.E. (1990). Matching-to-sample by an echolocating dolphin (Tursiops truncatus). *Journal of Experimental Psychology: Animal Behavior Processes, 16,* 85–95.

Romeo, F. (1984). Adolescence, sexual conflict, and anorexia nervosa. *Adolescence, 19,* 551–557.

Rosch, E.H. (1973). Natural categories. *Cognitive Psychology, 4,* 328–350.

Rosch, E.H. (1978). Principles of categorization. In E.H. Rosch & B.B. Lloyd (Eds.), *Cognition and categorization.* Hillsdale, NJ: Erlbaum.

Rosen, R.C., & Rosen, L. (1981). *Human sexuality.* New York: Knopf.

Rosenthal, D. (1970). *Genetic theory and abnormal behavior.* New York: McGraw-Hill.

Rosenthal, E. (1992, October 15). Headache? You skipped your coffee. *New York Times,* p. A8.

Rosenthal, R., Archer, D., DiMatteo, M.R., Koivumaki, J.H., & Rogers, P.L. (1974, September). Body talk and tone of voice: The language without words. *Psychology Today,* pp. 64–68.

Rosenthal, R., Hall, J.A., Archer, D., DiMatteo, M.R., & Rogers, P.L. (1979). The PONS test: Measuring sensitivity to nonverbal cues. In S. Weitz (Ed.), *Nonverbal communication* (2nd ed.). New York: Oxford University Press.

Rosenzweig, M.R. (1984). Experience, memory, and the brain. *American Psychologist, 39,* 365–376.

Rosenzweig, M.R. (1996). Aspects of the search for neural mechanisms of memory. *Annual Review of Psychology, 47,* 1–32.

Rosenzweig, M.R., & Bennett, E.L. (1976). Enriched environments: Facts, factors, and fantasies. In L. Petrinovich & J.L. McGaugh (Eds.), *Knowing, thinking, believing* (pp. 179–214). New York: Plenum.

Rosenzweig, M.R., Bennett, E.L., & Diamond, M.C. (1972). Brain changes in response to experience. *Scientific American, 226*(2), 22–29.

Rosenzweig, M.R., & Leiman, A.L. (1982). *Physiological psychology.* Lexington, MA: D.C. Heath.

Ross, C.A., Norton, G.R., & Wozney, K. (1989). Multiple personality disorder: An analysis of 236 cases. *Canadian Journal of Psychiatry, 34,* 413–418.

Ross, L. (1977). The intuitive psychologist and his shortcomings: Distortions in the attribution process. In L. Berkowitz (Ed.), *Advances in experimental social psychology* (Vol. 10). New York: Academic Press.

Ross, L., & Nisbett, R.E. (1991). *The person and the situation.* New York: McGraw-Hill.

Roth, D., & Rehm, L.P. (1980). Relationships among self-monitoring processes, memory, and depression. *Cognitive Therapy and Research, 4,* 149–157.

Roth, G. (1996, April 30). Eating less may bring longer life. *New York Times,* p. B8.

Rothbart, M., Evans, M., & Fulero, S. (1979). Recall for confirming events: Memory processes and the maintenance of social stereotypes. *Journal of Experimental Social Psychology, 15,* 343–355.

Rottenstreich, Y., & Tversky, A. (1997). Unpacking, repacking, and anchoring: Advances in support theory. *Psychological Review, 104*(2), 406–415.

Rotter, J.B. (1954). *Social learning and clinical psychology.* Englewood Cliffs, NJ: Prentice Hall.

Rovner, S. (1990, December 25). The empty nest myth. *Ann Arbor News,* p. D3.

Rowan, A., & Shapiro, K.J. (1996). Animal rights, a bitten apple. *American Psychologist, 51*(11), 1183–1184.

Ruberman, J.W., Weinblatt, E., Goldberg, J.D., & Chaudhary, B.S. (1984). Psychological influences on mortality after myocardial infarction. *New England Journal of Medicine, 311,* 552–559.

Rubin, K.H., Coplan, R.J., Chen, X., & McKinnon, J.E. (1994). Peer relationships and influences in childhood. In *Encyclopedia of human behavior* (Vol. 3, pp. 431–439).

Ruble, D.N., Fleming, A.S., Hackel, L.S., & Stangor, C. (1988). Changes in the marital relationship during the transition to first time motherhood: Effects of violated expectations concerning division of household labor. *Journal of Personality and Social Psychology, 55,* 78–87.

Ruffin, C.L. (1993). Stress and health–little hassles vs. major life events. *Australian Psychologist, 28,* 201–208.

Rumbaugh, D.M. (1977). *Language learning by a chimpanzee.* New York: Academic Press.

Rumbaugh, D.M. (1990). Comparative psychology and the great apes: Their competence in learning, language, and numbers. *Psychological Record, 40,* 15–39.

Rumbaugh, D.M., & Savage-Rumbaugh, E.S. (1978). Chimpanzee language research: Status and potential. *Behavior Research Methods and Instrumentation, 10,* 119–131.

Rumbaugh, D.M., Savage-Rumbaugh, E.S., & Sevcik, R.A. (1994). Biobehavioral roots of language. In R.W. Wrangham, W.C. McGrew, F.B.M. de Waal, & P.G. Heltne (Eds.), *Chimpanzee cultures* (pp. 319–354). Cambridge, MA: Harvard University Press.

Rumbaugh, D.M., von Glaserfeld, E., Warner, H., Pisani, P., & Gill, T.V. (1974). Lana (chimpanzee) learning language: A progress report. *Brain and Language, 1,* 205–212.

Rumelhart, D.E., & McClelland, J.L. (Eds.). (1986). *Parallel distributed processing: Explorations in the neurostructure of cognition.* Cambridge, MA: MIT Press.

Rushton, J.P. (1995). *Race, evolution, and behavior.* New Brunswick, NJ: Transaction.

Rushton, J.P. (1997). Race, IQ, and the APA report on the Bell Curve. *American Psychologist, 52*(1), 69–70.

Russell, D.E.H. (1986). The incidence and prevalence of intrafamilial and extrafamilial sexual abuse of female children. *Child Abuse and Neglect, 7,* 133–146.

Russell, J.A. (1991). Culture and the categorization of emotions. *Psychological Bulletin, 110*, 426–450.

Russell, M.J., Switz, G.M., & Thompson, K. (1980). Olfactory influences on the human menstrual cycle. *Pharmacology, Biochemistry, and Behavior, 13*, 737–738.

Russell, T.G., Rowe, W., & Smouse, A.D. (1991). Subliminal self-help tapes and academic achievement: An evaluation. *Journal of Counseling and Development, 69*, 359–362.

Russo, N.F. (1985). *A woman's mental health agenda*. Washington, DC: American Psychological Association.

Russo, N.F. (1990). Overview: Forging research priorities for women's mental health. *American Psychologist, 45*, 368–373.

Russo, N.F., & Denmark, F.L. (1987). Contributions of women to psychology. *Annual Review of Psychology, 38*, 279–298.

Russo, N.F., & Sobel, S.B. (1981). Sex differences in the utilization of mental health facilities. *Professional Psychology, 12*, 7–19.

Rutter, M.L. (1997). Nature-nurture integration: An example of antisocial behavior. *American Psychologist, 52*, 390–398.

Salthouse, T.A. (1991). Mediation of adult age differences in cognition by reductions in working memory and speed of processing. *Psychological Science, 2*(3), 179–183.

Sanford, R.N. (1937). The effects of abstinence from food upon imaginal processes: A further experiment. *Journal of Psychology, 3*, 145–159.

Sarason, I.G., & Sarason, B.R. (1987). *Abnormal psychology: The problem of maladaptive behavior* (5th ed.). Englewood Cliffs, NJ: Prentice Hall.

Sarter, M., Berntson, G.G., & Cacioppo, J.T. (1996). Brain imaging and cognitive neuroscience: Toward strong inference in attributing function to structure. *American Psychologist, 51*, 13–21.

Satow, K.K. (1975). Social approval and helping. *Journal of Experimental Social Psychology, 11*, 501–509.

Sattler, J.M. (1992). *Assessment of children* (3rd ed.). San Diego: Jerome M. Sattler.

Savage-Rumbaugh, E.S. (1990). Language acquisition in a nonhuman species: Implications for the innateness debate. *Developmental Psychobiology, 23*, 599–620.

Savage-Rumbaugh, E.S. (1993). *Language comprehension in ape and child.* Chicago: University of Chicago Press.

Savage-Rumbaugh, E.S., McDonald, K., Sevcik, R.A., Hopkins, W.D., & Rubert, E. (1986). Spontaneous symbol acquisition and communicative use by pygmy chimpanzees (Pan paniscus). *Journal of Experimental Psychology: General, 115*, 211–235.

Savage-Rumbaugh, S., & Brakke, K.E. (1996). Animal language: Methodological and interpretative issues. In M. Berkoff & D. Jamieson (Eds.), *Readings in animal cognition.* Cambridge, MA: MIT Press.

Saxe, L. (1994). Detection of deception. Polygraph and integrity tests. *Current Directions in Psychological Science, 3*, 69–73.

Scarr, S. (1993). Ebbs and flows of evolution in psychology. *Contemporary Psychology, 38*, 458–462.

Scarr, S. (1995). Inheritance, intelligence and achievement. *Planning for Higher Education, 23*, 1–9.

Scarr, S., & Weinberg, R. (1983). The Minnesota Adoption Study: Genetic differences and malleability. *Child Development, 54*, 260–267.

Schaal, B. (1986). Presumed olfactory exchanges between mother and neonate in humans. In J.L. Camus & J. Conler (Eds.), *Ethology and psychology.* Toulouse: Private IEC.

Schachter, S. (1971a). Some extraordinary facts about obese humans and rats. *American Psychologist, 26*, 129–144.

Schachter, S. (1971b, April). Eat, eat. *Psychology Today*, pp. 44–47, 78–79.

Schacter, D.L., Cooper, L.A., Tharan, M., & Rubens, A.B. (1991). Preserved priming of novel objects in patients with memory disorders. *Journal of Cognitive Neuroscience, 3*, 117–130.

Schaefer, H.H., & Martin, P.L. (1966). Behavioral therapy for "apathy" of hospitalized patients. *Psychological Reports, 19*, 1147–1158.

Schaie, K.W. (1984). Midlife influences upon intellectual functioning in old age. *International Journal of Behavioral Development, 7*, 463–478.

Schaie, K.W. (1994). The course of adult intellectual development. *American Psychologist, 4*, 304–313.

Schally, A.V., Kastin, A.J., & Arimura, A. (1977). Hypothalamic hormones: The link between brain and body. *American Scientist, 65*, 712–719.

Schanberg, S.M., & Field, T.M. (1987). Sensory deprivation stress and supplemental stimulation in the rat pup and preterm human neonate. *Child Development, 58*, 1431–1447.

Schatzman, E.L. (1992). *L'outil theorie*. Paris: Eshel.

Scheier, M.F., & Carver, C.S. (1993). On the power of positive thinking: The benefits of being optimistic. *Current Directions 2*, 26–30.

Scherer, K.R., & Wallbott, H.G. (1994). Evidence for universality and cultural variation of differential emotion response patterning. *Journal of Personality and Social Psychology, 66*, 310–328.

Schiffman, H.R. (1982). *Sensation and perception: An integrated approach* (2nd ed.). New York: Wiley.

Schleidt, M., & Genzel, C. (1990). The significance of mother's perfume for infants in the first weeks of their life. *Ethology & Sociobiology, 11*, 145–154.

Schlenker, B.R., & Weigold, M.F. (1992). Interpersonal processes involving impression regulation and management. *Annual Review of Psychology, 43*, 133–168.

Schlenker, B.R., Weigold, M.F., & Hallam, J.R. (1990). Self-serving attributions in social context: Effects of self-esteem and social pressure. *Journal of Personality and Social Psychology, 58*(5), 855–863.

Schnurr, P.P., Rosenberg, S.D., & Friedman, M.J. (1993). Preliminary MMPI scores as predictors of combat-related PTSD symptoms. *American Journal of Psychiatry, 150*(3), 479–483.

Schoenthaler, S.J., Amos, S.P., Eysenck, H.J., Peritz, E., & Yudkin, J. (1991). Controlled trial of vitamin-mineral supplementation: Effects on intelligence and performance. *Personality and Individual Differences, 12*, 251–362.

Schroeder, S.R., Schroeder, C.S., & Landesman, S. (1987). Psychological services in educational setting to persons with mental retardation. *American Psychologist, 42*, 805–808.

Schulz, D.A. (1984). *Human sexuality* (2nd ed.). Englewood Cliffs, NJ: Prentice Hall.

Schwartz, B. (1989). *Psychology of learning and behavior* (3rd ed.). New York: Norton.

Schwartz, G.E. (1974, April). TM relaxes some people and makes them feel better. *Psychology Today*, pp. 39–44.

Schwartz, J., Stoessel, P., Baxter, L., Martin, K., & Phelps, M. (1996). Systematic changes in cerebral glucose metabolic rate after successful behavior modification treatment of obsessive-compulsive disorder. *Archives of General Psychiatry, 53*, 109–113.

Schwartz, J.E., Friedman, H.S., Tucker, J.S., Tomlinson-Keasey, C., Wingard, D.L., & Criqui, M.H. (1995). Sociodemographic and psychosocial factors in childhood as predictors of adult mortality. *American Journal of Public Health, 85*, 1237–1245.

Schwartz, P. (1994, November 17). Some people with multiple roles are blessedly stressed. *New York Times.*

Schweickert, R., & Boruff, B. (1986). Short-term memory capacity: Magic number or magic spell? *Journal of Experimental Psychology: Learning, Memory, & Cognition, 12*(3), 419–425.

Schweinhart, L.J., Barnes, H.V., & Weikart, D.P. (1993). *Significant benefits: The High/Scope Perry Study through age 27* (Monographs of the High/Scope Educational Research Foundation, No. 10). Ypsilanti, MI: High/Scope Press.

Scott, C., Klein, D.M., & Bryant, J. (1990). Consumer response to humor in advertising: A series of field studies using behavioral observation. *Journal of Consumer Research, 16*, 498–501.

Scott, K.G., & Carran, D.T. (1987). The epidemiology and prevention of mental retardation. *American Psychologist, 42*, 801–804.

Scupin, R. (1995). *Cultural anthropology* (2nd ed.). Englewood Cliffs, NJ: Prentice Hall.

Seamon, J.G., & Kenrick, D.T. (1992). *Psychology*. Englewood Cliffs, NJ: Prentice Hall.

Sears, D.O. (1994). On separating church and lab. *Psychological Science, 5,* 237–239.

Seddon, J.M., Willett, W.C., Speizer, F.E., & Hankinson, S.E. (1996). A prospective study of cigarette smoking and age-related macular degeneration in women. *Journal of the American Medical Association, 276,* 1141–1146.

Seligman, J., Rogers, P., & Annin, P. (1994, May 2). The pressure to lose. *Newsweek,* pp. 60, 62.

Seligman, M.E., & Schulman, P. (1986). Explanatory styles as a predictor of productivity and quitting among life insurance sales agents. *Journal of Personality and Social Psychology, 50,* 832–838.

Seligman, M.E.P. (1972). Phobias and preparedness. In M.E.P. Seligman & J.L. Hager (Eds.), *Biological boundaries of learning.* Englewood Cliffs, NJ: Prentice Hall.

Seligman, M.E.P. (1995). The effectiveness of psychotherapy: The *Consumer Reports* study. *American Psychologist, 50*(12), 965–974.

Seligman, M.E.P. (1996). Science as an ally of practice. *American Psychologist, 51*(10), 1072–1079.

Seligmann, J., et al. (1992, February 3). The new age of Aquarius. *Newsweek,* p. 65.

Sell, R.L., Wells, J.A., & Wypij, D. (1995). The prevalence of homosexual behavior and attraction in the United States, the United Kingdom and France: Results of national population-based samples. *Archives of Sexual Behavior, 24,* 235–238.

Selman, R. (1981). The child as friendship philosopher. In S.R. Asher & J.M. Gottman (Eds.), *The development of children's friendships.* New York: Cambridge University Press.

Selye, H. (1956). *The stress of life.* New York: McGraw-Hill.

Selye, H. (1976). *The stress of life* (rev. ed.). New York: McGraw-Hill.

Semrud-Clikeman, M., & Hynd, G.W. (1990). Right hemispheric dysfunction in nonverbal learning disabilities: Social, academic, and adaptive functioning in adults and children. *Psychological Bulletin, 107,* 196–209.

Shalev, A., & Munitz, H. (1986). Conversion without hysteria: A case report and review of the literature. *British Journal of Psychiatry, 148,* 198–203.

Shapiro, D., & Shapiro, D. (1982). Meta-analysis of comparative therapy outcome studies: A replication and refinement. *Psychological Bulletin, 92,* 581–604.

Shapiro, K. (1991, July). Use morality as basis for animal treatment. *APA Monitor,* p. 5.

Shaywitz, B., Shaywitz, S., Pugh, K., Constable, R., Shudlarski, P., Fulbright, R., Bronen, R., Fletcher, J., Shankweiler, D., Katz, L., & Gore, J. (1995). Sex differences in the functional organization of the brain for language. *Nature, 373,* 607–617.

Shepard, R.N, & Metzler, J. (1971). Mental rotation of three-dimensional objects. *Science, 171,* 701–703.

Shepard, R.N. (1978). Externalization of mental images and the act of creation. In B.S. Randhawa & W.E. Coffman (Eds.), *Visual learning, thinking, and communicating.* New York: Academic Press.

Shepherd, G.M. (1994). *Neurobiology* (3rd ed.). Oxford: Oxford University Press.

Sherin, J.E., Shiromani, P.J., McCarley, R.W., & Saper, C.B. (1996). Activation of ventrolateral preoptic neurons during sleep. *Science, 271,* 216–219.

Shiffrin, R.M., & Cook, J.R. (1978). Short-term forgetting of item and order information. *Journal of Verbal Reasoning and Verbal Behavior, 17,* 189–218.

Shimamura, A.P., Berry, J.M., Mangels, J.A., Rusting, C.L., & Jurica, P.J. (1995). Memory and cognitive abilities in university professors: Evidence for successful aging. *Psychological Science, 6*(5), 271–277.

Shneidman, E. (1989). The Indian summer of life: A preliminary study of septuagenarians. *American Psychologist, 44*(4), 684–694.

Shriver, M.D., & Piersel, W. (1994). The long-term effects of intrauterine drug exposure: Review of recent research and implications for early childhood special education. *Topics in Early Childhood Special Education, 14*(2), 161–183.

Siegel, L. (1993). Amazing new discovery: Piaget was wrong. *Canadian Psychology, 34,* 239–245.

Siegel, R.K. (1977). Hallucinations. *Scientific American, 237,* 132–140.

Siegel, R.K. (1982). Cocaine smoking. *Journal of Psychoactive Drugs, 14,* 271–359.

Sigman, M. (1995). Nutrition and child development: More food for thought. *American Psychological Society, 4*(2), 52–56.

Simon, H.A. (1974). How big is a chunk? *Science, 165,* 482–488.

Simon, H.A. (1979). *Models of thought.* New Haven, CT: Yale University Press.

Simpson, H.B., Nee, J.C., & Endicott, J. (1997). First-episode major depression. Few sex differences in course. *Archives of General Psychiatry, 54*(7), 633–639.

Singer, J.L. (1975). *The inner world of daydreaming.* New York: Harper Colophon.

Singer, J.L., & Singer, D.G. (1983). Psychologists look at television: Cognitive, developmental, personality, and social policy implications. *American Psychologist, 38,* 826–834.

Singh, G.K., & Yu, S.M. (1995). Infant mortality in the United States: Trends, differentials, and projections, 1950 through 2010. *American Journal of Public Health, 85*(7), 957–964.

Singular, S. (1982, October). A memory for all seasonings. *Psychology Today,* pp. 54–63.

Sinha, P. (1996). I think I know that face . . . *Nature, 384,* 404.

Sinnott, J.D. (1994). Sex roles. In *Encyclopedia of human behavior* (Vol. 4, pp. 151–158).

61% of Americans call drug use "immoral," survey reports. (1990, February 27). *Ann Arbor News,* pp. A1, A9.

Skaalvik, E.M., & Rankin, R.J. (1994). Gender differences in mathematics and verbal achievement, self-perception and motivation. *British Journal of Educational Psychology, 64,* 419–428.

Skeels, H.M. (1938). Mental development of children in foster homes. *Journal of Consulting Psychology, 2,* 33–43.

Skeels, H.M. (1942). The study of the effects of differential stimulation on mentally retard children: A follow-up report. *American Journal of Mental Deficiencies, 46,* 340–350.

Skeels, H.M. (1966). Adult status of children with contrasting early life experiences. *Monographs of the Society for Research in Child Development, 31*(3), 1–65.

Skinner, B.F. (1938). *The behavior of organisms.* New York: Appleton-Century-Crofts.

Skinner, B.F. (1948). *Science and human behavior.* New York: Macmillan.

Skinner, B.F. (1953). Some contributions of an experimental analysis of behavior to psychology as a whole. *American Psychologist, 8*(2), 69–78.

Skinner, B.F. (1957). *Verbal behavior.* Englewood Cliffs, NJ: Prentice Hall.

Skinner, B.F. (1987). Whatever happened to psychology as the science of behavior? *American Psychologist, 42,* 780–786.

Skinner, B.F. (1989). The origins of cognitive thought. *American Psychologist, 44,* 13–18.

Skinner, B.F. (1990). Can psychology be a science of mind? *American Psychologist, 45,* 1206–1210.

Skrzycki, C. (1995, November 24). Is it pure or just pure nonsense? *Washington Post,* pp. F1, F4.

Smith, C.T. (1985). Sleep states and learning: A review of the animal literature. *Neuroscience & Biobehavioral Reviews, 9,* 157–168.

Smith, C.T., & Kelly, G. (1988). Paradoxical sleep deprivation applied two days after end of training retards learning. *Physiology & Behavior, 43,* 213–216.

Smith, C.T., & Lapp, L. (1986). Prolonged increase in both PS and number of REMS following a shuttle avoidance task. *Physiology & Behavior, 36,* 1053–1057.

Smith, E.P., & Davidson, W.S., II. (1992). Mentoring and the development of African-American graduate students. *Journal of College Student Development, 33*(6), 531.

Smith, G.P., & Gibbs, J. (1976). Cholecystokinin and satiety: Theoretic and therapeutic implications. In D. Novin, W. Wyrwicka, & G. Bray (Eds.), *Hunger: Basic mechanics and clinical implications*. New York: Raven Press.

Smith, J.F., & Kida, T. (1991). Heuristics and biases: Expertise and task realism in auditing. *Psychological Bulletin, 109*, 472–489.

Smith, K.H., & Rogers, M. (1994). Effectiveness of subliminal messages in television commercials: Two experiments. *Journal of Applied Psychology, 79*, 866–874.

Smith, M.L., & Glass, G.V. (1977). Meta-analysis of psychotherapy outcome studies. *American Psychologist, 32*, 752–760.

Smith, M.L., Glass, G.V., & Miller, T.I. (1980). *The benefits of psychotherapy*. Baltimore: Johns Hopkins University Press.

Smith, P.B., & Bond, M.H. (1994). *Social psychology across cultures: Analysis and perspectives*. Boston: Allyn & Bacon.

Smollar, J., & Youniss, J. (1989). Transformations in adolescents' perceptions of parents. *International Journal of Behavioral Development, 12*, 71–84.

Snodgrass, S.E. (1992). Further effects of role versus gender on interpersonal sensitivity. *Journal of Personality and Social Psychology, 62*, 154–158.

Snyder, H.N. (1996). The juvenile court and delinquency cases. *Future Child, 6*(3), 53–63.

Snyder, M. (1987). *Public appearances/private realities: The psychology of self-monitoring*. New York: Freeman.

Snyder, M., & Cunningham, M.R. (1975). To comply or not comply: Testing the self-perception explanation of the "foot-in-the-door" phenomenon. *Journal of Personality and Social Psychology, 31*, 64–67.

Snyder, M., & Swann, W.B., Jr. (1978). Behavioral confirmation in social interaction: From social perception to social reality. *Journal of Experimental Social Psychology, 14*, 148–162.

Snyder, M., & Tanke, E.D. (1976). Behavior and attitude: Some people are more consistent than others. *Journal of Personality, 44*, 501–517.

Snyder, S.H. (1977). Opiate receptors and internal opiates. *Scientific American, 236*, 44–56.

Snyderman, M., & Rothman, S. (1987). Survey of expert opinion on intelligence and aptitude testing. *American Psychologist, 42*, 137–144.

Solomon, D.A., Keitner, G.I., Miller, I.W., Shea, M.T., & Keller, M.B. (1995). Course of illness and maintenance treatments for patients with bipolar disorder. *Journal of Clinical Psychiatry, 56*, 5–13.

Sommers, C.H. (1994, April 3). The myth of schoolgirls' low self-esteem. *Wall Street Journal*, p. 4.

Sommers-Flanagan, R., Sommers-Flanagan, J., & Davis, B. (1993). What's happening on music television? A gender role content analysis. *Sex Roles, 28*, 745–754.

Sorensen, R.C. (1973). *Adolescent sexuality in contemporary America*. New York: World.

Southern, S., & Gayle, R. (1982). A cognitive behavioral model of hypoactive sexual desire. *Behavioral Counselor, 2*, 31–48.

Spanos, N.P. (1986). Hypnotic behavior: A social-psychological interpretation of amnesia, analgesia, and "trance logic." *Behavioral and Brain Sciences, 9*, 449–502.

Spanos, N.P., & Chaves, J.F. (1989). *Hypnosis. The cognitive-behavioral perspective*. Buffalo, NY: Prometheus Books.

Sperling, G. (1960). The information available in brief visual presentations. *Psychological Monographs, 74*, 1–29.

Sperry, R.W. (1964). The great cerebral commissure. *Scientific American, 210*, 42–52.

Sperry, R.W. (1968). Hemisphere disconnection and unity in conscious awareness. *American Psychologist, 23*, 723–733.

Sperry, R.W. (1970). *Perception in the absence of neocortical commissures. In Perception and its disorders* (Res. Publ. A.R.N.M.D., Vol. 48). New York: The Association for Research in Nervous and Mental Disease.

Sperry, R.W. (1988). Psychology's mentalists paradigm and the religion/science tension. *American Psychologist, 43*, 607–613.

Sperry, R.W. (1995). The future of psychology. *American Psychologist, 5*(7), 505–506.

Spettle, C.M., & Liebert, R.M. (1986). Training for safety in automated person-machine systems. *American Psychologist, 41*, 545–550.

Spiegel, D. (1995). Essentials of psychotherapeutic intervention for cancer patients. *Support Care Cancer, 3*(4), 252–256.

Spiegel, D., & Moore, R. (1997). Imagery and hypnosis in the treatment of cancer patients. *Oncology, 11*(8), 1179–1189.

Spiegel, D., Bierre, P., & Rootenberg, J. (1989). Hypnotic alteration of somatosensory perception. *American Journal of Psychiatry, 146*, 749–754.

Spitzer, R.L., Skodal, A.E., Gibbon, M., & Williams, J.B.W. (1981). *DSM-III case book*. Washington, DC: American Psychiatric Association.

Spitzer, R.L., Skodal, A.E., Gibbon, M., & Williams, J.B.W. (1983). *Psychopathology: A casebook*. New York: McGraw-Hill.

Spoendlin, H.H., & Schrott, A. (1989). Analysis of the human auditory nerve. *Hearing Research, 43*, 25–38.

Springer, S.P., & Deutsch, G. (1989). *Left brain, right brain* (3rd ed.). New York: Freeman.

Squire, L.R., & Ojemann, J.G. (1992). Activation of the hippocampus in normal humans: A functional anatomical study of memory. *Proceedings of the National Academy of Sciences, 89*, 1837–1841.

Squire, L.R., & Zola-Morgan, S. (1991). The medial temporal lobe memory system. *Science, 253*(5026), 1380–1386.

Squire, L.R., Knowlton, B., & Musen, G. (1993). The structure and organization of memory. *Annual Review of Psychology, 44*, 453–495.

Squire, S. (1983). *The slender balance: Causes and cures for bulimia, anorexia, and the weight loss/weight gain seesaw*. New York: Putnam.

Sridhar, K.S., Ruab, W.A., & Weatherby, N.L. (1994). Possible role of marijuana smoking as a carcinogen in development of lung cancer at a young age. *Journal of Psychoactive Drugs, 26*, 285–288.

Stack, S. (1994). Divorce. In *Encyclopedia of human behavior* (Vol. 2, pp. 153–163).

Stancliffe, R.J. (1997). Community residence size, staff presence and choice. *Mental Retardation, 35*, 1–9.

Steele, C.M., & Josephs, R.A. (1990). Alcohol myopia: Its prized and dangerous effects. *American Psychologist, 45*, 921–933.

Steinberg, K.K. et al. (1991). A meta-analysis of the effect of estrogen replacement therapy on the risk of breast cancer. *JAMA, Journal of the American Medical Association, 265*(15), 1985–1990.

Steiner, J.A., (1972). A questionnaire study of risk-taking in psychiatric patients. *British Journal of Medical Psychology, 45*, 365–374.

Steiner, J.E. (1979). Facial expressions in response to taste and smell stimulation. In H.W. Reese & L.P. Lipsitt (Eds.), *Advances in child development and behavior* (Vol. 13). New York: Academic Press.

Steinhauer, J. (1997, July 6). Living together without marriage or apologies. *New York Times*, p. A9.

Steinhausen, H.C., Willms, J., & Spohr, H. (1993). Long-term psychopathological and cognitive outcome of children with fetal alcohol syndrome. *Journal of the American Academy of Child and Adolescent Psychiatry, 32*, 990–994.

Stern, L. (1985). *The structures and strategies of human memory*. Homewood, IL: Dorsey Press.

Stern, R.M., & Koch, K.L. (1996). Motion sickness and differential susceptibility. *Current Directions in Psychological Science, 5*, 115–120.

Stern, R.M., Breen, J.P., Watanabe, T., & Perry, B.S. (1981). Effect of feedback of physiological information on responses to innocent associations and guilty knowledge. *Journal of Applied Psychology, 66*, 677–681.

Sternberg, R.J. (1982, April). Who's intelligent? *Psychology Today*, pp. 30–39.

Sternberg, R.J. (1985a). *Beyond IQ: A triarchic theory of human intelligence*. New York: Cambridge University Press.

Sternberg, R.J. (1986). *Intelligence applied*. Orlando, FL: Harcourt Brace Jovanovich.

Sternberg, R.J. (1992). Ability tests, measurements and markets. *Journal of Educational Psychology, 84*, 134–140.

Sternberg, R.J. (1993). *Sternberg Triarchic Abilities Test*. Unpublished test.

Sternberg, R.J. (1997). Educating intelligence: Infusing the triarchic theory into school instruction. In R.J. Sternberg & E. Grigorenko (Eds.), *Intelligence: Heredity and environment*. New York: Cambridge University Press.

Sternberg, R.J., Conway, B.E., Ketron, J.L., & Bernstein, M. (1981). People's conceptions of intelligence. *Journal of Personal and Social Psychology, 41,* 37–55.

Sternberg, R.J., & Davidson, J.E. (1985). Cognitive development in the gifted and talented. In F.D. Horowitz & M. O'Brien (Eds.), *The gifted and talented: Developmental perspectives*. Washington, DC: American Psychological Association.

Sternberg, R.J., & Davidson, J.E. (Eds.). (1986). *Conceptions of giftedness*. New York: Cambridge University Press.

Sternberg, R.J., & Lubart, T.I. (1996). Investing in creativity. *American Psychologist, 51*(7), 677–688.

Sternberg, R.J., & Wagner, R.K. (1993). The g-ocentric view of intelligence and job performance is wrong. *Current Directions in Psychological Science, 2,* 1–5.

Stevens, G., & Gardner, S. (1982). *Women of psychology: Expansion and refinement* (Vol. 1). Cambridge, MA: Schenkman.

Stevenson, H.W. (1992). Learning from Asian schools. *Scientific American,* 70–76.

Stevenson, H.W. (1993). Why Asian students still outdistance Americans. *Educational Leadership,* 63–65.

Stevenson, H.W., Chen, C., & Lee, S.-Y. (1993). Mathematics achievement of Chinese, Japanese, and American children: Ten years later. *Science, 259,* 53–58.

Stevenson, H.W., Lee, S.-Y., & Stigler, J.W. (1986). Mathematics achievement of Chinese, Japanese, and American children. *Science, 231,* 693-697.

Stewart, R.H. (1965). Effect of continuous responding on the order effect in personality impression formation. *Journal of Personality and Social Psychology, 1,* 161–165.

Stiles, W.B., Shapiro, D.A., & Elliott, R. (1986). "Are all psychotherapies equivalent?" *American Psychologist, 41,* 165–180. (from Myers, 1992)

Stock, M.B., & Smythe, P.M. (1963). Does undernutrition during infancy inhibit brain growth and subsequent intellectual development? *Archives of Disorders in Childhood, 38,* 546–552.

Stone, R.A., & Deleo, J. (1976). Psychotherapeutic control of hypertension. *New England Journal of Medicine, 294,* 80–84.

Stone, W.F., Lederer, G., & Christie, R. (1993). Introduction: Strength and weakness. In W.F. Stone, G. Lederer, & R. Christie (Eds.), *The authoritarian personality today: Strength and weakness*. New York: Springer-Verlag.

Stoner, J.A.F. (1961). *A comparison of individual and group decisions involving risk*. Unpublished master's thesis, School of Industrial Management, MIT Press.

Straub, R.O., Seidenberg, M.S., Bever, T.G., & Terrace, H.S. (1979). Serial learning in the pigeon. *Journal of the Experimental Analysis of Behavior, 32,* 137–148.

Strickland, B.R. (1989). Internal-external control expectancies. From contingency to creativity. *American Psychologist, 44,* 1–12.

Strupp, H.H., & Hadley, S.W. (1977). A tripartite model of mental health and therapeutic outcomes: With special reference to negative effects on psychotherapy. *American Psychologist, 32,* 187–196.

Study links alcohol use to earlier death. (1990, October 2). *Ann Arbor News,* p. C1.

Stunkard, A.J., Harris, J.R., Pedersen, N.L., & McClearn, G.E. (1990). The body-mass index of twins who have been reared apart. *New England Journal of Medicine, 322,* 1483–1487.

Subotnik, R.F., & Arnold, K.D. (1994). *Beyond Terman: Contemporary longitudinal studies of giftedness and talent*. Norwood, NJ: Ablex.

Sue, S., Zane, N., & Young, K. (1994). Research on psychotherapy with culturally diverse populations. In A.E. Bergin & S.L. Garfield (Eds.), *Handbook of psychotherapy and behavior change* (4th ed., pp. 783–820). New York: Wiley.

Suedfeld, P.E. (1975). The benefits of boredom: Sensory deprivation reconsidered. *American Scientist, 63,* 60–69.

Suedfeld, P.E., & Borrie, R.A. (1978). Altering states of consciousness through sensory deprivation. In A. Sugerman & R. Tarter (Eds.), *Expanding dimensions of consciousness*. New York: Springer.

Suga, N. (1990, June). Bisonar and neural computation in bats. *Scientific American,* 60–66, 68.

Suls, J., & Fletcher, B. (1983). Social comparison in the social and physical sciences: An archival study. *Journal of Personality and Social Psychology, 44,* 575–580.

Swaab, D.F., & Hoffman, M.A. (1995). Sexual differentiation of the human hypothalamus in relation to gender and sexual orientation. *Trends in Neuroscience, 18,* 264–270.

Swaab, D.F., & Hofman, M.A. (1995). Sexual differentiation of the human hypothalamus in relation to gender and sexual orientation. *Trends in Neuroscience, 18,* 264–270.

Swan, G.E., Dame, A., & Carmelli, D. (1991). Involuntary retirement, Type A behavior, and current functioning in elderly men: 27-year follow-up of the Western Collaborative Group Study. *Psychology & Aging, 6*(3), 384–391.

Symonds, A. (1979). The wife as a professional. *American Journal of Psychoanalysis, 39*(1), 55–63.

Tagano, D.W., Moran, D.J., III, & Sawyers, J.K. (1991). *Creativity in early childhood classrooms*. Washington, DC: National Education Association.

Takaki, A., Nagai, K., Takaki, S., & Yanaihara, N. (1990). Satiety function of neurons containing CCKK-like substance in the dorsal parabrachial nucleus. *Physiology & Behavior, 48,* 865–871.

Takami, S., Getchell, M.L., Chen, Y., Monti-Bloch, L., & Berliner, D.L. (1993). Vomeronasal epithelial cells of the adult human express neuron-specific molecules. *Neuro Report, 4,* 374–378.

Tan, D.T.Y., & Singh, R. (1995). Attitudes and attraction: A developmental study of the similarity-attraction and dissimilarity-repulsion hypotheses. *Personality and Social Psychology Bulletin, 21*(9), 975–986.

Tanner, J.M. (1973). Growing up. *Scientific American, 235,* 34-43.

Tanner, J.M. (1978). *Foetus into man: Physical growth from conception to maturity*. Cambridge, MA: Harvard University Press.

Tanofsky, M.B., Wilfley, D.E., Spurrell, E.B., Welch, R., & Brownell, K.D. (1997). Comparison of men and women with binge eating disorder. *International Journal of Eating Disorders, 21*(1), 49–54.

Taylor, D.M., & Moghaddam, F.M. (1994). *Theories of intergroup relations: International social psychological perspectives*. Westport, CT: Praeger.

Taylor, S.E. (1983). Adjustment to threatening events. *American Psychologist, 38,* 1161–1173.

Taylor, S.E., & Armor, D.A. (1996). Positive illusions and coping with adversity. *Journal of Personality, 64,* 873–898.

Taylor, S.E., & Brown, J.D. (1988). Illusion and well-being: A social psychological perspective on mental health. *Psychological Bulletin, 103,* 193–210.

Taylor, S.E., & Brown, J.D. (1988). Positive illusions and well-being revisited: Separating fact from fiction. *Psychological Bulletin, 116,* 21–27.

Taylor, S.E., & Brown, J.D. (1994). Positive illusions and well-being revisited: Separating fact from fiction. *Psychological Bulletin, 116*(1), 21–27.

Taylor, S.E., Peplau, L.A., & Sears, D.O. (1994). *Social psychology*. Englewood Cliffs, NJ: Prentice Hall.

Telch, C.F., Agras, W.S., Rossiter, E.M., Wilfley, D., & Kenardy, J. (1990). Group cognitive-behavioral treatment for the nonpurging bulimic: An initial evaluation. *Journal of Consulting and Clinical Psychology, 58,* 629–635.

Terman, L.M. (1925). *Mental and physical traits of a thousand gifted children: Genetic studies of genius* (Vol. 1). Stanford, CA: Stanford University Press.

Terrace, H.S. (1979). *Nim: A chimpanzee who learned sign language*. New York: Knopf.

Terrace, H.S. (1985). On the nature of animal thinking. *Neuroscience and Biobehavioral Reviews, 9*(4), 643–652.

Thelen, E. (1994). Three-month-old infants can learn task-specific patterns of interlimb coordination. *American Psychological Society, 5*(5), 280–288.

Thelen, E. (1995). Motor development: A new synthesis. *American Psychologist, 50*(2), 79–95.

Thomas, A., & Chess, S. (1977). *Temperament and development.* New York: Brunner/Mazel.

Thompson, R.K.R. (1995). Natural and relational concepts in animals. In H. Roitblat & J.A. Meyer (Eds.), *Comparative approaches to cognitive science* (pp. 175–224). Cambridge, MA: Bradford Books, MIT press.

Thompson, T. (1993, November 21). The wizard of Prozac: A pilgrimage to the center of a medical debate. *Washington Post,* pp. F1–F5.

Thorndike, E.L. (1898). Animal intelligence. *Psychological Review Monograph, 2*(4, Whole No. 8).

Thorndike, E.L. (1903). *Heredity, correlation, and sex differences in ability: Vol. 11.* Columbia University contributions to philosophy, psychology, and education. New York: Columbia University Press.

Thorndike, E.L. (1911). *The elements of psychology* (2nd ed.). New York: A.G. Seiler.

Thorpy, M., & Glovinsky, P. (1987). Parasomnias. *Psychiatric Clinics of North America, 10,* 623–639.

Thurstone, L.L. (1938). Primary mental abilities. *Psychometric Monographs, 1.*

Tobias, R. (1994). *Education progress of students in bilingual and ESL programs: A longitudinal study.* (Research/Technical Report). Brooklyn, NY: New York City Board of Education.

Tolman, E.C., & Honzik, C.H. (1930). Introduction and removal of reward, and maze performance in rates. University of California Publications in *Psychology, 4,* 257–275.

Tomarken, A.J., Davidson, R.J., & Henriques, J.B. (1990). Resting frontal brain asymmetry predicts affective responses to films. *Journal of Personality and Social Psychology, 59,* 791–801.

Tooby, J., & Cosmides, L. (1990). The past explains the present: Emotional adaptations and the structure of ancestral environments. *Ethology and Sociobiology, 10,* 29–50.

Torgersen, S. (1983). Genetic factors in anxiety disorders. *Archives of General Psychiatry, 40,* 1085–1089.

Torrance, E.P. (1954). Leadership training to improve air-crew group performance. *USAF ATC Instructor's Journal, 5,* 25–35.

Torrey, E.F., Bowler, A.E., Taylor, E.H., & Gottesman, I.I. (1994). *Schizophrenia and manic-depressive disorder: The biological roots of mental illness as revealed by the landmark study of identical twins.* New York: Basic Books.

Tower, R.B., Singer, D.G., Singer, L.J., & Biggs, A. (1979). Differential effects of television programming on preschoolers' cognition, imagination, and social play. *American Journal of Orthopsychiatry, 49,* 265–281.

Tranel, D. (1994). Memory, neural substrates. *Encyclopedia of human behavior, 3,* 149–163.

Tranel, D., Damasio, A.R., & Damasio, H. (1988). Intact recognition of facial expression, gender, and age in patients with impaired recognition of face identity. *Neurology, 38,* 690–696.

Treaster, J.B. (1994, February 1). Survey finds marijuana use is up in high schools. *New York Times,* p. A1.

Treisman, A.M. (1960). Contextual cues in selective listening. *Quarterly Journal of Experimental Psychology, 12,* 242–248.

Treisman, A.M. (1964). Verbal cues, language and meaning in selective attention. *American Journal of Psychology, 77,* 206–219.

Treisman, A.M. (1986). Features and objects in visual processing. *Scientific American, 255,* 114–125.

Treisman, A.M., Cavanagh, P., Fischer, B., Ramachandran, V.S., & von der Heydt, R. (1990). Form perception and attention: Striate cortex and beyond. In L. Spillman & J.S. Werner (Eds.), *Visual perception.* San Diego, CA: Academic Press.

Trends in Education. (1995). *APA Education Directorate News,* Vol. II, (1), 2–3.

Triandis, H.C. (1994). *Culture and social behavior.* New York: McGraw-Hill.

Triandis, H.C., Bontempo, R., Villareal, M.J., Asai, M., & Lucca, N. (1988). Individualism and collectivism: Cross-cultural perspectives on self-ingroup relationships. *Journal of Personality and Social Psychology, 54,* 323–338.

Triandis, H.C., Leung, K., Villareal, M.J., & Clack, F.L. (1985). Allocentric versus idiocentric tendencies: Convergent and discriminant validation. *Journal of Research in Personality, 19,* 395–415.

Trice, A.D. (1986). Ethical variables? *American Psychologist, 41,* 482–483.

Trotter, R.J. (1983, August). Baby face. *Psychology Today,* pp. 12–20.

Tryon, R.C. (1940). Genetic differences in maze-learning abilities in rats. In *39th Yearbook: Part I. National Society for the Study of Education.* Chicago: University of Chicago Press.

Tulving, E. (1972). Episodic and semantic memory. In E. Tulving & W. Donaldson (Eds.), *Organization and memory.* New York: Academic Press.

Tulving, E. (1985). How many memory systems are there? *American Psychologist, 40,* 385–398.

Tulving, E., & Schacter, D.L. (1990). Priming and human memory systems. *Science, 247,* 301–306.

Tulving, E., Kapur, S., Markowitsch, H.J., Craik, F.I.M., Habib, R., & Houle, S. (1994). Neuroanatomical correlates of retrieval in episodic memory: Auditory sentence recognition. *Proceedings of the National Academy of Sciences of the U.S.A., 91,* 2012–2015.

Tupes, E.C., & Christal, R.W. (1961). *Recurrent personality factors based on trait ratings.* USAF ASD Technical Report, No. 61-97.

Turk, D.C., & Salovey, P. (1985). Cognitive structures, cognitive processes, and cognitive behavior modification: II. Judgments and inferences of the clinician. *Cognitive Therapy and Research, 9,* 19–34.

Turkheimer, E. (1991). Individual and group differences in adoption studies of IQ. *Psychological Bulletin, 110,* 392–405.

Turnbull, C.M. (1961). Observations. *American Journal of Psychology, 1,* 304–308.

Turnbull, S., Ward, A., Treasure, J., Jick, H., & Derby, L. (1996). The demand for eating disorder care. An epidemiological study using the general practice research database. *British Journal of Psychiatry, 169*(6), 705–712.

Tversky, A., & Kahneman, D. (1973). Availability: A heuristic for judging frequency and probability. *Cognitive Psychology, 5,* 207–232.

Tyrer, P. (1994). What are the borders of borderline personality disorder? *Acta Psychiatrica Scandinavica, 89*(Suppl. 379), 38–44.

U.S. Bureau of the Census. (1990). *Statistical abstract of the United States* (110th ed.). Washington, DC: U.S. Government Printing Office.

U.S. Merit Systems Protection Board. (1993). *Sexual harassment of federal workers: Is it a problem?* Washington, DC: U.S. Government Printing Office.

Uchino, B.N., Cacioppo, J.T., & Kiecolt-Glaser, J.K. (1996). The relationship between social support and physiological processes: A review with emphasis on underlying mechanisms and implications for health. *Psychological Bulletin, 119*(3), 488–531.

Uhl, G., Blum, K., Nobel, E.P., & Smith, S. (1993). Substance abuse vulnerability and D_2 dopamine receptor gene and severe alcoholism. *Trends in Neuroscience, 16,* 83–88.

Ulrich, R., & Azrin, N. (1962). Reflexive fighting in response to aversive stimulation. *Journal of Experimental Analysis of Behavior, 5,* 511–520.

Underwood, G. (1994). Subliminal perception on TV. *Nature, 370,* 103.

Underwood, G. (1996). *Implicit cognition.* New York: Oxford University.

Unger, R., & Crawford, M. (1992). *Women and gender: A feminist psychology.* New York: McGraw-Hill.

Usher, J.A., & Neisser, U. (1993). Childhood amnesia and the beginnings of memory for four early life events. *Journal of Experimental Psychology: General, 122,* 155–165.

Vaillant, G.E. (1977). *Adaptation to life.* Boston: Little, Brown.

Vaisse, C., Halaas, J.L., Horvath, C.M., Darnell, J.E., Stoffell, M., & Friedman, J.M. (1996). Leptin activation of Stat3 in the hypothalamus of wild-type and ob/ob mice but not db/db mice. *Nat Genet 14*(1), 95–97.

Valkenburg, P.M., & van der Voort, T.H.A. (1994). *Psychological Bulletin, 116,* 316–339.

van der Pompe, G., Duivenvoorden, H.J., Antoni, M.H., Visser, A., & Heijnen, C.J. (1997). Effectiveness of a short-term group psychotherapy program on endocrine and immune function in breast cancer patients: An exploratory study. *Journal of Psychosomatic Research, 42*(5), 453–466.

Van Natta, P., Malin, H., Bertolucci, D., & Kaelber, C. (1985). The influence of alcohol abuse as a hidden contributor to mortality. *Alcohol, 2,* 535–539.

Van Yperen, N.W., & Buunk, B.P. (1990). A longitudinal study of equity and satisfaction in intimate relationships. *European Journal of Social Psychology, 54,* 287–309.

Vauclair, J. (1996). *Animal cognition: An introduction to modern comparative psychology.* Cambridge, MA: Harvard University Press.

Vaughn, M. (1993, July 22). Divorce revisited. *Ann Arbor News,* p. C4.

Vignolo, L.A., Boccardi, E., & Caverni, L. (1986). Unexpected CT-scan findings in global aphasia. *Cortex, 22,* 55–69.

Virkkunen, M. (1983). Insulin secretion during the glucose tolerance test in antisocial personality. *British Journal of Psychiatry, 142,* 598–604.

Vogel-Sprott, M. (1967). Alcohol effects on human behavior under reward and punishment. *Psychopharmacologia, 11,* 337–344.

von Frisch, K. (1974). Decoding the language of the bee. *Science, 185,* 663–668.

von Hippel, W., Hawkins, C., & Narayan, S. (1994). Personality and perceptual expertise: Individual differences in perceptual identification. *Psychological Science, 5,* 401–406.

von Hofsten, C., & Fazel-Zandy, S. (1984). Development of visually guided hand orientation in reaching. *Journal of Experimental Child Psychology, 38,* 208–219.

Voyer, D., Voyer, S., & Bryden, M.P. (1995). Magnitude of sex differences in spatial abilities: A meta-analysis and consideration of critical variables. *Psychological Bulletin, 117*(2), 250–270.

Vygotsky, L.S. (1979). *Mind in society: The development of higher mental processes.* Cambridge, MA: Harvard University Press. (Original works published 1930, 1933, and 1935.)

Vygotsky, L.S. (1989). Concrete human psychology. *Soviet Psychology, 27*(2), 53–77.

Wachs, T.D., & Smitherman, C.H. (1985). Infant temperament and subject loss in a habituation procedure. *Child Development, 56,* 861–867.

Wagner, R.K., & Sternberg, R.J. (1986). Tacit knowledge and intelligence in the everyday world. In R.J. Sternberg & R.K. Wagner (Eds.), *Practical intelligence* (pp. 51–83). New York: Cambridge University Press.

Waid, W.M., & Orne, M.T. (1981). Cognitive, social, and personality processes in the physiological detection of deception. In L. Berkowitz (Ed.), *Advances in experimental social psychology* (Vol. 14). New York: Academic Press.

Waid, W.M., & Orne, M.T. (1982). The physiological detection of deception. *American Scientist, 70,* 402–409.

Waid, W.M., Orne, E.C., & Orne, M.T. (1981). Selective memory for social information, alertness, and physiological arousal in the detection of deception. *Journal of Applied Psychology, 66,* 224–232.

Waldman, H.B. (1996). Yes, overall crime statistics are down, but juveniles are committing more criminal offenses. *ASDC J. Dent Child, 63*(6), 438–442.

Walk, R.D., & Gibson, E.J. (1961). A comparative and analytical study of visual depth perception. *Psychological Monographs,* No. 75.

Wall, R.P., & Melzack, R. (Eds.). (1989). *Textbook of pain* (2nd ed.). Edinburgh: Churchill Livingston.

Walster, E., Walster, G.W., & Berscheid, E. (1978). *Equity: Theory and research.* Boston: Allyn & Bacon.

Walters, E.E., & Kendler, K.S. (1995). Anorexia nervosa and anorexic-like syndromes in a population-based female twin sample. *American Journal of Psychiatry, 152,* 64–67.

Walton, G.E., & Bower, T.G.R. (1993). Newborns form "prototypes" in less than 1 minute. *Psychologia Science, 4,* 203–206.

Walton, G.E., Bower, N.J.A., & Bower, T.G.R. (1992). Recognition of familiar faces by newborns. *Infant Behavior and Development, 15,* 265–269.

Warr, P., & Perry, G. (1982). Paid employment and women's psychological well-being. *Psychological Bulletin, 91,* 498–516.

Warrington, E.K., & Weiskrantz, L. (1970). Amnesic syndrome: Consolidation or retrieval? *Nature, 228*(272), 628–630.

Washburn, M.F. (1916). *Movement and mental imagery: Outlines of a motor theory of the complexer mental processes.* Boston: Houghton Mifflin.

Wasserman, E.A. (1993). Comparative cognition: Beginning the second century of the study of animal intelligence. *Psychological Bulletin, 113,* 211–228.

Wasserman, E.A., Kledinger, R.E., & Bhatt, R.S. (1988). Conceptual behavior in pigeons: Categories, subcategories, and pseudocategories. *Journal of Experimental Psychology: Animal Behavior Processes, 14,* 219–324.

Waterman, C.K., Bleubel, M.E., & Waterman, A.S. (1970). Relationship between resolution of the identity crisis and outcomes of previous psychosocial crises. *Proceedings of the Annual Convention of the American Psychological Association, 5*(Pt. I), 467–468.

Watkins, C.E., Campbell, V.L., Nieberding, R., & Hallmark, R. (1995). Contemporary practice of psychological assessment by clinical psychologists. *Professional Psychological Research & Practice, 26,* 54–60.

Watkins, P.C., Vache, K., Verney, S.P., Mathews, A., & Muller, S. (1996). Unconscious mood-congruent memory bias in depression. *Journal of Abnormal Psychology, 105,* 34–31.

Watson, D.L., & Tharp, R.G. (1997). *Self-directed behavior: Self-modification for personal adjustment* (7th ed.). Pacific Grove, CA: Brooks/Cole.

Watson, J.B. (1924). *Behaviorism.* Chicago: University of Chicago Press.

Watson, J.B., & Rayner, R. (1920). Conditioned emotional reactions. *Journal of Experimental Psychology, 3,* 1–14.

Waugh, N., & Norman, D.A. (1960). Primary memory. *Psychological Review, 72,* 89–104.

Wauquier, A., McGrady, A., Aloe, L., Klausner, T., & Collins, B. (1995). Changes in cerebral blood flow velocity associated with biofeedback-assisted relaxation treatment of migraine headaches are specific for the middle cerebral artery. *Headache, 35*(6), 358–362.

Weaver, M.T., & McGrady, A. (1995). A provisional model to predict blood pressure response to biofeedback-assisted relaxation. *Biofeedback and Self-Regulation, 20*(3), 229–240.

Webb, W.B., & Levy, C.M. (1984). Effects of spaced and repeated total sleep deprivation. *Ergonomics, 27,* 45–58.

Wechsler, H., Davenport, A., Dowdall, G., Moeykens, B., & Castillo, S. (1994). Health and behavioral consequences of binge drinking in college. *Journal of the American Medical Association, 272,* 1672–1677.

Wechsler, H., Fulop, M., Padilla, A., Lee, H., & Patrick, K. (1997). Binge drinking among college students: A comparison of California with other states. *Journal of American College Health, 45,* 273–277.

Wedeking, C., Seebeck, T., Bettens, F., & Paepke, A.J. (1995). MHC-dependent mate preferences in humans. *Proceedings of the Royal Society of London, B, 260,* 245–249.

Wehr, T.A., Giesen, H.A., Moul, D.E., Turner, E.H., & Schwartz, P.J. (1995). Suppression of men's responses to seasonal changes in day length by modern artificial lighting. *American Journal of Physiology, 269,* 173–178.

Weinberger, D.R. (1997). The biological basis of schizophrenia: New directions. *Journal of Clinical Psychiatry, 58*(Suppl. 10), 22–27.

Weinstein, R.S., Madison, W., & Kuklinski, M. (1995). Raising expectations in schooling: Obstacles and opportunities for change. *American Educational Research Journal, 32,* 121–160.

Weinstein, R.S., Soule, C.R., Collins, F., Cone, J., Melhorn, M., & Simantocci, K. (1991). Expectations and high school change: Teacher-researcher collaboration to prevent school failure. *American Journal of Community Psychology, 19,* 333–402.

Weinstein, S. (1968). Intensive and extensive aspects of tactile sensitivity as a function of body part, sex, and laterality. In D.R. Kenshalo (Ed.), *The skin senses.* Springfield, IL: Charles C. Thomas.

Weintraub, M.I. (1990). High-impact aerobic exercises and vertigo—A possible cause of vestibulopathy. *New England Journal of Medicine, 323,* 1633.

Weiskrantz, L. (1995). Blindsight–Not an island unto itself. *Current Directions in Psychological Science, 4*, 146–151.

Weiskrantz, L. Barbur, J.L., & Sahraie, A. (1995). Parameters affecting conscious versus unconscious visual discrimination with damage to the visual cortex (VI). *Proceedings of the National Academy of Science, U.S.A., 92*, 6122–6126.

Weiss, B.A., & Reynolds, S. (1992). Generation of neurons and astrocytes from isolated cells of the adult mammalian nervous system. *Science, 255*, 1707–1710.

Weissman, M.M. (1993). The epidemiology of personality disorders: A 1990 update. *Journal of Personality Disorders* (Suppl.), 44–62.

Weissman, M.M., & Olfson, M. (1995). Depression in women: Implications for health care research. *Science, 269*, 799–801.

Wells, G.L. (1993). What do we know about eyewitness identification? *American Psychologist, 48*, 553–571.

Werker, F.J., & Desjardins, R.N. (1995). Listening to speech in the 1st year of life: Experiential influences on phoneme perception. *American Psychological Society, 4*(3), 76–81.

Werker, J.F. (1989). Becoming a native listener. *American Scientist, 77*, 54–59.

Werner, E.E. (1995). Resilience in development. *American Psychological Society, 4*(3), 81–84.

Wheeler, C.G. (1993). 30 years beyond "I have a dream." *Gallup Poll Monthly, 337*, 2–10.

Whisman, M.A., & Kwon, P. (1993). Life stress and dysphoria: The role of self-esteem and hopelessness. *Journal of Personality and Social Psychology, 65*, 1054–1060.

Whitam, F.L., Diamond, M., & Martin, J. (1993). Homosexual orientation in twins: A report on 61 pairs and three triplet sets. *Archives of Sexual Behavior, 22*, 187–206.

White, J., Davison, G.C., & White, M. (1985). *Cognitive distortions in the articulate thoughts of depressed patients.* Unpublished manuscript, University of Southern California, Los Angeles.

Whorf, B.L. (1956). *Language, thought, and reality.* New York: MIT Press–Wiley.

Whyte, W.H. (1956). *The organizational man.* New York: Simon & Schuster.

Wickelgren, W.A. (1979). *Cognitive psychology.* Englewood Cliffs, NJ: Prentice Hall.

Widom, C.S. (1978). A methodology for studying noninstitutionalized psychopaths. In R.D. Hare & D.A. Schalling (Eds.), *Psychopathic behavior: Approaches to research.* Chichester: Wiley.

Wielkiewicz, R.M., & Calvert, C.R.X. (1989). *Training and habilitating developmentally disabled people: An introduction.* Newbury Park, CA: Sage.

Wiens, A.N., & Menustik, C.E. (1983). Treatment outcome and patient characteristics in an aversion therapy program for alcoholism. *American Psychologist, 38*, 1089–1096.

Wierzbicki, M. (1993). *Issues in clinical psychology: Subjective versus objective approaches.* Boston: Allyn & Bacon.

Wiggins, J.S. (Ed.). (1996). *The five-factor model of personality: Theoretical perspectives.* New York: Guilford Press.

Wilcoxon, H.C., Dragoin, W.B., & Kral, P.A. (1971). Illness-induced aversions in rat and quail: Relative salience of visual and gustatory cues. *Science, 171*, 826–828.

Wilder, B.J., & Bruni, J. (1981). *Seizure disorders: A pharmacological approach to treatment.* New York: Raven Press.

Will, G. (1993, April 6). How do we turn children off to the violence caused by TV? Wise up parents. *Philadelphia Inquirer*, p. A1.

Williams, J.E., & Best, D.L. (1990). *Measuring sex stereotypes: A multinational study.* Newbury Park, CA: Sage.

Williams, J.E., & Best, D.L. (1990). *Sex and psyche: Gender and self viewed cross-culturally.* Newbury Park, CA: Sage.

Williams, J.H. (1987). *Psychology of women: Behavior in a biosocial context* (3rd ed.). New York: Norton.

Williams, L. (1989, November 22). Psychotherapy gaining favor among blacks. *New York Times*.

Williams, L.M. (1994). Recall of childhood trauma: A prospective study of women's memories of child sexual abuse. *Journal of Consulting and Clinical Psychology, 62*(6), 1167–1176.

Williams, R.B., Barefoot, J.C., Califf, R.M., Haney, T.L., Saunders, W.B., Pryor, D.B., Hatky, M.A., Siegler, I.C., & Mark, D.B. (1992). Prognostic importance of social and economic resources among medically treated patients with angiographically documented coronary artery disease. *Journal of the American Medical Association, 267*, 520–524.

Williams, T.P., & Sogon, S. (1984). Group composition and conforming behavior in Japanese students. *Japanese Psychological Research, 26*, 231–234.

Willis, S.L. (1985). Towards an educational psychology of the elder adult learner: Intellectual and cognitive bases. In J.E. Birren & K.W. Schaie (Eds.), *Handbook of the psychology of aging* (2nd ed.). New York: Van Nostrand.

Willis, S.L., & Schaie, K.W. (1986). Training the elderly on the ability factors of spatial orientation and inductive reasoning. *Psychology and Aging, 1*, 239–247.

Wilson, G.D. (1987). An ethological approach to sexual deviation. In G.D. Wilson (Ed.), *Variant sexuality: Research and theory* (pp. 84–115). London: Croom Helm.

Wilson, R.S. (1983). The Louisville Twin Study: Developmental synchronies in behavior. *Child Development, 54*, 298–316.

Wilson, T.D., & Schooler, J.W. (1991). Thinking too much: Introspection can reduce the quality of preferences and decisions. *Journal of Personality and Social Psychology, 60*, 181–192.

Wilson, W., & Hunter, R. (1983). Movie-inspired violence. *Psychological Reports, 53*, 435–441.

Wincze, P., Hoon, E.F., & Hoon, P.W. (1978). Multiple measure analysis of women experiencing low sexual arousal. *Behavior Research and Therapy, 16*, 43–49.

Winerip, M. (1998, January 4). Binge nights: The emergency on campus. *Education Life (New York Times* supplement), Section 4A, pp. 28–31, 42.

Wing, H. (1969). *Conceptual learning and generalization.* Baltimore, MD: Johns Hopkins University.

Winn, P. (1995). The lateral hypothalamus and motivated behavior: An old syndrome reassessed and a new perspective gained. *Current Directions in Psychological Science, 4*, 182–187.

Winson, J. (1990). The meaning of dreams. *Scientific American, 263*(5), 94–96.

Winter, D.G. (1973). *The power motive.* New York: Free Press.

Witkin, A.H., Dyk, R.B., Faterson, H.F., Goodenough, D.R., & Karp, S.A. (1962). *Psychological differentiation.* New York: Wiley.

Witt, D.M., & Insel, T.R. (1991). A selective oxytocin antagonist attenuates progesterone facilitation of female sexual behavior. *Endocrinology (Baltimore), 128*, 3269–3276.

Wolberg, L.R. (1977). *The technique of psychotherapy* (3rd ed.). New York: Grune & Stratton.

Wolf, S.S., & Weinberger, D.R. (1996). Schizophrenia: A new frontier in developmental neurobiology. *Israel Journal of Medical Science, 32*(1), 51–55.

Wolpe, J. (1973). *The practice of behavior therapy* (2nd ed.). New York: Pergamon.

Wolpe, J. (1982). *The practice of behavior therapy* (3rd ed.). New York: Pergamon.

Wolpe, J., & Rachman, S. (1960). Psychoanalytic evidence: A critique of Freud's case of little Hans. *Journal of Nervous and Mental Diseases, 130*, 198–220.

Wolpe, P.R. (1990). The holistic heresy: Strategies of ideological challenge in the medical profession. *Social Science & Medicine, 31*(8), 913–923.

Wood, J.M., & Bootzin, R.R. (1990). The prevalence of nightmares and their independence from anxiety. *Journal of Abnormal Psychology, 99*, 64–68.

Wood, J.M., Nezworski, M.T., & Stejskal, W.J. (1996). The comprehensive system for the Rorschach: A critical examination. *Psychological Science, 7*(1), 3–10.

Wood, N.L., & Cowan, N. (1995). The cocktail party phenomenon revisited: Attention and memory in the classic selective listening procedure of Cherry (1953). *Journal of Experimental Psychology: General, 124,* 243–262.

Wood, P.B. (1962). *Dreaming and social isolation.* Unpublished doctoral dissertation, University of South Carolina, Columbia.

Wood, W., Wong., F.Y., & Chachere, J.G. (1991). Effects of media violence on viewers' aggression in unconstrained social interaction. *Psychological Bulletin, 109,* 371–383.

Woodward, K.L., & Springen, K. (1992, August 22). Better than a gold watch. *Newsweek,* p. 71.

Worchel, S., Cooper, J., & Goethals, G.R. (1991). *Understanding social psychology* (5th ed.). Pacific Grove, CA: Brooks/Cole.

Wright, J., Johns, R., Watt, I., Melville, A., & Sheldon, T. (1997). Health effects of obstructive sleep apnea and the effectiveness of continuous positive airways pressure: A systematic review of the research evidence. *British Medical Journal, 314,* 851–853.

Wright, R. (1994). *The moral animal: The new science of evolutionary psychology.* New York: Pantheon.

Wundt, W. (1874). *Principles of physiological psychology.* London: Macmillan.

Wyatt, W.J. (1993, December). Identical twins, emergenesis, and environments. *American Psychologist,* pp. 1294–1295.

Wynn, K. (1995). Infants possess a system of numerical knowledge. *American Psychological Society, 4*(6), 172–177.

Wyrwicka, W. (1988). Imitative behavior: A theoretical view. *Pavlovian Journal of Biological Science, 23,* 125–131.

Wysocki, C.J., & Meredith, M. (1987). *The vomeronasal system.* New York: Wiley.

Xitco, M.J., & Roitblat, H.L. (1996). Object recognition through eavesdropping: Passive echolocation in bottlenose dolphins. *Animal Learning and Behavior, 24*(4), 355–365.

Yahiro, K., Inoue, M., & Nozawa, Y. (1993). An examination of the Social Readjustment Rating Scale by Japanese subjects. *Japanese Journal of Health Psychology, 6*(1), 18–32.

Yalom, I.D. (1995). *The theory and practice of group psychotherapy* (4th ed.). New York: Basic Books.

Yamamoto, K., & Chimbidis, M.E. (1966). Achievement, intelligence, and creative thinking in fifth grade children: A correlational study. *Merrill-Palmer Quarterly, 12,* 233–241.

Yanovski, S.Z. (1993). Binge eating disorder. Current knowledge and future directions. *Obesity Research, 1,* 306–324.

Yerkes, R.M. (1921, 1982). *Psychological examining in the United States Army.* Millwood, NY: Kraus Reprint.

Yerkes, R.M. (1948). Psychological examining in the United States Army. In W. Dennis (Ed.), *Readings in the history of psychology* (pp. 528–540). New York: Appleton-Century-Crofts.

Yoder, J.D., & Kahn, A.S. (1993). Working toward an inclusive psychology of women. *American Psychologist, 48,* 846–850.

York, J.L., & Welte, J.W. (1994). Gender comparisons of alcohol consumption in alcoholic and nonalcoholic populations. *Journal of Studies on Alcohol, 55,* 743–750.

Zajonc, R.B. (1980). Feeling and thinking: Preferences need no inferences. *American Psychologist, 35,* 151–175.

Zajonc, R.B. (1984). On the primacy of affect. *American Psychologist, 39,* 117–129.

Zajonc, R.B., Murphy, S.T., & Inglehart, M. (1989). Feeling and facial efference: Implications of the vascular theory of emotion. *Psychological Review, 96.*

Zametkin, A.J., Nordahl, T.W., Gross, M., & King, A.C. et al. (1990). Cerebral glucose metabolism in adults with hyperactivity of childhood onset. *New England Journal of Medicine, 323,* 1361–1366.

Zaragoza, M.S., & Mitchell, K.J. (1996). Repeated exposure to suggestion and the creation of false memories. *Psychological Science, 7*(5), 294–300.

Zaragoza, M.S., Lane, S.M., Ackil, J.K., & Chambers, K.L. (1997). Confusing real and suggested memories: Source monitoring and eyewitness suggestibility. In N.L. Stein, P.A. Ornstein, B. Tversky, & C. Brainerd (Eds.), *Memory for everyday and emotional events.* Mahwah, NJ: Erlbaum.

Zeiller, B., & Barnoud, S. (1993). Enfants et adolescents criminels: Aspects psychopathologiques. (Delinquent children and adolescents: Psychopathological aspects). *Anal. Psicol., 11,* 87–98.

Zeki, S. (1992). The visual image in mind and brain. *Scientific American, 267*(3), 68–76.

Zeki, S. (1993). *A vision of the brain.* London: Blackwell.

Zigler, E., & Muenchow, S. (1992). *Head Start: The inside story of America's most successful educational experiment.* New York: Basic Books.

Zigler, E., & Styfco, S.J. (1994). Head Start: Criticisms in a constructive context. *American Psychologist, 49,* 127–132.

Zigler, E., & Styfco, S.J. (Eds.). (1993). *Head Start and beyond.* New Haven, CT: Yale University Press.

Zigler, E.F., & Hodapp, R.M. (1991). Behavioral functioning in individuals with mental retardation. *Annual Review of Psychology, 42,* 29–50.Banaji, M.R., & Hardin, C.D. (1996). Automatic stereotyping. *Psychological Science, 7*(3), 136–141.

Zola-Morgan, S.M., & Squire, L.R. (1990). The primate hippocampal formation: Evidence for a time-limited role in memory storage. *Science, 250*(4978), 288–290.

Zucker, R.A., & Gomberg, E.S.L. (1990). Etiology of alcoholism reconsidered: The case for a biopsychosocial process. *American Psychologist, 41,* 783–793.

Zuckerman, M. (1995). Good and bad humors: Biochemical basis of personality and its disorders. *Psychological Science, 6,* 325–332.

Zuckerman, M., Miyake, K., & Elkin, C.S. (1995). Effects of attractiveness and maturity of face and voice on interpersonal impression. *Journal of Research in Personality, 29,* 253–272.

Zwislocki, J.J. (1981). Sound analysis in the ear: A history of discoveries. *American Scientist, 245,* 184–192.

PHOTO CREDITS

NAME INDEX

Wilson, D., 557
Wilson, G.D., 524
Wilson, G.T., 353, 550, 551, 552
Wilson, M., 17
Wilson, M.I., 408
Wilson, R.S., 83
Wilson, T.D., 285
Wilson, W., 412
Wincze, P., 523
Winerip, M., 597
Wing, H., 336
Winn, P., 57
Winnik-Berland, N., 353
Winocur, G., 262
Winter, D.G., 365
Witherspoon, 236
Witkin, A.H., 131
Witt, D.M., 76
Wittchen, H., 514, 535
Wittlinger, R.P., 237
Wlodkowski, R.J., 327
Wolberg, L.R., 545
Wolf, S.S., 531
Wolkenstein, B., 188
Wolpe, J., 188, 203
Wolpe, P.R., 550, 551
Wolz, J.P., 290
Wonder, S., 449
Wong, F.Y., 360
Wood, J.M., 160
Wood, L., 358

Wood, L.A., 461
Wood, N.L., 229
Wood, P.B., 157
Wood, W., 360
Woodward, K.L., 432
Woodyard, E., 324
Woolf, V., 310
Worchel, S., 593
Word, L.E., 603
Works, J., 239
Worthley, J.S., 237
Wortman, C.B., 483
Wozney, K., 521
Wright, R., 10, 17
Wright, S.C., 360
Wrightsman, L., 590
Wundt, W., 12–13
Wu-Peng, X.S., 350
Wyatt, W.J., 83
Wynn, K., 401
Wypij, D., 356
Wyrwicka, W., 393
Wysocki, C.J., 117

Xitco, M.J., 290

Yahiro, K., 478
Yalom, I.D., 555
Yamamoto, K., 336
Yandell, B., 593
Yanovski, S.Z., 353

Yaw, A., 524
Yerkes, R.M., 326
Yoder, J.D., 25
Yong, M., 596
York, J.L., 168
Young, A.C., 53
Young, K., 571
Youniss, J., 418
Yu, S.M., 391
Yudkin, J., 324
Yuzda, E., 533

Zajonc, R.B., 97, 372, 373
Zametkin, A.J., 60
Zane, N., 571
Zaragoza, M.S., 241
Zarcone, V., 158
Zautra, A.J., 480
Zeki, S., 106
Zelkowitz, P., 526
Zhang, Y., 350
Zigler, E., 327, 334, 511
Zimmerman, R.R., 121, 358
Zubek, J., 325
Zucker, R.A., 168
Zuckerman, M., 459, 584
Zuroff, D.C., 554
Zusho, H., 117
Zwislocki, J.J., 114

SUBJECT INDEX

Anger, 369–70
  chronic, 492
  confrontation and, 485–86
  gender differences in, 377
Anger stage of dying, 434
Anima, 448
Animal behavior genetics, 81
Animal-rights groups, 36
Animals
  cognitive learning in, 217–18
  consciousness in, 290
  ethics in research on nonhuman, 35–36
  language and thought in, 289–93
Animus, 448
Anonymity, deindividuation and, 602
Anorexia nervosa, 352–54
Anosmia, 117
Anterior pituitary, 76
Anthromorphism, 289
Anthropologist, 11
Antianxiety drugs, 562, 564
Antidepressant drugs, 562, 563–64
Antigens, 492
Antimanic drugs, 562
Antiobsessional drugs, 562
Antipanic drugs, 562
Antipsychotic drugs, 562, 563
Antisocial personality disorder, 527–28
Anvil (ear), 112
Anxiety
  ability to remember and, 250
  desensitization therapy for, 188–89
  in Horney's theory, 450
  mathematics, 330
  separation, 406
Anxiety disorders, 514–18, 534
  causes of, 517–18
  stress-inoculation therapy for, 553
  in women, 535
Anxiety Disorders Association of America, 561
Aphasias, 65
Apnea, 160
Apparent movement, 137
Applied psychology, 37
Approach/approach conflict, 481, 482
Approach/avoidance conflict, 482
Aptitude, 305
Arbitrary inference, 513
Archetypes, 447–48
Artificial alterations in consciousness, 161–63
  hypnosis, 123, 149, 162–63
  meditation, 161–62
  sensory deprivation, 161
Asian students, academic performance of, 330–32
Assessment
  of mental retardation, 334–35
  personality, 465–69
    with objective tests, 466–68
    by observation, 466
    personal interview for, 465–66
    with projective tests, 468–69
Assimilators, cultural, 596
Associates degrees in psychology, career opportunities and, 37
Association, free, 542–43
Association areas, 58
Association for Children's Mental Health, 561
Association neurons. *See* Interneurons

Asylums, 506
Atherosclerosis, 492
Atropine, 53
Attachment
  children of dual-career families and, 427–28
  defined, 406
  development of, 406–7
Attention
  focused, 127
  information processing and, 228–29
  maintaining, 592
  strained versus effortless, 149
Attention-deficit/hyperactivity disorder (ADHD), 6, 532–33, 564
Attitudes, 586–95
  attitude change, 592–95
  behaviors and, 587
  toward death, 433–34
  defined, 586
  development of, 588
  nature of, 586–88
  prejudice and discrimination, 588–92
Attraction
  interpersonal, 584–86
  reward theory of, 585–86
Attractiveness
  physical, 419, 584–85
  sexual, 355–56
  stereotype of, 580–81
Attribution, 581–84
  biases in, 582–83
  across cultures, 583–84
Attribution errors
  fundamental, 583
  ultimate, 589
Attribution theory, 582
Audience
  attitude change and, 593
  imaginary, 415
Audiotapes, self-help, 97, 98
Auditory nerve, 94, 95, 113, 114
Auditory registers, 227–28
Authoritarian parents, 408
Authoritarian personality, 589
Authoritative parents, 408
Autistic disorder, 533
Autobiographical memory, 243–45
Autoimmune disorders, classical conditioning to treat, 189
Autokinetic illusion, 137
Autonomic nervous system, 71–74
Autonomous work group, 608
Autonomy, 407
  shame and doubt versus, 407, 452
Availability heuristic, 284
Aversion, taste, 189–91
Aversive conditioning, 551–52
Avoidance/avoidance conflict, 481–82
Avoidance training, 195–96
Avoidant personality disorder, 526
Awareness
  gender-role, 410
  self-awareness in animals, 290
Axon, 47
  myelinated, 47, 48
  spinal cord, 67–68

Babbling stage, 402–3
Bachelor's degrees in psychology, career and, 36

Backward conditioning, 206
Baldness, male-pattern, 80
Barbiturates, 170, 177
Bargaining stage of dying, 434
Basal age, 312
Basal forebrain, 252
Basic trust, development of, 406
Basilar membrane, 113, 114
Bats, hearing of, 113
Battered women, 358
Bayley Scales of Infant Development, 315
Beauty, 584
Beck's cognitive therapy, 554
Bee communication, 291
Behavior(s)
  adaptive, 85–86
  attitudes and, 587
  attributions explaining, 582
  biological basis of. *See* Biological basis of behavior
  gender differences in, reporting, 331
  genetics and, 81–84
  health, 518
  helping, 602–4
  heroic, 577–78, 583
  operant, 191
  organizational, 607–8
  reflexive, 184, 185–91, 209–10
  sex-typed, 410, 411
  superstitious, 197
Behavioral couple therapy, 556
Behavioral geneticists, 4
Behavior contracting, 552
Behavior genetics, 78–87
  animal, 81
  defined, 78
  evolution and, 84–85
  evolutionary psychology, 16–17, 78, 85–86, 152
  genetics. *See* Genetics
  social implications of, 86–87
Behaviorism, 14–15
Behavior modification, 218
Behavior tendencies, 587
Behavior therapies, 549–52, 565
  classical conditioning, 550–52
  effectiveness of, 559
  modeling, 550
  operant conditioning, 550
Beliefs. *See also* Culture(s)
  evaluative, 587
  irrational, 553–54
  normative, 598
  pain sensation and, 122
Bell Curve: Intelligence and Class Structure in American Life, The (Herrnstein and Murray), 328
Bereavement, extreme stress from, 495–96. *See also* Death and dying
Beta endorphin, 77, 121
Beta waves, 69
Bias(es)
  in attribution, 582–83
  confirmation, 284–85
  cultural, avoiding, 33
  experimenter, 30
  group tests and, 314–15
  in IQ tests, 319–20
  observer, 26, 27

response acquisition in, 198–99
  as selective, 189–91
  as therapy, 550–52
Classification schemes, ability to grasp complex, 400
Classroom, self-fulfilling prophecy in, 581
Claustrophobia, 187
Client-centered therapy, 545–47, 565
Clinical depression, 510
Clinical psychologists, 37
Clinical psychology, 5–6
Clinical settings, careers in, 37–38
Cloning, 86
Closure, perceptual organization based on, 126
Coca-Cola Company, 174
Cocaine, 53, 174–75, 177
Cochlea, 113
Cochlear implants, 115
Cocktail-party phenomenon, 229
Code of ethics, APA, 35
Coercion, sexual, 361–62
Cognition, 258–301
  building blocks of thought, 260–68
    concepts, 260, 263–68, 290
    images, 260, 262–63
    language, 260–62
  decision making, 281–86
  defined, 259
  language and thought, 286–93
    nonhuman, 289–93
  problem solving, 268–81
    becoming better at, 278–81
    interpretation of problems, 270–72
    obstacles to, 275–78
    producing and evaluating solutions, 272–75
  social, 578–86
    attribution, 581–84
    impression formation, 578–81
    interpersonal attraction, 584–86
Cognitive abilities
  estrogen and, 77
  gender differences in, 329–30
  twin studies of, 83
Cognitive-behavioral model of psychological disorders, 507–8
Cognitive behavior therapists, 553
Cognitive development
  in adolescence, 400, 415
  in adulthood, 428
    late adulthood, 432–33
  in infancy and childhood, 398–401
    television viewing and, 412
Cognitive dissonance theory, 594–95
Cognitive distortions, 513–14
Cognitive exercise, 428
Cognitive learning, 210–18
  insight and learning sets, 213–15
  latent learning and cognitive maps, 210–13
  learning by observing, 215–17
  in nonhumans, 217–18
Cognitive map, 212–13
Cognitive marital therapy, 556
Cognitive misers, 579–80, 589–90
Cognitive perspective on anxiety disorders, 517
Cognitive psychology, 16. *See also* Cognition
  development of, 260
Cognitive-social learning theories, 443, 462–65
Cognitive sources of prejudice, 589–90
Cognitive style, perception and, 131–32
Cognitive theory of emotion, 371

Cognitive therapies, 553–54, 559, 565
  Beck's cognitive therapy, 554
  defined, 553
  effectiveness of, 559
  rational-emotive therapy (RET), 553–54
  stress-inoculation therapy, 553
Cohabitation, 422–23
Cohesiveness of group, effectiveness and, 605–6
Cohort, defined, 389
Cohort differences, 389
Collective unconscious, 447
Collectivism, 363
  aggression and, 362
  conformity and, 598–99
  emotion and, 378
  helping behavior and, 604
College
  binge drinking on campuses, 598
  coping with stress at, 485
Color(s)
  primary, 107
  properties of, 106, 107
Color afterimage, 109
Colorblindness, 106, 108–9
Color constancy, 130
Color vision, 106–10
  in other species, 110
  theories of, 107–10
Combat
  extreme stress of, 496
  post-traumatic stress disorder (PTSD) and, 496, 497
Common sense, 10
Communication
  in animals, 290–91
  of emotion, 373–76
    nonverbal, 373–76
    verbal, 373
  responsibility and, 608
Communication model of persuasion, 593–94
Community mental-health centers, 567
Compensation, 449
Compensatory model, 282
Competence, social, 306
Competency to stand trial, 529
Competitiveness, 364
Complementary afterimages, 109
Complementary traits, 585
Complex cells, 128
Compliance, 599–600
  obedience and, 600–601
Componential intelligence, 308, 335
Compromise
  in conflict resolution, 424
  direct coping by, 486
Compulsions, 516–17
Computational neuroscience, 127–28
Computerized axial tomography (CAT or CT) scanning, 70
Computer simulation, 260
  of problem solving, 275
Concentration of flow state, 149
Concentration techniques of pain reduction, 123
Concepts, 260, 263–68
  fuzzy, 265–66
  nonhuman formation of, 290
Concrete operational stage, 399–400
Conditional positive regard, 456, 546
Conditioned food aversion, 189–91

Conditioned response (CR), 186–87, 188, 198, 199, 201
Conditioned stimulus (CS), 186–87, 188, 198, 199, 201
Conditioning, 14–15, 184. *See also* Classical conditioning; Operant conditioning
  aversive, 551–52
  backward, 206
  cultural lessons through, 596
Conductive hearing loss, 114–15
Cones (eye), 100–102
  color vision and, 106–10
  visual adaptation and, 102–4
Confidence, stress and, 483
Confirmation bias, 284–85
Conflict
  defined, 481
  stress from, 481–82
  types of, 481–82
Conflict resolution, steps for, 424–25
Conformity, 596–99
  across cultures, 598–99
  defined, 597
  gender differences in, 25
  prejudice and, 590
Confrontation, direct coping by, 484–86
Connections, tendency to see, 284
Conscientiousness, 459
Consciousness, 146–81
  in animals, 290
  artificial alterations in, 161–63
    hypnosis, 123, 149, 162–63
    meditation, 161–62
    sensory deprivation, 161
  defined, 147, 148
  drug-altered, 163–78
    depressants, 165–71, 177
    hallucinogens and marijuana, 175–78
    stimulants, 77, 171–75
    substance use, abuse, and dependence, 163, 164–65
  natural variations in, 148–60
    daydreaming and fantasy, 150
    sleep and dreaming, 150–60
    waking, 148
Consensus of others' similar behavior, 582
Conservation, principle of, 400
Consistency
  of behavior, 582
  of personality, 461–62
Constancy(ies)
  gender, 410
  perceptual, 128–30
Consumer Reports study of effectiveness of psychotherapy, 558
Contact
  need for, 121, 358
  reducing prejudice through, 591–92
Content of IQ tests, criticism of, 319–20
Content validity, 317–18
Contextual intelligence, 308, 309–10
Contingencies, 206–9
  in classical conditioning, 206–7
  in operant conditioning, 207–9
Contingency model of leader effectiveness, 606–7
Continuity, perceptual organization based on, 126
Continuous reinforcement, 207, 208
Contracting, behavior, 552
Contrapreparedness, 189

Direct coping, 484–86
Direct observation, 466
Discrepancy, attitude change and, 593–94
Discrimination, 203–4
    in classical conditioning, 203–4
    defined, 588
    frustration over, 481
    in operant conditioning, 204
    pitch, 114
    racism, 590–91
    sources of, 590
    against women in psychology, 18, 19
Disengagement, 432
Disorganized schizophrenia, 530
Displacement, 488, 489, 518
Display rules, 380
Dissociative amnesia, 520–21
Dissociative disorders, 520–22
Dissociative fugue, 521
Dissociative identity disorder, 521
Dissonance, cognitive, 594–95
Distal stimulus, 127
Distance, personal, 376
Distance cues, 139
Distance perception, 133–36
Distinctiveness of behavior, 582
Distortions, cognitive, 513–14
Distractions, memory ability and, 250
Distractor studies, 231
Divergent thinking, 279
Diversity, human, 8, 18–25
    mental abilities and, 329–32
        academic performance, culture and,
            330–32
        gender, 329–30
    psychology and, 23–25
    research methods and, 32–33
Divorce, 425–26
    cohabitation and, 422
    extreme stress from, 495
Divorce rate, 425
DNA (deoxyribonucleic acid), 79
Doctoral psychologists, career opportunities for,
    37
Dolly (sheep), cloning of, 86
Domestic violence, 358–59, 360
Dominant gene, 79–80
Door-in-the-face effect, 600
Dopamine, 51, 52, 53, 71
    antipsychotic drugs to block receptors for, 563
    nicotine and increase in, 173
    schizophrenia and, 51, 53, 531
Double-blind procedure, 165
"Downers," 170
Down syndrome, 79, 334
Dreams, 155–58
Dress, culture and, 595
Drive
    defined, 347
Drive-reduction theory, 347
Drives
    primary, 348–56
        hunger, 131, 348–54
        sex, 20, 354–56
    unconscious, 347
Drug abuse
    criminal activity among teens and, 421
    mental health resources for, 560
Drug-altered consciousness, 163–78
    depressants, 53, 158, 165–71, 177

hallucinogens and marijuana, 175–78
    stimulants, 77, 171–75
    substance use, abuse, and dependence, 163,
        164–65
Drugs
    methods of studying effects of, 164–65
    synapses and, 52–53
Drug therapies, 562–64, 570
    psychotherapy versus, 5–6
DSM-IV. See Diagnostic and Statistical Manual of
    Mental Disorders (DSM-IV)
Dual-career family, 427–28
Dysthymia, 510, 512

Ear, 112–13
Eardrum, 112
"Easy" babies, 393
Eating abusers, mental health resources for, 560
Eating disorders, 352–54, 419
Echolalia, 533
Eclecticism, 559
Economists, 11
Economy, prejudice and, 589
Ecstasy (MDMA), 173
ECT (electroconvulsive therapy), 565–66
Education
    bilingual, 264, 405
    normative, 598
    sex, 414
EEG (electroencephalograph), 69–70
EEG imaging, 70
Effect, law of, 192–93
Efferent neurons. See Motor (efferent) neurons
Ego, 444, 445
Egocentricity of preschool children, 399
"Egocentrism of formal operations," 415
Ego ideal, 445
Eidetic imagery, 247
Ejaculation
    first, 413–14
    premature, 523
Elaborative rehearsal, 233–34, 235
Elderly, sleep patterns in the, 154. See also Late
    adulthood
Electra complex, 446, 453
Electroconvulsive therapy (ECT), 565–66
Electroencephalograph (EEG), 69–70
    EEG imaging, 70
Electromagnetic spectrum, 100
Elevation, 134
Elimination, tactic of, 278
Elimination-by-aspects tactic, 283
Embarrassment, helping behavior and, 604
Emblems, 380–81
Embryo, 391
Emergency, bystander effect in, 602–4
Emotion(s), 367–81. See also Motivation
    basic emotional experiences, 368–70
    culture and, 370, 378–81
    defined, 346
    expression of, 373–76
    facial expression of, 370, 372–73, 375,
        379–81
    frontal lobe function in, 60
    gender differences in, 376–78
    hemispheric specialization and, 63–64
    hunger drive and, 350
    limbic system and, 67
    negative expressed, 532
    pain sensation and, 122

problem solving and, 276
    theories of, 370–73
Emotional deprivation, 528
Emotional labor, 378
Emotional stability, 458, 459
Empathy, 376
    helping behavior and, 603–4
Empathy training, 556
Employment. See Work
Empty chair technique, 548–49
Encoding
    in long-term memory, 234–35
    in short-term memory, 231
Encounter groups, 548
Endocrine glands, 74–78
Endocrine system, 46, 68, 74–78
Endorphins, 51, 52, 53
    beta endorphin, 77, 121
    nicotine and increase in, 172–73
    pain sensation and, 123
English language
    English only education, 264
    male-domination of, 288
Environment
    heredity versus (nature vs. nurture), 8, 78,
        356, 388–89
    home, personality and, 460
    intelligence and, 324–26
    neuron growth and, 55
    schizophrenia and, 531–32
Epidemiologists, 534
Epilepsy, corpus callosum and, 60
Epinephrine, 77–78
Episodic memory, 234, 237
Epithelium, olfactory, 116
Equity, 586
Erectile disorder, 522–23
Error
    in decision making, potential for, 285
    fundamental attribution, 583
    ultimate attribution, 589
Esalen Institute, 547–49
Escapism, 497
ESP, 99
Esprit de corps, 365
Estrogen, 76, 77
Estrogen replacement therapy, 430
Ethics
    ethical dilemmas in genetics, 86–87
    psychology and, 33–36
Ethnic identity, 23
Ethnicity. See also African Americans
    defined, 23
    IQ and, 326–28
    IQ tests and minorities, 319–20
Ethnic minority issues, 24
Evaluative beliefs, 587
Event-related potential (ERP), 70
Evoked potential (EP), 70
Evolution, 84–85
    facial expression and, 375
    pheromone communication and, 117
    taste aversion and, 190–91
    theory of, 12, 84–85
Evolutionary psychology, 16–17, 78, 85–86, 152
Exaggeration, 488, 489
Exchange, reward theory of attraction and,
    585–86
Excitation, threshold of, 49
Excitement phase of sexual response cycle, 354

emotion and, 378
helping behavior and, 604
Individuality in late adulthood, 432
Individual needs, adjustment accounting for, 497
Individual perspective on psychological disorders, 504
Induced movement, illusion of, 139
Industrial/organizational (I/O) psychology, 6–7, 607–8
Industry versus inferiority, 409, 452
Infancy and childhood, 396–413
  development in, 396–413
    cognitive development, 398–401
    language development, 402–5
    moral development, 401–2
    motor development, 396–98
    physical development, 396
    social development, 405–10
    television and, 410–13
  IQ and intervention programs in, 327
  malnutrition in, IQ scores and, 324
Infantile amnesia, 244
Inference
  arbitrary, 513
  schemata and, 579
Inferiority, industry versus, 409, 452
Inferiority complex, 449
Influence, social, 595–601
  compliance, 599–600
  conformity, 25, 590, 596–99
  cultural assimilators, 596
  cultural influence, 595–96
  hunger drive and, 350
  in mood disorders, 514
  obedience, 34–35, 600–601
Information processing
  initial processing, 228–29
  sequence of, 228
Information-processing model, 226
Information-processing view of memory, 226–45, 260
  long-term memory, 234–45
    autobiographical memory, 243–45
    encoding, 234–35
    implicit memory, 235–37
    language and, 286
    storage and retrieval in, 237–43
  sensory registers, 226–29, 245
    initial processing, 228–29
    sequence, 228
    visual and auditory registers, 227–28
  short-term memory, 229–34, 245
    capacity of, 229–31
    elaborative rehearsal, 233–34, 235
    encoding, 231
    retention and retrieval in, 231–32
    rote rehearsal, 232–33, 244
Information retrieval, 272
Inheritance, polygenic, 80. See also Genetics
Initial processing, 228–29
Initiative versus guilt, 407, 452
Inner working model, attachment and, 407
Insanity, 528
Insanity defense, 529
Insight, 213–15
  creative problem solving and, 279–80
  experiential intelligence and, 309
  learning sets and, 214–15
  in psychoanalysis, 544

Insight therapies, 542–49, 565
  client-centered therapy, 545–47, 565
  effectiveness of, 559
  Gestalt therapy, 547–49, 565
  psychoanalysis, 14, 37, 444, 454, 542–45, 565
  recent developments in, 549
Insomnia, 159–60
Instincts, 13, 347
  in psychoanalysis, 444
  sexual, 444, 445
Institute of Canadian Advertisers, 98
Institutionalization, 566–70
  alternative forms of treatment, 568
  deinstitutionalization, 506, 567–68
Institutional racism, 590
Instrumental conditioning. See Operant conditioning
Insulin, 75, 351
Integrity versus despair, 453
Intellectualization, 488, 489
Intelligence, 302–43
  bodily-kinesthetic, 310
  characteristics of, layperson versus expert views of, 306
  componential, 308, 335
  contextual, 308, 309–10
  creativity and, 336–38
  crystallized, 307
  defining, 305–6
  determinants of, 322–29
    environment, 324–26
    heredity, 322–24
    IQ debate, 326–29
  experiential, 308, 309
  extremes of, 332–36
    giftedness, 329, 335–36
    mental retardation, 329–30, 332–35, 533
  fluid, 307
  general, 311
  interpersonal, 310
  intrapersonal, 310
  linguistic, 310
  logical-mathematical, 310
  mental abilities and human diversity, 329–32
    academic performance, culture and, 330–32
    gender, 329–30
  musical, 310
  practical, 306
  spatial, 308–10
  theories of, 307–11
  verbal, 306
Intelligence quotient (IQ), 311
  criticisms of IQ tests, 319–22
  debate over, 326–29
  scores
    academic performance and, 320–21
    brain activity and, 71
    prenatal nutrition and, 324, 325
    race and, 25
    twin studies of intelligence and, 322–24
    use of, 320
  success and, 320–22
  television viewing and, 412
Intelligence tests, 305, 311–22
  criticisms of IQ tests, 319–22
  group tests, 314–15
  performance and culture-fair tests, 315–16, 319
  reliability of, 316–17

Stanford-Binet Intelligence Scale, 311–12, 313, 318, 319, 330
  validity of, 317–19
  Wechsler Intelligence Scales, 312–14, 317, 330
Intensification of facial expression, 380
Interaction styles, gender differences in, 411
Interference, long-term memory and, 238–39
Interference theory, 231–32
Intermittent pairing, 199
Intermittent reinforcement, 207
Internal attribution, 583
Internal locus of control, 462–63
International Association for Suicide Prevention, 560
International Society for Traumatic Stress Studies, 561
Interneurons, 48, 101, 104
Interpersonal attraction, 584–86
Interpersonal intelligence, 310
Interpretation of problems, 270–72
Intervention, 569
Intervention programs, IQ and, 327
Interview, personal, 465–66
  structured, 466
  unstructured, 465
Intimacy, interpersonal attraction and, 586
Intimacy versus isolation, 422, 452
Intimate partnerships, 422–23
  ending, 425–26
  parenthood and, 423–25
  resolving conflicts in, 424–25
Intonation, 403
Intrapersonal intelligence, 310
Intrinsic motivation, 348
Introspection, objective, 12–13
Introverts, 448, 458
Invulnerability, teenage sense of, 414, 415
Ions, 48, 49
IQ. See Intelligence quotient (IQ)
Iris, 99–100
Irony, 288–89
Irrational beliefs, rational-emotive therapy for, 553–54
Irrational individuals, 448
Isolation, intimacy versus, 422, 452

James-Lange theory of emotion, 370–71, 372–73
Japanese culture
  attribution in, 583–84
  collectivist orientation of, 378
  conformity in, 599
  management style and, 607
Jealousy, as adaptive, 17
Jet lag, circadian cycles and, 151
Jews, violence against, 589
Job performance, IQ and, 321
Just noticeable difference (jnd), 96
Just-world hypothesis, 583, 590

Kinesthetic sense, 119, 120
Knowledge, tacit, 309, 321
Koko (gorilla), 292–93
Korsakoff's syndrome, 168, 253

La belle indifference, 519
Lactate, blood, 162
Lana (chimpanzee), 292
Language
  body, 375–76, 571

as building block of thought, 260–62
emotions and, 370
figurative, 287–89
hemispheric specialization and, 60, 63
  gender differences in, 65
long-term memory and, 286
male-domination of, debate over, 288
sign, 261, 264
  chimp language studies and, 291–93
  deaf babies' babbling of, 402–3
thought and, 286–93
  nonhuman, 289–93
Language acquisition device, 404
Language development
  critical periods in, 405
  in infancy and childhood, 402–5
  second language (bilingualism), 404–5
  theories of, 404
Late adulthood, 430–35
  cognitive changes, 432–33
  facing end of life, 433–35
  physical changes, 430–31
  social development, 431–32
Latency period, 446
Latent content of dreams, 156
Latent learning, 210–13
  of cognitive maps, 212–13
Laudanum, 171
Law of effect, 192–93
Leadership
  across cultures, 607
  group decision making and, 606–7
  styles, 606
Learned helplessness, 197–98
  stress and, 483
Learning, 182–223
  classical conditioning, 184, 185–91, 209–10
    elements of, 186–87
    in humans, 187–89
    Pavlov's conditioning experiments, 185–86
    as selective, 189–91
  cognitive, 210–18
    insight and learning sets, 213–15
    latent learning and cognitive maps, 210–13
    learning by observing, 215–17
    in nonhumans, 217–18
  comparing classical and operant conditioning, 198–204, 209–10
    extinction and spontaneous recovery, 201–3
    generalization and discrimination, 203–4
    response acquisition, 198–200
  contingencies, 206–9
    in classical conditioning, 206–7
    in operant conditioning, 207–9
  cooperative techniques of, 591
  culture and, 595–96
  defined, 184
  new learning based on original, 204–6
  operant conditioning, 184, 189–98
    elements of, 192–93
    learned helplessness, 197–98, 483
    punishment, 194–96
    as selective, 196
    superstitious behavior, 197
    Thorndike's conditioning experiments, 192
    types of reinforcement, 193–94
  social, 596
  social learning theory, 215–17, 412
Learning sets, 214–15

Learning theories
  behavior therapies based on, 550
  cognitive-behavioral model of psychological disorders and, 507–8
  cognitive-social, 443, 462–65
Left visual field, 105
Lens (eye), 100
Leptin, 350
"Levelers," perception by, 132
Libido, 445–46
Lie detector, 374
Life events, as source of stress, 477–78, 479
Life expectancy, gender differences in, 430
Life functioning
  abnormal behavior and, 504–5
  agoraphobia and, 515
Life space, shrinkage in late adulthood of, 431–32
Life span
  night's sleep across, 154
  suicide rate across, 511
Life span development, 386–439
  adolescence, 413–22
    cognitive changes in, 415
    personality and social development of, 416–18
    physical changes in, 413–15
    problems of, 418–22
  adulthood, 422–30
    "change of life," 429–30
    cognitive changes, 428, 432–33
    facing end of life, 433–35
    late, 430–35
    love, partnerships, and parenting, 422–26
    personality changes, 428–29
    physical changes, 430–31
    social development, 431–32
    world of work, 426–28
  developmental psychology, 388
    methods in, 389–90
    recognition of, 24
  infancy and childhood, 396–413
    cognitive development, 398–401
    language development, 402–5
    moral development, 401–2
    motor development, 396–98
    physical development, 396
    social development, 405–10
    television and children, 410–13
  newborn baby, 392–96
    perceptual abilities, 394–96
    temperament, 393–94
    prenatal development, 390–92
Life-span psychologists, 4
Light, 100
Light adaptation, 103
Limbic system, 64–67, 355
Linear perspective, 133
Linguistic intelligence, 310
Linguistic relativity hypothesis, 286–87, 289
Listening skills, conflict resolution and, 424
Lithium, 564
"Little Albert," 14–15, 188
"Little Hans," 27
Loafing, social, 605
Lobotomy, prefrontal, 566
Locus of control, 462–63
Logical-mathematical intelligence, 310
Longitudinal study, 389, 390
Long-term memory (LTM), 234–45

autobiographical memory, 243–45
encoding, 234–35
implicit memory, 235–37
language and, 286
storage and retrieval in, 237–43
Long-term potentiation (LTP), 55
Losses, frustration over, 481. See also Memory loss
Loudness of sound, 111
Love, 422, 586
Lowball procedure, 599–600
Lucy (chimpanzee), 292
Lymphocytes, 492
Lynchings, 589, 601
Lysergic acid diethylamide (LSD), 175, 177
  synapses and, 52–53

Macroelectrode techniques, 69
Magnetic resonance imaging (MRI), 70
Magnetic source imaging (MSI), 70
Magnetoencephalography (MEG), 70
Magnification, 513
Mainstreaming, 334
Maintenance rehearsal. See Rote rehearsal
Major depressive disorder, 510–12
Male fertility, 413–14
Male menopause, 430
Male-pattern baldness, 80
Malnutrition during infancy, IQ scores and, 324
Management style, 607
Mania, 512
Manic depression, lithium for, 564
Manifest content of dreams, 156
Manipulation motive, 357–58
MAO inhibitors, 564
Marijuana, 53, 163, 176–78
Marital status, psychological disorder and, 535
Marital therapy. See Couple therapy
Marriage, 422–23
  child rearing and satisfaction in, 424
  ending. See Divorce
Masculine, use of term, 20–21
Masculinity-femininity scale on MMPI-2, 468
Masking, 228, 380
Masochism, sexual, 524
Mass media, as source of attitudes, 588
Master, 364
Master's graduates in psychology, career opportunities for, 37
Mate selection, adaptive behaviors in, 85–86
Mathematical skill, culture and, 330–32
Mathematics anxiety, 330
Maturation, 397
MDMA (Ecstasy), 173
Means-end analysis, 274
Medications. See Drug therapies; Psychoactive drugs
Meditation, 161–62
Medium, attitude change and choice of, 593
Medulla, 56, 61, 67
  adrenal, 77
Melancholia, 505–6
Melatonin, 75, 151
Mellaril (thioridazine), 563
Memory, 224–57
  alcohol and, 168
  biological bases of, 252–54
  cultural influences on, 245–46
  episodic, 234, 237
  explicit, 235

extraordinary, 247–48
eyewitness, 240–41
flashbulb, 246–47
improving, 248–52
information-processing model of, 226
limbic system and, 66–67
long-term (LTM), 234–45
 autobiographical memory, 243–45
 encoding, 234–35
 implicit memory, 235–37
 language and, 286
 storage and retrieval in, 237–43
marijuana use and, 176
perceptual constancy and, 129
reconstructive, 239
recovered, 241
schemata and, 579
semantic, 234, 237
sensory registers, 226–29, 245
 initial processing, 228–29
 visual and auditory registers, 227–28
short-term (SLT), 229–34, 245
 capacity of, 229–31
 elaborative rehearsal, 233–34, 235
 encoding, 231
 retention and retrieval in, 231–32
 rote rehearsal, 232–33, 244
Memory loss, 252–54, 522. *See also* Amnesia
 Alzheimer's and, 433
Menarche, 413
Menopause, 429–30
 male, 430
Menstrual cycle, ovulatory phase of, 77
Menstrual synchronicity, pheromones and, 117
Menstruation, 413
Mental abilities. *See* Intelligence
Mental age, 311, 312
Mental disorders. *See* Psychological disorders
Mental Health Counseling Hotline, 560
Mental Health Help Line, 561
Mental Health Info, 561
Mental-health professionals, perspective on psychological disorders, 504
Mental-health resources, 560–61
Mental imagery, memory improvement and, 251
Mental representations, 398–99
Mental retardation, 329–30, 332–35
 autism and, 533
 levels of, 333
Mercaptan, 115
Mescaline, 175
Mesmerism, 162
Metabolism
 thyroid gland and, 74
 weight loss and, 351–52
Metaphor, 288–89
Methamphetamines, 173
Microelectrode recording techniques, 69
Midbrain, 56, 61, 67
Middles Ages, supernatural view
 of abnormal behavior in,
 506
Midlife crisis, 428
Midlife transition, 429
Mild retardation, 333
Milner's syndrome, 253
Milwaukee Project, 327
Mind of a Mnemonist, The (Luria), 247
Mind versus body debate, 8
Minimization, 513

Minnesota Multiphasic Personality Inventory
 (MMPI), 467–68
Minorities, IQ tests and, 319–20. *See also* Ethnicity
"Minor tranquilizers," 170
Mr. Rogers (TV), 412
Mistrust, trust versus, 406, 452
MMPI (Minnesota Multiphasic Personality Inventory), 467–68
Mnemonics, 251
Mnemonists, 248
Mob behavior, 601–2
Modeling
 of aggression, 360
 as therapy, 550
Moderate retardation, 333
Money, as secondary reinforcer, 205–6
Monoamine oxidase inhibitors (MAO inhibitors), 564
Monoaural (single-ear) cues, 135
Monochromats, 108, 110
Monocular cues, 133–35
Mood, helping behavior and, 604
Mood disorders, 510–14, 534
 causes of, 512–14
Moral development, 23
 antisocial personality and, 528
 forms of moral reasoning, 603
 in infancy and childhood, 401–2
Moratorium, identity, 417
Morphemes, 261
Morphine, 53, 171
Mother(s). *See also* Parent-child relationships;
 Parents
 concepts of, 267–68
 sense of smell in, 118
Motherese, 403
Motion
 sensations of, 119–20
 stroboscopic, 137
Motion parallax, 134–35
Motion sickness, 119
Motivation, 344–67. *See also* Emotion(s); Motives
 of altruism, 603
 extrinsic, 348
 intrinsic, 348
 limbic system and, 67
 memory improvement and, 250
 pain sensation and, 122
 perception and, 131
 perspectives on, 347–48
 primary drives, 348–56
  hunger, 131, 348–54
  sex, 20, 354–56
 rewards and, 194
Motives, 356–67
 achievement, 364–65
 affiliation, 365–66
 aggression, 358–64
 defined, 346
 hierarchy of needs, 366–67
 power, 365
 sexual coercion and, 361
 social, 358, 364–66
 stimulus motives, 356–58
Motor cortex, primary, 59
Motor development, 396–98
Motor-development tests, 333
Motor (efferent) neurons, 48, 71

Mourning, 495–96
Movement
 apparent, 137
 biological, 137
 induced, illusion of, 139
 motion parallax, 134–35
 perception of, 136–37
 real, 136–37
 vestibular sense about, 119
Movement and Mental Imagery (Washburn), 19
Multimethod research, 30
Multiple intelligences, theory of, 308–10
Multiple personality, 521–22
Musical intelligence, 310
Myelinated neurons, 47, 48
Myelin sheath, 47, 48
Myocardial ischemia, 491
Myopia, alcohol, 167

Narcissistic personality disorder, 526
Narcolepsy, 160
Narcotics, 53
National Academy of Science, 98
National Advisory Mental Health Council, 348
National Alliance for the Mentally Ill, 561
National Association for Children of Alcoholics, 560
National Clearinghouse for Alcohol and Drug Information, 560
National Clearinghouse on Family Support and Children's Mental Health, 561
National Clearinghouse on Marital and Date Rape, 561
National Institute of Health (NIH), 36
National Institute of Mental Health, 561
National Institute on Alcohol Abuse and Alcoholism (NIAAA), 166
National Institutes of Health, 169, 571
National Mental Health Association, 561
National Mental Health Consumer Self-Help Clearinghouse, 561
National Opinion Research Center (NORC), 355
National Organization for Women, 561
National Resource Center on Homelessness and Mental Illness, 561
National Self-Help Clearinghouse, 560
Native Americans, therapy and, 570–71
Natural disasters, behavior during, 483
Naturalistic observation, 26–27, 31
Naturalistic view of abnormal behavior, 505–6
Natural selection, 84–85
Nature versus nurture, 8, 78, 388–89
 on sexual orientation, 356
Nazi Germany, 86
Needs. *See also* Motivation; Motives
 hierarchy of, 366–67
 individual, adjustment accounting for, 497
Negative expressed emotion, 532
Negative reinforcers, 193–94
Negative self-concept, 513
Negative transference, 544
Neonates, 392–96
Nerve (tract), 47
Nervous system, 46–74. *See also* Neurons
 central nervous system, 54–71
  brain, 54–67
  hemispheric specialization, 60–64
  limbic system, 64–67, 355
  reticular formation, 64, 113

Progressive Matrices, 316, 318
Projection, as defense mechanism, 487, 489
Projective tests, personality assessment with, 468–69
Prosopagonsia, 105
Protein synthesis during REM and NREM sleep, 156–57
Prototypes, 265–68
Proximal stimulus, 127
Proximity
    friendship and, 26
    interpersonal attraction and, 584
    perceptual organization based on, 126
Proximodistal motor development, 397
Prozac, 6, 53, 564
Pseudosciences, 11
Psychasthenia scale on MMPI-2, 468
Psychiatric Service Section, American Hospital Association, 561
Psychiatrist, 37
Psychoactive drugs, 562–64
    alteration of consciousness with, 163–78
        depressants, 165–71, 177
        hallucinogens and marijuana, 175–78
        stimulants, 77, 171–75
        substance use, abuse, and dependence, 163, 164–65
Psychoanalysis, 14, 37, 454, 542–45, 565
    defined, 444
Psychoanalytic model of psychological disorders, 507
Psychobiologists, 4
Psychodynamic psychology, 13–14
Psychodynamic theories of personality, 443–55, 465
    of Adler, 448–49
    of Erikson, 451–53
    evaluating, 453–55
    of Freud, 444–47
    of Horney, 449–50
    of Jung, 447–48
Psychodynamic theory, 14
Psychological disorders, 502–39. See also Therapies
    anxiety disorders, 514–18, 534, 535, 553
        causes of, 517–18
    childhood disorders, 532–33
    classifying, 508–10
    conflicting theories of nature, causes, and treatment of, 506–8
    cultural bias in diagnosing, avoiding, 33
    dissociative disorders, 520–22
    gender differences in, 533–35
    historical views of, 505–6
    mood disorders, 510–14, 534
        causes of, 512–14
    neurotransmitter imbalance and, 53
    personality disorders, 525–28
    perspectives on, 504–5
    prevalence of, 534
    psychosomatic disorders, 518
    schizophrenic disorders, 528–32, 534
    sexual disorders, 522–25
        gender-identity disorders, 525
        paraphilias, 523–24
        sexual dysfunction, 522–23
    somatoform disorders, 518–20
    suicide attempts and, 420
Psychologists for the Ethical Treatment of Animals (PsyETA), 36

Psychology
    academic, 37
    applied, 37
    careers in, 36–38
    clinical, 5–6
    cognitive, 16, 260
    counseling, 5–6
    defined, 8
    developmental, 2–4, 24, 389–90. See also Life span development
    enduring issues in, 7–8
    ethics and, 33–36
    evolutionary, 16–17, 78, 85–86, 152
    existential, 16
    experimental, 4–5
    fields of, 2–7
    history of, 12–18
    human diversity and, 23–25
    humanistic, 16
    industrial and organizational (I/O), 6–7, 607–8
    multiple perspectives of, 17–18
    personality, 5
    physiological, 4
    psychodynamic, 13–14
    as science, 8–12
    social. See Social psychology
Psychoneuroimmunology, 492
Psychopathic deviation scale on MMPI-2, 468
Psychosis, 528
    amphetamine, 173, 531
Psychosocial development, Erikson's theory of, 406–7
Psychosomatic disorders, 518
Psychostimulants, 562, 564
    for ADHD, 533, 564
    defined, 533
Psychosurgery, 566
Psychotherapeutic Drugs, 561
Psychotherapy, 541–59. See also Therapies
    behavior therapies, 549–52, 559, 565
    cognitive therapies, 553–54, 559, 565
    defined, 541
    drug therapy versus, 5–6
    effectiveness of, 542, 557–59
    group therapies, 554–57, 565
    insight therapies, 542–49, 559, 565
    short-term psychodynamic, 549
Psychotic, 512
Psychoticism, 458
PTSD (post-traumatic stress disorder), 361–62, 496–97, 517, 571
Puberty, 413
    early and late developers, 414
Punishers, 192
Punishment, 194–96
    extinction of behaviors learned through, 203
    learned helplessness and, 197–98
    vicarious, 215, 216, 217
Pupil (eye), 99–100
Pygmalion effect, 581

Questioning attitude toward problems, 281
Questionnaire, self-report, 467

Race
    defined, 22
    IQ scores and, 25
    suicide rate across life span and, 511
Racism, 590–91

Radioactive PET, 71
Random sample, 32
Rapid eye movement (REM) sleep, 153–54, 155
    changes in, across life span, 155
    dreams in, 155
    protein synthesis during, 156–57
    REM rebound, 157–58
Rational-emotive therapy (RET), 553–54
Rational individuals, 448
Reaction formation, 488, 489
Reality principle, 445
Real movement, perception of, 136–37
Recategorization, 591
Receptor cells, 94, 104
    of retina, 100–102
Receptors, stretch, 119
Receptor sites, 51
    drugs' effects on, 52–53
Recessive gene, 79–80
Reconstructive memory, 239
Recovered memory, 241
Recovery, spontaneous, 201–3, 557
Recovery stage of catastrophe, 496
Redefinition of problem, 280–81
Reflex action, spinal cord and, 68
Reflexes in newborn, 392
Reflexive behavior, 184, 185–91, 209–10
Refractory period, absolute versus relative, 49
Refugees, therapy for, 571
Regression, 488, 489
Regulations, federal, 35
Rehearsal
    elaborative, 233–34, 235
    rote, 232–33, 244
Reinforcement, 15
    cognitive-social learning theory and, 464
    language development and, 404
    schedule of, 207–9
    superstitious behavior and, 197
    types of, 193–94
    vicarious, 215, 216, 217
    withholding, 202–3
Reinforcers, 192
    negative, 193–94
    positive, 193–94, 195
    primary, 205
    secondary, 205–6
Relationship-oriented leadership, 606
Relative refractory period, 49
Relaxation exercises, memory and, 250
Relaxation techniques, teaching, 551
Reliability
    of DSM-IV, 508–9
    of intelligence tests, 316–17
Religion, 10
    immune system and service attendance, 494
Remote Associates Test (RAT), 337
REM rebound, 157–58
REM sleep. See Rapid eye movement (REM) sleep
Renewal effect, 202
Representation(s)
    mental, 398–99
    problem, 270–72
    symbolic, in animals, 290–91
Representativeness heuristic, 283–84
Representative sample, 32
Repression, 239
    as defense mechanism, 487, 489
Reproductive success, 17